JUVENILE SEXUAL OFFENDING

JUVENILE SEXUAL OFFENDING

Causes, Consequences, and Correction

NEW AND REVISED EDITION

Gail Ryan
Sandy Lane
Editors

JOSSEY-BASS
A Wiley Company
www.josseybass.com

Published by Jossey-Bass
A Wiley Imprint
989 Market Street, San Francisco, CA 94103-1741   www.josseybass.com

Jossey-Bass books and products are available through most bookstores. To contact Jossey-Bass directly call our Customer Care Department within the U.S. at (800) 956-7739, outside the U.S. at (317) 572-3986 or fax (317) 572-4002.

Jossey-Bass also publishes its books in a variety of electronic formats. Some content that appears in print may not be available in electronic books.

Library of Congress Cataloging-in-Publication Data

Juvenile sexual offending: causes, consequences, and
   correction/Gail Ryan and Sandy Lane, editors.—New and
rev. ed.
      p. cm.
   Includes bibliographical references and index.
    ISBN 0–7879–0843–6 (alk. paper)
    1. Teenage sex offenders. I. Ryan, Gail D. II. Lane, Sandy L.
  HV9067.S48J88 1997
  364.3'6—dc21
                                     96–50209
                                       CIP

Printed in the United States of America
SECOND EDITION
PB Printing 10 9 8

CONTENTS

Introduction   xi

Gail Ryan and Sandy Lane

PART ONE: THE PROBLEM OF JUVENILE SEXUAL OFFENDING

1   Sexually Abusive Youth: Defining the Population   3

Gail Ryan

2   Incidence and Prevalence of Sexual Offenses
Committed by Juveniles   10

Gail Ryan

PART TWO: THEORETICAL PERSPECTIVES

3   Theories of Etiology   19

Gail Ryan

4   Sexual Development in Infancy and Childhood   36

Floyd M. Martinson

5 Deviancy: Development Gone Wrong   59
    Brandt F. Steele and Gail Ryan

6 The Sexual Abuse Cycle   77
    Sandy Lane

7 Phenomenology: A Developmental-Contextual View   122
    Gail Ryan

8 The Families of Sexually Abusive Youth   136
    Gail Ryan

PART THREE: CONSEQUENCES OF SEXUAL ABUSE

9 Consequences for the Victim of Sexual Abuse   157
    Gail Ryan

10 Consequences for the Youth Who Has Been Abusive   168
    Gail Ryan

PART FOUR: INTERVENTION IN JUVENILE SEXUAL OFFENDING

11 The Evolving Response to Juvenile Sexual Offenses   179
    Gail Ryan

12 Program Development   183
    Fay Honey Knopp and Rob Freeman-Longo, with Sandy Lane

13 The Legal System's Response to Juvenile Sexual Offenders   201
    Joseph Heinz and Gail Ryan

14 Comprehensive Service Delivery with a Continuum of Care   211
    Steven Bengis

15 Assessment of Sexually Abusive Youth   219
    Sandy Lane

PART FIVE: TREATMENT OF SEXUALLY ABUSIVE YOUTH

16 Integrating Theory and Method   267

Gail Ryan and Sandy Lane

17 Special Populations: Children, Females,
    the Developmentally Disabled, and Violent Youth   322

Sandy Lane, with Chris Lobanov-Rostovsky

18 The Family in Treatment   360

Jerry Thomas

19 Creating an "Abuse-Specific" Milieu   404

Gail Ryan

20 Aftercare: Community Integration
    Following Institutional Treatment   417

William C. Greer

PART SIX: PREVENTION

21 Perpetration Prevention: Primary and Secondary   433

Gail Ryan

PART SEVEN: WORKING WITH SEXUAL ABUSE

22 The Impact of Sexual Abuse on the Interventionist   457

Gail Ryan and Sandy Lane

About the Editors   475

About the Contributors   477

Name Index   479

Subject Index   485

This book is dedicated to the memory of Fay Honey Knopp for her shepherding of workers in this field and to the young clients who have struggled with us to achieve understanding and change in order to stop the multigenerational cycle of sexual abuse.

INTRODUCTION

Sexual offenses encompass a wide spectrum of behaviors, in a variety of situations, with many types of victims. Sexual aggression in the form of violent or sadistic rape has long been feared and punished, and other deviant sexual behaviors or paraphilias have been shunned and prohibited. Moreover, sexual deviancy has generated many myths and misconceptions. Sex offenders have often escaped report and recrimination because of the lack of accurate information and the reluctance of many cultures to discuss sexual issues. Juvenile offenders have often been exempted from responsibility for their deviant behaviors and sexual aggression; many exploitative behaviors were considered "adolescent adjustment reactions" or "exploratory" stages and were thought to pass with age.

As society has recognized the incidence and prevalence of child sexual abuse, clinical work and research have demonstrated the negative impact of early sexual exploitation on the developing child. Legal, educational, and social service approaches have been mobilized to intervene on behalf of sexually abused children. The sexual abuse of children has been defined as a criminal offense for which perpetrators are accountable and punishable; mandatory reporting has been legislated to aid in earlier detection; prevention curricula have been developed to teach children how to resist and report sexual victimization; and treatment programs for victims, offenders, and families have been developed to address the issues of sexual abuse. The primary prevention of sexual abuse, however, is dependent on eliminating the danger or potential of sexual exploitation by stopping sexual offending. Effective intervention to prevent further offending by identified offenders and the development of new sexual offenders is ultimately the only proactive alternative in sexual abuse prevention. It is in asking the question, "Who are these sex offenders, and where do they come from?" that our attention turns to children and adolescents who are sexually abusive.

Concern has been growing since the early 1980s that sexually abusive behavior that begins in childhood or adolescence often continues on into adult years. The discouraging prognosis for adult sex offenders in treatment and the multiple victims they leave behind has led to earlier intervention in sexual offending, and so programs for sexually abusive youth developed rapidly in the 1980s. Current thinking on the treatment of sexually abusive youths is based on a combination of the applied implications of research with adult offenders and clinical experience and a small but growing body of research with children and adolescents.

Sexual abusers of all ages often are characterized by denial or minimization of their abusive behavior and resistance to intervention. Treatment is often most successful when it is court ordered rather than voluntary. Offense-specific programs combine many nontraditional approaches, and specialized training is required to conduct them. This book is designed to aid in the acquisition of the specific knowledge needed to understand the causes, consequences, and correction of juvenile sexual offending. It does not present specific program designs but explores the theory and concepts supporting practice in all settings.

The primary focus of this book is the sexual abuse of children; evidence indicates this to be the highest-frequency sexual offense, and those who engage in the sexual victimization of children have the largest number of victims. Rape and other deviant sexual behaviors are treated separately in the book only when theory or practice differs significantly. In general, we assume that all sexually exploitative behaviors are contained within a single continuum with more commonalities than differences. This assumption is supported by the findings that multiple paraphilias are often displayed by the same individual at different times and that abusers often progress from less intrusive to more intrusive or less coercive to more coercive behaviors over time (Abel, Mittelman, & Becker, 1983).

This book is designed to be of interest to clinicians already working in the field, and it is also specifically appropriate for graduate study in the university setting. Supplemental reading or study in sexual abuse, child development, sexuality, delinquency, sexual addiction, aggression, and clinical practice are suggested for those who are specializing in the treatment of sexually abusive youth.

After defining the problem of sexually abusive behaviors committed by juveniles and exploring its scope, the book provides a historical perspective and the rationale for intervention with this population. We address theories of etiology and the development of specialized programs, and then we present a developmental perspective by looking at sexuality, deviancy, and the role of sexuality and abusiveness in sexual offending. The consequences of sexual abuse are considered by looking at the impact of these behaviors on both the victims and the perpetrators, as well as the families of each. Next, we present a basic introduction to the system's legal and therapeutic responses and a foundation for specialized treatment approaches. This format provides a basis for understanding the development of both the problem and current approaches in treatment and prevention.

This second edition retains the common base of knowledge that the first edition promoted while incorporating new areas of thinking and advances in the field. It discusses the implications of recent research in both adult and juvenile work and evolving theoretical approaches. The constant growth of knowledge reflects both the curiosity and the science that drive us to continue working toward prevention and early intervention in order to reduce sexual victimization.

Acknowledgments

We acknowledge the tremendous sharing, caring support, and influence of our colleagues across the country, without whom this work would not have been possible. We are grateful to the Kempe Center secretary, Fran Dollard, for her hours of commitment to this manuscript and to the center's past and present directors, Richard Krugman and Susan Hiatt, for their faith in and support of efforts in this field.

We extend special thanks to Brandt Steele, John Davis, Connie Isaac, Vicki Agee, Jeff Metzner, Jerry Yager, and Pablo Zamora for their collaboration with and support of us during the early years of this work.

We express personal gratitude as well. From Gail Ryan: I thank Jim and Kacy, Carolyn and Patrick, my mother, my sisters, and my dad for their patience and nurturance. Also, I thank Henry Kempe, Helen Alexander, Pat Mrazek, Pamela McBogg, Jo Blum, Kim Oates, Rob Freeman-Longo, Doug Jones, and all my colleagues at the Kempe Center for their support. From Sandy Lane: I thank Dan for his patience and encouragement during the completion of this work and all of my family and friends who have encouraged and supported me in the risk of sharing knowledge and experience in this work.

Reference

Abel, G. G., Mittelman, M. S., & Becker, J. B. (1983, December 10). *Sexual offenders: Results of assessment and recommendations for treatment.* Paper presented at the World Congress of Behavior Therapy, Washington, DC.

February 1997

Gail Ryan
Denver, Colorado
Sandy Lane
Denver, Colorado

JUVENILE SEXUAL OFFENDING

PART ONE

THE PROBLEM OF
JUVENILE SEXUAL OFFENDING

CHAPTER ONE

SEXUALLY ABUSIVE YOUTH

Defining the Population

Gail Ryan

Sexually abusive behavior has been defined as any sexual interaction with person(s) of any age that is perpetrated (1) against the victim's will, (2) without consent, or (3) in an aggressive, exploitative, manipulative, or threatening manner. It may be characterized by one or more of a wide array of behaviors, and multiple paraphilias (more than one type of sexual deviancy) may be seen in a single individual. Molestation may involve touching, rubbing, disrobing, sucking, exposure to sexual materials, or penetrating behaviors. Rape may include any sexual act perpetrated with violence or force, although legal definitions often include penetration: oral, anal, or vaginal and digital, penile, or objectile. Hands-off offenses include exhibitionism (exposing one's genitalia), peeping or voyeurism (observing others without their knowledge or consent), frottage (rubbing against others), fetishism (such as stealing underwear, urinating on a victim, or masturbating in another's garments), and obscene communication (such as obscene telephone calls and verbal or written sexual harassment or denigration).

Definition of the acts that constitute sexual abuse cannot be approached in terms of behavior alone. Relationships, dynamics, and impact must be considered as well. Definition of rape relates primarily to force and lack of consent. In evaluating the sexual abuse of children by adults, age differential and behavior are adequate to define the problem. When concerns arise regarding sexual interactions involving two juveniles, however, age and behavior identifiers are often inadequate definitions, and further evaluation is required.

It is clear that an older adolescent's sodomizing a small child is sexual abuse, but as age differences narrow and the behaviors become less intrusive and less aggressive, the interaction and relationship between the two juveniles needs evaluation. In any sexual interaction, the factors that are useful when assessing the presence or absence of exploitation are equality, consent, and coercion.

Equality considers differentials of physical, cognitive, and emotional development, passivity and assertiveness, power and control, and authority. Physical differences such as size and strength may be assessed with some ease; cognitive and emotional differentials may be more reflective of life experience. Thus, in similar situations, one case of two children of the same age engaging in reciprocal genital touching may be exploitative due to either a delay in the development of one child or precociousness in the development of the other, whereas a case of two juveniles with an age difference of even three or four years engaging in the same behavior may not be exploitative if the two are developmentally equal. Similarly, power and control issues and passivity and assertiveness may be used to define the roles of two juveniles in an interaction in order to clarify the equality or inequality of the two in a particular situation. In some cases where all other factors appear equal, some subtle authority of one child over the other may exist. This authority may be explicit, as in the case of an older child who is put in charge of a younger one in a babysitting relationship or on an outing. Other examples of explicit authority are when one child is the "president of the club," the "parent," the "teacher," or the "hero" in a play situation. More subtle levels of authority may exist if one child has previously been held responsible for the other's misbehavior or due to the implications of family positions (for example, if the perpetrator is the older brother, favorite child, uncle, or so on) or due to differences in self-image related to popularity, competence, talents, and success. The juvenile who feels inferior in a peer relationship may be victimized by a peer as surely as a smaller child may be victimized by the older adolescent.

Consent as a legal definition is considered to be a concept beyond the competence of juveniles. Even older adolescents are seldom allowed to give legal consent in important decisions. In sexual issues, arbitrary ages have been considered the age of consent for engaging in sexual relationships. Assessing consent in interactions of juveniles, however, demands more than a legal definition or an age identifier. The elements of consent have been defined as follows:

> *Consent:* Agreement including *all* of the following: (1) understanding what is proposed based on age, maturity, developmental level, functioning, and experience; (2) knowledge of societal standards for what is being proposed; (3) awareness of potential consequences and alternatives; (4) assumption that

agreements or disagreements will be respected equally; (5) voluntary decision; [and] (6) mental competence. (National Task Force on Juvenile Sexual Offending, 1988, 1993)

Difficulties arising in the assessment of consent often stem from a basic confusion regarding the distinctions among compliance, cooperation, and consent. The apparent outcome may be identical in terms of behavior, but the intent, motivation, and perception are quite different, so the experience and impact are not the same. Whereas consent implies that both persons have similar knowledge, understanding, and choice, cooperation implies an active participation regardless of personal belief or desire and may occur without consent; compliance may mean passively engaging without resistance in spite of opposing beliefs or desires (Ryan, 1988).

Coercion, the third factor in defining exploitation in juvenile sexual interactions, refers to the pressures that deny the victim free choice. The factors already discussed as inequality are often the tools of coercion: perceptions of power or authority are often exploited to coerce cooperation, while size differentials may coerce compliance.

Another level of coercion involves secondary gains or losses that may result from the interaction. Secondary gains are employed in bribery to coerce cooperation or compliance in return for emotional or material gains. When money, treats, favors, or friendship are offered in return for sexual involvements, the bribe is the tool of coercion. Even more subtle secondary gains lie in the nurturance and caring that offenders offer within exploitative relationships. Secondary losses for lack of compliance may also be material, but most often they lie in the victim's fear of rejection or abandonment—the loss of love, friendship, or caring.

Finally, coercion extends into the realm of threats and overt violence. Threats of the losses previously discussed may be implicit, as when the victim thinks, "Maybe he won't like me if I don't do it," or explicit, as when an offender states, "I won't like you if you don't." Coercion may also be expressed through the threat of force. Threats of force or violence are more common elements of coercion than are actual acts of violence. Both threats and acts of violence are less common in the sexual abuse of children than in sexual assaults against peers or adults, since it is usually possible to coerce a child without resorting to violence or force.

To date, no profile has been identified that can be applied to every sexually abusive youth. It is possible, however, to paint a picture of the modal (or most often identified) offender and offense as a composite, and then describe the range of characteristics that may vary from the mode.

The Modal Sexually Abusive Youth

Several samples of sexually abusive youth have been studied, and the modal factors are similar in all samples (Chabot, 1987; Farrel & O'Brien, 1988; Kerr, 1986; Ryan, 1988; Ryan, Miyoshi, Metzner, Krugman, & Fryer, 1996; Wasserman & Kappel, 1985; Wheeler, 1986). The vast majority of currently identified youth are male (91 to 93 percent), and the modal age is fourteen. These youths are likely to be white and living with two parental figures at the time of the offense. They rarely have any previous conviction for sexual assault, but very often this conviction does not represent the first offense or first victim. They may have been a victim of sexual abuse themselves by an acquaintance, neighbor, or relative—or they may not have been. It is perhaps even more likely that they have been physically abused or witnessed domestic violence or a deviant sexual environment as a child. (Disclosures of one's own past victimization vary widely, for many reasons more fully discussed in Part Three.) There is also one chance in three that they have been convicted of nonsexual delinquent behavior prior to this arrest.

The modal offense scenario most likely involves a seven- or eight-year-old victim, and more likely a female who is not related to the offender by blood or marriage. The behavior is unwanted, involves genital touching and often penetration (over 60 percent), and is accompanied by sufficient coercion or force to overcome the victim's resistance.

The Range of Characteristics

Reports have been made of sexual abuse perpetrated by children as young as four and five, and juvenile offenses are perpetrated by youths through ages eighteen and nineteen. Although the majority of work with sexually abusive youth to date has focused on twelve- to eighteen-year-olds, concern in regard to sexually exploitative and aggressive behaviors in prepubescent and latency-age children (Cavanagh-Johnson, 1988; Isaac, 1986) has increased dramatically recently, and earlier identification of younger sexually abusive children is beginning to yield a broader range of characteristics (Bonner, Walker, & Berliner, 1996; Gil & Cavanagh-Johnson, 1993). Sexual offenses are perpetrated by juveniles of all racial, ethnic, religious, and geographic groups in approximate proportion to these characteristics in the general population. Although most of these youth are living in two-parent homes at the time of discovery (70 percent), over half report some parental loss, such as divorce, illness, or death of a parent or permanent or temporary separations due to placement or hospitalization of a child or parent. There is also speculation that adopted children may be overrepresented in this population, which might relate to either inconsistent care, parental loss, or to dysfunctional child-rearing experiences prior to adoption.

The majority of these juveniles are attending school and achieving at least average grades, although a significant number have been identified with special problems in school, such as learning disabilities, special education needs, truancy, or behavior problems. The range of social characteristics includes every type of youngster; any group of sexually abusive youth may contain the tough delinquent, the undersocialized youth, the social outcast, the popular star, the athlete, or the honor roll student. Fewer than 5 percent have been previously identified as suffering mental illness or psychosis, although there appears to be an overrepresentation of juveniles with emotional and behavior disorders, affective and attention deficit disorders, obsessive-compulsive disorder, or posttraumatic stress disorder (Ryan, 1993; Dailey, 1996). Only about 30 percent have been involved in chronic nonsexual delinquent or antisocial behaviors that might support a diagnosis of conduct disorder or antisocial personality. The remaining 65 percent appear to manifest their paraphilia without other observable personality or behavior characteristics that set them apart from their peer groups.

The Range of Offense Scenarios and Behaviors

The juvenile's stage for sexual exploitation is often the home of either the victim or offender, but it may be out-of-doors somewhere in the neighborhood. Sexual assaults against peers sometimes occur in the context of a date, or the victim may be sought out, stalked, and seized by the offender in a more typical rape scenario. Assaults on older persons often occur during the commission of a robbery or burglary, typically in the home of the victim. Children provide easy targets for the sex offender; they may seek out the attention of the perpetrator or be left in the care or company of the youth by unsuspecting adults. Over 95 percent of child victims of sexual abuse know the perpetrator as an acquaintance, friend, neighbor, or relative.

Many sexually abusive youth abuse the same victim on more than one occasion, sometimes over a period of months or even years prior to disclosure or discovery. In some instances, especially as public awareness has grown, juveniles are apprehended after their first offense or first victim, but more often they have multiple victims over time prior to their first arrest. The average number of victims of juvenile perpetrators is seven, although some juveniles disclose thirty or more. In most cases, however, an earlier age of identification correlates to a smaller number of victims and fewer offenses.

The range of behaviors these youths perpetrate is enormous. Often hands-off offenses such as peeping, flashing, and obscene communications may precede hands-on offenses, and sometimes they continue between assaults. It is important to note that nondeviant sexual experiences usually precede the juvenile's illegal behavior (Becker, Cunningham-Rathner, & Kaplan, 1986), which supports the view that the sexually abusive behaviors are not merely the "exploration" of curious youth.

Although these youth have engaged in similar behaviors and have many things in common, each is a unique individual. Describing the modal youth or the most common abuse scenario does not constitute a profile of the sexually abusive youth or act. Each case requires individual assessment to describe differential diagnoses and treatment plans.

References

Becker, J. B., Cunningham-Rathner, J., & Kaplan, M. F. (1986). Adolescent sexual offenders: Demographics, criminal sexual histories, and recommendations for reducing future offenses. *Journal of Interpersonal Violence, 4,* 431–445.

Bonner, B., Walker, E., & Berliner, L. (1996). *Children with sexual behavior problems: Research based treatment.* Paper presented at the Eleventh International Congress on Child Abuse and Neglect, Dublin, Ireland.

Cavanagh-Johnson, T. (1988). Child perpetrators: Children who molest children. *Child Abuse and Neglect: The International Journal, 12*(2), 219–229.

Chabot, H. (1987). *Interdisciplinary cooperation in juvenile justice's approach to child sexual abuse: Final report.* Tacoma, WA: Juvenile Sexual Assault Unit, Pierce County.

Dailey, L. (1996). *Adjunctive biological treatments.* Paper presented at the Twelfth Annual Conference of the National Adolescent Perpetrator Network, Minneapolis, MN.

Farrel, K. J., & O'Brien, B. (Eds.). (1988). *Sexual offenses by youths in Michigan: Data, implications, and policy recommendations.* Detroit: Safer Society Resources of Detroit, Michigan, Michigan Adolescent Sexual Abuser Project.

Gil, E., & Cavanagh-Johnson, T. (1993). *Sexualized children.* Washington, DC: Launch Press.

Isaac, C. (1986). *Identification and interruption of sexually offending behaviors in prepubescent children.* Paper presented at the Sixteenth Annual Child Abuse and Neglect Symposium, Keystone, CO.

Kerr, M. (Ed.). (1986). *An executive summary: The Oregon report on juvenile sexual offenders.* Salem, OR: Avalon Associates, Children's Services Division.

National Task Force on Juvenile Sexual Offending. (1988). Preliminary report. *Juvenile and Family Court Journal, 39*(2), 8.

National Task Force on Juvenile Sexual Offending. (1993). Revised report. *Juvenile and Family Court Journal, 44*(4).

Ryan, G. (1988, April). *The juvenile sexual offender: A question of diagnosis.* Unpublished data collected by the Uniform Data Collection System of the National Adolescent Perpetrator Network. Presented at the National Symposium on Child Victimization. Anaheim, CA.

Ryan, G. (1993). *Concurrent psychiatric disorders.* Paper presented at the Annual Conference of the National Adolescent Perpetrator Network, Lake Tahoe, NV.

Ryan, G., Blum, J., Law, S., Sandau-Christopher, D., Weber, F., Sundine, C., Astler, L., Teske, J., & Dale, J. (1989). *Understanding and responding to the sexual behavior of children: Trainer's manual.* Denver: Kempe Center, University of Colorado Health Science Center.

Ryan, G., Miyoshi, T., Metzner, J., Krugman, R., & Fryer, G. (1996). Trends in a national sample of sexually abusive youths. *Journal of the American Academy of Child and Adolescent Psychiatry, 35*(1).

Wasserman, J., & Kappel, S. (1985). *Adolescent sex offenders in Vermont.* Burlington, VT: Vermont Department of Health.

Wheeler, J. R. (1986). *Final evaluation of the Snohomish County prosecutor's Juvenile Sex Offender Project.* Olympia, WA: Department of Social Services, Juvenile Justice Section.

CHAPTER TWO

INCIDENCE AND PREVALENCE OF SEXUAL OFFENSES COMMITTED BY JUVENILES

Gail Ryan

Estimating the incidence and prevalence of sexual offenses has always been difficult because of the many unknown variables. Victims of sexual crimes have often been made to feel responsible for or guilty about their own victimization; rape victims have feared the publicity and accompanying trauma of testimony. For centuries, the incest taboo prevented disclosure more effectively than it prevented occurrence, and males who have been sexually victimized during childhood or adolescence have always been socialized to deny or minimize the nature of such experiences in order to preserve the image of male invulnerability. In the past decades, increasing numbers of both men and women have disclosed that they were sexually abused as children.

During the 1970s, child abuse reporting laws that had been passed in the 1960s were amended to address the needs of child sexual abuse victims for identification, intervention, and protection. As the public's awareness of the devastating impact of childhood sexual abuse increased, reports of this abuse rose at an alarming rate. In 1976 confirmed cases of sexual abuse represented only 3.2 percent of all child abuse reports; by 1982 these reports had increased to 6.9 percent of confirmed cases of child abuse (Russell & Trainor, 1984). The National Center on Child Abuse and Neglect (NCCAN, 1987) indicated that in 1986 there had been an estimated 2.25 million cases of child abuse reported and over 1.5 million cases confirmed that year alone, and that those reported cases indicated an incidence rate of child sexual abuse at 2.5 children per 1,000 annually, for a tripling of reported incidence since 1980. By 1993, reports for child protection investigation had increased to nearly 3 million per year nationwide, but the reported rates of sexual abuse had remained stable and the demographics had not changed significantly (Snyder, Sickmund, and Poe-Yamagata, 1996). Juveniles continue to be responsible for the perpetuation of approximately 30 percent of reports of child sexual abuse ((Finkelhor, 1996). These recent data suggest an incidence rate of 2 child sexual abuse cases confirmed by child protective services per 1,000 children per year in 1994 (American Humane Association, 1996). Underreporting continues to be a problem even today. The 1995 Gallup survey indicates that the true number may be as many as 19 per 1,000 per year (American Humane Association, 1996).

The NCCAN's studies begin to reveal the magnitude of the problem, but they do not fully define the incidence or prevalence of child sexual abuse because their data are limited to cases handled by child protective services agencies. This point is especially relevant to the incidence of sexual abuse of children by older juveniles because many cases of juvenile offenses are rejected by social service intake criteria, which often refer all extrafamilial or third-party cases to the law enforcement or criminal justice system, and we know that only a minority of the juvenile sexual offenses involve sibling incest. The Uniform Data Collection System of the National Adolescent Perpetrator Network reported that only 38.7 percent of the cases involved siblings and only 15 percent were crimes against peers or older individuals. The balance, 46.2 percent, were offenses against children not related to the young offender; such cases, involving neighbors, friends, and acquaintances, are seldom investigated by social service systems. Although the Uniform Data Collection System's sample ($N = 1,600$) contains an enormous amount of data on cases, it cannot contribute to our knowledge of incidence or prevalence because its data come from multiple treatment providers in many states, but not every provider in any one state. One area of information in that sample does, however, support the notion that all official data underreport the true incidence: the majority of these juveniles were being referred for "first offenses," and yet the average number of victims per offender was seven, indicating that already many unreported offenses had occurred (Ryan, 1988; Ryan, Miyoshi, Metzner, Krugman, & Fryer, 1996).

Another source of data that could be used to define further the incidence or prevalence of juvenile sexual offending might be federal statistics on juvenile crime and juvenile delinquency. The FBI Crime Index for both adults and juveniles does identify rape and other sexual offenses for both adult and juvenile perpetrators, but it reports on only cases charged, prosecuted, and found guilty. This index thus gives us scant dependable data on juvenile perpetration of child sexual abuse because many of these cases go undetected, others are never brought to the attention of the criminal justice system, many are referred to diversion or social service programs for treatment and no charges are filed, and still others are dismissed or rejected for prosecution for a variety of reasons, which will be explored in Chapter Thirteen.

The most reliable sources for true incidence figures on child sexual abuse appear to be in the self-reports of past and present victims and offenders. In a *Los Angeles Times* poll in 1985 (Timnick, 1985), an anonymous telephone survey of a random sample of over 2,600 American adults, 22 percent of the population (16 percent of all male respondents and 29 percent of all female respondents) reported having been sexually abused prior to age eighteen. It is not possible to extract from the poll what portion of cases involved a juvenile perpetrator, but several other studies note the proportions of reported victims who were abused by juvenile perpetrators. These studies indicate that 56 to 57 percent of the reported cases of sexual abuse of male children are perpetrated by teenagers (Rogers & Tremaine, 1984; Showers, Farber, Joseph, Oshins, & Johnson, 1983).

Since we know that 24 percent of the reported child sexual abuse victims in 1986 were male, we can estimate that approximately seventy thousand boys were reported sexually abused by juveniles during 1986. We can also expect that at least half of the adult male victims disclosed by the *Los Angeles Times* poll may have been abused by juvenile perpetrators, which would result in an estimate that 8 percent of all males in the general population are sexually abused by a juvenile prior to age eighteen.

Similarly, if we know that 15 to 25 percent of female sexual abuse victims were molested by a juvenile (Farber, Showers, Johnson, Joseph, & Oshins, 1984), then we might estimate that in 1986, 60,000 to 110,000 girls were victims of other juveniles and that approximately 5 to 7 percent of all females under age eighteen are sexually abused by a juvenile.

Even these approximations must remain suspect because it is likely that the incidence of child sexual abuse continues to be underreported in these national studies for many reasons, including the protective reactions of victims who experience disassociation and blocking of the memories of these experiences, fear of disclosure, and the likelihood that male victims continue to underreport experiences that may threaten their male image of invulnerability.

Several more specific studies of smaller samples in defined areas confirm the alarming magnitude of juvenile sexual offending and suggest that our estimates here are conservative. The Colorado Department of Social Services, reporting statistics on confirmed cases of child abuse in 1985, showed that 32 percent ($N = 2,115$) involved child sexual abuse. Of these cases, 18 percent ($N = 385$) were male children and 82 percent ($N = 1,727$) female. Of these victims, 24.4 percent were less than five years old, and 43 percent of these youngsters were molested by an unrelated third party; 45.9 percent were between six and twelve years old, and 37 percent of these were third-party cases. Approximately 30 percent were thirteen to seventeen years old, with only 28 percent of this older group molested by a third-party perpetrator. We may assume that part of the 41.3 percent who were abused by someone who was related by birth or marriage were molested by juvenile siblings or cousins and that some of the 37.6 percent abused by an unrelated person were the victims of juvenile offenders (Rosenthal, Beveridge, & Associates, 1986). The substantially higher proportion of males who were molested by an unrelated third party (51 percent, as compared to 32 percent of the females) correlates with findings in other studies that females are more at risk for sexual abuse in the family and males more at risk outside the family. If our observation in other samples of the percentage of reported sexual abuse cases involving juvenile offenders is applied to the Colorado sample, over 50 percent of the boy victims (or more than 190 cases) and at least 20 percent of the girl victims (or 345 cases) would likely be attributable to juvenile perpetrators in Colorado in 1985. Unfortunately, no data were available from Colorado on the number of identified perpetrators who were juveniles, but several other states have studied juvenile offenses in their states.

For 1983, California's Department of Youth Authority reported 2,575 felony arrests for sex offenses by people less than twenty years old, including 1,000 forcible rapes, and an additional 4,500 misdemeanor arrests for other sex offenses by those under twenty. Juvenile arrests of those under eighteen accounted for 1,850 of the felonies—600 of them for forcible rape and over 700 for lewd or lascivious conduct (State of California, 1986).

In Vermont, the Department of Health surveyed the Department of Social, Rehabilitation, and Corrections Services regarding known juvenile perpetrators and found 161 sex offenses reported during 1984. This figure represents approximately 1.6 sex offenses committed per year per 1,000 juveniles ages five to seventeen. Only about one in four of these cases was adjudicated or convicted, which would prevent the rest from being counted in the FBI Crime Index. In this sample, 90 percent were male and were known to their victims; the median age of the victims was seven; one-quarter of the victims were male; and the median age of these offenders was fifteen (Wasserman & Kappel, 1985).

In Oregon, 1,000 sexual offenses were reported committed by juveniles in 1985, although only 382 were arrested. With almost 500,000 juveniles ages five to seventeen in the state, this represents 2 per 1,000 reported for sexual offending in 1985. The modal age range of the perpetrators was thirteen to fourteen years old, and molestation was the most common sexual offense reported (Kerr, 1986).

In Washington State, two counties have published reports on juvenile sexual offending. In Pierce County, 200 cases were referred over the two years 1985 to 1987, although only 101 cases were charged. This represents a rate of 4.9 per

1,000 male juveniles ages ten to nineteen referred for a sexual offense in the two-year study (or possibly 2.45 per 1,000 per year). Of cases charged, 37 of these juveniles were charged with rape, 55 with indecent liberties, and 8 with incest. By Washington's definition, all categories could include child victims, and the victim population was 35 percent male and 65 percent female. This study specifically excluded reported cases involving an offender under age twelve and victims under age three without an eyewitness or medical evidence (Chabot, 1987).

Another Washington State county, Snohomish, working to increase prosecution and conviction of juvenile sex offenders, reported 201 referrals and 136 convictions over the two years 1984 to 1986. This represents a rate of over 7 per 1,000 male juveniles ages ten to nineteen referred for a sexual offense over the two-year period (or possibly 3.5 per 1,000 per year). Of the 201 cases, 49 juveniles were not charged for various reasons not reflective of guilt or innocence, but the conviction rate for those charged was 90 percent. Only 9 of 150 cases charged were for rape of a peer or older person; 27 of 150 were charged with other crimes, including deviant sexual intent; and 114 were charges relating to sexual contacts with victims under age fourteen, 27 percent under age six, and 63 percent under age nine, with a modal age difference for the whole sample of six years. Of the offenders in this sample, 91 percent were males committing 22 percent of the offenses against males and 70 percent against females (Wheeler, 1986).

The State of Michigan completed a survey of sexual offenses committed by juveniles in 1988. In this sample, 85 percent involved a victim younger than the offender; the average age of the victim was between five and seven, and the median age of offender was fourteen (Farrell and O'Brien, 1988). Drawing data from Child Protective Services, community service workers, and juvenile court officers, the state substantiated 731 cases out of 1,178 referrals in 1985. Approximately 6 percent involved sexual assault of a same-age peer, and only 8.3 percent were sexual assaults against an older person. More than half of the victims were ten or more years younger than the offender, and the rate of penetration or attempted penetration in the offenses was highest in crimes against victims under age three and over eleven years old, remaining above a rate of 50 percent from ages three to twelve and then decreasing somewhat. Forty percent were offenses against relatives or family members, and only 5 percent were against strangers. The age range of abusive youth on active caseloads of community service workers and juvenile court officers in 1986 was from seven to seventeen, 95 percent of them males; and rates increased rapidly from age nine to age fourteen, dropping off by age seventeen as offenders aged sixteen and older were moved out of the juvenile court into adult court. In this sample, 36 percent of victims under age ten were male, compared to only 14 percent of those over age ten.

While the FBI Crime Index does not adequately describe the offenses of sexually abusive youth, the Office of Justice reports that 6 percent of all juveniles, ages ten to seventeen, were charged in 1994 with sexual crimes: 6,000 for forcible rapes and 17,700 for other sexual offenses committed in the United States. Other studies using broader definitions of sexual assault than legal charges, such as Ageton's (1983), have estimated much higher rates of sexual abuse by adolescents.

Another source of information on the incidence of sexual offending by juveniles is found in the retrospective self-reports of convicted adult sex offenders. Several studies of adult offenders' self-reports have agreed that over half of adult offenders began committing sexual offenses prior to age eighteen (Abel, Mittelman, & Becker, 1985; Freeman-Longo, 1983). Most notably, Abel, Mittelman, & Becker (1985) report on a group of 240 adult offenders who, when guaranteed confidentiality, reported an onset of deviant sexual behavior prior to age eighteen and averaged 581 attempted or completed acts against an average of 380 victims per offender throughout their lifetimes. The range of number of offenses included adults with both much lower and much higher numbers of offenses and victims. (Subsequent studies have not replicated as high averages as Abel's 1986 study but nevertheless continue to demonstrate multiple victims and high rates of offending. Differences may be related to sample differences or differences in accuracy of self-reports.)

In recent studies using polygraph exams to improve the veracity of self-reports, the high rates of offenses committed by some sexually abusive youth have been corroborated. Chambers (1994) reports that 36 youth (ages 10 to 18) in treatment reported a total of 111 victims. When preparing for polygraph exams, the youth reported an additional 77 victims of 153 previously undisclosed incidents. Polygraph exams subsequently indicated that 50 percent of the youth were deceptive, and subsequent self-reports revealed 19 more victims of 349 incidents.

All of these estimates must be approached with extreme caution because of so many unknown factors. We do not know how many sex offenders are never reported or if those who are caught are representative of all. Also, just as the self-reports of victimization may be unreliable, the self-reports of sex offenders are highly suspect. Although it seems important to explore the question of incidence and relevance, the scope of this book is not concerned so much with the size of the problem but rather with its causes and how it may be corrected.

References

Abel, G. G., Mittelman, M. S., & Becker, J. B. (1985). Sex offenders: Results of assessment and recommendations for treatment. In H. Ben-Aaron, S. Hacker, & C. Webster (Eds.), *Clinical criminology: Current concepts.* Toronto: M&M Graphics.

Ageton, S. (1983). *Sexual assault among adolescents.* San Francisco: Lexington Books.

American Humane Association. (1996). *Fact sheet on child sexual abuse.* Denver: Author.

Chabot, H. (1987). *Interdisciplinary cooperation in juvenile justice's approach to child sexual abuse: Final report.* Tacoma, WA: Juvenile Sexual Assault Unit, Pierce County.

Chambers, H. (1994). Snohomish County Juvenile Court policy statement on use of poly-graph in treatment of juvenile sex offenders. *Interchange.* Denver, CO: National Adolescent Perpetrator Network.

Farber, E. D., Showers, J., Johnson, C. F., Joseph, J. A., & Oshins, L. (1984). The sexual abuse of children: A comparison of male and female victims. *Journal of Clinical Child Psychology, 13*(3), 294–297.

Farrell, K. J., & O'Brien, B. (Eds.). (1988). *Sexual offenses by youth in Michigan: Data, implications, and policy recommendations.* Detroit: Safer Society Resources, Michigan Adolescent Sexual Abuser Project.

Federal Bureau of Investigation. (1979). *National crime survey.* Washington, DC: Author.

Finkelhor, D. (1996, August). *Keynote address.* Presented at the International Congress on Child Abuse and Neglect, Dublin, Ireland.

Freeman-Longo, R. E. (1983). Juvenile sexual offenses in the history of adult rapists and child molesters. *International Journal of Offender Therapy and Comparative Criminology, 27*(2), 150–155.

Kerr, M. (Ed.). (1986). *An executive summary: The Oregon report on juvenile sexual offenders.* Salem, OR: Avalon Associates, Children's Services Division.

National Center on Child Abuse and Neglect. (1987, December). *Study of national incidence of child abuse and neglect.* Washington, DC: National Center on Child Abuse and Neglect.

Rogers, C., & Tremaine, T. (1984). Clinical intervention with boy victims of sexual abuse. In S. Greer & I. R. Stuart (Eds.), *Victims of sexual aggression: Men, women, and children.* New York: Van Nostrand Reinhold.

Rosenthal, J., Beveridge, J., & Associates (1986). *Reporting of child abuse to Colorado Central Registry.* Denver: Colorado Department of Social Services.

Russell, A. B., & Trainor, C. M. (1984). *Trends in child abuse and neglect: A national perspective.* Denver: American Humane Association.

Ryan, G. (1988, April). *The juvenile sexual offender: A question of diagnosis.* Unpublished data collected by the Uniform Data Collection System of the National Adolescent Perpetrator Network. Presented at the National Symposium on Child Victimization. Anaheim, CA.

Ryan, G., Miyoshi, T., Metzner, J., Krugman, R., & Fryer, G. (1996). Trends in a national sample of sexually abusive youths. *Journal of the American Academy of Child and Adolescent Psychiatry, 35*(1).

Showers, J., Farber, E. D., Joseph, J. A., Oshins, L., & Johnson, C. F. (1983). The sexual victimization of boys: A three-year survey. *Health Values: Achieving High-Level Wellness, 7,* 15–18.

Snyder, H., Sickmund, M., Poe-Yamagata, E. (1996). *Update on violence.* Washington, DC: Office of Justice.

State of California. Department of Youth Authority. (1986). *Sex Offender Task Force report.* Sacramento, CA: Author.

Timnick, L. (1985, August 25). The Times poll. *Los Angeles Times.*

Wasserman, J., & Kappel, S. (1985). *Adolescent sex offenders in Vermont.* Burlington, VT: Vermont Department of Health.

Wheeler, J. R. (1986). *Final evaluation of the Snohomish County prosecutor's Juvenile Sex Offender Project.* Olympia, WA: Department of Social Services, Juvenile Justice Section.

PART TWO

THEORETICAL PERSPECTIVES

CHAPTER THREE

THEORIES OF ETIOLOGY

Gail Ryan

Sexual aggression is a multidimensional problem without a clearly defined cause. Historically, there have been many theories advanced concerning both normative and deviant sexuality. Sexual exploitation and aggression have been considered truly deviant only in this century. Many ancient cultures viewed sexual behavior only in terms of reproduction or physical satisfaction, and thus it stood outside the context of relationships. Male dominance was the norm.

Today, however, sexual interactions are expected to be physically, emotionally, and psychologically meaningful in the context of a relationship. Exploitation, violence, and force are now considered both deviant and criminal. In the light of societal norms and the taboos and penalties associated with the sexual victimization of others, many hypotheses have been explored in regard to the etiology of sexually abusive behaviors.

The various theories that have received substantial attention in this century serve as a basis for understanding both the history of thinking about sexual offending and the historical basis of current approaches to treatment. Many aspects of these various theories are interwoven, and similar issues surface in the application of different theories to sexual offending. The descriptions of these theories that follow are brief; clinicians entering this field as a specialty may wish to explore more fully the works cited in each section.

Psychosis Theory

It is ironic that the most readily acceptable theories seem to account for the smallest portion of the problem. In terms of logic and humane sensibilities, the only acceptable explanation for rape and child sexual assault is that of psychosis. The notion that these perpetrators "must be crazy" or "sick in the head" is the oldest and most widely accepted theory in the community, and yet in the vast majority of cases, there is little basis for a diagnosis of mental illness (as a causal explanation) in the sense that other personality disorders are defined. In actuality, truly psychotic sex offenders account for less than 8 percent of the total population of perpetrators (Knopp, 1984). In those relatively rare cases where sexually abusive behaviors are associated with borderline, schizophrenic, or psychotic conditions, psychiatric hospitalization and treatment to control the underlying personality disturbance would be a prerequisite to any assessment of continued risk of sexual offense. It is not apparent in the scientific literature that psychotic features specifically support or promote sexually exploitative behavior; therefore, sexual offenses in this small proportion of cases may be symptomatic of the underlying illness rather than descriptive of the illness itself.

The psychotic offender's behavior has no less of an impact, however, than that of other offenders, and thus the concern for decisive intervention is not diminished. These offenders are the least likely to be served in the majority of specialized treatment programs and are therefore not the focus of this book.

Physiological Theory

Physiological explanations have been sought and explored to explain sexual aggression and deviancy. Neurological and hormonal factors seem to be the most promising areas for physiological research, as either would involve measurable and potentially alterable conditions. The attraction of a biological explanation is not entirely scientific, however, because any physiological cause would support a view that sex offenders are born rather than raised. This distinction is an important one because any inborn deviant, harmful, or repulsive condition can be approached with compassion and science without casting guilt on the postnatal environment. The notion that sexual offenders choose to behave as they do is so dissonant with our social sensibilities that an explanation that portrays the problem as beyond the control (and therefore the accountability) of offenders is in some ways especially palatable. If offenders are helpless to control their behavior because of an inborn condition, then society is also helpless, and neither can be held responsible. The burden of guilt shifts to the fates.

Physiological investigation is not without merit, however. Neurological research continues to offer new clues to human conditions and behavior, and hormonal factors are known to exert powerful influences on many aspects of psychological, emotional, and physiological functioning in ways that often affect feelings and behavior. To date, neurological factors have been linked to some elements of aggression, and some hypotheses related to learning and memory in the brain are possible, but no specific neurological explanation has been found for sexually aggressive behavior. In the 1980s researchers studying posttraumatic stress disorder demonstrated that for some individuals, the experience of overwhelming trauma may produce permanent changes in the way the brain secretes certain chemicals in response to subsequent events. This area of study appears to be potentially relevant to the understanding of many dysfunctional responses that have previously defied adequate explanation (Van der Kolk, 1986). Research in the basic sciences that has described and illuminated brain functions, especially the neurotransmitters relating to emotional states, has supported clinical applications of pharmacological interventions in the treatment of numerous psychiatric disorders, among them posttraumatic stress disorders, attention deficits, mood disorders, obsessive-compulsive disorders, and dissociative disorders. The importance of these advances will be discussed in Chapter Sixteen.

Hormonal factors have been investigated extensively in research on sexuality, but this book will not address those findings except as they concern the treatment of sexual offenders. Basically, antitestosterone drugs such as Depo-Provera have been used in the treatment of adult sex offenders to reduce the frequency and intensity of arousal. In some cases, elevated rates of sexual arousal are thought to be associated with compulsive sexual behaviors. For the offender who is bothered by too frequent or continual arousal, reduction of that physical condition may reduce the perceived need to engage in sexual behaviors and consequently may reduce the rate of offending (Berlin & Meinecke, 1981). Even so, only a small portion of adult sex offenders are treated with antitestosterone therapy during the course of treatment, and this therapy is not considered an exclusive treatment or a curative course; rather, it is one tool to aid the offender in reducing his arousal while he is learning to control subsequent behaviors.

The use of biomedical methods with sexually abusive youth is a very different area of consideration. Antitestosterone therapy has numerous side effects, the most troublesome of which is interference in growth and maturation. Because growth failure in an immature male is a significant risk, antitestosterones are rarely an option in the treatment of sexually abusive youth. Only in extreme cases would this course of therapy be considered, and only then if the juvenile is determined to have already attained his full stature.

The factors that might warrant consideration of hormone therapy for a juvenile would be extreme compulsivity (as is the case in some developmentally disabled offenders) or extreme violence. Occasionally a juvenile engages in sexual behaviors with such frequency and in such a manner that the behaviors interfere in virtually all areas of functioning, including participation in therapy. In these extreme cases, masturbation is excessive and often public and sometimes continues even in the presence of law enforcement personnel, therapists, and other investigators. At the same time, multiple paraphilias may be observed in the same individual, including hands-on and hands-off offenses. In this case, biomedical treatment to reduce arousal in an older juvenile may be indicated for a period of time in order to enable the offender to become engaged in therapy and in a less sexualized lifestyle.

The other possible exception that could warrant consideration of antitestosterone therapy would be an extremely violent older juvenile with a long record of offenses pairing violence and sexuality. For this client, other methods in treatment would be tried first, but for some period during the course of treatment, hormonal therapy might be added to sublimate sexual arousal in order for the youth to succeed in separating feelings of aggression and sexuality more definitively. In this extreme case, the supposition is that sexuality may have become so fused with aggression, for whatever reason, that the juvenile is virtually unable to distinguish one from the other.

Biomedical methods are not indicated for most sexually abusive youth and would never be undertaken without the close surveillance of medical professionals (National Task Force on Juvenile Sexual Offending, 1988, 1993). It is also important to consider that sexually abusive behaviors are often motivated by nonsexual needs, and there is no empirical research to prove that reducing arousal necessarily reduces the abusive behavior.

Intrapsychic Theory

Related to, but not synonymous with, the theory of psychosis are the early theories of sexual offending as a symptom of intrapsychic conflict. Stimulated by Freud's theories of personality development, psychoanalytic approaches were used exclusively for many years and will also relate to the developmental theories covered later in this chapter. Freud's theory of personality was based on the belief that people have two basic instincts: sexual and aggressive. These instinctual expectations for gratification and the external demands for socially acceptable behavior are often in conflict. Freudian theory suggests that three elements of personality (the id, the ego, and the superego) are in unconscious, internal conflict: the id, operating on the pleasure principle, seeks immediate gratification of sexual and aggressive impulses; the ego, working on the reality principle, attempts to direct impulses into socially acceptable channels; and the superego makes the moral and ethical judgments that produce shame and guilt. Freud's work advanced the theory that development from birth to maturity proceeds through various stages and that internal conflicts that interrupt this development might later manifest in dysfunctional behavior symptomatic of personality disorder.

Freud's views of the psyche are so rooted in sexuality and aggression that his theory appeared to be applicable to the manifestation of sexual aggression and was therefore a preferred starting point in attempting to understand and treat sexual offenders. Although psychoanalytic and psychodynamic therapy has taught us a great deal about the origins of deviancy, it has never been shown to be consistently effective in changing sexually abusive behavior when used as an exclusive method of treatment.

As the problem of childhood sexual abuse has been explored in more recent times, increased knowledge of child development has led to new scrutiny of Freudian theories. It is now thought that prior to the widespread publication of his theory, Freud was aware of the devastation and destruction of childhood sexual abuse as it was seen in the Paris morgue. As a medical student observing autopsies in the morgue, he was quite likely aware of the evidence of genital trauma in children, so prevalent in some of these young victims that a hypothesis that children were being sexually abused by their caregivers was suggested. Historians report that Freud had in his personal library the books of Brouardel (1909), Bernard (1886), and Tardieu (1878), which described sexual violence against children (Mason, 1985). The seduction theory (Freud, 1954) was built on the evidence that "real sexual traumas in childhood lay at the heart of neurotic illness" (Mason, 1985), and yet Freud later relegated clients' reports of sexual trauma in childhood to the realm of fantasy. It is very probable that Freud's colleagues were so outraged at the hypothesis that client symptoms might be sequelae of childhood sexual abuse that he retreated to a position dealing with sexual issues in childhood as fantasies symbolic of developmental stages and intrapsychic conflicts (Freud, 1954; Kiell, 1988). Thus, societal ignorance and the pervasive denial of the reality of childhood sexual abuse has a long history. It is also apparent that sexual conflicts of childhood have long been acknowledged to be intertwined with life's miseries, in both fantasy and fact.

As late as 1977, research into the etiology and treatment of sexual offending (see Groth, 1979) was investigating intrapsychic conflict as the causative factor in sexually exploitative behaviors. Groth conceptualized child molesters as either fixated or regressed pedophiles. Although this dichotomy has no scientific basis, it applies a Freudian style of thought to the development of the child molester. Groth and his colleagues recognized that some molesters had an exclusive interest in having sex with children, while others were also interested in sexual activities with age-mates. The resulting hypothesis was that the fixated pedophile had suffered a developmental arrest, which caused his sexual interest to remain in childhood, whereas the regressed pedophile had proceeded into adult development, but then some trauma or stress caused a regression to an earlier stage of sexual interest and behavior.

The notion that childhood trauma or adult conflicts are causal or explanatory of an adult's use of children as sexual partners is not entirely without substance, for it increases our understanding of the individual and also alerts us to the lessons of history, which can guide us toward earlier intervention and prevention. Nevertheless, the psychoanalytic approach to intrapsychic conflicts is inadequate by itself to correct the problem behavior because several other factors have also played a part in the development of sexual deviancy.

Learning Theory

Learning theory relates in a basic sense to the concept of the infant mind as a blank slate, which is imprinted by experience. Pavlov's dogs (1927) are the famous example of learned response patterns, where the simultaneous experience of a stimulus and a reward leads to a pairing of the two in a classical condition of learning. Instrumental learning theory (Skinner, 1974) illuminated the learning experience by correlating a sequence of events (a stimulus followed by a consequence). Bandura's theory of observational learning (1977) added modeling and imitation to the learning repertoire of social animals. These theories of learning have been applied to the exploration of sexual behavior and have important implications in consideration of the causes, consequences, and correction of sexually abusive behavior.

It is important to consider how learning theory may apply to the development of sexuality and sexual deviancy. Although the capacity for sexuality is inborn, and many biological factors create the preconditions necessary for sexual functions, the ways in which people manifest their sexuality are learned. The concepts of normal and deviant sexuality are based in societal norms and values, and thus evaluation of sexual behavior is based on learning what is acceptable within a given culture. The conditions that support or enable a sexual offender in the circumvention of social norms must be explored. If almost everyone is aware of sexually deviant behavior in the course of a lifetime, what conditions support or inhibit the manifestation of deviant behavior in the individual? Each of the learning theories offers a hypothesis.

Pavlov's theory of classical conditioning demonstrates a physiological response to the paired stimuli. In any sexual behavior, physiological arousal may be a variable. If sexual arousal is paired with deviant behavior, a condition exists whereby sexual deviance may occur. Repetition of deviant behavior would then reinforce the original pairing and support continuation of the behavior. In view of juvenile sexual offending, classical conditioning might relate to a child's early experiences of sexual arousal that occurred in the context of a deviant situation or an exploitative relationship. These conditions might include sexual victimization but could also be relevant to arousal that occurs in the context of exposure to sexually deviant or aggressive stimuli in the culture.

Similarly, Skinner's theory also pairs two factors: behavior and reward or punishment. In the scenario of instrumental conditioning, a sexual behavior might be reinforced by subsequent sexual arousal or inhibited by a negative consequence. An equally important consideration is that the reinforcement or inhibition of sexual behaviors may initially lie in nonsexual rewards or punishment. In applying this theory to the question of juvenile sexual offending, the child's early experience of sexual behavior may or may not have included sexual arousal but may have been paired with some reward or punishment.

Bandura's theory of learning through observation and imitation supports a hypothesis that learning may begin prior to experience. That one may learn through observing a model that is then practiced imitatively implies that sexual behaviors may be learned from the models available in the environment; thus, exposure to deviant models might result in the practice of deviant behaviors. It would then follow that the experience of imitating deviant models might incorporate a pairing of stimuli with either rewards or punishment that are present in the imitative experience. For the sexually abusive youth, this theory implies that the reinforcement of early imitative or reactive behaviors has led to a patterned response.

The social aspects of learning are particularly significant in regard to sexual behaviors because of the interpersonal conditions and societal judgments that define what is exploitative, and therefore criminal. Societies that do not protect their developing children from deviant modeling and experiences are at high risk of being plagued by deviant behaviors.

Learning theories are not entirely fatalistic. Research in learning addresses not only the origins of behavior but also its extinction or correction. Reduction of undesirable behaviors has been a focus of learning research; to unlearn what has been learned and to relearn more acceptable patterns has been central to behavior modification research. In sexually abusive behavior, reduction or extinction of deviant arousal patterns has been recognized as one of the necessary components in treatment, and behaviorists have applied learning theory to developing corrective techniques. Positive and negative reinforcers are employed to reshape physiological responses and decrease the likelihood of continued negative behaviors; punishment for criminal behavior attempts to override the positive reinforcers with a more powerful negative consequence, and case management often attempts to restrict or remove the offender from situations likely to reinforce continued deviant behavior.

Although psychotic, physiological, and intrapsychic theories offer partial understanding, learning theory has provided a number of areas for consideration in both prevention and correction or control. Many clinicians treating adult sex offenders have reached similar conclusions regarding the etiology of the problem. Groth (1979), Freeman-Longo (1982), Abel, Becker, Murphy, & Flanagan (1975), and Blanchard (1974) have all suggested that deviant arousal patterns develop as the result of learned behavior and social interactions, such as sexual victimization or sexually traumatic or deviant events. Observations that the sexually abusive youths may have learned a distorted or confused view of sexuality invoke classical, instrumental, and observational learning hypotheses. The question of origin in the learning framework is therefore, Where does the sex offender learn offending?

Application of learning theory to the exploration of any harmful or repulsive deviancy invites resistance because of the implication of responsibility. If the sex offender "learned" his deviancy from individuals or environmental conditions, then society is forced to examine its role and responsibility in the origins of the problem. This implication of some societal omission or commission—failure of function, neglect, or abuse—has motivated both personal and societal denial of the existence of sex crimes, especially the sexual abuse of children. The question of the origin of deviancy arises in every theory and hypothesis, and the role of sexual conflicts, learning, abuse, or trauma will be more fully explored as the various theories are integrated later in this book. It is clear that the implications of childhood learning and behavioral change are areas of importance for the exploration and understanding of the causes, consequences, and correction of juvenile sexual offending.

Developmental Theories

Developmental theories must be one focus of concern if the causal factors of sexual offending are to be understood and ultimately prevented. Many theories of child development have been advanced in this century and provide a basis for exploration of both normal and deviant development. Three of the more global and influential of these theories are Piaget's theory of cognitive development, Erikson's theory of psychosocial development, and Freud's theory of personality development. Each views development from birth to maturity in the context of stages, and in each case, the stages are dependent on the previous ones. Table 3.1 depicts these three primary theories as they relate age and developmental stages. The similarities of ages and stages are immediately apparent.

TABLE 3.1. THE DEVELOPMENTAL STAGES IN THE THEORIES OF PIAGET, ERIKSON, AND FREUD.

Age	Piaget	Erikson	Freud
1	Sensorimotor	Trust vs. Mistrust	Oral
2		Autonomy vs. Shame and Doubt	
3	Preoperational		Anal
4			Phallic
5		Initiative vs. Guilt	
6			
7		Industry vs. Inferiority	
8	Concrete Operations		Latency
9			
10			
11			
12	Formal Operations	Identity vs. Role Confusion	Genital
13			
14			
15			
16			
17			
18		Intimacy vs. Isolation	
19			
20			

Piaget (1928) begins with the sensorimotor stage, from birth to age two, in which the infant learns from interacting with the environment. Piaget asserts that the fundamental cognitive abilities develop in this earliest stage of life and that one cannot progress to subsequent stages until each stage of development is successfully completed. This concept of fixation in an unsuccessful stage of development is important in relation to Groth's concept of fixated pedophiles, and the concept that life views form in the first years of life will relate to the exploration of antisocial personality later in this book.

Several other areas of Piaget's work have important implications in the occurrence of sexual exploitation. Egocentrism in infancy directs all concern and behavior toward personal interests and needs; decentration, which should occur around age two, enlarges one's view to encompass a recognition of other people's feelings, ideas, and needs. These stages are especially relevant to the capacity for empathy within relationships, usually an identifiable deficit of abusers. Also, accommodation and assimilation, or the processing of new experiences on the basis of past experiences, relate to the learning theories previously discussed, adding the dimension that past experiences lay the foundation for incorporating or interpreting future experiences. Concerning the recurring question of exposure to deviancy in the history of sexually abusive youth, this aspect of Piaget's work would support the hypothesis of a deviant foundation for the accommodation and assimilation of future experiences.

Erikson's theory of psychosocial development describes a variety of crises through which individuals must pass in order to achieve a mature identity. The first of these crises occurs during the first months of life as the infant's experience inspires either trust or distrust depending on the ability of the nurturer. During Erikson's second stage, control issues such as feeding and toilet training must be successfully resolved to attain autonomy, or the child experiences shame and doubt regarding the failure. This concept leads to speculation that the control issues so prevalent among sexually abusive youth may relate to resolution failures in these early stages. Erikson's theories differ from Piaget's in that they suggest negative consequences of developmental failures rather than fixation; in other words, development does not stop, but the course of development is altered. Sexual identity is defined in Erikson's third stage with implications of sex role modeling by the parents. It may be assumed that parental dysfunction or loss may increase the risk of dysfunctional modeling.

Freud's theory of personality development is permeated with themes of sexual conflict: oral, anal, phallic, and genital stages are defined. The oral stage is related to adequate nurturing and gratification in feeding, the anal stage to control issues arising around bodily functions, the phallic stage to sexual identity and self-image, and the genital stage to heterosexual fulfillment. Freud's concept of a latency stage was that children were relatively free of sexual issues or interests from ages seven to eleven, although later research has disproven this (Ford & Beach, 1951). The implications of either unresolved earlier stages or traumatic sexual experiences during the oral, anal, phallic, or latent stages would be the expectation of conflict and subsequent dysfunction. The Freudian theory also advances the theory of fixation as a result of unresolved conflicts of the id, ego, and superego.

The application of development theory to the etiology of sexual offending was obvious in Groth's work. Also, Steele (1986) and Freeman-Longo (1982) have advanced the theory that early childhood experience is of vital concern, that the family and the environment are essential influences in the development of sexuality, and that the lack of empathic care, family trauma, physical and sexual abuse, neglect, scapegoating, undefined family roles and boundaries, and exposure to sexually traumatic experiences or explicit materials in the environment may contribute to the development of sexually deviant or abusive behavior.

Attachment Theories

Although the nature of the interpersonal relationship and interaction is definitive of abuse, theories related to relationships have not been widely applied to sexual abusers. Yet it is apparent that many of the early childhood variables are related to early relationships. It has been especially apparent in work with younger children that many of those with sexual behavior problems are also "attachment disordered," and Marshall, Hudson, and Hodkinson (1993) have applied attachment theories to the adolescent as well. Most recently, Ward, Hudson, Marshall, and Siegert (1995) have explored the relationship between intimacy deficits and sexually abusive behavior in adults.

Attachment models suggest that early relationships provide internal representations of relationships that affect self-image and expectations in relationships throughout the life span. Such theories provide an explanatory bridge between developmental theories and cognitive processes.

Drawing extensively on the concept of internal working models (Bowlby, 1969, 1973; Ainsworth, 1989; Main, Kaplan, & Cassidy, 1985) that represent one's view of self and others as positive or negative, Bartholomew (1990; Bartholomew & Horowitz, 1991) and others have described four categories of adult attachment—(1) secure, (2) anxious/ambivalent, (3) avoidant I, and (4) avoidant II—that affect an individual's ability to achieve intimacy in personal relationships. By applying these categories in the assessment of sexual abusers, Ward and others (1995) were able to differentiate adult sex offenders subgroups from each other in terms of motive, victim selection, grooming, coercion, and offense variables.

Ryan and colleagues (Ryan, Hagler, Short, & Eck, 1995; Ryan, Lindstrom, Knight, Arnold, Yager, Bilbrey, & Steele, 1993) have proposed a developmental-contextual approach that integrates theories relevant to growth and development (Strayhorn, 1988) along with phenomenological theories (Yochelson & Samenow, 1976) in a more individualized and holistic approach to understanding sexual abuse clients. Theories of developmental competence suggest that functional deficits and deviance are products of inadequate or dysfunctional growth. Contextual (or ecological) theories consider the interaction between individual experience and the environment as the basis of individual beliefs about self and others and the world. This model has been described by other theorists (Donovan & MacIntyre, 1990; Gilgun, 1996) and will be discussed in Chapter Seven.

Cognitive Theory

Whereas Piaget's theory addresses cognitive development, cognitive theory also has been applied to the assessment and treatment of sex offenders. One element

of sexual offending is the thinking that allows the person to imagine his or her behavior is acceptable, justifiable, or harmless. These cognitive distortions or irrational rationalizations are essential to the abusive individual's ability to overcome
the societal taboo against abusive behavior. Many criminal offenders think differently from nonoffenders, and it is suggested that this difference relates to those
earliest developmental stages where the infant first formed his view of the world
and accommodated his experiences.

Yochelson and Samenow published a singularly comprehensive theory of
cognitive distortions or "thinking errors" in *The Criminal Personality* (1976). Their
theory of antisocial thinking, as well as its application in cognitive restructuring
with sexually abusive youth, will be covered in depth in Chapter Sixteen. Although
only 30 to 35 percent of adult sex offenders are diagnosed as having antisocial
personalities (corresponding to similar numbers of sexually abusive youth diagnosed as conduct disordered), virtually all sex offenders, regardless of age, demonstrate some patterns of distorted thinking to support and excuse their behavior.
Distorted thinking patterns are also pervasive in their interpretations and reactions to other life experiences. Cognitive and behavioral techniques are therefore
thought to be useful in treatment that addresses the thinking that allows the behavior. Cognitive restructuring is based on changing the subject's thinking in order
to change his view of the world and it requires the individual to confront his basic
belief systems.

Addictive Theory

Because all sexual behaviors potentially include a physiological reward (intimacy,
arousal, orgasm, tension reduction), theorists have explored the "addictive" qualities of sexual offending. The reference to physiological rewards recalls Pavlov's
and Skinner's conditional learning theories and brings the compulsive qualities of
the problem to the forefront. Carnes (1983) proposed a continuum of compulsive
sexual behaviors, including legal, nuisance, and criminal behaviors, that become
problematic because of their unmanageability and interference in other areas of
functioning. Applying an addictive systems model to sexual behaviors, Carnes'
theory of sexual addiction considers faulty beliefs and impaired thinking (previously discussed in relation to cognitive theory) as a "distorted view of the world"
and "thinking errors." The sexual behaviors become unmanageable or out of control because of the offender's preoccupation, ritualization, compulsivity, and subsequent despair. The offender sees his behavior as beyond his control.

The addictive model explores the family of origin and current relationships
for coaddictive systems and patterns. This exploration includes boundaries and

role reversals, control battles, unrealistic expectations, and deviant modeling of sexual attitudes and behaviors. By the early 1990s, Carnes had started to recognize that childhood victimization is relevant to the etiology of sexual addictions, and began advocating greater collaboration in the addictions field regarding victimization, survivor, and offender issues. In the addictions model, distorted thinking and shamelessness are confronted, and individuals are made accountable for their behavior and its impact. Twelve-step models of group support similar to the various "Anonymous" groups (Alcoholics Anonymous, for example) have evolved from this theory to aid in controlling compulsive sexual behavior, both legal and criminal.

Family Systems Theories

For many years, intrafamilial sexual offending such as spousal rape and parent-child or sibling incest was seen as a family problem separate and distinct from other sexual offenses. Weiner surveyed the literature on incest in 1964 and reported that incest was viewed predominantly as a family dysfunction: (1) the incest perpetrator's behavior occurred "independent of general criminal tendencies," (2) the mothers "frustrate their husbands sexually while encouraging father-daughter intimacy," and (3) the victims "seldom resist or complain . . . and rarely experience guilt." All three statements are now believed to be false but are exemplary of the thinking prior to and through the 1960s. We now know that incest perpetrators often exhibit multiple paraphilias and antisocial behaviors, that wives often are powerless in these families but not equivocally responsible or even supportive of their husband's behavior, and that children often resist within the limits of their power to do so and indeed suffer long-term negative effects. One characteristic noted in the early literature on incest holds true: denial and distorted thinking to rationalize the childhood sexual abuse.

In the 1970s, the first shift in family systems thinking removed responsibility from the child victim, although mothers were still thought to play a colluding role. Giaretto (1978) continued to view incest as a family dysfunction but moved with the legal system to hold both parents accountable. Although the child was no longer considered a causal part of the problem, the family system and interrelations of the various dyads remained a focus, and marital problems were often blamed. Each family member's contribution to the pathological system that allowed and maintained the sexual abuse was explored. Zaphiris (1978) described the dynamics of the incestuous family as "conditioning" the family to allow and support the incestuous relations.

Not until the mid-1980s (see Conte, 1985; Finkelhor & Araji, 1983) were blame and responsibility for intrafamilial sexual abuse placed unequivocally with the perpetrator. This is not to say that family dynamics need not be understood and perhaps modified, but family therapy is now adjunctive to the first and primary responses of prosecution and offense-specific treatment for perpetrators and protection and therapy for child victims. Family dynamics and treatment issues will be explored in greater depth later in Chapters Eight and Eighteen.

Integrative Theories

None of the theories outlined so far is as simple as these brief synopses suggest; furthermore, all are interrelated through certain recurring themes. Integrating these theories has been an ongoing challenge, and today many offense-specific treatment specialists use eclectic approaches that incorporate aspects of many theories. Each theory offers something to our understanding of the causes, consequences, and control of sexually exploitative behaviors.

Although a few programs operate with a single, unadulterated theory, there are probably almost as many integrative approaches as there are programs. The integrations summarized here demonstrate how theorists have visualized various patterns or typologies as frames of reference; they are by no means exclusive of the possibilities.

One of the earliest conceptualizations was Groth's application of developmental and intrapsychic conflict theories to distinguish "fixated" and "regressed" pedophiles. Although his theory has been discounted, it serves as a reminder that child molesters have different motives, patterns, and treatment needs. The search for profiles has been continual and illuminating.

In the adult field, Lanning (1987) contributed a concept of profiles based entirely on behavior patterns and related solely to law enforcement investigation. He distinguishes a "situational molester" and a "preferential molester" and characterizes them according to personal characteristics, motivation, victim criteria, method of operation, and use of pornography. His is a useful model for investigation, although it does not speak to origins or correction.

Finkelhor and Araji (1983) have conceptualized a four-factor model of pedophilia that identifies four areas of explanation: (1) *emotional congruence,* which explores the reasons that an adult might find it satisfying to relate sexually to a child (possibilities include arrested development, mastery of victimization, and identification with aggressor); (2) *sexual arousal to children,* which explores the origin of sexual preference (for example, in childhood arousal, childhood sexual trauma, operant conditioning, modeling, or misattribution); (3) *blockage,* which explores factors that might prevent success in sexual relationships with equal and consenting age-mates (such as intrapsychic conflicts, fear, adult sexual trauma, and poor social skills); and (4) *disinhibitions,* which cover conditions that might interfere with normal inhibitions against such behaviors (examples include psychosis, substance use, senility, impulse disorders, rationalizations, and stress). This model expands the incorporation of multiple theories into a single framework to demonstrate the diversity and complexity of the problem. Although this model has significant implications in treatment, it specifically relates to assessment and explanation rather than correction.

Weissberg (1982) conceptualized a simplistic view of multiple maladaptive responses to stress, which included sexual abuse and incest (as well as spousal violence, substance abuse, child abuse, and suicide). His concept identified a stressful precipitant that caused normal functioning to fail, a stage of denial, disorganization and symptom formation, and a maladaptive behavioral response. The role of adaptation in these maladaptive responses appears to represent an irrational or distorted mode of coping. While considering both predispositions and precipitating factors, Weissberg focuses on not only a concept for understanding but a focus in treatment of "promoting (more) adaptive responses," which implies both cognitive and behavioral change.

Although Abel, Becker, Cunningham-Rathner, Rouleau, Kaplan, & Reich (1984) take a behavioral approach in treatment, they use a "lifeline" from birth to the present, pinpointing significant events, patterns, and escalation of dysfunction, especially experiences of victimization or loss, sexual fantasies and behaviors, and offenses, in order to explore etiology and progression.

Prentky, Knight, Rosenberg, and Lee (1989) use a decision tree for subtyping child molesters that sorts them according to (1) the "meaning of aggression in the offense" as instrumental or expressive; (2) the "manner of relating to the victim" as objective, related, or exploitative; and (3) the "prior level of achieved relations" as either fixated or regressed. This approach guides treatment planning and supports differential diagnosis and treatment. This work supports a taxonomic classification system with implications for prediction and prevention.

Many clinicians have explored the syndrome of sexually abusive behavior and the antecedents and sequence of these behaviors. (The concept of a sexual assault cycle is explored in depth in Chapter Six.) The notion that sexually abusive behavior does not occur randomly without an opportunity for choice implies hope for its control. The integration of various theories in practice promises the fullest understanding of the individual's personal patterns and potential for success in reducing sexual victimization.

References

Abel, G., Becker, J., Cunningham-Rathner, J., Rouleau, J., Kaplan, M., & Reich, J. (1984). *The treatment of child molesters*. Program description. [Brochure]. New York: Authors.

Abel, G., Becker, J., Murphy, W., & Flanagan, B. (1975). Identifying dangerous child molesters. In R. Stuart (Ed.), *Violent behavior: Social learning approaches.* New York; Brunner Mazel.

Ainsworth, M. D. S. (1989). Attachments beyond infancy. *American Psychologist, 44,* 709–716.

Bandura, A. (1977). *Social learning theory.* Englewood Cliffs, NJ: Prentice Hall.

Bartholomew, K. (1990). Avoidance of intimacy: An attachment perspective. *Journal of Social
and Personal Relationships, 7,* 147–178.

Bartholomew, K., & Horowitz, L. M. (1991). Attachment styles among adults: A test of a
four category model. *Journal of Personality and Social Psychology, 61,* 226–244.

Berlin, F. S., & Meinecke, C. F. (1981). Treatment of sex offenders with anti-androgenic
medication: Conceptualization, review of treatment modalities, and preliminary findings.
American Journal of Psychiatry, 138, 601–607.

Bernard, P. (1886). *Des attentats à la pudeur sur les petites filles.* Paris.

Blanchard, E. (1974). The role of fantasy in the treatment of sexual deviation. *Archives of
General Psychiatry, 30,* 467–475.

Bowlby, J. (1969). *Attachment and loss* (Vol. 1). New York: Basic Books.

Bowlby, J. (1973). *Attachment and loss* (Vol. 2). New York: Basic Books.

Brouardel, P. (1909). *Les Attentats aux moeurs.* Paris: Pref de Thionot.

Carnes, P. (1983). *Out of the shadows: Understanding sexual addiction.* Minneapolis: CompCare
Publications.

Carnes, P. (1990). Sexual addiction: Progress, criticism, challenges. *American Journal of Preventive Psychiatry and Neurology.*

Conte, J. (1985). The effects of sexual victimization on children: A critique and suggestions
for future research. *Victimology, 10,* 110–130.

Donovan, D., & MacIntyre, D. (1990). *Healing the hurt child.* New York: Norton.

Erikson, E. H. (1963). *Childhood and society* (2nd ed.). New York: Norton.

Finkelhor, D., & Araji, S. (1983). *Explanations of pedophilia: A four factor model.* Durham, NH:
University of New Hampshire Family Violence Research Program.

Ford, C. S., & Beach, E. A. (1951). *Patterns of sexual behavior.* New York: HarperCollins.

Freeman-Longo, R. E. (1982). Sexual learning and experience among adolescent sexual
offenders. *International Journal of Offender Therapy and Comparative Criminology, 26*(2), 235–241.

Freud, S. (1954). Letters to Wilhelm Fliess, drafts and notes: 1887–1902. In M. Ponparte, A.
Freud, & E. Kris (Eds.), *The origins of psychoanalysis* (E. Mosbacher & J. Strachey, Trans.).
New York: Basic Books. (Original work published 1897)

Freud, S. (1965). *Normality and pathology in childhood: Assessment of development.* New York: International University Press.

Giarretto, H. (1978). Coordinated community treatment of incest. In A. Burgess, N. Groth,
L. Holstrom, & S. Sgroi (Eds.), *Sexual assault of children and adolescents.* San Francisco:
Lexington Books.

Gilgun, J. (1996). Human development and adversity in ecological perspective: Part I and II.
Families in society. Manuscript submitted for publication.

Groth, A. N. (1979). *Men who rape.* New York: Plenum Press.

Groth, A. N., & Burgess, A. W. (1977). Motivational intent in the sexual assault of children.
Criminal Justice and Behavior, 4(3), 253–263.

Kiell, N. (1988). *Freud without hindsight.* Madison, CT: International Universities Press.

Knopp, F. H. (1984). *Retraining adult sex offenders: Methods and models.* Syracuse, NY: Safer
Society Press.

Lanning, K. V. (1987). *Child molesters: A behavioral analysis.* Quantico, VA: National Center for
Missing and Exploited Children.

Main, M., Kaplan, N., & Cassidy, J. (1985). Security in infancy, childhood, and adulthood: A move to the level of representation. In I. Bretherton & E. Waters (Eds.), Growing points in attachment theory and research. *Monographs of the Society for Research in Child Development, 50*, 66–166.

Marshall, W. L., Hudson, S. M., & Hodkinson, S. (1993). The importance of attachment bonds in the development of juvenile sex offending. In H. E. Barbaree, W. L. Marshall, & S. M. Hudson (Eds.), *Juvenile sex offending.* New York: Guilford.

Mason, J. M. (1985). *The assault on truth: Freud's suppression of the seduction theory.* New York: Penguin Books.

National Task Force on Juvenile Sexual Offending. (1988). Preliminary report. *Juvenile and Family Court Journal, 39*(2).

National Task Force on Juvenile Sexual Offending. (1993). Revised report. *Juvenile and Family Court Journal, 44*(4).

Pavlov, L. (1927). *Conditioned reflexes.* Oxford: Clarendon Press.

Piaget, J. (1928). *Judgement and reasoning in the child.* London: Routledge & Kegan Paul.

Piaget, J. (1963). The attainment of invariants and reversible operations in the development of thinking. *Social Research, 30*, 283–299.

Prentky, R., Knight, R., Rosenberg, R., & Lee, A. (1989). A path-analytic approach to the validation of a taxonomic system for classifying child molesters. *Journal of Quantitative Criminology, 5*, 231–257.

Ryan, G. (1995). *Treatment of sexually abusive youth: The evolving consensus.* Paper presented at the International Experts Conference, Utrecht, Netherlands.

Ryan, G., Hagler, S., Short, S., & Eck, B. (1995). *Treatment for sexually abusive youth: Program description.* Working draft. Larkspur, CO: Griffith Center.

Ryan, G., Lindstrom, B., Knight, L., Arnold, L., Yager, J., Bilbrey, C., & Steele, B. (1993). *Treatment of sexual abuse in the context of whole life experience.* Paper presented at the Twenty-first Annual Child Abuse and Neglect Symposium, Keystone, CO.

Skinner, B. F. (1974). *About behaviorism.* New York: Knopf.

Steele, B. F. (1986). Lasting effects of childhood sexual abuse. *Child Abuse and Neglect: The International Journal, 10*(2), 283–291.

Strayhorn, J. (1988). *The competent child.* New York: Guilford Press.

Tardieu, A. (1878). *Etude médico-légale sur les attentats aux moeurs.* Paris.

Van der Kolk, B. (1986). *Psychological trauma.* Washington, DC: American Psychiatric Press.

Ward, T., Hudson, S., Marshall, W., & Siegert, R. (1995). Attachment style and intimacy deficits in sexual offenders. *Sexual Abuse: A Journal of Research and Treatment, 7*(4).

Weiner, I. B. (1964). On incest: A survey. *Exerpta Criminologica, 4*, 137–155.

Weissberg, M. (1982). *Dangerous secrets: Maladaptive responses to stress.* New York: Norton.

Yochelson, S., & Samenow, S. (1976). *The criminal personality* (Vol. 1). Northvale, NJ: Aronson.

Zaphiris, A. (1978). *Incest: The family with two known victims.* Denver: American Humane Association.

CHAPTER FOUR

SEXUAL DEVELOPMENT IN INFANCY AND CHILDHOOD

Floyd M. Martinson

Sexuality is seldom treated as a strong or healthy force in the positive develop-ment of a child's personality in the United States. We are not inclined to be-lieve that our children are sexual or that they should be sexual in any of their behaviors. Although it is difficult to generalize in our pluralistic society, there is typically no permission for normal child sexual experiences. Children are not taught to understand their sexual experiences or to anticipate sexual experiences as enjoyable. Rather, they are taught to be wary of most sexual experiences, both interpersonally and intrapsychically.

There are conflicting and contradictory expectations in American society con-cerning sexuality. Despite the inhibition of sexual knowledge and experience, we expect adolescents to develop a secure sexual identity in preparation for healthy adult relationships. We demand that adolescents develop a healthy sexual matu-rity before engaging in learning experiences that make that maturity possible (Gadpaille, 1975). Our society's confusing expectations contribute to dysfunctional sexual attitudes and behaviors.

In the protective paradigm (Lee, 1980) that we have generally accepted as the proper perspective for rearing children, we attempt to protect children from even knowing there is such a thing as sexuality. This protection, as traditionally carried out, has meant that the child is shielded from all adult and adolescent, and most childhood, sexual experience. There is no modeling on the part of adolescents or adults, sex talk in the presence of children is avoided, nonlabeling or mislabeling of sexual parts and activities occurs, no sexual experimentation with peers or siblings is allowed, and no age-appropriate sex education for younger children is sanctioned. North American children know the least about sexuality, received their sexual knowledge at older ages, and are least prepared for adult sexual experience when compared with other English-speaking and with Swedish children (Goldman & Goldman, 1982).

Children nevertheless have capacities for sexual experiences and interactions, and they do express sexual behavior in a variety of ways. An increased understanding of the child's sexual development may enable us to increase our awareness of the role that sexuality plays in both sexually abusive behaviors and the development of deviant arousal. It also contributes to an understanding of the impact of sexual victimization at various ages, the ability to identify problems related to dysfunctional sexual development, and early identification of sexually abusive attitudes, interests, and behaviors.

The sexual development of the child is complex, involving a number of factors. During its intrauterine period, the fetus exhibits sensory development that continues through the neonatal stage. The neonate is developing the capacity for intimacy through its interaction with its mother or other primary caregiver. During this period, the capacities of both tactile responsiveness and sensual interaction are enhanced. In the first year, the child exhibits increased interest in bodily exploration, as well as autoeroticism and the development of orgasmic abilities. In early childhood, there is increasing social interaction, especially with peers, that involves experimentation with sexual behaviors and intimacy. Gender roles and continued interactional sexual experimentation continue to develop through the preadolescent years, and during adolescence youth appear to learn sexual and intimate behaviors that enable them to function as adults in sexual encounters.

Each child's development is markedly influenced by the cultural norms and expectations, familial interactions and values, and the interpersonal experiences encountered. Organic capacities, cognitive development and integration, and intrapsychic influences further determine the rate and extent of development of the sexual capacity. There are no predictable biological-psychological stages that occur during the stages of growing up. There is no universal ontogeny; there are no inborn, normal stages in the sexual development of the child. There are, however, identifiable capacities and behaviors that appear to contribute to the child's sexual development.

The sensory capacity for erotic experience begins to emerge during the intrauterine development of the human organism. Eroticism, the condition of being physically or psychically aroused, excited, or motivated, is an integral part of human sexual functioning. The sources of the capacity and motivation for eroticism are both organic and social in nature, whether one is aroused toward oneself (autoeroticism) or by and toward another person, including experiences of desire, tenderness, and passionate affection for and with another (alloeroticism). The rate and extent of erotic capacities are markedly influenced by social experiences. The capacities for eroticism, begun during the embryonic stage, continue to emerge and develop through fetal, neonatal, and infantile stages given favorable conditions. There is a developmental erotic continuum.

Sensory Development in Utero

Although children do not normally have a sufficiently strong, compelling, inborn sex drive that will overcome all social obstacles to its expression, they do have a significant sensory capacity, especially tactile responsiveness. All senses can be involved in erotic excitation and satisfaction. For humans, touch is more intimately related to erotic arousal and activity leading to orgasm than are the other senses, such as smell or taste. The potential for sensory capacity for touch appears to begin its development early. The fetus is responsive to pressure and touch; at times the fetus appears to move intentionally for the sensual reason of making itself more comfortable in the uterus. Just as children have the capacity to develop a very robust appetite for sexual experience, including orgasm, the fetus may also be experienced in autostimulation before birth.

The intrauterine period of development is an active one for the sensory development and experience of the human organism. One of the earliest sensory systems to become functional in the embryonic stage is the skin (Montague, 1978). The skin enables the human organism to experience its environment.

The fetus is massaged with each movement of the mother as she carries on her daily activities. Stroking, massaging, and rocking of premature infants who have missed the stimulating activity in the womb have dramatic results: significant increases in body weight and improved neurological and bodily functioning. Without stimulation and activity, normal growth and maturation are hampered. The fetus is active in the womb because movement is absolutely essential to full human development, and perhaps because activity reduces tensions and increases pleasurable feelings.

The areas of cutaneous reflex are generalized over the body (Langworthy, 1933). Although the embryonic response to tactile stimulation appears reflexive, the fetus may also engage in purposeful autostimulation before birth. Habituation and perhaps even some sensate learning take place even before birth, as well as the early development of a system of tensional outlets. Genital erectile capacity is in functional readiness during the fetal period (Calderone, 1983), and some fetal genital play is possible.

The fetus also becomes acquainted with its extrauterine environment through hearing. It can hear the mother's heartbeat and other organic sounds, hear the rhythm and tone of conversations between the mother and others, and detect the difference between male and female voices (Pines, 1982). Since the mother's voice will be the one the fetus hears most regularly, if the rhythm, intensity, and timbre of that voice provide a pleasant experience, it may well be that the fetus is prosocially primed to a positive relationship with that mother as a neonate.

Development of Attachment and Sensory Responsiveness in the Neonate

The newborn infant continues to develop responsiveness to sensory stimulation through contact with the mother. Beginning with the initial moments of contact with the mother, the first social experiences become the basis for future patterns of communication and intimacy. The neonate is capable of beginning a bond with the mother immediately on birth in spite of its total inability to fend for itself. Klaus and Kennell (1976), who coined the term *maternal sensitivity period,* see this sensitive period in the first minutes and hours after birth as vital for parent-infant attachment and the "wellspring for all the infant's subsequent attachments" to other individuals.

Infants are capable of interactional behaviors in spite of being almost totally dependent on the mother or other primary caregiver for food, protection, and early interaction. With favorable early attention and stimulation, babies respond to attachment behaviors (fondling, caressing, kissing, gazing at, looking *en face,* talking to, and being held close) by forming an attachment relationship. Eye-to-eye contact is an especially significant aspect of initial mother-neonate interaction since neonates lack definitive vocal symbols. A high degree of eye-to-eye contact between mother and infant has been observed to lead to the infant's immediate cessation of crying and a stronger bond with the mother (Clark-Stewart, 1973). Vocal interaction occurs between the mother and the neonate during the first few days of life, and the neonate's motor behavior becomes entrained by and synchronized with the speech behavior of the mother. Synchrony is an important element in mother-infant interaction. Establishing mutual attention is generally only the first step in a whole series of behaviors beginning the patterns of communication (Honig, 1982) and learning.

The true locus of intimacy is the dyad. Because of neonates' dependency and immobility, their first social experience is by necessity within a dyad, usually with the mother. The earlier, the more, and the better the time mother and infant spend together, the more intimate their relationship becomes. Attachment and intimacy result from the consistency of this relationship.

Neonates' interactive resources are meager indeed. They engage in infant-parent interaction, but it is not symbolic interaction. Neonates' initial motivations are not socially acquired; rather, they are physiological and psychological givens. In this first experience with others, babies are at a zero point as far as symbolic meanings are concerned, but they nevertheless have energy, capacities, some inherent predispositions, and needs. The neonate's interpersonal competency begins development through interaction with the parents and is enhanced by the variety and complexity of those interactions.

Although neonates are totally incapable of fending for themselves, it is not accurate to assume that they are only passive and receptive. Neonates from the moment of birth have a relatively advanced sensory system (Harris, Cassel, & Bamborough, 1974). They appear to have a "capacity for curiosity," and their first impulse appears to be the desire to establish contact with the outside world (Kanner, 1939). As a general principle, neonates appear to have an "instinct to master" (Hendrick, 1942), to want to do what they are able to do, a basic psychobiological impulse or urge to experience and to control as large a segment of the outside world as is compatible with their very obvious locomotive limitations, and their limitation in the use of symbols. Neonates appear to derive pleasure by the affective use of those sensory, motor, and intellectual functions physiologically available to them. Healthy infants appear to possess an immediate desire to use each ego function and to perfect it as soon as it becomes physiologically possible. The whole body of impulse can be regarded as a yet undifferentiated desire for physical, emotional, and intellectual satisfaction (Martinson, 1973). Those who observe newborns are struck with the active part, the initiative, that infants show in the development of attachment to others.

As a result of her observations, Ainsworth (1964) hypothesized that it is largely through an infant's own activity that attachment is effected with the mother rather than through stimulation by the mother or through her satisfying the neonate's creature comfort needs. The early attachment may be defined as a unique relationship between two people that is specific and endures through time. Mother-infant bonding behaviors such as fondling, kissing, cuddling, and prolonged gazing are seen as the indicators of attachment (Klaus & Kennell, 1976). Such behaviors serve both to maintain contact and exhibit affection toward an individual.

Early infant-mother interaction patterns are established at a fundamental bodily level of giving and receiving. Each partner is biologically primed to develop reciprocal contacts and interaction patterns (Honig, 1982). The physical involvement is intense, because the caretaking interaction involves extensive physical intimacy. Physical handling that is gentle, firm, close, and relatively frequent has a beneficial effect on the infant's attachment and responsiveness to the mother, as well as on cognitive and motor development (Clark-Stewart, 1973). Infants who have been held tenderly and carefully tend later to respond positively to close bodily contact as well (Honig, 1982). It is the nonanxious mother who is most likely to hold her baby tenderly and carefully.

Rossi (1978) suggests that we might distinguish among degrees of intimacy according to the sense organs involved in the interaction. Her continuum begins at one end with ear and eye contact between two persons, which can range from casual, distant contact to very close contact. Other sensory interaction involves the senses of scent, touch, and taste and requires physical nearness. Most intimate on Rossi's continuum is contact involving sexual organs: erotic contact of mouth, tongue, breasts, and genitals (Levinger, 1977). Using these criteria of sense organs involved, infant-mother intimacy is extremely close. It involves ears, eyes, nose, hands, mouth, lips, tongue, breasts, and some genital contact in caregiving to the baby. Only extensive and prolonged genital contact is normally excluded from intimate infant-mother interchanges.

Intimate-sensate dyadic relationships can become so intense, consuming, and concentrated as to appear almost hypnotic; indeed, they are sometimes referred to as "hypnotic role taking" (Burr et al., 1979). Activities such as those involved in sucking at the breast for the infant and coitus for the adult fall into this category of hypnotic role taking. *Ecstasy* is another term interactionists use to characterize activity that is intense and perhaps erotic. In an ecstatic state, a person is so "carried away" by the interaction that there is usually a suspension of voluntary action. Such ecstatic, intimate experience occurs at least on occasion for both infant and mother, and it may even be orgasmic for both. Lewis (1965) reports having observed such ecstatic behavior in infants eight to ten months old when "in a moment of apparent delight, the child clasps the mother and begins rapid, rotating pelvic thrusts" at a frequency of about two per second and lasting ten to fifteen seconds. Thrusting behavior is most characteristic of adult coital behavior.

The most physiologically charged interactions between infant and mother occur during breast feeding. Sucking at the breast is primarily a food-getting response for the neonate. The reactions, particularly of older babies, to breast feeding show signs of eagerness, including rhythmic motions of hands, feet, fingers, and toes that may occur along with the rhythm of sucking. With an older baby there is more than mouth-breast stimulation. Suckling infants often put their fingers into the mother's mouth; she responds by smiling. Babies also pat the mother's breast while sucking or during breaks in feeding, pat her face, turn a cheek to be kissed, clasp her around the neck, lay a cheek on hers, hug, and bite (Hurlock, 1950). Such scenes can be observed in endless variation in a mother-child interchange. The sensuous enjoyment of infant feeding is likely to increase the baby's desire to suckle frequently and fully, thus also stimulating the mother's secretion of milk. After feeding there is likely to be a relaxation that some observers characterize as being akin to that of the relaxation that occurs with the conclusion of satisfactory coitus among adults (Newton & Newton, 1967).

The physiological responses to coitus and lactation are closely allied. Uterine contractions occur during suckling and during sexual excitement; nipple erection occurs during both.

Emotions aroused by sexual contact with an adult partner and breast feeding of an infant both involve skin changes as well. Excitement causes marked vascular changes in the skin, and the breast-feeding act raises body temperature as measured in the submammary and mammary skin areas (Newton & Newton, 1967). There is a great increase in maternal touching during suckling, in many cases with the hand that is holding the baby while the free hand is used to prevent the breast from occluding the baby's nostrils (Dunn & Richards, 1977).

The sensory and sexual responses of infant and mother to their stimulating dyadic experiences appear to be almost wholly reflexive in nature, that is, neither planned nor intended. Although society generally disapproves of or is generally ambivalent about intimacy, it approves of intimate infant-mother interaction. Mothers expect that this interaction should be intimate and sensual. Infants are supposed to be stimulated, cuddled, fondled, and aroused by the mother from the moment of birth. Intimacy even at ecstatic and hypnotic levels is possible in physiologically and emotionally charged infant-parent interaction.

Developmental studies suggest that infants' emotional maturation depends on such stimulation. If one were to design an infant socialization model that was designed to lead to the development of full erotic potential and eventual capacity for intimacy, one could hardly improve on the model currently in vogue and recommended for the care of infants during the first year of life in the United States. Clinical studies credit insufficient physical contact between infant and parent as the cause of later inability to form attachments. It is suggested that if sexual identification is to develop in a child, parental attachments must evoke and encourage corresponding responses from the infant. On the other hand, case studies attest to the disastrous consequences of parental overstimulation and continued arousal, suggesting that the enactment of diffuse sexual actions that might bind dependency patterns is harmful.

Most activities associated with nurturance and hygienic care of neonates is intimate, and sexual as well, in that it involves contact with sensitive organs: lip, mouth, anus, and genitals. These activities include breast feeding, toilet training, diapering, and bathing. Such activities may not be purposely sensual or sexual so far as the parent or caretaker is concerned. Mothers generally do not attribute erotic motives to their neonate, even to an infant son who has erections. Roberts

(Roberts, Kline, & Gagnon, 1978) found that most mothers and fathers were thoroughly relaxed about self-stimulation, for instance, infants' touching their genitals, and most often described such self-exploration as "natural."

Bodily Exploration and Autoeroticism in the First Year of Life

During the first year of life, there is progression in infants' discovery of their body and manual exploration of parts of the body, including the genitals. By the age of five to six months, many infants have found their ears and appear to derive satisfaction from pulling them or sticking their fingers in them, although after six months, this behavior gradually diminishes (Levine, 1957). Most boys in one study (Galenson & Riophe, 1974) began genital play at six or seven months, and most girls began at ten or eleven months. This type of genital play involves fingering, simple pleasurable handling, and random exploration. Girls' genital play tended to disappear within a few weeks of onset, but boys continued casual play, adding visual and tactile exploration of the genitals at about eleven or twelve months. Large-muscle control is sufficiently coordinated as early as six months for infants to develop rocking behavior. An infant who is able to sit up may engage in many types of rocking, all of which appear to bring the infant a great deal of satisfaction. Some infants sit and sway rhythmically, some lift the trunk and pelvis and bounce up and down off the surface on which they are sitting, and some combine these movements. Elevating to hands and knees and rocking forward and backward appears to be the most frequent type of rocking and is not uncommon as early as six to twelve months (Levine, 1957).

Many infants form a pattern of rocking that is likely to be much more intensely rhythmic and repeated than is manual genital play. Infants may discover the pleasure of rhythmic genital sensation through rocking activity before they have adequate hand and arm control to masturbate. Rocking appears more satisfying, for infants engaged in manual genital play may be fairly easily distracted, in contrast to infants who rock with great vigor and tension and are not easily distracted. The majority of rockers engage in the activity before going to sleep and immediately on rising. Many cease the rocking behavior before they are eighteen months to two years old, but a few continue to age three or later (Levine, 1957).

There is an important distinction between genital play and masturbation in infancy. Infants in the first year of life generally are not capable of the direct volitional behavior required for the behavior pattern that we call the masturbatory act. Some pleasurable experience may result simply from pressing the thighs together, especially for girls. The greatest autoerotic satisfaction, and certainly the occurrence of orgasm, is dependent to a large extent on manipulations that are rhythmic and repeated. But rhythmic manipulation with the hand does not appear to occur until children are approximately two and a half to three years old, likely because small-muscle control is not sufficiently well developed (Levine, 1957). Some infants under one year old have the hand and muscle coordination necessary to masturbate and do stimulate themselves in that way. Kinsey, Pomeroy, and Martin (1948) reports one record of a seven-month-old infant and five infants under one year who were observed to masturbate. Nevertheless, the average infant is not innately motivated and lacks the muscular capacity for the degree of self-stimulation necessary to produce orgasm.

Do most infants have the physiological capacity for genital response and satisfaction? We know that erection in the male baby and vaginal lubrication in the female baby are present from birth. It is reported that during sleep, spontaneous erection or vaginal lubrication occurs every eighty to ninety minutes throughout the entire life span, but only erections in males have been observed and recorded in any systematic way (Sears, Maccoby, & Levine, 1957). In a study of nine male babies ages three to twenty weeks, Halverson (1938) noted that tumescence was exhibited at least once daily by seven of the nine. Tumescence was often accompanied by restlessness, fretting, crying, and stretching and flexing the limbs stiffly. Following the detumescence, the babies appeared to be more playful and relaxed. As early as 1883, Pouillet reported that if the edge of an infant's foreskin was tickled with a feather, the penis would swell and become erect, and the infant would grab at it with his hand. Kinsey et al. (1948, 1953) reported that orgasm is not at all rare among preadolescent boys or girls and has been observed in boys of every age from five months to adolescence and in girl infants from four months old.

Kinsey, Pomeroy, and Martin (1948) described stimulation to orgasm in nine male infants under one year of age as a series of gradual physiologic changes: the development of rhythmic body movements with distinct penis throbs and pelvic thrusts; an obvious change in sensory capacities; a final tension of muscles, especially of the abdomen, hips, and back; a sudden release with convulsions, including rhythmic anal contractions; followed by the disappearance of all symptoms. A fretful baby quiets under the initial stimulation, is distracted from other activities, begins rhythmic pelvic thrusts, becomes tense as climax approaches, and is thrown into convulsive action, often with violent arm and leg movements and sometimes with weeping at the moment of climax. After climax the child loses erection quickly and subsides into the calm and peace that typically follows adult orgasm. Thirty-two percent of boys two to twelve months old were able to reach climax. One boy of eleven months had been stimulated to ten climaxes in an hour, and another of the same age had fourteen climaxes in thirty-eight minutes, although for most there is some time required before erection could be induced again following climax. Halverson (1938) reviewed the findings and concluded that penile erection in infants can be a purely reflexive response resulting from mechanical stimulation.

Male infants have the capacity for sexual response. The stimulus for penile erection can be internal or external. A full bladder or a full bowel can initiate the reflexes; after evacuation, the erection slowly subsides. Strong sucking or frustration in attempting to get nourishment can initiate the same penile reflexive response. When the sucking stops or the milk is easily attained, the erection often subsides. Such erections, unlike the ones induced by external stimulation, are less likely to be accompanied by signs of intense pleasure followed by relaxation (Sears, Maccoby, & Levine, 1957). According to Spitz and Wolf (1946), autoerotic activity, that is, genital play, in the first eighteen months of life is a reliable indicator of the adequacy or inadequacy of parenting. They found that when the relationship between mother and infant was optimal, genital play on the part of the infant was present in all cases.

During the first year of life there are significant events that contribute to the child's erotic, sexual capacity: an attachment or bond that becomes the basis for later capacity for intimacy; an appreciation of and practice in the aspects of physical and emotional attachment and intimacy (hugging, kissing, clutching, petting, gazing, vocalization, stroking, sucking, and biting); sensory-erotic intimacy and response comparable to that of optimal sensory-erotic experience in adult love-making, but without the specific and direct genital stimulation and response; an awareness of one's body, including genitals, and the development of rhythmic, pleasure-inducing behaviors; and the capacity for orgasmic response, although the threshold of genital orgasm is generally too high to result from optimal infant-mother intimate behaviors and requires stimulation by another to occur.

Young Children

Young children continue to develop erotic capacity, in part through more purposeful autoerotic behaviors. They exhibit a capacity to fantasize and begin involvement in intimate relationships with others. From their observations, Riophe and Galenson (1981) hypothesize an endogenously rooted early genital phase that emerges early in the second year of life. In the child's interaction with self and others, the exploration of genitalia becomes increasingly influential in organizing the infant's development, especially in forming the basic core of sexual identity. It is different from the less organized genital awareness of infancy because it appears to occur in a regular developmental sequence, is characterized by psychological awareness of the genitals, and affects all areas of functioning.

Galenson and Riophe (1974) observed that genital manipulation at thirteen to sixteen months is accompanied by distinct signs of pleasure, including giggling and smiling, visual and tactile attention to the genital area, and definite affectionate gestures and behavioral signs of feeling directed toward other people. In boys, masturbation began at fifteen to sixteen months, whereas in girls a pattern of intermittent genital play was noted. Levine (1957) observes that most of the sexual activity at this young age remains genital play rather than true masturbation. He reports that most children, even through twenty-four to thirty-six months, indulge in genital play with a certain degree of satisfaction, but in most cases without any apparent emotional excitement or increased stimulation. During self-stimulation in the second year of life, both boys and girls frequently make affectionate gestures toward the mother and touch the mother's body during or subsequent to genital self-stimulation (Riophe & Galenson, 1981).

Masturbation appears to be a common experience in the development of normal infants and children and has long been recognized as nearly universal. At three years old, most boys masturbate manually by rubbing the penis or by wrapping the fingers around the erect penis and moving the hand. Other boys lie on their stomachs on a flat surface and writhe while engaged in other activities such as watching television. Some raise themselves slightly and propel themselves forward and backward, rubbing the genitals against the leg of a chair or other object, and derive satisfaction in that way. In girls at three years old, there are manifold varieties of masturbation: placing a soft toy or blanket between the legs in the region of the genitals and wriggling the body, manually titillating the clitoris, and, less frequently, inserting objects in the vagina (Levine, 1957). Following masturbation that leads to orgasm, children relax and sometimes go to sleep, although a few appear to be stimulated by the activity.

Masturbation, often observed among preschool-aged children (Dillon, 1934), is recognized as a tension reliever. It unquestionably increases during periods of emotional tension, but three-year-old children have also been observed to masturbate as an expression of delight when they are not tired, stressed, or unhappy (Levine, 1957).

The question is appropriately raised concerning the extent of eroticization in the young child. Do they see others as objects of sensory and sexual attention? Do they fantasize sexually? Within every person there is a constellation of thoughts, images, wishes, and fears that differ greatly in the degree to which they are fantastic to the individual (Pitcher & Prelinger, 1963). At whatever age fantasizing first occurs, it is the case that the fantasy life of an inexperienced person (a child) will not be as rich in content or as sexually explicit as will that of an experienced adult. In adolescence, and especially in adulthood, the sexual life is informed and organized by a store of experiences, actual and vicarious. The kind and content of prior sexual experiences influence, produce, and structure subsequent experiences of a sexual nature.

It is assumed that sometime in the first year, before beginning to speak, the infant probably fantasizes, for understanding precedes speech (Gardner, 1969). Riophe and Galenson (1981) observed that the affectionate touch of the mother during the infant's genital self-stimulation begins to disappear after a few weeks and is replaced by an "inward gaze and a self-absorbed look. This development would seem to indicate that a fantasy feeling state had now become a regular component of the genital self-stimulation and that this new type of genital activity is true masturbation."

Since little evidence can be collected until the child is old enough to talk, several studies relate to the fantasy content of children aged two years and older. Ames (1966) studied the themes or topics in stories told by two- and three-year-old children. He found that 60 percent of the boys and 68 percent of the girls had themes of violence. Among the other themes reported were food and eating, sleep, good and bad, possible sibling rivalry, possible castration, and reproduction. None of the group of two-year-olds described stories overtly concerning anal activities. Pitcher and Prelinger (1963) analyzed stories of children two to five years old and identified eight main themes: aggression, death, hurt or misfortune, morality, nutrition, dress, sociability, and crying. With boys, aggression tended to be much more violent than with girls, characterized by the two-year-olds in relationship to concerns about violation of body intactness, that is, some part of the body is broken or severed. This theme is almost absent in the stories of the three-year-olds.

What of themes that relate to the sensory and sexual experiences of life, such as intimacy, kindness, and eroticism? Ames (1966) found that although kind and friendly stories were uncommon at any age, they occurred most commonly at two and three years. Pitcher and Prelinger (1963) found that girls referred to love, courtship, and marriage, and they were more likely than the boys to express emotion and affect around a parental figure, particularly the mother. These authors found that the younger children appeared at times to make quite a transparent reference to the issue of pregnancy in their stories, but the connections of the various details tended commonly to be illogical or poorly motivated. They also observed that it was rare that the phenomenon of excitement and of aggression between a man and woman took place in the stories. A major flaw in these studies may be that American children learn early that they must not talk about sex, and that may be why the subject does not appear in their stories.

One of the most striking findings of Conn and Kanner's (1947) play interview study of two hundred children aged four to fourteen was the inability or unwillingness of the children to use words referring to sex. In the play interviews, Conn and Kanner found that sexual fantasies accompanying masturbation—

imagining sight or touch of genitals, buttocks, or breasts and thoughts of coitus—were reported by a very small number of boys below age nine and by no girls of any age. For instance, in play interviews, the children even as young as four years old spoke up unhesitatingly and without embarrassment of the boy's "thing" and the girl's "thing," but other distinctions had something secret or hidden about them. It was not so much that they did not know names for the genitals—in fact, these children used no fewer than sixty-one different names—but that they regarded the names as bad, nasty, or dirty and hence not to be uttered. Children with such inhibitions would be unlikely to report stories they have made up about sex or sexual activity.

That children who had more information available to them would likely fantasize about sex is evident in their questions. In Hattendorf's (1932) collection of sex questions, preschoolers asked the most questions (49.1 percent), those from six to ten asked 40.1 percent of the questions, and those ten to fourteen asked only 16.8 percent. The questions asked most frequently concerned the origin of babies, the coming of another baby, physical differences, organs and functions of the body, the process of birth, relation of the father to reproduction, intrauterine growth, and marriage. Apparently children want to know about these matters.

Two- to three-year-olds exhibit intimate involvement with others. Freud (1938) observed that children from three to five years old were capable of "evincing a very strong object selection which is accompanied by strong affect," but it can occur earlier than that. Kinsey, Pomeroy, Martin, and Gebhard's (1953) interviews with a small sample of two-year-olds and their mothers reveal a good deal of cuddling and kissing of parents and others by both boys and girls. Infants who are securely attached to a parent are compliant and cooperative by twenty-one months. Schvaneveldt, Frye, and Ostler (1970) report that children as young as three years old, when asked what "good" and "bad" parents do, report that good mothers kiss you and bad mothers do not, and a good father is one who kisses and hugs you and a bad father is one who is not nice to you.

By ages three to four, children are beginning to be socialized away from body contact with self as well as with others (Lewis, 1958). Children begin early to sense consciously that touching patterns (as part of their tactile communication system with their parents) have gradually become nonreciprocating. Blackman (1980) has shown that at least by the age of four, children no longer have permission to touch their parents. Beyond the age of infancy, it becomes quite apparent that parents hold gender-specific attitudes about intimacy and affectionate relationships with their children. There are a number of distinctions as to what body parts can be touched in interacting based on the gender of the child and the gender of the parent. "Too much" touching, especially among boys, causes discomfort for many parents (Roberts, Kline, & Gagnon 1978).

Even by eighteen to twenty-four months, infants have been observed to display a variety of forms of direct prosocial activity, such as helping and comforting peers, siblings, and parents (Johnson, 1982). Gesell and Ilg (1946) indicate that children three and a half years old are interested in marriage and marrying and may propose to their parents and others, of either sex. They use the expression "I love" frequently. Pitcher and Prelinger (1963) found that in their stories, the girls referred to love, courtship, and marriage. Children of this age begin to show an interest in babies and want to have one in their family. They like to look at and touch adults, especially mothers, and babies.

Children up to three years of age may show no marked distinction between sexes in play with peers. Some of the play with peers may be sexual if several children of this age are left together unsupervised with nothing else that interests them more. Their interest in sex play is episodic (Ilg & Ames, 1955). Spiro (1958) found that heterosexual behaviors between children of this age included simple embrace as its most common expression, followed in frequency by stroking and caressing, kissing, and touching the genitals. Bell (1902) divided manifestations of "the emotion of love between the sexes" into two stages. The first stage included children from three to eight years old and was characterized by "hugging, kissing, lifting each other, scuffling, sitting close to each other, confessions to each other and excluding others, grief at being separated, giving of gifts, extending courtesies to each other that are withheld from others, making sacrifices such as giving up desired things or foregoing pleasures, jealousies, etc." Moll (1913) also divided childhood into two phases, the first of which ends at age seven. This first phase is characterized by a process tending toward bodily and mental approximations to another individual but is more social (that is, less sexual) than the period from eight years old and up. Young children appear to prefer sex play with peers rather than with persons of older ages (Constantine & Martinson, 1981). It is a way of relating to others and can be enjoyable, providing coercion is not used. Child development experts generally believe that peer sex play is normal and is generally a harmless growing-up experience.

Preadolescence

Preadolescence, defined here as the ages from eight through twelve, is a period of anticipation and growth. This has long been considered a period of latency, during which sexual activity and interest is diminished, but it now appears that this concept has been overstressed. Sexual awakening—the beginning awareness of the self as a sexual being and of the opposite sex as potential affectional and erotic partners—is very real for many preadolescents. The sexual, psychological, and social changes that begin during these years and mature later are essential to the transition to full adult sexual functioning. Even in a sexually restrictive society such as ours, children go through stages of heterosexual involvement, in both fantasy and actuality, during the preadolescent years. Sexual-erotic responses and encounters occur more commonly than previously acknowledged.

Many children in preadolescence experience sexual awakening as their physiological sexual development occurs. The biological sexual changes—appearance of pubic hair, development of breasts, wet dreams, and so on—can be awesome to the child, who is often not sure how to react to such phenomena. Biological puberty, announced by the beginning of menarche in girls and by the capacity for ejaculation in boys, begins between the ages of eight and fifteen. Sexual development varies in timing and rate for each child and is different for boys and girls.

Children go through stages of heterosexual involvement in relationships that may not be characterized by overtly sexual behavior. In some communities, children begin these stages in preadolescence or earlier; in others they may begin in puberty or later. The youngsters begin to form attachments, or "crushes," on persons outside the family. The love feeling is expressed to the other person in a form that depends on the youngster's age, sexual and social maturity, and the permissiveness of the adults who supervise the child's behavior. It may appear in the form of roughhouse love play (hitting a boy, pulling a girl's hair), writing notes, inviting the other to a party, or simply walking home together. If the other person responds to this attention, the two may enter into the first of what often becomes, through adolescence, a series of close relationships with peers of the opposite sex. They also provide a set of learning experiences, such as learning how to kiss, how to dance, how to talk to a person of the opposite sex, as well as how to fondle and caress. The process of learning these skills is often exciting and dramatic, but it can also be painful and embarrassing.

A U.S. Office of Education Survey conducted in 1958 supports the observation that boys and girls do not appear to feel a need to separate from each other during preadolescence. In most schools, some dating begins as early as the fourth grade, and youth in grades four through six frequently asked for activities that would allow both boys and girls to participate. Boys groomed themselves (some beginning in the fourth grade), carried a comb and used it, washed their hands voluntarily, and occasionally wore a tie. Girls wore lipstick and nail polish and groomed their hair. A few children wore "going steady" rings. Broderick and Fowler's (1961) studies revealed that the majority of children in each primary grade claimed to have a sweetheart, and most of these children expected reciprocation. In the fifth grade, nearly 45 percent of the boys and 36 percent of the girls claimed to have had dating experience. By the seventh grade, nearly 70 percent of the boys and 53 percent of the girls claimed to have had at least one date. Some experience with kissing is common at these ages.

Broderick and Fowler (1961), and later Ruppel (1979), reported a pyramidally structured set of stages of social heterosexual maturation. This more-or-less orderly pattern or progression is discernible during the preadolescent years, and success or failure in each step appears to have consequences for more advanced stages of heterosexual development. Each stage is not an absolute prerequisite to the next, but the stages are closely interrelated. The beginning point seems to be the child's attitude, with the most advanced stage for preadolescents being going out on a date. The steps or stages they delineated in the process of heterosexual development are desire to marry someone, having a certain girlfriend or boyfriend, having been in love, preferring a companion of the opposite sex over one of the same sex or no companion at all when going to a movie, and having begun to date. There has been a marked trend toward greater heterosexual experience of preadolescents with their peers in the United States, as compared with studies in the 1920s and 1930s, which demonstrated that preadolescent boys were generally disinterested in sex and only covertly interested in girls.

Masturbation is much more common in preadolescent boys than is heterosexual experience. The incidence is not precisely known, although Ramsey's (1943) research indicates that masturbation occurs at some time in the sexual histories of nearly all males; 75 percent reported their first experience as occurring between the ages of ten and sixteen. In Ramsey's sample, 14 percent of eight-year-olds reported having masturbated, as did 23 percent of those nine years old, 29 percent of those ten years old, 54 percent of those eleven years old, 73 percent of those twelve years old, 85 percent of those thirteen years old, 95 percent of those fourteen years old, and 98 percent of those fifteen years old. Boys often learn of masturbation from each other; for girls masturbation may be less common, or may be less often self-reported to investigators.

Erection occurs more quickly in preadolescent boys than it does in adult males, and the capacity to achieve repeated orgasms in limited periods of time exceeds the corresponding capacity of teenage boys, who in turn are more capable of repeated orgasms than adult males are. The speed with which preadolescent males reach climax varies considerably, as it does in adult males. Ramsey (1943) found a wide variation in the erotic responsiveness of each preadolescent boy in his study. The following items are arranged in declining order based on the ratings as stimulants by the group as a whole: sex conversation, female nudity, obscene pictures, motion pictures, daydreams, burlesque or stage shows, nude art, motion when riding, literature, own body, male nudity, dancing, and music.

About 50 percent of the boys in Ramsey's study reported erections resulting from some type of nonerotic stimulus as well. The situation in which nonerotic responses occurred usually involved elements of fear, excitement, or other emotional experiences. The items reported as nonerotic stimuli included carnival rides, war motion pictures, being late to school, reciting before class, fast rides, playing a musical solo, band music, and fear of punishment. These responses were most frequently reported in boys aged ten, eleven, and twelve.

First experiments with copulation are not unusual between the ages of ten and fourteen. According to Kinsey, Pomeroy, and Martin (1948), by age twelve, approximately one boy in every four or five has at least tried to copulate with a female, and more than 10 percent of preadolescent boys experience their first ejaculation in connection with heterosexual intercourse. Kinsey's data on the active incidence for each year show that for boys who later attend college, heterosexual play of all kinds dropped off after about age ten, presumably in response to a redefinition of the meaning of this type of behavior. But among boys who did not finish high school, there was reportedly little withdrawal; rather, heterosexual activity continued at a high level through preadolescence and into adolescence.

Broderick and Fowler (1961) found some racial differences in the pattern of heterosexual development, with the most striking differences between black and white children noted during the preadolescence ages of ten and thirteen. At these ages, the white children showed the traditional pattern, with girls far more romantically oriented than boys, although at about the same level in terms of heterosexual interaction. Black boys, however, did not have the heterosexual reserve of the white boys and exhibited a higher level of heterosexual interaction at ages twelve and thirteen than did black girls.

The incidence of preadolescent heterosexual sex play at particular ages appears to be highest for girls in the younger years of preadolescence rather than the older. Some 8 percent of the females in the Kinsey, Pomeroy, Martin, and Gebhard (1953) sample recalled heterosexual play at ages five and seven, but fewer recalled it at later years of preadolescence, and only 3 percent reported having sex play just before pubescence. Few of the girls seemed to have developed any pattern of frequent or regular sexual activity. (Again, it is not possible to know to what extent girls might be reticent to self-report these behaviors.) Retrospective reports of adults appear to indicate more female activity in childhood than is reported in interviews with children (Ryan, Miyoshi, Metzner, Krugman, & Fryer, 1996). One girl for every seven boys reported having heterosexual play near the approach of adolescence. At each age of preadolescence, prepubertal boys report more sexual activity of every kind than do girls (Broderick & Fowler, 1961).

The marked differences in reported incidence of heterosexual sex play for boys and girls just prior to puberty may depend in part on the increased restraints that are placed on girls by their parents as the girls approach puberty—restraints that girls often resent after a carefree childhood (Martinson, 1973). Additionally the female subculture does not advocate sexual activity for girls as the male subculture does for boys.

Recent studies by Friedrich and others (1992) and Gil and Cavanagh-Johnson (1993) report on parental observations of children's sexual behaviors and confirm that children continue to engage in both autoerotic behaviors and sexual interactions with peers throughout childhood. Girls may be somewhat more active than in previous generations, although it is not possible to separate changes such as less secrecy and less parental denial from actual changes in behavior. Some differences seem likely in the light of the much greater exposure of children to sexual stimuli in the culture when comparing studies from the 1940s, 1960s, and 1980s; however, it is apparent that children have always been sexual and continue to be sexual. In some ways, it may be more surprising to note that the differences are not greater than they appear to be despite differing norms and exposure. This may provide some evidence that childhood sexuality is primarily affected by internal developmental processes.

In societies where children are permitted to do so, they increase rather than decrease their sexual activities during preadolescence. Sexual encounters first include genital autostimulation and mutual masturbation with the same and the opposite sex, but with increasing age, they are characterized more and more by attempts at heterosexual intercourse. By the time children reach puberty in sexually permissive societies, their expressions of sexuality consist predominantly of the accepted adult form of heterosexual intercourse, and they will continue to follow this pattern throughout their sexually active years of life (Ford & Beach, 1951).

Eroticization of Children

Child-parent intimate interactions in the United States are heavily circumscribed by social norms. In early infancy, mother-infant interaction is close, intimate, permissive, and highly sensual; society accepts that. As the child grows, the relationship moves further along the continuum toward role- and gender-based relationships (Douvan, 1977), and the parent represents a more demanding authoritative structure. The habits of sensory and sexual interaction are left behind, and the child is not expected to engage in these behaviors until later in life.

Although we do not yet have societal agreement about what constitutes age-appropriate child sexual behavior, we do have a universal norm that infants and children should not be sexually abused. It is generally agreed that adult and child sexual involvement is fraught with the greatest dangers for the child. The possibility of full eroticization of the relationship between a parent and child is great given the interactive opportunity and emotional access to each other (Rosenfeld, 1976; Rorty, 1972). Although intimacy at ecstatic and hypnotic levels is possible in child-parent encounters, it may also occur in erotically charged parent-child encounters. Sexual stimulation such as fondling, caressing, and masturbation are more common in erotic parent-child encounters; physical involvement to the point of coitus and the use of physical force are less common (Constantine & Martinson, 1981).

Erotic interactions that are seductive, exploitative, coercive, or manipulative and serve to use the child's sexual developmental behavior to meet the parent's needs have negative ramifications for a child.

Finkelhor (1978), in concentrating on the sexual dimension of family intimacy and affection, categorized families as sex positive and sex negative, and high-sexualized and low-sexualized. Family sexuality has at least three dimensions according to Finkelhor: a family's attitude toward sexuality (family culture), the actual eroticization of family relationships, and the family's respect for personal boundaries. In sex-positive families, children receive accurate information about sex, are given positive attitudes about their bodies, and are shown physical affection. In sex-negative families, sex and discussions about sex are loaded with anxiety and taboos. In high-sexualized families, members use one another as objects in their role playing. Each member tries to test out his or her powers of attraction and adequacy on the others. Low-sexualized families discourage sexual role playing and posturing from occurring inside the family. Regarding personal boundaries, one interpretation of clear boundaries is a family in which the privacy of each family member is respected. In such families, there is likely to be a clear differentiation of what the sex roles are between adults and children. In families with poor personal boundaries, family members intrude on one another, and child sexuality is not clearly distinguished from adult sexuality.

Unless eroticized by an older person, most children are more exploratory than goal (orgasm) oriented. Being affectionate is not the same as being eroticized, and being eroticized is not a pathology in and of itself. An erotic activity can have either adaptive or maladaptive potential, "depending on the child's flexibility and appreciation of reality" (Yates, 1978).

Cases of premature erotic awakening clearly support the appetitional theory of sexual motivation, that is, that motives are learned in association with affective experience. This can bring on early eroticization. Once true arousal has occurred, a host of acts may serve as sexual stimuli to the child. Some eroticized children calm themselves by masturbating in private; others make inappropriate advances toward others (Yates, 1978). Many prematurely awakened children are uncommonly erotic, easily aroused, highly sexually motivated, and readily orgasmic. They are easily aroused by a variety of circumstances and may not be able to discriminate erotic from nonerotic relationships. Being readily orgasmic, they can also maintain a high level of arousal without orgasm. They often appear to find sexual activity eminently pleasurable. "In fact, erotic expressions may be so gratifying that it is difficult to find comparable rewards to reinforce socially acceptable behavior" (Yates, 1978).

Many, but not all, eroticized children also demonstrate problems, such as anxiety, depression, underachievement, somatic complaints, and self-defeating behavior patterns. However, the eroticization process may be independent of these emotional disturbances. Not every child is severely traumatized by early sexual encounters with parents or with others. Constantine and Martinson's (1981) study concluded, "The more negative outcomes are associated with ignorance of sexuality; with negative attitudes towards sex; with tense situations; with force, brutality, or coercion; or with unsupportive, uncommunicative, or judgmental adult reactions."

Early erotic pleasure by itself does not damage the child. From a theoretical standpoint, it is clear that a major consequence of overt sexual experience is an increase in the specificity of acts that the child learns to perform in satisfying sexual needs. We would also expect an increase in desire to perform sexual acts and a greater degree of frustration when the acts are prevented from occurring (Sears, Maccoby, & Levine, 1957). Early eroticized sexual experiences appear to lead to activity, not latency. From a developmental perspective, a competency may be learned at a teachable moment, even though the experience or the competency may be judged morally and legally wrong.

That infants and small children have the physiological capacity for sexual response, that they are curious about their bodies and the bodies of others, and that they are attracted to intimate interaction with others have been established. With modeling, encouragement, and education, there appears to be no need for a cessation of sensory and sexual activity from first discovery through childhood. The capacity for sexual response is very much shaped by experience; thus, parents have the potential to help their children learn from their experiences to develop healthy sexual functioning later in life.

References

Ainsworth, M. D. (1964). Patterns of attachment behavior shown by the infant in interaction with his mother. *Merrill-Palmer Quarterly, 10,* 51–58.

Ames, L. B. (1966). Children's stories. *Genetic Psychology Monographs, 73,* 337–396.

Bell, S. (1902). A preliminary study of the emotion of love between the sexes. *American Journal of Psychology, 12,* 325–354.

Blackman, N. (1980). Pleasure and touching: Their significance in the development of the preschool child—An exploratory study. *Childhood and Sexuality: Proceedings of the International Symposium 1980,* 175–202.

Broderick, C. B., & Fowler, S. E. (1961). New patterns of relationships between the sexes among pre-adolescents. *Marriage and Family Living, 23,* 27–30.

Calderone, M. (1983, May–June). Fetal erection and its message to us. *Sex Education and Information Council of the United States* (Report).

Clark-Stewart, K. A. (1973). Interactions between mothers and young children: Characteristics and consequences. *Monographs of the Society for Research in Child Development, 38* (6–7, Serial No. 153).

Conn, A. & Kanner, L. (1947). In L. Kanner (Ed.), *Child Psychiatry* (5th ed.). Springfield, IL: Thomas.

Constantine, L. L., & Martinson, F. M. (1981). *Children and sex: New findings, new perspectives.* Boston: Little, Brown.

Dillon, M. S. (1934). Attitudes in children toward their own bodies and those of other children. *Child Development, 5,* 165–167.

Douvan, E. (1977). Interpersonal relations: Some questions and observations. In G. Levinger & H. L. Raush (Eds.), *Close relationships: Perspectives on the meaning of intimacy* (pp. 17–32). Amherst: University of Massachusetts Press.

Dunn, J. B., & Richards, M. P. M. (1977). Observations on the developing relationship between mother and baby in the neonatal period. In H. R. Schaffer (Ed.), *Studies in mother-infant interaction* (pp. 427–455). London: Academic Press.

Finkelhor, D. (1978).Psychological culture and family factors in incest and family sexual abuse. *Journal of Marriage and the Family, 4,* 41–49.

Ford, C. S., & Beach, F. A. (1951). *Patterns of sexual behaviors.* New York: HarperCollins.

Friedrich, W., Grambsch, P., Damon, L., Koverola, C., Wolfe, V., Hewitt, S., Lang, R., & Broughton, D. (1992). The Child Sexual Behavior Inventory: Normative and clinical comparison. *Psychological Assessment, 4*(3), 303–311.

Freud, S. (1938). *The basic writings of Sigmund Freud* (A. A. Brill, Trans. and Ed.). New York: Modern Library.

Gadpaille, W. J. (1975). Adolescent sexuality—A challenge to psychiatrists. *Journal of American Academy of Psychoanalysis, 3*(2), 163–177.

Galenson, E., & Riophe, H. (1974). The emergence of genital awareness during the second year of life. In R. C. Friedman, R. M. Richart, & R. L. Van de Wiele (Eds.), *Sex differences in behavior* (pp. 223–223). New York: Wiley.

Gardner, R. A. (1969). Sexual fantasies in childhood. *Medical Aspects of Human Sexuality, 3,* 121, 125, 127–128, 132–134.

Gesell, A., & Ilg, F. (1946). *The child from five to ten.* New York: HarperCollins.

Gil, E., & Cavanagh-Johnson, T. (1993). *Sexualized children.* Rockville, MD: Launch Press.

Goldman, R. I., & Goldman, L. D. G. (1982). *Children's sexual thinking.* London: Routledge and Kegan Paul.

Halverson, H. M. (1938). Genital and sphincter behavior of the male infant. *Journal of Genetic Psychology, 56,* 383–388.

Harris, P. L., Cassel, T. Z., & Bamborough, P. (1974). Tracking by young infants. *British Journal of Psychology, 65*(3), 345–349.

Hattendorf, K. W. (1932). A study of the questions of young children concerning sex: A phase of an experimental approach to parent education. *Journal of Social Psychology, 3,* 37–65.

Hendrick, I. (1942). Instinct and the ego during infancy. *Psychoanalytic Quarterly, 11,* 33–58.

Honig, A. S. (1982). Prosocial development in children. *Young Children, 37,* 51–62.

Hurlock, E. B. (1950). *Child development.* New York: McGraw-Hill.

Ilg, F. L., & Ames, L. B. (1955). *Child behavior.* New York: Dell.

Johnson, D. B. (1982). Altruistic behavior and the development of the self in infants. *Merrill-Palmer Quarterly, 28,* 379–388.

Kanner, L. (1939). Infantile sexuality. *Journal of Pediatrics, 4,* 583–608.

Kinsey, A. C., Pomeroy, W. B., & Martin, C. E. (1948). *Sexual behavior in the human male.* Philadelphia: Saunders.

Kinsey, A. C., Pomeroy, W. B., Martin, C. E., & Gebhard, P. H. (1953). *Sexual behavior in the human female.* Philadelphia: Saunders.

Klaus, H. M., & Kennell, J. H. (1976). *Maternal-infant bonding.* St. Louis: Mosby–Year Book.

Lang, R. (1972). *Birth book.* Ben Lomond, CA: Genesis.

Langworthy, 0. R. (1933). Development of behavior patterns and myelinization of the nervous system in the human fetus and infant. *Contributions to Embryology, 24,* 1–57.

Lee, J. A. (1980). The politics of child sexuality. In *Childhood and sexuality* (pp. 56–70). Montreal: Editions Etudes Vivantes.

Levine, M. L. (1957). Pediatric observations on masturbation in children. *Psychoanalytic Study of the Child, 6,* 117–124.

Levinger, G. (1977). Reviewing the close relationship. In G. Levinger & H. L. Raush (Eds.), *Close relationships: Perspectives on the meaning of intimacy* (pp. 137–161). Amherst: University of Massachusetts Press.

Lewis, G. M. (1958). *Educating children in grades 4, 5 and 6.* Washington, DC: U.S. Office of Education, Department of Health, Education and Welfare.

Lewis, W. C. (1965). Coital movements in the first year of life: Earliest anlage of genital love? *International Journal of Psychoanalysis, 46,* 372–374.

Martinson, F. M. (1973). *Infant and child sexuality: A sociological perspective.* St. Peter, MN: Book Mark.

Moll, A. (1913). *The sexual life of the child.* New York: Macmillan.

Montague, A. (1978). *Touching: The human significance of the skin.* New York: HarperCollins.

Newton, M., & Newton, M. (1967). Psychologic aspects of lactation. *New England Journal of Medicine, 272,* 1179–1197.

Pines, M. (1982). Baby you're incredible. *Psychology Today, 16,* 48–53.

Pitcher, E. G., & Prelinger, E. (1963). *Children tell stories: An analysis of fantasy.* Madison, CT: International Universities Press.

Pouillet, T. (1883). *Etude médico-psychologique sur uonanisme chez homme.* Paris: Delahaye et Lecrosnier.

Ramsey, G. V. (1943). The sexual development of boys. *American Journal of Psychology, 56,* 217.

Riophe, H., & Galenson, E. (1981). *Infantile origins of sexual identity.* New York: International Universities Press.

Roberts, E. J., Kline, D., & Gagnon, J. (1978). *Family life and sexual learning: A study of the role of parents in the sexual learning of children.* Cambridge, MA: Population Education.

Rorty, A. 0. (1972). Some social uses of the forbidden. *Psychoanalytic Review, 58,* 497–510.

Rosenfeld, A. A. (1976). Sexual misuse and the family. *Victimology: An International Journal, 2,* 226–235.

Rossi, A. (1978). A biosocial perspective on parenting. *Daedalus, 106,* 1–31.

Ruppel, H. J. (1979). *Socio-sexual development among preadolescents.* Paper presented at the International Symposium on Childhood and Sexuality. Montreal, Canada, University of Quebec.

Ryan, G., Miyoshi, T., Metzner, J., Krugman, R., & Fryer, G. (1996). Trends in a national sample of juvenile sex offenders. *Journal of the American Academy of Child and Adolescent Psychiatry, 35*(1), 17–25.

Schvaneveldt, J. D., Frye, M., & Ostler, R. (1970). Concepts of "badness" and "goodness" of parents as perceived by nursery school children. *Family Coordinator, 19,* 98–103.

Sears, R. R., Maccoby, E. E., & Levine, E. H. (1957). *Patterns of child rearing.* Evanston, IL: Row, Peterson.

Spiro, M. (1958). *Children of the kibbutz.* Cambridge, MA: Harvard University Press.

Spitz, R. A., & Wolf, K. N. (1946). Anaclitic depression. *Psychoanalytic Study of the Child, 2,* 313–342.

Wolff, P. H. (1959). Observations of newborn infants. *Psychosomatic Medicine, 21,* 110–118.

Yates, A. (1978). *Sex without shame: Encouraging the child's healthy sexual development.* New York: Morrow.

CHAPTER FIVE

DEVIANCY

Development Gone Wrong

Brandt F. Steele and Gail Ryan

Deviancy in its broadest sense refers to any quality, conduct, or thought that significantly diverges from a standard or norm. Deviancy may be determined by the laws, customs, or standards of any group and may refer to appearances, behavior, or beliefs. Society's concern with deviancy follows a continuum that often correlates with the impact of the deviancy.

Overall, divergent or nonconforming appearances are of little concern to society as a whole, and they may be tolerated as harmless or even valued within some subcultures. Modes of dress, customs, music, and language, for instance, may deviate from the norm in order to distinguish one subgroup from another and consequently act as descriptors of individual or group identity. Negative connotations may come to be attached to appearances because of the deviant's concurrent behavior or because of the perceptions of the beholder. Teenage fads, the homeless derelict, the bag lady, or the "biker" may conjure up fear or revulsion in others; the negative connotation is not based solely on the appearances of these individuals but stems as well from the values and experience of those who judge them. For some, the appearance of the uniformed police, the three-piece suit, or the cleric's collar may inspire similar fears or disgust for entirely different reasons. When the only deviant quality in a known individual is appearance, however, it is rarely of major social concern.

Deviant thinking may be valued or shunned. Creative or innovative thinking has been valued for its contribution to invention, science, art, and progress. Divergent beliefs have been defended throughout history as a right, and democracies have sought to accommodate thinking along a wide spectrum. Thought control has been labeled "brainwashing," and the lack of independent thought may be perceived as boring or even inhuman. The human intellect is inherently dependent on the ability to reason: to think differently in different situations and thereby to be deviant from other species.

It is one's behavior that has an impact on society and colors the evaluation of deviancy. Deviant behavior that benefits others by enhancing or improving the environment or the quality of life is valued; deviant behavior that has a negative or harmful impact on the self, others, or the environment is problematic. Every sphere of human behavior can demonstrate deviancy. In this chapter, we are concerned with deviant sexual behavior and the cognitive deviancy that supports or allows one to abuse or exploit others.

Sexual deviancy, like all other divergent qualities, may be valued or problematic. Being more "sexy" or sensual is considered an asset in most cultures, either openly or covertly. Sexual activity beyond the norm is often coveted, and extremes of sexual prowess are valued. Sexuality may become problematic if the deviancy is promiscuity, frigidity, or impotence, but the impact of these qualities for the most part is personal and of little concern to the fiber of society. Bizarre sexual thoughts are protected as one's right and may even be promoted, as in pornography and sexually explicit entertainment. It is sexually deviant behavior that has a negative impact on others—rape, assault, child abuse—that has drawn the attention of society as its incidence and prevalence have become known. Perverse sexual behaviors that misuse, debase, and corrupt others are considered negatively deviant and are therefore made illegal because of their impact. Cultural norms dictate where, when, and with whom sexual interactions are permitted or prohibited. In most modern cultures, sexual violence, sex without consent, incestuous relations, and child molestation are prohibited by custom and law.

Deviancy is identifiable because it stands out as abnormal. In an orderly society, differences that violate standards of behavior surprise and bewilder. It is assumed that all human development follows a similar course, which will produce a predictable pattern of growth and result in similar, acceptable characteristics. When occurrences blatantly violate these expectations, the questions that ultimately arise are "Why?" and "How?" Why did this happen? How can this occur? Where did this aberration come from?

In exploring the development of sexually deviant behaviors, both the norms of sexuality and the range of what is developmentally possible must be understood. Chapter Four has defined the range and progression of sexual development that may be seen in humans. The development of sexuality is shaped by cultural norms, familial and societal messages, and life experiences.

In many cultures, sexual behaviors in infancy and early childhood are repressed by parental and societal messages that deny, discourage, or punish displays of sexuality prior to puberty. "Latency" has long been considered a period of child development during which sexual issues diminish, and yet experience and research both counter that assumption. Sexuality prior to puberty may be effectively suppressed or it may be kept secret, but it is not naturally dormant or latent. Societal taboos, however, often prohibit any overt sexuality in children. Puberty and adolescence have been recognized as sexually active periods of development, but many cultures have sought to delay or repress sexual interactions prior to achievement of adult status. The child who is known to be sexual with self or others and the adolescent who defies repression have often been labeled deviant or promiscuous.

In recent years, recognition of women's rights and the "discovery" of child molestation have brought social concern to focus on sexual exploitation. Rape and child sexual abuse have been reported throughout centuries of history, and in many cultures sexual exploitation of women, children, and adolescents was the norm. Negative impacts were often minimized or denied, however, and blame was placed on victims more than offenders. Historically, sexual exploitation was seen as an interactional deviancy rather than a clear-cut crime. Rape was viewed as an interaction between a provocative female and an impulsive male, incest was considered a family problem, and hands-off behaviors such as voyeurism or exhibitionism were considered "victimless" crimes perpetrated by "sick" individuals. The social outcry against the sexual abuse of children has prompted tremendous change in societal perceptions, and a new view of sexual exploitation has evolved that holds offenders personally responsible for sexually abusive behaviors.

The capacity for sexual urges is inborn, but the ways in which sexuality is expressed are learned. Deviant sexual behavior is therefore a product of the environment, and its prevention lies in our understanding its origins. Work with sexually abusive youth offers a unique opportunity to explore the early manifestations of sexually exploitative behavior. Our hypothesis is that the origin of these behaviors lies in early childhood experience. The interaction of various factors is not always apparent in explaining why an individual manifests sexual deviancy rather than some other dysfunction, but it is usually possible in the exploration of the sexually abusive person's early life experience to see those factors that create the risk of major dysfunctions in intimate relationships.

Many child molesters, like other persons who maltreat children, have a history of significant family disruption, neglect, or abuse in their earlier years. We do not know well enough why some children who have been maltreated in early life grow up with persistent emotional problems, others to be physical abusers of their own children, others to be neglectful caretakers, and others to become sexually abusive, while at the same time many grow up with relatively little dysfunction (Ryan and others, 1993). What seems to be the most pervasive common element in those who maltreat children is the feeling of not having been adequately cared for or loved in the emotional sense; the mother or primary caregiver did not provide a good enough holding environment and was unable to help the child develop a solid, cohesive sense of a worthwhile self.

Similarly, the child who experiences significant family disruption, especially in the preverbal years, is failed by the environment. The child is left with a low self-esteem; an empty and yearning dependency; a wish for love, care, and respect; and an identification with the uncaring or absent parent. Such persons, as they grow up, are constantly searching in their interactions with other people for something that will assuage the emptiness and provide satisfaction of the need for self-enhancement. The particular way in which the growing and grown-up child chooses to try to resolve earlier traumatic experiences seems to be related to a large degree on other events in the child's life. The exposure to various forms of intrafamilial violence seems likely to predispose the child to become a physical abuser, while pervasive disregard and emotional neglect is more likely to lead to a depressive, withdrawn adult who may neglect a child or may create a failure-to-thrive syndrome. Similarly, exposure to developmentally inappropriate sexual stimuli or sexual trauma, especially the experience of being sexually abused as a child, may alter the child's development and suggest sexual behavior as a means to solve inner turmoil in later years. It is well recognized that many abusers experienced some form of abuse in their earlier years. Sexual trauma may occur as early as the first and second years of life, although it is more common between ages six and twelve.

Widom (1995) and Williams (1995) found that only 6.5 percent and 14 percent, respectively, of sexually abused children had been arrested for sexual offenses at twenty-year follow-up. In these studies, physically abused and neglected children appeared to be at equal or even higher risk than sexually abused children for arrest for sexual offenses. These results support the growing recognition in the field that a broad definition of maltreatment is more salient than the variable of sexual victimization alone in understanding why individuals become sexually abusive (Hunter, 1996).

In exploring the development of sexually abusive behaviors, three main threads of development can be traced that appear relevant to pedophilic behavior: an empty yearning and low self-esteem left over from early disregard or disruption in care, a lack of empathic modeling, and the sexualization of attempts to overcome inner conflict (Longo, 1982; Longo and McFadin, 1981; Steele, 1980, 1987, 1988). Case material helps to clarify these hypotheses.

Case 1: Regression in Times of Stress

Nineteen-year-old Robert was picked up by the police for molesting a little girl. During the course of the investigation, it developed that he had molested at least ten or twelve little girls around the age of four over the past year. He found his victims by hanging around housing projects where lonely children were often wandering around without adult supervision. He would talk to his victim, walk to a secluded spot, expose himself, and have the little girl look at his erect penis and touch it after he asked her, "Do you want to see something neat?" There were no attempts at genital manipulation of the victims or any request for fellatio. In one later episode, he ejaculated while putting his penis between the girl's legs. He confessed to authorities and expressed his strong sense of embarrassment, shame, and guilt, being quite aware that what he had done was unacceptable both socially and legally. At the same time, he was aware that there was some element in his thinking that led him to believe in some way that his "playing" with the little girls was perfectly okay and that nobody had ever told him that such activities were wrong.

Robert was born when his mother was sixteen. Two siblings from two or three different fathers had been given up for adoption. The man Robert calls his father was a stepfather who adopted him after marrying his mother when Robert was still a baby. They divorced when Robert was seven. He does not know what the trouble was but remembers some arguments and thinks that his father was much more serious and his mother much more frivolous. Since that time, his father has remarried a "nice woman" and has had two other children. His mother has been married twice and has had several other liaisons. Robert says his mother changes her man about every three years. Robert always assumed that there was a lot of sexual activity going on, but does not have a clear memory of actually witnessing any. Robert always felt the desire for a good father and never seemed to have any trouble with his stepfathers. He has had yearly visits with his father, but never a "good enough" relationship.

During his school years, Robert, with his mother and her current man, changed residences several times, to different countries and states. This meant many changes in Robert's schools, and he often felt like a stranger. He usually was treated as the "new kid" and sometimes was physically bullied. He never fought back, but became a very glib "salesman," and used his experiences to build up colorful stories of where he had been and what he had done. These gained him a certain amount of respect and acceptance, and he felt superior when he was believed.

During his childhood, Robert felt strongly that his mother did not really care about him. She never wanted to hear about any of the problems he was having and made all the household moves, which led to his problems in school, without consulting him or listening to his objections. He did not feel emotionally close to his mother, but did feel some necessity to make sure she was not upset: "She fed me and cared for me. She expected me to work and care for myself." He felt the lack of a father to turn to for guidance and support.

Over a period of several months from ages four to five, Robert had a close friendship with a same-aged neighbor, Jenny. He and Jenny often stayed overnight at one or the other's home, slept together, and engaged in a great deal of sex play, looking at and fondling each other's genitals. He recalls saying to her, "Want to see something neat?" and enjoying what he felt was her liking and approval. None of the parents interfered with or disapproved of these activities, and Robert assumed they were all right. Although Jenny and Robert occasionally saw each other during their school years, they never had further sexual activity. Robert still recalls the relationship with pleasure.

At fourteen, Robert was given the choice of living with a recently divorced stepfather and being under his control, living with his mother with no money, or being independent and earning his own keep. He took the last route with some moral support and a pat on the back, but no money from his mother. He found a job and paid his mother room and board for a few months until he moved out to his own quarters at the age of fifteen. He has been independent since that time, going to school and being self-supporting.

After his extensive sexual activity with the little girl at ages four to five, he had no further sexual experience with girls until age fourteen. At that time, he met a girl two years older and went steady with her for eight months. They had sexual intercourse about twice a week, with occasional oral activity. He found her very pleasurable and was slightly upset briefly after she ended the relationship. Two months later, he met a girl his own age, Annie, with whom he quickly developed a relationship. He was still living at home, and he and Annie would spend the night either there or at her home. Both sets of parents seemed to accept this relationship. When he left home to be on his own, Annie moved in with him, and they lived together for nearly three years.

Robert believes his interest in younger girls began when he was living with Annie and wonders if it was possibly the excitement of thinking of something different or forbidden. It was not related to lack of sexual activity with Annie. If he did not have sex with her, he would masturbate with the fantasy of having sex with some other girl he had seen, usually of his own age but occasionally of somewhat younger girls. He would also look at magazine pictures, which he described as dirty pictures of women (nudity). He does not describe any hard pornography (sexually explicit, exploitative, or involving children).

The relationship with Annie finally deteriorated when he found out that she was also going out with other boys, and she told him she was through with him. They broke up, and Annie moved out. Robert was devastated, feeling rejected by an unsympathetic, uncaring female, but he was not aware of or able to express any anger.

It was while feeling lonely and depressed over the loss of Annie that he first acted on a pedophilic impulse: seeking out a four-year-old girl and exposing himself to her. He repeated this behavior, despite feeling very scared, but thought he could control it and kept telling himself that each time was the last.

When he was arrested, Robert confessed freely to the police and prosecutors, expressing a clear sense of guilt and a great deal of remorse. He was convicted, his sentence was suspended, and he was placed on probation with the condition that he get psychiatric treatment. He began therapy in an atmosphere of gratitude for what role the therapist had in keeping him from having to face the terrors of jail. He appreciated having an outside organizing influence in his life, as well as feeling that someone was taking an interest in him and could help him guide his life more effectively.

Recurrent themes during therapy related to feelings that his mother had never really cared deeply about him or his welfare in any meaningful sense, and she had never responded to his deeper feelings. Neither his mother nor his father had ever talked to him about sexual matters or sexual behaviors, and he took their lack of concern about his behavior as a little boy as approval. Looking back, he thought that his sexual interaction with four-year-old Jenny in his preschool years was largely an attempt to resolve the feeling that his mother did not care. Jenny had expressed admiration in what he had to show her, and he experienced a sense of positive regard in the relationship.

As an adult, Robert developed his childhood expertise as a salesman, selling high-class china, crystal, and cutlery to families. Subsequently, it was when he failed to sell his wares to women that he would sometimes have an impulse to look for a little girl again. He did not act on these impulses during treatment and began to get in touch with the depth of his own neediness. He was aware that in some sense he had followed his mother's pattern of solving life's disappointments by sexual activity. In his dating activities, he had a tendency to become involved with lonely young women who were in some sort of difficulty, finding it easier to talk with them than with men or independent women. These young women responded to his concern for their troubles and his caring attitude. He became aware that he was not sure of his own masculinity and had worried that he might have homosexual tendencies. He gradually worked toward having a more adult relationship with a woman rather than rescuing the less mature girls he had been dating.

Robert was quite capable in his work and received awards for being a top salesman, but he became aware that it was not what he really wanted to do in life. He realized that he might never be able to satisfy his needs through material gains. He also became aware that the type of work he was doing was reflective of his old pattern of trying to get recognition and acceptance by showing off something "really neat" and hoping for validation. His customers' failure to buy recreated the old feelings of desertion and disregard he had felt with his mother, and his pattern was to seek sexualized methods to restore his self-esteem.

When Robert's father suddenly asked Robert to come to work with him at a good salary, Robert was entranced and excited. His father was at last offering to be the longed-for provider. Robert left treatment abruptly, before he and his therapist had discussed the new situation realistically. He sent a happy "everything is fine" letter to the therapist after a month, followed soon after by a note that things were not working out as well as he had hoped for and that he had moved from his father's home. The therapist heard nothing further, and a letter sent to him went unanswered. Three years later, a message from a defense attorney in a distant state revealed that he had been arrested for molesting another four-year-old girl. Details have not been made available.

Robert's life history was rather benign, and yet it demonstrates the suggested hypothesis that a lack of empathic modeling, an unfulfilled yearning for a sense of attachment, and sexualized models of compensation may support the development of sexual deviancy.

The following case is from the other end of the spectrum and pictures the development of sexual deviance during the course of an extremely chaotic, atypical life.

Case 2: Pervasive Sexual Deviance

Warren, charged with sexually molesting his own children as well as other young boys, was referred by social services for evaluation and possible treatment. He was a small, slender young man with dark horn-rimmed glasses. Although tense and embarrassed, he was trying to be cooperative and agreeable (reminding one of a furtive, obliging little gnome).

He is not sure of his age, either twenty-seven or twenty-nine. There is no original birth certificate, and although he obtained a copy that says he is twenty-nine, he believes this certificate is really for an older brother who died. As far as he knows, his mother gave him away sometime during his second or third year, accompanied by a short note that read, "Please take good care of John," with no last name or signature. He was placed in foster care and remembers being called John for several years, but sometime around the age of ten, his foster parents changed his name to Warren and gave him their last name. He had been told that a few months after his mother gave him away, she was sent to jail for seven years because she had given her older son a forty-eight-ounce bottle of beer and the child had died. He says, "I don't know if I had a father."

Warren's earliest memories relate to the time just before he was abandoned by his mother. He recalls lying alone on an attic floor, bleeding from the rectum after having a glass rod inserted into him. He also recalls a man trying to penetrate him rectally with his penis, a man's penis in his mouth, and being made to hold onto a man's penis. He tends to merge these memories into a single idea of all three things happening at one time. He also recalls lying on his back and having a menstruating woman sit on him with her vulva in his face. He became nauseated and vomited. He remembers playing outdoors without any clothes on, sleeping on a sofa, and playing with rats. He has been told that when he was placed with his foster parents, he had rat bites, measles, and rickets. It seems quite possible that these are the memories of a later age and that he was really older than two or three when he was placed in foster care. Attempts to corroborate these facts through social service records in the state where he grew up were fruitless.

Warren felt that his new foster home was wonderful: a nice, warm house with food, clothing, and a bed and caring, kind people. This paradise did not endure. After about six months, Warren got into a squabble with the neighbor boy, who hit him over the head with a branch, and he came home crying. His foster father was very angry with him and said if he was going to act like a girl, he would be dressed like a girl. Warren objected, but his foster father stripped him, hit him, dressed him in girls' clothes, and put him out in the yard. Other children saw him and made fun of him. Although he had not started school at the time, the children who saw him then remembered the incident later and ridiculed him throughout his school years.

He had thoughts of running away but never did. The father periodically dressed Warren in girls' clothes in the home, would talk to him about how he would go to the toilet, take down his pants, and urinate; the father would also reach up under the dress Warren was wearing and fondle his genitals. Soon Warren became aware that the foster father was also sexually molesting an older sister in the home who was the mother's child by a previous marriage.

When Warren was five or six, his foster father began having Warren and the sister come early in the morning to a restaurant he owned and do general cleaning work. They would then go to school and come back to the restaurant after school to work again until 7:00 P.M. before they could go home. The foster father was strict and demanding and often beat Warren with his fists or a belt if he did not work hard enough. Both the sexual molestation and physical punishment continued until Warren was about twelve or fourteen. At that time, the sister had hit the father on the head with a flower pot, and a year later Warren had a fistfight in which the father was knocked down. Following this incident, the abuse and molestation stopped. The foster father never really talked to Warren again except to say hello or goodbye and would often go into another room when Warren came in the house. Warren has felt that there was nobody really close to him or who cared about him during all those early years except possibly the sister, with whom he shared feelings about the abuse when they sat and cried together.

One of the interesting things about Warren's memories is that he can never recall the father physically abusing him when he was dressed in girls' clothes. He had a feeling of safety at such times. The sexual fondling had progressed to include some oral-genital contact but never any anal intercourse. Warren also observed the activity between the father and the sister in which the father would pull up her dress, fondle her, put fingers in her vagina, and then have alternating fellatio and cunnilingus. Warren also recalled some fuzzy memories of sexual activity between him and his sister, carried out at father's insistence. He remembers mostly being frightened about this because the father would say, "Do it or get your ass kicked."

Warren remembers being curious about sex; he liked a little girl next door who was about age three, and they looked at each other's genitals. He also liked to look at older girls and indicated he maintained some level of visual and possible tactile contact with girls until he was about eight or ten. Although he has vague recollections of sexual activity with the sister, he describes his first intercourse as being with a girl during his adolescence and says, "It did not work out very well."

Warren's foster mother is conspicuous by her absence in his life story. He describes her only as being somewhat more mellow but never interfering in any way with his foster father's abuse of him or the sister. She is only a vague presence in the background; there was no indication of any close relationship.

Warren graduated from high school with a C average and started working. He was rather shy, a loner, and a workaholic. He worked in a factory as a spray painter, teamed up with a young woman. They hardly spoke to each other for six months, but then began talking and eventually dated. After two or three months, they developed a sexual relationship and got married because "we both needed someone to hold on to." Sexual activity with his wife became comfortable and pleasurable. His wife brought with her a young boy from a previous marriage, and they had a daughter when the boy was about four years old.

Periodically throughout the marriage, Warren would dress in female clothing in the privacy of the home. His cross-dressing distressed his wife somewhat because she said the clothing made him look too feminine. She later decided that she did not mind because Warren seemed to feel much more secure when he was dressed that way. This sense of security seemed to be a derivative of his having felt safe because his father never beat him when he was dressed as a girl during childhood. In addition to the cross-dressing behavior, Warren used articles of female clothing as a sort of fetish. He loved the soft, silky texture of undergarments and even when not wearing them would hold them when he masturbated. At times he would wear a complete female outfit—not only underclothes but dress, stockings, and shoes. He never used any makeup.

During masturbation, from puberty to the present, Warren has had fantasies about women, usually involving straightforward intercourse, rarely any oral activity, and never any anal activity. He occasionally saw magazines like *Playboy* and had fantasies about the naked women pictured in them. He describes himself as having a strong sex urge, and says, "I don't seem to get enough sex." This is particularly referring to the present, although it also has reference to the past. He has masturbated a great deal for many years, apparently since the time the activity with his father stopped. He still either wears girls' clothing or has female garments to hold onto or to look at while masturbating. Sometimes he masturbates five to six times a day, other times only once a week. During the activity, he has a repetitive fantasy: "thinking of the kind of lady I'd like to have sex with." His ideal lady is "five feet seven inches tall; weighs around 120 or 130; has firm breasts, a nice spinal curve, narrow waist and expanded hips; is either naked or dressed, but preferably wears something soft like a negligee. She is never either younger or older than twenty-three. The colors of her hair and eyes make no difference. She knows just what to do in all kinds of activity, everything from backrubbing to oral activity, intercourse or whatever, according to her mood. She can both give and take." He denies having fantasies about children, either boys or girls.

Warren is very unsure of his identity. He wonders if he is genetically more female than male and really a female in a male body. Because of this sense that he might be female, he has wondered about homosexuality, although he has never had the desire to make love with a man. He tried once out of curiosity to have a homosexual relationship and fondled a man. This man wanted him to perform fellatio; he refused. He felt no interest in the relationship. He is also puzzled by his attraction to children, particularly to his own stepson. He feels that there is something in the back of his head that says, "Do as I did when I was a kid." He also feels he has two characters within him: one that pushes forward, the other that holds back. One is grown up, the other more childlike. He feels as if sometimes he goes back to being seven years old, then comes back to the present and hates himself.

Warren is not quite clear about how many children he has molested. Besides his stepson and daughter, he tells specifically of another boy and two girls and vaguely indicates that there may have been others. He describes the extrafamilial children as being wandering, alone, bereft, and looking for someone to care for them and love them. Apparently the sexual activity with his stepson began when the boy was about seven. It started with fondling and then progressed to include mutual masturbation and fellatio. Warren believes the son wanted him to manipulate the boy's genitals but the son never wanted to do as much for Warren. The son would often demand some reward for performing the activity for his stepfather. Warren says the son did not seem to mind when Warren put girls' clothes on him or object to the sexual activity associated with it, but he would get angry if his father pulled him away from some other activity that he was enjoying to undertake these sexual activities. Sometimes Warren dressed in girls' clothes to be sexual with the son, and sometimes he put the girls' clothes on the boy, but never had both of them dressed as females during sexual activities. Similar activities occurred with the neighbor boy, a friend of the stepson, who came over to visit with Warren when the stepson was away. The activity with his daughter, including looking and touching and possibly some oral activity, began when she was about four. He had done physical care of his daughter when she was younger but did not like to change diapers and did not seem to be aware of any sexual interest in her until later.

In the rest of his life, Warren was a rather quiet, unsociable person with few friends, but quite devoted to duty and hard work. He was in the army for several years, working as a mechanic. He received many commendations for excellent, careful work and was promoted several times. He brought these documents to show the therapist with a great sense of pride, as if to demonstrate he really was somebody worthwhile.

While on probation, Warren worked rather faithfully at several jobs in the restaurant business, sometimes quitting because he was treated rudely and abusively by superiors, and sometimes quitting because others did not keep up the high standards of cleanliness that he tried to maintain. He also worked as an assistant manager in a cheap men's rooming house in return for free rent. As a hobby, he worked at designing women's dresses, using his excellent talent as a draftsman. Occasionally he would get material, cut the dresses out, and have them sewn up by one of his girlfriends. Women admired his work. He did develop a few rather tentative friendships with women and occasionally had some sexual activity. He continued to masturbate occasionally. He did not report any interest in or fantasies about children. His wife was divorcing him, and he was under court order not to see his children.

At the beginning of treatment, one possibility, in view of his statements of his intense, irresistible sex drive, was to put him on antiandrogenic hormone treatments. After about the third session, however, he reported that his sex drive was becoming an insignificant part of his life. He intimated that therapy was his first experience in life of somebody seeming to care for him and about him and that this was a very rewarding situation. Although it is impossible to prove, it seemed as if the experience of someone's empathizing with his life troubles and talking with him about his feelings and desires diminished his drive to use sexuality to maintain esteem and identity. He lived alone, gradually trying to improve his work situation and developing a few social relationships, but disappeared after two years in treatment. Efforts to find other support groups had been fruitless.

The life histories of these two men are remarkably different in outward details—Robert was never physically or sexually assaulted; Warren was severely sexually and physically abused—yet both ended up exhibiting paraphilias including child molesting behaviors, and there are common themes in both histories. Both had the perception of not being cared about or respected in the earliest years, with the accompanying yearning for basic regard to build some sense of self-esteem and bolster an inadequate, fragmented identity. Early sexual activities, in addition to providing solutions for age-appropriate sexual curiosity and pleasure, became the available substitute for the missing empathic care and protection. Normal dependency issues became sexualized. In his repetitive sex play with Jenny, Robert found a replacement for the prevailing feelings of his mother's lack of empathy and involvement. His mother took effective though perfunctory care of his physical needs but left his emotional needs unfulfilled. His father figures were inadequate and distant. Jenny "rescued" him from an emotional wasteland. He remembers her warmly, and their relationship provided the pattern for pedophilic behavior whenever Robert felt bereft, unloved, and rejected by adult women in later life. He would have fantasies about a girl when he felt rejected during his therapy, but these were controlled by deterring thoughts of how wrong it was, how the girl would be hurt by it, and, especially, a strong fear of jail.

Warren, despite the sexual abuse in infancy, developed in later childhood an unconscious amalgamation combining sexuality, cross-dressing, and the sense of safety. Although the foster father was physically and sexually abusive, he was also the one who had rescued young Warren from the previous horrors and was kind and gentle when he dressed Warren in girls' clothes and sexually stimulated him. As an adult parent, Warren felt he could somehow prove himself loving and lovable by recreating his foster father's pattern of sexual activity with children. His unsureness of gender identity remained a source of confusion and unusual behavior. The apparent lack of fantasy about sex with children is unusual in view of his behavior, but he may have effectively blocked all sexual fantasies involving children in order to avoid the horrifying memories of his own early abuse and abandonment. He had no good models in his experience of being parented to guide him in appropriate parenting of his own children. The intensity of Warren's fantasies about a very specific adult female figure may reflect his fantasy of what he himself could be as an idealized sexual woman as much as it was a picture of a sexual object, the projection of himself as the loving and lovable female person.

Treatment was not successful for either Robert or Warren; their patterns of trying to solve deep-seated, lifelong problems were not adequately changed. This is not surprising in Warren's case. His personality disorders were severe and could not be changed in a short time, and legal and social controls were inadequate to complete treatment. It would be surprising if he did not offend again. Robert, on the other hand, had many ego strengths and adaptive abilities. Yet the failure of the hoped-for love of a caring father appears to have revived the old sense of emptiness and the pattern of relieving it by sexual expression that had been established at age four. He had seemed to be an ideal candidate for treatment, but the old behaviors had the strength to take control again.

In the adult cases presented here, the adult manifestations of deviancy and the developmental history were explored retrospectively. In the following juvenile cases, the history is closer at hand and development is still unfolding.

Case 3: Sexually Abusive Behavior in Childhood

Eight-year-old Billy was referred for evaluation after causing serious genital injury to his five-year-old sister. Adopted at age five, Billy's new parents had been told that he came from a "very dysfunctional family where there might have been some incest." Within weeks following his placement, Billy revealed to the adoptive parents graphic accounts of sexual intercourse between his mother and grandfather, as well as his own sexual abuse by them both.

Billy's new parents struggled to create a new life for him, but his relationships in the family were polarized from the beginning. His interactions with his father were distant and somewhat fearful, he was defiant and violent toward his mother, and he seemed to tolerate closeness only with the younger sister, who was medically disabled and developmentally delayed. The sister began complaining about Billy's touching during the first year, and the mother's attempts to limit his behavior and protect the younger child from his sexual advances escalated his anger and violence toward her.

A mental health worker enlisted to treat Billy was able to confirm the multigenerational incest and dysfunction in the family of origin, including Billy's failure to thrive in infancy. Billy arrived at the child abuse center for evaluation with the appearance of a small, bereft waif and a history of sexually abusing numerous children and assaulting his mother with a baseball bat. He showed little distress for himself, no appreciation of the harm he had caused others, and no defense for his behavior. Billy was a perfect image of the empty objectification he had experienced in an unempathic, sexualized world.

Treatment is still in progress. Billy's prognosis is poor, but his youth and the intensity of intervention are enhanced by his adoptive parents' continued commitment to him.

Case 4: Sexually Abusive Behavior During Puberty

Mickey, age twelve, was referred for treatment after molesting a four-year-old neighbor. Placed for adoption at age six, Mickey had lost his parents and siblings at age four. Mickey remembers his family of origin in idealized terms, although he reports knowing he was too young to be of any value except when caring for his younger sibling. He remembers fishing alone and wonders if his family looked for him or missed him when he was lost.

Within weeks of his placement, his new mother was concerned about his sexualized behaviors and enlisted counseling to help manage his behavior with the other children in the home. The healthy preplacement environment of the adoptive home became characterized by suspicion, and Mickey was never able to attach to the females in the home (or they to him).

After Mickey was removed from the adoptive home and placed in residential treatment, he finally revealed that he had been sodomized by an older boy in a preadoptive orphan asylum when he was five. Although he appeared capable of some empathy for himself and others, his ability to trust was minimal, and his sexual confusion was evident in conflicting fears and desires, including homophobic and homosexual incidents. His primary arousal to older women was accompanied by shame and revulsion in response to heterosexual fantasies. He was able to acknowledge his loneliness and sadness and his feeling that he did not know who he was, either sexually or personally. Multiple losses and betrayals made attachment and trust with adults difficult, and suspicion and lack of a worthwhile identity brought little depth to relationships with peers. Mickey's most enjoyable intimacy was with younger children, whom he was quite good at engaging, and he seemed to turn to them specifically when feeling rejected by peers. His deviant sexual behaviors were somewhat random manifestations in all his relationships with peers and adults as well as younger children.

Mickey was relinquished and is alone in the world again. He was believed to be at high risk for numerous dysfunctions, but his risk of molesting was moderated by his greater capacity to anticipate its harmfulness to others and its consequences for himself.

He was discharged from treatment at age fifteen and placed in a long-term foster placement with a single man whom he liked and appeared to trust. At age twenty-five, Mickey reported that he had not been sexually abusive again but that he had been arrested once for a group burglary while drinking with friends. He felt that he had fallen into a pattern of substance abuse, which was a factor in his making poor choices about peers and behavior. He indicated that he would consider seeking counseling for this. The foster father whom he had gone to live with at age fifteen continued to provide housing and a sense of family, which improves the prognosis for Mickey.

Case 5: Sexually Abusive Behavior in Adolescence

Chuck was arrested at age fourteen for the molestation of several cousins and his sister. Upon interrogation, he revealed that he had been sodomized by an older cousin when he was about six years old, although later, in view of his cousin's anger and denial, he became ambivalent as to whether this had really occurred or was "just a dream."

Chuck was the second of six children, born at a time when his mother's first marriage was both abusive and breaking up. His older brother and younger siblings appeared to have satisfactory relationships with their mother, but Chuck's mother stated she had "always felt different" about him and "never felt as close to him" as to the other children. Chuck had felt this difference, and he and his mother seemed to experience a distorted intimacy only around shared feelings of fear and guilt. His mother reported that Chuck had "always been a problem" and "never been trustworthy," acting up and being in trouble perpetually from age six. Lying, stealing, intimidating his siblings, and incidents that caused his mother to feel like a failure were common occurrences, although he was well liked by peers and had good social skills. The first-grade teacher had reported unusual sexual components in his artwork at age six. Chuck had been discovered trying to sodomize a younger sibling at that time and had gone to counseling for a brief period.

Chuck had felt set apart and different much of his life. His mother's preoccupation with a bad marriage at the time of his birth may have impaired her availability to him and precluded empathic care. Although he had no conscious memory of his natural father, there seemed to be some covert implication that he was like his father: untrustworthy, criminal, and a source of fear for his mother. He had never felt allowed to inquire about that father, and he felt some obscure sense of loss that he described as "an empty place" relative to his perceived abandonment or rejection by his father. In addition to his reported experience of sodomy at age six, he remembered learning about sex by eavesdropping when an older brother and his friends discussed sexual matters in the home.

Chuck showed little genuine affect and was quite unaware of the feelings of self or others. He had difficulty maintaining eye contact with adults and reported feeling very helpless and small, especially with his mother. Although his sexual abuse of boys was quite aggressive, his perception of the long-term molesting relationship he had with one female cousin was that it was a loving and intimate experience, and she agreed. In every molestation, however—and also in subsequent peer relationships—his victims were related to a fierce protector whom he feared: his mother, a very scary uncle, a crazy, gun-toting boyfriend, and so forth. It is possible that the experience of fear in his exploitative sexual relationships made him feel more alive and somehow connected him to that "missing part," which was the father figure whom his mother had feared.

Chuck's family was very involved and invested in treatment. Chuck completed treatment successfully and returned home for about one year before going away to college. While away, he was somewhat delinquent and was suspended from college due to grades. After a year or two on his own, he returned to his home town with a girlfriend and was doing well at follow-up when he was twenty-four years old.

Case 6: Sibling Incest

Jay, age fourteen, was referred for treatment following disclosure of a long-term incestuous relationship with his younger sister. Jay had lots of family: a natural father, a mother and a stepfather, grandparents, and siblings. His natural father and stepfather were recovering alcoholics, but everyone else appeared quite functional. The pervasive qualities in this family seemed to be distance and defense. Family members met financial and physical needs without any emotional connection. His mother was frequently absent due to business commitments, and his sister spent much of her childhood with relatives. In this case, it was the victim, Jay's sister, who had been set apart and different, with chronic patterns of acting out that may have filled some of the emotional void for all the family members. Although Jay was clearly exploiting the power in their relationship, his sister was easy prey, and both seemed to experience some intimacy in the relationship, although there did not appear to be much capacity for empathy.

After completing treatment, Jay was being sent away to boarding school, where he will be further disconnected from the family he yearns for and will likely engineer failure in the new school in order to return home. No legal constraints are in place to prevent his removal from treatment.

All of these cases demonstrate the common themes of emptiness, lack of empathic experience, and sexualized patterns of coping that are characteristic of sexual offenders. And yet every theme represented in the developmental history of these individuals is also reported by many persons who do not manifest sexual deviance or sexually abuse others.

In normal development, a child's dependency needs for empathic care, closeness, intimacy, and a sense of self follow a separate line from that of sexuality, although the two coexist and in some ways interact. The two lines of development are related but not merged. Throughout the life cycle of healthy persons, sexuality and intimacy can be expressed together or separately. Intimacy may occur in relationships that are not sexual, and sexuality can be expressed without intimacy. Ideally, both occur together in romantic relationships and can be enjoyed together, although they do not replace each other. For some people, however, there may be a merging of the two desires or drives during childhood, with sexuality being used to replace the ability to be truly empathic and intimate and to establish a sense of self and identity. Such merging is never truly successful and is never totally satisfying. It cannot replace the deficits of early childhood and has been referred to as counterfeit.

We are not suggesting that sexual activity per se in childhood leads to a fixation on children as sexual objects (Groth, 1979). Cultures in which there is free and open sexual activity all through childhood do not have any appreciable incidence of pedophilia (Constantine and Martinson, 1981). It is the incomprehensible or traumatic sexual exploitation of children who are seeking love and care that creates the false equation. The merging of sexuality and one's sense of self may lead to pedophilia and the repetition in adult life of identification with the kind of experience endured in childhood. Pedophilic behavior in both adolescent and adult life may be the attempt to satisfy through sexual activity the emptiness and yearning left over from the bleak early years. This is but one variation of the use of sexuality for nonsexual purposes that is also seen in rape (when sexuality is used to express hatred and hostility) and in the more commonly observed phenomena that many people enter sexual relationships or activity to satisfy more deeply felt needs for loving care and touching. As Warren said, it is important to have "someone to hold on to." Sexually exploitative behaviors reflect a basic inability to be empathic, appreciative of, and caring for another human being, a deficit that is a residue from early years of unempathic care.

References

Constantine, L. L., & Martinson, F. (1981). *Children and sex: New findings and new perspectives.* Boston: Little, Brown.

Groth, A. N. (1979). Sexual trauma in the life histories of rapists and child molesters. *Victimology, 4*(1), 10–16.

Hunter, J. (1996). *Working with children and adolescents who sexually abuse children.* Paper presented at the Eleventh International Congress on Child Abuse and Neglect, Dublin, Ireland.

Longo, R. E. (1982). Sexual learning and experience among adolescent sexual offenders. *International Journal of Offender Therapy and Comparative Criminology, 26*(2), 235–241.

Longo, R. E., & McFadin, B. (1981, December). Sexually inappropriate behavior: Development of the sexual offender. *Law and Order, 2*(9), 21–23.

Ryan, G. (Ed.). (1997). *The web of meaning: A developmental view of sexual abuse.* Manuscript submitted for publication.

Ryan, G., Lindstrom, B., Knight, L., Arnold, L., Yager, J., Bilbrey, C., & Steele, B. (1993). *Treatment of sexual abuse in the context of whole life experience.* Presentation at the Twenty-First Child Abuse and Neglect Symposium, Keystone, CO.

Steele, B. F. (1980). Generational repetition of the maltreatment of children. In
    E. J. Anthony & G. Pollock (Eds.), *Parental influences in health and disease.* Boston: Little,
    Brown.

Steele, B. F. (1987). Abuse and neglect in the earliest years: Groundwork for vulnerability.
    Zero to Three, 7(4), 14–15. (1988).

Steele, B. F. (1988). Psychodynamic factors in child abuse. In E. Helfer & R. Kempe *The bat-
    tered child* (4th ed.). Chicago: University of Chicago Press.

Widom, C. (1995). *Victims of child sexual abuse: Later criminal consequences.* Washington, DC: U.S.
    Department of Justice, National Institute of Justice.

Williams, L. (1995). *Juvenile and adult offending behavior and other outcomes in the cohort of sexually
    abused boys: Twenty years later.* Philadelphia: Joseph J. Peters Institute.

CHAPTER SIX

THE SEXUAL ABUSE CYCLE

Sandy Lane

The sexual abuse cycle represents the antecedents, components, patterns, and progression of sexually abusive behavior. The framework depicts the commonalities among numerous sexually abusive youth and abusive behaviors. When the cycle is personalized, the thoughts, circumstances, characteristics, reactions, feelings, and behaviors will vary from youth to youth, yet the commonalities will still be evident.

A youth who is aware of the thinking, affective reactions, and behaviors represented in the cycle is then able to cope differently with stress, thereby avoiding abusive behavior. The youth is also able to identify the particular stressors and typical coping styles that have contributed to the abusive behaviors. It is likely that these stressful issues and coping deficits have been reflected in other aspects of the sexually abusive youth's life.

The concept of the sexual abuse cycle presented in this chapter was developed at the Closed Adolescent Treatment Center (CATC) of the Colorado Division of Youth Services in 1977–1978 (Lane & Zamora, 1982, 1984). The initial cycle, called the rape cycle, was a synthesis of the commonalities observed among the adolescents with a history of sexually abusive behaviors who were incarcerated in the CATC program. Although each youth had unique perceptions, motivations, rationalizations, and justifications concerning his or her abusive behaviors, there seemed to be common abusive behavior elements, a common type of gratification, and a common style of thinking that supported the behavior. Moreover, there appeared to be a common pattern among the juveniles that was somewhat predictable and occurred antecedent to the behavior.

The observations of the initial youth were based on their daily behavior and interactions, review of their personal journals that described their perceptions and reactions to various events, their reports of ongoing urges to engage in sexually abusive behaviors, and their retrospective descriptions of abusive behaviors and associated thoughts. It appeared that the patterns represented by the sexual abuse cycle involved a maladaptive or dysfunctional coping response to problematic situations or interactions. The youths seemed to interpret the meanings of others' behaviors or various life events inaccurately, they made erroneous conclusions about themselves, and they seemed to have misconceptions about power and control as it related to self-perceptions of adequacy. Their responses (or their cycle) appeared to be compensatory, repetitive, and generally consistent for each youth.

Over time, the cycle was used and modified by staff from RSA, Inc., an outpatient treatment center for sexual offenders in Lakewood, Colorado. The concept has been valid for over three thousand offenders at RSA, regardless of age, gender, developmental capacity, or type of sexually abusive behavior. Youth with cognitive deficits benefit from more concrete adaptations of the cycle.

In the late 1970s and early 1980s, other clinicians observed similar patterns and offense components that were also presented in a cycle format (see Freeman-Longo & Bays, 1988; Wolfe, 1994). Several other clinicians have developed modifications or adapted the cycle concept to their clinical settings (Johnson, 1989; Kahn, 1990; G. Lowe, personal communication, 1984; O'Connor & Esteve, 1994; Ross, 1993; Ryan & Blum 1993; Ryan, Lane, Davis, & Isaac, 1987; Stickrod, 1988). Still others have adapted the cycle to other delinquent behaviors (Gray, 1996; Lane, 1985, 1991; Turner, 1994), psychiatric disorders (MacFarlane & Cunningham, 1996; Ryan, 1993), or dysfunctional behaviors (Ryan, 1989). By the 1990s the cycle was being used in the majority of programs, national and international, treating sexual abusers, and there are dozens of adaptations representing clinicians' and clients' personal understanding and articulation of the concept.

In the absence of a validated theoretical base, early clinicians relied on clinical experience and observation to develop treatment programs and strategies. The concept of the sexual abuse cycle has not been totally empirically validated, but research has begun to confirm various elements of the cycle concept (see Gilgun, 1988; Marshall & Barbaree, 1984; and Prentky and others, 1989, on developmental history; Fagan & Wexler, 1988; Fehrenbach, Smith, Monastersky, & Deischer, 1986; and Gilgun & Connor, 1989, on isolation; Hunter & Santos, 1990, on deviant arousal; and Becker, Hunter, Stein, & Kaplan, 1989, on fantasy and arousal).

Most recently, studies exploring the frequency and relationship of conflict, vulnerable emotions—such as loneliness and humiliation—and anger have seemed to validate the connection between negative affective states and deviant sexual fantasies, as well as with masturbation while fantasizing deviant behaviors (McKibben, Proulx, & Lusigna, 1994; Proulx, McKibben, & Lusigna, 1996). Pithers, Kashima, Cumming, Beal, and Buell (1988) previously reported that anger preceded abusive sexual behaviors, and Ward, Louden, Hudson, and Marshall (1994) have explored the emotional dysphoria (negative affect) that is apparent in the affective components of the sexual abuse cycle.

Overview of the Cycle

The abuse cycle is a construct representing cognitive, affective, and behavioral progressions occurring antecedent to, during, and subsequent to abusive behavior. It is described here in relation to sexually abusive behaviors, although it has also been found to be relevant to a broader spectrum of abusive behaviors. It is descriptive of a process and is not a causal representation. It is presented as a cycle because of the repetitive nature of the behavior sequence many youth report, as well as indications that previous abuse incidents often parallel and reinforce subsequent abusive patterns. The sequence of the cycle is based on the general progression of thoughts, feelings, and behaviors commonly described by youth. The labels are arbitrary terms that attempt to describe the experience typically associated with perceptions, thoughts, feelings, or behaviors described by these youth in treatment settings.

Briefly, the juvenile responds to an event, interaction, or problem that triggers negative perceptions and feelings of helplessness (the *event*). His life experience, personal view of the world, beliefs, and history influence his perceptions of the event as being stressful, and he assumes the future will be similar and thus unsafe (*negative anticipation*). He begins to feel hopeless and attempts to avoid the issue, his internal response, and the expected outcomes (*avoidance*). When this is unsuccessful, he begins to feel resentful and defensive and attempts to exert power over others in nonsexual ways (*power/control*). As the sense of being powerful or in control is brief, he begins to think of further power-based behaviors and other things (such as sex) that would make him feel good (*fantasy*). The exertion of control or dominance is eventually expressed sexually (*sexual abuse*); then the youth attempts to cope with the sexual abuse behavior and fear of consequences of being caught (*fugitive thinking*). He subsequently assimilates the behavior through a series of thinking errors (*reframing*). (See Figure 6.1.)

FIGURE 6.1. THE SEXUAL ABUSE CYCLE.

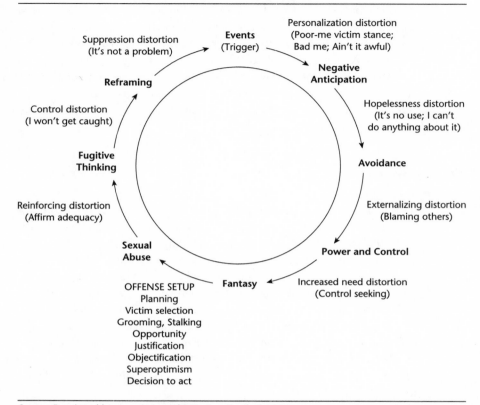

Source: Reprinted by permission of RSA, Inc. Revised 1996.

The sequential response appears compensatory in that it counters the perception of inadequacy and helplessness and reduces internal anxiety. The response appears to represent a coping mechanism, but it is an essentially maladaptive one because it is only a temporary measure and does not resolve the stressful issue.

Because movement through the cycle results in compensatory self-perceptions and anxiety reduction, cycle progression is not necessarily consistent for the individual or among various youth. It is seldom that a youth will progress through the cycle a step at a time, start to finish, nor does a sexual offense occur each time the youth's cycle is triggered. Progression in the cycle, in response to each trigger, will go only as far as is needed for the youth to experience some relief and an improved self-perception. Progression to the next stage will not occur until the first stopping point no longer relieves the youth. Interruptions or delays in the cycle might be called plateaus. In response to repeated triggers, the youth may progress to the same plateau several times and not move on to the next plateau until the current stage of the cycle fails to relieve anxiety or sufficiently counters negative self-perceptions. The stress may seem to dissipate temporarily, but in fact it accumulates over time.

As an example, a youth may respond to three different triggers and may progress only to a victim stance orientation; the youth externalizes responsibility, which reduces his anxiety, and he becomes somewhat self-righteous about being mistreated. Of the next three triggers, one progresses to a victim stance orientation, one to negative anticipation, and one to an avoidance behavior. At the same time, he is beginning to feel uncomfortable about the initial triggers and starts to personalize or think negatively about himself. The next two triggers feel more stressful to the youth, and both progress to the control-seeking stage of the cycle. The youth does not move to the sexual abuse behavior stage for five weeks, although his cycle was triggered twenty-seven times before he reached that point in the cycle.

The rate of progression through the cycle also varies among youth, depending on the strength of the maladaptive coping response, the individual's anxiety tolerance, and the associated thought process. It does seem, however, that the more frequently the maladaptive response style is used, the faster the rate of progression tends to become for the youth. Habituated perceptions or thoughts appear to be associated with a faster rate of cycle progression. The more habituated the use is of the coping response depicted in the cycle, the less tolerance the individual seems to have for precipitating events or problems and the further in the cycle the youth progresses in his initial response. For example, many youth who habitually rely on this pattern move quickly to the negative anticipation or control-seeking stages of the cycle. It also appears that the more the young offender relies on this type of coping, the less he relies on nonpower-based or nonsexual social competencies or coping strategies. The more the youth focuses on the gratification associated with the offense behavior, the less willing he becomes to struggle with anxiety to inhibit the behavior, and the more quickly he develops the plans and justifications.

Personalization of the cycle assists both the youth and the therapist in identifying problematic issues, maladaptive coping patterns, distorted thinking, social competency deficits, affective states, cues that herald cycle progression, and specific offense behavior styles. Effective therapeutic strategies can then be developed for the abusive behavior patterns, coexisting psychiatric disorders, unresolved trauma issues, or other dysfunctional behaviors. Some offense-specific treatment strategies will be common for each youth, but individual treatment needs and strategies may also be developed. Although the pattern and its function is similar, the interventions that will be most effective must be tailored for each particular youth. For example, one youth may need more assistance with misperceptions about others' behaviors, while another youth may have significant developmental deficits and may need to work with attachment issues.

Differential diagnosis and treatment planning occurs after careful analysis of the youth's whole life experience, including the sexual abuse behavior. Offense-specific treatment strategies common to each youth should be directed toward understanding and learning to control multiple offense-related aspects, eliminating power-based coping strategies, and developing the ability to empathize with others. The youth may also need to increase his ability to use social competencies that do not rely on the use of power, address unresolved trauma issues and family issues, improve the ability to perceive the motivations of others, strengthen relationship building and intimacy skills, and develop more accurate and positive self-perceptions.

Basic Assumptions Underlying the Sexual Abuse Cycle

The basic assumptions that underlie the various concepts of the sexual abuse cycle are important to keep in mind when using this cycle. A variety of aspects contribute to or support sexually abusive behaviors. Although the assumptions are derived from the commonalities exhibited by many sexually abusive youth, so far they are only theoretical. Future research will validate, clarify, or correct these assumptions. The assumptions are considered equally significant and are not listed in order of importance.

Sexual Abuse

Any sexual behavior that lacks consent and involves violation, exploitation, manipulation, trickery, coercion, or force of another is considered sexually abusive and may result in varying impacts to the victim. The behaviors involved in an offense are viewed as a sexualized expression of nonsexual needs at the expense of another individual. Sexual abuse behaviors are not viewed as impulsive acts; rather, the offender engages in some antecedent thinking or contemplation about the behavior.

Control Seeking and Dominance

Sexual abuse is viewed as a sexualized expression of power, control, and dominance. A misuse of power is involved in both the nonsexual and sexual abuse behaviors, cognitions, and offense setups exhibited in the cycle.

Essentially the cycle represents a maladaptive and dysfunctional power-based response style to problematic interactions or situations. The response style appears to provide a reduction of anxiety, a sense of well-being, positive self-regard, a sense of gratification, and a sense of mastery through efforts to control another or the environment. Power-based thinking and behaviors may be equally gratifying to the individual.

Through the misuse of power, the young offender seems to associate internal perceptions or experiences of adequacy, superiority, dominance, strength, empowerment, mastery, excitement, or a sense of control. The perceptions seem to be based in believing that retaliating for some affront, controlling another, or being in control of the circumstances proves to the perpetrator and others that he is "okay." The perceptions are based in erroneous cognitions.

These beliefs are illusory in that the expectation of being able to control another or one's total environment is unrealistic and the misuse of power does not improve one's adequacy. A control-seeking or dominating response does not solve a problem or resolve a situation. Nor does it contribute to developing self-control, improve an individual's interpersonal coping skills, or contribute positively to relationships or interpersonal interactions. Unfortunately, this type of response style is easily habituated and is eventually used in lieu of effective coping skills and social competencies that would involve communication, conflict resolution, empathic interactions, or equality.

Nonsexual expressions of power may be interpersonal (yelling, hitting, manipulating others, or overcompliance) or solitary (punching the wall, slamming doors, pouting, or walking away from a situation) and provide the offender with an inflated sense of self or a sense that his self-image is intact if he has somehow gained an upper hand. Power and control may be expressed in a passive, passive-aggressive, or aggressive manner.

Some degree of power thrust appears to be present in every type of sexual abuse behavior. At the least, the youth may experience a feeling of empowerment or mastery because he or she is directing the incident and is thus in control of the situation. A youth may experience a sense of dominance because he has gained the cooperation of a child, or an improved sense of self because a child victim exhibits acceptance of the perpetrator. Successfully surprising, enticing, or setting up a victim may induce feelings of competency, control, or empowerment. An offender who engages in forcible sexual behaviors, expressions of anger, or sadistic behaviors as part of an offense is exhibiting a more aggressive form of power or control. It is important to realize, however, that the behavior provides a sense of control or a perception of being powerful, which the youth seeks in response to his feeling powerless. Although many sexually abusive youth present as powerless and exhibit a victim stance orientation, in fact they are not powerless. Their sense of being powerless is based in distorted beliefs that indicate they should be able to control others or an occurrence they experience.

Compensatory Aspects

Many youth report temporarily experiencing an improved sense of well-being and positive self-regard when engaging in behaviors they believe are controlling or dominating. They describe an even greater sense of gratification while committing a sexually abusive behavior. Sexually abusive youth have described internal experiences of thrill, excitement, sexual arousal, risk, positive self-perception, a sense of getting away with something, superiority, and empowerment whether contemplating, anticipating, committing, or recalling a sexually abusive behavior. The experience is described as sufficiently pleasurable and self-enhancing that anxiety-provoking thoughts and feelings present prior to the abusive behavior are temporarily eliminated or diminished. As the behaviors are repeated, the compelling urges to repeat the behavior are based primarily on the juvenile's desire or perceived need to experience the feelings of control, empowerment, and the euphoric high, as well as the positive self-perceptions that are associated with their behavior. The reinforcements associated with the sexual aspect of the behavior will be discussed shortly.

The need for a compensatory experience appears to be evoked by feelings of helplessness or lack of control associated with problems, interactions, or events occurring antecedent to the abusive behavior. The youth may believe he is unable to control what happens to him, resulting in feelings of powerlessness; his psychological resources may be insufficient to cope with some situations; or he may perceive himself as inadequate because he is unable to prevent some occurrence or respond to some situation. Engaging in control-seeking or dominating behaviors gives the youth the impression that he is able to be effective and in control of his environment. He perceives the precipitating event or problem as having been resolved, less significant, or under control and believes that he has regained a sense of adequacy. Associated defense mechanisms may include reaction formation, compensation, suppression, and repression. Beliefs or cognitions such as those suggested by Yochelson and Samenow (1976) may support these perceptions.

A youth's cycle begins as he responds to an event, an interaction, or a problem that he perceives as distressing. Observation has indicated that the common affective reaction associated with the precipitating event, or trigger, is that of feeling helpless, powerless, controlled, or out of control. Frequently described events that elicit the experience of powerlessness include abandonment or perceived abandonment, physical abuse, sexual victimization, rejection, humiliation, loss, alienation, refusal, debasement, control, embarrassment, or betrayal. These triggers are perceived as a loss of control, which causes the youth to feel unsafe. The need for a defensive response arises from feeling vulnerable. Many sexually abusive youth report that either their current triggers, or those occurring prior to their abusive behaviors, are reminiscent of historical problems or situations that elicited nearly intolerable feelings of helplessness and have remained unresolved. Over time, many offenders are able to identify groups of similar precursor events or interactions that typically trigger the onset of their cycle progression. The following example concerns a youth who exhibits a sensitivity to triggers that involve loss:

When Dan was four years old, his grandfather died while the two of them were taking a nap. Dan, too young to understand death, felt scared and a sense of loss, and he believed that he had done something wrong that made his grandfather go away. When Dan was nine years old, his parents divorced, and his mother was granted custody of him. He felt sad, helpless, scared, and a sense of loss. He again believed that he was responsible, this time for his father's leaving home. Later in life when he experienced any kind of loss—when his friend moved away, his girlfriend broke up with him, he lost a job—he thought it was his fault and had similar thoughts and feelings. As time went on, he would become anxious if he lost anything—even if he misplaced his keys or papers at school. He also began to be sensitive to times when he felt put down and believed he had lost face.

The use of power-based behaviors or thoughts to define individual success, strengthen self-esteem, measure adequacy, or resolve interpersonal disputes is widely supported in our society. Our culture tends to promote such attitudes as these: "Don't get mad, get even," "Take care of number one," "Revenge is sweet," "Winning is what counts," "Rise to the top," and "All is fair in love and war." Similarly, the use of sexual thoughts or behaviors to boost self-esteem, reduce tension, or provide an image of adequacy are supported by our culture. Many youth begin to believe, "If I am sexual, I am macho," "Having sex will make me more popular," "Sex will solve my problems," and "Sex will make me feel better." These beliefs, and the perceived societal sanction for them, appear to support compensatory-power-based and sexual thoughts and behaviors for the youth.

Arousal Aspects

Sexual excitement or arousal is described by adolescents as occurring not only during the sexual abuse incident but also during antecedent contemplation, behaviors that set up the behavior, and during subsequent recall of abusive incidents. All sexual behaviors are supported, and preferences strengthened, by the associated intimacy, arousal, orgasm, and tension reduction. This is true of sexual abusive behavior as well. Arousal and orgasm are both psychologically and physiologically pleasurable and are therefore self-reinforcing. Urges to initiate abusive sexual behaviors reportedly intensify or become more frequent as the associated arousal increases.

It is believed that arousal is strengthened and sexual interest shaped by masturbatory behaviors associated with sexual fantasies. McGuire, Carlyle, and Young (1965) suggest that sexual interest is strengthened most by masturbatory fantasies, partly because individuals typically engage in sexual fantasies more frequently than in sexual behaviors. Adolescents who sexually abuse typically report either engaging in masturbatory fantasies or experiencing sexual excitement when contemplating or specifically imagining offense behaviors. Marshall (1979) and Abel and Blanchard (1974) suggest that masturbation to deviant fantasies occurs antecedent to sexually aggressive behavior. Some sexually abusive youth report strengthened arousal associated with thoughts and behaviors as they engage in masturbatory fantasies of offense incidents and behaviors. Although adolescents who are sexually abusive may also engage in nonabusive sexual fantasy and behaviors when they are not in the cycle, they may be at risk for increasing the arousal and interest associated with their sexually abusive behaviors to the extent that normative arousal and activity is diminished or precluded.

The specific elements of sexual arousal appear to be unique for each offender and probably result from associations with a wide variety and combination of cognitions, sensory experiences, and behaviors. Many youth in treatment report experiencing stronger arousal to antecedent or anticipatory thoughts and behaviors, as well as to their subsequent recall of the offense, than to the sexual abuse incident itself. It may be partly because when they are fantasizing, they are in total control and they imagine behaviors and reactions that are consistent with the anticipated outcomes of the behavior.

For some there appears to be a rush or some degree of excitement, thrill, and risk that is associated with and enhances anticipatory arousal or excitement. For others, there may be ideations of anticipated closeness, pleasure, acceptance, or intimacy that is further associated with anticipatory arousal. For still others, the expectation of dominance, control of another, or expression of anger and infliction of pain may be associated with antecedent arousal or excitement.

During subsequent recall, various cognitions may be associated with the juvenile's arousal. These cognitions may affirm the youth's adequacy or the victim's willingness to engage in the behavior. For some sexually abusive youth, the arousal associated with cognitions about the victim's characteristics or the offense style may become the preferred or exclusive way of becoming sexually excited if they continue abusive thoughts and behaviors over time.

The arousal associated with sexual abuse fantasies or behaviors appears to contribute to the compensatory process. It appears that sexual arousal, in association with other aspects of gratification, serves to provide some degree of soothing and positive self-regard. It is likely that the process of soothing oneself through sexual stimulation is learned quite young and may become a habitual response when distress or anxiety occur (see Money, 1986; Chapter Four in this book). Various cognitions may become associated with abuse-related arousal. Repetition of the cognitions and the arousing behavior or thoughts may support an eventual pairing, and these associations may become conditioned as the patterns are repeated. It is possible that abuse associations may have become paired with arousal in the context of victimization that the youth experienced in the past. One of the most insidious effects of sexual abuse for both victims and perpetrators may be the confusion of an experience that involves conflicting thoughts and feelings (Ryan, 1989).

Although most information and research descriptive of deviant arousal patterns refers to adults, sexually abusive youth are believed to exhibit similar patterns. Many youth (as well as some younger children and intellectually handicapped perpetrators) have described arousal associated with the antecedent thoughts and urges as well as offense behaviors. Becker and others (1989), Becker, Stein, Kaplan, and Cunningham-Ratherner (1992), and Hunter and Santos (1990) confirm the presence of deviant arousal for adolescent youth who had sexually abused. The development of pedophilic interests and arousal was reported as early as age ten in boys attracted to male children and age twelve in boys attracted to female children. It is believed that adolescents exhibit discriminate arousal and that many young offenders experience deviant arousal that may be as strong as that of adult offenders, although the adolescent typically has less history of engaging in sexually abusive behaviors, and these patterns may be less ingrained and less exclusive. Results of research by Kaemingk, Koselka, Becker, and Kaplan (1995) demonstrated that younger adolescents had erectile responses to a greater number of stimuli; these authors suggest that one possible explanation may relate to inhibited ability to modulate or inhibit erectile response because frontal lobe development is incomplete at this age. Research by Hunter and Goodwin (1992) indicated that younger sexually abusive youth tend to have more difficulty learning to control abuse-related sexual arousal.

Cognitive Aspects

A variety of cognitions, all labeled as cognitive distortions, are referred to in the sexual abuse cycle. Some cognitions refer to thinking errors or patterns of thought that contribute to or support criminal or antisocial behavior. Some justify, rationalize, or provide the youth with a way of making the sexual offense behavior seem reasonable to engage in. Still others reflect the beliefs or perceptions a youth may have about the motivations of others or the meaning of circumstances in his life. Other cognitions refer to assumptions, conclusions, and fears about the world or to the self-perceptions and self-statements the youth has.

The sexual abuse cycle appears to be triggered by perceptions of interactions or situations. If the events are interpreted as a threat to the youth's sense of control or the youth lacks adequate coping skills and believes he or she is unable to handle the situation, cycle progression may be initiated. If the youth were able to reexamine initial conclusions and depersonalize the meaning of the event, they would feel less need for a compensatory or control-seeking response. Often the individual's interpretation or experience of the triggering event may appear erroneous or extreme to others, but in the context of the youth's life experience, the reaction may be quite rational.

Yochelson and Samenow (1976) identified fifty-two patterns of thought, which they called thinking errors, that contribute to or support criminal or antisocial behavior. Berenson (in Knopp, 1982) described seventeen of these as typically present in young sexual offenders:

1. Victim stance
2. "I can't" attitude
3. Lack of concept of injury to others
4. Failure to put oneself in the place of others
5. Lack of effort
6. Refusal to accept obligation
7. No concept of trust
8. Unrealistic expectations
9. Attitude of ownership
10. Irresponsible decision making
11. Failure to plan ahead or think long range
12. Flawed definition of success and failure
13. Fear of being put down
14. Refusal to acknowledge fear
15. Anger used to control others
16. Power thrust
17. Pride or refusal to back down

When daily occurrences or traumatic experiences are interpreted through the filter of these patterns of thoughts, the individual's perceptions may be based on distorted beliefs, conclusions may be inaccurate, and the response may manifest in behaviors that involve a misuse of power. The sexually abusive youth's perception that a power-based response, sexual or nonsexual, is self-enhancing or is indicative of adequacy is based on such thoughts. These beliefs reflect an overgeneralization of defensive strategies and allow the youth to seek control over others, feel entitled to impose sexual interactions, objectify and depersonalize victims, consider their own needs as more important than others' rights, and believe that their behavior is warranted and reasonable. These patterns of thought might be called core distortions because they shape the way the individual perceives the world.

A variety of cognitions specifically justify, rationalize, or support the offender's sexually abusive behavior (Abel & Blanchard, 1974; Becker and others, 1990; Berenson, 1987; Lane & Zamora, 1978). Some of the distortions support a youth's belief in the victim's willingness or need to engage in the sexually abusive behavior, some shape the perception of the victim as obligated to meet the needs of the perpetrator, some construe the behavior as helpful, and still others allow the youth to objectify or depersonalize the victim. These distortions occur during contemplation of an offense, planning or setting up the offense, as well as subsequent to the offense to assist the youth in feeling somewhat comfortable about the behavior.

During childhood experience of traumatic events, or even confusing situations or interactions, the child strives to interpret and understand what has happened. The child may conclude that he or she has done something bad or that the experience occurred because of the child's behavior or some character deficit. The conclusions become negative self-statements and self-perceptions that the child reaffirms over time. Although the conclusions are generally inaccurate, they become the basis (as core issues) for misperceptions and the types of triggers or events that will initiate cycle progression.

Although there are common patterns of cognitive distortions that support cycle progression and abusive behavior, the development of specific distortions is unique for each individual. With repetition, the individual's thoughts become ingrained and develop into a belief system that supports a habitual response to many situations. The thoughts appear to become more automatic as they occur more frequently. The cognitions tend to be directed to only similar situations initially but later are generalized to an increasing number of situations. When the distortions become more ingrained and habitual, cycle progression is more rapid and abusive behaviors occur more frequently. As the cycle response becomes habituated through repetition, misinterpretation of events increases in both frequency and scope.

Compulsive or Addictive-Like Aspects

Many sexually abusive youth demonstrate impulse-control deficits and report that the urges to engage in abusive behaviors are difficult to deny or manage. They report repetitive cycle progressions and repeated offenses despite their decision to control or cease their sexually abusive behaviors. There are also reports of difficulty in delaying gratification of impulses to engage in the behavior.

Adolescents who engage in repeated sexual abuse report subsequent increases in the frequency and intensity of associated urges. Some have reported that their internal sense of excitement and control, as well as the associated arousal, seemed to diminish with repetition, and these youth indicated they begin to add elements of risk, increased power, or additional sexual behaviors to subsequent fantasies or abusive behaviors in order to maintain the same level of gratification.

Engaging in both sexual- and nonsexual-power-based thoughts and behaviors provides a significant degree of pleasure and relief of negative internal states. The behavior patterns are experienced positively and are thus likely to be repeated. As the youth develops a repetitive pattern, it may gradually become the favored, and eventually habitual, response to specific types of problematic emotions or situations. Because the response is maladaptive and does not truly resolve problems, the initial negative internal states return, and the response pattern reoccurs to reestablish a sense of well-being. These ineffective efforts may result in more frequent, and possibly more intense, anxiety experiences, and the process is again repeated. Concurrently the individual's tolerance for stress appears to diminish, and the compensatory process occurs more frequently. There is a tendency to strive for or rely less and less on more effective styles of resolving difficulties, eventually resulting in a paucity of social competencies or a failure to develop such skills.

Although the behavior patterns reflected in the sexual abuse cycle may not be true compulsions or addictions, there is a compulsive quality to the urges to engage in the behavior reported by young offenders. The need to increase the intensity of some aspects of the offense behavior has an addictive-like quality. Freeman-Longo (1982) and Carnes (1983) have indicated that because there is psychological and physiological reinforcement in sexually aggressive behavior, it may become an addictive disorder. There are many unanswered questions regarding compulsive or addictive aspects. Some of the associated variables that reinforce the behavior may include sexual arousal, thrill, risk, empowerment, anticipation, pleasure, and individual perceptions. There may also be physiological, biochemical, and neurological processes associated with the habituation of sexually abusive behaviors.

Components of the Sexual Abuse Cycle

A comprehensive, in-depth understanding of the sexual abuse cycle can be used to begin to predict the youth's future behaviors during treatment. The cycle also provides a framework for assessing the treatment needs of the youth. By developing an awareness of the individual's red flags (cues that indicate progression through various stages of the cycle), clinicians can assist the youth with learning to recognize and interrupt cycle progression. The therapist can also identify potential core issues (historical or trauma issues) that influence current functioning. When a youth understands his personalized cycle and the patterns associated with his abusive behaviors, he is able to develop strategies to cope with problems more effectively and control his sexually abusive behavior. For some youth, this is a welcome relief and provides hope for the future when they have perceived their behavior as unpredictable and, therefore, out of control.

When exploring the cycle, it is helpful to view it as occurring in three main phases:

1. *The precipitating phase.* The youth's initial cognitive and affective response to a problem, interaction, or occurrence; his sense of helplessness, dread, and hopelessness; and his attempts to avoid the issue.
2. *The compensatory phase.* The youth's attempts to compensate through nonsexual and sexual power-based behaviors and thoughts.
3. *The integration phase.* The youth's efforts to assimilate the abusive behavior without self-deprecation. The process culminates in suppression, which allows the youth to deny that his behavior is problematic or that he may be unable to prevent future recurrence.

The Precipitating Phase

During the precipitating phase, the youth is reacting to something that has happened. Essentially events are neutral; it is the meaning the youth attaches to them that dictates the affective and behavioral response. The initial interpretation of any situation, interaction, or event is based on the conclusions the individual has developed about the world and his or her self. Each youth has the choice of reacting to a problem as something to solve or something to avoid. Healthy responses include being aware of internal affective reactions, thinking clearly and accurately about the problem, and using a variety of social competencies and resources to cope with or solve the problem.

The response depicted in the precipitating phase of the cycle is maladaptive and unhealthy. The meaning of the problem is based on distorted thoughts. In the sequence of distorted perceptions, the youth concludes he is being treated unfairly or that there is something wrong with him. He then assumes that he will continue to experience similar or worse circumstances and specifically imagines the outcomes. He attempts to avoid the issue, the anticipated outcomes, and his current thoughts and feelings (see Figure 6.2). At times, each of us may initially respond to a situation in this way, but eventually we recognize and interrupt the process or arrive at an effective, nonabusive plan.

FIGURE 6.2. THE PRECIPITATING PHASE
OF THE SEXUAL ABUSE CYCLE.

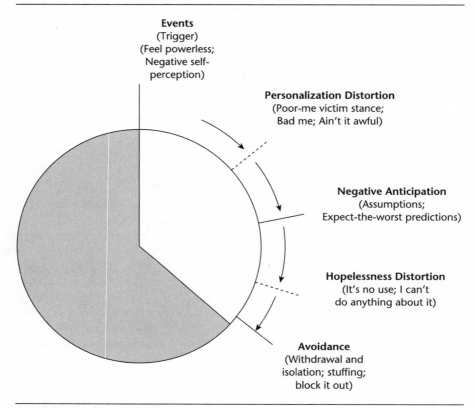

Source: Reprinted by permission of RSA, Inc.

When the young offender is first developing the distortions or thinking errors represented in this phase, the process may unfold quite slowly. The distortions may be based in adaptive defenses that developed during early childhood experience or may reflect the beliefs and defensive coping styles of others who have served as role models. Once the distorted or inaccurate perception becomes a habitual way of interpreting certain types of events, the process appears nearly automatic, and the initial phase can move so rapidly that the youth has little conscious awareness of the process. In fact, many youth who enter treatment initially indicate that they had no problems prior to their referring behavior. This may be due in part to the distorted beliefs and thoughts' being so ingrained and in part to defense mechanisms that help them avoid the discomfort associated with their thoughts and feelings.

Events. Interactions, experiences, problematic situations, trauma, and exposure to the difficulties of others are events that can trigger the sexual abuse cycle. Each individual will have an idiosyncratic perception of the meaning of any occurrence, based on his or her basic beliefs, life experience, and perceptions about the world. The nature of the event will vary significantly from youth to youth, but the common theme appears to be the kind of feeling that is evoked—most frequently, helplessness or lack of control, followed by a sense of abandonment or perceived abandonment.

Helplessness is the feeling of being overwhelmed and not being able to respond to or do anything about a situation. Feelings of helplessness underlie issues of abandonment as the individual is unable to do anything to prevent the loss of another. In fact, helplessness underlies many uncomfortable feelings. In the cycle, feeling helpless seems to be associated with such cognitions as, "I ought to be able to prevent this from happening," "I should be able to make them feel like I want them to," "I should get what I want," or "I should know what to do." Feeling helpless is not acceptable to many people, and they often deny it or mask it with anger. When it is masked with anger, the prevailing cognitions relate to a win-lose type of perception. The cognitions and feelings are quickly masked or suppressed, and the youth begins to personalize the event.

The event and associated feelings are interpreted by the youth in ways that result in negative self-perceptions. He may believe there is something wrong with him or view himself as weak, inadequate, incompetent, or deficient in some way, conclusions that result in decreased self-esteem. Each subsequent situation that the youth perceives as similar, and similarly interprets, strengthens the negative self-image and the distorted perceptions.

When the perceptions or conclusions about the original, or historical, event remain unchanged, the juvenile may suppress the issues to decrease anxiety. Subsequently there seems to be an increased sensitivity to any situation or event that is reminiscent of the original event (Lane & Zamora, 1982; Ryan, 1989). The reaction to the more current event may appear to be out of proportion to the situation because the juvenile is reacting to an accumulation of internal responses to past and current situations. The youth manages the anxiety associated with both historical and current events through the sense of control, empowerment, and temporary relief experienced in the maladaptive cycle. As the cycle is repeated, the oversensitive response occurs more frequently and is generalized to an increased variety of situations. More types of events remind the individual of the original situation, and there is less tolerance for any type of situation that evokes feelings of powerlessness. The pattern becomes more automatic and eventually becomes the habitual way of perceiving most occurrences. Consider a young child who observes his father being physically abusive to his mother. He is afraid of losing his mother and feels vulnerable. He tries to intervene but is shoved out of the way. He feels helpless and frightened. The child may later conclude, "I should have stopped him and protected my mom. I'm weak because I did nothing. I'm a failure. If I'm not strong enough, Mom gets hurt, and I'm not good enough." The conclusions are based on imagining that he should be able to control his father. This is clearly not a reasonable expectation, but it makes him feel less vulnerable. Subsequent events that are beyond the control of the youth may trigger similar feelings of weakness, inadequacy, and vulnerability. Over time, situations when the youth is challenged or criticized may evoke similar feelings and conclusions. He attempts to defend against these thoughts and feelings by trying to exert control in other ways.

The most frequently reported historical events that elicit feelings of helplessness are parental divorce; death of a significant person or pet; loss; change in environment; sexual, physical, or emotional abuse; family violence or dysfunction; rejection; public humiliation; being put down; betrayal; and awareness of family members' involvement in deviant sexual behaviors. It is likely that attachment issues and the style of parenting the youth experienced as a young child are also significant historical events that the youth may not be consciously aware of. Some youth report that loneliness or boredom triggers their cycle and that they find it intolerable to feel nothing when nothing is going on. This is a type of zero state that may result from years of defensive strategies that have effectively blocked emotions, for better and for worse. These experiences are not causal to sexual abuse behavior, but they are the stimuli for the child's development of coping styles.

In my initial work with sexually abusive youth, I believed that sexual victimization was the predominant historical experience that elicited feelings of helplessness, an assumption based on work with severely disturbed adolescent rapists, 98 percent of whom reported sexual victimization and the remaining 2 percent of whom had family members who had engaged in atypical sexual behaviors (Lane & Zamora, 1978). At that time, it was believed that young sexual offenders learned abusive behaviors through their experience of victimization. These assumptions have since been modified through subsequent work with a broader spectrum of youth who were not incarcerated and engaged in other types of sexually abusive behaviors. Although sexual victimization is a contributing factor for some, it is not characteristic of all. There are many ways children learn to be abusive. (Factors that may contribute to the development of sexually abusive behaviors are considered in Chapters Three and Five.)

Some youth have described historical events that involve distressing or incomprehensible sexual experiences. Some report exposure to sexual behaviors on the part of other family members, including fetish behaviors, pornographic involvement, or molestation. Others report poor sexual boundaries in the home, excessive nudity, parental sexual dysfunction, sexualized interactions with family members, or premature exposure to explicit and overstimulating sexual information. Others are known to have been sexually victimized and have failed to resolve, or at times even acknowledge, the experience. Some youth develop perceptions that there is something wrong with their family, and therefore with them. Others describe family attitudes or beliefs that justify their own sexual abuse behavior.

Events or situations that triggered the cycle prior to the youth's first offense or are current triggers are varied. Typical for juveniles are the experiences of moving, feeling put down or challenged, entering a new school, poor grades, being told no, rejection by a friend or a romantic liaison, parental conflicts and restrictions, criticism, parental remarriage, embarrassment, losing a game, a friend's moving away, feeling unaccepted, feeling that one cannot measure up, authority conflicts, and skill deficits. As his tolerance lessens, even more innocuous situations may affect the youth. Such events as being asked to wait, being told one is wrong, seeing someone laugh or stare and interpreting it as personal, failing to be acknowledged, not getting one's way, being ignored, or feeling bored may trigger the cycle. There is a common theme here: a lack of tolerance for feelings of helplessness and distorted conclusions about adequacy and power.

The Personalization Distortion.   The first cognitive distortion in the sexual abuse cycle strengthens the youth's sense of vulnerability, powerlessness, and inadequacy. This distortion represents how the youth has interpreted the event over some period of time. A young client called this PMS, "poor me syndrome," because many of the thoughts have a victim-stance orientation.

Each of the cognitions indicates some degree of personalization. The thoughts might include assuming responsibility for the event due to some perceived deficit, attributing negative and hurtful motivations to another for some behavior, perceiving it as some kind of an affront or an attack, believing one is a victim because of the event, focusing on the inconvenience that has occurred, believing it is not fair, or affirming the youth's worldview. The affective response involves uncomfortable emotions. The youth might feel guilty, ashamed, frustrated, hurt, helpless, sad, angry, controlled, persecuted, betrayed, inadequate, or embarrassed. There is a sense of unease and anxiety associated with the thoughts.

Consider a child whose parents divorce, and the custodial parent moves to the opposite side of town. The child experiences the loss of both parents' being present all the time, predictability and familiarity, a peer group, neighborhood, house, room, and so forth. He thinks, "They don't care about me. It's not fair. They're messing with me. I don't count. If only I had cleaned up my room. I trusted them. I didn't get a say in this." If the child does not successfully cope with the change, he will have difficulty with future changes as well. Over time, even minor disruptions in routine may be seen as having the same meaning as the historical situation and evoke similar feelings of powerlessness and thoughts of not being important.

Regardless of the way he personalizes, the youth will begin to question his ability to protect himself in the current situation. When the adolescent has a core belief that he should be able to stop or control threatening events, his adequacy is continually questioned and his negative self-concept is increased. This distortion is related to misattributions of the locus of control. The youth feels responsible for controlling things outside himself and fails to recognize his capacity for internal control. If such misattributions are not corrected, the youth may brood about the implications of the events, and their feelings of victimization and helplessness increase. The cycle progresses to the next stage as thinking begins to generalize.

Negative Anticipation. In this stage the youth begins to predict that the future will be the same as the past. There is a tendency to view situations as black or white, inflexible, and overwhelming, with limited options, explanations, or outcomes. The process is one of generalization, or making mountains out of molehills. The youth makes assumptions about potential outcomes, and the predictions become his expectations. He begins to feel defensive and think about how to handle what he knows is going to happen. There is a generalized increase in anxiety associated with feelings of dread, apprehension, helplessness, inadequacy, and hopelessness. During this phase, the young offender may feel incapacitated, depressed, and incompetent.

Statements reflecting thoughts in this stage of the cycle include words such as *always* and *never*. The predictions and assumptions are absolute and unyielding. Although the cognitions are distorted, to the youth they are solid beliefs. For example, the child whose parents are divorcing worries about the move and begins to think, "I'll never have friends over there. She'll never let me see my dad, and he won't have any place for me anyway. There will be nothing to do over there. She'll want me to stick around all the time. They will never care about my needs." He begins to feel down as he has these thoughts. He starts to think about the separation, and he feels pretty tense. If the youth fails to use communication, resolution, or coping skills so that he can challenge his assumptions, he will continue to progress through the cycle.

The Hopelessness Distortion. As the youth convinces himself that his situation will worsen in the future and that he will have no ability to prevent it, he becomes increasingly hopeless. Depression may increase as he feels more unable to protect himself. Anxiety increases to an uncomfortable level, and the groundwork is laid for defensive reactions.

Thoughts in this stage of the cycle are characterized by feelings of incapacity and incompetence. He may think, "I can't do anything about this," "I can't handle this," "I can't face it," "It's bigger than I am," "It's no use; it will never change," "I can't help it," and "Maybe it will go away if I don't think about it." As his sense of inadequacy and hopelessness grow, he may exhibit increased dependency or protection-seeking behaviors. The youth also exhibits decreased tolerance for conflict or problematic interactions. For example, a young girl watched television after school with her friends instead of doing her chores. When her mother got home from work, she scolded her and told her she was grounded and could not go to the mall with her friends on the weekend. The girl begins to think, "She doesn't let me to do anything. She doesn't want me to have friends. She doesn't care about me. No matter how hard I try, I can't please her. She wants me to look bad to my friends." As her thoughts generalize, she begins thinking, "I'll never be able to please her. She'll never be satisfied. She'll never let me do anything. She'll never care about my needs. Why should I even try anymore?" She cries and refuses to eat that night or the next morning. She is depressed and listless.

For some youth, the negative expectations and hopelessness are based in reality and may not be distorted because they have such developmental deficits that they lack the skills to achieve better outcomes. This situation has implications for treatment.

Avoidance. In his first attempt to cope with the situation as well as his negative thoughts and feelings, he tries to push it away by blotting it out, withdrawing, isolating himself, or avoiding thinking about it. Any success he may have with avoidance, however, is temporary, and the uncomfortable thoughts and feelings intrude again.

Commonly described avoidance behaviors include increased sleeping, substance abuse, spending more time in one's room, not answering the telephone, giving excuses to avoid activities, playing video games, listening to loud music, wearing earphones to avoid having to interact with others, extensive daydreaming, excessive reading, engaging in solitary activities, or doing hobbies alone. Many youths report active attempts to repress any thoughts associated with the trigger. Some effectively isolate by behaving in ways that irritate others to the extent that they stay away from the youth.

Instead of being able to escape the negative self-perceptions, fears, and uncomfortable feelings, the youth typically finds himself ruminating about the problem, his self-perceived shortcomings, or the negative motivations he has attributed to others' behaviors. Consider the following case example:

As the teacher is handing back the midterm math test to her class, she comments, "Willie, you have the worst score on this test; you must not pay attention in class." Willie feels embarrassed and begins to think, "Everyone knows how dumb I am. They are laughing at me. The teacher hates me. She's trying to make me look bad. I'm so stupid." As he looks around the class, he notices everyone staring at him, and some are snickering. He thinks, "They're going to make fun of me because I'm dumb. Everybody is going to think I'm dumb. I won't have friends anymore. The teacher isn't ever going to give me a chance. I'm going to get yelled at by my parents and be grounded for a long time." Willie stares at his desk during the rest of the class and doesn't talk to anyone. He decides he won't go to the mall with his friends after school because they will tease him, and besides, they wouldn't want to be seen with a stupid person.

After class, he races out and doesn't answer his best friend's calls to him. He heads to his locker and decides not to take his math book, thinking, "It's no use. I won't understand it anyway." He walks home by a different route than usual and goes straight to his room when he gets home. He turns on his video game and plays until his mother calls him to dinner. During the weekend, he spends a lot of time alone and doesn't talk much to his family. He takes a long, solitary bicycle ride and then goes fishing, also alone. He feels more and more lonely. Over the weekend, the picture of his teacher saying he's stupid pops into his mind constantly, but he keeps trying to push the thoughts away. When he can't, he thinks about how unfair she has been to him, and he dreads going to math class next week because she'll do it again. He decides he can sit in the back and keep his mouth shut so she won't notice him, and he'll call in sick the next time there is a test.

Because Willie doesn't correct his misperceptions, the hopeless, helpless feelings continue and are gradually replaced by anger. As the thoughts continue, there may be further avoidance attempts if there has been some relief of anxiety from previous isolation or withdrawal. When this process is no longer effective, he progresses further in the cycle to reduce anxiety and increase his sense of adequacy.

The Compensatory Phase

Elements of both sexualized and nonsexualized expressions of control and dominance are depicted in the compensatory phase of the cycle. Through the irresponsible use of power, the youth attempts to improve his self-perceptions. Power-based thoughts and behaviors provide a sense of mastery, empowerment, and excitement that compensate for previous feelings of inadequacy and helplessness. The youth believes that his issues are settled by lashing out at someone (retaliation) or that he is entitled to feel better (compensation).

The process begins with anger and blaming others; then the youth expresses the anger through nonsexualized power-based behaviors. The gratification is effective but temporary, and the youth experiences a need for further gratification. His thoughts initially meet that need; then he begins to engage in power-based behaviors that culminate in an abusive behavior to maintain the same level of gratification. Setting up the opportunity to be abusive involves a complex set of thoughts, behaviors, and reactions (see Figure 6.3).

FIGURE 6.3. THE COMPENSATORY PHASE OF THE SEXUAL ABUSE CYCLE.

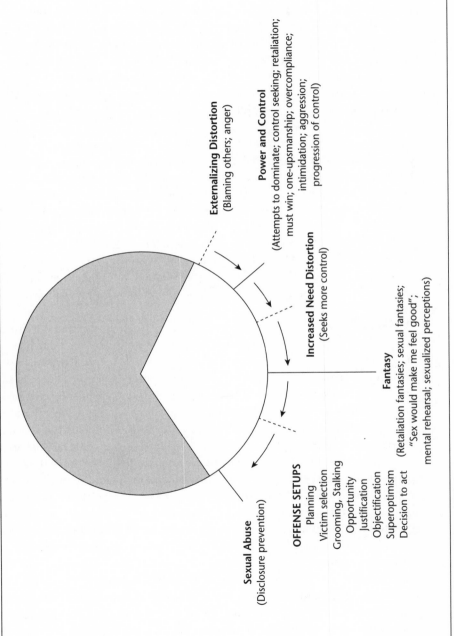

Externalizing Distortion
(Blaming others; anger)

Power and Control
(Attempts to dominate; control seeking; retaliation; must win; one-upsmanship; overcompliance; intimidation; aggression; progression of control)

Increased Need Distortion
(Seeks more control)

Fantasy
(Retaliation fantasies; sexual fantasies; "Sex would make me feel good"; mental rehearsal; sexualized perceptions)

Sexual Abuse
(Disclosure prevention)

OFFENSE SETUPS
Planning
Victim selection
Grooming, Stalking
Opportunity
Justification
Objectification
Superoptimism
Decision to act

Source: Reprinted by permission of RSA, Inc.

The rate of progression in this phase varies considerably among sexually abusive youth. A youth whose response pattern is more habituated will move quickly to nonsexualized control-seeking behaviors and more gradually toward an abusive sexual behavior. At times some offenders engage in blitz behaviors, with rapid and frequent progression toward an offense. This pattern appears to relate to the significance of the precipitating issues and the degree of internal distress. The process appears to be supported by beliefs that being powerless is equivalent to being weak, that one ought to be able to control external circumstances, and that demonstrations of power emphasize one's strength and adequacy.

The Externalizing Distortion. As the youth is ruminating about his situation, he becomes increasingly frustrated. Anger begins to build, and he blames someone for what he is experiencing. To blame himself would only strengthen his sense of powerlessness and inadequacy. His sense of outrage builds, and he begins to think about some form of retaliation or one-upmanship. He may think, "It's their fault I am feeling this way," "If it weren't for them I'd be fine," "They had no right to do this to me," "He deserves to pay for what he's done to me," "I'll show her she can't do this to me," and "They'll be sorry for this." The youth may begin to engage in some power-based fantasies that involve retaliation, humiliation of those he views as responsible, one-upmanship, or making others sorry for having mistreated him.

Power and Control. The first observable compensatory response consists of control-seeking behaviors. Juveniles who engage in power-based behaviors initially feel a sense of superiority, authority, or control. They seek a sense of adequacy and empowerment by trying to dominate or exert control over others; in some respects, the youth views control-seeking behaviors as a defensive reaction to prevent the things he assumes will occur or to retaliate against those whom he views as responsible for what he is feeling and thinking. The distorted sense of empowerment masks the prior experience of helplessness, vulnerability, and negative self-perceptions. Control-seeking behaviors may be expressed aggressively, passively, or passive-aggressively. The associated thinking involves a sense of anger, entitlement, and superiority. Misuse of power may involve efforts to dominate, direct, or control others; retaliation efforts; one-upmanship; initiating win-lose interactions; presenting oneself as the best or having the most; looking for a loophole to exploit; or sarcasm. It is common for the youth to exhibit a progression of control-seeking behaviors in this phase.

Sexually abusive youth have described behaviors such as having to win at games, arguing, slamming doors, walking out of a confrontation, needing to have the last word, pressing one's point until it is accepted, not following directions, a victim-stance response, derogatory statements, ignoring others, substance abuse (either to get away with something or to oppose parental expectations), obsequious or overcompliant reactions, lying, making others come to him to work things out, breaking rules, failing to do what was requested, manipulation, needing to do things one's own way or on one's own terms, tricking someone, not completing homework or failing to turn it in, intimidation, paybacks, put-downs, threats, fighting, oppositional behaviors, superior stance, bragging, being critical, challenging others, and setting others up to get in trouble.

Thoughts associated with these behaviors might include, "I showed them. They've been put in their place," "Now he knows not to mess with me," "That will stop her," and "I'm really something." The affect may be angry, arrogant, or resentful. Several young offenders have described an associated sense of thrill, excitement, and accomplishment when they feel they have successfully controlled another, as Willie did:

By Sunday evening, Willie felt angry at his teacher and dreaded going to class the next day. That evening he began picking on his younger sister by hiding her favorite toy and refusing to let her watch her regular television show. When his mom reminded him to take out the trash, he told her to wait. He later decided that his mother was being unfair by expecting him to do everything. He thought, "She can just do it herself," and went to his room.

On the way to school the next morning, he called his friend George "fatso." He was thinking that would teach him not to make fun of Willie or call him stupid. In his math class, he ignored the teacher's offer to give him help after school and did not turn in his homework. He sat in the back of the classroom and threw spit wads at some of the teacher's favorite students. He called one of the boys who answered a question a cheater. When he walked out of class he thought, "I'm better than all of the smart kids in that class. I really showed her she was wrong to front me off."

The sense of empowerment that results from power-based behaviors is fairly brief, lasting from a few minutes to a day. The more habituated the response patterns are, the briefer are the positive effects. It is difficult for the young offender to realize that his expression of power represents an ineffective and maladaptive coping response. Because interpersonal control behaviors do not really resolve issues, the juvenile is again faced with self-doubt, a victim-stance orientation, and negative assumptions. As his anxiety increases, the youth continues efforts to achieve empowerment through the misuse of power. When he is no longer able to manage his anxiety adequately or compensate for his thoughts and feelings, cycle progression will continue. If the youth is assisted with developing effective social competencies to manage or resolve the trigger, the cycle can be interrupted, and the youth would experience a more authentic sense of self-control and a more enduring sense of empowerment.

The Increased Need Distortion. This distortion is typically brief and is characterized by the youth's sense of not having adequately "shown" others that they had no right to treat him the way they have. Because the misuse of power does not create an enduring sense of control, his sense of anxiety returns, and the perceived need for control continues. It is also possible that the gratification from the expression of power-based behaviors is so satisfying that the youth wants to obtain more gratification. He then experiences an increased need for control. Although there is little overt acknowledgment of the need for more control, a typical thought is, "I really showed them, but it would show them even more if I were to _____ ."

Fantasy. The sequence of thoughts, or fantasies, in this stage of the cycle involves a progression from nonsexualized control-seeking thoughts, to sexual thoughts that involve some element of control, to contemplation of sexually abusive behaviors. The effect continues to be compensatory as the youth thinks of himself as powerful, heroic, irresistible, or invincible. He believes that because others do not know what he is thinking, he is somehow controlling that person. The fantasies may be brief, partial thought fragments or elaborate and detailed. Appropriate fantasies are an integral part of our lives. Fantasies that occur in the sexual abuse cycle serve a compensatory purpose and involve the misuse of power.

Nonsexualized control-seeking fantasies tend to be elaborations of previous power-based behaviors but often involve more expression of power, with themes of domination, retaliation, humiliation, and aggression. At times the fantasies can involve violence that appears to be out of proportion to the situation.

Frequently described control-seeking fantasies include being in charge of the world, school, the family, or others; being a star; placing snakes in the teacher's desk; beating someone up; being the most popular person around; putting sugar in a gas tank; being perfect; making someone crawl to beg forgiveness; being a millionaire; killing someone; or torturing someone. Associated thoughts tend to contribute to the young offender's sense of power. Examples include, "They'd be really sorry if I did that. That would really show them," "They don't even know what I'm thinking or could do. If they knew they'd be freaked. I'd love to see the look on his face if I did it. I bet they'd never mess with me again." The associated affect is often exuberant and smug.

The youth eventually begins to have sexual fantasies. Some sexually abusive youth report that they switch to sexual fantasy as they begin to realize that they would be unable to do the things they have been thinking of, and their sense of gratification and the enhanced self-perception diminish. As they begin to think of sexual matters, they experience an associated arousal experience, the gratification resumes, and the behaviors seem somewhat more plausible. Other youth report they begin thinking that sex would make them feel better. For juveniles who have a more habituated offense pattern, the switch to sexual fantasies occurs more quickly, and they experience stronger urges to do something sexual.

The sexual fantasies may initially appear to be normal fantasies, but close examination indicates that an element of control, dominance, or power is involved. Frequently described fantasies include being the most sexually desirable, a "superstud" or "hot pants"; having a sex partner who will do everything he or she is told to or who is interested only in meeting all of his needs; being so irresistible that the most popular person in school cannot help but be attracted to him; being sexual with a rock or movie star; indulging in bondage or sadistic behaviors; having perfect sexual abilities or performance; having an insatiable sex partner, a harem at his command, or a partner who is willing to be sexual in public or precarious places; or engaging in humiliating sexual behaviors.

When sexually abusive youth are having power-based sexual fantasies, they overtly exhibit increased sexual preoccupation. They may make more sexual comments than usual, tell more sexual jokes, exhibit an increased interest in pornography or pictures that have sexual meaning to them, engage in more masturbatory activity, or report increased sexualized perceptions. They begin to notice sexual cues and characteristics of others and may move in more sexualized ways. As they begin to sexualize others, there may be some misinterpretation of nonsexual cues. Frequently youth will begin to objectify others by noticing only sexual body parts, staring, or invading privacy.

Thinking of themselves as engaging in sexual behaviors provides an enhanced self-perception. The youth views himself as potent, adequate, desirable, and in control. The associated arousal and psychological pleasure contribute to a positive association with sexualized controlling thoughts that is more powerful and gratifying than the pleasure associated with nonsexualized power-based thoughts. Given the positive association, the youth is more likely to engage in similar fantasies in the future when he needs to perceive himself in a more positive light or needs to reduce internal discomfort.

The youth gradually begins to realize that his control-seeking sexual fantasies are not attainable either. The sense of needing more control remains and is perhaps increased if the youth begins to have negative self-perceptions when he realizes his fantasy is unattainable. He begins to shift his thoughts to sexual behaviors that are daring. Some juvenile offenders report that they begin to think of possible alternatives to engage in some sexual behavior. They think of ways to make it possible and consider who is most likely to cooperate.

As a youth begins to contemplate sexually abusive behavior, there is a "What if?" or "I wonder what it would be like?" quality. The majority of sexually abusive youth report that when they initially entertain the thought of some type of sexual abuse behavior and experience arousal, they reject the idea based on values or internal sanctions against such behavior. The thoughts may recur any number of times, the youth may masturbate to the ideations, and he may continue to reject the idea after each fantasy. It is believed that this process may contribute to the development of deviant arousal. The experience of arousal and orgasm associated with thoughts of controlling sexual behaviors or sexually abusive behaviors enhances the youth's feeling of well-being yet at the same time develops an association, and perhaps an eventual pairing. It appears to strengthen and reinforce inappropriate sexual arousal. This process continues to provide compensatory anxiety reduction and increased self-perceptions of being powerful or in control.

As the thoughts are repeated, the sense of excitement and gratification begins to wane. Sexually abusive youth report they begin to add elements to their fantasies to maintain the level of excitement and gratification: additional sexual behaviors, increased elements of control, or improved ways of making the behavior possible. Some youth begin to feel uncomfortable with their thinking and try to stop such thoughts or repress their fantasies. When they finally sexually abuse someone, they initially fail to recall previous sexual abuse thoughts and believe the idea just popped into their head. Other youths may continue to refine their fantasy until they arrive at an ideal scenario. They may repeat the ideal fantasy several times. Some youth have reported engaging in an ideal fantasy in a compulsive manner, even to the point of masturbating so vigorously that they cause penile irritation or injury. Still others engage in repetition of their original fantasy with little change in detail, although the imagined victim may vary from time to time. The fantasies and subsequent behaviors of some youth are rigid and ritualized and change very little over time. Some report a somewhat fixated scenario, often a re-creation of their own memory of being victimized but seeing themselves in the role of the aggressor in their fantasy. The repetition and refinement of the fantasies is the basis for planning and becomes a mental rehearsal for later behaviors. Here is an example

As Manuel rides his bike to football practice, he is still steaming at his coach for scheduling a scrimmage on a Saturday and spoiling his chance to go to the mall with his friends. He had been so mad he had slammed the telephone down when his coach called. While he was riding, he deliberately splashed gutter water on some little kid, and when he got to practice, he was sullen and talked back to the coach once. He was thinking of telling the coach what he really thought of him, getting the entire team to go on strike if there were any more Saturday practices, and deliberately giving the ball to the other team. The more he thought of these things, the better he felt. He began to think of trying some of them but realized he would get benched or lose his starting position. He now considers cutting the coach's brake lines on his precious van, or blowing up his house to show him he shouldn't mess with other people's plans, but as he thinks of it, he isn't sure what lines to cut or where to buy dynamite. Besides, he'd be in a jam if there wasn't a coach for his team.

After practice, while he is riding home, he begins to think about the girl down the street. He wishes she'd notice him; he could show her a good time. He knows where his parents keep an X-rated movie; he could make her watch it. She'd probably like it so much she'd kiss him. Maybe she'd even let him touch her breast. Then he remembers she has an older boyfriend who would beat him up if he even tried. He remembers the coach has two little girls. He starts thinking, "I bet he'd be sorry if something happened to those girls. I could babysit for him and touch them, but if they told, I could get caught. I could tell them if they ever told I'd shave their heads. They'd like it if I touched them. I bet I could even get them to suck me."

As Manual entertains these thoughts over the next few days, he is aroused and even masturbates once. About a week later, he decides that what he is thinking is sick and that he would never really try something like that because he'd be in a lot of trouble. He'd probably end up in some prison built just for jerks like him. A couple of weeks later, his friend sneaks a centerfold into practice, and all the guys ogle the picture. On his way home that night, he sees a woman walking alone on the bike path. He looks at her breasts and wonders if they look like the picture he saw. That evening he thinks that if he could find someone like her, only a little bit smaller, he could grab her breast and get away with it. He'd never be identified, and who would believe a kid would do something like that anyway? That night he thinks of trying it, masturbates, and has the best orgasm he has ever had. He thinks about grabbing her crotch and wonders what a lady's pubic hair feels like.

As the weeks go on, he imagines grabbing a lady and taking her to a bush where he could make her give him a blow job. Sometimes he imagines her thinking he is a stud and wanting to teach him all about sex. He begins to wonder if he really could pull it off. He can imagine how great he would feel. He begins to think of where he could do it. One time on the way home from practice, he even stopped by a bush and thought about the lady and got very aroused. He began to think of what kind of person he'd pick. He decides to watch for someone who isn't too alert and is small enough to handle—maybe someone who is kind of heavy so he can outrun her if he has to. He knows he'd never really do it, but he needs to have a real lady to picture when he thinks about it.

When the compensatory effects of fantasy begin to diminish, the youth progresses toward a sexual abuse behavior to maintain a level of compensatory gratification. Interrupting the cycle at this point requires that the youth develop abilities to interrupt and correct the thinking that justifies the behavior.

Offense Setups. In this stage of the cycle, the young offender lays the groundwork for committing a sexual abuse behavior. Through a series of thoughts and behaviors, the youth's fantasy becomes a plan, a victim is selected and objectified, the possibility of successfully engaging in the behavior is evaluated, an opportunity is developed or exploited, the behaviors are rationalized and justified, a belief in capability is reinforced, and a decision is made to engage in the behavior. Throughout the process, the youth feels a sense of thrill, empowerment, anticipation, and, for some, sexual arousal. Youths who have engaged in previous sexually abusive behaviors may move rapidly through this stage. It is difficult for the youth to stop the behavior during this stage due to the accompanying internal gratification.

Planning. Planning essentially involves refining the young offender's repetitive fantasy. The original scheme, or fantasy, becomes more explicit and is modified based on situational aspects. Sometimes the plan is completed as the offense evolves, and sometimes it occurs well before the offense. For some youths, the plans are elaborate and detailed, and for others they may consist of fragments or a vague outline of what they would like to do. The young offender becomes increasingly excited about the anticipated outcomes and continues to feel a sense of empowerment and mastery.

It is difficult for a youth to acknowledge having planned his abusive behavior. He may believe it sounds worse if it was not an impulsive act, or he may be struggling with the implications of the behavior to the extent that he needs to deny planning. He may be concerned that the consequences will be greater if the behavior was premeditated. The majority of sexually abusive behaviors occur in an area that allows the behavior to succeed, and there are elements of secrecy involved. This would suggest the presence of some planning that would support a successful offense. In fact, many clinicians think that a young offender would be more dangerous if he committed an offense without thinking about it at all.

Refining a plan might include thinking about strategies that would increase victim compliance or cooperation, selecting the most promising opportunity, and deciding what to do during the offense behavior. An integral part of planning is predicting the victim's thoughts and behaviors, as well as anticipating their own pleasurable experience. When a youth is thinking about an offense, he is in control and believes that how he hopes a victim will respond and think is how it will actually be when he engages in the behavior.

Juveniles who engage in repeated sexual abuse behaviors indicate that their offenses become less exciting or fulfilling over time. They tend to refine their plans to maintain excitement by introducing more intrusive sexual behaviors, manipulating the victim to agree to more sophisticated behaviors, adding to the amount of control or coercion involved, increasing the elements of risk, adding punitive aspects, choosing a new locale, or introducing rituals. Most offenders maintain elements of their original modus operandi, to which these elements are added.

Victim Selection. Victim selection is the process of choosing the individual who offers the greatest likelihood of complying with a sexual abuse behavior. The choice is based on the sexually abusive youth's perception of the victim's vulnerability. In fact, the victim may not be vulnerable, but the choice is based on the youth's perspective. Perceptions of vulnerability are based on victim characteristics that the youth believes he can use to exploit, manipulate, coerce, or overcome to engage in a sexual abuse behavior. A youth is less likely to abuse someone he does not believe he can control.

Other criteria related to choosing a victim are age, gender, personality traits, physical features, or interpersonal qualities. The sexually abusive youth may choose a victim who is outgoing because she relates to him in a way that makes him feel looked up to, or he may target a quiet child because he is less likely to tell. A youth may choose a prepubescent child because his skin is soft and he lacks pubic hair, an elderly victim because she will struggle less, or a peer who appears naive because she is less likely to understand what he is trying to do. Each youth has an idiosyncratic set of criteria for the type of victims selected.

The victim may be known to the youth or a stranger. It is more likely that child molestation and acquaintance rape behaviors will be committed with someone the youth knows and that hands-off offenses and some rapes will involve strangers. When the victim is known, the sexually abusive youth will develop a relationship or interaction with the potential victim and identify ways to complete the offense successfully. When the victim is a stranger, the youth may take advantage of an opportunity that presents itself, may stalk the victim, or may cruise for a victim.

Cruising, or searching for a victim, and at times an opportunity, is used primarily by youth who expose, peep, rape, molest young children, or make obscene telephone calls. When a youth is cruising, he is typically searching for someone he perceives as vulnerable, someone he believes will react in the way he has fantasized, someone in a location that will allow the offense to occur undetected, and someone who meets his idiosyncratic victim criteria. At times an offender may cruise for a locale, then watch for a potential victim to appear. Still others may join an organization or get a job (for example, the boy scouts, a youth group, food delivery to the elderly, or telephone solicitation) in order to gain access to potential victims.

One youth described programming his telephone to dial sequential numbers until he heard a younger female respond with irritation. He then called that number repeatedly to make obscene telephone calls. He believed that because he could "make the victim angry," he was controlling her. Some youth who expose report choosing "housewife" types or teenage girls because they assume these victims are less likely to report the experience, while others report choosing young children because the anticipated response is fascination and curiosity. Some youth who rape describe looking for someone who is isolated or lacks accessibility to assistance.

When the youth is fantasizing about an offense behavior, he assumes he has the ability to control a victim. When a victim has been selected, the youth's fantasies involve a quality of ownership of the victim. They begin to expect the victim to behave and react in the way they have fantasized. If the potential victim is known to the youth, he may become angry or attempt to exert nonsexual control if the victim is behaving differently than he expects.

Grooming or Stalking. Grooming or stalking behaviors are used by the sexually abusive youth to increase the likelihood that his offense behavior is successful. Stalking is the process of observing a potential victim to identify lifestyle patterns and habits. Grooming is a way of checking out victim responses to intrusive behaviors, directions, or boundary violations. It is also used to train a victim to be comfortable with the youth's behaviors. During either process, the victim is viewed as an object who is there to meet the youth's needs.

A power differential is often established by the youth when he is grooming the victim. In part, it is the power differential that the youth relies on to make the sexual abuse behavior successful. Power differential involves a lack of equality of knowledge, awareness, strength, experience, status, or authority.

Young males who commit acquaintance rape may groom a prospective victim with expensive treats, expressing expectations of obligation, controlling behaviors, and criticism. Youth who molest younger children might groom a potential victim by developing a special relationship involving trust or closeness; establishing an authority position by directing the child to do various behaviors, babysitting for the youngster and capitalizing on parental directives to obey him, or becoming an adviser to the child; developing a pattern of paying the child for favors; seemingly accidental genital touch during horseplay or wrestling; or being aggressive in nonsexual situations to make the child afraid and more willing to acquiesce to requests for sexual behaviors to avoid being harmed. At times, those who engage in hands-off behaviors may groom a victim to be fearful and react in a manner the sexually abusive youth desires through threatening notes or telephone calls. Each youth develops a unique way of grooming the victim.

The youth may distort the victim's responses to grooming behaviors in a way that meets some of his emotional needs. If a child becomes more trusting in response to the youth's behaviors, he may perceive the child as accepting, respecting, and looking up to him and feel accepted and more worthwhile. If a child follows his directives, he may feel adequate and capable. If a child exhibits fearful responses, he may feel more powerful. He may feel excited about getting away with something if he is able to trick a child.

Grooming involves deception that lessens the victim's resistance to, discomfort with, or awareness of the impending offense behaviors. A victim who may question invasive touch may be disarmed or confused by responses that it was unintentional. The youth may later use the same instance to induce guilt on the victim's part by pointing out that he or she did not question it previously. The youth may also use the same instance to convince himself that the victim did not mind, and maybe liked, the previous touch and thus would not object to more specific and overt sexual abuse behaviors. Thus, grooming also tends to increase the youth's comfort with the sexual behavior.

The sexually abusive youth learns about the potential victim's habits and routines through stalking. If the victim is a stranger, he may follow the person, gain access to a living situation through surreptitious means, or observe the victim over an extended period of time. He begins to identify the most likely situation or timing to sexually assault the victim successfully. Stalking may also occur with a known victim. In a home situation, the youth may violate boundaries and observed parental routines, establish victim patterns, and identify situations where he can successfully molest the victim. During the stalking process, the youth strengthens cognitions of victim ownership and entitlement.

Opportunity. Opportunity is the location or situation that affords the youth the best possibility for successfully committing his sexual abuse behavior. He may create the opportunity or take advantage of one that presents itself. An opportunity encompasses a location that is secluded or private, a victim who meets the offender's criteria, the probability that the offense can be committed, and the offender's readiness to engage in the behavior. Each youth has an idiosyncratic view of the ideal opportunity, and there is a tendency to seek similar criteria from offense to offense.

A youth might volunteer to babysit or to supervise younger children on a school outing to develop both victim access and an opportunity to molest a child. Other youth might cruise an amusement park or a bike path to look for a potential opportunity or develop a scheme to lure a potential victim to an isolated site. Still other youth may find themselves in an interaction where a potential victim suggests an activity that will afford an opportunity to engage in the behavior.

Readiness to engage in an offense will vary considerably among youth. Some will decide to commit an offense and work to develop the opportunity over a long period of time. Others may experience a strong urge to engage in the behavior and immediately search for the first available opportunity. Some youth may entertain a fantasy and reject acting on it, then find themselves in a situation where the offense could be easily accomplished and capitalize on the opportunity. Still other youths may prepare themselves through use of pornography or pictures that have sexual meaning to them and then use a situation that is usually available as the opportunity. Many youth report engaging in some rehearsal behaviors. They will practice various elements of the anticipated offense behavior to ensure success and maximize the opportunity.

On some occasions, the youth may believe that he has the right opportunity and prepares to commit the sexually abusive behavior. If an external deterrent prevents access and the opportunity is no longer possible, thus delaying the planned behavior, some youths will feel frustrated and escalate efforts to engage in the behavior, while others may feel irritated and wait for another potential opportunity. Planned deterrents can be a component of relapse-prevention planning.

As the sexually abusive youth engages in repeated sexual abuse behaviors, he appears to take more risks with the opportunity structure. Some might engage in behaviors when adults are nearby but not in the same room or in public with minimal cover. The increased risk adds an element of feeling that he has accomplished something or is slick. A greater degree of risk indicates the youth is experiencing distortions that normalize his behaviors, his entitlement to do what he wants, and an increased sense of empowerment.

Justifications. Justifications are rationalizations and distorted perceptions developed to support the youth's sexual abuse behavior. The distortions help the young offender to overcome or erode internal prohibitions against the behavior and make the offense behavior seem reasonable. The perceptions are not temporary; they are enduring beliefs that are difficult to correct.

The sexually abusive youth is aware that what he is considering doing would not be approved of by others, although he may not realize it is illegal. He has already accepted the notion that exerting control over others would make him feel good, he has begun to believe he is entitled to engage in the sexual fantasies he has had, and the thrill of contemplating something forbidden is exciting and empowering. These factors begin to outweigh internal prohibitions, and the distortions developed tend to eradicate his prohibitions and decrease the dissonance of the behavior. When the youth offends more habitually, the distortions are already in place, and the process becomes more automatic. Youth who have completed treatment indicate that one of the first things that begins to happen over time is a resumption of their belief in the justifications they had developed.

Justifications may involve reinterpreting or relabeling the behavior as not abusive, attributing positive motivations to his behaviors, viewing the victim as willing to participate, or perceiving the victim as deserving to be abused. Youth who are reinterpreting the offense might think, "I'm only trying to teach him sex so that he'll know what to do in the future," "I'm not doing anything wrong; I'm checking to see if her sore is better," "This isn't abuse; it's fun," "It's not abuse because I didn't use my penis, just my finger," and "I was just bathing him and making sure he knew good hygiene."

Thoughts that attribute positive motivations include, "This isn't wrong; I'm only trying to show her how much I care," "I need to try what I learned in sex education so I don't look dumb," "I want to share these pictures with them," "After all I've done for her, I'm entitled; I ought to be able to do what I want," and "I wanted him to feel better about himself, to feel accepted."

Examples of distorting the victim's willingness to engage in the offense behaviors include, "She loves me and wants to be close to me," "When she sits on my lap, she knows it arouses me so she must want to have sex with me," "He agreed to spend the night with me so he knows what I want," "They are tired and would like to relax," "He trusts me so he won't tell," "They like playing with me, so they'll like this," "She's loose and wants to have sex," "They are real sophisticated for their age so they'll enjoy this," and "He just wanted to do something gay."

Thoughts that view the victim as deserving might include, "She's dressed all sexy and is obviously asking for it," "She's a bitch; she deserved it," "It happened to me, so it should happen to him," "A nice girl wouldn't be out at this time of night, so she deserves it," "His parents messed with me, and he should pay for it," "I'm tired of all his crap; this will show him he should shut up," " He's a fag; he has no rights," "She looked me right in the eye; she was a slut," "They always get me in trouble," and "She was in the wrong place at the wrong time."

Objectification. Objectification is a way of viewing a victim as an object whose purpose is to satisfy the youth's wants and needs. It involves a process of depersonalization that allows the juvenile to forget that the individual is a whole person or someone he may have cared about. The victim's rights, wants, and needs are discounted and are viewed as having less importance than those of the youth's.

Some young offenders may exhibit sexual objectification of all females or younger children during this stage. They may become intrusive, violate individual privacy, or make demeaning sexual comments. Such behaviors might include disregarding closed bathroom or bedroom doors, looking down blouses, pulling someone's pants down, attributing sexual motives to others' behaviors, making catcalls, or telling sexual jokes. Victim behaviors and comments are often distorted by the youth as being sexual or supportive of the actions the youth wants to initiate. Many offenders will exhibit sexualized or nonsexual control-seeking behaviors that indicate a sense of superiority, ownership, or control over potential victims.

Superoptimism. Superoptimism is a strong belief that one can successfully engage in the sexually abusive behavior and attain the desired outcome without detection, interference, or consequence. It has been described by young children as "superman" thinking. The belief involves an overestimation of one's abilities and is accompanied by a sense of euphoria, confidence, and power. Typical thoughts might include, "I'm so slick," "Nothing can stop me now; she's all mine, only for me," and "I can get away with it. No one can catch me."

The belief in success extends to assuming that, if caught, the youth will experience no, or only minor, consequences. Even if there were consequences, the young offender overestimates his ability to handle them. When the youth is in this stage, he disregards internal prohibitions and underestimates potential deterrents. There is little, if any, cause-and-effect thinking. It is felt that the self-perceptions and affective reactions associated with this belief strengthen the compensatory aspects of the anticipated offense behavior.

The Decision to Act. The decision to act occurs immediately prior to the sexual abuse behavior and appears to involve several factors: excitement, sexual arousal, thrill, risk, superoptimism, anticipation, empowerment, eradication of remaining inhibitions, and entitlement. Many youth prefer to view their offense behavior as having "just happened" and initially deny that they made an active decision to cross the line and sexually abuse someone.

Many youth report an Adrenalin rush just prior to their offense. They report a rapid heartbeat, a heightened awareness, a sense of being focused, and increased alertness. Affective reactions of excitement, thrill, risk, boldness, and adventure are associated with the sensation. Thoughts include superoptimism, entitlement, fantasized expectations, and an "I want what I want when I want it" attitude. Many sexually abusive youth experience sexual arousal at various times during fantasizing and offense setups. They describe increased arousal as the time to commit the behavior nears. It is likely that arousal contributes to urges and a desire for immediate gratification just prior to sexual abuse behavior.

Some youth report substance abuse as being a contributor to the final decision. Although some sexually abusive youth try to blame drugs or alcohol for their behavior, most indicate that they abused some substance to reduce inhibitions and get the nerve to commit the act or felt that it would increase the enjoyment of the experience.

Anxiety, fear, and awareness of cause and effect are outweighed by the powerful and exhilarating feelings the youth has just before an offense. Most youth report some type of self-statement such as, "I might as well go for it; there won't be a better opportunity." Consider Theo's experience:

Theo has been fantasizing about exposing himself. He thinks, "It seems kind of weird, but I always wondered what it would be like to be naked outdoors. I could feel the sun better. It can't be too weird, I've heard of people who like to moon girls. It would be fun to try it in the park by my house. If I ever tried it, no one would ever have to know."

A few days later as he walks through the park, he sees a girl who is two years behind him in school. He thinks, "She looks like someone who would get off on a thrill. The way she's dressed, she'd appreciate seeing a little skin." He blushes and feels embarrassed as he walks home.

During the next week he thinks more about the girl and wonders how her face would look if he jumped out of a bush. He thought, "She'd be startled, but then she'd say, 'What a hunk.' Maybe she'd want to touch me. I wouldn't want to date a girl like her—too cheap." He starts walking home through the park. Each day he sees her walk home by the creek, but usually she is with a bunch of friends. He'd never do it in front of a lot of people; he'd be too embarrassed.

One weekend he walks down by the creek to see what it is like. He finds a big tree he could hide behind if he ever really wanted to do it. Later that week he even hid behind the tree while the girl and her friends walked by, and they never even knew he was there. He thinks, "This could work; too bad I'm too chicken to try it." About a week later he sees the girl enter the park by herself. He gets excited and thinks, "This could be it. She looks lonely; she could probably use a lift. Maybe this will brighten her day. I like making others feel happy." He feels turned on more than usual, and he imagines how seeing him will make her feel better. He runs down to the tree and decides to give it a try.

Sexual Abuse. Sexual behaviors that involve a misuse of power and occur without the consent of the victim are considered to be sexually abusive. The sexually abusive youth may use tricks, exploitation, manipulation, pressure, coercion, or force to gain the victim's compliance with the behavior. The youth experiences a sense of empowerment, mastery, and excitement when engaging in sexual abuse behavior.

Sexually abusive behaviors include exposing (flashing); voyeurism (peeping); frottage (rubbing one's genitals against another's body); obscene telephone calls or notes; grabbing sexual body parts in a crowd; simulating intercourse; genital fondling; oral-genital or oral-anal contact; effecting vaginal or anal penetration via digital, penile, or foreign object insertion; inflicting pain during sexual behaviors; taking pornographic pictures; showing a victim sexually explicit materials; providing sophisticated sexual information to a child; sexual harassment; or engaging in sex with animals.

Many youth report engaging in more than one type of offense behavior during the development of their offense behavior patterns. Some youth who engage in child molestation behaviors report prior experience with voyeurism, exhibitionism, and displaying sexually explicit materials to children before they first touched a child. Many youth who eventually rape report engaging in voyeurism, obscene telephone calls, breaking and entering (as a rehearsal or to steal underwear), or frottage prior to their first rape. The progression of behaviors likely occurs when the youth adds elements to increase his sense of control or to maintain previous levels of excitement, risk, thrill, or arousal. The development of additional sexual interests and arousal patterns may also be a factor.

The experience of arousal during the offense behavior varies among sexually abusive youth. Some report a loss of arousal and erectile dysfunction; they may have difficulty maintaining an erection or ejaculating. Other youth report remaining aroused throughout the offense. There may be greater arousal prior to the offense, and the youth may masturbate immediately before initiating the sexual abuse. Some describe experiencing more arousal subsequent to the offense and may masturbate during review or recall of the incident.

A variety of thoughts occurring during the offense is also reported. Some youths have indicated they were disappointed or angry at the victim's failure to respond in the way they had anticipated. Some report congratulating themselves for having planned well. Some maintain a distorted perception of the victim's pleasure about being involved in the offense. Some report not being aware of thinking but just experiencing the surge of Adrenalin and arousal. Many have reported having a backup plan in case the victim struggled or was difficult to control.

The style of the offense also varies. Some youths intend to inflict pain; during their offense, they might taunt or hit the victim. Others may perceive the victim as a romantic partner, and they may verbalize affection or reassurance. Some intend to express anger as part of the offense, so they may verbalize and act out anger. Some carry a weapon that they may or may not use during the offense. If a weapon is used, the youth may show it to elicit fear or compliance or use it to harm the victim. Some sexual abuse incidents may involve a ritual or a fetish behavior. The youth may wear certain clothing for each offense, request specific behaviors on the part of each victim, inflict mutilation or punishment that is consistent to each offense, or take a trophy, or souvenir, from each victim. Fetish behaviors involving clothing, urination, defecation, or cross-dressing might be part of an abusive ritual for the youth. Other behaviors that the youth considers arousing, amusing, or lucky may also be part of the behavior style.

There have been several reports of satanic ritualism occurring as part of an abusive behavior, but little is documented about the role of the sexually abusive youth.

Typically the young offender will do or say something to prevent disclosure on the victim's part during or immediately after the behavior. He may threaten the victim or play on a sense of guilt, loyalty, or victim responsibility to encourage the person not to tell—for example: "If you tell anyone, I'll be in big trouble," "I know where you live, and I'll kill you," "We'll both get in trouble if you tell," "Keep this a secret, or your family will be hurt," "Let's keep this a special secret between us," "I know you liked it; it's your fault as much as mine," "Don't tell; what you did would really upset your mom," or "Nobody will believe you if you tell." He may use some sort of disguise, such as a mask or a hat, to prevent being identified. Some rapists have forced victims to shower or douche in an attempt to eliminate evidence.

Many youths report that the effect of their justifications and distortions begins to diminish toward the end of the offense. Some wonder why they are doing this, others think what they are doing is wrong, and still others worry about being caught. They attempt to reassure themselves by thinking again of their justifications, or they direct some anger or frustration toward the victim, as Cassie did.

As Cassie arrived to babysit, she was excited. She couldn't wait for the parents to leave because tonight was the night. After she told the older boy it was okay for him to play outside until dark, she told the younger boy, Nathan, not to be upset because they would do something special. She turned the TV to a cable movie that had some sexual scenes in it and pulled Nathan next to her on the couch. When the couple on the screen kissed, she said, "I bet your girlfriend would like it if you knew how to kiss like that." He grinned, and she asked him if he had ever learned how. When he said no, she offered to teach him so that he could make his girlfriend happy. He looked eager, so she told him how to kiss and offered to let him practice on her so he could get it just right. She put her tongue in his mouth and told him to do that back to her. She put his hand on her breast and told him how to rub and squeeze it. Then she told him his girlfriend would probably touch his penis and offered to show him how. She began touching his penis over his clothes before he could answer her. As she pulled his pants down, she was explaining about how much girls preferred to touch a bare penis. She continued to touch him and then put her mouth on his penis. Then she told him that he always had to return the favor if he wanted to be popular with the girls. She took her pants off and showed him how to rub her genitals, then pulled his head down and told him to stick his tongue in her vagina. When he resisted, she told him he better do it or she would tell his mom about the extra cookies he had taken last time she babysat. He started crying, but he did it. Then she masturbated while she held him close and made him watch her. When she was done, she used a mean voice and told him that if he ever told, she would go to his classroom and for show and tell she would describe how he wet his bed every night. She told him to get out of the living room, then got something to eat while she watched a comedy on TV.

The Integration Phase

In this phase, the youth attempts to assimilate and integrate the experience of sexually abusing someone. When the excitement, thrill, arousal, and empowerment begin to diminish after the offense, the youth attempts to recapture a feeling of adequacy and satisfaction. After reinforcing the success of the sexual abuse, he begins to fear getting caught and potential consequences. The youth reassures himself but then begins to experience some ambivalence about what he has done. Hindsight raises some self-concerns that threaten his sense of adequacy, control, and empowerment. He struggles internally, then decides he is in control and suppresses his concerns (see Figure 6.4).

FIGURE 6.4. THE INTEGRATION PHASE
OF THE SEXUAL ABUSE CYCLE.

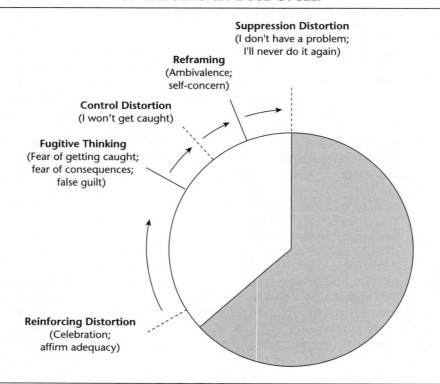

Source: Reprinted by permission of RSA, Inc.

The Reinforcing Distortion. The youth begins to question why the actual abuse did not measure up to his fantasies and expectations. Because he cannot afford to dilute his sense of control, he needs to reassure himself that he was adequate. He reviews his justifications for committing the offense and strengthens his sense of adequacy by celebrating or congratulating himself. The youth convinces himself that if there were any mistakes, the victim was at fault. Typical thoughts are, "I pulled it off. She was really shocked," "I really turned her on," "I sure made her pay," "He liked it, I could tell," "I showed her some good sex," "I did a good job; I feel good," and "It was great!"

Fugitive Thinking. After the youth reassures himself of his adequacy, his thoughts and concerns about getting caught begin to arise. He wonders if the steps he took to prevent disclosure were adequate or whether the victim will report the offense. He begins to think he should not have committed the offense, and his thoughts or statements appear to involve guilt or remorse. If the youth's statements are examined, however, what he is really describing are the potential consequences if he is caught. He knows he has done something that others view as wrong, and he is worried about how they will perceive or react to him. Sexually abusive youth describe little, if any, concern about victim impact or exploration of moral issues related to their offense.

In this stage of the cycle, typical thoughts include, "What if she tells? What kind of trouble could I get into?" "My friends will call me names," "My parents will disown me," "I could go to prison," " My name will be in the newspaper," and "I'll be grounded for life." The youth's affective reactions include fear and apprehension. Youth who have habitual offense patterns may move through this stage rapidly as their previously developed distortions become habitual perceptions. Those who are beginning sexual abuse behaviors report significant discomfort with this area. Interestingly, many youth have indicated they will worry for no more than three days. If they have not been reported by then, they believe they are safe.

The Control Distortion. The youth becomes convinced that the victim will not disclose the abuse. He may strengthen the belief that he is still controlling the victim, review his justifications for the offense behavior, reassure himself of his adequacy, or make an emotional bargain. He reaffirms the distortion that the victim enjoyed or deserved the offense and likes, trusts, or fears the offender enough that she or he will not report being sexually abused. Thoughts might include, "I really scared her, so she won't dare tell," "He promised he wouldn't tell so I'm okay," "He knows he'll be in just as much trouble as me so he won't even tell," "I don't have to worry; who'd believe a five-year-old over me?" and "Why sweat it? She won't even remember what I look like. There won't be any evidence and she knows I'll come back for her if she tells."

The youth may think of bargains: "If I don't get caught, I'll be nicer to my sister," "If I get away with it this time, then I'll go to church with my mom this Sunday," "If they don't tell, I'll never do it again," and "Not to worry, I won't get caught."

Reframing. When his fears are diminished, the sexually abusive youth begins to experience some ambivalence about himself and the abuse incident. Throughout this stage of the cycle, the youth is alternating between self-doubt and self-criticism or self-praise and reassurance.

The basis of his conflict can be variable. Some youth experience self-doubts or develop negative self-perceptions about having committed a sexually abusive behavior. Some label themselves weirdos or perverts and wonder if they are as bad as the "creeps" they hear about on the news. Those who have committed previous abusive behaviors and had promised themselves they would never repeat the behavior begin to doubt their ability to control themselves. They start questioning their ability to deny their urges to abuse and feel controlled by the compulsive quality of their behaviors. They wish they could just do it whenever they want to. Still others wonder if they have sufficiently controlled the victim, could have been more punitive, or should have asked the victim to do other behaviors. Although sexually abusive youth do not typically show extensive concern about the impact to the victim, some do question whether their behavior has been hurtful.

The conflict the youth experiences in this phase becomes the basis for further low self-esteem and feelings of inadequacy. The youth tries to counter each of his self-doubts, but the attempt is unsuccessful.

The Suppression Distortion. The final distortion in the sexual abuse cycle allows the youth to enhance his view of himself and his sense of self-control through self-deception and suppression. He convinces himself that he is in control of his behavior rather than driven by urges of some process of which he is unaware. He reminds himself he is an okay person who is quite different from those who really do sexually abuse others. He convinces himself that his self-doubts have no basis. Eventually he decides he does not have to worry about it because his behavior is not a problem, and, besides, he will never do it again anyway. There are some personality types who use this distortion to resolve these conflicts by deciding to be more aggressive in future offenses.

Thoughts characteristic of this distortion include, "It's no big deal; I'm in control," "I'll just stop doing this, and I won't have to worry about it," "They got something from me, so forget it," "I'm not weird; I care about them and I was gentle," "If I control this from now on, I'm not a bad person," "I'll never do it again," "I can forget all about it," and "I'm okay; I don't have to worry."

Despite the youth's suppression of his concerns, residual self-doubts continue to produce anxiety and a sense of inadequacy. When these feelings are coupled with the original sense of powerlessness and perceptions of inadequacy, the youth becomes more vulnerable to subsequent interactions or situations that may elicit similar perception. There is increased defensiveness and protection of the self, resulting in sensitivity and misinterpretation of more types of situations. Because of the gratification experienced with the compensatory response style, the pattern is repeated.

Conclusion

Therapists can use the sexual abuse cycle model to develop a clear understanding of the patterns of sexually abusive youths. They can then help the youth develop and use a variety of interventions to interrupt the progression toward an abusive behavior, as well as learn to modify the cognitions, arousal, and ineffective coping styles that have supported the behavior.

In working with sexually abusive youth, therapists need to consider additional treatment needs and each youth's unique characteristics, as well as offense-specific treatment for those factors identified in the sexual abuse cycle. Youths who have concurrent psychiatric diagnoses, learning disabilities, or unresolved trauma issues may require supplemental treatment approaches. Modified cycles may be used to assist individuals who require a more concrete explanation, and in every case, differential diagnosis and treatment should consider both the risks and assets of the individual.

References

Abel, G., & Blanchard, E. (1974). The role of fantasy in the treatment of sexual deviation. *Archives of General Psychiatry, 30,* 467–475.

Becker, J., Hunter, J., Stein, R., & Kaplan, M. (1989). Factors associated with erection in adolescent sex offenders. *Journal of Psychopathology and Behavioral Assessment, 11*(4).

Becker, J., Stein, R., Kaplan, M., & Cunningham-Rathner, J. (1992). Erection response characteristics of adolescent sex offenders. *Annals of Sex Research, 5,* 81–86.

Berenson, D. (1987). *Outline of the thinking errors approach.* Unpublished paper.

Carnes, P. (1983). *Out of the shadows: Understanding sexual addiction.* Minneapolis: CompCare Publications.

Fagan, J., & Wexler, S. (1988). Explanations of sexual assault among violent delinquents. *Journal of Adolescent Research, 58,* 281–291.

Fehrenbach, P., Smith, W., Monastersky, C., & Deischer, R. (1986). Adolescent sexual offenders: Offender and offense characteristics. *Journal of Orthopsychiatry, 56,* 225–233.

Freeman-Longo, R. E. (1982). Sexual learning and experience among adolescent sexual offenders. *International Journal of Offender Therapy and Comparative Criminology, 26*(2), 235–241.

Freeman-Longo, R. E., & Bays, L. (1988). *Who am I and why am I in treatment?* Orwell, VT: Safer Society Press.

Gilgun, J. (1988). *Factors which block the development of sexually abusive behavior in adults abused as children.* Paper presented at the National Conference on Male Victims and Offenders: Controversies in Treatment, Minneapolis, MN.

Gilgun, J., & Connor, T. (1989). *Isolation and the adult male perpetrator of child sexual abuse.* Unpublished manuscript.

Gray, A. (1996). Juvenile firesetters. In K. MacFarlane & C. Cunningham, *Treatment strategies for obsessive compulsive behavior problems.* Brandon, VT: Safer Society Press.

Hunter, J., & Santos, D. (1990). Use of specialized cognitive-behavioral therapies in the treatment of adolescent sexual offenders. *Journal of Offender Therapy and Comparative Criminology, 34,* 239–248.

Hunter, J., & Goodwin, D. (1992). The clinical utility of satiation therapy with juvenile sexual offenders: Variations and efficacy. *Annals of Sex Research, 5,* 71–80.

Johnson, S. (1989). *Branching out: The tree cycle.* Paper presented at the Fourth National Adolescent Perpetrator Network Meeting. Keystone, CO.

Kaemingk, K., Koselka, M., Becker, J., & Kaplan, M. (1995). Age and adolescent sexual offender arousal. *Sexual Abuse: A Journal of Research and Treatment, 7,* 249–257.

Kahn, T. J. (1990). *Pathways: A guided workbook for youth beginning treatment.* Orwell, VT: Safer Society Press.

Knopp, F. H. (1982). *Remedial intervention in adolescent sex offenses: Nine program descriptions.* Orwell, VT: Safer Society Press.

Lane, S. (1977). [Author's treatment notes from Closed Adolescent Treatment Center, Division of Youth Services, Denver, CO.] Unpublished.

Lane, S., & Zamora, P. (1978). [Syllabus materials from inservice training on adolescent sex offenders, Closed Adolescent Treatment Center, Division of Youth Services, Denver, CO.] Unpublished.

Lane, S., & Zamora, P. (1984). A method for treating the adolescent sex offender. In R. Mathias, P. Demuro, & R. Allinson (Eds.), *Violent juvenile offenders.* San Francisco: National Council on Crime and Delinquency.

Lane, S. (1985). *Treatment issues.* Presentation at the Fourteenth Annual Child Abuse and Neglect Symposium, Keystone, CO.

Lane, S. (1991). *Offense cycle: Adaptations to delinquent behavior.* Presentation to the Michigan Association of Children's Alliances, Detroit, MI.

MacFarlane, K., & Cunningham, C. (1996). *Treatment strategies for obsessive compulsive behavior problems.* Brandon, VT: Safer Society Press.

Marshall, W. L. (1979). Satiation therapy: Procedure for reducing deviant sexual arousal. *Journal of Applied Behavioral Analysis, 12,* 10–22.

Marshall, W. L., & Barbaree, H. (1984). A behavioral view of rape. *International Journal of Law and Psychiatry, 7,* 51–77.

McGuire, R. J., Carlyle, J. M., & Young, B. G. (1965). Sexual deviations as conditional behavior: A hypothesis. *Behavior Research and Therapy, 2,* 185–190.

McKibben, A., Proulx, J., & Lusigna, R. (1994). Relationships between conflict, affect and deviant sexual behaviors in rapists and pedophiles. *Behavior Research and Therapy, 32,* 571–575.

Money, J. (1986). *Love maps.* New York: Irvington Publishers.

O'Connor, B., & Esteve, J. (1994). Poster session presented at the Tenth National Conference of the National Adolescent Perpetrators Network, Denver, CO.

Pithers, W. D., Kashima, K. M., Cumming, G. F., Beal, L. S., & Buell, M. M. (1998). Relapse prevention of sexual aggression. In R. A. Prentky and L. L. Quincey (Eds.), *Human sexual aggression: Current perspectives* (pp. 244–260). New York : New York Academy of Sciences.

Prentky, R., Knight, R., Straus, H., Rokous, F., Cerce, D., & Sims-Knight, J. (1989). *Developmental antecedents of sexual aggression.* Paper presented at the Fourth National Adolescent Perpetrator Network Meeting, Keystone, CO.

Ross, J. (1993). Poster session presented at the Ninth National Conference of the National Adolescent Perpetrator Network, Lake Tahoe, NV.

Ryan, G. (1989). Victim to victimizer: Rethinking victim treatment. *Journal of Interpersonal Violence, 4*(3), 325–341.

Ryan, G. (1993). *Concurrent psychiatric disorders.* Paper presented at the Ninth Annual Conference of the National Adolescent Perpetrator Network, Lake Tahoe, NV.

Ryan, G., & Blum, J. (1993). *Managing chronic sexual behavior in understanding and responding to the sexual behavior of children* (rev. ed.). Denver: Kempe Center.

Ryan, G., Lane, S., Davis, J., & Isaac, C. (1987). Juvenile sexual offenders: Development and correction. *Child Abuse and Neglect, 3*(3), 385–395.

Stickrod, A. (1988). Preventing sexual abuse through treating juvenile sexual offenders. *Proceedings of the Adolescent Sex Offender's Symposium,* Salt Lake City, UT.

Turner, R. (1994). *Treating violent juvenile sex offenders.* Paper presented at the Tenth National Conference of the National Adolescent Perpetrators Network, Denver, CO.

Ward, T., Louden, K., Hudson, S., & Marshall, W. (1994). *A descriptive model of the offense chain for child molesters.* Paper presented at the Thirteenth ATSA Conference, San Francisco, CA.

Wolfe, S. (1994). Poster session presented at the Tenth National Conference of the National Adolescent Perpetrators Network, Denver, CO.

Yochelson, S., & Samenow, S. (1976). *The criminal personality.* Northvale, NJ: Aronson.

CHAPTER SEVEN

PHENOMENOLOGY

A Developmental-Contextual View

Gail Ryan

When we say these kids are committing inhuman acts . . . perhaps they have not experienced human development.

WHITAKER, 1990

Sexual abusers are not born abusive. The human infant is born with the capacity to be sexual, to grow and develop, and to become both attached and autonomous. Humans naturally strive to achieve a sense of personal competence and belonging based on safety, nurturance, and intimacy in relationships.

Human growth and development are influenced by internal and external factors that interact from birth in different ways to contribute to the unique individuality of each person. Individual development becomes problematic when it undermines successful independence or relationships.

From infancy to independence, human development is distinguished by the capacity to be intellectual, sensual, and emotional (Firestone, 1990). Personal competence is dependent on mastery of skills that facilitate, operationalize, and mediate human capacity in ways that contribute to independence and interrelatedness. Deviant developments are normally subjected to corrective experiences, which are the natural consequence of useless or destructive growth.

Human development continues throughout the life span and is subject to internal and external influences that shape and change the course of development. Values, beliefs, skills, interests, and concerns change over time, most rapidly early in life. Piaget's (1963) theory posits that each stage of development builds on what has gone before. In cognitive development, the child's understanding of current events is based on his or her beliefs and understanding of earlier events, and current perceptions become the basis for understanding future events.

Developmental-contextual theory focuses on the interaction of the individual's developmental status in the context of life experiences, which continually shape human functioning. What is developing internally is both a product of and an influence in what surrounds the individual externally.

The individual and the environment are each complex puzzles with infinite pieces. In order to begin to identify which pieces might be relevant to a particular problem—sexually abusive youth—it may be useful to conceptualize what categories (or factors) are involved by breaking the problem into definitive and more manageable pieces. The first step, then, in studying sexually abusive youth is to consider sexuality, abusiveness, and youth as three separate domains, each represented in the problem, each affording various opportunities for understanding and change.

Much of the development of offense-specific theory and intervention has focused on the sexual aspect of the sexually abusive youth's behavior. This parallels the tendency throughout the fields of child protection and criminology to separate sexual crimes from nonsexual crimes. This differentiation is reflected in all aspects of the work: laws, theories, case management, and treatment. The effect of the sexual component, which separates these crimes from all others, is likely related to several factors: the perceived intrusiveness of these crimes, the intensely personal violation of the victim, the strong historical incest taboos, and the interventionists' discomfort dealing with sexual issues. However, the sexual behavior is not what separates sexual abuse from normative sexual behaviors; it is the abusive nature of the interaction that makes the sexual behavior a crime.

Interventions for children and adolescents who have been sexually abusive have been motivated by a belief that there might be a better prognosis for change if treatment occurred while these individuals were still growing and developing, as compared to treating them as adults. It is the youth factor that is most significant in distinguishing work with sexually abusive youth from the treatment of adult sex offenders. Therefore, a developmental perspective is particularly compelling (National Task Force, 1993). However, even in this book, the sexual and criminal aspects attract much of the attention. In this chapter, the phenomenon of abusiveness and development will be the focus and the sexual aspect viewed as just one particular manifestation of abusive development.

In trying to imagine why one individual becomes a sexual abuser while another with similar experiences does not, it is necessary to conceptualize the interaction of experiences and perceptions in relation to deficits and deviance. On the one hand, there are the experiences illustrated in the developmental history, and on the other, there are the available models for interpreting and coping with those experiences. The first may be weighted with trauma and deficits or with good care and assets. The other may present a limited repertoire of coping behaviors, failed relationships, and dysfunctional experience, or successful relationships, effective coping skills, and developmental competency. The early life experience may be weighted with either adaptive or maladaptive patterns of coping, problem solving, and intimacy (Ryan and others, 1993, 1997; Steele, 1987; Steele & Ryan, 1991).

Research into the developmental factors associated with sexual deviance has lagged behind clinical knowledge. The prevention of sexually abusive behavior is inherently dependent on earlier identification of antecedents and encourages a developmental focus. As numerous clinical groups have begun to penetrate the denial of childhood sexuality (see Constantine & Martinson, 1981), researchers have begun to inquire into the early experiences and childhood perceptions of paraphiliacs. The early hypotheses of clinicians such as Groth (1979, regarding "fixated" versus "regressed" pedophiles), Longo & McFadin (1981) and Longo (1982, regarding the history of childhood victimization), and Steele (1980, 1987, regarding the quality of early life relationships) were tentatively validated in studies by Gilgun (1988) and Prentky and others (1989).

Gilgun's (1988) exploration of factors that block the development of sexually abusive behaviors in males who have experienced childhood sexual abuse described the *lack of a confidant* (someone in whom to confide personal matters) and a *nonnormative sexual environment* (either oversexualized or sexually repressive) as significant variables in the early childhood experience of sex offenders. That confidant may be the factor that mediates unempathic experiences and nourishes trust. Her description of a nonnormative sexual environment parallels Morris and Bolton's (1989) description of the extremes of sexuality. Gilgun (1988) has also described the isolation of these individuals, which we may relate to the emptiness and lack of intimacy, and which is also a characteristic in the abusive cycle. The sexual abuse cycle, described in Chapter Six, represents the dynamic pattern associated with abusive behavior. Within that cycle, distortions are often related to externalizing responsibility and control.

Prentky and colleagues (1989), in an ongoing empirical study of "developmental antecedents of sexual dangerousness," found that sexual and nonsexual aggression in an adult sample are related to "distinct aspects of developmental history." *Caregiver inconsistency* (disruptions in the parent-child relationship) is related to the incidence of sexual aggression, and *sexual deviation in the family* is related to increased levels of sexual aggression. They also found sexual victimization to be a significant risk factor. They suggest "that the quality (and consistency) of early interpersonal attachments and the experience of sexual abuse as a child may be important to understanding sexual aggression in adulthood."

Quinsey (1995) has discussed an actuarial model for predicting the risk of recidivism for sexual abusers that describes many variables relevant to deviant developmental history—for example, psychopathy, elementary school maladjustment, parental loss, never married, and age at first offense. Although Quinsey is quick to point out in presenting the model that these predictors are virtually unchangeable because they are historical, he urges a focus in treatment on *dynamic predictors* of sexually abusive behavior as the variables most likely to be changeable.

The cycle Lane describes in Chapter Six represents a dynamic process specifically related to sexually abusive behaviors. This same pattern is described elsewhere (Ryan, 1989) as related to all types of abusive behaviors (abuse of self, others, or property; physical, sexual, verbal), and similar patterned responses to stress are described by others in regard to many behavioral disorders (Wiessburg, 1982). These patterned responses represent maladaptive coping strategies within which the imagined solution is abusive. The pattern represents a common compensatory, externalizing response to stress, however, that is often temporarily adaptive if the imagined solution is not harmful to self or others—that is, if the behavior reduces the anger or tension produced by the stress without hurting someone. Examples of temporarily adaptive behavior include isolation, which provides a time-out effect by blocking awareness or providing containment until the individual is able to manage the stressful issue in a helpful fashion; fantasy, which works to replay the stressful event in a manner that either desensitizes the trigger or reaches a less stressful conclusion; and compensatory behaviors, which either provide self-nurturance or tension reduction and effectively increase a sense of self-efficacy. (Such time-outs are routine breaks in functioning, the fantasies are the vehicle of cognitive restructuring, and the compensatory behaviors are signs of competence.)

It is not the compensatory pattern per se that is dysfunctional but rather the overgeneralization of a defensive strategy or the choice of harmful behavioral solutions that cause a common coping strategy to become dysfunctional and abusive. Self-control, accepting responsibility, and escape-avoidance behaviors have been suggested as mediating or exacerbating variables in relation to outcomes for victims coping with the experience of abuse (Steele, Wilson, Cross, & Whipple, 1996). These variables seem congruent with aspects of the sexual abuse cycle described by Lane in Chapter Six.

In scrutinizing the abusive aspect, it appears that the most common dynamic in all types of abusers is the interaction of a deficit—*lack of empathy*—and a distortion—*misattribution of responsibility*. The individual who has learned deviance and lacks other inhibitions should be deterred from abusive behavior by empathy if he or she feels responsible for the behavior.

Attributions of Responsibility

In every relationship, the potential exists for an individual to imagine being abusive, and one's tendency is to project responsibility away from self, and toward some other—for example, "He made me so mad that I wanted to hurt him." Implicit in the effectiveness of any deterrent for behavior that is imagined is the assumption of control and the attribution of responsibility. If behavior were uncontrollable, then there could be no attribution of responsibility. However, even the lowest-level deterrents, such as restraints (jail or confinement, for example) or punishment (painful consequences), demonstrate that abusive behavior is controllable. It is the locus of control that varies across the continuum of deterrence, as shown in the following annotated list of the levels of deterrence.

Highest Level *(generalize across diverse situations)*

Empathic foresight and accountability	Imagining potential impact on others
	I am responsible for my behavior
Empathy	Others may feel differently than I do; therefore, I can only imagine how they feel based on the cues they communicate to me, and my hypotheses must be validated.

Higher Level *(Golden Rule)*

Sympathy	I assume others feel as I do; therefore, I do to them what I would like, based on how I would feel.

Midrange *(behavior modification)*

Positive association	Good memories: self-righteousness; positive self-image; positive feelings
Positive consequences	Respect-regard/esteem of others
	Rewards-tangible gains/privileges
Negative consequences	Disrespect-shame; loss of privilege
	Tangible losses
Negative association	Bad memory; something bad happens

Lower Level *(entirely dependent on external factors)*

Pain, punishment	Physical or emotional distress
Restraint	Confinement—fences, jail, locks, physical holding

The responsibility for control is attributed at one extreme to the actions of others and at the other extreme to the individual's own internal processes. Abusers frequently demonstrate misattributions of responsibility: internalizing the belief that they are responsible for controlling others while projecting or denying responsibility for themselves. They often perceive themselves as helpless, feeling responsible for many things beyond their control, and failing to accept responsibility for the things that are clearly part of their own behavior—for example, "My father beat me because I was bad" and "I beat my child because he was bad." In both instances, the child is beaten because the parent is abusive, yet responsibility is attributed to the child's "badness."

The denial commonly described as characteristic of abusers is often related to distorted attributions of responsibility, and the goal of accountability is to accept responsibility for one's own behavior.

Empathy

Empathy is the capacity to read the cues of others and thus imagine the experience of the other. Infants experience empathy from birth as their caregivers read the infants' cues and provide care that validates the infants' needs (food, stimulation, and comfort in response to cries of hunger, boredom, or distress). Infants who experience such empathic care (Steele, 1980) begin to demonstrate empathic reactions to the cues of others as early as eighteen months (Landry & Peters, 1992).

Empathy provides the highest level of deterrence for abusive behavior. It is most effective and most generalizable because it is based on a recognition that not every person has the same needs or feels the same, even in very similar circumstances. This assumption of difference (Bennett, 1979) distinguishes empathy from sympathy, which is based on an assumption of sameness. Bennett clarifies this distinction by pointing out that the Golden Rule works well when persons are similar but breaks down in the face of diversity. This distinction is especially relevant to understanding the limitations of sympathetic role taking or perspective taking (Davis, 1980, Hanson & Scott, 1995) as a deterrent for sexually abusive behavior because the abuser often believes that the victim's experience in the interaction is "the same" as his (for better or for worse). For example, the violent aggressor may attempt to dump or dilute his own fear and anger by giving it to (or sharing it with) the victim, or the seductive abuser may believe that the victim is experiencing the same pleasure from the intimacy or sexual arousal that the abuser feels. The abuser fails to see the cues that describe the victim's experience as different from his own.

Development

Three important developments that occur in the first two years of life are of critical importance in a developmental-contextual view of abusive behavior:

1. The infant's view of the world develops from birth and is profoundly affected by his or her view of self, view of others, and view of relationships.
2. Attachments develop as a product of interactions with caregivers and are the basis for the infant's view of self, view of others, and view of relationships.
3. Empathy develops as a result of the infant's experience in relationships with consistent, empathic caregivers.

The developmental markers of a healthy two-year-old are manifestations or evidence of these three developments. Small children's success or failure in achieving the ability to be both autonomous and attached, to establish the boundaries that separate them as individuals from others (separation-individuation), to enjoy basic trust (object relations), and to become empathic are cornerstones for psychological health. These developmental tasks are profoundly related to the nature of subsequent functioning, and especially the nature of interpersonal relationships.

Childhood attachments develop and become the working models or blueprints for subsequent relationships. The qualities represented in the working model are positive or negative views of self and others (Ainsworth, 1989; Bartholomew, 1990; Bowlby, 1977). The potential combinations are shown in Figure 7.1.

Marshall, Hudson, and Hodkinson (1993) and Ward, Hudson, Marshall, and Siegert (1995) have explored the relationship of the various attachment styles to the emotional loneliness and isolation that characterize deficits in the abuser's capacity for intimacy and have suggested that the individual's interpersonal goals and strategies (and therefore motives and modus operandi for offending) reflect the individual's internal working model.

Deviancy seems to result from imbalance and confusion in the earliest perceptions of the child combined with failures in normative developmental achievement. Pond and Brown (1996) have referred to a "Swiss cheese" effect to describe the holes in developmental competency, and Steele (1987) suggests that a sense of emptiness may result from disregard or loss, a lack of empathic care, objectification, or betrayal. The combination of incompetency and negative self-image creates a vulnerability: an incomplete state of development, which is a disabling condition. The outcome is subject to tremendous variation dependent on how stressful the environment is and what compensatory resources become available to the individual. Abusive or sexualized compensatory behaviors may be learned in

FIGURE 7.1. INTERNAL WORKING MODELS.

Positive Self Positive Other	Positive Self Negative Other
Negative Self Positive Other	Negative Self Negative Other

observation or experience early in life, or remedial interventions may provide models for more adaptive coping or opportunities for new growth and development.

Gilgun (1996b) has suggested a model for considering the balancing effect of assets and risks, which promises to illuminate the understanding of how the positives and negatives of early life experience enter into an equation that may help to explain outcomes. Whereas the concept of resiliency has been a subject of study in relation to many life stresses and outcomes, Gilgun's model posits four quadrants (Figure 7.2), each of which might be explanatory, diagnostic, and changeable. In this model, *assets* may be developmental competencies or positive contextual factors, and *risks* may be developmental deficits or negative contextual factors. Gilgun suggests that treatment goals should seek to increase assets and either decrease or moderate the effects of risks.

Developmental competence refers to the skills that support optimal human functioning. Strayhorn (1988, pp. 28–29) describes sixty-two skills in nine areas that maximize human potential:

- Closeness, trust, relationship building
- Handling separation and independence
- Handling joint decisions and interpersonal conflict
- Dealing with frustration and unfavorable events
- Celebrating good things, feeling pleasure
- Working for delayed gratification
- Relaxing, playing
- Cognitive processing through words, symbols, images
- An adaptive sense of direction and purpose

The definition of observable components in healthy functioning provides a basis for differential diagnosis and treatment planning to address the deficits that

FIGURE 7.2. GILGUN'S MODEL FOR COMBINATIONS OF ASSETS AND RISKS.

Low Asset Low Risk	High Asset Low Risk
Low Asset High Risk	High Asset High Risk

exacerbate risk, as well as supporting a more holistic view of the process of growth and development. The success of intervention in childhood and adolescence is thought to be partially related to the developmental opportunities of youth.

Context

Contextual theories refer to the *view of the world,* which is the individual's unique way of understanding and anticipating life experiences based on diverse life experiences and the beliefs and perceptions of the individual.

It may be helpful to conceptualize an overlay of the components: sexuality, abusiveness, development, and context (see Figure 7.3). It is also possible to conceptualize the possible outcomes in each domain: for development, they may be competence, deviance, deficits, or disability. For context, they may be a positive or negative view of self, others, or the world. The path of development is growth, and the path of context is experiential perception.

As each of the domains represented in Figure 7.1 (view of self and others), Figure 7.2 (risks and assets), and Figure 7.3 (development and context) is overlaid, the complexity of the developmental contextual view is multiplied exponentially. Accommodation and assimilation of experiences from birth also have an impact on the phenomenological perception of the individual. The desirability of differential diagnosis and treatment is more and more apparent.

Yochelson and Samenow (1976) described differences in the "criminal" view of the world and characterized particular patterns of thinking as thinking errors and distortions. A contextual view facilitates the exploration of this phenomenon (phenomenology) but reframes the understanding of patterns of thinking as reflective of the individual's perceptual experience; rather than assuming distortion, such thoughts may reflect a different reality.

FIGURE 7.3. INTERACTION OF DEVELOPMENT AND CONTEXT.

Abusive Development Deviant Sexual Context	Abusive Development Normative Sexual Context
Nonabusive Development Deviant Sexual Context	Nonabusive Development Normative Sexual Context

Abusive behaviors may develop as a defensive strategy when the individual's sense of competence and control is jeopardized. When individuals experience levels of stress that overwhelm their ability to cope, defense mechanisms act as an adaptive response to protect the individual. The following list describes defense mechanisms relevant to the cycle.

Dissociation: Separation of some mental or behavioral processes from one's perception in order to avoid overwhelming emotion

Identification with the aggressor: Assuming the patterns of thought or behavior of another person who represents an external source of frustration

Intellectualization: Using reasoning and logic to distance oneself from anxiety

Isolation: Separation of feeling from an idea or memory

Projection: Placing blame or responsibility on another in order to avoid internal or external sources of anxiety or conflict

Rationalization: Using logic to explain or justify irrational thoughts or behavior

Regression: Partial or total return to an earlier pattern of adaptation

Repression: An unconscious process that keeps unacceptable mental content out of consciousness

Sublimation: Channeling frustrated or intolerable energy into more gratifying activity

Suppression: Conscious repression

Withdrawal: Retreat or avoidance of sources of anxiety

(Adapted from Koplau & Sadock, 1985, p. 498)

Defenses initially protect humans from insanity by mediating stress, but in doing so, those attributes that distinguish humanness and enrich relationships (sensuality, intellect, and emotion) are diminished (Firestone, 1990). When defenses are overgeneralized or chronic stress requires dependence on a consistent defensive mode, the individual may become isolative and disempowered.

When the environment is unsafe or uncaring, energy that the growing child should direct into developing human competency may be expended on defenses in order to survive, and his or her growth may be retarded. The developmental context therefore illuminates understanding of the imbalance of resources (Donovan & MacIntyre, 1990). The youth may demonstrate overdeveloped skills in some areas and deficits in others. If the world has been unsafe and relationships have jeopardized survival rather than nurtured growth, the youth's dependence on the compensatory cycle may be a sign of a necessary survival strategy.

When events are deviant, their assimilation into the individual's perception of self and others may distort subsequent development and contribute to patterns of thought and beliefs that support deviant behavior. When new information and experience is dissonant with the youth's prior life experience, it may be difficult for the youth to accommodate. A new defensive strategy may develop to manage the dissonance. The more defensive layers that the individual adopts, the slower growth and change can occur, and the more restricted the individual becomes in terms of optimal functioning.

Implications

The implications of developmental and contextual factors are already shaping research, practice, and prevention efforts. In research with adult sex offenders, Ward, Hudson, Marshall, and Siegert (1995) have demonstrated significant relationships between adult attachment styles (the internal working models that describe one's view of self and others) and the characteristics of the abusive pattern, and Marshall, Hudson, and Hodkinson (1993) have related attachment theory to sexually abusive adolescents as well. Numerous researchers (for example, Beckett & Fisher, 1994; Bumby & Hanson, 1996; and Marshall & Pithers, 1995) are struggling to define and measure the construct of empathy, and clinicians are rethinking interventions that have been aimed at increasing the offender's "victim empathy." In the literature, the ecology of abuse is being described in relation to the environmental habitat of the individual, and the interaction of what individuals bring to their life experience and what surrounds them is being explored in relation to many relevant aspects of family and culture (Gilgun, 1996a). Hypothesizing that individuals are uniquely diverse from birth, are endowed with qualities that profoundly affect their lives, and then are subject to be profoundly affected by each life experience supports both optimism and alarm—optimism that many of the risks are changeable and alarm that so many youth are not being protected from the known risks.

Similarly, the hypothesis that deviance is both understandable and predictable supports both optimism and alarm as well. Refinement of the definition of variables that might deter abusive behavior (such as the empathy and accountability) informs treatment planning as well as prevention efforts.

The most significant contribution of the application of developmental-contextual theory to the treatment of sexually abusive youths may be in developing a more comprehensive and holistic view of these youths that supports both differential diagnosis and treatment and values the need to nurture growth while decreasing deviance. The youth who leaves treatment without the psychological health skills to support functional competence is likely to remain at greater risk for relapse (Whitaker, 1990). Humane behavior is a reflection of human qualities that are the optimal outcome of growth and development.

References

Ainsworth, M. D. S. (1989). Attachments beyond infancy. *American Psychologist, 44,* 709–716.

Bartholomew, K. (1990). Avoidance of intimacy: An attachment perspective. *Journal of Social and Personal Relationships, 7,* 147–178.

Bartholomew, K., & Horowitz, L. M. (1991). Attachment styles among adults: A test of a four category model. *Journal of Personality and Social Psychology, 61,* 226–244.

Beckett, R., & Fisher, D. (1994). *Assessing victim empathy.* Paper presented at the Thirteenth Association for the Treatment of Sexual Abusers Conference, San Francisco, CA.

Bennett, M. (1979). Overcoming the golden rule: Sympathy and empathy. In D. Nimmo (Ed.), *Communication yearbook* (3rd ed.). New Brunswick, NJ: Transaction.

Bowlby, J. (1977). The making and breaking of affectional bonds. *British Journal of Psychiatry, 130,* 201–210.

Bumby, K., & Hanson, K. (1996). *Victim empathy enhancement.* Paper presented at the Fifteenth ATSA Conference, Chicago, IL.

Constantine, L. L., & Martinson, F. (1981). *Children and sex: New findings and new perspectives.* Boston: Little, Brown.

Davis, M. (1980). *Interpersonal reactivity index.* Washington, DC: American Psychological Association.

Donovan, D., & MacIntyre, D. (1990). *Healing the hurt child.* New York: Norton.

Firestone, R. (1990). *The universality of emotional child abuse.* Los Angeles: Glendon Association.

Gilgun, J. (1988). *Factors which block the development of sexually abusive behavior in adults abused as children.* Paper presented at the National Conference on Male Victims and Offenders, Minneapolis, MN.

Gilgun, J. (1996a). Human development and adversity in ecological perspective: Part I and II. *Families in society.* Manuscript submitted for publication.

Gilgun, J. (1996b, September). *Clinical instruments for children with sexually inappropriate behaviors.* Paper presented at the Conference on Psychosocial Intervention: Social Work's Contribution, Bethesda, MD.

Groth, A. N. (1979). Sexual trauma in the life histories of rapists and child molesters. *Victimology, 4*(1), 10–16.

Hanson, K., & Scott, H. (1995). Assessing perspective-taking among sexual offenders, nonsexual criminals, and nonoffenders. *Sexual Abuse: A Journal of Research and Treatment, 7*(4).

Koplau, H., and Sadock, B. (Eds.). (1985). *Comprehensive textbook of psychiatry* (4th ed.). Baltimore: Williams & Wilkins.

Landry, S., & Peters, R. (1992). Toward an understanding of a developmental paradigm for aggressive conduct problems. In R. Peters, R. McMahon, & V. Quinsey (Eds.), *Aggression and violence throughout the life span.* Thousand Oaks, CA: Sage.

Longo, R. E. (1982). Sexual learning and experience among adolescent sexual offenders. *International Journal of Offender Therapy and Comparative Criminology, 26*(2), 235–241.

Longo, R. E., & McFadin, B. (1981, December). Sexually inappropriate behavior: Development of the sexual offender. *Law and Order, 2*(9), 21–23.

Marshall, W. L., Hudson, S. M., & Hodkinson, S. (1993). The importance of attachment bonds in the development of juvenile sex offending. In H. E. Barbaree, W. L. Marshall, & S. M. Hudson (Eds.), *Juvenile sex offending.* New York: Guilford.

Marshall, W., & Pithers, B. (1995). *Enhancing victim empathy.* Paper presented at the Fourteenth ATSA Conference, New Orleans, LA.

Morris, L., & Bolton, F. (1989). *Males at risk: The other side of sexual abuse.* Thousand Oaks, CA: Sage.

National Task Force on Juvenile Sexual Offending. (1993). Revised report. *Juvenile and Family Court Journal, 44*(4).

Piaget, J. (1963). The attainment of invariants and reversible operations in the development of thinking. *Social Research, 30,* 283–299.

Pond, A., & Brown, J. (1996). *Disclosure: Obtaining sexual histories from developmentally disabled youth.* Paper presented at the Twelfth Annual Conference of the National Adolescent Perpetrator Network, Minneapolis, MN.

Prentky, R. A., Knight, R. A., Straus, H., Rokou, E., Cerce, D., & Sims-Knight, J. (1989). Developmental antecedents of sexual aggression. *Development and Psychopathology, 1,* 153–169.

Quinsey, V. (1995). *Actuarial prediction of sexual dangerousness.* Paper presented at the Fourteenth ATSA Conference, New Orleans, LA.

Quinsey, V., Rice, M., & Harris, G. (1995). Actuarial prediction of sexual recidivism. *Journal of Interpersonal Violence, 10*(1).

Ryan, G. (1989). Victim to victimizer: Rethinking treatment. *Journal of Interpersonal Violence, 4,* 325–341.

Ryan, G. (1997). The sexual abuser. In E. Helfer & R. Kempe (Eds.), *The battered child* (5th ed.). Chicago: University of Chicago Press.

Ryan, G., and Associates. (1997). *The web of meaning: A developmental view of sexual abuse.* Manuscript submitted for publication.

Ryan, G., Lindstrom, B., Knight, L., Arnold, L., Yager, J., Bilbrey, C., & Steele, B. (1993). *Treatment of sexual abuse in the context of whole life experience.* Paper presented at the Twenty-First CAN Symposium, Keystone, CO.

Steele, B. F. (1980). Generational repetition of the maltreatment of children. In E. J. Anthony & G. Pollock (Eds.), *Parental influences in health and disease.* Boston: Little, Brown.

Steele, B. F. (1987). Abuse and neglect in the earliest years: Groundwork for vulnerability. *Zero to Three, 7*(4), 14–15.

Steele, B. F. (1997). Psychodynamic factors in child abuse. In E. Helfer & R. Kempe (Eds.), *The battered child* (4th ed.). Chicago: University of Chicago Press.

Steele, B. F., & Ryan, G. (1991). Deviancy: Development gone wrong. In G. D. Ryan & S. L. Lane (Eds.), *Juvenile sexual offending: Causes, consequences, and correction*. San Francisco: New Lexington Press.

Steele, J., Wilson, G., Cross, H., Whipple, H. (1996). Mediating factors in the development of psychopathology. In Victims of childhood sexual abuse, *Sexual Abuse: A Journal of Research and Treatment, 8*(4).

Strayhorn, J. (1988). *The competent child*. New York: Guilford Press.

Ward, T., Hudson, S., Marshall, W., & Siegert, R. (1995). Attachment style and intimacy deficits in sexual offenders. *Sexual Abuse: A Journal of Research and Treatment, 7*(4).

Whitaker, M. (1990). Personal communication to the National Task Force on Juvenile Sexual Offending regarding competency-based treatment models.

Wiessburg, M. (1982). *Dangerous secrets: Maladaptive responses to stress*. New York: Norton.

Yochelson, S., & Samenow, S. (1976). *Criminal personality*. Northvale, NJ: Aronson.

CHAPTER EIGHT

THE FAMILIES OF SEXUALLY ABUSIVE YOUTH

Gail Ryan

The exploration of various theories, development of sexuality, deviance, and the dysfunctional cycle suggests that many risk factors converge within the juvenile's early life experience. The family's role in shaping the beliefs and behavior patterns of its children is recognized as a primary influence in child development. It is within this earliest holding environment that the infant's view of the world and basic assumptions are formed. The early caregivers may enhance or hamper the child's growth and development either overtly or covertly. As the child's world expands and experiences broaden, extrafamilial influences have an impact on development and continue to shape the individual's beliefs and behavior, but the infant's earliest experience remains the core and is thought to be the source of the internal working model.

Some theorists, such as Yochelson and Samenow (1976), disregard infant experiences and family influences in the development of the irresponsible patterns that support criminal behavior. Their view is based on observation of discrepant outcomes among siblings raised in the same family. The notion that criminal and noncriminal children emerging from the same family negates the role and influence of early life fails to recognize the unique experience and individuality of each child. Siblings are not identical at birth, and each child is born into circumstances and expectations that are unique (Klaus & Kennell, 1976). Although external factors may remain constant, personal and internal circumstances do not. The most dysfunctional or inadequate family may produce a very successful child, while a family that appears more adequate and functional may raise a very deviant child. Each dyadic relationship within the family is unique, and each child's needs and perceptions are personal.

The hypotheses that suggest risk factors for the development of sexually abusive behavior include a nonnormative sexual environment in the home (Gilgun 1988), sexualized models of compensation (see Chapter Five in this book), or the experience of sexual victimization, humiliation, or trauma (Freeman-Longo 1982; Prentky and others, 1989), combined with a lack of empathic care (Steele, 1987), early parental loss (Ryan, 1987), inconsistent care (Prentky and others, 1989), and the lack of a confidant in childhood (Gilgun, 1988). Most recently, in their prospective studies of child abuse victims, Widom (1996) and Williams (1995) found that physically abused and neglected children were even more at risk to manifest sexually abusive behaviors than sexually abused children. Hunter (1996) suggests that all forms of maltreatment represent a risk of abusive outcomes. These factors point either inclusively or exclusively to early childhood experience and parental influences. The dysfunctional cycle (Ryan, 1989) points specifically to factors reminiscent of earlier life experience as well as cognitive behavioral patterns that reflect maladaptive coping styles. Many of these issues were discussed in Chapter Seven. The author does not suggest that parents are directly causal, but rather that circumstances, experiences, and parental models in the early life environment may allow or support the development of sexual deviance or fail to develop the empathy and inhibitions that prevent exploitative behavior.

This chapter examines some of the common characteristics of families of sexually abusive youth and explores the potential of family involvement in treatment. The author of Chapter Eighteen suggests a five-stage model to assess and treat the family.

Research

Family variables in one thousand cases of sexually abusive youth referred to specialized treatment programs are described by the Uniform Data Collection System of the National Adolescent Perpetrator Network at the Kempe Center in Denver. This database reports parental loss in 57 percent of cases and describes overrepresentations of family dysfunctions that are likely to have an impact on child development. Parental violence is reported by 28 percent, and over half of those juveniles have witnessed spousal abuse. Substance abuse is reported for 27 percent of the mothers and 43 percent of the fathers. Only 27.8 percent of the juveniles were living with both natural parents at the time of their offense. The evaluating clinicians rated family functioning as "below average," "inappropriate," or "dysfunctional" in 86 percent of their caseload (Ryan, 1988; Ryan, Miyoshi, Metzner, Fryer, & Krugman, 1996).

Lankester and Meyer (1986, 1988), reporting on the families of 153 sexually abusive youth seen at the University of Washington in Seattle, found that 64 percent of family members had been physically or sexually abused as children. They urge that families be assessed for the "meaning of the sex offense behavior" within the context of the family dynamics and structure. They suggest dynamic distinctions between chaotic and rigid families and structural distinctions in single-parent and blended families. Kaplan, Becker, and Cunningham-Rathner (1988) describe the parents of twenty-seven male adolescent incest perpetrators from the New York City ghettos and report that these parents underreport the physical and sexual abuse of their sons, were often victims of abuse in their own childhood, and deny the incestuous behavior of their sons. Smith and Israel (1987), studying the family characteristics of twenty-five sibling incest perpetrators, describe distant, inaccessible parents; parental stimulation of the sexual climate in the home; and family secrets, especially extramarital affairs.

O'Brien (1989) notes important similarities and differences in family characteristics when comparing sibling incest perpetrators, juvenile extrafamilial child molesters, and juveniles who assault peers or adults. In his study, over half of the families in all three groups reported substance abuse. Mothers of the sibling incest perpetrators were significantly more likely to have been victims of sexual abuse than the mothers in the two other groups. Sexual abuse (in addition to current juvenile offending) was more common in the incestuous families than the other two groups but was present in only a minority of families (22.4 percent of sibling incest group). Physical abuse was most prevalent in the incestuous group (61.2 percent), somewhat less in the extrafamilial molester group (44.69 percent), and even less in the nonchild perpetrator group (36.8 percent). Case managers (using Beaver's levels of family functioning as a guide) rated less than 14 percent of the families in the study "healthy," with 52.5 percent of the incestuous group, 45.5 percent of the extrafamilial group, and 34.5 percent of the nonchild perpetrator group rated "severely disturbed" (O'Brien, 1989).

Murray (1996) explored the relationship between natural fathers and their sons in a sample of eighteen sexually abusive youths and found evidence of strained relationships lacking in warmth, closeness, and nurturing. He notes that many sexually abusive youths have no relationship at all with their natural fathers—often having never met them and sometimes not even knowing their name.

Research to date is seriously deficient concerning the role of family variables, as is evaluation of the impact of family therapy in the treatment of sexually abusive youths. There is no evidence of direct causation on a one-to-one basis but rather a cluster of factors that appear to play some role. Further empirical research is needed in order to distinguish whether family variables increase the risk of sexually deviant development. There is, however, a wealth of published information that describes incestuous family dynamics, and clinical experience provides a basis for describing similarities and differences among the families of sexually abusive youth. Many theorists have contributed to the conceptualization of distinctive variables among families. This chapter addresses only the relevance of family dynamics that seem to accompany juvenile sexual offending. Although early sexual risk factors may be present within the family, the exploration and understanding of the family system seem less related to the development of deviant sexual arousal patterns and more related to the tolerance of abusive, unempathic relationships and patterns of maladaptive coping.

A Conceptual Typology

The family system includes the beliefs and expectations of its members and is the holding environment for the developing child. Conte (1986), in his critical analysis of the family system's approach to the problem of sexual abuse, stated that the system "describes function but is not causal." The literature on incest has described family dynamics that are common to the problem of sexual abuse in general. Some of these dynamics may relate to the developmental history of individuals who become victims or perpetrators, some relate to the roles and interactions that become internal working models for future relationships, and some relate to the system that allows or supports the occurrence of sexually deviant experience or behavior. Maladaptive coping styles are often multigenerational.

Common Family Characteristics

Some of the common characteristics of the families of sexually abusive youths are emotional impoverishment, lack of appropriate affect, dangerous secrets, distorted attachments, and a history of disruptions in care and function. The juvenile's role in the family has often been to act as a receptacle for negative feelings in the family (especially shame, guilt, and anxiety), and the sexual abuse may become the presenting symptom in a long history of acting-out behaviors.

Many family members show no affect at all—only stone faces that avoid eye contact or carry a blank gaze. Sometimes one or more family members show extreme affect inappropriate or out of context to the situation at hand (such as a perpetual smile and chuckle without depth or relevance or hysterical reactions out of proportion to the most minor difficulties). In both extremes, the family is not emotionally supportive or nourishing; feelings have been denied, suppressed, or distorted until family members have few labels attached to emotions. Affective cues are either absent or incongruent, making it difficult to assess how others are feeling.

The juvenile's behavior reflects the myths, secrets, and beliefs of the family that have served to mediate, elicit, rationalize, or suppress various behaviors in the family members. Faulty beliefs and incorrect information have not been available for validation and correction because of the denial of feelings and secrecy regarding behavioral dysfunctions.

The secrets that fester within these families are often pervasive and span generations. The proverbial skeletons in the closet include more than just sexual abuse. Denial may have protected many forms of dysfunction, including substance abuse; physical, sexual, and emotional abuse; criminal records; mental illness; physical infirmities; and social, marital, and vocational failures. Not only are these secrets kept within the family, they are kept from the family itself. It is not only extrafamilial judgment that is feared but also the secret itself. The family is often superstitious and rigid in the belief that the secrets will be more painful and powerful if they are acknowledged or discussed. The family believes the secrets are dangerous not in the keeping but in the telling.

Although the degree of attachment in the parent-child relationship may vary tremendously, the attachments that exist within the family are often distorted. Negative attachments result from role reversals, sexualized attention (Haynes-Seman & Krugman, 1989), and bonds that are rooted in negative, shared emotions. Intimacy may be misrepresented, tending to be exploitative rather than giving and sharing. Negative attachments may reflect the parents' own childhood dysfunctions or the current fearful affective state. Attachment alone fails to describe family function. It is the quality of attachment that becomes the issue.

Disruption in care may result from family crisis, illness, hospitalization, incarceration, out-of-home placement, divorce, abandonment, or death. Foster placements and adoption, as well as extended care by various relatives, are common. Maternal stress and depressive episodes in the early years, as well as paternal absence, are characteristic of instability and interruptions that affect family function. The resulting infant perception may well be one of chaos and isolation rather than connection and control. The juvenile's ability to form empathic relationships is hampered by affective parental neglect. (The issue of empathic development was discussed thoroughly in Chapter Seven.)

Other patterns frequently identifiable in the families of sexually abusive youth include sexualized problem solving or compensation, objectification and exploitation, and the pairing of intimacy and aggression. Sexualized models of coping may be a risk factor, and Smith and Israel (1987) have reported high rates of extramarital sexual relations in the families of sibling incest. Objectification refers to the depersonalization of individuals (being treated as an object, used to gratify the needs of others) and relates to the chronic exploitation of family members. Sexual objectification may be supported by exposure to pornographic materials. Exploitation may also relate to the imposition of roles, including role reversals, in order to meet the needs of the family. Intimacy and aggression are confused in the occurrence of physical abuse in the home, whether spouse abuse or child abuse.

These common characteristics in family structure and function relate to many of the families throughout the following typological conceptualization. Of course, not every sexually abusive youth's family fits any discrete category. Every family has its own unique history of strengths and weaknesses that can be discovered over the course of time. Nevertheless, some distinctions that may have implications relative to the origins and the correction of sexual abuse patterns may be made more clearly and can be useful in guiding the therapist's exploration of the client's history. These dynamics are not limited to incest families but seem to be present in many instances of extrafamilial child molestation, rape, and hands-off offense cases as well. Research is needed to further distinguish the significant variables.

The Exploitative Family

In the exploitative family, there is no unconditional love. Parents use their children to meet their own needs and may have very unrealistic expectations for their offspring. These expectations may be negative (the child is expected to be bad and fall) or extreme (the child is pushed to excel toward very high standards). Children's experience in the exploitative family is that they are cared for only to the extent that they are able to meet the needs of others. Because their validation is external, they fail to develop an internal sense of self-worth and instead develop a belief in an external locus of control. The common characteristic of objectification may be exaggerated into ownership thinking, and these parents may view family members as property. The juvenile experiences that relationships are bartered: every act of nurturance has its price. Needs are met through the manipulation of others, not as a result of communication and caring.

The Rigid or Enmeshed Family

These families are often secretive and isolated. The home is buttressed against intrusion, and there is very little social support or system contact. Family members collude in reassuring each other that they do not need or want extrafamilial contacts—that the family is self-sufficient. As one mother conceptualized enmeshment, "We feed off of one another." Inquiries or investigations are experienced as very intrusive.

The rigid family often has many secrets and taboos, which are quite binding and serve to protect the family system. Enmeshment clouds the boundaries and roles of family members. Parent-child relationships may be symbiotic, with separation and individuation issues very confused. The driving force seems to be extreme insecurity and codependency. Family members fear abandonment and believe changes and disclosures will literally tear the family apart.

Lankester and Meyer (1986) describe "almost no overt expression of affection" in these families. Moreover, mothers may become overly involved with the son in order to achieve emotional intimacy, and the repressed father may implicitly accept the son's aggressive behavior. In single-mother households, mother and son may maintain a codependency that produces a constant anxiousness. The sexual offense in some cases may represent an attempt by the son to create distance in the mother-son relationship (Lankester & Meyer, 1986) and overcome the rigid controls. These are often homes that seethe with anxiety, and intrusion from the outside threatens to send everything flying out of control. The parents impose rigid controls at home in an effort to hold everyone together because they feel helpless in relationships outside the family. Locus of control is extremely externalized, and extrafamilial occurrences are blamed on the fates. The juvenile may attribute anxiety to intimacy and perceive nonanxious periods as boring and intolerable. The youth's ability to enjoy relaxation may be very limited, and the absence of anxiety may reduce them to the "zero state," which Yochelson and Samenow (1976) note in some of the characteristics of criminal persons. Such a state is intolerable because the void of affect portends annihilation or death. For some, the anxiety associated with the risk of consequences for negative behavior may be a normalizing or reinforcing state rather than negative experience.

The Chaotic or Disengaged Family

The multiproblem family has often experienced chronic dysfunctions and perpetual crises. The chaotic qualities are often related to extreme immaturity as well as poor life skills. Parents set an example of acting-out behaviors that are reflected in the children's own dysfunctional coping. These families often lack attachments, and family members appear unconnected. Affectional relationships tend to be shallow and indiscriminate, and attachments are insecure or avoidant, placing members at risk for dangerous and exploitative encounters outside the family as well. Coaddictive patterns contribute to ineffective interventions within the family, and the disengagement may leave children bereft and adrift, without the secure base of healthy attachments. Supervision is often poor, and there is little expectation of order or control. In describing this type of family, Lankester and Meyer (1986) point out, "Generational boundaries and members' personal space are not respected . . . intrusiveness and lack of privacy are the norm . . . parents are grossly dysfunctional . . . [the child] is thrust into the role of parent . . . inappropriate modeling . . . no negative sanctions."

In a chaotic or disengaged family, the juvenile's experience may create anxiety because of the inconsistency and lack of structure, and the offense may represent an attempt to connect in a relationship perceived as controllable. Ritualization may create a structure in the abusive relationship that is reassuring to the young perpetrator, and the secrecy may be perceived as a welcome boundary around the youth.

The "Perfect" Family

The "perfect" family initially looks functional and appropriately concerned. The juvenile's sexually abusive behavior appears to be an aberration in an otherwise ideal family. The marriage, living arrangements, and work history are stable, with parents in traditional patriarchal roles. These are career fathers and "apple pie" mothers with good social skills and community involvement. The children are succeeding in school, although they may have identified learning disabilities and require some tutoring. Parents are genuinely concerned about their juvenile's problem and appear cooperative with authorities.

No family, however, can be perfect. Over time, assessment reveals that the initial appearance is an image that lacks quality and depth. Family members are invested in maintaining the "perfect" family, and each member plays out his or her assigned role with consistent dedication. Underlying the image of bliss and contentment is an intense fear of family breakdown. A nonverbal collusion exists that denies dissonance in the family, and a convenient amnesia wipes away unpleasant realities. Communication regarding emotionally charged issues is suppressed, and problem solving is dealt with at a superficial behavioral level. The roots of the family system are often the parents' own survival of an inadequate, abusive, or deprived childhood, which they have consciously vowed to overcome. These are parents who feel tremendous guilt and responsibility and are adamant in their defense of their current family.

The appearance of cooperation and compliance in arranging treatment for the sexually abusive youth meets a stone wall of resistance to working in treatment; control issues are paramount. Yet often this family eventually becomes able to overcome its distrust and engage in a meaningful exploration of change. These are families who are initially resentful of the intrusive allegations inherent in family therapy but often emerge from treatment with positive feelings. The sexually abusive youth has fulfilled the role of facilitating a necessary (though feared) period of growth for the family.

The Previously Adequate Family

Another family system that presents difficulties for treatment of sexually abusive youth is a blended family where, through marriage or adoption, a previously adequate family has become dysfunctional because of new dynamics. Lankester and Meyer (1986) note the dynamics of blended families wherein "older children perceive themselves losing status [and] jealousy or anger gets acted out" on the younger children. Perlmutter, Engel, and Sager (1982) have also considered "loosened sexual boundaries in remarried families," citing the lack of biological and developmental ties, as well as the sexual atmosphere during the new couple's romance as factors that may increase risk of sexual behavior in the household. Although these families' histories are unremarkable and the juvenile's sexual problems may have originated outside the current family system, the family arrives in treatment severely damaged and distressed. The defense mechanisms that protect individuals from the pain of chronic family problems may have been lacking, and family trust and function have often been severely affected by the discovery of the youth's sexually abusive behavior. These families are sometimes the hardest to engage in family therapy because they fail to acknowledge the impact of the juvenile's dysfunction on other family members. Adoptive parents are often the "walking wounded," who feel tremendous guilt in their failure to correct the problem behavior and are at risk for relinquishment, abandonment, or family dissolution if they cannot be engaged in the treatment process. The previously adequate family can be torn apart by the betrayal and distrust that are inherent in sexual abuse.

Implications of the Typology

Understanding as much as possible about the family of origin of the sexually abusive youth is important to his or her therapy. Conte (1986) suggests assessment of the pathology of individuals within the family, the pathology of interactions within the family, and the pathology of extrafamilial systems. Thus, a distinction evolves among those variables that may be causal (contributing to development or generation of the problem), supportive (allowing or maintaining the problem), or consequential (resultant or reactive to the problem). The causal variables may be most basic to the change process, the supportive variables most relevant to relapse prevention, and the consequential variables most pressing in crisis interventions.

Although this typology has focused on the dysfunctional elements within the families of sexually abusive youth, it is important to observe the strengths that are evident as well. Intense family loyalty is often a characteristic that can be mobilized on behalf of the juvenile in order to facilitate the treatment process. Defensive characteristics are evidence of the commitment of these families to survive the problems they face. The parents' own history may reveal severe abuse or adversity, and the strengths that have brought them through painful experiences may serve them now and be mobilized in the current crisis.

The parents' own survivorship may be the basis for hope in times that seem hopeless. The family's genuine concern often motivates its members to explore painful issues, and many are willing to participate in the treatment program. The juvenile's treatment is enhanced by tapping into the family's strengths and resources.

The disclosure of sexual perpetration by a son or daughter has a clear impact on the family. Parents who have consciously or unconsciously harbored concerns about their child's sexualized behavior have their worst fears confirmed. Parents who have successfully denied the child's progression into sexual deviance are shocked and dismayed, feeling a complete sense of helplessness relative to the discovery of the perceived aberration. The family dynamics that accompany the development of the behavior problem are often multigenerational, and the disclosure confronts the parents' denial of victimization and dysfunction in their own life experience. Families may initially shelter siblings from the painful disclosure in an effort to protect them; nevertheless, they most assuredly feel the anxiety and secrecy surrounding the perpetrator in the family.

Initial disclosures often only partially describe the extent and duration of the abuse. Sibling victims of the disclosed offending must wait to see if the bad things that the abusive sibling had threatened them with will occur, and nondisclosing sibling victims remain anxious regarding the possible discovery of their own victimization. The extreme reactions and overwhelming consequences of partial disclosure fuel the fear of further disclosures within the family. Typological characteristics are often revealed in the observation of the family's response to the crisis at hand.

The Potential Role of the Family in the Juvenile's Treatment

Four significant areas of the sexually abusive youth's treatment may be significantly enhanced by family involvement: the family is a rich source of developmental history, may be a primary source of supervision, may be able to support the juvenile's treatment and the maintenance of change, and may be capable of making alterations in the family structure and function that facilitate change and reduce risk situations for the juvenile. The full engagement and optimal work of the family in all of these areas may improve the prognosis of successful treatment and maximum relapse prevention. However, even less than full cooperation and minimal involvement of the family can be beneficial in facilitating understanding and change in the juvenile (Thomas, 1988). (Comprehensive family treatment is fully described in Chapter Eighteen.)

Developmental History

The abusive youth's developmental history provides a good basis for identifying his or her beliefs and assumptions, as well as sensitive risk factors, and thus helps to provide the phenomenological understanding of the sexually abusive youth described in Chapter Seven. Although it is possible to identify irrational beliefs through self-report or the inferences of behavior, many juveniles have difficulty articulating their thoughts and have poor writing and communication skills, so the identification of thinking patterns can be slow and arduous. The youth's difficulty in articulating thoughts is compounded by patterns of denial and a reluctance to report thoughts that are associated with painful or shameful memories or events. Some of the most illuminating keys to understanding the juvenile's view of the world may lie in preverbal memories or unspoken family beliefs, which are most difficult to define because they were experienced without language and may be recorded in perceptions and feelings that the youth has denied and left unlabeled for many years.

When the family of origin is available and can be engaged in a thorough report of the juvenile's infancy and early childhood, a wealth of information becomes available that may offer clues to the present and the past. Understanding in three major areas is facilitated: the client's view of the world, developmental deficits, and the origins of sensitive feelings and irrational beliefs. Much of the important developmental information may appear irrelevant to the current behavior problem and is reported by the family either in avoidance of the perceived problem areas or in annoyance or boredom with the therapist's apparently rambling investigation.

Worldview. The juvenile's view of the world has evolved from birth and is the basis for both conscious and unconscious decision making. This worldview is often a combination of the infant's experience and the parents' own views. The child who is born into a nurturing and trustworthy home experiences the world as a logical and empathic place wherein struggles are rewarded, consequences are consistent, and needs are satisfied through communication, perseverance, and patience. It may not be as important that the caregiver succeeds in meeting every need of the infant as that the infant perceives the caregiver's appreciation of and concern for the infant's needs and his or her willingness to struggle with the infant to achieve adequate communication and care. However, the infant who is born into crisis or confusion, whose needs are not appreciated, and whose struggle to communicate needs meets with inconsistent responses, a lack of regard, or painful consequences experiences the world as incomprehensible and uncontrollable, learns that struggles are not rewarded, and comes to believe that he must take what he needs without regard from others. The infant who achieves trust and empathy may later be betrayed, but the view of the world remains more functional than the infant whose worldview lacks basic trust and empathy.

Developmental Deficits. Lack of trust and empathy are developmental deficits that originate in infancy and may be revealed in the family's reports of circumstances surrounding the juvenile's birth. Many sexual abuse issues and developmental deficits are related to the preoperational stages of development, which are difficult for the juvenile to recall. The control-seeking function of the sexual abuse cycle may relate to issues of autonomy and control that are reminiscent of the toddler's association of genital shame regarding diapering, toilet training, and early sexual expression or to control issues related to feeding, bathing, and independence. Autonomy and competency are affected by separation and individuation issues, and the preschool years contain the early experiences of role taking, fantasy, and rule making or breaking. The origins of control issues may become apparent, as in the case of the twelve-year-old whose mother proudly reported that as an infant, he had been prevented from walking until she had returned from a long hospitalization so she would not miss his first steps. She reported this as evidence of their closeness, but the toddler's perception can be imagined: bound (rather than bonded) to the parent in order to meet the parent's needs.

Origins of Cognitive and Emotional Distortions. Patterns of thought and shared emotions may be revealed in every interaction with the juvenile and his family. Distortions, rationalization, denial, and unrealistic expectations have been described as common family characteristics and may be revealed as chronic patterns of shared belief among family members. Beliefs about power, sexuality, relationships, and coping may be accessible to the therapist, as well as the patterns of distorted thinking that support abusive behavior. Especially important may be the shared emotions within the family, which often describe the nature of attachments for better or worse. These shared emotions are often negative feelings, such as fear, shame, or guilt, that the family has experienced as closeness and may explain a secondary gain in the negative feelings associated with offending. The child whose early need to feel connected to others has been met within an environment of negative shared emotions may be reinforced rather than inhibited by the guilt and shame associated with early abusive behaviors.

Implications of Developmental History. Efficient gathering of developmental clues can contribute to the treatment process by identifying patterns of thought and emotional reactions that previously defied explanation. The juvenile who has felt a lack of control can achieve tremendous relief from the knowledge that there are identifiable explanations for how he arrived at his current situation. His faith in the therapist increases when correlations and explanations are forthcoming, even when he does not fully understand the concepts or rationale of the associations. Although no developmental antecedent can be allowed to excuse or rationalize the offender's abuse of others, the therapist's ability to imagine the early life experiences of the juvenile is a powerful demonstration of empathy, and by enabling the youth to apply empathy to himself, the therapist may help him find in himself empathy for others.

The cognitive restructuring required to break the dysfunctional cycle is inherently dependent on the definition of the beliefs and assumptions that arise from the client's view of the world. Although the thinking errors that allow or support sexual abuse can be identified and confronted on the basis of expert definition (Yochelson & Samenow, 1976; Berenson, 1987), the process of change is made easier when the client is helped to see the origin of the thinking pattern. It is often possible to acknowledge that the distortion or denial may have been temporarily adaptive, protective, or rational in its origin but that its generalization to subsequent functioning has become maladaptive and dysfunctional.

When developmental delays can be understood intellectually, the feelings of shame and incompetency can be addressed by direct intervention. Failure to achieve autonomy and the control issues subsequent to that failure may be more accessible to change when their origins become clear. The youth who understands the childhood dilemmas that prevented successful mastery and maturation may now be much more open to acknowledgment and disclosure and more amenable to corrective exercises and resolution, cognitive restructuring, and acceptance of accountability for more responsible functioning. The toddler's intimidation or the preschooler's inability to find functional and trustworthy role models need not continue to control the adolescent's functioning. Negative attention seeking; intimacy through fear, dominance, or shame; sexualized compensation; and dysfunctional patterns of adaptation and coping are more easily addressed when self-understanding allows empathy and acceptance rather than continued defense. Fantasies and compensatory thinking become less shameful when the youth understands the early learning processes and is given credit for survival of earlier difficult experiences.

The developmental history helps to unravel the defenses and mysteries of the individual and focuses treatment more rapidly on the trigger issues and deficits. The therapist's understanding of the child's dilemmas in the family of origin simultaneously reveals the family's own difficult circumstances and dilemmas, facilitating the engagement of parents in the change process.

Supervision

The juvenile's removal from the home during treatment and subsequent return is sometimes dependent on the family's ability to provide adequate supervision. The National Task Force on Juvenile Sexual Offending (1988, 1993) has stressed that intrafamilial sexual abuse should always result in some period of removal of the abusive child in order to provide physical and psychological safety for the victim(s) and to avoid assigning a *watchdog* role to the parents, which may further erode existing levels of trust within the family. However, for the youth who has sexually abused outside the home and is in outpatient treatment or the juvenile returning home from residential treatment or correctional placement, the need for parental supervision is clear. Therapists, teachers, and probation and parole officers cannot fully monitor the juvenile's activities in the community. Parents have the maximum opportunity to supervise and monitor their child.

The family's inability to see the juvenile's behavior is often the first obstacle to appropriate supervision (Thomas, 1988). The juvenile's abusive patterns have often developed in an environment that has failed to acknowledge problem behaviors at all. This pervasive denial is a common characteristic, although families may report underlying concerns of long-standing duration. Even in families that have recognized early behaviors as problematic, minimization or ineffective interventions have often characterized their patterns of response. Just as victims should not be expected to believe that disclosure and entry into treatment will protect them from further abuse (Ryan, 1989), therapists must not assume adequate supervision will be forthcoming in the home following disclosure.

Parents must be educated to see and recognize the juvenile's behavior—not only the overtly abusive acts but the antecedent indicators of risk or progression. The family's ability and motivation to provide adequate supervision are improved by their involvement in the juvenile's treatment. Parental perceptions of sexual abuse are often as clouded by distorted beliefs and ignorance as is the offender's own perception. Hopelessness and helplessness contribute to the parental perception that the sexual offense is an aberration that occurred without warning and is beyond prediction and control.

In order to protect both the abusive youth and the community from the consequences of additional abuse, the parents must be motivated and educated. Very specific instructions must be given and enforced to ensure that apparently unrelated decisions do not increase risk or continue denial of relapse cues. The parents must be given the rules of supervision without any presumptions, or it is likely that the environmental factors that have either supported or allowed sexual abuse will remain unchanged.

The youth's access to past and potential victims is a major concern and must be specifically prohibited. It is not unusual for the parent who knows one child has been sexually abused to leave the abusive youth alone with (or even in charge of) another child. For example, a fourteen-year-old male who had molested his twelve-year-old sister for two years was encouraged to continue bathing the four-year-old sibling at bedtime. In another case, the twelve-year-old had molested a four-year-old sibling and was sent to live with relatives who had a four-year-old child of their own. In many cases, the youth who molests children has been seen as "very good" with children or having "very special" relationships with many children. Both victim and nonvictim children may be very attached to the youth who abuses them and may express feelings of loss when access is curtailed; nevertheless, all of the abusive youth's access to children should be restricted initially. Even interactions with children in view of the parents should be forbidden until treatment progress indicates the victim's sense of safety; decreased risk of deviant fantasy, arousal, and grooming behavior by the abusive juvenile; and the adequacy of supervision and control is assessed.

Covert levels of exploitation and sexualization are often pervasive in many relationships of the sexually abusive youth. Until the juvenile and the parents are both educated to see and change exploitative sexualization, even peer relations must be evaluated as suspect. Parents must be cautioned against assuming their child's interest in more "acceptable" sexual objects (that is, opposite-sex peers) is automatically a sign of progress. Concrete rules must be set up for the parents regarding the juvenile's access to potential victims, and detailed reporting of activities and situations must be encouraged.

Access and exposure to sexually explicit materials is another area that requires supervision. Many juveniles have access to pornography within their own home, and the culture is full of sexually explicit and exploitative models. Some popular music, album covers, and posters are permeated with sexual messages and images, many of them glorifying incest, rape, sexual violence, and sadomasochism (Parents Music Resource Center, 1988). Television, even prime-time programming, is another source of sexual messages (National Coalition on Television Violence, 1988). Recently, sexually explicit content on the Internet has caused concern about juvenile access as well (Laws, 1996). It is not unusual for parents to be completely unaware of their children's access to sexually explicit materials in their own home, and it is important to be specific about monitoring sexually explicit material in order to establish the role they play in the juvenile's concept of sexuality and sexual arousal. Education and communication are important for the juvenile and the parents in this regard.

Ideally the supervisory role of the parents should include the monitoring of their child's progress and behavior in school, as well as in all other activities and responsibilities. Collateral sources of information (for example, teachers, case workers, and so on) must always be used to verify the validity of the parents' reports. Patterns of irresponsible behavior are often so pervasive that parents are desensitized and unable to recognize many signs of concern.

Participation in the Juvenile's Treatment

Another potential role of parental involvement is support for the juvenile's treatment. Some families are unable to support treatment at all, and if they completely deny the need for or sabotage the juvenile's participation, legal interventions or out-of-home placement may be necessary. However, families who can acknowledge the juvenile's need to get help and make changes, even minimal ones, can be educated in specific and nonthreatening ways to encourage the juvenile's participation in treatment and to help maintain the changes that are made. Optimally families will participate in family treatment with the juvenile in order to be actively involved in changes within the family structure and function that support the juvenile's treatment and decrease stress and risk factors within the home environment.

Family: Absent, Impossible, or Amenable

Every juvenile enters treatment with a family history. Whether absent, distant, functional, or dysfunctional, the family raises issues that must be addressed, and the therapist must assess the potential for family involvement. For some sexually abusive youth, family involvement appears unlikely because of absence. The situations of juveniles who have been disowned or abandoned, have been placed outside their community for treatment or incarceration, or have lost their parents due to other circumstances appear to preclude family involvement in the treatment process. Creative thinking about what is needed from families, however, may reveal alternate sources and methods.

A family orientation is crucial in terms of the client's place in the human family (Thomas, 1988). The juvenile's developmental history may be available from extended family members, such as older siblings or grandparents, or it may be obtained through correspondence with previous caregivers. Absent or distant parents may be willing to provide a biography of the juvenile or respond to specific questions by mail or telephone. Every source of information may offer different perspectives and pieces of understanding that complement or contradict each other. Collateral sources can be cross-checked, and diverse opinions help to identify sources of distortion and confusion.

Current caregivers can be vital observers and informants and may be educated to spot trigger situations and antecedents that are a part of the juvenile's dysfunctional cycle. These caregivers must be educated for supervision of the sexually abusive youth and may be engaged in supporting and reinforcing participation in treatment and positive change. For the juvenile who will return to a distant family, creative involvement is imperative and may include marathon family therapy weekends, conference calls, or additional family therapy in the home community. For the juvenile who has lost his family or will not be returning home, developmental history provides a basis for dealing with the dysfunction and the loss as well as future familial relationships.

For some sexually abusive youth, an "impossible" family may be even more difficult than an absent or distant one. The "impossible" family is often chaotic and has manifold problem areas, frequently involving a multigenerational history of interpersonal violence and sexual abuse. The family may be absent or distant or painfully present, sabotaging treatment overtly and/or covertly. Family denial, rationalization, and distortions may be pervasive, and the family may feel threatened and intruded on by the disclosure of the sex abuse. Although they may be willing to share developmental perceptions, these families may never be even minimally supportive in the treatment of the youth. Many times these juveniles are unable to become engaged in treatment or participate in meaningful change until they are removed from the family's influence. In some cases, the family's refusal to allow or support change makes it impossible for the juvenile to return home.

Most frustrating of all are the cases where it is not possible to remove a juvenile from a family that discourages his involvement in treatment or contributes to the risk of further abusive functioning. In difficult family dilemmas, therapists should seek the help of attorneys in the field, who will be able to communicate an understanding to the court of the detrimental effect a particular family will have on the juvenile's treatment and eventual rehabilitation. In many of these situations, therapists can only document the problems and communicate their concerns to the courts and to the juvenile. Expectations for change must be realistic. In some cases, the juvenile is able to participate in treatment in spite of family resistance, and the therapist can be direct in acknowledging the dilemma and supporting the juvenile's personal strengths. The therapist's ability to establish a consistent, dependable relationship may enable the juvenile to trust and confide, benefiting from the treatment experience by seeing that there are other ways to view the world that are different from those he has learned in his family.

The amenable families are those who are able to go beyond provision of history and education for supervision to support the juvenile's treatment and participate in meaningful family therapy as well. Chapter Eighteen will explore the family involvement process in five stages: (1) crisis intervention, (2) assessment, (3) family therapy, (4) reconstruction, and (5) transition and aftercare. Crisis intervention and family assessment are applicable to every juvenile referral. The potential and prognosis for family therapy are not immediately apparent but emerge over time in response to early attempts to work with the family of the sexually abusive youth.

A family orientation is both possible and desirable in approaching every case (Thomas, 1988). Each piece of understanding that becomes available from family contacts must be appreciated for its contribution to the therapist's work with the juvenile.

References

Berenson, D. (1987). Choice, thinking and responsibility: Implications for the treatment of the sex offender. In G. Ryan (Ed.), *Interchange*. (Newsletter of the National Adolescent Perpetrator Network). (pp. 1–8). Denver: Kempe National Center.

Conte, J. (1986). Sexual abuse and the family: A critical analysis. In T. Trepper & M. Barrett (Eds.), *Treating incest: A multimodal systems perspective*. New York: Hawthorn Press.

Freeman-Longo, R. E. (1982). Child molestation: The offender and the assault. *Proceedings of the 112th Annual Congress of Correction*. Toronto, Canada: American Correctional Association.

Gilgun, J. (1988). *Factors which block the development of sexually abusive behavior in adults abused as children*. Paper presented at the National Conference on Male Victims and Offenders, Minneapolis, MN.

Haynes-Seman, C., & Krugman, R. (1989). Sexualized attention: Normal interaction or precursor to sexual abuse? *American Journal of Orthopsychiatry, 59*(2), 238–245.

Hunter, J. (1996, November). *The juvenile offender: Different challenges and approaches*. Paper presented at "National Summit: Promoting Public Safety Through Management of Sex Offenders in the Community," Office of Justice, Washington, DC.

Kaplan, M. S., Becker, J. V., & Cunningham-Rathner, J. (1988). Characteristics of parents of adolescent incest perpetrators: Preliminary findings. *Journal of Family Violence, 3*(3), 183–191.

Klaus, H. M., & Kennell, J. H. (1976). *Maternal-infant bonding*. St. Louis: Mosby–Year Book.

Lankester, D., & Meyer, B. (1986). *Relationship of family structure to sex offense behavior*. Paper presented at the First National Conference on Juvenile Sexual Offending, Minneapolis, MN.

Lankester, D., & Meyer, B. (1988). Sex gone wrong. *Networker*, pp. 1, 5, 7.

Laws, R. (1996). Panel moderated at the Sixteenth Association for the Treatment of Sexual Abusers Conference, Chicago, IL.

Murray, M. (1996, August). *Exploratory study of the relationship between national fathers and their sons in cases of adolescent sexual offenders.* Paper presented at the Eleventh International Congress on Child Abuse and Neglect, Dublin, Ireland.

National Coalition on Television Violence. (1989). [Data sheet.] *NCTV News, 10,* 2–3.

National Task Force on Juvenile Sexual Offending. (1988). Preliminary report. *Juvenile and Family Court Journal, 39*(2), 13.

National Task Force on Juvenile Sexual Offending. (1993). Revised report. *Juvenile and Family Court Journal, 44*(4).

O'Brien, M. (1989). *Sibling incest.* Brandon, VT: Safer Society Press.

Parents Music Resource Center. (1988). *Rising to the challenge* [Videotape]. Alexandria, VA: Author.

Perlmutter, L., Engel, T., & Sager, C. (1982). The incest taboo: Loosened sexual boundaries in remarried families. *Journal of Sex and Marital Therapy, 8*(2).

Prentky, R., Knight, R., Straus, H., Rokous, F., Cerce, D., & Sims-Knight, J. (1989). Developmental antecedents of sexual aggression. *Development and Psychopathology, 1,* 153–169.

Ryan, G. (1987). Getting at the facts. *Interchange.* (Newsletter of the National Adolescent Perpetrator Network). (pp. 6–7). Denver: Kempe National Center.

Ryan, G. (1988). *The juvenile sexual offender: A question of diagnosis.* Presentation of unpublished data at the National Symposium on Child Victimization, Anaheim, CA.

Ryan, G. (1989). Victim to victimizer: Rethinking victim treatment. *Journal of Interpersonal Violence, 4*(3), 325–341.

Ryan, G., Miyoshi, T., Metzner, J., Fryer, G., & Krugman, R. (1996). Trends in a national sample of sexually abusive youth. *Journal of the American Academy of Child an Adolescent Psychiatry, 35*(1).

Smith, H., & Israel, E. (1987). Sibling incest: A study of the dynamics of 25 cases. *Child Abuse and Neglect, 11*(2), 101–108.

Steele, B. F. (1987). Abuse and neglect in the earliest years: Groundwork for vulnerability. *Zero to Three, 7*(4), 14–15.

Thomas, J. (1988). *Multifamily group work with juvenile sexual offenders.* Paper presented at the National Training Conference, Long Beach, CA.

Widom, C. S. (1996). Childhood sexual abuse and its criminal consequences. *Society, 33*(4), 47–53.

Williams, L. M. (1995). *Juvenile and adult offending behavior and other outcomes in a cohort of sexually abused boys: Twenty years later.* Philadelphia, PA: Joseph J. Peters Institute.

Yochelson, S., & Samenow, S. (1976). *The criminal personality* (Vol. 1). Northvale, NJ: Aronson.

PART THREE

CONSEQUENCES OF SEXUAL ABUSE

CHAPTER NINE

CONSEQUENCES FOR THE VICTIM OF SEXUAL ABUSE

Gail Ryan

Sexual abuse is problematic not only because of the occurrence of a sexual behavior but because of the abusive nature of the interaction. Although the impact of the behavior is not what defines abuse, the impact is what causes the concern. The consequences of sexual abuse for those involved encompass the immediate qualities of the experience, the short-term effects, and the long-term outcomes. For both victims and offenders, the occurrence of a sexual assault triggers a sequence of subsequent problems. This chapter and the next examine the experience and impact of the event itself at a personal level for both victims and offenders and the families of each.

The Experience of Sexual Victimization

The experience of any victimization is always one of helplessness (Hiroto, 1974). For the sexual abuse victim, the experience is particularly intrusive because of the assault on both body privacy and the psychic self. However, sexual abuse does not occur in a vacuum; the experience and impact are affected by all that has gone before and everything that follows. The nature of the victimization only partially defines the victim's experience (Hindman, 1989; Briere, 1992). A full understanding of the experience considers each victim's own perception at a very personal level.

Variables affecting the victim's experience include virtually every experience and perception of the individual since birth, and the impact of the experience will differ on that basis, as well as in the many variables of subsequent life experience (Ryan, Wagstaff, Pullen, & Wand, 1989; Ryan and Associates, 1997). The most important caution therefore is that it cannot be assumed that every victim's experience is the same or that the impact or outcome will be the same. This has become apparent, although not always acknowledged, in the assessment of victims at the point of disclosure, as well as in the consideration of intervention and long-term outcomes.

Although assumptions about the individual's experience cannot be made, a range of factors documented in the literature alert us to areas of consideration. These become very important in discussions with youth in treatment regarding the impact of their abusive behaviors, as well as victimization in their own life experiences.

Vulnerabilities to Abuse

Some sexual victimization occurs in the context of an entirely random victim selection. Many rapes of adults are perpetrated by assailants unknown to the victim, a small percentage of child molestations are committed by strangers, and many of the hands-off abuses occur somewhat randomly. However, most child sexual abuse and many acquaintance rapes occur within relationships that have either revealed or groomed a vulnerability in the victim. Preexisting conditions of neglect, parental loss, inferior self-image, and lack of nurturance may make potential victims, especially child victims, vulnerable to the advances of sexual perpetrators. When the youth's advances or grooming process fulfill an "emotional need for nurturance" (Summit, 1983), the victims are made vulnerable because resistance or disclosure will cost the victim a relationship that is meeting some emotional need. These *secondary gains* have been reported in some victims' experience, but it should also be recognized that secondary gains are only as powerful as the needs of the victim.

Prior Life Experience

Vulnerability is based in earlier life experiences, but many other factors also affect the impact of the experience. The degree to which the victimization is dissonant with the individual's view of the world may affect the level of trauma, as well as the method of coping. The victim who has experienced the world as a safe, empathic place may be more traumatized by, but less accepting of, the abuse than a victim whose worldview lacks safety. Similarly, the existing repertoire of coping mechanisms may vary in accord with past coping models and experiences. Coping styles may range from denial and disassociation to problem solving and resolution. Passivity and assertiveness, distorted or rational belief systems, and empathic or exploitative patterns may all be preexisting qualities—products of early life experience.

Betrayal

Sexual victimization is often perpetrated by someone whom the victim trusts, and the betrayal of that confidence is paramount. The level of trauma in the experience of sexual abuse may also relate to prior life views in the perception of betrayal as dissonant or expected. The basic development of trust or distrust emphasized in infant development contributes to the quality of all relationships, and the victim's level of trust in the exploited relationship affects the perception of betrayal. The victim whose prior experiences have been a trade-off of exploit-and-be-exploited may experience less betrayal in the sexual victimization than the victim who has believed the world is a safe, trustworthy place. The sexually abusive youth's lack of regard for the victim's needs (Willock, 1983; Steele, 1986) will be perceived in the context of earlier experiences of empathy or disregard.

The Relationship

The relationship that exists prior to the sexual abuse is not always easily definable. Although it has been assumed that the closer the relationship, that is, family versus friend, the greater the impact of the betrayal, it is the victim's perception of trust and dependency in the relationship that must be considered. The father who has been emotionally absent or distant, unempathic, and inconsistent has a very different relationship with the child than does the older cousin who has always catered to and doted on the child. Assumptions about impact on the basis of relationship must therefore be approached from the perception of the victim.

Developmental Stages

Another area that is thought to relate to the child's experience of sexual abuse is that of developmental stage. Not only is the experience of sexual abuse developmentally inappropriate (Conte, 1984), but the developmental stage of the victim may vary not only according to age but also in regard to success or failure in earlier developmental tasks. The experience of victimization or trauma creates a developmental crisis that may arrest future development or trigger regression to an earlier developmental phase. The assault is not only on the body of the child but also on basic trust and worldview. Development of interpersonal relationships is almost certain to be adversely affected, and the child's subsequent development may be distorted.

Sexuality

The "traumatic sexualization" (Conte & Brown, 1985) that the victim experiences is the product of exposure to deviant sexuality, which may be incomprehensible to a child (Summit, 1983). Concepts of sexuality relate to genitalia, arousal, and relationship. Sexual victimization may include genital injury or the perception of injury. Children who have been penetrated often believe their bodies are subsequently different from those of other children and permanently damaged. This "damaged goods" syndrome may lower self-esteem, devalue the sense of self, and discourage self-protection in the future. At the same time, the experience of sexual arousal may be present in any sexual interaction, and the resultant confusion may lead victims to conclude themselves guilty and stigmatized (Conte, 1984). For the victim who experiences pleasure in either the physical closeness of hugging and petting or in the sexual arousal associated with the experience of abuse, the subsequent pairing of fear and guilt, pain, and pleasure must be accommodated at a cognitive level. The victim's thinking is then likely to incorporate the perpetrator's own distorted rationalizations, and the risk of deviant sexual development is high. The victim who experiences arousal without pain is even more likely to accept a personal stigmatization, and the victim who experiences pain from the sexual behavior without arousal may pair the behavior with aggression.

Gender Issues

For the male victim who is sexually abused by a male, the whole issue of homosexuality arises. The male victim may conclude that the experience causes or defines him to be homosexual. The opposite conclusion may result in an extreme homophobia that impairs all future same-sex relationships (Breer, 1987). The male victim may deny his arousal in the abuse or translate himself into the role of aggressor. When males are sexually exploited by a female, they are especially likely to convince themselves they were not really a victim.

The female victim's sexuality may be perceived as tarnished or perverted. Her acceptance of guilt and responsibility may lead her to interpret her victimization as deserved and lead to increased risk of further abuse, promiscuity, or self-degradation. She may feel that her virginity is forever gone and that she is therefore undeserving of nonexploitative sexual relationships in the future. For the smaller proportion of female victims who are sexually abused by a female perpetrator, concerns regarding homosexuality may also arise.

Secrecy

One of the most pervasive common elements in the experience of sexual victimization may be that of secrecy, and it is the factor that supports the helplessness of the victim and the power of the abuser. Secrecy isolates the victim (Finkelhor, 1986), separates the experience from the mainstream of life, and prevents validation of the nature of the experience. As long as the abuse remains secret, the victim is unable to express feelings or seek verification of perceptions. The secret protects the sexually abusive youth, and the victims may be led to believe that it protects them as well. In the isolation imposed by the secret, the offender's distortions and rationalizations are the victim's only source of interpretation for the experience, and the secret gains power over time as the abuse continues.

Accommodation

The victim's experience of sexual abuse must be reconciled with his or her view of self and of the world. Summit (1983) has addressed the child victim's dilemma as the "child sexual abuse accommodation" syndrome, a concept that bridges the span from experience through disclosure. Because the secret has bound the victim in a helpless complicity, disclosure may be delayed indefinitely. Even when the victim discloses the abuse, the accusation may be so tentative and exploratory as to be unconvincing. Victims may "test" the reality of the outside world and find that the immediate response is much like the youth had warned. When disclosure triggers a sequence of embarrassments, disbelief, or trouble, victims sometimes retract statements in order to escape the impact and stigma of the system's response. The victim whose disclosure is not believed or for whom the results of disclosure are ineffective in providing safety and protection from further abuse is recaptured by the power of the perpetrator and left even more helpless. Even when the victim's disclosure is believed and intervention takes place, the victim's removal from the home, loss of the relationship with the perpetrator, and intrusive interviews with strangers may seem a high price to pay for protection from the unwanted sexual experience.

The Short-Term Impact of Sexual Abuse

The short-term impact of sexual abuse on the victim is a demonstration of the methods of coping: emotional reactions, psychological functioning, and behavioral change. In all reactions to trauma and stress, males are more inclined to externalize reactions; females tend to internalize them. These reactions are thought to be a product of sex role modeling and socialization, which teaches females to manifest emotions and males to deny them. In the experience of sexual abuse, the female victim is more likely to internalize the experience, feeling somehow personally responsible, guilty, and deserving of abuse. Male victims, on the other hand, are more likely to externalize the experience: discounting negative feelings, depersonalizing the abuse, and identifying with the aggressor (Summit, 1983). The female victim may appear more sad, depressed, and anxious, while male victims appear more angry, distrustful, and aggressive.

The immediate goal for the victims is to protect themselves from the painful aspects of the abuse. All the perceptions discussed in regard to the experience of victimization must be interpreted, accepted, or rejected in relation to the victim's sense of self and view of the world. In order to protect themselves from the painful meaning of the abuse, many victims' immediate style of coping is denial. Disassociation, blocking the memory of the abuse, imagining that it did not occur or that it was only a dream, or minimizing the exploitative or sexual nature of the interaction are all effective forms of denial that protect the victim from being overwhelmed by the experience (Conte, 1988).

The second goal for the victims in coping is to regain what was lost. The victim experiences the powerlessness as a loss of control and must either accept helplessness or master it. One of the immediate reactions is retaliatory thinking, which is often modeled for the victim by those who discover the abuse. Upon disclosure of abuse, uninvolved family members as well as those involved in the systems that intervene are often consumed by their own anger and the betrayal of their own basic trust in people, and they may model retaliation as a means of coping. The victim's own inclination to "get back" is thus supported by the parent who expresses the desire to incarcerate, castrate, or kill the perpetrator (Ryan, 1989).

Observations throughout the literature of children who have been sexually abused include reports of acting-out behaviors (Friedrich, Urquiza, & Bielke, 1986). These behaviors are thought to represent attempts to master the experience of helplessness by seeking control in subsequent situations (Ryan, 1984). The cognitive processes that accompany these acting-out behaviors often reflect the distortions the victim was exposed to in the course of the abuse.

The victim who acts out continued helplessness, engages in "tempting" others with seductive behavior, or participates in behavior that puts him or her at risk of injury or further abuse is said to be displaying a learned helplessness. That profile of powerlessness may actually be a very empowering mechanism for the victim, however, by (1) reassuring the victim that he or she was truly unable to prevent the abuse and is therefore guiltless and by (2) coping with the fear of reabuse by controlling its occurrence and thereby avoiding the sense of betrayal in future situations. The "delusions" of persecution noted in the literature (Adams-Tucker, 1980) may therefore actually be "illusions" supportive of the victim's coping style. The victim who acts out aggressively, on the other hand, may be attempting to master rather than accommodate the experience of helplessness and betrayal. Risk taking, fighting, and perpetration may be attempts to regain the power and control lost in the experience of abuse and are easily defined as control mechanisms that Lane refers to as power thrusting (Ryan, Lane, Davis, & Isaac, 1987).

In either method of coping (continued helplessness or power thrusting), the thinking that supports the reaction reflects the patterns of distorted rationalization present in the experience of abuse. These short-term aberrations of thought and behavior may serve to protect the victim from being overwhelmed by the experience and are therefore temporarily adaptive methods of coping (Conte, 1988). Failure to resolve these issues rationally, however, may lead to lifelong patterns of thought and behavior that support long-term dysfunctions (Ryan, 1989).

Not every victim's perception of sexual victimization is the same, and the process of adaptation, accommodation, and coping may also be very different for different individuals. Resolution is similarly variable and requires differential diagnosis and treatment interventions. Terr (1983, 1985a, 1985b) and others have studied the traumatic nature of the experience, which for some victims seems to create a subsequent posttraumatic stress syndrome. The posttraumatic stress symptoms are particularly resistant to resolution, as they seem to seek control by freezing the experience: reenacting the experience in fantasy or behavior that is increasingly elaborate, ritualistic, and secretive and becomes more rigid over time without any resolution. This condition or syndrome may exist for years and hamper long-term mental health.

Long-Term Sequelae of Sexual Abuse

Adolescent and adult survivors of childhood sexual abuse are overrepresented in many dysfunctional populations. The long-term impacts are apparent in the subsequent miseries perpetuated in the victim's own life, as well as that which is perpetrated on others.

Sexual Dysfunctions

Many sexual dysfunctions may result from the premature or traumatic sexual experience. Hypersexual dysfunctions may include promiscuity, sexual addictions, compulsive masturbation, or elevated or deviant arousal patterns. Sadistic or masochistic characteristics may manifest in either consensual or exploitative relationships and are frequently present in the dynamics of prostitution and marital difficulties. Hyposexual dysfunctions may include inhibited desire or arousal and manifest in frigidity, impotence, or sexual aversions, which are also dynamics in marital difficulties. Victimless fetishes too, such as cross-dressing, may relate to the impacts of childhood sexual abuse.

Somatic Complaints and Anxiety

The pervasive fears and helplessness (Sanford, 1987; Weiss, Rogers, Darwin, & Dutton, 1955) inherent in the experience of abuse may be manifest throughout the life span and, in combination with the "damaged-goods" perception previously described, may lead to somatic complaints and nonspecific anxiety. The somatic disorders may represent a hypervigilance of one's physical condition, while the anxieties relate to the lost trust and betrayal that manifest in distrust of the environment and an uneasiness in interpersonal relationships. In the extremes, these characteristics may make it impossible for survivors ever to feel entirely well or completely comfortable.

Affective Disorders and Suicide Risk

The chronic feelings of fear and anxiety may contribute to feelings of depression and a profound sense of hopelessness. In childhood, these qualities may manifest in either sadness and worry or hyperactivity and attention deficits. With maturity, depressive disorders increase the risk of self-destructive behaviors and suicidal ideation. Self-destruction may relate to a control-seeking cycle, with suicide representing the ultimate control.

Substance Use and Abuse

The dynamics and thinking patterns present in the abuse of alcohol or drugs may relate to either a self-medication of somatic or depressive conditions or an escape from hypervigilance and anxiety in order to feel more relaxed. In either case, the substance use may represent the same control-seeking cycle as other dysfunctions, whereby the user feels isolated and separate from others and imagines that substance use will result in his or her feeling better. This pattern of seeking external sources of control in order to feel less helpless is supported by the same patterns of distorted thinking experienced in the sexual abuse (Ryan, 1989).

Eating Disorders

Extreme food behaviors have long been observed in abused, neglected, and deprived populations (Ryan, 1978). Treatment of eating disorders has pointed to the addictive properties as well as the control-seeking qualities of such conditions as anorexia and bulimia. The search for autonomy and body control is manifest in these binge-and-purge behaviors, and eating disorders have been associated with childhood sexual abuse by Oppenheimer, Howells, Palmer, and Challoner (1985) and others. When these disorders appear in adolescent or adult survivors, the same control-seeking cycle earlier related to sexual abuse, suicide, and substance abuse may apply, and similar distorted thinking patterns and developmental deficits support the disorder. The eating disorders of sexual abuse survivors may extend into the next generation; we see nonorganic failure to thrive manifest in the infants of some mothers who were victims of incest (Haynes-Seman, 1987). The betrayal of nurturance may explain these mothers' inability to feed their infants successfully, or the feeding interaction may become a field for the power and control issues raised by the sexual abuse.

Communication, Learning, and Relationships

The failure of communication and learning has been documented in the sexually abused population that is seen in special education and learning-disabled groups (Blum & Gray, 1987; Conte, 1984). These problems significantly alter functioning and subsequent feelings of competency. Interpersonal relationships and self-image are often fragile or ambivalent. Failed marriages, parent-child conflicts, and an inability to maintain close friendships may characterize adult experience, and intimacy may always be difficult. Communication failures hamper treatment as well as relationships, and every new experience may be perceived with distrust.

The Victim's Family

Many of the issues and reactions for the parents and siblings of sexual abuse victims are similar to those of the victim. The violation of a family member in many ways violates the family as well. Betrayal of trust, intrusion, and retaliatory thinking may resonate throughout the family system. Family members' coping styles are often cast from the same die as the victim's, and thus, denial, dissonance, accommodation, and reactive behaviors are potentially similar.

For the family that has previously experienced intrafamilial sexual abuse (incest) in the current or previous generations, the disclosure of the child's abuse may be less traumatic and more a fulfillment of the expected or the feared. For the family that experiences extrafamilial sexual abuse of the child, the disclosure may be so dissonant that its validity is denied or be so traumatic that family function fails.

The family is affected by the disclosure of the abuse, and their subsequent reactions to the disclosure have a further impact on the victim. Disbelief and inadequate protection add to the victim's original confusion and validate the threats and distortions of the offender. Belief and subsequent protection supports the victim's disclosure but at the same time acknowledges the legitimate helplessness of the victim and the family's original failure to protect. The family's sense of violation and confusion mirror the victim's own confusion and require family interventions.

Implications

The consequences of sexual victimization for the victim include the potential for infinite miseries throughout the life span, although many survivors do very well. The experience may alter the course of subsequent development and jeopardize future relationships. Multiple dysfunctions may result from a failure to cope effectively, and sexual deviancy may reappear in many forms. When the victim takes on the role of victimizing others, the intergenerational cycle of abuse is perpetuated by the sexually abusive youth's cycle of maladaptive coping.

Comprehension of the victim's experience of sexual abuse has many implications in the treatment of sexually abusive youth. Victim empathy is imperative to prevention of further abuse and is relevant to the victims whom the youth has abused, as well as the offender's own past victimization. In exploration of the victim-to-victimizer transition, parallel issues and characteristics have been identified in the victim's experience and the youth's perpetration of sexual abuse. In addition to dealing with the impact of their behaviors, sexually abusive youth who have experienced victimization require treatment intervention. These parallels (suggested in Ryan, 1989) have implications throughout this book in relation to treatment and prevention.

An important distinction can be drawn in defining the issues of sexual abuse separate from the ways in which the issues become characterized in the personality of the individual or manifested in behavior, either immediately or in the future (Ryan, 1989). If the issues inherent in the experience of abuse are helplessness, depersonalization, and betrayal, then treatment of sexual abuse must address the issues rather than focus on the characteristics or behavior of the offender.

References

Adams-Tucker, C. (1980). *Sex abused children: Pathology and clinical traits*. Paper presented at the Annual Meeting of American Psychiatric Association, San Francisco, CA.

Blum, J., & Gray, S. (1987). *Strategies for communicating with young children*. Paper presented at the Sixteenth Annual Child Abuse and Neglect Symposium, Keystone, CO.

Breer, W. (1987). *The adolescent molester*. Springfield, IL: Thomas.

Briere, J. (1992). *Child abuse trauma*. Thousand Oaks, CA: Sage.

Conte, J. (1984). The effects of sexual victimization on children: A critique and suggestions for future research. *Victimology: The International Journal, 10,* 110–130.

Conte, J. (1988). *The effects of sexual abuse on the child victim and its treatment.* Paper presented at the Fourth National Symposium on Child Sexual Abuse, Huntsville, AL.

Conte, J., & Browne, A. (1985). The traumatic impact of child sexual abuse: A conceptualization. *American Journal of Orthopsychiatry, 55*(4), 530–541.

Finkelhor, D. (1986). Initial and long-term effects: A review of the research. In D. Finkelhor (Ed.), *Sourcebook on child sexual abuse.* Thousand Oaks, CA: Sage.

Friedrich, W. N., Urquiza, A., & Bielke, R. (1986). Behavioral problems in sexually abused young children. *Journal of Pediatric Psychology, 11*(2), 47–57.

Haynes-Seman, C. (1987). *Impact of sexualized attention on the preverbal child.* Paper presented at the Sixteenth Annual Child Abuse and Neglect Symposium, Keystone, CO.

Hindman, J. (1989). *Just before dawn.* Oregon: Alexandria Press.

Hiroto, D. (1974). Locus of control and learned helplessness. *Journal of Experimental Psychology,* p. 1022.

Oppenheimer, R., Howells, K., Palmer, R., & Challoner, D. (1985). *Adverse sexual experience and clinical eating disorders: A preliminary description.* Unpublished manuscript, University of Leicester, England.

Ryan, G. (1978). Extreme food behavior in abusive families. *Child Abuse and Neglect: The International Journal, 2,* 117–122.

Ryan, G. (1984). The child abuse connection. *Interchange.* (Newsletter of the National Adolescent Perpetrator Network). (pp. 1–4). Denver: Kempe National Center.

Ryan, G. (1989). Victim to victimizer: Rethinking victim treatment. *Journal of Interpersonal Violence, 4*(3), 325–341.

Ryan, G., and Associates. (1997). *The web of meaning: A developmental contextual view of sexual abuse.* Manuscript submitted for publication.

Ryan, G., Lane, S., Davis, J., & Isaac, C. (1987). Juvenile sexual offenders: Development and correction. *Child Abuse and Neglect: The International Journal, 11*(3), 385–395.

Ryan, G., Wagstaff, B., Pullen, C., & Wand, S. (1989). *Sexual abuse in the context of whole life experience.* Paper presented at the Eighteenth National Symposium on Child Abuse and Neglect, Keystone, CO.

Sanford, L. (1987). Pervasive fears in victims of sexual abuse: A clinician's observations. *Preventing Sexual Abuse, 2*(2), 3–5.

Steele, B. F. (1986). Lasting effects of childhood sexual abuse. *Child Abuse and Neglect: The International Journal, 10*(2), 283–291.

Summit, R. (1983). The child sexual abuse accommodation syndrome. *Child Abuse and Neglect: The International Journal, 7*(2), 177–193.

Terr, L. (1983). Chowchilla revisited: The effects of psychic trauma four years after a school-bus kidnapping. *American Journal of Psychiatry, 140,* 1543–1550.

Terr, L. (1985a). Play therapy and psychic trauma: A preliminary report. In C. Schaefer & K. O'Connor (Eds.), *Handbook of play therapy.* New York: Wiley.

Terr, L. (1985b). Therapy and psychic trauma: A preliminary report. In C. Schaefer & K. O'Connor (Eds.), *Handbook of play therapy.* New York: Wiley.

Weiss, J., Rogers, E., Darwin, M., & Dutton, C. (1955). A study of girl sex victims. *Psychiatric Quarterly, 29*(l), 1–27.

Willock, B. (1983). Play therapy with the aggressive, acting out child. In C. Schaefer & K. O'Connor (Eds.), *Handbook of play therapy.* New York: Wiley.

CHAPTER TEN

CONSEQUENCES FOR THE
YOUTH WHO HAS BEEN ABUSIVE

Gail Ryan

In order to understand the motivation and reinforcement of sexually abusive behavior, as well as to facilitate an empathic experience in treatment, it becomes necessary to explore what the sexually abusive youth's experience has been relative to the sexual abuse. It is also important to understand the immediate and long-term impacts of the experience. The implementation of corrective interventions in treatment is dependent on understanding the individual who is being treated and appreciating both the past experience and the future risk factors associated with sexually deviant behavior.

The Abusive Experience

Whether child molesting, rape, or more covert assaults, the sexually abusive behaviors set the perpetrator apart from the norms of his culture and his peers. The deviancy carries its own stigma, and the sexually abusive youth's self-image is affected by his evaluation of the behavior. The values of the culture are known to him and assert themselves in defining him as an aberration. In spite of his rationalizations, he learns he must keep his thoughts and behavior hidden in order to avoid consequences, but the secrecy fails to defend against the fear and guilt that intrude on his self-image.

Fantasy

It is unclear (and probably variable) at what point the fantasy or thought of sexual behavior occurs within the individual relative to the first occurrence of abusive sexual behavior. However, it is the author's firm belief that interactive sexual behavior does not occur without thought.

Sexual feelings are present even in the preverbal infant (see Chapter Four). It is possible to imagine that the thoughts that emerge from and accompany those earliest experiences of sexuality are self-centered. As the child begins to individuate, thoughts of interactive sexual relationships become possible. In a nurturing environment, caregivers shape the child's perception through the modeling of empathic adult interactions and limit the child's early imitative role taking and behavior in line with the cultural norms.

A young child growing up in a nonnormative sexual environment—one that is rigid and condemning, avoidant or absent, oversexualized, or sexually abusive (Bolton, Morris, & MacEachron, 1989; Gilgun, 1988a; Haynes-Seman, 1985; Haynes-Seman & Krugman, 1989)—may process early sexual feelings through a nonnormative view and experience them as aberrant, evil, overwhelming, painful, frightening, or incomprehensible. If early sexualized behavior has been encouraged by caregivers as cute or novel, discouraged by severe punishment, exploited by a perpetrator, or is a reenactment of early abusive experiences, the child's perceptions may be extremely confused. Early offending may seem normal ("That's just something we all did") or aberrant, ("I must be different from other kids"). At some point, however, whether by others' labeling the behavior directly or by the youth's own growing awareness of cultural norms, meaning becomes attached to the deviance.

Individuals who are seeking counseling to deal with troublesome sexual fantasies afford some appreciation of the self-doubt and confusion that may accompany deviant thoughts even in the absence of behavioral manifestations. The presence of deviant sexual fantasies may isolate the individual from the mainstream as he imagines a unique quality to his thoughts. In some cases, the individual experiences a constant shift from feeling superior and all powerful when imagining the experience of the deviant sexual fantasy to a zero state when he realizes the likelihood that the fantasy will not be met. The constant shift from feeling immensely capable and feeling utterly hopeless is anxiety producing and takes a toll. The fantasy preceding a first sexual assault may seem routine, exhilarating, or troubling to the individual in the light of its dissonance or consistency with the youth's sense of self and view of the world.

Whether experiential or observational, the origins of deviant sexual fantasy are the first element present in the experience of being sexually abusive. The risk factors described relative to sexual abusing are observed by the mind and the body, and the patterns of thought that accompany early experience move the individual toward the manifestation of deviance. The fantasy that occurs prior to sexually abusive behavior is part of the compensatory thinking that imagines a solution to the unmet needs of the individual. These thoughts are a product of life experience, and it is the youth's perception and accommodation of the past that shapes sexual fantasy and allows or inhibits behavior. For some individuals who have experienced sexual victimization or trauma, fantasies may be replicating that earlier experience, and the initial abusive behaviors may mirror their own victimization (Freeman-Longo, 1982). For others, arousal may be associated with more normative fantasies that appear unfeasible or inaccessible to the individual, and rationalizations or distortions work to alter the thoughts into a plan for abusive behaviors.

The First Occurrence of Sexually Abusive Behavior

The first occurrence of sexually abusive behavior may be accompanied by anxiety or fear, which is overcome by the individual's sense of entitlement. Arousal and excitement temporarily subdue fear, and the youth is able to depersonalize the victim, objectifying and using him or her without regard. His thoughts are for himself, and immediacy foils the inhibitions that normally preclude such behavior. As he exerts his plan and acts to commit the behavior, a sense of empowerment and control may emerge. In moving from the realm of fantasy into the manifestation of behavior, the youth may experience fulfillment or a sense of mastery. On the other hand, many sexually abusive youth report the perception of a lack of control over the behavior: "It just happened." It is sometimes unclear whether this report is a conscious minimization of responsibility or an inability to remember the deviant thoughts and associated choices that preceded the behavior. Physiological arousal and satisfaction are powerful experiences that counter the youth's prior sense of helplessness and neediness. He has achieved some satisfaction in life. However, the good feelings associated with the physical pleasure and the sense of power do not last, and he is now at risk to repeat the behavior in an attempt to reexperience the pleasure.

Subsequent Occurrences of the Behavior

Over time, the youth's narcissistic orientation and the ability to objectify others serves to increase isolation and interpersonal alienation as these perceptions become generalized to all areas of the youth's life. As sexually abusive behaviors recur over time, the offender may experience a chronic sense of confusion as new patterns of arousal become reinforced and the behaviors seem to assume a compulsive quality. Then arousal associated with abusive behaviors may become the predominant interest, beginning to outweigh normative interest and arousal, leaving the youth increasingly dissatisfied or bored with previously pleasurable experiences or with those that peers seem to enjoy. The compulsive quality is experienced as being beyond the control of the youth and becomes yet another factor that contributes to poor self-concept, helplessness, and anxiety.

Failure to suppress the behavior has a further impact on the sense of self, and the fantasies may become more intrusive, distracting the youth from previously satisfying pastimes. Thinking patterns become altered in order to process the deviant behavior and may succeed in distorting normal inhibition even more.

For some youths, these patterns of arousal may progress over time into an addictive model (Carnes, 1983), which drives the abusive cycle forward. The behavior that initially empowered the youth may become overpowering and unmanageable. Increasingly elaborate distortions and rituals defend the youth against his feared loss of control. For others, the power-thrusting aspects of abusing become self-perpetuating, and the rationalization of retaliatory and abusive behavior supports continued abusive behavior. A distinctive differentiation may emerge between the more aggressive youth whose beliefs support criminal values and the more compulsive sex addict whose beliefs support paraphiliac behavior. Both become characterized by the depersonalization of the victim, personalization of the behavior, and patterns of distorted thinking that allow and support continued abusiveness (Yochelson & Samenow, 1976).

A narcissistic self-centeredness allows these youths to overlook the pain they cause to others in their attempts to stabilize their own emotional disequilibrium, but the behavior in turn "contributes to the core feelings of inadequacy and worthlessness ... increasing hypersensitivity and [subsequent] emotional disequilibrium" (Gilgun, 1988b). At the same time, separation of affect and intellect divide the sense of self (Gilgun, 1988b).

The Short-Term Impact

Early occurrences are followed by a resurgence of anxiety. As described relative to the sexual abuse cycle, thoughts following sexual abuse may reflect a temporary feeling of guilt relative to the failure of the behavior to promote an enduring sense of control and well-being. In the absence of a confidant (Gilgun & Connor, 1990), there is no external source for validation or correction of thoughts or behavior.

In the aftermath of the assault, fears of discovery and consequences produce an immediate anxiety, as the implications of the occurrence attack the youth's self-image. The immediate effects include a perception of powerlessness due to the confusion—"Am I a pervert?" "Am I homosexual?" "Can I control this aspect of myself?"—that accompanies attempts to accommodate this newly manifest view of self.

In the short term, declarations of reform ("I won't do this again") attempt to suppress and deny the meaning and problematic nature of the sexual deviance, but as similar behavior recurs, the youth must assimilate the deviant self. Isolation prevents normal learning and development of interaction with age-mates and fosters shame regarding deviant thoughts and behavior (Gilgun & Connor, 1990).

The Long-Term Impact

Prior to discovery, the fear of disclosure may be overwhelming, and the youth's efforts to protect the secret may be extreme. The preoccupation with the deviance may interfere with other areas of functioning, the victim relationship takes precedence over all other relationships, and the youth's self-image is under constant self-scrutiny. Over time, as the sexually abusive youth assimilates the role of perpetrator into his sense of self, his justification of the behavior becomes routine. Even so, an awareness that others do not share his beliefs alienates him further from nonexploitative relationships, and his deviance may become an all-encompassing identity.

As the process continues, the youth is increasingly isolated, expending energy in maintaining the identity and becoming more closed to input or learning that is dissonant with the abusive lifestyle. He feels increasingly empty inside and loses the ability to view anything except through the filter of who is dominant in any situation and striving to keep himself in that position. When he meets a sufficiently traumatic experience, he has no alternative internal resources to rely on except to seek an expression of greater power. Gilgun and Connor (1990) describe intrapersonal, interpersonal, and existential isolation as significant and pervasive in the life span of adult sexual abusers. This isolation contributes to the diminished likelihood of self-correction of behavior.

Some sexually abusive youth report the belief that they are "more sexual" than normal people, a rationalization in which some sense of a lack of control over the behavior is evident. Others define their whole life experience in terms of sexual abuse, and their identity is that of an unprotected victim and a rejected victimizer. One fourteen-year-old described his past as follows:

Age three | Sexually abused by brother

Age five | Sexually abused by sister (removed from home)

Age seven | Sexually abused by foster brother and physically abused by foster parents

Age eight | Sexually abused younger child in the home (sent to a new foster home)

Age ten | Called a liar and sex offender by foster parents

Age eleven | Sexually abused foster parents' grandchild (sent to a secure facility)

Age twelve | Called a "baby raper" by older sex offenders in the treatment group

Age thirteen | Sexually assaulted a younger peer on a pass

Age fourteen | Sent to a residential sex offender program

At seventeen, it was still difficult to elicit any reports from this young man of any life history or personal characteristics not associated with sexual abuse.

Following disclosure or discovery, the young person's initial fear of consequences often proves to have been an underestimation, and the youth may be devastated to learn the extent of his consequences. Police investigation and formal court proceedings, removal from his home for residential treatment or incarceration, probation, and restitution may represent a far greater intrusion into his life than his worst expectations. Many juveniles have little concept that the sexually abusive behavior is actually illegal and have not anticipated the public embarrassment and intrusion that may follow (Metzner & Ryan, 1995). At the same time, the consequences they had anticipated—shame, guilt, stigma, parental disapproval, threats and punishment, victim recriminations—are occurring as well, so they feel impacts on many levels simultaneously. As one twelve-year-old stated, "I knew it was wrong and that I would be in trouble. . . . I always got in trouble for sexual behavior, . . . but I never knew it was illegal. . . . I didn't know the police would come. . . . I thought I'd be grounded. . . . I never imagined my parents would kick me out. I lost my family."

For those who enter treatment, the treatment process is long, time-consuming, and uncomfortable. Yet even treatment does not complete the consequences. The youth is told that there is no "cure," only tools for him to use to control his behavior, and he subsequently realizes that he will always be a suspect when a sexual assault occurs in his vicinity. Many states have enacted laws that require sexual offenders to register with local police for many years each time they change residences, and in some areas, public notification laws inform neighbors of the youth's history of sexual offenses (Freeman-Longo, 1996). Although some youth may pose such a risk to community safety that such measures seem justified, these laws fail to discriminate among youth on any basis of differential diagnosis or changes resulting from participation in treatment. The implications in terms of stigma and impediments to returning to a more normative course of development are clear. For some, the hopelessness of their past circumstances stretches out before them endlessly into the future.

The Youth's Family

The disclosure of sexual abuse may be dissonant or congruent within the abuser's family, just as it was for the victim's family. The dissonance of the occurrence supports shock and denial, whereas the family that has a history of sexual abuse may be defensive but less surprised. In many cases, the family of the sexually abusive youth has had an underlying sense of the deviance prior to the first disclosure of the abusive behavior, but the disclosure usually exceeds their worst fears. Regardless of its history and experience, the family is hit by the disclosure and subsequent intrusion into the home. Fears related to the meaning of the disclosure and its implication on the home environment are accompanied by the anxiety relative to the immediate consequences for their child. Often parents were not aware of the legal consequences of such behavior.

For families experiencing intrafamilial sexual abuse, ambivalent feelings for the victims and the perpetrator create confusion. The need to protect the victim may hang in the balance along with the need to defend the abuser. The family's dilemma is exacerbated by the anger and betrayal associated with such a breach of trust.

For the family whose child has been abusive outside the family, denial may prevent their acceptance of the facts or minimize the seriousness of the behavior. They may be at risk to engage in retaliatory actions against those making the allegations, or they may expend tremendous resources in the defense of their child. As the reality becomes clear, however, their fear of consequences and the implications on the home environment are similar to other parents' reactions to such a disclosure.

Parents are often frustrated in attempts to obtain appropriate treatment for their child and may be forced into financial burdens that stress the family even more. It is important that families acknowledge the impact of sexual abuse by a family member on the other members of the family in order to receive help for everyone.

Implications of Understanding the Youth's Experience

Yochelson and Samenow (1976) have described a technique designed to anticipate an offender's denial and minimization. It begins the therapeutic relationship
by the therapist's describing the individual to himself on the basis of commonalities among sexually abusive persons. By defining the variables of concern as they
relate to the experience and subsequent impacts of being abusive and of being
identified as an abuser, the therapist assures the youth from the outset that (1) he
is not alone and unique as he had believed, (2) the therapist "knows" him in a way
that prevents denial, and (3) there may be hope for self-understanding and change.
The therapist's ability to identify cues that describe the youth's experience and to
form reasonable hypotheses for the youth about what the experience has been becomes the basis for empathic interactions in the therapeutic relationship.

References

Bolton, F., Morris, C., & MacEachron, A. (1989). *Males at risk.* Thousand Oaks, CA: Sage.

Carnes, P. (1983). *Out of the shadows: Understanding sexual addiction.* Minneapolis: CompCare
Publications.

Freeman-Longo, R. (1982). Sexual learning and experience among adolescent sexual offenders. *International Journal of Offender Therapy and Comparative Criminology, 26*(3), 235–241.

Freeman-Longo, R. (1996). Feel good legislation: Prevention or calamity? *Child Abuse and
Neglect: The International Journal, 20*(2).

Gilgun, J. (1988a). *Factors which block the development of sexually abusive behavior in adults abused as
children.* Paper presented at National Conference on Male Victims and Offenders, Minneapolis, MN.

Gilgun, J. (1988b). Self-centeredness and the adult perpetrator of child sexual abuse. *Comparative Family Therapy, 10*(4), 216–234.

Gilgun, J., & Connor, T. (1990). Isolation and the adult male perpetrator of child sexual
abuse. In A. L. Horton, B. L. Johnson, L. J. Roundy, & D. Williams (Eds.), *The incest perpetrator: A family member no one wants to treat* (pp. 74–87). Thousand Oaks, CA: Sage.

Haynes-Seman, C. (1985, May). *Impact of sexualized attention on the preverbal child.* Paper presented at the Sixteenth Annual Child Abuse and Neglect Symposium, Keystone, CO.

Haynes-Seman, C., & Krugman, R. (1989). Sexualized attention: Normal interaction or precursor to sexual abuse? *American Journal of Orthopsychiatry, 59,* 238–245.

Metzner, J., & Ryan, G. (1995). Sexual abuse perpetration. In G. Sholevar (Ed.), *Conduct disorders in children and adolescents* (pp. 119–146). Washington, DC: American Psychiatric Press.

Yochelson, S., & Samenow, S. (1976). *The criminal personality* (Vol. 1). Northvale, NJ: Aronson.

PART FOUR

INTERVENTION IN JUVENILE SEXUAL OFFENDING

CHAPTER ELEVEN

THE EVOLVING RESPONSE
TO JUVENILE SEXUAL OFFENSES

Gail Ryan

Historically, denial and minimization of sexually exploitative behaviors in childhood and adolescence prevented specific intervention while protecting and enabling the development of abusive behaviors. Societal denial of all childhood sexuality and a standard of repression of sexuality during adolescence has contributed to the problem of sexual abuse in several ways. First, children experience at least disapproval and often overt punishment for early genital exploration or sexual interests, and consequently they learn early in life that sexuality is a secret matter. In this climate of denial, childhood sexual learning often occurs without reliable sources of information or feedback, and sexual interests or feelings may come to be associated with guilt. Children who do not receive guidance regarding normative sexual behavior are not protected from deviancy, and children without norms for sexuality represent optimal targets for child molesters. The advances of the offender may appear to promise education and satisfaction in an arena no one else will discuss. The secrecy associated with sexual abuse is actually the only aspect of sexual experience that the child has prior knowledge of and is congruent with the societal message that sexuality is secret and not discussed. This secrecy allows children to be victims and abusers to continue offending.

The same societal denial, minimization, and repression come into play when juveniles are discovered initiating any sexual interactions, consensual or exploitative. The response has not historically been evaluative but rather repressive or dismissive. Juveniles engaging in masturbation, sexual exploration with peers, and sexual exploitation of others have generally been met with equal reactions of disapproval, punishment, or dismissal. Until recent years, juveniles engaging in behaviors that were clearly both sexual and criminal were often dismissed with a "boys will be boys" attitude or a slap on the hand by parents, teachers, and judges alike (Ryan, 1986).

Occasionally juvenile sexual behaviors that were deviant, persistent, and apparent prompted referrals for counseling or psychotherapy in private one-on-one sessions where the sexual behaviors were usually not specifically discussed. In the Freudian tradition, accounts of sexual victimization or sexual offending were often seen as fantasies symptomatic of intrapsychic conflicts, and the realities of sexual abuse were denied. Young offenders were often diagnosed as suffering from "adolescent adjustment reaction" and, more recently, as "conduct disordered."

Although the disclosure or discussion of the sexual abuse of children has long been taboo, the behavior has not. Sexual victimization has occurred for centuries. Sexual use of children, especially male children, is depicted in the art and graphics of ancient cultures, and Tardieu (1860) documented children with genital injuries in France in coroners' reports as early as the mid-1800s. The reality of early evidence was so abhorrent, however, that the Freudian attribution of childhood sexual issues to the imagination or the unconscious mind remained the norm for years.

Beginning in the late 1800s, isolated cases of the physical abuse and neglect of children in the United States began to attract the attention of humanitarians, and early child protection advocates invoked the standards of care for domestic animals on behalf of abused children (Riis, 1892). By the 1940s, several pediatricians and radiologists had begun to document cases of child abuse (such as Caffey, 1946), and the publication of "The Battered Child Syndrome" (Kempe, Silverman, Steele, & Droegemuller, 1962) forced society and medical practitioners to realize that children are sometimes maltreated. As standards for the care of children improved, legislation began to allow greater surveillance of and intervention in the rearing of children, which led to the discovery of the alarming incidence of sexual abuse of children. By the 1970s, the sexual exploitation of children had been addressed in both the civil and criminal statutes, and research on the adult perpetrators of such abuse had increased.

In the late 1970s, numerous studies were reporting a dismal prognosis in treatment for adults who molested children. Recognition that this was a problem requiring control rather than cure led to exploration of new techniques to facilitate change better, but many clinicians treating adult sex offenders reached the same conclusion: "We have to get these guys sooner" (Abel, Becker, & Mittelman, 1985; Groth, 1977). Studies indicating that over half of the adult offenders had begun sexually abusive behaviors prior to age eighteen confirmed the need for earlier identification and intervention. Simultaneously workers in juvenile corrections and human sexuality programs began to see that many of the juveniles committed or referred on lesser complaints had actually committed serious sexual offenses. Looking to the adult field for direction, clinicians struggled to develop the first offense-specific programs for adolescent sex offenders (Knopp, 1982). As work increased with sexually abusive youths, and older teenagers began to reveal their own histories, the dictate for earlier intervention continued, and the field expanded to encompass prepubescent children who sexually abuse younger children or peers. By the 1980s the definition of a juvenile sex offender had come to be any youth who sexually abuses (National Task Force, 1988).

As is often the case, the pendulum of change swings wide. Challenging denial of the sexually abusive behavior of youth has supported earlier identification and intervention, but the change has led to such sensitivity regarding this issue in the community that reactions are swinging to an opposite extreme. Whereas the goal of early intervention and treatment for sexually abusive children and adolescents is to interrupt the developmental trajectory of sexual deviance and abusive patterns of behavior, public concern regarding the risks such youths pose in the community is fueling more punitive and repressive responses. Many states are now labeling sexually abusive youth as "special offenders" and enacting tougher sentencing, registration, and, in some areas, public notification. Such responses arise from legitimate concerns and the communities' desire to control sexual abuse, but they are untested to date. There is no evidence to determine whether such actions protect children or deter potential or chronic abusers (Berliner, 1996; Freeman-Longo, 1996a, 1996b).

Practitioners must now be concerned that current responses that stigmatize and isolate these youths may actually work against the treatment process. Although it is becoming apparent that some of these youths are at risk to continue sexually abusing despite intervention, it is equally clear that many are able to return to a more normative course of development and can avoid further sexually abusive behaviors (Ryan, 1995). The challenge is now to be able to differentiate responses based on the unique characteristics of each youth who is identified, differential diagnosis and treatment, measurement of change, predictive risk assessment, and relapse-prevention planning. This challenge is addressed by advocating that offense-specific treatment must consider and address the developmental and contextual realities of these youths (National Task Force, 1993), an approach that is more holistic and requires more individualized treatment planning.

References

Abel, G. G., Becker, J. B., and Mittelman, M. (1985). Sex offenders: Results of assessment and recommendations for treatment. In H. Ben-Aaron, S. Hacker, & C. Webster, *Clinical criminology: Current concepts.* Toronto: M&M Graphics.

Berliner, L. (1996). Community notification: Neither a panacea nor a calamity. *Sexual Abuse: A Journal of Research and Treatment, 8*(2).

Caffey, J. (1946). Multiple fractures in the long bones of infants suffering from chronic subdural hematoma. *American Journal of Roentgenology, 56*(2), 163–173.

Freeman-Longo, R. (1996a). Feel good legislation: Prevention or calamity. *Child Abuse and Neglect: The International Journal, 20*(2).

Freeman-Longo, R. (1996b). Public notification: Prevention or problem. *Sexual Abuse: A Journal of Research and Treatment, 8*(2).

Groth, A. N. (1977). The adolescent sex offender and his prey. *International Journal of Offender Therapy and Comparative Criminology, 21*(3), 249–254.

Kempe, H., Silverman, E., Steele, B. F., & Droegemuller, W. (1962). The battered child syndrome. *Journal of the American Medical Association, 181*, 17–24.

Knopp, F. H. (1982). *Remedial intervention in adolescent sex offenses: Nine program descriptions.* Orwell, VT: Safer Society Press.

National Task Force on Juvenile Sexual Offending. (1988). Preliminary report. *Juvenile and Family Court Journal, 39*(2).

National Task Force on Juvenile Sexual Offending. (1993). Revised report. *Juvenile and Family Court Journal, 44*(4).

Riis, J. (1892). Little Mary Ellen's legacy. In *The children of the poor.* London: Sampson, Low, Marston.

Ryan, G. (1986). Annotated bibliography: Adolescent perpetrators of sexual molestation of children. *Child Abuse and Neglect: The International Journal, 10*, 125–131.

Ryan, G. (1995). *Treatment of sexually abusive youth: The evolving consensus.* Paper presented at the International Experts Conference, Utrecht, Netherlands.

Tardieu, A. (1860). Etude médico-légale, sur les sevices et mauvais traitements exercés sur des enfants. *Ann. D. Hyg. Publ. et Med. Leg., 13*, 361–398.

CHAPTER TWELVE

PROGRAM DEVELOPMENT

Fay Honey Knopp and Rob Freeman-Longo, with Sandy Lane

The few programs in the mid- to late 1970s that attempted to develop treatment approaches specifically for sexually abusive youth typically functioned in isolation, without the benefit of networking to share information or validate experiences. There was little awareness in the juvenile field of the newer developments occurring in work with adult sex offenders, and written resources were difficult to obtain. Knopp's *Remedial Intervention in Adolescent Sex Offenses: Nine Program Descriptions* (1982) provided the first recognition of the pioneering work in this fledgling field.

At the time of the book's publication in 1982, Knopp had identified 22 programs nationally that offered specialized approaches for treatment of these youth. Within two years, the number of programs had multiplied ten times. By 1986 there were 410 identified programs (Knopp, Rosenberg, & Stevenson, 1986), and by October 1988, 645 specialized programs were available nationwide for sexually abusive adolescents and preadolescents (Knopp & Stevenson 1989). In only two years, there was a 66 percent increase in the number of specialized programs.

Since 1986, the Safer Society Foundation has conducted a comprehensive survey every other year of all identified adolescent and adult sexual offender treatment

---

Note: In the first edition of *Juvenile Sexual Offending*, this chapter was coauthored by Fay Honey Knopp. Honey passed away on August 10, 1995.

programs. Beginning with the 1994 survey, the Nationwide Survey was expanded to include programs treating prepubescent children as well. The 1994 Nationwide Survey of Treatment Programs and Models Serving Abuse-Reactive Children and Adolescent and Adult Sex Offenders (Freeman-Longo, Bird, Stevenson, & Fiske, 1995) identified 684 programs treating sexually abusive adolescents and 390 programs treating younger children. The growth of these specialized programs as tracked by the Safer Society Foundation is shown in Table 12.1.

Early Developments

In the late 1970s and early 1980s, identification of sexually abusive youth began to improve in communities that had specialized programs. Nationally, reports of sexually abusive incidents had already begun to increase due to educational efforts of victim advocacy programs and improved laws requiring reporting of child abuse. Investigators, through education and experience, were becoming more aware of the aggressive, intrusive, and patterned aspects of sexual victimization.

Courts were more frequently charging youth who had committed these offenses with an actual sexual offense rather than reducing the charges to criminal mischief, assault, or disturbing the peace, and they were beginning to mandate specialized treatment for perpetrators. Despite these trends and the increasing reports of sexual victimization committed by adolescents (Showers Farber, Joseph, Oshins, & Johnson, 1983), underreporting and inaccurate identification of behavior continued to occur in localities without specialized programs. National crime statistics consequently failed to reflect the significant numbers of juveniles involved in sexually abusive behaviors or the extent to which intervention was needed.

TABLE 12.1. NUMBER OF PROGRAMS TREATING SEXUAL OFFENDERS SINCE 1986.

Year	Adult	Juvenile	Child	Total
1986	297	346	—	643
1988	429	573	—	1,002
1990	541	626	—	1,167
1992	745	755	—	1,500
1994	710	684	390	1,784

Source: Freeman-Longo, Bird, Stevenson, & Fiske (1995).

Note: Data for 1994 are based on a 65 percent return of questionnaires by the cutoff date.

In the 1970s even the pioneers in this field were only beginning to grasp the scope of the problem. There was growing awareness that the onset of sexually abusive behaviors frequently occurred shortly after puberty, though it could appear as early as ages seven or eight. Many youths involved in these programs were reporting multiple undetected offenses, more than one type of offense, patterns indicating a progression from less intrusive to more aggressive behaviors, as well as a variety of developmental factors that seemed to contribute to the impetus for committing sexual offenses. There were increasing indications that early intervention could offer preventive benefits and that rehabilitative treatment could be effective.

Earlier studies had paralleled many of the new findings. Studies by Doshay (1969), Apfelberg, Sugar, and Pfeffer (1944), Markey (1950), and Atcheson and Williams (1954) identified sexual offense behavior occurring as early as age seven, advised remedial treatment, and proposed some causal factors. Doshay advocated preventive approaches and introduced the notion that orthodox psychoanalytic methods were not effective in the treatment of young sex offenders. Markey suspected that family trauma was a source of sexual maladjustment, and Atcheson and Williams proposed that both community and residential programs offer early, specialized, remedial approaches for this population. Studies by Maclay (1960) suggested that these youth came from homes that failed to give them adequate emotional support. Unfortunately, the studies before 1970 were frequently based on the perception that sexual abuse and sexual promiscuity during adolescence were comparable behaviors, a view that contributed to later confusion about the nature of offense behaviors.

Studies that investigated youth who molested younger children (for example, Shoor, Speed, & Bartelt, 1966) concluded that the young molester was a loner who had distorted family relationships and was socially and sexually immature. The youth in these studies were engaged in few age-appropriate social activities with peers, preferred playing with younger children, and exhibited maladjusted personality patterns. These studies encouraged professionals not to minimize offense incidents and made distinctions between treatment approaches and settings for aggressive and passive child molesters. Ageton (1981) reported on the first large sample of adolescents who reported either offense or victimization experiences. In an attempt to develop a model predictive of sexual assault, it was suggested that sexually assaultive youth differed from other youth in the study in that they (1) associated with and were committed to a delinquent peer group that provided support for sexually aggressive behaviors, (2) appeared to be more estranged from conventional settings, especially home and school, (3) were more delinquent in general, and (4) held attitudes that facilitated engaging in physically violent or rough behavior.

Early Programs

One of the first comprehensive, organized programs developed to assess adolescent sex offenders began in the fall of 1975 at the Adolescent Clinic of the University of Washington's School of Medicine. The community-based treatment component was largely delayed until 1978 because of funding difficulties. As for many of the programs that followed, the impetus for the development of the program was professional concern over increasing numbers of adolescents who were exhibiting an onset of sexually abusive behaviors soon after puberty. Many of their clients were identified in the course of child protection work with incest cases, and their treatment approaches relied heavily on a family systems model. As staff experience in evaluation and treatment grew, the program was inundated with numerous requests to share its findings, help design programs, and train program staff. This program had a significant impact on the development of many other adolescent sex offender treatment programs.

Simultaneously, other pioneers were working with less support and recognition in isolated areas around the country. Groth and his colleagues, working in the eastern United States, had become aware of the adolescent histories of their adult sex offender clients. They began to describe adolescent perpetrators (Groth, 1977) and to suggest specialized assessment and treatment strategies (Groth, Hobson, Lucey, & St. Pierre, 1981; Groth & Loredo, 1981). Similarly, researchers in New York City and many of the adult treatment programs in Oregon were turning their attention to adolescent offending and applying a more behavioral orientation to the development of offense-specific treatment approaches. Fueled by the presence of the University of Minnesota's Program in Human Sexuality, community-based programs were springing up in Minnesota that approached the problem of juvenile sexual offending in the context of promoting healthier sexual expression.

In juvenile correctional settings, in addition to youth committed for sexual crimes, workers were beginning to identify many sexual offenses in the histories of some violent and delinquent youth who had been committed on lesser charges of assault or property crimes as a result of plea bargaining. Several programs began in correctional facilities, including the Hennepin County Home School in Minnesota and the Colorado Division of Youth Services. These programs were somewhat eclectic, with a more cognitive-behavioral model emerging in Colorado. Cases were identified in mental health, child protection, and delinquency intervention processes.

Because there were no scientifically based theories or model programs to guide their development, most of the early programs developed their own understanding of sexually abusive youth and designed treatment approaches through trial and error. Interestingly, there were many similarities in the philosophies and approaches among the diverse programs. As the similarities began to be shared among the various programs, the basis of many current treatment programs began to evolve.

Factors that were similarly described by many programs in the initial Knopp study (1982) included the youth's dysfunctional or chaotic family system; a lack of knowledge about positive and consensual sexuality; a history of earlier sexual victimization; a deficit of skills for managing anger, aggression, and feelings of powerlessness; acceptance of sex role stereotyping; expression of prevailing negative social and personal attitudes toward human sexuality and power; inadequacies in father-son relationships; and low self-esteem. The consistency of many of these factors among various programs seemed to strengthen the validity of the observations. Although there was, and still is, a lack of research validating these observations or identifying in a systematic manner the relationships among these factors, the empirical studies beginning to appear have supported many clinical assumptions.

Program Components

Knopp's 1982 study included descriptions of both community-based and residential treatment settings. Program structure and intensity tended to increase as the seriousness of the offense or expression of violence by the offender increased. Several programs used various types of peer culture approaches to remedy low self-esteem and social skill deficits. Many programs used some combination of family, group, and individual therapies. The most common program mode at that time was an educational model. Many programs found that eclectic techniques and approaches were most effective. Some of the techniques most frequently used were role plays, psychodrama, transactional analysis, rational emotive therapy, Gestalt therapy, and Yochelson and Samenow's (1976) approaches to identifying and countering thinking errors.

At that time, program components typically included family therapy, education regarding human sexuality, victim awareness, interpersonal social skills development, anger management, grief work, survival skills, sex role education, and journal recording of thought and behavior patterns. Various programs emphasized one or two program components over the others.

By 1984 the most common components of psychoeducational programs used in community-based treatment were social skills training, education in human sexuality and values, victim awareness, responsibility and empathy, anger management, appropriate sex role expectations versus stereotyping, and victim counseling for clients who had suffered emotional, physical, or sexual trauma. A few programs were beginning to offer various types of arousal conditioning through behavioral techniques.

Program distribution at the time of the Knopp (1982) publication indicated that over half the identified programs were located in four states: Washington, California, Minnesota, and Oregon. Many states, particularly in the Southeast, were entirely without identified, specialized programs. The most recent survey (Freeman-Longo, Bird, Stevenson, and Fiske, 1995) shows that services remain unevenly distributed geographically. The eastern North-Central, south Atlantic, and Pacific states offer the greatest number of juvenile services, while the eastern South-Central states are the most poorly endowed of all regions. New York and Ohio offer the highest concentration of all services nationwide, and New Mexico and Alabama have the least number of programs serving adolescent sex offenders (see Table 12.2).

Community-based outpatient programs made up 80 percent of the available services; residential treatment settings accounted for the remaining 20 percent. Of the 134 residential settings in 1994, 66 (49 percent) were public, and 68 (51 percent) were private. Twenty-one (15 percent) of the residential programs were located in juvenile prisons, 35 (26 percent) in mental health facilities, 68 (51 percent) in private facilities, and 10 (8 percent) in court-related facilities. Of the 550 community-based or outpatient services, 194 (35 percent) programs were public, and 356 (65 percent) were private. Mental health services were associated with 167 (30 percent) of the programs, 27 (5 percent) were court-related services, and there were no community-based, prison-related services. Private services constituted 424 (62 percent) of combined residential and community-based services. Despite support for the desirability of a continuum-of-care model (Bengis, 1986) for each state, eight (16 percent) states (Arkansas, Delaware, Georgia, Hawaii, Iowa, Maryland, and Mississippi, as well as Washington, D.C.) had no residential services (see Table 12.3).

Program Models

From the 1988 survey until 1994, it was believed that there was a need, in addition to identifying treatment and program components, to (1) clarify how service providers identify, define, and name the treatment models they use, (2) identify which specific modalities were associated with those models, and (3) determine which modalities were most widely used. It was already evident from prior surveys that group therapy and psychosocio-educational modalities were the predominant treatment approaches and that the use of behavioral methods, cognitive

TABLE 12.2. PROGRAMS FOR SEX OFFENDERS, BY REGION.

South Atlantic Region	Child	Juvenile	Adult	Total
Maryland	8	11	13	32
Delaware	3	3	4	10
District of Columbia	3	4	3	10
West Virginia	2	3	2	7
North Carolina	18	28	24	70
South Carolina	2	6	8	16
Georgia	2	3	3	8
Florida	17	23	24	64
Virginia	14	21	28	63
Total	69	102	109	280
	18 percent	15 percent	15 percent	16 percent

West: North Central Region	Child	Juvenile	Adult	Total
Minnesota	10	23	23	56
Iowa	8	7	9	24
Missouri	8	13	12	33
North Dakota	2	4	4	10
South Dakota	2	4	5	11
Nebraska	3	4	3	10
Kansas	5	8	10	23
Total	38	63	66	167
	10 percent	9 percent	9 percent	9 percent

East: North Central Region	Child	Juvenile	Adult	Total
Michigan	20	30	28	78
Ohio	25	45	34	104
Indiana	7	11	13	31
Wisconsin	2	10	14	26
Illinois	13	21	21	55
Total	67	117	110	294
	17 percent	17 percent	16 percent	16 percent

East: South Central Region	Child	Juvenile	Adult	Total
Kentucky	3	7	8	18
Tennessee	6	10	7	23
Alabama	0	1	1	2
Mississippi	2	2	2	6
Total	11	20	18	49
	3 percent	3 percent	3 percent	3 percent

East: Mid-Atlantic Region	Child	Juvenile	Adult	Total
New York	27	51	58	136
Pennsylvania	12	25	41	78
New Jersey	6	16	10	32
Total	45	92	109	246
	11 percent	13 percent	15 percent	14 percent

TABLE 12.2. PROGRAMS FOR SEX OFFENDERS, BY REGION, Cont'd.

Mountain Region	Child	Juvenile	Adult	Total
Montana	6	8	7	21
Wyoming	1	3	3	7
Colorado	7	16	13	36
New Mexico	0	1	3	4
Idaho	4	8	7	19
Nevada	4	5	6	15
Utah	2	7	8	17
Arizona	7	11	10	28
Total	31	59	57	147
	8 percent	9 percent	8 percent	8 percent

New England Region	Child	Juvenile	Adult	Total
Maine	3	7	9	19
New Hampshire	5	8	10	23
Vermont	4	12	10	26
Massachusetts	13	25	21	59
Connecticut	5	11	10	26
Rhode Island	1	3	3	7
Total	31	66	63	160
	8 percent	10 percent	9 percent	9 percent

Pacific Region	Child	Juvenile	Adult	Total
Alaska	3	8	10	21
Hawaii	1	3	4	8
Washington	17	37	40	94
Oregon	16	25	27	68
California	24	35	40	99
Total	61	108	121	290
	16 percent	16 percent	17 percent	16 percent

West: South Central Region	Child	Juvenile	Adult	Total
Arkansas	2	2	3	7
Louisiana	2	5	5	12
Oklahoma	2	3	4	9
Texas	31	47	45	123
Total	37	57	57	151
	9 percent	8 percent	8 percent	9 percent

Total Programs and Percentages	Child	Juvenile	Adult	Total
	390	684	710	1784
	22 percent	38 percent	40 percent	100 percent

Source: Freeman-Longo, Bird, Stevenson, & Fiske (1995).

Note: Data compiled from program providers' responses to a questionnaire.

restructuring, and relapse-prevention strategies had been increasing. The 1986 survey indicated a lack of consensus, indeed even some confusion, regarding the nature of behavioral treatment methods for this population. Some concern still exists regarding the use of phallometry, behavioral treatment, vicarious sensitization, and other arousal-reduction therapies.

Respondents to the 1994 survey were asked to identify which one of nine models defined by the Safer Society could be identified most closely with their program model (Freeman-Longo, Bird, Stevenson, & Fiske, 1995):

Behavioral-cognitive: A comprehensive structured treatment approach based on sexual learning theory using cognitive restructuring methods and behavioral techniques. Behavioral methods are primarily directed at reducing arousal and increasing pro-social skills. Peer groups and educational classes are employed. Draws from a variety of counseling theories.

Relapse prevention: A three-dimensional, multimodal approach specifically designed to help clients maintain behavioral changes by anticipating and coping with the problem of relapse. Relapse Prevention (1) teaches clients internal self-management skills, (2) plans for an external supervisory component, and (3) provides a framework within which a variety of behavioral, cognitive, educational, and skill training approaches are prescribed in order to teach the sexual offender how to recognize and interrupt the chain of events leading to relapse. The focus of both assessment and treatment procedures is on the specification and modification of the steps in this chain, from broad lifestyle factors and cognitive distortions to more circumscribed skill deficits and deviant sexual arousal patterns. The focus is on the relapse process itself.

Psychosocio-educational: A structured program utilizing peer groups, educational classes, and social skills development. Does not use behavioral methods. Draws from a variety of counseling theories.

Psychotherapeutic: The primary emphasis is on individual and/or group therapy sessions addressing the client's own history as a sexual abuse victim and its relationship to subsequent perpetration of others. Draws from a variety of counseling theories.

Family systems: The primary emphasis is on family therapy and the inclusion of family members in the treatment process. Draws from a variety of counseling theories.

Sexual-addictive: A structured program using peer groups and an addiction model. Often includes Twelve-Step and Sexual Addiction groups.

Behavioral: Focused exclusively on reducing deviant arousal using plethysmography and various reconditioning techniques.

TABLE 12.3. JUVENILE SEX OFFENDER PROGRAMS AND TREATMENT PROVIDERS, BY STATE AND SETTING.

State	Tot. Pro.	Tot. Res.	R/MH	R/A	R/C	R/P	Total Com.	C/MH	C/A	C/C	C/P
Alaska	8	3	3	0	0	0	5	3	2	0	0
Alabama	1	1	0	1	0	0	0	0	0	0	0
Arkansas	2	0	0	0	0	0	2	1	1	0	0
Arizona	11	5	1	2	0	2	6	2	4	0	0
California	35	6	1	2	1	2	29	6	22	1	0
Colorado	16	3	0	3	0	0	13	4	9	0	0
Connecticut	11	1	0	1	0	0	10	1	8	1	0
District of Columbia	4	0	0	0	0	0	4	1	3	0	0
Delaware	3	0	0	0	0	0	3	2	1	0	0
Florida	23	6	3	3	0	0	17	3	14	0	0
Georgia	3	0	0	0	0	0	3	0	3	0	0
Hawaii	3	0	0	0	0	0	3	0	3	0	0
Iowa	7	0	0	0	0	0	7	4	3	0	0
Idaho	8	3	1	2	0	0	5	0	5	0	0
Illinois	21	6	0	5	0	1	15	4	11	0	0
Indiana	11	3	1	1	0	1	8	4	4	0	0
Kansas	8	2	0	0	1	1	6	6	0	0	0
Kentucky	7	2	2	0	0	0	5	1	4	0	0
Louisiana	5	2	1	1	0	0	3	0	3	0	0
Massachusetts	25	7	3	4	0	0	18	7	11	0	0
Maryland	11	0	0	0	0	0	11	2	8	1	0
Maine	7	1	1	0	0	0	6	1	5	0	0
Michigan	30	5	2	2	0	1	25	12	10	3	0
Minnesota	23	3	0	3	0	0	20	10	10	3	0
Missouri	13	3	1	2	0	0	10	3	4	3	0
Mississippi	2	0	0	0	0	0	2	0	2	0	0

	Tot. Pro.	Tot. Res.	R/MH	R/A	R/P	R/C	Tot. Com.	C/MH	C/A	C/C	C/P
Montana	8	2	0	2	0	0	6	0	6	0	0
North Carolina	28	1	1	0	0	0	27	14	13	0	0
North Dakota	4	1	0	1	0	0	3	2	1	0	0
Nebraska	4	1	0	1	0	0	3	1	2	0	0
New Hampshire	8	1	0	0	0	1	7	2	5	0	0
New Jersey	16	2	1	1	0	0	14	7	5	2	0
New Mexico	1	1	1	0	0	0	0	0	0	0	0
Nevada	5	1	0	0	0	1	4	0	4	0	0
New York	51	5	0	1	2	2	46	14	30	2	0
Ohio	45	9	1	6	1	1	36	19	15	2	0
Oklahoma	3	1	0	0	1	0	2	0	2	0	0
Oregon	25	2	0	2	0	0	23	9	12	2	0
Pennsylvania	25	5	1	1	3	0	20	4	11	5	0
Rhode Island	3	2	1	1	0	0	1	1	0	0	0
South Carolina	6	3	0	2	0	1	3	0	3	0	0
South Dakota	4	1	1	0	0	0	3	1	2	0	0
Tennessee	10	5	1	4	0	0	5	1	4	0	0
Texas	47	10	2	7	0	1	37	2	34	1	0
Utah	7	3	0	3	0	0	4	2	2	0	0
Virginia	21	2	0	0	0	2	19	3	16	0	0
Vermont	12	4	2	1	0	1	8	3	5	0	0
Washington	37	5	3	1	0	1	32	1	27	4	0
Wisconsin	10	3	0	2	0	1	7	2	5	0	0
West Virginia	3	1	0	1	0	0	2	1	1	0	0
Wyoming	3	1	0	0	0	1	2	1	1	0	0
Total	684	134	35	68	10	21	550	167	356	27	0

Note: Tot. Pro. = total treatment providers; Tot. Res. = total residential programs; R/MH = residential/mental health; R/A = residential/private; R/C = residential/provided by the court; R/P = residential/prison; Tot. Com. = total community based; C/MH = community based/mental health; C/A = community based/private; C/C = community based/provided by the court; C/P = community based/prison.

Psychoanalytic: The primary emphasis is on client understanding of the psycho-dynamics of sexual offending, usually through individual treatment sessions using psychoanalytic principles.

Biomedical: The primary emphasis is on the medical model, disease processes, with a major emphasis on treatment with medication.

Two hundred eighty-one respondents (41 percent) indicated they used a behavioral-cognitive model. Two hundred forty-seven respondents (36 percent) identified relapse prevention as the model of choice. The remaining models were identified as follows: psychosocio-educational, 94 (14 percent); psychotherapeutic, 37 (5 percent); family systems, 16 (2 percent); sexual-addictive, 4 (1 percent); behavioral, 1(0.5 percent); psychoanalytic, 4 (1 percent); and biomedical, 0.

Tables 12.4 and 12.5 reflect the eclecticism and diversity of the various models and treatment modalities categorized by the respondents. The range of models and modalities being used by the respondents is impressively broad. When the survey was first conducted, the majority of the respondents routinely applied a "whatever works" approach to treatment, choosing from a rich and creative repertoire of methods. Others, equally creative, are involved in attempting to develop distinct, comprehensive, and testable treatment models for specific types of sex offenders. As consensus emerges on such models, it will be possible to determine their efficacy only when longitudinal outcome studies are designed and funded. Until that time, the refining and uniform categorizing of specialized treatment models for specific juvenile and adult sex offenders is a worthwhile agenda for this developing discipline.

For the 1994 survey, the Safer Society Foundation elected to assess treatment modalities used with both male and female adolescent sexual abusers because the number of identified female adolescent sexual abusers was increasing. The professionals who treat sexual abusers have begun developing treatment techniques that might be useful for these clients' particular needs (Turner & Turner, 1994).

Recent Developments

Over the past decade some important developments have contributed to this young field. A significant amount of networking has been ongoing. The National Adolescent Perpetrator Network at the Kempe Center in Denver began networking twenty-two members in 1984 and now includes a multidisciplinary membership of more than one thousand professionals working with sexually abusive children and adolescents. The Safer Society Foundation networks specialized

TABLE 12.4. TREATMENT MODELS USED BY PROVIDERS.

Treatment Models	Child	Juvenile	Adult	Total
Behavioral-cognitive	157 (40 percent)	281 (41 percent)	270 (38 percent)	705 (40 percent)
Relapse prevention	138 (35 percent)	247 (36 percent)	280 (40 percent)	662 (37 percent)
Psychosocio-educational	47 (12 percent)	94 (14 percent)	86 (12 percent)	224 (13 percent)
Psychotherapeutic	31 (8 percent)	37 (5 percent)	47 (6 percent)	114 (6 percent)
Family systems	11 (3 percent)	16 (2 percent)	11 (2 percent)	37 (2 percent)
Sexual-addictive	3 (.8 percent)	4 (1 percent)	12 (2 percent)	18 (1 percent)
Behavioral	1 (.5 percent)	1 (.5 percent)	0 (0 percent)	2 (.5 percent)
Psychoanalytic	2 (.7 percent)	4 (1 percent)	4 (0 percent)	9 (.5 percent)
Biomedical	0	0	0	0
Total	390	684	710	1,784

Source: Freeman-Longo, Bird, Stevenson, & Fisk (1995).

Note: Each identified program received the 1994 survey questionnaire and the Safer Society Program (SSP) list of models and definitions. Survey participants were instructed to select the one model that most accurately described their programs. Several respondents selected more than one model. When more than one model was selected (or if the program did not select a model), the program questionnaire was reviewed and a single model identified for the program that most closely fit SSP definitions based on the program's responses on the questionnaire.

TABLE 12.5. TREATMENT MODALITIES USED
WITH JUVENILE SEX OFFENDERS.

Treatment Modalities	Male	Female	Average Male and Female
Victim empathy	660 (96 percent)	356 (96 percent)	96.0 percent
Sex education	635 (93 percent)	352 (95 percent)	94.0 percent
Social skills	632 (92 percent)	346 (94 percent)	93.0 percent
Anger/aggression management	644 (94 percent)	337 (91 percent)	92.5 percent
Communication	606 (89 percent)	342 (92 percent)	90.5 percent
Cognitive distortions	601 (88 percent)	330 (89 percent)	88.5 percent
Assertiveness training	586 (86 percent)	383 (87 percent)	86.5 percent
Personal victimization/trauma	578 (85 percent)	325 (88 percent)	86.5 percent
Relapse cycle	592 (87 percent)	313 (85 percent)	86.0 percent
Preassault/assault cycle	580 (85 percent)	307 (83 percent)	84.0 percent
Victim apology	569 (83 percent)	304 (82 percent)	82.5 percent
Positive/prosocial sexuality	561 (82 percent)	307 (83 percent)	82.5 percent
Conflict resolution	551 (81 percent)	310 (84 percent)	82.5 percent
Relapse-prevention plan	579 (85 percent)	292 (79 percent)	82.0 percent
Frustration tolerance and impulse control	556 (81 percent)	307 (83 percent)	82.0 percent
Thinking errors (Samenow)	551 (80 percent)	305 (82 percent)	81.0 percent
Relaxation techniques/ stress management	540 (79 percent)	304 (82 percent)	80.5 percent
Sexually transmitted diseases	527 (77 percent)	290 (78 percent)	77.5 percent
Values clarification	513 (75 percent)	288 (76 percent)	75.5 percent
Dating skills	497 (73 percent)	282 (76 percent)	74.5 percent
Journal keeping	491 (72 percent)	275 (74 percent)	73.0 percent
Sex role stereotyping	470 (69 percent)	260 (70 percent)	69.5 percent
Autobiography	388 (57 percent)	200 (54 percent)	55.5 percent
Fantasy work	391 (57 percent)	186 (50 percent)	53.5 percent
Reality therapy	354 (52 percent)	201 (54 percent)	53.0 percent
Relapse contract	356 (52 percent)	187 (51 percent)	51.5 percent
Victim restitution	336 (49 percent)	187 (51 percent)	50.0 percent
Employment/vocational issues	345 (50 percent)	175 (47 percent)	48.5 percent
AA (Alcoholics Anonymous)	295 (43 percent)	154 (42 percent)	42.5 percent
Core relapse-prevention group	315 (46 percent)	124 (34 percent)	40.0 percent
Addictive cycle	268 (39 percent)	149 (40 percent)	39.5 percent
Rational emotive therapy	242 (35 percent)	148 40 percent)	37.5 percent
NA (Narcotics Anonymous)	238 (35 percent)	135 (36 percent)	35.5 percent
Covert sensitization	247 (36 percent)	105 (28 percent)	32.0 percent
Art therapy	195 (29 percent)	131 (35 percent)	32.0 percent
ACOA (Adult Child of Alcoholics)	138 (20 percent)	91 (25 percent)	22.5 percent
Experiential therapies	153 (22 percent)	80 (22 percent)	22.0 percent
SAR (sexual attitude reassessment)	130 (19 percent)	89 (24 percent)	21.5 percent
Masturbatory training	151 (22 percent)	63 (17 percent)	19.5 percent
SA (Sexaholics Anonymous)	128 (19 percent)	65 (18 percent)	18.5 percent
Modified aversive behavioral rehearsal	133 (19 percent)	62 (17 percent)	18.0 percent
Polygraph	122 (18 percent)	64 (17 percent)	17.5 percent
Verbal satiation	120 (18 percent)	54 (15 percent)	16.5 percent

TABLE 12.5. TREATMENT MODALITIES USED
WITH JUVENILE SEX OFFENDERS Cont'd.

Treatment Modalities	Male	Female	Average Male and Female
Dissociative state therapy	79 (12 percent)	63 (17 percent)	14.5 percent
Masturbatory satiation	119 (17 percent)	37 (10 percent)	13.5 percent
Masturbatory (orgasmic) conditioning	101 (15 percent)	34 (9 percent)	12.0 percent
Hypnosis	71 (10 percent)	51 (14 percent)	12.0 percent
Sexual arousal card sorts	77 (11 percent)	32 (8 percent)	9.5 percent
Aversive techniques (olfactory)	73 (11 percent)	25 (7 percent)	9.0 percent
Minimal arousal conditioning	73 (11 percent)	29 (8 percent)	9.5 percent
Sexual arousal measures	79 (12 percent)	18 (5 percent)	8.5 percent
Phallometry, biofeedback	50 (7 percent)	27 (7 percent)	7.0 percent
Shaming	20 (3 percent)	14 (4 percent)	3.5 percent
Bodywork, massage therapy	13 (2 percent)	11 (3 percent)	2.5 percent
Aversive techniques (Faradic)	18 (3 percent)	8 (2 percent)	2.5 percent
Psychopharmacologic agents			
Prozac	150 (22 percent)	66 (18 percent)	20.0 percent
Lithium carbonate	136 (20 percent)	55 (15 percent)	17.5 percent
Minor tranquilizers	124 (18 percent)	52 (14 percent)	16.0 percent
Major tranquilizers	108 (16 percent)	48 (13 percent)	14.5 percent
Anafranil	95 (14 percent)	46 (12 percent)	13.0 percent
Buspar	89 (13 percent)	41 (11 percent)	12.0 percent
Serotonin reuptake blockers	86 (13 percent)	40 (11 percent)	12.0 percent
Depo-Provera (hormonal)	35 (5 percent)	9 (2 percent)	3.5 percent

Source: Freeman-Longo, Bird, Stevenson, & Fisk (1995).

Note: Of the respondents, 684 were treating males and 370 treating females.

programs for developmentally disabled offenders and female offenders. Further, organizations originally designed around adult sex offender treatment and research have begun to incorporate adolescent treatment into the scope of their meetings and work. Developments in Canada have been significant as well (Mathews & Stermac, 1989), and other countries (such as England, Australia, New Zealand, Ireland, and the Netherlands) are joining efforts in this concern. State and regional networks (modeled after the Oregon State Network) meet to facilitate professional cooperation and peer support at the local level. In state and regional networks, workers gather to share experiences, data, and techniques. Training is available in all regions of the United States, and several major conferences annually provide multiple levels of training. Experienced consultants are now available to guide new programs. In addition to the collaboration between those who work with adult and those who work with adolescent offenders, there is also a move toward interagency cooperation between those who work with victims and those who work with offenders. These developments have supported the infrastructure that facilitates continued development of research and quality treatment in the field.

During the past few years, some crucial concepts have been proposed. The comprehensive vision of the continuum-of-care philosophy for each community is significant (Bengis, 1986). The suggested risk criteria and offender typologies (see Abbot, 1984; Gray & Wallace, 1992; O'Brien & Bera, 1985; Ross & Loss, 1987; Wenet & Clark, 1983), the sexual abuse cycle (Lane & Zamora, 1978), relapse-prevention strategies (Pithers, Marqus, Gibat, & Marlatt, 1983), and the matrix of treatment interventions used by the Oregon Department of Family Services (Kerr, 1986), which is based on the O'Brien and Bera typologies, are all significant contributions. The Uniform Data Collection System of the National Adolescent Perpetrator Network offers a rich resource of data from participating members. The 1993 *Revised Preliminary Report* from the National Task Force on Juvenile Sexual Offending of the National Adolescent Perpetrator Network provides a consensus that reflects the current thought and practice of those who work with sexually abusive youth. This consensus-building process allows the field to move closer to establishing guidelines for monitoring professional expertise and service delivery.

Researchers are beginning to produce studies that test the theories, practices, and results from various parts of the country. There have also been developments in work with various special populations, such as developmentally disabled offenders (Murphy, Coleman, & Haynes, 1983), female offenders (Grayson, 1989), and the child perpetrator (Cavanagh-Johnson, 1988, 1989; MacFarlane & Cunningham, 1988). Both primary and secondary perpetration-prevention concepts are being developed to promote the primary prevention of offending (Ryan and others, 1988; Ryan, 1989; Strong, Tate, Wehman, & Wyss, 1986).

The availability of programs is not enough. A body of research must be created to support or refine current knowledge and practice. Replicable models must be developed and tested to ensure optimal effectiveness and to define their necessary components more coherently. Longitudinal studies are needed to evaluate outcomes, and services must be made available throughout the country. Public legislation is needed to advocate intervention with sexually abusive youths and to develop funding for treatment. Such efforts should reflect an expectation that many of these youths can stop abusive behaviors and avoid labeling them all offenders for life without differentiating their prognoses. Undergraduate and postgraduate training for professionals entering the field must be developed and promulgated. Perpetration-prevention curricula must be disseminated, and professionals at all levels of involvement with children must be educated to respond to behaviors indicating the early stages of abusive behaviors. Further development of effective programs for habituated, antisocial offenders is also imperative.

The field is on the brink of formalizing and clarifying the work of the past few years. The work to date has challenged dominant ideologies, untangled a web of myths, and broken the silence about sexually abusive behaviors of juveniles. As future developments refine and clarify knowledge, the potential exists to provide a safer society through effective responses to sexual abuse and eventually the prevention of sexual offending.

References

Abbot, B. (1984). *Guidelines for assessment of adolescent sexual offenders and their families.* San Jose, CA: Institute for the Community as Extended Family.

Ageton, S. S. (1981). *Sexual assault among adolescents: A national survey* (Summary Progress Report). Washington, DC: National Institute of Mental Health.

Apfelberg, B., Sugar, C., & Pfeffer, A. Z. (1944). A psychiatric study of 250 sex offenders. *American Journal of Psychiatry, 100,* 762–770.

Atcheson, J. D., & Williams, D. C. (1954). A study of juvenile sex offenders. *American Journal of Psychiatry, 111,* 366.

Bengis, S. (1986). *A comprehensive service delivery system with a continuum of care for adolescent sexual offenders.* Orwell, VT: Safer Society Press.

Cavanagh-Johnson, T. (1988). Child perpetrators: Children who molest children. *Child Abuse and Neglect: The International Journal, 12*(2), 219–229.

Cavanagh-Johnson, T. (1989). *A curriculum in human sexuality for troubled families.* Los Angeles: Children's Institute.

Doshay, L. (1969). *The boy sex offender and his later career.* Montclair, NJ: Patterson Smith. (Original work published 1943)

Freeman-Longo, R. E., Bird, S., Stevenson, W. F., & Fiske, J. (1995). *1994 nationwide survey of treatment programs and models: Serving abuse reactive children, adolescent and adult sex offenders.* Brandon, VT: Safer Society Press.

Gray, A. S., & Wallace, R. (1992). *Adolescent sexual offender assessment packet.* Brandon, VT: Safer Society Press.

Grayson, J. (1989). Female sexual offenders. *Virginia Child Protection Newsletter, 28,* 1–12.

Groth, A. N. (1977). The adolescent sex offender and his prey. *International Journal of Offender Therapy and Comparative Criminology, 21*(3), 249–254.

Groth, A. N., Hobson, W., Lucey, K., & St. Pierre, J. (1981). Juvenile sex offenders: Guidelines for treatment. *International Journal of Offender Therapy and Comparative Criminology, 25*(3), 265–272.

Groth, A. N., & Loredo, C. (1981). Juvenile sex offenders: Guidelines for assessment. *International Journal of Offender Therapy and Comparative Criminology, 25*(1), 31–39.

Kerr, M. (Ed.). (1986). *An executive summary: The Oregon Report on Juvenile Sexual Offenders.* Salem, OR: Avalon Associates, Children's Services Division.

Knopp, F. H. (1982). *Remedial intervention in adolescent sex offenses: Nine program descriptions.* Orwell, VT: Safer Society Press.

Knopp, F. H. (1989). *New directions in program development.* Paper presented at the National Training Conference on Juvenile Sex Offending, Salt Lake City, UT.

Knopp, F. H., Rosenberg, J., & Stevenson, W. (1986). *Report on nationwide survey of juvenile and adult sex-offender treatment programs and providers: 1986.* Orwell, VT: Safer Society Press.

Knopp, F. H., & Stevenson, W. (1989). *Nationwide survey of juvenile and adult sex offender treatment programs and models: 1988.* Orwell, VT: Safer Society Press.

Lane, S., & Zamora, P. (1978). [Syllabus materials from inservice training on adolescent sex offenders.] Denver, CO: Closed Adolescent Treatment Center, Division of Youth Services.

MacFarlane, K., & Cunningham, C. (1988). *Steps to healthy touching.* Mt. Dora, FL: Kids Rights Publishers.

Maclay, D. T. (1960). Boys who commit sexual misdemeanors. *British Medical Journal, 51*(67), 186–190.

Markey, O. B. (1950). A study of aggressive sex misbehavior in adolescents brought to juvenile court. *American Journal of Orthopsychiatry, 20,* 731.

Mathews, F., & Stermac, L. (1989). *A tracking study of adolescent sex offenders.* Toronto, Ontario: Central Toronto Youth Services.

Murphy W., Coleman, E., & Haynes, M. (1983). Treatment and evaluation of the mentally retarded sex offender. In J. G. Greer & I. R. Stuart (Eds.), *The sexual aggressor.* New York: Van Nostrand Reinhold.

National Task Force on Juvenile Sexual Offending. (1988). Preliminary report. *Juvenile and Family Court Journal, 39*(2).

National Task Force on Juvenile Sexual Offending. (1993). Revised report. *Juvenile and Family Court Journal, 39*(2).

O'Brien, M., & Bera, W. (1985). *The PHASE typology.* Minneapolis: Program for Healthy Adolescent Sexual Expression.

Pithers, W., Marqus, J., Gibat, C., & Marlatt, G. (1983). Relapse prevention with sexual aggressives: A self-control model of treatment and maintenance of change. In J. G. Greer & I. R. Stuart (Eds.), *The sexual aggressor.* New York: Van Nostrand Reinhold.

Ross, J., & Loss, P. (1987). *Assessment factors for adolescent sexual offenders.* New London, CT: Ross, Loss, & Associates.

Ryan, G. (1989). Victim to victimizer: Rethinking victim treatment. *Journal of Interpersonal Violence, 4*(3) 325–341.

Ryan, G., Blum, J., Sandau-Christopher, D., Law, S., Weher, F., Sundine, C., Astler, L., Teske, J., & Dale, J. (1988). *Understanding and responding to the sexual behavior of children: Trainer's manual.* Denver: Kempe Center, University of Colorado Health Science Center.

Shoor, M., Speed, M. H., & Bartelt, C. (1966). Syndrome of the adolescent child molester. *American Journal of Psychiatry, 122,* 783–789.

Showers, J., Farber, E., Joseph, J., Oshins, L., & Johnson, C. (1983). The sexual victimization of boys: A three-year survey. *Health Values: Achieving High-Level Wellness, 7,* 15–18.

Strong, K., Tate, J., Wehman, B., & Wyss, A. (1986). *Sexual assault facts and effects.* Cumberland, WI: Human Growth and Development Program.

Turner, M. T., & Turner, T. N. (1994). *Female adolescent sexual abusers: An exploratory study of mother-daughter dynamics with implications for treatment.* Brandon, VT: Safer Society Press.

Wenet, G., & Clark, T. (1983). *Juvenile sexual offender decision criteria.* Seattle: Juvenile Sexual Offender Program, University of Washington Adolescent Clinic.

Yochelson, S., & Samenow, S. (1976). *The criminal personality* (Vol. 1). Northvale, NJ: Aronson.

CHAPTER THIRTEEN

THE LEGAL SYSTEM'S RESPONSE TO JUVENILE SEXUAL OFFENDERS

Joseph Heinz and Gail Ryan

As the incidence and prevalence of rape and child molestation have become known, public awareness and concern have grown. Increased reporting by victims has resulted in an increase in successful prosecutions for abusive sexual acts. In some jurisdictions, petitions alleging criminal sexual misconduct have risen dramatically in recent years.

Corrections systems in many jurisdictions around the country have been inundated with sex offenders. In many cases, local and state juvenile corrections systems were ill prepared for this dramatic increase of sexually abusive youth in their populations.

The Question of Incarceration or Treatment

The question of what should be done with these youth has been a debated issue. The public's outcry for community protection has led to some juveniles' being certified as adults and sentenced to adult correctional facilities where there is no pretense of treatment. In other localities, early attempts to treat these youth in their own local community led to severely negative community reaction. These reactions reflect legitimate concerns for community protection as well as the community's repulsion toward sexual crimes.

It is not difficult to understand why many people want these youth punished and kept in a secure environment. When people hear about sexual abuse, the most dominant emotions evoked are fear and anger toward the perpetrator, not compassion.

The public's view that sex offenders should be incarcerated was supported by reports from researchers who found in many early studies that treatment of adult sex offenders did not prevent recidivism. At the same time, treatment programs in correctional facilities have always been pointed to as schools of crime. Critics of juvenile justice contend that incarceration, regardless of whether there is treatment, increases the risk the youth poses in the community by association with deviant peers. Even treatment practitioners were initially skeptical that sexually abusive youth would change. The message that emerged was that sex offenders could not be "cured."

Over time, practitioners and correctional workers were learning more and more about the characteristics of these youth and the nature of the problem. Community treatment programs developed, but many practitioners minimized or discounted the dangerousness of their clients. Often these clients were in outpatient programs not because they did not present a danger to the community but because it was the first time they had been caught. Many juveniles reoffended while on furloughs they had earned in institutional systems when furloughs had been granted in return for program compliance but without regard for the safety of the community.

In reaction to early failures and the poor prognosis for adult sex offenders in treatment, researchers and therapists in the 1970s were saying treatment did not work. People from all sectors of the community advocated incarceration instead of treatment. States passed laws to force therapists to report new victims, and many laws mandated incarceration to keep sex offenders off the streets. The battle raged over treatment versus incarceration.

As new methods and techniques developed, however, programs began to show better success in controlling sexually abusive behaviors. In 1986, the Hennepin County Home School in Minnesota was reporting that over 90 percent of program graduates were not reoffending. Using models that stress performance and change in treatment and accountability for community safety, professionals now believe that sexually abusive youth can change; they can learn how to control their behavior and become motivated to do so. The choice between incarceration or treatment has given way to the belief that treatment sometimes requires incarceration. Although many youth may be treated effectively and safely in outpatient settings, some need to be incarcerated. These are not just needy clients, but in many cases also dangerous clients. There is now recognition of the need for a continuum of legal and therapeutic responses. Just as legitimate concerns regarding community protection must be recognized, the limits of incarceration must be considered.

Far from being a way to protect community safety, incarceration without treatment may further jeopardize community safety. Thirty-five to 80 percent of sex offenders released from prisons where they have not been treated commit more sexual crimes. Some of their new victims are then at risk to become perpetrators, because experiencing victimization is one of the ways children learn to be abusive.

Far from being a deterrent, incarceration without treatment fosters the very conditions that lead to further sexual acting out: high stress, no outlets for healthy expression of feelings, no healthy sexual outlets, isolation from family supports, inadequate supervision, availability of victims—the conditions present in every prison.

Treatment is expensive, but there is also a price of not treating. Twenty-four offenders released from the Hennepin County Home School had reported 726 offenses (Heinz, Gargaro, & Kelley, 1987). Without treatment, these same youth might well have continued their sexual offenses as adults. The Oregon State Hospital has reported that one sample of 53 adult offenders had committed over 25,000 sexual offenses ranging from rape and child molestation to obscene telephone calls. Without treatment, the costs are multiplied again and again. Advocating a continuum of treatment settings, community safety, and victim rights dictates that good treatment sometimes requires incarceration.

Legal Ramifications

The legal system's response to the sexual behaviors of juveniles has changed drastically in recent years, although it continues to vary tremendously by jurisdiction. Rape of an unknown age-mate or adult victim has always received some consideration for prosecution in the legal system, even though the sexual nature of these acts was often denied or minimized by the practice of plea bargaining to nonsexual charges, and many of these offenses were excused by a "boys-will-be-boys" attitude. At the same time, consensual activity that violated community values was often dealt with harshly as status offenses. Hands-off offenses and child molestation were frequently attributed to curiosity, experimentation, or "adolescent adjustment reactions." Responsibility for acquaintance rape was frequently attributed to foolish or seductive victims.

There was tremendous ambivalence in regard to labeling any juvenile behavior a sexual offense. This reticence was likely due in part to the discomfort adults felt in discussing the sexuality of children, as well as the global denial of the sexual abuse of children. The legal reactions and implications can be better understood in the context of the history of juvenile justice.

The Juvenile Court System: A Historic Overview

The juvenile court system evolved from the ideology of childhood: that children are not the same as adults and have unique developmental needs for nurturance and protection. Historically, the juvenile court was conceived as an intermediate intervention between parental authority and criminal sanctions. The juvenile court's intent was to act in loco parentis (or in the absence or breakdown of parental care and/or control of the child). This court's role was to be that of guardian and guide.

From 1899 until the mid-1960s, the misbehavior of children was attributed to causes outside themselves, and they were believed incapable of predicting the negative impacts of their behavior. Many theoretical considerations contributed to the rationale that supported the child's need to be "saved" from evil influences and redirected toward responsible behavior. Throughout that period, the goals of juvenile court intervention were remediation and rehabilitation. The court had broad discretion, which was sometimes beneficial but sometimes abused.

In the late 1960s and 1970s, along with the concern about the civil rights of minority adult populations, the legal rights of children also became an issue. In the context of this new scrutiny of human rights, children were given new status, and juvenile courts were forced to develop new standards to balance the protection of juveniles from environmental influences against protection of the juvenile from intrusive legal procedures. The traditional juvenile court system had invoked complete control over juveniles in its care without regard for due process or legal representation.

During this time, labeling theorists were suggesting that legal processing of juveniles was creating criminals by so labeling their behavior and that the "misbehavior" of children should be decriminalized wherever possible. It evolved that many of the misbehaviors of children and adolescents were labeled "status offenses," that is, behaviors that would not be illegal for adults but required intervention due to the childhood status of the perpetrator. At the same time, serious offenses were defined as delinquency.

Of the range of juvenile sexual offenses, only forcible rape was included in the "serious" category (National Council of Juvenile and Family Court Judges, 1984). Promiscuity, prostitution, and consensual sexual intercourse prior to age sixteen were eventually considered status offenses; nonviolent sexual crimes such as hands-off offenses and child molestation fell into a gray area, where they received less attention and intervention. (For a thorough review of the evolution of the juvenile court response to delinquency, see Empey, 1982.)

With the distinction between status offenses and criminal behavior, the most serious delinquents became subject to the prevailing theory regarding all criminal behavior, which at that time had abandoned its earlier focus on causation and prevention and was under pressure to punish rather than rehabilitate (the "just desserts" model). This model was a reaction to the poor outcomes documented in early studies on the effectiveness of rehabilitation efforts, and it led to incarceration without remedial interventions.

Over time, probably because of the accumulated understanding of criminal behavior and the development of more focused interventions, it was demonstrated that some early interventions in childhood and adolescence can significantly reduce delinquent and criminal behavior (Gendreau & Ross, 1987). In the 1980s, as law enforcement and the judiciary began to hear from treatment providers that the sexual offenses of juveniles tend to become chronic and that these youth benefit from being held legally accountable and mandated to complete specialized treatment programs, legal systems became more responsive. There was a gradual but significant shift, with the result that more cases were being charged and successfully prosecuted.

Between 1977 and 1986, forcible rape charges brought against juveniles increased 22 percent, while other juvenile sex offense charges increased 32 percent (U.S. Department of Justice data reported in Speirs, 1989). Even so, many juvenile offenses continued to be handled informally without delinquency proceedings. Juveniles who sexually abused a family member were only half as likely to be charged, and although only 26 percent of violent sexual crimes were disposed of informally, only 22 percent of those offenders were placed outside the home for incarceration or residential treatment. Minority youth were much more likely to be charged and to be incarcerated for their sex offenses than were majority offenders. About 5 percent were remanded to the criminal courts to be tried as adults. At the same time, disposition in 48 percent of violent sex offense referrals did not result in any court-ordered supervision (Speirs, 1989).

As specialized treatment programs began developing in various settings, legal disposition was frequently determined by the availability of treatment rather than any uniform legal or clinical criteria. In some jurisdictions, treatment was accessible only in juvenile correctional settings, while other counties' treatment services might be in social service or mental health agencies. The need to fund programs within state agencies or to contract with private facilities for treatment often was a consideration in where treatment was most likely to occur. These considerations continue to affect the disposition of these cases.

Legal Responses in the 1980s and 1990s

During the 1980s, numerous states conducted surveys to determine the rate of sexual offending by juveniles and began to document the system's response.

Reports of such surveys came from Oregon, California, Utah, Michigan, Vermont, Ohio, and Maine, and others have since followed. Canadian interest has paralleled the U.S. efforts, with the Central Toronto Youth Services reporting on a tracking survey of adolescent sex offenders (Mathews & Stermac, 1989). Most recently, England, Holland, Ireland, Scotland, Australia, New Zealand, and some other European countries have found a similar incidence of sexual abuses committed by children and adolescents. In the United States, the rates for both rape and other sexual offenses committed by juveniles remained relatively stable between 1985 and 1990 and then rose between 1990 and 1993 (Snyder, Sickmund, & Poe-Yamagata, 1996).

These reports make it clear that identification of sexually abusive youth has improved in many areas (although such cases are probably still underreported) and that systems are struggling to respond to these cases. However, the legal responses vary tremendously across jurisdictions. The array of potential dispositions for documented cases of sexual offending by juveniles still falls along a continuum from no legal response to extreme legal consequences (for example, lengthy incarceration, lengthy probation, public notification, and so on).

The Legal Process

The legal system involves several steps of involvement. Insufficient evidence may end the legal response at any point.

Law Enforcement

The first step in the legal process is the police investigation, which may or may not result in an arrest. Police officers in the past were often discouraged by parents, as well as by the implications of labeling theory, from investigating or arresting juveniles for sexual offenses. Further discouragement was likely due to a lack of training in the evaluation of sexual interactions. Law enforcement's confusion paralleled the dilemma of adults in the community, who were often unaware of or unwilling to acknowledge the sexually abusive nature of some behaviors. Legislation has clarified the definition of sexual offenses. Officers are now trained to investigate and encouraged not to minimize sexual offenses, and arrests have become more consistent.

Diversion or Prosecution

Following an arrest, the district attorney may decline to prosecute due to insufficient evidence, divert the case from prosecution into a diversion program, or file charges to be brought to court.

Diversion programs are sometimes available to juvenile delinquents who are admitting their offense and are willing to agree to comply in some remedial course of action in order to avoid the court process and the subsequent record of the incident. In some jurisdictions, the only specialized treatment for juvenile sex offenders is available through diversion programs, making this course of action appear desirable. However, diversion from the filing of charges may support minimization of the seriousness of these offenses; moreover, it is also important for there to be a record of sexual offense history (National Task Force on Juvenile Sexual Offending, 1988, 1993). For these reasons, district attorneys have been discouraged from diversion of these cases.

The Defense

If charges are being filed, the juvenile has the right to be represented by an attorney. Defense attorneys are hired to represent the best interests of the client and therefore seek to minimize the legal consequences by asking for a reduction of charges or a finding of not guilty. In this process, plea bargains may result in the youth's entering a guilty plea to a lesser charge than that describing the actual offense.

Unfortunately, a reduction in charges corresponds with the youth's own pattern of redefining his behavior in more acceptable terms. For this reason, a reduction in charges may not only decrease the likelihood of an adequate treatment referral and resources to pay for services, but it also supports the youth's denial of the problem. The better course is for charges to reflect the nature of the actual behavior as nearly as possible, with no plea bargains resulting in nonsexual charges (National Task Force 1988, 1993). Moreover, it is in the best interest of the juvenile who has engaged in sexually abusive behavior to seek a disposition that will facilitate treatment; it is clearly not in the client's best interest to continue offending.

Adjudication

When charges are filed, the case usually is brought before a judge in juvenile court. Increasingly, more and more cases involving adolescents are being remanded to adult criminal court, but the lack of treatment in that system discourages this practice. Recent legislative changes in some jurisdictions, reflecting the community's concern about the dangers of juvenile crime, have lowered the age for remand to adult court to as low as age twelve.

The juvenile court judge may accept a guilty plea or may hear the case and arrive at a finding of guilt or innocence. If guilt is not established, the case is dismissed. With a finding of guilt, the court is then in a position to order remedial intervention, restitution, or punishment (or all three). It is within the court's discretion to order specialized assessments prior to sentencing in order to consider the rehabilitation of the offender and the protection of the community. Sentencing may order compliance with a recommended course of treatment or may be deferred on the condition that the youth comply with and successfully complete the recommended course of treatment.

Court orders may include incarceration or placement in residential treatment facilities, probation, and parental cooperation or involvement in treatment and may well prescribe the actual conditions of treatment and restitution. Because sexually abusive youth are unlikely to face the discomfort of the treatment process without an external mandate to do so, the court's involvement in ordering completion of specialized treatment is crucial. The court is also most able to protect the community with specific orders for placement, supervision, and follow-up.

In one model program in Washington State, treatment providers and prosecutors worked together to improve the referral, screening, charging, and disposition of juvenile sex offenses (Wheeler, 1986). In addition to effective prosecution of these cases, the Snohomish County prosecutor's Juvenile Sex Offender Project emphasized improved services for the juvenile offender's victims, evaluation and treatment of the youth, coordination of services between agencies, and public and professional education regarding juvenile sex offenses. Over the two-year grant period of this project, Snohomish County prosecutors significantly improved the prosecution rate while following a strict policy prohibiting plea bargaining: 91 percent of charges filed resulted in convictions, 91 percent of convictions ordered offense-specific evaluations, 76 percent of the youth were treated in community-based programs while supervised by the court, and 23 percent were committed to institutional treatment programs. The changes made in the system's response continued beyond the grant period, although no additional data have been published.

It is clear to treatment providers in this field that the court's involvement is crucial in supporting the development of effective treatment resources, as well as in facilitating the treatment process. The desirability and implications of central registries regarding child molestation and the tracking of juvenile offenders as they become adults are ongoing dilemmas. These are two areas that require additional study and research.

Many jurisdictions have enacted registry or notification laws in reaction to public outcry following extraordinary cases of recidivism and heinous crimes committed by known sexual offenders who were poorly placed or had been released in the community. Such reactions come despite evidence that recidivism rates are not extraordinary, professional concern that stigma and isolating conditions may exacerbate the risk for some abusers and have no deterrent effect on most (see Berliner, 1996; Freeman-Longo 1996a, 1996b), and the lack of any research to indicate such laws and practices increase community safety.

The central registries of alleged perpetrators of child abuse that were developed in most states during the 1970s and 1980s were specifically designed to be held confidential, with access usually limited to investigators of subsequent allegations to establish patterns of abuses and to agencies hiring adults to educate or care for children in order to prevent known abusers from being placed in positions of trust with children.

Recent trends, which require registries and long periods of tracking of sex offenders and public notification, have caused discomfort to many professionals in the field, and it has become increasingly difficult to balance the need for legal accountability and the court's control and supervision with the long-term implications of such laws, especially in regard to young persons who are motivated to work in treatment, demonstrate relevant changes in behavior, and appear to be at a low risk to reoffend following treatment. Many practitioners experienced in treating sexually abusive youth believe that most can be dissuaded from continuing to abuse and that only a minority might be indicated for lifelong tracking and supervision. Such decisions should be informed by differential consideration of risk and response to treatment. Research continues to be needed to evaluate current case management and community protection practices and to further the courts' understanding of factors relevant to risk after treatment.

References

Berliner, L. (1996). Community notification: Neither a panacea nor a calamity. *Sexual Abuse Journal of Research and Treatment, 8*(2).

Empey, L. T. (1982). *American delinquency: Its meaning and construction.* Florence, KY: Dorsey Press.

Freeman-Longo, R. (1996a). Feel good legislation: Prevention or calamity. *Child Abuse and Neglect: The International Journal, 20*(2).

Freeman-Longo, R. (1996b). Public notification: Prevention or problem. *Sexual Abuse: A Journal of Research and Treatment, 8*(2).

Gendreau, P., & Ross, R. (1987). Revivication of rehabilitation: Evidence from the 1980s. *Justice Quarterly, 4*(3), 349–407.

Heinz, J., Gargaro, S., & Kelley, K. (1987). *A model residential juvenile sex offender program: Hennepin County Home School.* Brandon, VT: Safer Society Press.

Mathews, F., & Stermac, L. (1989). *A tracking survey of adolescent sex offenders.* Toronto, Ontario: Central Toronto Youth Services.

National Council of Juvenile and Family Court Judges. (1984). The juvenile court and serious offenders [Special issue]. *Juvenile and Family Court Journal.*

National Task Force on Juvenile Sexual Offending. (1988). Preliminary report. *Juvenile and Family Court Journal, 39*(2), 10–20.

National Task Force on Juvenile Sexual Offending. (1993). Revised report. *Juvenile and Family Court Journal, 44*(4).

Speirs, V. (1989). The juvenile court's response to violent crime. *Juvenile Justice Bulletin.* Washington, DC: U.S. Department of Justice.

Snyder, H., Sickmund, M., & Poe-Yamagata, E. (1996). *Juvenile offenders and victims: 1996 update on violence.* Washington, DC: Office of Justice.

Wheeler, J. R. (1986). *Final evaluation of the Snohomish County prosecutor's Juvenile Sex Offender Project.* Olympia, WA: Department of Social Services, Juvenile Justice Section.

CHAPTER FOURTEEN

COMPREHENSIVE SERVICE DELIVERY WITH A CONTINUUM OF CARE

Steven Bengis

Since the early 1980s, there has been virtual unanimity among professionals treating sexually abusive youth that successful intervention requires specialized diagnostic evaluations and specialized treatment (Bengis, 1986; Knopp, 1982, 1985). Given the consequences to innocent victims of diagnostic and treatment mistakes, many practitioners adopted the following assumptions as a guide to their work:

1. Treatment of sexually abusive youth must be specifically directed at preventing further victimization of innocent members of the community.
2. Legal accountability for sexually abusive behavior is part of an overall treatment approach. Legal accountability and treatment are not mutually exclusive principles.
3. Client evaluation must include a diagnostic assessment by a specialist trained to work with sexually abusive youth.
4. Treatment in peer groups designed specifically for youth who have been sexually abusive is the treatment of choice.

These assumptions were validated by the consensus reached by the National Task Force on Juvenile Sexual Offending (1988, 1993).

Victim protection, legal accountability, specialized diagnosis, and group treatment are the four fundamental operating principles that have guided practitioners operating in the field. For these approaches to be truly effective, however, they must be implemented across a carefully constructed service delivery system with a continuum of care that guarantees both a range of residential and outpatient alternatives and a consistent therapeutic approach across the treatment continuum (Bengis, 1986).

The Continuum of Care

A continuum of care is based on recognition of both the similarities and differences of sexually abusive youth. It reflects those similarities by adhering to the basic concepts that abuse is abuse, irregardless of the form it takes, and that all abusive youth must be held accountable for a commitment to change. The differences are a reflection of differential diagnosis regarding risk to others and the treatment needs of the individual. The continuum model allows placements and service delivery to be either more or less restrictive and offense-specific strategies to be either more or less intense.

Sexually abusive youth who come to the attention of the service system early in the development of sexually abusive patterns of behavior and who have not used violence in their offenses may be treatable in outpatient settings. Although these youth will generally neither self-refer nor agree to treatment unless it is mandated by the courts, successful intervention can occur in outpatient groups. The prognosis for this group improves if the client's family also enters treatment.

Youth whose diagnostic assessments reveal a rather lengthy history of sexually abusive behaviors, delinquent behaviors, or violent sexual assault generally require more secure settings. Some of these youth will be treatable in staff-secure residential programs that are community based. Others, who are very high risk or have engaged in particularly violent sexual acts, require a physically secure site. Without such a locked setting, innocent community members may face the risk of becoming the future victims of these youth, who initially neither intend to nor are able to stop their sexual assaults. Exposing the community to such a serious and unnecessary risk is unacceptable. Therefore a comprehensive service delivery system with a continuum of care should include the following components:

1. Locked residential treatment facilities
2. Unlocked staff-secure residential treatment units
3. Alternative community-based living environments (such as foster care, group living homes, mentor programs, or supervised apartments)

4. Outpatient groups, day programs, and special education schools
5. Diagnostic centers and services specifically designed to provide sex offender–specific as well as traditional diagnostic assessments

This same treatment continuum should be replicated for developmentally disabled clients who have sexually offended. These clients cannot be integrated with more cognitively capable adolescents or with nonabusive disabled clients, because of the risks they pose and their special treatment needs (see Part Five).

Services are sometimes developed to distinguish different levels of risk or to separate youth by arbitrary categories such as age or referral criteria. Consideration of services without attention to the content creates two problems:

1. A continuum of services may lack a consistent treatment orientation and philosophy that remains constant as a youth progresses along the continuum.
2. A continuum of services may fail to maintain relationship bonds over time between primary caregivers (teachers, clinicians, other direct care personnel), peers, and the youthful client.

Without a continuum of care, a youth who enters the system in a highly secure residential setting and moves through less restrictive residential programs (foster care, home placement, or a supervised apartment) may be confronted with a variety of treatment approaches, intervention styles, clinical strategies, and programmatic philosophies. Direct care personnel, clinicians, and teachers may change with each new placement. This sort of inconsistency is thought to contribute to recidivism in the general population of emotionally disturbed juveniles, and it is particularly risky for sexually abusive youth.

Even with a specialized approach that is consistently implemented over time by treatment staff whom these youth know and trust, these young offenders experience great difficulty in freeing themselves from deeply imprinted behavior responses. These responses tend to reassert themselves if the youth finds himself under stress or pressure or dealing with disappointment, failure, or highly emotional encounters. To avoid regression and new abusive behavior, these youth need to have their new behaviors and new coping mechanisms reinforced over and over again in a consistent and predictable manner. If any of the service providers along the care continuum fails to support and reinforce the principles and practices of abuse-specific treatment (such as specialized groups, confrontation of abusive patterns and distortions, and legal accountability), the denial, minimization, and acting-out that brought the adolescent into the system may be reinforced. The consistency and predictability of approach, central elements in the treatment of these clients, can be guaranteed only when service providers at all levels of the service delivery system are committed to a common treatment philosophy.

Thus, a comprehensive service delivery system with a continuum of care must contain the components listed above and be guided by the following basic premises:

1. That each youth moving through the system be treated with a consistent approach regardless of his residential or outpatient placement. Although different placements might require a modification of technique, objectives, or strategies, the basic treatment orientation should remain the same.
2. That every effort be made to maintain certain staff-client-peer relationships as a youth moves from one placement to another. In other words, a youth would continue to work with the same therapist, group leader, or day program staff as he changes residential placements and moves along the continuum from secure treatment to independent living.

Offense-Specific Residences

By establishing a continuum of care based on the five components and two principles outlined above, communities create the optimal conditions for meeting both their own needs and the needs of this specific client population. However, one additional question needs to be addressed: Can sexually abusive youth be successfully placed in programs designed to serve emotionally or behaviorally disturbed adolescents who are not known to have been abusive? This question is particularly pertinent when considering the need to create new services versus the utilization of existing ones and the difficulties and ethical issues raised by attempting to site a residence specifically designed for sexually abusive youth within the community.

In addressing this question, Knopp, Rosenberg, and Stevenson reported in 1986 that "most residential programs do not provide separate cottages or quarters for sex offenders. Usually, they live in the general population, but meet in separate offense-specific groups at least once per week." Knopp and other service providers suggest that such an arrangement may not be optimal. Some programs that have evolved from the mixed-population model into one of separate housing for sex offenders have reported considerable advantages for both staff and residents in housing sexually abusive youth in separate cottages. Before they were separated, staff were sometimes intimidated by the manipulative and victimizing behaviors of these abusive youths. They found that these youth could divide staff detrimentally on issues regarding their treatment. Training for staff to be specialists in offense-specific treatment had to cover the staff of the entire institution.

By separating the sexually abusive youth from the general population, all staff could be trained to relate to the abuse issues, but training could be intensified in the specific cottages, and the staff there could specialize.

Sexually abusive youth in offense-specific units may create a stronger treatment culture when all the members are working on similar issues. In effect, it permits them to implement their program twenty-four hours a day. When all the youngsters are dealing with manipulative and intimidating behaviors, they can recognize them more readily in others and help one another deal with them. Because the treatment culture is stronger and the focus can be on the sexual or abusive issues all day, length of stay may be shortened, and the supportive atmosphere can ease the difficulty of exploring sensitive issues such as homosexuality and masturbation.

The author's own experience in working with this population in a mixed-diagnostic residential setting suggests additional reasons for creating offense-specific residences. First, low-ego-functioning youth and younger adolescents (ages thirteen to fifteen) who do not have any history of sexual acting-out behaviors but are struggling to carve out an identity and to be seen as acceptable group members by their adolescent peers often mimic behaviors and attitudes of offenders, a highly undesirable consequence of mixing client groups. Second, sexually abusive youth are often aggressive and intimidating. Psychotic and borderline youth are often unable to protect themselves from their more aggressive peers. As a result, these more seriously emotionally disturbed youth may be either psychologically or physically abused by abusive peers. Such experiences recreate their own histories of physical and sexual abuse and seriously hamper their treatment. Occurrences of physical abuse cannot always be blamed on the incompetency of staff. Even in the most secure, locked correctional facilities, covert abuses are common. In adolescent treatment units that are also attempting to provide normalized environments, such abuse by any youth determined to find a victim cannot always be prevented simply through staff vigilance.

Some major residential programs for juvenile sex offenders have remained committed to maintaining a client mix. Some of these programs serve the more violent adolescents who have committed both sex crimes and other offenses. During much of the day, these youth, who may be housed in individual locked rooms, are treated together. These programs provide groups specifically for sexually abusive youth as well as other subgroups for work on other issues, and the general population milieu stresses responsible behavior and thinking for all residents.

Particularly in large correctional systems, this model is sometimes feasible. Other programs that have both a mixed-diagnostic client population and the offense-specific treatment model may be found in facilities that serve severely emotionally or behaviorally disturbed adolescents. Further experience in locked settings, such as hospitals and intensive residential treatment programs, suggests that a highly structured day program can provide all the juveniles with certain positive treatment experiences without risking the negative outcomes. In addition, mixed-population educational day programs may be suitable for clients who can be served in unlocked, community-based, residential facilities, including clients placed in such facilities subsequent to treatment in a locked specialized residence.

A mixed-diagnostic educational day program may have positive features. One is that some sexually abusive youth do well in an educational setting. They are behaviorally compliant (that is, they can move through the school routines with relative ease without disruptively acting out, since their serious acting out is specifically sexual), and they are often educationally advanced in comparison to other emotionally disturbed clients. Therefore, they may provide positive role models for other students in an educational setting while themselves benefiting from the normalized social interactions.

An educational environment generally focused on emotionally neutral subject matter with a highly structured setting seems to help these youths regulate their oversexualized lifestyle and preoccupation with sexual issues. These issues may be aggravated by leisure time and residential environments such as bedrooms and common living areas.

Finally, school can serve as a bridge between residential placement and a return to the community for youth who will have to cope with both their own sexually abusive histories and a nonabusive community population. Within the structure of the school, they can practice community-appropriate behaviors in an environment that includes male and female peers and teachers. If the staff have been specially trained to work with sexual abuse issues, they can confront any inappropriate behaviors and work on them immediately.

Thus, a mixed-diagnostic category day program can provide the type of structured environment suited to helping sexually abusive youth move along the care continuum toward more independent living.

During the 1980s there was much debate with regard to homogeneous versus heterogeneous secure and community-based residential placements for sexually abusive youth. It has become apparent that special-needs groups of children and adolescents are at risk to have been and to be sexually abused or abusive (or both). These issues are not always the symptom of record but are frequent enough to warrant significant anticipatory planning for safety and prevention in every juvenile setting (Thomas, 1996). The abuse-specific milieu presented in Chapter Nineteen addresses this need.

Given the risk factors in mixing abusive and nonabusive youth, mixed-diagnostic residential programs should develop strict criteria and procedural guidelines to ensure the safety of all of their client populations. In addition, certain categories of youth who are known to have been abusive (for example, youth who have committed serious hands-on offenses for which they have never been adjudicated, who are in denial, and who will not voluntarily agree to participate in offense-specific treatment) may pose too high a risk for unlocked community-based placements.

Minimally, all residential, day program, and educational staff should be provided with extensive training in the management of sexual abuse issues. In addition, these programs should be provided with sufficient resources for consultation and supervision by a qualified treatment specialist and for one-to-one staffing of abusive youth during initial assessment periods and times of crisis. Without such basic safeguards, the placement of sexually abusive youth in residential and other community-based programs that have not been designed to serve them raises serious legal and ethical issues should another client be sexually victimized while in treatment in these same sites (Freeman-Longo & Ryan, 1990).

The lack of adequate resources or other administrative or political realities may prevent the implementation of the entire service delivery system at any one time, but a minimum commitment of resources allocated for training can facilitate the initiation of specialized groups and offense-specific evaluation and treatment planning in residential programs and outpatient clinics where personnel trained in general assessment and group treatment techniques already practice.

In order to create all of the components of the care continuum, many states need only to redesign portions of their existing delivery systems. By allocating resources to training and evaluation and by mandating offense-specific treatment, they can address the sexually abusive behaviors of this client population directly and specifically during adolescence with a better prognosis and fewer victims.

References

Bengis, S. (1986). *A comprehensive service delivery and a continuum of care for adolescent sexual offenders.* Orwell, VT: Safer Society Press.

Freeman-Longo, R., & Ryan, G. (1990). *Tort liability in treatment of sexually abusive juveniles.* Denver: Interchange National Adolescent Perpetration Network, Kempe Center.

Knopp, F. H. (1982). *Remedial intervention in adolescent sex offenders.* Orwell, VT: Safer Society Press.

Knopp, F. H. (1985). *The youthful sex offender: Rationale and goals for treatment.* Orwell, VT: Safer Society Press.

Knopp, F. H., Rosenberg, J., & Stevenson, W. (1986). *Report on nationwide survey of juvenile and adult sex-offender treatment programs and providers: 1986.* Orwell, VT: Safer Society Press.

National Task Force on Juvenile Sexual Offending. (1988). Preliminary report. *Juvenile and Family Court Journal, 39*(2).

National Task Force on Juvenile Sexual Offending (1993). Revised report. *Juvenile and Family Court Journal, 44*(4).

Thomas, J. (1996). *Safety in residential settings.* Paper presented at the Twelfth Annual National Adolescent Perpetrator Network, Minneapolis, MN.

CHAPTER FIFTEEN

ASSESSMENT OF SEXUALLY ABUSIVE YOUTH

Sandy Lane

Assessment of sexually abusive youth is a complex process. In the initial assessment, the clinician is asked to identify behavior patterns and determine the youth's potential to reoffend, amenability for treatment, the recommended treatment setting, the type of treatment needed, community safety issues, risk factors, monitoring considerations, and the potential risk if the youth has any contact with the victims or other vulnerable persons. The assessment of the youth also seeks to identify psychiatric, individual, and family treatment needs. For many clinicians, the assessment is disturbing. It requires them to use a more directive and educational interaction than may typically be used in an initial contact with a client. Some clinicians may find it difficult to discuss sexual matters openly, and they may have uncomfortable reactions as they listen to the details and the youth's perceptions of his sexually abusive behavior. Often the interviewer needs to observe and analyze the youth's anxiety reactions or style of interacting with the therapist rather than intervene to alleviate discomfort or attempt to build rapport.

Clinicians subsequently share the information they obtain with each of the legal, mental health, family service, placement, and treatment agencies involved. Some clinicians struggle with confidentiality issues because professional standards

Note: Although the concepts described in this chapter apply to both male and female youths who sexually abuse, we have used the masculine pronoun to facilitate readability.

identify client confidentiality as an ethical responsibility. Waiving confidentiality (National Task Force on Juvenile Sexual Offending, 1988, 1993) in the interest of community safety and client monitoring is difficult for many clinicians because it places the needs of others over the needs of the client. This is thought to be in the best interest of the client in the long run but may feel uncomfortable for the professional at the time.

The youth's level of motivation for therapy may also be problematic. Rarely does a juvenile or a parent initiate contact to request help with sexually abusive behavior patterns without some external pressure to do so. It is more likely that a youth has been reported or apprehended and has been referred by an agency or the court for the assessment. The youth may be embarrassed, defensive, ashamed, or self-protective. His initial motivation for involvement in the assessment or treatment is likely either minimal or related more to fear of consequences than to any desire to change. Family members may also struggle with minimization, denial, or protective issues.

Prior to the 1980s, assessment of youth who had committed sexually abusive behaviors often failed to address the sexual abuse issue in any specific or relevant fashion. When workers in the field shared their experiences in the early 1980s, the focus of the effort was to decrease minimization of sexually abusive behaviors and to identify and articulate offense-specific treatment needs. By concentrating on the sexually abusive behavior, professionals learned a great deal about assessment and treatment techniques specifically relevant to the referring problem. Many extremely thorough and highly structured specialized offense-specific assessments were developed (for examples, see Fehrenbach, Smith, Monastersky, & Deisher, 1986; Kerr 1986; O'Brien & Bera, 1985; Ross & Loss, 1987). Unfortunately, there was a tendency for practitioners to view offense-specific treatment objectives as a priority and to minimize the importance of other issues in the lives of the youth. Often other problems were put on hold until objectives related to the sexual abuse behavior were met, and other life factors (for example, victimization issues, pharmacological needs, or early childhood trauma) were not always integrated into the work. As this field evolves, it is becoming apparent that many aspects of development, life experience, and functioning are relevant to both the youth's success in treatment and the risks of reoffending. Offense-specific assessment protocol and treatment approaches are becoming more comprehensive, and the identification and prioritization of treatment needs involve assessment of all relevant issues, not just those related to sexual abuse behaviors.

Because treatment of sexually abusive youth is viewed as a preventive intervention in the development of sexual deviance, there has been a sustained interest in trying to identify antecedents related to the risk of sexual deviance and abusive behavior. As both clinical and empirical research unfolds, it has become apparent that there is no single causative path and that many of the risks are associated with the antecedents described in the cycle prior to the emergence of the sexual aspects of the pattern; many of those risk factors are related to deficits in attachment, developmental competence, and concurrent disorders (Gilgun, 1988; Hunter, 1996; Marshall, Hudson, & Hodkinson, 1993; Prentky et al., 1989). Therefore, treatment providers now believe that an effective approach to assessment considers sexual abuse behavior patterns, safety issues, concurrent psychiatric disorders, family issues, interpersonal capacities, developmental history, traumatic experiences, and social competencies (National Task Force on Juvenile Sexual Offending, 1993). An important component of assessment is the evaluation of the interaction of the various issues in the life of the youth and their influence on his ability to function effectively, as well as their impact on his sexually abusive behavior patterns.

As the field continues to evolve, it becomes increasingly important to develop and use tests that objectively measure aspects related to the behaviors and factors that contribute to their development. Other than the reported initial research for the Sex Offender Scale (SOS) (Phipps, 1996), there are no known tests that effectively discriminate sexually abusive youth from those who have not been involved in such behaviors. Several tests do provide information that will help the clinician with gaining an understanding of various aspects of the youth's personality, interactional, attitudinal, behavioral, interpersonal and sexual abuse behavior characteristics. *Assessing Sexual Abuse: A Resource Guide for Practitioners* (Prentky & Bird, 1997) provides an excellent compilation of available tests and what they are intended to measure. It is more effective to complete the testing protocol prior to the initial clinical interview with a youth. The results will assist the clinician in identifying specific issues to be discussed. Many agencies select tests that assess personality characteristics, depression, anxiety, self-concept, attachment, traumatization, psychiatric symptomatology, interpersonal competency, empathy, anger management, sexual functioning, attitudes, paraphilias, and honesty.

Assessment of sexually abusive behavior is an ongoing, dynamic process that occurs throughout the youth's involvement with legal and treatment agencies. There are five phases of involvement (National Task Force on Juvenile Sexual Offending, 1993):

Phase 1: Pretrial (investigative)

Phase 2: Presentence (dangerousness, risk, placement prognosis)

Phase 3: Postadjudication clinical assessment (treatment issues, modality)

Phase 4: Release and termination of treatment (community safety, successful application of treatment tools)

Phase 5: Monitoring and follow-up (ongoing treatment needs, life adjustment)

This chapter focuses on the presentence and clinical assessments. Although the information is presented in segments, the assessment of the youth and his sexually abusive behavior should be holistic. The initial assessment may be used for sentencing as well as initial placement, monitoring, and treatment decisions. The clinician must remain aware that the initial assessment will likely be incomplete, given that youth who sexually abuse present with varying degrees of minimization, denial, and other psychological defenses related to their behavior. For most youth, some pieces of information are not disclosed or evident until the youth has progressed in treatment. The clinical assessment and the analysis of the youth's sexually abusive behavior patterns will continue to emerge during treatment and monitoring. The challenge for providers is to integrate the various aspects of assessment into a comprehensive and flexible assessment that considers differential diagnosis and treatment recommendations.

Preparation for Assessment

Prior to undertaking an assessment of a youth who has sexually abused, the clinician needs to develop a clear definition of abuse and a thorough understanding of sexually abusive behavior. Understanding the sexual abuse cycle can provide a framework for areas to explore with the youth and assist with analyzing the information provided (or denied) by the youth (see Chapter Six). An awareness of typologies (O'Brien & Bera, 1985), risk criteria (Groth & Loredo, 1981; Johnson, 1995; Ross & Loss, 1987; Steen, 1996; Wenet & Clark, 1983), guidelines to assessment (Abbot, 1984; Gray & Wallace, 1992; National Task Force on Juvenile Sexual Offending, 1988, 1993; Ross & Loss, 1987; Steen, 1996), and information related to placement criteria (Bengis, 1986; Kerr, 1986; National Task Force on Juvenile Sexual Offending, 1988, 1993) can assist with developing an effective plan for safety and treatment (as an example of assessment guidelines, see Table 15.1).

Reviewing collateral data is essential to the assessment process. Police reports, victim statements, victim therapist reports, agency investigation summaries, and presentence investigation reports should be requested and reviewed prior to interviewing the youth. It is helpful to talk with investigators to identify any information omitted from the report (such as, observations of nonverbal behaviors or the investigator's impressions). The data in these reports will assist the clinician with evaluating the youth's honesty, degree of ownership, areas of denial, attributions of responsibility, and sexual abuse behavior style. Psychological evaluations, school records, placement or treatment summaries, criminal records, and summaries of agency involvement will assist the clinician with identifying psychotherapeutic needs, concurrent psychiatric disorders, developmental and social competencies or deficits, and family treatment needs.

TABLE 15.1. TWENTY-ONE FACTOR GUIDE TO ASSESSMENT.

Factor 1:	The offender's cooperation with the assessment process
Factor 2:	Honesty and self-initiated disclosure
Factor 3:	The degree of aggression or overt violence in offenses
Factor 4:	The frequency and duration of offenses
Factor 5:	The length, nature, and progression of history of sexual aggression
Factor 6:	Offense characteristics other than sexual aggression
Factor 7:	Number of victims in relation to amount of victim access
Factor 8:	Victim selection characteristics
Factor 9:	Personal responsibility for offending behavior
Factor 10:	The precipitating factors to offenses
Factor 11:	Other exploitative or addictive behaviors
Factor 12:	Family system functioning
Factor 13:	School and/or employment stability
Factor 14:	Social relationships
Factor 15:	Nonoffending sexual history and past victimization
Factor 16:	External motivation for treatment
Factor 17:	Internal motivation for treatment
Factor 18:	Response to confrontation
Factor 19:	Treatment history
Factor 20:	Criminal arrests, convictions, and incarceration history
Factor 21:	Current degree of access to present, past, or potential victims

Source: Adapted from Ross and Loss (1991).

Collateral interviews with parents, and sometimes siblings, assist the clinician in assessing familial attitudes related to the offense and the youth's developmental history, current functioning, family dysfunctions, and risk factors. Collateral contacts with teachers, prior therapists, physicians, or adults who supervise the youth's activities may provide additional perspectives. The victim may wish to offer information, directly or through his or her therapist, which could provide significant information about the youth that may not have been considered pertinent to the criminal investigation.

Prior to the interview, the clinician's approach to the youth needs to be considered. It is the author's suggestion that the interactional style models a non-judgmental, win-win orientation that is respectful of the youth as an individual, while maintaining an awareness of the youth's motivation to manipulate the interview. Some clinicians advocate assuming control of the interview (Ross & Loss, 1991; Gray & Wallace, 1992). This means directing the content and being clear about expectations and the outcomes if a youth chooses not to meet expectations. It does not mean intimidating or degrading the youth or engaging in power struggles with him. If the clinician models control seeking, the youth also may exhibit this behavior. If a clinician misuses power in interactions with the young sexual abuser, the juvenile is likely to become defensive, his cycle may be triggered, and he will be reluctant to participate fully in the assessment process. Helping the youth have some sense of control might be achieved through offering choices such as, "Would you rather discuss this aspect now or later in the interview?" The clinician can gather valuable information by observing the youth's resistance, denial, defensiveness, or manifestations of anxiety. Rather than terminating the process until the youth is cooperative, the clinician can use such information for making decisions regarding appropriate treatment settings, safety considerations, and treatment strategies to assist the youth with these areas.

In my experience, an honest, direct, calm, matter-of-fact approach is most effective. Questions about whether or why the youth committed the offense are not helpful. Other than knowing it felt good, the youth does not really know why he sexually abused someone, and he is likely prepared to deny the behavior or say what he thinks the interviewer wants to hear. More constructive questions request specific details about the behaviors and the associated thoughts and feelings—for example: "When you did _____ ?" "What were you _____ ?" "What do you think contributed to _____ ?" "How did you decide _____ ?" or "How long did you _____ ?" Because they require more consideration than yes or no questions, the youth is encouraged to reveal more, and thus they elicit more detailed information. Information provided from the youth's perspective allows a more accurate assessment of his motivations, cognitions, and patterns.

At times, an educational approach increases the youth's comfort with providing information. Statements such as, "People usually do some thinking about what they are going to do. When did you start thinking about doing something sexual with [the victim]?" may normalize something that the youth had feared would be compromising if it were known. Questions such as, "Did you fantasize?" may seem accusatory to the youth, and he may refuse to acknowledge abusive thoughts in hopes of receiving greater acceptance from the interviewer or less stringent consequences for his behavior. Learning that there are some predictable cognitive and behavioral patterns may be encouraging to the youth and the family.

Confronting a discrepancy between the victim's account and the youth's version allows assessment of his response to criticism and disagreement, as well as the degree of responsibility he is taking. Assertive questioning is encouraged rather than attacking or demeaning confrontation. Discrepancies that remain after probing and encouragement should be articulated and identified as areas that will become clearer in treatment—for example, "The discrepancy between your memory and your sister's memory of the incident will need to be resolved during treatment if you and she are going to be able to make sense of this." Any defensive reactions will depict the style of attribution of responsibility the youth is utilizing. At times allowing silence until the youth interrupts it will provide clues about how he handles anxiety. Asking for information in several different ways, particularly when the youth is not acknowledging some aspect, helps to assess denial issues.

It is important to empathize with any demonstration of a sense of shame, embarrassment, or fear of consequences. Although the youth's associated cognitions may be somewhat distorted, validating his feelings lays the groundwork for him to improve his awareness of internal reactions and his capacity for empathy during treatment. Offering support for the youth to disclose may acknowledge the difficulty the youth may be having about sharing offense information without minimizing the seriousness of his behavior or the impact to the victim.

Being honest with the sexually abusive youth during the interview models a behavior expected of the juvenile during treatment and facilitates the development of a therapeutic alliance. When he appears to be lying, it is acceptable to say, "I'm having a hard time believing you because _____ ; help me understand," or "I don't like what you did, but I am willing to work with you to help you learn to control abusive behaviors." If a youth asks about potential consequences for disclosing or not cooperating with the assessment, it is important to provide accurate information as well as to acknowledge the youth's right to choose how he will be involved. During their initial contact, the youth and family should be informed of the assessment protocol and the intent to share information obtained, and conclusions developed, with the agencies involved as well as themselves.

Assessment of the Abusive Behavior

Assessment of the sexually abusive behavior for which the youth is initially referred provides information about the cognitions, emotions, and behaviors involved in the offense. Comparison between the referring behavior and other sexually abusive behaviors the youth reports becomes the basis for identifying patterns, progression of behaviors, and degree of habituation. The intent is to explore in depth everything the youth did, thought, or felt that related to the abusive behavior.

Interview Content

The youth is more likely to explore the abusive behavior if the clinician relates as a nonjudgmental individual who understands that there are many thoughts and behaviors that typically occur during sexual abuse. It is also likely that the youth will be more open if his family members are not in the room during this portion of the interview.

Requesting the youth to describe the incident initially and then asking questions that elicit more detail is an effective approach. As the youth describes the incident from his perspective, observe nonverbal cues, any discrepancy with the victim's or investigator's reports, manifestations of anxiety or defensiveness, minimization, and any aspects the youth avoids. If he is acknowledging some portion of the sexually abusive behavior, offer some recognition of how difficult it is to assume responsibility and some education about how his acknowledgment is the first step toward learning to control the behavior. Although the client may deny the accuracy of some of the information about the abuse, the clinician can assess issues of sensitivity, minimization, or denial more comprehensively by asking for more detail.

Among the questions that provide the necessary information and tend to elicit detail are these:

- How did the youth get the victim to cooperate?
- What did he say during the sexual abuse?
- What specific behaviors did he do during the abuse incident (sexual and nonsexual)?
- What did the victim do or say during the abuse?
- How did the victim seem to feel during the abuse, and how did the offender react?
- What did he do or say to encourage the victim not to tell?
- What did he do immediately afterward?
- What was he doing just before the sexual abuse?
- What was most attractive about the victim?
- At what point in the abuse did he become aroused?
- Did he ejaculate or masturbate during the abuse (or before or after)?
- How did he set up the situation, and what was involved in deciding where to do it?
- How did he choose the victim?
- What made the victim seem to be someone who would cooperate?
- Did he do anything different during the sexual abuse from what he had thought about doing beforehand?
- Was anything about the sexual abuse disappointing?
- How long had he thought about it before the sexual abuse occurred?
- What had he done to make it more likely for the victim to be involved?
- What is he thinking about the sexual abuse behavior now?
- What was most gratifying about doing the sexual abuse?
- How had he expected the victim to react?
- If the victim reaction was different from his expectation, how did he feel, and how did he respond?
- How is he feeling about the abuse behavior now?

- How did he get caught?
- In what ways did he threaten the victim?
- What did he wear, and did the clothing have any specific meaning to him?
- Did he have a weapon with him?
- How did he avoid interruption or detection?
- What thoughts and feelings did he have during the sexual abuse?
- Did he ask the victim to do anything that increased his arousal?
- Did he do anything before the offense to increase his arousal?
- What did he do to set up the opportunity?
- What reasons did he give himself that made the behavior seem reasonable at the time?
- Did he take anything from the victim or record the offense in any way?

The youth will likely feel vulnerable subsequent to in-depth questioning and may need to process some of his reactions. Observe how he handles the feelings that arise. Some youth will become more distant, hostile, or nontrusting, while others may exhibit some withdrawal or a depressed affect. Still others may become somewhat more open during the rest of the interview.

A portion of the interview with the youth's parents assesses their perceptions and awareness of the sexually abusive behavior. Unless the youth has acknowledged his behavior to his parents, it is likely that they will exhibit some minimization, justification, or attribution of responsibility to the victim. Providing some educational information to parents at this time is effective. Questions about the youth's relationship to and style of interacting with the victim can help assess the power differential and possible grooming behaviors. Additional questions might include their view of the incident, what they know of the sexually abusive behavior, ways their child has been secretive or deceptive with them, and any awareness of their child's use of pornography or sexual preoccupation. If the abuse has occurred within the family, sensitivity to the parents' struggle with meeting the needs of both the perpetrator and the victim is critical.

Denial

Some youth who sexually abuse may exhibit partial or extensive denial. Denial is a self-protective process and may be an intentional deception or a psychological defense mechanism. Most youth exhibit some level of denial at some point during their assessment or treatment, depending on various internal or external circumstances.

Denial may exist to protect self-image, decrease anxiety, or avoid thinking about the offense. It may serve as protection from external social consequences (retaliation, rejection, ridicule, isolation, and stereotypes) and legal consequences (prosecution, severity of sentencing, treatment, or placement). It can also protect against internal consequences of negative self-perception (lack of control, deviancy, or "bad me") or negative emotions of shame, embarrassment, fear, and grief. It may also serve to maintain a sense of acceptance from others. For still others, the sexually abusive behavior may be so ego dystonic that the youth is unable to acknowledge the offense, even to himself. There are several layers of denial to consider, and some youth exhibit more than one type of denial.

- *Justification* is partial denial in that the youth acknowledges having engaged in the behavior but identifies reasons that allowed, or "made," him do the behavior. The reasons often parallel those the youth gives himself before he engages in the sexually abusive behavior—for example: "I wouldn't have done it if I wasn't drunk" or "She's a prick tease; she came on to me and then cried rape."
- *Minimization* is partial denial that allows the youth to lessen the seriousness of the sexually abusive behavior. He may describe the behavior as less extensive than the victim has reported or may minimize the impact of the behavior to the victim—for example: "It was just one little touch," "He said he would do it, so it couldn't have bothered him," or "It wasn't like I was cruel or anything; I didn't even penetrate."
- *Denying abusive aspects* while acknowledging the behavior is typically based on cultural beliefs or cognitive distortions. If a youth is raised in a multigenerational incest family, he may believe that being involved with a sibling sexually is normal and does not constitute an abusive behavior. Believing that a three-year-old who sat on a perpetrator's lap and wiggled was aware of the youth's arousal and was inviting a sexual response, or mislabeling a sexually abusive behavior as educational, are distorted perceptions.
- *Denial of sexual intent* involves perceiving the sexually abusive behavior as based on some other motivation, with the sexual aspects occurring coninciden-tally—for example: "I was just trying to make him feel better about himself, and we got carried away," "I never had an erection during it," "I only wanted to feel close," "I was just playing a game," or "I was just giving a massage."
- *Denial of part of the abusive behavior* may protect the youth from feelings of shame or embarrassment. The youth may admit the sexually abusive behavior in general but omit some part that he believes will cause others to ridicule him—for example: "I molested her and that was wrong, but I didn't try to have intercourse with her; she must have been confused about when I rubbed against her genital area." It is common for many youth to initially deny planning or contemplating the sexually abusive behavior beforehand.

- *Denial of potential recurrence* is common among youth who sexually abuse. In part, this type of denial stems from the suppression effect at the end of the cycle, and in part it helps the individual disregard his need for treatment—for example: "Now that I know it is illegal, I'd never do it again," "I never want to be locked up again, so of course I'd never do it again," or "Now I know how bad it hurt the victim, I couldn't even think of it."

- *Denial of history* includes denying any similar behaviors, or other types of sexually abusive behaviors, even if there are reports of other behaviors. The youth may believe that if he acknowledges other incidents, he will receive increased consequences. Some youth feel a sense of control if they know of another sexually abusive behavior they have done that the therapist is unable to get them to admit to. Some youth may mislabel other types of behaviors as nonabusive or may be unable to face the issue that their sexually abusive behavior patterns are more extensive.

- *Denial of victim harm* helps the youth avoid identifying the consequences of his behavior to himself or others. The youth may believe that because there was no physical damage, the behavior was not hurtful to the victim. Some youth deny emotional impact because the victim still talks to him. Others may think that the behavior was not hurtful because he was not trying to hurt the victim, or because the victim was young, he or she will forget the abuse. Sometimes the victim has stated that he or she "forgives" the abuser, and the youth believes that is an indication that whatever harm was done is healed.

- *Denial of deviant sexual arousal* associated with attraction to children or aggressive sexual behaviors is common among youthful sexual abusers. It is difficult for some youth to acknowledge anticipatory arousal or pedophilic interests. Other youth may normalize attraction to children or eliminate the sexual meanings of behaviors—for example: "I pictured her as my girlfriend while we did it," "We were naked in the bed, but he was just hiding there," or "I wasn't aroused when I was looking at those ads; they just made me think of doing it."

- *Inability to recall the details* of the sexual abuse behavior may seem to the youth to absolve him of responsibility for it—for example: "We were napping on the couch and my hand must have moved; I'm not responsible for what I do when I'm asleep" or "I was so loaded I don't remember a thing."

- *Denial of habituation* is common among youth. Even when acknowledging several sexually abusive behaviors and a progression of types of behaviors, many youth continue to believe that they can stop any time without having to be in treatment or avoiding risk factors. Most youth prefer to believe they are totally in control of their sexually abusive behaviors and are not driven by any urges or nonsexual needs.

- *Denial of the referring sexual abuse behavior* is less frequently observed, but some youth will acknowledge previous sexually abusive behaviors and deny the instant behavior. There is generally some circumstance that makes it difficult to acknowledge the behavior, such as fear of consequences or discomfort with the age of the victim.

- *Total denial* means that the youth will deny having engaged in any aspect of the sexually abusive behavior or even being present when the sexual abuse occurred. Some youth who persistently deny the behavior exhibit an angry, hostile affect, and others remain calm and logical. At times they will blame the victim for lying or retaliation and present themselves as the injured party.

If a youth is completely denying any responsibility for a sexually abusive behavior, he will not benefit from offense-specific treatment, nor will he be able to manage his sexual abuse behavior patterns. This does not mean that the youth should not be treated. Efforts during the assessment to interrupt or decrease denial will help ascertain what type of treatment setting would be most appropriate. Engaging in a power struggle with the youth to force him to admit to the behavior may strengthen his denial. It is more effective to begin with a nonconfrontational approach such as asking him to identify why the victim might lie about him, posing questions about other interactions with the victim, or asking him to share what he imagines the reactions of others would be if he had committed the offense. Processing through some of his fears or helping him identify what he could gain by acknowledging the behavior is often effective. It is important to confront the behavior as opposed to the individual when pointing out inconsistencies in the youth's version. The youth's tendency to misinterpret or perceive confrontation as a personal threat is heightened when he is defensive and denying.

Assessment of the Abusive Pattern

Sexual abuse behavior patterns encompass:

- The various types of behaviors the youth has committed
- Indications of progression over time
- Level of aggression
- Frequency of behaviors
- Style and type of victim access
- Preferred victim type
- Associated arousal patterns
- Changes in the sexual abuse behaviors or related thinking

- The youth's intent and motivation
- The extent of the youth's openness and honesty
- Internal and external risk factors
- Characteristics of the sexually abusive behaviors

By the time a youth who sexually abuses is known to the system, it is likely that he has engaged in some prior sexual abuse behaviors (Becker, Cunningham-Rathner, & Kaplan, 1986; Ryan, Miyoshi, Metzner, Krugman, & Fryer, 1996; Smith & Monastersky, 1986). He may have been involved in similar behaviors, less intrusive versions of the referring behavior, or other types of sexual abuse behaviors. Sexually abusive behaviors include molestation, rape, hands-off offenses, obscene communication, harassment, or exploitative behaviors. Typically the younger that youth are at the time of their first attempt to abuse sexually, the greater the variety of behaviors they have tried. Each abuse behavior and behavior type acknowledged by the youth needs to be examined in a manner similar to the referring sexual abuse behavior. Analysis of the differences and similarities of sexually abusive behaviors, locations of the behavior, victim characteristics, thinking, and associated circumstances will provide an initial understanding of the youth's abusive behavior patterns.

Sexually Abusive Behavior Types

During the interview, the youth needs to be questioned about other types of sexually abusive behaviors he has engaged in. It is helpful to inform the youth that the purpose of the questions is not intended to increase consequences but rather to understand the full extent of his sexually abusive behavior history, because such knowledge allows for more comprehensive treatment and safety planning. Most youth will be somewhat reluctant to share such information and may not disclose their entire history until they have progressed in treatment.

Simply asking the youth if he has done any other type of sexual abuse behavior will likely result in denial. A more helpful approach is to ask about behaviors or thoughts related to each possible type of sexual abuse behavior. Educational information about the commonality of multiple paraphilias among sexually abusive youth may increase the youth's willingness to share such information. One way to begin this exploration is to ask the youth to explain how the referring incident (which you have just discussed) is similar to and different from other sexual experiences and behavior.

Molestation behaviors typically involve a younger child. Legal definitions of the age difference varies from more than two to four years younger than the perpetrator, depending on the state in which the youth resides. Victims may be relatives, acquaintances, or strangers. Behaviors may involve touching, rubbing, kissing, "humping," penetration, or sucking, clothed or unclothed.

Rape or sexual assault behaviors involve force, coercion, violence, intimidation, and aggression. Victims may be of any age and may be a stranger or an acquaintance. Behaviors may involve penetration, touching, rubbing, kissing, sucking, biting, hitting, pain infliction, anger discharge, torture, or sadism.

Hands-off behaviors include exhibitionism and voyeurism. Unfortunately, these are typically viewed as nuisance behaviors and are often minimized by the youth and the community. *Exhibitionism* is displaying one's genitals or nude body to a victim of any age. *Voyeurism* is an attempt to observe someone unclothed or involved in sexual or hygiene behaviors without their knowledge. *Obscene communication* is obscene telephone calls or written messages to a victim of any age. *Frottage* is rubbing one's genitals against a victim. The behavior typically occurs in a crowded location (school hallways, elevators, buses, subways), although some perpetrators will grab a victim from behind in an isolated area, commit frottage, and run away. *"Grabbage"* is grabbing breasts, buttocks, or genitals of a victim of any age. The behavior may occur in a crowded location or an isolated area.

Harassment means unwelcome sexual advances, requests for sexual favors, or other verbal, written, or physical conduct of a sexual nature that continues without permission or in spite of the victim's distress or requests to stop. It may include gender harassment, seductive behaviors, sexual bribery, sexual coercion, or gross sexual imposition. It is of particular concern when the behavior occurs where the victim works or attends school, or in a peer group, and when submission is a criterion for decisions regarding privilege, status, or advancement.

Exploitation includes exposure to sexual materials beyond the victim's age or developmental level (such as showing a nine-year-old an X-rated video or describing sodomy to a six-year-old), enticing a victim to pose for nude photographs or child pornography, encouraging a younger child to wear or display certain clothing for the youth's sexual gratification, engaging a known sexual abuse victim in complying with sexual requests, providing alcohol or drugs to an individual to decrease the person's resistance to a sexual interaction, or taking advantage of a developmentally delayed individual's desire to be accepted in order to be sexual with that person.

Some behaviors are not legally defined as a sexual offense but may be associated with the youth's sexually abusive behavior patterns. Some youth engage in bestiality, or sex with animals, which is legal in some jurisdictions and not in others. Some youth may have sexual fantasies or arousal related to this behavior, and others may be aggressive or sadistic while involved in bestiality. Some youth steal undergarments from women or children for use as stimuli for masturbatory fantasies or to strengthen their perception of being secretly in control of the victim.

Behaviors involving some fetishes may be reported as part of the youth's development of arousal patterns or as part of an offense behavior. Examples include requiring a victim to wear some article of clothing during the sexual abuse to arouse the perpetrator, observing the victim urinate, or defecating at the scene of the offense behavior. Cross-dressing during voyeuristic behaviors or during masturbatory abuse fantasies has been reported by some youth. Some youth who have eventually been involved in rape have reported breaking and entering to stand in a victim's room while the person is sleeping and fantasize of raping, to take something of a victim's to enhance a feeling of empowerment, or to masturbate and ejaculate on a potential victim's bed or article of clothing when the victim is absent. Some youth report use of pornography preliminary to their sexual abuse behavior, during subsequent recall of the incident, or as part of the behavior. Pornography refers to sexually explicit pictures, videos, or stories; some youth report use of nonsexual materials such as catalog pictures, advertisements, art magazines, pictures depicting nudity of people from various cultures, or objects belonging to children that have sexual meaning for them.

Occasionally youth have been observed smelling girls' or children's chairs after they were occupied. Youth involved in this behavior describe experiencing a sense of ownership of the person who had been sitting there or using the behavior to make a potential victim feel uncomfortable. Some youth include rituals, behaviors that are characterized by rigid repetition of a series of steps, as part of their sexually abusive behavior. Examples include returning to the same site for each abusive behavior, repeating the same preparations each time, wearing the same clothing during each incident, or requiring each victim to say specific words or do a certain behavior during each abusive behavior. Fire setting may be present in the history of some sexually abusive youth and may be associated with destruction of pornographic materials or victimized animals (Law, 1987). Involvement in group-affiliated abuse where the youth appears to be acting in accordance with a group belief is occasionally reported. Association with a group may provide a youth with a sense of belonging, safety, or control, but it is possible for a perpetrator to use the norms of the group to coerce a victim or accomplish the abuse. Examples are multifamily or multigenerational sexual abuse, gang rapes, and ritualistic abuse. Ritualistic patterns have been noted in some prepubescent youth who are thought to be reenacting their own victimization as part of a posttraumatic syndrome (Cavanagh-Johnson, 1988; Ryan, 1989).

Progressive Aspects

Over time, youth who commit repeated sexual abuse behaviors exhibit some degree of progression of behavior types, elements of the behavior, or associated thoughts. Even if a progression of behaviors is apparent, some youth may engage in more than one type of sexual abuse behavior in the same time period. Identifying progressive aspects provides information about the youth's risk for reoffense, the presence of habituated sexual abuse behavior patterns, and the extent of danger to the community.

The youth should be asked about the age of onset of his first thought of sexually abusive behavior, when his first attempt occurred, and what thoughts and behaviors were involved. Of the abuse behavior types acknowledged by the youth, questions should be related to the sequence of behavior types, length of involvement, and what was involved in deciding to try another type of behavior. If the youth has not acknowledged additional sexual abuse behavior types, sharing that many youth exhibit a progression from one type of behavior to another may increase his willingness to explore this area.

Although there is no known longitudinal study confirming clinical observation, it appears that some juveniles who later commit rape or sexual assault behaviors have previously engaged in voyeurism, frottage, obscene telephone calls, or breaking and entering. Similarly, clinical observation indicates that some juveniles have engaged in voyeuristic and exhibitionistic behaviors prior to the onset of child sexual abuse behaviors. At least two studies have confirmed that a prior history of less intrusive sexual abuse behaviors occurs in adolescence prior to adult convictions for more intrusive offense behaviors (Longo & Groth, 1983; Longo & McFadin; 1981).

There also appears to be a progression over time of the elements of the sexual abuse: the behaviors, the amount of power thrust, or the risks a perpetrator is willing to take. The clinician can ask detailed questions about what motivated the addition of various elements and what changed about their gratification experience.

For some youth a progression of behaviors may be evidence of becoming more confident about their ability to commit a sexually abusive behavior. For example, a youth's first child sexual abuse behavior may consist of touching the child's genital area over clothing. He may have been fearful of being caught, he may have needed to see the child's reaction, or it may have been as much as he dared to do. The next two incidents may be similar; in the third episode, he touches the child's bare genitals under clothing because he is less fearful and it is more exciting. For other youth, the progression of behaviors may be to maintain or increase the initial sense of gratification. Repetition of the same behaviors may become boring for these youth. Occasionally a youth may exhibit a less intrusive behavior for a period of time. For example, a youth may have exposed for thirteen months, then began molesting a sibling. Eventually he began to feel badly about being involved sexually with a sibling or fearful of being detected, so he quit the behavior and resumed exposing.

A progression of the amount of power thrust may include increased intrusiveness or increased coercion. For example, a youth who initially used a game of playing house to involve his victim in sexual behaviors may subsequently order the child to do the behavior or threaten to get the victim in trouble if he or she does not comply. Eventually abuse behaviors with the same child may only involve forcing the victim's head to his genital areas. Increased objectification of the victim often parallels the progression of power thrust.

Progression of the degree of risk a youth takes could represent an attempt to increase his sense of empowerment about being "slick" (a grandiose self-perception of being a good planner and being able to get away with anything he attempts), normalization of the behavior in his perception, increased distortions about the victim's willingness to be involved in the behavior, or increased super-optimism. For example, a youth who exposes might initially display his penis through an open garage door while potential victims walk by. During subsequent incidents, he may make a noise causing them to look his way. Eventually he may call a potential victim to his garage and then expose.

Progression of associated thoughts may involve increasingly sophisticated or aggressive fantasies of sexually abusive behavior. Although the youth may not yet exhibit a progression of behavior, the progression of thoughts indicates he is experiencing some need to progress behaviorally. A fruitful avenue during the interview is an exploration of what has kept the youth from acting on the thoughts, what precipitated the progression of thoughts, and what it would take to disinhibit him sufficiently to try some of the new behaviors he has been thinking about.

A more subtle form of progression involves changes in victim selection. A youth may initially peep any time he finds an opportunity, then begin to search for opportunities that involve females close to his age. Over time, the youth may begin to search for opportunities that involve younger children and eventually molest a child.

Level of Aggression

The sexually abusive youth can exhibit a range of aggression—emotional pressure, harassment, coercion, force, violence, cruelty, or sadism—in any type of sexual abuse behavior. Police reports and victim statements will likely provide details of alleged aggressive behaviors and the victim's perception of his or her response to the perpetrator. Information about the level of aggression is pertinent to assessing the youth's dangerousness. Knight and Prentky (1990) developed typologies for adult rapists and child molesters that included differentiation of various aggressive behaviors associated with sexually abusive behaviors. Although their research does not pertain to sexually abusive youth, the range of aggressive behaviors described is similar to that observed in some of these youth.

Some youth may use fear-inducing tactics or harassment with a victim or a potential victim, such as repeated obscene telephone calls to the same victim, then leaving a note indicating that the perpetrator knows where she lives. Some youth exhibit significant verbal or physical discharge of anger during an offense. They might make derogatory statements, or punch, threaten, beat, or wound the victim. Some youth carry a weapon in case it is needed to subdue or control the victim; others carry and show a weapon to induce a fearful reaction. Still others may use a weapon to inflict pain or mutilate the victim. Occasionally a youth will torture a victim or commit sadistic behaviors.

Issues to identify during the interview include the youth's affective state and thinking during the abuse; perception of self-gratification; expectations regarding victim response; the youth's perception of and attitude toward the victim; the nature of any aggressive behaviors occurring during the abuse; any intent to inflict pain, torture, humiliate, or degrade the victim; fear-inducing tactics; presence or use of a weapon; any discharge of anger during the offense; sadistic or mutilative behaviors; the degree of responsibility the youth assumes for aggression; attitudes toward people who are vulnerable; the youth's justification for aggressive behaviors; and the perception of and response to any expression of distress by the victim during the sexually abusive behavior. The clinician should identify whether aggressive behaviors were premeditated or reactive to the victim's resistance or failure to respond in the way the youth expected and then compare the extent of aggression involved in the abusive behavior to the level of force or intimidation required to gain victim compliance (based on victim statement descriptions compared to the youth's description). For example, the youth may hold a knife to the victim's throat, threaten to kill the victim, and then cut the victim's neck despite the victim's repeated statements of her willingness to cooperate and pleas to the youth not to hurt her.

Frequency of Abusive Behaviors

During the assessment, the youth should be questioned about the number of his sexually abusive behaviors, the number of repeated behaviors with the same victim, and the frequency of successful and attempted incidents. The clinician can explore the extent to which available opportunity affected frequency, evaluate the relationship of how often triggers for the youth's cycle contributed to frequency, and determine to what extent habitual reactions affected frequency. Information about frequency provides clues to the extent that a habituated pattern has developed, opportunistic or predatory style, the extent that stressors in the youth's life affect sexual abuse behavior patterns, and risk potential.

Ross and Loss (1991) suggest evaluating frequency relative to the amount of access the youth has to potential victims. A youth who sexually abuses young children will have more access if he has siblings, regularly babysits, or swims at the local pool daily than a youth who sees young children only when visiting relatives or attending church activities. A youth with significant amounts of free time may use that time to develop an opportunity to engage in an offense behavior.

Some youth engage in their sexually abusive behavior on a regular basis, weekly, monthly, or daily. Some youth may seize every opportunity that occurs to abuse sexually. Others commit their offenses episodically depending on victim access and opportunity. Still others exhibit a blitz pattern, refraining from committing a sexual abuse behavior for several weeks or months and then abusing daily for a period of time. Blitzing is reported more frequently by youth who commit exhibitionistic, voyeuristic, and rape behaviors.

Preferred Victim Type

The victims of sexually abusive youth who engage in repetitive abuse behaviors often exhibit similar characteristics, although the similarities may be difficult to identify. The youth develops a perception of the individual he chooses to abuse that has an intrinsic meaning. Developing an understanding of the youth's process and thoughts related to victim selection allows more comprehensive treatment and safety planning.

Initial questions relate to identifying characteristics that made a victim seem attractive, pleasing, or vulnerable to the youth—for example, physical aspects, personality traits, behaviors, styles of interacting with the youth or others, or developmental conditions (age, gender, intellectual capacity, disabilities, and so forth). It is common for victim selection to involve several characteristics. For example, the youth may choose to molest a prepubescent boy because his skin is smooth, he smells good, he is shy, he has an engaging smile, he seems needy, he appears to be naive and innocent, and he acts as if he admires and cares about the perpetrator.

Preferred victim type should be assessed in relationship to both victim access and opportunity structure. For example, if the youth tends to develop an opportunity to attract a specific victim type, he is likely to have a more predatory style. If a youth who has had rape fantasies is walking through a park and sees someone isolated and small enough for him to control, and then rapes that person, his style is more situational or opportunistic. Assessing the perceived degree of risk associated with the victim selected, versus other possible victims also provides significant information. A youth may overlook a sibling whom he knows is fearful of him and likely will not report the abuse in favor of one who may or may not tell because the increased risk is more exciting for him.

Arousal Assessment

The gratification a youth experiences when he is anticipating, setting up, committing, or recalling a sexually abusive behavior appears to reinforce the behavior.

Despite societal and individual taboos against sexual abuse, there is an impact on the perpetrator that is sufficiently positive that such prohibitions are outweighed and the behavior is often repeated. The impact appears to have several components, including sexual arousal, orgasm, excitement, thrill, an adrenalin rush, and self-enhancing perceptions. Each sexually abusive youth has a unique combination of the elements involved in the gratification experience associated with the sexually abusive behaviors.

Although tests are available that measure or estimate the degree of associated sexual arousal, there are no known measurements of the other aspects of the youth's internal response to committing a sexually abusive behavior. During the interview, the youth should describe what he experienced internally before, during, and when reminiscing about his sexually abusive behavior and describe any self-enhancing self-perceptions he had, even if they were brief or were overshadowed by later cognitions. Many youth report self-perceptions related to empowerment, skill, slickness, mastery, control, and capability. There may also be some perceptions of the victim's response or view of the perpetrator that seem positive to the youth.

The research related to sexual arousal involving adult sexual offenders has been extensive. Some studies have indicated that one predictor of recidivism is an indication that the perpetrator exhibits chronic sexual arousal associated with his preferred sexually abusive behavior (Quinsey, Rice, & Harris, 1995). Research with juveniles who sexually abuse (Becker, Hunter, Stein, & Kaplan, 1989; Becker, Stein, Kaplan, & Cunningham-Rathner, 1992; Hunter & Santos, 1990) demonstrates that some youth have significant arousal preferences associated with their sexually abusive behaviors, while others may exhibit preference for partner characteristics or behaviors that are different from the characteristics of their sexually abusive behaviors. Other youth may demonstrate less differential in their sexual arousal, that is, nearly equivalent arousal to both deviant and normative and abusive and nonabusive sexual behaviors and interactions. The congruence or disparity between what is most arousing for the youth and the characteristics of victim selection and offense behaviors has important implications in sorting out the process between fantasy and behavior. For example, the youth who is most aroused by thoughts of similar-aged female peers but has molested a small child may have had elaborate fantasies and cognitive processes that enable him to imagine the child as an acceptable and justifiable partner, whereas the process may be much more straightforward if the youth is most aroused by children. The implications of such information in relation to risk assessment and treatment interventions are clear. It is possible that arousal patterns may also be a factor in predicting reoffense potential for youth who sexually abuse, particularly those who are primarily attracted to younger children or violence. Programs need to assess arousal aspects in order to provide comprehensive treatment plans for youth who do exhibit offense-related arousal.

Measurements of arousal vary among programs that treat sexually abusive youth. Many clinicians rely on self-reports, asking the youth if he was aroused during the abuse, whether he had an erection, and if he ejaculated before, during, or after the behavior. Other programs use testing that prioritizes deviant and normal sexual interests and fantasies (such as card sort tests), or tests that involve self-reports of interest and arousal (Prentky & Bird, 1997). Recent research by Kaufman, Henning, Daleiden, and Hilliker (1995) indicates that their sexual fantasy questionnaire may have some validity. Still other programs use physiological assessment of sexual interests using the plethysmograph or the recently developed Abel Assessment (Abel & Warberg, 1996). Resources and access are often factors in choosing arousal assessment measures.

Known published research on plethysmograph assessment involves males, although it has been used with both male and female juveniles. There has been some concern relative to whether arousal assessment by means of plethysmograph will influence the development of a youth's sexual interests. There is no known research indicating the age that a child begins to exhibit discriminate arousal interests or at what age a youth has fully developed his sexual interests. The Association for the Treatment of Sexual Abusers (ATSA) currently suggests fourteen years as the minimum age for physiological assessment. In every instance, it is suggested that use of plethysmography be based on individual treatment needs and that clinicians should reach thoughtful decisions regarding why they do or do not recommend physiological assessment with the youth they treat.

When physiological assessments of arousal were initially used with sexually abusive youth in the 1980s, the protocol was to use both visual and auditory stimuli. But there were concerns about graphic visual stimuli being shown to juveniles, and as a result most practitioners have ceased using visual stimuli. The current acceptable protocol is to use a standardized set of auditory stimuli approved by the ATSA. The stimuli are similar to those developed by Becker and Kaplan (Hunter & Santos, 1990). The auditory stimuli consist of several specific, brief descriptions of various abusive and nonabusive sexual behaviors with a variety of partner criteria. Results appear to provide gender, behavior, and age interests. All agencies that use physiological assessment should have both a procedural protocol that provides for privacy, respect, and safety for the youth and an orientation protocol that fully informs the youth and his parents or guardians of the nature and purposes of the procedure and possible side effects. The consent of both the youth and his parents or guardians should be obtained prior to conducting the procedure. Results obtained must not be misused by professionals. The physiological assessment provides objective data suggestive of the youth's sexual interests;

it does not measure motivation to act on such interests, nor does it determine guilt or innocence regarding previous sexually abusive behaviors. It is suggested that any protocol follow the guidelines developed by the ATSA.

The Abel Assessment is designed to identify age- and gender-specific sexual interests. The testing protocol uses a set of slides that the youth views and a written test. The slides are not sexually explicit but are divided among various age, gender, and racial (Caucasian and African American) groups. The assessment is based on the interest exhibited when viewing material that is affect laden for that youth. Abel and Warberg (1996) report that initial research indicates that the results are as valid as plethysmograph results with adult subjects. Additional slides indirectly suggest types of sexually abusive behaviors; however, research is still in progress regarding the validity of this aspect of the test. The written test consists of questions typically used in an interview with a youth about sexual development, sexually abusive behavior interests, and cognitive distortions. The protocol is less intrusive than a physiological assessment and reportedly does not require parental consent; however, agencies wishing to use the protocol must be licensed by Abel, and the results are scored at his facility.

Intent and Motivation

Although sexually abusive behaviors involve an effort to control or dominate and serve to compensate for nonsexual issues, these aspects are not typically part of the youth's conscious motivation or intent when he engages in sexual abuse. In addition to the justifications a youth develops to support his abusive behavior, he is attempting to achieve some anticipated goal. The goals vary among sexually abusive youth.

During the interview, questions about anticipated victim reactions and what the youth hoped to achieve will help clarify what the youth believed was his motivation at the time—for example, he was bored and wanted to feel some excitement, sought to feel close to someone, thought the victim would enjoy the experience and want to become his girlfriend, was vindictive toward females, or wanted to learn about female bodies. Although the goals may be based on rationalizations, it is important to understand what the youth believed to be his intent in committing the sexual abuse behavior and how it relates to issues identified in the youth's life experience.

Honesty

There is a level of deception and self-protection exhibited by most sexually abusive youth who are referred for a specialized assessment. Some youth, depending on how safe they feel in their assessment or treatment situation, may disclose additional information about the extent and nature of their sexually abusive behavior history and their life experience. Others may never do so unless they are apprehended for another sexual abuse behavior. Lacking full information may result in treatment plans that fail to address all issues.

The use of polygraph examination with sexually abusive youth for assessment and monitoring purposes has increased recently. Polygraph examinations during the assessment process or the early months of treatment are designed to assist the youth with fully disclosing the range of his sexually abusive behavior history. Many clinicians believe some youth experience a beneficial relief when they have "come clean" or have given up all the secrecy regarding past abusive behaviors. The relief may contribute to improved self-perceptions. What is revealed may indicate additional treatment needs or suggest additional relapse-prevention components.

Monitoring polygraph examinations occur during treatment or aftercare and are designed to encourage accountability and monitor compliance with safety plans and structure developed to minimize reoffense. Examinations during treatment are designed to assist the youth with developing accountability and beginning to manage his life and activities in ways that help him avoid further abusive behaviors. Polygraph monitoring for a period of time following treatment is designed to help the youth be honest with himself regarding lapses and avoidance of high-risk situations. It is a tool to be used for the benefit of the youth in succeeding in his desire to change and become responsible. Polygraph examinations cannot be used for legal purposes such as proving guilt or innocence and should not be used against the youth to revoke probationary status or terminate him from a treatment facility.

Polygraphers with computerized polygraph systems often videotape the sessions and use software developed and tested at the Harvard Medical School to assess results (Amich & Jenks, 1994). The polygraph measures a variety of physiological responses (respiratory functioning, galvanic skin response, and cardiac functioning) that indicate that the individual is reacting differently to certain questions. The clinician can then challenge the youth to explore and explain the reactions to sensitive issues. Such challenges may jeopardize defenses that the youth has erected to preserve his sense of self, and the process can stir up issues that may increase triggers and subsequent risk while the work is in progress. It is widely believed that the youth's knowledge that he will be unable to hide dishonesty facilitates much of the beneficial disclosure of secrets prior to polygraph examinations; some youth, however, may be at increased risk for isolation, running away, or even suicidal ideation when they feel their secrets are about to be exposed.

Programs that wish to use polygraph examinations should ensure that the maximum benefits are derived and the process is helpful to the youth. An orientation and consent protocol should be developed and presented to the youth and his parents or guardians prior to the examination. It is helpful to meet with district attorneys, social services, and probation or diversion supervisors to orient them to the purpose and structure of the examinations. Many communities work together to adjust policies that will avoid prosecution for newly disclosed sexually abusive behaviors (that are similar to the referring behavior) if the youth success-fully completes treatment and legal or agency supervision. Specific questionnaires should be developed for each type of examination completed and reviewed with the youth prior to his examination. Often this process will result in increased dis-closure prior to the actual examination. It is helpful to assist the youth with pro-cessing fears, concerns, and grief that may arise as he completes this process, as well as new information that is disclosed.

Polygraphers selected should comply with the established standards, practice, and ethics of the American Polygraph Association and should be thoroughly trained in issues relevant to juvenile sexually abusive behaviors. There should be clear agreement between the polygrapher and the program about what informa-tion is requested and what the preexamination will include, and all questions de-veloped should be able to be answered clearly with yes or no.

Risk Factors and Sexual Abuse Behavior Characteristics

A risk factor is an internal thought or feeling or an external set of circumstances that increases the likelihood that a sexually abusive behavior may occur. (Internal risk factors are addressed in the next section.) A review of all known offenses of the sexually abusive youth should look for similar situations of victim access and opportunity for the sexual abuse behavior. Such situations should be addressed when suggesting safety plans and supervision of the youth in the assessment re-port and with the youth's parents, guardians, or caregivers.

Offense characteristics are the general style and quality of the sexually abusive behaviors committed by the youth, as well as particular elements unique to the individual. Evaluating the whole range of the youth's behaviors assists the clini-cian in identifying the least restrictive setting that can be recommended for treat-ment in order to maximize victim and community protection.

Developmental-Contextual Assessment

Developing an understanding of how the youth functions as a whole person is crucial to devising a treatment plan that encompasses all pertinent factors, ad-dressing both offense-specific treatment needs and the youth's capacity to live a fulfilling life while managing sexually abusive behaviors. The context of the youth's life in which the sexual abuse occurred affects the clinician's assessment of offense patterns, the type and extent of treatment needs, and the development of initial relapse prevention strategies.

The developmental-contextual assessment of the youth seeks to identify the following elements:

- The stressors or triggers the youth is attempting to cope with through the compensatory process, including the ability to cope with stress and anxiety
- Family structure, dysfunctions, issues, norms, and strengths
- The ability to form and maintain relationships, including style of interacting with peers, adults, and authority figures
- Developmental history, including the youth's capacity for intimacy, attachment issues, and the quality of caretaking provided during early childhood
- Social competencies, including his ability to get his needs met in an assertive manner
- Trauma history
- Nondeviant sexual history, including dating skills, gender identity, and self-perception of sexual functioning
- Temperament
- Self-concept, including self-perceptions and ego strength
- Medical history, including any concurrent psychiatric disorders, character pathology, or medical disorders
- Cultural, ethnic, and environmental issues
- Capacity for empathy
- Locus-of-control issues
- Previous treatment history
- Substance abuse history
- Depression, grief, and suicide ideation
- Worldview and perspective, including extent of misattribution regarding others' behaviors or motives
- Intellectual capacities, including learning abilities or deficits
- The quality of his expression and management of anger and conflict

There are several assessment tools that can assist in evaluating many of the areas of concern (Prentky & Bird, 1997).

Coping Ability

Identifying what is stressful to the youth, how the stressor is perceived, the youth's affective and cognitive reactions, and the style of managing his reactions contributes to an understanding of what triggers the youth's sexual abuse cycle, unresolved issues that need to be addressed in treatment, and internal risk factors. As the youth is questioned about what he was experiencing prior to each abuse incident, an identifiable cluster of issues may begin to emerge. The pattern of issues will provide clues about the youth's self-perception and core issues or traumatic and discomforting experiences that continue to have a negative impact on his daily functioning and worldview. Issues that repeatedly trigger the youth's cycle may be indicative of competency deficits, psychiatric disorders, or internal conflicts and can be addressed in treatment to increase the youth's capacity to cope in a healthier, nonabusive manner.

Previous chapters have identified several factors that affect the youth's development, environmental experiences, perceptions, and level of functioning. Questioning should relate to these factors. The clinician needs to maintain an awareness that problematic issues are painful for the youth to describe and that the initial phases of the cycle have helped him attempt to avoid or defend against the feelings and thoughts associated with the issues. A youth is unlikely to simply say he felt distant from his father or was neglected during his childhood. More likely the youth will describe anger with his father or exhibit some sensitivity to situations where he believes that his needs are not being considered.

During the assessment interview, the clinician can question the youth about what he was experiencing immediately prior to each sexual abuse behavior and for the preceding three to six months. If the youth denies any problems during that period, indirect questions about relationships with others or incidents that may have provoked victim stance thinking or negative self-perceptions may elicit responses indicating problematic areas. Information pertaining to issues may be obtained throughout the assessment as the youth's adjustment to school, interactions with others, and family history are explored. Some issues will not be identified until a youth has progressed in treatment. Youth who are unable to identify any event that triggers their cycle may be exhibiting denial of painful issues or a habituated offense pattern that is symptomatic of a chronic defensive strategy; it may be helpful to ask about life experiences prior to the initial sexual abuse behaviors rather than the more recent behaviors.

Keeping in mind that the cycle represents a compensatory, power-based style of coping, the youth can be questioned about various ways he might address a specific problem. The intent is to develop an understanding of the youth's range of coping strategies, problem-solving abilities, or the extent to which he relies on power-based coping strategies. If the youth consistently indicates his coping style is "to get even," "pay them back," or some type of one-upmanship, the clinician can ask several questions about other ways the youth can think of to handle the situation. If the only affective response described is anger, questions about other feelings underlying anger, even to the point of describing what another individual might feel, can help assess the youth's awareness of the range of his affective reactions. So can questions about how anxiety is experienced, when the youth feels anxious, and how he tends to handle anxiety, as well as other emotions that typically elicit anxiety (such as sadness, loss, fear, grief, or helplessness).

It is helpful to inform the youth, his parents, and other professionals working with the youth that the issues identified are not an excuse for or necessarily causal to the sexual abuse, but they may have contributed to the youth's development and be related to current functioning.

Family

Assessing the youth's family is accomplished by developing an understanding of how family factors influenced the youth's development, the family's potential to be protective or threatening, and identification of treatment needs. The family has a profound impact on the youth's development, which can include positive and negative aspects (see Chapters Five and Eight). If it becomes apparent that the family has supported the development of dysfunctional coping or beliefs or sexually abusive behaviors, or has exposed the youth to a life experience that is traumatic or models dysfunction, the family unit will need assistance with identifying, resolving, and correcting these issues (see Chapter Eighteen). It is likely that assessment of family issues will continue throughout the youth's involvement in treatment.

Although various combinations of family members may be interviewed together for different aspects of the assessment, it is helpful to meet with the entire family at least once to observe their interactions and evaluate the responses of each family member. Efforts should be directed toward gaining an understanding of a number of elements:

- Family roles and structure
- Quality and style of interactions
- How various affective reactions are expressed
- How caretaking, nurturing, authority, and discipline are conveyed
- The developmental history of the family
- How the family interacts with the community
- The quality and style of communication among family members
- Styles of coping with conflict
- Family issues and how individual family members address them
- Apparent strengths and apparent deficits
- The family's environment
- How responsibilities are allocated
- Family beliefs, values, and traditions

Family assessment also involves identifying ways that the family may have modeled or reinforced behaviors and beliefs that have supported the youth's development of compensatory patterns or sexually abusive behaviors. Exploring family norms about privacy, boundaries, sexuality, dissemination of sexual information, aggression, misuse of power, problem solving, perceptions, attitudes about others, and coping techniques will assist in this process. Identifying other victimizations (sexual and nonsexual) in the immediate and extended family, any degree of eroticization of family relationships, how adult sexuality is distinguished from child sexuality, if family members test attraction with each other, or the presence of any dysfunctional sexuality is helpful. Factors such as family instability or disruptiveness, poor models of aggression, or sexual deviancy within the family may be identified. Some research has suggested that such factors may be developmental antecedents to sexual aggression (Prentky et al., 1989).

The reaction of family members to the youth's sexually abusive behavior can help or hinder treatment progress. Identifying the family's initial response to the disclosure of the offense, the family's perceptions about the offense and the victim, whether they expect the youth to be accountable for his sexual abuse behavior, and how they view the youth in the context of his behavior provides an opportunity to evaluate what assistance family members need to help them appropriately support their child in treatment.

Because family members may be responsible for supervising the youth at some point during treatment or aftercare, evaluation of their ability to be sensitive to community safety and supporting the youth with relapse-prevention strategies is important. Questions that identify any parental minimization of the behavior or attribution of responsibility to the victim, ability to accept the potential of reoffense despite the youth's promises to avoid future behaviors, attitude about potential risk to siblings or other children, current style of providing supervision and protection, and parenting capabilities help provide useful information.

Relationships

Most sexually abusive youth exhibit deficits in building or maintaining relationships and limited abilities to be intimate with others. Research by Gilgun (1988) suggested that the experience of loneliness and lack of a confidant may be significant in the development of sexually abusive behaviors. Ward, Hudson, Marshall, and Siegert (1995) have also addressed the issue of relationships as it relates to the internal working model of relationships, which is the product of the attachment process. Many clinicians have identified social isolation and poor relationship skills as characteristic of sexually abusive youth. Clinical observation indicates that dysfunctional peer and family relationships can contribute to a higher risk for reoffense during or after treatment. Research by Murray (1996) suggested that the extent of a father's involvement in his son's treatment and the quality of their relationship affect the youth's success or failure in managing abuse behaviors. Constructive relationships can provide support, validation, and enjoyment to the youth.

During the assessment process, the clinician should evaluate how the youth relates to the interviewer in various situations and attempt to identify the age range and gender of peers the youth associates with. If friends tend to be younger, the youth may have some difficulty with social competencies involved in developing age-appropriate relationships or some perceptions that decrease his willingness to risk involvement with age-appropriate peers, or he may be seeking offense opportunities. Asking the youth to describe his best friend, the quality of their relationship, what they talk about, and their activities can help to identify the youth's capacity for interpersonal closeness and whether he is able to confide in a friend sufficiently to share problems and painful emotions. Youth who tend to have superficial relationships or relate to friends in a power-based manner tend to distance others and experience isolation, alienation, or rejection. The conversation can explore whether the youth has a variety of friends or tends to be somewhat isolated, how long he has maintained friendships, if he has ever lost a friend and what caused that, what his cognitive and affective reactions were to that loss, whether he has any gang affiliation, how he expresses anger toward friends, what activities are fun for him to do with friends, what he believes he offers to friends, how he would know a friend needed help, and how he would help that friend. Maintain awareness that the youth may have no friends at all and may fabricate information.

Identifying the quality of the youth's interactions with adults and authority figures is important. Many youths who exhibit delinquent behaviors do not trust adults based on previous traumatic or rejecting experiences; others see adults as people to manipulate, exploit, or deceive. The therapist can explore how the youth perceives criticism, correction, support, or information that adults offer. Some youth may exhibit misattributions regarding the motivations of adults and defend against expected harm, embarrassment, or control. The therapist can ask what adults the youth feels he can confide in, what type of adult he respects, and what he feels adults can offer him. The interviewer can question his reactions to authority figures, how he behaves and what he thinks when he gets in trouble with a teacher or a coach, or what he thinks about rules.

The youth's relationship with each family member needs exploration. It is helpful to ask the youth three things he likes, dislikes, would change, and would keep about each family member. Answers tend to provide clues about relationship issues that can then be explored in more depth. The youth can be asked to describe his most satisfying and most traumatic memories of interactions with each family member. The exploration can seek to determine the extent the youth discounts or heeds advice or support from each family member. Because many sexually abusive boys perceive their fathers as distant, weak, emotionally unavailable, or difficult to please, how he perceives his father and their relationship is important. The evaluation can examine how close he feels, how he manipulates, and whether he feels supported or accepted in relationship to each parental figure and assess the youth's reactions to parental authority or discipline and how he manages anger, disagreement, or conflict with each parent. (Chapters Eight and Eighteen in this book explore additional family dynamics and treatment issues.)

Developmental History

Understanding how the youth's development contributed to his current belief system, his capacity for attachment and intimacy, his coping style, his competency to relate to others effectively, and the life experiences to which he was exposed is critical in identifying the issues that underlie the sexually abusive behaviors and developing effective treatment approaches. Inquiring about parental experiences at the time the youth was born and during infancy, maternal-child interactions during the first year, and what was frustrating for the parents at that time may provide information about the youth's bonding experience and the quality of interaction between the youth and his caretakers. This understanding may help identify early attachment and nurturing experiences. Youth who have experienced healthy attachments with caretakers during infancy and young childhood tend to be more secure, comfortable relating to others, trusting, able to use a range of social competencies, and able to cope with stress. Clinical observation indicates that most sexually abusive youth tend to have significant deficits in each of these areas. Steele (1987) and Marshall, Hudson, and Hodkinson (1993) suggest a causal relationship between poor attachment experiences and factors relevant to the development of sexually abusive behaviors.

Exploring the quality of the home environment, the experiences during the youth's childhood, the quality of parenting and type of supervision the youth experienced, as well as the youth's maturation, provides further information about the influences that have shaped the youth's worldview and his behaviors. Questions could focus on assessing the youth's adjustment to new situations, functioning in the family and at school, disciplinary tactics in the home, parental views about child rearing, the youth's life experience, and family characteristics. Attention should also be given to any indications of arrested development, which may be a clue in identifying victimization or trauma and the onset of the compensatory pattern. Identifying the origin of the dysfunctional cycle and the earliest manifestations of the sexualization of that pattern may be important because preoccupation with such behaviors may interrupt or slow development for the youth.

Temperament

Temperament traits are usually rather stable and continuous across the life span, although the influence of temperamental qualities may be moderated or exacerbated by factors in the environment, relationships, and experiences. Temperament traits are usually apparent from birth and may be gleaned from the reports of parents regarding how the infant interacted with the environment and reacted to care, change, limits, and schedules early in life. Identifying difficult temperament traits is important in order to distinguish them from defenses and resistance in the therapeutic process (Ryan, 1995).

Parents can supply information about how the youth reacted to changes as an infant and toddler, how easy it was to redirect his attention or behavior, how the infant was able to calm himself, and overall disposition. The youth can explain his perceptions of himself in comparison to others and how such qualities or characteristics have affected his relationships and functioning.

Social Competencies

Most sexually abusive youth exhibit a paucity of effective social competencies. If a youth is unable to manage various problems or relate to others effectively, he is more likely to feel helpless or inadequate and to rely on a compensatory pattern involving misuse of power to cope with his feelings and self-perceptions. Strayhorn (1988) and Whitaker (1987) suggest that a variety of social competencies are critical to successful and adaptive functioning. Youth who exhibit a habituated abuse behavior pattern, a concurrent diagnosis of conduct disorder, or a history of other delinquent or abusive behaviors tend to rely on power-based social competencies almost exclusively. Youth who lack relationship-building skills tend to feel insecure about developing friendships or being close to others, resulting in isolation and increased potential for abusive behaviors.

There are a number of areas of concern regarding social competency:

- Conflict resolution
- Assertiveness
- Relating with others in a win-win manner
- Communication
- Social interaction
- Negotiation

- Initiating interactions
- Managing criticism or rejection
- Refusal to involve oneself in negative behaviors
- Disagreement
- Accepting and giving compliments
- Problem solving
- Listening
- Compromise
- Asking for or offering help
- Self-discipline
- Stress management
- Anger management
- Perspective taking
- Decision making
- Leisure management
- Delayed gratification
- Managing frustration
- Tolerance
- Empathy

Although many youth may initially appear to have varied social competencies, closer examination indicates the youth may be attempting to manipulate how he is perceived and his competencies are actually power based. At times, questions related to potential experiences or requesting the youth to provide examples of ways he has managed certain issues elicit information that allows a more accurate assessment of the youth's range of social competencies than does asking the youth if he knows how to do a specific skill. As an example, the youth might be asked how he would let someone know he did not like a particular behavior, how he might verify an assumption that he has about why someone did something, or how he would decide to resolve a disagreement. Efforts should be made to identify areas of strength as well as deficits.

Trauma History

Traumatic experiences may have a significant impact on the youth's current functioning or the development of sensitivities that may trigger the sexual abuse cycle. When this area is considered in the context of the youth's developmental history and family characteristics, the therapist can begin to identify deficits arising from disruption of the child's cognitive, affective, social, and adaptive development. Identified deficits and issues may suggest specific treatment needs. For example, a child who was maltreated within the family may have difficulty with trust, betrayal issues, intimacy, and social competencies. A youth exposed to a natural disaster or chronic community violence may have difficulty feeling safe, even outside of relationships.

A range of overt or covert experiences may be traumatic or perceived as traumatic by the youth. Information should be sought about maltreatment, including victimization (sexual, physical, or emotional), neglect, or abandonment. Other issues include significant loss (by death, family separation, or moving), witnessing violence, exposure to dysfunctional or abusive interactions in the home, a sexualized environment, hospitalization or extended illness, placement out of the home, or an unsafe environment. The assessment interview can explore how traumatic experiences have affected the youth over time and the extent of the impact on the youth's current functioning. Recurring memories, nightmares, startle responses, and a sense of threat or dread may be signs of trauma effects.

Sexual History

The youth has likely had some nondeviant sexual experience prior to or during the time he was engaged in sexually abusive behaviors. In treatment it is important to assist the youth with developing or strengthening healthy sexuality. Gaining an understanding of the youth's nondeviant sexual history assists in assessing social competency development, self-perceptions, and additional treatment needs.

The clinician should ask the youth about:

- Sexual experience
- Sexual development
- Gender identity
- Gender orientation
- Capacity for sexual intimacy
- Dating experience
- Apprehension or confidence related to sexual functioning
- Fetishes
- Sexual stereotypes
- Conditions that affect sexual functioning
- Genital injuries or abnormalities
- Self-perceptions of sexual functioning
- Use of or exposure to pornography
- Sexual knowledge

Sexual history questionnaires completed prior to the interview can assist in identifying specific areas to explore further. The clinician's comfort with discussing these subjects may contribute to the youth's ability to share this sort of information.

Self-Concept

The youth's self-perception, ego strength, and self-concept underlie the sexually abusive behavior history, potential to prevent further behaviors, and the capacity to develop healthy functioning. Self-concept is influenced by the youth's life experience and the beliefs developed based on experience (see Chapters Three, Five, and Seven). Because the sexually abusive behavior apparently occurs partly in response to how the youth views himself, it is important to understand issues related to the youth's self-concept. In addition to conducting specific testing, the interviewer could explore how the youth describes himself, self-perceptions, and self-statements.

Cultural Issues

Many youth are influenced by cultural, ethnic, or environmental issues. Youth who are raised in an urban area may develop different views of the world from someone raised in a rural area. Youth who are raised in an inner city may develop different norms and values about violence or their potential for the future from those raised in a suburban area. Youth of color may be subjected to overt or covert racism or prejudice, which may influence their levels of trust, expectations, or self-perceptions. It is important to develop an understanding of the youth's behavior within the sociocultural context in which it occurs (McIntyre, 1993).

Behaviors may be interpreted differently by different cultures and ethnic groups. Sexual practices or norms may vary among cultures or ethnic groups. What may be perceived as intimidating by one group may be viewed as a normal aspect of flirting or seduction by another group. It is important during the interview to question the meaning of various behaviors to the youth, to identify cultural or ethnic views, and to assess the impact of the environmental situation. Youth of varying ethnicity may have specific beliefs or practices that need to be considered when developing treatment recommendations.

Minority youth tend to be overrepresented in institutional and detention settings. This may be due in part to professionals' failure to explore fully the meanings of behaviors and attitudes to the youth or developing interpretations without considering the sociocultural context. Clinicians need to be aware of their own biases in interpreting behaviors and attitudes.

Capacity for Empathy

The development of the ability to be empathic may be one of the important changes that need to occur for the youth to develop an ability to prevent future abusive behaviors (see Chapter Seven). It is important to discriminate between empathy, based on an assumption of difference, and sympathy, based on an assumption of sameness or likeness (Bennett, 1988). Empathy means being aware of others' cues in order to imagine how they are feeling; sympathy means assuming another person would experience the same feelings as oneself in the same situation. Although it is unlikely the sexually abusive youth is being empathic to the victim at the time of the initial assessment, identifying the youth's ability to empathize in other situations assists in understanding his capacities or deficits in this area.

A variety of psychological measures test perspective taking and sympathetic responses. To date, measurement of one's ability to see and accurately interpret the cues of others relies primarily on clinical observations. The inquiry into empathic capacity should explore the youth's awareness of internal and external cues associated with his own needs and emotions, as well as his ability to describe the range of cues that let him know how other persons feel. The clinician might present situations and ask him what he thinks the participants would feel, or ask the youth to describe a situation when he was able to identify a friend's emotions.

Specific victim-empathy assessment focuses on the youth's awareness of signs that were present at the time of the offense indicative of the harm he was causing or the victim's distress. The clinician can ask the youth what he thinks the victim was experiencing, and then challenge him to describe the signs that support his beliefs.

Other Issues

Locus of control refers to the extent to which a youth has developed internal controls or responds to external controls and prohibitions to make decisions about behaviors. In some respects, it indicates superego development or the development of a conscience. Clues to the youth's locus of control may be reflected in the accuracy and completeness of attributions of responsibility related to the abusive behavior, but it is helpful to examine other areas as well. Questions that explore why a youth might choose to avoid a certain behavior or how he decides whether something is wrong may provide further information about whether the youth relies on internal or external influences to guide his decisions and behaviors. Locus of control is measured by many psychological tests.

Previous treatment history provides information relative to the youth's amenability to treatment and risk potential. Analysis of the nature of previous treatment as well as the youth's response to it may be identified through review of summaries by prior treatment providers and by exploring with the youth what was helpful and what was discounted or resisted. If the youth has reoffended after participating in treatment for sexually abusive behaviors, the clinician can explore what he believes contributed to this, what tools or knowledge he did not use or felt did not pertain to his situation, and whether he believes additional treatment will change his risk. The clinician can observe for indications of any previously undiagnosed psychiatric disorder.

Screening the youth for *substance use or abuse history* may assist the clinician in identifying whether use of drugs or alcohol was part of the abusive behaviors, reflects a tendency to self-medicate to manage feelings or physiological experiences, is part of social interaction, expresses rebellion or disregard for authority, or whether the youth is chemically dependent. The results may be important to monitoring, placement, and treatment recommendations.

Some youth may exhibit *depression, suicide ideation, or grief* during the initial assessment related to fear of consequences, shame, loss of control, or a concurrent psychiatric disorder. If the youth has been placed out of home or incarcerated recently, the risk of suicide gestures or attempts may be higher. Some degree of depressive symptoms may be expected in response to the youth's situation, but the history and chronicity of such symptoms should be explored. Some youth may exhibit grief related to the loss of being able to continue to engage in sexually abusive behaviors. Screening should relate to current functioning and ideation as well as past history and family history.

Screening to identify the youth's *intellectual capacities* and any learning disabilities assists in identifying the type of treatment, monitoring, and individualized interventions will be most beneficial to the youth. For example, youth with lower functioning may require a more concrete treatment style, and youth who have an auditory perception deficit might require more visual or written information.

Assessing *anger management* includes identifying the quality of the youth's expressions of anger, anger management strategies, and how the youth resolves issues that anger him. The intent is to identify any incidents of discharge of anger or rage, what the youth views as appropriate expression of anger, whether there is any modulation of anger, how the youth cools himself down, the extent of persistent angry affect, and retaliatory aspects versus resolution aspects. Anger associated with manic mood swings may be indicative of a bipolar disorder and signal the need for psychiatric assessment.

Assessment of Concurrent Psychiatric Disorders

Many sexually abusive youth exhibit concurrent diseases or psychiatric disorders that can have an impact on the extent to which a youth is able to benefit from treatment, the ability to use tools to manage abusive behaviors, interpersonal interactions, and self-concept. Some conditions may have had an impact on the youth's actual execution of abusive behaviors. If these conditions are not recognized and addressed in treatment, the potential for positive change may be impaired.

Some diseases, such as diabetes or epilepsy, may have a negative impact on a youth's self-perception. Some diseases may affect behavior and affective reactions. For example, youth who have hypoglycemia or thyroid disorders may exhibit increased irritability, impulsivity, lethargy, low frustration tolerance, and aggressive outbursts. Youth who have asthma or cardiac conditions may feel different because they have less endurance or energy than their peers have or activity restrictions. Sexually transmitted diseases may be present and may have implications for the victim or for management of the sexually abusive youth. Diagnoses of neurological disorders and fetal alcohol syndrome are not unusual in this population, and a high percentage of youth have chemical dependency diagnoses or report extensive substance abuse (Ryan, Miyoshi, Metzner, Krugman, & Fryer, 1996).

Many sexually abusive youth who have failed in some treatment settings or appeared to have a poor prognosis have subsequently been found to have a concurrent psychiatric disorder (Ryan, 1993). Posttraumatic stress disorder may be present in youth who have been victimized or traumatized. This disorder has significant physiological effects due to the extent of anxiety experienced, as well as psychological symptoms (van der Kolk, 1994). Attention deficit hyperactive disorder is overrepresented in this population (Ryan et al., 1996) and affects the youth's ability to concentrate and control impulses. Some youth exhibit mood disorders, particularly dysthymia (Dailey, 1996). These youth may appear untreatable and exhibit sleep problems, self-injurious behaviors, hypomanic episodes, irritability, physiological complaints, negative self-perceptions, and difficulty modulating anger. When appropriately medicated, these youth often become more amenable to treatment and able to succeed in work that they could not otherwise tolerate. Anxiety disorders and depressive disorders are also common. Dailey (1996) has identified several youth in residential treatment who suffer from obsessive-compulsive disorders that appear to drive their paraphilic behaviors. In addition to repetitive behaviors and thoughts, these youths' sexually abusive fantasies are so pervasive that they interfere with other activities and may be associated with compulsive masturbation. Dailey reports a decrease in excessive fantasies and sadistic aspects of those fantasies when the youth are appropriately medicated. Some youth also exhibit bipolar depression, paraphilias, Tourette's syndrome, eating disorders, dissociative disorders, or conduct disorder diagnoses. Screening for current and past suicide ideation and identifying any history of suicide gestures or attempts is also imperative.

Identification of concurrent psychiatric disorders may have implications in assessment relevant to placements, treatment needs, level of risk, and prognosis. It is also critical in understanding the phenomenology of the youth and appreciating how such disorders may have increased the risks associated with the compensatory cycle. Such disorders do not, however, explain or minimize the meaning of the sexually abusive history. The goal is to help the youth succeed in treatment and improve future functioning, not to excuse behaviors.

Analysis of Information

The information gathered during the assessment process is used to develop a comprehensive treatment plan that addresses all identified needs of the youth and considers community safety. The recommendations consider offense-specific treatment and family, psychological and psychiatric, developmental, and safety needs. Each area is considered equally. The concern is to provide safety and treat the youth in a way that preserves the family (if appropriate) and provides a treatment structure that the youth can benefit from. The goal is for the youth to develop sufficiently healthy, adaptive, prosocial functioning so that he can internally manage life's stresses and avoid sexually abusive behaviors.

Community Safety Needs

Community safety needs involve monitoring or supervising the youth in a way that protects potential and known victims. Limiting access to potential opportunities is protective of the youth as well. Determining the extent of supervision a youth requires to prevent further behaviors involves analysis of the youth's psychological makeup, internal and external risk factors and assets, and sexually abusive behavior patterns to determine the potential level of risk for further abusive behaviors. Identification of the setting and type of treatment required is also a factor.

Predicting potential risk for reoffense is a difficult process. Many professionals have used clinical experience, intuition, and the risk checklists developed in the early 1980s to assist in identifying risk potential, but no tools are research based. Quinsey, Rice, and Harris (1995) have suggested the development of an actuarial model of predicting reoffense that considers static (unchangeable or historical) and dynamic (variable or current) predictors. Their initial analysis of follow-up studies of adult sexual offenders is promising. Some current research studies are attempting to validate risk assessments for sexually abusive youth.

At this time, however, the best predictor is past behavior; thus it must be assumed the youth is at risk to repeat the behavior. Research related to violent and criminal behavior with adults has demonstrated that individuals who have committed such behaviors are more likely to commit them again in the future. Although it is likely that some sexually abusive youth would not continue their behaviors (or not be caught for subsequent behaviors), it is not known at this time which youth will cease their behavior on their own. In an effort to protect potential victims and provide community safety, treatment plans and supervision that offer such protection by assuming the risk for repeated behaviors are suggested for all sexually abusive youth.

The risks and strengths of a number of factors must be evaluated in determining risk potential. For example, a youth who has committed repeated sexually abusive behaviors, attributes responsibility to the victims or others, exhibits deviant sexual arousal preferences, has used excessive force during the abuse behaviors, exhibits antisocial or obsessive features, has severe problems with impulse control, appears resistive to treatment, and whose family minimizes, reinforces, or denies the abusive behaviors would be considered a high risk to reoffend and would likely require intensive supervision during treatment. A youth who denies the sexual aspect of the behavior, exhibits a habituated behavior pattern, is socially isolated, is interested in treatment, and has a family history of sexualized and violent behaviors would also be considered high risk to reoffend and might require strict supervision during treatment. A youth whose family responded to the abuse by increasing supervision and protective measures, who acknowledges having engaged in two different types of sexually abusive behaviors, who has some close friends, is impulsive, appears amenable to treatment, and recently disclosed extrafamilial sexual victimization might be at moderate risk to reoffend and require moderate supervision during treatment. A youth who committed a sexually abusive behavior subsequent to a sexual education class, appears ashamed, assumes responsibility for the abusive behavior, exhibits empathy in most situations, has several close friends, whose family appears appropriately protective, is close to his parents, and is mildly resistive to treatment might be at low risk to reoffend and might require less intensive supervision during treatment.

Another aspect of risk potential involves identifying and developing plans to limit access to potential victims and opportunities. If the sexual abuse occurred within the family, the sexually abusive youth and the victim should be separated, at least during the initial phases of treatment for each. Even if the youth vows not to continue sexually abusive behaviors and the parents appear protective and capable of consistent eyes-on supervision, the power differential remains. Until issues related to the power differential are clarified and resolved, the victim will likely continue to be fearful and may experience continued emotional impacts if the victim and offender are not separated. If the assessment of the youth indicates a specific age preference, victim-aged children in the home may be at risk, and decisions will need to be made relative to thorough education of the parents and risk potential to those children.

The degree of and type of supervision required to monitor the youth's risk factors may occur in the youth's home, a relative's home, a foster home, a group home, a residential setting, a locked facility, or a secure residential setting.

Monitoring may be accomplished by placement in a secure setting, electronic monitoring, eyes-on supervision, supervision in certain situations, polygraph examinations, activity and curfew restrictions, frequent contact with probation or diversion supervisors, or a relapse-prevention team. If the youth will remain in the community, it is imperative that recommendations include specific education to the parents or guardians and caretakers about what sexually abusive behaviors entail and what various levels of supervision require.

If it is determined that a sexually abusive youth is appropriate for community-based placement or remains in the home, safety plans need to be suggested related to the type and extent of limitations that decrease victim access or opportunity potential. Restrictions might include avoiding locations that previously provided opportunities, avoiding unsupervised access to children, requiring that the youth be accompanied by someone familiar with his abusive behavior pattern when he attends certain activities, limiting driving privileges, or activity restrictions. Communication should be established between parents, supervising personnel, and treatment personnel to strengthen safety and supervision.

Recently several states have enacted statutes that require mandatory registration or mandatory reporting for community safety. Mandatory registration typically requires registration with police agencies, and mandatory reporting requires informing neighbors or organizations involved with potential victims of the youth's sexually abusive behavior history. It is suggested that decisions related to these issues make every effort to ensure that information is used to monitor and supervise rather than increase the youth's isolation or debasement.

Offense-Specific Treatment

Offense-specific treatment needs refer to identifying treatment requirements based on analysis of the youth's sexually abusive behavior patterns. It involves assessing treatment amenability and identifying the intensity and structure of treatment a youth needs to develop an adequate understanding of his sexually abusive behavior patterns and to develop sufficient awareness and skills to manage associated thoughts, feelings, and behaviors to prevent future abusive behaviors.

Clinicians have relied on clinical experience, research-based assessment tools, and typologies developed in the 1980s to analyze sexually abusive behavior patterns and develop treatment plans. Knight and Prentky (1993) have suggested applying the taxonomy they developed for adult sexual offenders to sexually abusive youth. They have demonstrated areas that may be applicable through statistical analysis of adult offenders who report a juvenile sexual abuse behavior history. As they continue their research, the results may assist in identifying more discriminate treatment needs.

The youth's amenability to treatment may be identified based on the degree of accountability versus denial related to the sexually abusive behavior, the extent to which the behavior patterns or associated cognitions are ingrained, concurrent psychiatric disorders, intellectual capacities, and the youth's perceptions about treatment.

The National Task Force on Juvenile Sexual Offending (1988, 1993) identified several components of offense-specific treatment that are applicable to each sexually abusive youth and components that are applicable to some sexually abusive youth, depending on specific treatment needs. In general, youth who exhibit high-risk potential; a history of other delinquent or nonsexual aggressive behaviors; significant disruption, deprivation, or trauma in their development; habituated sexually abusive behavior patterns; or disabling concurrent psychiatric disorders will likely require more intensive and more comprehensive treatment. Youth who exhibit low-risk potential, have a positive developmental history, and appear fairly well adjusted may not require such intensive treatment. Youth who exhibit different assets and deficiencies may require more emphasis in one area or another. For example, a youth whose sexually abusive behaviors have unique characteristics (such as fetishes or sadistic aspects) may require additional treatment approaches. A youth who exhibits a set of negative self-perceptions that appear ingrained may need extra work with cognitive restructuring, self-esteem, and victimization treatment. A youth who is developmentally disabled may need a more concrete and experiential approach. As the field of treating sexually abusive youth continues to evolve, more discriminate treatment objectives need to be identified and recommended.

It is likely that treatment intensity will vary according to the setting. For example, a residential setting might offer milieu therapy or daily group sessions, and an outpatient treatment program for a youth living in the community may offer services that range from day treatment to one group session per week.

Psychological and Psychiatric Needs

Psychological and psychiatric needs are related to any identified concurrent psychiatric disorder and the indicated treatment, specific symptomatology, deficits identified in the youth's developmental-conceptual assessment, and basic needs. Indicated treatment might include specialized treatment approaches, individual therapy, or medication. Adjunct treatment may occur concurrent to offense-specific treatment, and some may need to occur prior to offense-specific treatment for the youth to receive maximum benefit. For example, if the youth exhibits a severe posttraumatic stress disorder, initial work may need to occur before a youth is capable of addressing sexually abusive behavior patterns, or if a youth exhibits active psychotic symptoms, medication and stabilization may need to occur prior to offense-specific treatment.

Some facilities that treat sexually abusive youth refuse youth who have pharmacological needs (often believing that the youth will be less able to learn to manage his abusive behavior or has been medicated only for manageability). If a specific disorder is identified (such as dysthymia) and it is unlikely the youth will benefit from treatment without receiving appropriate medication, it would seem unethical not to afford the youth the best opportunity to be successful in treatment.

Family Needs

Family needs include educational needs, intervention related to understanding the scope of the youth's sexually abusive behavior, and specific treatment needs for any identified dysfunction or deficit.

Each parent or guardian needs assistance with understanding the nature and scope of sexually abusive behavior in order to provide adequate supervision of and support to their child. Part of the family's healing will include communication about their child's sexually abusive behavior. If the abuse occurred within the family, victim and perpetrator sessions should also be recommended.

Family deficits, dysfunctions, or issues that may have contributed to the youth's sexually abusive behaviors that were identified during the assessment will require specific treatment intervention (see Chapter Eighteen).

Conclusion

Data obtained from the interviews, testing results, and collateral material are the basis of the recommendations that are developed and are typically presented in a written report that describes data obtained, interpretations, and recommendations. Comprehensive recommendations cover a number of areas:

- Needs relevant to the sexually abusive behavior
- Treatment setting, intensity, and type
- Risk potential
- Risk factors and safety plans
- Intensity and nature of supervision
- Placement considerations
- Adjunct treatment and concurrent disorders
- The family's treatment and educational needs
- The victim's protection, resolution, and treatment needs

It is helpful to avoid jargon that individuals who do not typically work with sexually abusive youth may misinterpret, as well as some educational information supporting conclusions and opinions. It is also important to indicate that assessment is an ongoing process that will need to continue throughout treatment and during aftercare.

References

Abbot, B. (1984). *Guidelines for assessment of adolescent sexual offenders and their families.* San Jose, CA: Institute for the Community as Extended Family.

Abel, G., & Warberg, B. (1996). *Assessing juvenile sex offenders with the new Abel assessment.* Paper presented at the Twelfth Annual Conference of the National Adolescent Perpetrator Network, Minneapolis.

Amich, D., & Jenks, J. (1994). *Current state of the art polygraph examinations for sexual offenders.* Paper presented to RSA, Inc., Lakewood, CO.

Becker, J., Cunningham-Rathner, J., & Kaplan, M. (1986). Adolescent sexual offenders: Demographics, criminal, and sexual histories and recommendations for reducing future offenses. *Journal of Interpersonal Violence, 1,* 431–443.

Becker, J., Hunter, J., Stein, R., & Kaplan, M. (1989). Factors associated with erection in adolescent sex offenders. *Journal of Psychopathology and Behavioral Assessment, 11*(4).

Becker, J., & Kaplan, M. (1988). The assessment of sexual offenders. *Advances in Behavioral Assessment of Children and Families, 4,* 97–118.

Becker, J., Stein, R., Kaplan, M., & Cunningham-Rathner, J. (1992). Erection response characteristics of adolescent sex offenders. *Annals of Sex Research, 5,* 81–86.

Bengis, S. (1986). *A comprehensive service delivery system with a continuum of care for adolescent sexual offenders.* Orwell, VT: Safer Society Press.

Bennett, M. (1988). Overcoming the golden rule: Sympathy and empathy. *Communication Yearbook, 3,* 408–422.

Cavanagh-Johnson, T. C. (1988). Child perpetrators: Children who molest children: Preliminary findings. *Child Abuse and Neglect: The International Journal, 12*(2), 219–229.

Dailey, L. (1996). *Adjunctive biological treatments with sexually abusive youth.* Paper presented at the Twelfth Annual Conference of the National Adolescent Perpetrator Network, Minneapolis.

Fehrenbach, P., Smith, W., Monastersky, C., & Deisher, R. (1986). Adolescent sexual offenders: Offenders and offense characteristics. *American Journal of Orthopsychiatry, 56,* 225–233.

Gilgun, J. (1988). *Factors which block the development of sexually abusive behavior in adults abused as children.* Paper presented at the National Conference on Male Victims and Offenders: Controversies in Treatment, Minneapolis.

Gray, A., & Wallace, R. (1992). *Adolescent sexual offender assessment packet.* Brandon, VT: Safer Society Press.

Groth, A., & Loredo, C. (1981). Juvenile sex offenders: Guidelines for assessment. *International Journal of Offender Therapy and Comparative Criminology, 25*(1), 31–39.

Hunter, J. (1996). *Understanding the impact of trauma on children: When victimization leads to victimizing.* Paper presented at the Eleventh International Congress on Child Abuse and Neglect, Dublin, Ireland.

Hunter, J., & Santos, D. (1990). Use of specialized cognitive-behavioral therapies in the treatment of adolescent sexual offenders. *Journal of Offender Therapy and Comparative Criminology, 34,* 239–248.

Johnson, T. C. (1995). *Treatment exercises for child abuse victims and children with sexual behavior problems.* Pasadena, CA: Author.

Kaufman, K., Henning, B., Daleiden, E., & Hilliker, D., (1995). *Assessing the sexual history and fantasies of adolescent sexual offenders.* Paper presented at the Fourth National Colloquium of the American Professional Society on the Abuse of Children, Chicago.

Kerr, M. (Ed.). (1986). *An executive summary: The Oregon Report on Juvenile Sexual Offenders.* Salem, OR: Avalon Associates, Children's Services Division.

Knight, R., & Prentky, R. (1990). Classifying sexual offenders. In W. Marshall, D. Laws, & H. Barbaree (Eds.), *The handbook of sexual assault: Issues, theories, and treatment of the offender* (pp. 27–52). New York: Plenum Press.

Knight, R., & Prentky, R. (1993). Exploring characteristics for classifying juvenile sex offenders. In H. Barbaree, W. Marshall, & S. Hudson (Eds.), *The juvenile sex offender* (pp. 45–83). New York: Guilford Press.

Law, S. (1987). [Clinical notes from client interviews.] Unpublished.

Longo, R., & Groth, A. (1983). Juvenile sexual offenses in the histories of adult rapists and child molesters. *International Journal of Offender Therapy and Comparative Criminology, 27,* 150–155.

Longo, R., & McFadin, B. (1981). Sexually inappropriate behavior: Development of the sexual offender. *Law and Order, 29,* 21–33.

Marshall, W., Hudson, S., & Hodkinson, S. (1993). The importance of attachment bonds in the development of juvenile sex offending. In H. Barbaree, W. Marshall, & S. Hudson (Eds.), *The juvenile sex offender.* New York: Guilford Press.

McIntyre, T. (1993). Reflections on the new definition for emotional and behavioral disorders of children and youth. *Behavioral Disorders, 18,* 148–160.

Murray, M. (1996). *An explorative study into the relationship between natural fathers and their sons in cases of adolescent sexual perpetrators.* Unpublished master's thesis, University of Ulster and Queen's University, Belfast, Ireland.

National Task Force on Juvenile Sexual Offending. (1988). Preliminary report. *Juvenile and Family Court Journal, 39*(2).

National Task Force on Juvenile Sexual Offending. (1993). The revised report. *Juvenile and Family Court Journal, 44*(4), 28.

O'Brien, M., (1994). *The PHASE manual: Assessment and treatment of adolescent sex offenders.* St. Paul, MN: Alpha PHASE.

O'Brien, M., & Bera, W. (1985). *The PHASE typology.* Minneapolis: Program for Healthy Adolescent Sexual Expression.

Phipps, A. (1996). *The Sex Offender Scale.* Paper presented at the Twelfth Annual Conference of the National Adolescent Perpetrator Network, Minneapolis.

Prentky, R., & Bird, S. (1997). *Assessing sexual abuse: A resource guide for practitioners.* Brandon, VT: Safer Society Press.

Prentky, R., Knight, R., Straus, H., Rokous, F. Cerce, G., & Sims-Knight, J. (1989). *Developmental antecedents of sexual aggression.* Paper presented at the Fourth National Adolescent Perpetrator Network Meeting, Keystone, CO.

Quinsey, V., Rice, M., & Harris, G. (1995). Actuarial prediction of sexual recidivism. *Journal of Interpersonal Violence, 10*(1), 85–105.

Ross , J., & Loss, P. (1987). *Assessment factors for adolescent sexual offenders.* New London, CT: Ross, Loss, & Associates.

Ross, J., & Loss, P. (1991). Assessment of the juvenile sex offender. In G. Ryan & S. Lane (Eds.), *Juvenile sexual offending* (pp. 199–251). San Francisco: New Lexington Press. *Ross and Loss 21 Factor Guide to Assessment* was featured in the first edition of *Juvenile Sexual Offending: Causes, Consequences, and Correction.* In the mid-1980s, Ross and Loss were active in providing training to many clinicians. We are grateful for their contributions to developing the field of assessment and treatment of juvenile sexual offenders. Their assessment materials can be obtained from Jonathan E. Ross, P.O. Box 428, Mt. Pleasant, SC 29465.

Ryan, G. (1989). Victim to victimizer: Rethinking victim treatment. *Journal of Interpersonal Violence, 4*(3), 325–341.

Ryan, G. (1993). *Concurrent psychiatric disorders.* Paper presented at the Ninth Annual Conference of the National Adolescent Perpetrator Network, Lake Tahoe, NV.

Ryan, G. (1995). *The difficult client: Temperament or resistance?* Paper presented at the Eleventh Annual Conference of the National Adolescent Perpetrator Network, St. Louis, MO.

Ryan, G., Miyoshi, T., Metzner, J., Krugman, R., & Fryer, G. (1996). Trends in a national sample of sexually abusive youth. *Journal of the American Academy of Child Adolescent Psychiatry, 35*(1), 17–25.

Smith, W., & Monastersky, C. (1986). Assessing juvenile sexual offenders' risk for reoffending. *Criminal Justice and Behavior, 13*, 115–140.

Steele, B. (1987). Abuse and neglect in the earliest years: Groundwork for vulnerability. *Zero to Three, 7*(4), 14–15.

Steen, C. (1996). *Assessment of adolescent sex offenders.* Paper presented at the Twelfth Annual Conference of the National Adolescent Perpetrator Network, Minneapolis.

Strayhorn, J. (1988). *The competent child.* New York: Guilford Press.

van der Kolk, B. (1994). *The body keeps the score: Memory and the evolving psychobiology of post traumatic stress.* [On-line]. Paper on the Trauma Info Pages Bookshelf Home Page, Harvard Medical School, HRI Trauma Center.

Ward, T., Hudson, S., Marshall, W., & Siegert, R. (1995). Attachment style and intimacy deficits in sexual offenders. *Sexual Abuse: A Journal of Research and Treatment, 7*(4).

Wenet, G., & Clark, T. (1983). *Juvenile sexual offender decision criteria.* Seattle: Juvenile Sexual Offender Program, University of Washington Adolescent Clinic.

Whitaker, M. (1987). Behavioral goal areas. *An overview of Allegheny Intensive Treatment Program.* [Brochure]. Pittsburgh, PA: Allegheny Intensive Treatment Program, Youth Services Training Center.

PART FIVE

TREATMENT OF SEXUALLY ABUSIVE YOUTH

CHAPTER SIXTEEN

INTEGRATING THEORY AND METHOD

Gail Ryan and Sandy Lane

The emphasis in program development for sexually abusive youth throughout the 1980s was clearly to develop treatment interventions that would specifically address the problem of sexually abusive behavior. In this decade of specialization, sexually abusive behavior was studied intensely, and offense-specific treatment strategies were developed, incorporating a variety of techniques to address sexual deviance and the attitudes, beliefs, and distortions that support and rationalize these behaviors. Treatment approaches for sexually abusive youth were profoundly influenced by research and experience with adult sexual offenders, and many of the offense-specific techniques were adapted to work with younger clients. Most of the techniques that distinguish offense-specific programs from other treatment programs for juveniles originated in the work with adults, with the exception of the sexual abuse cycle (see Chapter Six).

The sexual abuse cycle demonstrates a specific behavioral manifestation of a compensatory response style in a general dysfunctional cycle (Lane, 1977; Lane & Zamora, 1984; Ryan 1989; Ryan & Lane, 1991; Ryan, Lane, Davis, & Isaac, 1987). Following the conception of the original cycle depicting the pattern described by young rapists (Lane & Zamora, 1978), clinicians working in various programs have used the cycle in many ways, adapting the concept relative to a broad spectrum of sexually abusive behaviors, as well as its application to other control-seeking dysfunctions (Freeman-Longo & Bays, 1989; Johnson, 1989; G. Lowe, personal communication, 1984; Ryan, 1989; Smith, 1987; Stickrod, 1988). In its broader context, sexual abuse is one of many negative behaviors that might result from a similar cognitive behavioral syndrome. Because the cycle considers situations, thoughts, feelings, and behaviors and because of its versatility and applicability to dysfunctional patterns generally and sexually abusive patterns specifically, it has been an ideal framework for understanding eclectic approaches to treatment of sex offenders and is used widely (Freeman-Longo, Bird, Stevenson, & Fiske, 1995; National Task Force on Juvenile Sexual Offending, 1988, 1993).

Many adult programs use the cycle as well (Freeman-Longo & Bays, 1988, 1989; Pithers & Gray, 1996); it is compatible with the cognitive-behavioral approaches and relapse-prevention concepts that formed the foundations of sex offender treatment, research, and practice throughout the 1980s. The work with adults typically focused on fantasies, grooming, deviant sexual arousal, and abusive behavior. Although the immediate precursors (stresses) and the cognitive justifications have been addressed in adult programming, there has tended to be less emphasis on the historical and affective elements in the cycle model. In fact, many practitioners believed that exploration of the etiological risk factors and the vulnerable feelings reflected in the beginning phase of the cycle might encourage offenders to excuse and justify their abusive behaviors. Intense controversy came to focus on the pros and cons of dealing with childhood victimization in the course of offense-specific treatment, with some programs prohibiting that work entirely and others specifically limiting that work to modules separate from the offense-specific work, often at the end of the treatment process.

It is likely that a variety of factors contributed to the maintenance of an intense focus on sexual deviancy (and the exclusion of the broader implications of the cycle). Most obvious, the sexual behavior was the reason for referral, and specialized techniques dealing with sexual deviance were clearly what distinguished offense-specific treatment from traditional, generalist treatments. The relative lack of scientific knowledge and techniques to treat sexual aggression and deviant arousal prior to the 1980s dictated a need for basic and applied research to focus on the sexual aspect of the problem. Additionally, the crimes of sexual offenders are so abhorrent for clinicians to contemplate that some resistance to compassionate understanding of the phenomenology and developmental influences was inevitable. Clinicians did not want to confront the possibility that sex offenders are more similar to than different from other people (Marshall, 1996).

The life histories of many perpetrators are so horrendous that the temptation to avoid painful issues associated with abuse, neglect, and trauma was a parallel issue for both the therapist and the client. If the sexual arousal, fantasies, and behaviors could be addressed in isolation, a mechanistic approach could apply cognitive and behavioral interventions without going through the painful affective issues and without even forming a therapeutic relationship (Blanchard, 1995).

Most people have been associated with the impact of sexual abuse in their own lives or the lives of someone they know or care about. For decades people have struggled to understand the behavior, identify how and why such a thing could occur, grasp what really happens during sexual abuse, or come to terms with feelings of shame, guilt, and fear. Perhaps some of the focus was, in part, a vehicle for self-reassurance or healing, or to provide the relief (or sense of control) that ensues when one feels an understanding of a particularly puzzling and affect-laden problem.

Perhaps the juvenile field was forced to confront childhood experiences because the clients were still children, or perhaps the earlier aspects of the cycle were more apparent in interventions with youth because the sexual aspects were less habituated and the manifestations of the cycle moved more slowly. Or perhaps the drive to understand the developmental pathway in order to illuminate primary and secondary prevention strategies (Gilgun, 1988; Hunter, 1996; Prentky et al., 1989; Ryan, 1984a, 1984b, 1989) provided the impetus for juvenile treatment providers to explore the experiential, developmental, and etiological antecedents of sexually abusive behavior, or perhaps it was simply curiosity. In any case, work with sexually abusive youth began to contribute to a developmental-contextual understanding, which has led to important changes in therapeutic approaches (Gilgun, 1996; Ryan, 1995b; Whitaker, 1987). Many clinicians have come to believe that for many sexually abusive youth, the sexual deviance is secondary to the abusive nature of the problem and that exposure to sexual deviance is less relevant than the developmental deficits and phenomenological context in terms of risk. Research by Hunter (1996) seems to suggest some validation of the notion that a more holistic, developmental approach may be indicated, a belief articulated by growing numbers of theorists and clinicians (National Task Force, 1993; Ryan et al., 1993; Bremer, 1992; Whitaker, 1987; Marshall, 1996).

Although some sexually abusive youth do have significantly deviant sexual fantasies and arousal (Hunter & Becker, 1994; Kaemingk, Koselka, Becker, & Kaplan, 1995), some research suggests that the beliefs, attitudes, and sexual interests of many persons in the nonoffender population are not so different from those of many abusive youth (Malamuth, 1984, 1986; Prentky et al., 1989; Hunter, 1996). Appreciation of the powerful reinforcers associated with sexual behavior (intimacy, arousal, orgasm, and tension reduction) may explain why the sexual deviance becomes more apparent and more influential over time, requiring intense interventions for the more habituated offender. The sexual deviance may be somewhat less the focus in interventions that occur earlier in the development of the behavior. Nonetheless, assessment and treatment techniques specifically targeting the sexual components of the cycle (sexual fantasies, interests, arousal, and behavior) remain imperatives in treating sexually abusive youth and distinguish offense-specific programs. Recent trends in the field reflect the challenge of integrating offense-specific techniques into more holistic, developmental-contextual approaches that address differential diagnosis and treatment in a more comprehensive fashion.

This chapter reflects the need to address the unique needs of individual youth and the global patterns of functioning that are the developmental and contextual phenomena associated with the manifestation and continuation of sexually abusive behaviors. The goal is to help clinicians integrate offense-specific interventions along with more comprehensive approaches that support differential diagnosis and goal-oriented interventions. Treatment strategies must address the sexual, the abusive, and the youthful characteristics of the sexually abusive youth and explore the developmental and contextual phenomena in order to identify both risks and assets (Gilgun, 1996). The goal is to decrease the deficits and deviance and increase the youth's competent functioning and nonabusive relationships. Treatment modalities include peer groups, individual and family therapies, psychoeducation and skill building, and nurturance of growth and development within caregiving milieus or the family.

Cycles of Functioning

As we grow, everything we encounter is assimilated into the worldview that we develop. Each of us is probably most affected by our earliest experiences during infancy and childhood as we develop our initial perceptions and beliefs about our surroundings and react to what we encounter. Our perceptions and reactions to subsequent experiences are influenced by our experience, and we incorporate all of the information into a current belief system. As we test our environment, try to get our basic needs met, and react to those experiences, we gather and assimilate further information. We begin to identify what responses or behaviors elicit the things we like and the things we do not like. We begin to develop predictions, assumptions, and expectations about the world and ourselves. Over time, we tend to rely on certain responses in certain situations because we think we know what the outcome will be. At times our responses are self-protective, at times we want to obtain what we want, and at times we want to reach out to others. If our responses achieve the intended purpose, we feel content and may feel a sense of control; if they do not, we feel unhappy, confused, or helpless, and we reassess our situation. We may try another response or repeat the same response in an effort to reach our goal. If we perceive ourselves as successful in meeting our needs and goals, we will continue to do the same things. We may modify some of our beliefs, perceptions, or responses as we receive new information or have different experi-

ences. Over time our beliefs, perceptions, and responses that have been successful become more ingrained and may become habitual. Some of our patterns may
be healthy and some may be unhealthy, but they are all part of our individual
style. The whole process represents our uniqueness, our personality characteristics, and our adaptive style.

The concept of the cycle is based on this process of human development and
functioning. It is intended to facilitate an understanding of behavior in the context of life functioning, both generally and specifically, and to assist in distinguishing situational, cognitive, affective and behavioral elements. The sexual abuse
cycle (Figure 16.1) represents a general style of responding to certain situations.
The response that sexually abusive youth have developed appears compensatory
and involves a misuse of power that may ultimately result in an abusive expression of a sexual behavior. The general response style appears to be similar among
most sexually abusive youth, although the elements are unique to each individual's

FIGURE 16.1. A SIMPLISTIC ADAPTATION OF THE ABUSE CYCLE.

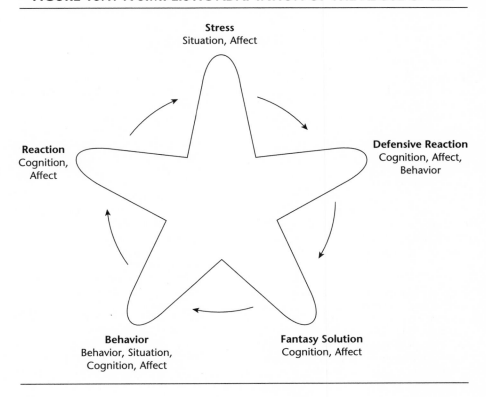

development and life experience. Current patterns have their roots in each youth's earlier life experience. Their history often reveals the origins of dysfunctional coping patterns, unresolved sources of affective stress, the nature of problem behaviors, beliefs that influence reactions, and models of compensation.

The various elements of the cycle constantly interact and result in the functioning observed by others. Cognitive and affective elements occur in response to, and are influenced by, situational elements, and the cumulative process influences behavioral elements, which in turn stimulate cognitive and affective elements. The various elements interact in a cyclical process that influences the youth's future experience. When treatment interventions are developed, they are directed toward modifying these elements (Table 16.1).

Historical elements are the important factors that have had an impact on the youth. Many of the youth who abuse have been subjected to maltreatment, trauma, or a lack of consistently nurturing and empathic care during their development. These historical elements or experiences contribute to their basic beliefs and the capacities they develop to cope with the world. Their maladaptive or dysfunctional coping strategies are readily observable to those who work with them.

TABLE 16.1. ELEMENTS OF THE ABUSE CYCLE.

Historical Elements

Development history
Early childhood attachment
View of world, basic beliefs
Stressors: abuse, neglect, loss, trauma
Consistency of care
Significant relationships

Situational Elements

Home, family role models
Peer expectations, acceptable
Structure, control, predictability
Success, failure, expectations
Relationships, events
Supervision, opportunity

Affective Elements

Helplessness, powerlessness, lack of control
Degradation, humiliation, embarrassment
Abandonment, fear, distrust
Guilt, blame, shame
Victimization, persecution
Lack of empathy, insecure attachment,
  affective memories, connectedness

Cognitive Elements

View of world, basic beliefs, self-image
Distortions, rationalizations, thinking errors
Denial, minimization, overoptimism
Blaming, projection, irresponsibility
Failure to consider consequences
Unempathic, depersonalization, retaliatory
Unrealistic, negative expectations
Decision making, problem solving, choice
Fantasies, imagination
Personalization

Behavioral Elements

Impulsivity, compulsivity
Aggression, passivity
Control seeking, dominating
Violence, exploitation, manipulation
Isolation, withdrawal, avoidance
Sexual arousal, sexual behaviors
Self-destructive behaviors, abusive behaviors
Risk taking, thrill seeking
Interactions, social competencies, deficits
Addictive behaviors

Children initially tend to mimic or learn from coping and interactional models that they are exposed to and incorporate those models in their belief system as being representative of relationships. The youth's ability to develop, and capacity to maintain, relationships is based on the quality of his initial relationships with his caretakers. Youth who are exposed to more positive experiences in their development are more resilient and flexible, and they have a wider range of competent coping skills.

The *situational* elements are external events and circumstances experienced by the youth and his family, the home and community environment the youth is exposed to, the nature of the guidance and structure provided by the youth's caretakers, and the quality of role models and interactions with family members, peers, and associates.

When a sexually abusive behavior occurs, situational elements have contributed to the development of the behavior itself, and they have played a role in the onset of that specific behavior. The sensitivity to the trigger that precipitates the onset of a response style or the abuse cycle is based in the youth's life experience. Over time, many situations will arise that are reminiscent of the circumstances about which the youth was initially sensitive.

When we observe the youth in his current situation, we may see him begin to progress through the cycle as he reacts to being told "no." His sensitivity to the interaction is based in some prior experience of being told "no" by an authority figure. Some treatment interventions are geared toward assisting the youth in recognizing what he is sensitive to, identifying the developmental experience that contributed to the sensitivity, and modifying the extent of his sensitivity. Other interventions address situational variables that increase access to vulnerable persons or decrease the level of supervision.

Affective elements are the feelings or emotions the youth has as he progresses through the cycle. Some of the feelings occur when he reacts to a situation or interaction or when his abuse cycle is triggered. These feelings are reminiscent of emotions or feelings that the youth experienced in reaction to the original historical occurrence, and they are anxiety producing or discomforting. Most of the emotions are feelings the youth would prefer not to experience, although because they are familiar, a youth may feel comfortable with the feelings. There is a tendency for vulnerable feelings to be masked by angry feelings (anger typically elicits less of a sense of vulnerability), or the youth may become angry about the memories or feelings he is experiencing. It is believed that the youth seeks to decrease the anxiety or discomfort by seeking to feel more empowered—a compensatory response.

Other feelings the youth experiences as he progresses through the cycle occur in reaction to or association with the behavioral and cognitive elements in the cycle. They may be elating, comfortable, or uncomfortable. Treatment intervention is geared toward helping the youth recognize, allow himself to experience, label, express, and manage his sensitive feelings. Therapeutic efforts are also geared toward increasing the youth's capacity to feel empathy. By becoming more aware of cues related to his own needs and feelings, he becomes better able to recognize and interpret those of others.

Cognitive elements occur throughout the abuse cycle and interact with each element. Thoughts and feelings form a chain, with every thought influencing the subsequent feelings and every feeling being interpreted in subsequent thought. Similarly, thought and behavior form an interlocking path with every behavior that occurs in the cycle. All behavior is preceded by some contemplation and decision to engage in the behavior, although the process may become so rapid for more habitual behaviors that the youth is not even aware of the thought. Cognitive elements influence the development of abuse behavior and play a role in the sensitivity of the trigger at the onset of the response pattern. They are also reminiscent of the original historical occurrence and influence how the current trigger is perceived. Thoughts occur in each stage of the abuse cycle.

Cognitive elements include personalizing or self-deprecatory thoughts, assumptions and expectations, perceptions, beliefs, control-seeking and retaliatory thoughts, fantasies, plans, decisions, anticipations, assessment, and interpretations. The sequence of cognitions represented in the cycle seems to drive or perpetuate the cycle as one type of cognition stimulates the next one.

Treatment intervention is geared toward recognizing thought patterns associated with current or historical triggers and modifying the perceptions that contribute to the youth's discomfort. Efforts are also geared toward assisting the youth in assuming accountability, interrupting the sequence of cognitions associated with the abuse behavior, modifying self-deprecatory cognitions and negative assumptions, modifying beliefs that support misattribution of responsibility or sanction abusive behavior, influencing decision making, and managing fantasies.

Behavioral elements are the actions that the youth does and the qualities associated with the actions. These elements interact with the other elements in the abuse cycle and may occur in reaction to any part of the cycle or to achieve some type of gratification. The actions in the cycle include isolating, controlling, dominating, interacting, grooming or stalking, and the sexual abuse behavior itself. The associated qualities include impulsivity and compulsivity, risk taking and thrill seeking, aggression and passivity, violence and exploitation, and self-defeating behaviors. Sexual arousal and masturbation fall within the behavioral realm as well. The associated qualities are characteristics or traits of the youth that developed as part of or in response to life experience. The qualities depicted in the abuse cycle are those that support the response style and characterize the compensatory and abusive behaviors.

Sexual arousal provides a positive interaction and experience of cognitive and affective elements for the youth. It is believed that it is one of the compensatory aspects that the youth hopes to achieve to diminish the negative experience at the onset of the cycle. Sexual arousal and masturbation play are often associated with cognitive elements related to anticipation and contemplation. Sexual arousal is integral to the sexual aspect of the abusive behavior and is associated with many of the behaviors that set up the abuse and the associated cognitions. Treatment is geared toward assisting the youth in controlling and preventing behaviors that are hurtful to others, recognizing and modifying behaviors that are self-defeating, understanding the associated qualities, and decreasing or managing the arousal that is associated with abusive behavior.

Because so many different elements contribute to an abusive sexual expression of power, treatment interventions comprise multiple elements. Developmental questionnaires gather historical details from the parents' recollections, and family sessions illuminate the experiential understanding of the juvenile's life perceptions. Client and family may work together to create a family tree or genogram that facilitates discussion of intergenerational patterns of behavior and belief systems. In the context of the family, divergent perceptions of shared memories may reveal the shared emotions and define role expectations. A youth who creates a lifeline can use it to integrate past and present perceptions (Figure 16.2).

It is often in the process of revealing childhood experiences that offenders are first able to access and acknowledge the feelings of vulnerability and helplessness that they have denied in their more recent experiences. It is also relative to childhood memories that the group members are first able to express some empathy for each other, and through that experience of empathic responses the client becomes able to express some empathy himself for the child he was. Cognitive and experiential techniques can then work to confront the negative reinforcers and challenge the underlying beliefs.

The juvenile whose lifeline is shown in Figure 16.2 engaged in lying, stealing, and sneaky behavior from the time he was very young. His older and younger siblings had never displayed these irresponsible patterns. At the time of his birth, his mother's first marriage was disintegrating, and his father was both physically and emotionally abusive. An older sibling took on the role of nurturer and protector, and the mother dealt first with her fear and guilt relative to the bad marriage and subsequently with her fears relative to separating and becoming self-sufficient. Her issues were compounded by the guilt she felt that her children were inadequately cared for when she returned to work. She described her relationship with the client as always "different" from those she had with her other children; she said she never felt close to this child.

As a result of identifying the chronic pattern of misbehavior, hearing accounts of the client's feeling fearful of his mother's anger and guilty about her anguish

FIGURE 16.2. LIFELINE OF A SEXUALLY ABUSIVE YOUTH: THE SITUATIONAL, COGNITIVE, AFFECTIVE, AND BEHAVIORAL ELEMENTS.

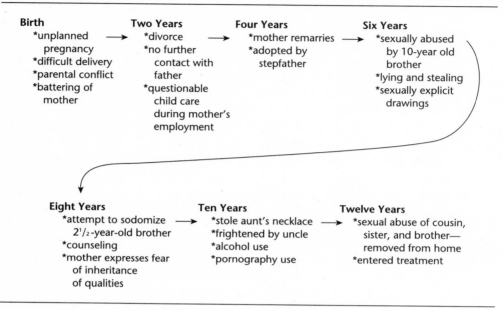

over him, and hearing the mother describe her fear that this child was "like his father" and her guilt at not being a good enough mother, the therapist realized that the shared emotions in this parent-child dyad were fear and guilt. Not surprisingly, work with the sexual assault cycle revealed that one of the primary triggers for sexual assault was fear, and the consequent guilt following the client's negative behaviors, including the sexual assaults, was actually a reinforcer because it connected him to his mother's concern for him.

When emotional triggers and reinforcers are identified, their role in the cycle can be illustrated relative to the sexual abuse and other problem behaviors as well. This particular client described "feeling very small" whenever his mother confronted him, and that small, fearful feeling became one of his primary indicators of risk. Feeling small seemed to encompass the vulnerability, helplessness, and lack of importance regarding his early life experience. In family and group sessions, his body language would convey this "small" feeling as he seemed to diminish visibly when confronted. The fact that this sixteen-year-old was now strong, athletic, and almost six feet tall was part of the ironic unfolding of his self-image. As he restructured his thinking, he became able to maintain his stature and more able to own and control his responses to fear; as he experienced competency and pride, he became less at risk and more self-satisfied.

The Therapeutic Relationship

In defining sexual abuse, it has been stated that it is not the sexual behavior that defines sexually abusive behavior but rather the abusive qualities of the interaction and the relationship. Specifically, consent, equality, and coercion are the definitive factors, and the relationship of victim and perpetrator is often characterized by coercive and exploitative patterns of interaction that demonstrate a lack of regard for the victim's needs and feelings. This lack of regard reflects the abusive youth's experience of relationships and constitutes a lack of empathy. Also, in describing the phenomenology of the youth in terms of the individual's internal working model for relationships being the basis for one's view of the world, it is apparent that the youth's earliest relationships and attachment models are profoundly relevant to the problem of abusive relationships and therefore to the treatment process. Some new or corrective experience must occur to challenge the youth's view of self, others, and relationships. Much of the resistance in treatment may be related to the therapist's attempting to change the client's view of the world (cognitive restructuring) without providing any evidence that the change is rational. To change the youth's beliefs about the nature of relationships, the clinician must be willing to enter into a corrective experience, that is, a therapeutic relationship, with the client. Every intervention with the sexually abusive youth provides an opportunity to model empathic relationship skills that challenge the youth's beliefs about self and others.

Blanchard (1995) provides a rich discussion of the therapeutic relationship in treatment with sexually abusive clients. It has always been apparent that the treatment of involuntary clients poses a challenge for creating a therapeutic relationship. The unique conditions of the relationship are imposed by the nature of the referral and the treatment needs and are present before the therapist and client meet.

First is the issue of consent: the relationship cannot be defined as consensual because of the involuntary nature of the referral. The court-ordered client is clearly coerced by the power of the court and usually faces some negative consequence if he fails to participate in treatment. In addition, the power of parents and caseworkers, as well as the power of the therapist as authority and agent of the court, may be overwhelming evidence of the imbalance of power in the relationship. With these three factors—lack of consent, lack of equality, and the pressure of coercion in the relationship—there is a high risk that the youth will perceive the relationship with the therapist as potentially abusive. The discomfort is exacerbated by several other nontraditional factors, again present prior to entering the relationship: victim advocacy, a lack of confidentiality, a lack of trust, and confrontation.

Offense-specific treatment is based on several underlying assumptions that affect the therapeutic relationship and direct the course of treatment. Basic to our understanding of the process is that the purpose is to prevent sexual abuse. Sexual perpetration is not a personal problem in the sense that it is a private concern of the perpetrator; it is a social and legal concern as well. It is based on long-standing patterns that have developed over time, and so it is not an isolated dysfunction that can be addressed in isolation.

Victim Advocacy

Victim advocacy drives the treatment of sexually abusive youth. Although this statement seems simple enough, its implications in treatment are complex. The National Task Force on Juvenile Sexual Offending stated in its 1993 report, "Protection of the community . . . is the highest priority of intervention in sexual offending. The community is the ultimate client" (p. 12). The nature of the therapeutic relationship is clearly affected, and decision making is based in the second assumption of the task force's report: "Community safety takes precedence over any other consideration, and ultimately, is in the best interests of the offender" (p. 12).

In practice, these assumptions require the therapist to consider the needs and rights of others in priority over the needs and rights of the client. Issues of victim contact, where the youth can reside, the type of treatment setting, and accountability are dictated by these concerns. This is not a large step for those working in corrections, but it is a giant step for those working in mental health.

Placing community protection in the forefront requires a shift in the therapist-client relationship toward monitoring and accountability. In addition, the message to the youth carries a powerful therapeutic lesson: the need to consider others. The therapist's demonstration of concern for victim protection and community safety parallels the goals of treatment and is congruent with the treatment process. In this light, the youth's treatment is enhanced by victim advocacy, as are the immediate advantages of reducing risk of additional offenses, which is clearly in the best interest of the client as well.

Confidentiality

Confidentiality is the next area requiring special consideration in the treatment of sexually abusive youth. Again, this concept is a small step for corrections people and a large step for traditional therapists. The National Task Force reports (1988, 1993) state, "Confidentiality cannot apply in the treatment of this population because it promotes the secrecy which supports offending" (p. 37).

By requiring that the juvenile client (and parents) sign a complete waiver of confidentiality prior to acceptance for treatment, the therapist not only maximizes communication regarding the client's functioning in the community but also makes a clear, therapeutic statement to the client: "You must be willing to give up the secrecy that supports your problem, and you must be accountable for controlling your behaviors." This waiver allows the treatment provider to validate the juvenile's self-reports of functioning and to communicate concerns with the other professionals involved in the care, education, and supervision of the youth.

Trust

Trust surfaces as the next special concern in treatment. Not surprisingly, the priority of community safety and the waiver of confidentiality are overt statements reflecting the provider's distrust of the client's behavior and self-reports. These are obvious and understandable factors, directly stemming from the referring problem. Because the youth has engaged in abusive behaviors that have hidden aspects and has denied and minimized the harm of those behaviors in order to maintain his gratification, the immediate situation supports distrust in these areas.

There are, however, two underlying issues that more subtly influence trust in the therapeutic relationship. The first lies within the youth: an inability to trust. Many sexually abusive youth have never achieved basic trust or have experienced loss or betrayal that severely impairs their ability to trust. (Recall the development of deviancy discussed in Chapter Five and the developmental theories in Chapters Three and Seven.) They may hope for someone who is trustworthy, but it is not their expectation, and it is unlikely that they would risk trusting early in the therapeutic relationship. It is more likely that they will take a defensive or manipulative posture initially, based on their life experience.

The second underlying trust issue lies within the therapist: the desire to trust. The unconditional acceptance that is a basic element of relationship-based treatment can conflict with the need to challenge and confront the denial, minimization, and distortions of the abusive youth. The therapist, bringing to the relationship the capacity for basic trust that the youth lacks, may be tempted to model trust in spite of the untrustworthy nature of the client. It is a mistake, however, to imagine that trust will be warranted, reciprocated, or respected. It would be irrational for the treatment provider to trust the self-control or self-report of clients who demonstrate a lack of control and rely on exerting power over others to meet their needs. The therapist may adopt an orientation of unconditional positive regard that communicates respect to the youth as an individual as well as an expectation of accountability.

Therefore, trust is a long-term goal in this therapy, not an immediate or necessary condition. The initial goal is developing a therapeutic alliance based on direct communication of expectations and goals. The client must begin to behave responsibly, control behaviors, and risk nonpower-based behaviors before the therapist can model trust, and the client must begin to understand the nature and value of trust before he will risk trusting others. It would be naive to imagine that a youth who has never known a trusting relationship would ever be able to trust the therapist who had so little understanding of the client as to trust (even superficially) the client who is not trustworthy. Yet most therapists have been trained to establish trust first and then do the work of treatment.

So how can the therapist create a condition that will enable growth and development and change in the absence of trust? It is suggested that the same conditions that enable the infant to develop basic trust are the basis for the development of trust and trustworthiness in all relationships. Briggs (1975) describes these conditions as a "psychologically safe relationship" with the following elements:

1. Focused attention (listening, seeing, reading cues)
2. Nonjudgmental (judging behavior separate from identity)
3. Owning feelings (personal expression of sympathy)
4. Recognition of diversity (the individual's unique developmental context)
5. Empathy (interpreting and validating cues)
6. Trustworthiness (no abuse of power, authority, faith)

In the context of a psychologically safe relationship, the therapist is able to convey the understanding and unconditional acceptance of the youth as a worthy person, capable of change, and able to achieve control. Acceptance of person must be carefully distinguished from acceptance of thoughts, words, and behaviors. Finally, it is imperative that the therapist demonstrate his or her own trustworthiness throughout the process, never abusing the privilege and power of the therapist's role in the youth's life.

As the layers of deceit and self-deception begin to be discarded and the client begins to experience the self-confidence that accompanies more functional and responsible living, the client becomes able to experience confidence in others. At that point, the provider's own accountability becomes a model for the building of trusting relationships. The growth of trust in the relationship is a parallel process—a product of consistent empathic interactions. This experience of an empathic relationship enables the youth to consider new models of relationships, which change his view of self, others, and the world.

Finally, the need for the therapist to challenge the client's perceptions and beliefs rather than work from a position of unconditional acceptance is also unusual for many therapists. The offense-specific treatment process dictates the direction and scope of treatment and is dependent on confrontation and accountability. The locus of responsibility and change must lie within the client, who is usually resistant given his desire to protect a behavior pattern that provides a significant sense of empowerment, safety, and adequacy. The youth must begin to feel uncomfortable with his behavior if he is to change. As he works to develop empathy and personal responsibility, the client goes through periods of intense discomfort (shame, guilt, grief, and remorse) and must confront many painful issues. Feeling responsible for increasing a client's distress is also an uncomfortable feeling for the therapist, who must understand and validate the client's resistance.

Being aware of these conditions is imperative for the therapist to be able to monitor and manage his or her own reactions in the relationship and be able to validate the client's experience. The resistance and defensive posturing of the youth can be viewed as rational and adaptive protective strategies. As the therapist articulates the cues that indicate the client's expressions, expresses his or her own feelings and shares thoughts about the reasons that it may be hard to feel safe and comfortable in the relationship, and clarifies that the uncomfortable conditions stem from the nature of the work and not because of who the client is or who the therapist is, the therapist is modeling *communication, empathy,* and *accountability,* the tools for creating a sense of psychological safety and empathic interactions (Ryan et al., 1988).

There has been a tendency among practitioners to avoid the process of creating a therapeutic relationship; to look for interventions that could be applied in an educational, didactic, or impersonal fashion; and to create the illusion of safety by imposing tight structure and rules in the treatment setting. It is our belief, however, that the struggle to create psychologically safe relationships (and to model the empathic care that is missing in the youth and puts him most at risk of abusing others) is an important part of treatment.

The therapist's willingness to struggle to create a sense of safety in relationships is one of the new experiences that challenges the client's view and is also directly relevant to the cycle: demonstrating that someone who feels unsafe in interaction with others can struggle to create psychologically safe relationships and succeed rather than isolate and rely on the externalized control seeking and compensatory solutions of the cycle. Therapists should not be discouraged by the struggle it takes to create relationship but should view it as a critical component of treatment.

The Developmental-Contextual Framework

By pairing a comprehensive view of life span development with a similarly comprehensive view of life experience, the complexity of each unique individual becomes apparent (see Chapter Seven). The implications for treatment become the basis for caregiver interventions to affect the client's growth and experience (see Chapter Nineteen).

In trying to understand the effects of developmental and experiential risk factors, clinicians must also consider premorbid risk factors, such as temperament traits, neurological impairments, physiological problems, or chronic illness.

Temperament

One important aspect to understand about the unique phenomenology of the youth is temperament. Temperament traits are characteristics that describe the "how" of behavior, that is, how the individual behaves as opposed to what the behavior is or why the behavior occurs. They encompass the following traits (Thomas, Chess, & Birch, 1977):

- Activity (the typical motor level, for example, restlessness or impulsivity)
- Intensity (level of energy in reactions; reactivity)
- Rhythmicity (level of regularity, predictability)
- Adaptability (response to newness or change; adjustment)
- Threshold (level at which stimulation evokes a response)
- Persistence (level of attention or pursuit despite obstacles)
- Distraction (level at which stimuli interrupt or redirect attention)
- Responsivity (approach or withdrawal patterns regarding newness and change)
- Mood (typical affective state—positive, negative, or neutral)

Research on temperamental qualities has focused on what makes certain traits "difficult" (Ryan, 1995a). It is usually the extremes of too little or too much that cause any trait to be considered difficult. Consideration of difficult temperament traits may be particularly useful for therapists who are treating sexually abusive youth; although "sex offenders are not born sex offenders, they may have been born difficult" (Ryan, 1995a). Some of the difficult aspects of treating abusers that we attribute to resistance may actually be temperament.

Controversies in the research on temperament include questions of heritability, stability, and continuity, which have implications regarding whether such characteristics are changeable. What appears most reasonable at this time is that temperament traits are relatively stable across the life span but can be moderated or exacerbated by environment and experience. Temperament traits are probably especially salient in considering fit or lack of fit for children in the family system, school, and community as important factors in the phenomenology of the youth. Even more important may be to understand how these traits manifest in the treatment setting and potential relationships between these traits and the cycle.

The difficultness of these traits is usually described in terms of how difficult it is for other people to deal with the person (Turecki, 1985); however, equally important for the therapist is to understand how these difficult traits have made life difficult for the youth. For example, the youth who has a high activity trait may have chronic negative assessment from others, which affects his self-esteem; the youth who has difficult rhythmicity but lives in a world based on predictability may experience a lack of fit, which makes it very difficult for others to be empathic. (The infant who has very irregular hunger and sleep patterns may frustrate caregivers and be chronically invalidated.)

Temperament is just one piece in the puzzle of phenomenology and context, but difficult traits may profoundly affect the youth's experience of the world and view of self. The youth's cycle may develop as a compensatory strategy and may also reflect these traits. For example, the intensity trait may contribute to how overwhelming the triggers are, as well as how overbearing the power and control behaviors are. Overreactions may be related to the intensity trait, or the youth with a low threshold may be easily triggered and may carry sensory memories of caregiving touches that he perceived as aversive. The persistence trait may contribute to the rigid or ritualized nature of the cycle pattern, whereas the rhythmicity trait may contribute to a less predictable pattern and a greater sense of being out of control.

Concurrent Psychiatric Disorders

In order to appreciate and validate the unique phenomenology of each youth and the implications of differential diagnosis and treatment, the provider must not lose sight of concurrent psychiatric disorders. Several are particularly prevalent among sexually abusive youth (that is, overrepresented in this population compared to nonclinical peers). Attention deficit disorder (ADD) (with or without hyperactivity), affective (mood) disorders (especially anxiety, depression, and bipolar disorders), and posttraumatic stress disorders (PTSD) are of special note (Becker, Kaplan, Tenke, & Tartaglini, 1991; Ryan, Miyoshi, Metzner, Krugman, & Fryer, 1996). Although statistics are not available to suggest what portion of sexually abusive youth manifest a dual diagnosis, estimates are that a sizable number of more serious and chronic youth may benefit from a medical-psychiatric-neurological evaluation (Dailey, 1987; Lewis, Shanok, & Pincus, 1979, 1981) and that many juveniles who initially appear unable to participate and benefit from treatment may become able to do so when underlying attention deficits, anxiety, or depressive conditions are managed with appropriate medications or adjunct treatment. The importance of recognizing and treating concurrent psychiatric disorders became apparent as psychiatric interventions (especially pharmacology) began to demonstrate that youth who were failing in treatment programs were often eventually diagnosed and treated for these concurrent disorders, and then they became able to complete the offense-specific program's work (Dailey, 1987; Sczechowicz, 1988).

One of the obstacles to effective integration of psychiatric evaluations, consults, and pharmacological treatments in working with sexually abusive youths has been the differences in professional terminology between offense-specific therapists and generalist psychiatrists. Therapists often fail to communicate adequately the symptoms that describe concurrent disorders, and psychiatrists' diagnostic summaries are often viewed as irrelevant to the specialists' understanding of the youth. This language barrier often results in a breakdown in services that may be critical to the youth's success. Maletzky (1996) cites thirteen reasons for the lack of collaboration between psychiatry and sex offender treatment, several of which seem related to poor communication. In an effort to create better communication, Ryan (1993) proposed a psychiatric view of the cycle that simplistically suggests psychiatric terms that may be relevant to the different elements of the cycle and symptomatic of the characteristics of the youth (Table 16.2)

Both disciplines must be accountable regarding the need for better communication. It can be useful for the request for a psychiatric evaluation to include a description of the characteristics of the youth's patterns that are particularly problematic and articulation of whatever has led the therapist to suspect some concurrent disorder may be manifest in the youth's behavior or posing an impediment in therapy. If medication is indicated, the intent is to modulate the symptomatology biochemically, not to sedate the client to make him easier to manage. It is imperative that monitoring of medication trials provides the prescribing doctor with relevant details in order to assist him or her in determining whether a dosage adjustment is needed or to determine the medication is not providing the desired effect and another medication should be tried. The obvious implication for appropriate monitoring and documentation of medication effects is that all caregivers, therapists, and special educators need to know what the medication is expected to change, as well as potential side effects. It would be difficult to say whether a medication is having the desired effect without such knowledge; therefore, programs should have available the fourth edition of the *Diagnostic and Statistical Manual of Mental Disorders* (DSM-IV) and a current *Physician's Desk Reference*

TABLE 16.2. PSYCHIATRIC SYMPTOMATOLOGY ASSOCIATED WITH THE ELEMENTS OF THE CYCLE.

History

Trauma
Unresolved losses, rejection
Family history of affective disorders
Family history of substance abuse
Family history of suicide
Head injuries
School reports of attention deficit/
    hyperactivity disorder, learning
    disabilities, and so on
Prenatal drug or alcohol exposure
Complications at birth
Enmeshed or intrusive parenting
Attachment disorders
Disruptions in early care
Developmental disability, deviance

Trigger

Flashbacks
Flooding
Overwhelming affect

Victim stance

Paranoia
Anxiety
Helplessness

Hopelessness

Depression
External locus of control
Disorganized thinking
Distortions

Isolation

Dissociation
Withdrawal
Avoidant behavior

Anger

Defensiveness
Projection
Externalizing
Mania
Hysteria

Fantasy solution

Ruminating
Intrusive thoughts
Grandiosity
Suicidal ideation
Paraphiliac ideation
Homicidal ideation

Plan

Ritualized
Defensive

Decision

Impulsive
Dissociated
Irrational

Behavior

Disordered
Habituated
Reinforcing
Aggressive
Self-destructive

Anxiety

Attention deficits
Distractibility
Hypervigilance

Promises

Grandiosity
Magical thinking

Denial

Amnesia
Dissociated

Source: Ryan (1993).

(PDR), and therapists should ask the prescribing doctor for specific information on what treatment providers would consider a positive or negative response (Dailey, 1996). Similarly, psychiatrists who consult on these cases will enhance their role by learning something about the treatment providers' programs and working to break down the communication barriers.

Knowledge arising from research and practice in psychiatry in the past decade, particularly in relation to child psychiatry's understanding of neurological functioning associated with ADD after puberty, depressive disorders in childhood and adolescence, PTSD, and, most recently, obsessive-compulsive disorders, is exciting and holds much promise in regard to treatment of the hardest-to-treat youth (those who have sometimes been labeled "untreatable" because we did not yet know how to treat them). Medication studies are producing results demonstrating not only which agents are most effective for particular disorders, but which work on particular symptoms best (for example, some medications are particularly effective in reducing intrusive fantasies, some are particularly helpful in reducing the affective flooding associated with PTSD triggers, some are useful in reducing disorganized thinking, and others address impulsive urges). Many studies are looking at combinations of disorders, such as ADD and hyperactivity with Tourette's syndrome, or depression with ADD (Dailey, 1996; Spencer et al., 1996). It is especially important for clinicians working in specialist programs and their consulting psychiatrists to review the literature routinely and consistently. In addition to the pharmacological studies, treatment for the various concurrent disorders must be understood in relation to the usual interventions (Eth & Pynoos, 1985; James, 1989; Jancin, 1995; Spiegel, 1993; Terr, 1990; VanderKolk, 1987).

Developing an understanding of the characteristics and nature of the concurrent psychiatric disorder will improve differential treatment approaches. Particular disorders will influence the youth's way of thinking about or reacting to a given situation. Some disorders may be manifest in ways that appear to be part of the abuse cycle when in fact they are not; at other times, the manifestation may be triggered by cycle progression. For example, a youth who has been diagnosed as dysthymic and is not sleeping well may be manifesting associated hyperactivity rather than responding to anxiety associated with his current treatment work. Another youth may be extremely upset about exploring the specifics of his abuse behaviors, and that may trigger an increase in obsessive thoughts and fantasies as he tries to cope with the anxiety. Youth who are exhibiting increased defensiveness or irritability may be manifesting behaviors associated with elements of the cycle, they may be exhibiting a reaction to a flashback as part of PTSD symptomatology (Spiegel, 1993), or their blood sugar may be too low. As the provider becomes increasingly aware of how a youth's particular disorder interacts with the elements of the cycle, treatment for that youth will become increasingly specific.

It is not possible to adequately review here all the information on psychiatric interventions relevant to work with sexually abusive youth, but practitioners are encouraged to look beyond the offense-specific field to benefit from other relevant work in progress.

Goal-Oriented Interventions

As the field continues to evolve, there is increasing awareness that every element in the cycle is manifested in diverse and unique ways by each youth. Differential diagnosis and treatment is based in acknowledgment of the specific needs of each youth and the awareness that diverse strengths and deficits will have an impact on the type of intervention required. Certainly some interventions are common to the needs of each youth, but there are multiple interventions that may apply to fewer youth or situations. The use of goal-oriented interventions allows the specificity required to provide differential treatment.

Although the repertoire of treatment interventions currently available may appear to provide a shotgun approach (where we present everything we know and hope some of it works), in fact, each of the interventions has a specific goal and is designed to target a specific element represented in the sexual abuse cycle. In treatment planning, identifying the goal (the youth's specific treatment needs), the process of meeting the goal (specific interventions to address the goals), desired outcome (behavioral, cognitive, affective, or situational changes), and the measurement of progress (how we will know change has occurred) allows providers to be more focused in the treatment process. Identification of progress or lack thereof and the need for modification or addition of interventions is based on more objective data. As the health care field continues to change, the demand for more discrete treatment practices grows. The challenge to practitioners is to begin to identify how to modify the current interventions to each youth's needs and to identify adjunct interventions that address some of the diverse qualities.

The specialized goals that address sexually abusive behavior are to stop all sexually abusive behavior, protect members of society from further victimization, prevent other aggressive or abusive behaviors that the youth may manifest, and assist the youth in developing more functional relationship skills (National Task Force Report, 1993). Those broad goals are addressed in specialized offense-specific treatment, which focuses on areas of particular concern in the sexual abuse behavior and the youth's functioning. These goals include creating a physically and psychologically safe environment in the treatment setting; operationalizing, communication, empathy, and accountability; consistent definition of abusive interactions; acknowledgment of risk; recognition of the dysfunctional cycle; ability to interrupt the cycle; and demonstrating changed patterns of functioning and increased empathy in the treatment setting and daily life. Goal-oriented interventions address each of the areas of concern.

Treatment may occur in various settings: institutional settings, residential facilities, psychiatric hospitals, probation offices, schools, churches, or a private therapist's offices. Offense-specific treatment typically occurs in a group or individual sessions, but a considerable amount of treatment occurs in the youth's milieu. The milieu provides feedback to the youth about how he is perceived relative to his functioning, challenges behavior and statements that maintain his abuse behavior, and holds him accountable for using the tools he has learned or maintaining behavioral changes. In a more formalized setting, the milieu might be a therapeutic community or a positive peer culture (see Chapter Nineteen), but the community supervision team, relapse-prevention team, the youth's network, and the family also provide a milieu experience.

Many of the common characteristics associated with sexually abusive behavior are most effectively addressed in a group setting with male and female cotherapists. Group membership models and promotes relationship development, and it is a safe testing ground for practicing new ways of interacting. As the youth hears others describe experiences and behaviors similar to his own, he may be able to adjust his negative self-perceptions, such as thinking he is a bad person because he is the only youth who ever did such an awful behavior. When the youth hears the distortions and minimizations of another, he is able to begin to recognize the lack of logic or objectifying aspects without defensiveness and then is more able to begin to question his own thinking. Observing another youth risk sharing painful experiences or being able to hear and use constructive feedback may facilitate a decision to take similar risks. Sexually abusive youth can sometimes identify denial and minimization in each other's accounts more quickly and accurately than the therapist can because of the similarity of their experiences. A male and female cotherapy team offers modeling of healthy interactions and heterosexual relationships that are equal, nonabusive, and communicative. In the group process, clients manifest their unique strengths, patterns, and vulnerabilities.

The Treatment Group

As a milieu is achieved in the group, the clients are encouraged to report their daily experiences and provide information about themselves. The various elements of the cycle can be addressed in a group setting. Within any group of sexually abusive youth, whether homogeneous or diverse, each member's cycle will be unique, and the techniques that are most relevant, useful, and tolerable for the individual become apparent over time. By using various components and modalities with the group, the cotherapists provide each member the opportunity to explore, experience, and benefit from a wide range of ideas and interventions. One juvenile may prove most competent in the cognitive areas, another might make best use of behavioral methods, and yet another could make significant affective changes. For some, educational components work to correct faulty beliefs or skill deficits, while others accept one or more specific techniques and become adept at averting themselves from the progression of cycle. The experience of individuals through this group process not only exposes them to understanding the interventions relevant to all the elements of the cycle, but also demonstrates the individuality of each member, increasing their capacity for empathy and appreciation of each individual's unique needs and competency.

In the treatment group, consistent labels for the various points on the sexual abuse cycle create a common language within the group that the therapist begins to relate to each client's reports of past and current functioning. As they begin to understand and define the elements of the cycle, group members begin to take on the role of identifying the cycle in the accounts of their peers, and finally they begin to be able to see similar patterns and common characteristics in themselves. Over time, the youth understands the various concepts and labels and sees how they apply to his own situation, thoughts, feelings, and behavior. The cycle is used to promote understanding of past and present patterns, as well as to identify risk in the future and develop more functional response patterns. The various interventions apply to each element in the cycle. Descriptors for the elements and stages of the cycle may be simplified to suit the client's intellectual and conceptual ability.

The twelve-part cycle depicted in Figure 16.3 is useful in working with ten- to eighteen-year-old youths, because it uses very simple terms and creates an association with the face of a clock.

It is often in the process of revealing his life history and describing childhood experiences that the youth is first able to access and acknowledge the feelings of vulnerability and helplessness that he denies in more recent experiences. It is also relative to childhood memories that the group members are first able to express some empathy for each other. Through that experience of empathic responses, the client becomes able to express some empathy himself for the child he was. The group process provides a forum for defining and labeling body language and affect, challenging unempathic responses, sharing perceptions, and defining painful or shameful emotions such as embarrassment, sadness, humiliation, and helplessness. Client-centered psychotherapy techniques aid in the identification and labeling of feelings, and the group milieu demonstrates empathic relationships. The goal of exploring and defining the full range of emotions—both positive and negative—is to clarify for the individual the role of his emotions in triggering or

FIGURE 16.3. TWELVE-PART ABUSE CYCLE.

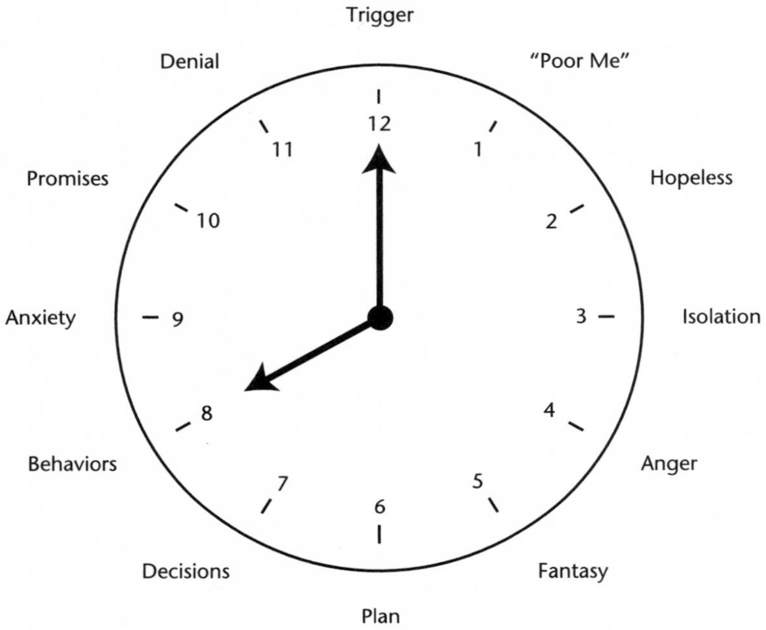

reinforcing behavior while helping the client learn healthy aspects of experiencing and coping with the feelings.

Cognitive work requires the ability to describe thoughts separate from the associated situations, feelings, and behaviors, even though they interact together in the youth's functioning. The denial, rationalizations, and distortions that are so characteristic of sexually abusive youth are cognitive processes. In the group process, existential, rational emotive, Adlerian, and reality-based approaches help to access and confront the thoughts of the youth. Many of the historic and affective techniques make important contributions to the understanding of patterns of thought and the individual's view of the world. Other cognitive techniques include visualization exercises and the psychoeducational components.

Ultimately treatment works toward self-monitoring and self-control, and the cycle is primarily a tool in long-term risk management. As the youth identifies his experience and personalizes the elements in his cycle, he is developing an awareness that will allow him to identify the red flags that alert him to the need to use some tool to interrupt the progression through the cycle or to reject a particular thought or behavior. He begins to identify specific situations he must avoid and those he must leave if his red flags begin to appear. Situational elements are also affected by those aspects of treatment that change the individual's thoughts and behaviors in interaction with others. When the youth identifies triggers and reinforcers, their role in the cycle can be illustrated relative to the sexual abuse and other problem behaviors as well. Throughout treatment, the youth receives the message that there are many situations he cannot control; therefore, the focus of treatment is to learn to control himself in all situations.

Confrontation

The combination of confrontation and support is most useful as it originates in the peer group. Adolescents are less resistant when challenged by their peers than in similar interactions with adults. Each intervention or interaction with the youth is likely to involve an element of feedback or challenge of the youth's beliefs or behaviors. The role of confrontation in the treatment of sexually abusive youth is clear, but the technique is often misinterpreted. The group function frequently involves the confrontation of peers, especially confrontation of the cognitive elements of the cycle. The process and distortions that allow abusive behaviors must be confronted, and the beliefs that support risk must be challenged. Confrontation is the tool that guides the client's process of change.

Confrontation is one of the least understood techniques in this field of treatment. Often the confusion seems to relate to the misattributions of anger, degradation, and shame to the process. The goal of confrontation is to provide feedback to help the clients be aware of the nature of their thoughts and behaviors and reach a breakthrough that illuminates their understanding of a concept and helps them to own the thought or behavior in question. When confrontation is based in anger and shame and expressed through yelling, name calling, and put-downs, it may be a powerful experience that influences the client's thinking, but the change may increase defensiveness and self-protection rather than understanding by triggering the client's sense of victimization, helplessness, and poor self-image. It is the authors' belief that shame and victimization are inherent in the problem; they are not the solution. Confrontation should be a calm and rational process in a direct and purposeful progression toward an identified goal.

It is imperative for the clinician to be aware of the client's historic experiences of assault. These youth have often been battered, both verbally and physically, and frequently they expect to be maligned and threatened. The goal of confrontation is to challenge dishonest or distorted thoughts and exploitative behavior. The youth needs to become uncomfortable with irresponsible thoughts or behavior, but further damage to self-image is counterproductive. Confrontation should be undertaken only to help the client's change process, never as a vehicle for the clinician's own anger, frustration, or vicarious control issues (Davis, 1989).

Three factors are crucial in regard to confrontations: timing, relationship, and impact. The timing of confrontation must consider the therapist's preparedness, the constraints of the treatment session, and the youth's readiness to hear the issues. If the therapist is angry or frustrated or has personalized the client's behavior, it is wise to delay a confrontation in order to clarify the youth's needs and allow the therapist to formulate a clear and rational course. Supervision or collegial discussions are useful in clarifying the goal and strategy of an anticipated confrontation. Another aspect of the time factor is that of having adequate time; effective confrontation needs to proceed without distraction and may require some follow-up time to monitor the impact and process the material with other group members. It is better to wait until a later session to begin than to be interrupted in the process. Also, if a youth is just beginning to learn about power and control, confrontation should point out when it is occurring but not be directed at the client's failure to use a more effective solution.

The second factor relative to confrontation is relationship. In order to avoid the "battered client syndrome" (Davis, 1989), confrontation must convey a genuine sense of empathy and concern and provide helpful information. Coming from either the clinician or the peer group, the desired change is unlikely to occur outside a respectful and supportive relationship. Without a positive relationship, confrontation may be experienced as an assault. Care must be taken that indiscriminate confrontation does not inadvertently reflect a dynamic of scapegoating within the peer group.

The effectiveness of confrontation is increased by accurate definition of the specific thoughts that must be confronted, sensitivity to the youth's ability to hear feedback at a particular time, and the youth's readiness or willingness to risk self-examination. This readiness is increased and the confrontation is more likely to be heard and considered if some positive feedback regarding associated thoughts is included (for example, "I think you are absolutely right about . . . but where I see a problem is. . . .").

Finally, the impact of confrontation may well be the most important variable. The appropriate level of confrontation is determined by the impact it is having on the client (Ross, 1987). Although the level may exceed what the therapist is personally comfortable with or may raise resistance in other group members, it is the impact on the person being confronted that must be used to gauge the appropriate level. The youth's discomfort with his or her own thoughts or behaviors must become sufficient to motivate the desired change.

The role of cotherapy is especially important when confrontation is employed. While the confronting therapist encourages the desired change, his or her attention is best focused on the youth who is being confronted in order to follow the cognitive progression and monitor the impact. The cotherapist can observe the confrontation while staying tuned in to the reactions and resistance of other group members in order to be prepared to process issues with the group. Cotherapists may also need to trade roles occasionally if a client becomes engaged in a standoff. Sometimes the observing therapist is able to comment on a standoff and suggest an alternative thought or approach, taking over to complete the desired progression when the original therapist has hit a brick wall. Some cotherapists trade off in a "good guy–bad guy" parlay wherein one confronts and the other resolves. The key word here is *trade* so that neither therapist is cast permanently in the "bad guy" role.

Different clients and different situations may require different levels of confrontation. Think of these levels on a continuum of assertiveness rather than force. The mildest confrontation may simply identify the area of concern and wonder about it, seeking clarification and understanding from the client (for example, "I hear you saying _____ . I wonder if you can help me understand") The client may achieve the desired change under the challenge of explaining himself.

The moderately assertive confrontation may identify the concern and challenge more directly (for example, "I hear _____ . That has not been my experience. How can you explain?"). In a major confrontation, the therapist again identifies the concern and confronts the denial or distortion with disparate facts (for example, "I hear _____ and yet I know _____ "). In this most assertive confrontation, the challenge may be for honesty more than a cognitive shift relative to the identified concern, and the therapist must convey expectations relative to the therapeutic relationship while acknowledging the youth's dilemma (as in, "We have to be honest with each other. I know that it may be difficult to believe this process is helpful" or "You seem to be seeing it like _____ but it appears to me that _____ ").

It is important to recognize that defensiveness is a normal reaction to confrontation. When confrontation is perceived as a threat to one's self, instinct dictates flight or fight. When confrontation is unavoidable, it is natural to defend one's self. The clinician must remove the perceived threat and model nonexploitative resolution (Davis, 1989).

Early confrontations in the treatment process may be related to the behavior of record and may draw on police reports and victim statements in confronting the youth's denial or minimization of abusive behavior. Sometimes confrontation may include new information and be part of the educational process. In other instances, the process of confrontation may lead the therapists to their own "aha!" experience by demonstrating a lack of knowledge or understanding by the client that requires more basic education. As treatment progresses, confrontations are often related to old patterns' reappearing or the failure to generalize treatment concepts to current situations, choices, and functioning.

Let us say that in exploring the elements of abuse, a therapist defines coercion as the continuum of pressures that are brought to bear on the victim. The client states, "Well, I never threatened anybody." The goal is to confront the client's denial of coercion and help him own his exploitative tactics. Here is how the discussion might ensue:

Therapist: What did you say would happen if she didn't do it?
   Client: Nothing.
Therapist: Then why do you suppose she went along?
   Client: I don't know.
Therapist: What do you think she thought would happen?
   Client: Maybe that I wouldn't like it.
Therapist: Did you say you wouldn't like it?
   Client: Yes.
Therapist: Do you think she thought you wouldn't like her?
   Client: Maybe.
Therapist: Did you say you wouldn't like her?
   Client: I said if she loved me she would.
Therapist: So do you suppose she thought you wouldn't love her if she wouldn't?
   Client: Maybe.
Therapist: You were a pretty important person to her?
   Client: Yeah. I was the one who always stuck up for her and did things for her. She always came to me.
Therapist: So, what do you think it meant to her to think you might not love her if she didn't do it?
   Client: I don't know.
Therapist: Do you think not being loved by you would be pretty bad for her?
   Client: Yes.
Therapist: So you think not loving her anymore was a threat?
   Client: Maybe.
Therapist: So do you think maybe you did threaten her?
   Client: Yes.

When the therapist is confronting the client's inadequate participation in treatment, the consequences of nonparticipation need not lie within the group but rather are presented relative to the client's being clear about the choices he is making regarding current and future conditions; that is, violation of the court orders for treatment and risk of reoffense.

Introduction to Treatment

At the outset, the rules and expectations of the treatment provider, the group, and the program must be discussed. Group rules may cover confidentiality, behavior, and participation, and the group should clearly define the consequences of noncompliance. Similarly, the therapists must explain the limits of their own confidentiality, define their role within the group, and convey their basic expectations regarding group participation, assignments, and attendance. The program may have more global expectations relative to behavior within the agency, components of treatment, and family involvement, which should also be made clear.

Equally important is the juvenile's introduction of himself to other group members and they to him. Most programs require at least a disclosure of the charges and some description of the referring abuse behavior at the first group session. Introductions do not need (nor is it advisable to encourage) full, detailed descriptions of the sexual aspects of the offense. The focus of the group will be on the abusive aspects of offenses, not the sexual aspects. The introductions begin to establish accountability, and the focus of the group is offense specific. Preparation for this first session is usually part of the assessment and intake process.

Initial sessions must also address the same issues that any other group therapy must. Clients—not even voluntary and motivated clients—do not arrive in treatment knowing how to be clients. Anxiety and inexperience hamper every new client's first group experience; and for juvenile offenders, suspicion and reluctance to give up their behaviors compound the problem. The therapist may outline the goals of the program and empathize with the client's understandable anxiety. Reassurance is possible, however, as the therapist is able to reveal his or her understanding and experience relevant to the client's problems and offer encouragement that new information and understanding will be available to the client. In all fairness, the therapist must warn the client that the treatment process will often be emotionally painful and that he will often wish to quit, but that if he successfully completes treatment, he may feel better and display fewer problem behaviors. Early assignments might include clarifying why the client is in the program, what he hopes to get out of treatment, definition of short-term and long-term goals, and group expectations and goals.

Definition of Sexual Abuse. Many sexually abusive youth arrive in treatment without clearly understanding what sexual abuse is. Although they know what behavior was involved and the legal consequences, they have little understanding as to why the behavior was considered abusive. When a significant age difference or extreme force was involved, they may believe those are the only criteria for definition of abuse. Just as adults have historically been confused in the evaluation of the sexual interactions of children and the meaning of hands-off offenses, the juvenile is similarly confused. The youth are often relieved to hear that the sexual behaviors involved in the abuse are normal human behaviors (usually). The therapist identifies the behavior but pursues the definition regarding why the interaction was abusive.

The factors that must be understood are consent, equality, and coercion. Group discussion should result in correct definitions:

Consent: (1) understanding what is proposed without confusion or trickery, (2) knowing the standard for the behavior in the culture, the family, and the peer group, (3) awareness of possible consequences including stigma, punishment, pain, and disease, and (4) respect for agreement or disagreement without repercussions.

It is imperative that therapist and client distinguish consent, cooperation, and compliance. *Cooperation* implies participation without regard for one's personal beliefs or desires. *Compliance* implies allowing without regard for one's personal beliefs or desires. Neither cooperation nor compliance equals consent:

Equality: Equal authority, power, and control within a relationship.

Although significant age or size differentials are clearly indicators of inequality, there are many more subtle indicators of inequality: intellectual or strength differentials; sexual knowledge and experience differentials; assertiveness, popularity, and self-image differentials; and delegated authority differentials such as big brother, baby-sitter, leader, and boss.

Coercion: Pressures—either explicit or implied—that are exerted in order to get someone else to do something.

These pressures may include subtle threats such as loss of love, attention, or friendship; covert manipulation, trickery, and bribes; overt threats and peer pressure; as well as physical force and violence. Juveniles must understand the whole continuum of coercion in order to define fully the exploitative nature of their behavior.

Assignments can be given to challenge clients to define these terms and apply them to their own experience. Subsequent group discussion should continue to refine definitions. Assignments might include defining how the youth obtained the cooperation or compliance of their victims; identifying situations in which they consented, complied, or cooperated during a given week; or describing in detail pressures they brought to bear on their victims and the nature of the power inequalities between themselves and the victim.

As the juveniles begin to understand the definition of abuse, they are likely to become aware of other experiences and behaviors in their history that were also abusive. New disclosures of additional behaviors and their own victimization are common following this process. As the youth become aware of the elements of consent and inequalities of power, they should be held accountable through feedback and confrontation to eliminate the behaviors involved in all interactions.

Consequences, Deterrence, and Empathy.

In communicating the expectation that the client control sexually abusive behaviors during treatment, it must be made clear from the beginning of treatment what the consequences of reoffense might be for each youth personally, in the group, and in the legal system. Definition of these potential consequences can be the basis of assignments to be discussed in the group. Deterrence can be discussed in terms of external restraint, limited access, punishment, aversion, and empathic development. (See also Chapter Seven.)

External restraints may include removal from the home and placement in residential or correctional facilities; limited access may be imposed by supervision and conditions that restrict contact with potential victims; punishment may be imposed by the family or the courts. Discussion of legal definitions of sexual abuse is typically enlightening to the youth.

Aversion and empathy are internal deterrents that will be goals of the treatment process. Aversive deterrence is the result of the discomfort a youth experiences when he is aware of the potential consequences of a behavior. Empathic deterrence is based in awareness of the harmfulness of an imagined behavior and is the highest form of deterrence. This is a long-term goal of treatment and is unlikely to occur in a meaningful sense until much later in the treatment process as the youth develops empathic skills. For some, aversive deterrence may be the highest level achieved. Early work related to victim sympathy may include assignments requiring the youth to imagine the impact of his behavior on his victim. Immediate, short-term, and long-term consequences can be explored.

It may be helpful in discussing the various levels of deterrence to relate to common learning experiences. External restraint may be demonstrated in the example of a parent's putting a fence around the play area to prevent the child from running into the street. Limited access would be the parent's putting a fence around the swimming pool in order to keep the child from falling in. Learning as a result of punishment occurs not only in spanking but also in learning not to touch the hot stove as a result of being burned. Learning to stay away from skunks is the best example of aversive conditioning, wherein that which initially looks cute and cuddly proves itself noxious by its odor.

These examples also demonstrate how learning situations may inadvertently teach lessons other than that which is desirable. For instance, the child who must learn about hot stoves by being burned may also learn that the world is a dangerous place rather than a safe, protected environment. Similarly, the child who is spanked or beaten as a deterrent to further misbehavior may learn that physical force and violence are methods of achieving control over others. Another lesson of aversion demonstrates aversive experiences as a betrayal of one's trust in one's own perception. This lesson can also be related to the victim's experience of betrayal in a relationship that appears to be good and then proves to be exploitative. These parallels provide a basis for these youths' discovery of the origins of their own distorted perceptions, beliefs, and dysfunctional patterns.

Early discussions of deterrence relative to reoffense may later be recalled in social skills training and relationship building as the group explores the ways in which they deter others from getting close enough to form friendships and achieve intimacy. At that time, assignments may challenge group members to identify their own obnoxious or distancing patterns of behavior, as well as confronting these same patterns in the peer group. Self-control can be discussed in terms of deterring themselves from negative behavior, as well as not deterring others from desirable interactions. Assignments might include completing a decision matrix that identifies the positive and negative outcomes for both sexually abusing and choosing not to engage in this behavior. Completion of the same matrix toward the end of treatment can highlight the youth's awareness of his own deterrent factors.

Learning to Use the Cycle

The concept of the cycle is introduced very early in treatment in a didactic framework, likening it to an algebra formula that must be learned before it can be applied. Just as mathematical terms must be understandably defined before the equation makes sense, the elements of the cycle must also be defined. Assignments can help the juvenile learn to distinguish situations, thoughts, feelings, and behavior. These early assignments may include such activities as making lists of feelings, describing situations, reporting thoughts, and recording the behavior of others. Clients might be instructed to observe others in a public place where they do not have knowledge of other persons' thoughts or feelings in order to clarify behavior and to notice those things we infer about thoughts and feelings on the basis of body language. Group members can analyze the incidents that the client describes to the group in order to separate the various elements.

As group members become able to distinguish these elements, their reporting of thoughts and descriptions of feelings are enhanced by writing assignments such as journal and letter writing. Cognitive and affective statements can be differentiated throughout the group process by the therapist's observations as well as direct questions. Traditional psychotherapeutic techniques can be used with a focus on the relationship of the cycle (for example, "I hear you saying that you think _____ . Now tell me what you feel about _____ ." or "It sounds as if you are feeling _____ . Can you tell me what thoughts make you feel that way?"). This exchange can be followed by pointing out for the group the presence of both thoughts and feelings in the client's report. As the youth describes problems he encounters or cognitive or affective aspects, it is helpful to write those on the board to assist the group with beginning to see how the various elements of the cycle interact. It is important for the youth to begin to recognize that he exhibits cycle progression to some plateau level several times each day.

In preparation for teaching the client to use the cycle, the therapist may collect anecdotal information that demonstrates the elements of the cycle from group discussions. The therapist then shows the application to the cycle by making connections between current material and the cycle that is being discussed. A blackboard may be helpful in illustrating the cycle for the group. For example, the therapist can say, "Let's see if we can relate the incident Shane described in our last group to the cycle. Shane reported that he and his mother had a big fight because his stereo was too loud. But what had happened before the fight? I find that blasting one's parents with the stereo is often a power-and-control behavior, so let's see if we can make the cycle work here." Beginning with the power-and-control behavior, the therapist helps the group recall other things Shane had said about the incident and helps Shane describe his thoughts and feelings, filling in key words and phrases in the appropriate places on the cycle being drawn on the blackboard:

Situation:	Mother says she does not want Shane to spend the weekend with her because she has a lot to do.
Triggers:	Feeling disappointment and hurt.
Victim-stance perception:	"She doesn't think I can help her."
Negative expectation:	"She will never let me help her with anything."
Feeling:	Rejection.
Isolation and withdrawal:	Going in his room alone.
Power-and-control behaviors:	Slamming door, blasting his stereo, arguing with mother about the volume.
Fantasy:	"Maybe I should run away."
Retaliatory thought:	"Then she'll feel sorry."
Plan:	None.

Further discussion can then explore how the feelings might have been expressed directly instead of through behavior (for example, "Mom, when you say you don't want me with you, it makes me feel hurt. I'm disappointed that you don't want me to help you this weekend") or how feelings might have been changed by restructuring thoughts (for example, "Just because I can't help her this weekend doesn't mean I can't do something else helpful"). The implications of the fantasy for Shane and the consequences of acting on the fantasy can be discussed. Finally, the retaliatory thought can be shown to parallel the trigger feeling: that making someone else feel bad would somehow "get back" for the youth's own bad feeling.

In this illustration, the cycle did not run its full course, but the issues were not resolved. Mother and Shane fought about the volume of the stereo but did not resolve Shane's issues. This event would be considered unresolved, leaving Shane at risk in future situations.

As each aspect of the cycle is explained, it is helpful to assign the client the task of monitoring his thoughts, feelings, or behavior during the week and listing examples of ways he exhibited the concept. It is helpful to use copies of the form shown in Exhibit 16.1, instructing the youth to write a brief description by each term. Review of the homework in the group helps group members to begin recognizing their own manifestations of each stage in more depth. When the youth appears to have adequate understanding and recognition of each element, it is helpful to suggest assignments that represent the daily manifestation of cycle progression. Requesting the group members to list three examples of incidents that occurred during the week that elicited a feeling of helplessness and identifying the progression of thoughts and behaviors through the fantasy or planning stages assist the clients with recognizing when the process is currently occurring. Group discussion of these assignments should always include the identification of nonpower-based solutions or ways of coping with the situation, as well as identification of the failure of the power or control behaviors to solve the dilemma or make the client feel better in an enduring way.

After the group has been involved in a few illustrations of the cycle, they can be challenged to begin assignments relating the cycle to their sexually abusive behaviors. The client is asked to identify current issues occurring prior to the offense, his reactions to the event, and his subsequent thinking. By this time, the client will be fairly accurate with identification through the initial aspect of the fantasy portion but may be somewhat uncomfortable with the specific sexual content. Providing examples of sexual fantasies or working with this phase in the group typically decreases the client's reticence. The client is then asked to identify each element involved in contemplating, planning, or setting up the abuse, describing in detail the coercive actions used to gain the victim's cooperation or compliance,

EXHIBIT 16.1. JUVENILE GROUP CYCLE.

Situation: _____

_____

Feelings: _____

_____

Thoughts: _____

_____

How do you feel now?   What bad thing did you expect?*

_____   _____

_____   _____

Did you get caught?*   Did you isolate?*

_____   _____

_____   _____

What did you think would happen?   What were you angry about?*

_____   _____

_____   _____

Did you hurt someone?   Power struggles: _____

Yourself? _____   _____

Property? _____

What was your plan?*   What did you imagine to make
                                        you feel better?*

_____   _____

_____   _____

*What were you thinking?

signs of resistance and distress he ignored, any threats or promises made to keep the victim from disclosing, and the cognitive aftermath. Typically this process reduces any residual denial or minimization of the abusiveness of the behavior, and hearing other youth do the work encourages more detailed sharing. Later the client will be asked to identify historical issues that may have affected his sensitivity to the current issues occurring prior to the sexual assault, as well as patterns of thinking, situations, or feelings associated with other fantasies of sexual abuse or other incidents that may have occurred. The youth is also encouraged to identify progressions in his abusive patterns and crossover behaviors and, if possible, to identify the first onset of any sexually abusive or humiliating behavior. Much of this work is maximized through ongoing homework assignments asking the client to identify each aspect being considered. Typically, youth will spend time reflecting and recalling but may write minimally. When the group discusses each individual's assignment, the client becomes more willing to share some of the thoughts he did not write down.

For youth who have difficulty identifying trigger situations or events or cognitive aspects, or who seem to have compulsive patterns of fantasizing about sexual abuse, journal keeping may be of benefit. This assignment should be done daily to be most effective with helping the therapist and the client identify patterns. Initially, the youth might be requested to detail situations that elicit feelings of helplessness, control, or anger and then to write down his associated thinking. Detailing what the situation meant to the client, his retaliatory thoughts, or his negative expectations will begin to help the youth identify the early phases of the cycle. The youth might then be asked to include retaliatory or control behaviors and fantasies that include sexual thinking. Providing clarifying questions or feedback when reviewing the journal can be helpful to the client. As treatment progresses, feedback can be directed toward healthy alternatives and accountability. Initially, it is quite risky for the client to disclose his thinking and uncomfortable for the therapist to hear or read it.

It is important to respect the client's vulnerability with this assignment unless clear safety issues are apparent. Some youth benefit from short-term use of this technique, and others may benefit from keeping a journal throughout the entire treatment. It is important, however, to monitor the sexual content of journal work. Because fantasies of sexually abusive behaviors are very reinforcing, journal work describing sexual interactions should focus on defining the abusive aspects of sexually abusive thoughts rather than sexually explicit descriptions of arousal and orgasm, which are more usefully incorporated into nonabusive fantasies describing consensual interactions.

If treatment takes place in an outpatient setting, it is beneficial to help the youth identify high-risk factors that could increase the chance of reoffense as soon as he has taken responsibility for the offense. For youth who are in residential treatment, this process may be used later. The client is asked to determine the types of situations that are high risk and conducive to engaging in abusive behaviors, associated thinking that increases cycle progression, and antecedents that occur earlier in the cycle that could alert him that he is at risk. The client is assisted with developing safety plans that involve specific behavioral and thinking alternatives or self-imposed restrictions that would strengthen his ability to prevent reoffense. Use of cognitive and behavioral rehearsal of reactions to potential situations strengthens this ability for the client. Any apparent grooming, stalking, planning, or fantasizing that occurs needs to be dealt with as seriously as a reoffense might be handled. Issues of supervision or restriction previously discussed might be implemented and the youth assigned to do assignments that help him identify the progression that he may have missed or the basis for deciding to place himself in a high-risk situation. In a residential program, accountability for controlling these factors might be increased levels of supervision or loss of privileges when the youth fails to stop the process.

Having established the offense-specific group and helped the youth to define the problem, understand the pattern of the cycle, and think about deterrents and the goals of treatment, the therapist can relate every subsequent intervention back to one or more of those concepts. Individual treatment plans will become more and more specific as the therapist ascertains more details about the risks and assets, sexuality and abusiveness, and the developmental and contextual framework of the youth. Interventions that address the contextual phenomenology of the youth will be relevant to the client's sense of safety and expectations of self and others, and so they are relevant to the early phase of the cycle. Interventions that address growth and development will be relevant to the youth's sense of self-esteem and competence and will counter negative expectations of failure and rejection. Interventions that address sexuality will be relevant to sexual thoughts and behaviors. Interventions that address abusive attitudes and behaviors are clearly relevant to the abusive cycle, and interventions that plan for future risk management are relevant to relapse prevention.

Therapists, staff, teachers, and parents will do well to be creative in developing interventions based on a goal orientation, and treatment providers must be prepared to articulate the relationship between the referring problem, the intervention, and the goals of treatment. Courts, social services, and managed care companies cannot be expected to understand the relationship of these elements without the therapist's being able to explain the connections.

In describing the relationship between treatment interventions and treatment goals, the primary offense-specific goal is to change the abusive cycle. Therefore, it is useful to think about what elements of the cycle might be affected by various interventions. Table 16.3 provides a useful outline.

TABLE 16.3. GOAL-ORIENTED
INTERVENTIONS FOR ABUSE CYCLE ELEMENTS.

Historical Elements	Cognitive Elements
Family therapy	Phenomenological reporting, journaling
Psychotherapy (person-centered, humanistic)	Cognitive restructuring
Biography, memories	Confrontation, accountability
Family tree, genograms	Thought stopping
Lifeline	Covert sensitization
Role definition	Social skills, relationship building
	Visualization, guided fantasies
Situational Elements	Problem solving, decision making
Supervision, structure restrictions	Empathy training
Family therapy	Group process
Competency, self-image	Psychotherapy (existential, rational emotive therapy, Adlerian, and reality-based)
Risk management, risk taking	
Temperament	Risk taking, expectations
Peer culture	Values clarification
Psychotherapy	
	Behavioral Elements
Affective Elements	Supervision, structure, restrictions
Identification and labeling	Positive and negative reinforcers
Journaling	Logical consequences, impulse control
Group process	External controls, group process
Psychotherapy (traditional, rational emotive)	Arousal conditioning
	Behavior modification, social skills
Anger management	Systematic sensitization and desensitization
Empathy training	Psychotherapy (reality, behavioral)

Education and Assignments

Meaningful participation in the offense-specific group process and the demonstration of understanding and change relevant to the sexual abuse cycle are enhanced by a variety of structured, psychoeducational components. The specific components are eclectic and are designed to develop the youth's ability to control cycle progression and thus prevent further sexually abusive behaviors. Each technique selected is directed toward a specific aspect of the cycle.

The client must understand that he is responsible for his treatment; he is the only one who can implement control of the cognitive, affective, and behavioral aspects that have previously been problematic. The statement that treatment is designed to help the youth achieve control over his own behavior not only defies the myth of a cure but also says that treatment is not something the therapist does to the client; rather, it is something the client does for himself. It is ultimately a message that imparts control to the client.

Although the needs and deficits of each individual vary, some of the more common areas of treatment are presented here with suggestions of topics and assignments. Equally important are techniques that improve social skills and competence. The assignment of homework not only reinforces the educational components of treatment but also intensifies the process by extending the juvenile's attention to his problems and maintains application of concepts between treatment sessions. The expectation that the client will complete work outside the sessions can clarify that developing the ability to control the problem is the client's responsibility.

Educational, psychotherapeutic, vocational, or recreational programs may be indicated to address skill deficits, psychological conditions, and competency issues that are unique to the individual but not relevant to the offense-specific elements of treatment. Drawing on community resources to improve the client's overall functioning and competency supports the treatment process and demonstrates the therapist's concern for the client's future success.

Cognitive Restructuring

Cognitive restructuring is a critical aspect of work with sexually abusive youth. In order to develop the maladaptive response of exerting power over others, the youth has to have a different view of the world from those who do not accept that style of functioning. The sexually abusive youth thinks differently from other youth. Developing control of sexually abusive behaviors involves changing the way he thinks. Thinking errors, distortions, and beliefs about the client's rights must be modified. Berenson (1987) indicates the youth must attack his ways of making decisions, his worldview, and his thinking errors.

Continual feedback and challenging of beliefs may occur in the group process. It is important to challenge thoughts that indicate that the youth is perceiving himself as superior to others or is exhibiting attempts to dominate others. Any power-thrust thinking or behavior needs to be pointed out and examined by group peers, and the underlying belief that the world owes the youth or is his to control must be challenged. Indications that the youth is exhibiting a victim-stance orientation, which is typically based on the juvenile's belief that others have no right to criticize, interfere with what he wants to do, or establish his own rights, needs to be challenged as ineffective and inaccurate and contrasted with more accurate perceptions and beliefs. The client needs to assume responsibility for what he does or how his behavior affects others in a way that elicits responses. In order to provide challenges to the youth's thought patterns, the therapist must listen, observe, and examine how each youth does think about or view the world. Autobiographies, journals that log perceptions of each occurrence the youth encounters, and identifying daily experiences in the framework of the cycle can provide clues for the client and the therapist about individual thinking styles.

A particularly useful technique to help youth correct thinking errors was developed by Ellis (1962) and other cognitive therapists. Rational emotive therapists suggest learning to counter thoughts through a structured process that challenges the client to identify the irrationality of his perceptions and assumptions. The process alters affective response based on the change in perception of a situation (see Figure 16.4).

It is helpful to instruct the group members in the technique initially and then require them to do extended assignments to correct their distortions and irrational thoughts. Initially many youth claim they have no distorted thoughts because their way of thinking seems so reasonable to them.

Supplemental assignments that detail types of thinking errors and expect the client to identify his way of exhibiting similar thinking errors, as well as identifying the thinking errors represented in the sexual abuse cycle, increase the juvenile's awareness. Providing models of more rational and healthier ways of thinking or viewing the world can begin to help the youth be aware of differences. As this process becomes clearer to the client, expectations of accountability for using the technique to correct his irrational thoughts needs to increase.

Approaches that increase the client's ability to relate to others in a reciprocal way, increasing his awareness of the impact of his behavior on others, and developing an ability to be interdependent with others are also important. Learning to solve problems and make decisions that are not based on unrealistic expectations or faulty assumptions improves the client's ability to function in a way that does not involve domination of others. Learning to interrupt his ability to corrode deterrents, to cut off fear, or to allow superoptimism (thinking that he is capable of getting away with anything he wants) is critical to interrupting the immediate antecedents to sexual abuse. Some programs use the techniques of Yochelson and Samenow (1976) in these processes, such as the moral inventory, disposing of criminal thinking by reasoning, and preempting criminal thinking through the development of anticipatory mental strategies for replacing thinking errors. Critical to the success of these strategies is the client's ability to develop self-disgust with his behaviors and cognitions. It is not effective to approach the client in a punitive or angry way to develop this self-disgust because that will challenge the assumptions of superiority and elicit defensiveness or power-based retaliation and the youth will not be receptive to new ideas. Instead, techniques should be directed toward rational and informative approaches that facilitate the development of an open channel (Berenson, 1987).

FIGURE 16.4. COGNITIVE RESTRUCTURING.

*The youth counters the provoking thought with one that promotes the desired feeling.

It was suggested in Chapter Seven that the beliefs referred to as thinking errors are often very rational in the context of the youth's reality. The best confrontation of such distortions is through the experience of a new reality in treatment.

Empathy

The overwhelming majority of programs report that work on victim empathy is a critical component in treatment. Many techniques have been described in the field for developing victim empathy; however, in developing research methodologies to measure empathy during the early 1990s, several controversies arose.

First, the definition of the construct itself is not always clear, although most often researchers have discussed role taking or perspective taking as markers of empathic skills. Perspective taking, however, is only related to one's ability to be empathic; it is not definitive of empathy, which we have defined in this book as *reading cues, interpreting to attribute meaning,* and *validation of the interpretation.* Perspective taking is the basis for sympathetic responses (imagining the experience or feeling of another based on similar experiencing of oneself). It has been pointed out that sympathy is based in the "assumption of sameness" but that empathy is based on the "assumption of difference" (Bennett, 1988). One of the critical issues for the sexually abusive youth is the need to understand that not everyone sees or feels as he does; for example, he cannot assume that another person is enjoying sexual contact just because he is.

Victim awareness—increasing the youth's understanding of the negative impacts of abuse—may be an important step in motivating the abuser to work in treatment to change abusive patterns and to use relapse-prevention skills throughout his life (Pithers & Gray, 1996). Empathy, however, is a critical psychological health skill, and it is vital to all future relationships. Whereas victim awareness work may ask the youth to imagine what the victim was feeling or to describe the ways victimization may continue to affect the victim in future relationships, victim empathy work will ask the youth: "What signs did the victim give you? What cues did you miss? How did you misinterpret that cue?" Similarly, the youth can be helped to develop empathy for self and others by getting in touch with his own cues. Questions like, "What was your body telling you? What was your heart feeling?" can help the youth recognize his own cues.

In treatment, the goal of empathy is to begin to see the youth noticing the cues of self and others, being willing to struggle to interpret the cues accurately (without jumping to conclusions), and becoming able to validate interpretations. Empathic skills should become noticeable and observable before treatment ends. To expect less is to settle for lower-level deterrents, which may be less generalizable. Youth who do not learn to demonstrate these skills, either because of developmental deficits or because of lack of sufficient time in treatment, must be considered to be at a higher risk, and external sources of deterrence continue to be necessary.

Victim Awareness

The process of developing an awareness of how sexually abusive behaviors affect others is critical to countering the distortions that support abusive behavior and the belief that the youth can impose control over others. It is critical to personalize the victim as a human being: validating the victim's right to safety using the victim's first name in introductions while respecting privacy by not using the last name and challenging expressions such as "my victim" that objectify or assert ownership of the victim. When victim awareness is fostered too early in the treatment process (prior to understanding the distortions or power thrust involved), there may be a tendency to use this new awareness to strengthen the youth's sense of ownership and empowerment.

Videos and books regarding child victims and adult survivors may be used to broaden the group's appreciation of the impact of sexual abuse. The youth's own experiences of victimization can also be the basis for achievement of victim empathy. It is often useful to provide general information first, having clients define general impacts and then personalize the information by trying to imagine the impacts for the victims they abused. Concrete exercises in how one imagines what others are feeling are necessary and prepare the way for confrontation of the denial and justification the youth has used regarding his abusive behavior.

Having the youth write a description of the abuse incident from the victim's point of view, having the youth write a letter to himself from the victim's perspective, and writing detailed apologies to the victim that specify the abuse is entirely the client's responsibility and detailing how he misused power and misinterpreted consent are all helpful assignments. Letters are always reviewed in the group; they may be sent if appropriate to the case. Singer and Sermabeikian (1995) have demonstrated the use of doll-play reenactments as a vehicle to increase victim awareness.

Victim-perpetrator clarification sessions—with the specific victim when the victim is in the family and reunification is a goal, or when such sessions are requested by a victim therapist for a third-party offense—can be useful, but they must be carefully prepared for and must always be responsive to the victim's need for such a session. Emphasis on developing healthy sibling relationships is important in family abuse cases.

Sometimes victim-perpetrator sessions can be arranged by having a group of perpetrators and a group of victims meet together to allow the youth to hear first-hand about the impacts. These sessions require extensive preparation and guidance regarding how to answer victim questions, and they should not be attacking to perpetrators or threatening to victims. Consent, equality, and lack of coercion are guidelines for such sessions, so victim groups would be the same age or older than the abusive youth they are meeting with, and both groups would require consent. The rules for such sessions are always based in accountability and empathy.

The hope is that understanding the impact of sexual victimization will foster empathy and motivate the youth to consider the feelings of others. Learning about the impact provides the basis for challenging the distortions that justify abusive behaviors.

Societal Messages and Myths

Although the major focus of treatment is on identifying and restructuring the client's beliefs and thinking patterns that allow and enable sexually abusive behavior, it is also important to explore the role of external systems in supporting the client's thinking. Remembering Conte's (1986) suggestion that we first explore the pathology of the individual, then the pathology of the family, and then the pathology of external systems, it is important to sensitize the client to the societal messages and myths that seem to support sexually abusive patterns. The attitudes demonstrated by the peer group, the community, and the culture have been part of the client's learning process and experience.

At the same time that the client is very aware of the external controls that have been implemented within his immediate environment (such as no access to children and pornography), he must begin to be aware of the more pervasive influences in the culture that contribute to sexually exploitive thinking. An exploration of the functions and methods of relevant social learning and the origins of attitudes and beliefs help to explain the current myths. Socialization, stereotyping, and role expectations demonstrate the ways in which individuals become depersonalized and objectified. Each of these areas can be discussed in terms of the attitudes of others that have a negative impact on the client, as well as their contribution to attitudes of the client that have had a negative impact on others. For example, male socialization suggests that males are tough and able to protect themselves (therefore they are not victims), males are sexually aggressive (therefore they are always willing in sexual interactions), and males are dominant (therefore they are always in control of others). The client's experience has often been a contradiction of many of these myths; he may have been victimized or sexually confused, and he may often feel helpless and out of control. At the same time, sexually aggressive behaviors have often been supported by these messages and yet have violated the culture's laws and customs. Stereotypes, prejudice, and role expectations depersonalize the client as well as his victims and contradict the need to appreciate the needs and feelings of others as unique individuals. For example, the older adolescent male is stereotyped as one of the strongest, most virile, and most aggressive members of the community, yet adolescent males between the ages of fifteen and twenty are more often victims of both violent and personal crimes than any other segment of the community (National Criminal Justice Information and Statistics Service, 1995). The subsequent lack of protection and empathy for the male adolescent is in direct conflict with the client's needs and experience. More globally, attitudes and myths relevant to sexual aggression include many exploitative and depersonalizing messages that support male domination, victim culpability, and deviant sexuality.

The client's attitudes and beliefs may be defined within the group's discussion or more specifically through administration of such testing instruments as the Burt Rape Myth Acceptance Scale, Buss-Durkee Hostility Inventory, Attitudes Toward Women Scale, Phase Sexual Attitudes Questionnaire, and the Multiphasic Sexual Inventory—Juvenile. Assignments designed to identify and sensitize group members to the messages that support their attitudes may include definitions of sexually derogatory language, the portrayal of stereotypes in advertising and movies, sexual objectification in pornography, biases in news reporting, and the glorification of sexual deviance and exploitation in song lyrics and entertainment.

Confrontation of sexually exploitative thinking must include sensitization to the pervasiveness of supporting messages within the culture. The client's understanding of advertising techniques that influence behavior, such as the repetition of visual and auditory images that subconsciously influence the choices we make in buying detergent, choosing a restaurant, or preferring a particular brand of jeans or shoes, can be generalized to acceptance of sexual myths and subsequent risk of behavior. By challenging the client's acceptance and awareness of these messages in the cultural environment, the suggestion is made that the client may choose to control the influence that these things have on his thinking rather than being subconsciously controlled by external messages.

Sexuality

Basic to the process of reducing the risk of sexually exploitative behaviors is the client's need for correct sexual information, dating skills and relationship building, definition and acceptance of his own sexual identity, and developing values that support reciprocal and consensual sexual interactions. Sex education curriculums may be used, and assignments may include reading and reporting on relevant physiological and relationship aspects. Many videos relevant to sex education, dating skills, responsible sex, and acquaintance rape are available for group discussions. Values-based sex education challenges the youth to identify values regarding nonconsensual interactions, sexual fantasies, arousal patterns, masturbation, and homosexuality, all areas deserving open group discussion and examination. Many sexually abusive youth are confused about the implications of their abusive behavior and their own victimization in defining their sexual preference and identity. Reassurance that fantasy and experience need not dictate future sexuality is comforting and enables more open discussion of fears and perceptions. Assignments include logging arousal, reporting on fantasies, and creation of nonexploitive fantasy material.

Clients must understand the reinforcing mechanism of masturbation and appreciate the danger of masturbating to deviant fantasies. Rules can be set up for masturbation:

YES!   Only when I am feeling good, have privacy, and have caring thoughts

NO!   Not in public, when I am angry or upset, or when I am having thoughts of abusive interaction or an inappropriate partner

HELP!   To stop thoughts and behavior, think of the consequences, and talk to staff or parent

Emphasis in the group is on identifying covertly exploitative elements of fantasy material and support of nonexploitative material. Deviant material should be minimized by constant restructuring to more normative thinking. Therapists must be alert to the reinforcement of group members' prurient interest in deviant material and vigilant to arousal and subsequent masturbatory behaviors. Clients who have not achieved understanding of the exploitative elements of fantasy or are unable to use consensual, nondeviant fantasies should be restricted from opportunities for masturbation in order to minimize continued reinforcement of problematic arousal patterns and deviant sexual preferences. More compulsive masturbators must be helped to redirect their time and energy into nonsexual activities in order to achieve a less sexualized lifestyle.

As a whole, providers have been much more conscientious about addressing sexual deviance than sexual health. Conscious efforts must always be to reinforce the positive aspects of sexuality and relationships.

Controlling Arousal

All of the work in treatment is relevant to avoidance or interruption of future dysfunctional cycle progression, but many therapists use at least two techniques early in treatment. Covert sensitization and arousal-conditioning techniques are used to decrease deviant arousal, and cognitive restructuring techniques are used to help the youths correct the justifications that supported their offense behavior as well as the distortions that support cycle progression. Either can be implemented as soon as clients have applied the cycle to their situation or have identified the thinking that supports their offense behavior and the immediate antecedents occurring prior to the sexual abuse.

Covert sensitization is a self-conducted technique that develops uncomfortable associations with behavior and thinking that has occurred immediately antecedent to the client's offense behavior. The process interrupts the pleasurable association and anticipation that the youth has previously experienced. There are several indirect effects that appear beneficial, including improved impulse control or decision making, decreased deviant or inappropriate arousal, decreased strength of previous cognitive distortions, and an improved sense of self-control. Although most research substantiating the effectiveness of this technique has been related to work with adult offenders (Abel, Becker, Cunningham-Rathner, Kaplan, & Reich, 1984; Quinsey & Marshall 1983), research by Hunter and Santos (1990) and Becker, Hunter, Stein, and Tartaglini (1989) describes the effective use of this technique with adolescents. Many programs presume the presence or risk of deviant arousal and use this technique based on the client's reports; however, the protocol sanctioned by the Association for the Treatment of Sexual Abusers (ATSA) recommends that a physiological assessment of the individual's arousal patterns be conducted initially.

Physiological assessment of arousal patterns and sexual interests is most typically done with a penile plethysmograph, a physiological recorder that measures changes in penile tumescence (increase in the circumference of the penis) and detumescence (decrease in the circumference of the penis) that occur in response to a sexual stimulus (Davis, 1988). The stimulus materials used vary among programs. Recent recommendations from ATSA are to use auditory stimulus materials and that clients be at least fourteen years of age. The assessment measures the differential response of the individual to the varied sexual stimuli presented in each scenario in order to identify the client's arousal and interest patterns (such as prepubescent children versus age-appropriate peers and forceful versus consenting sexual behaviors). Plethysmograph evaluation of male tumescence is used to understand to what degree the subject is interested in deviant and appropriate sexual behavior and to understand the client's arousal pattern so that interventions of specific treatments can be applied to alter a deviant sexual arousal pattern (Davis, 1988).

There was initially some controversy regarding the use of physiological evaluations with adolescents, primarily based on concerns that the juvenile may be exposed to new, deviant stimuli. The National Task Force on Juvenile Sexual Offending (1988) indicated the following assumption: "If arousal patterns indicate significant or fixated interest in deviant and/or criminal sexual behaviors, it is in offender's best interest to change or control his arousal" (p. 46). A similar statement was repeated in the task force's 1993 report (p. 80). Becker, Hunter, Stein, and Kaplan (1989) and Hunter and Santos (1990) cite the use of auditory stimulus material that has been specifically developed for the assessment of adolescent sex offenders.

Clinicians who teach clients covert sensitization techniques must educate them initially regarding the expected outcomes and effects. The technique is used to teach the patient to pair antecedent fantasy and behaviors with mentally aversive stimuli through a structured sequence. Because the technique is not useful if it is not done correctly and because the client may resist completing the required number of sessions, the client is asked to record the sessions on audiotape in some programs or to complete the assignments in the treatment setting in other programs. The client is provided feedback regarding his technique, and the audiotapes (if used) are erased. According to research by Abel, Becker, Cunningham-Rathner, Kaplan, and Reich (1984) the most effective results are obtained if four hours of this technique are completed in twenty-minute segments. It is useful to request the juvenile to complete twelve twenty-minute segments, at a rate of not more than four per week.

A typical protocol would include repeating three to four sets of three scenes for a twenty-minute session. The scenes are the deviant scene, the aversive scene, and the escape-reward scene. The deviant scene is a one- to two-minute scene describing the sequence of thoughts and behaviors occurring immediately antecedent to the client's sexual acting out. The youth switches to the aversive scene at the point where the thought of sexually abusive behavior occurs, prior to describing specific sexual behavior. The aversive scene is a three-minute description of strongly personal and aversive social consequences that have occurred or could occur as a result of sexually abusive behavior. During this scene, the client makes three to four references as to why these aversive consequences are occurring (perhaps because of their abusive sexual thoughts or sexually abusive behaviors). This process strengthens pairing of the consequences with the antecedent thoughts and behaviors described in the deviant scene. The client then switches to the escape-reward scene, which is a one- to two-minute description of expected positive outcomes of the youth's developing control of the behaviors or descriptions of nondeviant sexual interactions with consenting age-mates. Throughout the escape-reward scene, the youth makes three to four references to these things being possible because he no longer engages in sexually abusive behaviors or is in control of his sexual thoughts and behaviors.

Assignments might include developing the chains of thoughts and behaviors, identifying the most aversive consequences and most rewarding outcomes that the youth can identify that would affect him, and writing scenarios that could be used in the scenes. The client is instructed that any time he experiences himself beginning to engage in deviant sexual fantasies or is engaging in any of the antecedent behaviors, he should repeat the aversive scene cognitively to interrupt the process.

Satiation techniques have been used in some programs to decrease the client's arousal to deviant behaviors and stimuli. The satiation procedure is based on an extinction model designed to eliminate the erotic aspects through boredom (Hunter & Santos, 1990). Most programs that include satiation techniques use Abel's protocol (Abel et al., 1984). Essentially, the process involves repeating the deviant fantasy for specified periods of time until it becomes boring. The repetition may be accompanied by masturbation or may consist of only verbal repetition. Each satiation session typically lasts for one hour and consists of one five- to ten-minute scene describing consensual activity with an appropriate-aged partner, followed by fifty to fifty-five minutes of repeating a specific, arousing component of a deviant sexual behavior. Approximately six to eight sessions are required for beneficial results. This technique has not been popular in the field because of parental resistance, difficulty in monitoring, and limited research.

Additional arousal conditioning techniques might include fantasy management to develop appropriate, arousing sexual fantasies; thought-stopping techniques to interrupt deviant fantasy; or aversive conditioning.

Family Dynamics and Influence

The need to explore family dynamics, role expectations, beliefs, and myths is obviously relevant to understanding the phenomenology of the youth. (Chapters Eight and Eighteen discuss family history and involvement relevant to the treatment of juveniles.) Similarities of family dynamics can be brought to light within the group, and parallels of family functions and role expectations are often demonstrated within the group as well. Role plays of both past and anticipated future family interactions can be enacted in the group.

Even clients who have no family available or involved in the treatment program can be helped to see the relevance of family discussions to both their history and their future. All clients benefit from definition of family role expectations, parent-child interactions, and appreciation of early parental influences. Ideally, responsible sex discussions include pregnancy prevention and the implications of parenthood.

Parent education and child development information relate not only to the client's own childhood experience and empathy for his child victims, but also to his potential in future marriage, family, and parent roles. The intimacy of family relationships is always an area of concern and is often basic to the client's abusive behavior because the achievement of intimacy is often relevant to the early motivations in sexual relationships.

Treatment issues relevant to family functioning that deserve special note and are often overlooked in evaluations of family dynamics are (1) the incidence and prevalence of physical, emotional, and psychological abuse and intimidation among siblings, (2) the incidence and prevalence of physical, emotional, and psychological abuse and intimidation perpetrated by baby-sitters, and (3) the incidence and prevalence of physical, emotional, and psychological abuse and intimidation perpetrated on family pets. Sibling conflicts are often normalized by parents, who say, "All kids fight." It has become apparent in many cases, however, that sibling relationships may have been pervasively abusive long before the sexual abuse triggered an intervention. Similarly, abuse of pets often goes unnoticed as well.

The implications of sibling violence and animal cruelty must be seen and the relevance of these incidents considered in treatment planning. In the search to identify both risks and assets in the past, present, and future, therapists must ask of families: "Who nurtures whom?" and "Who hurts whom?" For better and for worse, sibling relationships are likely to represent the youth's internal working models of attachment and can profoundly illuminate the phenomenology.

Treatment of Concurrent Psychiatric Disorders

The goals of interventions to address concurrent psychiatric disorders are (1) to manage the effects that might impede success in the offense program, (2) to achieve resolution of or develop a life span management perspective of effects that might impede success in relationships, (3) to achieve optimal global functioning, and (4) to achieve understanding and acceptance of those disorders that are unchangeable. Some disorders, especially those associated with traumatic experience, are resolvable if the client is able to tolerate the work and short-term use of medications that may aid the process. Some disorders appear more transitory or situational and may be more easily resolved. Some disorders are heritable and chronic and will require lifelong management. Usually pharmacological interventions are most successful when used in combination with other therapeutic interventions.

Individual Therapy Sessions

Although group treatment is recommended for all sexually abusive youth (National Task Force, 1988, 1993), many youth can benefit from adjunctive individual therapy as well when resources allow for both. It is imperative, however, that individual therapies also be conducted by specialists who are trained in sexual abuse issues and are part of an integrated team approach. Purposeful thought should be given to articulating the goals and boundaries of each therapeutic modality. Individual therapy can be particularly useful in demonstrating the differential boundaries of various types of relationships. Individual sessions can also be intensely empathic, and they may be a more appropriate setting for detailed disclosures of victimization and perpetration in order to keep group work focused on health rather than deviance.

Individual sessions are sometimes indicated in the early stages of treatment to help draw out the painfully shy client who is unable to speak freely in the group. Individual sessions are also occasionally warranted in the course of therapy to address uniquely personal concerns or to conduct physiological testing, facilitate understanding or application of concepts, monitor medical interventions, or confront destructive group dynamics.

Individual sessions may be routine, weekly, hour-long appointments or may be called for on a case-by-case basis, from day to day, in either shorter or longer time frames, to address particular issues that arise. As is always suggested, all components should be congruent with the common concepts and treatment philosophy (see Chapter Fourteen).

Relapse Prevention

The relapse-prevention model (Pithers, Marques, Gibat, & Marlatt, 1983) may be included throughout the treatment process, but it is especially important during the final phases of treatment, during aftercare, and as a long-term support following treatment. Relapse prevention adds another dimension to the dysfunctional cycle by focusing on the apparently irrelevant decisions that result in the youth's being in a high-risk situation or in a situation that provides the opportunity for offending.

The relapse-prevention model requires a high level of accountability for thinking and personal choices, recognizing high-risk factors, internal or external, and averting the dysfunctional cycle. By examining the choices and decisions that support the client's being in a high-risk situation and cognitively rehearsing ways to interrupt the cycle progression, the client learns to implement more responsible thinking and foresight throughout daily living.

It can be useful to help clients integrate the relapse-prevention model and the sexual abuse cycle models. The concepts of relapse prevention are especially supportive of the client's awareness of the continued risk of reoffense, and the model calls for external sources of monitoring for the abuser after treatment. In combining the two models (Ryan, 1996b) it is suggested that the process of relapse should be changed by the treatment process. Prior to treatment, abusers do not experience the abuse as dissonant with their self-image until after committing the offense, when the anxiety arises regarding the meaning and possible consequences of abusing and elaborate distortions are used to suppress and deny the problem. However, the goal in treatment should be for the abuser to experience that dissonance at the first thought of being abusive because abusive fantasy is no longer congruent with self-image. If thoughts (fantasies) of being abusive do not become dissonant, then the individual's risk of reoffense may continue to warrant external sources of supervision.

Recently researchers have raised some interesting questions about the relapse-prevention model (Ryan, 1996b; Ward, Hudson, & Siegert, 1995), and an entire issue of the ATSA journal, *Sexual Abuse: A Journal of Research and Treatment* (Vol. 8 no. 3, July 1996) was devoted to various authors' work with this model. Of particular interest was the observation by Pithers and Gray (1996) that abusers become more motivated to learn and use relapse-prevention strategies if they have completed work on victim awareness first.

Successful outcomes of the treatment process carry with them certain inherent dangers. As the client begins to feel better and experience a greater sense of control and competence, there is a tremendous temptation to deny any further risk of relapse. The client's understanding of the role of negative feelings and expectations moves him toward a more consistent sense of hope and anticipation. Continued treatment begins to be experienced as an undertow—a downward pull back into the pain and despair of the past. During this period of treatment, the client may appear resistant or exhibit the previous patterns, or client and therapist may both be inclined to terminate because the client appears to be so much improved. It is in this final phase that relapse prevention supports the concept of long-term risk management within a framework that confirms the impending end of formal treatment.

The relapse-prevention model is also a useful framework for ongoing aftercare and support groups following termination from the intensive treatment program. The expectation of the need for ongoing support and reminders of the lessons of treatment should be a consistent message throughout the treatment process. Long-term follow-up and support protects both the client's investment in the work of treatment and the community's investment of treatment resources.

At the end of the youth's participation in offense-specific group treatment, a group celebration is appropriate to congratulate him on succeeding in treatment and to emphasize his lifelong commitment to a nonabusive lifestyle. Successful graduation represents a transition from intense treatment to a personal aftercare plan that is tailored to the specific risks and needs of the individual. The youth's ability to celebrate growth and development, while still acknowledging risk, is an important sign of success.

References

Abel, G., Becker, J., Cunningham-Rathner, J., Kaplan, M., & Reich, J. (1984). *The treatment of child molesters: A manual.* Unpublished manuscript.

Becker, J., Hunter, J., Stein, R., & Kaplan, M. (1989). Factors associated with erection in adolescent sex offenders. *Journal of Psychopathology and Behavioral Assessment, 11*(4).

Becker, J., Kaplan, M. S., Tenke, C. E., & Tartaglini, A. (1991). The incidence of depressive symptomatology in juvenile sex offenders with a history of abuse. *Child Abuse and Neglect, 15,* 531–536.

Bennett, M. (1988). Overcoming the Golden Rule: Sympathy and empathy. *Communication Yearbook, 3,* 408–422.

Berenson, D. (1987). Choice, thinking, and responsibility: Implications for treatment (pp. 1–12). *Interchange.* (Newsletter of the National Adolescent Perpetrator Network). Denver: Kempe National Center.

Blanchard, G. (1995). *The difficult connection.* Brandon, VT: Safer Society Foundation.

Bremer, J. (1992). Serious juvenile sex offenders: Treatment and long term follow-up. *Psychiatric Annals, 22*(6), 326–332.

Briggs, D. C. (1975). *Your child's self esteem.* New York: Doubleday.

Conte, J. (1986). *Sexual abuse and the family: A critical analysis.* In T. Trepper & M. Barrett (Eds.), *Treating incest: A multimodal systems perspective.* New York: Hawthorne Press.

Dailey, L. (1987). *Utilizing psychiatric consultation: Implications of dual diagnosis.* Paper presented at the Fourth National Adolescent Perpetrator Network Meeting, Keystone, CO.

Dailey, L. (1996). *Biomedical treatments.* Paper presented at the Twelfth Annual Conference of the National Adolescent Perpetrator Network, Minneapolis.

Davis, D. (1989). *Counseling techniques with reluctant clients: Core curriculum training manual for sex offender counselors.* Louisville: Kentucky Department of Social Services.

Davis, J. (1988). *Sexual arousal and related treatment.* Presentation handout at the What Is the Plethysmograph? workshop, National Conference on Juvenile Sex Offenders, Long Beach, CA.

Ellis, A. (1962). *Reason and emotion in psychotherapy.* Secaucus, NJ: Citadel Press.

Eth, S., & Pynoos, M. (1985). *Post traumatic stress disorder in children.* Washington, DC: American Psychiatric Press.

Freeman-Longo, R., & Bays, L. (1988). *Who am I? And why am I in treatment?* Shoreham, VT: Safer Society Press.

Freeman-Longo, R., & Bays, L. (1989). *Why did I do it again?* Orwell, VT: Safer Society Press.

Freeman-Longo, R., Bird, S., Stevenson, W., & Fiske, J. (1995). *1994 nationwide survey of treatment programs and models.* Brandon, VT: Safer Society Press.

Gilgun, J. (1988). *Factors which block the development of sexually abusive behavior in adults abused as children.* Paper presented at the National Conference on Male Victims and Offenders, Minneapolis.

Gilgun, J. (1996). Human development and adversity in ecological perspective: Part I and II. *Families in Society.*

Hunter, J. (1996). *Understanding impact of trauma on children: When victimization leads to victimizing.* Paper presented at the Eleventh International Congress of the Society for the Prevention of Child Abuse and Neglect, Dublin, Ireland.

Hunter, J. A., & Becker, J. (1994). The role of deviant arousal in juvenile sexual offending: Etiology, evaluation and treatment. *Criminal Justice and Behavior, 21*(4).

Hunter, J., & Santos, D. (1990). Use of specialized cognitive-behavioral therapies in the treatment of adolescent sexual offenders. *Journal of Offender Therapy and Comparative Criminology, 34,* 239–248.

James, B. (1989). *Treating traumatized children.* San Francisco: Lexington Books.

Jancin, B. (1995, December). SSRI's may bring deviant fantasies to heel. *Clinical Psychiatry News,* pp. 3–4.

Johnson, S. (1989). *Branching out: The tree cycle.* Paper presented at the Fourth National Adolescent Perpetrator Network Meeting, Keystone, CO.

Kaemingk, K., Koselka, M., Becker, J., & Kaplan, M. (1995). Age and adolescent sexual offender arousal. *Sexual Abuse: A Journal of Research and Treatment, 7*(4).

Lane, S. (1978). [Author's treatment notes from Closed Adolescent Treatment Center, Division of Youth Services, Denver]. Unpublished.

Lane, S., & Zamora, P. (1978). [Syllabus materials from inservice training on adolescent sex offenders, Closed Adolescent Treatment Center, Division of Youth Services, Denver.] Unpublished.

Lane, S., & Zamora, P. (1984). A method for treating the adolescent sex offender. In R. A. Mathias, P. Demuro, & R. Allinson (Eds.), *Violent juvenile offenders: An anthology* (pp. 347–354). San Francisco: National Council on Crime and Delinquency.

Lewis, D., Shanok, S. S., & Pincus, J. (1979). Juvenile male sexual assaulters. *American Journal of Psychiatry, 136*(9), 136–139.

Lewis, D. O., Shanok, S. S., & Pincus, J. H. (1981). Juvenile male sexual assaulters: Psychiatric, neurological, psychoeducational, and abuse factors. In D. O. Lewis (Ed.), *Vulnerabilities to delinquency* (pp. 67–88). Jamaica, NY: Spectrum Publications.

Malamuth, N. (1984). *Pornography and sexual aggression.* New York: Academic Press.

Malamuth, N. (1986). Predictors of naturalistic sexual aggression. *Journal of Personality and Social Psychology, 50,* 953–962.

Maletzky, B. (1996). Treatment by degrees. *Sexual Abuse: A Journal of Research and Treatment, 8*(2).

Marshall, W. (1996). The sexual offender: Monster, victim or everyman? *Sexual Abuse: A Journal of Research and Treatment, 8*(4), 317–336.

Marshall, W. L., Hudson, S. M., & Hodkinson, S. (1993). The importance of attachment bonds in the development of juvenile sexual offending. In H. Barbaree, W. Marshall, & S. Hudson (Eds.), *The juvenile sex offender.* New York: Guilford Press.

National Criminal Justice Information and Statistics Service. (1995). *Criminal victimization in the United States.* Washington, DC: U.S. Government Printing Office.

National Task Force on Juvenile Sexual Offending. (1988). Preliminary report. *Juvenile and Family Court Journal, 39*(2), 10, 26, 46.

National Task Force on Juvenile Sexual Offending. (1993). Revised report. *Juvenile and Family Court Journal, 44*(4).

Pithers, W., & Gray, A. (1996). Utility of relapse prevention in treatment of sexual abusers. *Sexual Abuse: A Journal of Research and Treatment, 8*(3).

Pithers, W., Marques, J., Gibat, C., & Marlatt, G. (1983). Relapse prevention with sexual aggressives. In I. Stuart & J. Greer (Eds.), *The sexual aggressor.* New York: Van Nostrand Reinhold.

Prentky, R., Knight, R., Straus, H., Rokou, F., Cerce, D., & Sims-Knight, J. (1989). Developmental antecedents of sexual aggression. *Development and Psychopathology, 1,* 153–169.

Quinsey, V., & Marshall, W. (1983). Procedures for reducing inappropriate sexual arousal. In I. Stuart & J. Greer (Eds.), *The sexual aggressor.* New York: Van Nostrand Reinhold.

Ross, J. (1987). *Treating the adolescent perpetrator.* Paper presented at the Sixteenth National Symposium on Child Abuse and Neglect, Keystone, CO.

Ryan, G. (1984a). [Panel presentation at the University of Minnesota, Program in Human Sexuality, Minneapolis]. Unpublished.

Ryan, G. (1984b). The child abuse connection. (pp. 1–4). *Interchange.* (Newsletter of the National Adolescent Perpetrator Network). Denver: Kempe National Center.

Ryan, G. (1989). Victim to victimizer: Rethinking victim treatment. *Journal of Interpersonal Violence, 4*(3), 325–341.

Ryan, G. (1993). *Concurrent psychiatric disorders.* Paper presented at the Tenth Annual Conference of the National Adolescent Perpetrator Network, Lake Tahoe, NV.

Ryan, G. (1995a). *Difficult clients in treatment: Temperament or resistance.* Paper presented at the Eleventh Annual Conference of the National Adolescent Perpetrator Network, St. Louis, MO.

Ryan, G. (1995b). *Treatment of sexually abusive youth: The evolving consensus.* Paper presented at the International Experts Conference, Utrecht, Netherlands.

Ryan, G. (1996a). The sexual abuser. In E. Helfer & R. Kempe (Eds.), *The battered child* (5th ed.). Chicago: University of Chicago Press.

Ryan, G. (1996b). A response to the critical comment on Pither's relapse prevention model. *Sexual Abuse: A Journal of Research and Treatment, 8*(2).

Ryan, G., & Lane, S. (1991). *Juvenile sexual offending* (1st edition). San Francisco: New Lexington Press.

Ryan, G., Lane, S., Davis, J., & Isaac, C. (1987). Juvenile sexual offenders: Development and correction. *Child Abuse and Neglect: The International Journal, 11*(3), 385–395.

Ryan, G., Blum, J., Law, S., Christopher, D., Weher, F., Sundine, D., Astler, L., Teske, J., & Dale, J. (1988). *Understanding and responding to the sexual behavior of children: Trainers manual.* Denver: Kempe National Center.

Ryan, G., Lindstrom, B, Knight, L., Arnold, L., Yager, J., Bilbrey, C., & Steele, B. (1993). *Treatment of sexual abuse in the context of whole life experience.* Paper presented at the Twenty-first Annual Child Abuse and Neglect Symposium, Keystone, CO.

Ryan, G., Miyoshi, T., Metzner, J., Krugman, R., & Fryer, G. (1996). Trends in a national sample of sexually abusive youth. *Journal of the American Association of Child and Adolescent Psychiatry, 35,* 17–25.

Sczechowicz, E. (1988). *Residential programming for adolescent sexual offenders.* Presentation at the Fifth Annual Conference of the National Adolescent Perpetrator Network, Anaheim, CA.

Singer, K., & Sermabeikian, P. (1995). *Using doll reenactments to increase victim empathy.* Unpublished manuscript.

Smith, T. (1987). *You don't have to molest that child.* Chicago: National Committee for Prevention of Child Abuse.

Spencer, T., Biederman, J., Welens, T., Harding, M., O'Donnell, D., & Griffin, S. (1996). Pharmacotherapy of attention-deficit hyperactivity disorder across the life span. *Journal of the American Academy of Child and Adolescent Psychiatry, 35*(4).

Spiegel, D. (1993). *Dissociative disorders.* Lutherville, MD: Siedran Press.

Strayhorn, J. (1988). *The competent child.* New York: Guilford Press.

Stickrod, A. (1988). [Presentation handout from Preventing Sexual Abuse Through Treating Juvenile Sexual Offenders workshop, Proceedings of the Adolescent Sex Offenders Symposium, Salt Lake City.] Unpublished.

Terr, L. (1990). *Too scared to cry.* New York: Harper & Row,

Thomas, A., Chess, S., & Birch, A. (1977). *Temperament and development.* New York: Brunner Mazel.

Turecki, S. (1985). *The difficult child.* New York: Bantam Books.

van der Kolk, B. (1987). *Psychological trauma.* Washington, DC: American Psychiatric Press

Ward, T., Hudson, S., & Siegert, R. (1995). A critical comment on Pithers' relapse prevention model. *Sexual Abuse: A Journal of Research and Treatment, 7*(2).

Whitaker, M. (1987). [Program description.] Allegheny Intensive Treatment Program, Philadelphia.

Yochelson, S., & Samenow, S. (1976). *The criminal personality* (Vol. 1). Northvale, NJ: Aronson.

CHAPTER SEVENTEEN

SPECIAL POPULATIONS

Children, Females, the Developmentally Disabled, and Violent Youth

Sandy Lane,
with Chris Lobanov-Rostovsky

The special populations that are the subject of this chapter—young children, female, developmentally disabled, and violent youth—are sexually abusive youth who have some unique characteristic that requires special consideration or modifications in treatment approaches. In the past, fewer specialized services were available for these youth or, because of their unique characteristics, their abuse behaviors were often minimized or discounted. At times, systemic reactions to the abusive behavior of these youth were disproportionate. In some respects, these youth were viewed by some as untreatable or unlikely to have committed sexually abusive behaviors. Each of these populations has exhibited an ability to benefit from comprehensive treatment that considers all aspects of their life experience, their developmental history, and their abusive behavior.

Exciting developments have occurred in work with each of these populations. Increasing numbers of treatment programs are available, several books and articles have been published, and several research studies are in progress or have been published. It also appears that a greater number of agencies identify the need for assessment, intervention, and reporting for each of the populations. There are still controversies, and at times the abuse behaviors are still minimized or misconstrued, but the efforts to identify effective approaches, developmental antecedents, and program development are important and ongoing.

Children with a Sexual Abuse Behavior Problem

A survey conducted within the membership of the National Adolescent Perpetrator Network (NAPN) (Rogers, 1992) elicited twenty-five responses from clinicians who work with young children with sexual abuse behavior problems. Approximately half of the respondents indicated concern about social service agencies that respond only to intrafamilial sexual abuse. Additional dilemmas included lack of research to guide practice, placement issues, making a clear differential definition of normative and nonnormative sexual behaviors, and balancing victimization and perpetration issues. Many of the dilemmas have begun to be addressed.

In the most recent survey of programs conducted by the Safer Society Foundation, 390 programs were identified that work with children with sexual behavior problems (see Chapter Twelve), and there has been increased focus on a number of areas:

- Refining and further defining a variety of treatment approaches
- Identifying through research the characteristics of children with a sexual abuse behavior problem and their response to various treatment approaches (NCCAN grants have been made to Pithers and Gray and to Bonner, Walker, and Berliner)
- Increased exploration of various etiological theories (Gil, 1993)
- The development of assessment tools, including the Child Sexual Behavior Inventory (Friedrich, Grambsch, Broughton, Kuiper, & Beilke, 1991) and the Child Sexual Behavior Checklist-R and a suggested typology for children who molest (Johnson, 1993, 1995)
- Research related to differentiating between normative and nonnormative sexual behaviors (Friedrich et al., 1992)
- Increased sharing among clinicians about treatment techniques and intervention strategies related to preadolescent children who have a sexual abuse behavior problem.
- Resources developed to help parents (Gil, 1987; Pithers, Gray, Cunningham, & Lane, 1993; Ryan & Blum, 1994).

Some preschools have begun to seek information about what behaviors to identify and be concerned about. Particularly encouraging has been an increased use of developmental-contextual assessments and the exploration of developmental antecedents. It is beginning to be more apparent that issues of attachment and the associated outcomes of disrupted or dysfunctional attachment may contribute to the development of abusive behaviors (Marshall, Hudson, & Hodkinson, 1993).

Although jurisdictional and budgetary constraints continue to limit some social service agencies to intrafamilial intervention, it appears that there is improved awareness, identification, consideration, and intervention with reported sexual abuse behaviors by children. Behaviors are viewed more seriously and evaluated more consistently. Many professionals continue to struggle with balancing safety considerations with the child's developmental need to be with the family. Many treatment programs also face these difficult struggles. In Colorado social services is oriented toward family preservation, and several agencies throughout the state have attempted to identify strategies to integrate safety, treatment, and the child's needs.

In the field there continue to be controversies about labeling children, diverse beliefs about the etiology of the behavior, diverse treatment approaches, and healthy discussions and explorations about the direction of the field. This situation is somewhat reminiscent of what clinicians who worked with sexually abusive adolescents experienced in the early 1980s.

In our own work with treating young children with sexual abuse behavior problems, we are fairly eclectic; we use bits and pieces from most theories and suggested approaches, integrated with our own perceptions and beliefs. Our treatment and assessment is based in the abuse cycle concepts (see Parts Two and Four in this book). Implicit to the theoretical concepts underlying this approach is the belief that the child is initially responding to something about which he or she feels helpless (Finkelhor and Associates, 1986; Porter, 1986). The young child may be reacting to early childhood maltreatment, a traumatic experience, some type of victimization, neglect, a disrupted environment, dysfunctional models of coping, or a lack of nurturing, empathic, or consistent care. The development of the child's worldview, belief system, coping ability, and internal reactions is influenced by that child's experience. It is believed that the eventual coping mechanism the child uses involves a compensatory misuse of power that is eventually sexualized or expressed sexually. When we assess a child, we attempt to identify unresolved issues that relate to early development and the related deficits, as well as assessment of the abusive sexual behavior. We are not concerned just with compensatory misuse of power or the abuse behavior; resulting treatment plans focus on all problematic areas. Although the overview of our program primarily describes the treatment components oriented toward the abuse behavior, the child and the family also receive treatment for symptomatology related to any contributing unresolved issues, deficits in functioning, and adjunct therapy for any concurrent psychiatric disorders.

Our work with young children with sexual abuse behavior problems began in the mid-1980s as we became increasingly concerned about the frequent reports we heard from adolescents about their initial abusive behaviors at about eight or nine years old. Our initial work looked at prevention in an effort to help young children avoid developing sexually abusive behavior problems. The initial group consisted of six children who ranged from seven to nine years old and exhibited a constellation of behaviors and symptoms that we believed to be predictive of eventual sexual abuse behaviors. Within the first two months, we learned that each of the group members was already engaged in abuse behaviors, and at least two reported the onset of their behaviors as occurring as early as ages four and five. We began to think that some youth may exhibit a progression of sexual abuse behavior over time, and our group became a treatment group rather than a prevention effort (initially described by Isaac, 1986), although we had little idea then as to how to treat young children with sexual abuse behaviors. Over time, we learned from the children, much as we had learned from adolescents in the mid-1970s.

Initially we were intrigued by how similar the pattern of thoughts, feelings, and behaviors of the antecedents and the actual abuse were to the adolescent and adult offenders we were working with. The children were much less sophisticated and somewhat less calculating, but the elements were the same, so we used the abuse cycle concepts as a basic approach with the children. We had to adapt the concepts to the children's cognitive level and consider the children's developmental level and learning abilities in the presentation of treatment concepts. We also learned that the children exhibited symptoms of traumatic experiences of developmental disruptions more overtly, and we needed to develop treatment approaches to address those issues. We learned that involvement of the family and caretakers was critical. Because of the similarity of the abuse pattern to that of adolescents, we continue to be concerned that there may be a potential for some young children to progress in the development of more ingrained abuse behavior patterns without intervention.

During the early years, we struggled with numerous reactions of disbelief that children so young could exhibit sexually abusive behaviors and even, at times, that children that young were exhibiting any sexual behavior. The children we were working with had extremely dysfunctional backgrounds and behaviors, and it was easy for some to view those children as exceptions rather than indicative of a more widespread problem. Over time, people have become more aware of the frequency of the problem in this population, and several programs for young children have been developed in our community and nationally.

We have worked with over one hundred young children and are in the early stages of analyzing the data we have accumulated on each child. In retrospect, we wish we had been more systematic in the earlier years about using consistent tests and structured interviews or collecting specific demographic data so that comparisons would be more beneficial. We suggest that any newer programs consider these aspects because part of helping the field continue to develop is sharing data. Several pioneers in this field have provided examples (see works by Friedrich, MacFarlane, Johnson, Cunningham, Berliner, Gil, Gray, Bonner, Rasmussen, Burton, and Christopherson) of suggested data collection and testing.

Assessment

Differentiating between normative and nonnormative sexual behaviors of the children referred to our agency has been based on information developed by Friedrich, Beilke, & Urquiza (1988), Friedrich, Grambsch, Broughton, Kuiper, & Beilke (1991), Friedrich et al. (1992), Johnson (1988a, 1988b, 1993, 1995), and Ryan (1989), our understanding of sexual development, and the sexual abuse cycle. We also explore issues related to the equality of power (Isaac, 1986; Ryan, 1989), developmental-contextual history, family, and risk factors.

We currently identify our population as children with sexual abuse behavior problems in an attempt to emphasize both the children's needs and the nature of the behavior for which they have been referred. The behavior is viewed as harmful to others and to themselves. Although we do not believe the child decides to hurt or exert power over another, the behavioral manifestation of the child's coping response involves an expression of sexual and nonsexual control-seeking or dominating behavior. Power differential involves contrasting the levels of experience, sophistication, knowledge, secrecy, age, size, authority, personality characteristics, intellectual capacity, and developmental aspects of the participants in the abuse behavior.

Characteristics

The children have been divided into two age groups for treatment purposes: seven to nine years old (and occasionally six years old) and ten to twelve years old. Less mature or more sophisticated children may be assigned to a group that does not match these age categories. Slightly more than half of the children we have worked with are in the younger age group. The majority of the children are male, and about two-thirds of the children have been Caucasian. Nearly half of the children were living in their own home at the time of referral.

Over two-thirds of the children exhibited a history of sexual, physical, or emotional victimization or abandonment experiences. Slightly less than two-thirds of the children were exposed to disruptive or dysfunctional home environments. About one-third of the children exhibited concurrent psychiatric disorders (the most prevalent diagnosis was attention deficit hyperactivity disorder), learning disabilities, and medical problems. Slightly more than one-quarter of the youth also had engaged in nonsexual behaviors that would be considered delinquent if they were older.

Slightly over half of the children fully acknowledged the abuse behavior, and over one-third exhibited some form of partial denial. The older children had a greater tendency to deny their behavior completely. About one-fourth of the children appeared quite ashamed or embarrassed about their behavior.

Characteristics Related to the Abuse Cycle

During the early groups, the concept of the sexual abuse cycle was not introduced to the children, although the facilitators operated on assumptions based on the concept. About two years after we began working with this population, one of the children was trying to explain to the group a situation in which he had nearly repeated a sexual abuse behavior; he began to describe his experience as a set of stair steps. The other children in the group began to relate to him about their experience of steps and described some of their experiences. The steps they described were remarkably similar to the sexual abuse cycle developed for adolescents and adults.

In subsequent groups the "stair-step" cycle was used for the younger group. The younger children seemed more comfortable using the steps to discuss their behavior, and it began to be easier to introduce the notion of intervention and prevention in terms of learning how to "get off the steps" or "stop myself from going higher." (See Figure 17.1 for one child's step cycle.) With the younger children, developing experiential activities has increased their awareness. When they play, they often set chairs up like stair steps, jump from chair to chair, and then practice jumping off safely. They draw pictures of getting off the stairs, and we use an outside open staircase that goes to the second floor of the building to talk about how scary it is to get too high on the steps.

The children have exhibited the same lack of tolerance for feelings of helplessness, powerlessness, abandonment, rejection, or humiliation identified in older sexually abusive youth. The vocabulary they use to describe their affective experience is more simplistic and representative of their age level, but they appear to communicate beliefs that what they have experienced is outside of their realm of control and they try to account for why these things have happened. Often they assume they are somehow responsible because they have been bad. In our population, approximately two-thirds of the children had experienced some type of victimization, and approximately two-thirds had experienced some disruption in their home (the same children were not necessarily exposed to both situations).

FIGURE 17.1. ONE CHILD'S STEP CYCLE.

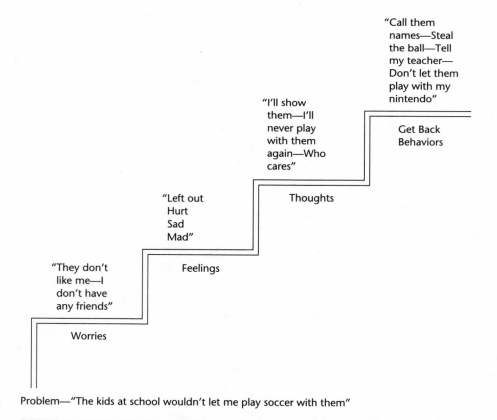

"Call them
names—Steal
the ball—Tell
my teacher—
Don't let them
play with my
nintendo"

Get Back
Behaviors

"I'll show
them—I'll
never play
with them
again—Who
cares"

Thoughts

"Left out
Hurt
Sad
Mad"

Feelings

"They don't
like me—I
don't have
any friends"

Worries

Problem—"The kids at school wouldn't let me play soccer with them"

Source: Reprinted by permission of RSA, Inc.

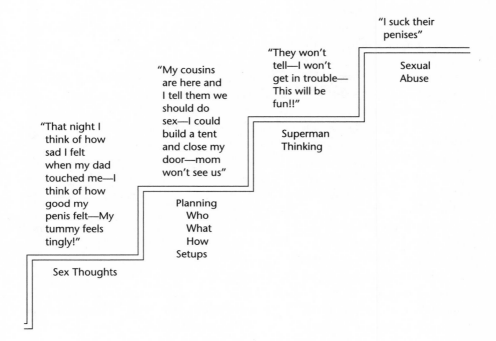

"I suck their
penises"

Sexual
Abuse

"They won't
tell—I won't
get in trouble—
This will be
fun!!"

Superman
Thinking

"My cousins
are here and
I tell them we
should do
sex—I could
build a tent
and close my
door—mom
won't see us"

Planning
Who
What
How
Setups

"That night I
think of how
sad I felt
when my dad
touched me—I
think of how
good my
penis felt—My
tummy feels
tingly!"

Sex Thoughts

The experiences they were exposed to in the home included physical violence, sexual problems, boundary violations, significant loss, neglect, a move in the prior year, attachment disorders, frequent moves, and family enmeshment. When asked to draw pictures of their families, many of the children failed to include eyes, mouths, or ears.

Many of the children have exhibited poor self-esteem, a lack of self-confidence, and negative self-statements. The children often seem needy or dependent, and they seek reassurance. They personalize statements, feedback, and discipline. There have been frequent statements by many of the children indicating that they believe others' behaviors are intended to harm them, make them look bad, or reject them. The most frequently described life experiences or symptoms are depression, social isolation, social alienation, enuresis, thoughts of drinking or using drugs, excessive fears, nightmares, communication problems, eating problems, and self-mutilation.

Most of the children have exhibited social competency deficits. They seem to have difficulty with joining in, asking for help, handling failure or mistakes, apologizing, compromising, building friendships, sharing, problem solving, handling embarrassment, accepting compliments, playing with others, impulse control, empathy, intimacy, handling conflicts, making decisions, delaying gratification, anger management, or accepting no. They tend to be socially isolated in school situations, and few have close friends.

The children have also exhibited a tendency to rely on a compensatory coping style that involves a misuse of power or control in many situations. The style we have observed is less sophisticated than in older sexually abusive youth, but it appears similar in nature. During group sessions the children have exhibited a need to be first or best or to win. If they are playing a game, they will often cheat or change the rules in their favor in the middle of a game if they believe they are losing. If they lose, their comments are self-deprecatory. They have exhibited frequent retaliatory and manipulative behaviors, and some have described thinking they would like to be in a gang because they would feel strong and safe. Parents and school personnel have described frequent power-based behaviors: fights, disruptive behaviors, disobeying rules, tantrums to get their own way, challenging statements, oppositional behaviors, testing limits, an inability to accept confrontation, low frustration tolerance, provoking younger children, provoking peers, hitting, and whining.

Many of the children exhibit sexualized behaviors or sexual preoccupation, particularly when they seem confused, stressed, or angry. They also exhibit sexualized behaviors and curiosity normative to their developmental level. They may perceive or react to benign, nonsexual situations in a sexualized manner, describe sexual experience in a way that seems to be self-enhancing, make sexual observations, or describe sexual behaviors in a more sophisticated manner than is typical of their age or developmental level. Episodically, they report a preoccupation with sexual thoughts or masturbation; many have described engaging in "humping" behaviors on their bed or with stuffed animals, as well as genital self-touch. During play we have observed boundary violations and intrusive touch.

The majority of the children we have worked with describe early arousal experiences. This was another topic that was not introduced to early groups until three of the eight- and nine-year-old boys raised the issue about two years after we started. They asked if they could talk about something adults do not like to talk about. Interestingly, while the elected spokesman asked the question, the other two were drawing pictures. One drew several knives and the other an alligator with very large, sharp teeth. The boy said that the three of them had talked, and they all had a problem. The problem was that none of them wanted to do another abuse behavior, but they kept having a problem with their penis getting hard when they thought about sex, and it made them want to do sex with their siblings. One said that he had tied strings on his penis or used rubber bands to try to make the hardness go away. Another had placed his penis under the tub faucet and turned the cold water on as hard as it would go to make it "get normal" again, and the other slapped and hit his penis. The boys were frustrated because nothing they had tried had worked, and they believed that having an erection caused their abuse behavior.

Although we had talked some about healthy sexuality, it was apparent that it was time to discuss arousal and clarify misconceptions and confusion with the group members. Some group members said that they had tried masturbation to control arousal feelings. Various group members described arousal as "a tingly feeling," "butterflies in the stomach," "an erection," "feeling good," "having a queasy stomach," "feeling happy," and "a penis that is sort of hard." Nearly all of the children have said they experience these feelings when they have "sex thoughts" or "touching thoughts" and that they occur "near the top of the steps."

Sexual abuse behaviors have included genital fondling, vaginal and anal intercourse, fellatio, attempted intercourse, "humping," cunnilingus, "french kisses," rubbing chests, digital vaginal and anal penetration, exhibitionism, voyeurism, rubbing penis against genitals, fondling buttocks, and object penetration. Over two-thirds of the victims were either siblings or nonrelative children who were visiting in the home. Of the sibling victims, about one-quarter were half- or step-siblings, and the remaining were full biological siblings. About one-third of the victims were neighbors or schoolmates. The numbers of victims varied considerably (from one to more than fifty), but most children reported involvement in three to six different abuse incidents. Over half of the behaviors involved taking advantage of an opportunity that occurred in a home when an adult was in another room, asleep, or outside. The children expressed more concern about getting to do the behavior without being interrupted than about someone finding out what they have done. The frequency of the behaviors ranged from daily to once every three or four months.

Fantasies about sexual abuse behavior are thoughts. They may be brief thought fragments, mental images, or more detailed thoughts. Most of the young children describe brief fantasies. About two-thirds of the children we have worked with report some thoughts that occurred prior to their abuse behavior. The children are not asked about fantasizing but rather about what they thought about before the abuse. They are then asked to show where on the stair steps the thoughts occurred. Of the children who have reported fantasies, about one-third indicated they had sexual thoughts. Some of the thoughts were wondering about babies, some were related to things they had seen or heard, some were recall of previous sexual behaviors, and some were memories of sexual victimization. Slightly over half of the children who reported fantasies said they thought about the abuse behavior. About half of those thought of what they could do, and about half thought of what they could do and who they would do it with. About one-fourth reported experiencing urges to do the behavior, about a third reported masturbation or genital self-touch during the thoughts, and a few said they thought of using sexual behaviors to get back at their parents when they were angry.

The children have talked about how they got the victim to do what they wanted. They developed a list of types of grooming behaviors—ways of increasing the likelihood of the victim's cooperation or testing victim reactions. The children's list includes threats, bribery, buttering up, tricks, playing games, pressure, force, and authority (like being bossy). About half of the children acknowledged grooming the victim, and about one-fourth described grooming a parent or caretaker. A few youth described specific planning. One youth said that when he was five, he thought of doing a sexual behavior with a small child in the home, but he knew people would not like it so he figured out how to connect the alarm on his radio to his earphones and set it for the middle of the night when everyone would be asleep and only he would hear it. He got up in the middle of the night to engage in this behavior two or three times without getting caught.

The children have expressed justifications for their sexual abuse behavior. Examples include, "She wanted me to do it," "Well, she took her clothes off first," "But my cousin asked me to do it before I did anything," "He liked it just as much as I did, so it's both our faults," "She pushed me on the bed; I don't see why everyone is mad at me," and "Well, I had to do it; I was mad at my dad." The children also seem to attempt to come to terms with the offense (as depicted in the reframing part of the abuse cycle) to lessen the bad feelings they have when they are caught and consequently punished. They do not see this process as part of the steps, however, and it may be that the concept of suppression or denial of the problem is too abstract for most of the younger children to work with. We try to approach this concept indirectly by helping them identify ways they can request help from parents or other adults to help them avoid behaviors, situations they need to walk away from, and choices they make.

Treatment

For most children in the program, treatment is divided into weekly group sessions, with family sessions and individual sessions as indicated. The group sessions are geared toward goals related to the abuse behavior:

- Developing an understanding of the behavior
- Developing internal controls and external resources to avoid further behaviors
- Identifying behavioral, cognitive, and affective antecedents and learning to recognize and interrupt them
- Cognitive restructuring related to negative self-perceptions and expectations
- Correcting social competency deficits to improve the child's coping resources, socialization, and decision making
- Strengthening capacity for empathy and intimacy
- Improving awareness of cause and effect related to improving impulse control
- Exploring the consequences of the abuse behavior
- Working with distressing developmental, traumatic, or victimization experiences

Family sessions are both psychoeducational and therapeutic. The parents or caretakers are required to attend educational sessions to develop an understanding of the abuse behavior, the concepts their child will learn, protective supervision, and how to assist their child during and after treatment. Family therapy sessions are geared toward assisting the parents with implementing supportive measures, dealing with current problems, and addressing family dysfunctions that may contribute to the child's functioning. Individual sessions are geared toward improving self-image, addressing current problems, working with traumatic experiences and developmental deficits, strengthening assets, and improving avoidance of further abuse behaviors.

When a child enters the program, he or she signs a brief contract that refers to ten specific rules the child will follow related to controlling his abuse behavior. The concreteness and specificity of the rules seem to be helpful to the child and the parents or caretakers during the initial stages of treatment and are the basis for the child's eventual relapse strategy. They are also part of the initial safety structure developed to avoid further behaviors. The rules support boundaries, use of adults and parents as a resource for control, and avoidance of stimuli that may support the abuse behavior.

Group Structure. Because so many of the children have short attention spans or exhibit hyperactivity, the hour-and-a-half group time is split into segments to decrease distraction, boredom, and disruptiveness. Topics are focused on for two to four weeks; then another topic is addressed. Nearly all topics are revisited once or twice over the course of the nine- to fifteen-month treatment to increase the children's understanding and retention. In addition to presenting concepts at the children's developmental and cognitive levels, efforts are made to provide as many experiential activities as possible for each topic to make them memorable to the children. Several publications assist in suggesting activities (Berliner & Rawlings, 1991; Cunningham & MacFarlane, 1991, 1996; Gray, 1991; Johnson, 1995). The groups typically have six group members and two staff. One of the facilitators is male because so many boys with sexual abuse behavior problems have problematic relationships with their fathers (Murray, 1996).

The first segment of the session is labeled "sharing something important" or "happy-mad-sad things," depending on the age level or stage of group development. Each child is asked to share issues of concern and a positive experience that occurred during the past week. It is a warm-up that serves to focus the group, encourage sharing, develop empathy capacity, establish feeling recognition, promote problem solving, improve listening skills, and provide an opportunity to seek or share feedback about a problematic issue. As they share, we become more aware of what concerns the child has, how the child views the situation or issue, and the child's coping response.

The second segment is labeled "learn something new." During this segment, specific treatment concepts and strategies are presented in a psychoeducational or experiential manner or through a structured activity. The child identifies how a particular concept applies to his situation, and the group talks about reactions to the concept.

The third segment is labeled "play time." All young children need a period of play to express reactions, work out issues, and expend some energy. Educational activities, games, or fun therapeutic activities may be used. During the children's interactions, problematic behaviors or statements receive immediate feedback, and support is offered to encourage the use of a variety of social competencies. Compliments, praise, and affirmation are offered if the child handles a situation in a prosocial manner in an effort to strengthen a sense of internal control and promote positive self-regard.

The last segment is labeled "group clean-up and feedback." All group members and facilitators are involved in a cooperative manner. This portion encourages taking responsibility, boundaries, cooperation, equality, and the ability to help others. The younger children have a feedback chart, but both groups offer information about behavior and interactions, encourage feelings of accomplishment, and emphasize the ability to make appropriate choices to develop self-control.

The younger group has developed a chart for feedback that lists each group member's name and four categories: following group rules, participation, use of correct words, and control behaviors. Each child is allowed two control behaviors during group sessions until the latter portion of treatment. Group rules are listed on a posterboard chart and posted in the group room. The group rules are: not hurting others, doing what one is asked to do, listening without interrupting others, and following directions. A happy face stamp is used to mark each category that the youth has been successful with during the session. The determination is based on peer discussion and staff input. Each child who receives at least one happy face is congratulated.

At the end of group, each child is given a homework assignment: practicing a behavior, an interaction, or a specific style of self-talk that is based on the concepts presented that day. The children are assigned to complete their homework one to three times during the next week, and their parents or caretakers are asked to assist their child and provide feedback about their child's homework. At the close of group, the children receive a small nutritional snack.

During the earlier segments, peer pressure is used to keep the group focused and to conform to the structure. A certain amount of disruption is tolerated, and the limits that are emphasized are carefully chosen. Excessive disruptive behaviors are handled by labeling the behavior and requesting the child to cease the behavior. A child who continues the behavior is given reminders that a request was made to stop and an expression of dissatisfaction that the child has failed to stop. The play time is a potent motivator for the children to encourage each other to make choices about stopping the behavior in time for play time. The consistent expectation is for the child to choose alternatives that will help him control inappropriate behaviors. In the past we used a modified time-out procedure for aggressive behaviors. Time-out occurred in the room; the child was excluded from active participation in the group, while remaining in hearing range and visual contact, for a short period of time (two to five minutes), followed by an opportunity to rejoin the group if the child was ready to control the behavior. Group members would express disappointment or sadness if the child did not choose to return at the earliest opportunity. This type of time-out procedure seems to contribute to the development of using internal control and conveys the message that power-based behaviors result in distancing rather than being in control, yet it does not foster a sense of rejection. It also limits retaliatory thoughts or masturbatory behaviors that may occur when the child is isolated from the group. We have not had to use the time-out procedure for about five years, probably because there is usually at least one youth who has been in the group for some time who models group norms to newer group members.

Group Content. During the "learn something new" segment, a variety of issues are addressed. Content is offered with some verbal explanation and some catch-word that gives the children a quick way of identifying a particular concept. Learning exercises, stories, experiential activities, role playing, puppets, art, movement, and group discussions may be used to make the content more meaningful and memorable. Books that have been popular with the children include *A Very Touch-ing Book* (Hindman, 1983), *No No Seal* (Patterson, 1986), *Steps to Healthy Touching* (MacFarlane & Cunningham, 1989), and *Good Touch, Bad Touch* (Deniger, 1987).

The abuse behaviors are addressed openly, beginning with the child's introduction to group. The group members introduce themselves to new members by providing demographic information, describing why they are in the group, and sharing interests and skills. The attempt is to provide an atmosphere that is comfortable and safe in which to discuss the behaviors that have occurred and to help the children become aware that they are not different, bad, or the only child who has ever engaged in such behaviors. The emphasis is on problematic behavior that is separate from personhood. Over time the children are encouraged to take accountability for their abuse behavior and work with diminishing the shame, embarrassment, and fear reactions to their behavior.

The group works with developing an understanding that their behaviors are hurtful and that there are differences between abuse behaviors and nonhurtful sexual behaviors. When the harm the abuse behavior caused is explored, descriptors are used that the young child may understand, such as, "The abuse causes a pain in the victim's heart," "It makes the victim sad," or "It is scary and confusing to the victim." An effort is made to help the children understand that sex is not bad and to assist them in becoming aware that they lack a full understanding of sex at this time and are not ready for sexual behaviors older people engage in. They draw a parallel between readiness for sexual interactions and readiness to drive a car; they know that people drive and have some idea of what it involves, but they do not really know how to drive themselves and they are not big enough to reach the pedals and still see out the window.

Emphasis is placed on understanding that sex is typically private and that respect for others involves respect for boundaries and the individual's right to be asked if he or she wants to be sexual. Issues of boundaries and privacy are specifically identified, and the children participate in activities to rehearse respecting boundaries. Concepts of personal body space are used to demonstrate the distinction of invasive behaviors.

The stair step cycle is used with the younger group and a modification of the abuse cycle is used with the older group to help the children become aware of the thoughts, feelings, and behaviors antecedent to their sexual abuse behavior (Figure 17.2).

As the children begin to identify clues that they are moving up the steps (or through the cycle), they develop strategies to help them interrupt the process. The younger children initially describe picturing themselves walking backward down the stairs, turning around and walking down the stairs to something that is good, or jumping off the stairs. Regardless of the perception that is helpful to each child,

FIGURE 17.2. MODIFICATION OF THE SEXUAL ABUSE CYCLE USED WITH TEN- TO TWELVE-YEAR-OLD CHILDREN.

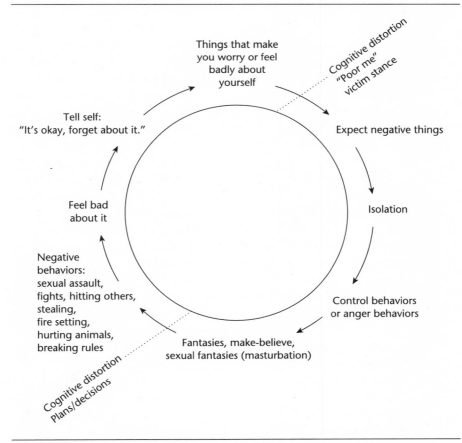

Source: Reprinted by permission of RSA, Inc.

the importance lies in their ability to learn to interrupt the progression by identifying the types of thoughts and behaviors they need to become aware of and learn to correct or interrupt. The thoughts and behaviors are tagged as "red flags" or "red lights." During the group discussions and through applying cycle progression to their own situation, the children begin to experience a sense of self-control and pride at their ability to prevent the abuse behavior. As they try new ways of handling problems, they begin to experience good feelings when they can handle a problem effectively or relate to others in a constructive way.

The children work on identifying body or thinking clues related to moving up the steps, and practice ways of reacting when they recognize the signs. For example, a child might identify that he is angry and is moving up the steps when he recognizes that he is getting a stomachache and clenching his fist or beginning to think of not sharing a toy with his sister. He might decide to tell his mom when he recognizes these signs.

They learn thought-stopping techniques that involve saying or thinking "Stop" or "No" to interrupt their inappropriate thoughts or contemplation of sexual abuse behaviors. They practice a type of cognitive self-talk in which they explain to themselves why they should decide to avoid an abuse behavior. They typically describe a desire not to hurt someone or to avoid getting in trouble. The self-talk is useful early in the contemplation or planning process but has less impact as the child moves closer to doing an abuse behavior.

Telling themselves to stop is one of the most difficult things for the children to do when they are feeling excited or experiencing some arousal or anticipation. It does not make sense to them to stop something that feels good and exciting. Some children try to develop substitution behaviors that help them slow the process and distract them, as well as develop more functional options to help them feel good about themselves. The child identifies something that makes him feel almost as good and excited as the sexually abusive behaviors made him feel. Some of the children pick playing ball, riding a bicycle, or running, while others choose special time with family members. It is helpful to consider contingencies because the child takes his substitute quite literally. For example, one child did not use his option of playing basketball because it was dark and he could not see the basket, so he decided it was okay to do something sexual. The child may contract with the group to engage in this activity to interrupt the times he begins to contemplate, fantasize, or masturbate to sexual abuse thoughts. It is important not to assume that the substitution process will decrease sexual arousal; it simply slows the progression and gives the child time to control the urges that are occurring. The child is complimented about his choice to attempt to control thoughts and behaviors when he or his caregivers report following his contract. Other children develop a plan to inform their parents or caregivers when they are feeling urges and to request help in avoiding abuse behaviors.

Acknowledging how good the arousal feels or that the abuse behaviors may have felt good for a short time validates the children's perception and helps decrease their confusion and anxiety. The arousal aspects are openly discussed to improve the children's ability to recognize physical warning signs and to enable them to initiate interruption or control techniques.

If a child reports masturbating to abuse thoughts and his parents approve of masturbation, he is encouraged to develop masturbatory habits that will not strengthen abusive urges. The children learn that masturbation is a behavior some people do but that it makes their problem with sexual touching or sexual abuse harder to control. They identify times that are wrong to masturbate, which include when they are moving up the stairs (progressing toward a sexually abusive behavior), when they are angry, when they are thinking about any sexual abuse behavior, and when they seek to feel better about some problem. They learn that the behavior should occur in the privacy of their bedroom or the bathroom when they are feeling good or want to think about sex in the context of future consensual relationships. They are encouraged when they choose to masturbate to think of neutral scenes that make them feel good about themselves and specifically scenes that do not involve animals, younger children, or any coercion. They are also instructed that if they begin to think of sexual abuse behaviors while masturbating, they should use the thought-stopping technique, switch scenes, or stop the masturbatory behavior. This process is difficult to monitor because the children typically report hiding masturbatory behaviors from their parents and caregivers. We encourage open communication about the behavior and attempt to help the children feel comfortable letting their parents know when they are thinking about masturbating.

In an attempt to assist the development of improved impulse control, a modified form of covert sensitization techniques has been used with the older group; a frequent benefit associated with the technique is the reduction of deviant arousal patterns. Although the effect has been documented with adult and adolescent offenders, there is no known objective verification for the child who is too young to assess arousal. The children report, however, that use of this technique seems to decrease the frequency of their thoughts. The adaptation that has been most successful is helping the children write two to three sentences that they carry with them and read when they think of abuse—for example, "I'm thinking about touching my sister. STOP. I don't want to do this. I got in trouble last time, and I felt bad. I know if I stop myself, I'll feel good, and my mom will be real proud of me. When she tells me, 'Good job,' I feel good." When they report having said these things to themselves to interrupt thoughts, they are complimented by their parents and group members.

Throughout their involvement in group, the children work with improving their sense of self-esteem. They focus on positive characteristics, giving themselves permission to make mistakes, separating their sexually abusive behavior from their definition as a person, and learning that they can make choices to do things they feel good about. A variety of techniques are used, ranging from group discussions to stories and structured exercises, as well as feedback that interrupts and reinterprets negative self-statements. They discuss what types of things they are and are not able to control, with the emphasis being on their ability for self-control and making choices and decisions about their own behaviors. They learn that they can request changes from others but that they are not able to control the decisions of others. The children also work on not making negative conclusions about themselves. They work on identifying that uncomfortable feelings are a sign they are unhappy with a situation or themselves, but that they can learn to talk about the feelings and try to solve the problem instead of thinking something is wrong with them. The children often report that they assume they are bad when they are disciplined or receive corrective feedback at home or school.

The children are encouraged to develop positive self-talk when they are making negative statements about themselves or negative assumptions about the motives of others. Although they do well when practicing, it seems to be a difficult habit to develop. The children need to be reminded when they make a negative self-statement to stop and say something positive about themselves. When the child makes a statement that is a negative assumption, he is assisted in gaining perspective of the situation and encouraged to check things out or learn to wait and think before reacting to something. When working with positive self-talk, group members practice saying something like, "Stop. I'm telling myself I'm bad, but I know I am good at helping my mom," or, "Stop. I'm thinking my mom hates me because she won't let me do what I want. I know that's not true because she reads to me before bedtime, and she always tells me she loves me." The older children discuss what might actually be occurring, such as, "My mom thinks that would be bad for me so she's trying to help me." This process appears to help the children develop a more realistic perception of many of their problems and to manage their feelings in a more productive way.

The children work on developing problem-solving skills to increase their sense of empowerment. The group members learn to identify the problem, brainstorm solutions, and offer each other suggestions. They use a formula: Is the solution safe? Will it hurt anyone? Will it work? Can I do it by myself? The children enjoy doing this work with puppet shows. When the children begin work with this area, many identify retaliatory solutions and are resistant to other alternatives. The children who seem to struggle most with this area have families who use similar strategies to solve problems, and it should be expected that change may take some time and some work in family sessions. As children begin to develop more skill with facing problems directly and thinking of solutions, their internal reactions are contrasted with the short-term relief of power-based alternatives.

The children work with problematic issues that have been identified in their developmental history and their life experience. They seem to have the most discomfort with this aspect. Talking about painful feelings or maltreatment is anxiety producing. At times a child may need to do nonverbal work or play therapy to work with these issues. It has been more effective to work with control of the abuse behavior initially and address historical issues as the child is ready. Some of this work may occur in individual or family sessions. The children begin to identify areas of confusion and recognition of how the experience affected them. Efforts are also geared toward helping them learn ways to handle memories and feelings. They are encouraged to share what they are experiencing, and parents are assisted in responding in supportive and constructive ways. The children work with validating their perceptions and affective reactions, talking about confusing aspects, developing accurate attributions of responsibility, and learning how the experience has affected them.

The child may need to be involved in a clarifying talk with the victim if the abuse occurred within the family or if it is likely that there will be future interactions with the victim. Parents and each child's therapist should be involved in meetings, and the focus could be directed toward clarifying information for the victim, identifying power inequities used in the abuse (for example, "I bribed you with a stick of gum, and that's not fair"), and establishing future boundaries.

Safety plans are developed at various points during treatment with the child and the caretakers. Plans include supervision needs and strategies, and they identify how to assist the child when he experiences thoughts or urges to do a sexual abuse behavior. By the end of treatment, children exhibit increased self-confidence, openness, and socialization, and they seem more able to handle problems without misusing power. These characteristics appear to assist them in preventing further sexually abusive behaviors. Caretakers are encouraged to continue to reinforce treatment concepts and to be alert to warning signs as the child matures.

Developmentally Disabled Youth

Although the incidence of youth who are developmentally disabled and engage in sexually abusive behaviors is still not known, it appears that there has been a gradual increase in recognition that these youth do engage in abusive sexual behaviors and do require specific treatment. There appears to be more effort to provide differential assessment and treatment for this population and less tendency to assume that institutionalization or incarceration are the only options when behaviors are repetitive (Abrams & Brecht, 1996; Baker, 1996; Myers, 1991; Pond & Brown, 1996; Stermac & Sheridan, 1993; Stoops & Baiser, 1996). Organizations that specifically work with developmentally disabled youth seem more knowledgeable about the potential of sexual abuse behaviors in this population and more creative in developing strategies for supervision and to assist with generalization of treatment concepts. Since the Americans with Disabilities Act was implemented in 1990, we have received more inquiries about programs that address the needs of these youth. As programs struggle to address the treatment needs of this population, it becomes even more necessary for a sharing of clinical experience and the development of research related to this population to occur.

Several years ago, the literature concerning the treatment of developmentally disabled adult offenders tended to focus on biochemical treatment, specifically the use of medications that reduce sex drive. More recently several publications have focused on more differential determination of the use of biochemical treatment and have suggested additional diverse and creative treatment approaches (Griffiths, Quinsey, & Hingsburger, 1989; Haaven, Little, & Petre-Miller; 1990; Knopp & Lackey, 1987b; National Task Force Report, 1993).

Abuse Behaviors

Clinical observation indicates numerous similarities but also some unique differences between sexually abusive behavior of disabled and nondisabled youth. The range of behaviors, the types of sexually abusive behaviors, and the elements of the behavior appear similar, while the associated cognitive process, the context of the behaviors, and the level of sophistication exhibit some differences.

A survey conducted by the Safer Society Program (Knopp & Lackey, 1987b) identified 3,355 offenses committed by slightly more than 1,500 developmentally disabled adults and adolescents that included a full range of types of sexually abusive behaviors. For some youth, the frequency may be higher than it is for nondisabled youth because the behavior tends to be repeated more frequently. These youth may be at risk for a greater degree of habituation. The youth describe contemplation of their abuse behavior, elements of planning, and associated arousal and excitement. Statements such as, "I got real excited and thought I'm a pretty smart fella when I did it" or "I feel real big when I do it" suggest there is a compensatory dynamic involved similar to that of nondisabled youth.

Physiological assessment of arousal interests by plethysmograph indicates that these youth do exhibit discriminate and offense-related arousal interest. Clinical observation indicates that some youth may have difficulty differentiating the abusive nature of some behaviors (Comte, 1988; Murphy, Coleman, & Haynes, 1983). It is possible that when these youth listen to audiotaped stimuli for plethysmography, some may begin to react to and think about the sexual nature of the cues and may not attend to the rest of the language. During an arousal assessment, many of these youth exhibit age discrimination, but in actual situations, many appear to have difficulty estimating the age of the victims.

Reports of fantasy antecedent to the abuse behavior are similar to those of nondisabled youth, but the cognitive style of developmentally disabled youth appears to be somewhat different. Many of these youth indicate that when they start thinking of a sexual behavior, they are often unable to interrupt the thought. They describe perseverative thinking patterns that interfere with activities at times.

Victims are more likely to be known to these youth or to be someone they have observed in their living, school, or recreational sphere. A victim who is a stranger is more likely to be selected from situations that are part of the youth's daily routine. The victim selection process appears to be similar to that of nondisabled youth in terms of perceiving vulnerable qualities or identifying characteristics that are appealing. Clinical observation indicates that there is less gender preference involved in victim selection; it is possible that victim selection may be based more on access. A significant degree of objectification of victims has been observed. There appears to be more of a tendency for either the victim to be a repeat victim or the location of the abuse to become the preferred location for subsequent behaviors. There appear to be fewer grooming behaviors exhibited by this population, but there have been several self-reports of returning to the same victim to attempt to become friends with the person or offering bribes such as candy, money, or presents in an attempt to engage in further behaviors. At times these youth misjudge their ability to control the victim, and if the victim resists, they seem to be equally likely to become more aggressive or to run away to seek another victim.

Justifications reported by some youth appear to be ingrained, narcissistically based, and influenced by their perceptions of what is considered normal (that is, of being a "real man"). Offenses tend to be more opportunistic, but some youth have described specific attempts to isolate a victim or lure the person to a specific location. Reports of planning appear somewhat akin to the level of sophistication exhibited by children with sexual abuse behavior problems. The developmentally disabled youth tend to underestimate the problems that may occur, but they do report thinking about what they want to do and how to make it happen. There seems to be more of a tendency for these youth initially to deny involvement in abusive behaviors.

Characteristics

The developmental history and life experience of many developmentally disabled youth suggest significant disruption. Some youth are placed out of home when they are quite young, and attachment issues may be prevalent in this population. Many youth who have been placed report exploitative and victimizing experiences by other residents or their caretakers. Several youth report social isolation, social alienation, and humiliation during school and recreational experiences. Many exhibit low self-esteem and a lack of confidence.

This population appears to experience life management interventions that may foster an external locus of control and the perception that they have little control over their environment and limited opportunity for choices. Recently there appear to be more efforts to inform youth of their options and acknowledge their preferences. The youth tend to exhibit impulsivity and less inclination to consider potential outcomes of choices they make.

There appear to be significant social competency deficits for many of these youth, and their interactional styles may invite rejection or ridicule on occasion rather than acceptance. Many of these youth seek affirmation and acceptance by "normal" youth or exhibit a desire to be perceived as normal. Given the concreteness of their cognitive processes, some youth may misunderstand, misinterpret, or overemulate what they observe nondisabled youth do. For example, one youth wanted to dress similarly to a youth he wanted to be friends with, so he wore a leather jacket everywhere, nine rings with skulls on them, and five earrings in one ear. Several youth have described believing that if they are sexual, they are like other youth; this perception may also be influenced by media.

Many of these youth exhibit a paucity of sexual knowledge. They appear to be well educated about birth control or safer sex and exhibit familiarity with the mechanics of sexual intercourse. Information about relationship or reciprocal aspects of sexual interactions, and social-sexual norms about age, consent, or privacy seem more limited.

Special Needs in Treatment

The level of functioning may vary significantly among youth referred for treatment or assessment. Most youth who are accepted for treatment in various community-based and residential programs are reported to have full-scale intelligence quotients ranging from 65 to 90. This information may imply that these youths' style of thinking is more concrete, their information about the world may be more restricted, and their learning styles may require special approaches. Their ability to manage various daily living activities, level of sophistication, and the ways they have learned to adapt to their environment must be assessed separately. These factors have a significant impact on decisions about management during treatment and the style of treatment intervention required.

The risk of reoffense during treatment appears to be somewhat higher for this population based on the potential of habituation, perseverative thinking, impulsivity, and issues related to immediate gratification. Whether the youth is considered to be appropriate for community-based or residential treatment, it is important that caretakers and supervisors be thoroughly trained and aware of the youth's sexual abuse behavior characteristics and patterns. Consistent, frequent communication about the issues that arise for the youth and current treatment objectives need to occur to enhance safety for the youth and community, as well as ensure that treatment concepts are reinforced and practiced by these youth in their living situation.

When practitioners adapt offense-specific treatment concepts to this population, they must consider style of learning. Because the attention span of these youth may be shorter, concepts presented in several brief segments and reinforced by an experiential activity may be effective. An experiential activity tends to link an affective component to the information, which may increase retention. Care must be taken with the language that is used to explain concepts because the youth will hear information in a concrete, literal manner. For example, if one explains that inappropriate touch is unacceptable, the youth may hear, "I'm not supposed to touch anybody," and miss the implication that sexually abusive touch is being discussed, or he may not understand the word *inappropriate* and tune out or ignore the concept. The process of providing information must be slower to give the youth time to think about what is being presented. It appears that comprehension is best when one style of presentation is used at a time, such as verbally one time and visually another. Associations with familiar objects will provide more meaning and improve retention. Such associations might involve sports concepts, traffic lights, or concrete objects.

Concepts must be presented in a repetitive manner, and revisited over time, to encourage internalization and retention. Generalizations must be taught through describing similarities and applications of various concepts. Attempts must be made to cover all aspects and avoid leaving loopholes that the youth may exploit. Whitaker (1986) suggests, "Present concrete information or concepts by providing an experiential presentation that is dramatic and includes powerful repetitions of information that involve descriptions or discussions of how the concept is experienced. Practice application of the concepts through role playing or games; expect application of concepts and provide feedback regarding situations the concept applies to, or assist the youth with identifying when and how to use the concept." Abrams and Brecht (1996) suggest using relational, repetitive, and rehearsal strategies.

Developmentally disabled youth appear to benefit from the same offense-specific treatment concepts used with nondisabled youth if the presentation of the concepts is adapted to their learning style. Sexual abuse cycle concepts are useful, but they are more easily understood if there are fewer steps and the information is presented in a linear format. It has been beneficial to include choices as part of the cycle and to refer consistently to choices. Intervention techniques are designed to develop better internal control, and the external structure expects the youth to apply intervention techniques when indicated. The development of effective coping skills allows these individuals to experience mastery and improved self-perception.

Female Youth

There have been several developments in work with female youth who sexually abuse. In 1993 the Safer Society Foundation and the National Institute of Mental Health supported a meeting of several practitioners to explore current knowledge, theories, and practices regarding adult and adolescent female offenders. At that time, there were 497 community-based and 61 residential programs offering treatment for this population (Safer Society Program, 1993).

The incidence of female adolescents who sexually abuse remains unknown. (Unfortunately there is a paucity of information and research on female offenders of any age, but especially concerning adolescent females.) Some studies have attempted to estimate the prevalence based on retrospective victimization reports of various populations, and some programs have shared data about the female youth they have worked with. In a survey of forty-four treatment providers who work with female perpetrators (Knopp & Lackey, 1987a), fifteen females below age eleven and thirty-five females aged eleven to seventeen were identified as currently receiving treatment services. Another study described thirteen sexually abusive girls, aged four to thirteen, who constituted 21.6 percent of the children treated by the Support Program for Abuse Reactive Kids (SPARK) (Johnson, 1988c); another study offered data on fourteen female offenders, aged twelve to eighteen, who constituted 2 percent of the adolescent offenders treated by the Program for Healthy Adolescent Sexual Expression (PHASE) (Mathews, 1987). Female youth constituted 2 percent of the adolescent offenders treated by the University of Washington Adolescent Clinic (Fehrenbach, Smith, Monastersky, & Deisher, 1986). A national survey of 1,600 youth involved in treatment for sexual abuse behaviors identified 2.6 percent as female youth, and 22 percent of youth indicating they had been sexually victimized identified a female as the perpetrator (Ryan, Miyoshi, Metzner, Krugman, & Fryer, 1996). Female youth have constituted less than 1 percent of the youth who have been treated at our facility, but retrospective reports of adults and youth suggest a much higher percentage of abuse committed by females.

In the most recent data available, the Oregon report on sexually abusive youth (Kerr, 1986) indicated that in 1985, nineteen (5 percent) of the youth arrested for sexual offenses were female. The report on adolescent sex offenders in Vermont (Knopp & Lackey, 1987a) indicated that in 1984 twelve female youth (8 percent) were known to the social Rehabilitation Services or the Corrections Department.

The Utah Report on Juvenile Sex Offenders (1989) indicated that 7 percent of the youth referred to the juvenile court for sexually abusive behaviors during a five-year period were female.

It has been speculated that the actual incidence and prevalence of offenses committed by this population are not reflected by the numbers of female youth known to the system or involved in treatment services. The revised report from the National Task Force on Juvenile Sexual Offending (1993) indicates that

> identification and reporting of female perpetrators may be inhibited by many factors. The legitimate authority, and primary relationships that females have with children in our society may make it especially difficult for victims to report due to dependency needs and ambivalence in the relationship. The legitimate genital contacts females have with children as a function of child care may also increase the child victim's confusion in defining the abuse. Discovery of ongoing abuse perpetrated by females may be impeded by stereotypic views of female sexuality which support denial in potential reporters, while the easy access female caregivers have to potential victims may decrease suspicion at the same time it creates opportunity.

One study comparing adult women and men who sexually abuse children (Allen, 1991) suggests that recognition and reporting are inhibited because sexual abuse by females is perceived as unacceptable and that these perceptions are supported by an overestimation of the strength of the incest taboo, overextension of feminist explanations of child sexual abuse, and overgeneralization that the occurrence is rare. He roughly estimates that as many as 3.1 million children have been abused by females.

Characteristics

A high percentage of sexually abusive females are reported to have a history of sexual victimization as compared to estimates or reports of sexually abusive males. Allen's study (1991) confirmed this finding and also indicated that the females in his study reported a higher incidence of physical abuse as children than the males reported. He also noted that females have more conflictual relationships with their mothers, which parallels the widespread observation that male youth who sexually abuse have problematic relationships with their fathers. A history of intrafamilial sexual abuse (mothers' having been sexual abuse victims) and physical abuse by the father figure in the home appear to be prevalent factors for the female youth (R. Mathews, personal communication, 1993). The limited population we have worked with have identified victimization, problematic parental relationships,

perceived abandonment, family separation (usually through out-of-home placement), school performance, and relationship difficulties with peers as some of the
issues they have struggled with. Many of the developmental experiences are similar to those identified in the history of male youth, although they may be experienced differently by female youth based on gender, socialization, and role
expectations.

These experiences would significantly affect the developmental experience of
the female youth. Mathews, Matthews, and Speitz (1989) suggest that the developmental experience may have a severe impact on identity development. They
suggest that treatment models incorporate developmental, cultural, and stereo-
typic sex role issues regarding females and that treatment issues include experiencing their sexuality and sexual identity (which they may have denied in order
to protect themselves from male victimization), dealing with male dependency,
and work that facilitates moving beyond shame. Issues of social isolation and victimization are viewed as primary treatment issues by Larsen and Maison (1987).
Turner and Turner (1994) suggest that females who abuse identify with the traits
of the aggressor, and their abusive behaviors usually reflect an effort to maintain
or establish relationships.

Abuse Behavior Characteristics

The range of sexually abusive behaviors is comparable to that of adolescent males
who sexually abuse. The respondents to the Safer Society survey indicated that
68 percent of the 44 identified offenses committed by female children under age
eleven were hands-on behaviors that ranged from child molestation to rape. There
were slightly more female victims than male victims; half of the victims were relatives, and the remainder were acquaintances. Of the 247 offenses committed by
the female youth aged eleven to seventeen, 76.5 percent were hands-on behaviors
involving child molestation or rape; there were 28 percent more female victims
than male victims. Acquaintances were 67 percent of the victims, 28 percent were
relatives, and 5 percent were strangers. Approximately 90 percent of the female
youth identified in the survey had been adjudicated for a sexual abuse behavior.
Hands-off behaviors included obscene telephone calls, voyeurism, exhibitionism,
and fetishism. Other offense behaviors were bestiality, prostitution, child pornography, and adult pornography (Knopp & Lackey, 1987a). In another study
(Hunter, Lexier, Goodwin, Browne, & Dennis, 1993), 40 percent of the females
abused strangers, and 60 percent abused both male and female victims.

The various studies previously cited and clinical observation indicate that
hands-on sexual abuse behaviors of female youth include sexual kissing, simulated
intercourse, breast fondling or sucking, genital fondling, digital or object penetra-

tion of the vagina or anus, cunnilingus, fellatio, and intercourse. The majority of the reported incidents involved the female's acting alone, although a small percentage coparticipated in the behavior with a male or another female. A higher percentage of adult female offenders are reported to have committed their sexual offenses with male coparticipants (Mathews, 1987).

Female adolescents are viewed as generally nonviolent as part of their offense behaviors (Johnson & Shrier, 1987; Marvasti, 1986; Wolfe, 1985). Denial is characterized as ranging from being predominant in some females who sexually abuse (Larsen & Maison, 1987), or nonexistent in that "males minimize the effects of their offenses, females don't" (Mathews, Matthews, & Speitz, 1989). The majority of the female youth we have worked with have acknowledged their abuse behavior at the time of referral.

Clinical observation has indicated that elements of offense behavior and sexual abuse cycle progression are described similarly by female youth and male youth, although the impacts of societal socialization, role expectations, and gender differences in perceptions, affective reactions, and internal experience are identifiable. In general, observations were confirmed by Hunter, Lexier, Goodwin, Browne, and Dennis (1993). The female youth identified compensatory aspects, nonsexual misuse of power, and retaliatory fantasies, although the expression of control-seeking behaviors appeared gender or role biased. They report antecedent sexual and sexually abusive fantasies and associated arousal. Most also reported associated masturbatory activity. The extent to which arousal is associated with female sexual abuse behavior is unknown because the use of arousal assessment with females is limited. The majority of the females had more than one victim and more than one occurrence of their behavior. Interestingly, the more common justifications related to doing something to get out of an intolerable situation or desiring to hurt their parents for something the parents had done. Many indicated they counted on the victim's reporting the behavior, and if necessary, they were prepared to facilitate the child's disclosure. During contemplation of the abuse, anticipations included feeling close, accepted, and aroused. Three of the females we have worked with indicated they had a specific intent to inflict harm or sexual humiliation as part of their abuse behavior. Several of the youth described grooming behaviors as being based on establishing trust and offering reassurance that they would never hurt the victim. A few described threats to the victims regarding disclosure, but most assumed the child would not tell because of the nature of their relationship.

Subsequent to the abuse behavior, the female youth report significant internal struggles with shame and embarrassment. They seem to sympathize more with the victim's experience sooner than most male youth who sexually abuse. However, many male youth who have also been victimized exhibit a similar capacity when their victims are male.

Female youth who sexually abuse appear to benefit from the same offense-specific, individual, and family treatment approaches identified in previous chapters. Adjunct treatment issues unique to females involve autonomy and socialization issues. Continued work with improved identification of this population and development of specific intervention techniques and approaches is anticipated.

The Violent Youth

The Safer Society Foundation facilitated and partially financed a gathering of a subcommittee of National Task Force on Juvenile Sexual Offending members in 1991 and 1992 who were experienced in the treatment of violent, hard-core youth. The purpose was to identify issues, theories, needs, characteristics, and intervention strategies and to develop recommendations about the most effective treatment approaches for these youth (National Task Force on Juvenile Sexual Offending, 1993).

Violent, hard-core offenders are defined as youth who manifest extreme and abhorrent offenses, attitudes, dynamics, and behaviors. Clusters of behaviors reflect a total disregard for the safety and welfare of others, and may include the use of weapons to injure another, sadism, ritual abuse, or murder. Their attitudes often include an intent to cause physical injury, degrade, humiliate, torture, maim, and intimidate another for self-pleasure. Their interactive relationships are purely for self-gain, and their lifestyles show high levels of violence, aggression, and thrill seeking.

These are the youth who fit the extremes of adolescent diagnostic criteria, exhibit extensive psychopathy, and if they were adults would have antisocial, narcissistic, and sexual sadism diagnoses or be perceived as potential serial offenders. These youth are rarely treated in the community unless legal sentencing and supervision terms have expired or they are making the transition from secure or intermediate residential placements. In placement settings, these youth commit repeated, impulsive assaults and typically exhibit little progress.

The subcommittee developed a suggested continuum of care, based on the tendency of these youth to make some progress, then regress, then make some progress (Table 17.1). This pattern is reflected over and over during treatment. Movement up and down the placement continuum appears to be critical for these youth because their risk potential and dangerousness increase during regression, and movement is viewed as a leveraging tool that assists the youth in beginning to recognize cause and effect, assuming accountability for choices, and understanding that prosocial choices are required to live in less restrictive environments.

The following preamble accompanies the document:

For 15 years, the treatment community has developed a comprehensive intervention approach to work with juvenile sex offenders that includes consequences, accountability, and treatment. A crucial segment of this offending population has been excluded: those who have been labeled "untreatable," based on the particularly heinous nature of the crimes they have committed.

It is the position of this task force that all offenders, regardless of the severity or nature of their offense(s) or their personality traits or characteristics, must have access to all appropriate intervention and resources, including specialized treatment. Based on these assumptions, we are guided by the following principles of logical consequences, accountability, and treatment:

Logical Consequences and Accountability

People are ultimately responsible for the decisions they make to engage in offensive behavior regardless of possible predisposing environmental factors and circumstances.

Our society has a common standard: If an individual does something wrong, he/she is accountable for these actions and there is a logical consequence for his/her behavior.

The logical consequence should have a relationship to the nature of the offense.

The logical consequences in these cases, removing the individual from the community, precedes treatment. Sex offender specific treatment should be perceived not only as an opportunity to the offender to change, but also as an additional consequence that mandates him/her to face what he/she has done.

Treatment

Every human being has the potential for humanization and change. Since we don't know what clients will maximize this potential, just as the offender has a responsibility, we have an obligation to provide treatment to all clients.

The violence, trauma, abuse, and neglect to which most of these individuals have been exposed have been major factors in the development of their offending behaviors. Many of their offenses may have been prevented had society provided the necessary identification and intervention early in their development. While that failure does not excuse their behavior, it does obligate the society to provide them with the opportunity to change.

TABLE 17.1. PROPOSED TREATMENT AND MANAGEMENT CONTINUUM FOR VIOLENT YOUTH.

Variable	Conforming *Facility Secure*	Adaptive *Partial Secure*	Staff-Assisted Responsibility *Staff Secure*	Self-Responsibility *Client Secure*	Autonomous *Community*
	• 24-hour custody • Individual rooms • Isolated • Fenced • Sex offender specific unit	• Staff secure • Locked • Individual rooms • Electronic surveillance	• Individual room /roommate • Unlocked	• Halfway house • Alternative structure living	• Independent living
Aggression	Conformity to rules re: no overt victimizing, verbal aggression, physical aggression, overt violence	Accepting staff initiative; exploring alternatives to victimizing; identify precursors; risk factors	Evaluates potential harm and intercepts by demonstrating progressive social competencies: • Assertive verbal expression • Conflict resolution skills • Negotiation skills	Effective, consistent application of skill under stress, thus preventing potential harm	Self-management with nonaggressive social competencies
Routine related	Following staff instructions, policies, procedures	Responds to less external control by following routines without prompting	Creates own routine during unstructured time; appropriate use of leisure time	Adapts routines to changing situations; self-management of leisure time	Creates independent routines; leisure time
Cognitive	Learns about cognitive distortions to recognize misperceptions/distortions	• Explores personal cognitive distortions/misinterpretations identified by others • Learns process of countering cognitive distortions/misconceptions	Implements correction of distortions and misperceptions with staff assistance	• Self-initiated identification and correction of distortions, misperceptions, and thinking errors • Initiates requests for feedback	Management of tendencies to revert to use of cognitive distortions and misperceptions

Cognitive, affective	Conforms to staff initiated: • conflict resolutions • problem solving • decision making Learns about process for: • problem solving • decision making	Acknowledges need to: • resolve conflicts • solve problems • make decisions through nonpower-based positions	Correctly identifies the need and seeks assistance in attempting to: • resolve conflicts • solve problems • make decisions	Self-initiates processes for: • resolving conflicts • solving problems • making decisions	Continues to consistently utilize processes for: • problem solving • decision making as related to self and others
Affective	Learns about the concepts of feelings	• Identifies feelings by linking concepts of feeling with own internal feelings with staff assistance • Learns processes for expecting in addressing feelings	Acknowledges, expresses, and experiences feelings with staff assistance: • explore the origins of personal feelings • identify cognitions that precede feelings	• Develops an understanding of personal feelings experienced • Feelings experienced are congruent (relative) to the situation • Spontaneous expression of feelings	• Cognitive modification of affective thoughts
Control of behavior	• Accepts external limits • Acquires skills for intervention	• Begins internal control development • Recognizes antecedent buildup	Rehearsal of skills and controls	Spontaneous use of intervention	Generalized use of interventions
Interpersonal relations	• Rudimentary interactions • Teach communication skills	• Interactive conversation • Negotiates to change routines and requests	• Identification of potential nonexploitative relationships • Recognition of diverse relationships	• Establish prosocial relationships • Differentiates relationship levels	• Initiating/developing nonexploitative reciprocal relationships • Maintaining ongoing relationships
Offense specific	Acknowledge offense	Explore level of denial	Accountability of offense behaviors; explore • offense identity patterns • impact of crime on victims • acquire skills to interrupt offense/RP skills	• Victim reparation • Utilizes support in preventing offense buildup • Use of community support group when needed to support lapses (see aggression, control of behavior)	• Self-initiated relapse prevention maintenance • Consistent use of coping strategies • Accesses support supervision

TABLE 17.1. PROPOSED TREATMENT AND MANAGEMENT CONTINUUM FOR VIOLENT YOUTH, Cont'd.

Variable	Conforming *Facility Secure*	Adaptive *Partial Secure*	Staff-Assisted Responsibility *Staff Secure*	Self-Responsibility *Client Secure*	Autonomous *Community*
Variable	• 24-hour custody • Individual rooms • Isolated • Fenced • Sex offender specific unit	• Staff secure • Locked • Individual rooms • Electronic surveillance	• Individual room/roommate • Unlocked	• Halfway house • Alternative structure living	• Independent living
Personal trauma	Education	Acknowledge, therapeutic intervention	Relates to own history and triggers to victimizing pattern Continues therapeutic intervention	Accepts/acknowledges issues	Accesses report
Sexuality	Clarification of consent vs. coercive, exploitative sexual interaction	• Acknowledges own coercive/exploitative sexual interactions • Values-based sex education	• Develops age-appropriate dating skills • Develops body awareness • Appropriate fantasy management • Distinguishes sensuality vs. sexuality	Clarification of sexual values: • gender stereotypes and biases, sexual orientation, sexual preferences	Responsible, non-abusive, consensual interactions
Treatment approach	• Psychoeducational: confrontation observations staff modeling • Relationship development: basic control staff-resident resident-resident • Pre-release prevention education	Participatory psychoeducational • confrontive disclosure (surrendered disclosure) • increased requirements for self-responsibility • relationship development • exploratory • dependency development • relapse-prevention education	Engaging in planned individual treatment: • self-initiated disclosure • integration of sexual offense constructs Relationship development • attachment (adaptive) • consistency and continuity of care staff Application and practice of relapse-prevention principles	Independent self-generating problem solving • understanding self Relevance of constructs Relationship maintenance • recognition of primary attachments • generalization of relationship building skills Self-application of relapse-prevention principles	Ongoing maintenance relationship detachment • formation of other relationships • content specific Reflexive use of relapse prevention

Criteria movement/evaluation	Accomplishment of goals related to foci of treatment	Accomplishment of goals related to foci of treatment	Accomplishment of goals related to foci of treatment	Accomplishment of goals related to foci of treatment	N.A.

Staff training development	• Prevention and management of aggressive behavior
	• Physical containment of impulsive aggression
	• Impression management of suicide
	• Suicide
	• Victimizing behavior
	• Offender awareness training
	• Team dynamics
	• Interviewing
	• Concrete level of supervision
	• Staff self-presentation
	• Crisis intervention
	• Cultural diversity
	• Criminal personality
	• Prosocial role modeling
		Relapse-prevention (Model)
		• Offense-specific content (see Glossary)
		• Therapeutic relationships
		• Physical containment for emotive expression
		• Sexual-abuse cycle antecedents
		• Levels of denials residents
		• Victimization training
		• Sex education
		  • sex orientation
		  • sex preferences
		  • gender stereotypes
		• Conflict resolution
		• Milieu training
			Treatment planning process assessment
			Therapeutic relationships
			• Social skills training
			• Relapse-prevention (internal management)
			Assertion training
			• Family therapy
				Transition resource training
				RPIII (external supervision)
				Community networking
					N.A.

Prevention team	• Identification • Education • Networking • Development	• Visitation with relapse-prevention goals • Disclosure-feedback process • Feedback • Setting contracts for roles, visits, and confidentiality • Networking	Client-team • Situation analysis • Negotiating relapse prevention • Support client as teacher • Standards for community contact • Clarifying feedback • Provides community needs, perspectives • Modeling and networking • Team self-monitoring	• Maintenance and review of relapse-prevention contacts • Consistent reporting effort/team: among team members and authorities • Contact schedules increase • Modeling and networking • Team resources as teacher or contributor	• Ongoing availability as a resource • Modeling • Expect reciprocal contacts • Maintains networking in lapse conditions

Source: Unpublished presentation of the violent offender subcommittee of the National Task Force on Juvenile Sexual Offending: Gary Lowe (Chairperson), Janis Bremer, Steve Bengis, David Berenson, Alison Stickrod Gray, Faye Honey Knopp, Sandy Lane, Rob Freeman-Longo, Brian Scrub, Ken Singer, and Mike Whitaker.

The rationale for treatment with this population also includes the following:

We can only learn about the development of violent behaviors by individuals by studying them. In the process, we will also learn about offenders who have committed less heinous crimes, thereby contributing to prevention.

The offender has violated the public trust and must demonstrate behaviors, values and competencies that indicate they can be trusted in the community safely.

The offender has the obligation to change if he wants to reenter the community. We should not assume the failure of the client to change indicates that they are untreatable; we must rethink and redesign failed treatments. However, if change does not take place, the offender has not exhibited readiness to reenter society (National Task Force on Juvenile Sexual Offending, 1993).

References

Abel, G., Becker, J., & Cunningham-Rathner, J. (1984). How a molester perceives the world. *International Journal of Law and Psychiatry, 7,* 89–103.

Abrams, R., & Brecht, B. (1996). *Using the three r's in outpatient therapy with developmentally delayed adolescent sexual offenders.* Presentation at the Fourteenth Annual Association for the Treatment of Sexual Abusers Research & Treatment Conference—Marching Into the Future: Challenges, Directions, Solutions. New Orleans, LA.

Allen, C. M. (1991). *Women and men who sexually abuse children: A comparative analysis.* Brandon, VT: Safer Society Press.

Baker, S. (1996). *Integrating youth with special needs into outpatient adolescent sex offender group treatment.* Presentation at the Twelfth Annual Conference of the National Adolescent Perpetrator Network—Sexually Abusive Youth: Developmental Dilemmas and Opportunities, Minneapolis.

Berliner, L., & Rawlings, L. (1991). *A treatment manual: Children with sexual behavior problems.* Seattle: Harborview Sexual Assault Center.

Comte, M. (1988). *Treating the intellectually disabled sexual offender.* Paper presented at the First National Conference on the Assessment and Treatment of Intellectually Disabled Juvenile and Adult Sexual Offenders, Columbus, OH.

Cunningham, C., & MacFarlane, K. (1991). *When children molest children: Group treatment strategies for young sexual abusers.* Brandon, VT: Safer Society Press.

Cunningham, C., & MacFarlane, K. (1996). *When children abuse: Group treatment strategies for children with impulse control problems.* Brandon, VT: Safer Society Press.

Deniger, L. (1987). *Good touch bad touch.* Norristown, PA: Rape Crisis Center of Montgomery County.

Fehrenbach, P., Smith, W., Monastersky, C., & Deisher, R. (1986). Adolescent sexual offenders: Offender and offense characteristics. *American Journal of Orthopsychiatry, 56*(2).

Finkelhor, D., and Associates (1986). *Sourcebook on child sexual abuse.* Thousand Oaks, CA: Sage.

Friedrich, W., Beilke, R. L., & Urquiza, A. J. (1988). Behavior problems in young sexually abused boys. *Journal of Interpersonal Violence, 3,* 1–12.

Friedrich, W., Grambsch, P., Broughton, D., Kuiper, J., & Beilke, R. (1991). Normative sexual behavior in children. *Pediatrics, 88*(3), 92–100.

Friedrich, W., Grambsch, P., Damon, L., Koverola, C., Wolfe, V., Hewitt, S., Lang, R., & Broughton, D. (1992). The child sexual behavior inventory: Normative and clinical comparisons. *Psychological Assessment, 4*(3), 303–311.

Gil, E. (1987). *Young sexual offenders: A guide for press.* Rockville, MD: Launch Press.

Gil, E. (1993). Etiologic theories. In E. Gil and T. C. Johnson (Eds.), *Sexualized children.* Walnut Creek, CA: Launch Press.

Gray, A. S. (1991). *Setting a context: A balanced approach* [Audiotape]. Address given at the First National Conference on Sexually Aggressive and Sexually Reactive Children—Seeking a Balanced Approach, Burlington, VT.

Grayson, J. (Ed.) (1989). Female sex offenders. *Virginia Child Protection Newsletter, 28*(1), 5–7.

Griffiths, D., Quinsey, V., & Hingsburger, D. (1989). *Changing inappropriate sexual behavior: A community-based approach for persons with developmental disabilities.* Baltimore, MD: Paul H. Brooks Publishing.

Haaven, J., Little, R., & Petre-Miller, D. (1990). *Treating intellectually disabled sex offenders: A model residential program.* Brandon, VT: Safer Society Press.

Hindman, J. (1983). *A very touching book.* Durkee, OR: McClure-Hindman Associates.

Hunter, J. A., Lexier, L. L., Goodwin, D. W., Browne, P. A., & Dennis, C. (1993). Psychosexual, attitudinal, and developmental characteristics of juvenile female sexual perpetrators in a residential treatment setting. *Journal of Child and Family Studies, 20*(3).

Isaac, C. (1986). *Identification and interruption of sexually offending behaviors in prepubescent children.* Paper presented at the Sixteenth Annual Child Abuse and Neglect Symposium, Keystone, CO.

Johnson, R., & Shrier, D. (1987). Past sexual victimization by females of male patients in an adolescent medicine clinic population. *American Journal of Psychiatry, 144*(95), 650–652.

Johnson, T. C. (1988a). *Assessing the pre-pubescent offender.* Paper presented at the National Training Conference—Implementing an Intervention Continuum for the Youthful Sex Offender, Long Beach, CA.

Johnson, T. C. (1988b). Child perpetrators—Children who molest other children: Preliminary findings. *Child Abuse and Neglect, 12,* 219–229.

Johnson, T. C. (1988c). Female child perpetrators: Children who molest other children. *Child Abuse and Neglect: The International Journal, 13*(3).

Johnson, T. C. (1993). *Preliminary findings.* In E. Gil and T. C. Johnson (Eds.), *Sexualized children.* Walnut Creek, CA: Launch Press.

Johnson, T. C. (1995). *Treatment exercises for child abuse victims and children with sexual behavior problems.* Pasadena, CA: Author.

Kerr, M. (Ed.) (1986). *An executive summary: The Oregon report on juvenile sexual offenders.* Salem, OR: Avalon Associates, Children's Services Division.

Knopp, F. H. (1989). *Selected bibliography: Sexual offenders identified as intellectually disabled.* Brandon, VT: Safer Society Press.

Knopp, F. H., & Lackey, L. B. (1987a). *Female sexual abusers: A summary of data from forty-four treatment providers.* Brandon, VT: Safer Society Press.

Knopp, F. H., & Lackey, L. B. (1987b). *Sexual offenders identified as intellectually disabled: A summary of data from forty treatment providers.* Brandon, VT: Safer Society Press.

Larsen, N., & Maison, S. (1987). *Psychosexual treatment program for female sex offenders.* Shakopee, MN: Minnesota Correctional Facility.

MacFarlane, K., & Cunningham, C. (1989). *Steps to healthy touching.* Mount Dora, FL: Kids' Rights Publishers.

Marshall, W. L., Hudson, S. M., & Hodkinson, S. (1993). The importance of attachment bonds in the development of juvenile sex offending. In H. E. Barbaree, W. L. Marshall, & S. M. Hudson (Eds.), *The juvenile sex offender.* New York: Guilford Press.

Marvasti, J. (1986). Incestuous mothers. *American Journal of Forensic Psychiatry, 7*(4), 63–69.

Mathews, R. (1987). *Female sexual offenders: Treatment and legal issues.* Minneapolis: PHASE-Genesis II.

Mathews, R., Matthews, J., & Speitz, K. (1989). *Female sexual offenders—An exploratory study.* Brandon, VT: Safer Society Press.

Monastersky, C. (1986). *Program components for preadolescent sexually abusive/reactive kids.* Paper presented at Treating the Juvenile Sexual Abuse Perpetrator Training Conference, Minneapolis.

Murphy, W. D., Coleman, E. M., & Haynes, M. R. (1983). Treatment and evaluation issues with the mentally retarded sex offender. In J. G. Greer & I. R. Stuart (Eds.), *The sexual aggressor: Current perspectives on treatment* (pp 22–41). New York: Van Nostrand Reinhold.

Murray, M. (1996). *An explorative study into the relationship between natural fathers and their sons in cases of adolescent sexual perpetrators.* Unpublished dissertation, University of Ulster and Queen's University, Belfast, Ireland.

Myers, B. A. (1991). Treatment of sexual offenses by persons with developmental disabilities. *American Journal on Mental Retardation, 95*(5), 563–569.

National Task Force on Juvenile Sexual Offending (1988). Preliminary report. *Juvenile and Family Court Journal, 39*(2).

National Task Force on Juvenile Sexual Offending. (1993). The revised report. *Juvenile and Family Court Journal, 44*(4).

Patterson, S. (1986). *No no seal.* New York: Random House.

Pithers, W. D., Gray, A. S., Cunningham, C., & Lane, S. (1993). *From trauma to understanding: A guide for parents of children with sexual behavior problems.* Brandon, VT: Safer Society Press.

Pond, A., & Brown, J. (1996). *Levels of disclosure: A dynamic model for obtaining sex offender histories with developmentally disabled youths.* Presentation at the Twelfth Annual Conference of the National Adolescent Perpetrator Network—Sexually Abusive Youth: Developmental Dilemmas and Opportunities, Minneapolis.

Porter, E. (1986). *Treating the young male victim of sexual assault: Issues and intervention strategies.* Brandon, VT: Safer Society Press.

Rasmussen, L. A., Burton, J. E., & Christopherson, B. J. (1990). *Interrupting precursors to perpetration in males ages four to twelve.* Paper presented at the Fifth Annual Training Conference—Confronting Sexual Offending, Albany, NY.

Rogers, N. (1992). Results of a survey regarding the treatment of preadolescent sexually abusive behavior (pp. 4–8). *Interchange.* (Newsletter of the National Adolescent Perpetrator Network). Denver: Kempe National Center.

Ryan, G. (1989). Victim to victimizer: Rethinking victim treatment. *Journal of Interpersonal Violence, 4,* 325–341.

Ryan, G., & Blum, J. (1994). *Childhood sexuality: A guide for parents.* Denver: Kempe Children's Center, University of Colorado Health Sciences Center, Department of Pediatrics.

Ryan, G., Blum, J., Sandau-Christopher, D., Law, S., Weher, F., Sundine, C., Astler, L., Teske, J., & Dale, J. (1989). *Understanding and responding to the sexual behavior of children: Trainer's manual.* Denver: Kempe National Center, University of Colorado Health Sciences Center.

Ryan, G., Miyoshi, T. J. Metzner, J. L., Krugman, R. D., & Fryer, G. E. (1996). Trends in a national sample of sexually abusive youths. *Journal of the American Academy of Child and Adolescent Psychiatry, 35*(1), 17–25.

Safer Society Program. (1993). *Juvenile and adult female sex offender treatment programs identified by Safer Society Program* [Information sheet]. Brandon, VT: Safer Society Program.

Stermac, L., & Sheridan, P. (1993). The developmentally disabled adolescent sex offender. In J. E. Barbaree, W. L. Marshall, & S. M. Hudson (Eds.), *The juvenile sex offender.* New York: Guilford Press.

Stoops, A. L., & Baiser, M. L. (1996). *Bridging the gap in services for the adolescent sex offender with mental retardation.* Presentation at the Fourteenth Annual Association for the Treatment of Sexual Abusers Research and Treatment Conference—Marching Into the Future: Challenges, Directions, Solution. New Orleans.

Task Force of the Utah Network on Juveniles Offending Sexually. (1989). *The Utah report on juvenile sex offenders.* Salt Lake City: Author.

Turner, M. T., & Turner, T. T. (1994). *Female adolescent sexual abusers: An exploratory study of mother-daughter dynamics with implications for treatment.* Brandon, VT: Safer Society Press.

Whitaker, M. (1986). *The low-functioning client.* Paper presented at the Second National Training Conference, Atlanta.

Wolfe, F. (1985). *Twelve female sexual offenders.* Paper presented at Next Steps in Research on the Assessment and Treatment of Sexually Aggressive Persons (Paraphiliacs), St. Louis, MO.

CHAPTER EIGHTEEN

THE FAMILY IN TREATMENT

Jerry Thomas

J ust as treatment providers agree that a nontraditional therapy approach is necessary to intervene effectively with the sexually abusive youth, treatment of the family also necessitates an approach that changes the usual concepts of family therapy, therapist, and sometimes even the definition of family

Every adolescent enters treatment with a family attached. Whether the family is absent, distant, functional, or dysfunctional, family issues must be addressed, the potential for family involvement must be assessed, and a family systems perspective must be maintained. This focus allows the therapist to help the adolescent come to terms with what family means in his or her life.

Every individual has a basic need for family—for connectedness with significant others. Maintaining a family perspective helps the adolescent not only deal with his current family issues but also prepares him to function as a positive participant in his future adult family. Therapy with a family focus may help to break the cycle of multigenerational dysfunction.

The Meaning of Family Therapy

Family therapy can mean working with the biological family or the institutional family. It can be as basic as using a family for a resource or as complex as integrating into a complicated family system. It can also mean preparing adolescents for independence and for being adult members of their families.

Family therapy for the sexually abusive youth may mean separating from the family of origin and dealing with issues of grief and loss. It sometimes means teaching the adolescent how to function as part of a family that is dysfunctional. It can also mean that the youth learns to identify and use familial role models from his surroundings.

For some sexually abusive youth, a nonsupportive family may be even more difficult than an absent or distant one. The "impossible" family is often chaotic and multiproblem; it frequently has a history of multigenerational interpersonal violence and sexual abuse. The impossible family may be absent or distant or painfully present, sabotaging treatment both overtly and covertly. Family denial, rationalization, and distortions may be pervasive, and the family may feel threatened by the disclosure of the sexual abuse. Although they may be willing to share social history information, these families may never be even minimally supportive in the treatment of the youth. Many times, these adolescents are unable to become engaged in treatment or participate in meaningful change until they are removed from a nonsupportive family's influence. In some cases, the family's refusal to support change makes it necessary for the adolescent not to return home.

In other cases, the adolescent is able to participate in treatment in spite of family resistance. Then the therapist can be very direct in acknowledging the dilemma and supporting the adolescent's personal strengths. The therapist's ability to establish a consistent, dependable relationship may enable the adolescent to trust and confide in the therapist, benefiting from the treatment experience by seeing that there are other ways to view the world from those he or she experienced in the family. Thus, the adolescent learns how to deal with the family without letting the family dynamics determine his or her response to life.

Sometimes it is impossible to engage a family in treatment or have an adolescent removed from a nonsupportive family that prevents his involvement in treatment. This is often a distressing situation personally and professionally for the therapist because of the risk it poses to both the family and the community. In these cases, therapists can only document the problems and communicate their concerns to the courts, the adolescent, and the family.

The therapist must keep in mind that families may be supportive or nonsupportive, caring or rejecting, distant or nonexistent. They may be biological, adoptive, foster, or institutional family, and they can even be familial substitutes. They can strengthen the treatment or sabotage it. They may absent themselves either emotionally or physically. The therapist's plan for treatment must take all of these contingencies into account. Every adolescent who enters treatment must work with his or her own unique family circumstances.

The Family Therapist

The professional working with these families often serves as director, crisis manager, systems organizer, teacher, guide, advocate, and resource person, as well as a supportive and confrontive therapist. This expanded role of the treatment professional serves to address the multitude of problems these families present. Without a broad range of assistance, increased defensiveness, self-protection, discouragement, disillusionment, poor compliance with treatment, and premature termination from treatment are likely. A comprehensive family treatment approach is preferable here to the usual traditional family therapy model. It is difficult for one person to be responsible for all the perspectives, processes, information, and resources required by these cases and simultaneously cope with the complexities of conducting actual treatment. It is suggested, therefore, that the family therapist serve as case manager of a multidisciplinary treatment team that includes the family's individual and group therapists, as well as other agencies, disciplines, or systems regularly involved in treatment.

This expanded role is difficult and stressful for therapists, who may not be fully prepared to assume it. In addition to basic academic and practicum preparation for work in the mental health field, these practitioners also need expertise in family therapy and specialized training in the provision of offense-specific treatment. Professional training for this kind of work is not offered in graduate school, so clinicians must supplement their traditional training through self-directed reading and study of current literature, attendance at professional seminars and workshops, supervised clinical experiences with other professionals whose expertise is in this area, and networking with therapists who specialize in services for sexually abusive youth.

Therapists in this field must have a broad awareness of sexual abuse issues, research trends, community resources, risk factors for offending, social effects of abuse and disclosure, and susceptibilities by type of youth to the various treatment applications. In addition, skill and specialization must include a comprehensive understanding of child sexual abuse, a knowledge of the theories and techniques of family therapy, and the theories, techniques, and applications for working with sexually abusive youth and their families. Finally, a knowledge of the laws and procedures for investigating and validating child sexual abuse, as well as multidisciplinary approaches to intervening and interacting with the relevant social systems, is essential.

In addition to professional training and knowledge, there are personal qualities that contribute to the ability of some people to work with families whose lives have been affected by child sexual abuse—for example:

- The ability to be both nurturing and confrontational
- The ability to set limits and consequences without being controlling
- Acceptance of and comfort with sexuality (one's own and that of others)
- An ability to convey a feeling of strength without being aggressive
- The ability to allow transference without fostering dependence
- The ability to use power productively without abusing it
- Openness to hearing sexual information that includes deviancy
- An ability to establish trustworthy relationships

Perhaps the most important skill that family treatment providers must have is an individual perceptive framework that is an internalization of family systems theory. More than anything else, the family will need the treatment provider to be able to put all the pieces together, to make the chaos in their lives comprehensible, to show that control is possible, and to facilitate healing change. Surviving the tremendous mental and emotional strain in dealing with these families is a personal challenge. The family treatment provider must also be capable of emotional, logical, rational, and radical self-disengagement. A lack of any of these qualities might prevent a therapist from ever being effective in this field.

Because of the intensive, fast-paced nature of family therapy, it is definitely preferable to have a cotherapist team work with families. It is often difficult for one person to keep up with the verbalizations as well as the personal and familial dynamics in this situation. When there is a cotherapy team, it is certainly beneficial to have both genders represented, to give the family an opportunity to see the cotherapists role-model nonsexist attitudes, mutual cooperation, trust and respect, as well as the ability to be intimate without being sexual. In order to be effective as a team, the cotherapists need to spend time prior to working together to determine if they are compatible both philosophically and in their personal styles of therapy.

The Theoretical Approach

Most specialists treating sexually abusive youth agree that a nontraditional approach is required for successful intervention with this population. This nontraditional approach is typically called "offense specific," which means that clients are often nonvoluntary, confidentiality is limited, treatment may be mandated, the therapist must often be directive and take a value stance, and the treatment focus is on those problem areas that are relevant to the problems of sexually abusive youth. Numbers of programs incorporate elements of many theories into a multimodal, multifactor model that is influenced by family systems theory, juvenile delinquency studies, and techniques developed in work with incest families.

Components of a Comprehensive Family Treatment Program

The components of a comprehensive family treatment program may include individual family therapy as well as a multifamily therapy group; a psychoeducational or support group; weekend retreats; working visits in the facility, community, and home; and a family informational packet or manual. One prerequisite must always be that the sexually abusive youth is in offense-specific therapy as well. If the victim is a sibling of the youth, then part of the treatment plan should be that the victim participate in victim-specific therapy. In addressing the needs of the nonoffending parents, victims, and the sexually abusive youth, it is important not to forget the nonabused or nonabusive siblings, who often are significantly affected by the disclosure of abuse within the family.

The five-stage model proposed here outlines the optimal work that the family component of treatment for sexually abusive youth should include. For every family, the crisis of disclosure and intervention is initially present, and engagement of the family is imperative for any assessment to occur. The first stage is therefore relevant to every new referral and is the basis for the second stage, where evaluation can occur and a preliminary structure for the family's involvement in treatment is formulated. Although family assessment continues throughout the adolescent's treatment, the third stage outlines the range of issues that family therapy most commonly addresses and suggests techniques for facilitating recognition, understanding, and change within the family.

The last two stages of family therapy are most relevant to the adolescent who will remain with the family after treatment, although they do have implications for caseworkers, foster parents, and group home parents as well. Stage IV involves issues of reconciliation and reconstruction that are especially relevant to adolescents who have abused family members or have been out of home during treatment. Stage V, the transition from active treatment into aftercare, has a strong focus on the family's role in relapse prevention.

Stage I: The Crisis of Disclosure

Sexual victimization is one of the most difficult and stressful experiences that families can face. When confronted with allegations or evidence of sexual abuse, families frequently react with a combination of shock, disbelief, and confusion, followed by intense feelings of shame, anger, guilt, and depression. When the sexual abuser is one's own child, the pain and confusion are intensified. When the perpetrator and victims are children within the same family, parents have difficulty even believing that their son or daughter could have engaged in this type of deviant behavior against a sibling. They struggle with questions of whether, how, and why this could have happened to them. Knowing that trust and loyalty have been betrayed, the whole family is in crisis. The family therapist's ability to provide crisis intervention that the family will experience as helpful and supportive improves the likelihood of family involvement and cooperation throughout the treatment process. Ideally, family therapists should become involved soon after the initial disclosure of sexual abuse, when the crisis provides an opportunity to engage the family, provide stability and structure, and assess family functioning.

It is important to connect and bond with the family by demonstrating an understanding of abuse, a willingness and capacity to deal with the family's intense feelings, acceptance and care for them as a family, and a genuine interest in assisting them toward recovery. The family may feel humiliated and shamed by the disclosure and expect the therapist to contribute to their humiliation and shame by blaming them as well.

Because parents will perceive themselves as failures and believe they will be judged and found guilty, they are likely to project these feelings on the therapist. Whether or not they are ordered into treatment, they often feel resentful and resistant. The necessity of open communication between systems often makes them suspicious of the therapist's motives. It becomes difficult for them to distinguish the mental health, juvenile justice, and child protection systems, which they perceive as colluding in their loss of autonomy and privacy.

In the face of this distrust, the therapist needs to help the family to share their feelings by providing a perspective for normalization. He or she also needs to allow the family to ventilate while remaining nonjudgmental and nonaccusatory. By providing an intellectual understanding of what has occurred, the therapist begins to build the family's confidence that professionals can and will be helpful and reassures them that familial healing is possible.

During this time, the therapist can demonstrate empathy for the family's feelings of helplessness and loss of control and help them regain some control by giving them concrete ways they can help themselves and their children. Much of crisis intervention must focus on these feelings of helplessness and lack of control. As the parents become informed of the facts and see the relevance of therapeutic interventions, they begin to experience some sense of control by choosing to participate in treatment. Learning what crises the family has faced in the past and how they have solved them, the therapist can begin to identify where the strengths are in the family and mobilize those strengths to deal with this crisis as well. Acknowledgment of strength apparent in the family's history that will help them with the current situation begins to restore the family's self-esteem and reduces their defensiveness and fear of intervention.

If the family has successfully resolved problems in the past, they are more likely to manage this one. Identifying the strong family members and the extrafamilial support systems will enable the therapist to encourage the family to use their resources now. If they have not weathered crises well in the past, learning why not will help the therapist work with the family to make better choices now.

Informing them of the many families that have had similar problems and the therapist's experience and expertise in working with those families encourages the family's cooperation. While helping them anticipate what they can expect from the legal and social service systems, the therapist can assure them of help in dealing with these systems. Predicting some of the emotional reactions they can expect can help them feel less overwhelmed. When families are feeling fearful and helpless, it is beneficial for them to know that they can be healed and that the therapist will be there throughout the healing process. The strengths of the family should be stressed, as well as the part the therapist will play in helping the family to weather this crisis.

Helping families to identify and label their feelings, to know what they can expect legally, socially, and emotionally, contributes to the family's confidence in the therapist's expertise. As parents learn that other families have experienced similar crises and have benefited from treatment, they are able to become more hopeful and the initial helplessness and depression abate. Availability of other parents through parent groups is particularly helpful in normalizing the experience during this early stage. The therapist can help the family to identify and find support systems. If this is an isolated family system, the therapist may need to be particularly creative and especially encouraging.

The crisis stage may be the time when family members are most open in revealing themselves and discussing their history because this is a time of intense personal questioning for them. Although the initial shame and distrust often raises a wall of denial and silence, parents are usually searching internally for answers to explain this deviant development within their family. The therapist's ability to identify and frame their feelings and articulate unspoken questions can tap into the family's anguish to facilitate early disclosures, engagement, and continued assessment.

Accountability is a desired treatment goal, but support and empathy are important at the crisis point. Any confrontation of family denial now must be gentle because confrontation is most effective after an alliance has been forged between the therapist and the family. Confrontation of family denial in the beginning is best accomplished through nonthreatening means, such as presenting didactic information through bibliotherapy, videotapes, lectures, and other psycho-educational means.

During this phase, it is necessary to monitor for signs of depression. Family members may experience mood swings and serious clinical depression. They may report trouble sleeping, feeling physically sick, recurring thoughts and nightmares, and a general feeling of self-blame and loss of control. The therapist should be cognizant of these reactions so that appropriate referrals may be made for medical or psychiatric help.

The disclosure period is a time of crisis for the family. Considerable support, accurate and clear information, and directive guidance are greatly needed. The seriousness and gravity of the abuse must be emphasized and understood, but a sense of hope and a promise of a life after treatment must also be conveyed.

Stage II: Family Assessment

Because the family is so influential, it is important to look at how the family has participated either overtly or covertly in shaping the behavior of the adolescent. Conversely, the family system may also contribute to change and support nonabusive behavior. These tenets are congruent and integral to understanding the family's role in the sexually abusive youth's treatment.

The family's role in the initial assessment is to provide information relative to the individual disposition of their child's case. Much of that information is relevant to treatment planning for the family as well. It is important that the initial assessment process reinforce the family's willingness to cooperate in further assessment and treatment. When the adolescent's evaluation is complete and he is accepted for treatment, an additional and distinct family assessment is needed to provide the basis for family treatment planning and to set goals for the family's involvement.

Ideally, the potential family therapist will participate in the initial evaluation in order to begin the bonding process. Nevertheless, many times the initial evaluation may precede the placement decision, and the family therapist must begin with the information already obtained and expand it to include an assessment of the family.

A major goal of the family assessment is the development of the fullest possible understanding of the juvenile and the family circumstances. Both formal and informal assessment procedures may be used to obtain the information necessary to determine the nature and scope of the problems in the family, identify the primary problem areas, and assess the immediate health and safety of the family, particularly in terms of risk of more abusive behavior. This assessment must also generate hypotheses regarding the youth and the family that can be tested and revised throughout the course of treatment.

The sexually abusive youth may present with a variety of family characteristics and dynamics that can range all the way from reasonably normal to very pathological. The abuse can be intrafamilial, extrafamilial, or both; abuse can entail a wide range of behaviors, including molestation or rape; and intergenerational abuse may have occurred. Some families will be intact, others single or blended, and others disengaged or absent.

This section reviews the assessment information that is most relevant to and necessary in the family component of treatment. Much of this information may have been discovered in the earlier evaluation and can be reviewed with the family as the treatment process begins. By sharing the previously recorded information with the family, the therapist is able to expedite the establishment of a mutual base of understanding with the family, gently confront any discrepancies in different reports, and see how distortion and denial have changed the family's statements over time. The sharing of information also demonstrates a climate of openness and begins to confront the patterns of secrecy that have supported the problem.

The following characteristics are areas of concern that need to be evaluated during initial and ongoing family assessment:

1. *Overinvolvement or enmeshment.* The physical, emotional, psychological, and sexual boundaries in the family may be blurred or nonexistent.

2. *Isolation.* The outside world may be seen as hostile, and so the family has closed itself off, which has led to family secrecy, loss of perception or reality checks, and a lack of support systems in the community.

3. *External and internal stress.* The family has a large number of intra- and extrafamilial problems, including debt, illness, legal difficulties, and extended-family conflict. Constant exposure to stress weakens family resources. Coping mechanisms may be poor or maladaptive.

4. *Intergenerational sexual or physical abuse.* The youth or other family members may have been victims of abuse or may have been abusive, sometimes dating back generations. It is not uncommon for the sexually abusive youth to have been abused by older family members and for his parents to have been victimized as well.

5. *Impaired communication styles.* Communication patterns tend to be indirect, with feelings and thoughts expressed through behavior or in such obscure ways that family members often misunderstand one another.

6. *Conflicting parental relationship styles.* Relations may be too close or too distant (for example, the father is sometimes emotionally distant while the mother is enmeshed). There is often inadequate control, and limit setting may be erratic.

7. *Emotional deprivation.* Emotional needs for nurturance and closeness typically are not met, and family members' skills in this area are limited.

8. *Abuse of power.* Family members, particularly parents, may not know how to use power, and they may react to external stimuli rather than respond from an internal value system.

The assessment should include all immediate family members, as well as extended-family members who live in the home or are significant in the juvenile's life. It may not be practical or feasible to interview all family members, but telephone contacts and correspondence with family members can prove quite helpful in determining the assets, liabilities, and pertinent dynamics of the environment in which the youth lives.

The family is the richest source of information about the youth and his or her development of sexually abusive behaviors, but not all youth are residing with their family of origin at the time of referral. Some have been placed in foster homes, agencies, or correctional settings. Nevertheless, information about the family is still needed. Reports and records from secondary sources such as previous care providers, child protection agencies, and foster or group home staff may be able to provide at least some background information. Persons who share the youth's current living arrangements should also provide information about the youth's current level of functioning, quality of interactions, lifestyle, recent stress, coping mechanisms, relationships, and other environmental influences. They also may have access to other valuable and pertinent information about the youth's developmental and family backgrounds. It will be particularly difficult to alter unacceptable relationships and patterns if the therapist is unable to obtain background on early relationships and experiences. Breaking the cycle of intergenerational abuse may be dependent on maintaining a family perspective, even if the family of origin is not available or willing to participate.

The accuracy and reliability of historical information are almost always in question. Falsification, distortion, and alteration of information are not uncommon. Because the level of defensiveness and stress is extremely high, the therapist can expect at least some misrepresentation and confusion. Comparison of facts across time and among informants can help determine the most accurate description of circumstances, dynamics, and individuals. Reports and information from collateral sources are useful in this regard. Many times, details about the abuse and the family are not made clear until the later stages of treatment, and sometimes it is impossible to unravel the true circumstances. The level of cooperation and engagement usually correlates highly with the reliability and accuracy of the data.

It is helpful to remember, however, that much of the information relevant to understanding the juvenile's early life experience and the development of deviance is not as dependent on the facts as on the perceptions of the individuals. Discrepancies in reports often provide the keys to understanding family roles, characteristic distortions, and patterns of denial and miscommunication.

The initial assessment typically includes interviews of the sexually abusive youth, the parents or stepparents, and possibly any older, nonvictimized siblings or extended-family members living in the home. In addition to assessing the need for crisis management and engaging the family in the treatment process, the therapist may have obtained information regarding several major areas of concern:

1. *Family members' perceptions of the sexual abuse.* What happened and how did it happen? What do they think the consequences ought to be, and why? What are the respective and overall levels of denial or minimization? Who knows, and who does not know, about the sexual abuse? Do the parents insist uninformed siblings not be told, or perhaps be told only minimizing accounts?

2. *Reaction of the family to disclosure.* Whom do they support, and why? Are they taking adequate steps to support and protect the victim and to get help for the sexually abusive youth? Are there any new indications of other victims or potential victims who need protecting?

3. *Reaction of extended family or significantly involved others.* Whom do they support, and why? What is the strength and nature of their interaction with the juvenile and family? What potential treatment resources or unhealthy influences do these people bring to the treatment plan?

Initial contacts with the family often result in more questions than answers. First impressions and initial hypotheses must be tested and revised as the assessment and treatment process continues. A detailed psychosocial history of the youth and family should be completed soon after treatment is initiated. A psychosocial assessment provides basic information about the family and includes the following primary components:

1. *Demographics.* Who are the participants? What is their relationship to the sexually abusive youth? What is their attitude toward the events that led to treatment and the treatment process itself, including legal and social service interventions?

2. *Family environment.* What are the significant processes, intra- and extra-familial relationships, marked alliances and alienations, discipline patterns, parenting style, socioeconomic environment, and sleeping arrangements?

3. *Problem presentation.* What does the family perceive as the reason for its inclusion in the treatment? How do they describe their specific problems, and what are their reactions to the causal events?

4. *Historical data.* What historical patterns are revealed? What information is available on the criminal, correctional, psychiatric, and medical histories of the adolescent and significant family members?

5. *Abuse history.* Has there been victimization of the sexually abusive youth and other family members, other sexual offenses, physical or emotional violence in the home, and significant lapses of self-control or accountability (that is, addictive, obsessive, or chronically depressive behavior)?

6. *Psychological data.* Have any family members received mental health services in the past? If so, what were the reasons for these services? Did they perceive benefit, help, or change as a result of these services? Has the family or any subgroup of its members ever been in family therapy or treatment programs before? (Corroboration of these reports is important, if at all possible. Former therapists or service programs can be very useful but may be unpredictably cooperative or uncooperative.)

7. *Family background.* What is the family history? This area covers number of siblings by generation and developmental stage, birth orders, character of intra-familial relationships, religious environment and influences, socioeconomic stability of home(s), perceptions and expressions of sexuality, and disruptions such as single-incident violence, death, divorce, abandonment, financial hardship, long-term or forced separation of family members, and behavior problems.

8. *Developmental and medical histories of the youth.* What information is available concerning prenatal health, birth and delivery, any unusual problems or complications, hospitalizations, developmental patterns and phenomena, physical and psychological trauma, remarkable illnesses, and any suspected or known physical or emotional abuse?

9. *Medical and developmental histories of family members.* What evidence is there of physical trauma (treated and untreated), accident proneness, enuresis and encopresis, psychosomatic complaints, venereal disease, addictive or obsessive neuroses, and developmental problems?

10. *Educational histories.* What are the family members' educational backgrounds and respective levels of cognitive sophistication? Does the juvenile have any noteworthy educational or disciplinary problems in school?

11. *Sexuality histories.* What is the family's perception of the sexual development of the youth? What or who are the sexual influences and models within the

family? Are there instances of sexual acting out within the family? What is the level of comfort in the family with the subject and specifics of sexuality? What is the sexual relationship of the parents? Are there any dysfunctions in this relationship? Is the sexually abusive youth (or any siblings) known to be sexually active?

12. *Leisure time.* How do the youth and the family spend leisure time? (Investigate community activities, isolation, and sociability factors.)

13. *Legal history of family members.* What contacts with the legal system has the family had?

14. *Substance use.* What are the medical and recreational drugs of choice within the family? And what are the drug of choice's effects? Is the drug use illegal? What effects has it had on the person and family? How do family members see the others' drug usage? Has there ever been drug treatment? Is an additional substance abuse assessment necessary?

Through the process of gathering the sociodemographic, psychosocial, and developmental information, a common frame of reference for the family and therapist is established, and a relationship may be formed that will facilitate family treatment. Identification of family patterns such as exploitation, lack of empathy, distortions, denial, and maladaptive coping styles helps to relate the current abusive patterns to the adolescent's life patterns. Especially important are the family members' reports of occurrences and perceptions during the adolescent's preverbal years since these are extremely difficult for the adolescent to understand and report without external information. These reports may help the therapist to understand some of the belief systems and patterns of trust or distrust of the youth and to begin to identify attachment styles.

The search for developmental clues and familial patterns continues throughout family treatment. The exploration of shared emotions, meaning, and perceptions, as well as conflicts and problems, continues in individual, family, and group treatment. This will lead to understanding the family, which will lead to the establishment of realistic expectations and goals and an improvement in the prognosis for a helpful outcome.

Stage III: Family Therapy Interventions

The goals of family therapy are to provide support for the sexually abusive youth to continue in treatment; to identify and interrupt the family patterns that allowed or supported the sexual abuse; to improve family relationships and maximize family strengths; and to provide the information needed for the family's participation in relapse prevention. The ultimate goal, of course, is the prevention of additional sexual abuse.

Sometimes, in spite of good therapeutic intervention, some families will not be amenable to change or even willing to participate in assessment and evaluation; others will be very motivated to learn specific ways in which they can facilitate and support the adolescent's own change process. Some will be able to make significant changes in the family system and functioning, and some will choose not to do so.

All therapists want to facilitate the growth of a truly healthy family system: one characterized by positive interactions, appropriate allocation of power, non-exploitative role models, direct communication, effective problem solving, and a tolerance for change and growth. This is a family with a sense of belonging and attachment, appropriate boundaries, shared values and beliefs, mutual trust and confidence, humor, enjoyment, and a sense of psychological and physical safety. However, it is imperative that family therapists be realistic in their expectations and goals. A less than perfectly healthy family can still be very functional and inhibit the recurrence of sexual abuse, which is the most important issue. If treatment providers are realistic, the family and the clinician can avoid a sense of failure when less than perfect results are the outcome.

Family Treatment Plan

The purpose of a treatment plan is to help the therapist develop an organized approach to the treatment process. The plan is individualized for each family and is based on that particular family's assessment and evaluation. The therapist then collaborates with the family and adolescent in the formulation of the plan. The treatment plan will typically encompass identified problems, short- and long-term goals, interventions, the party responsible for the intervention indicated, an inventory of family strengths and liabilities, discharge and aftercare plans, and estimated length of treatment. The goals should be observable, measurable, time limited, target dated, realistic, and relevant. The interventions must be specific, not vague, and should specify treatment modalities, services, activities, frequency of intervention, and the party responsible for the intervention. A treatment plan is a working document and must be continually reviewed and updated to allow for changes in treatment because of progress or regression, or new assessment findings. Some problems will be resolved during the course of treatment, and others will be added. Both the family and the client must be kept informed of the progress or lack of progress made toward reaching goals or in indicating new goals.

The interventions identified in the family treatment plan will be influenced by the treatment setting. Treatment providers who are part of an extensive outpatient, residential, or inpatient program may have access to adjunctive groups that treatment providers working alone or in small programs do not. Therefore, treatment planning must consider the therapist's resources as well as the family's needs. The approach the therapist can use may be dependent on the size of the program, the staff, and the available resources. In every case, community resources can be drawn on to supplement the youth's offense-specific program.

The treatment plan is developed and implemented recognizing the many constellations within the family: the family as a whole, as individuals, as subgroups, and as extended family. Indeed, a family treatment plan can also be based on the development of substitute familial relationships for the youth.

Treatment Issues

There are treatment issues that transcend the other variables that enter into treatment with this group. Not all of these issues will be present in all of the families, but many of these issues affect most of these families. The degree to which each of these issues is relevant is determined by the individual family dynamics as well as those of the abusive youth. The treatment issues within the system are similar to those seen individually in victims and offenders and play themselves out within the context of the system. Some, but not all, of these treatment issues will be discussed here.

Denial, Minimization, and Projection of Blame. These three characteristic behaviors of sexually abusive youths are often reflected in their families as well. The first reaction of parents to the news that their child has been sexually abusive is generally disbelief. It is difficult for any family to believe that their child would be capable of the sexually abusive acts he is accused of having perpetrated. Feelings of parental denial will be closely followed by minimization of the behavior, particularly if the youth encourages and supports the parents' denial. Some parents are so upset that they choose to believe the youth rather than the victim's statements so they will not have to deal with the problem. Even when the victim is within the home, they may find it easier to see this as a problem of the victim, who they think is making things up to get someone in trouble, than to acknowledge that their child has molested or raped. Parents often believe that if their child has molested or raped, then obviously they are failures as parents.

The parents' next reaction will often be that the therapist is overreacting. Because the therapist is the available person and is often either associated with or is the bearer of bad news, this person becomes the object of the family's anger and blame. The therapist is often seen as the person who keeps the problem alive and will not allow the family to bury it and so is the person responsible for their continued suffering and humiliation. At this point, therapists are sometimes accused of inventing the entire phenomenon of child sexual abuse because without it they would not have a job. The following therapeutic interventions should lead to a successful resolution of this stage in the therapy:

1. *Confrontation.* Confrontation should always be framed as an act of caring: direct and firm but never shaming or humiliating. Parents will probably not respond to the confrontation of denial by the therapist unless some therapeutic alliance exists. While this alliance is forming, the therapist may confront family denial indirectly by giving the family appropriate reading material. Good books are *The Silent Children* (1980) by Linda Sanford, *A Guide for Parents of Young Sex Offenders* (1986) by E. Gil, and *Pathways for Parents* (1990) by T. Kahn. Videos that depict victim interviews are also helpful. Participation in educational groups will give parents an opportunity to hear didactic material that is less threatening than personal information, which attacks their self-esteem as parents and human beings.

2. *Empathy.* The therapist can let the family know he or she understands and sympathizes with their denial and that denial is natural at this point. It is often possible to share with them some of the feelings and reactions seen in similar other families and some helpful ways of dealing with those reactions.

3. *Support.* Family support groups and multifamily therapy groups can be instrumental in helping families deal with denial because parents are often able to listen to other families when they are not willing to listen to someone in a perceived authority position.

4. *Disclosure.* If adolescents are in residential treatment programs where they are separated from families who are in denial, it is possible for significant treatment progress to take place with the youth separate from the family. If he is accepting responsibility without projection of blame or minimization, then a family session can be arranged to have the youth tell his parents about his abusive behavior, giving explicit details, sharing feelings, and taking full responsibility. In the face of their child's responsible behavior, it is difficult for parents to continue in their denial, although sometimes they will accuse the therapist of having coerced the child to confess. The therapist can prepare for this reaction by generalizing this reaction to experiences with other parents prior to the session.

An important aspect of the youth's own treatment is to become able to tell the parents exactly what happened, that he or she and no one else was responsible for that deed, and that he knows the consequences of abusing. The youth should also be able to tell them that he is learning how to break the cycle of abuse but needs their help and support in doing that. Of course, these verbalizations may not all come in a single session, but they are important to both the youth's acceptance of responsibility and their impact on the family's denial. This also demonstrates the adolescent's new understanding of more open and direct communication patterns and the ability to use these patterns in an effective manner. Parents are often confused about details of what took place. Having the child explain without minimization will help. Parents are generally not aware of the deviant fantasies, the extensive planning, the extent of the coercion, the physical threats, or the length and extent of the abuse. The use of euphemisms does not help parents understand the full extent of the abuse.

5. *Educational group.* This group discusses sexual abuse in didactic terms and often decreases denial. Also, the use of didactic material and other parents or educators to confront family denial removes the therapist from the "bad guy" role.

6. *Personalization.* Helping family members to speak for themselves using "I" statements encourages direct and assertive communication and helps individuate family members, thus decreasing the strength of the denial.

7. *Victim statements.* Use of the victim's statement in police reports or the audio recording of these statements will have an impact on family denial by giving the victim's perspective and personalizing the victim as a human being.

Lack of Empathy. Families whose child has abused outside the home tend to block their feelings for the victim in order to support their denial that a family member could be abusive. Even when the victim is another child within the home, there can be a lack of empathy for the victim, particularly if the sexually abusive youth is the favored child and the victim is the family scapegoat. It is often easier to believe that one child is a liar than to accept that the other child has molested or raped. Since lack of empathy among family members parallels the youth's own lack of empathy, this characteristic, which supports abusive behavior, must be a major focus in treatment.

Many of the interventions used by the therapist for denial, minimization, and projection of blame are also relevant for dealing with lack of empathy. Here are some others:

1. *Victim perspective.* The victim's own report often facilitates empathy. For family members, it can be directly given with the support of the victim's therapist. It is important that family members are prepared to hear the victim's disclosure and understand the damage that may be done by not supporting their victimized child. For victims outside the family, it is often possible to use the victim's statement or audiotapes of the victim recounting the offense. If one of the parents has experienced sexual victimization, then sometimes getting in touch with that victimization will personalize some of the hurt and pain, as well as what it felt like to be unsupported and unprotected.

2. *Survivor accounts.* Literature written by survivors describing their victimization, their reaction to it, and its effect on their lives may promote empathy. Videos with survivors' describing their experience can be shown with the family and therapist so that the therapist can process any feelings that occur as a result of seeing the film. An excellent video is *Once Can Hurt a Lifetime* (VanDerBur-Atler,

1990). Films may be a catalyst for releasing feelings that are blocked because they show actual victims sharing their experiences on a feeling level. Personal accounts of survivors in multifamily therapy group can make this even more real.

3. *Modeling empathic care.* The consistent priority given to the victim's physical and psychological safety demonstrates appropriate regard. If the victim is within the home and receiving no support, child protective services will often aid in the removal of that child to a place where support is available. In every interaction with the family, the therapist's labeling of the affective cues of each family member and validating the needs and feelings of each is the best modeling.

4. *Role playing.* Having one parent play the role of the victim while the therapist recounts what happened can provide a powerful discovery of empathy. This is most effectively done in an ongoing group where senior members are able to facilitate participation.

5. *Multifamily groups.* Other families who have dealt with their own denial and lack of empathy can confront families who are stuck in this stage very effectively. Sometimes the therapist can guide them to do this by asking them to help another family deal with their feelings. Family members sometimes have to discover empathy for someone else in the multifamily group who has been victimized before they can feel empathy for the victim of their own child.

Abuse of Power, Powerlessness, and Empowerment.

Behind the abuse of power are feelings of powerlessness. The goal of the therapist is to confront the abuse of power, identify the feelings of powerlessness, and provide the necessary education and guidance for family empowerment. Empowerment, the ability to examine one's thinking and correct false assumptions that may control subsequent feelings and actions, must be based in reality. Empowerment for families is found in clear role boundaries, internal controls, and rational thinking.

Empowered parents are in charge of and responsible for the care of their children. If families feel powerless, they will either abdicate responsibility or engage in constant power struggles with the therapist or their children in their search for some semblance of control. The therapist is responsible for avoiding those power struggles by refusing to engage in them, constantly reframing his or her relationship to the family as guide, advocate, and counselor. The lesson to impart to families is this one: "You may not be in control of what happens to you, but you are in control of what you do about it." There are many decisions that are important for them to reestablish control of their actions.

The abuse of power in families can encourage or support abusive behaviors. For the sexually abusive youth, feeling helpless and out of control can trigger an assault. When families are out of control, an adolescent has no external boundaries to guide the control of his behavior. As families attempt to regain control by intellectualizing or analyzing, the therapist must redirect them to a reality-based situation where feelings and behavior are concerned.

When families do become empowered, children are initially unhappy and will attempt to split the therapist and family in order to avoid unknown territory. Therapists must expect and prepare for this situation. The following are useful guidelines for effecting family empowerment:

1. Family empowerment begins with the initial assessment when the therapist emphasizes parents' right to make decisions, beginning with whether they will cooperate in treatment. It continues throughout treatment as the therapist presents the family with options and increasingly engages the family in more and more decision making. In a residential setting, the program should incorporate this guideline.
2. If a program does not provide a parenting skills group, one can be located in the community or incorporated into individual family sessions or a multi-family education group. Staff can role-model these skills or invite parents to spend time in the program learning by watching staff. It is important for the therapist and staff to model good parenting skills.
3. The therapist can aid family decision making and problem solving by assigning tasks and responsibilities. One example is the development of a behavior contract with the child.
4. Involving the parents in an assertiveness training class helps them understand the positive use of personal power.
5. After parents begin experiencing some feelings of empowerment, they will make bad decisions as well as good ones. They should be prepared for this outcome and for dealing with their feelings about those bad decisions.
6. The therapist's job is to model the appropriate use of power and empowerment. It is essential that the therapist never abuse power with families. The therapist must be continually vigilant about this.
7. Assertiveness training, self-esteem building, and anger management all lead to empowerment. These skills are trained in groups, access to which can be provided if the youth is in a structured program. Smaller programs may draw on community resources, educational booklets, or videotapes to expose parents to these skills.

Anger Management. Anger is often a central issue for families who act out their feelings rather than share them. The therapist must explore how anger is handled by the family. Is it bottled up or explosive? The therapist's aim is to teach families to control their anger, not contain it, and learn to express it safely without victimizing others and to work through it to resolution. There are certainly some things that it is right to be angry about and that one needs to be angry about. Sharing those feelings in a nonabusive way can be learned. However, it is possible to work with underlying feelings of hurt or helplessness before they turn into anger. When families learn to share feelings rather than act them out, psychological safety becomes possible. The following are ways family members can effect this process:

1. *Writing.* Release of anger can be accomplished by writing or tape recording negative feelings. These receptacles of anger can be kept and reviewed periodically. Then the writer can symbolically let go of the anger by throwing away the letter or tape when ready to do so.

2. *Role playing.* Families can learn to share their feelings of anger with each other by role playing with the therapist or group members until they are ready to communicate more directly with family members. In family therapy, clients can begin practicing with family members how to deal with angry feelings toward someone outside the family group. This rehearsal facilitates the learning process while preparing the family members to test this with each other.

3. *Literature.* Family members can find useful advice in appropriate literature, such as *Overcoming Anger and Frustration* (Hauch, 1974) and *The Angry Book* (Rubin, 1969).

4. *Artwork.* When angry feelings are blocked, artwork can allow each member's expression of angry feelings and facilitate sharing with the family what the artwork has elicited.

5. *Assertiveness training groups.* Family members who are aggressive or passive-aggressive can be helped to develop skills to deal with those feelings assertively.

6. *Relaxation therapy.* Guided imagery and relaxation exercises can be useful tools to learn to control explosive outbursts until one is able to resolve angry feelings and communicate in nonhurtful ways. Family members must learn to be responsive rather than reactive.

7. *Exercise.* Physical activity is a tried and true way of dealing with tension associated with anger. The goal here is to use physical activity not to dissipate angry feelings but to deal with them. Relieving tension does not resolve the issues that fuel the tension, so physical activity is only a temporary solution in anger management.

Intergenerational Abuse. Sometimes the disclosure of child sexual abuse can trigger remembrance of the parents' own previously unremembered abuse, and sometimes the abuse may have been remembered but never disclosed or dealt with. Sometimes, intergenerational abuse is a norm and not thought to be unusual or damaging. For children who live in families where intergenerational abuse is present, the dynamics of abuse are compounded. The symptoms of abuse—anger, inability to trust or bond, depression, and isolation—are part of the family dynamics. Sometimes the disclosure of the abuse of a sibling may be a catalyst for the disclosure that the perpetrator was abused by one of the parents.

Parents who have not dealt with or resolved their own abuse may be powerless to deal with their children's abuse because they will have to acknowledge and face their own.

If the mother was abused, she may use the abusive youth as the target for all her own unresolved issues about the abuse. These are sometimes mothers who reject children when they abuse, or (if mother was abused by a sibling) she may put her son in positions that support fulfillment of her expectation that he will abuse. If the disclosure is that one or both parents have been abusive, then a report must be made. Therapists must prepare every family for the necessity of this at the time of the initial referral in order to be able to do this without breaking therapeutic ties. Whether or not it destroys the therapeutic alliance, it is necessary, not only for legal and ethical reasons but for the therapeutic reasons of accountability.

Families in which intergenerational abuse is an issue require very careful treatment planning and coordination with numerous therapists and agencies. Two considerations must be kept in mind at all times in such cases:

1.   *Referrals.* The therapist must assess the necessity of referring family members to individual and group therapy for their own treatment, as well as the necessity for hospitalization if any members exhibit extreme posttraumatic stress reactions. Releases and staffings must be arranged to coordinate all aspects of therapy in progress with various providers.

2.   *Accountability.* All family members must be held accountable for their own behavior. Abusive incidents must be owned, as well as failure to respect and protect each other.

Family Secrets.   Often the issues that families do not want to talk about are the most important ones. Clues to the nature of these family secrets may be found in an examination of prior assessments, evaluations, and reports, particularly if any discrepancies are found. Family secrets may involve shared information or information that is differentially shared. Secrets may be kept to prove loyalty, show power, strengthen boundaries and alliances within the family, or protect members from painful memories or consequences. The consequences of secret keeping result in the distortion of information and the loss of communication in relationships and can be a critical element in child sexual abuse. Incest is possible only in secrecy. The therapist must be careful not to enter into secrets with either individual family members or the family as a whole when they wish to align the therapist with them against others. There are both practical and ethical consequences when this happens. The following considerations have proven useful:

1. *Expectations.* When the therapist initially informs the family about the therapeutic process and his or her role in that process, the therapist must discuss the need for openness and honesty in treatment, as well as the problems caused by keeping secrets in relationships. In the therapeutic process, secrets decrease effectiveness.

2. *Confrontation.* Deep family secrets often surface only by consistent confrontation of discrepancies between what is said and what is not said but is apparent in behavior, interactions, or family history. Initially, the family is able to tolerate only gentle confrontation. After a therapeutic alliance is established, confrontation can be very strong and direct.

3. *Disclosures.* When family secrets do emerge, the therapist should expect a grieving process characterized by anger, denial, acceptance, sadness, and grief. Getting past the denial of past and present secrets is imperative if the family is to change.

4. *Insights.* The therapist can observe the dynamics that occur when a secret is kept and share these with the family: the sense of responsibility, powerlessness, the fear for loss of love and protection, the fear for the safety of others, the fear of the breakup of the family. These discussions and disclosure of secrets will raise anxiety and resistance. Prepare the family to deal with this anxiety.

5. *Letting go.* Families will feel ambivalent about giving up their secrets. It may be helpful for the therapist to role-play the struggle over keeping the secret. By having someone who is suspected of keeping a secret role-play with another family member, the common dilemmas and feelings of keeping secrets become more apparent and reinforce the desirability of letting go.

Blurred Role Boundaries. In families in which children are acting out, there is often evidence of role confusion. Parents and children are in constantly changing roles with one another. Parents sometimes behave like children and children like parents. If there are to be clear, effective role boundaries, parents need to parent, and children need to experience childhood with reasonable external controls. In order to have a healthy family, these boundaries must be intact. The following interventions are suggestions for increasing effective role boundaries:

1. When the father is distant or physically abusive, treatment strategies may focus on building a nurturing relationship and increasing paternal involvement.
2. When the mother is enmeshed or passive, treatment strategies may focus on strengthening her boundaries and facilitating individuation.
3. Family sculpting is a good technique to use in individual family and multifamily therapy. For families that are rigid and enmeshed, having family members create a human sculpture in which the various persons place themselves in ways that represent the family's functioning helps to see where these alliances are and to demonstrate the discomfort of entanglements.

Human Sexuality. Confusion about sexuality in general and positive sexuality in particular is a common characteristic of sexually abusive youth and their families as well. In fact, it is difficult to grow up in America without being confused about sexuality. Distinctions between healthy and pathological sexuality are not taught or defined. In addition, many of these family members have been victims of intergenerational sexual abuse and have a particularly skewed attitude toward sexuality. Because the family's attitude toward sex helps to shape the adolescent's attitude, it is important that the family develop healthy sexual values and attitudes.

Sexual issues are difficult for most families to deal with openly and honestly. The ability to decrease the family's anxiety about approaching sexual topics comes only after the family therapist has established a comfortable relationship with the family members, and even then it can be difficult.

It is the family who must give the adolescent permission to know about the positive and healthy sexuality that is a natural part of life. The youth needs to hear that it is not sex that is bad but the abuse of it. Families perceive sexuality very differently, depending on their personal, cultural, or religious backgrounds. These differences can be understood and respected while encouraging a positive view of sexuality. Some particularly difficult issues for parents to discuss are their child's early sexualization, gender identity issues, sexual arousal, and the sexually abusive behaviors of their child.

Because sexuality is an important part of life, discussions about it cannot be limited to a sex education group. Although this type of group can be important in preparing parents to talk with their children openly and honestly, issues about sexuality are topics for individual family therapy, multifamily therapy, dyadic therapy, and family education and support groups. Sex education can be excellent preparation for necessary discussions.

Adolescents and adults alike are embarrassed by talking about sex. Therapists can discuss this unease openly, prepare for the embarrassment as natural, and give permission for it to occur. The following suggestions should prove useful:

1. *Human sexuality and sex education.* In many areas of the country, it is even important what this element of treatment is called. *Sex education* is a red-flag word in the Bible Belt; *human sexuality* is less threatening. Sexuality units or classes for parents should mirror the content of the classes for the youth, with careful planning for simultaneous group and individual family therapy around human sexuality. The purpose of sex education is to provide clients with accurate information about sex, correct misconceptions and myths, define familial sexual values, and promote healthy sexual development. Parents must learn how to talk with their children about sexual behavior. The therapist can address problem areas before the parents are brought into discussions with the children. Sex education may be

part of the parent education group, a group by itself, or part of individual family therapy.

It is important not to get too complicated about facts and details, yet to be accurate in providing information and confronting misconceptions. The author is reminded of the five-year-old who asked what the cramps were and received a detailed discussion of the menstrual cycle. Afterward, he said, with amazement, "Jimmy has cramps when he swims."

A basic outline for sex education might include but not be limited to the following topics:

> Male and female anatomy
>
> Reproductive process
>
> Consensual versus exploitative sexuality
>
> Venereal disease
>
> AIDS
>
> Sexual myths and misconceptions
>
> Birth control
>
> Values and attitudes
>
> Masturbation
>
> Sexualization of behavior, feelings, and fantasies
>
> Uses and misuses of sex
>
> Communicating with children about sexuality

2. *Relationships.* Family therapy provides an opportunity to discuss the ways that love is shown by family members. The therapist may ask family members to demonstrate how love and affection are currently shown, as well as how family members would like to have it shown. Asking family members to demonstrate brings this to a concrete operational level. In individual family and multifamily therapy, members can brainstorm all the different ways that people have of showing affection, care, and love for each other.

3. *Role definition.* Individual family sessions are the place to deal with sex roles within the family, exploring how sex is used or misused to meet emotional needs. The family can begin by objectively listing all the uses and misuses of sex in general and then apply them specifically to their family.

4. *Responsible sexuality.* Planned Parenthood is a good resource for slides, literature, and audiovisual material, as well as curriculums. It is often willing to provide or loan materials. Inviting Planned Parenthood volunteers to speak on birth

control, physiology, and other related topics is helpful because parents become desensitized by the representative's professional, carefully neutral presentations. However, even an entire sex education series does not replace open discussion of sexual issues and child sexual abuse.

5. *Sexual preference and gender.* Sexual orientation is often a family concern when children are sexually abused by someone of their own sex, sexually abuse someone of their own sex, or seriously question their gender identity. This topic may come up spontaneously; it becomes the therapist's responsibility to bring it up if the topic is avoided. Advocacy of any particular orientation is not the business of the therapist; rather, the job is to give the family factual information and provide the basis for as objective a discussion as possible of sexual options. For example, many parents and adolescents do not realize that there are normal periods of homosexual interest during childhood and puberty and that these do not define sexual orientation. Many do not know that molesting a younger prepubescent, same-sex child does not necessarily correspond with homosexual interest in age-mates. Understanding developmental issues will relieve both parent and child that decisions about orientation are not confirmed at age thirteen or fourteen years or even in later teens.

Sibling Involvement. When there are one or more children with serious problems in a family, it is easy to forget or minimize the needs of the other children. Families would prefer to believe that siblings who have not been abused or abusive are not aware of what has happened and that they can protect them from knowing. This is usually a mistake; the fears of these children can be worse than knowing the reality.

Siblings often have many thoughts and feelings they need to share—issues of guilt, self-blame, anger, and confusion. They wonder why they were not chosen to be abused and what they should or could have done to protect a sibling. They may feel anger toward the victim for disclosing because of the consequent disruption of family life. They may be ready to see the abusive sibling return home long before the victim is ready and be very resentful of his absence. If they are the ones who told and their sibling was removed from the home and prosecuted, they may feel a great deal of guilt. Often their friends will be unkind or be forbidden to associate with them. The family's financial status may change, with loss of home, school, and resources. Everyone is affected by these significant events, and therefore everyone should be involved in family treatment. All of the following should be kept in mind during the course of family therapy:

1. All siblings must be assessed regarding their need for individual therapy and referred as necessary to a child sexual abuse specialist.

2. All siblings need to participate at some point in individual family therapy. The amount of time and level of involvement depends on the individual. Some will need more involvement than others. Age and relationship are important factors.

3. The therapist must create an atmosphere for the family in which they can communicate safely, siblings can express their fears and anxiety, and parents can be honest and open. Siblings often have many questions regarding the sexual abuse that they have been afraid to ask.

4. Siblings should be aware of the sexually abusive youth's relapse-prevention program, the family's support of it, and their part in it.

5. As family contracts are made, the siblings need to be involved. As the family grows healthier, boundaries become clearer, and limit setting and accountability more established, siblings may act out against what they see as an infringement on their freedom. When this occurs, it is natural for them to blame other siblings.

Divided Loyalty. When the sexual abuse is committed by one child against another in the family, the family quite naturally will have feelings of divided loyalty. Parents and siblings usually love both children and will be confused about how to show that caring in this circumstance. There is a great deal of pressure to keep the family intact by dealing with the problem within the family.

The extent of the family's reaction will depend on several variables: the age of the children, the type of sexual contact, whether force was used, and the consequences for both the victim and the abusive youth. Families tend to want to dismiss most sexual activity between children as sexual exploration or curiosity and have to be educated regarding the definition and seriousness of sexual abuse for both the abused child and the abusive youth.

The sexually abusive youth tends to capitalize on divided loyalty as much as possible by expressing confusion and remorse, saying he did not mean to hurt anyone, was only fooling around, and will do anything they ask if they will just allow him to remain in the family and keep this secret. The victim will often feel guilty for disclosing if the abusing sibling has to leave home and there are legal consequences.

Parents need help in determining how they can meet the needs of all their children and the family. What may be seen as punishment can be reframed as consequences that will help the youth be motivated to deal with his problem so that he can lead a normal life. Real caring is often doing what is best rather than what is easy.

Behavior Contracts. The importance of logical consequences in the treatment of disturbed adolescents is critical. Dysfunctional adolescents typically view freedom as a condition of no restrictions, no limits, and no consequences. They frequently demand freedom, seldom realizing that they already possess all the freedom that any other person has: the freedom to choose. Adolescents often think that the freedom to make choices means choices without the fear of consequences.

One effective way for families to be clear and specific with one another about familial expectations and responsibilities, as well as privileges and consequences, is through the use of a behavior contract. The use of a contract to guide and govern behavior is a common concept in our society and one we use frequently in everyday life. Parrish (1985) identifies three advantages to using a behavior contract: (1) the contract serves to clarify parental beliefs, values, and expectations while preventing arguments, misunderstanding, and manipulation about those expectations; (2) it will keep parents from having to reiterate rules over and over again; and (3) the adolescent will learn that each behavior has a consequence, either positive or negative, and that these consequences are predictable.

Family contracts are most effective when everyone participates in making them. The process of involving the adolescent in suggestions and decision making concerning the contract is one way to get his investment and commitment. It also reduces his sense of powerlessness over his own destiny, a feeling that with sexually abusive youth often leads to the abuse of power. Although the adolescent needs to be an active participant in this process, it is understood that the parents must have the final approval. When young people participate in decision making in this way, they are often very fair and reasonable and sometimes will make rules that are more difficult than even their parents would expect to be followed. In this case, it is the parents' responsibility to keep the rules realistic.

A behavior contract is based on a system of discipline rather than punishment. Punishment is what a frustrated adult does to an adolescent to decrease the adult's feeling of frustration. It is rarely effective as a method of instilling values or lasting changes. Discipline, on the other hand, is feedback that signals to the adolescent that his choice was inappropriate or destructive (or appropriate and positive) and that his approach to living is functional or dysfunctional.

Behavior contracts are made to be changed as the adolescent's behavior changes and the need for structure and feedback decreases. The family should agree on a regular time during the week to meet and discuss the contract and make any modifications necessary. Modifications are not made on the spur of the moment or in the heat of an argument. When the term of the contract is ambiguous or unclear, the parent and child should meet to make an interpretation and clarify.

The sexually abusive youth in the very early stages of treatment needs structured feedback, determined by his developmental maturity level. A more externally controlled adolescent requires significant structure and specific behavioral feedback in order to bring the abusive behavior under control. A more internally controlled adolescent, perhaps in treatment longer, needs less structure and less specific behavioral feedback. Feedback should stimulate internal processing of dysfunctional behavior.

Behavioral contracts need to be divided into four distinct components. The first part is used for explanations and for the parties to describe the contract and put it into perspective, perhaps with a statement of family philosophy or goals for the individual and the family to achieve.

The second section addresses expectations and responsibilities. The components are rules and consequences. Breaking rules into categories and differentiating major from minor offenses—or what we call, respectively, bottom-line behaviors and rule infractions—is helpful. Each rule should be followed by a statement setting out the consequences for breaking it, as well as the privileges supported by compliance. Some effective consequences to use with adolescents are verbal redirection, the loss of privileges, the use of restriction, and restitution. For example, a rule might specify that the adolescent may have the right to use the telephone for no more than thirty minutes daily. His responsibility is not to use the telephone after 8:00 P.M. or when he is responsible for other duties. For his first violation of this rule, he loses the right to use the telephone for two days; for the second infraction within one week, he loses the right to use the telephone for one week. A bottom-line rule might be that the adolescent cannot use alcohol or drugs, and the consequences for breaking this rule might be a number of things: (1) being reported to a probation officer, (2) being grounded to the house for two to four weeks, (3) losing significant privileges, such as the freedom to attend school dances, (4) being reported to the police, or (5) losing the privilege to live at home.

Generally consequences should be as natural as possible and related to the violation of the behavior contract. Short-term consequences are usually more effective than long-term ones. Unlimited restriction leaves the adolescent hopeless and feeling as if there is nothing to lose by continuing to violate the contract.

The final section is for the signatures of all parties. Signing means that both the adolescent and the parents understand the terms of the contract and agree to abide by them.

Two types of contracts are useful with sexually abusive youths: one specifically related to the youth's relapse-prevention plan and the other related to typical adolescent behavior and adolescent issues. These can be separated or combined.

Substance Abuse. It is rare to find an adolescent who has not experimented with alcohol and drugs, and sexually abusive youth are no exception. Since drugs are a disinhibitor, it is important to view substance use as a risk factor with these youngsters. The initial assessment should have determined to what extent the adolescent and the family use or abuse drugs, and part of the individual and family treatment plan should deal with that problem.

Sexually abusive youth and their families will fall on the continuum from nonusers all the way to chemically dependent. If a youngster is chemically dependent, the youth must be chemical free for a sufficient period of time to ensure that the presence of drugs does not interfere with therapeutic interventions. Chemical dependency treatment should always be congruent with treatment for sexual abuse issues. However, both issues are closely interrelated and may be treated concurrently with success.

Chemical dependency is understood by substance abuse experts as a family issue. Therefore, the family's involvement in treatment for substance abuse problems is as critical as it is for the sexual abuse issues. The following therapeutic interventions should be considered:

1. *Prevention and education.* Material on basic prevention of substance abuse can be obtained at no charge from the local alcohol and drug abuse council, board of education, or area treatment programs. Many communities offer free seminars for parents and adolescents. It may be difficult to motivate the family to attend them on their own because it is hard to deal with a potential future problem when today's problem is overwhelming.

2. *Parental substance abuse.* If the parents have a problem with substance abuse, then addressing this issue directly is essential to the adolescent's recovery. Confrontation of parental denial of substance abuse can be very tricky. Parents want to deal with problems outside themselves and will avoid looking at problems they consider unrelated to the sex offense. The adolescent may have been troubled for some time about parental substance abuse but was afraid to raise the subject. The therapist's support of the sharing of these feelings with parents often gives the youth the courage to do this. Referrals to treatment programs such as Alcoholics Anonymous and Al Anon/Alateen, may be indicated. When a family member continues to abuse substances, the youth must be helped to recognize the dilemma and depersonalize the issue so that he does not feel responsible for controlling the family member's behavior.

3. *Child substance abuse.* Just as parents of sexually abusive youth frequently have to deal with denial, parents of adolescents who abuse substances or are chemically dependent may be resistant to accepting that their child has a problem. Even more difficult for a parent is to accept any responsibility in the adolescent's abuse or recovery. Utilization of support groups that focus specifically on dealing with the problems associated with being close to someone with a substance abuse problem, such as Al Anon, can be especially beneficial. With the support of others, parents can learn to face the associated feelings. These groups can also

support a change in the parents from denial and enabling of the problem behaviors to effective limit setting and support that can augment the treatment and recovery of the chemically dependent adolescent.

When the Abusive Youth Is a Daughter. As difficult as it is to accept that one's child has been sexually abusive, it is even more difficult when that child is a daughter. Traditionally women have been the primary caretakers of children. The idea of a female's hurting a child carries with it a role reversal that is particularly repugnant. Also, women traditionally are thought to be sexually aroused by someone bigger and stronger, while males are thought to be attracted to what is seen as the weaker, smaller sex. Thus, for a daughter to sexually abuse someone she is supposed to protect is incomprehensible to many parents.

The author's clinical experience of working in inpatient and residential programs with male and female adolescents is that there is very little difference in the dynamics and characteristics of the two genders of sexually abusive youth, and the treatment interventions are basically the same. One distinction, of course, is the specific gender issues to be taken into account. Another distinction is in the area of parent support and education. Parents of sexually abusive female youth find it virtually inconceivable that their daughter has committed a sexual offense. This being the case, the treatment provider must address the issue by means of parent education concerning causes of sexually abusive behavior, current information about female offending, and any available resources. If possible, providing a parent support group will give the parents of sexually abusive female youth an opportunity to express their feelings of anger, frustration, and disbelief with other families who face or have faced the same concerns. Such a group is also an excellent venue to dispel myths regarding sexual abuse.

Adjunctive Family Groups

Adjunctive family groups not only augment individual family therapy but also enrich it by giving individual families an opportunity to practice newly learned relationship skills in a group setting. Group settings are often likened to families in composition and so are valuable for modeling and learning family roles under the direction of skilled group therapists.

These adjunctive groups include, but are not limited to, multifamily therapy groups, multifamily education groups, multifamily support groups, and sibling groups for children not involved in the sexual abuse. These supplement but do not replace group treatment for the victim and the sexually abusive youth.

Some programs and providers involve the entire family system in these groups, others divide them by subsystems, and still others make education and support a part of their individual family therapy sessions. The way a practitioner chooses to employ these tools may depend on the size of the program, the size of the staff, and the availability of resources, as well as the individual case. Although in most programs multifamily education and support groups run concurrently with those for the sexually abusive youth, in some cases it might be useful to hold them jointly. Whether family education takes place in a distinct and separate multifamily format or as a part of individual therapy, it is important to every treatment program for sexually abusive youth.

Some programs expect a commitment from parents or surrogate parents to participate in the family components of the program before they will accept the adolescent into treatment. A comprehensive family component should include individual family therapy, a multifamily education group, a multifamily therapy group, and a multifamily support group. The timing of each family's presence in these different groups is based on individual case management decisions.

The Multifamily Education Group. Although a multifamily education group in no way replaces individual or multifamily therapy, it often is as therapeutic for the parents as any other component of treatment. Treatment issues can be addressed didactically in a personally nonthreatening way, which prepares families for dealing with these issues personally, and in individual family therapy.

Family education is part of almost every encounter with the family, beginning with the initial interview and family assessment and continuing throughout treatment in informal telephone calls and formal family therapy sessions, as well as in the organized education groups.

Families also benefit from carefully selected information packets that include basic as well as comprehensive information about child sexual abuse and sexually abusive youth. The family education packet should include books and pamphlets at different developmental levels so that it will be useful to all family members regardless their reading level.

There are many excellent materials available today and the selection is increasing. Some programs and providers prefer developing their own. Some suggestions are *The Silent Children* (Sanford, 1980), *Child Sexual Abuse: Let's Talk About It* (O'Hyde, 1987), and *He Told Me Not to Tell* (Fay, 1979). For parents, articles on local and national resources relevant to child sexual abuse and *A Guide for Parents of Young Sex Offenders* (Gil, 1986) may be helpful. This information may be supplemented with special prevention and education materials, including special materials for young children and information on parenting skills, anger management, grief and loss, assertiveness, and so forth. Some programs maintain a resource library for families to check out materials, and others develop packets of information meant to be shared by all family members. The resource library may include videotapes and audiotapes, as well as literature.

The multifamily education group as a separate group may run from thirty minutes to an hour and is often most helpful when it immediately precedes therapy sessions. The facilitator can use a combination of lectures, videotapes, and slides to impart information. It is suggested that any family education group cover the following topics:

Definition of abuse

Sex education and human sexuality

Treatment issues and approaches

Characteristics of adolescent sex abuse victims and sexually abusive youth

Family problems and coping strategies common to child sexual abuse

Abuse cycles

Risk factors

Relapse-prevention concepts

Parent Support Groups. The parent support group differs from multifamily therapy in that the adolescents are not involved. This is an opportunity for parents to support one another and decrease their feelings of isolation and alienation. There is sometimes information parents want to share with each other that is not appropriate for sharing with adolescents, and so it is helpful for them to meet alone. They often learn that their feelings of shame, humiliation, and failure are understood by others. They have an opportunity to discuss the ways their families have been affected by the disclosure of child sexual abuse and how relationships have changed. When parents realize that it is natural and common to wish the disclosure had never been made, they feel less guilt and shame and can accept their humanity. When the parent support group is open-ended, parents can see families in all stages of treatment. This encourages optimism and motivates participation in the treatment process.

The support group may stand alone or come after a multifamily therapy group. The multifamily therapy group is so intense and draining that parents often need the support that they can give to one another in an accepting, caring environment afterward. In a positive sense, parents become peer counselors and help each other, although a therapist or facilitator is always present.

Multifamily Therapy. Bringing families together to discuss mutual concerns seems logical. Multifamily therapy brings together several families with similar problems into a therapeutic group. This treatment modality, which has been used for over twenty years in psychiatric settings, is particularly useful in working with families of adolescent victims and sexually abusive youths for the same reason that the group setting is the treatment modality of choice for these two populations.

The benefits of multifamily group therapy are obvious. It is an efficient use of the therapist's time as well as being cost-effective. It gives the therapist an opportunity to see the adolescent in the context of his family system and the family system in the context of society.

This kind of experience is good for any family but seems to work particularly well with families of sexually abusive youth because it addresses the following issues: the degree of isolation, rigidity, and enmeshment often found in these families; the high degree of internal and external stresses and poor coping mechanisms; faulty communication patterns; unmet emotional needs for closeness and nurturance; feelings of hopelessness and helplessness; feelings of failure as parents; and the weight of the imagined condemnation of the world around them for their failure as parents.

Multifamily therapy decreases the alienation and isolation that isolated families feel when they see other families with similar feelings and problems, and thus it decreases the anxiety that often immobilizes these families. For enmeshed families, it provides an opportunity to engage in meaningful encounters as they relate to other families—the children as well as the adults. The child with a single parent and the child with no parents are also served by the availability of parental substitutes in a multifamily group. It is not necessary to live without familial affection and guidance if one can learn to build family and extended-family relationships with those encountered in daily life. The opportunity to experience the universality of human needs and emotional ties acts as a catalyst for adults and adolescents to be genuine with one another both within family boundaries and across those boundaries with other families.

A multifamily group presents some practical considerations due to the size of the group. These include setting, time, group composition, control of content, and limitation of group size.

The setting needs to be large enough to accommodate a group that could at times contain over thirty people. A group of eight families with two parents and one youth each is twenty-four people. With the addition of a few siblings and extended-family members, the group can easily grow to thirty-five. It is also possible that guests of the participants or the therapists may be included, raising the total attendance even further.

To allow for maximum family participation, refreshments before or after the group are helpful for parents who come immediately from work, and a social period can also serve as an icebreaker.

Not all families can benefit from multifamily therapy, and so screening is necessary before inviting families to join such a group. Each treatment program can develop its own screening criteria based on what is best for them. In general, heterogeneous groups are better than homogeneous in that they bring more energy and information into the group setting. Relationships form based on the universality of human emotion and needs rather than external similarities. Later-generation parents, stepparents, and foster parents all have something unique to give and benefits to gain.

Two basic prerequisites for admission to the group are a recommendation from the individual family therapist and adequate reality contact. Contraindications for involvements are very chaotic families, families who are keeping secrets from each other and refuse to share these secrets except with therapists, very young children, and parental incest families where the perpetrator is in denial and the nonoffending parent is unsupportive of the treatment process.

Because of the size of this group, it is necessary to consider the number of therapists. A male and a female cotherapists are a minimal requirement, with other staff added as needed. For a group of thirty-five, four therapists are helpful. Multifamily group therapists should have a good sense of timing, be creative in handling new situations, be able to adjust to cases of unusual group malfunction, and show initiative in their choice of previously unusual approaches to critical situations. The therapists are much like the conductors of large symphony orchestras who must know the score and be able to direct as needed.

The therapists' tasks in multifamily therapy are similar to those in individual family therapy, but on a larger scale. The first task is to establish a climate of respect and trust, and the use of role modeling is critical here. Families that are not functioning well within their own systems will not function well within societal systems—of which the multifamily group is a microcosm. To establish respect and trust, the therapist consistently models an attitude of accepting the person while rejecting the behavior; caring for the person, while abhorring the act. The therapist demonstrates how to do this while confronting negative behaviors and supporting positive ones, promoting sharing on a feeling level, careful listening, and honest response. The goal is for this to be a self-directed group, so therapist control of the group must be subtle, with the therapist more a guider and facilitator than group leader. It is useful to clarify the work and goals of the group, serve as a resource person, summarize and process group efforts, and be a catalyst where needed.

Because these groups are emotionally draining, debriefing among cotherapists after group is essential. There will be time to laugh together, cry together, be angry together, and disagree vehemently on either strategic interventions or family dynamics. Group therapists may number between two and six, so these therapists form a microcosm of another family system. Careful attention to the family dynamics in the cotherapist group will aid in modeling the behavior of families within the multifamily group. As human beings, as well as mental health professionals, therapists must be watchful of their own dysfunctional family behavior;

transference and burnout are prevalent in this profession. Helping each other with these issues can serve to keep therapists functioning effectively.

There will be some aspects of the group that the group itself needs to control. For the group to be in control here is quite different from abusive control. This is another quality that therapists must role-model for the multifamily group, because control and abuse of control are significant therapeutic issues. Setting guidelines from the beginning is one way of keeping the group in control of the session content. For example, although there are no taboo subjects for this group, some subjects should be addressed first in individual family therapy. During introductions is not the time for an adolescent to disclose that he was abused by his grandfather, although some adolescents who wish to strike back at their parents for nonprotection may choose this avenue.

The group itself will make up its own rules as they discover what is helpful and what is not, and often those rules will be what the therapists have modeled for them: "It's okay to cry." "Confidentiality is important so we can trust one another." "Rocking your chair or cracking your knuckles distracts me from the work of the group." These kinds of statements will often be reflected back to new group members as "rules of the group."

Rituals are also important. Introductions and farewells are parameters established by the therapists, and the group will establish their own forms within these. Group members who are designated as peer parent counselors play an important role in helping to keep the group rules, rituals, and tasks.

Some parents evolve into the role of peer parent counselors as they progress through treatment and become able to provide encouragement and education to their peers. The therapist does not create an expectation that this must occur (as not every parent will become able to be effective in such a role), but the therapist does reinforce and provide recognition of helpful behavior.

The therapeutic processes include learning by analogy and indirect interpretation. A father hugs his child after hearing the child say he feels unloved and that he needs to feel his father's love. The therapist or a group member interprets how difficult it is for adult males to demonstrate their love for each other, and other fathers in the group become willing to take that risk as well. Thus, the family models part of the behavior, and the therapist models another part (for example, talking about why it is so hard to show love). This process of modeling extends from behavior to healthier coping patterns as families demonstrate what they have learned about handling angry feelings within the family, establishing limits, sharing feelings, changing communication patterns, and so forth. Learning through identification happens when one family sees another identify and cope with a problem that may be the same one they are denying and exacerbating by that denial. Learning through trial and error happens as families begin practicing what they have seen work. In order to learn by these previously described processes, it is sometimes necessary for the therapist to break the intrafamilial code to interpret what certain behaviors or words mean in one particular family. Through amplification and modulation of signals, the group then interprets what the therapist is saying.

There are basically three therapeutic stages in multifamily groups and for new families becoming part of the group. The first is fear of and resistance to being in the group. The therapist can deal with this fear by offering good support to the family as well as imparting an understanding of what happens in the group to the new family before the first session. A peer family counselor can be assigned to offer support and initiate the new members into the group. The support of other families is important for the new family to see that other families have hope and have regained control of their lives and that the adolescents in these families are making positive changes.

The second stage is characterized by increased openness and self-confidence. This shows in a willingness to take risks in group by sharing feelings, thoughts, and experiences. It is during this period that some families will disclose their own personal abuse. The third stage is the point at which increased self-esteem as a family allows its members to become peer counselors and role models for other families.

Among the therapeutic interventions that are particularly suited to multifamily groups are gestalt techniques, psychodrama, role plays, and the use of reflection and connection, as well as reconstruction and normalization. Honesty checks and art therapy can also be good activities for these groups.

The goals for multifamily therapy are the same as with all offense-specific treatment: the prevention of future victimization.

Stage IV: Reconstruction and Reunification of the Family

For the youth who has been out of the home and will return home to live with a sibling victim, reunification work is clearly indicated. This is often a complicated and difficult task for the therapist, the youth, and the family. The therapist must consider the possibility of reunification and plan for it from the beginning of treatment. The family assessment evaluates the potential for reunification, and the treatment plan outlines the necessary steps. If there is no careful planning, the risks to the family and the victim can be very serious.

There is considerable professional disagreement about when, if, and how to approach reunification. Opinions vary from reunification in all cases to reunification in no cases. It is this author's opinion that reunification should be viewed as a continuum, with levels ranging from full reunification into the family system, to partial reentry, to minimal or even no contact. Many jurisdictions are beginning to require that all treatment plans include the reunification of child and family. Although this author believes strongly in the preservation of the family, it is not always in the best interest of every family.

The reality, nevertheless, is that even youth who do not return to live with family often do reestablish contact after the system's control ends. Therefore, although this section is written in support of the many sexually abusive youth who do reunite with families, many of these concepts should also be considered when the client is not expected to return home and when the youth has remained at home throughout the treatment process.

Reunification is really not an event but a process with three steps: clarification, reconciliation, and reintegration. The process involves the systematic restoration of family relationships and a step-by-step reunification within the various subsystems in the family. It is time-consuming, work intensive, and physically and emotionally draining for all involved. The commitment to do the work despite these difficulties recognizes the importance of family in everyone's life and particularly listens to the voice of the child who says, "I just wanted the abuse to stop. I didn't want to lose my family."

Reconstruction is the bridge to reunification, and a major consideration in developing a reconstruction plan is the psychological readiness of the individual members. The sexually abusive youth and other members of the family will not be ready for reconstruction steps at the same time. Individual therapists and other professionals working with the subsystems within the family must assess the readiness of each family member. The sexually abusive youth is often involved in more intensive and extensive treatment than the rest of the family and therefore may to be ready for family reconstruction sooner than the others.

When the sexual abuse has occurred between siblings, particular caution must be exercised in determining the victim's readiness to be with the sibling who abused him or her. The safety and well-being of the victim always take precedence over the needs of the sexually abusive youth and the rest of the family (National Task Force on Juvenile Sexual Offending, 1988, 1993).

At the risk of sounding contradictory, however, one must be cautious of not being overprotective of the victim, thus sending the message to the victim and the rest of the family that he or she is not capable of being assertive enough to encounter the perpetrator. Empowering and fortifying the strengths of the victim are part of the healing process. Issues in deciding the readiness of the victim include a basic understanding of what has occurred, a reduction of acute symptoms, an increased feeling of support, an alliance with parents and therapists, and a basic ability to withstand the stress of the session.

The reunification process typically occurs in a series of steps. Initial sessions are usually conducted with various subsystems within the family. As relationships between the members of each subsystem are reestablished and fortified, the various subgroupings gradually can be joined. The process may be more complicated and protracted with larger families, more extensive abuse, multiple perpetrators or victims, and family members with more pervasive pathology.

The basic foundation for reconstruction of the family is developed during the course of treatment. Early family sessions typically involve the sexually abusive youth and the parents. As treatment progresses, consideration is given to the inclusion of other family members. Sessions that include the parents and the nonabusive siblings are helpful in assessing their readiness for the work of reconstructing the family. Such sessions provide an opportunity to share information about treatment issues and to assist the family members in dealing with unresolved feelings and concerns. Family therapy sessions that involve the entire family will be safe and productive only when the preliminary work has already been accomplished with the various subsystems within the family.

The first session between the victim and perpetrator is a clarification session. These are always intense and stressful but can be productive and helpful to everyone. When the sexually abusive youth accepts full responsibility for the abuse and is able to demonstrate empathy for the victim, the risk to the victim is substantially reduced. Parents and other family members need to have established a strong alliance with the victim and demonstrate a clear understanding of who is responsible for the abuse. Even so, the family therapist always retains the option to end the session if blaming, shaming, or intimidation occurs. During the initial meetings, clear and direct messages from the supportive family members such as parents and nonvictimized siblings regarding the responsibility for the abuse are helpful.

The resolution and reconstruction phase is always more difficult when the sexual abuse victim is a member of the family or when other family members have been sexually or physically abusive. With the high number of sexually abusive youth who report being sexually abused, it is not surprising that many have been victimized by siblings, parents, grandparents, or other relatives. In these cases, decisions have to be made regarding which family members to include and at what time. The same concerns and principles apply with the more complicated family situations as were described for less complicated ones. Establishing basic alliances within the family is very important. Victims need to perceive themselves as being supported and assisted in drawing on their strengths. With each successive unification of the various subgroups, the goals are to resolve problems and resistances, strengthen the sense of family, and promote a willingness to work together to prevent relapse and revictimization and restore stability and health to the family.

The preconditions that support effective reunification are that the sibling who has been abusive has learned to manage the sexual aggression, the family has eliminated the patterns that supported or encouraged abusive behavior and developed patterns that support or encourage empathic behavior, and the sibling victim feels supported, safe, and empowered.

The resolution and reconstruction process must be modified if the sexually abusive youth is not able to rejoin the family or return home. In these cases, families can still be involved and benefit from participation in rebuilding efforts. Clarifying and strengthening of family bonds, resolution of feelings about the abusiveness and the subsequent changes in the family, and a redefinition of relationships are goals of these efforts. Additionally, the families may need assistance in addressing feelings of grief associated with the loss of the youth from the family and the alterations of the family system. The ultimate goal of family treatment is to establish a functionally healthy family system in which further abuse is unlikely.

The sexually abusive youth who cannot be reintegrated into his or her family of origin needs assistance in learning to function safely and effectively as a member of a family group. Developing and strengthening abilities to express feelings, relate intimately, resolve conflict, and work cooperatively forms the foundation for being an adult member of his or her own future family system. Maintaining a family perspective allows the therapist, even when working with the sexually abusive youth apart from the family of origin, to address the pertinent issues and problem areas that relate to functioning as a healthy family member. The goal of these efforts is to break the cycle of dysfunctional family relationships and abuse. Foster families or "borrowed" families from the institution or agency that is working with the youth can provide positive experiences and practice in relating in a family-like constellation. Similarly, youth often report the development of a sense of family from their experience in group therapy, particularly when the group is led by male and female cotherapists. Although work in group is not typically considered part of family therapy, the "family" within the group may be the only available resource for dealing with family relationship issues. In these cases, group therapy may be an adjunctive mode of family treatment.

Issues related to separation, loss, grief, and abandonment are common with these youth and their families. Unless they are addressed and resolved, treatment can reach an impasse. Most individuals have a basic need for connectedness with a family. Treatment must include corrective experiences of this nature in order for the youth to function effectively with their families of origin and their future adult families. The multigenerational repetition of abuse is a risk if these issues are ignored.

Reconstruction cannot be accomplished with all families. At times, the sexually abusive youth is so fixated, disturbed, or unwilling to alter his or her behavioral pattern that he or she cannot be safely returned to the family. In other cases, one or more of the family members is unable or unwilling to address and work through personal issues related to the abuse to allow resolution and reconstruction to occur. Similarly, the individual pathology, cognitive deficits, or abusiveness of significant family members may hinder or prevent the family environment from being a safe place for the youth. Despite these possible limitations, many families overcome the obstacles if the members can be helped to address pertinent feelings and issues, are provided adequate instruction and support, and have a sincere willingness to resolve the problems and rebuild the family relationships.

Stage V: Termination and Aftercare

Relapse prevention is the ultimate goal of the offense-specific treatment program. Work on a plan begins at the start of treatment and continues with the culmination of the plan in written detail prior to discharge and the monitoring of its continued use after discharge.

Relapse prevention has its roots in substance abuse treatment and was later modified for use with sexual offenders at the Vermont Treatment Program for Sexual Aggressors by Pithers, Marques, Gibat, and Marlatt (1983). This model is based on the premise that there is no cure for sexual deviancy; sexual offenders must continue to practice intervention strategies if they are to avoid committing other sexual crimes. Not only is it important for the individual to practice relapse prevention, but for the adolescent in the care of his family, the family must be committed to this concept as well. The idea that even after completing treatment, the adolescent still has the potential to reoffend can be a bitter fact for parents to face. Parents certainly would prefer to believe that their adolescent who had been sexually abusive received treatment and was forever cured. Since there are no data to support this for adolescents, therapists are conservative in predicting continued risk and ask these youth to commit themselves to a relapse-prevention plan along with their parents' support. Just as parents of chemically dependent youngsters must accept their responsibility to participate in relapse prevention for their youngster, so must the parents of the sexually abusive youth.

The offender's family is an important part of his support and prevention team. In order for them to fulfill this role, it is necessary that everyone understands the concept of relapse prevention and what it requires of them. There are two ways that this can happen: (1) the therapist can plan special sessions to teach the family about relapse prevention using the adolescent as a resource for information, or (2) the family may participate in a relapse-prevention psychoeducational group designed for parents. Learning the relapse-prevention model is a commitment the family must make if they are to be a part of the resident's support team while the juvenile is in the program and after discharge.

Relapse prevention for the family means that they will have to understand their adolescent's sexual abuse cycle and how to help interrupt that cycle, his risk factors and high-risk situations for him, and methods for coping with lapses so they do not become relapses. It is important for the family to understand that high-risk situations can occur internally for their child or externally in the family. Parents must learn to identify the family dynamics that may have contributed to or supported the child's progression into abusive behavior and commit to changing those dynamics. The adolescent's responsibility is to share his relapse-prevention plan with his family and help educate them in its implementation. Parents must identify and agree to change the family dynamics that increase risk, such as diffused role boundaries, poor communication, cognitive distortions, abusiveness, lack of parental limit setting, lack of emotional support, or poor supervision.

The use of a written relapse-prevention contract between the parents and adolescent is useful in identifying the signs of relapse, the relapse-prevention approach, and the stages of intervention to prevent relapse. This contract should be specific and individualized for each family based on its own relapse-prevention needs as identified by both the therapist and family during the treatment process. It is important that the family rather than the therapist be the guide in establishing this contract so that the family will have ownership of it.

As part of such a contract, the family members can set up a system of monitoring themselves on successful use of relapse-prevention methods so they can identify problem areas that need support or help before they become unmanageable. One way to do this is for the family to establish a weekly meeting for the purpose of reviewing the contract, identifying current problems, and establishing goals and objectives for the following week. The therapist also establishes a system of posttreatment monitoring that includes the family's returning for follow-up monitoring for an unspecified time.

Termination

When the time approaches for termination or transition of family therapy, it is common for both the adolescent and the family to regress. Violations of treatment contracts and various acting-out behaviors may occur that seem to challenge the validity of earlier progress. Regression sometimes signals a need to slow the termination process, and at other times it is simply symptomatic of a healthy level of anxiety regarding the impending change. Occasionally some lingering family secret emerges and demands attention.

The child regresses because the treatment group and the therapist have become so important. The family regresses for much the same reason, coupled with their ambivalence about their ability to parent alone without the therapist's constant guidance and support. Families often feel that their emotional strength and parenting skills are not up to the task ahead. When this happens, individuals often avoid what they perceive as loss and abandonment by withdrawal, distancing, blaming the therapist, denying the importance of treatment, or dropping out altogether. This appears to be true whether the adolescent is currently at home or in a treatment program preparing to go home.

If the youth has been in a residential program where the therapist, staff, and program have provided major resources of support, structure, and self-esteem, then the letting go is particularly difficult and best approached in stages. The relapse-prevention model provides a gradual transition for families who will continue with the same therapist, but on a much less intense scale, identifying transition issues as well as termination ones. As the family regresses, therapist and staff may have ambivalent feelings as well as to whether this family can really parent this child.

It is up to the therapist to assist the client and family by preparing them for the difficulty of termination and transition through exploration of their feelings and expressions of confidence in their readiness. Families need to be reminded of situations they have handled well and to review with the therapist what they have learned in order to support positive family self-esteem. In reviewing the changes in the child and family, family members are able to see their progress and take credit for their part in it. At the same time, families must be prepared for reality. The future will not be perfect, and setbacks must be anticipated and managed.

If the child has been in a residential treatment program, home visits should become progressively more frequent and for longer periods. These home visits should have goals and objectives and should be processed with the family at their conclusion. It is important that the therapist express and demonstrate confidence and support of the family at this time to increase the family's confidence that they can parent the child at home. The therapist must make these goals and objectives realistic so that home visits are really practice time.

For the family leaving a treatment center and beginning outpatient treatment with another therapist, there needs to be sufficient preparation and transition time. This includes sharing of information and perhaps the receiving therapist's sharing in some of the final family sessions.

Aftercare

The concept of aftercare for sexually abusive youths means that treatment never really ends. The youth and family must be prepared to be responsible for this as the therapist or program gradually disengages and the family becomes empowered. The therapist and the therapy program continue to monitor treatment stability as long as necessary or possible. Unfortunately, there are no data to indicate what "as long as necessary" means. The number, length, and duration of aftercare services are treatment issues best determined by individualized treatment monitoring.

Aftercare services provided by the treatment provider may include, but are not limited to, individual therapy, group therapy, multifamily therapy, and family therapy. Participation is based on each individual family's needs as assessed by the therapist and the family. For some families, this will mean only check-in appointments for monitoring; for others, participation on an as-needed basis; and for still others, frequent, regularly scheduled appointments.

The therapist should be responsible for providing or making referrals for aftercare services and for monitoring the family's ongoing functioning by establishing a pattern and system of aftercare follow-up. Limited access and lack of resources for long-term aftercare may be obstacles to successful follow-up care. However, an encouragement to the family to keep in touch by way of an occasional phone call and to give notification of address and phone changes does not require resources so much as commitment to follow-up on the part of the therapist. An inquiry regarding current conditions, a genuine expression of caring and concern, and an offer of referral information for additional services takes only a few minutes and may be a nice reminder to families to continue to be vigilant.

The use of carefully chosen parents as peer counselors can be a practical resource in the design of aftercare services. Peer counseling is good as a reinforcement for the parents themselves, who are committed to being a resource for other families. At the same time, parents who receive peer counseling have the opportunity to see a family that is successfully coping and is practicing relapse prevention. Parents as peer counselors provide other families with the hope that there is life after treatment.

Most treatment providers encourage clients to return for help if problems arise. It is important to stress early interventions and encourage clients to call back before committing an offense. The responsibility must be placed very clearly with the clients to ask for help if they need it. The therapist's encouragement and confidence in the clients' progress must be tempered with caution. The consistent expectation of participation in aftercare supports recognition of the continued risk and holds the youth accountable for his own future.

References

Fay, J. (1979). *He told me not to tell.* Seattle: King County Rape Relief Center.

Gil, E. (1986). *A guide for parents of young sex offenders.* Walnut Creek, CA: Launch Press.

Hauch, P. (1974). *Overcoming anger and frustration*. Philadelphia: Westminster Press.

Kahn, T. (1990). *Pathways for parents*. Syracuse, NY: Safer Society Press.

National Task Force on Juvenile Sexual Offending. (1988). Preliminary report. *Juvenile and Family Court Journal, 39*(2).

National Task Force on Juvenile Sexual Offending. (1993). Revised report. *Juvenile and Family Court Journal, 44*(4).

O'Hyde, M. (1987). *Child sexual abuse: Let's talk about it*. Philadelphia: Westminster Press.

Parrish, L. (1985). *Behavioral contracting: Description and guidelines*. Unpublished manuscript.

Pithers, W., Marques, J., Gibat, C., & Marlatt, G. (1983). Relapse prevention with sexual aggressives. In L. Stuart & J. Greer (Eds.), *The sexual aggressor*. New York: Van Nostrand Reinhold.

Rubin, J. (1969). *The angry book*. Hackensack, NJ: Popular Press.

Sanford, L. (1980). *The silent children*. New York: Anchor Press, Doubleday.

VanDerBur-Atler, M. (1990). *Once can hurt a lifetime* [Videotape]. Washington, DC: One Voice.

CHAPTER NINETEEN

CREATING AN "ABUSE-SPECIFIC" MILIEU

Gail Ryan

The vast majority of at-risk youth in settings designed to provide remedial interventions have victimization and/or perpetration issues. Such settings include treatment programs that specifically address sexually abusive behaviors, violent assaultive behaviors, firesetting, vandalism, substance abuse, eating disorders, self-injurious behaviors, suicidal behaviors, and other chronic behavioral acting out. Youth with these issues may be housed in remedial settings such as residential, group, or foster care, and schooled in special education classrooms or alternative school settings. The abuse issues of youth put them at risk for victimization and perpetration in current and future interactions and benefit from an abuse-specific approach. Such an approach should arise from a developmental and contextual understanding of the unique history and needs of each youth, and it should be congruent with the treatment needs of all youth in the milieu

Note: The author acknowledges the role of three residential programs' participation in the development of the abuse-specific milieu model: Denver Children's Home (a long-term residential program with a mixed population); Synergy at Fort Logan Mental Health Hospital (a long-term residential substance abuse program for teenagers); and Falcon Lodge at Griffith Center (a long-term "offense-specific" residential unit for sexually abusive teenagers). Jerry Yager was particularly supportive in piloting the model during the late 1980s, and Susan Haglar, Stephanie Short, and Bill Ek helped with writing an earlier draft of the model in 1994.

and with other treatment services, which are provided in individualized treatment plans.

In Chapter Fourteen, Steven Bengis discussed the range of settings in which sexually abusive youth might require services and the pros and cons of those settings' segregating or integrating the sexually abusive youth from or with youth who have other referring problems. Although it is clear that some sexually abusive and some violent youth pose a danger to similar-age peers and must be segregated in settings designed to manage those risks (see Chapter Seventeen), the majority of sexually abusive youth do not appear to pose any greater risk to peers than do many other delinquent or acting-out adolescents. The youth who abuses smaller, vulnerable children or engages in hands-off offenses against adults or strangers is often treated in outpatient, day treatment, or mixed population settings.

At the same time, many youth in special-needs settings have experienced multiple risk factors, which put them at risk to have victimization or perpetration issues. Sometimes it is known that such youth have been abused, but the referral into treatment is related to current behavior problems, which are not viewed as abuse related; sometimes victimization issues are very apparent in the referral, but the risk of becoming abusive has not been recognized; and sometimes youth are referred for unrelated behavior problems, and it is not known until they settle into treatment that they have also been abused or abusive.

The prevalence of abuse issues in special-needs settings is sufficient that it has been suggested that such settings must acknowledge the risk of children abusing other children while in care and must purposefully plan risk-management strategies to moderate those risks (Freeman-Longo & Ryan, 1990; National Task Force, 1993; Thomas, 1996)

Planning for Safety

Freeman-Longo and Ryan (1990) have written about the need for planning:

> Whereas in the past, the abuse of one child by another may not have been a foreseeable risk, the growing body of literature on juvenile sexual offending supports the need to anticipate the risk of such behavior. In addition to the risk of perpetration by juveniles identified as sexual offenders, it has been noted that children who have been victims of sexual abuse and children in out-of-home care may be at an increased risk for sexual behaviors which may become abusive.

Current awareness of the incidence and prevalence of sexual offending by juveniles requires re-examination of policies, procedures, practice, and liability coverage in all institutions educating or caring for children and/or adolescents in order to ensure the safety of all. Negligence suits arise from a lack of purposeful planning, lack of defined policy and procedure, lack of on-going risk assessment, and lack of adequate documentation of preventive and interventive strategies.

It is suggested that decisions relevant to policy, procedure, and practice in juvenile service settings be made in consideration of the risk of sexually abusive behavior, and:

1. Clearly define policy and procedure
2. Implement team decision-making
3. Document prevention and intervention strategies
4. Follow ethics and standards of care wherever relevant standards exist and apply
5. Keep informed of current professional knowledge including new practice discoveries
6. Make appropriate referrals and placements
7. Seek consultation in difficult or unusual circumstances
8. Exercise due care in selecting, training, and supervising all adult employees including volunteers and student interns
9. Know and follow all mandatory reporting laws
10. Consult an attorney routinely and in cases or events which raise questions of liability or civil rights

Policy and procedure should clearly define the limits of confidentiality in order to foster open communication among staff and administration and minimize the secrecy which enables sexual abuse. At the same time, reporting and disclosures of information must be carried out with caution and respect for the rights and safety of all involved.

Documentation of routine care, treatment sessions, and incidents occurring during the treatment process is crucial to both daily practice and one's potential defense against suit. Documentation should include:

- Incidents during treatment (or care)
- Non-compliance
- Less than adequate resources
- System or family not following recommendations

- Termination of treatment without successful completion
- Continued risk factors and recommended follow-up

> Routine care decisions should be a part of written policies and procedures, and emergency situations requiring immediate decisions by individuals should be anticipated. Overall, team decision-making (preferably multidisciplinary) regarding deviations in the course of treatment, supervision, crisis management, expulsion/termination/completion of treatment, passes, privileges, consequences, etc., protects both individuals and agencies from negligence suits. Decision-making is strengthened by numbers and documentation [Freeman-Longo & Ryan, 1990, pp. 2–3].

Thomas (1993, 1996) has suggested that agencies must address the risks of staff abusing children, children abusing other children, and children abusing staff. She further details the need to examine the physical plant and staffing patterns, in addition to the policies and programming, from a risk-management perspective. Staff cannot adequately supervise and protect children if they cannot see them, do not have adequate backup, or do not have the training to understand the risks and implement preventive strategies.

Abuse-Specific Programming

Planning for safety acknowledges the immediate risks in the special-needs setting, but the issues that create the risk must be addressed within the programming in order to decrease the risks for these youth throughout their life span. Many of the issues related to victimization are the same as those related to perpetration (Ryan, 1989), and the same dysfunctional pattern is apparent in relation to behaviors that are abusive to self, others, or property. Abuse is abuse, whether it is physical, sexual, emotional, psychological, or verbal. With these concepts in mind, it becomes possible to see the similarities more than the differences in the abuse issues of youth referred for the wide range of behavioral problems already noted and found in special-needs populations.

Creating an abuse-specific milieu in all special-needs settings is advantageous for youth who have been victims of violence or sexual abuse, youth who have witnessed violence and abuse in their homes and communities, and youth who have become abusive to themselves, others, or property. An abuse-specific milieu enables abuse issues to be addressed in mixed populations, as well as in the care and schooling of youth who are segregated into offense-specific treatment programs due to a known history of sexually abusive or violent behavior.

Key Concepts in the Abuse-Specific Milieu

In creating a milieu in care settings or classrooms, staff and clients are introduced to fundamental concepts that underlie the expectations in the milieu. The abuse-specific milieu is dependent on staff and clients operationalizing the following key concepts.

"Abuse Is Abuse"

Abuse is defined as behaviors that occur without consent or equality or with coercion. Because informed consent requires regard for the standards and the potential consequences of decisions, behaviors that pose a risk of harm or stigma for one's self must be defined as abuse, just as behaviors that cause harm or stigma for others are abusive. In discussing treatment of victims and perpetrators of abuse, Thomas (personal communication, 1987) stated, "I hold victims and perpetrators equally accountable for their behaviors." To excuse or minimize self-abusive behaviors fails to protect individuals from harm as surely as their exposure to abuse by others.

Defining all abusive behaviors as problematic in the milieu allows the staff to hold all youth equally accountable and to build an expectation that every individual is worthy of safety and protection from abuse.

Abusive Cycles

The abusive cycle represents a dysfunctional coping strategy, and within that pattern, defensive reactions prevent resolution of stressful issues while the individual imagines a temporary solution to compensate for or get back a sense of control. Because the expanded definition of the "abuse is abuse" concept applies to all of the behaviors reflected in the dysfunctional cycle, the cycle becomes the second piece in the foundation of the abuse-specific milieu.

Learning, Reinforcement, and Deterrence

Sexual behaviors may be learned through direct experience or observation. (In this culture, all youth are exposed to both normative and deviant sexual information and stimuli.) All sexual behaviors are intrinsically reinforcing due to the presence of intimacy, arousal, orgasm, or tension reduction, powerful reinforcers that make it likely that behaviors will be repeated unless something occurs to deter repetition. The other behaviors that are defined as abusive to self, others, or property tend to become habituated or chronic as well, due to the intrinsic reinforcers associated with each. Reinforcement from physical sensations may result from either the introduction of foreign substances into the body or from substances generated in the brain as a result of certain behaviors. Psychological reinforcement results from the person's perception that the behavior in some way increases pleasure or efficacy or decreases negative factors in the individual. The more potent the physical and psychological reinforcers are, the more likely it is that the behavior will be repeated.

People may be deterred from imagined behavior by external factors: physical restraints that block opportunity; punishments, negative consequences, or negative associations that are more powerful disincentives than the perceived reinforcers for the behavior; or positive consequences associated with restraint that are perceived as more beneficial than the behavior. People may be deterred from behaviors that are harmful to themselves by internal cues that make clear the negative effects of the behavior. They may also be deterred from behaviors that are harmful to others by internal factors: sympathy, which assumes that others will feel as the individual does and may deter behavior perceived as unpleasant; empathy, which notices the other's signs of distress; or empathic foresight, which accurately predicts how behavior will affect others and avoids behavior perceived as distressing to others. Empathy is believed to be the highest and most lasting deterrent for abusive behavior.

Risk versus Identity

Youth who have engaged in sexually abusive behavior in the past are at risk to be abusive in the future, although a history of such behavior does not dictate future behavior. Some youth may give up abusive sexual interactions spontaneously as they mature, others may avoid further abusive interactions as a result of consequences or treatment interventions, and others may continue to be abusive despite all attempts to stop such behavior. There is no evidence at this time to distinguish which group a particular sexually abusive youth will be in. The consequences for victims and for the youth who engages in abusive sexuality are so serious that every case warrants some preventive intervention to attempt to reduce the risk that the behavior will continue.

The abuse-specific milieu recognizes the risk of repetition of abusive behaviors and addresses it very directly but does not label these youth as sex offenders for life. Differential evaluation and treatment provides each youth with new options in the future if he or she chooses to resist further abusive behavior. (Many are able to develop more normative sexual interests and arousal patterns; youth who work hard in treatment but continue to experience abusive fantasies and arousal require long-term relapse-prevention plans.) Similarly, youth who steal, deface, or vandalize property are considered at risk for criminal behaviors but are not labeled criminal for life on the basis of delinquent behaviors. Youth who abuse alcohol or drugs during adolescence are not labeled addicts for life, but are considered at risk for substance abuse. Labeling the *risk of recurrence* of past behaviors encourages vigilance and a sincere commitment to change. Labeling the *person* on the basis of past behavior implies that change is not possible or expected and perpetuates hopelessness. Early interventions are driven by the hope that children can return to more normative developmental paths.

Growth and Development

Youth are continuing to grow and change throughout their time in treatment, acquiring new developmental skills, accommodating to the environment of the milieu, and assimilating new experiences into their view of themselves, others, and the world. The bad things that have been a part of their past experience become proportionately smaller as new experiences are integrated, and deviancy and deficits can be replaced with more normative growth and development. Growth and development are fostered in a psychologically safe environment and facilitated by empathic nurturance, education, and new experiences of the world and of relationships. Growth is interspersed with regressions, which enable the individual to push forward in trying new things but also to slip back into more comfortable patterns of the past.

In the milieu, a physically and psychologically safe environment increases the opportunity for growth and development. Therefore, physical and psychological safety are the first goals in the abuse-specific milieu, demonstrating staff's commitment to a nonabusive lifestyle.

Physical Safety

It is imperative that the milieu be a haven of physical safety in the life experience of youth who have often been hurt or hurtful in relationships, and who have witnessed violence or experienced a pervasive sense of being unsafe and unprotected. Physical safety is the most basic need. It must be met before other needs can be recognized and met. At the same time, the abuse-specific milieu recognizes that the very nature of the problem that leads to referral to the program (a history of abusive behavior) describes a population of youth who pose a danger to themselves and/or others in that they are abusive and remain at risk of being abusive even as they begin to benefit from the treatment program. Therefore, program staff expect that some abusive dynamics will occur among peers and toward staff, and staff are trained to minimize the risks posed to physical safety in the milieu. *Preventing abusive behavior is the highest priority of the program.* Establishing physical safety in the milieu is the first step, and the efforts spent struggling to maintain such safety are both therapeutic and instructive for youth in the program.

Deescalation. The emphasis in managing aggressive or assaultive behavior that threatens the physical safety of youth or staff in the program is always on deescalation. Staff are trained to speak in a nonthreatening manner and to attempt to slow the escalation toward a youth's acting out. Every attempt is made to validate the youth's emotions with words and to encourage him to talk it out or take a time-out to slow things down. Peers may be asked to suspend their own activities or to refrain from any interaction or provocation with a youth who is struggling to maintain self-control. Understanding that the cycle that leads to behavioral acting out is functioning to help the youth regain a sense of control, staff can give the youth an opportunity to be in control (without being abusive) by asking: "What can we do to help you not lose control?"

Physical Restraints. Staff should be trained in an approved method of physical restraint as a last resort to prevent a youth from causing physical harm to self or others. However, physical restraints are the lowest level of deterrence for behavior and are likely to be perceived by the youth as a loss of control, which exacerbates the control issues he is trying to resolve in treatment. Therefore, physical restraints are viewed as an extreme (rather than routine) intervention, which is carefully documented. Every incident is processed by staff on duty (and, to the extent possible, with the youth and peers) in order to attempt to predict and prevent further need for such controls. Staff must be very sensitive to the difference between a protective restraint and a coercive or punitive restraint.

Isolation. Program administration should provide a method for the isolation of some youth in some circumstances related to clinical or behavioral needs. Isolation is an individualized clinical intervention designed to give a high level of intense therapeutic intervention to a particular youth who is jeopardizing safety in the milieu. The goal is to slow the process for the youth in order to enable him to be safe in the milieu. Isolation is not the same as a time-out. Time-outs are brief periods during which a competent person is able to calm himself and rethink a situation. Many of these youth are not able to use time-out effectively early in treatment because they lack the skills to calm themselves or to rethink.

A youth in isolation should not be left alone for long periods of time, to avoid a parallel with the isolation we see in the cycle or trigger issues of neglect or rejection. Staff's willingness to be with the youth when he is too upset to interact, and to work with him to understand his behavior in relation to the cycle when he is able, are powerful demonstrations of care, which are part of the new experience of relationship in treatment.

Milieu Closures. Closures occur only when the physical and psychological safety of the milieu is being jeopardized by a significant number of residents, and staff and peer culture interventions have been unable to reestablish a safe environment. Closure represents a group intervention that is designed to reestablish safety in the milieu. By necessity, staff take control of the milieu, and the whole group is held accountable to a very tight structure and limits in order to slow the interactions in the milieu and reestablish safety. Internally, closures are about group accountability and are a powerful demonstration of staff commitment to the needs of the youth to be and feel safe. Externally, closures significantly limit interaction with other persons and programs in the community and discourage intrusion into the milieu. Closure precludes involvement in all other activities and programs; meals are brought in, education is by in-house tutorial assistance, and recreational activity is limited to activities the whole group is able to participate in together. The tight limitations of closures facilitate intense interventions into the relational system of youth and staff with a constant goal of the earliest possible return to normal programming. Such interventions demonstrate staff's relentless commitment to creating a safe environment, another new experience for many youth.

Legal Interventions. If any youth physically or sexually assaults or uses a weapon to threaten physical harm to any other youth or any staff, law enforcement must be called immediately. Such assaults are defined by law, and youth must be legally accountable. Youth who commit felonious assaults against peers or staff in the milieu may need to be discharged in order to ensure the safety of the milieu. Policies regarding the bottom lines that will result in legal consequences or discharge must be made clear on entry into the program, as well as any conditions for consideration of readmission.

Sexual Behavior

Sexual contact between peers in any milieu is forbidden by state regulations and must always be reported as required by regulation. Any sexual contact between peers in the abuse-specific milieu is usually specifically counterproductive in relationship to the treatment needs of the youth who are struggling to understand and manage sexual issues. Staff must be trained and the milieu programming designed to minimize the access and opportunity for sexual contacts to occur among peers. Any sexual contact that is discovered or disclosed as occurring within the milieu is first evaluated in relation to the legal definitions of sexual assault, and then in relation to the program's definition of abusive interactions. Legal and clinical interventions are based on this evaluation. The rules regarding sexual contact should be explicitly defined as youth are admitted to the milieu. At the same time, the dilemma these rules pose for youth in restricting normative sexual expressions also must be acknowledged.

Behavior Modification

Physical safety is clearly related to behavior control. Reinforcement of behavior through rewards and extinction of behaviors through aversive conditioning processes are effective in achieving temporary behavior change. However, such interventions should be viewed as temporary solutions and the control as superficial. Genuine control will be a product of internal changes and developmental growth.

Level systems, which grant or deny privileges as rewards or consequences, should be viewed as descriptive of the proportion of responsibility and control over behavioral safety and decision making shared by staff and youth. Levels are best not earned, given, or negotiated; they should be demonstrated. The consistent demonstration of a high level of personal responsibility is a goal of treatment. Progress toward that goal may be sporadic, with movement between levels anticipated in both directions. Stated level changes are a form of communication among staff, and between staff and youth, which enables everyone to recognize changing roles and responsibilities from day to day. Levels should be assessed by two or more staff at the end of each day in order to document observations that demonstrate different levels of responsible behavior. Signs of vulnerability or risk should result in higher levels of supervision.

Youth who have not demonstrated self-management skills rely on staff for close supervision, whereas youth who have been able to demonstrate high levels of personal responsibility may need less close supervision. Levels should be thought of as related to the level of care, not as punishment. Rewards and negative consequences associated with behavior management strategies must be carefully reviewed. It is important to distinguish privileges, which are given or revoked, from the legitimate needs of youth, which are related to healthy growth and development. For example, staff are often tempted to use recreation, peer interactions, pleasurable activities, and special foods as tools of behavior management. Yet healthful pursuits, learning to benefit from prosocial interactions, and signs of nurturance are needs of the growing child. Deprivation of needs is counterproductive to growth and also may trigger issues related to past deprivation.

At the same time, youth who need to learn tension-reduction and relaxation skills but are deprived of activities that meet those needs, such as being told they cannot play basketball, go on the hike, or listen to music, because of rule violations may escalate their dysfunctional pattern rather than learn to enjoy healthy activities. Just as parents are taught to "catch kids being good," behavior management systems should be designed as win-win strategies, with perhaps tokens or marks given that eventually accumulate for some reward (beyond the legitimate needs of the youth).

Consistently labeling abuse as the highest-priority issue and psychological safety as the goal helps staff and clients be clear about why they are working together. Because the youth are there to work on abuse issues, it is expected that abusive patterns will be manifest in the milieu, but the consequence of abusive patterns is that they are consistently labeled as treatment issues. As such, the youth eventually realize that they will need to stop abusive behaviors and demonstrate nonabusive coping strategies and empathic interactions in order to succeed in the program. This keeps the focus where it needs to be.

In the milieu, the daily goals are to prevent abusive behaviors (abuse of self, others, and property) and promote growth. Staff must struggle within themselves and with peers in the milieu to depersonalize abusive behaviors so they do not perceive themselves as victims. Consistent attribution of responsibility for such behaviors to the youth who is acting out in an abusive fashion is imperative.

Goals

The ongoing goals of the abuse-specific milieu are communication, empathy, and accountability: the ability to articulate rather than act out, the ability to participate in empathic interactions, and the accurate attribution of responsibility. These are referred to as *universal goals* that promote the sense of safety that enables growth and change. In such an environment, differential treatment plans can identify developmental goals, and staff can work to promote healthy functioning.

The focus of the milieu should be on health. Deviance can be addressed specifically in treatment interventions with clinicians (group, individual, and family sessions), but the milieu is the arena for living and growing. It becomes the surrogate for the family and home, which nurtures and protects, encouraging growth and development. In the mixed milieu, all youth can be encouraged and supported in healthy human development, and the abuse-specific concepts that (1) define abuse, (2) identify dysfunctional patterns, and (3) promote empathic interactions are operationalized. The milieu becomes the new learning environment for experiencing and practicing nonabusive lifestyles. Becoming able to experience pleasure, succeeding in creating safe relationships, and developing evidence of self-efficacy and esteem increase the youth's prognosis for avoiding deviancy.

Milieu Staff

Milieu staff should be highly trained regarding the concepts of "abuse is abuse," the cycle, the universal goals, and developmental competence, and be encouraged, supported, and supervised to be accountable for operationalizing those concepts in every interaction and intervention in the milieu.

The abuse-specific milieu model has several advantages for staff in segregated offense-specific programming. First, it offers a more holistic approach, viewing the youth as whole human beings rather than "sex offenders." Second, it keeps the focus on the abuse issues but without the constant vicarious exposure of staff and peers to the traumas and deviance of abuse. Third, it helps to provide some containment around the issues that escalate the youth's acting out by labeling and referring the manifestations of the cycle back into the clinical components of treatment. For example, when staff intervene in an escalating abuse cycle, they may identify important clues about triggers, cognitive distortions, or fantasy material. However, the issue is referred to the clinical components of the day—for example: "Saul, I noticed that you were kind of shut down right before you blew up at Pete. It might be helpful to talk to your group today about what kind of thoughts you were having," or "Sara, I noticed you had a strong reaction when we walked past the stairwell. You might want to look at what that trigger was when you go to group today." The fourth advantage is the clear distinction of role boundaries between direct care staff and clinicians and the reduced risk of burnout from chronic exposure to deviance. Representatives from the milieu staff may participate in clinical components, attending groups or joining the family session, but the role is to provide a supportive bridge for communication between clinicians and the milieu.

The abuse-specific milieu has several advantages for mixed population settings as well. By relating a single model to the dysfunctions of all the youth, staff and peers can see their similarities and avoid stigmatizing some behaviors as "worse" than others. The goal orientation of safety and growth meets the needs of all youth, and the intervention style of communication, empathy, and accountability represents universal goals for healthy, empathic relationships. For staff, the containment of deviant exposure and the more heterogeneous population reduces the high risks of burnout associated with offense-specific work. The youth seem to benefit from the experience of a mixed population as well (see Chapter Fourteen).

Staff have three primary roles in the milieu: to protect, to nurture, and to observe. Protection is demonstrated in the struggle to achieve physical and psychological safety. Nurturance focuses on developmental competency (Strayhorn's "Psychological Health Skills" describe sixty-two specific skills in nine areas of development and can be a good framework for conceptualizing developmental goals for staff to nurture; see Chapter Seven). Observation is the primary measure available in the program to inform differential diagnosis and treatment planning. Although psychological tests may illuminate understanding of many aspects of the youth's functioning, it is only through informed observation that treatment providers can see the developmental context, the cues, and the changes over time, which are the basis for determining treatment needs, progress, and outcomes.

Milieu staff must be trained to observe and document the evidence that indicates the youth's progress and must use goal-oriented strategies to help the youth succeed in becoming able to:

- Consistently define abuse
- Acknowledge ongoing risks
- Recognize the cycle
- Demonstrate the ability to interrupt the cycle
- Demonstrate functional coping skills
- Demonstrate an increased ability to be empathic

By containing the work on offense-specific deviance and other behavioral disorders in the clinical components of treatment, the milieu can focus on health and growth, creating a basis for a new contextual phenomenology and the skills for more normative functioning.

References

Freeman-Longo, R., & Ryan, G. (1990). Tort liability in treatment of sexually abusive juveniles. *Interchange*. (Newsletter of the National Adolescent Perpetrator Network). Denver: Kempe National Center.

National Task Force on Juvenile Sexual Offending. (1993). Revised report. *Juvenile and Family Court Journal, 44*(4).

Ryan, G. (1989). Victim to victimizer: Re-thinking victim treatment. *Journal of Interpersonal Violence, 4*(3).

Strayhorn, J. (1988). *The competent child*. New York: Guilford.

Thomas, J. (1993). *Safety in residential programs*. Presentation at the Ninth Annual Conference of the National Adolescent Perpetrator Network, Lake Tahoe, NV.

Thomas, J. (1996). *Safety in residential treatment settings*. Paper presented to the Twelfth Annual Conference of the National Adolescent Perpetrator Network, Minneapolis, MN.

CHAPTER TWENTY

AFTERCARE

Community Integration Following Institutional Treatment

William C. Greer

The ultimate test of treatment success is the sexually abusive youth's ability to control abuse behaviors in the community after treatment. He or she must use the multiple behavioral, emotional, attitudinal, interactional, cognitive, and physiological changes effected to maintain control of his or her behaviors. In the past, before recognition of the ingrained, habitual, and defensive nature of sexually abusive behavior patterns of some youth, there were numerous post-treatment failures. Aftercare planning, relapse-prevention techniques, and follow-up services were increased or developed to support the growing awareness that a gradual decline (not a sudden termination) of contact, support, and treatment intervention encourages the offender to continue applying new techniques and concepts to manage his behaviors in a new environment. Although many sexually abusive youth can be treated in outpatient programs, many others require institutional or residential treatment. Although all programs should develop an aftercare program, this chapter focuses on aftercare subsequent to release from an institutional treatment program.

Aftercare is that portion of comprehensive adolescent sexual perpetrator treatment intervention that takes place in the community after the youth is released from the institution. It is the area of the rehabilitative intervention process that involves supervision and continued treatment of the client after release from secure custody, residential treatment, or inpatient care. Aftercare philosophies recognize that the offender is not cured in the traditional sense and acknowledge the compulsive nature of the sexually abusive behaviors. Aftercare is the part of the treatment plan that most directly connects with the client's future and thus deserves to be as integral a part of treatment planning and the rehabilitative process as other components.

Aftercare is a significant conjunct to offense-specific treatment for three primary reasons. First, an aftercare program assists the youth with acknowledging that he continues to be at risk of offending; his behavior problem is still part of him and has not magically vanished on release or discharge. Aftercare encourages the youth to continue to use the tools acquired to prevent reoffense and focuses on strengthening behavior management. Clients experience more difficulty with maintaining these abilities while reentering the community than in an institutional program. The world they return to after leaving a residential program lacks the controls, structure, treatment intervention, and type of support that they have become accustomed to. Aftercare supervision provides a therapeutic link of continued accountability for offense behavior management.

Second, aftercare provides a clear-cut method for monitoring the youth's behavior after release. The aftercare supervisor can observe clients for any resumption of behaviors or thinking errors that could become dangerous to others or themselves and can often intervene before the behaviors progress or the client can reoffend. Aftercare or follow-up providers monitor high-risk behaviors, involvement in high-risk situations, irresponsible decision making, denial or minimization, substance abuse, placement difficulties or failure, decompensation, and abusive behavior antecedents. In order to monitor the client's behavior adequately, the aftercare provider must maintain close contact with the youth, his family, and close friends or any significant others in the offender's life. The aftercare supervisor becomes more of an ombudsman than a therapist (Freeman, 1979). The development of a team approach to supervision, in which the client and those in his or her environment are part of the team, can help in the control or the discovery of any reoffense or potential of reoffense.

The third benefit of an aftercare program is that of helping the youth establish a community-based locus pairing, or association of the therapeutic messages received by the offender with the locus of the community. Prior to release, the youth's locus is the residential or closed-custody facility. When the youth is released, the change of locus and custody status may precipitate a new level of denial. The youth may begin to believe, "The problem doesn't exist for me anymore. I'm cured. I've dealt with it so there will be no more problems. That solution only applied to lock-up. I can handle this risk." Often treatment staff in residential treatment facilities, particularly in juvenile correctional systems, unwittingly support this type of subtle denial when attempting to prove to a parole board or other discharge authority that the youth now presents an acceptable risk for release or discharge. The message implicitly, and sometimes explicitly, is that the client is now cured, which is inaccurate. In fact, the youth is more likely to be of higher risk subsequent to release and may exhibit some regression while coping with change and transition issues.

The youth who has been able to master adequate behavior management techniques to lessen his risk to others is simply a lower risk. Most clinicians and a growing number of researchers are realizing that the youth is not cured any more than a chemically dependent person or an alcoholic is cured. The compulsivity of the sexually abusive youth is in remission at the time of discharge or release; he or she is better able to recognize and interrupt the signs of potential reoffense and better able to master the appropriate behavior management techniques required to prevent reoffense incidents. These abilities should enable the youth to live in the community safely. Establishing a community-based locus helps to reinforce the therapeutic messages and interventions received by the youth prior to release and return to the community.

Goals and Objectives of a Prototype Aftercare Program

An aftercare program that I designed and implemented in San Francisco in April 1985, under the auspices of the California Youth Authority, was subsequently replicated throughout California. The San Francisco Aftercare Program was designed to receive sexually abusive youth who were released on parole status from Youth Authority facilities and returning to the community. The program design demonstrates the importance of an aftercare process as a conjunct to treatment and provides guidelines for those who are developing similar programs.

The primary goal of the San Francisco program was the protection of public safety through adequate treatment and supervision of the sexually abusive youth. The second goal was to assist the youth with developing effective management strategies to control sexually aggressive behavior during both the short and the long term. The program was referred to as one for behavior management rather than rehabilitation because the word *rehabilitation* connotes that the youth is cured of deviant tendencies, ideation, or behaviors. Even implication of the term *cure* gives both the youth and the public a false sense of security. Viewing the sexually abusive youth as a chronically compulsive person appears to be much more accurate.

The third goal was to develop a model of interagency cooperation and information sharing that included representatives from the local police, parole board, probation office, district attorney's office, public defender's office, child protective services, rape crisis center, and local victim witness assistance agencies. The fourth goal was to focus clearly on the concerns of the victims of the sexually abusive youth and to address community victim issues.

Supervision

Initially supervision and surveillance, a normal part of a parole program, was intensified to help control and monitor the youth's behavior during the short term to provide the greatest possible safety to the public. The intensified level of supervision and surveillance was accomplished in a variety of ways.

Local Law Enforcement. A dynamic linkage was established between the program staff and local law enforcement officials, including face-to-face contact and frequent telephone contact. With the assistance of local law enforcement, we were able to monitor closely the behavior of the youth assigned to the Aftercare Program through police field interviews documented in the police computer system and information on recent contacts or arrests. Clients were confronted when they exhibited dangerous behavior, as well as behavior that brought them closer to acting out old, dangerous behavior patterns, such as loitering around children's playgrounds, "cruising" with negative or gang-oriented peers, drinking, or substance abuse. Our cooperative relationship with local law enforcement officials allowed a higher level of "surveillance availability"—that is, observation of the youth's accountability in public areas, where he hangs out and with whom, and identification of high-risk factors.

Cooperation between local law enforcement and the sexually abusive youth's field supervisor (parole or probation officer) helps to maintain an attitude of expecting accountability from the offender. The field supervisor can check police field interviews and other police contacts with the youth, as well as keeping current with other intelligence, such as gang intelligence or sighting of the youth in high-risk situations or areas. Law enforcement connections are vital to soliciting assistance when apprehending an offender who is at high risk or is missing. Additionally, a close relationship with the local police authorities can be helpful in assuaging negative public reaction to the release of the youth to the community following treatment or incarceration.

Local Probation Departments. It is equally important for local probation departments to establish specific supervision programs for sexually abusive youth. In California, as in many other states, the difference between probation and parole supervision is one of jurisdiction. Probation supervision typically is the responsibility of a local agency, usually at the county level, and it commonly takes place prior to and in lieu of a court's committing the youth to a state facility. Parole supervision involves a state agency and takes place after the youth is released from a state correctional facility. Since sexually abusive youth often go through the probation system before entering parole supervision, continuing contact between probation and parole field supervisors limits the loss of information concerning the youth's developmental history, community ties, family problems, and prior victims.

In San Francisco, probation and parole staff worked together to share information about sexually abusive youth who, because of their risk to the community, were moved from one system of custody and supervision to the other. In this way valuable treatment time was not wasted reinventing the wheel. Through access to the youth's behavior profile prior to entering treatment in either residential treatment or treatment at a correctional facility, continuity of treatment is fostered. Additionally, if a youth under either probation or parole supervision is convicted of less serious offenses, the field supervisor can often suggest appropriate sentencing alternatives to the court.

Contact with Offenders and Families. Correctional community release programs often predetermine guidelines for client contact, typically weekly during a thirty-day reentry phase and once or twice monthly during the subsequent case management phase. These guidelines, however, fail to consider the compulsive nature of sexually abusive youth. The field supervisor needs to be flexible enough to increase the level of contact as the client's needs indicate. Typical parolee contact schedules may be doubled and maintained at that level throughout the youth's parole program. Some youth may be seen twice or three times per week and sometimes daily during crisis periods.

More important than frequency of contact is the quality of the contact. The field supervisor encourages a network of information sharing with the youth, his family, and significant others in the youth's environment. The field supervisor creates a team atmosphere in which he or she acts as the coordinator of the team and individual members of that team (the youth, parents, girlfriend or boyfriend, teachers, and employers) are encouraged to share information concerning behaviors that may indicate the youth is returning to a high-risk state. The message to the team members is that sharing such information is not "snitching" but helps the youth to manage behaviors for long-term successful adjustment.

Contact with Previous Victims. From the beginning, victims must be an integral part of the program. The field supervisor initiates contact with the victim or victims at the time of the youth's removal from the community and again at the time of the youth's reentry to the community. The victim's feelings and requests are shared with the parole board at both the time of sentencing and the time of release. Appropriate referrals are made to victims for counseling, reparation of damages, or other needed services. Victim tracking may be aided through victim witness agencies, Department of Motor Vehicles records, and the victim's own efforts to maintain contact with the program.

Care should be taken not to place sexually abusive youth near their victims when releasing them to the community. Initiating contact with the victims soon after the youth's commitment to the correctional agency ensures that the victim has had an adequate chance to voice his or her concerns to the sentencing and release authorities. Additionally, this type of personal contact with the victim allows the field supervisor the opportunity to give victims and their families appropriate referrals to community services.

Community-based treatment components need to be in place for the sexually abusive youth at the time of his release and reentry into the community. These components include a specialized field supervisor, access to continuing offense-specific treatment, and specific supports for managing and controlling offense behaviors. Critical to the design of an aftercare program is an effective assessment protocol, a treatment delivery system, and the relapse-prevention model.

Risk Assessment

Risk assessments are tools used to determine appropriate placement for treatment, an adequate reentry plan, risk for reoffense, and the type of support a youth will need to assist him or her with maintaining treatment philosophies and using treatment techniques. Exhibit 20.1 contains an example of the risk assessment scale used in the San Francisco program (Lowe, 1986). This scale, like similar other assessment scales (see Groth & Laredo, 1981), relies on somewhat subjective means to define a client as a low-, medium-, or high-risk offender. However, the focus on such issues as violent content of assault, denial or minimization of the offense, and empathy for the victim are consistent with other widely used risk assessment scales.

Treatment Programs

The treatment used in the San Francisco program is consistent with that generally recognized as effective for sexually abusive youth and described in the National Task Force Report on Juvenile Sexual Offending (1988, 1993). The treatment of choice for most sexually abusive youth is offense-specific treatment using techniques that are discussed in Chapter Sixteen. Counseling sessions focus on the specifics of the sexual abuse, as well as the antecedent behaviors and thinking. For the aftercare client, the field supervisor may contribute a detailed community assessment

EXHIBIT 20.1. SEX OFFENDER RISK ASSESSMENT SCALE.

1. Documented Offenses

   L First offense

   M First or second sexual offense with a history of other non-sexual criminal behaviors

   H Extensive history of sexual offenses

2. Nature of Offense

   L Offense seems uncharacteristic or spontaneous

   M Offense is premeditated with associated masturbatory fantasies

   H Offense involves stalking the victim(s) and frequent masturbatory fantasies about violence/sexual assault

3. Violence

   L No violence and/or physical force associated with offense(s)

   M Threats of violence and/or physical force associated with offense(s)

   H Offenses are violent in nature, with use of weapons, and may be becoming increasingly violent

4. Personal Responsibility

   L Admits involvement and personal responsibility

   M Minimizes or denies involvement, may blame victim, drug/alcohol use or other external sources

   H Total denial of involvement and personal responsibility

5. Attitude Toward Victim(s)

   L Expresses empathy toward victim, feels remorse

   M Objectifies victim, expresses little empathy, depreciates victim's hurt

   H No concern for injuries caused, may blame victim

6. Age:

   L Under age 15

   M Age 16–18

   H Above 18 years old

7. Family Background

   L Supportive prosocial family

   M Little family support, family may be overprotective with strong puritanical morals code

   H Family either nonexistent or deviant

8. Abuse Background

   L No history of abuse, physical or sexual

   M Background of abuse, physical or sexual

   H Severe history of abuse and victimization

Source: Lowe (1986). *Sex offender risk assessment.* Preston, CA: Oak Specialized Counseling Program, Preston School of Industry, California Youth Authority. Reprinted by permission.

Note: L = low-risk offender; M = medium-risk offender; H = high-risk offender.

of the youth's adjustment to family, friends, and school or employment to assist the treatment agent in focusing on transition and current risk issues.

There has been an adversarial relationship between those who treat sexually abusive youth and those who are responsible for their supervision. Turf issues and distrust, particularly regarding confidentiality, are all too common. Some sexually abusive youth are masters at using this dichotomy to their advantage, playing the therapist against the field supervisor, until no effective treatment is accomplished. Supervision is also hampered when there is little coordination or cooperation as vital information relevant to the youth's current level of risk may not be received or considered in monitoring strategies.

The approach to this dilemma is similar to that endorsed in the preliminary and revised reports of the National Task Force on Juvenile Sexual Offending and used by most offense-specific treatment programs. In aftercare, there is no confidentiality between contracted therapists and the field supervisor concerning the youth's behavior or issues that place a client at a high risk for reoffense. This expectation is made clear to the client both verbally and in writing prior to starting treatment.

A good system of information sharing and communication between the therapist and field supervisor strengthens both the treatment and the supervision processes. Most state laws require therapists to inform law enforcement officials of a client's reports of reoffense. Operational policy with contracted therapists should neither require nor encourage them to maintain confidentiality with clients. This approach is controversial and may inhibit self-disclosure when clients are in the initial stages of treatment; however, clients typically begin to self-disclose any return to dangerous behavior patterns as they become more involved with the treatment process. Of course, the field supervisor and the therapist cannot rely solely on the client's self-report of high-risk thinking or behavior. This is the reason it is so important to establish a network of information sharing with others in the youth's environment. It is far more likely that the client's parents, girlfriend, teacher, or neighbor will disclose high-risk behaviors or attitudes. In recent years, some treatment programs have used periodic monitoring polygraph examinations to encourage the youth to be accountable. Sometimes a youth will disclose his involvement in high-risk behaviors.

Sexually abusive youth need to evaluate and explore each failure or success. When providing supportive confrontation to the youth, it is important to minimize one's own emotive content. The client must realize that the confrontation or support is not given because the therapist or field supervisor is a friend or an enemy, or that the client has been "good" or "bad." Anger and power and control issues are usually primary areas of behavioral deficit and serve a self-protective or empowering function. These emotions should not be modeled in the therapist's or field supervisor's approach to the client's exhibiting an inability to use appropriate coping and response skills with interpersonal conflicts or situations that elicit strong emotions. Supportive confrontation should be done with a matter-of-fact attitude and a manner that is noncritical yet expectant of accountability for control of abusive behaviors. Even explicit statements such as, "I am not confronting you because I am angry with you," are helpful in separating the client's behavior from his or her value as an individual. This approach elicits a higher level of cooperation from the youth.

Relapse Prevention

The San Francisco program uses a modification of the Brownell et al. (1986) relapse-prevention model developed initially for use with chemically dependent individuals and originally modified for sex offenders by Pithers, Marques, Gibat, and Marlatt (1983). The outline of the effectiveness criteria looks at measures of both positive and negative behavior and is used for both relapse prevention and monitoring purposes:

Measures of Negative Behavior

1. Reoffense versus recidivism

   Clients still under supervision: Check local police files and with youth's significant others

   Clients out of supervision: Check local, state, and national criminal data files

   Check state and local registering files

2. Frequency and content of deviant fantasy
3. Return to high-risk behavior

   Return to denial or minimization

   Inadequate or inappropriate cooperation with therapy

   Apparently irrelevant decisions

   Substance abuse

   Placement failure

   Decompensation

Measures of Positive Behavior

1. Employment
2. School attendance
3. Appropriate behavior in therapy

4. Avoidance of high-risk behavior
5. Development of workable coping strategies for high-risk situations
6. Positive relationships with family and significant others, friends and peers

The focus is on helping the youth identify the components of his high-risk behavior and thinking. The more that these clients can recognize their progression from low-risk to high-risk behavior and can identify the feeling states and internal dialogue associated with each stage of the progression, the better they can learn to manage their behavior effectively.

Review of the literature and clinical experience indicate that sexually abusive youth, particularly rapists, report an increase in the urge to be sexually abusive when they are bored (Marshall, Earls, Segal, & Darke, 1983). Although many other factors may trigger increased urges, this seems to be true of adolescents. Boredom may be a defense against experiencing uncomfortable thoughts or feelings. Deviant fantasies and behavior also seem to increase when sexually abusive youth are using intoxicants. Alcoholism can compound denial issues, making effective treatment more difficult (Nichols & Haines, 1978). Alcohol and intoxicant ingestion can inhibit social judgment or recognition of inappropriate sexual cues involving force or violence or any associated urges and fantasies. These issues commonly arise in the treatment of sexually abusive youth and are addressed by counseling components that teach appropriate life skills. During aftercare, aggressive field supervision can help to minimize intoxicant consumption and ensure the youth's participation in therapy. It can also hold the youth accountable for using his time positively (for example, in employment or academic and vocational training).

The goal in aftercare planning is to replicate the treatment messages given to the youth in residential treatment and pair those messages with the locus of the community, demanding accountability while monitoring the client for any return to high-risk behavior patterns. Leveraging techniques include encouraging the youth to seek periodic "treatment boosters" from the original source of treatment when he is exhibiting higher-risk thinking patterns or to participate in aftercare groups, twelve-step programs, or ongoing long-term support groups. When the youth is facing problematic situations, increased supervision is warranted and supports the youth's efforts to manage his abusive behaviors. At times the youth may require short periods of confinement to interrupt a return to previous behavior patterns. Aftercare promotes accountability for using new behaviors and avoiding reoffense.

Communication Between Aftercare and Residential Treatment Staff

The same type of dynamic linkage achieved between aftercare staff and the probation department also helps treatment and field supervision staff to avoid reinventing the wheel when establishing treatment plans. The same effect can be seen when a similar linkage is developed between aftercare staff and those who provided treatment in the institution or residential facility. The client does not magically change when he is released from a residential facility to aftercare supervision, and neither should the treatment strategy for the client. When staff from residential treatment facilities and aftercare programs maintain effective communication with each other, the treatment message can be consistent, and client data are more likely to be accurate.

In the San Francisco program, the aftercare field supervisor makes monthly visits to the institutions to talk to incarcerated youth and the staff responsible for their treatment. The field supervisor participates in the monthly case reviews held at the institution for these youth and provides input for release and aftercare planning.

Public Information Sharing

One of the problems that correctional and parole authorities involved in approving the release of sexually abusive youth continually face is negative reaction by community officials and the public when a high-profile perpetrator is released. The national publicity given to the public outcry over the release of rapists William Archie Fain and Lawrence Singleton in California illustrates the problem. When sexually abusive youth are incarcerated or placed in institutions or residential treatment facilities, it is as if they are out of sight and out of mind. The public and their elected or appointed officials generally do not know about, and rarely trust even if they do, the state-of-the-art treatment processes used with sexually abusive youth. This lack of awareness helps to fuel the public distrust of release decisions made for these youth and can make community placement difficult.

The aftercare field supervisor is in a unique position to keep public officials informed of the treatment progress that high-profile perpetrators make while incarcerated and in treatment. Maintaining an information-sharing relationship with the judge, district attorney, public defender, and police investigators who were involved in the arrest and conviction process of a sexually abusive youth helps those officials understand that something positive and constructive is indeed happening with the youth while in custody. The field supervisor can also share information about the treatment progress of released youth with similarly appropriate professionals who work with the client. This communication helps to minimize distrust in an often complicated and misunderstood correctional process and fosters a spirit of interagency cooperation and support. In the light of recent laws related to mandatory registration and reporting, the field supervisor can encourage those involved to recognize the youth's progress and to use the information only for monitoring purposes.

Assessing Effectiveness

All programs need a set of objective evaluation criteria. The effectiveness of after-care programs can be measured by assessing the youth's behavior for the presence of negative and positive indicators, including indicators of high-risk or lower-risk status. There have been few studies of reoffense or recidivism for sexually abusive youth. Two studies that may assist in identifying indicators for this population are Bremer (1992) and Schram, Milloy, and Rowe (1991).

A word should be said about reoffense and recidivism. Both are indicators of a sexually abusive youth progressing to a high-risk status; however, *reoffense* means new instances of sexually aggressive behavior, whether or not the new offense is similar to prior sexual aggression. *Recidivism* refers to the incarceration of the youth for any number of criminal or dangerous behaviors that the aftercare field supervisor or the criminal justice system discovers. Instances of reoffense clearly indicate that the client is unable to manage his sexually aggressive behavior effectively and should return to secure custody. Recidivism measures more than the failure on the part of the youth to control his behavior. It can also measure the ability of the aftercare program staff's ability to assess accurately a client's return to more dangerous risk levels and to return the client to custody before that client sexually abuses another victim. Traditional measures of effectiveness used in corrections systems have often seen recidivism as a sign of staff failure. If aftercare program staff aggressively supervise and provide treatment for the youth, then recidivism, particularly temporary detention of the youth to refocus the client on the treatment contract, is a sign of successful program management. Indications of a client's reoffense or an arrest for other crimes can be identified by searching the databases available through local law enforcement agencies. Additionally, sexually abusive youth are required to register their whereabouts in many states. To the extent that the youth complies with this regulation, the registration laws provide a system of tracking their behavior long after their release from treatment and supervision.

It is well documented in the literature on sexual abuse that sexually deviant fantasies commonly precede deviant behavior. Usually the deviant content of these fantasies, reinforced by masturbation to orgasm, increases as the client's control dissipates. Monitoring the client's fantasies through log keeping, group counseling, or involvement in aftercare groups can help provide clues to a youth's behavior management progress. The indicators of high-risk behavior listed previously are based on the relapse-prevention model.

The measures of positive behavior listed previously are typical of appropriate behavior of sexually abusive youth in treatment. Full employment or attendance at academic or vocational training programs indicates the youth's ability to manage positively his or her time and to interact appropriately with others. Appropriate behavior in therapy indicates a spirit of cooperation with the therapeutic process. Recognizing high-risk situations and developing adequate skills to manage them is a clear indication that the youth is learning to manage his life in order to control tendencies toward sexual abuse. Having clearly established indicators for both positive and negative client behavior, the aftercare program staff helps the youth develop long-term successful behavior management strategies.

Summary

Repeated experience with treating sexually abusive adolescents has shown that previous patterns of behavior typically begin to recur as the youth reenters the community from closed security, residential, or inpatient treatment programs. Aftercare monitoring and supervision is an important conjunct to treatment in facilitating successful transition of treatment concepts and strategies to a youth's life in the community. The answer lies in a systems intervention that provides a continuity of supervision, treatment, and public protection and a comprehensive intervention team that includes a treatment team and custodial, aftercare, and community professionals. If there is cooperation, information sharing, and planned intervention with the youth and those involved, successful adjustment can be achieved and the youth's efforts to manage his behaviors can be strengthened.

Probation or parole services should be delivered to a sexually abusive youth by a consistent specialist who is involved with the case from the point of initial contact with the judicial system. The specialist provides information at intake, sentencing, admission to a treatment program or correctional facility, release planning, and after release. The specialist becomes the team supervisor in the community and coordinates any intervention needed subsequent to release. The intent is to hold the youth accountable for managing his offense behaviors using those strategies developed during treatment and to assist the youth with establishing a successful community transition.

Although the San Francisco program has been successful and has been replicated in various localities, several areas have been identified that could increase success. An improved system of classification is needed that could be used by all agencies involved with the youth to improve continuity and placement. Minimum training standards and provision of training for those who work with sexually abusive youth would improve consistent effective responses to the youth and increase the available resources for intervention when the youth requires assistance. Youth who engage in sexual abuse are not ordinary delinquency cases and need to be monitored and assisted differently from other delinquents. Their unique characteristics require specific intervention and approach, typically best provided by those who have had special training. With coordinated and intense supervision, sexually abusive youth can successfully control any reoffense behavior.

References

Bremer, J. F. (1992). Serious juvenile sex offenders: Treatment and long-term follow-up. *Psychiatric Annals, 22,* 326–332.

Brownell, K., Mariatt, G., Lichtenstein, E., & Wilson, G. (1986). Understanding and preventing relapse. *American Psychologist, 4*(7), 765–782.

Freeman, A. M. (1979). Planning community treatment for sex offenders. *Community Mental Health Journal, 1*(2).

Groth, A. N., & Loredo, C. M. (1981). Juvenile sex offenders: Guidelines for assessment. *International Journal of Offender Therapy and Comparative Criminology, 2*(l), 31–39.

Lowe, G. (1986). *Sex offender risk assessment.* Preston, CA: Oak Specialized Counseling Program, Preston School of Industry, California Youth Authority.

Marshall, W. L., Earls, C. M., Segal, Z., & Darke, J. (1983). A behavioral program for the assessment and treatment of sexual aggressors. In K. Craig & R. McMahon (Eds.), *Advances in clinical behavior therapy.* New York: Brunner/Mazel.

National Task Force on Juvenile Sexual Offending. (1988). A preliminary report. *Juvenile and Family Court Journal, 39*(2), 36–37.

National Task Force on Juvenile Sexual Offending. (1993). The revised report. *Juvenile and Family Court Journal, 44*(4), 28.

Nichols, F. L., & Haines, D. (1978). The difficulties of dual denial of treatment of sex offenders with alcoholism. *International Journal of Offender Therapy and Comparative Criminology, 22*(2).

Pithers, W., Marques, J., Gibat, C., & Marlatt, G. (1983). Relapse prevention with sexual aggressives. In J. Greer & L. Stuart (Eds.), *The sexual aggressor.* New York: Van Nostrand Reinhold.

Schram, D. D., Milloy, C. D., & Rowe, W. E. (1991). *Juvenile sex offenders: A follow-up study of reoffense behavior: A research study.* Olympia: Washington State Institute for Public Policy.x

PART SIX

PREVENTION

CHAPTER TWENTY-ONE

PERPETRATION PREVENTION

Primary and Secondary

Gail Ryan

It is clear that sexually abusive behaviors do not suddenly appear in adolescence but rather have developed over time—often from early in childhood. Many sexually abusive youth in treatment have been able to identify, in retrospect, abusive patterns of thinking and behavior that were present as early as age five (Law, 1987). Historically, the literature relevant to behavior problems in childhood has included reference to sexual behaviors, and the increased sexual acting out of children who have experienced sexual abuse has been well documented (Conte, 1985; Friedrich, Urquiza, & Bielke, 1986; Ricci & Watson, 1989).

Reports of very young sexual perpetrators have supported the development of treatment programs for sexually abusive children (Cantwell, 1988; Cavanagh-Johnson, 1988; Isaac, 1987). In this book, Chapter Sixteen identified very young and prepubescent children as special populations needing offense-specific treatment. The identification of these sexually abusive children nevertheless tends to recognize only the most severe cases, and specialized treatment for sexually abusive

Note: The author wishes to acknowledge the contributions of J. Blum, D. Sandau-Christopher, S. Law, F. Weber, C. Sundine, L. Astler, J. Teske, and J. Dale to the concepts of primary perpetration prevention in childhood and of A. Junk, M. L. Waitz, and P. Beach in applying these concepts to adolescence. The author also wishes to acknowledge her debt to the members of the multiagency Study Group on the Development of Sexual Offending in Denver and to Toni Cavanagh-Johnson for their contributions to the concepts of secondary prevention.

children is still unavailable in many communities. Yet even the early identification of children who are sexually abusing other children is only a tertiary intervention, aimed at preventing the continuation of sexually abusive behavior by an identified perpetrator.

Although tremendous resources have been enlisted to respond to the incidence and impact of both child sexual abuse and adult sexual assaults, intervention strategies have failed to prevent the occurrence, and prevention strategies have usually been aimed at potential victims. Certainly self-protection and defense, reporting, prosecution, and treatment programs are called for in response to this problem, but the ultimate solution is to prevent the development of new offenders so that future generations are no longer at risk. The only proactive approach to sexual abuse prevention is perpetration prevention rather than the descriptive and reactive intervention responses that have been most common.

Primary perpetration prevention requires social, cultural, and familial change in order to alter the earliest learning experiences of children in the family and in the community at large. Secondary perpetration prevention requires specialized intervention with children in groups known to be at increased risk to develop sexually aggressive or deviant behavior.

Primary Perpetration Prevention from Birth in the Family and the Community

Although research has illuminated a variety of negative experiences that may increase the risk of the manifestation of abusive behaviors, every risk factor identified to date is also experienced by many who do not become abusive. It is the author's belief that the two most common characteristics among all types of abusers are the lack of empathy and the misattribution of responsibility. These are not so much a product of deviant experience as they are deficits in human development, that is, the absence of something healthy, more than the presence of something deviant.

Empathy develops from birth in infants who are cared for by consistent, empathic caregivers and should begin to be seen in the infant's interactions very early in life. Empathy is characterized by reading cues that indicate the needs or emotions of the individual, interpreting the cue (attributing meaning), and validating the need or emotion. Infants learn these three skills first in the experience of empathic care and then become able to read, interpret, and validate their own and others' cues.

Unfortunately, much of the advice given to and the practice of parents today is aimed at meeting the needs of babies according to the caregiver's agenda rather than the infant's cues. Parents are often advised by pediatricians, parenting instructors, and other parents to disregard the infant's cues in order to prevent "spoiling" the child and in the interest of developing discipline and schedules. The most blatant examples are evident in feeding schedules (rather than demand feeding) and in regard to interpretation of the baby's distress when seeking intimacy, attention, or reassurance.

The notion that parents should control the infant's care rather than be controlled by the infant's expression of needs is a fundamental cultural mind-set. The parent who struggles to understand and respond to the baby's cues of distress is often chastened as "doting on" or "spoiling" the child and is admonished regarding the need to avoid being "manipulated" by the child.

The community's empathy for the newborn's cry rapidly gives way to judgment regarding the parent and the child. Such judgments often distort attributions of responsibility and encourage coercive styles of parenting. Friends and family, pediatricians and health professionals, and even strangers in the community are quick to offer advice in the form of rules for the parent that are often designed to manipulate the child without regard for the child's legitimate need for empathic care. Of course, the community is not unaware of the needs of children, and so it sanctions parents who "abuse" or "neglect" their child (although there is often intense controversy in defining those terms). Parents often receive mixed messages regarding their role in caring for the infant.

Those parents who bring to their relationship with the infant the developmental assets of empathy, secure attachment models, and a positive, assertive sense of self are usually able to provide a consistent empathic experience that is responsive to the infant's unique needs (often in spite of advice to the contrary). However, parents whose own internal representations of self and relationships are less secure or who lack empathic skills and sensitivity may rely on the "rules" of parenting, and although the child appears well fed, clean, comfortable, and cared for, the child's expression of needs may diminish over time from lack of reinforcement. Thus, an appearance of health may exist despite the absence of empathic care. Such children may be at risk to lack empathy in their own subsequent functioning, and therefore they may be less aware of their own needs and less sensitive to the needs of others. Other children do not experience consistent empathic care due to abuse or neglect and may be even more at risk. Child protection should include perpetration prevention efforts with child victims of maltreatment or neglect as a priority.

Such a deficit may not be manifest in any deviant functioning as long as the environment remains somewhat consistent and predictable and the individual's needs are not unusual. However, there is a risk that deviant exposure, stress, trauma, or unpredictable environmental factors may overwhelm the individual's internal resources. Failure to interpret their own needs accurately and attribute control and responsibility accurately puts them at risk of being similarly insensitive to the unique needs of others, including their own children as they become parents. Those who have not experienced validation and reinforcement of their own cues may be at risk for many harmful outcomes.

Consider, for example, the infant who is taught through experience to disregard hunger as a cue for eating; this child might be at risk of developing eating disorders—either overeating or undereating—without regard for the body's cues regarding how much nutrition is needed. Such disorders might be subclinical (that is, not meet diagnostic criteria) throughout the life span or might become clinically apparent in the extremes. Similarly, sexual functioning might not be affected as long as the environment and individual experience proceed along a normative, predictable course, but sexual functioning might become deviant when stress, trauma, or deviant exposure overwhelms the individual's internal resources to read cues, interpret, and attribute responsibility accurately in sexual experiences.

Without empathic parenting, the parent's disregard of the child's ability and responsibility to communicate his or her own needs may shift the locus of control early in life from the individual to the environment, creating a condition of risk for the external control seeking that is manifest in the abusive cycle, combined with the lack of empathy and misattributions of responsibility that are manifest in the extreme in abusive individuals. These risks may be exacerbated by changes in the culture and the community that expose more individuals to deviance or stress, as well as attitudes about violence, sexuality, and relationships. Certainly the infant who has not experienced or developed empathy and is then exposed to the risk factors already described in this book may be at greater risk to become abusive.

Although these ideas are speculative and theoretical at this time, it may be useful for the community to be encouraged to be more empathic in the care of infants and toddlers. If parent education, advice, and practice would emphasize the value of respecting and responding to an infant's cues, perhaps more empathic interactions will result. An example would be for the advice to say how much food one might expect the infant to need in a day and what cues might indicate when the baby is hungry, rather than advising "8 ounces every 4 hours" as a schedule. Similarly, parents might be encouraged to provide nourishing snacks between mealtimes when the child expresses hunger and to pay attention to the child's lack of hunger as well rather than avoiding snacks and then forcing the child to clean the plate at meals. This very basic respect for children's ability to express feelings and needs may provide the basis for children to recognize the needs of others.

Despite studies indicating that children should acquire and demonstrate empathy early in life, many early childhood educators state that they do not expect

children to be empathic because they believe that empathy requires abstract thinking. If educators and caregivers do not expect children to be empathic, they are not
likely to model or promote empathic interaction as the optimal level of functioning.

A parallel concern for parent educators should be the normalizing of aggression in sibling relationships. Parents often dismiss sibling violence, saying "All
kids fight." Distinctions must be made, however, between *sibling rivalry*, which is an
assertion of uniqueness that facilitates personal boundaries; *sibling conflicts*, which
are the products of disagreements or conflicting needs and are resolved through
mediation and compromise; and *sibling abuse*, which is physical or verbal attacks
that model a lack of empathic care. Sibling relationships may be an early indicator of internal working models for parenting, and the adults should correct coercive, intimidating, and abusive patterns.

Primary Perpetration Prevention in Relation to Childhood Sexuality

Primary perpetration prevention must next consider sexual development in the
general population of all children. Recognizing that many sexually abused children are not identified, that all children are exposed to sexualized messages and
information in the media and entertainment that seem to condone or even glo-
rify sexual exploitation, and that models of sexualized compensation pervade
many cultures, it is clear that children experience sexual learning throughout childhood. It is also clear that the development of sexuality begins in infancy and progresses throughout childhood (see Chapter Four). Yet many cultures traditionally
have denied sexuality in childhood, redirecting and deterring children from open
sexual exploration and discouraging acquisition of sexual information.

Sex education often has taught the process of reproduction with little or no
mention of sexual behavior or relationships. The interactions explicit in sexual
relationships have been learned in secrecy and colored by guilt. Early childhood
arousal has been defined as "genital discovery" and "genital exploration," and
sexual feelings during childhood have been denied. It is not surprising that the
majority of boys and girls who have been sexually exploited in childhood have
preserved the secret of their abuse and that victims may internalize enormous
burdens of guilt if they experience pleasure or arousal while being exploited.

Sexual learning prior to puberty has occurred within a social vacuum, without the influence of societal norms, for better and for worse, so it is not surprising
that children are often confused by sexual information, experiences, and feelings
that occur without opportunity for validation, explanation, or correction. The secrecy surrounding sexuality during childhood not only protects the perpetrators of

child sexual abuse but also prohibits both normative and corrective learning for children.

The traditional responses (or nonresponses) of ignoring, repressing, or punishing sexual behavior in childhood have failed to recognize the psychological and physiological motivations and reinforcements that are inherent in sexual interactions. Intimacy, arousal, and orgasm are powerful rewards in the process of sexual learning, so it is likely that sexual behaviors will persist and increase. Arousal patterns and sexual thoughts develop and progress over time. Knowledge and understanding of adolescent sexual offending has many implications in the consideration of prevention, and both primary and secondary models that specifically address the risk of deviant sexual development are possible.

Throughout the 1980s adult awareness of the sexual behavior of children increased as it was suggested that sexual behaviors might be diagnostic of a child victim's deviant experience. Unfortunately, when viewed as a symptom of child sexual abuse, all sexual behavior was seen as deviant, and so management and modification were entirely reactive. However, childhood sexuality is not a pathological condition. The capacity for sexual arousal and function is inborn, and the ways in which people behave sexually are learned: products of the environment and life experience. The motivation for sexual behaviors in early childhood is not always clear and may not be the same for every child. The initial behavior may be exploratory, imitative, or reactive, but the question of origin or motivation in no way minimizes the need for understanding.

Having defined sexual abuse in terms of unlawfulness and harm; intimidation, coercion, and force; inequality; and lack of consent (National Task Force on Juvenile Sexual Offending, 1988), it becomes possible to differentiate problem behaviors from the normal range of sexual behavior in childhood (Ryan et al., 1988).

The Range of Behavior

Children exhibit a wide range of sexual behaviors, from the curious exploration of self and others in "playing doctor" to the aggressive seven-year-old who demanded sex at gunpoint in the school yard ("Boy, 7, Demands Sex at Gunpoint," *Rocky Mountain News*, 21 September, 1988; Denver, Colorado). Definition of this range of behaviors comes from the observations of caregivers and educators (Ryan et al., 1988), the self-reported memories of childhood sexual experiences by adults (Ryan, Krugman, & Miyoshi, 1988), reports of childhood sexual behavior by sexually abusive children (Cantwell, 1988; Cavanagh-Johnson, 1988; Law, 1987), and an extensive review of the literature on childhood sexuality. It is apparent that children do engage in sexual interactions with their peers, as well as solitary sexualized behaviors. Additional studies of the range of sexual behavior in both clinical samples and general population controls have validated these earlier efforts (Friedrich, Grambsch, Broughton, Kuiper, & Beilke, 1991; Friedrich et al., 1992).

In exploring the range of behavior observed in nonclinical samples, Cavanagh-Johnson (1988) noted that these behaviors normally occur alone or between similar-aged peers, without coercion, and that the affect of the children is usually fun and teasing. Masturbation is common in toddlers and preschoolers, and attempts to touch or see the genitals of others commonly accompany the genital discovery and exploration of toddlers. The sexual behavior of young, sexually abused children may deviate from the norm in duration and frequency as a child appears preoccupied with sexual themes for an extended period of time. These "sexually reactive" behaviors may include more explicit and precocious demonstrations and intensified masturbation, and they are often accompanied by confused or anxious affect (Cavanagh-Johnson, 1989).

The full range of sexual behaviors of children can be placed along a continuum from normal to abusive (Table 21.1). Within the normal range, adult responses may be indicated to educate, redirect, or limit behavior, but the behavior itself is not deviant. As the behaviors move away from the norm however, some evaluation and corrective responses become desirable. It is important to note that many of the behaviors in the middle of this continuum may be seen in many children occasionally as they experiment and imitate things they have seen or heard. Even so, these behaviors should be attracting attention and activating a response from adults and caregivers.

As in any other area of learning, the child's expectation is that adults will validate or correct behavior. An adult's failure to respond specifically to sexual behavior may confuse the child or be perceived as acceptance or approval. Most adults have considered the impact of the myths of their own upbringing and have moved toward a less judgmental response. Telling children they are "nasty" or bad because they touch their genitals or threatening to cut off the penis or the hand that masturbates are not thought to be helpful in managing these behaviors. As a result, adults' responses have become less specific and less punitive, but no less disapproving and no more enlightening. Children have continued to be confused about an area of information that rightfully concerns them. While acknowledging the need for more informed responses, adults have been confused in the evaluation of sexual interactions involving same-aged children, as well as the management of solitary sexualized behaviors.

In considering the range of behavior in childhood, it becomes clear that most of these behaviors are not deviant in our culture. It is the relationship and interaction that define sexual abuse rather than an isolated behavior that occurs out of context. When the sexual abuse of children was first defined, age and behavior were the only factors considered. Even the sexual abuse of children by adolescents

TABLE 21.1. THE RANGE OF SEXUAL BEHAVIORS OF CHILDREN.

Normal	Genital or reproduction conversations with peers or similar-age siblings
	Show me yours/I'll show you mine with peers
	Playing "doctor"
	Occasional masturbation without penetration
	Imitating seduction (i.e., kissing, flirting)
	Dirty words or jokes within cultural or peer group norms
Yellow flags	Preoccupation with sexual themes (especially sexually aggressive)
	Attempting to expose others' genitals (i.e., pulling other's skirt up or pants down)
	Sexually explicit conversation with peers
	Sexual graffiti (especially chronic or impacting individuals)
	Precocious sexual knowledge
	Single occurrences of peeping, exposing, obscenities, pornographic interest, frottage
	Preoccupation with masturbation
	Mutual masturbation or group masturbation
	Simulating foreplay with dolls or peers with clothing on (for example, petting, french kissing)
Red flags	Sexually explicit conversations with significant age difference
	Touching genitals of others
	Degradation or humiliation of self or others with sexual themes
	Forced exposure of other's genitals[a]
	Inducing fear or threats of force
	Sexually explicit proposals or threats, including written notes
	Repeated or chronic peeping, exposing, obscenities, pornographic interests, frottage
	Compulsive masturbation, task interruption to masturbate
	Masturbation, including vaginal or anal penetration
	Simulating intercourse with dolls, peers, animals (i.e., humping)
No questions	Oral, vaginal, anal penetration of dolls, children, animals
	Forced touching of genitals
	Simulating intercourse with peers with clothing off
	Any genital injury or bleeding not explained by accidental cause

Source: Ryan et al. (1988).

[a]Although "force" is usually a factor in the "no question" range, restraining an individual in order to pull down pants or expose breasts does occur in the context of hazing among peers.

has been defined on the basis of age and behavior (it is not difficult to know that a seventeen-year-old sodomizing a four-year-old is abuse). However, with younger perpetrators and smaller age differences between victim and aggressor, additional criteria are needed. The relationship of the involved children and the nature of the interaction must be evaluated.

Evaluating Sexual Interactions

In order to evaluate the interaction and relationship of two or more children who are involved in a sexual behavior, three factors must be considered: *consent, equality, and coercion.*

Because the consent of minors is not legally acknowledged, the elements of consent must be defined:

1. Understanding what is being proposed without confusion, misconception, or misattribution (that is, not being tricked or fooled)
2. Knowing the standard for the behavior in the family, the peer group, and the culture (that is, both parties have similar knowledge)
3. Having an awareness of possible consequences, such as punishment, pain, stigma, pregnancy, or disease (that is, both parties' being similarly aware)
4. Having respect for agreement or disagreement without repercussions

It is important to distinguish consent, cooperation, and compliance. Whereas consent is based in one's beliefs and desire, cooperation implies participation without regard for personal beliefs or desires, and compliance implies allowing without resistance in spite of personal beliefs or desires. It is important to realize that cooperation or compliance does not equal consent.

The second factor, equality, relates to the balance of power and control in the relationship and interaction of the involved children. Some indicators of inequality may be obvious, such as size differential, weight differential, age differential, or extreme differences in intellectual development. Some indicators of a power differential may be more subtle, however, and may have been demonstrated prior to the sexual interaction. For example, a strength differential may have been established in earlier wrestling, fighting, or play. Also, some arbitrary labels designate unequal power such as the peer group's empowering a "leader" or "boss," as well as fantasy roles of play, such as, "I'll be the king, and you be the slave" or "I'll be the doctor, and you be the patient." These may be subtle distinctions whereby one child assumes a position of greater power over the other. This same dynamic underlies the concern regarding children who reenact their own experience of abuse with dolls or animals, assuming the role of perpetrator in their play.

Internal factors may also be unequal. It is important to recognize the power inherent in popularity and self-image. The differentials of more popular or less popular, assertive or passive, confident or insecure, and so forth may be indicators of the inequality that defines vulnerability and exploitation.

Finally, the element of coercion must be assessed. The pressures that are brought to bear on one child by another to achieve compliance constitute the third factor in the evaluation of the interaction. These pressures can be placed along a continuum (see Figure 21.1).

At the low end of the continuum may be the subtleties of implied authority, manipulation, trickery, or peer pressure. Farther along the continuum may lie more explicit coercion, threats, and bribes; and at the far end are physical force, threats of harm, and overt violence.

There is also a perceptual shift that tends to occur along this same continuum from privacy to secrecy. Within the normal range, children may be embarrassed to be discovered engaging in a sexual behavior, which is perceived to be personal and private. Secrecy, however, prohibits the validation and correction necessary for social learning and prevents external feedback or intervention. The child's affect may be fearful or shameful.

The evaluation of sexual interactions is therefore dependent on these factors:

1. Consent versus cooperation or compliance
2. Equality of power and control
3. Pressure or coercion or force

It is important at this point to clarify the ways in which language may contribute to children's confusion. Distinctions must be made among privacy, secrecy, and surprise. The word *secret* is often misused to mean "a delay of awareness that enables a surprise" but may also be used to mean "exclusivity" or the "denial of sharing." Most accurately, a secret is binding and inhibiting-prohibiting external verification or feedback and protecting those involved from the consequences of disclosure. A *surprise*, on the other hand, is a temporary condition inherently dependent on disclosure. *Privacy* most accurately reflects a "rightful lack of sharing" and "protection from intrusion" and implies self-ownership.

FIGURE 21.1. RANGE OF COERCION.

No Pressure	Authority Manipulation Trickery	Coercion Threats Bribes	Physical Force Threat of Harm Violence

While sexual abuse prevention programs for children have emphasized the "no more secrets" concept, adults have not been similarly educated to the "no secrets" rule. Secrecy can be a hard habit to break; Christmas presents and surprises have too often been referred to as secrets. It is important for all adults to observe the "no secrets" rule with the understanding that adults cannot be sure children are safe if there are secrets. Secrecy allows sexual abuse to occur and to continue. Secrets protect perpetrators.

Responding to the Sexual Behavior of Children

Having identified a sexual behavior of concern and having evaluated the interaction, the educator or caregiver must then respond in ways designed to decrease the risk of abusive behavior and support healthy, prosocial development. It is very important to realize that many sexual behaviors, especially those falling in the middle of the continuum, may be exhibited by many children once or occasionally, and even frequently among abused children.

It would not be helpful to overreact to a child who might be imitating language or behavior seen on television, talked about by others, or even experienced by the child. But it must be remembered that children look to the adults in their lives for verification and validation of what they are learning. They expect that adults will correct negative behavior. Failure to respond to sexually exploitative behavior may covertly support it. When no response occurs, the child's perception may be that the adult condones such behavior. When a nonspecific response occurs, the child may be confused. At the same time, the responses that have been suggested (Ryan et al., 1988) are specifically intended to be nonjudgmental, to label the behavior without labeling the child, and to foster universal goals that are not value laden or based on personal opinions. These universal goals are *communication* (articulating with words), *empathy* (recognition of affective cues), and *accountability* (accurate attributions of responsibility), and they have been well accepted as a model for consistent goal-oriented responses (Ryan & Blum, 1994).

A progressive range of response is suggested, as the continuum in Figure 21.2 shows.

FIGURE 21.2. RANGE OF RESPONSE.

The first response should always be to label the behavior and react at a personal level. The label is specific: what is seen ("I see you touching Johnny's penis") or what is heard ("I hear from Johnny that you touched his penis"). This labeling gives the child the language to discuss the behavior, avoids confusion concerning what behavior is problematic, and lets the child know that adults can discuss such matters. The reaction in the first response is nonjudgmental and not prohibiting. The reaction comes from a personal and empathic level: personal feelings ("It makes me feel uncomfortable") and cues that are apparent reflections of others' feelings ("It looks as if it makes Johnny uncomfortable too"). The goal is primarily to foster empathic thought and consideration of others—to attach feelings to the behavior.

Fostering empathic thought requires that we demonstrate and verbalize empathy in our own reactions. It is important that adults be honest and at the same time nonjudgmental in reacting to sexual behaviors—placing responsibility rather than blame and not making assumptions about what the child is thinking or feeling. Too often adult demonstrations of empathy tell the child what the adult thinks the child and others are feeling or thinking but fail to empower the child in their own processes to identify and communicate feelings for themselves. The instinct is to minimize or deny the realities of negative feelings in children in order to preserve the myths of their carefree innocence and the adults' omniscient protection. In order to raise responsible people, adults must empower children with their own feelings and thoughts, so they are allowed to express both anxiety and hurt and can be directed toward safe and empathic means of expression.

If the same or similar exploitative behaviors recur, the second response would be to confront and prohibit. The confrontation conveys the adult's concern that empathy has not been sufficient to control the behavior. The label and reaction are reinforced with the addition of serious concern, and a rule is invoked to prohibit further recurrences—for example, "I am very concerned because I see you touching Johnny's penis. I told you before that makes me uncomfortable and Johnny is upset. You need to stop doing that."

This second response is still not judgmental but now adds the prohibition. By putting the emphasis of the first response on communication and empathy and reserving the prohibition for the second response, learning is possible, which has been unlikely in repressive and suppressive reactions. Holding off on prohibiting the behavior is also the hardest part of the response for adults today. In the past, adult reactions to the sexual behavior of children have been prohibition without discussion ("Don't let me catch you doing that again!"), which may have contributed to the behavior's continuing in secret and discouraged opportunities for education, validation, or correction.

The monitoring is equally important: to increase observation and supervision between responses in order to prevent the continuation and reinforcement of undetected, exploitative behaviors, as well as to prevent victimization of other children. The monitoring phases might include further discussion and interventions, such as these:

1. Talking with the child about thoughts and feelings associated with the behavior of concern
2. Exploring information deficits and identifying confusion in order to provide accurate information and sex education
3. Demonstrating and encouraging empathy
4. Watching for patterns of behavior antecedent to the concerning behaviors
5. Setting limits on solitary, private behaviors ("Masturbation is private, and this is not a private place.")
6. Redirecting away from preoccupation or compulsive sexual behavior and aggression by occupying the child with new activities and positive interpersonal experiences
7. Drawing the child away from isolation and withdrawal
8. Empowering the child by allowing choices and reinforcing competency
9. Managing the risk of abusive behaviors by limiting access to potential victims and imposing restraint, if necessary

In cases of extremely harmful or abusive behavior, the second response may occur shortly after the first, without waiting for any subsequent occurrence. For instance, a few minutes after the response, one might seek out the child in a private setting and say, "Sally, I am very concerned about what happened this morning. I told you then that I felt very upset. Pushing a stick inside Susi's bottom is very dangerous. You must never do that again." This response may continue with additional interventions, such as, "I am going to need to talk to some other grownups about what happened too. I need to be sure that Susi is okay. I want you children to be safe. If you have questions about bodies, you can ask me."

Victim Interventions

Many of the behaviors defined as beyond the normal range of sexual behavior in childhood may be indicators of a child's own experience of abuse or exposure to incomprehensible sexual stimuli. When children are already known to the system as victims of sexual abuse, the response to their sexual behavior is a part of a comprehensive intervention response, and the teacher or caregiver may be communicating their concerns to other caregivers and therapists. When concerns arise about the sexual behavior of children not previously involved in child protective services, however, careful consideration must be given to the need for a social services report. On the one hand, the child who is exhibiting deviant or exploitative sexuality may have been (or is currently being) abused. If the behavior is sufficient to warrant a report when considered alone or in combination with other indicators, a report to police or social services should be made. On the other hand, the current behavior may have created new victims who also need intervention. If other children have been victimized or exposed to incomprehensible sexual ideas, a report should also be made. Behaviors defined as characteristic of sexual abuse (the far end of the continuum) always warrant a report and may benefit from both a legal and a therapeutic response.

Although the first concern may be to manage the sexually exploitative behavior of children, a focus on the behavioral manifestation or symptoms of sexual abuse is a temporary intervention. Aggressive and unempathic behaviors, as well as isolating and self-destructive behaviors, are manifestations of abuse issues, not definitive of the issue itself. The issues of sexual abuse lie deep in the experience of helplessness, betrayal, confusion, and fear (Ryan, 1989). (Treatment of sexually abusive children is addressed in Chapter Sixteen; see also Gil and Cavanagh-Johnson, 1993, and Cavanagh-Johnson, 1989.)

Primary Perpetration Prevention in Adolescence

Many differences exist in the range of behaviors that are considered normal, deviant, and abusive. Some behaviors that are deviant in childhood become normal in adolescence, while others that were of lesser concern in childhood become problematic for the adolescent. The concept of a continuum of behavior is again relevant.

Not surprisingly, many new areas of information and education need to be addressed with adolescents. As genital contact becomes more normal and the adolescent moves toward the establishment of adult relationships (Gadpaille, 1975), moral, social, and familial values and rules are applied to the consideration of sexual behavior. Health and reproduction are two areas that require specific cautions in order to prevent sexually transmitted diseases (including HIV) and unplanned pregnancy. It is important to note, however, that these issues are parallel to, but separate from, our consideration of sexually exploitative behavior. The identification of abusive behaviors and evaluation of abusive interactions in adolescence is possible within the same model applied to childhood sexual behavior (see Table 21.2).

After considering the normality or deviance of the behavior, evaluation of the interaction again considers consent, equality, and coercion. In this assessment, cooperation or compliance may mask a lack of consent with even more subtlety than in childhood, and adolescent victims may be less able to assert their personal

TABLE 21.2. THE RANGE OF ADOLESCENT SEXUAL BEHAVIOR.

Normal	Sexually explicit conversations with peers Obscenities and jokes within the cultural norm Sexual innuendo, flirting, and courtship Interest in erotica Solitary masturbation Hugging, kissing, holding hands Foreplay (petting, making out, fondling)[a] Mutual masturbation[a] Monogamist intercourse (stable or serial)[a,b]
Yellow flags	Sexual preoccupation, anxiety Pornographic interest Polygamist sexual intercourse (promiscuity)[c] Sexually aggressive themes, obscenities Sexual graffiti (especially chronic or impacting individuals) Embarrassment of others with sexual themes Violation of others' body space Pulling skirts up/pants down Single occurrences of peeping, exposing, frottage with known age-mates Mooning and obscene gestures[d]
Red flags	Compulsive masturbation (especially chronic or public) Degradation or humiliation of self or others with sexual themes Attempting to expose others' genitals Chronic preoccupation with sexually aggressive pornography Sexually explicit conversation with significantly younger children Touching genitals without permission (grabbing, goosing) Sexually explicit threats (verbal or written)
Illegal flags	*(illegal behaviors defined by law)* Obscene phone calls, voyeurism, exhibitionism, or frottage Sexual contact with significant age difference (child sexual abuse) Forced sexual contact (sexual assault) Forced penetration (rape) Sexual contact with animals (bestiality) Genital injury to others

[a]Moral, social, or familial rules may restrict, but these behaviors are not abnormal, developmentally harmful, or illegal when private, consensual, equal, and noncoercive.

[b]Stable monogamy is defined as a single sexual partner throughout adolescence. Serial monogamy indicates long-term (several months or years) involvement with a single sexual partner that may be preceded or followed by similar long-term monogamous relationships.

[c]Polygamist intercourse is defined as indiscriminate sexual contact with more than one partner during the same period of time.

[d]Mooning and obscene gestures have been called "Americana." Although many of the yellow flags are not necessarily outside the normal range of behavior exhibited in teenage peer groups, some evaluation and response is desirable in order to support healthy and responsible behavior.

beliefs or desires because of misattributions and the perception that the behavior is expected or approved by the peer group. Equality continues to be affected by very subtle differences in internal and external strengths, and coercion includes tremendous peer pressures and the threat of lost relationships or esteem.

Just as was true of children's behaviors, normal behaviors may occur in the wrong place and require limits, and many of the behaviors of concern may be exhibited occasionally by many adolescents. The expectation that adults will validate and correct continues to apply to the process of sexual learning in adolescence.

The goals of response to the adolescent's sexual behavior also remain the same as the suggested response for children: to foster communication, empathy, and accountability in order to prevent exploitative behavior. This response again requires the adult's expression of feelings. The adolescent may be cognitively more open to discussion, and intervention within the peer group is often desirable and possible. The peer culture's acceptance of sexually aggressive norms is an area of major concern.

Sexuality in adolescence is more apparent, and in some ways the adult response may be more difficult. The conflicts characteristic of normal adolescent development sometimes make it even harder for adults to communicate their feelings and for adolescents to acknowledge theirs. Moral, social, and familial values influence the adult's beliefs, and the adolescent's expectation is often that an adult's response to sexual behavior will be judgmental rather than empathic. An adult response that encourages communication and focuses on feelings is unexpected and may be initially unacknowledged or met with resistance and denial. By stressing one's feelings rather than rules or beliefs in the initial response, continued communication becomes more likely, and adults may have an opportunity to articulate their personal beliefs in a more didactic discussion at a later time.

In some communities, perpetration prevention curricula have been introduced into the classroom in order to educate middle school and high school students in the avoidance of sexually exploitative attitudes (Kassees & Hall, 1987; Strong, Tate, Wehman, & Wyss, 1986), and numerous videotapes have been produced for adolescent audiences regarding responsible sexual behavior, identification of past victimization, and prevention of acquaintance rape.

In responding to the sexual behavior of adolescents, concerns regarding past victimization may again lead to a social services report, and current abusive behaviors may warrant involvement of law enforcement and the courts as well. Appreciation of the sexual learning and confusion of youth in this culture is accelerated by awareness of the prevalence of sexually exploitative themes in the media, but the goals of accountability and empathy remain constant.

Parental Guidance

Evaluation of sexual behavior problems has attracted enormous attention in the past decade, and there is a reasonable level of consensus among professionals who specialize in these issues that is congruent with the model just described. However, there has been a tremendous temptation among untrained professionals and parents to look for a simple checklist to define problematic behaviors. This is understandable but of concern because it has been very apparent that the evaluation of children's sexual behavior must consider many contextual factors. Therefore, dissemination of the range of behavior (see Table 21.1) and evaluation criteria was limited to professional audiences and conveyed primarily through interactive workshops rather than print mediums.

In 1993, a new model was developed specifically for parents and lay people in a published format (Ryan & Blum, 1994). Rather than describe a specific range of behavior, the new model simplifies the evaluation of children's sexual behaviors by posing a series of questions designed to determine if the behavior is problematic and, if so, what kind of problem it presents.

When Is Sexual Behavior a Problem?

- Behavior may be a problem for the child who is doing it if the behavior puts the child at risk, interferes with other developmental tasks, interferes in relationships, violates rules, is self abusive, or if the child believes the behavior is a problem.
- Behavior may be a problem for others if the behavior causes others to feel uncomfortable, behavior occurs in the wrong time or place, behavior conflicts with family or community values or rules, or behavior is abusive.
- Behavior may be abusive if the behavior involves other children without consent, or if two children are not equal, or if one child is pressured or coerced by another child [pp. 12–13].

The response is then more apparent based on the nature of the problem. This model has been very useful to educators, caregivers, and parents and is a good framework for case management as well as care and treatment planning. This model, in combination with the universal goals described earlier in this chapter—communication, empathy, and accountability—provides very explicit yet non-judgmental options for parents. The booklet additionally describes adult interventions for secondary prevention in chronic acting-out patterns based on the high-risk cycle.

Secondary Perpetration Prevention for High-Risk Groups

Whereas the concepts of primary perpetration prevention, as well as the specialized treatment of sexually abusive children, are reacting to the child's manifestation of sexual behavior, it is possible to infer that some individual children and some groups of children may be at risk for sexually deviant development before any behavioral manifestation occurs. There are multiple risk factors that may, alone or in combination, increase the likelihood of sexually abusive behavior. Children who have been sexually abused or otherwise maltreated, exposed to overstimulating or incomprehensible sexuality, or exposed to sexualized models of compensation, as well as those who have been emotionally neglected, physically abused, abandoned, rejected, institutionalized, or undersocialized, may constitute a group at risk for deviant development, including sexually abusive patterns of behavior. This recognition identifies a target population for secondary perpetration prevention in order to decrease this risk. These children may be overrepresented (and, therefore, accessible) in treatment programs for maltreated children, special education and emotionally/behaviorally disturbed (EBD) programs, foster care and adoptions, and residential facilities. Groups of children who have experienced sexual, physical, or emotional abuse; parental loss, abandonment, or rejection; disruptions in early care and relationships; and exposure to nonnormative or incomprehensible sexual learning may be at risk to develop patterns of deviant or exploitative sexual behavior (Cavanagh-Johnson, 1989). Perhaps most important, children who fail to develop positive attachment models and empathic relationship skills in the early years may be at risk for exploitative and dysfunctional relationships. When these individual children are referred to therapeutic services and specialized programs are made available to groups of these children, an opportunity exists for preventive intervention.

An identifiable cluster of issues has been defined that may manifest in a variety of dysfunctional behaviors (Ryan, 1989). In the same way that the sexual assault cycle focuses treatment on the combination of situations, thoughts, feelings, and behaviors that precede the abusive behavior, intervention with high-risk groups may identify similar patterns of coping and defense that support behaviors harmful to one's self or others (Figure 21.3) and more functional responses become the goal.

Helplessness, powerlessness, and a lack of control are issues that may trigger this dysfunctional cycle (Ryan, 1989). Children who are trying to regain a sense of control and well-being often harbor negative or unrealistic expectations in anticipation of interpersonal failures. These expectations may be fulfilled or avoided, resulting in the child's isolation or withdrawal. Attempts to regain control are often primitive and unsuccessful, increasing the child's frustration and anger while reinforcing helplessness and poor self-image. As the child struggles to achieve control, the fantasy may be that some external source of gratification will compensate for negative experiences or that some behavior will "get back" what is missing. In this compensatory or retaliatory mode, the child imagines a solution, develops a plan, and decides to act. The behavior that follows may be self-abusive, reabusive, or abusive of others. Simplistically, the victim who continues to operate within a victim identity maintains a victim stance that supports a worldview in which interactions will always or usually be abusive. The options are limited to revictimization, self-victimization, or victimization of others. For this child, the only adaptive response imaginable is to take control of the anticipated abuse rather than be betrayed or helpless.

Understanding the progression of thinking that supports the choice of behavior (see Figure 21.3) adults can intervene earlier in the pattern and help break the habituation of the cycle (Figure 21.4). The therapist can focus intervention on more adaptive responses to the trigger situation. These children must retrace developmental stages, experience new relationships, and become competent both affectively and socially in order to reframe their worldviews, restructure their thinking, and experience success. Critical elements of intervention with these children must be consistent safety, accountability, and empathy. For many children, the opportunity to discuss their worries and confusion and to develop a less sexualized lifestyle is welcome. Whether they have abused others or themselves or risked abuse by others, children must be accountable for their own behavior and become empathic to themselves and others.

Conclusions

Perpetration prevention in childhood is not so different from the adult modeling, teaching, and responses that shape responsible behavior in other areas. Adults must resist the temptation to accept or excuse the child's exploitative behavior as symptomatic of the culture or the child's experience and must confront the beliefs that support abusive patterns of behavior. Dispelling the secrecy, communicating openly, expressing empathy, and holding children accountable for behavior are basic to the prevention of exploitative sexuality.

By propagating understanding of the range of sexual behavior and evaluation of the coercive and exploitative nature of some interactions, perpetration prevention seeks to promote empathic interventions and thus prevent the development of new perpetrators.

FIGURE 21.3. THE HIGH-RISK CYCLE.

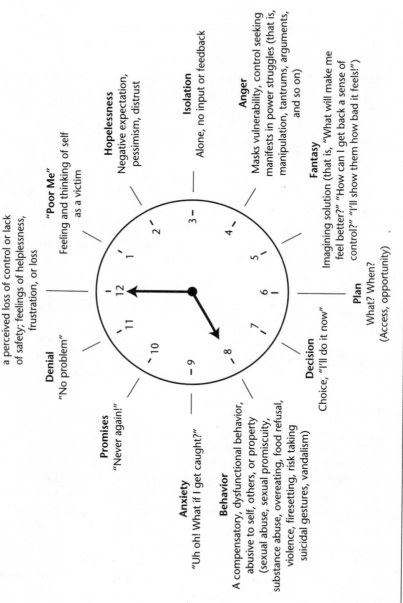

Trigger
A situation or event evokes
a perceived loss of control or lack
of safety; feelings of helplessness,
frustration, or loss

"Poor Me"
Feeling and thinking of self
as a victim

Hopelessness
Negative expectation,
pessimism, distrust

Isolation
Alone, no input or feedback

Anger
Masks vulnerability, control seeking
manifests in power struggles (that is,
manipulation, tantrums, arguments,
and so on)

Fantasy
Imagining solution (that is, "What will make me
feel better?" "How can I get back a sense of
control?" "I'll show them how bad it feels!")

Plan
What? When?
(Access, opportunity)

Decision
Choice, "I'll do it now"

Behavior
A compensatory, dysfunctional behavior,
abusive to self, others, or property
(sexual abuse, sexual promiscuity,
substance abuse, overeating, food refusal,
violence, firesetting, risk taking
suicidal gestures, vandalism)

Anxiety
"Uh oh! What if I get caught?"

Promises
"Never again!"

Denial
"No problem"

Source: Ryan and Blum (1994, pp. 29–36).

FIGURE 21.4. ADULT INTERVENTIONS IN THE HIGH-RISK CYCLE.

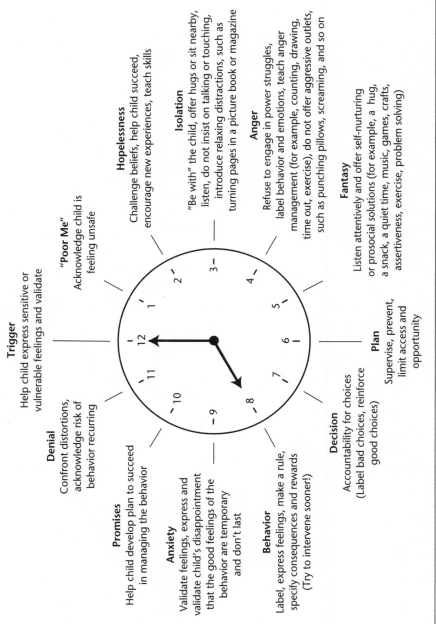

Trigger
Help child express sensitive or vulnerable feelings and validate

"Poor Me"
Acknowledge child is feeling unsafe

Hopelessness
Challenge beliefs, help child succeed, encourage new experiences, teach skills

Isolation
"Be with" the child, offer hugs or sit nearby, listen, do not insist on talking or touching, introduce relaxing distractions, such as turning pages in a picture book or magazine

Anger
Refuse to engage in power struggles, label behavior and emotions, teach anger management (for example, counting, drawing, time out, exercise), do not offer aggressive outlets, such as punching pillows, screaming, and so on

Fantasy
Listen attentively and offer self-nurturing or prosocial solutions (for example, a hug, a snack, a quiet time, music, games, crafts, assertiveness, exercise, problem solving)

Plan
Supervise, prevent, limit access and opportunity

Decision
Accountability for choices (Label bad choices, reinforce good choices)

Behavior
Label, express feelings, make a rule, specify consequences and rewards (Try to intervene sooner!)

Anxiety
Validate feelings, express and validate child's disappointment that the good feelings of the behavior are temporary and don't last

Promises
Help child develop plan to succeed in managing the behavior

Denial
Confront distortions, acknowledge risk of behavior recurring

Source: Ryan & Blum (1994, p. 37).

References

Cantwell, H. (1988). Child sexual abuse: Very young perpetrators. *Child Abuse and Neglect: International Journal, 12*(4), 579–582.

Cavanagh-Johnson, T. (1988). Child perpetrators: Children who molest children. *Child Abuse and Neglect: The International Journal, 12*(2), 219–229.

Cavanagh-Johnson, T. (1989). *Human sexuality curriculum for parents and children.* Los Angeles: Children's Institute International.

Conte, J. (1985). The effects of sexual victimization on children: A critique and suggestions for future research. *Victimology: The International Journal, 10*(1), 10–30.

Friedrich. W., Damon, L., Hewitt, S., et al. (1992). The Child Sexual Behavior Inventory: Normative and clinical comparison. *Psychological Assessment, 4,* 303–311.

Friedrich, W., Grambsch, P., Broughton, D., Kuiper, J., & Beilke, R. (1991). Normative sexual behavior in children. *Pediatrics, 88*(3), 456–464.

Friedrich, W., Urquiza, A., & Bielke, R. (1986). Behavioral problems in sexually abused young children. *Journal of Pediatric Psychology, 11*(2), 47–57.

Gadpaille, W. J. (1975). Adolescent sexuality—A challenge to psychiatrists. *Journal of American Academy of Psychoanalysis, 3*(2), 163–177.

Gil, E., & Johnson, T. (1993). *Sexualized children.* Walnut Creek, CA: Launch Press.

Isaac, C. (1987). *Identification and interruption of sexually offending behaviors in prepubescent children.* Paper presented at the Sixteenth Annual Child Abuse and Neglect Symposium, Keystone, CO.

Kassees, J., & Hall, R. (1987). *Adolescent Sexual Abuse Prevention Project: Program curricula.* Wilmington, DE: Parents Anonymous of Delaware.

Law, S. (1987). [Clinical notes from client interviews.] Unpublished raw data.

National Task Force on Juvenile Sexual Offending. (1988). Preliminary report. *Juvenile and Family Court Journal, 39*(2).

Ricci, L., and Watson, R. (1989). *Sexualized behavior seen by a child sex abuse diagnostic program in Maine.* Presentation of unpublished manuscript at trainers' workshop, Bar Harbor, ME.

Ryan, G. (1988). *Juvenile sexual offender: A question of diagnosis.* Paper presented at the National Symposium on Child Victimization, Anaheim, CA.

Ryan, G. (1989). Victim to victimizer: Rethinking victim treatment. *Journal of Interpersonal Violence, 4*(3), 325–341.

Ryan, G. (1995). *Treatment of sexually abusive youth: The evolving consensus.* Paper presented at the International Experts Conference, Utrecht, Netherlands.

Ryan, G., & Blum, J. (1994). *Childhood sexuality: A guide for parents.* Denver: Kempe Center, University of Colorado Health Sciences Center.

Ryan, G., Blum, J., Sandau-Christopher, D., Law, S., Weber, F., Sundine, C., Astler, L., Teske, J., & Dale, J. (1988). *Understanding and responding to the sexual behavior of children: Trainer's manual.* Denver: Kempe Center, University of Colorado Health Sciences Center.

Ryan, G., Krugman, R., & Miyoshi, T. (1988). *Results of the Early Childhood Experience Survey.* Paper presented at the National Symposium on Child Abuse and Neglect, Keystone, CO.

Ryan, G., Lane, S., Davis, J., & Isaac, C. (1987). Juvenile sexual offenders: Development and correction. *Child Abuse and Neglect: The International Journal, 11*(3), 385–395.

Strong, K., Tate, J., Wehman, B., & Wyss, A. (1986). *Sexual assault facts and effects.* Cumberland, WI: Human Growth and Development Program.

PART SEVEN

WORKING WITH
SEXUAL ABUSE

CHAPTER TWENTY-TWO

THE IMPACT OF SEXUAL ABUSE
ON THE INTERVENTIONIST

Gail Ryan and Sandy Lane

Professionals who interact with dysfunctional populations are at risk personally, socially, and professionally. These risks stem from the realities, the beliefs, and the attributions of each individual and how each meets the challenges posed in the integration of this experience into his or her own worldview. Working in the area of sexual victimization raises issues on many different levels. These issues flow into each other, alternating from external to internal and personal to interpersonal. Each individual's experience of the impacts of this work proceeds along a different course in terms of the ordering and processing of the issues, but most workers face similar questions as their experience evolves.

In many ways, the impact of this work parallels the impact of sexual abuse itself, and these effects have often been defended against in ways that parallel the dysfunctions of sexual abuse. Denial and rationalization, secrecy and avoidance, disbelief, and victim blaming are all reactions that have supported the failure to define the risks of this work and prevented adequate protection and intervention on behalf of the professionals and paraprofessionals who work with sexual abuse cases. Burnout has been accepted as inevitable, and the involved systems have accepted staff turnover as if it were beyond control. Workers have experienced dysfunctional impacts in their own lives without understanding the nature of their reactions. The acceptance of detrimental effects has been so pervasive that little has been done to confront the problem and protect workers from burnout or to identify healthy management strategies.

This chapter explores the worker's experience and anticipates impacts in hopes of promoting greater awareness and defining the mystery of burnout in order to promote healthier adaptation and coping. Burnout not only causes trained people to leave work, but also supports dysfunction in their work and personal lives. Just as intervention with the victims and offenders of sexual abuse must ultimately be based in accountability and empathy, systems and workers who intervene in sexual abuse must also apply accountability and empathy in their own functioning. Prevention can occur only through definition and understanding of the potential problems.

Relevant Concepts

Burnout has been described in general terms by theorists and clinicians in many fields of work. In the areas of mental health, social services, and the helping professions, Maslach (1978), Maslach and Florian (1988), Warnath and Shelton (1976), and Spaniol (1986) are a few of the authors who have explored the symptomology of burnout. Seligman's (1974, 1975) research on learned helplessness has been applied to understanding the depression that characterizes burnout. These theorists describe physical, psychological, and functional characteristics. Spaniol (1986) describes somatic aches and pains and reduced energy and fatigue, and Seligman notes the loss of appetites for food, sex, and social contact. Outwardly, workers begin to slow down and retreat from their work, spending less time, initiating fewer voluntary responses, minimizing client contact, vacillating in decision making, avoiding confrontation of issues, and distancing themselves emotionally and intellectually. Internally, disillusionment, powerlessness, and apathy contribute to lower and lower expectations (Warnath & Shelton, 1976), and a negative cognitive set thwarts curiosity and decreases learning (Seligman, 1975).

Functioning and feelings are both affected by one's perception of control. Helplessness is the psychological state that results when events seem uncontrollable (Seligman, 1974). When the outcome of one's work is controlled by others, the risks of detachment and depression increase.

Whereas in many clinical, remedial, or rehabilitative settings, measurable results are expected and possible (improvement or cure), the treatment of sex offenders does not suggest cure, and outcomes are difficult to measure. As Yochelson and Samenow (1976) stated in regard to the outcomes of treatment with criminal personalities, "Only time will tell." There is little immediate gratification in the treatment of sex offenders, and long-term feedback is more likely related to failures than success. The client who is not known to have been rearrested cannot be assumed successful because measures of recidivism are so unreliable. When the offender is told that he or she will always be at risk, the clinician is also denied any closure.

Warnath and Shelton (1976) describe the "Sisyphus syndrome" as a state of doom associated with the constant repetition of doing the same job again and again. The relentless procession of new sexual abuse cases may constitute the persistent assault on the clinician's assertiveness and adaptive coping that Richter's (1957) research parallels in terms of one's willingness to struggle to survive. The professional's willingness to leave the work may result from this inability to struggle against feelings of hopelessness and doom.

Theorists have also suggested strategies of intervention and prevention. Seligman (1975) suggests that prevention is supported by teaching adaptive responses and escape mechanisms prior to exposure to uncontrollable situations. Spaniol (1986) concentrates on more primary prevention of risk rather than responses to the occurrence. This primary prevention of burnout includes awareness (correct information), adequate training and skills, adequate support from peers and colleagues, personal health and assertiveness, and shared responsibility and decision making. Others have suggested open communication, administrative empathy and support, and time away (vacations and sabbaticals) as other preventive measures. In many ways, these preventive measures parallel the primary prevention of victimization by defining consensual involvement, balancing power and control, and eliminating coercion. For the professional, knowing what the work involves, evaluating the possible consequences, and making an informed choice to expose oneself to the risks counters the potential perception of a lack of control in the experience. Seligman's theory regarding teaching adaptive coping skills in advance might be viewed as a secondary level of burnout prevention that parallels secondary prevention concepts regarding sexual abuse.

Clinicians must recognize the defenses they use in their work. Many of the dysfunctional patterns of sex offenders evolve from a maladaptive coping with their own victimization (Ryan, 1989). Just as it is recognized that many responses to sexual abuse that were initially healthy, adaptive defenses for the victim become problematic when generalized over time (Conte, 1985), clinicians are at risk to overgeneralize defenses in ways that become maladaptive. The details of sexual abuse are painful to hear and may be incomprehensible or overwhelming for the counselor. It is not only necessary but adaptive for therapists to defend themselves against this painful information. As these defense mechanisms are defined in Table 22.1, it is easy to conceptualize how each of the defenses may be used by therapists in order to remain objective and functional in the course of exposure to the details of sexual victimization or offending. It is initially adaptive and healthy to protect oneself from being overwhelmed by the experience. Nevertheless, coping does not equal resolution, and overgeneralization of defense mechanisms becomes maladaptive over time. Clinicians must face and resolve the painful and confusing aspects of their work in order to prevent personal and professional dysfunction.

TABLE 22.1. DEFENSE MECHANISMS.

Denial	Refusing to acknowledge consciously or perceive either internal or external realities that produce anxiety
Displacement	Redirection of distressing emotional energy toward less dangerous objects than the source of the distress
Dissociation	Separation of some mental or behavioral processes from one's perception in order to avoid overwhelming emotion
Identification with the aggressor	Assuming the patterns of thought or behavior of another person who represents an external source of frustration
Intellectualization	Using reasoning and logic to distance oneself from anxiety
Isolation	Separation of feeling from an idea or memory
Projection	Placing blame or responsibility on another in order to avoid internal or external sources of anxiety or conflict
Rationalization	Using logic to explain or justify irrational thoughts or behavior
Regression	Partial or total return to an earlier pattern of adaptation
Repression	An unconscious process that keeps unacceptable mental content out of consciousness
Sublimation	Channeling frustrated or intolerable energy into more gratifying activity
Suppression	Conscious repression
Withdrawal	Retreat or avoidance of sources of anxiety

Source: Adapted from Koplau & Sadock (1985, p. 498).

When the risks of the work are not managed and the worker becomes symptomatic, the effects become more difficult to counter and more resistant to intervention. The counselor who is experiencing burnout may become isolated from colleagues or seek out similarly affected peers in attempts to escape painful feelings. Denial and cynicism are frequent, and escape mechanisms may parallel the dysfunction of clients. Drug and alcohol abuse, eating disorders, or promiscuity by workers may represent attempts to escape or avoid the issues and "feel better."

Maladaptive coping becomes self-perpetuating, and the counselor's own responses may be similar to the dysfunctional cycle of the client. Seligman (1974) suggests that interventions with burnout must be very directive to both teach and practice more functional coping patterns. Many professionals are lost to the field entirely when burnout occurs. However, even leaving the work does not constitute a cure. The individual's mental health is jeopardized until the issues are resolved.

Defining the Issues

Acquiring the knowledge necessary to anticipate and counter negative impacts requires careful exploration of the issues that sexual abuse work entails. In work with any criminal problem, issues of community safety, victim protection, and personal safety are legitimate concerns that place tremendous responsibility on therapists and decision makers. These are the obvious worries of those who counsel the sex offender, but there are also many covert issues attached to the work. Awareness of the risks these clients pose in the community, the vulnerability of potential victims, and the impact of abuse translates into a personal knowledge of one's own vulnerability and sensitivity to danger. Additionally, all sexual abuse work brings up issues from the past related to one's own sexual learning and experience, interpersonal relationships, and beliefs about humanity.

Many people who work in the field of child protection were themselves abused as children. In several surveys of participants at professional child abuse conferences, 45 percent of the multidisciplinary respondents reported histories of childhood sexual abuse (Ryan & Miyoshi, 1988). Others have chosen to work with dysfunctional problems because they have been touched by these problems in their relationships with others in their family or community. For some, working in the field of sexual abuse is motivated by the dissonance of abuse with their own view of the world. Many professionals enter social services, mental health, special education, or justice work and find that sexual abuse is a component in a majority of their cases.

One's own exposure to sexual abuse is the most recognized of covert issues, and there are both advantages and disadvantages to having prior victims working in this field. Workers who are motivated to work with offenders by retaliatory or compensatory drives because of their own unresolved experiences with sexual abuse are ill advised to pursue this line of work. Survivors of sexual trauma may be particularly vulnerable due to posttraumatic stress reactions that may be triggered by this work. For those who choose or are chosen to become involved in the treatment of victims and offenders, a capacity for empathy and understanding and a desire to create a safer society support that choice.

Less obvious issues from the past involve memories of childhood sexual learning and the development of one's own sexuality. Ultimately, definition of deviancy in the sexual abuse client forces interventionists to question the normality of their own sexuality, sexual fantasies, and sexual experience. When forced to examine and question one's own experience, misinformation and lack of information regarding sexuality throughout life may raise many unanswerable questions. In the broadened definitions of Bolton, Morris, and MacEachron (1989), Haynes-Seman and Krugman (1989), and Finkelhor and Browne (1985), the abuse of sexuality, sexualized attention in family relationships, and traumatic or incomprehensible sexual experiences abound with such frequency in individual experience and the culture that few individuals are untouched by potentially abusive stimuli. Sexual abuse work confronts the defenses and assumptions that protect the average individual from being overwhelmed by the sexual fears and confusion of the times.

At every level of intervention—legal, medical, and psychological; education, investigation, prosecution, and correction; case manager and caregiver—all interventionists are exposed to a Pandora's box of sexual abuse issues. For some, the risks of this exposure are managed by the boundaries or the role of the profession and the definition of their own involvement with the problem. For others, distancing from the perceptual experiences of victims and offenders serves to insulate them from the personal implications of the subject. However, in a survey of caseworkers, supervisors, and members of sexual abuse teams involved with incest cases at social service agencies, respondents reported many negative impacts that they attributed to the unpredictable and intrusive aspects of their work. Difficult aspects of the work included "pain, sadness, nonsupportive systems, lack of recognition, inability to set boundaries, feelings of hopelessness, exhaustion, and distortion of power" (Corman & Smith, 1986). Workers described changes in their sexuality and sexual fantasies, increased levels of anger, and a variety of sleep disturbances and psychosomatic complaints. These descriptions parallel those voiced by interventionists who work with both victims and perpetrators of sexual abuse.

Counselors of victims and perpetrators are exposed to the intimate perceptions and dysfunctions of their clients. When the dynamics of dysfunction become reflected in the professional's own perceptions and functioning due to existing personal issues or through transference and countertransference in the therapeutic or correctional setting, the helping professional may become personally distressed or therapeutically ineffective. The risk of burnout in the helping professions (and especially in work with interpersonal violence and sexual abuse) has been acknowledged. It is interesting to note, however, that this risk is recognized much more than the pervasive and insidious effects of this work that change the individual's life in less obvious but more permanent ways.

External Issues

The external risks of working with sex offenders are the worries that one loses sleep over: the incidence and prevalence of sexual abuse, the system's inability to protect potential victims, incidents of reoffending that may occur during treatment, and the system's failure to remove dangerous offenders from the community. On a personal level, these facts make therapists more aware of their own vulnerability, oversensitive to dangerous situations, and overprotective of children and other loved ones. These personal worries may be countered by locking doors, carrying disabling sprays, and educating children in self-protection, but the worry nevertheless persists. Contrary to popular belief, fear of the known may in this case be greater than fear of the unknown. Knowing the logic, rationale, and tactics of sex offenders can only increase one's fear of their behavior. At the same time, confronting the distorted rationalizations of these offenders strips away many of one's own cognitive defenses and may leave therapists feeling vulnerable.

At a more global level, the external worries of the sexual abuse worker are for the community: awareness of the risks these clients pose in the community, how sexual abuse occurs, the unpredictability of victimization, and the impact of abuse on the social structure. Therapists may become over-sensitized to violence and explicit sexually exploitative influences in the culture and become more and more afraid for the community and of the community. They may experience television, movies, popular music, and advertising as aversive, and consider the attitudes and humor of relatives and peers to be intolerable. Also, at the external level the sex offender therapist sees the developmental antecedents of sexually abusive behavior and must be afraid for all children who are experiencing similar developmental crises. Awareness of the vicious, unrelenting transmission of abusive behaviors from one generation to the next can be the most overwhelming of the external impacts.

Workers may experience a sense of alienation in the community or workplace, as those who work with sexual assault victims often assume the sex offender worker is a protective advocate of sex offenders. Many who work with perpetrators confront hostility and emotional, volatile conflicts with those who are treating victims. Peers and coworkers may challenge or belittle the worker's belief in treatment by advocating severe punishment and alienation of sex offenders. Those close to the interventionist may be unwilling or unable to be supportive because of their own personal issues. This sense of alienation gives rise to a defensiveness that isolates therapists of offenders even further.

Because many of these external issues are based in the culture, the community, and the systems outside the therapeutic setting, the workers' frustrations and hopelessness are increased. As with many other problems, the gap between knowledge and collective applications is a time of frustration for those who suggest solutions. This is not unique to sexual abuse work; consumer advocate Ralph Nader has stated, "We have more problems than we deserve and more solutions than we apply." Much is known about the prevention and treatment of sexual abuse; much less is implemented and widely available to those who need it (Krugman, 1990). When the toll of this dilemma is measured in human suffering, the lack of access and resources supports helplessness and burnout.

Internal Issues

Therapists must recognize that their own powerful emotions and beliefs may become issues in the therapeutic relationship. Every intervention takes place within the context of a relationship between the interventionist and the client. Whether distant, professional, or intimate, every relationship adds to the worldview and perceptions of the parties involved. There are many internal issues that arise during work with sexual abuse clients.

Ambivalent Emotions. As the therapist is exposed to the offender's rage, fear, and disregard of others, the professional's own affective memories are stirred and may become problematic. Reactions of rage, revulsion, fear, and disbelief arise from the therapist's own life experience and are processed through the fibers of the individual's own worldview. At the same time, the offender's victim stance, poor self-image, and deprived life history trigger empathy, tolerance, and nurturance that may go beyond the safe, rational, or therapeutic. The ambivalence between one's personal abhorrence of sexually abusive behavior and the desire to help an individual gain control can be stressful. The emotional tug-of-war that ensues can be frightening and exhausting for the therapist who loses perspective and is drawn into the negative or unrealistic expectations of offenders. Denial of these emotions puts therapists at risk for covert expressions of victimization.

Victim or Aggressor Identification. Transference and countertransference may occur in various phases of treatment. It is difficult to listen to the minute details of the process of victimization without reacting. Reactions may lead to identification with the victim and elicit feelings of fear, helplessness, or rage. At other times, identification with the aggressor may engender feelings of anger, confusion, dominance, or guilt. Some interventionists may identify with the offender's power thrust and begin to believe that they are able to control the client. The counselor may experience these identifications with the offender through their interactions and the sharing of perceptions. As the randomness of victim selection and the pervasiveness of exploitative dysfunctions becomes apparent, a therapist can easily feel overwhelmed. Identification with either the victim or the aggressor serves as a coping mechanism. This reaction is typically maladaptive and may be expressed in the worker's interpersonal interactions if the underlying issues are not resolved.

Power and Control. Exposure to power-based interactions and behaviors is unavoidable because that is the means that sex offenders use to deal with their world (Lane, 1986). The client comes unwillingly into treatment due to the coercion or control of others, and the treatment setting becomes a new setting in which manipulation and exploitation are tested. The offender continues to engage in power and control interactions that boost his sense of adequacy and self-esteem. The therapist is often opposed, demeaned, or subtly victimized. There are times when it can become difficult to avoid engaging in the power game, and there are times when workers overidentify with power-based behaviors.

In some instances there is a qualitative difference in the reaction of offenders to confrontations from males and from females, possibly based on the perpetrator's perceived ability to control females and subsequent need to discount more of her input in order to maintain that assumption (Lane, 1986). Inequality or conflict in the male-female cotherapy team may result from or be exacerbated by the power and control dynamics.

Power struggles and control battles with clients may also be replicated in interactions with the various intervening professionals and systems and may leave therapists feeling discounted, ineffectual, or helpless. The temptation for rules, control seeking, and structure is great, as is the risk of retaliatory or compensatory reactions.

Examination of Beliefs. As the therapist pursues the relentless scrutiny of the offender's thoughts and beliefs, the examination of one's own worldview follows. It can be distressing to discover similarities to the offender in one's own patterns of coping, defenses, and beliefs; nevertheless, acknowledgment of one's own dysfunctional behaviors can increase the therapist's patience and empathy in work with offenders. The constant reexamination of one's beliefs and behavior supports changes in the therapist's own tolerance and accountability in personal relationships.

The worker's previous standards may become dissonant with new understandings acquired in the process of treating dysfunction. Disruptions in one's personal life lead the worker to question the assumptions that guide both work and personal decisions. As Maslach (1978) warns, sharp distinctions between personal and professional standards contribute to the risk of burnout.

Sexuality. Therapists cannot be repeatedly exposed to the ideation of sexual abuse without experiencing some effects on their own sexuality. The therapist who has been a victim of any part of a sexual act by a perpetrator may become distressed and need to work on that issue in his or her own therapy. The therapist who has unresolved adolescent sexuality issues may feel threatened or uneasy helping a youth with similar issues. Therapists with sexual dysfunctions of their own will become more aware of and more anxious about that area. Female workers who are covertly victimized during the process of treatment may transfer their fear or rage to all males they encounter or to the significant males in their lives. Male therapists who are covertly victimized may experience issues related to homo-sexuality, power, or even gender guilt (Lane, 1986).

Sex offender therapists may experience disinterest in sex at times, increased arousal at other times, or a complete shutdown of sexual desires. Deviant sexual images may intrude on fantasy or thought, and physiological arousal may occur in response to these images. When therapists experience arousal in response to a client's description of a sexually abusive behavior, it is usually associated with the therapist's own memory of a sexual behavior, such as digital penetration, penile thrusting, vaginal secretions, erections, and the like. The therapist must be able to distinguish the normality of that association and response from the deviance of the behavior occurring in the context of an exploitative or violent interaction. Therapists working with victims or offenders must anticipate that the sexual component of their work puts them at risk for sexual dysfunction, intrusive sexual images, and deviant fantasies and arousal. Both primary and secondary prevention concepts must be employed to support their own health and self-image and to counter the intrusion of work into their own sexual interactions. In almost every instance, the same techniques the therapist has used to help clients manage sexual thoughts and arousal or to restructure sexual fantasies can be used to manage the negative effects experienced by the interventionist.

As therapists working with victims come to think of them as potential perpetrators, a proactive approach works toward prevention. Many issues relevant to offending must be explored with victims. Workers must be aware that they are simultaneously being oversensitized to sexual issues and exposed to vicarious sexual victimization.

Sexual arousal and intrusive sexual images are not the only issues to arise from the sexual nature of this work. Therapists may also struggle with feelings of intrusiveness and voyeurism when they inquire into the thoughts and feelings of victims and offenders. The therapist's discomfort and the subsequent self-examination are both useful in evaluating one's work but should not automatically change the course of the treatment strategy. There is a very real need and a strong theoretical basis or rationale that supports the therapist's intrusive inquiry. Acknowledgment of one's own discomfort and empathy for the client's experience of the intrusive elements of the treatment process are appropriate and beneficial for the therapeutic relationship.

Much of the definition and restructuring of sexual thinking can be accomplished in anticipation of the client's needs in a more educational and informational format that minimizes the amount of intrusive investigation into the sexual thinking of the client. It is not possible, however, to treat sexual deviance without hearing from the individual the thoughts and fantasies that support and fuel the behavior. The intrusive and voyeuristic qualities associated with this aspect of the work are minimized in the context of an effective therapeutic group wherein alliances are less intimate; the client's self-disclosure is encouraged, and the defenses that allow self-observation are respected. While defining deviance and exploitation in his or her work, the therapist nevertheless recognizes that normal, healthy sexuality is a goal for the client. Workers must maintain some perspective of normality and celebrate healthy sexuality in their own lives (O'Brien, 1990).

Role Taking. The intervening systems assign workers various roles that often include overlapping or conflicting functions. The boundaries of one's role may at times be clear and at other times become enmeshed or rigid.

There is a tendency for those in victim services to assume that their role is victim advocacy and that those working with offenders are in a corresponding role as advocates for the perpetrator (and his behavior). The betrayal of trust and intrusion inherent in sexual abuse may be expressed by workers' becoming suspicious, rigid, intolerant, or oversensitive in these different roles. This conflict stems from the failure to think about all sexual abuse work in terms of prevention. The treatment of offenders is typically motivated by the desire to reduce further victimization, and the common denominator in the roles of all who intervene is victim advocacy. There are times, however, when therapists of offenders must actively pursue resources and support in order to have the potential to succeed in the treatment of their clients. Treating the perpetrator is a preventive measure, not advocacy for sexually abusive behavior.

The unfortunate dilemma of inadequate resources for both victim services and remedial programs for offenders is very real. Prioritizing time and dollars creates a debate regarding cause and effect similar to the proverbial dilemma of the chicken and the egg. If it is possible through treatment to stop offenders from victimizing, then there will be fewer victims and a corresponding reduction in the demand for victim services. On the other hand, if it is possible to intervene successfully with victims, their negative experience may be resolved without risk of long-term dysfunctions, including sexual perpetration against others. It is obvious why the allocation of limited resources fuels the role conflicts in this work.

Many workers are cast into multiple roles, working with victims and perpetrators, as well as with the systems and families involved. Work with each aspect may create an internal struggle that undermines the objectivity of the workers. The boundaries and conflicts become internalized within an individual, and the subsequent dilemmas become very personal in the context of the therapeutic alliances that form. Cotherapy relationships may support or exacerbate these conflicts or may be helpful in separating the issues.

At still another level, the therapist of offenders is often cast into rigid and conflicting roles by the client (Lane, 1986). At this level role definition goes beyond the function and attacks the identity of the interventionist. The role assignments of offenders are often extreme. The therapist may be seen as either all good or all bad: madonna or whore, macho or effeminate, protector or abuser, advocate or foe. These role assignments are based in the offenders' worldviews and beliefs, as are their definitions of their own roles in relationships. It is easy for the therapist to respond to the projection in dysfunctional ways. The challenge for the therapist in modeling more flexible roles is to maintain healthy boundaries and facilitate boundary respect among group members as well. Challenging the stereotypes that facilitate objectification is an aspect of treatment with sexual abuse clients that must also be a part of supporting healthy interactions among the interventionists.

Interpersonal Issues

The internal and external implications may be expressed in one's interpersonal relationships. Interpersonal impacts occur related to basic trust and empathy, responsibility, and accountability. Interactional difficulties are apparent in the multiplicity of roles that may lead to role confusion, blurring of personal and professional boundaries, and perceptual alienation among colleagues, family, and friends.

Being sensitized to exploitation and dysfunction opens one's eyes to the pervasiveness and risk of these negative qualities in all human relations. The dysfunctions that support or allow sexual offending are not black-and-white configurations, nor are they qualities that differ extensively from the personal characteristics of many who do not offend. The dynamics fall along a continuum from perfect to perverse. Cognitive manipulations of self and others are a constant part of our self-image and interactions. Emotional and physical gratification are powerful reinforcers that motivate each of us in our relationships with others, as well as in our personal behavior. It is empathy that deters exploitation, and one's own capacity for empathy increases rather than diminishes sensitivity to the pervasiveness of dysfunction.

Dissonance in one's personal and professional standards can be problematic. Defining sexual abuse in terms of nonconsent, inequality, and coercion goes beyond sexual behavior into the realm of interactions and relationships.

In exploring the quality of the offender's relationships, the therapist also examines his or her own personal relationships. In the therapeutic setting, workers must be sensitive to coercion and manipulation in their own interactions. This sensitivity follows them back to work and home. The style and tactics that have been the basis for giving and receiving nurturance in long-term relationships may be reevaluated in the light of the worker's increased understanding and fall short of his or her new standards regarding empathy, control, and trust. Faults and shortcomings in self and others may become dissonant in the light of the greater emphasis on accountability.

Challenging the defenses of the client increases the likelihood of similar challenges of one's own defenses, as well as those of friends, colleagues, and family members. As workers examine dysfunction in the life of clients, they are likely to reexamine their own life experiences as well. Sensitizing oneself to see the elements of the dysfunctional cycle in the daily lives of the clients leads to the discovery of those same elements in one's own functioning. This discovery can shake the interventionists' view of their own competence and health, as well as their evaluation of others. Negative expectations, isolating behaviors, cognitive distortions, and control seeking may seem pervasive as the risk or presence of negative behavior is revealed in the daily functioning of self and others. Workers may begin to fear the presence of secret negative behavior in those close to them.

Being aware of the continuum of functionality, workers must accept that normal functioning is not perfect. Most functioning falls along the middle of that continuum without clear delineation of the points that define optimal, acceptable, and unacceptable levels of responsibility. Similarly, most relationships are less than perfect as well. Differentiating between the dynamics of sexual abuse and the dynamics of one's own interactions and relationships is critical.

As the therapist becomes more and more sensitive to the issues, is propelled by curiosity and self-examination, or is excited by the positive implications and potential for change, his or her interpersonal relationships may be challenged, threatened, or jeopardized by the changes in his or her beliefs and expectations. One's spouse, partner, children, friends, and colleagues may be overwhelmed by what seem to them to be rapid changes, and they may complain about the impact on their relationships. Workers must be cautious of overgeneralizing the techniques and expectations of their work into their personal relationships and at the same time be willing to accept the inevitable need for change in some aspects of their lives.

Agency Issues

Agencies that specialize in sexual abuse work, as well as interagency teams, are also at risk for dysfunction. Understanding that defense mechanisms are adaptive responses that protect individuals from being overwhelmed by adversity, stress, and painful experiences, it becomes clear that therapists must call on a variety of defenses to maintain their objectivity and function while dealing with the abhorrent details of sexual abuse. At the same time, knowing that the overgeneralization of defenses becomes problematic over time and supports dysfunctional outcomes, teams must be vigilant in order to avoid taking on the very characteristics present in the functioning of their clients. In their exposure to the details of sexual abuse, therapists experience sexual victimization and offending vicariously and are at risk to mirror the client's issues in their own interactions. Agencies specializing in the treatment of family dysfunction are at risk to function in similar roles within the agency. Incest programs have often reported discovery of victim, perpetrator, abuse-tolerant, and abuse-supportive dynamics occurring in staff relationships. Somatic complaints regarding the organization are evident, and working conditions are maligned, with responsibility attributed to administrators, directors, and ancillary staff. O'Brien (1990) notes that even buildings become symptomatic in the perception of the workers, as if lack of space or old carpet were or could be responsible for one's stress. Those dynamics clearly contribute to the risk of burnout and high rates of staff turnover when workers' distortions of the impacts cause them to believe they are being victimized by the agency.

Professional staff are also at risk of overidentifying with their clientele to the extent that a process of normalization may occur. Staff may exhibit increased minimization of behaviors or reactions, rescuing, or acceptance of the client's victim stance. Normalizing may initially serve as an empathetic or coping response but may result in blurred professional roles or changes in agency orientation. Agencies must work to keep perspective of safety and accountability issues yet maintain a balance of intolerance of abusive sexual behaviors with supportive therapeutic interactions with the client.

Prevention and Intervention

Just as models have developed to support understanding, risk assessment, intervention, and prevention with victims and offenders, it is also possible to manage the risks associated with the work itself. To do so requires an understanding of the experience, recognition of symptoms, and purposeful planning for both prevention and intervention. Corman and Smith (1986), in processing the results of their survey on the effects of sexual abuse on staff, concluded that the manifestation of symptoms from the effects of sexual abuse work is not a measure of one's ability or inability to do the work, but rather that workers must monitor the impact on themselves and their coworkers and take responsibility for dealing with the stress.

In entering any challenging endeavor, the balance of risk and gain must be considered. One cannot accept a challenge without some anticipation of change. When accepting the sex offender into treatment, the professional evaluates the needs and strengths of the individual and, on the basis of this assessment of amenability for treatment, the client is urged to accept the challenge to change. Workers and those who hire them must similarly evaluate the potential employee's own amenability to facilitate change and to accept the inevitable challenges, impacts, and personal change. The potential worker's qualifications are an area of controversy in the field, and many agencies and organizations are exploring the criteria of some minimal level of training, knowledge, and experience that would measure one's ability to work with juvenile sex offenders. It has been suggested that some combination of clinical and specialized training is required, but at a more personal level the individual's potential long-term success in this work is likely to be more related to personal characteristics than to the simple acquisition of skills and knowledge. Some of the qualifications that may be worth considering in preemployment decisions include a genuine enjoyment of adolescents, comfort with one's own sexuality, an innate curiosity, and a good sense of humor. Just as the client's functioning reflects the influences of his or her whole life experience, the worker's ability to succeed is influenced by his or her life experience as well. It is the stability and consistency of the individual's experience and self-image, along with positive sources of validation and correction of change, that seem to mediate the risk of detrimental experiences' having a negative outcome.

Just as prevention and intervention work with offenders considers the situational, affective, cognitive, and behavioral aspects of their cycle and implements different strategies to counter each element of risk, burnout prevention must address each of these elements as well.

Situational variables present in the structure of the agency (as well as the specific therapeutic setting) can facilitate identification and management of many of the impacts. The atmosphere should support sharing of knowledge and responsibility and prohibit secrecy and scapegoating. Forums for learning, sharing, and conflict resolution (for example, study groups, case processing, supervision, and staff retreats) offer opportunities for open exploration of issues rather than denial. A clear statement of mission and goals that encompasses some vision of future directions counters the negative expectations and cynicism that support burnout. A peer culture based in accountability and empathy provides collegial support while allowing staff to both comfort and confront their peers. A consistent, shared awareness of the predictable issues facilitates recognition and intervention in symptoms as they arise.

Teamwork reduces isolation and allows for immediate validation or correction of erroneous perceptions and tough decisions. Cotherapy, outside consultation, and supervision reduce the worker's isolation. Networking with other programs and agencies reduces the secrecy and isolation that increases the risk of incestuous and exploitive dynamics among staff. Conferences and in-service training provide continuing education and support feelings of competence. The danger that similarly affected persons will reinforce maladaptive coping is countered by an open exchange of academic ideas in study groups, journal clubs, and book reviewing. Clinical dilemmas must be acknowledged at both the affective and cognitive levels, in a climate of curiosity that encourages exploration, resolution, and change.

Affectively, colleagues must facilitate sharing of emotional issues in a climate of empathy, openness, and permission. Minimization or denial of one's own feelings supports the denial of the feelings of one's colleagues, and pervasive minimizing of affect objectifies the interventionist. Lack of empathic peer support feeds the abuse-tolerant dynamic. Appropriate sharing encourages all staff to identify impacts and develop effective coping and resolution strategies. One of the strengths of those who work with children and adolescents is the good humor and enjoyment that supports both the clinician and the client in what might otherwise be intolerably painful circumstances. The collegial culture must monitor itself, however, for subtle shifts away from good humor into cynicism and sarcasm, which when pervasive support objectification of clients and a lack of empathy for colleagues. Failure to interrupt this type of shift can develop into hurtful interchanges between staff members. The source of the hurt very often parallels the affective triggers of the clients. Scapegoating, helplessness, and a lack of validation support hopelessness and feelings of doom. An ongoing process of feedback and insight provides validation and paves the way for intervention.

Cognitively, workers must constantly reconcile their own view of the world with the very different beliefs of the client. Colleagues must monitor professional interactions for subtle cognitive shifts away from accountability and empathy. While exposed to the sometimes overwhelming evidence of deceit and exploitation that pervade the life histories and the current functioning of the client, workers must remain grounded in their own experience of more rational and functional relationships.

Either consistently or intermittently, workers should seek out opportunities to work with or be exposed to nonclinical age-mates of their client population in order to maintain a sense of normality. The thoughts, feelings, and behaviors of young offenders are usually extremes or deviations and must not become one's measure of normalcy.

Although an emotional tug-of-war may result from the therapist's dual roles with victims and offenders, purposefully planned involvement in victim services can be beneficial in maintaining one's perspective, as well as countering the polarization of workers. The mutual exchange of workers from victim and offender programs promotes mutual goals and counters alienation, while providing external sources of validation and correction for both.

Behaviorally, the symptoms of burnout often manifest in power and control behaviors and the abuse of self or others. Agencies can facilitate behavioral accountability by providing clear expectations and open communication. Workers can monitor themselves and each other for retaliatory or compensatory plans. Colleagues must be willing to confront their peers when client dysfunction is being reflected in current behavior. The culture within the agency should process problems as they arise and assist workers in recognizing the need for intervention and obtaining the help they need.

Conclusions

It may be that the risks of personal and professional impacts in the treatment of juvenile sex offenders are predictable and manageable. Preemployment screening, appropriate ongoing training, peer consultation and supervision, and the open sharing of issues and responsibility minimize the negative risks of this work. It is equally important to acknowledge the unique individuality of each interventionist, appreciating the defenses that protect them in this work and supporting the strengths that keep them healthy. Each worker must find his or her own personal answers in order to survive in this work.

In explaining the challenge of staying sane while surrounded by misery, Hawkeye Pierce of the television series *M.A.S.H.* referred to the need for "mental anesthesia" with the following explanation: "If you get caught up in their misery too deeply, you can get into a hole you can't get out of." At the same time, anesthesia must be balanced with conscious, creative thinking. Always questioning what the current intervention can reveal about prevention is a good way to promote optimism and maintain health. Hopelessness and powerlessness must be countered by noticing and nurturing inner strengths and appreciating the importance of small changes in individual clients. Celebrating healthy relationships, positive sexuality, and peaceful pursuits are critical in the worker's ability to remain stable and grounded in a positive worldview.

Brandt Steele, in a personal communication with his staff (1990), suggests that one is never really expert: "We are only curious people struggling to understand suffering and overcome it." Sexual abuse workers must give themselves permission to leave the work behind either temporarily or permanently. Sexual abuse has enough casualties. Colleagues must take care of themselves and of each other.

References

Bolton, F., Morris, C., & MacEachron, A. (1989). *Males at risk.* Thousand Oaks, CA: Sage.

Conte, J. (1985). The effects of sexual victimization on children: A critique and suggestions for future research. *Victimology: The International Journal, 10*(1), 10–30.

Corman, C., & Smith, H. (1986). Effects of sexual abuse on staff. *Colorado's Children, 5*(3), 1–3.

Finkelhor, D., & Browne, A. (1985). The traumatic impact of child sexual abuse: A conceptualization. *American Journal of Orthopsychiatry, 55*(4), 530–541.

Haynes-Seman, C., & Krugman, R. (1989). Sexualized attention: Normal interaction or precursor to sexual abuse? *American Journal of Orthopsychiatry, 59*(2), 238–245.

Koplau, H., & Sadock, B. (Eds.). (1985). *Comprehensive textbook of psychiatry.* Baltimore: Williams & Wilkins.

Krugman, R. (1990). *Child sexual abuse.* Paper presented at the Twenty-second Ross Round-table on Critical Approaches to Common Pediatric Problems, Washington, DC.

Lane, S. (1986). Potential emotional hazards of working with sex offenders. *Interchange.* (Newsletter of the National Adolescent Perpetrator Network). Denver: Kempe National Center.

Maslach, C. (1978). Job burnout: How people cope. *Public Welfare, 36*(1).

Maslach, C., & Florian, V. (1988). Burnout, job setting and self-evaluation among rehabilitation counselors. *Rehabilitation Psychology, 33*(2).

O'Brien, M. (1990). *Child and adolescent perpetrators.* Paper presented at the Sexual Abuse Treatment Symposium, Breckenridge, CO.

Richter, C. (1957). On the phenomenon of unexplained sudden death in animals and man. *Psychosomatic Medicine,* 19, 191–198.

Ryan, G. (1989). Victim to victimizer: Rethinking victim treatment. *Journal of Interpersonal Violence, 4*(3), 325–341.

Ryan, G. R., & Miyoshi, T. (1988). *Results of the Early Childhood Experience Survey.* Paper presented at the Seventeenth National Symposium on Child Abuse and Neglect, Keystone, CO.

Seligman, M. (1974). Depression and learned helplessness. In R. J. Friedman & M. M. Katz (Eds.), *The psychology of depression.* Washington, DC: Winston and Sons.

Seligman, M. (1975). *Helplessness: On depression, development, and death.* New York: Freeman.

Spaniol, L. (1986). Program evaluation in psychosocial rehabilitation: A management perspective. *Psychosocial Rehabilitation Journal, 1*(1).

Warnath, C., & Shelton, J. (1976). The ultimate disappointment: The burned out counselor. *Personnel and Guidance Journal, 55*(4).

Yochelson, S., & Samenow, S. (1976). *The criminal personality* (Vol. 1). Northvale, NJ: Aronson.

ABOUT THE EDITORS

Gail Ryan, M.A., is a program director at the Kempe National Center for the Prevention and Treatment of Child Abuse and Neglect, University of Colorado Health Sciences Center, with a faculty appointment to the Department of Pediatrics. On staff since 1975, she has worked with abusive parents and abused children and is currently treating eleven- to seventeen-year-old males who have molested children. Her primary interests have been in the correlation between early life experience and dysfunctional behavior, with an emphasis on the development of sexual offending in high-risk groups. She is founder and facilitator of the National Adolescent Perpetrator Network, has served as facilitator of the National Task Force on Juvenile Sexual Offending (1986–1993), and is on the advisory boards for several relevant projects. She is director of the Perpetration Prevention Project and a specialist for the Kempe Center's Clinical Resource Center. She is an experienced trainer and consultant and has published widely in the field.

Sandy Lane, B.S.N., is the treatment coordinator at RSA, Inc., one of the largest private treatment agencies for sex offenders in Colorado, where she has been working since 1984 with male and female preadolescent, adolescent, developmentally disabled, and adult sex offenders. In addition, she has provided extensive consultation services to programs for sexually abusive youth and therapists. As a psychiatric nurse, she was one of the pioneers who codeveloped the sex offender component of the Closed Adolescent Treatment Center program in the

Colorado Division of Youth Services during the late 1970s. She was appointed to the National Task Force on Juvenile Sexual Offending in 1987 and to the Colorado Department of Corrections Therapeutic Community Advisory Board in 1996, and she has been listed in *Who's Who in American Nurses.* She has an extensive background in residential, community, day treatment, individual, and family mental health treatment.

ABOUT THE CONTRIBUTORS

Steven Bengis, Ed.D., is codirector, with Penny Cunningham, of the New England Adolescent Research Institute in Massachusetts, where he works with severely emotionally disturbed and violent adolescents. He is coordinator of the Massachusetts Adolescent Sex Offender Coalition and was appointed to the National Task Force on Juvenile Sexual Offending in 1987. He is also a trainer and consultant, and the author of *Comprehensive Service Delivery and a Continuum of Care for the Adolescent Sexual Offender* (1986).

Rob Freeman-Longo, M.R.C., L.P.C., is the director of the Safer Society Foundation and an international consultant on the assessment of sexual offenders and treatment program development. He has published over twenty-five articles and chapters on sexual aggression. As coauthor of many books and through his appearances at numerous media presentations, he has helped to educate the public about sexual abuse and sex offender treatment. He has worked with both victims and juvenile and adult sexual abusers in residential, hospital, prison, and community-based settings since 1976.

William C. Greer, a community service consultant for the California Youth Authority, works with multicounty juvenile detention programs. He has successfully demonstrated and implemented specialized parole aftercare for juvenile sexual offenders and was appointed to the National Task Force on Juvenile Sexual Offending in 1987.

Joseph Heinz, M.S.W., who has more than twenty years of experience in the field of corrections, was superintendent of the Hennepin County Home School, a 132-bed residential juvenile correctional facility near Minneapolis. He is cofounder and former director of the Juvenile Sex Offenders Program and the author of *A Model Residential Juvenile Sex Offender Treatment Program* (1987).

Fay Honey Knopp was founder and director of the Safer Society Program in Vermont, honorary chairperson of the National Task Force on Juvenile Sexual Offending, and author of numerous publications, including *Remedial Intervention with Adolescent Sexual Offenders* (1982) and *The Youthful Sexual Offender* (1985, 1991). She died in 1995.

Chris Lobanov-Rostovsky, M.S.W., is the clinical director of RSA, Inc., in Colorado. He has provided training and consultation on the evaluation and treatment of children and adolescents involved in sexually abusive behavior and participates in numerous policymaking committees on the state and local levels. He has worked with juvenile and adult sexual abusers in residential, diversion, and community-based settings since 1986.

Floyd M. Martinson, Ph.D., is research professor in sociology at Gustavus Adolphus College, St. Peter, Minnesota. He was a recipient of the 1988 Alfred C. Kinsey Award and a Fulbright Research Scholar to Sweden in 1980–1981. He is listed in the *International Who's Who in Sexology,* is a member of the board of the Foundation for the Scientific Study of Sex, and is a member of the International Academy of Sex Research. He was a guest researcher at the Center for Child Research in Norway, 1984–1985. He is also author of numerous publications on marriage, family, and human sexuality, including *Children and Sex: New Findings, New Perspectives* (1981).

Brandt F. Steele, M.D., is professor emeritus, Department of Psychiatry, University of Colorado Medical Center; psychiatric consultant to the Kempe National Center; honorary advisor to the National Task Force on Juvenile Sexual Offending; and author of numerous chapters and articles on child abuse and neglect.

Jerry Thomas, M.Ed., is a consultant, trainer, and program evaluator in private practice. She was program administrator at the Charter Lakeside Residential Treatment Center in Memphis, Tennessee, from 1982 to 1991 and was appointed to the National Task Force on Juvenile Sexual Offending in 1987. She is an expert on safety in institutions, inpatient program development, mixed psychiatric settings, and multifamily group work. She is past president of the board of directors for the Memphis/Shelby County Child Sexual Abuse Council.

NAME INDEX

A

Abbot, B., 198, 199, 222, 261
Abel, G., 26, 33, 34, 86, 89, 119, 239, 240, 261, 312, 313, 318, 356
Abel, G. G., *xiii*, 15, 180, 181
Abrams, R., 341, 345, 356
Adams-Tucker, C., 162, 166
Ageton, S. S., 15, 185, 199
Ainsworth, M. D., 40, 55
Ainsworth, M.D.S., 29, 34, 129, 133
Allen, C. M., 347, 356
Ames, L. B., 47, 49, 55, 56
Amich, D., 241, 261
Anthony, E. J., 75
Apfelberg, B., 185, 199
Arajii, S., 31, 32, 34
Arnold, L., 29, 35, 75, 134, 320
Astler, L., 200, 320, 358, 433, 454
Atcheson, J. D., 185, 199

B

Baiser, M. L., 341, 359
Baker, S., 341, 356
Bamborough, P., 40, 56
Bandura, A., 24, 25, 34
Barbaree, H., 78, 120, 262, 319
Barbaree, H. E., 35, 134
Barret, M., 153, 318
Bartelt, C., 185, 200
Bartholomew, K., 29, 34, 128
Bays, L., 78, 119, 267, 268, 318–319
Beach, E. A., 28, 34
Beach, F. A., 53, 56
Beach, P., 433
Beal, L. S., 79, 120
Becker, J., 26, 33, 34, 78, 87, 89, 119, 120, 231, 238, 239, 261, 269, 283, 312, 313, 318, 319, 356
Becker, J. B., *xii*, 8, 15, 180, 181
Becker, J. V., 138, 153
Beckett, R., 132, 133
Beilke, R., 323, 326, 356, 357, 439, 454
Bell, S., 49, 55
Ben-Aaron, H., 15, 181
Bengis, S., 186, 198, 199, 211, 212, 217, 222, 261, 355, 405
Bennett, M., 127, 133, 253, 261, 307, 318
Bera, W., 198, 200, 220, 222
Berenson, D., 88, 89, 119, 148, 153, 305, 306, 318, 355
Berlin, F. S., 21, 34
Berliner, L., 6, 8, 181, 182, 208, 209, 323, 326, 334, 356
Bernard, P., 23, 34
Beveridge, J., 13, 16
Biederman, J., 321
Bielke, R., 162, 167, 326, 433
Bilbrey, C., 29, 35, 75, 134, 320
Birch, A., 282, 321
Bird, S., 184, 188, 191, 199, 221, 239, 243, 262, 268, 319
Blackman, N., 48, 55
Blanchard, E., 26, 34, 86, 89, 119
Blanchard, G., 268, 277, 318
Blum, J., 78, 120, 165, 166, 200, 320, 323, 358, 433, 443, 449, 454
Bolton, F., 124, 132, 169, 175, 461, 473
Bonner, B., 6, 8, 323, 326
Bowlby, J., 29, 34, 128, 133
Brecht, B., 341, 345, 356
Breer, W., 160, 166
Bremer, J., 269, 318, 355

Bremer, J. F., 428, 430
Bretherton, I., 34
Briere, J., 157, 167
Briggs, D. C., 280, 318
Brill, A. A., 56
Broderick, C. B., 50, 51, 52, 55
Brouardel, P., 23, 34
Broughton, D., 56, 323, 326, 357, 439, 454
Brown, J., 128, 134, 341, 358
Browne, A., 160, 167, 462, 473
Browne, P. A., 348, 349, 357
Brownell, K., 425, 430
Buell, M. M., 79, 120
Bumby, K., 132, 133
Burgess, A., 34
Burgess, A. W., 34
Burr, 41
Burton, J. E., 326, 358

C

Caffey, J., 180, 182
Calderone, M., 38, 55
Cantwell, H., 433, 438, 454
Carlyle, J. M., 86, 120
Carnes, P., 30, 34, 90, 119, 171, 175
Cassell, T. Z., 40, 56
Cassidy, J., 29, 34
Cavanagh-Johnson, T., 6, 8, 52, 56, 198, 199, 233, 261, 433, 438, 439, 446, 450, 454. *See also* Johnson, T. C.
Cerce, D., 120, 134, 154, 262, 320
Chabot, H., 6, 8, 13, 15
Challoner, D., 165, 167
Chambers, H., 15
Chess, S., 282, 321
Christopher, D., 200, 320
Christopherson, B. J., 326, 358
Clark, T., 198, 200, 222, 263
Clark-Stewart, K. A., 39, 41, 55
Coleman, E. M., 198, 200, 342, 358
Comte, M., 342, 356
Conn, 47, 56
Connor, T., 78, 119, 171, 172, 175
Constantine, L. L., 49, 53, 55, 75, 124, 133
Conte, J., 31, 34, 138, 144, 153, 159, 160, 162, 165, 167, 309, 318, 433, 454, 459, 473

Corman, C., 462, 470, 473
Craig, K., 430
Cross, H., 125, 135
Cumming, G. F., 79, 120
Cunningham, C., 78, 119, 120, 198, 200, 323, 326, 334, 336, 356, 357, 358
Cunningham-Rathner, J., 8, 33, 87, 119, 138, 153, 231, 238, 261, 312, 313, 318, 356

D

Dailey, L., 7, 8, 255, 261, 283, 284, 286, 318
Dale, J., 200, 320, 358, 433, 454
Daleiden, E., 239, 262
Damon, L., 56, 357, 454
Darke, J., 426, 430
Darwin, M., 164, 167
Davis, D., 292, 293, 318
Davis, J., 78, 120, 163, 167, 267, 312, 313, 318, 320, 454
Davis, M., 127, 133
Deisher, R., 78, 119, 220, 261, 346, 356
Deniger, L., 336, 356
Dennis, C., 348, 349, 357
Dillon, M. S., 46, 56
Donovan, D., 29, 34, 132, 133
Doshay, L., 185, 199
Douvan, E., 53, 56
Droegemuller, W., 180, 182
Dunn, J. B., 42, 56
Dutton, C., 164, 167

E

Earls, C. M., 426, 430
Eck, B., 29, 35, 404
Ellis, A., 306, 318
Empey, L. T., 204, 209
Engel, T., 144, 154
Erickson, E. H., 26, 27, 28, 34
Esteve, J., 78, 120
Eth, S., 286, 318

F

Fagan, J., 78, 119
Farber, E. D., 12, 16, 184, 200
Farrell, K. J., 6, 8, 13, 16

Fay, J., 390, 402
Fehrenbach, P., 78, 119, 220, 261, 346, 356
Finkelhor, D., 11, 16, 31, 32, 34, 54, 56, 161, 167, 324, 364, 462, 473
Firestone, R., 122, 132, 133
Fisher, D., 132, 133
Fiske, J., 184, 188, 191, 199, 268, 319
Flanagan, B., 26, 34
Florian, V., 458, 474
Ford, C. S., 28, 34, 53, 56
Fowler, S. E., 50, 51, 52, 55
Freeman, A. M., 418, 430
Freeman-Longo, R., 26, 28, 170, 174, 175, 181, 182, 208, 209, 217, 267, 268, 318–319, 355, 405, 407, 416
Freeman-Longo, R. E., 15, 16, 34, 78, 90, 119, 137, 153, 183, 184, 188, 191, 199. *See also* Longo, R.
Freud, A., 34
Freud, S., 22, 23, 27, 28, 34, 48, 56
Friedman, R. C., 56
Friedman, R. J., 474
Friedrich, W., 52, 56, 323, 326, 356, 357, 433, 439, 454
Friedrich, W. N., 165, 167
Frye, M., 48, 57
Fryer, G. E., 6, 9, 11, 52, 57, 138, 154, 231, 255, 263, 283, 320, 346, 358

G

Gadpaille, W. J., 36, 56, 446, 454
Gagnon, J., 43, 48, 57
Galenson, E., 43, 45, 46, 47, 56, 57
Gardner, R. A., 47, 56
Gargaro, S., 203, 209
Gebhard, P. H., 48, 52, 56
Gendreau, P., 205, 209
Gessell, A., 49, 56
Giaretto, H., 31, 34
Gibat, C., 198, 200, 316, 320, 399, 403, 425, 430
Gil, E., 6, 8, 52, 56, 323, 326, 357, 375, 390, 402, 446, 454
Gilgun, J., 29, 34, 78, 119, 124, 129, 132, 133, 137, 153, 169, 171, 172, 175, 221, 246, 261, 269, 270, 319
Goldman, L.D.G., 37, 56

Goldman, R. I., 37, 56
Goodwin, D. W., 87, 119, 348, 349, 357
Grambsch, P., 56, 323, 326, 439, 454
Gray, A. S., 78, 119, 198, 199, 222, 223, 261, 268, 307, 317, 320, 322, 326, 334, 355, 357, 358. *See also* Stickkrod, A.
Gray, S., 165, 166, 222
Grayson J., 198, 199, 320, 357
Greer, J. G., 200, 358
Greer, S., 16
Greer, W. C., 417
Griffin, S., 321
Griffiths, D., 342, 357
Groth, A., 222, 261
Groth, A. N., 23–24, 26, 28, 32, 34, 75, 124, 134, 180, 182, 186, 199, 234, 422, 430
Groth, N., 34

H

Haaven, J., 342, 357
Hacker, S., 181
Hagler, S., 29, 35, 404
Haines, D., 426, 430
Hall, R., 448, 454
Halverson, H. M., 44, 45, 56
Hanson, K., 127, 132, 133, 134
Harding, M., 321
Hattendorf, K. W., 48, 56
Harris, G., 238, 256, 262
Harris, P. L., 40, 56
Hauch, P., 379, 403
Haynes, M., 198, 200, 342, 358
Haynes-Seman, C., 140, 153, 165, 167, 169, 175, 461, 473
Heinz, J., 201, 203, 209
Helfer, E., 75, 134, 135, 320
Hendrick, I., 40, 56
Henning, B., 239, 262
Hewitt, S., 56, 357, 454
Hilliker, D., 239, 262
Hindman, J., 157, 167, 336, 357
Hingsburger, D., 342, 357
Hiroto, D., 157, 167
Hobson, W., 186, 199
Hodkinson, S., 29, 35, 128, 132, 134, 221, 248, 319, 324, 358
Holstrom, L., 34
Honig, A. S., 39, 40, 41, 56

Horowitz, L. M., 29, 34
Horton, A. L., 175
Howells, K., 165, 167
Hucker, S., 15
Hudson, S., 35, 221, 248, 262, 263, 321
Hudson, S. M., 29, 35, 79, 120, 128, 132, 134, 135, 246, 317, 319, 324, 358
Hunter, J., 62, 75, 78, 87, 119, 137, 221, 238, 239, 261, 262, 269, 312, 313, 314, 318, 319, 348
Hunter, J. A., 319, 348, 349, 357
Hurlock, E. B., 41, 56

I

Ilg, F. L., 49, 56
Isaac, C., 6, 8, 78, 120, 163, 167, 267, 320, 325, 326, 357, 433, 454
Israel, E., 138, 140, 154

J

James, B., 286, 319
Jancin, B., 286, 319
Jenks, J., 241, 261
Johnson, B. L., 175
Johnson, C. F., 12, 16, 184, 200
Johnson, D. B., 49, 56
Johnson, R., 349, 357
Johnson, S., 78, 119, 267, 319
Johnson, T. C., 222, 262, 323, 326, 334, 346, 357, 449, 454. *See also* Cavanagh-Johnson, T.
Johnson, V. E., 57
Joseph, J. A., 12, 16, 184, 200
Junk, A., 433

K

Kaemingk, K., 87, 120, 269, 319
Kahn, T., 375, 403
Kahn, T. J., 78, 120
Kanner, L., 40, 47, 55
Kaplan, M., 33, 78, 87, 119, 120, 231, 238, 239, 261, 269, 283, 312, 313, 318, 319
Kaplan, M. F., 8
Kaplan, M. S., 138, 153, 313, 318
Kaplan, N., 29, 35

Kappel, S., 6, 9, 13, 16
Kashima, K. M., 79, 120
Kassees, J., 448, 454
Katz, M. M., 474
Kaufman, K., 239, 262
Kelley, K., 203, 209
Kennell, J. H., 39, 40, 56, 136, 153
Kempe, H., 180, 182
Kempe, R., 75, 134, 135, 320
Kerr, M., 6, 8, 13, 16, 198, 199, 222, 262, 346, 357
Kiell, N., 23, 34
Kinsey, A. C., 44, 48, 52, 56
Klaus, H. M., 39, 40, 56, 136, 153
Kline, D., 43, 48, 57
Knight, L., 29, 35, 75, 134, 320
Knight, R., 33, 35, 120, 154, 235, 258, 262, 320
Knight, R. A., 134
Knopp, F. H., 20, 34, 88, 120, 181, 182, 183, 187, 188, 199, 211, 214, 217, 346, 348, 357
Koplau, H., 131, 134, 460, 473
Koselka, M., 87, 120, 269, 319
Koverola, C., 56, 357
Kris, E., 34
Krugman, R. D., 6, 9, 11, 52, 57, 138, 140, 153, 154, 169, 175, 231, 255, 263, 283, 321, 346, 358, 438, 454, 462, 463, 473, 474
Kuiper, J., 323, 326, 357, 454

L

Lackey, L. B., 342, 346, 348, 357
Landry, S., 127, 134
Lane, S., 77, 78, 89, 93, 94, 120, 125, 163, 167, 183, 198, 200, 219, 263, 267, 319, 320, 322, 323, 355, 358, 454, 457, 464, 465, 466, 467, 474
Lang, R., 56, 57, 357
Langworthy, O. R., 38, 57
Lankester, D., 138, 142, 144, 153
Lanning, K. V., 32, 34
Larsen, N., 348, 349, 357
Law, S., 200, 233, 320, 358, 433, 438, 454
Laws, R., 150, 153
Lee, A., 33, 35
Lee, J. A., 36, 57

Levine, E. H., 44, 45, 55, 57
Levine, M. L., 43, 44, 57
Levinger, G., 41, 56, 57
Lewis, D., 283, 319
Lewis, D. O., 283, 319
Lewis, G. M., 48, 57
Lewis, W. C., 41, 57
Lexier, L. L., 348, 349, 357
Lichtenstein, E., 430
Lindstrom, B., 3, 29, 35, 134, 320
Little, R., 342, 357
Lobanov-Rostovsky, C., 322
Longo, R., 234
Longo, R. E., 62, 63, 75, 124, 134.
    See also Freeman-Longo, R. E.
Loredo, C., 186, 199, 222, 261,
    422, 430
Loss, P., 198, 200, 220, 222, 223,
    236, 263
Louden, K., 79, 120
Lowe, G., 78, 267, 355, 422, 430
Lucey, K., 186, 199
Lusigna, R., 79, 120

M

Maccoby, E. E., 44, 45, 55, 57
MacEachron, A., 169, 175, 461, 473
MacFarlane, K., 78, 119, 120, 198,
    200, 326, 334, 336, 356, 357
MacIntyre, D., 29, 34, 132, 133
Maclay, D. T., 185, 200
Maison, S., 348, 349, 357
Main, M., 29, 35
Malamuth, N., 269, 319
Maletzky, B., 284, 319
Mariatt, G., 430
Markey, O. B., 185, 200
Marlatt, G., 198, 200, 316, 320,
    399, 403, 425, 430
Marques, J., 198, 200, 316, 320,
    399, 403, 425, 430
Marshall, W., 35, 79, 120, 132, 134,
    135, 221, 246, 248, 262, 263,
    268, 269, 312, 319
Marshall, W. L., 29, 35, 78, 86, 120,
    128, 134, 319, 324, 358, 426,
    430
Martin, C. E., 44, 48, 52, 56
Martinson, F., 75
Martinson, F. M., 36, 40, 49, 52,
    53, 55, 57, 124, 133

Marvasti, J., 349, 358
Maslach, C., 458, 465, 474
Mason, J. M., 23, 35
Mathews, F., 197, 200, 206, 209
Mathews, R., 346, 347, 348, 349,
    358
Matthews, J., 348, 349, 358
McFadin, B., 62, 124, 134, 234
McGuire, R. J., 86, 120
McIntyre, T., 252, 262
McKibben, A., 79, 120
McMahon, R., 134, 430
Meinecke, C. F., 21, 34
Metzner, J. L., 6, 9, 11, 52, 57, 138,
    154, 173, 175, 231, 255, 263,
    283, 320, 346, 358
Meyer, B., 138, 142, 144, 153
Milloy, C. D., 428, 430
Mittelman, M. S., *xiii*, 15, 180, 181
Miyoshi, T. J., 6, 9, 11, 52, 57, 138,
    154, 231, 255, 263, 283, 320,
    346, 358, 438, 454, 461, 474
Moll, A., 49, 57
Monastersky, C., 78, 119, 220, 231,
    261, 263, 346, 356, 358
Money, J., 87, 120
Montague, A., 38, 57
Morris, C., 169, 175, 461, 473
Morris, L., 124, 134
Mosbacher, E., 34
Murphy, W., 26, 34, 198, 200
Murphy, W. D., 342, 358
Murray, M., 138, 154, 247, 262,
    334, 358
Myers, B. A., 341, 358

N

Nadar, R., 463
Newton, M., 42, 57
Nichols, F. L., 426, 430
Nimmo, D., 133

O

O'Brien, B., 6, 8, 13, 16
O'Brien, M., 138, 154, 198, 200,
    220, 222, 262, 467, 470, 474
O'Connor, B., 78, 120
O'Connor, K., 78, 119
O'Donnell, D., 321
O'Hyde, M., 390, 403

Oppenheimer, R., 165, 167
Oshins, L., 12, 16, 184, 200
Ostler, R., 48, 57

P

Palmer, R., 165, 167
Parrish, L., 386, 403
Patterson, S., 336, 358
Pavlov, I., 24, 25, 30, 35
Perlmutter, L., 144, 154
Peters, R., 127, 134
Petre-Miller, D., 342, 357
Pfeffer, A. Z., 185, 199
Phipps, A., 221, 262
Piaget, J., 26, 27, 28, 29, 35, 122,
    134
Pincus, J. H., 283, 319
Pines, M., 39, 57
Pitcher, E. G., 46, 49, 57
Pithers, B., 132, 134
Pithers, W., 198, 200, 268, 307,
    316, 317, 320, 399, 403, 425,
    430
Pithers, W. D., 79, 120, 323, 358
Poe-Yamagata, E., 11, 16, 206,
    210
Pollock, G., 75
Pomeroy, W. B., 44, 48, 52, 56
Pond, A., 128, 134, 341, 358
Ponparte, M., 34
Porter, E., 324, 358
Pouillet, T., 44, 57
Prelinger, E., 46, 49, 57
Prentky, R., 33, 35, 78, 120, 137,
    154, 221, 235, 239, 243, 246,
    258, 262, 269, 320
Prentky, R. A., 124, 134
Proulx, J., 79, 120
Pullen, C., 158, 167
Pynoos, M., 286, 318

Q

Quincey, L. L., 120
Quinsey, V., 124, 134, 238, 256,
    262, 312, 320, 342, 357

R

Ramsey, G. V., 51, 57
Rasmussen, L., 326, 358

Raush, H. L., 56, 57
Rawlings, L., 334, 356
Reich, J., 33, 312, 313, 318
Ricci, L., 433, 454
Rice, M., 238, 256, 262
Richards, M.P.M., 42, 56
Richart, R. M., 56
Richter, C., , 459, 474
Riis, J., 180, 182
Riophe, H., 43, 45, 46, 47, 56, 57
Roberts, E. J., 42, 43, 48, 57
Rogers, C., 12, 16
Rogers, E., 164, 167
Rogers, N., 323, 358
Rokous, F., 120, 134, 154, 262, 320
Rorty, A. O., 53, 57
Rosenberg, J., 183, 199, 214, 217
Rosenberg, R., 33, 35
Rosenfeld, A. A., 53, 57
Rosenthal, J., 13, 16
Ross, J., 78, 120, 198, 200, 220, 222, 223, 236, 263, 292, 320
Ross, R., 205, 209
Rossi, A., 41, 57
Rouleau, J., 33
Roundy, J., 175
Rowe, W. E., 428, 430
Rubin, T., 379, 403
Ruppel, H. J., 51, 57
Russell, A. B., 10, 16
Ryan, G., 3, 5, 6, 7, 8, 9, 10, 11, 16, 19, 29, 35, 52, 57, 59, 62, 75, 78, 87, 93, 120, 122, 124, 125, 134, 135, 136, 137, 138, 149, 153, 154, 157, 158, 162, 163, 164, 166, 167, 168, 173, 175, 179, 180, 181, 182, 198, 200, 201, 217, 231, 233, 249, 255, 263, 267, 269, 281, 282, 283, 284, 317, 320, 323, 326, 346, 358, 404, 405, 407, 416, 433, 438, 443, 446, 449, 450, 454, 457, 459, 461, 474

S

Sadock, B., 131, 134, 460, 473
Sager, C., 144, 154
Samenow, S., 29, 30, 35, 84, 88, 120, 130, 135, 136, 142, 148, 154, 171, 175, 187, 200, 306, 321, 458, 474

Sandau-Christopher, D., 200, 358, 433, 454
Sanford, L., 164, 167, 375, 390, 403
Santos, D., 78, 87, 119, 238, 239, 262, 312, 313, 314, 319
Schaffer, H. R., 56
Schram, D. D., 428, 430
Schvaneveldt, J. D., 48, 57
Scott, H., 127, 134
Scrub, B., 355
Sczechowicz, E., 284, 320–321
Sears, R. R., 44, 45, 55, 57
Segal, Z., 426, 430
Seligman, M., 458, 459, 460, 474
Sermabeikian, P., 308
Sgroi, S., 34
Shanok, S. S., 283, 319
Shelton, J., 458, 459, 474
Sheridan, P., 341, 359
Sholevar, G., 175
Shoor, M., 185, 200
Short, S., 29, 35, 404
Showers, J., 12, 16, 184, 200
Shrier, D., 349, 357
Sickmund, M., 11, 16, 206, 210
Siegert, R., 29, 35, 128, 132, 135, 246, 263, 317, 321
Silverman, E., 180, 182
Sims-Knight, J., 120, 134, 154, 262, 320
Singer, K., 308, 321, 355
Skinner, B. F., 24, 25, 30, 35
Smith, H., 138, 140, 154, 462, 470, 473
Smith, T., 267, 321
Smith, W., 78, 119, 220, 231, 261, 263, 346, 356
Snyder, H., 11, 16, 206, 210
Spaniol, L., 458, 459, 474
Speed, M. H., 185, 200
Speirs, V., 205, 210
Speitz, K., 348, 349, 358
Spencer, T., 286, 321
Spiegel, D., 286, 321
Spiro, M., 49, 57
Spitz, R. A., 45, 58
Steele, B. F., 28, 29, 35, 59, 62, 75, 76, 124, 127, 134, 135, 137, 154, 159, 180, 182, 248, 263, 320, 473
Steele, J., 125, 135
Steen, C., 222, 263

Stein, R., 78, 87, 119, 238, 261, 312, 312, 318
Stermac, L., 197, 200, 206, 209, 341, 359
Stevenson, W., 191, 199, 214, 217, 268, 319
Stevenson, W. F., 183, 184, 186
Stickrod, A., 78, 120, 267, 321. *See also* Gray, A.
Stoops, A. L., 341, 359
St. Pierre, J., 186, 199
Strachey, J., 34
Straus, H., 120, 134, 154, 262, 320
Strayhorn, J., 29, 35, 129, 135, 249, 263, 321, 415, 416
Strong, K., 198, 200, 448, 454
Stuart, I. R., 16, 200, 320, 358
Stuart, R., 34
Sugar, C., 185, 199
Summit, R., 158, 160, 161, 162, 167
Sundine, C., 200, 320, 358, 433, 454

T

Tardieu, A., 23, 35, 180, 182
Tartaglini, A., 283, 312, 318
Tate, J., 198, 200, 448, 454
Tenke, C. E., 283, 318
Terr, L., 163, 167, 286, 321
Teske, J., 200, 320, 358, 454
Thomas, A., 282, 321
Thomas, J., 146, 149, 151, 153, 154, 216, 218, 360, 405, 407, 408, 416
Timnick, L., 12, 16
Trainor, C. M., 10, 16
Tremaine, T., 12, 16
Trepper, T., 153, 318
Turecki, S., 283, 321
Turner, M. T., 194, 200, 348, 359
Turner, R., 78, 120
Turner, T., 194, 200, 348, 359

U

Urquiza, A. J., 162, 167, 326, 356, 433, 454

V

VanDerBur-Atler, M., 376, 403
van der Kolk, B., 21, 35, 255, 263, 286, 321
Van de Wiele, R. L., 56

W

Wagstaff, B., 158, 167
Walker, E., 6, 8, 323
Wallace, R., 198, 199, 222, 223, 261
Wand, S., 158, 167
Warberg, B., 239, 240, 261
Ward, T., 29, 35, 79, 120, 128, 132, 135, 246, 263, 317, 321
Warnath, C., 458, 459, 474
Wasserman, J., 6, 9, 13, 16
Waters, E., 34
Watson, R., 433, 454
Weber, F., 433, 454
Webster, C., 15, 181
Weher, F., 200, 320, 358
Wehman, B., 198, 200, 448
Weiner, I. B., 31, 35

Weiss, J., 164, 167
Weissberg, M., 33, 35, 125, 135
Welens, T., 321
Wenet, G., 198, 200, 202, 263
Wexler, S., 78, 119
Wheeler, J. R., 6, 9, 13, 16, 208, 210
Whipple, H., 125, 135
Whitaker, M., 122, 133, 135, 249, 263, 269, 321, 345, 355, 359
Widom, C. S., 62, 75, 137, 154
Williams, D., 175
Williams, D. C., 185, 199
Williams, L. M., 62, 75, 137, 154
Willock, B., 159, 167
Wilson, G., 125, 135, 430
Wolf, K. N., 45, 58
Wolfe, F., 349, 359
Wolfe, V., 56, 357

Wolfe, S., 78, 120
Wolff, P. H., 45, 58
Wyss, A., 198, 200, 448, 454

Y

Yager, J., 29, 35, 75, 134, 320, 404
Yates, A., 54, 58
Yochelson, S., 29, 30, 35, 84, 88, 120, 130, 135, 136, 142, 148, 154, 171, 175, 187, 200, 306, 321, 458, 474
Young, B. G., 86, 120

Z

Zamora, P., 77, 89, 93, 94, 120, 198, 200, 267, 319
Zaphiris, A., 31, 35

SUBJECT INDEX

A

Abandonment, 326; perceived, 70, 251, 348

Abuse, 123; behaviors of, 125, 131; of children, 137, 180; development of, 123; emotional, 123; neglect as, 62, 137; physical, 62, 120, 137, 138; and risk management strategies for prevention of, 405, 405–407. *See also* Sexual abuse

Abuse specific milieu, 404–416; goals in, 414, 416; programming for, 407

Abusiveness, 125, 127, 132, 138, 269, 277, 295

Accommodation and assimilation, 28, 30, 118, 130, 132, 161, 170, 172

Accountability, 31, 61, 127, 212, 241, 274, 280, 295, 297, 305, 316, 336, 350, 412, 418, 420, 425, 429

Affective reaction, 220, 240, 268, 273–274, 286, 289, 299, 327, 336, 340, 349, 366; self-awareness of, 244–245, 274, 289–290

Aftercare, 316, 401–402, 417–430; interagency cooperation in, 419, 420–421, 424, 426, 427, 428; risk factors monitored during, 418, 419, 420, 422, 425–426, 428, 429; supervision and monitoring during, 417, 418, 420, 421, 424, 425–426; transition from treatment to, 417, 419, 426–427

Aggression, 22–23, 310, 350, 411; in abuse behavior, 232, 235–236, 274, 350; paired with sexuality, 22

Alabama, 188

American Humane Association, 11, 15

Americans with Disabilities Act, 324

Anger, 98, 236, 273, 292, 332; style of managing, 254, 330, 377

Antisocial characteristics, 7, 30, 31, 350

Anxiety, 79, 81, 87, 96, 101, 142, 170, 171, 245, 295; reduction of, 80, 81, 84, 104

Arousal. *See* Sexual arousal

Assessment of sexually abusive youth, 219–261, 323, 326, 344, 422–424; collateral information in, 222, 227; consent for, 239, 242; developmental contextual aspects of, 242–256, 259–260, 323; identifying risk factors in, 242, 256–261, 282–287, 302–303, 308, 315, 326, 405, 407; identifying supervision needs in, 242, 256, 257–258, 260, 297, 303, 344–345; identifying treatment needs in, 258–261; interviewing in, 223–227; offense specific aspects of, 220, 225–242, 258–259; placement decisions in, 242, 257, 278, 297, 344, 350; preparation for, 222–225; purpose of, 219, 222; tests used in, 221, 310. *See also* Family assessment

Association for the Treatment of Sexual Abusers (ATSA), 239, 312, 317

Attachment, 29, 40, 132, 140, 142, 147, 246, 315, 323–324, 343;

disruption of, 221, 371; early, 248, 435; infant, 39–43, 45, 48, 435; interpersonal, 29, 39, 45, 50, 124, 128; maternal-infant bonding and, 39–41, 45; models of, 29, 277, 435

Attributions, 78; displacing blame in, 81, 100, 230; of responsibility, 81, 95, 124, 125–127, 227, 236, 414

Avoidance of problems, 91, 97

B

Behavioral: interventions, 25–26, 312–314, 317, 453; modification, 413–414, 444; reinforcement, 408–409

Bestiality, 113, 232, 348

Burnout, 457–473; agency intervention in, 457, 469–470; prevention of, 470–472; signs of, 462–469

C

California, 13, 188, 206; Department of Youth Authority in, 13, 419; San Francisco Aftercare Program in, 419, 420, 422, 425, 427; Support Program for Abuse Reactive Kids (SPARK) in, 346

Canada, 197, 206; Toronto in, 45, 206

Child abuse. *See* Abuse or Sexual abuse

Child protective agencies, 11, 323, 324

Children with sexual abuse behavior problems, 323–341; characteristics of, 326–333; identification of, 324, 326; responding to sexual behaviors of, 452; role of parents in treatment for, 333, 341, 452–453; treatment content for, 333–341

Coercion, 5, 6, 277, 296, 442

Cognitive, 299; development, 122; distortions, 30, 80, 83–84, 87–89, 147–148, 171, 225, 240, 288, 291; restructuring, 30, 148,

191, 274, 276–277, 290, 291, 300, 305–307, 312

Colorado: Closed Adolescent Treatment Center in, 77; Denver Children's Home in, 404; Department of Social Services in, 12, 324; Division of Youth Services in, 77, 186; Falcon Lodge, Griffith Center in, 404; Fort Logan Mental Health Center in, 404; Rocky Mountain News in, 438; RSA, Inc., in, 78; Synergy in, 404

Community: protection of, 150, 201, 202–203, 208, 212, 278, 419, 429; public awareness and education of, 434–437; safety of, 220, 256–258, 278, 410–411

Comprehensive service delivery: assumptions regarding, 211; day treatment in, 216; mixed populations in, 214–216; outpatient treatment in, 212; safety planning in, 216–217; secure facilities in, 212

Compulsive aspects, 30, 31, 89–90, 104, 118, 171, 255, 274, 302, 418, 419, 421

Concurrent diagnoses, 7, 221, 254–256, 283–284, 315–316, 324, 326–327; of attention deficit disorders, 255, 283, 286, 327; of conduct disorders, 30, 255; of depression, 254, 255, 286, 367; of dysthymia, 255, 286; of medical disorders, 255, 327; of neurological disorders, 21, 255, 286; of obsessive compulsive disorders, 255, 286; of posttraumatic stress disorder, 255, 283, 286; of psychiatric disorders, 21, 255, 283–287

Confidant: lack of, 246, 247

Confidentiality: issues, 219–220, 278–279, 295, 406; waiver of, 220, 279, 424

Confrontation, 279, 291–295, 375, 424–425; in assessment, 224, 230; group role in, 291; in treatment, 279, 291

Consent, 4–5, 49, 277–278, 296; evaluating, 4–5, 441; lack of, 3,

82; versus compliance, 5, 296, 441; versus cooperation, 5, 296, 441

Consequences, 173, 297; fear of, 220

Consistency: by care givers, 434, 443; in early life, 434

Continuum of care, 212–214, 405, 429; consistency of treatment in, 213–214, 421, 426; range of components in, 212–213, 417; specialized housing in, 214–215

Coping, 77, 93–94, 123, 129, 158, 243–245, 270, 271–272, 290, 324, 372; maladaptive style of, 33, 70, 78, 81, 83, 97, 101, 123, 125, 139, 142, 271–272, 290, 324, 372, 436, 460; sexualized style of, 62, 82, 140–141, 248–249; strategies for, 123, 125, 159, 162–163, 165, 244, 300, 338, 340, 459

Cotherapy, 288–289, 293, 334, 363, 393

Cross dressing, 114, 233

Culture, 85, 132, 252; meanings of sexual behaviors in, 24, 60, 252; norms of, 37, 50, 52, 53, 59, 60, 252

Cure: lack of, 180, 202, 304–304, 399, 417, 419

D

Defense mechanisms, 84, 92, 94, 118, 131–132, 227, 244, 291, 293, 306, 457, 459, 460, 462

Delinquency, 6, 327

Denial and minimization, 127, 220, 222, 288, 290, 293, 302, 308, 349, 366, 367, 368, 374–376, 418, 457; and intervention, 179, 230, 279, 325; of risk, 202, 367; types of, 227–230

Deterrence, 126, 208, 297, 307, 409; levels of, 443–444

Development, 122, 129, 269, 410; assets in, 123, 129–139, 371, 435; of child, 23, 128, 136, 270–271, 275–277, 324, 325, 351, 410; of competence, 29, 122, 128, 129, 147, 221, 305,

372; deficits in, 24, 74, 97, 123, 128, 129, 147, 148, 250–251, 269, 305, 324, 341, 372, 435; environmental effects on, 6, 25, 61–62, 124, 132, 248, 251, 252, 270–271, 326, 371; factors of, 6, 30, 38, 42, 62, 94, 122, 124, 137, 185, 246, 347, 372; history of, 61, 84–85, 94–95, 123, 124, 146–147, 158, 220, 248–249, 275, 289, 326, 340, 343, 347–348, 351, 366, 371, 372, 404, 421; life experience in, 6–7, 25, 28, 37, 42, 61, 84–85, 88, 89, 123, 129, 132, 146–147, 158, 220, 244, 248, 250–251, 268, 270–272, 282, 289, 298, 327–330, 343–344, 347–348; markers of, 23, 27, 128; pre-occupation with abuse, effects on, 172; risks factors in, 42, 129–130, 434–436; stages in, 27, 40, 159

Developmental-contextual approach, 29, 39, 122, 123, 132, 181, 248–249, 268, 269, 270–271, 282, 298, 326, 351, 404

Developmentally disabled youth, 341–346; characteristics of, 343–344; sexual abuse behaviors of, 342–343; treatment issues of, 259, 344–346

Deviancy, 23, 59–60, 122, 125, 128, 137, 268, 269; case studies of development of, 63–66, 66–70, 71–74; definition of, 59, 60; manifestations of, 170

Diagnostic and Statistical Manual of Mental Disorders (*DSM-IV*), 284

Differential diagnosis and treatment, 8, 33, 81–82, 119, 129, 133, 181, 222, 259, 270, 283, 287, 303, 409, 416

Disinhibition, 32–33, 235, 306

E

Education: of care givers, 152, 258, 344; of parents, 149, 257, 258, 323, 333, 364, 376, 379, 390, 435, 436, 449, 452–453; in

treatment, 187, 281, 289, 293, 294, 304–318

Empathy, 74, 127, 128, 132, 148, 225, 252–253, 274, 297, 307–308, 409; cues, 127, 253, 307, 434–435; developmental lack of, 74, 124, 125, 139, 147, 330, 376, 435–436; foresight, 409; function in group of, 289; modeling of, 62, 225, 280–281, 375, 377, 437, 444; in nurturing, 127, 128, 283, 434–435; versus sympathy, 127, 253, 297, 307; for victims, 166, 307

Equality, 4; differentials of, 4, 277, 441; evaluation of, 4, 441

Etiological theories, 19–33, 268; addictive, 30–31; attachment, 29; cognitive, 29–30; developmental, 26–28, 434–435; family systems, 31–32, 363, 364; integrative, 32–33; intrapsychic, 22–24; learning, 24–26; physiological, 20–22; psychosis, 20

Exhibitionism, 3, 113, 232, 237, 331, 348

Exploitation, 4, 113, 232, 310

F

Families of sexually abusive youth, 136–153, 245–246, 326, 360–402; affective qualities in, 139–140, 142, 147–148, 365, 370; attitudes in, 138, 370; characteristics of, 28, 54, 137–138, 187; conceptual typology of, 139–145; disclosure of abuse, impact on, 145, 174, 246, 365, 367, 375; disruption in, 62, 140, 326, 365; dynamics in, 30–31, 140–144, 314–315, 361, 368–369, 372; dysfunction in, 28, 31, 138, 140, 187, 368–369; influence on child's development, 136, 245, 314–315; quality of relationships in, 138, 140, 248, 347, 368; role in youth's treatment of, 145–151, 259, 275, 325, 333, 365, 371; roles in, 140, 143, 315, 360, 367; secrets in,

140, 142, 368, 380, 442; sexual dimension in, 2, 137, 140–141, 150, 169; strengths in, 145; supervision ability of, 149–151, 246

Families of victims, 165–166

Family assessment, 144, 245–246, 315, 362–372; of boundaries, 30, 143, 144, 246, 368, 371, 381; of parenting, 367; of perceptions of child's abusive behavior, 247, 370; of relationships, 246, 247–248, 368, 369, 371–372; of risk factors, 28, 246, 251, 361, 368–369, 371; of sexual attitudes, 31, 37, 246, 371, 382; of sexual dimension, 30–31, 54, 246, 251, 368, 371, 372

Family therapy, 152, 341, 360–402; comprehensive components of, 364; crisis of disclosure in, 365–367; goals of, 372, 373; meaning of, 360–362; multi-family groups, 377–389, 391–394; reconstruction and re-unification in, 395–399; termination from, 361, 399–400; therapist role in, 362–363, 365; treatment interventions in, 365–367, 372–389

Fantasies, 23, 46–47, 86, 102–105, 125, 232, 286, 300, 314; aggressive, 102; appropriate, 46–47, 86, 102; of children with sexual abuse behavior problems, 332; nonsexualized, 102, 300; sexualized, 102–104, 300; about sexually abusive behavior, 86, 103–105, 238, 302; of sexually abusive youth, 86, 102–105, 169–170, 238, 269, 302, 343, 349, 428; of young children, 46–48

Federal Bureau of Investigation (FBI), 16; Crime Index by, 11–12, 13, 14

Federal Office of Justice, 14

Female youth who sexually abuse: characteristics of, 347–348; sexual abuse behaviors of, 348–350, 389; underreporting of, 347

Fetish, 3, 113, 233, 348
Frottage, 3, 113, 232

G

Gallup survey, 11
Gender: identity, 70, 251, 311, 384;
    orientation, 251, 311, 384
"Grabbage," 113, 232
Grooming: of caretakers, 31, 332;
    of victims, 5, 108–109, 158,
    227, 302, 332, 349

H

Hands-off offenses, 3, 113, 232. *See
    also* Exhibitionism; Obscene
    communication; Voyeurism
Harassment, 113, 232, 235–236
Helplessness, 80, 84, 93, 96, 127,
    149, 270, 275, 289, 310, 324,
    327, 366
Honesty, 225; assessment of,
    240–242, 369
Hormonal factors, 20, 21–22

I

Impulse control: deficits in, 89
Intervention, 123, 185; goal ori-
    ented, 270, 287–288; historical
    overview of, 123, 179–181; ver-
    sus incarceration, 202, 203
Intimacy, 74, 123, 315; capacity for,
    39, 42, 45, 246, 466; deficits,
    124, 128, 330; locus of, 39; ma-
    ternal-child, 40–42, 45, 53
Isolation, 172, 246, 247, 258, 281,
    330, 343, 348, 411; and aliena-
    tion, 463; feeling of emptiness in,
    62, 124, 128, 172; interpersonal,
    124, 185; loneliness, 128, 246

J

Justifications, 87–89, 110–111, 172,
    308, 312, 332, 349

K

Kempe National Center for Preven-
    tion and Treatment of Child
    Abuse and Neglect, 137

L

Legal response to sexually abusive
    youth, 322, 372; changes in,
    11, 186, 201, 205; conviction
    rate of, 11, 14, 205; denial and
    minimization in, 202, 203, 204,
    206; disposition in, 206–208;
    diversion as a, 207; historic
    overview of, 204–206; incon-
    sistent response by, 206, 322;
    investigative role in, 206, 208;
    plea bargaining in, 186, 203;
    referral to adult court in,
    207
Locus-of-control, 96, 126–127, 142,
    253, 344
Low functioning. *See* Developmen-
    tally disabled youth

M

Maine, 206
Mandatory reporting, 202, 258,
    427, 446, 448; in child abuse
    laws, 10, 406; public notification
    and, 174, 208, 209, 258, 427;
    and registration, 173, 208–209,
    258, 427, 428
Masturbation, 274, 311, 349, 428;
    in adolescence, 447; by children,
    43–44, 46, 331, 438–440; com-
    pulsive, 255, 311, 314, 439;
    development of, 43–44, 45–46;
    excessive, 22; versus genital
    play, 43–46; as part of offense,
    86, 104, 114, 311; in preadoles-
    cence, 51; tension relief from,
    45, 46
Memories, 464
Michigan, 14, 206; Child Protective
    Services in, 14
Minnesota, 186, 188; Hennepin
    County Home School in, 186;
    Human Sexuality Program in
    the University of, 186, 202, 203;
    Program for Healthy Adoles-
    cent Sexual Expression
    (PHASE) in, 346
Motivation: for abusive behavior,
    22, 32; for treatment, 220; for
    work in this field, 461

N

National Adolescent Perpetrator
    Network (NAPN), 10, 194, 198,
    323
National Center on Child Abuse
    and Neglect (NCCAN), 10–11,
    16, 323
National Coalition on Television
    Violence, 150, 154
National Council of Juvenile and
    Family Court Judges, 204, 209
National Criminal Justice Informa-
    tion and Statistics Service, 310,
    320
National Institute of Mental
    Health, 346
National Task Force on Juvenile
    Sexual Offending, 5, 9, 22, 35,
    123, 134, 149, 154, 181, 182,
    198, 207, 211, 217, 220, 221,
    259, 262, 268, 278, 279, 287,
    313, 316, 320, 347, 350, 356,
    358, 396, 405, 416, 422, 424,
    438, 454
New Mexico, 188
New York: New York City in, 186,
    188

O

Objectification, 111, 128, 141, 235,
    308, 309, 310
Obscene communications, 3, 113,
    232, 348
Offender. *See* Sexually abusive youth
Offense. *See* Sexual abuse behavior
Ohio, 188, 206
Oregon, 13, 186, 188, 198, 206,
    346; Department of Family Ser-
    vices State Network in, 197;
    State Hospital in, 203

P

Paraphilias: multiple, 3, 22, 31, 231
Pedophilia, 62, 74–75; and fixated
    pedophile, 23–24, 27, 32, 124;
    four factor model of, 32; and
    regressed pedophile, 24, 27,
    32, 124; sexual interest in, 87,
    229

Perceptions, 87–88, 237, 247, 270–271; of self, 78, 81, 83, 84, 89, 93, 96, 97, 102, 108, 117, 160, 169, 235, 238, 251, 274, 288, 340

Perpetration prevention, 198, 269; definition of, 434; goals of, 434, 443; prevention of abusive behavior in, 434, 446–448; primary, 434–445, 449; primary, in adolescence, 446–448; primary, in childhood, 434–435; secondary, 434, 445–446, 450–454; victim interventions in, 445–446

Personalization, 87–88, 292, 308, 330

Perspective taking, 127, 253, 307

Pharmacology in treatment, 21, 284–285, 316; antitestosterone drugs, 21–22, 342

Phenomenology, 29, 122–133, 255, 269, 277, 283

Physician's Desk Reference (PDR), 284–286

Plethysmography, 239–240, 312–313, 342

Polygraphy, 15, 241–242, 424

Pornography, 109, 150–151, 227, 233, 251, 309, 310; use of nonsexual materials as, 233

Power and control, 78, 98, 100–102, 143, 165, 171, 223–224, 249, 279, 283, 292, 293, 305, 424; differential of, 3, 4, 108, 227, 257, 296, 324, 326, 341, 441; misuse of, 82–84, 271, 280, 292, 330, 369, 377–378; nonsexual expressions of, 83, 98, 100–102, 299; perceived lack of, 31, 84–85, 148, 171, 172, 187; retaliation, 98, 300, 306, 330; seeking of, 28, 40, 79, 81, 82–84, 100–102, 107–108, 127, 147, 162–163, 2240, 270, 281, 330, 349, 451; self-perceptions associated with, 83, 170; in sexual abuse, 105–115, 277, 308; sexualized expression of, 79, 83–84, 275; thrust, 83, 100–102, 163, 234–235, 305; unequal, 4, 296

Predicting risk, 124–125, 213, 256–257, 325, 350, 405, 409, 419–420, 428; dynamic variables, 126, 256, 302–303, 452; of dangerousness, 234, 235, 350; historical variables, 124–125, 256, 315, 441; of recidivism, 238, 308, 428; of reoffense, 234, 236, 238, 247, 253, 256–257, 302–303, 308, 315, 317, 428

Programs. *See* Comprehensive service delivery; Treatment programs

R

Racial disparity in incarceration, 205

Rape, 3, 113, 232, 233, 237, 348, 426

Recidivism, 213; versus reoffense, 428

Relapse, 133, 150, 317; prevention model, 110, 144, 307, 316–318, 399–400, 422, 425–426; risk factors indicating potential of, 229, 237, 242, 246, 247, 253, 281, 302–303, 317, 318, 400, 405, 425–426; strategies for prevention of, 191, 241, 243, 273, 278, 288, 290–291, 297, 303, 410, 417

Relationships, 29, 50, 53, 128, 246–248, 273, 277, 281, 288, 298, 306, 311, 348; effect of victimization on, 165, 298; empathic aspects of, 280–281, 434–435; quality of, in early life, 124; sexualized, 246; therapeutic, 277–281

Research, 21, 323; needs for, 20, 138–139, 187, 194, 198, 209, 325–326, 342, 429

Responsibility, 31–32, 305

Rituals, 114, 143, 233

Ritualistic, 114, 233

S

Safer Society Foundation, Inc. , 183, 194, 323, 342, 346, 348, 350

Safety plans, 222, 237, 242, 257, 258, 260, 281, 302–303, 341, 405–407

Self-concept, 4, 128, 169, 172, 252, 292, 317, 330; inadequacy in, 78, 80, 97, 118; low self-esteem in, 62, 81, 93, 117–118, 187, 291, 330, 339–340, 343; negative, 89, 93, 96, 101, 128, 171; view of others, effects on, 128

Sensory development: of infant, 37, 43–45; in utero, 37, 38–39, 371; of neonate, 37, 39–43, 434; of tactile responsiveness, 38, 48

Sex education, 311, 382, 391, 437

Sexual abuse: of children, 10–15, 23, 53–55, 231; definition of, 3, 83, 295–296, 431–433; extrafamilial, 11, 13; in history of client, 6, 26, 187; intrafamilial, 11, 13, 31, 53–54, 376, 385; multigenerational, 228, 233, 379–380; sibling incest, 11, 13, 31, 227, 234

Sexual abuse behavior, 372, 387, 388; age at onset of first, 234, 302; anticipated victim response; 106, 114, 236, 349; behavior type and range of, 7–8, 113, 231–233, 331; characteristics of, 3, 114, 242; decision to engage in, 20, 112, 234; definitions of, 3, 83, 231–233, 441–443; developmental factors contributing to development of, 6–7, 28, 29, 31, 61–62, 74–75, 84–85, 89, 93–95, 124, 220, 268, 269, 272, 323; disclosure prevention in, 114, 302; evaluation of, 3, 37, 225–242; frequency of, 22, 236–237; gratification of, 81, 84, 85–87, 90, 106, 234, 237–238, 274, 281; group affiliated, 233; habituated patterns of, 229, 234, 236; incidence of, 10–15, 342, 346–347; intent and motivation for, 240; location of, 109; modal, 6; multiple, 113, 231, 302; opportunity for, 109–110, 236, 237, 331–332; patterns of, 90, 230–242; planning for, 106,

228, 300, 332; prevalence, of, 10–15; progression in, 113, 185, 233–235, 273, 325; reinforcement of, 25, 79; repetition of, 79, 84, 89, 106, 117, 202, 237; risktaking in, 235, 237; self-reports of, 7, 15, 185, 247; setups for, 105–113, 300; underreporting of, 11, 184; victim selection for, 7, 106–108, 237, 302, 333

Sexual abuse cycle, 33, 77–119, 152, 221, 229, 244, 256, 267–268, 270–277, 286, 288, 324, 349, 405; adaptations of, 78, 327–329, 337, 345, 408, 451, 454; affective aspects of, 79, 80, 84, 93–94, 95, 96, 97, 100, 106, 112, 117, 273–274, 276; behavioral aspects of, 90, 100–101, 108–109, 114–115, 274–275; cognitive aspects of, 80, 81, 87–89, 91, 92, 93–94, 95–97, 101, 102, 103, 106, 108–109; compensatory aspects of, 78, 80, 83, 84–85, 88, 100–115, 170, 272, 281, 281, 324, 411; components, 79, 92, 99, 116; development of, 77–78, 246, 248–249, 269, 452; habituation in, 81, 100, 110, 234; historical elements in, 272–273, 302; interruption of, 77, 96, 98, 101, 119, 281, 289, 290–291, 300, 316, 327, 337–338; maladaptive coping response in, 81, 83, 90, 101, 105, 119, 408; progression of, 79, 80–81, 90, 286, 299, 300, 302; related research, 78, 79; situational elements of, 273; triggers of, 80–81, 93–95, 241, 243–244, 250, 273, 274–275, 276, 283, 291, 302; uses of, 81–82, 118–119, 289, 290–291, 298–303

Sexual Arousal, 54–55, 85–87, 238–240, 274, 331; antecedent to abuse behavior, 85, 86, 112; anticipatory, 86, 221, 237; assessment of, 237–240, 312; cognitions associated with, 86, 87, 104, 466; conditioning of, 25, 87; control of deviant patterns of, 312–314, 339; covert sensitization and, 312, 313–314, 339; development of, 26, 41, 42, 44–45, 86, 104, 239, 466; deviant, 26, 87, 104, 269, 312, 313; measurement of, 239; paired with stimuli, 25, 87, 104, 314; sexual interest and, 24, 85, 86, 238, 239, 240, 269; and sexually abusive youth, 87, 113–114, 170–171, 229, 238–239, 312–313, 338–339, 342, 349. *See also* Plethysmography

Sexual behavior, 19, 412; of adolescents, 447; of children, 37, 51–53, 54–55, 323, 330–331, 438–440; deviant, 19, 53–54, 408; evaluation of, 441–442; gratification of, 54, 269, 408; nondeviant, history of, 251–252; normative, 8, 19, 179, 251–252, 323, 330, 408, 438–440, 443, 447; responding to, 443–445, 448, 452–454

Sexual development, 24, 28, 36–53, 61; of adolescent, 37; of children, 37, 45–49, 431–440; genital exploration in, 43–44, 45–46, 47; genital response, 38, 42, 43, 44–45, 51–52; history, 251–252; identity in, 36, 42, 45, 311, 348; of infant, 37, 39–43, 43–45, 47; in utero, 37, 38–39, 371; lack of information during, 36, 37, of preadolescent, 37, 49–53; and puberty, 50

Sexual experience: distressing, 53–55, 465–466; early, 25, 52, 53–55

Sexual play, 49, 50, 52; exploration in, 438–440

Sexual harassment, 3, 113, 232

Sexuality, 61, 348, 382; capacity for, 24, 37, 38, 54–44, 437; development of, 24; deviant, 19; eroticism in, 37–38, 41, 42, 43–45, 46, 49–50, 54–55; eroticization of children and, 53–55; healthy, 437; normative, 19, 28

Sexually abusive youth: abusive experience of, 112, 127, 168–175, 277, 317; age at onset of behavior of, 185, 186, 231, 325; characteristics of, 6–7, 185; developmentally disabled, 322, 341–346; female, 194, 322, 346–350; identification of, 184; modal, 5–6; narcissistic orientation of, 170, 171, 305; normalization of abuse by, 169, 309; numbers of victims of, 6, 11, 12; preadolescent, 6, 14; stigmatization of, 168, 174, 258, 409–410, 427; superoptimism of, 111–112, 306; taxonomy of, 33, 258; typologies of, 32; urges experienced by, 89–90; victim stance orientation by, 83, 305; victimization history of, 6, 124, 268, 272, 291, 297, 310, 323, 397; violent, 322, 350–356

Social competencies, 49, 50–51, 83, 90, 101, 133, 187, 247, 248, 249–250, 300, 305, 306, 330, 340, 344

Society, 25, 61, 351; influences of, 24, 26, 85, 123, 309–310; myths in, 309–310, 347, 437; norms of, 19, 24, 36–37, 48, 53, 61, 169; taboos of, 10, 19, 30, 61, 123, 180, 238, 347, 427; view of abusers, 168, 180, 201–202, 206, 208, 268, 325, 347, 427; view of child sexuality, 36–37, 48, 53, 61, 124, 179–181, 185, 203, 325 437

Stalking, 108, 109

Stealing undergarments, 233

Substance abuse, 97, 112, 138, 164, 254, 255, 372, 387, 388, 410, 426

Suicide risk, 164, 241, 254. *See also* Assessment

Supervision, 242, 281, 288, 303, 413; by family, 399–400; after treatment, 208–209

T

Temperament traits, 249, 282–283

Thinking errors, 79, 88–89, 130, 148, 305, 306, 307

Trauma, 89; history of, 61–62, 250–251, 272, 291

Treatment intervention, 273, 274, 275, 287–318, 350; amenability for, 230, 253, 258, 259; assignments in, 295, 296–297, 298–299, 300, 302, 303, 304, 318, 335; communication about, 279, 281, 303, 345; developmental-contextual approach in, 268–270, 282–287, 295–303, 314–316, 418; eclectic approaches in, 290, 299; goal oriented interventions in, 270, 287–288, 295–318; groups in, 288–291, 334–335; history of prior, 253–254, 255; modalities in, 270, 288, 316, 334; offense specific approach in, 123, 269, 270, 278, 281, 287–288, 295–303, 418, 422; psychiatric aspects of, 284–287, 315–316; settings for, 288; techniques used in, 302; termination and, 318, 407; therapeutic relationship in, 268, 277–281, 292

Treatment programs for sexually abusive youth: approaches defined, 191–194; components of, 187–188; development of, 183–187; models of, 188–198, 404; networking by, 197; regional distribution of, 187–188

Trust, 247, 251, 279–281, 365

U

Uniform Data Collection System of the National Adolescent Perpetrator Network, 11, 137, 198

United States, 206; Department of Justice of the, 14, 205; Office of Education of the, 50

Utah Report on Juvenile Sex Offenders, 347, 359

V

Vermont, 206, 346; corrections services in, 13, 346; Department of Health in, 13; Department of Social Rehabilitation in, 13, 346; Treatment Program for Sexual Aggressors in, 399

Victim: advocacy of, 278, 362; awareness of impact to, 307, 308–309, 317; empathy for, 307–308; and perpetrator clarification sessions, 309, 396–398; protection for, 149, 256–258, 278, 419–420, 420–421

Victim experience of abuse: arousal in, 160; of betrayal, 159; confusion in, 160; in context of life experience, 158, 257; and damaged goods, 160; developmental stage and, 160; powerlessness in,

31, 157, 161, 162; and responsibility, 10; and secrecy, 161; sexual trauma in, 160

Victim impact, 10, 12, 37, 53–55, 62, 117, 145, 269, 307; and blocked memories, 12, 251; disassociation as a, 12, 162; and eating disorders, 164–165; learned helplessness and, 162; posttraumatic stress syndrome, 163; sexual dysfunction, 163

Victims: female, 12, 13, 14, 161–162, 348; male, 10, 12, 13, 14, 161–162, 348; numbers of, 10–15

Violent sexually abusive youth, 350–356

Voyeurism, 3, 113, 232, 237, 331, 348

Vulnerability, 158, 227, 237, 268, 273, 275, 289, 302, 457

W

Washington, 13–14, 188, 208; Adolescent Clinic, School of Medicine at the University of, 186, 346; Pierce County in, 13–14; Snohomish County in, 14, 208

Worldview, 87–88, 89, 91, 93, 122, 128, 130, 132, 136, 146–147, 158, 270, 305, 324, 361, 457, 465

Health Psychology
Through the Life Span

Health Psychology
Through the Life Span
Practice and Research Opportunities

Edited By

Robert J. Resnick
Ronald H. Rozensky

AMERICAN PSYCHOLOGICAL ASSOCIATION
WASHINGTON, DC

Published by the
American Psychological Association
750 First Street, NE
Washington, DC

Copies may be ordered from
APA Order Department
P.O. Box 92984
Washington, DC 20090-2984

In the United Kingdom and Europe, copies may be ordered from
American Psychological Association
3 Henrietta Street
Covent Garden
London WC2E 8LU
England

Typeset in Goudy by Innodata Corporation, Publishing Services Division, Hanover, MD

Printer: Automated Graphic Systems, Inc., White Plains, MD
Cover designer: Minker Design, Bethesda, MD
Technical/production editors: Liliana Riahi and Valerie Montenegro

Library of Congress Cataloging-in-Publication Data
Health psychology through the life span : practice and research
  opportunities / edited by Robert J. Resnick and Ronald H. Rozensky.
      p.   cm.
    Includes bibliographical references and index.
    ISBN 1-55798-378-X (cb : acid-free paper). — ISBN 1-55798-391-7 (pb :
  acid-free paper)
    1. Clinical health psychology.   I. Resnick, Robert J.
  II. Rozensky, Ronald H.
    [DNLM: 1. Preventive Psychiatry.   2. Health Promotion.   WM 31.5
  H434   1996]
  R726.7.H439   1996
  616.89—dc20
  DNLM/DLC
  for Library of Congress   96-41438
                                                                                    CIP

British Library Cataloguing-in-Publication Data
A CIP record is available from the British Library.

Printed in the United States of America
First edition

CONTENTS

List of Contributors ix

Foreword xi
  Jane E. Brody

Acknowledgments xvii

1. Introduction 1
   Robert J. Resnick and Ronald H. Rozensky

PART I: OVERVIEW

Part Introduction 9

2. Psychology as a Health Care Profession: Its Evolution
   and Future Directions 11
   Russ Newman and Geoffrey M. Reed

3. The New Structure of Health Care and a Role for
   Psychology 27
   Nicholas A. Cummings

4. A Life-Course Perspective on Physical and Psychological
   Health 39
   James S. Jackson

5. Aging, Health, and Behavior: The Interplay Between
   Basic and Applied Science 59
   Denise C. Park

6. A Proposal for an Expanded View of Health and
   Psychology: The Integration of Behavior and Health 77
   Cynthia D. Belar

PART II: PSYCHOLOGISTS IN PRIMARY CARE SETTINGS

Part Introduction 85

7. Psychologists as Primary Care Practitioners 89
   James H. Bray

8. Collaborative Practice: Psychologists and Internists 101
   Garland Y. DeNelsky

9. Psychologists and Pediatricians in Collaborative
   Practice 109
   Carolyn S. Schroeder

10. Behavioral Health Care in Primary Care Settings:
    Recognition and Treatment of Anxiety Disorders 133
    *David H. Barlow, Jonathan A. Lerner, and
    Jeanne Lawton Esler*

11. Catching Depression in Primary Care Physicians'
    Offices 149
    Lynn P. Rehm

12. Helping Physicians Make Useful Recommendations
    About Losing Weight 163
    Daniel S. Kirschenbaum

13. Substance Use Problems in Primary Care Medical
    Settings: Is There a Psychologist in the House? 177
    Bruce S. Liese, Belinda A. Vail, and Kimberly A. Seaton

14. Attention Deficit Hyperactivity Disorder and
    Learning Disabilities in the Pediatrician's Office 195
    Jan L. Culbertson

PART III: PSYCHOLOGISTS IN TERTIARY CARE SETTINGS

Part Introduction 211

15. Pediatric Oncology: Medical Crisis Intervention 213
    Gerald P. Koocher

16. Establishing a Role for Psychology in Respiratory
    Medicine 227
    Bruce G. Bender

17. The Role of Clinical Neuropsychology in the
    Assessment and Care of Persons With Alzheimer's
    Disease 239
    Alfred W. Kaszniak

18. Quality of Life and Adjustment in Renal Disease:
    A Health Psychology Perspective 265
    Petra Symister and Ronald Friend

19. Health Psychology and the Field of Urology 289
    Steven M. Tovian

20. Touch Therapies for Pain Management and Stress
    Reduction 313
    Tiffany M. Field

21. Treatment Adherence and Clinical Outcome:
    Can We Make a Difference? 323
    Jacqueline Dunbar-Jacob and Elizabeth A. Schlenk

**PART IV: PSYCHOLOGISTS IN DISEASE PREVENTION
AND HEALTH PROMOTION**

Part Introduction 347

22. African American Women, Their Families, and
    HIV/AIDS 349
    *Debra Greenwood, José Szapocznik, Scott McIntosh,
    Michael Antoni, Gail Ironson, Manuel Tejeda,
    Lavonda Clarington, Deanne Samuels, and Linda Sorhaindo*

23. Revolution in Health Promotion: Smoking Cessation
    as a Case Study 361
    James O. Prochaska

24. Reducing College Student Binge Drinking:
    A Harm-Reduction Approach 377
    G. Alan Marlatt

25. Strategies to Reduce the Risk of HIV Infection, Sexually
    Transmitted Diseases, and Pregnancy Among African
    American Adolescents 395
    John B. Jemmott III and Loretta Sweet Jemmott

PART V: PSYCHOLOGISTS AS HEALTH CARE PROVIDERS

Part Introduction 425

26. Expanding Roles in the Twenty-First Century 427
    Patrick H. DeLeon, William C. Howell, Russ Newman,
    Anita B. Brown, Gwendolyn Puryear Keita, and
    John L. Sexton

Index 455
About the Editors 463

CONTRIBUTORS

Michael Antoni, *University of Miami*
David H. Barlow, *Center for Anxiety and Related Disorders at Boston University*
Cynthia D. Belar, *University of Florida Health Science Center*
Bruce G. Bender, *National Jewish Center for Immunology and Respiratory Medicine*
James H. Bray, *Baylor College of Medicine*
Anita B. Brown, *U.S. Army*
Lavonda Clarington, *University of Miami*
Jan L. Culbertson, *University of Oklahoma Health Sciences Center*
Nicholas A. Cummings, *Foundation for Behavioral Health, Scottsdale, Arizona*
Patrick H. DeLeon, *U.S. Senate Staff*
Garland Y. (Gary) DeNelsky, *Cleveland Clinic Foundation, Cleveland, Ohio*
Jacqueline Dunbar-Jacob, *University of Pittsburgh*
Jeanne Lawton Esler, *Center for Anxiety and Related Disorders at Boston University*
Tiffany M. Field, *University of Miami School of Medicine*
Ronald Friend, *State University of New York at Stony Brook*
Debra Greenwood, *University of Miami*
William C. Howell, *American Psychological Association*
Gail Ironson, *University of Miami*

James S. Jackson, *University of Michigan*
John B. Jemmott III, *Princeton University*
Loretta Sweet Jemmott, *University of Pennsylvania*
Alfred W. Kaszniak, *University of Arizona–Tucson*
Gwendolyn Puryear Keita, *American Psychological Association*
Daniel S. Kirschenbaum, *Center for Behavioral Medicine,*
    Chicago, Illinois, and Northwestern University Medical School
Gerald P. Koocher, *Harvard Medical School*
Jonathan A. Lerner, *Center for Anxiety and Related Disorders at*
    Boston University
Bruce S. Liese, *University of Kansas Medical Center*
G. Alan Marlatt, *University of Washington*
Scott McIntosh, *University of Miami*
Russ Newman, *American Psychological Association*
Denise C. Park, *University of Michigan*
James O. Prochaska, *University of Rhode Island*
Geoffrey M. Reed, *American Psychological Association*
Lynn P. Rehm, *University of Houston*
Robert J. Resnick, *Randolph-Macon College (formerly of the*
    Health Sciences Center, Virginia Commonwealth University)
Ronald H. Rozensky, *Evanston Hospital and Northwestern University*
    Medical School
Deanne Samuels, *University of Miami*
Elizabeth A. Schlenk, *University of Pittsburgh*
Carolyn S. Schroeder, *Chapel Hill Pediatrics, Chapel Hill, North Carolina*
Kimberly A. Seaton, *University of Kansas Medical Center*
John L. Sexton, *U.S. Navy*
Linda Sorhaindo, *University of Miami*
Petra Symister, *State University of New York at Stony Brook*
José Szapocznik, *University of Miami*
Manuel Tejeda, *University of Miami*
Steven M. Tovian, *Evanston Hospital and Northwestern University*
    Medical School
Belinda A. Vail, *University of Kansas Medical Center*

FOREWORD

As any intelligent person can see from the changes that have already occurred in our health care system and the even more profound changes likely to occur in the not-too-distant future, every American will be increasingly obliged to take care of his or her own health. Medical care is likely to become harder and costlier to obtain, particularly for illnesses that are deemed to be self-inflicted.

It is likely that in the future there will be more and more triaging done in deciding who should—and who should not—undergo costly, heroic medical treatments in a desperate attempt to prolong life. Triaging may not be limited just to catastrophic measures like transplants or bypass surgery. It is possible that more commonplace treatments, such as drugs to lower cholesterol or to control asthma, will also be decided on the basis of who most deserves them. Chances are, people with self-inflicted ailments are going to find themselves increasingly out on a limb, medically speaking, while those who work the hardest to stay healthy get the most help from the medical profession. What would you do with an asthmatic who smokes two packs of cigarettes a day? Supply her with inhalants, hospitalize her for every breathing crisis, or insist that she first quit smoking?

It should be obvious to anyone involved directly or indirectly with medical care that most of the costly, chronic diseases that afflict Americans today are largely a consequence of how they live their lives: what and how much they eat, how they move their bodies, how they manage stress, whether they abuse alcohol or drugs or smoke cigarettes, and even whether they use seat belts. If you take an honest look at how Americans live, you might be forced to conclude that most have a death wish. Far worse, though, than dying is living longer while ill. Chronic, debilitating, and fun-robbing diseases tarnish far too many Americans' so-called golden years.

This, now, is the challenge facing psychologists in the late twentieth century and beyond: How to help people adopt and stick with lifestyle changes that foster continuing good health. We all can, if we choose to, achieve the goal established for humanity by the ancient Greeks: to die young—as late in life as possible.

We are unlikely to get much help from physicians, most of whom are not schooled in behavior modification. Psychologists have the largest role to play in improving the nation's health because psychologists are specialists in understanding behavior and how to change it. Psychologists probably know better than any health professional how to get inside a person's mind, how to change attitudes from helpless and hopeless to the determined optimism of *The Little Engine That Could.* Self-belief is the essential foundation for action.

Cigarette smoking is a good example. Nicotine is an addictive drug, and smoking is an addictive behavior. The use of tobacco is the single most health-damaging and costly habit in America today. But it is more than just health robbing, life shortening, and expensive. Many people find it to be disgusting and antisocial. If you walk the streets of any metropolitan area during working hours, you would think there's been an explosion of prostitution in America. In nearly every doorway, there are young women standing around puffing on cigarettes.

We will make little or no progress in curbing this noxious behavior without the input of psychological principles and techniques, first, to help convince people that they can quit; next, to inspire them to want to quit; then, to help them actually quit; and, finally, to help them repeat the process if they should backslide.

Smokers persist in their habit because it makes them feel better immediately. To quit, it helps to focus on the immediate benefits of becoming a former smoker. These include loss of odor from hair, clothes, house, car, and breath; increased stamina and reduced fatigue; relief from that nagging, chronic cough and coughed-up phlegm; greater resistance to respiratory infections like colds and flu (not just for the smoker who quits but also for the smoker's family and coworkers); and money saved. I know one former smoker who put the money she used to spend on cigarettes into a piggy bank. Before she knew it, she had saved enough to take a trip to Europe!

The same applies to other health-promoting habits: eating properly, exercising regularly, and controlling stress. I think the secret to progress in these areas is to dwell not on long-term benefits, but on the immediate rewards of a healthier lifestyle. These rewards include looking better, feeling better, having more energy, becoming more productive, and being a nicer person to live with and work with.

Of course, before one can help others achieve these goals, he or she would do well to set a good example by adopting a healthier lifestyle. I hear two common complaints about living healthfully. One is, "I don't have time"; the other is, "A healthy life really isn't any longer, it just seems that way." I submit that neither of these excuses has any real validity. I and millions of others like me have proved that a healthy life is not a life of deprivation and self-denial. Rather, it is a full, satisfying, and enjoyable life, filled with delicious, belly-filling foods, pleasurable activities, and rewarding work, with ample time left for rest and relaxation.

I never say "never." The hallmarks of a successful, healthful diet are moderation, not deprivation; variety, not limitation; and gradual, evolutionary change, not revolution. Revolutions only inspire counter-revolutions. I advise people to change just 1 meal a week. Assuming that most people eat 15 to 21 meals a week, within just 4 months, they will be eating significantly better. And they will be far less likely to miss eating the old way and less apt to fall back into their former, disease-promoting habits.

The best way to convince people that exercise is worth the effort is to focus on the immediate rewards of becoming physically active: more energy, greater productivity, improved appearance, higher self-esteem, less stress, and less depression. Exercise doesn't take time, it makes time, by making one a more efficient person, able to accomplish more in less time with less fatigue. Plus, a person can then eat more! Not only does exercise use extra calories while one exercises, but it also increases caloric burn after one stops exercising. Exercise helps a person shed body fat and put on lean muscle tissue. Pound for pound, muscle uses far more calories than fat does. So one can eat more without gaining or can lose weight without going on a diet. Also, pound for pound, muscle tissue takes up less room than fat tissue does, so even if a person does not lose an ounce, she or he will lose inches and sizes by becoming well-muscled instead of well-fatted.

Of course, psychologists do not have to be told about the value of physical activity in countering depression, the emotional epidemic of the late twentieth century. I know a number of therapists who decline to treat depression unless the patient agrees to participate in a regular exercise program. Physical activity helped my husband not only in quitting smoking, and, I might add, quitting without gaining a significant amount of weight, but also in overcoming depression. If more people reached for their running shoes instead of the cookie jar when they felt in need of a lift, there would be far fewer overweight, unhappy people in this country.

Perhaps from the perspective of a psychologist, the most critical aspect of a healthful life is stress management. Regular physical activity has helped me change from a Type A person to a Type A minus! I might like to be a Type B, but it's just not my style. However, Type A minus is a lot better than Type A. Whereas I used to allow 15 minutes to get someplace that took 20 minutes to get to—always trying to do one more thing before I left and being late and anxious even before I started out—I now allow 30 minutes instead. That way, if anything occurs en route to delay me, I will still most likely arrive on time. And if the delay is great enough to make me late, I can say to myself, "It's not my fault. I did everything reasonable to get there when I was supposed to." And that little message to myself can almost always avert a health-damaging stress reaction.

People also must learn to put distressing matters into perspective. Medical evidence strongly indicates that it is not so much the major stressors like death and divorce that are health robbing. It is, rather, how people react to nitty-gritty everyday annoyances that wears down their body's ability to resist disease. I have, for the most part, learned that when things go wrong, I try to fix what I can fix, and if it is something out of my control, I seek a way around it or try to ignore it. Currently, far too many Americans use cigarettes, alcohol, and drugs to help control stress and, in the process, undermine their health even more than the damage caused by the stress itself.

A final thought: Many people are very fatalistic about their health. In former times, they might have said, "It's all in the cards," suggesting that their medical fate is predetermined. Today they say, "It's all in my genes, and there's nothing I can do about it." At this point, at least, changing one's potentially health-robbing genes is not a readily available option, although in the not-too-distant future, it may become a reality for more and more people. For now, it is important to remember that the vast majority of unhealthy genes do not predict certain doom. Rather, they establish a predisposition. Predispositions need a conducive environment in which to express themselves. If you do not give your unhealthy genes a chance to act, they may never do their dirty work, at least not before you are good and ready to depart this world. A "bad" family medical history should not be considered a portent of doom. Rather, it should be welcomed as an opportunity to do whatever you can to keep those nasty genes from ever expressing themselves.

Psychologists have the tools to help people realize that opportunity. Now, go to it!

JANE E. BRODY
Personal Health columnist
The New York Times

ACKNOWLEDGMENTS

We would like to thank the following people, whose hard work helped to make this volume possible: Drs. Norman B. Anderson, Thomas J. Boll, James H. Bray, Sandra Haber, Jean Kristeller, Alan I. Leshner, Ruby Takanishi, and Diane J. Willis, as well as Jane E. Brody, William Coltellaro, Joanne Zaslow, Judy Strassburger, Mayella Valero, and Liz Kaplinski.

1

INTRODUCTION

ROBERT J. RESNICK and RONALD H. ROZENSKY

> Disease is not the accident of the individual, nor even of the genera-
> tion, but of life itself. In some form, and to some degree or other,
> it is one of the permanent conditions of life.
>
> *Henry David Thoreau*

Across the life span, in all developmental stages, we must face challenges to our health and our well-being. These personal challenges can include ensuring a healthy lifestyle or can be a direct reaction to the demands of coping with illness. As a profession, psychology has long been in the forefront of the scientific inquiry into the understanding of health and heath care, as well as the treatment of those suffering from acute illnesses and chronic or terminal disease.

The decade of the 1990s began with a call to psychologists to become involved in both psychological health care practice and scientific investigation beyond our traditional role as experts in mental health. VandenBos, DeLeon, and Belar (1991) stated that psychology "must be viewed, at a minimum, as a physical health *and* mental health profession—or in short, as a health profession" (p. 444). From a health policy standpoint, DeLeon (1991) highlighted the importance of psychology becoming clearly seen as a health care profession with his reminder that health and well-being are still equated with medicine and physicians and, thus, allocation of funding for clinical training, research, and even direct services will tend to go in the direction of those professions identified with health. Reviewing the trends in the field, DeLeon (1991)

1

noted that "psychology's survival (and astonishing growth) within medical settings has very significant ramifications for all elements of the profession and shows very good promise for our probable future" (p. 616).

COLLABORATIVE PRACTICE AND HEALTH PSYCHOLOGY

In answer to this challenge of professional redefinition and identity, Newman and Rozensky (1995) pointed out that "psychologists have functioned as *de facto* primary care providers during a sizable part of our discipline's history" (p. 3). Supporting this point, Bray and Rogers (1995) detailed a collaborative practice model for psychologists and physicians in primary care medicine, whereas Morris and Barron (1996) pointed out that for decades, in rural America, psychologists have been involved with primary health care. Psychologists have come to increasingly see primary care physicians as allies. Pace, Chaney, Mullins, and Olson (1995) described how "primary care physicians have access to patients in need of psychological services and are concerned for the health and welfare of these patients" (p. 129). By maintaining appropriate communications, educating physicians about psychological services, and focusing on a problem-oriented method of consultation (Pace et al., 1995), the psychologist can enhance coordination of services in the primary care medical setting. This certainly benefits the patient and his or her family, as well as enhancing the viability of, and visibility of, psychology as a health care profession.

McDaniel (1995) reminded us that much can be done to heal the mind–body split in the day-to-day practice of health care, even though the Cartesian view of the separate mind and body "remains dominant in our society today" (p. 117), both philosophically and in clinical practice. Melamed (1995) looked to researchers, as well, to help heal this duality by asking the "biomedical and psychological research communities to gather indices of each other's spheres of interest so that causal relationships can be examined" (p. 230). Carr (1996) challenged psychologists to not perpetuate the mind–body segregation and to help physicians, through their medical education, bridge the gap between biological and psychological functioning.

Matarazzo (1994) pointed to this bridge, noting that "after a century of benign neglect, physicians and psychologists have rediscovered a common ground in the arena labeled health and behavior" (p. 7). Illustrating this growth in collaborative practice between medicine and psychology, Siegel (1995) reported that "psychologists in medical settings are no longer housed exclusively within departments of psychiatry or psychiatric units. Instead, they are associated with almost every medical subspecialty that is present in health care settings" (p. 342). Furthermore, Holloway

(1995) and Liese, Shepherd, Cameron, and Ojeleye (1995) described how psychologists actually have shaped the practice of clinical medicine as faculty members in formal educational programming for physicians in medical schools and residencies. Reflecting this foothold in health care settings, in 1993, almost 35% of psychologists who paid the American Psychological Association special assessment identified themselves as engaged in full- or part-time practice in hospitals, clinics, or medical–psychological group practices (American Psychological Association Office of Demographic, Employment, and Educational Research, 1993).

In 1995, there were 65 identified doctoral training programs in health psychology (American Psychological Association Division of Health Psychology, 1995). In 1995, 327 of the 525 accredited internship sites had a rotation in behavioral medicine or health psychology (J. Kahout, personal communication, January 18, 1996). Additionally, the number of postdoctoral training opportunities in health psychology is approaching 600 (A. Wiens, personal communication, January 18, 1996). Relevant divisions within the American Psychological Association—for example, Health Psychology, Neuropsychology, and Rehabilitation Psychology—have enjoyed substantial growth in the 1990s, again reflecting broad interest in psychological health care. Dorken, Stapp, and VandenBos (1986) reported that in the decade prior to their report, there was a 125% increase in the number of psychologists who practice in health care settings. Clearly, the integration of mind–body, of psychology and health, has been occurring and is continuing to occur not only in training sites but in employment settings as well.

ORGANIZATION OF THIS TEXT

Frank and Ross (1995) reminded us that "emerging health care delivery systems require a professional psychologist who has broad skills to treat health problems" (p. 524). Toward that end, the 1995 Presidential Miniconvention, "To Your Health: Psychology Through the Life Span," held as part of the 103rd Annual Convention of the American Psychological Association, brought together over 60 psychologists with expertise in various aspects of life span development, health, illness, and behavior. Discussion ranged from prevention of illness to health care solutions, from psychologists working alongside primary care physicians to the broad scope of practice of psychologists found in tertiary care facilities, from psychologists treating medically ill children to the practice of geriatric psychology. The excellent attendance and active participation of attendees during this 3-day event again speak to the interest and importance of psychologists' roles in all areas of health care.

This book was inspired by the exciting discussions that took place during the Miniconvention. The major purpose of this book is to provide the reader with a survey of clinical and scientific issues across a wide range of practice and research topics in health care. It offers a variety of approaches and perspectives from research-based clinical programs to scientific challenges, to help clarify basic and applied health care problems; from clinically based health care programs and strong opinions on present-day issues of care to future trends in health care and the evolution of psychology from a mental health field to a profession that addresses the full spectrum of health care concerns.

The practicing health psychologist should find a useful review of primary and tertiary care treatment and research areas within the context of a developmental or life span approach to health. The practicing clinical psychologist who wishes to begin to explore expanding practice opportunities into health care will find a survey of topics that highlights the depth of knowledge necessary to successfully and ethically expand her or his scope of practice with medically ill patients and their families. The student, intern, or postdoctoral fellow will be able to explore a wide range of practice and research opportunities that will help shape their educational goals and training experiences, as well as help clarify issues related to career choices and direction. Readers of this text who work exclusively in the realm of research will have the opportunity to read about those clinical challenges in search of research answers as well as research topics in need of further study.

Beyond this introduction, the book is divided into five sections. Part I: Overview presents a discussion of the evolution and future directions of the field of psychology as a health care discipline, not just a mental health profession. This section of the book focuses on a life-course perspective while attending to the realities of the changes in health care financing. Part II: Psychologists in Primary Care Settings provides eight chapters that first describe the concepts of collaborative practice and the practical issues psychologists should address when practicing with physicians in medical settings. Prevalent health care issues in primary care—such as anxiety, depression, weight control, substance abuse, and attention deficit hyperactivity disorder—are discussed by experts in those fields, who offer the reader both clinical and scientific reviews of those topics, along with practical, clinical programming suggestions. Part III: Psychologists in Tertiary Care Settings highlights seven of the areas of clinical care in which psychologists are making substantial contributions to the scientific and clinical understanding, as well as treatment, of long-term illnesses. Experts in such clinical areas as pediatric oncology, respiratory medicine, Alzheimer's disease, renal disease, urological diseases, pain and stress management, and compliance to treatment offer a picture of both the wide range of services provided by psychologists and the scientific knowledge supporting that practice. In the four chapters in Part IV: Psychologists in Disease Prevention and Health Promotion, the clinical and research activities of psychologists in enhancing healthy lifestyles are presented. Experts in smoking cessation, reduction of binge drinking, teen pregnancy prevention, and HIV/AIDS and sexually transmitted disease reduction present the reader with answers to present-day problems. Finally, in Part V: Psychologists as Health Care Providers, the reader is challenged to approach psychology from a public policy vantage point, for the betterment of both society and our profession. Leaders in practice, science, and education offer comments to help direct psychology's continued evolution as a health care profession.

REFERENCES

American Psychological Association, Division of Health Psychology. (1995). *Doctoral training programs in health psychology* (3rd ed.). Washington, DC: Author.

Bray, J. H., & Rogers, J. C. (1995). Linking psychologists and family physicians for collaborative practice. *Professional Psychology: Research and Practice, 26*, 132–138.

Carr, J. E. (1996). Psychology and mind–body segregation: Are we part of the problem? *Journal of Clinical Psychology in Medical Settings*, 141–144.

DeLeon, P. H. (1991). Afterword. In J. J. Sweet, R. H. Rozensky, & S. M. Tovian (Eds.), *Handbook of clinical psychology in medical settings* (pp. 615–618). New York: Plenum.

Dorken, H., Stapp, J., & VandenBos, G. (1986). Licensed psychologists: A decade of major growth. In H. Dorken & associates (Eds.), *Professional psychology in transition: Meeting today's challenges* (pp. 3–19). San Francisco: Jossey-Bass.

Frank, R. G., & Ross, M. J. (1995). The changing workforce: The role of health psychology. *Health Psychology, 14*, 519–525.

Holloway, R. L. (1995). Building a primary care discipline: Notes from a psychologist in family medicine. *Journal of Clinical Psychology in Medical Settings, 2*, 7–20.

Liese, B. S., Shepherd, D. D., Cameron, C. L., & Ojeleye, A. E. (1995). Teaching psychological knowledge and skills to family physicians. *Journal of Clinical Psychology in Medical Settings, 2*, 21–38.

Matarazzo, J. D. (1994). Health and behavior: The coming together of science and practice in psychology and medicine after a century of benign neglect. *Journal of Clinical Psychology in Medical Settings, 1*, 7–40.

McDaniel, S. H. (1995). Collaboration between psychologists and family physicians: Implementing the biopsychosocial model. *Professional Psychology: Research and Practice, 26,* 117–122.

Melamed, B. G. (1995). The interface between physical and mental disorders: The need to dismantle the biopsychosocialneuroimmunological model of disease. *Journal of Clinical Psychology in Medical Settings, 2,* 225–231.

Morris, J. A., & Barron, J. (Eds.). (1996). *Rural hospital primer for psychologists.* Washington, DC: American Psychological Association.

Newman, R., & Rozensky, R. (1995). Psychology and primary care: Evolving traditions. *Journal of Clinical Psychology in Medical Settings, 2,* 2–6.

Pace, T. M., Chaney, J. M., Mullins, L. L., & Olson, R. A. (1995). Psychology consultation with primary care physicians: Obstacles and opportunities in the medical setting. *Professional Psychology: Research and Practice, 26,* 123–131.

Siegel, L. J. (1995). What will be the role of psychology in health care settings of the future? *Professional Psychology: Research and Practice, 26,* 341–365.

VandenBos, G. R., DeLeon, P. H., & Belar, C. D. (1991). How many psychologists are needed? It's too early to know! *Professional Psychology: Research and Practice, 22,* 441–448.

I

OVERVIEW

INTRODUCTION

Health care is changing, driven by improved clinical techniques that are based on a growth in scientific inquiry into health and wellness as well as spurred on by dramatic shifts in health care financing. Psychology, as a major health care field, is being influenced greatly by, as well as helping to shape, these changes. The overview section of this book is designed to set the stage for the following chapters, which focus on specific clinical or research topics that relate to psychology's place in the overall health care enterprise.

Four major themes are set forth in this section. The first is that the profession of psychology is evolving into a true health care profession, and the Cartesian mind–body split will have limited utility in any comprehensive understanding of health or health care. The second theme is that, in regard to both wellness and illness, a life-course perspective that focuses on all developmental stages of human growth and health is a key in building that comprehensive understanding. The third theme is that the balanced approach to building that comprehensive knowledge base should be founded on the interplay between scientific and clinical practice. This interaction not only defines psychology but also makes it a powerful profession in shaping the health care field. The final theme is that no matter how sound the clinical practice or scientific knowledge base, there are both political and financial realities that any psychologist must attend to in order to keep the field and his or her practice or research opportunities viable.

In chapter 2, "Psychology as a Health Care Profession: Its Evolution and Future Directions," Russ Newman and Geoffrey M. Reed look briefly at our field's evolution as a health care profession and the economic forces influencing clinical practice. They then provide an optimistic, visionary depiction of the strong future role psychologists will being taking as primary care professionals. On the basis of the profession's successful history of advocating for mental health care, Newman and Reed describe psychology's transition in defining itself as a (primary) health care discipline, a task that will be difficult, necessary, and ultimately successful.

From a more somber, business-oriented, vantage point, Nicholas A. Cummings, a pioneer in managed behavioral health care, details his view that psychology lost its opportunity to control managed care in the 1980s, in chapter 3, "The New Structure of Health Care and a Role for Psychology." However, he believes that in the near future, through the building of megaprovider organizations, those practitioners who are most adaptable to changes in both financial incentives and practice patterns will regain control of health care.

In chapter 4, "A Life-Course Perspective on Physical and Psychological Health," James S. Jackson presents a new perspective on health, which takes the patient's life course and development into consideration. The author uses minority life-course issues to illustrate his overall appeal for a scientific understanding of how the economic, social, and psychological lives of all individuals are understood and explained in the context of a historical context, structural disadvantages in the environment, and blocked mobility opportunities.

In chapter 5, "Aging, Health, and Behavior: The Interplay Between Basic and Applied Science," Denise C. Park clearly illustrates how basic and applied science evolve together with significant utility for both the scientist and practitioner. This chapter heightens the reader's awareness of some of the issues surrounding our aging population. The author focuses on her own scientific work on the psychosocial and cognitive components of medication adherence in older adults, emphasizing how behavioral science can maintain health and vitality into later life.

Cynthia D. Belar, in chapter 6, "A Proposal for an Expanded View of Health and Psychology: The Integration of Behavior and Health," completes the overview by reiterating and expanding on data, perspectives, and information presented in earlier chapters. She challenges the reader to look at the integration of mind and body and avoid any separation of behavioral health from health in general. This then prepares the reader to take an expanded view of the role of both psychological principles and the roles of psychologists in all areas of health care. This chapter forms a natural stepping-off point to look at the role of psychology in primary care, tertiary care, and prevention and wellness.

2

PSYCHOLOGY AS A HEALTH CARE PROFESSION: ITS EVOLUTION AND FUTURE DIRECTIONS

RUSS NEWMAN and GEOFFREY M. REED

In this chapter, we examine the ways in which health care and health care policy in the United States have changed over time. We look at how psychology has responded, in turn, shaping the system. We consider the implications of this history for the current and future direction of psychology as a field and for individual practitioners. This chapter is not intended as a history of how our body of knowledge and clinical skills have evolved over time and now apply to various aspects of health care, topics well covered in other chapters of this book. Rather, our intention is to illuminate the current status of psychology as an evolving health care profession, by examining some of the forces acting on it, and to consider the implications for the future path of our profession.

PSYCHOLOGY AND MENTAL HEALTH POLICY

As has been both pragmatic and appropriate, policy development, to date, in the field of psychology has focused primarily on mental health.

Before the mid-twentieth century, mental health policy had been seen as a state issue and a welfare issue (Kiesler, 1992). Federal policy focusing on mental health began to develop with the establishment of the National Institute of Mental Health (NIMH) in the late 1940s and the Joint Commission on Mental Health and Illness in the 1950s. It was not until the passage of the Community Mental Health Centers Act of 1963, however, that mental health policy was separated from state mental hospitals. This legislation was intended to make mental health care readily available to all Americans through community-based clinics. It made the community mental health system and NIMH the primary players in mental health policy. This lasted until 1981, when the Omnibus Budget Reconciliation Act effectively eliminated both the federal government's commitment to a formal community mental health system and the NIMH role in mental health service delivery.

Perhaps the ultimate achievement of mental health advocacy was the inclusion of mental health in both Medicare and Medicaid legislation passed in 1965. Largely based on this precedent, efforts to gain recognition and reimbursement for mental health services from private insurance carriers were quite successful during the 1960s and 1970s (Cummings & VandenBos, 1983). Mental health services were also included in the Health Maintenance Organization (HMO) Act of 1973. To qualify for federal subsidies, HMOs were required to offer outpatient mental health services, crisis intervention services, and drug and alcohol abuse treatment (DeLeon, VandenBos, & Bulatao, 1991). This has become increasingly important for psychology as progressively larger proportions of the private insurance market and the Medicare and Medicaid populations have been shifted to HMO-based care.

Pursuing the strategy of advocating for, and attempting to exercise influence in, the area of mental health policy has made sense for psychology. As a young and developing profession, psychology's strongest case for inclusion in service delivery could be made in the area of mental health; and we were able to make it quite successfully. However, in this chapter, we argue that to view our development and influence as a mental health care profession as the end goal for psychology will ultimately be unnecessarily limiting. For example, although the inclusion of psychologists in mental health services is well established under Medicare, only 3% of Medicare funding is spent for mental health services (Kiesler, 1992). Although the diagnosis and treatment of mental illness is a centrally important undertaking that must remain an integral component of psychology, we suggest that our self-conception as a mental health profession should be viewed as but a step on the way to much broader involvement and influence.

The next step is to develop patterns of practice, marketplace activity, and supporting policy that position psychology as a true health care profession. This will, no doubt, be a difficult transition, both within and outside the profession. Yet, this step is critical to the continued growth—if not survival—of psychology at a time when health care is becoming increasingly integrated and a past emphasis on specialty care is being replaced with an emphasis on primary care. This step will challenge psychologists "to look beyond diagnostic categories and disciplinary boundaries, beyond the dysfunctional distinction between mind and body, and beyond traditional psychotherapeutic interventions" (Friedman, Sobel, Myers, Caudill, & Benson, 1995, p. 509). Only by doing so will psychology be able to have a voice in how to most effectively and efficiently provide services in the presently evolving health care system.

A BRIEF HISTORY OF HEALTH CARE

VandenBos (1993) provided a history of the health care system in the United States. As he indicated, health care was considered a personal responsibility before about 1920, although those without the ability to pay for it could receive charity care (VandenBos, Cummings, & DeLeon, 1992). Voluntary health insurance began to grow rapidly after the Great Depression (Falk, 1964) and shifted rapidly to employer-paid health plans during World War II, when such benefits were considered exempt from anti-inflationary restrictions on wage increases. By 1960, 69.2% of the U.S. population was covered by some form of health insurance. During the 1960s, health policy was characterized by attempts to expand access to health care, and this decade saw the passage of Medicare, Medicaid, and other legislation designed to extend coverage to those without resources.

These efforts to increase access to and expand consumption of health care were quite effective. Health care spending rose from $27.1 billion in 1960 to $675 billion in 1990. In 1990, health care represented 12.2% of the gross national product, more than double the percentage in 1960. In constant dollars, this represents an increase of over 400% (see VandenBos, 1993). According to cross-national comparisons, the United States spends more on health care than any other nation in the world. Yet, we know that our health care system covers a smaller proportion of our population and does not provide demonstrably better care to those it does cover than those of many other industrialized nations who spend less.

During this period of rapid growth in expense, health insurance was characterized by a fee-for-service indemnity system. Clinical or treatment aspects of care received nearly exclusive focus. Providers and patients alike concerned themselves with the care that they believed necessary, and insurance companies paid the bill as long as services were generally covered. Neither providers nor consumers had much incentive to pay attention to the financial aspects of care. This was a key contributor to the explosion in health care costs.

In addition, health care policy during this period emphasized coverage for acute care, short-term general hospital care, and surgery. Thus, Kiesler (1992) argued that national health policy has represented general hospital policy, not health policy. This pattern has distorted the balance between inpatient and outpatient care, favoring hospitalization and expensive inpatient procedures. Providers have actually had economic disincentives to emphasize prevention, early intervention, and treatment in less restrictive environments and, in general, to mount serious initiatives to maintain health, as opposed to providing medical interventions focused on existing symptoms or illness. At a systemic level, this has been described as another major contributing factor to escalating costs.

Managed Care and Cost Containment

It was against this backdrop that an entire industry, the managed care or health care cost-containment industry, developed, to focus on the costs of health care, which were quickly spreading out of control. Although certain forms of managed care, in particular, HMOs, have historical roots in the early 1900s, these were populist in flavor and minor players by comparison (see DeLeon et al., 1991). The managed care movement changed in character and expanded rapidly after Congress passed the HMO Act of 1973. The HMO Act provided $325 million over a 5-year period to support the development of new HMOs and required that employers with more than 25 employees offering health benefits had to offer an HMO option if a federally qualified HMO was available in their area and requested inclusion in the benefits plan. This law also allowed the participation of profit-making corporations, which had not been part of the movement up to this time, in the development and operation of HMOs. In effect, this law and subsequent regulatory changes created the infrastructure that enabled HMOs and other managed care plans to expand rapidly during the late 1970s and 1980s (see DeLeon et al., 1991, for a detailed discussion), in the hope of slowing the country's rapidly escalating health care costs. The pendulum seemed to have radically shifted away from an almost exclusive emphasis on treatment and services to a comparable singular focus on costs, financial issues, and economic resources in the provision of health care.

Managed Care and Mental Health

From the late 1960s to the mid-1980s, the costs of mental health care also skyrocketed. The media had popularized mental health services, reducing stigma and increasing demand. More important, fee-for-service medical benefit structures that favored more expensive inpatient treatment had been applied to the mental health area as well. For-profit specialty psychiatry and chemical-dependency inpatient facilities had mushroomed as a result. As pressure to cut costs began to grow, the need for more comprehensive-care management of mental health benefits became apparent. One response to this situation was simply to begin eliminating mental health benefits. Professional associations and patient advocates objected vigorously and further argued that managing care for patients with mental health and substance abuse disorders required specialized knowledge and skills different from those needed to manage general medical care (Freeman & Trabin, 1994). There was a concern that if mental health benefits were not separated from medical benefits, mental health benefits would be sharply reduced. Medical systems under pressure to operate in more efficient and cost-effective ways might divert dollars from programs for patients with mental health needs to the medical–surgical side of care.

In response to these forces, a new subsection of the managed care industry was born. Separate companies that focused exclusively on what came to be called *managed behavioral health care* began to form (see Freeman & Trabin, 1994). Under these systems, mental health services are offered by administratively and functionally separate entities that contract directly with payors or subcontract with medical provider systems and assume responsibility for the management and delivery of services defined as belonging to the mental health side of care. This model gained significant momentum between 1986 and 1993, and the percentage of large employers offering separate "carve-out" insurance products for mental health and substance abuse has continued to rise. In 1994, 44% of companies with 20,000 or more employees offered such programs (Foster Higgins, 1995). Carve-out systems have been successful, in that they have permitted larger companies to see that behavioral health care costs can indeed be managed and have, thus, allowed some form of mental health benefits to remain.

INTEGRATED DELIVERY SYSTEMS

Throughout the 1980s and until quite recently, managed care has focused almost exclusively on supply-side strategies such as altering access, managing utilization, decreasing practice variation, and limiting technology. The demand side has been largely unaddressed (Friedman et al., 1995). However, a number of market forces are beginning to change the structure and nature of managed care delivery systems and have important implications for the direction and future opportunities for psychology. These forces are most obvious in more mature, competitive health care markets in which managed care currently dominates. The first is the need for managed care companies to begin competing with one another, now that they can no longer gain market share at the expense of indemnity plans. It is no longer sufficient to offer a health plan at a lower price; companies are being forced to demonstrate that they offer a better product as well. Thus, the bottom line is shifting from cost to value, as managed care companies compete with one another on price and service. Shortell, Gillies, and Anderson (1994) defined value as "being able to provide additional quality-enhancing features that purchasers desire for a given price, or, conversely, being able to provide a given set of quality attributes or outcomes for a lower price" (p. 48).

The second force, and perhaps the most important trend in the current health care marketplace, is the increasing dominance of *capitated* systems. Capitation-based health care provides care to a defined number of enrollees at a capitated, or fixed, rate per member per month. All of a provider's or a system's revenue is earned up front, when contracts are negotiated. All of a system's components (e.g., hospitals, physician groups, and clinics) become cost centers to be managed. In a marketplace that emphasizes value, capitation creates incentives for keeping people well by emphasizing prevention and health promotion. When people do become ill, there are incentives for treating them at the most cost-effective location (in contrast to earlier policies favoring hospital-based acute care).

These forces are driving what is now the dominant characteristic of health care systems: increasing levels of integration. Assuming health care continues in this direction, the best way to control health care value, that is, cost and service, is to control all of the organization, financing, and delivery of health care as closely as possible, in ways that are responsive to regional demographics and economics. Thus, the traditional lines separating hospitals, providers, and insurers have begun to blur. This is also in keeping with the strong consumer demand for what might be termed *one-stop shopping*. Only integrated delivery systems can offer a seamless, coordinated continuum of health care.

Shortell et al. (1994) defined an integrated delivery system as "a network of organizations that provides or arranges to provide a coordinated continuum of services to a defined population and is willing to be held clinically and fiscally responsible for the outcomes and the health status of the population served" (p. 47). Such systems encompass primary care providers, specialists, ambulatory-care centers, home health care agencies, hospitals, and so on. These networks may be formed in a variety of ways. Sometimes they are owned by or closely associated with an insurance product. Some may grow out of established HMOs. Provider service networks (e.g., alliances of physicians, hospitals, and home health care agencies) are a more recent basis for integrated delivery systems.

These systems have arisen primarily in response to local market forces, not in response to legislative reform. More mature markets are characterized by a greater degree of capitated payment and tend to be further along in the development of integrated delivery systems. On the basis of a systematic study of these markets, Shortell et al. (1994) concluded that more integrated systems perform better on a variety of measures of business performance than do their competitors. Current legislative proposals, such as more flexible application of antitrust laws, are likely to extend the incentives to form such systems to areas that are currently less far along. In spite of the need for more comprehensive measures of clinical performance and more research comparing different models of delivery, neither the market nor legislative policy is likely to wait until all the evidence is in before moving forward.

As systems move toward integration, it has become clear that many existing delivery systems have far more than the required number of specialty physicians and hospital beds and far fewer than the needed number of primary care providers. Shortell et al. (1994) described a variety of signposts of increasing integration:

> Present research suggests that the types of behavior that one should observe in more integrated health systems include significant downsizing of acute care capacity; consolidation of programs and services; development of cross-institutional clinical service lines such as in cardiovascular care, oncology care, behavioral medicine, and women's health; expansion of the number of primary care physicians; growth in both primary care and multispecialty group practices; development of clinical protocols, pathways, and care management systems; acceleration of the clinical applications of continuous quality improvement and expansion to the entire continuum of care; development of outcome measures; and . . . (a) balanced scorecard approach to assessing system performance. One should also observe much closer ties between such systems and local public health and social welfare agencies, schools, prisons, police departments, and related organizations. (pp. 62–63)

Psychologists have much to contribute to health care delivery systems that undertake responsibility for the health of populations and emphasize value as the bottom line. We have known for a long time that the provision of psychological services results in the reduction of overall health care costs (e.g., Cummings & Follette, 1968; Pallak, Cummings, Dorken, & Henke, 1995), yet until now, this message has fallen largely on deaf ears where policymakers are concerned. In addition, psychologists have developed treatment protocols for a variety of physical conditions that are at least as effective and far less costly than surgical interventions (e.g., for chronic back pain; see Turk & Stacey, in press) and even compare favorably to long-term medication use aimed at the same conditions (e.g., for hypertension; see Fahrion, Norris, Green, Green, & Schnar, 1987). Psychological research can provide a basis for behavior-change technologies and education methodologies that will significantly enhance health-promotion efforts. Integrated systems create incentives for liaison and treatment-coordination activities that psychologists are well positioned to provide. If integrated delivery systems are to be held responsible for the health status of populations, they will need to do a better job of assessing the needs, demands, and preferences of their populations. Such assessments will need to focus on community wellness and health promotion, and not exclusively on perceived or diagnosed illness (Shortell et al., 1994). The expertise of psychologists in clinical assessment can be brought to bear on the outcome assessments and quality-assurance systems that health care systems will need, to assess quality of care and cost-effectiveness.

HEALTH PSYCHOLOGY

Although the scope of the emerging opportunities for psychology is new, health care does not represent a new area of expertise for professional psychology. In fact, the marketplace developments described above have occurred simultaneously with the rise of health psychology as a research and clinical discipline. This has occurred within a remarkably short period of time. Although its foundations extend much further back, Division 38 (Health Psychology) of the American Psychological Association (APA) was founded in 1978. By 1990, health psychology had become the most popular area of clinical research in APA-accredited clinical psychology doctoral programs, with nearly twice as many schools, faculties, and grants devoted to this area as any other (Sayette & Mayne, 1990).

Psychologists have directed their efforts toward understanding the psychosocial contributors to and consequences of physical disease. We have focused on health promotion and disease prevention, as well as on the development of psychological and behavioral technologies for the treatment of various medical problems. These efforts have made it clear that our clinical and research expertise has relevance for far more than treating individuals with diagnosed mental health disorders:

> As health professionals, . . . psychologists are involved in research, assessment, intervention, consultation, teaching, and administration related to management of pain, coping with stressful medical procedures, control of pharmacological side effects, training in self-examination and health monitoring, recovery from illness and surgery,

cognitive rehabilitation, behavioral health, adherence to health care regimens, organ transplant decisions, health care staff stress and burnout, physician–patient relationships, and work-site prevention programs. (VandenBos, DeLeon, & Belar, 1991, p. 443)

Moreover, a large body of work has focused on behavioral contributors to health and disease. Indeed, U.S. Department of Health and Human Services officials have pointed out that all of the seven top health-risk factors in the United States—tobacco use, diet, alcohol, unintentional injuries, suicidal behavior, violence, and unsafe sex—are behavioral (cf. VandenBos et al., 1991). Behavioral factors make significant contributions to the development of chronic diseases (e.g., heart disease, cancer, and diabetes), currently the most serious and most costly threat to the nation's health. In addition to being actively involved in prevention efforts, psychologists have developed and presented empirical data on the efficacy of behavioral interventions aimed at a wide range of medical problems, such as coronary artery disease, stress disorders, essential hypertension, migraine headaches, and chronic back pain (Cummings & VandenBos, 1983).

Even more recently, the field of psychoneuroimmunology (PNI) has developed and expanded. Psychoneuroimmunology is concerned with the anatomical and chemical pathways through which the nervous system (especially the brain) and the immune system communicate with one another and with the implications of this communication for the pathogenesis and course of physical disease (Kemeny, Solomon, Morley, & Herbert, 1992). As part of this study, PNI focuses on the impact of psychosocial factors on the immune system. The rapidly growing literature in this area has established that exposure to stressful events can have adverse effects on the immune system and that specific psychological states, such as depression, can also be associated with changes in immunity (see Herbert & Cohen, 1993). Furthermore, research suggests that such immune-system changes may have an impact on the course of immunologically mediated or resisted diseases, including viral and bacterial infections, autoimmune diseases, certain forms of cancer, and HIV-related illness (see Kemeny, 1994). Thus, there is substantial evidence that psychological factors can have an impact on health and disease in ways that are not mediated by behavior. Whether such processes can be influenced through psychological interventions is currently being explored. Currently available data suggest that specific psychological interventions may have an impact on the course of certain types of cancer (Fawzy et al., 1993; Spiegel, Bloom, Kraemer, & Gottheil, 1989) and the course of HIV progression (e.g., Antoni et al., 1991; Esterling et al., 1992), although the mechanisms of these effects are still unclear.

PSYCHOLOGY AS A HEALTH CARE PROFESSION

None of this is to say that all psychologists will need to become health psychologists and immunologists or that there will cease to be a demand for psychologists who provide services directed at the amelioration of psychological distress and psychological disorders. However, one implication of the broader trends we have described is that technologies developed by health psychologists will need to be more fully integrated into professional education. Another is that many professional psychologists may need to become more flexible regarding the settings in which they practice and more collaborative with other health care disciplines.

The potential role of psychology in primary care settings provides an important illustration. Much of the research in this area has examined symptom presentation in primary medical-care settings, rather than focusing on populations with specific diagnoses. For example, one recent study involved the analysis of records for over 1,000 patients followed over 3 years in an internal medicine clinic (Kroenke & Mangelsdorff, 1989). For the 14 most commonly presented complaints, a clear organic etiology was established in less than 16% of the cases. Significant psychological distress was present in over 80%. A large and growing body of literature indicates that both the presence of psychologists as members of the primary care team and a variety of specific psychological interventions reduce unnecessary medical visits, reduce overall health care costs, and enhance patient care (see Friedman et al., 1995; Kenkel, 1995, for recent reviews).

Yet, if psychology is to be taken seriously as a health care profession, there are major challenges that must be met. One of the most important is the development of more sophisticated models and better technologies for health-related behavior change and maintenance. As behavioral risk factors for a variety of diseases have been identified, psychologists have developed and tested theoretically based interventions for modifying those behaviors. Although such interventions have often produced initial change, they have been less successful in maintaining behavior change. Models are needed that acknowledge the complex determinants of behavior, including sociocultural influences and irrational processes, and new interventions that are based on those models must be developed. This is particularly critical in areas like HIV prevention, where the best predictor of safer sexual behavior—whether following interventions, education campaigns, or antibody testing—is consistently found to be past sexual behavior (e.g., Aspinwall, Kemeny, Taylor, Schneider, & Dudley, 1991; McCusker et al., 1990). Although we may argue successfully that psychologists are the experts in behavior, the health care system will demand increasing accountability. We must begin to deliver programs that foster lasting behavior change in areas such as primary prevention, behavioral risk factors for the incidence of progression of disease, and treatment adherence.

A second, overlapping, priority is the management of chronic disease. Two major trends contribute to this priority (Chesney, 1993). The first trend consists of rapidly developing technologies for testing and screening and for identification of genetic risk. With early identification come opportunities for intervention to reduce or eliminate the risk of illness, as well as the need for treatments that address the psychological sequelae of risk identification. The second trend is related to the rapid growth of the aging population. By the year 2020, it is expected that over 50 million U.S. citizens will be age 65 or older. The great majority of these people are likely to have at least one chronic illness such as hypertension, heart disease, arthritis, or diabetes (U.S. Bureau of the Census, 1996). Psychologists will need to form partnerships with medical scientists and practitioners to develop programs for supporting healthy living, managing chronic conditions, and sustaining quality of life (Chesney, 1993). Increasingly, such programs will need to incorporate individual, community, and public health levels of intervention.

POLICY RECOMMENDATIONS

There are a number of general policy recommendations that are important in supporting the development of psychology in the directions described. First and foremost, psychologists must work toward general recognition of psychology as a health-care profession and psychologists as health-service providers. The involvement of psychological practice in health care—in health promotion and disease prevention, as team members in primary care settings, or in interventions directed toward conditions generally considered medical in nature—is not well known to policymakers, either at the local market or legislative level. For the most part, when policymakers think about health, they think about medical interventions provided by physicians (see, e.g., Kerrey & Holfschire, 1993). Advocacy materials and public messages should highlight psychological services related to the prevention, treatment, and rehabilitation of both psychological and physical health problems. Although the tremendous need for psychological expertise in the planning and delivery of health services may be clear to us, we must approach these efforts with a "deep appreciation both for the truly interdisciplinary nature of health care and the very tenuous nature of psychology's participation in its . . . planning" (DeLeon, O'Keefe, VandenBos, & Kraut, 1982, p. 480).

A central part of this effort will be to support and participate in the creation of clinically integrated health care delivery systems.

Psychologists can be key advocates for the elimination of mind–body dualism in health policy. Legislation, insurance, and health-plan-benefits language and the administrative structures of health care systems should be scrutinized for instances in which such dualism impedes the creation of integrated health systems. For example, behavioral health carve-outs may pose obstacles to the integration of psychology into health care service delivery, to the ability of systems to realize and track medical-cost offsets as a function of psychological services, and to the application of psychological and behavioral technologies to health promotion and treatment (see Belar, 1995).

To ensure that our opportunities within the health care system are as broad and varied as possible, it is important that common economic incentives be created for various levels of care (e.g., hospitals, primary care settings, and home health) to work together. As mentioned, this involves more flexible application of antitrust laws as they relate to health care systems and the dismantling of policies and benefit structures that favor hospitalization and acute care. For psychologists, restrictions on licensure and certification requirements and other legal barriers to participation in interdisciplinary groups must be removed. Legislative advocacy also can be used to promote cross-training and the use of clinical outcomes and patient satisfaction data in decisions regarding what services psychologists provide. It is important that our ability to provide services not depend on a diagnosis of psychopathology.

We can also encourage more integrated provision of care through promoting greater and more informed consumer choice of health plans and treatment options. For example, the APA has been quite active in supporting requirements for individual choice of plans and out-of-network service options at a legislative level. Similar efforts at a state and local level are at least as important.

The movement toward increasingly integrated systems will require policies and procedures that increase the supply of needed professionals (e.g., primary care providers). Within our own educational system, we must begin to address the disjuncture between the current "product" of our universities and professional schools and the needs of the delivery system. In parallel to our potential collaborators, our own education should include greater emphasis on learning and working in teams, systems thinking, quality improvement and outcomes assessment, the use of protocols and critical pathways, the analysis of cost-effectiveness, clinical epidemiology, program evaluation, and population-based health-status assessment.

THE CHALLENGE TO PSYCHOLOGY

The forces we have described present professional psychology with both great opportunity and great risk. The opportunity is for psychology to take its place as a health care profession, with mental health as a subset of expertise rather than its defining characteristic. The next several years will be a critical period in which to do so. Patterns of health care delivery and supporting policy are more open to reconceptualization, redesign, and renegotiation than at any point in recent history. Current systems are shifting away from previous policies that have favored hospital-based and acute care and have limited the participation of professional psychology. The management of health care delivery systems will become far more interdisciplinary, incorporating medical, nursing, public health, business, legal, and psychological perspectives.

In making this shift, psychology has a strong ally in the public. In preparation for its public education campaign, the APA recently sponsored a random survey of over 1,200 American men and women. More than 8 in 10 people surveyed endorsed the belief that good psychological health plays an important role in maintaining good physical health. Over 80% indicated that they would be more inclined to use a physician who worked with a psychologist over one who did not. Nearly half reported that they would be "much more inclined." A separate series of consumer focus groups revealed that the public believes strongly in a connection between the mind and the body and saw psychological services as an important part of treatment for physical illness and disease, enhancing both the ability to cope with the disease and recovery from it.

We can begin by taking practical and incremental steps toward changing the way we practice our profession. For example, an early step might be to develop group practices of psychologists. This will help to render the diversity within our profession an advantage, rather than a liability, and will relieve us of feeling overwhelmed and burdened by the sense of having to know everything. A second step might be to establish links with other health care providers, particularly with primary care physicians. A third step might be the development of multidisciplinary group practices with psychologists as integral members.

Building these relationships can strengthen referral bases, educate us about the needs for our services that exist on the front lines of health care, and prepare us to participate in integrated health care delivery systems. For most of us, this will involve shifting our frame sufficiently that we are able to conceptualize and incorporate a much wider range of needs and outcomes. Under fee-for-service models, the expanded application of psychological technologies to medical problems pitted psychologists against all of organized medicine (Cummings & VandenBos, 1983). Integrated delivery systems offer far greater opportunities for collaboration, but such collaboration will require more systematic training in health promotion and in the detection and treatment of more medically based problems and the ability to work closely in more flexible ways with other specialists.

The risks of this transition are also great. Perhaps the greatest risk to our profession is that by failing to resolve our internal struggles and anxiety related to this professional role transition, we may fail to develop coherent and well-coordinated models and messages that will carry us into the next century. In addition, the effective communication of these more complex messages to policymakers and payors will be a difficult task for a profession that has not historically articulated its knowledge base to outsiders (Newman & Vincent, 1996). Along with our message that the provision of psychological services as a routine part of medical care can reduce overall medical costs, we need to define what specific services are cost-effective for which individuals under what circumstances (Friedman et al., 1995). By clinging exclusively to traditional models of practice, we may fail to demonstrate our competence to do anything beyond the capabilities of less well trained—and cheaper—mental health providers.

Seizing the opportunity requires that two critical challenges be met simultaneously: differentiation and integration. By differentiation, we mean that psychology must demonstrate clearly the uniqueness of our training and experience and of the contribution we can make to health care delivery. By integration, we mean that providers acting alone or in loose affiliation, without strong interdisciplinary collaborative ties, will have great difficulty participating in the delivery of the full continuum of health care. The model of health care delivery will be the team. We must learn to become team players while maintaining our unique identity. Throughout this shift in our patterns of practice and our definition of ourselves, we must not lose sight of the ultimate purpose of all health care interventions. This is a principle for which psychologists have long been passionate advocates: to improve the quality of human life.

REFERENCES

Antoni, M. H., Baggett, L., Ironson, G., LaPerriere, A., August, S., Klimas, N., Schneiderman, N., & Fletcher, M. A. (1991). Cognitive-behavioral stress management intervention buffers distress responses and immunological changes following notification of HIV-1 seropositivity. *Journal of Consulting and Clinical Psychology, 59,* 906–915.

Aspinwall, L. G., Kemeny, M. E., Taylor, S. E., Schneider, S. G., & Dudley, J. P. (1991). Psychosocial predictors of gay men's AIDS risk-reduction behavior. *Health Psychology, 10,* 434–444.

Belar, C. D. (1995). Collaboration in capitated care: Challenges for psychology. *Professional Psychology: Research and Practice, 26,* 139–146.

Chesney, M. A. (1993). Health psychology in the 21st century: Acquired immunodeficiency syndrome as a harbinger of things to come. *Health Psychology, 12,* 259–268.

Cummings, N. A., & Follette, W. T. (1968). Psychiatric services and medical utilization in a prepaid health setting: Part II. *Medical Care, 6*, 31–41.

Cummings, N. A., & VandenBos, G. R. (1983). Relations with other professions. In C. E. Walker (Ed.), *Handbook of clinical psychology: Theory, research, and practice* (Vol. 2, pp. 1301–1327). Homewood, IL: Dow Jones–Irwin.

DeLeon, P. H., O'Keefe, A. M., VandenBos, G. R., & Kraut, A. G. (1982). How to influence public policy: A blueprint for activism. *American Psychologist, 37*, 476–485.

DeLeon, P. H., VandenBos, G. R., & Bulatao, E. Q. (1991). Managed mental health care: A history of the federal policy initiative. *Professional Psychology: Research and Practice, 22*, 15–25.

Esterling, B. A., Antoni, M. H., Schneiderman, N., Carver, C. S., LaPerriere, A., Ironson, G., Klimas, N. G., & Fletcher, M. A. (1992). Psychosocial modulation of antibody to Epstein–Barr viral capsid antigen and human herpesvirus type-6 in HIV-1 infected and at-risk gay men. *Psychosomatic Medicine, 54*, 354–371.

Fahrion, S., Norris, P., Green, E., Green, A., & Schnar, R. (1987). Biobehavioral treatment of essential hypertension: A group outcome study. *Biofeedback and Self-Regulation, 11*, 257–278.

Falk, I. S. (1964). Medical care: Its social and organizational aspects. Labor unions and medical care. *The New England Journal of Medicine, 270*, 22–28.

Fawzy, F. I., Fawzy, N. W., Hyun, S. C., Elashoff, R., Guthrie, D., Fahey, J. L., & Morton, D. L. (1993). Malignant melanoma: Effects of an early structured psychiatric intervention, coping, and affective state on recurrence and survival 6 years later. *Archives of General Psychiatry, 50*, 681–689.

Foster Higgins, A. (1995). *National survey of employer-sponsored health plans.* New York: Author.

Freeman, M. A., & Trabin, T. (1994). *Managed behavioral healthcare: History, models, key issues, and future course* (CMHS, SAMHSA Report No. #4692). Rockville, MD: U.S. Department of Health and Human Services.

Friedman, R., Sobel, D., Myers, P., Caudill, M., & Benson, H. (1995). Behavioral medicine, clinical health psychology, and cost offset. *Health Psychology, 14*, 509–518.

Herbert, T. B., & Cohen, S. (1993). Stress and immunity in humans: A meta-analytic review. *Psychosomatic Medicine, 55*, 364–379.

Kemeny, M. E. (1994). Stressful events, psychological responses, and progression of HIV infection. In R. Glaser & J. Kiecolt-Glaser (Eds.), *Handbook of human stress and immunity* (pp. 245–266). New York: Academic Press.

Kemeny, M. E., Solomon, G. F., Morley, J. E., & Herbert, T. L. (1992). Psychoneuroimmunology. In C. B. Nemeroff (Ed.), *Neuroendocrinology* (pp. 563–591). Boca Raton, FL: CRC Press.

Kenkel, M. B. (Ed.). (1995). Psychology and primary care/family practice medicine [Special section]. *Professional Psychology: Research and Practice, 26*, 117–146.

Kerrey, B., & Holfschire, P. J. (1993). Hidden problems in current health care financing and potential changes. *American Psychologist, 48*, 261–264.

Kiesler, C. A. (1992). U. S. mental health policy: Doomed to fail. *American Psychologist, 47*, 1077–1082.

Kroenke, K., & Mangelsdorff, D. (1989). Common symptoms in ambulatory care: Incidence, evaluation, therapy, and outcome. *American Journal of Medicine, 86*, 262–266.

McCusker, J., Westenhouse, J., Stoddard, A. M., Zapka, J. G., Zorn, M. W., & Mayer, K. H. (1990). Use of drugs and alcohol by homosexually active men in relation to sexual practices. *Journal of Acquired Immune Deficiency Syndromes, 3*, 729–737.

Newman, R., & Vincent, T. (1996). Balancing expertise with practical realities. In R. P. Lorion, I. Iscoe, P. H. DeLeon, & G. R. VandenBos (Eds.), *Psychology and public policy: Balancing public service and professional need* (pp. 203–206). Washington, DC: American Psychological Association.

Pallak, M. S., Cummings, N. A., Dorken, H., & Henke, C. J. (1995). Effect of mental health treatment on medical costs. *Mind/Body Medicine, 1*, 7–12.

Sayette, M. A., & Mayne, T. J. (1990). Survey of current clinical and research trends in clinical psychology. *American Psychologist, 45*, 1263–1266.

Shortell, S. M., Gillies, R. R., & Anderson, D. A. (1994). The new world of managed care: Creating organized delivery systems. *Health Affairs, 13*, 46–64.

Spiegel, D., Bloom, J. R., Kraemer, H. C., & Gottheil, E. (1989). Effect of psychosocial treatment on survival of patients with metastatic breast cancer. *Lancet*, 888–891.

Turk, D. C., & Stacey, B. R. (in press). Multidisciplinary pain centers in the treatment of chronic back pain. In J. W. Frymoyer, T. B. Ducker, N. M. Hadler, J. P. Kostiuk, J. N. Weinstein, & T. S. Whitecloud (Eds.), *The adult spine: Principles and practices* (2nd ed.). New York: Raven Press.

U.S. Bureau of the Census. (1996). 65+ in the United States. In *Current Population Reports*, (Special Studies Report No. P23-190). Washington, DC: U.S. Government Printing Office.

VandenBos, G. R. (1993). U. S. mental health policy: Proactive evolution in the midst of health care reform. *American Psychologist, 48*, 283–290.

VandenBos, G. R., Cummings, N. A., & DeLeon, P. H. (1992). A century of psychotherapy: Economics and environmental influences. In D. K. Freedheim (Ed.), *History of psychotherapy: A century of change* (pp. 65–102). Washington, DC: American Psychological Association.

VandenBos, G. R., DeLeon, P. H., & Belar, C. D. (1991). How many psychologists are needed? It's too early to know! *Professional Psychology: Research and Practice, 22*, 441–448.

3

THE NEW STRUCTURE OF HEALTH CARE AND A ROLE FOR PSYCHOLOGY

NICHOLAS A. CUMMINGS

Psychotherapists have had more than one occasion to counsel a patient who was lamenting a lost opportunity and expressing no insight into his or her responsibility in missing that opportunity. Still in denial, the patient is full of rage and self-pity, crying that never again will such favorable circumstances repeat themselves. It is incumbent on the psychotherapist to point out that a wonderful feature of life is that it presents repeated opportunities. But if, when the next opportunity occurs, the patient is still in denial, some time in the future the patient and psychotherapist will be repeating this conversation.

Psychology clearly missed the opportunity to own or control the behavior managed care industry. But as the first decade of managed behavioral health care draws to a close, there are megatrends emerging that signal that the second decade will see the restoration of the provider as paramount, albeit in a manner different than anything that has previously existed. Given the determination to respond appropriately, psychology is faced with a new frontier and yet another opportunity (N. A. Cummings, 1995a).

THE FIRST DECADE OF MANAGED BEHAVIORAL HEALTH CARE

In spite of wishful thinking to the contrary on the part of most practitioners, managed care has succeeded in reducing costs (Rich, 1995). In most cases, the cost containment has been in the form of deceleration of the inflationary spiral by as much as 30%, whereas in a few instances, there is an active reduction in the cost of providing health care. The marketplace, which is the final arbiter of the controversy, clearly perceived a significant cost saving, and the number of persons covered by managed care soared in 10 years from under 5% of insured Americans to 67%. This is more than just growth: It is a stampede. In the process, much got trampled, and among the casualties were some quality, much of solo practice, and all of psychoanalysis.

The question now remains of whether managed care companies have outlived their usefulness (Oss, 1995). With most of the fat wrung out of behavioral health care, they may maintain only a layer of bureaucracy that is no longer needed. This does not mean the end of managed care, for now that the industrialization of health care has occurred, for all time, when someone else pays the bill, care will be managed.

WHY CARVE-OUTS ARE OUT

Ten years ago, when I heralded the emergence of the managed behavior health care industry (N. A. Cummings, 1986), it was because existing structures and mechanisms lacked the expertise to control spiraling costs. The federal government in its promulgation of diagnosis-related groups (DRGs) had managed to tether medical–surgical hospital costs, but it did not know how to write DRGs for mental health and chemical-dependency (MH–CD) hospitalization. As DRGs emptied medical–surgical beds, hospitals converted the space to MH–CD, touted these services on radio and television, and MH–CD hospitalization soared out of control and became the new driving force in the inflationary spiral.

Clearly what was needed was expertise outside the then-current health industry, and companies such as American Biodyne (now MedCo. Behavioral Care Corporation) sprang up and flourished. In just 7 years, Biodyne went from 0 to 14.5 million eligible by carving out MH–CD from existing health plans, and a host of competitors also experienced phenomenal growth. It was not long before similar companies followed

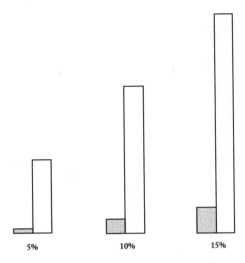

Figure 1. Potential savings in billions of dollars for mental health and chemical-dependency treatment at the 5%, 10%, and 15% levels (shaded columns) and for corresponding savings in all health expenditures (unshaded columns).

American Biodyne's lead, and because of the outside expertise or separate organizal structure of these contractors, they came to be known as "behavioral care carve-outs," or just plain "carve-outs." The carve-out was a necessary first step in tethering MH–CD costs, but now that all the carve-outs are doing essentially the same thing with similar degrees of success, their time may be passing, inasmuch as everyone has learned the technology, which is now also available to practitioner groups. Along with solo practice, long-term therapy, and psychoanalysis, it, too, may have become a dinosaur. But carve-outs have become a gigantic industry, and paleontology has taught us that not all the dinosaurs died at once. A probable scenario is the following, which will usher in the second decade of managed behavioral health care: the era of the *megaprovider*.

WHY CARVE-INS ARE IN

The cost containment that can be realized in MH–CD pales by comparison with the cost containment that lies potentially in medicine and surgery. Dollar amounts tend to obscure the importance of the comparison inasmuch as practitioners have become inured to large monetary sums being bandied about. Figure 1 is startling in that it dramatically shows the difference for 5%, 10%, and 15% cost savings in MH–CD (shaded columns) versus the same percentages in total health care (unshaded columns). All are in billions of dollars, and a 10% savings in total health care is equivalent to all MH–CD expenditures in the United States.

Medical-cost offset is the reduction in overuse or inappropriate use of medicine and surgery by introduction of behavioral health care to address somatization by those 60% of physician visits that are either translating emotional distress into physical symptoms or have a real physical illness that is either complicated by psychological factors or brought on by lifestyle. The figures 5%, 10%, and 15% were chosen because most medical-cost-offset studies report those kinds of savings (Pallak, Cummings, Dörken, & Henke, 1993). A 10% medical-cost offset is modal and readily achieved in settings organized to facilitate such savings (N. A. Cummings, 1994).

Carve-outs are antithetical to conducting medical-cost offset because, by definition, they are not part of the delivery system in which the overuse of medicine and surgery is occurring. The best medical cost offset takes place when the research and the delivery system are so integrated that it is totally unobtrusive (N. A. Cummings, 1994).

THE EMERGENCE OF THE MEGAPROVIDER

One of the few surviving ideas of Ira Magaziner, the architect of the defunct Rodham–Clinton health care proposal, is that of the purchasing alliance. In large metropolitan areas, communities are forming consortia of insurers, employers, consumers, providers, and other volunteers. These consortia have the authority not only to purchase health care delivery but also to bypass the managed care companies and contract directly with regional provider groups. Without the onerousness of government sanctions, these community groups are availing themselves of expertise in outcomes research and quality measures. Contracts will be awarded either to managed care companies or directly to provider groups, whichever has the best value (quality plus price) as demonstrated by real outcomes research. This is schematically shown in Figure 2, where independently conducted outcomes research is fed back to the purchasing alliance, which then makes purchasing decisions accordingly.

The groups of providers who are forming nationally and contracting directly with purchasers cover the entire spectrum of health care, not just MH–CD. They are variously called regional group practices (RGPs; N. A. Cummings, 1995b) or community-accountable health care networks (CAHNs; Neer, 1994). They are organized and owned by providers, and although they demonstrate business organization and acumen, they are clinically driven. The managed care companies, on the other hand, have essentially become isolated from their clinical roots and have become largely business driven.

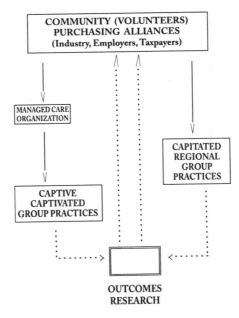

**COMMUNITY (VOLUNTEERS)
PURCHASING ALLIANCES**
(Industry, Employers, Taxpayers)

MANAGED CARE
ORGANIZATION

CAPITATED
REGIONAL
GROUP
PRACTICES

CAPTIVE
CAPTIVATED
GROUP PRACTICES

OUTCOMES
RESEARCH

Figure 2. Flowchart illustrating the ability of the purchasing alliances to contract with managed care organizations (MCOs) or directly with regional group practices, with the employment of outcomes research to determine renewals or future contracts.

The salient feature of these emerging provider groups is the physician equity model, in which the practitioners are participant owners in their own delivery systems. Physician equity has been the cornerstone of the world's most successful health maintenance organization (HMO) the Kaiser-Permanente system. The Mullikin Group has extended the physician equity concept to include all health care professionals (De Lafuente, 1993) and has become the prototype of the new practitioner groups.

The health care landscape was replete in the 1980s with physician-owned managed care companies that went bankrupt. Formed as the physician's answer to the encroachment of managed care, they lacked the sophistication and expertise to compete in the business world, and they did not survive. These new groups, whether RGPs or CAHNs, are successful businesses that, nonetheless, retain their ability to be clinically driven. These features, added to the physician equity component, render them a real threat to the existing managed care companies. Forrester (1994) refers to the physician equity model as the "dark horse contender to dominate healthcare delivery in the future" (p. 1). For-profit practitioner groups can "forge an entrepreneurial trail with zeal and speed"

(Forrester, 1994, p. 1) not possible in nonequity systems. It is important that psychologists begin now to assure equity in these systems of the future. Those psychologists who succeed will very likely be those who are involved in the initial formations of CAHNs.

The managed care companies, recognizing the threat from provider groups, are rapidly buying group practices, hoping to capture the field. It is now a race between the emerging provider groups, who have trouble raising capital, and the managed care companies, who have access to expansion dollars. Consequently, the provider groups can no longer be content to remain relatively small entities. Mergers, acquisitions, and consolidations, the steps the fledgling managed care companies had to traverse years ago, now must be the *modis operandi* of the provider groups, eventually forging megaproviders to counter the *megameds*, the name I gave (N. A. Cummings, 1995b) to the giant managed care entities.

The first megaprovider was formed with the acquisition of the Mullikin Group by MedPartners ("Physician Management," 1995). It is the prediction of several observers of the health care industry that the megaproviders will, over the next 10 years, overtake the managed care companies whose overlay of bureaucracy has outlived its usefulness (N. A. Cummings, 1995a; Neer, 1994; Oss, 1995). The health care delivery systems for the year 2000 will be the CAHNs and the HMOs, which are in actual practice their own kind of CAHN.

THE FUTURE IS IN BEHAVIORAL HEALTH

Psychologists, accustomed to pressure from above (psychiatry), are ill prepared to accept pressure from below (master's level practitioners). The fact that master's level psychotherapists will replace doctor's level psychotherapists is in keeping with this megatrend in all health care, involving midwives, nurse practitioners, and physician assistants. In addition, specialization will be curtailed in favor of more general practitioners in the trenches.

More than 15 years ago, with VandenBos (Cummings & VandenBos, 1979), I saw the psychologist as the behavioral primary care physician of the future. In enunciating the "General Practice of Psychology," we anticipated the current era and delineated the parameters, one of which was the psychologist as embodiment of the extinct, caring general practitioner of old, who never refused a house call, related to all the family as a concerned counselor, and coordinated and oversaw the family's health and well-being. Since the disappearance of the "family doctor" in the age of overspecialization, there has been a void, and who is better able to fill this role than the psychologist as primary care giver?

The most powerful economic argument for mental health benefits is the evidence that they reduce inappropriate medical care utilization (N. A. Cummings, 1991; Goldman & Feldman, 1993). In the 130 million Americans now covered by managed behavioral health care, most of the economic "fat" has been effectively wrung from the mental health system. There remains the far greater economic drain in the medical–surgical sectors resulting from the use of services by the millions of physician visits by somaticizing patients (N. A. Cummings, 1993). Thirty years of research have demonstrated the medical-cost-offset effect in organized settings: The reduction of inappropriate medical–surgical care by the use of psychological interventions. The current rediscovery of the medical-cost-offset phenomenon indicates that the future of the doctoral-level psychologist will be found in health psychology.

The doctorally trained psychologist is in a unique position to plan, research, and implement intervention programs for both the somaticizers and the noncompliant chronically physically ill (N. A. Cummings, 1995b; Pallak et al., 1993), as well as behavioral programs for the millions who demonstrate faulty living habits. But in the fact that the interventions of the future will be derived from empirical-outcomes research, resulting in treatment protocols, there is an even broader role for the doctoral-level psychologist.

Somatization

The translation of psychological conflict and stress into physical symptoms takes a heavy economic toll on our health system. Beyond that, there is the fact that when 60% of all visits to a physician are somaticized complaints, the patients are not receiving the appropriate behavioral treatment to ameliorate their pain and suffering. Repeated visits to a physician who attempts to reassure the patient by repeating medical test only strengthen the patient's conviction that a physical illness exists and will be found during the next round of tests.

Psychologists functioning in behavior health have the expertise to design systems and interventions that bring relief to the patient and reduce the strain of overutilization on the medical and surgical system. Somatization not only can mimic any physical condition, it can exacerbate an existing illness. Primarily, however, it challenges the frontiers of medicine. The less certainty regarding a syndrome, the greater the incidence of somatization.

Thirty years ago, the most frequent form of somaticized response was what physicians called "neurotic heart." As cardiology became more sophisticated, this gave way to lower back pain. With increased knowledge in back centers, there was a surge in the little-understood conditions of hypoglycemia and yeast infection. Now, carpal tunnel syndrome is exploding in frequency. Carpal tunnel syndrome demonstrates the critical features of somatization: (a) It challenges the frontiers of medicine, and (b) the extensive use of computer keyboards (i.e., repetitive movement) provides a social rationalization for the "disease." Consider, however, that the old typewriter required much more pressure and the type of repetitive movement that ostensibly contributes to the current wave of carpal tunnel syndrome complaints. The critical feature remains that medicine lacks certainty regarding the syndrome, inasmuch as the state of medical knowledge does not readily allow a differentiation between the somaticized symptom and the genuine physical disorder.

Similarly, patients challenge the frontiers of psychology, and the profession has not adequately addressed this "psychotizing." Thirty years ago, Joanne Woodward won the Academy Award for her performance in *The Three Faces of Eve*, a movie about a woman with multiple personality disorder. Woodward also married Paul Newman. There followed an epidemic in America of female patients manifesting multiple personality disorder. In due time the "epidemic" died out, and multiple personality disorder remained rare for many years, until the popularization of the case of Sybil, after which multiple personality disorder became epidemic again.

It is even as if psychotherapists contribute to the proliferation of multiple personality disorder. I recall how a small rural center of my managed care company was treating more multiple personalities in that center than the entire national delivery system combined. I was baffled until the center director, receiving a significant promotion, was moved to a larger center several states away. Within 60 days, his new location became the multiple personality center of the system.

Unfortunately, iatrogenic "neuroses" are not rare. Borderline personalities can mimic any condition in which a well-meaning therapist shows undue interest. Furthermore, those with personality disorders may plunge into "psychosis" when it suits their purpose, only to emerge when they have gotten their way, somewhat as a diver who emerges from the swimming pool. The unfortunate schizophrenic does not have this capacity, but unwitting therapists fall prey to borderline patients for whom hospitalization is a way out of the consequences of their lifestyle. Other therapists are easily blackmailed by severe personality disorders who will use the threat of suicide as a manipulation device.

We have failed to address scientifically the real parameters of posttraumatic stress disorder, repressed memories, false memories, and a number of other phenomena that challenge the frontiers of psychology, to say nothing of our professional embarrassment with colleagues who seriously treat the trauma resulting from ostensible abduction by space aliens. While helping medicine cope with the somatization, let us not neglect the challenges to the frontiers of psychology. Our future and credibility depend on it.

The Psychotherapy of the Future

When VandenBos and I (1979) described our general practice of psychology, we advocated multimodal group practices whose psychotherapists had combined dynamic and behavioral therapies into interventions designed to ameliorate the presenting life program. We postulated that throughout the life span, the client has available brief, effective interventions designed to meet specific conditions as these may or may not arise. Later termed *brief, intermittent psychotherapy throughout the life cycle* (N. A. Cummings & Sayama, 1995), this approach currently has over 30 years of clinical experience and empirical treatment of choice in the present U.S. health care environment.

As previously stated, most of the hands-on behavioral treatment will be conducted by master's level therapists working with empirically derived treatment protocols of targeted, focused interventions. Research, experience, and the nature of human diversity have shown that protocols serve only about 30% to 35% of the persons suffering from each condition being addressed. The master's level therapists will need the clinical acumen of the doctorally trained therapists for the remaining 65% to 70% of patients.

Outcomes research is beginning to demonstrate that many psychological conditions respond more effectively to group therapy than to individual therapy. In addition, a growing body of evidence indicates that preventive services in the form of psychoeducational groups reduce the demand for both psychotherapy and inappropriate medical–surgical utilization. These psychoeducational groups range from stress management, parenting programs, and smoking cessation to programs designed to improve compliance with medical regimens in hypertensives, diabetics, and other chronic diseases in which noncompliance is rampant. Outcomes research has identified well over 100 potentially useful psychoeducational approaches.

It is very likely, as the result of empirical findings, that only 25% of the psychotherapy of the future will be individual. It is anticipated that another 25% will be group therapy, whereas half of the psychological interventions will be preventive services in the form of structured psychoeducational programs involving small-group participation. The doctoral psychologist will be conducting the empirical research on which the eventual design and implementation of these therapies will rest. Note that the 25:25:50 ratio, or something resembling it, will be the result of tested effectiveness and not primarily a drive for further cost containment.

The Psychologist as Health Economist

The single most important characteristic that will define the successful psychologist of the future will be the ability to predict one's costs, not only for MH–CD and all behavioral care services but also for medicine and surgery. This will make the group to which he or she is a participant owner eligible for capitation or other forms of prospective reimbursement. Without the ability to predict and control costs, no provider group will be in a position to assume risk. It also follows from ongoing outcomes research that the psychologist will be pivotal in a system that constantly evolves toward ever-increasing efficiency (cost containment) and improved effectiveness (treatment and prevention).

Managed care companies have achieved cost containment by addressing the supply side of health care. Precertification, utilization review, case management, and other such techniques are intended to save money by shrinking the supply, a straightforward business approach that serves most industries well. However, this does not address demand, and therein lies the dilemma for the business-driven, as opposed to the clinically driven, system. The following example will illustrate.

In a given month, 23 patients presenting for psychiatric hospitalization manifest suicidal thoughts. None of these demonstrate severity of symptoms sufficient to warrant hospitalization other than possibly for a suicidal aspect. Yet, experience has shown that only 2 or 3 of these are actually lethal. The dilemma becomes who to hospitalize. To deny hospitalization to someone who then goes home and commits suicide is likely to result in a malpractice suit. To play it safe by hospitalizing most, if not all, 23 is costly and inefficient. These are all supply-side questions and dilemmas.

In a clinically driven system, the approach is one of *prevention*, which is another word for the demand side of the equation. By increasing the amount of brief psychotherapy, psychoeducational groups, outreach with early detection and treatment, the demand for hospitalization markedly decreases (J. L. Cummings, 1996; Pallak & Cummings, 1992). Furthermore, a great deal of ambulatory care can be provided for far less than the cost of one day of hospitalization. If prevention is appropriately and intensively provided, it is likely that 5 persons will present for hospitalization in that month, instead of 23. With this reduced demand, all 5 could be hospitalized without an overutilization of inpatient care and without concern for an error in diagnostic judgment.

SUMMARY AND CONCLUSION

Psychologists possess the skills, knowledge, and expertise to create and participate as owners in the provider groups that are likely to replace the current managed care carve-outs that have outlived their usefulness. These provider groups will consolidate into megaproviders and dominate the industry during the second decade of this health care industrial revolution.

Psychologists who participate in this megatrend will do so as participant–provider–owner. It will not be lack of knowledge or skills that stand in the way of the 50% of the psychologists who will not survive this century (N. A. Cummings, 1988) but, rather, outmoded attitudes. Important paradigm shifts are required to transcend the old order into the new, and the reader would do well to review these (N. A. Cummings, 1995b). In the words of Alvin Toffler, "The illiterate of the future are not those who cannot read or write, but those who cannot learn, unlearn and relearn" (cited in N. A. Cummings, 1995a, p. 10).

REFERENCES

Cummings, J. L. (1996). Managing suicidal patients: The ultimate test in overcoming outmoded attitudes. In N. A. Cummings, M. S. Pallak, & J. L. Cummings (Eds.), *Surviving the demise of solo practice: Mental health professionals prospering in the era of managed care* (pp. 253–267). Madison, CT: Psychosocial Press.

Cummings, N. A. (1986). The dismantling of our health system: Strategies for survival of psychological practice. *American Psychologist, 41*, 426–431.

Cummings, N. A. (1988, September). *The future of inpatient and outpatient mental health practice: A series of predictions.* Keynote address to the First Annual *Behavioral Healthcare Tomorrow* conference, San Francisco.

Cummings, N. A. (1991). Arguments for the financial efficacy of psychological services in health care settings. In J. J. Sweet, R. H. Rozensky, & S. M. Tovian (Eds.), *Handbook of clinical psychology in medical settings* (pp. 113–126). New York: Plenum.

Cummings, N. A. (1993). Somatization: When physical symptoms have no medical cause. In D. Goleman & J. Gurin, (Eds.), *Mind–body medicine* (pp. 221–230). Yonkers, NY: Consumer Reports Books.

Cummings, N. A. (1994). The successful application of medical offset in program planning and clinical delivery. *Managed Care Quarterly, 2*(2), 1–6.

Cummings, N. A. (1995a). Behavioral health after managed care: The next golden opportunity for professional psychology. *Register Report, 20*(3), 1, 30–33.

Cummings, N. A. (1995b). Impact of managed care on employment and training: A primer for survival. *Professional Psychology: Research and Practice, 26*, 10–15.

Cummings, N. A., & Sayama, M. (1995). *Focused psychotherapy: A casebook of brief, intermittent psychotherapy throughout the life cycle.* New York: Brunner/Mazel.

Cummings, N. A., & VandenBos, G. R. (1979). The general practice of psychology. *Professional Psychology, 10*, 430–440.

De Lafuente, D. (1993, June). California groups join for survival: Mullikin Healthcare Partners exemplify trend. *Modern Healthcare*, pp. 24–26.

Forrester, D. (1994, March). The "physician equity model." *Integrated Healthcare Report*, pp. 1–4.

Goldman, W., & Feldman, S. (Eds.). (1993). Managed mental health care. *New Directions for Mental Health Services, 59*, 1–112.

Neer, H. M. (1994, July). *The future of occupational medicine*. Address to the *National Workers' Compensation and Occupational Medicine Seminar*, Hyannis, MA.

Oss, M. (1995). As quoted by Saeman, H., An interview with Monica Oss. *National Psychologist, 4*(3), 2–3.

Pallak, M. S., & Cummings, N. A. (1992). Inpatient and outpatient psychiatric treatment: The effect of matching patients to appropriate level of treatment on psychiatric and medical–surgical hospital days. *Applied and Preventive Psychology, 1*, 83–87.

Pallak, M. S., Cummings, N. A., Dörken, H., & Henke, C. J. (1993, Fall). Managed mental health, Medicaid, and medical cost offset. *New Directions for Mental Health Services*, pp. 27–40.

Physician management merger deal: Medpartners–Mullikin would lead industry. (1995, August 18). *New York Times*, Section D, pp. 1, 8.

Rich, S. (1995, March 19). Study finds savings in some HMOs. *The Washington Post*, p. A20.

4

A LIFE-COURSE PERSPECTIVE ON PHYSICAL AND PSYCHOLOGICAL HEALTH

JAMES S. JACKSON

The purpose of this chapter is to outline a general theoretical and research framework for studying health over the individual life course. A life-course perspective is conducive to psychological research and practice, as well as the implementation of health relevant public policy. This framework encompasses consideration of the continuities and discontinuities over the individual life course and focuses on important developmental and aging related processes, cohort influences, and period events needed to understand physical and psychological health at different points in the individual life span.

Human development, aging, and the life course are the central concepts in any approach to truly comprehending physical and psychological health. A life-course approach is relevant not only in the developmental sciences, but in all areas of cognitive, social, personality, organizational, clinical, and physiological study. Individual, structural, and societal change transform the phenomena of interests in all these areas of psychological science and practice. Age divisions in the study of psychologically meaningful material are no longer tenable, if they ever were (Baltes, 1987).

The life-course framework assumes that individuals have divergent life experiences, beginning at conception, due to genetic, biological, sociostructural, socioeconomic, and cultural factors (Driedger & Chappell, 1988). These differing experiences will have significant positive and negative influences on individual, family, and group well-being at all stages of the life course, ultimately influencing the adjustment to successive major life transitions (e.g. puberty, loss of spouse, retirement, and disability) in adolescence and early, middle, and late adulthood.

A life-course framework is imperative in exploring how environmental factors influence and interact with group and personal resources to both impede and facilitate the health and quality of life of successive cohorts of individuals over their individual life spans and in the nature of their individual human development and aging experiences (Baltes, 1987; Burton, Dilworth-Anderson, & Bengtson, 1991). It is the premise of a life-course perspective that already-born and aging cohorts have been exposed to the conditions that will profoundly influence their social, psychological, and health statuses as they reach middle and older ages in the years and decades to come (Baltes, 1987; Barresi, 1987).

Some recent work on emotional selectivity (Carstensen, 1993) and successful aging (e.g. Mariske, Lang, Baltes, & Baltes, 1995) is beginning to provide testable hypotheses of life-course-related processes in human development and aging. Building on decades of work by interdisciplinary scholars (e.g., Rigle, Hagestad, Brim, Riley, Overton, Neugarten, Havinghurst, Birren, Troll, & Schaie), these new models help to organize what has been more a world view and testament of faith rather than organized theory with the power to generate testable predictions.

THE SIGNIFICANCE OF BIRTH-COHORT AND STRUCTURAL CHANGES

> The health of the Negro today is both an expression and the result of the social and economic burdens imposed upon him. His health is inseparably connected with poor housing, unemployment, and inadequate education. . . . Yet there is insufficient data, as well as a paucity of studies, designed to answer many of the questions confronting us. (Cornerly, 1967, p. 653)

This quotation is taken from the first Nationwide Conference on the Health Status of the Negro in 1967 at Howard University. Its content is still applicable today, to both Blacks and the larger population. During the conference, reports on the widening health gap between Blacks and Whites pointed specifically to fetal death rates, life expectancy, childhood health risks, and disease specific causes of death, all indicating significant increased risks in the Black population (Cornerly, 1967). Since this notable conference, there have been both improvements in Black health status over the early and middle stages of the life course and continued deficits to that found among the general population.

In this chapter, as an illustrative example, consider the health status in 1996 of those middle-aged and young Black people of 1967, and speculate on where they and subsequent birth cohorts might be in the twenty-first century, the millennium right around the corner. This birth cohort perspective highlights the importance of life-span continuity in the aging experiences in America. This experience is reflected in (a) cumulative individual and social deficits; (b) the strength of birth-cohort experiences for all Americans, especially certain racial–ethnic groups; and, (c) the important effects that the processes of human development and aging, and period events (e.g. The Older Americans Act and Medicare) may have in reshaping the future of existing cohorts of middle- and upper-middle-aged people. This characterization of today's older cohorts as the middle aged of 1967 also illuminates the vast heterogeneity in lifestyles; attitudes; and physical, social, and economic preparation for older age among individuals who are now 55 years of age and older. This chapter also addresses the context of the changing demography of older populations and the changing age structure. Both of these structural changes will have profound effects on the physical and psychological health of all Americans. Assuming the middle projection series of the United States Census Bureau (1.9 ultimate lifetime births per woman, mortality life expectancy of 79.6 years in 2050 and annual net immigration of 450,000), it is projected that sustained growth will occur in the over-65-year age group until 2010. From 2010 through 2030, the postwar baby boom cohorts will increase the over-65-year age group from 39 million to 65 million. By the year 2030, every fifth American will be over 65 years of age (Seigel & Taeuber, 1986).

It is quite clear to us who work in this area that life circumstances at younger years have significant influences on the quality (and quantity) of life in the latter stages of the life course. Environmental, social, and economic conditions early in the life course have significant influences on later social, psychological, and biological growth (J. J. Jackson, 1981). These accumulate over the individual life span and, when combined with the concomitants of older age itself, eventuate in higher levels of morbidity and mortality at earlier years in old age.

For example, and as a way of highlighting life-course influences, Blacks have greater disability and morbidity at every point of their individual life spans (J. J. Jackson, 1981). In infancy, this is marked by higher mortality figures as well as accident and disease rates. In adolescence, young adulthood and thereafter, Blacks are characterized by comparatively higher homicide deaths than Whites. Middle age and early old age show increased disability, earlier retirement, and, ultimately, higher death rates in the Black community as compared with the general population. It is only after the ages of 75 to 80 that Blacks tend to show increased longevity in comparison with whites (Manton, 1982; Manton, Poss, & Wing, 1979; Markides, 1983). In support of the substance of this observed crossover, it has been suggested that genetic and environmental factors act in tandem on a heterogeneous Black population to produce hardier older Blacks (Gibson & Jackson, 1987; Manton et al., 1979). One direct implication of this explanation is the existence of the differential aging processes within Black and White populations (Manton, 1982).

More generally, socioeconomic status (SES) has been proposed as a major risk factor and implicated in the effects of other risk factors as well in physical and psychological health (e.g., Haan & Kaplan, 1985). Impressive evidence exists that SES plays a major role in a wide variety of diseases, such that higher SES is associated with better health and lowered morbidity. This effect has been shown at both the individual and the ecological levels on blood pressure, general mortality, cancer, cardiovascular heart disease and cerebrovascular disease, diabetes, and obesity. What has not been shown is how SES status from point of origin in the life course affects these health outcomes (James, 1985).

Work in illness behavior and behavioral medicine, for example, also points to the independent role of cultural and lifestyle differences in accounting for behavioral, physical, and psychological health outcomes (Cooper, 1984, 1991; Dressler, 1985, 1991; Driedger & Chappel, 1988; Richardson, 1990).

Riley and her colleagues (J.W. Riley & Riley, 1994; M.W. Riley, 1994a, 1994b; M.W. Riley & Loscocco, 1994; M.W. Riley & Riley, 1994) have for a number of years proposed that cohort succession and structural lag must be considered in any model of aging and human development, including psychological ones. Their main argument has been that as people age, they encounter changing role opportunities and circumstances in society. At the intersections of lives and structures, lives influence structures, and structures influence lives. This interplay between individual lives and role opportunities for individuals can never be in synchrony; there must always be asynchronies. Thus, there must always be structural lags, that is "changes in social structures that provide role opportunities and norms [that] do not keep pace with the 20th century metamorphoses in people lives" (J. W. Riley & Riley, 1994, p. 17).

This notion of structural lag highlights the problem of allocating education, work, and leisure time over peoples' lives. As one example, the rapid technological advances in medicine and related scientific fields may quickly outstrip the original training of physicians, making them unqualified for continual practice over a long career without extensive re-education and training. Similar examples can be pointed to in highly sophisticated fields, like computer technology. Models of age integration that effectively intersperse work, education, and leisure at every point of the adult life course are needed.

Although the exact shape of the future is difficult to dictate, what is clear is that structural change will continue to be asynchronous with the course of peoples' lives. Thus, there must be developed flexible structures and processes for changes in opportunity and norms that are responsive to structural lags and the course of individual lives.

One of the areas briefly touched on in the Rileys' work on structural lag and age integration is the role of the family as an important mediator in the relationship between individuals and social structure. For many individuals in this country and, in fact, many countries around the world, age integration is accomplished not so much by individuals and their direct relationship in complex social structures, but instead through family systems that provide productive relationships and connections across the age span. Some of these functions have been formal, such as the assumption of leadership positions with age in complex tribal and family economic systems. Many of these role functions have been informal, involving important work within the family, as counselors, helpers for the youngest and most dependent, or sources of informal work, contributing to the economic and social well-being of the family. This has certainly been true among many American racial–ethnic groups.

Now, because of some of the structural changes that Riley and her colleagues have discussed, these formal and informal familial arrangements are in danger. These changes thus threaten to remove one important buffer and facilitator in the lives of many Americans—a buffer that has shielded them from some of the negative consequences of the structural changes that Riley and Riley discuss.

Among African Americans, the family has been an important, stable asset in a hostile and uncompromising world, insulating against the continuing, pernicious effects of racism, especially in its institutional forms (e.g., Jim Crow), that transcend the types of structural changes that have occurred. In fact, the continuing oppression of prejudice, racism, and discrimination interacts with structural changes to make it even more difficult to cope. For example, the technological revolution and its impact on aging individuals are bad enough. But imagine a situation in which systematic barriers to education existed for some groups (e.g., racial–ethnic groups)—barriers that affect not only the aging cohort members but also their offspring. This is exactly the situation that we have in the United States. In fact, it is much more widespread than just education. M. W. Riley (1994b) suggested the following:

> However, other segments of older people in future cohorts may be less advantaged than their predecessors, as, for example their lives will reflect their earlier experience with the deteriorating economic conditions of today, the rise of disadvantaged minorities, the loosening family structure, the spreading use of drugs, and the increasing proportions of younger people who are failing to meet acceptable standards of academic achievement. (p. 1216)

What is notable about this quotation is that in every example, racial and ethnic groups are disadvantaged: deteriorating economic conditions, the weakening of family strengths, spreading use of drugs, increasing poor educational and technical training. Significant improvements in the life situations of many groups (Farley, 1987), particularly health, have occurred over the last 40 years (J. J. Jackson, 1981). On the other hand, recent literature (e.g. Farley, 1987; Gibson, 1986; Jaynes & Williams, 1989) documents the negative life events and structural barriers, especially for impoverished groups, that still exist. These problems include the difficulties of single-parent households, high infant mortality and morbidity, childhood diseases, poor diets, lack of preventive health care, deteriorating neighborhoods, poverty, adolescent violence, unemployment and underemployment, teen pregnancy, drug and alcohol abuse, and broken marriages. Although the exact causal relationships are not known (Williams, 1990), clearly these are predisposing factors for poor physical and psychological health across the entire individual life span (Dressler, 1991; Haan & Kaplan, 1985).

PHYSICAL AND PSYCHOLOGICAL HEALTH OVER THE LIFE COURSE

Cohort succession, aging processes, and the life course are the central concerns in any approach to understanding physical and psychological health patterns over the individual life span. Our overall framework has assumed that different groups have divergent life experiences because of SES and cultural reasons (Driedger & Chappel, 1988). These different experiences will have profound influences, both positive and negative, on the individual, family, and group well-being at all stages of the life course, ultimately influencing the adjustment to major life transitions in older age (e.g., loss of spouse, retirement, and disability). We have tried to understand and empirically demonstrate how these variables provide important coping and adaptive mechanisms in alleviating the distinct socioeconomic and psychological disadvantages of categorical ethnic and racial membership (Stanford, 1990).

We are attempting to develop a coherent life-course framework within which the nature of the economic, social, and psychological lives of all Americans can be understood and explained in the context of historical and current structural disadvantage and blocked mobility opportunities (J. S. Jackson, 1991; J. S. Jackson, Antonucci, & Gibson, 1990a, 1990b). Our research has addressed the question of how structural disadvantages in the environment are translated into physical, social, and psychological aspects of group and self at different points in the individual and group life course. This work has focused on such things as self-esteem, personal efficacy, close personal and social relationships, neighborhood and family integration, physical and mental health, group solidarity, and political participation.

Our theoretical lens has been focused on understanding the interaction and intersection of age-related processes, period events, and cohort-related phenomena, as they influence the family and individual experiences. Thus, we have oriented our studies to examine how the adaptation and quality of life of individuals, families, and larger groups of Americans are influenced by (a) the age cohort into which individuals are born; (b) the social, political, and economic events that occur to cohorts born together; and (c) the individual aging process at different points in a person's life course. For example, African Americans born before the 1940s faced very different environmental constraints and have experienced a very different set of life tasks, events, opportunities, and disappointments than those born in the 1970s (Baker, 1987). Health care advances, family changes, urban migration, and macroeconomic influences, in addition to significant changes in the legal structure, all differed dramatically for these very different birth cohorts, as they will for future cohorts (Richardson, 1990).

Genetic and biological differences also play significant roles in disease, morbidity, and mortality in older ages. In general, members of different ethnic–racial groups evidence varying patterns of disease and limiting health conditions in older ages. These are differentiated due to subpopulation differences, gender as well as heredity, and are influenced by cultural patterns and socioeconomic differences. Although the exact mechanisms of how SES and gender may play a role are not known, the negative effects of low SES are unequivocal. Also, an important overlooked factor has been the patterning and co-occurrence of disease and chronic conditions, especially among racial–ethnic groups. For example, it has been reported that for Native Americans, diabetes is a risk factor, along with malnutrition, fatigue, and crowded living conditions, in the incidence and mortality effects of tuberculosis (McCabe & Cuellar,

1994). Alcohol abuse among Native Americans is a well-known phenomenon, although research on elders in this group is not extensive. McCabe and Cuellar (1994) reported significant differences among tribes. Whereas hypertension has been long recognized as a prevalent disorder among Blacks, recent work shows a dramatic increase among the current generation of Native Americans, especially Navajos, suggesting that the next generation over 65 may show an increase in its prevalence (McCabe & Cuellar, 1994).

Genetic and biological differences may also play a significant role in disease, morbidity, and mortality in older ages. Differential bone mass between Black and White elderly, for example, may play a significant role in predisposition to breaks in older ages (Richardson, 1990). Morioka-Douglas and Yeo (1990) indicated racial–ethnic group differences in drug sensitivity and tolerance among Asian Americans in comparison with other groups. Differential rates of diabetes, cerebrovascular problems, heart problems, and alcoholism may all have significant genetic and physiologic components in accounting for observed differences among groups.

On the other hand, culturally determined differences in beliefs and behaviors related to health may also account for large differences. For example, Yu, Liu, and Kyrzeja (1985) reported that on some measures of preventive health-promoting activities (e.g., well-baby examinations and early physician visits), Asian and Pacific Islander rates exceed those of the general population. Kuo (1984) noted, however, that Asian Americans tend to underutilize services and that the negative consequences of such underutilization differ among specific Asian American groups. Yu et al. (1985) reported that cultural factors related to family ties and health beliefs (e.g., use of herbal prescriptions or balance of hot and cold elements of the body) play a significant role in the health status of the elderly in these groups. Among Native Americans, several indicators of health prevention and promotion approximate those of the general population. The lack of sensitivity to cultural differences, however, lowers the quality of service delivery and utilization by Native American Indians (National Indian Council on Aging, 1984).

How different birth cohorts, historical and current environmental events, and individual differences in aging processes interact with one another must form the overall context of our psychological research, interventions, and public policy. Thus, whereas one focus is on scientific aspects of phenomena, such as political behavior, mental disorder, or service provision, the overarching framework is one that contextualizes these individual and group experiences by birth cohort, period events, and individual aging processes. The following are examples of selected areas of research.

Socially Supportive Processes

Descriptive studies of social support suggest that a life-course perspective is particularly useful for understanding specific events or behaviors. To understand current social participation and supportive exchanges, it is best to view the present within the context of past experiences and exchanges. In addition, research has shown that demographic factors, such as socioeconomic status, sex, marital status, and age, also affect supportive behaviors. For example, a lifetime of limited economic resources does not provide the same capability of building a tangible support reserve, that is, a history of having provided tangible resources to others so that they might provide the same or similar to you in some future time of need (Antonucci, 1985). However, the research does suggest that exchanges do occur among disadvantaged groups (e.g., Stack, 1974) using the more limited tangible and perhaps more bountiful emotional and affective resources that are available, creating special, mutually supportive, intergenerational, though not necessarily linear, exchanges (Mutran, 1985; Stevens, 1988).

Similarly, because structural position affects socially supportive arrangements, people of lower SES are more likely to have exclusively family-linked networks and to have multiple relations with fewer people. Because spouses are important support resources, especially for men, the decreased availability of a spouse, for example, among older Filipino men or older Black women, has negative effects on support relationships. Sex differences in social support (women have more complex and qualitatively superior relations) seem to hold across ethnic and racial groups. Thus, both minority and nonminority women without spouses are better able than men without spouses to develop substitute or compensatory support relationships.

On the other hand, many racial–ethnic groups, while showing deficits in comparisons to majority groups in some areas, have developed alternative sources of support. For example, for many Blacks, the church is an important alternative source of support to that of family and friends (Ortega, Crutchfield, & Rushing, 1983). (Religion as social support should not be confused with religiosity—the intrinsic value of religion.)

Another major area of investigation has been the function of social network and social support in alleviating the effects of stress, promoting effective health behaviors, and influencing health outcomes (Berkman, 1988). Some work (e.g., Krause, 1987) shows that the causal effects among stress, social support, and a variety of health and effective function outcomes in the elderly are highly complex and differ among groups. Other studies (e.g., James, 1985) suggest the following: (a) Social disorganization is related to elevated stroke mortality rates, (b) individuals within strong families are at reduced risk for elevated blood pressure, and (c) there is a positive role of social ties and support in reducing elevated blood pressure. In summary, it seems indisputable that social networks and social support have etiologic and buffering roles in health and well-being over the individual life course (Berkman, 1988).

Intellectual Functioning and Cognitive Potential

A great deal of research has been conducted on intellectual functioning. Theorizing by Perlmutter (1988) suggests that a belief in an inevitable decline in cognitive potential in late life is even less defensible than a view of inevitable decline with increased age in intellectual abilities (Baltes, 1987; Schaie, 1983). As has been suggested by an impressive body of empirical work (e.g., Baltes, 1987; Schaie, 1983), some abilities decline, some remain the same, and some improve with chronological age. The direction of change depends on the specific ability under investigation and the prevalence of risk factors, such as educational level and decline in the ability of the spouse. The fact that some groups (e.g., ethnic and racial cultural groups) show such marked differences on standardized measures of cognitive ability among the young may make for an interesting comparison with patterns of lifelong changes in these abilities found in other groups. It remains to be seen if there is lifelong continuity or a crossover effect, as compared with Whites, in the intellectual functioning among racial–ethnic groups.

The work of Labouvie-Vief (1985) stresses the importance of cultural evolution in considering adult cognitive development, suggesting a critical role of the opportunity structure and the definition of adaptive roles by elders within these structures. This view of adult cognitive development seems compatible with perspectives on behaviors that emphasize coping capacities and adaptive skills in the face of real systemic constraints (J. S. Jackson, 1988, 1991). One of the most fruitful areas of study is the role of how opportunity-structure variables interact with individual difference factors (e.g., capacity and motivation) and with family and formal support systems, to influence health and effective functioning over the life course. Recent advances in experimental work designed to explicate the role of retrieval, encoding, and decoding processes in the learning of meaningful material (Perlmutter, 1988) also shows promise. The investigation of cultural and ethnic factors (contextual factors) related to changes in learning and memory over the life span could be a very fruitful area of study, a point also made in a recent Institute of Medicine report (Lonergan, 1991).

Personality and Motivation

The construct of control has assumed an important role as an organizing framework in aging research (Lachman, 1995; Rodin, 1989).

Rodin (1989) suggested that the relations between health and control may strengthen with increased age. She speculated that this may occur because: (a) control experiences increase with age, (b) the association between control and health may be altered by aging, or (c) age may influence the association between control and health-related behaviors. Recent research by Krause (1987) and Lachman (1995), for example, on the pivotal role of control beliefs and self-conceptions as important mediators in social support effects is in keeping with these observations. My own work with Toni Antonucci on personal efficacy and social support also gives control beliefs a central theoretical position in understanding the mechanisms that may underlie the influence of socially supportive behaviors (Antonucci & Jackson, 1987). More empirical research, however, is needed on the distribution of control perceptions, and their etiology and relationship to health and mental health outcomes among different groups over the life course.

Personality and motivational research has shown that a distinction between personal and general control beliefs is necessary and leads to different behavioral predictions. In particular, externality, defined in terms of sensitivity to social system determinants, predicts greater rather than less effectiveness (Gurin, Gurin, Lao, & Beattie, 1969; J. S. Jackson, Tucker, & Bowman, 1982). Enhanced control, shown experimentally under certain conditions to have positive relationships to health and well-being in White elderly persons (Rodin, 1989), may not be as effective for—in fact, may be detrimental to—the adjustment of some groups of ethnic and racial group adults.

Another related area that appears fruitful for understanding how race and ethnic statuses serve as contextual variables is age-related changes in self-conceptions, particularly self-esteem (Bengtson, Reedy & Gordon, 1985). Self-esteem has been found often to be positively correlated with age. Similarly, positive racial ethnic group identity is also positively correlated with age, though we find that a complex interaction with region and education is also present (e.g. Broman, Neighbors, & J. S. Jackson, 1988).

Psychopathology, Social Pathology, and Mental Health

Epidemiological research reveals few differences in the distribution of the major mental disorders among the full age populations of groups (Roberts, 1987). A great deal of research on Americans of racial and ethnic background points to important cultural distinctions that make the assessment and treatment of mental disorders difficult (J. S. Jackson, Chatters, & Neighbors, 1982). Differences in cultural expression, distribution of disorders, differential reactions to environmental factors, and differential responsiveness to treatment modality all have been found to be related to ethnic and racial background.

Some race and ethnic differences in paranoia, suicide, and depression may exist. Alcoholism, neuroses and schizophrenia decrease, for example, while depressive and organically based psychiatric disorders increase in successively older age groups (LaRue, Dessonville, & Jarvik, 1985). A given disease, in fact, can manifest itself differently among the young and old (Minaker & Rowe, 1985), and individuals at midlife, in contrast to those at older ages, may be at higher risk for stress reactions and perhaps depression due to major life losses, such as divorce and death of loved ones.

Stress events, responses, consequent adaptation, and ways in which these factors are interrelated also differ across age (Schaie, 1981). The personal resources of the elderly, for example, appear to insulate against or buffer stress in ways that may be different from the young (e.g., Kasl & Berkman, 1981). Age also changes relationships between mental health status and selected variables. For example, risks for nervous and mental disorders are greater for Black than White men age 24 to 64, but less for Black than White women age 65 to 69—young black men are at greater risk for certain mental disorders than older Black women (Manton, Patrick, & Johnson, 1987). These findings suggest complex interactions among age, race, gender, and the risk for developing mental disorders. Heterogeneity in physical and mental health and functioning increases in successively older age groups (Rowe & Kahn, 1987). For example, Manton et al. (1987) found that the relationship between age and mental illness diagnoses and mental status, is nonlinear in older age groups of Black women. Thus, caution must be taken in extrapolating the psychiatric epidemiology of one age group to another.

Age group, aging processes, and cohort membership have special effects on mental health status; aging is clearly pivotal in the interpretation of any model of stress and adaptation (Gibson, 1986). Adaptation to stressors and stress, in fact, could vary at different ages or points in the life span, among different cohorts, and in different sociohistorical periods. This makes it clear that the mental status and functioning must be examined within a theoretical model that takes a life-course perspective (Barresi, 1987).

The examination of physical and psychological health status and functioning has been conducted in a relative life-course vacuum. Although several authors have indicated the necessity of considering life-course models (e.g., Baltes, 1987; Barresi, 1987; Manton & Soldo, 1985) and history, cohort, and period effects in the nature of physical and psychological health status and functioning, few have actually collected the type of data or conducted the types of analyses that would shed any light on this process. (Schaie's and the Baltes' work on intellectual and cognitive functioning and successful aging are exceptions.) This has been as much the fault of a lack of good conceptual life-course models of physical and psychological health status and functioning as it has been the lack of quality data over time on sizable numbers of representative samples.

SUMMARY AND CONCLUSIONS

Older age among the general population is not a time of inevitable decline (J. S. Jackson et al., 1990a; Rowe, 1985). Changes in lifestyles, environmental risk reductions, and medical interventions can have positive influences on the quantity and quality of physical and psychological health in late life among older adults, even given the negative life-course experiences I have outlined. Some data (e.g., Gibson & Jackson, 1987) show that many historically disadvantaged older groups are free from functional disability and limitations of activity due to chronic illness and disease. For example, after the age of 65, Blacks and Whites, within sex groups, differ very little in years of expected remaining life. Health care has improved significantly for older adults, and consecutive cohorts have been better educated and better able to take advantage of available opportunities. On the other hand, without extensive environmental interventions, it is highly likely that a significant, and undoubtedly growing, proportion of older adults of the year 2051, those being born in 1996, are at severe risk for impoverished conditions, and poor social, physical, and psychological health in old age.

A convergence of theory and research derived from resource-based, life-course models of health and effective functioning is emerging (e.g., Baltes & Baltes, 1990). The data briefly reviewed in this chapter suggest directions that new psychological theory and research on physical and psychological health over the life course might take (Barresi 1987; Carstensen, 1993; Fry, 1988; Holzberg, 1982; Mariske et al., 1995; Rosenthal, 1986).

The life-course framework holds great promise. There is a need, however, for a greater infusion of cultural considerations in life-course theorizing and research in human development and aging (Fry, 1988; Gelfand & Barresi, 1987). Theories, research paradigms, service delivery models, and public policies continue to be developed that are not sensitive to the ever-increasing, large, ethnically and culturally diverse segments of our population. Culture and lifestyle differences are of fundamental importance in psychological constructs, theories, and interventions (Holzberg, 1982; J. J. Jackson, 1985; Rosenthal, 1986). Some studies have shown how recognition and sensitivity to cultural and racial factors in service delivery programs can increase the effectiveness and reduce the cost of delivering services to some populations (J. S. Jackson, Burns, & Gibson, 1992). It also has been suggested that the infusion of cultural content has positive effects on the health of the nation more broadly, regardless of whether the direct focus of that work is on specific racial–ethnic groups (Cooper, Steinhauer, Schatzkin, & Miller, 1981)

A positive future for psychological, life-course research, practice, and policy related to aging and age related changes in physical and psychological health, lies in the increased emphasis on the important contextual variables of race, culture, ethnicity, gender, and social and economic statuses (J. S. Jackson et al., 1990a). A recent Institute of Medicine and National Institute on Aging report on aging research in the behavioral and social sciences (Lonergan, 1991) concluded that during the last 40 years an impressive acquisition of knowledge on the nature of aging in sensory, behavioral, and cognitive systems has occurred, indicating that: (a) People do not age the same way—Individuals differ greatly in age-related declines (and increments) in physical, behavioral, and cognitive functioning; (b) some aging processes and the probability of aging well are modifiable; and (c) observed functional differences across individuals are greatly influenced by societal, environmental, and health-related statuses, and, most important, by the background and makeup of the individual. Thus, we now know the following: (a) Cognitive declines are not universal with age, some intellectual abilities are actually maintained or improve with age; (b) positive social and psychological change is possible through interventions among older adults and, in fact, at every point of the life span; (c) intergenerational models of aging and human development are of critical importance in understanding individual aging trajectories; (d) there is a causal role of period events and cohort membership on aging-related physical and psychological health processes; and (e) we must conceptualize aging-related changes in physical and psychological health processes within individual, family, cultural, and societal life-course frameworks.

Our work, and the work of many others, is attempting to extend the life-course framework to encompass an integrated model that includes historical, cohort, and cultural influences on successful social, physical, and psychological development and aging. The relevance, power, and importance of comprehensive life-course models in psychological research, practice, and public policy cannot be overstated. It is the key to the evolution of comprehensive theory, appropriate research, and successful interventions and programs to ameliorate poor physical and psychological health conditions at every point in the life course.

REFERENCES

Antonucci, T. C. (1985). Personal characteristics, social networks, and social behavior. In R. H. Binstock, & E. Shanas (Eds.), *Handbook of aging and the social sciences* (pp. 94–128). New York: Van Nostrand Reinhold.

Antonucci, T. C., & Jackson, J. S. (1987). Social support, interpersonal efficacy and health. In L. Carsstensen & B. A. Edelstein (Eds.), *Handbook of clinical gerontology* (pp. 291–311). New York: Pergamon Press.

Baker, F. M. (1987). The Afro-American life cycle: Success, failure, and mental health. *Journal of the National Medical, 7,* 625–633.

Baltes, P. B. (1987). Theoretical propositions of life-span developmental psychology: On the dynamics between growth and decline. *Developmental Psychology, 23,* 611–626.

Baltes, P. B., & Baltes, M. M. (Eds.) (1990). *Successful aging: Perspectives from the behavioral sciences.* Cambridge, England: Cambridge University Press.

Barresi, C. M. (1987). Ethnic aging and the life course. In D. E. Gelfand & C. M. Barresi (Eds.), *Ethnic dimensions of aging* (pp. 18–34). New York: Springer.

Bengtson, V. L., Reedy, M. N., & Gordon, C. (1985). Aging and self-conceptions: Personality processes and social contexts. In J. E. Birren & K. W. Schaie (Eds.), *Handbook of the psychology of aging* (pp. 544–593). New York: Van Nostrand Reinhold.

Berkman, L. F. (1988). *The changing and heterogenous nature of aging and longevity: A social and biomedical perspective.* Unpublished manuscript, Yale University, School of Medicine, New Haven, CT.

Broman, C. L., Neighbors, H. W., & Jackson, J. S. (1988). Racial group identification among Black adults. *Social Forces, 67,* 146–158.

Burton, L. M., & Dilworth-Anderson, P., & Bengtson, V. L. (1991). Creating culturally relevant ways of thinking about diversity. *Generations, 15,* 67–72.

Carstensen, L. L. (1993). Motivation for social contact across the life span: A theory of socioemotional selectivity. In J. Jacobs (Ed.), *Nebraska symposium on motivation: Vol. 40. Developmental perspectives on motivation* (pp. 209–254). Lincoln: University of Nebraska Press.

Cooper, R. (1984). A note on the biological concept of race and its application in epidemiological research. *American Heart Journal, 108,* 715–723.

Cooper, R. (1991). Celebrate diversity—Or should we? *Ethnicity and Disease, 1,* 3–7.

Cooper, R., Steinhauer, M., Schatzkin, A. & Miller, A. (1981). Improved mortality among U.S. Blacks, 1968–1978: The role of antiracist struggle. *International Journal of Health Services, 11,* 511–522.

Cornerly, P. B. (1968). The health status of the Negro today and in the future. *American Journal of Public Health, 58,* 647–654.

Dressler, W. (1985). Extended family relationships, social support, and mental health in a Southern Black community. *Journal of Health and Social Behavior, 26*, 39–48.

Dressler, W. W. (1991). Social class, skin color, and arterial blood pressure in two societies. *Ethnicity and Disease, 1*, 60–77.

Driedger, L., & Chappell, N. (1988). *Aging and ethnicity: Toward an interface.* Toronto, Ontario, Canada: Butterworths.

Farley, R. (1987). Who are Black Americans?: The quality of life for Black Americans twenty years after the civil rights revolution. *Milbank Memorial Fund Quarterly, 65* (Suppl. 1), 9–34.

Fry, C. (1988). Theories of aging and culture. In J. E. Birren & V. L. Bengston (Eds.), *Emergent theories of aging* (pp. 447–481). New York: Springer.

Gelfand, D. E. & Barresi, C. M. (Eds.). (1987). *Ethnic dimensions of aging.* New York: Springer.

Gibson, R. (1986). Blacks in an aging society. *Daedalus, 115*, 349–372.

Gibson, R. C., & Jackson, J. S. (1987). Health, physical functioning, and informal supports of the Black elderly. *Milbank Memorial Fund Quarterly, 65* (Suppl 1), 1–34.

Gurin, P., Gurin, G., Lao, R. C., & Beattie, M. (1969). Internal–external control in the motivational dynamics of Negro youth. *Journal of Social Issues, 25*, 29–53.

Haan, M. N., & Kaplan, G. A. (1985). *The contribution of socioeconomic position to minority health.* In *Report of the Secretary's Task Force on Black and Minority Health: Volume II. Crosscutting issues in minority health.* Washington, DC: U.S. Department of Health and Human Services.

Holzberg, C. S. (1982). Ethnicity and aging: Anthropological perspectives on more than just the minority elderly. *Gerontologist, 22*, 249–257.

Jackson, J. J. (1981). Urban Black Americans. In A. Harwood (Ed.), *Ethnicity and medical care.* Cambridge, MA: Harvard University Press.

Jackson, J. J. (1985). Race, national origin, ethnicity, and aging. In R. B. Binstock & E. Shanas (Eds.), *Handbook of aging and the social sciences* (pp. 264–303). New York: Van Nostrand Reinhold.

Jackson, J. S. (1988). *The Black American elderly: Research on physical and psychological health.* New York: Springer.

Jackson, J. S. (Ed.). (1991). *Life in Black America.* Newbury Park, CA: Sage.

Jackson, J. S., Antonucci, T. C., & Gibson, R. C. (1990a). Cultural, racial, and ethnic minority influences on aging. In J. E. Birren & K. W. Schaie (Eds.), *Handbook of the psychology of aging* (3rd ed., 103–123). San Diego, CA: Academic Press.

Jackson, J. S., Antonucci, T. C., & Gibson, R. C. (1990b). Social relations, productive activities, and coping with stress in late life. In M. A. P. Stephens, J. H. Crowther, S. E. Hobfoll, & D. L. Tennenbaum (Eds.), *Stress and coping in later life families* (pp. 193–212). Washington, DC: Hemisphere.

Jackson, J. S., Burns, C., & Gibson, R. C. (1992). An overview of geriatric care in ethnic and racial minority groups. In E. Calkins, A. B. Ford, & P. R. Katz (Eds.), *Practice of geriatrics* (2nd ed., pp. 57–64). Philadelphia: W. B. Saunders.

Jackson, J. S., Chatters, L. M., & Neighbors, H. W. (1982). The mental health status of older Black Americans: A national study. *Black Scholar, 13,* 21–35.

Jackson, J. S., Tucker, M. B., & Bowman, P. J. (1982). Conceptual and methodological problems in survey research on Black Americans. In W. T. Liu (Eds.), *Methodological problems in minority research* (pp. 11–39). Chicago: Pacific/Asian American Mental Health Research Center.

James, S. A. (1985). Coronary heart disease in black Americans: Suggestions for future research on psychosocial factors. In A. M. Ostfield (Ed.), *Measuring psychosocial variables in epidemiologic studies of cardiovascular disease* (pp. 499–508). Bethesda, MD: National Institutes of Health.

Jaynes, G. D. & Williams, R. M. (Eds.). (1989). *A Common Destiny: Blacks and American society.* Washington, DC: National Academy Press.

Kasl, S. V., & Berkman, L. F. (1981). Some psychosocial influences on the health status of the elderly: The perspective of social epidemiology. In J. L. McGaugh & S. B. Kiesler (Eds.), *Aging, biology and behavior* (pp. 345–385). San Diego, CA: Academic Press.

Krause, N. (1987). Life, stress, social support, and self-esteem in an elderly population. *Psychology and Aging, 2,* 349–356.

Kuo, W. H. (1984). Prevalence of depression among Asian Americans. *Journal of Nervous and Mental Disease, 172,* 449–457.

Labouvie-Vief, G. (1985). Intelligence and cognition. In J. E. Birren & K. W. Shaie (Eds.), *Handbook of the psychology of aging* (pp. 500–530). New York: Van Nostrand Reinhold.

Lachman, M. E. (1995, August). *Maintaining a sense of control over physical and mental function.* Presentation at the 103rd Annual Convention of the American Psychological Association, New York.

LaRue, A., Dessonville, C., & Jarvik, I. (1985). Aging and mental disorders. In J. Birren & K. Schaie (Eds.), *Handbook of the psychology of aging* (pp. 664–702). New York: Van Nostrand Reinhold.

Lonergran, E. T. (Ed.). (1991). *Extending life, enhancing life.* Washington, DC: National Academy Press.

Manton, K. G. (1982). Differential life expectancy: Possible explanations during the later years. In R. C. Manual (Ed.), *Minority aging: Sociological and psychological issues* (63–70). Westport, CT: Greenwood Press.

Manton, K. G., Patrick, C. H., & Johnson, K. W. (1987). Health differentials between Blacks and Whites: Recent trends in mortality and morbidity. *Milbank Memorial Fund Quarterly, 65,* 129–199.

Manton, K. G., Poss, S. S., & Wing, S. (1979). The Black/White mortality crossover: Investigation from the perspective of the components of aging. *Gerontologist, 63,* 177–186.

Manton, K. G., & Soldo, B. J. (1985). Dynamics of health changes in the oldest old: New perspectives and evidence. *Milbank Memorial Fund Quarterly, 63,* 206–285.

Mariske, M., Lang, F. R., Baltes, P. B., & Baltes, M. M. (1995). Selective optimization with compensation: Life-span perspectives on successful human development. In R. A. Dixon & L. Backman (Eds.), *Psychological compensation: Mananging losses and promoting gains.* Hillsdale, NJ: Erlbaum.

Markides, K. S. (1983). Aging, religiosity and adjustment: A longitudinal analysis. *Journal of Gerontology, 38,* 621–625.

McCabe, M., & Cuellar, J. (1994). *Aging and health: American Indian/Alaska natives* (Working Paper No. 6). Stanford, CA: Stanford University, Stanford Geriatric Education Center, Division of Family & Community Medicine.

Minaker, K. L., & Rowe, J. W. (1985). Health and disease among the oldest old: A clinical perspective. *Milbank Memorial Fund Quarterly, 63,* 324–349.

Morioka-Douglas, N., & Yeo, G. (1990). *Aging and health: Asian/Pacific Island elders* (Working Paper No. 6). Stanford CA: Stanford University, Stanford Geriatric Education Center, Division of Family & Community Medicine.

Mutran, E. (1985). Intergeneratinal family support among Blacks and Whites: Response to culture or to socioeconomic differences. *Journal of Gerontology, 40,* 382–389.

National Indian Council on Aging. (1984). Indian and Alaskan natives. In E. B. Palmore (Ed.), *Handbook on the aged in the United States* (pp. 269–278). Westport, CT: Greenwood Press.

Ortega, S. T., Crutchfield, R. D., & Rushing, W. A. (1983). Race differences in elderly personal well-being. *Research on Aging, 5,* 101–118.

Perlmutter, M. (1988). Cognitive potential throughout life. In J. E. Birren & V. L. Bengtson (Eds.), *Emergent theories of aging* (pp. 247–268). New York: Springer.

Richardson, J. (1990). *Aging and health: Black elders* (Working Paper No. 4). Stanford, CA: Stanford University, Stanford Geriatric Education Center, Division of Family & Community Medicine.

Riley, J. W., & Riley, M. W. (1994, June). Beyond productive aging: Changing lives and social structure. *Aging International,* pp. 15–19.

Riley, M. W. (1994a). Aging and society: Past, present, and future. *Gerontologist, 34,* 436–446.

Riley, M. W. (1994b). Changing lives and changing social structures: Common concerns of social science and public health. *American Journal of Public Health, 84,* 1214–1217.

Riley, M. W., & Loscocco, K. A. (1994). The changing structure of work opportunities: Toward an age integrated society. In R. P. Abeles, H. C. Gift, & M. C. Orey (Eds.), *Aging and the quality of life* (pp. 235–252). New York: Springer.

Riley, M. W., & Riley, J. W. Jr. (1994). Age integration and the lives of older people. *Gerontologist, 34,* 110–115.

Roberts, R. E. (1987, December). *Depression among Black and Hispanic Americans*. Paper present at the National Institutes of Mental Health Workshop on Depression and Suicide in Minorities, Bethesda, MD.

Rodin, J. (1989). Sense of control: Potentials for intervention. *Annals of the American Academy of Political and Social Science, 503*, 29–42.

Rosenthal, C. J. (1986). Family supports in later life: Does ethnicity make a difference? *Gerontologist, 26*, 19–24.

Rowe, J. W. (1985). Health care of the elderly. *New England Journal of Medicine, 312*, 827–835.

Rowe, J. W., & Kahn, R. L. (1987). Human aging: Usual and successful. *Science, 237*, 143–149.

Schaie, K. W. (1981). Psychological changes from midlife to early old age: Implications for the maintenance of mental health. *American Journal of Orthopsychiatry, 51*, 199–218.

Schaie, K. W. (Ed.). (1983). *Longitudinal studies of adult psychological development*. New York: Guilford Press.

Seigel, J. S., & Taeuber, T. C. (1986). Demographic dimensions of an aging population. In A. Pifer & L. Bronte (Eds.), *Our aging society: Paradox and promise* (pp. 79–110). New York: Norton.

Stack, C. B. (1974). *All our kin*. New York: Harper & Row.

Stanford, E. P. (1990). Diverse Black aged. In Z. Harel, E. A. McKinney, & M. Williams (Eds.), *Black aged: Understanding diversity and service needs* (pp. 33–49). Newbury Park, CA: Sage.

Stevens, J. H. (1988). Social support, locus of control, and parenting in three low-income groups of mothers: Black teenagers, Black adults, and White mothers. *Child Development, 59*, 635–642.

Williams, D. R. (1990). Socioeconomic differentials in health: A review and redirection. *Social Psychology Quarterly, 53*, 81–99.

Yu, E. S. H., Liu, W. T., & Kyrzeja, P. (1985). Physical and mental health status indicators for Asian-American communities. In Department of Health and Human Services (Ed.), *Black and minority health: Vol. II. Cross-cutting issues in minority health* (pp. 255–286). Washington, DC: U.S. Department of Health and Human Services.

5

AGING, HEALTH, AND BEHAVIOR: THE INTERPLAY BETWEEN BASIC AND APPLIED SCIENCE

DENISE C. PARK

The composition of American society is changing. Besides a dramatic increase in racial and ethnic heterogeneity, perhaps an even more striking change is the massive shift in the age distribution of the population. Americans are getting old. The baby boomers are on the crest of late adulthood. By the year 2030, it appears that there will be as many elderly people in this country as there are children. To fully appreciate the magnitude of the demographic shift, consider that in the year 1900, only 4% of the U.S. population was over 65, whereas children constituted 40% of the population (Task Force on Aging Research, 1995). Thus, in 1900, there were 10 children for every elderly adult, and by 2030, that will have shifted to a 1:1 ratio of adult to child. It may chill you to recognize that the shift I am describing will happen in the lifetimes of most of you who are reading this book.

Preparation of this chapter was supported by National Institute on Aging Grants AGO6265-08, AGO9868-02, and P5011715-01. I thank Natalie Davidson and Maria Brinks for their assistance.

On the basis of just these few statistics, it should be apparent that at the least, the graying of America represents an amazing social and economic challenge for our society. What needs to be emphasized is that this problem is certain, and virtually on us, and that Social Security and Medicare were predicated on a large number of young adults to maintain the system. As government resources become more scarce, it seems likely that the successful adaptation of any given individual to the aging process will be tremendously influenced by his or her health behavior. It has become increasingly evident that health is not just a result of genetic and environmental contributions, but the behavior of the person plays a critical role in disease prevention as well as health outcomes once a disease process has begun. The focus of this chapter is twofold: First, I discuss the critical role that development of the behavioral sciences can play in maintaining health and vitality into late adulthood, with an emphasis on the importance of fostering both basic and applied behavioral research and the interplay between the two. Second, I follow this discussion with a concrete example of how my own research program on the psychosocial and cognitive components of medication adherence in older adults evolved from a long-term basic research program on mechanisms associated with age-related changes in memory function.

THE LINKAGE OF BEHAVIORAL RESEARCH TO HEALTH OUTCOMES

Behavior is the fundamental link between medical knowledge, services, and technology and successful health outcomes. Behavioral issues permeate all aspects of medical care and treatment. For example, it seems self-evident that health can be maintained only if people engage in preventive behaviors. What is less recognized is that successful treatment of illness requires that individuals both understand and follow relevant medical advice, once treatment is initiated. Moreover, effective treatments can be administered only to the extent that health care professionals understand the needs, attitudes, and goals of their clients. Finally, the individual cannot adjust his or her health behaviors in a direction that leads to adaptation and to successful aging if he or she does not know what behaviors prevent disease. It is only through behavioral research that we can address the issues raised thus far and then isolate and disseminate information to the general public and health care professionals that will lead to the maintenance of health in late adulthood.

The ominous developments in the recent past with respect to changes in Medicare and gatekeeping of access to health care make it eminently clear that baby boomers should be particularly concerned that they maintain their health. When the baby boomers are old, there

TABLE 1
Behavioral Recommendations Associated With Each Research Domain in the Report of the Task Force on Aging Research

Research domain	No. goals	No. goals with a behavioral component	Proportion
Biological processes	25	5	.20
Diseases and disabilities	42	24	.57
Mental disorders	12	12	1.00
Health care	27	22	.81
Social & behavioral functioning	16	16	1.00
An aging society	13	10	.77
Economic security	9	3	.33
Social & supportive services	12	11	.92
Special populations	18	17	.94
Research & data resources	18	11	.61
Total	192	131	.68

will be increasing competition for scarce medical resources, and many boomers also will have limited pension resources. Thus, health and vitality are likely to become even more important predictors of well-being in late adulthood than is the case at present. We need to know what behaviors lead to good health. Until the very recent past, the focus of most research within the National Institutes of Health has been on basic disease mechanisms and treatment, with much less attention being paid to behavioral factors. This is changing, especially with respect to health issues associated with the aging process.

Behavioral research and targeted behavioral objectives are permeating the goals of the National Institute on Aging. The National Institute on Aging has released a document prioritizing research objects for the future with respect to aging (Task Force on Aging Research, 1995). Categories of emphasis are divided into 10 research domains, as shown in Table 1. Within each domain, there are a series of research objectives and goals. There are a total of 192 goals specified across the 10 domains. What is particularly exciting is that 131 of them (68%) have a behavioral component or objective. Of course, one would expect categories such as social and behavioral functioning to have behavioral objectives. But what is most telling is that behavioral goals permeate every category, even basic medical objectives. For example, in the category of "diseases and disabilities," there are numerous goals that are primarily behavioral, including "frailty prevention"; "exercise, strength training, and metabolism"; "cancer prevention and early detection in older persons"; and "the effect of aging on biomechanical efficiency." Under the category of "health care," behavioral objectives include "compliance with health promotion and disease prevention measures"; "prevention of falls";

"smoking cessation"; and "autonomy in health-care decision making." There are many other goals that mandate the assessment of preferences and decision-making processes on the part of older adults with respect to health services, housing, and caregiving—these are all goals that have primarily behavioral science objectives. This report demonstrates conclusively that there is at last recognition that understanding disease mechanisms is entirely insufficient without understanding both the psychological mechanisms underlying the use of and adherence to treatments and the prevention behaviors individuals can engage in so that they will not need to be treated at all—they will stay healthy!

It is essential never to lose sight of the role that basic research plays as the foundation for applied, outcome-based research. It is our understanding of basic cognitive functioning and psychosocial processes that is the foundation for all of the prevention and intervention research that permits us to determine how to maintain sustained vitality into late adulthood. There are innumerable important questions about health and aging that psychologists are poised to answer, and some important developments have already occurred. The Human Capital Initiative is a scientific advocacy effort undertaken by the American Psychological Society. Under the auspices of this initiative, psychological scientists have prepared a series of reports based on their consensual opinions. The reports prioritize the important scientific questions that will have significant impact on society that psychologists are able to address now. One of these reports focused on aging and was developed in collaboration with the American Psychological Association. It is entitled "Vitality for Life: Psychological Research for Productive Aging" (Cavanaugh & Park, 1993). The report presents four major research objectives: (a) understanding relationships about health and behavior, (b) securing more information, much of it with health objectives, about the oldest old, (c) addressing issues associated with aging and the workplace, and (d) developing a better understanding of well-being in late adulthood and treatment for mental disorders in older adults. These priorities are very similar to many research objectives identified in the Task Force on Aging Research report (1995). It is very encouraging to see that there is considerable agreement about research priorities on aging for the future among both research scientists and representatives of federal agencies. Both reports emphasize areas where breakthroughs are possible due to the assembled corpus of basic knowledge and the fact that there are already beginnings of applications of that information to real-world problems.

FROM BASIC TO APPLIED RESEARCH: COGNITIVE FUNCTION AND MEDICATION ADHERENCE

One of the most highly researched basic areas in the psychology of aging that has tremendous implications for adaptation to aging is the understanding of aging and cognitive function. The knowledge base in cognitive aging is sufficiently developed that there are beginning to be substantial applications of basic behavioral work to areas of health and aging. In an effort to illustrate the link between basic laboratory research and effecting changes in health behavior, I devote the remainder of this chapter to presenting an overview of how basic research in the laboratory on aging and memory has led to the development of a substantial research program on aging and medication adherence, including intervention-based work. I close with a summary of important areas for future development in the area of health, behavior, and aging.

Cognition and Aging

I have spent the past 16 years studying memory function across the life span—from young adulthood to very late adulthood. In this work, my colleagues and I, along with many other researchers, have found convincing evidence that older adults perform more poorly on cognitive tasks that are measures of processing speed or processing resource. By this I mean that we have evidence that older adults process information more slowly than young adults (Park et al., 1994), that they have less *working memory* capacity (working memory is the ability to simultaneously process new incoming information while storing and retrieving old information), and that they have poorer recall abilities (Park & Shaw, 1992; Park, Smith, Morrell, Puglisi, & Dudley, 1990).

At the same time, we have demonstrated a number of cases in which older adults perform comparably to young adults on some types of memory tasks. For example, as Figure 1 illustrates, we have found that older adults have comparable picture-recognition abilities to young adults across a range of conditions (Park, Puglisi, & Smith, 1986), whereas Figure 2 demonstrates that age deficits observed in *direct, explicit recall* (recall items that one has studied) are not observed when indirect or implicit measures of recall are used (Park & Shaw, 1992). We have also found evidence for age invariance on some types of spatial memory and vocabulary abilities (Park et al., 1994). We believe that memory deficits occur when a memory task is high in its demands for mental effort (e.g., recall of information from memory, speeded measures of cognitive function, measures of maximal working memory capacity). In contrast, age deficits are minimized when a task requires less mental effort (e.g., recognition of pictures, implicit memory, and other processes requiring less direct, effortful memory search) or when it relies on world knowledge, which grows rather than decreases with age (e.g., vocabulary). On the basis of these premises, we have attempted to develop conditions where we can facilitate cognitive function of older adults by minimizing the processing resources required in a task. Figure 3 demonstrates that age differences for recall of pictures are markedly attenuated in a cued-recall

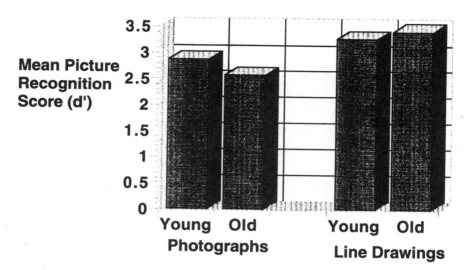

Figure 1. Picture-recognition scores (*d'* values) for old and young adults for photographs and line drawings of real-world scenes. Data derived from "Picture Memory in Older Adults: Does an Age-Related Decline Exist?" by D. C. Park, J. T. Puglisi, and A. D. Smith, 1986, *Psychology and Aging, 1*, 11–17.

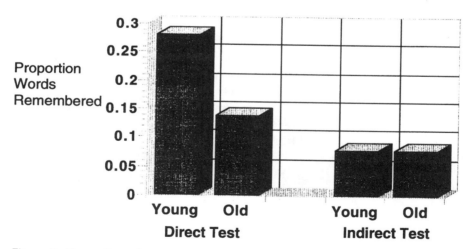

Figure 2. Proportion of words recalled in a stem-completion task as a function of age and type of memory test (direct or indirect). Data derived from "Effect of Environmental Support on Implicit and Explicit Memory in Young and Old Adults" by D. C. Park and R. Shaw, 1992, *Psychology and Aging, 7*, 632–642.

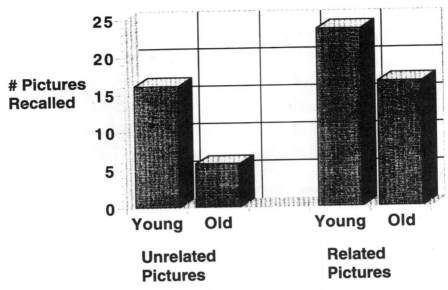

Figure 3. Number of items recalled in a cued-recall task when subjects were presented with unrelated compared with weakly related pictures. Data derived from "Effects of Contextual Integration on Recall of Pictures in Older Adults" by D. C. Park, A. D. Smith, R. W. Morrell, J. T. Puglisi, and W. N. Dudley, 1990, *Journal of Gerontology: Psychological Sciences, 45,* 52–58.

task when the cue is weakly related to the target word (e.g., spider–ant), compared with unrelated pictures (cherry–ant), because subjects can use their intact world knowledge to help them recall the words (Park et al., 1990). We also found that providing subjects with pictorial illustrations of an action represented in a sentence that they were to remember resulted in disproportionately greater improvement for older adults compared with younger adults, as shown in Figure 4 (Cherry, Park, Frieske, & Smith, in press).

The findings reported thus far probably appear to have little to do with health behaviors. However, as this basic laboratory work on memory and aging progressed, I became increasingly interested in understanding the meaning of these findings for a memory problem of practical significance to older adults.

Remembering to take medications correctly seemed to be a practical problem of great significance to older adults, as they consume more prescription medications than any other age group and are frequently placed in a situation where they must manage a complex regimen consisting of multiple medications. It has been estimated that medication nonadherence results in costs of $100 billion a year in the United States in terms of direct medical costs as well as lost time (Robbins, 1990). Thus, based on the importance of the problem and the significant role that memory and cognitive function appeared to play in this health

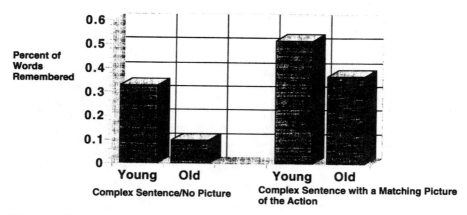

Figure 4. The percentage of target words remembered in a complex sentence when it was presented alone or with a matching picture of the action described in the sentence. Data derived from "Verbal and Pictorial Elaborations Enhance Memory in Younger and Older Adults" by K. E. Cherry, D. C. Park, D. A. Frieske, and A. D. Smith, 1996, *Aging, Neuropsychology, and Cognition, 3*, 15–29. Used with permission.

behavior, I embarked on a program of research on medication adherence, along with my colleague, Roger Morrell. *Medication adherence* can be defined as taking medication correctly, in the right amount, at the right time, and according to any special instructions, such as "take with food" (Park & Jones, in press). We hypothesized that there were four major cognitive components involved in the accurate use of medications: (a) comprehension of the individual instructions for each medication, (b) integration of the instructions across multiple medications to form a temporal plan—a working memory task; (c) remembering (or writing down) the plan—a long-term memory task; and (d) remembering to carry out the plan, that is, to take the medication—a prospective memory task (Park, 1992).

Laboratory Work on Medication Adherence

The initial work we conducted on this topic was a straightforward translation of our basic work in the laboratory into paradigms that examined age differences in comprehension and memory for medication information. We found evidence for significant age differences in both comprehension and memory for medication information (Morrell, Park, & Poon, 1989), with older adults remembering less information than young adults. This pattern of findings occurred even under conditions of unlimited study time. On the basis of the finding of age invariance for picture recognition presented in Figure 1, we attempted to design more memorable prescription labels for older adults by designing medication labels where information was presented pictorially. We then tested how memorable young and old adults found these redesigned pictorial labels compared with verbal labels (Morrell, Park, & Poon, 1990). We found that the pictorial labels were superior to verbal labels for young but not old adults, whereas old adults functioned better with the more familiar verbal labels.

As this work progressed, we became more interested in learning how older adults functioned with their own medications rather than with unfamiliar medication information designed for laboratory studies. Thus, for our next study, we focused on understanding how existing memory aids for organizing and taking medications were used with patients' actual medications. In this study, we presented patients with three types of medication organizers, commercial memory aids sold over-the-counter, designed to help facilitate the individual's medication-adherence behavior (Park, Morrell, Frieske, Blackburn, & Birchmore, 1991). We tested 45 arthritis patients taking multiple medications and asked them to load their own medications into three different types of organizers: one had merely 7 compartments, 1 for each day of the week; another was a medication wheel with 12 slots for 12 hours of the day; and a third had 28 compartments in which to place pills, created by crossing the 7 days of the week with 4 times during the day (morning, noon, dinner, and evening). We found that more errors were made in loading the first two organizers than with the third (the 28-compartment organizer). These findings, at the least, suggested that patients who loaded their organizers incorrectly were unlikely to be helped by these alleged memory supports.

Medication Adherence Outside the Laboratory

Although we were concerned that two of the organizers were loaded incorrectly, we were also intrigued by the finding that the error rate for the 28-compartment organizer (the 7-day organizer with 4 times per day) was below 5%. We were becoming increasingly interested in measuring what older adults actually did with their medications in the real world and in assessing the effect of a cognitive intervention, such as the use of a medication organizer, on adherence. We were concerned that verbal reports or diaries might not be accurate measures of adherence behavior, so we located a system based on bar-coding technology that we could use to monitor medication-taking behaviors outside of the laboratory. To implement the bar-coding measurement system, we provided 64 older adults with unique bar-coding stickers for each of the medications they were taking and put the stickers in a wallet. We also gave subjects a credit-card-sized bar code scanner with the wallet. The subjects were instructed to keep the wallet with their medications and scan the bar code, which was clearly labeled with the medication name, whenever they took that medication. The date and time of the scan were recorded

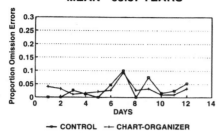

YOUNG-OLD ADULTS
MEAN - 65.87 YEARS

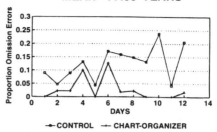

OLD-OLD ADULTS
MEAN - 77.80 YEARS

Figure 5. Mean adherence rates for young-old and old-old adults in a control condition compared with subjects receiving a chart and medication organizer. Reprinted from "Medication Adherence Behaviors in Older Adults: Effects of External Cognitive Supports" by D. C. Park, R. W. Morrell, D. Frieske, and D. Kincaid, 1992, *Psychology and Aging, 7,* 252–256. Copyright 1992 by the American Psychological Association.

in the tiny bar-coding device, and when the subject returned the device to us, we downloaded a complete record of their adherence behaviors for a 2-week period. The 64 older adults we studied were all taking multiple medications for various disorders, and they were randomly assigned to one of four groups. The first set of subjects was assigned to a control group where no intervention occurred. A second group of subjects was assigned to a chart condition, where they were provided with a chart in the form of a poster or booklet that provided them with an hour-by-hour, day-by-day account of which medications they should take for a 2-week period. There was a check-off space for them to record when they did take the medication. We hypothesized that this type of intervention would reduce the comprehension, working memory, and long-term memory components of medication adherence. A third group received the 28-compartment organizer, with their medications loaded in it by the experimenter. The organizer also facilitated the same cognitive components of medication adherence as the chart, but the medications were actually physically organized for the subject in the device, unlike the chart, where the medications remained in their original bottles. A final group received both aids: the medication chart and organizer. Results are displayed in Figure 5 for the control group and the group receiving the two interventions (Park, Morrell, Frieske, & Kincaid, 1992). The results indicate that young-old adults, those age 60–77, evidenced nearly perfect adherence, as shown in the left panel of Figure 5. An intervention was not effective for these subjects because they were making so few errors that there was no need to intervene. For old-old adults, however, the subjects receiving the two interventions made fewer medication errors than subjects in control conditions. The findings suggest that very old community-dwelling adults' medication adherence could be facilitated by cognitive aids.

In a subsequent study, we followed 48 adult hypertensives age 35 to 75 (Park, Morrell, Lautenschlager, & Firth, 1993) and found once again that the oldest old were most nonadherent and, as in Park et al. (1992), that young-old adults were the least nonadherent. Intermediate levels of nonadherence were evidenced by middle-aged adults. The poor adherence of the middle-aged subjects combined with the good adherence of the young-old adults caused us to reconceptualize medication-adherence behavior as involving more than merely remembering to take medications. We believe the nonadherence of the oldest old is a function of declines in working memory and long-term memory function that we have seen in the laboratory. In contrast, we hypothesize that the middle-aged show nonadherence due to the contextual press and high engagement of their lives. The high degree of obligations characteristic of middle age results in prospective forgetting, that is, subjects know what to do with their medications but cannot remember to take them. We also believe that young and middle-aged subjects may have had beliefs that were incompatible with adherence. In other words, they might have thought that they were not ill or that the medication was not useful, or they simply may have felt invulnerable and did not prioritize taking hypertension medication very highly. In contrast to these two groups, the young-old had both intact cognitive function and appropriate belief systems about medication and illness that led to high rates of adherence.

Psychosocial Aspects of Medication Adherence

On the basis of this work, we became very interested in understanding the joint contributions of cognitive function and psychosocial constructs to medication adherence (see Park & Mayhorn, in press, for a detailed discussion of the psychosocial aspects of medication adherence, and Park & Kidder, 1996, for an extended discussion of the role of prospective memory in medication adherence). We focused on the social psychological underpinnings of medication-adherence behavior and the self-regulatory framework of illness management and medication adherence espoused by Leventhal and Cameron (1987). Leventhal and Cameron argued that it is an individual's representation of her or his illness that drives illness behavior, rather than objective measures of illness status and function. In a sense, the Leventhal and Cameron view contrasts with our view of adherence, in which we view nonadherence simply as a cognitive–memory problem. At the same time, we recognized the views to be complementary rather than contradictory, because both health representations and cognitive function can contribute jointly to nonadherence. Based on the work described thus far, we reached three conclusions. These conclusions are quite likely generalizable to many aspects of aging, health, and behavior research:

1. The statistical techniques and methodologies we had used to date were inadequate to determine causality as well as to evaluate simultaneously the contributions of multiple constructs to adherence behaviors. The limitations imposed by collecting actual medication behaviors of patients at home over prolonged periods of time added to the complexity of the problem, because the dependent measures of the behavior of interest were also complex. Finally, we were unable to assess in a causal fashion the consequences of adherence. For example, do people who take medication for hypertension have measurably lower blood pressure, or do individuals with arthritis who take nonsteroidal anti-inflammatory drugs (which have numerous side effects of some consequence) actually function better and feel better? We concluded that to better address complex issues of this sort, we needed to use structural equation modeling techniques in our work, to permit the determination of complex causal relationships and the development of complex models that allow for the simultaneous and relative contributions of multiple constructs to a behavior (Jöreskog, 1993). Structural equation modeling techniques would allow us to examine the joint roles of cognitive function and illness representation, as well as other constructs to medication-adherence behaviors. Although the measurement requirements of constructs can be formidable for structural equation models (e.g., it is desirable to have three measures or indicators of every construct used in the model), these techniques are much better suited to addressing complex real-world problems than analysis of variance and even regression approaches.

2. We concluded that disease-specific approaches are necessary to understand medication-adherence behaviors. In other words, we believe that the adherence behaviors for individuals who have a silent disease like hypertension, where there are no obvious consequences of nonadherence except over the very long term, might be quite different from those of an individual with osteoarthritis, who has difficulty moving about without the use of pain-relieving medications.

3. We hypothesized that basic cognitive function was a factor in forgetting to take medications only for the very old and that belief systems, contextual press, and emotional states were more important for younger adults in determining

medication adherence. From this view, forgetting in younger adults would be caused by prospective memory failure, whereas in older adults, the focus would be on basic comprehension, working memory, and long-term memory function.

To address these issues in a systematic fashion, Roger Morrell and I developed a multidisciplinary research team that had the expertise to design a research program congruent with the conclusions described above. We now have a research team that consists of Howard Leventhal, a social psychologist who has been a key figure in the development of both theoretical and empirical tests of self-regulatory models of health behavior; Christopher Hertzog, a noted methodologist with expertise in both cognitive aging and structural equation modeling; Elaine Leventhal, a geriatric physician whose primary research interests are in aging, health, and behavior; and Daniel Birchmore, a practicing rheumatologist at the Wilmington, Delaware, Veterans Administration Hospital.

We have developed a model of medication adherence, portrayed in Figure 6, that integrates the roles of beliefs about illness and medications and cognitive function, as well as the role of external supports, as determinants of medication adherence. We are also interested in the relationship between medication adherence and well-being and physical function. We have elected to study two related populations across the adult life span: rheumatoid arthritis patients and osteoarthritis patients. In the case of rheumatoid arthritis, which is a serious, systemic autoimmune disorder, adherence to medications quite likely can prevent disease progression and the associated severe disability. In contrast, osteoarthritis is a local disorder specific to individual joints, and medications can only relieve pain, have relatively serious side effects, and in no way can prevent disease progression. Thus, we have somewhat similar disorders where in one case, it is in the patient's best interest to be highly adherent but in another case, it is in the patient's best interest to use as little medication as possible to avoid stomach ulcers and renal disease.

We have developed a complex psychosocial and cognitive battery for rheumatoid and osteoarthritis patients and are administering this, as well as measuring adherence behaviors for more than a month, using accurate microelectronic monitors. We are testing the role of cognitive interventions on nonadherent subjects, including devices such as beeping bottle caps on the medication and programmable reminder watches. We also are examining beliefs and adherence behaviors in a sample of Black hypertensives in a health clinic for low-income individuals. Our data are preliminary, and it is well beyond the scope of the present work to present a detailed description of it. Nevertheless, from the corpus of this work to date, we are able to conclude that it is a myth that older adults

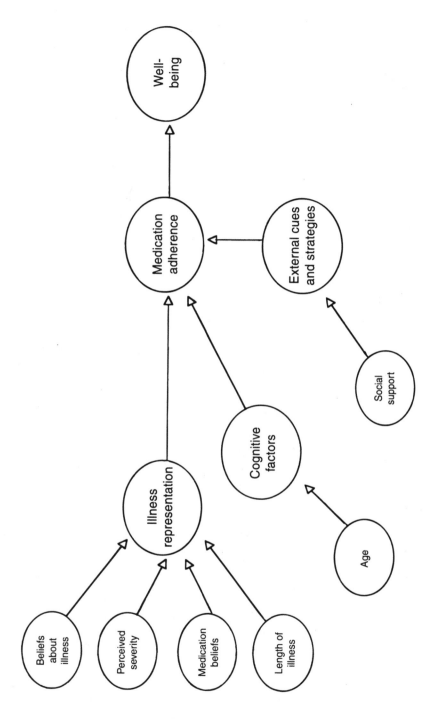

Figure 6. A conceptual model for medication adherence that integrates the role of beliefs and cognitive functions. From "Medication Adherence and Aging" by D. C. Park and T. R. Jones, in *Handbook of Human Factorss and the Older Adult*, edited by A. D. Fiske and W. A. Rogerss, in press, San Diego, CA: Academic Press. Copyright 1966 by Academic Press. Reprinted with permission.

are highly nonadherent with their medications. We consistently find evidence that the most adherent group is young-old adults, those age 60–75. It is also a myth that low-SES Black samples are highly nonadherent. We find evidence that our subjects, all of whom have hypertension, are highly adherent, recognizing at the same time that they are in a clinic situation where they receive structured, supportive information from a caring physician. We have not found strong evidence at this point that cognitive function plays a critical role in determining medication adherence. Rather, we find evidence that subjects' beliefs about their medications, strategies for coping with illness, and strategies for remembering to take medications are strong predictors of nonadherence. Finally, the most nonadherent group of subjects are the very elderly: those age 75 and above. We expect that as our sample increases, we will find evidence for cognitive function being related to nonadherence behavior.

CONCLUSION

The work presented is a long way from basic laboratory research on memory function. At the same time, the fundamental ways the basic work has informed, and continues to impact on, the applied work on medication adherence should be evident. The problem of medication adherence is one example of many dozens of issues that have tremendous implications for the effectiveness of treatment of older adults and judicious use of increasingly limited medical resources. How older adults make treatment decisions, what information they take away from an encounter with a physician, and how information can be structured to be maximally comprehended by older adults are just a few examples of critically important behavioral questions related to work on cognitive function and aging. Despite the threats to funding of research efforts, this is a very promising time to conduct socially important research that will result in sustained health and vitality for older adults and improve the overall productivity and well-being of our older population, resulting in increased gains of human resources to the social fabric of the lives of our citizens.

REFERENCES

Cavanaugh, J. & Park, D. C. (1993). *Vitality for life: Psychology research for productive aging* [A component of the Human Capital Initiative of the American Psychological Society]. Washington, DC: American Psychological Society.

Cherry, K. E., Park, D. C., Frieske, D., & Smith, A. D. (in press). Verbal and pictorial elaborations enhance memory in younger and older adults. *Memory & Cognition.*

Jöreskog, K. G. (1993). Testing structural equation models. In K. A. Bollen & J. S. Long (Eds.), *Testing structural equation models* (pp. 294–316). Newbury Park, CA: Sage.

Leventhal, H., & Cameron, L. (1987). Behavioral theories and the problem of compliance. *Patient Education and Counseling, 10,* 117–138.

Morrell, R. W., Park, D. C., & Poon, L. W. (1989). Effects of the quality of instructions on memory and comprehension of prescription information in young and old adults. *The Gerontologist, 29,* 345–353.

Morrell, R. W., Park, D. C., & Poon, L. W. (1990). Effects of labeling techniques on memory and comprehension of prescription information in young and old adults. *Journal of Gerontology: Psychological Sciences, 45,* 166–172.

Park, D. C. (1992). Applied cognitive aging research. In F. I. M. Craik & T. A. Salthouse (Eds.), *The handbook of aging and cognition* (pp. 449–493). Hillsdale, NJ: Erlbaum.

Park, D. C., & Jones, T. R. (in press). Medication adherence and aging. In A. D. Fiske & W. A. Rogers (Eds.), *Handbook of human factors and the older adult.* San Diego, CA: Academic Press.

Park, D. C., & Kidder, D. P. (1996). Prospective memory and medication adherence. In M. Brandimonte, G. Einstein, & M. McDaniel (Eds.), *Prospective memory: Theory and applications* (pp. 369–390). Hillsdale, NJ: Erlbaum.

Park, D. C., & Mayhorn, C. B. (in press). Remembering to take medications: The importance of nonmemory variables. In D. Herrman, M. Johnson, C. McEvoy, C. Hertzog, & P. Hertel (Eds.), *Research on practical aspects of memory* (Vol. 2) Hillsdale, NJ: Erlbaum.

Park, D. C., Morrell, R. W., Frieske, D., Blackburn, B., & Birchmore, D. (1991). Cognitive factors and the use of over-the-counter medication organizers by arthritis patients. *Human Factors, 33,* 57–67.

Park, D. C., Morrell, R. W., Frieske, D., & Kincaid, D. (1992). Medication adherence behaviors in older adults: Effects of external cognitive supports. *Psychology and Aging, 7,* 252–256.

Park, D. C., Morrell, R. W., Lautenschlager, G., & Firth, M. (1993, March). *Electronic monitoring of medication adherence hypertensives: Nonadherence is predicted by advanced age.* Paper presented at the meeting of the Society of Behavioral Medicine, San Francisco.

Park, D. C., Puglisi, J. T., & Smith, A. D. (1986). Picture memory in older adults: Does an age-related decline exist? *Psychology and Aging, 1,* 11–17.

Park, D. C., & Shaw, R. (1992). Effect of environmental support on implicit and explicit memory in young and old adults. *Psychology and Aging, 7,* 632–642.

Park, D. C., Smith, A. D., Lautenschlager, G., Earles, J., Frieske, D., Zwahr, M., & Gaines, C. (1994). Mediators of long-term memory across the life span. *Psychology and Aging.*

Park, D. C., Smith, A. D., Morrell, R. W., Puglisi, J. T., & Dudley, W. N. (1990). Effects of contextual integration on recall of pictures in older adults. *Journal of Gerontology: Psychological Sciences, 45,* 52–58.

Robbins, J. (1990). Schering report SVI—"OBRA '90' ": *Pharmacists not only count, but they also make a difference.* Kenilworth, NJ: Shering Laboratories.

Task Force on Aging Research. (1995). *The threshold of discovery: Future directions for research on aging.* Washington, DC: U.S. Government Printing Office.

6

A PROPOSAL FOR AN EXPANDED VIEW OF HEALTH AND PSYCHOLOGY: THE INTEGRATION OF BEHAVIOR AND HEALTH

CYNTHIA D. BELAR

Various chapters in this text describe the prevalence of psychological and behavioral problems (e.g., anxiety, depression, attention deficit hyperactivity disorder, substance abuse, obesity, and domestic violence) in persons seeking treatment by physicians. There is little doubt that biomedical treatments alone are not sufficient in the management of these well-known mental health and behavioral problems and that psychological services must be available if treatment is to be successful.

Overall, it has been estimated that some 25% of all visits in primary care are for mental health problems (Kamerow, Pincus, & MacDonald, 1986; Magill & Garrett, 1988). In addition, we have known for nearly 3 decades that 60% of all physician office visits fail to result in a confirmed biological diagnosis (Cummings & Follette, 1968; Follette & Cummings, 1967). It has been repeatedly stated that 60% of ambulatory-care visits involve problems with psychosocial components, and research reviews note that up to 80% of medical patients have evidence of significant psychological distress (Barskey, 1981).

However, the point of my discussion is that in actuality, it is not 25%, or 60%, or 80% of medical visits that should be considered psychological in nature. I am asserting that 100% of all medical visits are psychological and that Cartesian mind–body dualism simply does not belong in any conceptualization or implementation of the health care system. Behavior and health are inextricably intertwined, and psychology as the science of behavior has much to offer in both research and practice.

For example, we know that medical illness per se may precipitate emotional distress. Research has demonstrated that emotional distress can complicate medical treatment and thus elevate medical cost and that psychological interventions targeted to those with chronic diseases (e.g., diabetes, respiratory disorders, or hypertension) can actually reduce medical costs (Levenson, 1992; Schlesinger et al., 1983). In fact, there is an extensive body of knowledge concerning the medical cost offset of psychological services that in and of itself has been used to argue for the availability of psychological services in health care (e.g., Mumford et al., 1984).

However, the need for appropriate treatments of mental health problems and the potential for cost savings if psychological interventions are provided for chronic illness are only part of the total health care picture. In this discussion, I provide some sketchy outlines within a larger portrait, some of which will be more carefully drawn within other chapters of this text.

Over the last 2 decades, the body of knowledge in health psychology and its clinical applications has mushroomed. For example, psychological interventions have been developed to facilitate the management of a wide variety of health problems. Take coronary heart disease—the major cause of death and disability in the Western world. One of the most comprehensive studies of behavioral interventions in severe heart disease patients demonstrated significant and clinically meaningful decreases in low-density lipoprotein cholesterol (37%), systolic blood pressure (134 to 127 mmHg), angina pain (90%), and vessel blockage on angiogram in 18 of 22 patients. Over the same year, the control group receiving standard medical treatment experienced a 165% increase in angina pain, and angiograms revealed increased artery blockage in nearly half the patients (Ornish et al., 1990).

Research also demonstrates that psychological interventions have improved a number of troublesome physical symptoms, including but not limited to the following:

1. asthmatic episodes
2. pain during dressing change in burn patients

3. fecal and urinary incontinence
4. cramping and diarrhea in irritable bowel syndrome
5. anticipatory nausea with chemotherapy
6. vasospasms associated with Raynaud's disease
7. dyspnea with chronic obstructive pulmonary disease
8. headache severity, frequency, and duration
9. muscle spasms
10. insomnia and other sleep disorders
11. itching in neurodermatitis

Psychological support groups have helped patients and families deal with cancer, arthritis, disability, and bereavement. In addition to decreases in subjective distress and improved quality of life, there are some data to suggest health benefits in terms of reduced mortality and morbidity, especially for postmastectomy and heart attack patients (e.g., Spiegel, Gottheil, Kraemer, & Bloom, 1989).

With respect to even such overtly technical medical procedures as surgery, a meta-analysis of 191 studies involving both major and minor surgery revealed that brief presurgical psychological intervention has been consistently associated with fewer postsurgical complications, less medical usage, and an average of 1.5 fewer hospital days (Devine, 1992).

Traumatic injuries are major causes of morbidity and mortality and account for utilization of enormous amounts of some of our most expensive health care resources. Almost all injuries have behavioral risk factors: reckless driving, poor body mechanics, falls, substance abuse, failure to wear seatbelts or helmets, access to firearms, unsafe storage of toxic substances, interpersonal violence, and child and elder abuse.

Adherence to health care regimens is integral to virtually every service area. Noncompliance, a behavior, is a major issue throughout health care. In fact, it is estimated that half of the 1.6 billion prescriptions dispensed annually are taken incorrectly (Levy, 1989). Compliance is also especially important in smoking cessation, safe sex practices, exercise, dietary management, control of HIV and other infectious diseases, immunization programs, dental hygiene, and clinical trial research. As an example, some have noted that the incidence of polio can be directly related to a behavioral variable: failure to obtain vaccination.

In examining psychological and behavioral issues in a medical visit, it is also important not to focus too narrowly on the patient him- or herself. Health care outcomes can also be affected by family members' and service providers' behavior, on which there is also a substantial literature. The literature on physician–patient communication is especially illustrative of the latter.

Other provider determinants are infection-control procedures, which are essentially behavioral in nature. Although important, they are not always followed. For example, one author found a 50% failure rate in hand washing before seeing patients in a pediatric ambulatory-care setting (Lohr, Ingram, Dudley, Lawton, & Donowitz, 1991). Health systems are most concerned about the development of effective behavior-change programs for staff in areas such as promotion of hand washing and prevention of needle sticks.

At a more macro level, as public "report cards" for hospitals and health care plans become increasingly common and the health care industry becomes increasingly competitive, the interest in consumer behavior (e.g., satisfaction and appointment keeping) will increase, and there will be more focus on developing user-friendly systems marked by congenial staff behavior. The increased corporatization of health care also brings with it more focus on leadership behavior, personnel management (including concerns re staff burnout), and practice patterns.

In my opinion, one of the most positive features about health psychology in our discipline is that it is an area of research and practice to which virtually every area of psychology can contribute:

- From the behavioral epidemiologist to the behavioral geneticist
- From the experimental psychologists conducting basic pain research to the clinical health psychologist providing services
- From the human-factors engineer designing surgical-suite safety systems to the environmental psychologist designing user-friendly, and health-enhancing, spaces
- From the industrial psychologist providing executive management consultation and consumer studies to social and community psychologists developing community-based interventions
- From the basic scientist to the service provider to the policy advocate for health-promoting legislation and health care reform

So, back to my original perspective of the medical visit. Is there really any medical visit that is not psychological or that is impervious to behavioral influences? I cannot think of any. As stated before, behavior and health are inextricably intertwined, and psychology as the science of behavior has already demonstrated its potential for contributions to knowledge and practice.

REFERENCES

Barsky, A. J. (1981). Hidden reasons some patients visit doctors. *Annals of Internal Medicine, 94*, 492–498.

Cummings, N. A., & Follette, W. T. (1968). Psychiatric services and medical utilization in a prepaid health plan setting: Part II. *Medical Care, 6,* 31–41.

Devine, E. C. (1992). Effects of psychoeducational care for adult surgical patients: A meta-analysis of 191 studies. *Patient Education and Counseling, 19,* 129–142.

Follette, W. T., & Cummings, N. A. (1967). Psychiatric services and medical utilization in a prepaid health plan setting. *Medical Care, 5,* 25–35.

Kamerow, D. B., Pincus, H. A., & MacDonald, D. I. (1986). Alcohol abuse, other drug abuse and mental disorders in medical practice. *Journal of the American Medical Association, 255,* 2054–2057.

Levenson, J. L. (1992). Psychosocial interventions in chronic medical illness: An overview of outcome research. *General Hospital Psychiatry, 14S,* 43S–49S.

Levy, R. A. (1989, March). Improving compliance with prescription medications: An important strategy for containing health care costs. *Medical Interface,* pp. 34–41.

Lohr, J. A., Ingram, D. L., Dudley, S. M., Lawton, E. L., & Donowitz, L. (1991). Handwashing in pediatric ambulatory care settings: An inconsistent practice. *American Journal of Disease of Children, 145,* 1198–1199.

Magill, M. K., & Garrett, R. W. (1988). Behavioral and psychiatric problems. In R. B. Taylor (Ed.), *Family medicine* (3rd ed.), pp. 534–562). New York: Springer-Verlag.

Mumford, E., Schlesinger, H. J., Glass, G., Patrick, C., & Cuerdon, B. A. (1984). A new look at evidence about reduced cost of medical utilization following mental health treatment. *American Journal of Psychiatry, 141,* 1145–1158.

Ornish, D., Brown, S. E., Scherwitz, L. W, Billings, J. H., Armstrong, W. T., Ports, T. A., McLanahan, S. M., Kirkeeide, R. L., Brand, R. J., & Gould, K. L. (1990). Can lifestyle changes reverse coronary heart disease? *Lancet, 336,* 129–133.

Schlesinger, H. J., Mumford, E., Glass, G., Patrick, C., & Sharfstein, S. (1983). Mental health treatment and medical care utilization in a fee-for-service system: Outpatient mental health treatment following the onset of a chronic disease. *American Journal of Public Health, 73,* 422–429.

Spiegel, D., Bloom, J. R., Kraemer, H. C., & Gottheil, E. (1989). Effect of psychosocial treatment on survival of patients with metastatic breast cancer. *Lancet, 2*(8668), 888–891.

II

PSYCHOLOGISTS IN PRIMARY CARE SETTINGS

INTRODUCTION

As we pointed out in the introductory chapter to this book, psychologists have been practicing in primary health care settings for a significant portion of our field's history. Similarly, as primary care providers, psychologists have been involved in the comprehensive health care of patients and their families as well as serving as experts in practice areas such as internal medicine, family medicine, and pediatrics. In this section, again we see psychology defined by the interplay of the scientific study of clinical topics and the application of those research findings in the provision of health care services. We first learn about several collaborative-practice models in which psychologists and physicians work closely together to enhance the health care system. The section then goes on to elucidate the scientific and clinical understanding and treatment of various disorders found in primary care practice.

James H. Bray, in chapter 7, "Psychologists as Primary Care Practitioners," offers a description of a training program, detailing how psychologist–practitioners and physicians can, and do, work together successfully. This chapter offers a practical definition of primary care and elaborates on some of the findings of the American Psychological Association's Committee for the Advancement of Professional Practice's Primary Care Task Force. The collaborative-practice model discussed is based on defining the psychologist provider in primary care as a generalist.

In chapter 8, "Collaborative Practice: Psychologists and Internists," Garland Y. (Gary) DeNelsky offers general guidelines on how the practicing psychologist can produce and sustain a quality relationship with an internist. On the basis of DeNelsky's successful clinical practice experience and discussions with physicians, he also suggests that there are research and administrative opportunities that will enhance practice-based relationships.

In chapter 9, "Psychologists and Pediatricians in Collaborative Practice," Carolyn S. Schroeder offers a practical practice model for interfacing with pediatricians who are the primary gatekeepers for children's behavioral health care needs. On the basis of her successful pediatric psychology practice, Schroeder details the extent of problems seen in practice and clinical activities ranging from assessment and community consultation to parent "Call-In Hour" and from various treatment interventions to training models and research opportunities in pediatric practice.

David H. Barlow and colleagues describe the prevalence of the most common behavioral disorder that might be encountered in a primary care setting. In chapter 10, "Behavioral Health Care in Primary Care Settings: Recognition and Treatment of Anxiety Disorders," they offer information on the efficacy of psychological treatments of, and a model for intervention with, anxiety disorders that is applicable for psychologists working in or wishing to work in primary health care settings.

In chapter 11, "Catching Depression in Primary Care Physicians' Offices," Lynn P. Rehm focuses on the high incidence of depressive disorders found in primary care physicians' offices. He suggests that much can be done by psychologists to aid in the appropriate diagnosis of depression, given its high base rate but low and inaccurate detection rate in primary care settings. With health care moving to a "one-stop shopping" orientation with the growth of capitated care, Rehm encourages the psychologist to become involved in primary care settings in order to provide both accurate diagnosis of and effective psychotherapeutic intervention for depression.

Daniel S. Kirschenbaum, in chapter 12, "Helping Physicians Make Useful Recommendations About Losing Weight," provides valuable information for what psychologists can teach physicians about how to help patients who suffer from obesity. Rates of obesity are steadily climbing. Kirschenbaum uses both his research findings and clinical experience to detail a treatment strategy based on a six-step approach in counseling patients in successful weight loss.

In chapter 13, "Substance Use Problems in Primary Care Medical Settings: Is There a Psychologist in the House?" Bruce S. Liese and colleagues describe how substance abuse problems evidence themselves in primary care settings. The etiology of various drug problems are detailed by the authors, as are various diagnostic and treatment approaches.

The reader is offered useful suggestions on how to establish practice relationships with primary care physicians by marketing psychological services to physicians who will encounter substance abuse problems on a daily basis in their practices.

Jan L. Culbertson details the prevalence of attention deficit hyperactivity disorder and learning disabilities, two of the most common neurodevelopmental disorders of childhood. She discusses, in chapter 14, "Attention Deficit Hyperactivity Disorder and Learning Disabilities in the Pediatrician's Office," the need for a broad-based assessment of these problems, which often are first presented in the pediatrician's office. There is often less stigma if these problems are seen by parents within the context of a medical approach than when directly diagnosed or treated by a psychologist. Thus, with a strong working relationship with the pediatrician, the psychologist can establish alliances that facilitate information sharing in the community, cross-referral, and assistance in diagnosis and management of these disorders.

7

PSYCHOLOGISTS AS PRIMARY CARE PRACTITIONERS

JAMES H. BRAY

Psychologists are expanding their roles in the delivery of behavioral health services in a variety of health care settings. With the implementation of health care reform and the expansion of managed health care, psychologists are being forced to change their practices from providing only mental health services to offering a broad array of behavioral health services (Gaus & DeLeon, 1995). Psychologists have practiced in general medical settings for some time and have offered psychosocial interventions for both mental disorders and medical problems. With the new emphasis on primary health care, psychologists have additional opportunities to expand their role in the diagnosis and treatment of patients. However, this shift in practice will require an expanded knowledge base of primary care medicine and new skills in caring for primary care patients. This chapter reviews the definition of primary care and the role of psychologists in this setting and outlines the components of a training

Work on this chapter was supported partially by National Institute of Alcoholism and Alcohol Abuse Grant RO1 AA08864.

model intended to teach psychologists and physicians how to work in collaborative practice.

DEFINITION OF PRIMARY CARE

What is primary care, and who provides it? This has become a very controversial and "hot" topic because of the recent moves toward emphasizing primary care as the entry point and major provider of health care services. Primary care was defined by the Institute of Medicine as follows:

> the provision of integrated, accessible health care services by clinicians who are accountable for addressing a large majority of personal health care needs, developing a sustained partnership with patients, and practicing in the context of family and community. (Donaldson, Yordy, & Vanselow, 1994, p. 15)

The American Academy of Family Physicians defined primary care as follows:

> a form of medical care delivery that emphasizes first-contact and assumes ongoing responsibility for the patient in both health maintenance and therapy of illness. It is personal care involving a unique interaction and communication between the patient and the physician. It is comprehensive in scope and includes the overall coordination of the care of the patient's health problems, be they biological, behavioral, or social. The appropriate use of consultants and community resources is an important part of effective primary care. (American Academy of Family Physicians, 1994, p. 1)

Primary care is a form of delivery of medical care which encompasses the following functions:

1. It is "first-contact" care, serving as a point-of-entry for the patient into the health care system;
2. It includes continuity by virtue of caring for patients over a period of time, both in sickness and in health;
3. It is comprehensive care, drawing from all the traditional major disciplines for its functional content;
4. It serves a coordinative function for all the healthcare needs of the patient;
5. It assumes continuing responsibility for individual patient follow-up and community health problems; and
6. It is a highly personalized type of care. (American Academy of Family Physicians, 1975, p. 14)

A more common determination of a primary care provider is whether the provider takes care of routine health problems—such as checking patients' blood pressure and caring for common illnesses, such as colds, infections, depression, or hypertension. There are three medical specialties that are the core providers of primary care: family physicians, general internal medicine physicians, and pediatricians. Other specialties that are sometimes included are obstetrics/gynecologists and family nurse practitioners.

PSYCHOLOGISTS IN PRIMARY CARE

Where do psychologists fit within primary care? Are psychologists primary care providers? According to Rakel, one of the originators of the family physician movement,

> Primary care, to be done well, requires extensive training specifically tailored to problems frequently seen in primary care. These include the early detection, diagnosis, and treatment of depression, . . . and the care of those with chronic and terminal illnesses. (Rakel, 1995, p. 7)

These are clearly areas in which psychologists can provide services.

Although psychologists are usually not trained to take blood pressure or treat the common cold, they are trained to treat the most common behavioral health problems, such as depression and anxiety, and to provide behavioral interventions to prevent or intervene with major health problems, for example, cardiovascular disease or cancer, through lifestyle modification, weight management, smoking cessation, or stress management (Million, Green, & Meagher, 1982). In addition, many of the chronic diseases, such as diabetes, hypertension, or chronic back pain, can be helped or treated effectively through behavioral interventions (Holland & Rowland, 1989; Routh, 1988; Stager & Fordyce, 1982). Thus, psychologists are able to provide primary care behavioral health services and to diagnose or manage a number of health problems seen in primary care settings.

The American Psychological Association Committee for the Advancement of Professional Practice convened a Primary Care Task Force to examine the role of psychologists in primary medical care (1995). The core assumption of the task force is that psychology is defined as a health profession and not just a mental health profession. The task force believes that psychologists and psychological services are essential to the primary health care team to deliver cost-effective and clinically effective comprehensive care.

The task force discussed several models of psychology in primary care. One concept that gained support was that psychologists should provide comprehensive care. This type of care is provided over time, is coordinated with other members of the health care team, and uses specialists and subspecialists as needed. Comprehensive care makes use of community resources and recognizes the role of systems such as families and contextual factors in health and illness. Primary comprehensive health care teams emphasize prevention, education, consultation, and treatment. Furthermore, this care rests on a growing fund of knowledge and the science that underlies collaboration and the biopsychosocial, or systemic, model.

What kinds of characteristics do psychologists that work in primary care have? The Primary Care Task Force identified three major characteristics: First, the psychologist works in a primary care setting. This could be a clinic, group practice, or with an individual medical practitioner. This could also include both clinical and educational services, such as teaching in a family medicine residency.

Second, the psychologist is capable of working with all patients seen in the setting. This means that the psychologist can work with the broad range of behavioral and mental health problems found in primary care settings. In addition, the psychologist may serve as a consultant to the other primary care providers, such as family physicians or nurse practitioners, regarding patient-care issues, doctor–patient issues, or system issues. Furthermore, the psychologist is able to provide interventions for behavioral components of medical problems, such as facilitating compliance to medical regimes, lifestyle changes, or reducing complications due to surgery.

Third, the psychologist contributes to the patient's total health care, both in sickness and in health. Psychologists in primary care are not limited solely to the assessment and treatment of mental disorders. In essence, this model of psychology requires that the psychologist provider be a generalist and be able to treat the full range of problems, from birth to death, with individuals and families, that present in these settings.

COLLABORATIVE-PRACTICE MODEL

There is a critical need for the appropriate diagnosis and treatment of common types of behavioral health problems seen in primary care settings. Despite the high prevalence of certain mental disorders, such as anxiety and depression, in primary care settings (Katon & Sullivan, 1990), primary care physicians often overlook these types of problems and focus on diagnosis and treatment of physical health symptoms (Eisenberg, 1992). The expense of not diagnosing and treating these types of problems can be staggering. For example, the costs associated with depression have been recently estimated as high as $43.7 billion a year (Greenberg, Stiglin, Finkelstein, & Berndt, 1993). In addition, anxiety and depression result in higher medical utilization rates and costs (Simon, Ormel,

VonKorff, & Barlow, 1995). Furthermore, Kroenke and Mangelsdorff (1989) found that of patients from an internal medicine clinic, only 16% had clear organic causes of their problems, 10% had clear psychological problems, but nearly 80% of patients had significant psychological distress. These facts point to the need for psychological services in primary care settings.

With the increase in managed health care and integrated health care systems, primary care physicians have added pressures to diagnose and treat a broad spectrum of biomedical and psychosocial problems. Thus, they could benefit from greater access to behavioral health practitioners (Coleman, Patrick, Eagle, & Hermalin, 1979; MacDonald, Baloun, & McKenna, 1995). Collaborative practice between psychologists and physicians is one method to meet the multiple needs of primary care patients (Bray & Rogers, 1995; Clinical psychology, 1991; McDaniel, Hepworth, & Doherty, 1992). However, psychologists are not regularly trained to work with primary care physicians and often do not have access to the general health care system (Bray & Rogers, 1995).

Primary care physicians are the front-line medical providers and are frequently the first health care professionals to encounter patients with mental health or psychosocial problems ("Mental Health," 1995; Higgins, 1994). Unfortunately, psychologists are often isolated from the primary care medical system. Thus, the professionals best trained to assess and treat psychosocial problems may not be available to medical professionals and their patients who need these services. The change from psychologists as mental health providers to health care providers will require special training on how to work closely with primary care physicians.

Collaboration between psychologists and physicians is hampered by factors such as differences in theoretical orientations (biomedical vs. psychosocial), lack of a common language (medical jargon vs. psychological jargon), different practice styles, lack of accessibility to the different providers, and varying expectations for assessment and treatment (Bray & Rogers, 1995; McDaniel et al., 1992). Even with these cultural and practice difficulties, there are excellent examples of fruitful collaboration between psychologists and other medical professionals (Abraham et al., 1991; Biaggio & Bittner, 1990; Coleman, Patrick, Eagle, & Hermalin, 1979; Dym & Berman, 1986; Glenn, 1985; Hepworth & Jackson, 1985; McDaniel et al., 1992; McDowell, Burgio, Dombrowski, Locher, & Rodriguez, 1992; Natvig, 1991; Sargent, 1985). Most of these examples occurred in traditional medical settings, such as hospitals, group practices, or in educational settings.

A demonstration project that trained psychologists and family physicians for collaborative practice was recently reported by Bray and Rogers (1995). The Linkages Project developed a training model for psychologists and family physicians to facilitate collaborative practice that focused on treatment of alcohol and other drug abuse problems in rural areas. This section reviews the training program and general principles that were learned from this demonstration project (Bray & Rogers, 1995, in press).

The training included two 1-day workshops for pairs of psychologists and family physicians. The first day of training provided updated material on current information on the diagnosis and treatment of alcohol and other drug abuse problems, models of collaborative practice, and methods for developing linkages between professionals. This session included both didactic and experiential training.

Psychologists and physicians met in small groups to discuss training and "cultural" differences between psychologists and physicians. The psychologist trainer provided information to the physician group regarding training and educational backgrounds of psychologists, differences between psychologists and other mental health professionals, practice styles and issues, differences between psychological and medical practices, collaboration and referral recommendations, and financial issues. In addition, issues concerning differences in methods of handling confidentiality and sharing patient records between the professions were discussed. At the same time, the physician trainer discussed similar issues with the psychologist group concerning physicians and medical practice. The trainers discussed stereotypes of each profession and factors that might obstruct collaborative practice. The trainers switched groups to answer questions from their professional group and to discuss experiences and concerns that were raised in the other group. Also, the trainers initiated group discussion to develop possible solutions to concerns about collaboration raised by the participants.

Training was also provided on how to make successful referrals. This discussion included information about how to prepare a patient for a referral to a psychologist, how to include the psychologist in the evaluation of the referral, and how to communicate expectations concerning the referral to the psychologist. Differences in expectations about referral by the two provider groups were discussed. This part of the training focused on the etiquette of collaboration and the potential forms of collaboration.

Experiential exercises and role plays on cases were provided to demonstrate how the different professionals approach patient care and to practice diagnosing and referring patients. Questions about the cases were raised to reveal differences in assessment strategies between psychologists and physicians. In addition, participants explored in greater depth the differences between the two professions with regard to language, theoretical models, confidentiality, time constraints, and turf issues.

The last part of this training was for the participants to develop a linkage plan for establishing and maintaining collaborative practices between the professionals. The trainers provided several options: having regular meetings or phone contacts, establishing referral routines, and clarifying referral and treatment expectations. Regular contact between the professionals was strongly recommended, as was the development of expectations and methods for communicating about referrals. This part of the training emphasized the need for accessibility and the etiquette of collaboration for fostering collaborative relationships. This ended the first day of training.

The second day of training occurred about 6 months after the initial training session. The first part of the day reviewed the collaboration that developed after the initial training. The participants evaluated the initial training and provided feedback on areas that needed to be changed. Participants gave specific case examples of how their linkage plan worked or did not work and examples of successful and unsuccessful collaboration. Problems and concerns that hindered successful collaboration were also reviewed.

The participants were trained to use the process and stages of change model (Prochaska, DiClemente, & Norcross, 1992) and the motivational enhancement therapy model (Miller, Zweben, DiClemente, & Rychtarik, 1992) for treating alcohol and other drug abuse problems. The model seemed particularly relevant for family physicians because they often encounter patients who have behavioral and addictive problems. However, the patients are not necessarily seeking treatment for those specific problems and may not be ready to change their behavior. The model was expanded to be applicable to a wide range of medical and psychosocial problems. The trainers presented videotape examples of these models and discussed specific application of the models in primary care settings.

The training program was successful in linking providers and in enhancing the level and quality of collaborative practice between these professionals. The predominant changes in the collaborative relationship was from self-contained, independent practitioners to independent practices with mutually exclusive skills and from no relationship to limited referral and some consultation between professionals. In most cases, this type of arrangement was a step forward, but the training did not result in fully integrated forms of practice.

The participants indicated that collaboration enhanced the effectiveness of each professional and resulted in better diagnosis and treatment of medical and psychosocial problems. Participants reported that the linkage improved their own sense of efficacy and satisfaction in working with patients. In addition, through the collaboration, patients were provided enhanced treatment options for their problems. Although this project focused on rural practitioners, it appears that most of the training is applicable to both rural and urban practitioners. We are currently undertaking another demonstration project on linking psychologists and primary care physicians in an urban area.

There were several factors that facilitated or hindered the development of a collaborative practice between providers (Bray & Rogers, 1995). Developing a specific collaboration plan was a key factor in the development of a working relationship. Professionals who had regular contact with each other were most likely to consult and refer patients to each other. Practicing in close proximity also enhanced the linkage between providers. Participants who had regular meetings with each other or practiced in the same building were the most successful in establishing a collaborative relationship. Regular meetings included scheduled telephone contacts, lunch or breakfast appointments, use of faxes to make referrals, or shared hospital rounds.

Several factors can interfere with collaboration. Lack of proximity and regular settings for contact were major components that hindered referrals. In many cases it takes a special effort to develop the relationship, and it is necessary to have a regular setting or routine for continuing the collaboration. Psychologists may need to take the lead in developing and maintaining this relationship. Managed care and reimbursement issues are ongoing problems that interfere with collaborative practice. Not being on the hospital staffs where physicians practice further interferes with collaboration. Because many psychologists do not practice in general hospital settings, a convenient place for informal and formal consultations between providers, the opportunities for collaboration are decreased.

CONCLUSION

With the move from specialized medical care to primary medical care and the increase in integrated, managed health care services, it is essential that psychologists expand their practices into the general health care area. Psychologists can provide important diagnostic and intervention services, which enhance treatment options to patients in primary care settings. In addition, psychologists can provide valuable systems consultation to primary health care teams and providers (McDaniel et al., 1992).

Psychologists need to gain additional training and experience in working in primary care settings to be effective providers in these areas (Bray & Rogers, in press). This type of training needs to be offered in both graduate psychology programs and in continuing education programs, to familiarize psychologists with primary health care and psychological interventions for primary care patients. Finally, psychologists will need to shift their focus from an exclusively psychosocial orientation to a biopsychosocial orientation, to fully integrate into the general health care system. The movement from mental health to health care provider is an exciting opportunity to expand the roles and areas of practice for psychologists.

REFERENCES

Abraham, I. L., Thompson-Heisterman, A. A., Harrington, D. P., Smullen, D. E., Onega, L. L., Droney, E. G., Westerman, P. S., Manning, C. A., & Lichtenberg, P. A. (1991). Outpatient psychogeriatric nursing services: An integrative model. *Archives of Psychiatric Nursing, 5*, 151–164.

American Academy of Family Physicians. (1975). *Official AAFP definition of family practice and family physician* (AAFP Publication No. 303). Kansas City, MO: Author.

American Academy of Family Physicians. (1994, February). AAFP revises primary care definition and exhibit. *AAFP Reporter,* p. 1.

American Psychological Association, Committee for the Advancement of Professional Psychology. (1995, July). *Primary Care Task Force working recommendations.* Washington, DC: Author.

Biaggio, M. K., & Bittner, E. (1990). Psychology and optometry: Interaction and collaboration. *American Psychologist, 45*, 1313–1315.

Bray, J. H., & Rogers, J. C. (1995). Linking psychologists and family physicians for collaborative practice. *Professional Psychology: Research and Practice, 26*, 132–138.

Bray, J. H., & Rogers, J. C. (in press). Training mental health professionals for collaborative practice with primary care physicians. *Families, Systems, and Health.*

Clinical psychology and general practice. (1991). *Drug and Therapeutics Bulletin, 29*, 9–11.

Coleman, J. V., Patrick, D. L., Eagle, J., & Hermalin, J. A. (1979). Collaboration, consultation, and referral in an integrated health–mental health program at an HMO. *Social Work in Health Care, 5*, 83–96.

Donaldson, M., Yordy, K., & Vanselow, N. (Eds.) (1994). *Defining primary care: An interim report. Committee on the Future of Primary Care* (Part 3, pp. 15–33). Washington, DC: National Academy Press.

Dym, B., & Berman, S. (1986). The primary health care team: Family physician and family therapist in joint practice. *Family Systems Medicine, 4*, 9–21.

Eisenberg, L. (1992). Treating depression and anxiety in primary care: Closing the gap between knowledge and practice. *New England Journal of Medicine, 326*, 1080–1084.

Gaus, C. R., & DeLeon, P. H. (1995). Thinking beyond the limitations of mental health care. *Professional Psychology, 26,* 339–340.

Glenn, M. L. (1985). Toward collaborative family-oriented health care. *Family Systems Medicine, 3,* 466–475.

Greenberg, P. E., Stiglin, L. E., Finkelstein, S. N., & Berndt, E. R. (1993). The economic burden of depression in 1990. *Journal of Clinical Psychiatry, 54,* 405–418.

Hepworth, J., & Jackson, M. (1985). Health care for families: Models of collaboration between family therapists and family physicians. *Family Relations, 34,* 123–127.

Higgins, E. S. (1994). A review of unrecognized mental illness in primary care. *Archives of Family Medicine, 3,* 908–917.

Holland, J. C., & Rowland, J. H. (Eds.). (1989). *Handbook of psycho-oncology: Psychological care of the patient with cancer.* New York: Oxford University Press.

Katon, W., & Sullivan, M. D. (1990). Depression and chronic medical illness. *Journal of Clinical Psychiatry, 51,* 3–11.

Kroenke, K., & Mangelsdorff, D. (1989). Common symptoms in ambulatory care: Incidence, evaluation, therapy, and outcome. *The American Journal of Medicine, 86,* 262–266.

MacDonald, A. S., Baloun, E. T., & McKenna, Q. L. (1995). Emerging models of integrated health systems. *GFP Notes, 8,* 1–5.

McDaniel, S. H., Hepworth, J., & Doherty, W. J. (1992). *Medical family therapy.* New York: Basic Books.

McDowell, J., Burgio, K. L., Dombrowski, M., Locher, J. L., & Rodriguez, E. (1992). An interdisciplinary approach to the assessment and behavioral treatment of urinary incontinence in geriatric outpatients. *Journal of the American Geriatric Society, 40,* 370–374.

Miller, W. R., Zweben, A., DiClemente, C. C., & Rychtarik, R. G. (1992). *Motivational enhancement therapy manual: A clinical research guide for therapists treating individuals with alcohol abuse and dependence* (DHHS Publication No. ADM 92-1894). Rockville, MD: National Institute of Alcohol Abuse and Alcoholism.

Million, T., Green, C., & Meagher, R. (Eds.). (1982). *Handbook of clinical health psychology.* New York: Plenum.

Natvig, D. (1991). The role of the interdisciplinary team in using psychotropic drugs. *Journal of Psychosocial Nursing and Mental Health Services, 29,* 3–8.

Mental health: Does therapy help? (1995, November). *Consumer Reports,* pp. 734–739.

Prochaska, J. O., DiClemente, C. C., & Norcross, J. C. (1992). In search of how people change: Applications to addictive behaviors. *American Psychologist, 47,* 1102–1114.

Rakel, R. E. (1995). The family physician. In R. E. Rakel (Ed.), *Textbook of family practice* (5th ed., pp. 3–19). Philadelphia: W. B. Saunders.

Routh, D. K. (Ed.). (1988). *Handbook of pediatric psychology.* New York: Guilford Press.

Sargent, J. (1985). Physician–family therapist collaboration: Children with medical problems. *Family Systems Medicine, 3,* 454–465.

Simon, G., Ormel, J., VonKorff, M., & Barlow, W. (1995). Health care costs associated with depressive and anxiety disorders in primary care. *American Journal of Psychiatry, 152,* 352–357.

Stager, J., & Fordyce, W. (1982). Behavioral health care in the management of chronic pain. In T. Million, C. Green, & R. Meagher (Eds.), *Handbook of clinical health psychology* (pp. 467–498). New York: Plenum.

8

COLLABORATIVE PRACTICE: PSYCHOLOGISTS AND INTERNISTS

GARLAND Y. DENELSKY

It has been estimated that a large percentage of the patient visits to internists and primary care physicians are driven by primarily psychological problems. A number of estimates have been made that more that 50% of patients seen by primary care physicians are somatizers (Wickramasekera, 1989). Because proper psychological interventions may result in substantial improvement in patients' physical health, it becomes mutually advantageous for psychologists and internists to form close working relationships as a means of enhancing patient care.

The purpose of this chapter is to consider some of the factors that can contribute to smooth, harmonious working relationships between psychologists and internists. Much of what will be discussed is based on my own experiences of nearly 25 years at the Cleveland Clinic, a large, tertiary (and primary) care hospital and outpatient clinic. In addition, several internists and primary care physicians at the Cleveland Clinic were interviewed to capture their views of what they are expecting when they refer a patient to a psychologist, what criteria they use to decide whether to refer to a psychologist or a psychiatrist, and what type of communication process between psychologist and physician is most valued by them. This chapter outlines important areas that psychologists should focus on to create a positive collaboration with internists, including communication, the referral process, briefing, and the ongoing relationship.

COMMUNICATION

Several factors can facilitate smooth working relationships between psychologists and internists. Perhaps the most important, and certainly one of the most basic, is a friendly, collegial relationship between the two individual professionals. Quite frequently, some of the most valuable communication takes place informally: at a lunch table, in the corridors, on the phone. This type of contact is particularly helpful in discussing patient progress, talking over whether a particular patient would be an appropriate referral, and similar issues. But this type of informal contact also helps build an atmosphere of trust and cooperation, critically important ingredients in a sound, collaborative relationship between internist and psychologist. Put another way, the physician comes to view the psychologist as a reasonable person who does sensible and useful things to help his or her patients. The psychologist comes to appreciate the challenges to the internist who is trying to manage the patient's physical health, precisely what the physician is trained to do. Not infrequently, management of the patient's health is seriously complicated by psychological and emotional difficulties, something the internist may be neither trained nor interested in handling!

The actual process of collaboration between psychologist and internist begins with discussion and agreement on the types of patients most likely to benefit from psychological interventions. It has been noted that this collaboration is even more effective if the psychologist's office is on site, with an office on or near the service where patients are seen; such an arrangement can also permit a better understanding of the stressors and other situational factors in a patient's life (Cummings, 1992). But solid working relationships can be developed even when psychologist and physician are geographically separated. The communication process is the crucial ingredient; it is important at this stage for the psychologist to create realistic expectations as to the benefits (and limitations) of psychological interventions.

THE REFERRAL PROCESS

Each internist that I interviewed for this chapter described slightly different criteria for referral to a psychologist. One common denominator was that the patient had significant emotional or psychological issues that were either not responding or were not expected to respond to the internist's interventions. Antidepressant and anxiolitic medications were the most commonly used interventions of the internists. Brief counseling was the second most used tool, although the internists varied considerably with regard to how much counseling they typically employ.

The matter of whether to refer to a psychologist or a psychiatrist elicited some interesting comments. The common thread in several internists' comments was that they refer to a psychiatrist when they feel that medication is necessary and they feel that their knowledge of medications may be insufficient, either because it has not worked thus far or there are reasons to suspect that it will not work. Some internists mentioned that if the patient is clearly suicidal and is suspected to "need medications," then the referral is more likely to go to a psychiatrist. This is particularly interesting in view of the finding that suicidal patients not infrequently use their medications as a means of attempting suicide (Antonuccio, Danton, & DeNelsky, 1995). But the internists interviewed indicated a clear preference for psychologists when the primary problem seemed to involve interpersonal problems, inadequate coping skills, situational adjustment issues, chronic internal conflicts, or one of a variety of other primarily psychological problems. One internist confided that he refers to a psychiatrist when he suspects that a patient may be unworkable psychologically and that only medications or some other somatic therapy has any chance of making a dent!

When the internist refers a patient to a psychologist, that physician is pretty certain that psychological and emotional factors are relevant. Perhaps the most common exception here is when a physical condition exists that is suspected to be functional (e.g., a conversion, psychophysiologic, or somatization disorder) for which no physiopathology can be established. In these cases, internists often turn to other ways of verifying their suspicions before actually making a referral; psychological testing can be a particularly useful step here. When the internist orders psychological testing on the patient, the message begins to be conveyed to the patient that psychological factors are suspected to be playing some role in the patient's physical complaints. When the internist next orders a psychological consult, that message is strengthened. If the psychologist's conclusions are in keeping with the internist's hypothesis, the message is strengthened further. One internist specifically mentioned that the psychologist may need to help convince the patient of the role of psychological factors, if in fact psychological factors are felt to be fundamental. If this process has developed correctly, and if the patient feels that indeed a comprehensive medical evaluation of the patient's physical condition has been performed, the patient is much more likely—though not necessarily certain—to accept a psychological formulation of the problem.

BRIEFING THE INTERNIST

After the psychologist receives the referral, meets the patient, and performs a consultation, the findings must be communicated. Timeliness is a most important factor here; it is important for the psychologist to be able to respond reasonably promptly to requests from the physician and to communicate her or his findings fairly quickly. Excessive delay anywhere in this process can lead to a rapid diminution of referrals. The communication process is quite vital; the physician frequently is not as interested in a lengthy, comprehensive report so much as a succinct statement of the problem and the psychologist's plan for managing it. Brief phone or face-to-face discussions of the patient are frequently more satisfying and relevant for both parties than more formal reporting. But a more formal report is necessary as well.

The internists interviewed varied a good deal with regard to what they like to see in reports. One stated quite clearly, "I want a brief, concise report—the fewer words, the better!" Another indicated a preference for lengthier reports, "I like a more detailed report, one that teaches me something about the patient. I like to learn something new." Still another confessed, "I like it when there's a little 'gossip' about the patient—it lets me know that the psychologist has really come to know my patient!" Different preferences regarding reporting style may to some degree reflect gender differences. It has been noted that women physicians talk more with patients and ask more questions about psychosocial issues than male physicians (Hall, Irish, Roter, Ehrlich, & Miller, 1994). But even the internists who preferred longer reports agreed that they strongly desire a brief, succinct summary as well. That summary should include a formulation, a diagnosis (which may or may not be a product of the *Diagnostic and Statistical Manual of Mental Disorders* [American Psychiatric Association, 1994]), and a set of recommendations, which in many cases will include a treatment plan. If that plan is to include follow-up psychological interventions, the specifics of who, when, and where need to be delineated as well. Several internists expressed dismay about getting the patient back from a mental health professional's consultation with the conclusion "no psychiatric illness," and no additional comments or plan offered. On the other hand, one internist emphasized the value of honesty, "If psychological issues are not suspected to be playing a role, the psychologist should say so!"

THE ONGOING RELATIONSHIP

In most cases where the internist requests psychological involvement, the physician's expectations are that the psychologist will provide ongoing treatment as required, or arrange for such treatment to be delivered by someone else. Internists not infrequently voice frustration when they refer a patient to a mental health professional only to find that the patient has been given an initial evaluation with no provision made for further involvement. In these times when patients have complex (and frequently limiting) arrangements with third-party payers, however, the issue of who will be reimbursed for treatment can, of course, become quite complicated.

Note that there is the potential for complexities and conflicts whenever psychologists collaborate with physicians. Medical centers, both outpatient clinics and hospitals, are now and historically have been controlled by physicians. Psychologists may find themselves disadvantaged in medically dominated health care systems because they do not have the knowledge of disease that physicians have (Miller & Swartz, 1990). Psychologists may be tempted to permit devaluation of their expertise for the sake of harmonious working relationships and may find themselves at a decided disadvantage in terms of power issues between the two professions (Miller & Swartz, 1990). Yet these and other similar problems need not develop if the environment supports true teamwork, characterized by open communication and shared leadership (Lowe & Herranen, 1981). Although such teamwork is the ideal, the reality is that especially in the inpatient setting, most commonly the physician is the captain of the team, who is viewed as ultimately responsible for patient care (Shaw, 1986). In facing these complexities, psychologists need to be appropriately assertive with regard to patient management and treatment recommendations, but should avoid the extremes of passivity or aggressiveness, to maximize their contributions to patient care.

THE BENEFITS OF COLLABORATION WITH INTERNISTS

In addition to providing direct clinical services with physicians in primary care and internal medicine settings, there are numerous opportunities for research and teaching, as well as administration (Belar, 1989). Collaboration between psychologist and internist in such endeavors further enhances the working relationship between the two professionals.

Another benefit of such collaboration is personal but potentially quite significant; truly satisfying relationships can and often do develop between psychologists and physicians. Psychologists report "doubling their efforts to make their reports and opinions meaningful and helpful because of the fine level of professional acceptance they experienced" (Cummings, 1992, p. 78).

A strong case can be made that graduate education and training programs need to do much more than they are now doing to help prepare psychologists to develop and maintain solid working relationships with internists in medical settings, much as research psychologists are prepared for "grantsmanship" in their graduate education (Belar, 1989). As health care is increasingly restructured toward cost containment and prevention, the role of the psychologist can and should become increasingly prominent. It is well known that appropriate psychological care for patients with psychological and emotional problems can reduce medical utilization and that psychologically based health interventions (e.g., smoking cessation programs) can have a dramatic impact on reducing future morbidity and mortality.

CONCLUSION

Facilitating a solid working relationship with internists requires the psychologist to provide reasonable access; thorough evaluations, which include specific treatment recommendations; appropriate and timely reporting; and the willingness to continue working with difficult patients when appropriate. When a smooth, harmonious working relationship is established, the patient, the psychologist, and the physician all benefit. The patient gets enhanced health care, the psychologist gets interesting (and frequently challenging) cases, and the physician gets assistance in dealing with some of his or her most difficult and time-consuming patients. Such collaboration benefits psychology, it benefits medicine, and most important, it benefits the patient and the patient's physical health and psychological well-being.

REFERENCES

American Psychiatric Association. (1994). *Diagnostic and statiscal manual of mental disorders* (4th ed.). Washington, DC: Author.

Antonuccio, D. O., Danton, W. G., & DeNelsky, G. Y. (1995). Psychotherapy vs. medication for depression: Challenging the conventional wisdom with data. *Professional Psychology: Research and Practice, 26,* 574–585.

Belar, C. D. (1989). Opportunities for psychologists in health maintenance organizations: Implications for graduate education and training. *Professional Psychology: Research and Practice, 20,* 390–394.

Cummings, J. W. (1992). Psychologists in the medical surgical setting: Some reflections. *Professional Psychology: Research and Practice, 23,* 76–79.

Hall, J. A., Irish, J. T., Roter, D. L., Ehrlich, C. M., & Miller, L. H. (1994). Gender in medical encounters: An analysis of physician and patient communication in a primary care setting. *Health Psychology, 13,* 384–392.

Lowe, J. I., & Herranen, M. (1981). Understanding teamwork: Another look at basic concepts. *Social Work in Health Care, 7*, 1–11.

Miller, T., & Swartz, L. (1990). Clinical psychology in general hospital settings: Issues in interprofessional relationships. *Professional Psychology: Research and Practice, 21*, 48–53.

Shaw, B. (1986). Improving the management of illness behavior by changing roles within multidisciplinary treatment teams. In S. McHugh & T. M. Vallis (Eds.), *Illness behavior: A multidisciplinary model* (pp. 59–70). New York: Plenum.

Wickramasekera, I. (1989). Somatizers, the health care system, and collapsing the psychological distance the somatizer has to travel for help. *Professional Psychology: Research and Practice, 20*, 105–111.

9

PSYCHOLOGISTS AND PEDIATRICIANS IN COLLABORATIVE PRACTICE

CAROLYN S. SCHROEDER

Most parents are likely to talk initially to a pediatrician when they have concerns about their children's behavior or development (Clarke-Stewart, 1978; Schroeder & Wool, 1979). Thus, pediatricians are the first professionals most likely to encounter children's behavior problems. It has been estimated that 20% of pediatric primary care patients have biosocial or developmental problems, which, for the pediatrician seeing a total of 27 patients a day, translates into 4 patients per day (American Academy of Pediatrics, 1978). Clearly, the primary care setting offers unique opportunities for clinical psychologists.

The idea of psychologists and pediatricians working together is not new. Drotar (1995), in his recent book, *Consulting with Pediatricians: Psychological Perspectives*, gave a nice review of the evolution of collabora-

Parts of this chapter appear in Schroeder, C. S. (in press). Mental health services in pediatric primary care. In M. Roberts (Ed.), *Model programs in service delivery in child and family mental health*. Hillsdale, NJ: Erlbaum. Used with permission.

tion among psychologists and pediatricians. As early as 1964 (in his presidential address to the American Academy of Pediatrics), Wilson stated that "one of the things that I would do if I could control the practice of pediatrics would be to encourage groups of pediatricians to employ their own clinical psychologists" (p. 988). Indeed, Haggerty (1986), an influential leader in pediatrics who directed the William T. Grant Foundation from 1980 to 1992, referred to childhood behavioral and school problems as the new morbidity, requiring pediatricians to collaborate with mental health professionals. Work in a primary health care setting does, however, require a shift in the way that mental health services have traditionally been offered: (a) More clients are seen; (b) less time is spent with each client; (c) clients generally present with less debilitating disorders (Wright & Burns, 1986). The focus is thus on prevention and early intervention rather than on treatment of severe psychopathology. Although this approach is especially reasonable for parents and children, it is not widely practiced and has not received a great deal of attention in the literature or in the training of child mental health workers.

One of the earliest reports on a clinical collaboration in primary pediatrics appeared in a 1967 issue of *Journal of Pediatrics* in an article by two pediatricians and a psychologist (Smith, Rome, & Freedheim, 1967). They described the psychologist providing services in the pediatric office for half a day each week with a monthly meeting of the psychologists and pediatricians. They felt that the more visible pediatrician–psychologist collaboration reduced parent resistance to referral to a psychologist.

The practice model to be described in this chapter is based on work in a primary pediatric practice in Chapel Hill, North Carolina, that has evolved over a period of 22 years. In addition to developing a variety of preventative programs and clinical services, we have been able to coordinate our work with other community agencies that serve children, as well as to engage in professional training and research. These activities have been described, in part, in other publications (e.g., Hawk, Schroeder, & Martin, 1987; Kanoy & Schroeder, 1985; Mesibov, Schroeder, & Wesson, 1977; Routh, Schroeder, & Koocher, 1983; Schroeder, 1979; Schroeder & Gordon, 1991; Schroeder, Gordon, Kanoy, & Routh, 1983). This chapter will provide an overview of the population served, the clinical services offered, and the research opportunities in this setting. The chapter ends with a discussion of the issues surrounding collaborative practice.

POPULATION SERVED

Chapel Hill Pediatrics is a private group practice with 8 pediatricians serving approximately 20,000 patients in a small university town. Mental health professionals have been involved with the practice since 1973, offering services that have evolved out of the needs of the children and their parents. Although our clients are primarily from the pediatric practice, anyone in the community may use our services, and no referral from a pediatrician is necessary. The population served is primarily well educated, middle class, and White. Contracts with the Department of Social Services and other community agencies have given us an opportunity also to work with a more diverse cultural, ethnic, and economic population.

From 1973 to 1982, the services offered focused on prevention and early intervention (parent groups, brief face-to-face contacts, and telephone consultation), so the population served was primarily a well-child one, with about 17% of the clients referred for more in-depth assessment and treatment (Schroeder et al., 1983). In 1982, when a wider range of services was offered, the population served expanded to include children presenting with the full range of behavioral and emotional problems. In a descriptive study of a random sample of new clients (304 out of 681 referrals) seen over a 5-year period, from 1982 to 1987, Hawk et al. (1987) reported that 48% were girls and 52% were boys. The percentages of referrals by age were as follows: birth to 5 years, 34%; 6 to 11 years, 45%; and 12 to 20 years, 20%. The ages with the highest number of referrals were 7 years (11.4%) and 5 years (10.8%). The most frequent problems were negative-behavior and child management issues (24.4%); learning problems (18.4%); divorce, stepparenting, and adoption issues (11.5%); and developmental or medical problems (11.4%). There were also a substantial number of children who had suffered a sudden loss of a parent or sibling through death or disappearance.

Hawk et al. (1987) found that the number of sessions (1 hour per session) spent with families varied rather significantly, depending on the problem. Developmental issues such as sleep, toilet training, enuresis, and encopresis took an average of 2.19 sessions; negative behaviors required an average of 5.35 sessions; and specific fears and anxieties took an average of 6.75 sessions. Children with multiple problems required more sessions. For example, a child who had sleep problems as well as negative behavior was seen for an average of 7 sessions. A child who exhibited problems that were more pervasive and occurred across a number of settings required an average of 54 hours spent with child, parents, school, and other community agencies.

Schroeder (1992), in a review of all new referrals (714) for the years 1989 and 1990, reported that 54% were boys and 46% were girls. The percentage of referrals by age were as follows: birth to 5 years, 22%; 6 to 10 years, 44%; 11 to 15 years, 21%; and 16 years and older, 13%. Compared with the Hawk et al. (1987) data for the 5-year period (1982 to 1987), this represented a significant decrease in children seen from birth to 5 years (22% vs. 34%) and an increase in the children seen who were 11 or more years old (34% vs. 20%). The age distributions for the older group differed for the two studies (10 years and older; 11 years or older), which could account for part of the discrepancy for that age group. The increased number of services for the older age group (groups and family therapy) and the parents' greater awareness of the range of psychological services being offered in the practice could also account for the increase in the number of initial referrals at these ages. Certainly, the number of new referrals, 714 in a 2-year period versus 681 in a 5-year period, attests to the increased use of the psychological services over time. Currently, new referrals average 37 per month, or approximately 444 in a year. The addition of more preventive and early-intervention services (e.g., prenatal classes, free ongoing support and information groups for parents with infants and toddlers, more anticipatory guidance handouts, a daily on-call nurse) could account, in part, for the decrease in referrals for the birth to 5-year-old age range. The pediatricians also have indicated that through their close collaboration with the psychology staff, they have become more adept at handling developmental and behavioral issues in this age range and, therefore, could be decreasing the number of younger children who are either referred by them or their parents.

The most frequent problems seen in 1989 and 1990 were negative behavior (18%); anxiety (15%); attention deficit hyperactivity disorder (ADHD; 12%); learning problems and school problems (17%); divorce and separation (9%); peer- and self-esteem (7%); depression (6%); child abuse (6%); and developmental or medical problems (3%). This represents a shift to an increase in the number of internalizing problems and a decrease in the developmental or medical problems being referred to the psychology clinic. It is not clear if the rate at which the children with developmental or medical problems are referred has decreased or if the primary referral question for these children is now a behavioral or emotional problem versus the chronic illness or disability. When we began our work in the pediatric office, we anticipated that we would be seeing a significant number of children with chronic diseases or developmental disabilities. We, however, have learned over the years that most of the children seen in outpatient pediatric practices do not have major medical or developmental problems. This is especially true in our demographic area, given that there are two major medical schools within 10 miles of each other. The care provided by specialized clinics in the medical centers (often with their own pediatric or medical psychologists) decreases the number of children with significant medical or developmental problems followed in the primary care setting. Thus, while we call ourselves pediatric psychologists, the role is reflected more by the setting than the types of problems that are being addressed. Our goal as pediatric psychologists in the primary care setting is to enhance the development of all children and to reduce the number of children with significant emotional and behavioral problems through early identification and intervention.

The length of time clients are seen has remained fairly stable over the years, with five sessions being the mean for 1989–1990 and 13% of the clients seen for one session. Given the sheer number of referrals, our goal has been to provide short-term treatment with a quick turnover of clients. We have thus been faced with the dilemma of deciding what types of problems are best suited to the primary care setting as opposed to a setting geared to handling longer term clients. Although we could try to focus only on short-term clients, the reality is that in a population of 20,000 pediatric patients, there are probably 200 children at any one time who have serious emotional or behavioral problems. We have discovered that neither the parents nor the pediatricians want us to refer these children out of the practice. They argue for continuity of care and working with people with whom they have come to trust. Thus, there are an increasing number of children and families that require more extensive and extended treatment.

In addition to new referrals, we have discovered that a number of children and parents return for help at different points in the children's development. Initially, we felt that perhaps we had not done a thorough enough assessment and treatment the first time around, but the clinical and consumer satisfaction data have indicated that the initial treatment goals were accomplished. Indeed, these children appear to be more vulnerable to the occurrence of stressful events, and their parents periodically seek help in managing a developmental stage or particular event in their life. The stresses can be developmental problems; traumatic experiences, such as sexual abuse or the death of a parent; environmental instability; parental psychopathology; or behavioral or emotional problems that persist at a subclinical level but are exacerbated by a certain developmental stage. We have come to accept that successful treatment at one point in time does not automatically mean a "cure" for these children, nor does it mean that continuous long-term treatment is necessary. As in the moving-risk model described by Gordon and Jens (1988), these children appear to need help at different points in their life; with this periodic help, they are able to learn the necessary skills to cope with the stresses of life.

STAFF AND PERSONNEL

The mental health staff include 5.5 full-time–equivalent PhD clinical child psychologists, 1 full-time person with an MS degree in child development as well as training in marriage and family therapy; a part-time adult and child psychiatrist, and a part-time social worker. In addition, there are 3 full-time office staff and a group administrator. At various times, there are also research students, psychology practicum students, interns and postdoctoral fellows from universities and medical schools.

I began the practice alone and, within a year, began training other psychologists who already had their doctorates or were finishing graduate school, to help with the preventative services, diagnostic testing, school consultation, parent–child training, and treatment of behavior problems. The training necessary for psychologists to work in this type of setting and with this client population includes a strong background in clinical child psychology with an emphasis on a developmental perspective and the opportunity to work with preschoolers, children, and youth developing along a normal continuum; an internship or postdoctoral fellowship in a multidisciplinary clinic or hospital setting; and a strong background in behavioral approaches to treatment. Given the range of problems and issues, the quick pace, and the number of contacts the psychologist confronts on a daily basis, experience in an ambulatory pediatric setting is imperative. If a person is lacking this experience, then they must be prepared to spend some time in training and have supervision readily accessible. It is also important to understand and know the services available to children and families in the community and establish a network with the professionals in those service agencies. In addition, in our clinic, each psychologist brings a unique expertise to the practice (e.g., family therapy, substance abuse, assessment of learning disabilities and ADHD, school consultation, assessment and treatment of sexual abuse, public relations skills, or supervisory skills).

Professional staff have been selected to join the practice on the basis of patient-identified needs for services. For example, with an increased number of parents being referred for individual work, we added the clinical social worker. The child development specialist was added for her expertise in parent education, and the psychiatrist was added in response to the increased number of children and parents presenting with severe psychopathology and the need for a physician knowledgeable in psychotropic drugs.

The office staff is an integral part of the practice. They must not only perform the routine office tasks but also route a myriad of calls to the proper staff member or community agency, score questionnaires, manage the parent library and requests for parent handouts, interface with the pediatric staff and personnel, keep the individual and various clinic appointments straight, deal with the increasing number of managed care groups, and handle the consumer satisfaction questionnaires. A friendly, composed, and efficient person is a prerequisite, and time for proper training is also a necessary part of the job. We added the group administrator, who manages the business and office staff of both the pediatric and the psychology practices, to help streamline the business aspects of the practices and to determine more accurately the financial issues involved in providing a full array of free and fee-based services. This role is increasingly important as we enter the era of health care reform.

PEDIATRIC PSYCHOLOGY SERVICES

The work in the private pediatric office was initially developed in 1973 as an opportunity for graduate and postgraduate students in psychology, social work, nursing, pediatrics, and psychiatry to do preventive and early-intervention work with parents whose children were developing along a normal continuum. The primary placement for these students was in a developmental disabilities clinic at the University of North Carolina Medical School. A randomly selected group of parents from the pediatric office was surveyed by telephone, to assess the need for mental health services and the types of services desired to meet these needs. As a result of that survey, three services were developed: (a) a "Call-In Hour" twice a week, when parents could ask questions about child development and behavior; (b) weekly evening parent groups, which focused on different ages and stages of development; and (c) a "Come-In" time 2–4 hr a week, to give parents an opportunity to discuss their child-related concerns in greater depth. These services, 6 to 8 hr a week, were provided free by the psychologists, social workers, and nurses and their students from the hospital-based clinic.

In 1982, as a result of requests for more in-depth assessment and short-term treatment as well as the need to demonstrate the viability of a practice in this setting on a fee-for-service basis, I joined the pediatric practice on a full-time basis. Clinical services, community consultation, training, and research have always been integral parts of the psychological practice, with each part stimulating the activities of the other parts. Each of these aspects of the practice will be described separately.

Clinical Services

We use a behavior theory orientation with a transactional–developmental perspective in our clinical work. The clinical services cover a range of preventive work, screening, assessment, and short- and long-term treatment.

Preventive Services

Preventive services offered include the evening parent groups, a parent library, the Call-In Hour, and parent handouts. The evening parent groups, which have been ongoing since 1973, are 1.5-hr sessions that focus on different ages and stages in development. For example, a month of sessions might focus on toddlers, with the following topics: Ages and Stages, Toilet Training, Preventing Power Struggles, and Survival Tactics: Dinner Through Bedtime. For adolescents, the topics might be Adolescence: What to Expect, Balancing Their Needs: Independence and Rules, and Tips for Parenting During the Adolescent Years. The sessions are limited to 20 parents each and are organized to include a didactic presentation of material, an opportunity for questions and answers, and the use of handouts that focus on the presented materials. These sessions are advertised in the community as well as in the pediatric examination rooms; parents must register in advance for individual sessions, and there is a charge. We have not formally evaluated the effectiveness of the groups, but consumer satisfaction questionnaires have high ratings. Their popularity often results in two separate sessions on the same topic in order to accommodate the number of parents who wish to attend. The pediatricians offer prenatal parent groups, and there are ongoing groups for parents of newborns to 6-month-olds and parents of 7-month-olds to 24-month-olds. These latter groups are free for the parents, with the pediatricians paying the psychology practice to run them.

A parent library is another preventive service offered free of charge to the parents. Parents' first choice of an information source is books or reading material (Clarke-Stewart, 1978), although there is little empirical evidence on the usefulness of books (Bernal & North, 1978). Our parent library was developed in response to the continual requests of parents for reading material on child-related issues. The parent library is located in the receptionist's office, and an annotated list of books (organized by topic) in a three-ring notebook is kept in the waiting area. The books can be checked out for 2 weeks at no charge. The books that are included in the library have been selected from the "Books for Parents and Children" section of the *Journal of Clinical Child Psychology* (see, e.g., Schroeder, Gordon, & McConnell, 1987). This section was published several times a year from 1984 to 1990 and included reviews of books on divorce, sexuality education, sexual abuse prevention, learning disabilities, developmental disabilities, general parenting, behavior management, stepparenting, single parenting, death, and medical problems. These books are widely used by the general pediatric clientele, in addition to being used as adjuncts to treatment. The psychology practice buys and maintains the books.

The Call-In Hour, offered free twice a week, is a time when parents can ask psychologists about common child development and management concerns. From the inception of this program in 1973, a log has been kept of the phone calls received, the nature of the parents' concerns, and the advice given to them. Reports on the types and frequency of problems, as well as the effectiveness of the advice given, have been published in a number of sources (Kanoy & Schroeder, 1985; Mesibov et al., 1977; Schroeder et al., 1983). In general, the suggestions given to parents usually focus on environmental changes, punishing (using time-out by isolation or removing privileges) or ignoring inappropriate behavior, and rewarding and encouraging appropriate behavior. An important part of the program is to share information on appropriate developmental expectations and behaviors, so that the parents can put their children's behavior in perspective.

Telephone follow-up indicated that in general, the Call-In Hour and specific suggestions were rated highly by parents (Kanoy & Schroeder, 1985). Suggestions for socialization problems (e.g., negative behavior, sibling or peer difficulties, or personality or emotional problems) were rated more effective than those for developmental problems (e.g., toileting, sleep, or developmental delays). Only about 25% of the suggestions for sleep and toileting difficulties were rated between 4 and 5 on a 5-point scale (1 = *not helpful*, and 5 = *very helpful*), whereas about 75% of those for socialization problems were rated between 4 and 5. None of the scores for any behavior category, however, were rated below 3.

Kanoy and Schroeder (1985) found that parents were much more likely to use both the Come-In service and the Call-In Hour when they had concerns about socialization (about 50% used both services), as compared with developmental problems (fewer that 30% used both services). The increased contact with professionals could account for the parents' finding the suggestions for socialization concerns more helpful. With developmental problems, the parents were concerned about a skill or ability their children had failed to acquire by the age the parents believed was normal. We found that providing only support and developmental information did not decrease parents' concerns but that when this information was combined with suggestions for specific actions, the ratings for both developmental information and suggestions increased. The effectiveness of giving specific suggestions was evident for socialization problems (most often behaviors children had acquired that were undesirable). Suggestions such as time-out and rewarding appropriate behaviors with stars gave parents specific strategies to use. These findings led to the development of a series of handouts that are sent to parents who use the Call-In Hour, to reinforce specific suggestions. Further follow-up studies will have to be done to determine parents' perceptions of the effectiveness of the handouts.

One concern that we had with the Call-In Hour was determining when a parent should be referred for more in-depth assessment or treatment. If a problems or concern did not remit after two or three contacts, the parents and child were referred elsewhere. In addition, referrals were made when any of the following constellations of problems was evident:

1. a parent had serious personal problems (e.g., depression or marital problems);
2. a child had multiple emotional and behavioral problems that occurred across settings (e.g., home, school, and neighborhood);
3. a family had multiple psychological problems or stress events (e.g., several children with problems);
4. a child exhibited behavior that had caused (or could cause) significant harm to self or others or serious property damage;
5. there was evidence or suspicion of child abuse, which was reported to appropriate authorities for further investigation;
6. an infant or preschool child showed delayed development, which had been targeted through standardized developmental screening tests and had not responded to stimulation recommendations within a 3–6-month period;
7. a child's general development or academic achievement was below the child's, parent's, or teacher's expectations.

As previously stated, over the years, about 17% of the parents using the Call-In Hour have been referred for further assessment or treatment. Those parents who did follow through with the referral rated the suggestion very highly, but 33% of the parents who had been referred did not use the referral suggestion. Now that more clinical services are being offered in the pediatric setting, it is rare that a parent does not follow through with the recommendation for referral.

The number of parents who called in with concerns regarding developmental delays led to the routine use of the Denver Developmental Screening Test (Frankenburg & Dodds, 1967) for all children at their 3-year checkup. In this way, parents could get direct feedback on how their children were developing, and the number of calls regarding this concern has accordingly dropped.

It had been planned that the handouts developed for the Call-In Hour also would be used in conjunction with well-child physical examinations. For example, the toilet training handout was to be included in the 18-month physical examination. We have discovered, however, that unless the nurses remember to include it with the chart, the pediatricians do not routinely give these to the parents. It is usually a parent's request for information that results in a handout being given. Although this has been rather disappointing, particularly given this group of pediatricians' interest in and support for anticipatory guidance, it is not an atypical problem. One observational study (Reisinger & Bires, 1980) of 23 pediatricians found that the time spent on anticipatory guidance averaged a high of 97 seconds for children under 5 months and a low of 7 seconds for adolescents! One way to ensure that certain areas are discussed with parents both before and after the birth of a baby is to include forms in the patient's medical chart that include the physical and psychosocial areas to be covered at the well-child visit (Christopherson & Rapoff, 1979). Without such a system, it is not likely that this information will be shared with parents at the proper anticipatory time. It would also be important to study the effect of such an anticipatory guidance system on parents' behavior versus just giving the handouts to them or giving the handouts only when they request them.

Direct Clinical Services

In 1982, when the services offered were expanded to include more in-depth assessment and short-term treatment, we were not quite certain about the types of problems that would be referred for these services. The number of referrals made from the Call-In Hour was small and primarily focused on developmental delays, learning problems, and negative behavior. The earlier Population Served section reviewed the number and types of problems that have been referred over the years. Although the number and types of problems are probably not significantly different from those referred to mental health centers, given the number of clients seen for only one session (13%) and a mean of five sessions for assessment and treatment, the presenting problems appear to be less severe than those referred to more traditional mental health settings. Parents appear to be more willing to talk to mental health workers in the pediatric setting and, consequently, more willing to seek help before the problem becomes clinically significant. This, however, is an empirical question that has to be answered by comparing the data from our clinic on numbers, types, and severity of referred problems to other mental health care settings with comparable socioeconomic populations.

Our group offers a full array of clinical child psychology assessment and treatment services. This section gives a brief overview, with a focus on services or methods developed primarily by virtue of our working in the pediatric primary care setting.

Assessment. Assessment is recognized as an integral part of every contact, whether it be talking to a parent who has called for a suggestion on how to handle a specific problem, determining the need for treatment, or gathering and integrating information from multiple sources and with multiple methods to answer specific questions about a child or family. We use a behaviorally oriented system for assessment that is based on

Rutter's (1975) work, which we call the comprehensive assessment-to-intervention system (CAIS). The CAIS is described in detail in Schroeder and Gordon (1991). It focuses on the specifics of the behavior of concern, as well as taking into account other characteristics of the child, family, and environment that influence the behavior. It also provides a framework for choosing instruments or techniques for gathering information and for summarizing the assessment data. This leads to a judgment about the significance of the behavior problem for the child, family, or wider community and, if necessary, the appropriate areas to be considered for further assessment or treatment. The CAIS was developed initially as a systematic way to quickly assess and offer suggestions to parents who used the Call-In Hour, and it allows us to get an understanding of the dimension of the problem without needing to attach a label or initially categorize the problem with a system such as the fourth edition of the *Diagnostic and Statistical Manual of Mental Disorders* (American Psychiatric Association, 1994). This is particularly important in our setting because many of the referral problems would not be considered clinically significant or pathological, although they may be significantly impacting on the child or family's life.

An issue frequently presented to pediatricians by parents is the diagnosis of ADHD and the appropriateness of treating the disorder with stimulant medication. In the light of the controversies surrounding the use of stimulant medication, as well as the limited contact they have with the patient to make such determinations, the pediatricians in our practice felt ill equipped to make assessments regarding diagnosis and treatment. In fact, they refused to prescribe medication without some formal assessment of the problem. Thus, if a child is suspected of having ADHD, we work not only with the child but also with the child's pediatrician, the school, and the parents to assess the behavior through formal psychometric testing, direct behavioral observations, parent and teacher questionnaires, and daily observational data. If the child is determined to have ADHD or attention problems, a behavioral program is developed with the parents and teachers. After this work has commenced, it may be determined that a trial of medication is indicated. At this point, a double-blind, placebo-controlled multimethod assessment of the effects of high and low doses of medication, which includes teacher and parent questionnaires, laboratory measures of attention, and academic analogue tasks, is carried out over a 3-week period. This practice-based clinical protocol is based on a research protocol developed by Barkley (1990). The clinical data of over a 100 children receiving the protocol in our practice have been analyzed with a focus on its effectiveness and ways to streamline the protocol to make it more cost-effective (Riddle, 1993). For example, we initially included a baseline session (insisted on by a parent of a child who had ADHD who also happened to be a clinical researcher for a drug company!) but learned that it essentially duplicated the results from the placebo trial. We have also been able to reduce the time for an evaluation session from 60 minutes to 30 minutes, by selecting the tests most sensitive to treatment. This approach not only has proven to be clinically effective in determining the child's response to medication but also has been very positively received by the children and parents, who feel it has given them a better understanding of the effects of the medication. It also presents the opportunity for long-term follow-up on the cognitive functioning of children on stimulant medication. We are now considering the use of similar protocols for assessing the feasibility of other medications or the effect of medications used for conditions such as seizure disorders.

The pediatric clinic serves as the county medical evaluation center for children who have been neglected or abused. One of the pediatricians in the practice (Charles Sheaffer) is responsible for much of the work on behalf of physically and sexually abused children in North Carolina, and after we joined the pediatric practice, he was instrumental in getting the state to fund psychological evaluations for children for whom abuse or neglect is suspected or has been substantiated. We now are part of the statewide Child Mental Health Evaluation Program, which involves answering a wide range of referral questions. We may be asked, for example, "Has the child been abused?" "What are the effects of the abuse?" "Is the mother or father capable of protecting the child?" "Does the child need treatment?" "How will the child be affected by going to court?"

Our clinical work in the area of sexual abuse led us to engage in research on memory issues with colleagues from the university. This work, done in the pediatric office, has been extensively published (e.g., See Baker-Ward, Gordon, Ornstein, & Clubb, 1993; Gordon et al., 1993; Ornstein, Larus, & Clubb, 1991). Furthermore, the clinical implications of this empirical work resulted in the development of guidelines for clinicians to use when interviewing children suspected of being sexually abused (Gordon, Schroeder, Ornstein, & Baker-Ward, 1995).

Treatment. We have found ourselves involved in a number of roles in the process of providing intervention services to children and families, including the following:

1. Educator: giving specific information, sharing books and other written material, offering parent groups, or helping parents or teachers to develop more realistic expectations;
2. Advocate: speaking for the child in court, helping the parents negotiate with the educational system, or advocating for the child's needs within the family system;

3. Treatment provider: giving direct treatment to the child or family or providing indirect treatment (e.g., intervention in the environment);
4. Case manager: accessing and networking services to meet the needs of the child and family.

The role of case manager is particularly pertinent to the primary care setting. This involves networking the often fragmented and specialized services of the community, to meet the individual needs of the child and family. This approach, as described by Hobbs (1975), involves looking for unique ways to use the available services, as well as for creative ways to develop services that are needed but unavailable. Children with developmental disabilities are most often thought of as in need of case managers, but this is an important role in work with most children and parents. It requires the clinician to be very familiar with the resources in the community and to become skilled in negotiating cooperation between agencies.

The practice offers individual treatment for children and parents as well as couple and family therapy. The treatment protocols for common childhood problems—such as enuresis, encopresis, sleep, negative behavior, bad habits, and anxiety—and for stressful events—such as death, divorce, and sexual abuse—have been published in a book by Schroeder and Gordon (1991), *Assessment and Treatment of Childhood Problems: A Clinician's Guide*. The empirical literature indicates that we should be able to meet the needs of parents and children in a more cost-effective and efficient manner through groups, and this would appear to be particularly true in the primary care setting. Although we have offered group treatment for both parents and children, which has focused on specific problem areas or life events, such as ADHD, divorce, social skills, sexual abuse, and stepparenting, it has actually been very difficult to provide a variety of group treatments on an ongoing basis. We have had difficulties with scheduling and finding the right mix and number of children or parents at the right time. The treatment group for parents of ADHD children has been successful, given the number of children who are evaluated for this problem and for the use of medication. The parents in this group meet for four consecutive sessions and then may attend a once-a-month support group. The staff is also very involved in the local parent groups focusing on these children.

In cooperation with the local department of social services, we developed a group-treatment program for children who had been sexually abused and their parents. The goal was to help the children and families deal with the complex emotional sequelae of the abuse and to find ways to cope effectively with the aftermath of the abuse. The children's groups were divided into preschool, elementary school, and adolescent ages.

They met for 10 weekly sessions, focusing on the issues of traumatic sexualization, stigmatization, betrayal of trust, and powerlessness (Finkelhor & Browne, 1986; Walker, Bonner, & Kaufman, 1988). The parents met separately and focused on the effects of abuse, the role of the legal system in abuse cases, problem solving for ways to meet their individual needs, and learning about ways to prevent the abuse from recurring. At the end of these sessions, a determination was made for each child and family regarding the need for further treatment. Although the predata and postdata, plus the consumer satisfaction questionnaires, indicated that the program was effective in treating these children and their families, the funding for the program was cut.

Community Consultation

Being in a primary care setting gives the professional a great deal of visibility in the community and also a great deal of responsibility to advocate for children. We have discovered that when the newspaper wants information about a particular issue (e.g., "Is it morally right to tell children there is a Santa Claus?") or the court system wants information on a particular problem, they are just as likely to call the pediatric office as are parents. We have, thus, increasingly found ourselves in the position of having to interface with the community on a number of levels.

As noted earlier, in the late 1960s and early 1970s, a pediatrician in the practice became the coordinator for all of the community agencies involved with children who were physically or sexually abused. Regular meetings were held with representatives from the pediatric office, the police department, the schools, and the department of social services, together with mental health professionals from the community. The focus of the meetings was initially educational, but it quickly moved to case management issues. Problems of roles and responsibilities were worked out (sometimes hammered out!), and the result has been an ongoing coordinated community effort on behalf of these children. At times the system falters, especially when new people are added to one of the agencies or new regulations change the nature of the services. However, the short- and long-term benefits of this work cannot be underestimated, as is demonstrated by the statewide Child Mental Health Evaluation Program and the contract with the local department of social services to provide group treatment for children in our county who have been sexually abused.

Another example of community involvement is that we first convinced and then consulted with the school system to include sex education and sexual abuse prevention at all grade levels. In addition, both pediatricians and psychologists have been asked to provide training for the North Carolina Guardian Ad Litem program, district judges, district attorneys, the department of social services, the rape crisis center, the Young Men's Christian Association, day care centers, and many other community groups that are involved in the lives of children. We have discovered, however, that all of this work is made possible by the community interaction concerning a particular child or family, which identifies problems and solutions that can then be applied to the benefit of other children in the community. In the real world, where one must juggle time, economic issues, and altruism, this is as it should be.

Training

Training has always been part of the work in the pediatric office. From 1973 to 1982, graduate students, interns, and postdoctoral fellows in psychology; graduate students in social work; and medical students and residents participated in all aspects of the program. In 1982, the Division of Community Pediatrics at the University of North Carolina at Chapel Hill Medical School began a training program for all 1st-year pediatric residents and 4th-year medical students taking an ambulatory pediatrics elective (Sharp & Lorch, 1988). The goals of the program were to introduce the pediatric trainees to community resources for children and to increase their knowledge of the factors affecting a child's development. The pediatric psychology practice was one of 25 community agencies involved in this training. This is a unique approach to training pediatricians in the biosocial aspects of development, and in 1984 the program won the prestigious American Academy of Ambulatory Pediatrics Excellence in Teaching Award. The residents and medical students each spent 1 day a week for a month in our office; they learned about the types of developmental and behavioral problems parents bring to the pediatric office, how to interview parents and to develop intervention strategies for common problems, and what a psychologist has to offer in a primary health care setting and when children should be referred to them. It was hoped that we would alert these residents at an early stage in their careers to the value of psychologists! We plan to do a survey of graduates of this program to determine how they now interface with psychologists; however, we already know that a number of them (three in our area alone) have psychologists in their practices. Unfortunately, in 1992, the funds for this training program were cut, and we have not had the opportunity to train residents since that time.

Clinical psychology graduate students have continued to participate in the Call-In Hour and to provide treatment one afternoon a week. We have also had a 2-year postdoctoral fellow in psychology, who was jointly sponsored by our practice and the University of North Carolina Medical School Department of Pediatrics. Interns from the University of North Carolina Psychiatry Department spend a day a week for a 3-month rotation in the ADHD clinic, doing the drug protocol evaluations.

Training in a busy private clinic takes time and effort, which in part can be recouped by the trainees' work in the community or with families who cannot afford the full fee for service. The ultimate benefit is having more mental health professionals trained to work in primary care settings and pediatricians who are more aware of mental health issues and the desirability of having psychologists in their practices.

Research

The primary health care setting is a fertile ground for psychological research. The sheer number of available children who are developing along a normal continuum offers opportunities for interesting developmental research, and the smaller number of children who have chronic physical and behavioral or emotional disorders encourages research on treatment effectiveness as well as longitudinal research on these problems. The primary health care setting also offers the opportunity to evaluate the effectiveness of primary and secondary prevention programs. To do this work, one has to demonstrate credibility within the system by offering a range of high-quality services.

The first 5 years of the expanded practice (1982–1987) were devoted to developing the clinical services, and as we entered another 5-year era, we began to look at the research issues that were raised by the clinical practice. One study, done as a doctoral dissertation in the University of North Carolina School of Public Health Department of Epidemiology, compared a group of 2- to 7-year-old children who had received treatment for noncompliance with a control group matched for age and level of noncompliance (Martin, 1988). In view of the number of children identified with this potentially persistent problem, and the desire to provide early intervention to change the course of the behavior, the research questions were whether the treatment would be effective and (given the age of the children) whether the behavior of the untreated control group would improve without intervention. The parent-training program for the negative behavior was based on the work by Eyberg and Boggs (1989) and Forehand and McMahon (1981). Martin found that at a 3-month follow-up, the 31 children in the treatment group showed clinically and statistically significant decreases in both the number and frequency of behavior problems. The behavior of the 22 untreated control children did not improve over the same time period. Further follow-up of these children will provide more information about the course of this behavior.

Current work involves the collaboration of developmental and clinical psychologists in the study of the questions raised by our work with sexually abused children. We quickly discovered that questions asked by the legal system exceeded our knowledge in this area. We were asked, for example, "Can we believe what young children tell us about what has happened to them?" "Can children remember and report events as completely and as accurately as adults, especially when events may have been traumatic?" "Are children particularly vulnerable to suggestive and leading questions?" "What are the effects of repeated questioning on children's abilities to remember particular events?"

To begin answering these questions, we first looked at the role of prior knowledge. A common belief among professionals who testify in court on behalf of preschoolers who have been abused is that young children's knowledge of sexuality is limited and, therefore, that these children cannot describe sexual acts unless they have actually experienced them. To provide empirical evidence for this belief, we studied 192 nonabused children (age 2–7 years) to determine their knowledge of gender identity, body parts and functioning, pregnancy and birth, adult sexual behavior, private parts, and personal safety skills (Gordon, Schroeder, & Abrams, 1990a). There were significant age differences in children's knowledge of all areas of sexuality, but under the age of 6 or 7 years, children had little knowledge of adult sexual behavior. The children's sexual knowledge was directly related to their parents' attitudes about sexuality: Parents with more restrictive attitudes had children who knew less about sexuality than parents who had more liberal attitudes. A second study examined sexual knowledge of children for whom sexual abuse had been substantiated and an age-matched control group of non-abused children (Gordon, Schroeder, & Abrams, 1990b). This study indicated that sexually abused children do not necessarily have greater knowledge of sexuality than nonabused children of the same age. The children who were sexually abused, however, gave qualitatively unusual responses to the stimulus materials. For example, a 3-year-old withdrew in fright when presented with a picture of a child being put to bed by an adult.

A second line of research focused on factors that influence the accuracy of children's testimony. This research initially was supported by a National Institute of Mental Health grant. It examined children's memory for a personally experienced event, a physical examination (an analogue to sexual abuse). The purpose of this research was to establish baseline data for children's memory over varying periods of time and to examine factors that influence children's memory (e.g., repeated interviews, use of props in interviews, reinstatement, prior knowledge of visits to the doctor, painful procedures, and traumatic injuries). This research has been presented and published extensively (e.g., Baker-Ward et al., 1993; Baker-Ward, Hess, & Flanagan, 1990; Gordon et al., 1993;

Ornstein, Gordon, & Larus, 1992). Gordon et al. (1995) documented the clinical implications of this work for testimony of young children with guidelines for interviewing young children and evaluating their responses. This basic research, born out of our clinical work and carried out by necessity in the primary care setting, is an excellent example of the type of research that can be done in natural settings.

IMPLEMENTATION ISSUES

In recent years, pediatric practices have advertised for psychologists, but usually, it is the psychologist who must approach the pediatricians to set up a collaborative relationship. The published description of the psychologist's role in the Chapel Hill Pediatrics practice and other publications (e.g., Drotar, 1993; Wright & Burns, 1986) have served to present the positive benefits of such a relationship. More psychologists and pediatricians in private practice are developing collaborative relationships, as evidenced by the Society of Pediatric Psychology's Special Interest Group on Psychologists Working in Primary Care Settings (Division 12, Section V, American Psychological Association). As more psychologists doing this work are identified, we will, hopefully, be able to provide more information on the nature of these relationships and the variety of services offered in these settings.

Setting up a pediatric psychology practice in a primary health care setting is not dissimiliar to establishing a private practice, but the options available to the psychologist in a primary health care setting will depend on the particular health care setting and the relationship the psychologist wants with the other professionals in that setting. It is usually not possible for a psychologist to be a partner in another professional group (e.g., pediatrics); thus, other options for association must be considered. A psychologist may be employed by a pediatric practice, and may have a fixed salary or a salary based on a percentage of the collected receipts or may pay a fixed percentage of collected receipts to the pediatric practice. Another option is for the psychologist to establish an independent practice within the health care setting, with overhead paid by the psychologist. The administrative functions may be contracted to the pediatric practice or handled independently by the psychologist. Establishing an independent practice within the health care setting gives the psychologist the options of sole proprietorship, a partnership (if more than one psychologist is involved), or a corporation. The pediatric psychology practice described in this chapter was established as an independent corporation. For the first 2 years, I paid the pediatric practice for overhead costs. As the pediatric psychology staff grew, we hired a secretary, obtained separate phone numbers, did our own billing, paid a fixed rent, and so forth, while still being physically located within the pediatric setting. Due to space constraints, the mental health part of the practice moved to a building directly behind the pediatricians, keeping one office in the pediatrician's space. This decision was a difficult one for all involved, but we felt that our long-term collaboration would survive the short physical distance separating us. Only time will tell how well this arrangement works. We have agreed, however, that if we all survive managed care, we will eventually move to a building that will house both the pediatricians and the mental health professionals. The parents have actually appreciated the physical separation; they state that it provides them greater privacy and that the atmosphere is more conducive to mental health work.

The space available in the primary health care setting is geared to medical rather than psychological needs; it is therefore important to negotiate for space that will permit privacy, as well as flexibility to serve small children and families for diagnosis and treatment. It has been our experience that private pediatric offices are under renovation every 5 to 8 years, so although the clinician may have to start with less-than-optimal space, a goal to improve the space options as the value of the practice is demonstrated is usually realistic.

As described in previous sections, the types of services offered and the staffing patterns were the direct result of identified client needs and the interests of the psychologists and pediatricians in the practice. Keeping careful records of our work and doing follow-ups to determine consumer satisfaction have always been a part of our practice. Also, by taking the time to share the importance of certain research topics with the pediatricians, staff, parents, and children, we have had the opportunity to research some interesting questions. My association with a university and the availability of university students and staff to help carry out the research are key to being able to do this work. Doing any type of research in the primary setting presents obstacles: lack of sufficient time on the part of the doctors, nurses, and patients to collect extensive data; getting representative subject samples, which usually requires gathering data from several offices in several communities; lack of instruments that focus on the kinds of concerns reflected in a primary care setting; developing collaborative relationships with the physicians, which takes time; and lack of time and money on the psychologist's part to carry out the work. The importance of doing this work, however, is reflected in National Institute of Mental Health and the Agency for Health Care Prevention and Research funding research on mental health services in primary health care settings. With the increased interest in providing mental health services for children and parents in this area, new approaches should be forthcoming. The work by the American Academy of Pediatrics

Task Force on the Coding of Mental Health in children should help to better identify mental health disorders in primary care settings and generate further training, clinical services, and research in the primary care setting.

CONCLUSION

The collaboration of psychologists and pediatricians provides a unique opportunity to enhance children's and parents' lives over the trajectory of the child's development. The focus is on promoting the child's healthy development through services that focus on prevention and early intervention rather than the treatment of severe psychopathology. The collaborative practice described in this chapter has also included training opportunities for both pediatricians and psychologists as well as opportunities for research. Although special training to work in a pediatric primary care setting is necessary, psychologists working with children and adolescents have a great deal to offer in this setting.

REFERENCES

American Academy of Pediatrics, Task Force on Pediatric Education. (1978). *The future of pediatric education.* Evanston, IL: Author.

American Psychiatric Association. (1994). *Diagnostic and statistical manual of mental disorders* (4th ed.). Washington, DC: Author.

Baker-Ward, L. E., Gordon, B. N., Ornstein, P. A., & Clubb, P. A. (1993). Young children's long-term retention of a pediatric examination. *Child Development, 64,* 1519–1533.

Baker-Ward, L. E., Hess, T. M., & Flanagan, D. A. (1990). The effects of children's involvement on children's memory for events. *Cognitive Development, 4,* 393–407.

Barkley, R. A. (1990). *Attention deficit hyperactivity disorder: A handbook for diagnosis and treatment.* New York: Guilford Press.

Bernal, M. E., & North, J. A. (1978). A survey of parent training manuals. *Journal of Applied Behavior Analysis, 11,* 533–544.

Christopherson, E. R., & Rapoff, M. A. (1979). Behavioral pediatrics. In O. F. Pomerleau & J. P. Brady (Eds.), *Behavioral medicine: Theory and practice* (pp. 99–123). Baltimore: Williams & Wilkins.

Clarke-Stewart, K. A. (1978). Popular primers for parents. *American Psychologist, 33,* 359–369.

Drotar, D. (1993). Influences on collaborative activities among psychologists and pediatricians: Implications for practice, training, and research. *Journal of Pediatric Psychology, 18,* 159–172.

Drotar, D. (1995). *Consulting with pediatricians: Psychological perspectives*. New York: Plenum.

Eyberg, S. M., & Boggs, S. R. (1989). Parent training for oppositional–defiant preschoolers. In C. E. Schaefer & J. M. Briesmeister (Eds.), *Handbook of parent training: Parents as cotherapists for children's behavior problems* (pp. 105–132). New York: Wiley.

Finkelhor, D., & Browne, A. (1986). Initial and long-term effects: A conceptual framework. In D. Finkelhor & associates (Eds.), *A sourcebook on child sexual abuse* (pp. 180–198). Beverly Hills, CA: Sage.

Forehand, R. L., & McMahon, R. J. (1981). *Helping the noncompliant child: A clinician's guide to parent training*. New York: Guilford Press.

Frankenburg, W. K., & Dodds, J. B. (1967). The Denver Developmental Screening Test. *Journal of Pediatrics, 71*, 181–191.

Gordon, B. N., & Jens, K. G. (1988). A conceptual model for tracking high-risk infants and making services decisions. *Developmental and Behavioral Pediatrics, 9*, 279–286.

Gordon, B. N., Ornstein, P. A., Nida, R. E., Follmer, A., Crenshaw, M. C., & Albert, G. (1993). Does the use of dolls facilitate children's memory of visits to the doctor? *Applied Cognitive Psychology, 7*, 1–16.

Gordon, B. N., Schroeder, C. S., & Abrams, J. M. (1990a). Children's knowledge of sexuality: Age and social class differences. *Journal of Clinical Child Psychology, 19*, 33–43.

Gordon, B. N., Schroeder, C. S., & Abrams, J. M. (1990b). Children's knowledge of sexuality: A comparison of sexually abused and nonabused children. *American Journal of Orthopsychiatry, 60*, 250–257.

Gordon, B. N., Schroeder, C. S., Ornstein, P. A., & Baker-Ward, L. E. (1995). Clinical implications of research in memory development. In T. Ney (Ed.), *Child sexual abuse cases: Allegations, assessment and management* (pp. 99–124). New York: Brunner/Mazel.

Haggerty, R. J. (1986). The changing nature of pediatrics. In N. A. Krasnegor, J. D. Arasteh, & M. F. Calaldo (Eds.), *Child health behavior: A behavioral pediatric perspective* (pp. 9–16). New York: Wiley.

Hawk, B. A., Schroeder, C. A., & Martin, S. (1987). Pediatric psychology in a primary care setting. *Newsletter of the Society of Pediatric Psychology, 11*, 13–18.

Hobbs, N. (1975). *The futures of children*. San Francisco: Jossey-Bass.

Kanoy, K., & Schroeder, C. S. (1985). Suggestions to parents about common behavior problems in a pediatric primary care office: Five years of follow-up. *Journal of Pediatric Psychology, 10*, 15–30.

Martin, S. L. (1988). *The effectiveness of a multidisciplinary primary health care model in the prevention of children's mental health problems*. Unpublished doctoral dissertation, University of North Carolina, Chapel Hill.

Mesibov, G. B., Schroeder, C. S., & Wesson, L. (1977). Parental concerns about their children. *Journal of Pediatric Psychology, 2*, 13–17.

Ornstein, P. A., Gordon, B. N., & Larus, D. M. (1992). Children's memory for a personally experienced event: Implications for testimony. *Applied Cognitive Psychology, 6,* 49–60.

Ornstein, P. A., Larus, D. M., & Clubb, P. A. (1991). Understanding children's testimony: Implications of research on the development of memory. In R. Vasta (Ed.), *Annals of child development* (Vol. 8, pp. 145–176). London: Jessica Kingsley.

Reisinger, K. S., & Bires, J. A. (1980). Anticipatory guidance in pediatric practice. *Pediatrics, 66,* 889–892.

Riddle, D. B. (1993, August). *Double blind protocol research within a pediatric practice.* Paper presented at the 101st Annual Convention of the American Psychological Association, Toronto, Ontario, Canada.

Routh, D. K., Schroeder, C. S., & Koocher, G. P. (1983). Psychology and primary health care for children. *American Psychologist, 38,* 95–98.

Rutter, M. (1975). *Helping troubled children.* New York: Plenum.

Schroeder, C. S. (1979). The psychologist in a private pediatrics office. *Journal of Pediatric Psychology, 1,* 5–18.

Schroeder, C. S. (1992, August). *Psychologists working with pediatricians.* Paper presented at the 100th Annual Convention of the American Psychological Association, Washington, DC.

Schroeder, C. S., & Gordon, B. N. (1991). *Assessment and treatment of childhood problems: A clinician's guide.* New York: Guilford Press.

Schroeder, C. S., Gordon, B. N., Kanoy, K., & Routh, D. K. (1983). Managing children's behavior problems in pediatric practice. In M. Wolraich & D. K. Routh (Eds.), *Advances in developmental and behavioral pediatrics* (Vol. 4, pp. 25–86). Greenwich, CT: JAI Press.

Schroeder, C. S., Gordon, B. N., & McConnell, P. (1987). Books for parents and children on behavior management. *Journal of Clinical Child Psychology, 16,* 89–94.

Schroeder, C. S., & Wool, R. (1979, March). *Parental concerns for children one month to 10 years and the informational sources desired to answer these concerns.* Paper presented at the annual meeting of the Southeastern Psychological Association, New Orleans, LA.

Sharp, M. C., & Lorch, S. C. (1988). A community outreach training program for pediatrics residents and medical students. *Journal of Medical Education, 63,* 316–322.

Smith, E. E., Rome, L. P., & Freedheim, D. K. (1967). The clinical psychologist in the pediatric office. *Journal of Pediatrics, 21,* 48–51.

Walker, C. E., Bonner, B. L., & Kaufman, K. L. (1988). *The physically and sexually abused child: Evaluation and treatment.* Elmsford, NY: Pergamon Press.

Wilson, J. L. (1964). Growth and development in pediatrics. *Journal of Pediatrics, 65,* 984–991.

Wright, L., & Burns, B. J. (1986). Primary mental health care: A "find" for psychology. *Professional Psychology: Research and Practice, 17,* 560–564.

10

BEHAVIORAL HEALTH CARE IN PRIMARY CARE SETTINGS: RECOGNITION AND TREATMENT OF ANXIETY DISORDERS

DAVID H. BARLOW, JONATHAN A. LERNER, and
JEANNE LAWTON ESLER

Community surveys indicate that anxiety disorders are the single most prevalent class of mental disorders in the population at large, with 1-year estimates ranging from 13% to 17% (Kessler et al., 1994; Regier et al., 1984). This makes the prevalence of anxiety disorders greater than other major classes of disorders, including addictive disorders or mood disorders.

DO PATIENTS WITH ANXIETY DISORDERS SEEK TREATMENT IN PRIMARY CARE SETTINGS?

For many years, we had difficulty estimating the number of individuals with anxiety disorders presenting to primary care settings. More recently, information gleaned from various surveys indicates that these numbers are substantial, although the objectives of these surveys have typically varied widely. For example, Regier et al. (1993) reported that individuals with anxiety disorders seek out treatment in primary care settings and other medical facilities as often as they present to mental health providers. Barrett, Barrett, Oxman, and Gerber (1988), while examining more specifically the types of patients found in rural primary care settings, found that fully 21.3% of all patients met research diagnostic criteria (Spitzer, Endicott, & Robins, 1978) for anxiety disorders, depressive disorders, or mixed anxiety–depressive syndromes, including masked (suspected) depression and mixed anxiety–depression.

More recently, the fourth edition of the *Diagnostic and Statistical Manual of Mental Disorders* (*DSM–IV*; American Psychiatric Association, 1994) Task Force examined the distribution of anxiety disorders, as well as anxious symptoms sufficient to be impairing but not reaching definitional threshold for one or more of the anxiety disorders, in five primary care settings. Three of the five primary care settings were in the United States, one in Australia, and one in Paris. All patients filled out a brief screening instrument designed to detect the possible presence of anxiety and related symptomatology. Two thirds of the sample were chosen from patients falling above a cutoff point, indicating the possible presence of anxious or dysphoric symptoms, whereas one third were chosen from patients falling below the cutoff point. For this reason, the numbers in this study do not reflect absolute prevalence of anxiety disorders in primary care settings but do give a good idea of the distribution of specific problems. Patients were then carefully assessed with semistructured interviews to determine the presence and nature of a disorder, if any. Results showed that very high percentages of patients received diagnoses of generalized anxiety disorder (11.9%), social phobia (13%), and specific phobia. In addition, 8% of patients fell under a category labeled *not otherwise specified* (NOS) consisting of patients presenting with mostly anxious symptoms or symptoms of negative affect that did not meet definitional criteria for one disorder or another. Patients met criteria less frequently for panic disorder (4.3%), obsessive–compulsive disorder (1.2%), posttraumatic stress disorder (4.5%), and dysthymia (1.1%). Major depressive episode was diagnosed in 7.9% of patients, and fully 34.7% of patients were given a diagnosis of no mental disorder (see Zinbarg et al., 1994). The symptoms of negative affect, which are present in most anxiety disorders as well as depressive disorders, form the basis for a proposed new category in *DSM–IV*, termed mixed anxiety–depressive disorder (Zinbarg et al., 1994). This group would most likely encompass Barrett et al.'s (1988) categories of masked (suspected) depression, mixed anxiety–depression, and other depressive content.

More recent estimates indicate that the presence of anxiety-related symptoms and disorders in primary care settings may even be higher than previous numbers. For example, Fifer et al. (1994) discovered that 33% of over 6,000 eligible patients completing an up-to-date screening instrument in the offices of 75 physicians in a large mixed-model health maintenance organization reported elevated symptoms or disorders of anxiety. Shear, Schulberg, and Madonia (1994) also found high prevalence rates of anxiety disorders in primary care centers when primary care patients were assessed by semistructured interviews. Specifically, fully 11% of unselected patients in primary care settings met criteria for panic disorder and 10% for generalized anxiety disorder.

Approaching the issue from another direction, Katerndahl and Realini (1995) conducted a community survey to identify patients who had experienced panic attacks, to ascertain whether they had sought treatment for their attacks and, if so, where they went for treatment. Only 59% of the participants had ever sought care from the health care system for their panic attacks. Information on the specific health and mental health sites from which these patients sought help is presented in Table 1. These data are broken down by the percentage of patients seeking out various sites the first time that they presented for help with panic attacks and any time they presented for help, including subsequent episodes of panic. As one can see, medical settings are used far more frequently than mental health settings to care for panic attacks, even after the initial contact, where presumably the problem is identified as anxiety or panic related. Specifically, 49% of these patients sought out, and continue to seek out, medical settings, compared with 26% receiving help from mental health practitioners. The breakdown of type of medical setting or type of mental health practitioner or setting is also provided. In addition, fully 13% of this sample, located in south Texas, sought help from alternative sources of care such as telephone help lines or clergy. Of course, many participants used more than one site, so the percentages are not mutually exclusive.

From these surveys, it would seem that symptoms of anxiety and anxiety disorders are highly prevalent in primary care settings. Furthermore, because these disorders are chronic in nature, typically displaying patterns of exacerbation and remission often associated with life stress, the observation that these patients form a substantial core of the practices of primary health care practitioners gains credence (Barlow, 1988; Brown & Barlow, 1995).

ARE PATIENTS WITH ANXIETY DISORDERS RECOGNIZED IN PRIMARY CARE SETTINGS?

Although only 32.2% of patients with anxiety disorder seek treatment, approximately half of these patients seek treatment in primary

TABLE 1
Sites Selected by Patients Seeking Treatment for Panic Attack

Treatment site	% of patients presenting at any time ($N = 97$)	% of patients presenting for episode of initial contact ($N = 53$)[a]
Medical health care settings	49	85
Emergency department	32	43
Minor emergency center	11	7
Clinic	9	7
Physician's office		
General/family physician	35	35
General internist	3	6
Cardiologist	9	6
Otolaryngologist	3	6
Ambulance	19	15
Mental health care settings	26	35
Psychiatrist	24	22
Psychologist	10	13
Social worker	5	4
Mental health clinic	11	7
Alternative care settings	13	19
Telephone help line	10	6
Clergy	8	7
Folk healer/*curandero*	8	7
Chiropractor	6	6

Note: Subjects may have presented to >1 site, so percentages may not total 100.
[a]Only the 57 patients who presented to at least one site were included. Four of these subjects did not respond to this question.
Data are from "Where Do Panic Attacks Sufferers Seek Care?" by D. A. Katerndahl and J. P. Realini, 1995, *Journal of Family Practice, 40,* 237–243. Copyright 1995 by Appleton & Lange, Inc. Used with permission.

care settings. Because anxiety disorders are the most prevalent class of mental disorders, the number of individuals seeking treatment in primary care settings is enormous, with estimates in the range of 6 million (Regier et al., 1993).

It is now well recognized that approximately half of patients presenting with emotional disorders, such as anxiety or mood disorders, are not recognized or diagnosed by primary care physicians (e.g., Broadhead, 1994; Fifer et al., 1994; Shear & Schulberg, 1995). Because, as Ford (1994) pointed out, at least 50% of patients with psychological disorders receive all or part of their care from primary care physicians, lack of recognition is a source of major concern. In the Fifer et al. (1994) study, as noted above, 33% of the patients screened positive for anxiety symptoms and possible anxiety disorders. As represented in Figure 1, fully 56% of these patients were unrecognized and untreated, and only 44% were recognized as presenting with anxiety and were treated in

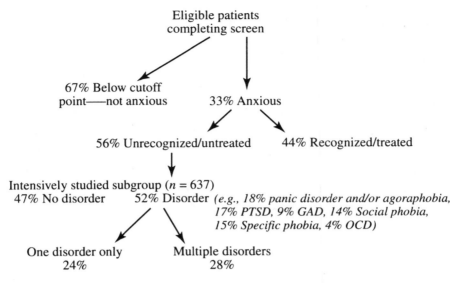

Eligible patients
completing screen

67% Below cutoff
point——not anxious   33% Anxious

56% Unrecognized/untreated   44% Recognized/treated

Intensively studied subgroup (*n* = 637)
47% No disorder   52% Disorder *(e.g., 18% panic disorder and/or agoraphobia,*
17% PTSD, 9% GAD, 14% Social phobia,
15% Specific phobia, 4% OCD)

One disorder only   Multiple disorders
24%   28%

Figure 1. Anxiety in primary care settings. PTSD = posttraumatic stress disorder, GAD = generalized anxiety disorder, OCD = obsessive–compulsive disorder. From "Untreated Anxiety Among Adult Primary Care Patients in a Health Maintenance Organization," by S. K. Fifer et al., 1994, *Archives of General Psychiatry, 51,* p. 743. Copyright 1994 by the American Medical Association. Adapted with permission.

some fashion or other. The figure of 44% recognized and treated is somewhat higher than estimates from community samples, in which data suggest that only 25% of individuals diagnosed with anxiety disorders are receiving any kind of treatment, and many of these treatments would also not necessarily be efficacious. Data on recognition of anxiety disorders in the Fifer et al. study may actually be an overestimate, because practitioners in this mixed-model health maintenance organization were provided some specific training in recognizing and treating these disorders. Katon, Vitaliano, Russo, Jones, and Anderson (1987) found that over 30% of patients in a primary care practice had experienced at least one panic attack during the previous year, and because somatic symptoms are such a heavy component of panic attacks, panic and anxiety were not recognized in the large majority of these patients. Returning to the Fifer et al. study, approximately half (*n* = 637) of the individuals unrecognized and untreated for anxiety symptoms or disorders were available for more intensive study. As reflected in Figure 1, 52% of these patients presented with a recognizable anxiety disorder upon semistructured interviewing. Approximately half of the individuals constituting this 52% (24%) presented with only one disorder, whereas the remainder presented with more than one anxiety disorder. Percentages of specific disorders were very similar to other surveys (e.g., Shear & Schulberg, 1995): Large percentages of patients presented with panic disorder with or without agoraphobia, posttraumatic stress disorder, generalized anxiety disorder, social phobia, and so on. On the other hand, 47% of these intensively studied individuals did not meet definitional criteria for a disorder but clearly presented with substantial anxious symptomatology. As we have seen above in the Zinbarg et al. (1994) study, many of these patients probably presented with generalized symptoms of negative affect that might meet criteria for the newly proposed diagnostic category of mixed anxiety–depressive disorder. Most of these patients also presented with substantial functional impairment that was as great as those meeting all criteria for one or more anxiety disorders. These patients are very much in need of treatment due to the chronic and recurring nature of this symptomatology (Zinbarg et al., 1994).

IMPAIRMENT

Several studies have addressed the issue of functional impairment associated with anxious or depressive symptoms in primary care settings. For example, Wells et al. (1989) reported on the functional status and well-being of patients with depressive disorders or depressive symptoms. They found that these patients were at least as impaired, and in some cases more impaired, than patients with chronic medical conditions. For example, individuals with symptoms of depression, or more generalized negative affect, were more impaired than patients with chronic pulmonary disease, diabetes, arthritis, back problems, and gastrointestinal disorders. Only coronary artery disease produced as much impairment. Although anxiety symptoms and disorders were not specifically identified in this study, more recent efforts, which included symptoms and disorders of anxiety, have essentially replicated these findings (K. B. Wells, January 12, 1994, personal communication).

COMPLAINTS OF ANXIOUS PATIENTS IN PRIMARY CARE SETTINGS

Patients presenting to primary care settings who are ultimately diagnosed with severe anxiety often somatize their complaints in some characteristic ways. Most often, the pattern of symptoms is not well explained by identifiable physical illnesses. For example, Van Hemert, Hengeveld, Boek, Rooijmans, and Vandenbroucke (1993) compared patients whose symptoms were explained by a known physical illness to those presenting with vague symptoms that were not well explained. Fully 38% to 45% of those patients presenting with symptoms that were not well explained by a known physical illness were later identified to have a psychological disorder, as compared with 15% of those whose symptoms were well explained. The majority of these disorders were anxiety or mood disorders.

Other common presentations include chest pain in the absence of clinical evidence of cardiac disease. For example, Yingling, Wulsin, Arnold, and Rovan (1993) found that 17% of 229 patients seeking treatment for chest pain at an emergency department met criteria for panic disorder. These individuals were significantly more likely than individuals without panic disorder to have visited an emergency department for chest pain at least once in the past year. Of individuals identified with panic disorder, fully 27% had made at least three emergency department visits for chest pain in the previous year.

Finally, Ford (1987) found that those patients presenting with atypical chest pain were four times as likely to have panic disorder than those without chest pain. Katon (1984) found that 89% of 55 primary care patients with panic disorder had initially presented to their general practitioners with somatic complaints and had been misdiagnosed with physical problems. The most common somatic complaints reported by individuals in this sample included cardiac symptoms, gastrointestinal symptoms, and neurological symptoms. In a 1986 study of panic in primary care settings, Katon et al. found that panic disorder patients had an average of 14.1 somatic symptoms, as compared with 7.3 symptoms in a control group. Katon et al. (1987) pointed out that the somatic focus of many individuals with panic disorder often leads to misdiagnosis. Other symptomatic presentations associated with anxiety include dizziness, joint pain, and breathlessness (e.g., Shear & Schulberg, 1995).

Of course, correctly identifying anxiety and mood disorders or anxiety and depressive symptoms not meeting definitional criteria for disorders in the context of the enormous complexity of the presentation of the variety of physical disorders is a very difficult task indeed. Broadhead (1994) noted that the presentation of psychological symptoms may be somewhat different in primary care settings compared with more traditional mental health settings and that cultural variations in the expression of anxiety symptoms often confuse the picture further for the primary care health practitioner. Indeed, expressions of anxiety are often tightly integrated with specific cultural idioms that may vary greatly from one culture to another, requiring some knowledge of these cultural expressions (Barlow, 1988).

ARE PATIENTS WITH ANXIETY DISORDERS APPROPRIATELY TREATED?

Recent studies have suggested that patients with anxiety disorders are seldom treated and, when they are treated, often receive ineffective

TABLE 2
Utilization of Effective Psychological Treatments in Cases of
Panic and Phobic Disorders

Study	N	Total % receiving effective psychological treatment
Breier (1986)	60	16%
Goisman et al. (1993)	231	38% (93% of these receiving medication)
Taylor et al. (1989)	794	15% (50% of these receiving counseling and hospitalization)

Note: Data are from Barlow (1994).

treatments. As noted above, findings from the epidemiologic catchment area study (Regier et al., 1993) suggested that only approximately 1 in 3 patients with a diagnosed anxiety disorder was receiving any treatment at all, let alone an effective treatment. More recent studies suggest that little has changed. Three studies, summarized in Table 2, surveyed patients presenting to emergency rooms or other primary care facilities with panic and phobic disorders, regarding their experiences with psychosocial treatments. Although it has been recognized since the time of Freud that some sort of exposure-based treatment is essential for phobic disorders, only between 15% and 38% of the patients had ever experienced an exposure-based treatment. A somewhat greater percentage had received counseling or relaxation treatments, and an even larger percentage had received some sort of medication. Although effective medications exist for some anxiety disorders (Liebowitz & Barlow, 1995), a number of studies suggest that medication is often prescribed inappropriately or at an incorrect dosage (Shear & Schulberg, 1995).

The status of treatment of psychological disorders in primary care settings was recently dramatically demonstrated by Schulberg et al. (in press), who identified 276 primary care patients meeting criteria for a current major depressive episode. These patients were then randomized to either usual care on the part of the primary care physician or one of two treatments delivered by a mental health professional: pharmacotherapy (nortriptyline) or interpersonal psychotherapy. Because all therapists, including the primary care physician, were informed that the patient was suffering from a major depressive episode, the fact of recognizing the disorder did not play a role in subsequent treatment strategies. After 8 months of treatment, the results indicated that approximately 70% of the patients receiving one of the treatments from a mental health professional were essentially asymptomatic on the Hamilton Rating Scale for Depression (Hamilton, 1960). In comparison, only 20% of the patients receiving usual care from the primary care physician were asymptomatic, a highly significant difference. Further inquiry revealed that most primary care physicians did not intervene actively or in a structured way to treat the depressive episode, even with an effective pharmacological agent, despite being aware of the diagnosis. This study and other similar findings (e.g., Sturm & Wells, 1995) would suggest that patients with psychological disorders, particularly emotional disorders such as anxiety and mood disorders, are not being well treated at the present time in primary care settings.

MODELS OF PSYCHOLOGICAL TREATMENT IN PRIMARY CARE SETTINGS

Highly effective psychological treatments have been developed for most psychological disorders. In most cases, clinical trials have demonstrated that these treatments are not only more effective than no-treatment or waiting list controls but also more effective than credible alternative psychological treatments or drug placebos (Barlow, 1994). A recent review indicates that we now have effective psychological treatments meeting the above criteria for all of the anxiety disorders (Barlow & Lehman, in press). In view of the enormous numbers of patients presenting with psychological disorders in primary care settings, one of the major problems facing psychologists and other mental health practitioners today is the dissemination of effective psychological treatments to those who need them.

In the United States, health care policy and the delivery of health care are undergoing revolutionary changes (e.g., Cummings, 1995). Although few agree at the present time on the end result of these changes, it is clear to all that mental health practitioners will have to adapt to remain important players in the delivery of mental health care (Barlow, 1994; Barlow & Barlow, 1995). There is also wide agreement that primary care settings will become an increasingly important arena for the delivery of behavioral health care and that psychologists and other mental health professionals need to come to grips with changes and practice patterns that would allow effective participation in primary care settings (DiBartolo, Hofmann, & Barlow, 1995; Liebowitz & Barlow, 1995).

Evidence has already been reviewed on the clinical and cost-effectiveness of mental health practitioners such as psychologists working in primary care settings (Schulberg et al., in press; Sturm & Wells, 1995). Various models are also under development for the delivery of effective psychological treatments in these settings. Because there is wide agreement that the number of people presenting with anxiety disorders in these settings far exceeds the capabilities of psychologists and other mental health professionals using traditional one-on-one models of treatment delivery, alternative, more efficient models are being developed. Within the anxiety disorders, one recent report by Swinson, Solios,

Cox, and Kuch (1992) examined the effects of treatment for patients presenting to emergency room settings with panic attacks. In this study, 33 patients presenting to the emergency room with panic attacks were identified, and they agreed to random assignment to two treatment conditions as well as follow-up. Seventeen patients ultimately received exposure instructions, in which patients were told that the most effective way to reduce fear and phobic behavior was to confront the situation in which the attack had occurred. These instructions were delivered in the course of one session. The other group of 16 patients were simply provided with reassurance that what they had suffered was a panic attack and that no serious physical or psychological consequences were anticipated. This also occurred in one session. Patients were then followed up at 3 months (midpoint) and 6 months (end point). Those people who had received exposure instructions had significantly less avoidance, as well as fewer panic attacks in the previous week, than the group receiving reassurance only. Clearly, this is a very cost-effective intervention, which takes advantage of the fact that most of these patients were in the very early stages of what might have become a more severe case of panic disorder with agoraphobia if left unchecked. Thus, it seems that structured psychological interventions, even minimal interventions, may be effective if delivered early enough to less severe patients in primary care settings.

As noted above, effective psychological treatments now exist for all anxiety disorders. Most of these treatments are available in manual or workbook form, so that they can be handed directly to the patient working under the supervision of a psychologist (e.g., Barlow & Craske, 1994). Thus, these treatments can be prescribed much like a medication, in the context of good general psychological care and attention to idiosyncratic problems that arise during the course of this treatment (Craske & Barlow, 1989). Evidence is accumulating that supports the viability of this type of approach to specific psychological disorders, even with minimal therapist contact (e.g., Cote, Gauthier, Laberge, Cormier, & Plamondon, 1994). Other studies have indicated that structured psychological interventions can be delivered in briefer format than has been customary, with beneficial results for a number of patients (e.g., Craske, Maidenberg, & Bystritsky, 1995). However, it is very likely that individuals presenting with severe levels of interference and symptomatology may require more substantial degrees of therapist involvement than afforded by brief treatments. In one study conducted in the Center for Stress and Anxiety Disorder, University at Albany, people suffering from panic disorder with agoraphobia did not benefit from self-administered manualized treatment but did benefit once a therapist was introduced into the process (Holden, O'Brien, Barlow, Stetson, & Fantino, 1983).

In another notable effort in a primary care setting, White, Brooks, and Keenan (1995) randomized 62 patients meeting criteria for an anxiety disorder to one of three conditions. The first condition was no intervention, in which patients were placed on a waiting list for a 3-month period. The second condition was advice only, in which patients met with a therapist once and were offered advice on ways of coping with anxiety. In the third condition, patients were given a self-help information package, containing a brief manual explaining the nature of stress and anxiety and ways of developing appropriate coping mechanisms. Patients were then placed on a 3-month waiting list for brief individual treatment. During this 3-month period, they were assessed monthly by mail. Results from the General Severity Index of the Symptom Distress Checklist (Derogatis & Melisaratos, 1983) are presented in Figure 2.

As one can see, patients receiving the manual (stress pack) had improved significantly more in 3 months than patients receiving advice only or patients on the waiting list. Furthermore, on entering individual treatment, patients receiving the manual required fewer appointments (approximately four) than patients receiving alternative interventions, who required approximately six sessions. Eight patients who had received the manual felt that they did not require additional therapy, whereas almost all patients in the other two conditions entered treatment. Finally, it seems that receiving the manual provided a "boost" to individual treatment, because patients at the end of individual therapy who had received the manual had done significantly better than the other groups.

White et al. (1995) carried out this evaluation in Scotland in the context of the National Health Service, where the number of patients suffering from these problems is substantial and the waiting list for treatment by psychologists is very long indeed. Thus, any psychological program that improves the efficiency of the therapist, as well as the clinical outcome, a very positive development. Furthermore, these results were maintained at a 12-month follow-up.

SUMMARY AND IMPLICATIONS

All indications point to an important and increasing role for psychologists in primary care settings. First, the number of patients suffering from psychological disorders in primary care settings or in the behavioral health care system as a whole, for that matter, is enormous and far outstrips current capacities to provide treatment. Second, the majority of patients suffering from anxiety and other psychological disorders in primary care settings are not recognized, and even fewer are treated effectively. Evidence exists that behavioral health care providers, particularly psychologists, are more clinically effective and more cost-effective

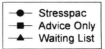

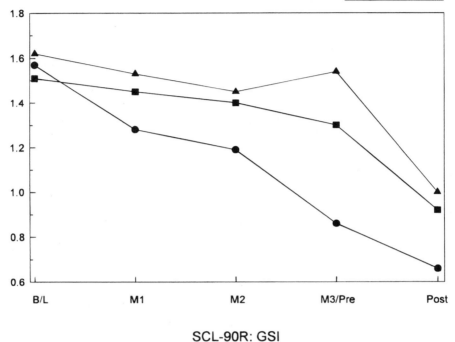

SCL-90R: GSI

Figure 2. Results of study by White (1995), as measured by General Severity Index (GSI) of the revised Symptom Checklist–90 (SCL-90-R). B/L = baseline; M1 = first month of manual; M2 = second month of manual; M3 = third month of manual; Pre = pre individual treatment; Post = post individual treatment.

From "Stresspac: A Controlled Trial of a Self-Help Package for the Anxiety Disorders," by J. White, 1995, *Behavioural and Cognitive Psychotherapy, 23,* 89–107. Copyright 1995 by the British Association for Behavioural and Cognitive Psychotherapies. Adapted with permission.

in the provision of behavioral health care in these settings than overburdened primary care physicians. Because the large number of these patients will preclude individual assessment and intervention, more efficient models for the delivery of behavioral health care must be developed, and some preliminary evidence suggests what these models may look like. One possible model is presented in Figure 3. In this model, psychologists and other behavioral health care professionals will supervise appropriate but cost-effective screening and assessment of all patients coming into primary care settings. These professionals will then triage patients with less severe psychological disorders or symptoms of anxiety into cost-effective self-help programs or programs administered largely by parapro-

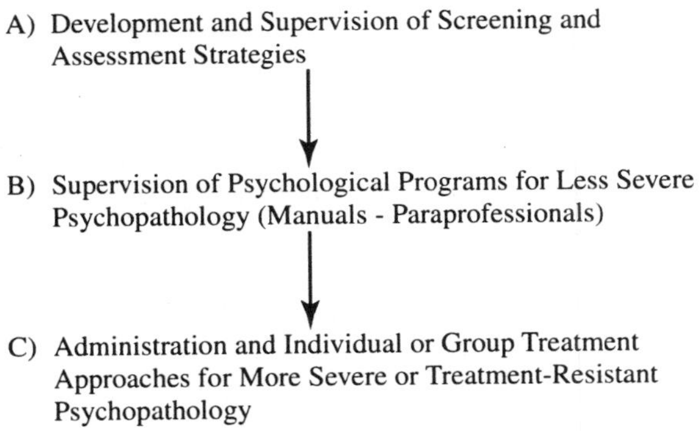

A) Development and Supervision of Screening and
   Assessment Strategies

B) Supervision of Psychological Programs for Less Severe
   Psychopathology (Manuals - Paraprofessionals)

C) Administration and Individual or Group Treatment
   Approaches for More Severe or Treatment-Resistant
   Psychopathology

Figure 3. The role of psychologists in primary care settings.

fessionals working under the supervision of psychologists. Patients will continue to be assessed by means of cost-effective screening instruments, and those individuals not benefiting from the less costly interventions because of severity, or some other treatment-resistant feature, will be candidates for individual therapeutic approaches with doctoral-level psychologists having expertise in these areas.

It is very likely, as these models develop, that we will discover fairly sensitive predictors of response to the various stepped levels of care that will allow early identification of patients and more immediate assignment to appropriate treatment methods. Much of the necessary data to develop this model more fully have yet to be collected, and when they are collected, it is likely that psychologists will be in the best position to develop this information.

REFERENCES

American Psychiatric Association. (1994). *Diagnostic and statistical manual of mental disorders* (4th ed.). Washington, DC: Author.

Barlow, D. H. (1988). *Anxiety and its disorders: The nature and treatment of anxiety and panic.* New York: Guilford Press.

Barlow, D. H. (1994). Psychological interventions in the era of managed competition. *Clinical Psychology: Science and Practice, 1,* 109–122.

Barlow, D. H., & Barlow, D. G. (1995 May/June). Practice guidelines and empirically validated psychosocial treatments: Ships passing in the night? *Behavioral Healthcare Tomorrow,* pp. 25–76.

Barlow, D. H., & Craske, M. G. (1994). *Mastery of your anxiety and panic: II.* Albany, NY: Graywind Publications.

Barlow, D. H., & Lehman, C. (in press). Advances in the psychosocial treatment of anxiety disorders: Implications for national health care. *Archives of General Psychiatry.*

Barrett, J. E., Barrett, J. A., Oxman, T. E., & Gerber, P. D. (1988). The prevalence of psychiatric disorders in a primary care practice. *Archives of General Psychiatry, 45,* 1100–1106.

Breier, A., Charney, D. S., & Heninger, G. R. (1986). Agoraphobia with panic attacks: Development, diagnostic stability, and course of illness. *Archives of General Psychiatry, 43,* 1029–1036.

Broadhead, W. F. (1994). Presentation of psychiatric symptomatology in primary care. In J. Mirandra, A. A. Hohmann, C. C. Attkisson, & D. B. Larson (Eds.), *Mental disorders in primary care* (pp. 139–162). San Francisco: Jossey-Bass.

Brown, T. A., & Barlow, D. H. (1995). Long-term outcome in cognitive–behavioral treatment of panic disorder: Clinical predictors and alternative strategies for assessment. *Journal of Consulting and Clinical Psychology, 63,* 754–765.

Cote, G., Gauthier, J. G., Laberge, B., Cormier, H. J., & Plamondon, J. (1994). Reduced therapist contact in the cognitive–behavioral treatment of panic disorder. *Behavior Therapy, 25,* 123–145.

Craske, M. G., & Barlow, D. H. (1989). *Mastery of your anxiety and panic.* Albany, NY: Graywind Publications.

Craske, M. G., Maidenberg, E., & Bystritsky, A. (1995). Brief cognitive–behavioral vs. non-directive therapy for panic disorder. *Journal of Behavior Therapy and Experimental Psychiatry, 26,* 113–120.

Cummings, N. A. (1995). Impact of managed care on employment and training: A primer for survival. *Professional Psychology: Research and Practice, 26,* 10–15.

Derogatis, L. R., & Melisaratos, N. (1983). The Brief Symptom Inventory: An intoductory report. *Psychological Medicine, 13,* 595–605.

DiBartolo, P. M., Hofmann, S. G., & Barlow, D. H. (1995). Psychosocial approaches to panic disorder and agoraphobia: Assessment and treatment issues for the primary care physician. *Mind/Body and Medicine, 1,* 1–12.

Fifer, S. K., Mathias, S. D., Patrick, D. L., Majonson, P. D., Lubeck, D. P., & Buesching, D. P. (1994). Untreated anxiety among adult primary care patients in a health maintenance organization. *Archives of General Psychiatry, 51,* 740–750.

Ford, D. (1987). *The relationship of psychiatric illness to medically unexplained chest pain.* Paper presented at the research conference, Mental Disorders in General Health Care Settings, Seattle, WA.

Ford, D. E. (1994). Recognition and underrecognition of mental disorders in adult primary care. In J. Miranda, A. A. Hohmann, C. C. Attkisson, & D. B. Larson (Eds.), *Mental disorders in primary care* (pp. 186–205). San Francisco: Jossey-Bass.

Goisman, R. M., Rogers, M. P., Steketee, G. S., Warshaw, M. G., Cuneo, P., & Keller, M. B. (1993). Utilization of behavioral methods in a multi-center anxiety disorders study. *Journal of Clinical Psychiatry, 54,* 213–218.

Hamilton, M. (1960). A rating scale for depression. *Journal of Neurology, Neurosurgery, and Psychiatry, 23,* 56–62.

Holden, A. E., O'Brien, G. T., Barlow, D. H., Stetson, D., & Fantino, A. (1983). Self-help manual for agoraphobia: A preliminary report of effectiveness. *Behavior Research and Therapy, 14,* 545–556.

Katerndahl, D. A., & Realini, J. P. (1995). Where do panic attacks sufferers seek care? *Journal of Family Practice, 40,* 237–243.

Katon, W. (1984). Panic disorder and somatization: Review of 55 cases. *American Journal of Medicine, 77,* 101–106.

Katon, W., Vitaliano, P. P., Russo, J., Cormier, L., Anderson, K., & Jones, M. (1986). Panic disorder: Epidemiology in primary care. *The Journal of Family Practice, 23,* 233–239.

Katon, W., Vitaliano, P. P., Russo, J., Jones, M., & Anderson, K. (1987). Panic disorder: Spectrum of severity and somatization. *The Journal of Nervous and Mental Disease, 175,* 12–19.

Kessler, R. C., McGonagle, K. A., Shanyang, Z., Nelson, C. B., Hughes, M., Eshleman, S., Wittchen, H.-U., & Kendler, K. (1994). Lifetime and 12-month prevalence of *DSM–III–R* psychiatric disorders in the United States: Results from the National Comorbidity Survey. *Archives of General Psychiatry, 51,* 8–19.

Liebowitz, M., & Barlow, D. H. (1995). Panic disorder: The latest on diagnosis and treatment. *Journal of Practical Psychiatry and Behavioral Health, 1,* 10–19.

Ormel, J., VandenBrink, W., Koeter, M. W. J., Giel, R., Vander Meer, K., VandeWillige, G., & Wilmink, I. W. (1990). Recognition, management and outcome of psychological disorders in primary care: A naturalistic follow-up study. *Psychological Medicine, 20,* 909–923.

Regier, D. A., Myers, J. K., Kramer, M., Robins, L. N., Blazer, D. G., Hough, R. L., Eaton, W. W., & Locke, B. Z. (1984). The NIMH Epidemiologic Catchment Area: Historical context, major objectives, and study population characteristics. *Archives of General Psychiatry, 41,* 934–941.

Regier, D. A., Narrow, W. E., Rae, D. S., Manderscheid, R. W., Locke, B. Z., & Goodwin, F. K. (1993). The deFacto US mental and addictive disorders service system: Epidemiologic catchment area prospective 1-year prevalence rates of disorders and services. *Archives of General Psychiatry, 50,* 85–94.

Schulberg, H. C., Block, M., Madonia, M., Scott, C., Rodriguez, E., Imbero, S., Perel, J., Laze, J., Houck, P., & Coulehan, J. (in press). Treating major depression in primary care practice: Eight-month clinical outcomes. *Archives of General Psychiatry.*

Shear, M. K., & Schulberg, H. C. (1995). Anxiety disorders in primary care. *Bulletin of the Menninger Clinic, 59,* A73–A85.

Shear, M. K., Schulberg, H. C. & Madonia, M. (1994, September). *Panic and generalized anxiety disorder in primary care.* Paper presented at a meeting of the Association for Primary Care, Washington, DC.

Spitzer, R. L., Endicott, J., & Robins, E. (1978). *Research diagnostic criteria: Rationale and reliability. Archives of General Psychiatry, 35,* 773–782.

Sturm, R., & Wells, K. B. (1995). How can care for depression become more cost-effective? *Journal of American Medical Association, 273,* 51–58.

Swinson, R. P., Solios, C., Cox, B. J., & Kuch, K. (1992). Brief treatment of emergency room patients with panic attacks. *American Journal of Psychiatry, 149,* 944–946.

Taylor, C. B., King, R., Margraf, J., Ehlers, A., et al. (1989). Use of medication and in vivo exposure in volunteers for panic disorder research. *American Journal of Psychiatry, 146,* 1423–1426.

Van Hemert, A. M., Hengeveld, M. W., Boek, J. H., Rooijmans, H. G. M., & Vandenbroucke, J. P. (1993). Psychiatric disorders in relation to medical illness among patients of a general medical out-patient clinic. *Psychological Medicine, 23,* 167–173.

Wells, K. B., Stewart, A., Hays, R. D., Burnam, M. A., Rogers, W., Daniels, M., Berry, S., Greenfield, S., & Ware, J. (1989). The functioning and well-being of depressed patients: Results from the Medical Outcomes Study. *Journal of American Medical Association, 262,* 914–919.

White, J. (1995). Stresspac: A controlled trial of a self-help package for the anxiety disorders. *Behavioural and Cognitive Psychotherapy, 23,* 89–107.

Yingling, K. W., Wulsin, L. R., Arnold, L. M., & Rouan, G. W. (1993). Estimated prevalences of panic disorder and depression among consecutive patients seen in an emergency department with acute chest pain. *Journal of General Internal Medicine, 8,* 231–235.

Zinbarg, R. E., Barlow, D. H., Liebowitz, M., Street, L., Broadhead, E., Katon, W., Roy-Byrne, P., Lepine, J.-P., Teherani, M., Richards, J., Brantley, P. J., & Kraemer, H. (1994). The *DSM–IV* field trial for mixed anxiety–depression. *American Journal of Psychiatry, 151,* 1153–1162.

11

CATCHING DEPRESSION IN PRIMARY CARE PHYSICIANS' OFFICES

LYNN P. REHM

The scenario for this topic is fairly clear. Depression is presented in primary care medical settings at a high frequency with substantial disability to the patient. Detection is poor, and many patients are not treated or are treated inappropriately. If detection and treatment in primary care settings can be improved, patient well-being can be improved and medical costs can be reduced. Psychology and psychologists should be inserted into the system, to develop efficient means of detection and screening, to provide treatment for depression, and to offer prevention services to head off depression at its earliest signs. Psychology has developed efficient assessment, effective treatment, and promising prevention programs. Its value to the primary care system should be obvious, and its participation should be welcome. It sounds like a simple and straightforward proposal, but let me examine the individual components of the argument and point out some of the problems and complications.

PREVALENCE OF DEPRESSION

Depression is presented in primary care medical settings in substantial proportions. For example, in a report of the Agency for Health Care

149

Policy and Research (AHCPR; Depression Guideline Panel, 1993), John Rush and his colleagues reviewed 11 studies in primary care settings in which major depression was diagnosed by means of structured diagnostic interviews, usually after paper-and-pencil screening. Estimates of the point prevalence of major depression ranged from 4.8% to 8.6%, with a median of around 6.5%. Other mood disorders such as dysthymia, minor depression, or intermittent depression brought totals up to around 10%. A new study (Coyne, Fechner-Bates, & Schwenk, 1994) found an estimated prevalence of 13.5% for major depression and 22.6% for all depressive disorders. Patients who are frequent users of primary health care have a particularly high rate of psychiatric comorbidity (54% in one study). Mood disorders, identified in 24% of cases, and anxiety disorders, identified in another 24% of cases, are the most prevalent among these diagnoses (Karlsson, Lehtinen, & Joukamaa, 1995).

Substantial disability is associated with untreated depression. Figures from the medical outcomes studies (Depression Guideline Panel, 1993; Sturm & Wells, 1995) indicate that patients with depression have substantial problems in life functioning. For example, in one study, 23% of depressed patients reported that their health kept them in bed all or most of the day at least once in the past 2 weeks, as compared with 5% of the general population. Patients with major depression report 11 days of disability per 90 days, as compared with 2.2 days for the general population. Their decrements in functioning equal or exceed those of patients with chronic medical illnesses (Hays, Wells, Sherbourne, Rogers, & Spritzer, 1995). Depressed patients also report poorer intimate relations, less satisfying social interactions and poorer general health. Health care use is increased for these patients.

Depressed patients represent a disproportionate cost to the health system. In a major study of computerized records in a large-staff-model health maintenance organization (Simon, VonKorff, & Barlow, 1995), patients were identified as depressed either by a depression diagnosis recorded at an index visit or by a pharmacy record of a prescription for an antidepressant medication. A sample of 6,257 such patients was compared with an individually matched sample of 6,257 controls. For the 12 months after the index visit, depressed patients cost the health maintenance organization an average of $4,246, in comparison with $2,371 for the control sample. Costs for depressed patients were elevated in every category (primary care, specialty care, medical inpatient, pharmacy, and laboratory). Mean pharmacy costs were nearly three times greater for the depressed sample ($632 vs. $231), and only $194 of this was attributable to antidepressants. The depressed sample was found to have a higher index of chronic medical illness, but even when this was statistically controlled, their medical costs were higher. Depressed patients were a greater economic burden to the system at every level of chronic medical illness severity. In summary, the problem is of large proportion, the disability is considerable, and the economic impact on the medical system is substantial.

PROBLEMS OF DETECTION IN PRIMARY CARE

Depression is often poorly detected and treated in primary care settings. A number of studies suggest that physicians underdetect and undertreat depression in primary care settings. A general estimate is that one third to one half of depressed patients are diagnosed with the disorder (Depression Guideline Panel, 1993). Coyne, Fechner-Bates, and Schwenk (1995) identified a sample of depressed patients in a primary care setting by screening with the Center for Epidemiological Studies Depression Scale (CES–D; Radloff, 1977) and structured clinical interviews. Of the sample they diagnosed, family physicians had detected 35% of cases of major depression and 28% of cases of any mood disorder.

Coyne et al. (1995) highlighted another problematic dimension to the detection issue. They pointed out that the undetected patients tended to be mildly depressed and highly functioning. Such patients may not actively seek treatment and may not accept treatment recommendations and referral. When these mildly depressed patients are treated, they may benefit from relatively minimal interventions. Level of depression may be an important variable for differential treatment recommendations. Severe depression may require hospitalization, and medication may be required with severe outpatients, who may not be amenable to the effort involved in psychotherapy. Psychotherapy appears to be useful across most ranges of depression, but mild depression may well benefit from minimal interventions such as bibliotherapy.

High base rates and low detection rates lead to an assumption that appropriate assessment and treatment will improve effective treatment outcomes and produce a cost offset in medical utilization. Improved detection and treatment in primary care is the purpose of the AHCPR guidelines (Depression Guideline Panel, 1993), which were written to guide physicians in making appropriate decisions in treating depression. Within the guidelines, the panel recommended an interview when history or other vulnerability factors indicated risk. Self-report depression scales were also recommended for screening, with a note that they may be lacking in specificity and that some authorities suggest increased cutoff scores in primary care to decrease false positives. Fechner-Bates, Coyne, and Schwenk (1994) examined the power of the CES–D to detect depression in primary care. Most distressed patients did not meet criteria for mood diagnoses, and the scale was as predictive of anxiety disorders as it is of depression. Fechner-Bates et al. concluded that the CES–D measured general distress rather than depression per se. Any screening program in a primary care setting must look not only at depression but at other common psychological problems that may accompany or complicate medical visits. Differentiating among problems and making accurate diagnoses require a second step after a paper-and-pencil measure such as the CES–D. Brief physician interviews, as recommended by the AHCPR guidelines, may not be sufficient. Differential diagnosis is important not only between depression and anxiety disorders, but also among these disorders. Differentiations between unipolar and bipolar depression have important treatment implications, as does differentiation between panic disorder and obsessive–compulsive disorder. Psychological treatment modalities also vary considerably in their appropriateness for depression or anxiety diagnoses.

In part, the issue is one of the reliability of detection and of the criterion for depression. Diagnosis by the fourth edition of the *Diagnostic and Statistical Manual of Mental Disorders* (American Psychiatric Association, 1994) is but one criterion, and it, too, has a reliability of less than one. Detection by one instrument may not be perfectly correlated with detection by another instrument or method. Both false negatives and false positives will occur if instruments are compared. To detect clinically meaningful depression in efficient ways in primary care settings, alternative criteria and how specific criteria might be related to intervention strategies must be recognized. Self-report scales such as the CES–D may not be specific to *DSM–IV* Major Depression, but distress should be examined seriously, and appropriate interventions should be evaluated. It might be more effective to ask patients about the nature of the problems that are producing distress, how they are coping, and whether they are coping effectively. Psychological interventions might be matched more exactly to the patient by the nature of the coping problems than by *DSM–IV* diagnosis. The review, later in this chapter, of treatment strategies for depression illustrates the different treatment foci of each approach.

Adding to the problems of lack of detection are the problems of inaccurate detection or misdiagnosis. Patients who are detected may not receive proper treatment. Sturm and Wells (1995), in examining the data from the large RAND study of medical outcomes (Tarlov et al., 1989), found that in general medical settings, the probability of severe depression being detected was 49%, but the probability that it was treated with minor tranquilizers, rather that antidepressants or counseling, was 36%. Treatment with minor tranquilizers was associated with a poorer, more deteriorating outcome in terms of ability to function 1 year later than was no treatment at all. A fairly extensive and sophisticated evaluation, preferably by a mental health expert, may be required to make these distinctions accurately.

Referral to a mental health practitioner raises other issues. The AHCPR guidelines encourage the primary care practitioner to be the first line of treatment. Referral for psychotherapy is recommended as a secondary alternative. Patients often do not follow through on referrals, and it has been suggested that primary care physicians thus may become discouraged in making referrals of depressed patients to mental health professionals (Munoz & Ying, 1993).

In their 1995 study, Sturm and Wells addressed the question of whether treatment outcomes in current settings with current resources could be improved. Sturm and Wells looked at actual outcome in primary care and in mental health settings for patients in multiple types of practices, in three cities. They found that three treatment factors were associated with improved functioning of depressed patients. *Functioning* was defined as serious limitations in daily life (i.e., not able to work at a paying job; not able to do housework; not able to do strenuous exercise, such as lawn mowing; or not able to do moderate exercise, such as climbing stairs). The three factors that improved outcomes were increased use of counseling, increased use of appropriate antidepressants, and avoidance of regular minor tranquilizer use. Counseling and antidepressants were found to add to total costs, but they improve the value of care because each dollar spent provided more benefit in terms of health and functioning improvements. Sturm and Wells (1995) also concluded that "in contrast with the effects of more appropriate care for depression, the trend away from mental heath specialty care and toward general medical provider care under current treatment patterns reduces cost, worsens outcomes, and does not increase the value of health care spending in terms of health improvement per dollar" (p. 51). That is, the direction taken by the AHCPR guidelines may save money, but at the expense of better outcomes.

Where Sturm and Wells (1995) found the combination of antidepressants and counseling to be the most effective treatment strategy, an article by Wexler and Cicchetti (1992) addresses the larger issue of the relative efficacy of pharmacotherapy, psychotherapy, and their combination for the treatment of depression. They question the often-made recommendation that the combination of treatments is best. Their review of the literature on treatment success and failure rates and on dropout rates indicates that the combined treatment offers no advantage over psychotherapy alone and only minimal advantage over medication alone. The difference in the two conclusions may have to do with the fact that Sturm and Wells had a very minimal definition of counseling— essentially, any record of some time spent discussing the patient's problems—whereas, Wexler and Cicchetti were reviewing studies of carefully administered forms of psychotherapy compared with trials of medication.

When a full course of an effective psychotherapy is administered, medications appear to add little to outcomes.

If effective intervention is to be instituted in primary care settings, it appears that a mental health component would best be integrated into the health system. Initial screening might lead to better diagnosis if the psychologist or other mental health worker was involved at the point of diagnosis. Treatment recommendations might be more acceptable to the patient if they were made by the appropriate expert, and patients might be more likely to follow up on referral if it did not require contacting another professional in another setting. Patients would be more likely to comply with treatment if a range of treatments were available to match severity and problem type.

MODELS OF TREATMENT

Much needs to be done if we are to actualize the scenario for improved detection and treatment of depression in primary care settings. In an article critiquing the AHCPR guidelines, Munoz, Hollon, McGrath, Rehm, and VandenBos (1994) pointed out some serious limitations to the guidelines. To begin with, they underestimate the problems in detection and diagnosis, some of which I mention above. The AHCPR guidelines acknowledge, but underestimate, the problems of generalization of studies in research mental health settings to primary care settings and systems. Treatments that are effective in trials in mental health settings may not be as effective in primary care settings where acceptability of psychiatric diagnosis may be less and where patients may not be persuaded of the necessity or utility of treatment. Research needs to be done in primary care settings or with primary care patients in collaborating settings. We need to find out what treatments are effective in these settings. Psychotherapy, for example, may need to be offered in formats acceptable and affordable to patients in primary care. We may need to adapt treatments to match patients' beliefs about their problems and about what they think they need to do to make changes. We need to take into account issues of diversity and the efficacy and acceptability of treatment to different groups.

It is clear that severity level has to be taken into account. Differential diagnosis is very important at moderate-to-severe levels of depression. At milder levels, the differentiation of distress into depression or anxiety may be difficult, and treatment options may need to be different than those for more severe levels of disorder. Intervention at milder levels may also be effective as a prevention strategy to ward off more severe depression. Munoz and Ying (1993) provided an example of a treatment program for patients with mild depressive symptoms in a preventative treatment program. They argued that treating mild symptoms of depression may prevent more serious disorder and disability later on. Their San Francisco Depression Prevention Project screened 700 primary care patients at two hospitals and identified 150 who showed symptoms of depression but did not meet diagnostic criteria for a clinical disorder. The research sample of adults was diverse with regard to ethnicity, age, and socioeconomic status. Participants were randomly assigned to either a prevention class, an informational-videotape minimal-intervention comparison group, and a no-treatment control. Classes were available in Spanish- and English-language versions. The classes consisted of eight weekly sessions aimed at an eclectic set of topics drawn from the cognitive–behavioral treatment literature. Topics included the effect of thoughts and behavior on feeling, ways to change thinking and increase positive thoughts, ways to increase pleasurable activities, and ways to improve interpersonal relationships. Outcome was assessed on a number of variables, including symptoms and diagnosis of depression, sense of well-being, life stress, cognitive and behavioral mediators of depression, and medical utilization. The group sessions were found to have a greater effect on symptoms, well-being, mediators, and life stress. Prevention of depression diagnosis was not demonstrated, largely because in the 1-year follow-up, few patients in any of the conditions developed the full syndromal disorder. Similarly, the study was not able to detect differences in subsequent medical utilization, largely due to small numbers in gross utilization indices. This study is exemplary in many ways. It is one of the few intervention studies in a primary care setting. It identified a diverse sample and provided a short-term, state-of-the-art intervention. Results were measured on a variety of relevant variables. On the other hand, the study also illustrates that it is difficult to demonstrate prevention and reduction of medical utilization in an intervention study. Such effects require very large numbers, like those in the naturalistic, retrospective studies of treatment outcomes cited above.

A number of treatment strategies have been shown to be useful in treating depression in efficacy studies. These are primarily cognitive–behavioral therapies that have been tested in controlled clinical trials. These treatments are based on therapist manuals that increase the replicability and portability of the therapies, although, of course, they do not ensure therapist skill or competence with the treatment. I will provide a brief overview of the major treatment models for those readers unfamiliar with this area.

Behavioral Model

The behavioral model of depression is primarily identified with the work of Lewinsohn. Lewinsohn (1974) posited that depression was the result of a loss or lack of response-contingent positive reinforcement. Loss of a loved one or loss of a job is seen as removing a source of reinforcement that maintains multiple chains of behavior. It is the resulting reduction in behavior that constitutes depression. Early approaches to depression treatment by Lewinsohn's group focused on developing therapy modules aimed at ameliorating specific forms of reinforcement loss. Modules focused on increasing previously enjoyable activities, on increasing skills to elicit positive reinforcement from the environment, and on decreasing social anxiety that might interfere with experiencing social reinforcement. Later versions of the therapy program have combined the various modules into a psychoeducational therapy program. The program takes participants through a series of lessons and homework assignments, related to components of depression, organized around the general theme of increasing contingent positive reinforcement. Munoz and Ying's (1993) intervention relied heavily on the basics of the Lewinsohn behavioral model.

The current program is well suited to use in primary care health care settings. It has evolved for use in an economical group format. A therapist manual is available for group leaders (Lewinsohn, Antonuccio, Breckenridge, & Teri, 1987). A participant's textbook has been developed for the course (Brown & Lewinsohn, 1984a), and a self-help version of the program has been published as well (Lewinsohn, Munoz, Youngren, & Zeiss, 1978). This is one of the few programs for which an evaluation has been done of the effectiveness of the program in bibliotherapy format (Brown & Lewinsohn, 1984b) and in group versus individual formats (Brown & Lewinsohn, 1984b). A version of the program has also been developed for use with adolescents (Clarke, Lewinsohn, & Hops, 1991) and their parents (Lewinsohn, Rohde, Hops, & Clarke, 1991). A number of assessment instruments have been developed by Lewinsohn's group to evaluate sources of reinforcement and their availability and frequency in the patient's environment. These instruments could be helpful in determining whether this strategy would be a fit with a particular patient's deficits as well as being appropriate measures of treatment progress. In general, depressions that seem to be typified by a withdrawal from previously pleasurable activities might best be targeted by this approach.

Social Skills Model

A number of approaches, including Lewinsohn's behavioral program, have viewed depression as a result of certain skill deficits or of insufficient skill level to deal with specific types of interpersonal stressors (cf. Gotlib & Colby, 1987). A number of different strategies arise from this basic approach. Hersen, Bellack, Himmelhoch, and Thase (1984) evaluated a traditional assertiveness-oriented approach with a depressed population. Nezu, Nezu, and Perri (1989) argued for a problem-solving approach to depression that sees depression as a series of deficits in interpersonal problem-solving deficits. They demonstrated in one study (Nezu, 1986) that a treatment strategy based on this approach was superior to placebo therapy and waiting list controls. This approach is best suited to depressed patients who perceive their interpersonal circumstances as uncontrollable when faced with a situation that could be defined as a problem to be solved.

Beach and O'Leary (1986) and Jacobson (1984) have made a case for depression as an interpersonal problem in the context of marriage and have illustrated marital therapy interventions as appropriate treatments for depression. Dysfunctional marriages may be detected in primary care as a focus for treatment of depression.

From a more psychodynamic perspective, Klerman, Weissman, Rounceville, and Chevron (1984) provide a manual for interpersonal therapy. Interpersonal therapy is based on the idea that current interpersonal problems, whether they be relational or due to a loss of relationship, should be the priority targets for therapy for depression. Interpersonal therapy was one of the psychotherapies evaluated in the National Institute of Mental Health Collaborative Treatment of Depression study (Elkin et al., 1989), where it was found to be equivalent to a tricyclic antidepressant medication and to cognitive therapy.

Cognitive Therapy Model

At present, the best researched model of therapy for depression is Beck's cognitive therapy. Cognitive therapy is based on the assumption that depression is based in a systematic, negative cognitive distortion of the person's experience. Depressive cognitive schema filter experience to create depressive inferences and interpretations of everyday experiences. These distortions are relatively automatic and are based on unspoken and unexamined assumptions that underlie views of self, world, and future. Cognitive therapy was also evaluated in the National Institute of Mental Health national collaborative study (Elkin et al., 1989). Cognitive therapy appears to be widely suited to depression and other problems. It can be seen as an approach to viewing problems as much as a particular set of therapy strategies.

Two additional cognitive conceptions of depression deserve note, although they have not led to specific forms of therapy. Seligman's learned helplessness theory has evolved through several forms (Abramson, Seligman, & Teasdale, 1978; Alloy, Abramson, Metalsky, & Hartlage, 1988; Seligman, 1975). The essential feature of the theory is the assumption that one path to depression is a negative interpretive style whereby depression-prone people attribute negative events to internal, stable, and global causes. Thus, "an aversive event happened because of me, because of something constant about me, and because of something about me that applies to everything I do." As a vulnerability theory, learned helplessness may be particularly applicable to prevention programs.

Nolen-Hoeksema (1987) focuses on sex differences between women and men and presents a case that higher rates of depression in women may be due to women's greater likelihood of having a cognitive style of ruminating about negative events, in contrast to men's tendency to distract themselves from rumination. Again, the vulnerability aspect of the theory suggests an application to prevention, especially with women.

Self-Management Model

My own work on psychotherapy for depression (Rehm, 1984) has been based primarily on a self-control or self-management model of depression (Rehm, 1977). The model began as an attempt to integrate elements of prior theories under a self-control framework but has, as a defining feature, a focus on how people organize their thinking and behavior around long-term goals. Resistance to depression is seen as an ability to sustain efforts toward long-term goals in the face of current negative events and contrary reinforcement contingencies. This is accomplished by providing oneself with overt or covert rewards contingent on progress toward goals. The behavior of the depressed person deteriorates because of a loss of organization of behavior by immediate external contingencies that do not occur regularly for long-term goals. The approach has empirical support for the theory (Rehm, 1988) and for the psychoeducational, group-format therapy that has been derived from the model (Rehm, 1984). Adaptations of the program have been developed for children (Stark, 1990). In application to primary care settings, the program is applicable to prevention and to cost-effective treatment because of the group-therapy format.

RESEARCH NEEDS AND FUTURE DIRECTIONS

Today we can feel confidant that efficacy of several treatments for depression have been empirically demonstrated (Task Force on the Promotion and Dissemination of Psychological Procedures, 1995). That is, several approaches or strategies have been demonstrated to be more effective than placebo therapy or no treatment. This does not, however, answer the question as to whether these programs are going to be effective in nonresearch settings, such as primary care. Many conditions differentiate research studies from clinical practice (Seligman, 1995). More diverse patient populations with multiple problems may not respond as well as the carefully defined and delimited samples in research studies. We badly need effectiveness research in practical settings such as primary care.

We also need to disseminate these valid treatments. Although consumer surveys tend to show public satisfaction with the unspecified forms of treatment that are in use in the practice world, utilization and training in the better validated treatment methods is sparse (Task Force on the Promotion and Dissemination of Psychological Procedures, 1995). It is one thing to say that empirically validated treatments are available for application or testing in primary care settings, but it is quite another to say that psychologists or other mental health practitioners are ready to offer these programs.

We need to study and validate our treatments in primary care and our screening and detection methodologies as well. In the long run, the inclusion and integration of psychological assessment and intervention in primary care will depend on our ability to demonstrate valid outcomes that benefit patients. To be persuasive to primary care systems, we need to show that instituting screening and intervention not only improves the health, both mental and physical, of patients but also improves their functioning and reduces unnecessary use of medical services.

With the changes that are taking place in our health care system, it is important to consider the economics of the delivery of treatments for depression in primary care settings. This consideration, however, needs to take into account not only the costs of treatments but also the costs of lack of treatment and the value of treatment. Value can be measured in terms of medical cost offset, in terms of improved health, and in terms of improved life functioning.

Psychology needs to be better integrated into primary care settings. As health care change moves us toward capitated, integrated health care systems with "one-stop shopping," psychology needs to be in place in primary care settings, to set up programs of detection and treatment of patients with depression and other debilitating psychological disorders. Psychology will be able to do so to the degree that its value can be demonstrated in improving health in dollars and cents.

REFERENCES

Abramson, L. Y., Seligman, M. E. P., & Teasdale, J. (1978). Learned helplessness in humans: Critique and reformulation. *Journal of Abnormal Psychology, 87*, 49–74.

Alloy, L. B., Abramson, L. Y., Metalsky, G. I., & Hartlage, S. (1988). The hopelessness theory of depression: Attributional aspects. *British Journal of Clinical Psychology, 27*, 5–21.

American Psychiatric Association. (1994). *Diagnostic and statistical manual of mental disorders* (4th ed.). Washington, DC: Author.

Beach, S. R. H., & O'Leary, K. D. (1986). The treatment of depression occurring in the context of marital discord. *Behavior Therapy, 17*, 43–49.

Brown, R. A., & Lewinsohn, P. M. (1984a). *Participant workbook for the coping with depression course.* Eugene, OR: Castalia.

Brown, R. A., & Lewinsohn, P. M. (1984b). A psychoeducational approach to the group treatment of depression: Comparison of group, individual, and minimal contact procedures. *Journal of Consulting and Clinical Psychology, 52*, 774–783.

Clarke, G., Lewinsohn, P. M., & Hops, H., (1991). *Adolescent coping with depression course: Leader's manual for adolescent groups.* Eugene, OR: Castalia.

Coyne, J. C., Fechner-Bates, S., & Schwenk, T. L. (1994). The prevalence, nature, and comorbidity of depressive disorders in primary care. *General Hospital Psychiatry, 16*, 267–276.

Coyne, J. C., Fechner-Bates, S., & Schwenk, T. L. (1995). Nondetection of depression by primary care physicians reconsidered. *General Hospital Psychiatry, 17*, 3–12.

Depression Guideline Panel. (1993). *Depression in primary care: Volume 1. Detection and diagnosis, clinical practice guideline, number 5.* (AHCPR Publication No. 93-0550) Rockville, MD: U.S. Department of Health and Human Services, Public Health Service, Agency for Health Care Policy and Research.

Elkin, I., Shea, T., Watkins, J., Imber, S., Sotsky, S., Collins, J. F., Glass, D. R., Pilkonis, P., Leber, W. R., Docherty, J. P., Fiester, S. J., & Parloff, M. B. (1989). National Institute of Mental Health treatment of depression collaborative research program: General effectiveness of treatments. *Archives of General Psychiatry, 46*, 971–982.

Fechner-Bates, S., Coyne, J. C., & Schwenk, T. L. (1994). The relationship of self-reported distress to depressive disorders and other psychopathology. *Journal of Consulting and Clinical Psychology, 62*, 550–559

Gotlib, I. H., & Colby, C. A. (1987). *Treatment of depression and interpersonal systems approach.* New York: Pergamon, Press.

Hays, R. D., Wells, K. B., Sherbourne, C. D., Rogers, W., & Spritzer, K. (1995). Functioning and well-being outcomes of patients with depression compared with chronic general medical illnesses. *Archives of General Psychiatry, 52*, 11–19.

Hersen, M., Bellack, A. S., Himmelhoch, J. M., & Thase, M. E. (1984). Effects of social skills training, amitriptyline, and psychotherapy on unipolar depressed women. *Behavior Therapy, 15*, 21–40.

Jacobson, N. S. (1984). Marital therapy and the cognitive–behavioral treatment of depression. *The Behavior Therapist, 7*, 143–147.

Karlsson, H., Lehtinen, V., & Joukamaa, M. (1995.) Psychiatric morbidity among frequent attender patients in primary care. *General Hospital Psychiatry, 17*, 19–25.

Klerman, G. L., Weissman, M. M., Rounceville, B. J., & Chevron, E. S. (1984). *Interpersonal psychotherapy for depression.* New York: Basic Books.

Lewinsohn, P. M. (1974). A behavioral approach to depression. In R. M. Friedman & M. M. Katz (Eds.), *The psychology of depression: Contemporary theory and research.* New York: Wiley.

Lewinsohn, P. M., Antonuccio, D. O., Breckenridge, J. L., & Teri, L. (1987). *The coping with depression course.* Eugene, OR: Castalia.

Lewinsohn, P. M., Munoz, R. F., Youngren, M. A., & Zeiss, A. M. (1978). *Control your depression.* Englewood Cliffs, NJ: Prentice Hall.

Lewinsohn, P. M., Rohde, P., Hops, H., & Clarke, G. (1991). *Adolescent coping with depression course: Leader's manual for parent groups.* Eugene, OR: Castalia.

Munoz, R. F., Hollon, S. D., McGrath, E., Rehm, L. P., & VandenBos, G. R. (1994). On the AHCPR depression in primary care guidelines: Further considerations for practitioners. *American Psychologist, 49*, 42–61.

Munoz, R. F., & Ying, Y. (1993). *The prevention of depression: Research and practice.* Baltimore: Johns Hopkins University Press.

Nezu, A. M. (1986). Efficacy of a social problem-solving therapy approach for unipolar depression. *Journal of Consulting and Clinical Psychology, 54*, 196–202.

Nezu, A. M., Nezu, C. M., & Perri, M. G. (1989). *Problem-solving therapy for depression: Theory, research and clinical guidelines.* New York: Wiley.

Nolen-Hoeksema, S. (1987). Sex differences in unipolar depression: Evidence and theory. *Psychological Bulletin, 101*, 259–282.

Radloff, L. S. (1977). The CES-D scale: A self-report depression scale for research in the general population. *Applied Psychological Measurement, 1*, 385–401.

Rehm, L. P. (1977). A self-control model of depression. *Behavior Therapy, 8*, 787–804.

Rehm, L. P. (1984). Self-management therapy for depression. *Advances in Behavior Therapy and Research, 6*, 83–98.

Rehm, L. P. (1988). Self-management and cognitive processes in depression. In L. B. Alloy (Ed.), *Cognitive processes in depression* (pp. 143–176). New York: Guilford Press.

Seligman, M. E. P. (1975). *Helplessness: On depression, development, and death.* San Francisco: W. H. Freeman.

Seligman, M. E. P. (1995). The effectiveness of psychotherapy: The *Consumer Reports* study. *American Psychologist, 50*, 965–974.

Simon, G. E., VonKorff, M., & Barlow, W. (1995). Health care costs of primary care patients with recognized depression. *Archives of General Psychiatry, 52*, 850–856.

Stark, K. D. (1990). *Childhood depression: School-based intervention.* New York: Guilford Press.

Sturm, R., & Wells, K. B. (1995). How can care for depression become more cost-effective? *Journal of the American Medical Association, 273,* 51–58.

Tarlov, A., Ware, J. E., Greenfield, S., Nelson, E. C., Perrin, E., & Zubkoff, M. (1989). The Medical Outcomes Study: An application of methods for monitoring the results of medical care. *Journal of the American Medical Association, 262,* 925–930.

Task Force on the Promotion and Dissemination of Psychological Procedures. (1995). Training in and dissemination of empirically-validated psychological treatments: Report and recommendations. *The Clinical Psychologist, 48(1),* 3–23.

Wexler, B. E., & Cicchetti, D. V. (1992). The outpatient treatment of depression: Implications of outcome research for clinical practice. *The Journal of Nervous and Mental Disease, 180,* 277–286.

12

HELPING PHYSICIANS MAKE USEFUL RECOMMENDATIONS ABOUT LOSING WEIGHT

DANIEL S. KIRSCHENBAUM

Imagine that you are a successful San Francisco internist in 1992. Rock icon Jerry Garcia walks into your office for a checkup. After telling the Grateful Dead guitarist that you love his music and you even love his ties, you begin to scold him.

"Look, Mr. Garcia—"

"Hey, Doc, no one calls me Mr. Garcia! Call me Jerry."

"OK, Jerry. Between your smoking, drug use, and excess pound-age, you are going to kill yourself. If you don't make some big changes soon, your 'long, strange trip' might get a lot shorter than you'd like."

Jerry Garcia died in the summer of 1995. He was 53 years old.

Physicians generally receive inadequate training regarding the nature and treatment of obesity. Inadequate knowledge often combines with the notoriously refractory nature of the problem, to produce frustration. Frustration, in turn, can become manifested in negative doctor-to-patient communications. Such communications have little chance of helping people lose weight. The present article provides alternatives to guilt-inducing negative communication, through several specific suggestions. Physicians can learn, quite readily, how to confront denial, acknowledge efforts toward change, and construct a practical treatment plan with their overweight patients. This approach should increase commitment, improve the alliance between physician and patient, and promote more effective change. Psychologists can also provide physicians with information that they can then offer to patients, to help them achieve their weight-loss goals. This chapter reviews both communica-

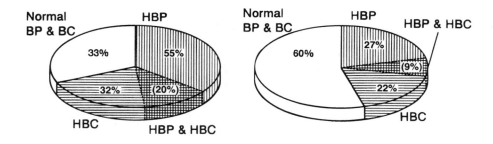

OVERWEIGHT MEN   NON-OVERWEIGHT MEN

Figure 1. The prevalence of high blood pressure (HBP; ≥140/90 mmHg or on hypertensive medication) and high blood cholesterol (HBC; ≥240 mg/dL) among overweight men compared with nonoverweight men (according to the 1976 to 1980 National Health and Nutrition Examination Survey; National Heart, Lung, and Blood Institute, 1992).

tion strategies and behavioral interventions that psychologists can teach physicians who work with overweight patients. This information can, in turn, help patients find weight-loss programs that may exist outside the physician's office.

PREVALENCE AND HEALTH RISKS OF OBESITY

Rates of obesity in the United States are climbing steadily, currently affecting approximately 1 in 3 adult Americans (Williamson, 1995). Obesity is generally defined as 20%+ over ideal weight based on health data (see Andres, 1989; Blackburn & Rosofsky, 1992). Some estimates suggest that the total costs of obesity include approximately $45 billion for direct costs associated with such diseases as diabetes, cardiovascular disease, musculoskeletal disease, and cancer; indirect costs have been estimated at $23 billion (Wolf & Colditz, 1994). These extraordinary costs coincide with a proponderance of scientific evidence that indicates that obesity often has widespread and serious adverse consequences on physical health (e.g., Berg, 1993; Bray, 1985; Pi-Sunyer, 1993). For example, Figures 1 and 2 show that according to data from the 1976 to 1980 National Health and Nutrition Examination Survey, obesity is associated with very clear differences in two key health-risk factors (high blood pressure, defined as greater than or equal to 140/90 mmHg or on antihypertensive medication; and high blood cholesterol, defined as total cholesterol levels greater than or equal to 240 mg/dL; Berg, 1993; National Heart, Lung, and Blood Institute, 1992).

Research also suggests that even modest weight losses (e.g., 5% to 10% of initial weight) can result in substantial improvements in a variety

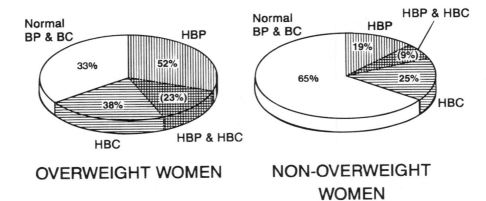

Figure 2. The prevalence of high blood pressure (HBP; ≥140/90 mmHg or on hypertensive medication) and high blood cholesterol (HBC; ≥240 mg/dL) among overweight women compared with nonoverweight women (according to the 1976 to 1980 National Health and Nutrition Examination Survey; National Heart, Lung, and Blood Institute, 1992).

of health-risk factors (see, for review, Kirschenbaum & Fitzgibbon, 1995). Because physicians are on the front line of combating this very serious epidemic, their patients and society at large would benefit tremendously if they could adopt communication strategies that would help overweight people improve their commitments to change.

APPROACHES TO WEIGHT LOSS

The research evidence clearly indicates that complex, chronic, multifaceted difficulties, such as obesity, change in slow, refractory, and sometimes imperceptible ways for most people most of the time (Meichenbaum & Turk, 1987). This scenario frustrates physicians, particularly in an economic climate in which increasing demands are made of them to see increasing numbers of patients for limited amounts of time. The inevitable frustration this situation produces often leads to ineffective and rather negative communication by physicians with their overweight clients (e.g., Shapiro, Boggs, Melamed, & Graham-Pole, 1992). This negativity, sometimes emerging as scolding or guilt-inducing diatribes, tends to increase patients' anxiety and distress (e.g., Shapiro et al., 1992); decrease the accuracy of their memory for information conveyed (Shapiro et al., 1992); and decrease the probability of effective change (e.g., Hall, Roter, & Katz, 1988; Korsch & Francis-Negrete, 1972). Alternative approaches to communication, by physicians, particularly as it pertains to this very common and substantial health problem, may increase the probability of healthful change by their patients (Sweet, Rozensky, & Tovian, 1991).

I have worked closely with physicians in medical centers and in private practice for more than 20 years, focused on the treatment of obesity. This experience, coupled with guidance from the empirical literature (e.g., Kirschenbaum & Flanery, 1984; Putnam, Finney, Barkley, & Bonner, 1994), has resulted in some specific suggestions to offer physicians. These suggestions should enable physicians to decrease their frustrations and potential negativity when communicating with their obese clients about how to make changes in their life. Before I describe these suggestions, three key assumptions are worth reviewing.

First, most physicians know very little about nutrition or weight loss. Relatively little information is provided in their medical school curriculum, and they are usually too busy to focus on this issue when they begin their practice. Second, most physicians also seem quite responsive to information about this problem. They see many patients who are overweight and often seem frustrated and lost when directing them toward effective solutions. Third, physicians seem to respond best to relatively brief and well-encapsulated words of advice that they can use in a practical way immediately.

EFFECTIVE WEIGHT CONTROL

Brownell (1993) summarized the results of a survey involving more than 20,000 readers of *Consumer Reports* who have attempted to lose weight. He noted that of those who reported losing a significant amount of weight (M = 34 lb) and maintaining those losses, "72% had done so on their own compared to 20% in commercial programs, 3% with diet pills and only 5% in a hospital or university based program" (Brownell, 1993, p. 339). Population surveys indicate that of that 72% who attempt to lose weight on their own (or perhaps more in the wider population of people who do not read *Consumer Reports*) approximately 15%–25% may achieve very good results (Jeffery & Wing, 1983; Orne & Binik, 1987; Schachter, 1982).

These findings suggest that physicians could play a role in pointing the many individuals who attempt to lose weight on their own in the direction of effective approaches. Perhaps with a little guidance from a health professional, many of these self-directed weight controllers could do so more efficiently and effectively. On the other hand, studies of self-help materials suggest that only a modest percentage of people are likely to be successful when attempting to lose weight on their own (e.g., Meyers, Cuvillier, Stalgaitis, & Cooke, 1980). In addition, commercially available weight-control programs provide relatively little evidence of long-term effectiveness (e.g., Fatis, Weiner, Hawkins, & Van Dorsten, 1989; Volkmar, Stunkard, Woolston, & Bailey, 1981).

Although some people can lose weight and maintain weight loss remarkably well with relatively little professional guidance (Brownell, 1993), a higher percentage of people achieve good outcomes when they participate in long-term intensive cognitive–behavioral treatments (Kirschenbaum & Fitzgibbon, 1995; Perri, Nezu, & Viegener, 1992). Such programs are usually directed by psychologists. They include the following elements: (a) a thorough initial assessment of psychological issues, (b) a complete cognitive–behavioral therapy component, (c) a complete nutritional component, (d) a clear emphasis on increasing exercise, (e) staff who are well trained in cognitive–behavioral therapy, (f) at least weekly sessions for at least 1 year, (g) assistance provided for promoting support and otherwise managing social environments, and (h) use of protein-sparing modified fasting when appropriate. Some recent evidence also indicates that the impact of programs with these eight elements could be augmented by the appropriate use of modern appetite-suppressant drugs (see, for reviews, Bray 1993; Silverstone, 1993).

Relatively few programs have included all of these eight (or nine) elements, and fewer still have evaluated their combined impact (Kirschenbaum & Fitzgibbon, 1995). Nonetheless, some programs that have included many of these elements have demonstrated some remarkable outcomes. Brownell and Jeffery (1987) noted that average weight losses in the outcome studies they reviewed in the 1980s almost doubled those obtained in studies in the 1970s. This trend seems to be continuing into the 1990s. For example, participants in programs that combined protein-sparing modified fasting and behavior therapy lost more than 40 pounds (on average) and maintained more than 20-pound weight losses 1.5 years posttreatment; these numbers are based on a review that included all 11 studies published before 1990 of such interventions that included at least 1.5-year follow-ups (Conviser, Kirschenbaum, & Fitzgibbon, 1990). Several recent reports of long-term cognitive–behavioral interventions also presented evidence suggesting that most people can lose and maintain substantial weight losses (e.g., Beliard, Kirschenbaum, & Fitzgibbon, 1992; Perri et al., 1988; Perri, Nezu, Patti, & McCann, 1989; Wadden, Foster, Letizia, & Stunkard, 1992).

Length of treatment deserves special emphasis; the evidence that supports treating obese people for years, instead of weeks, includes experimental research (e.g., Baum, Clark, & Sandler, 1991; Perri et al., 1989) and meta-analytic results (e.g., Bennett, 1986). Another argument for length and intensity of cognitive–behavioral treatments is provided in the clinically derived stages-of-change model that my colleagues and I developed recently (Kirschenbaum et al., 1992). Figure 3 shows the three primary stages, or those posited as experienced by most weight controllers during their first 2 years in intensive treatment, and the three secondary

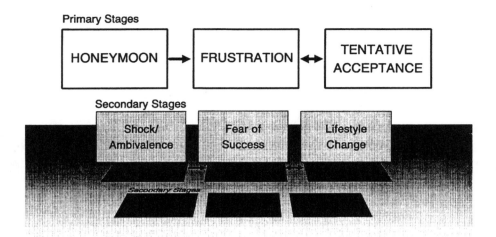

Figure 3. A model of the primary and secondary stages of change in long-term weight control. From *Weight Loss Through Persistence: Making Science Work for You* (p. 36), by D. S. Kirschenbaum, 1994, Oakland, CA: New Harbinger Publications. Copyright 1994 by D. S. Kirschenbaum.

stages, those that seem to occur regularly, but for a minority of participants. The behaviors, thoughts, and feelings that Kirschenbaum et al. (1992) viewed as characterizing the stages make it clear that participants usually struggle for long periods of time to persist at this highly challenging process of life change. First, the relatively easy honeymoon stage passes into the much more difficult, but ostensibly inevitable, frustration stage. Fortunately, many people, with the help of the relationship with a professional therapist, cognitive–behavioral techniques, and the other weight-loss-treatment elements listed earlier in this section, find their way to the peaceful sense of resolve and behavioral consistencies of supernormal eating and exercising that characterize tentative acceptance. Some weight controllers even develop the aggressive self-protectiveness of lifestyle change ("unwilling, and adamantly so, to place [themselves] in a position to become 'mindless' . . . again about eating, exercise, and weight"; Kirschenbaum et al., 1992, p. 627). Another way of describing this transition through stages of change is to suggest that long-term, intensive cognitive–behavioral treatments may help people reach the often elusive but potentially critical goal of obsessive–compulsive self-regulation (Kirschenbaum, 1987; Kirschenbaum & Tomarken, 1982).

A HIERARCHICAL WEIGHT-CONTROL PLAN DIRECTED BY PHYSICIANS

Exhibit 1 shows an example of a handout for physicians that outlines six hierarchical steps for weight control. The steps are ordered from least

EXHIBIT 1
Weight-Loss Recommendations

1. Self-directed attempts?
2. Increase exercise (Join club? Walk?)
3. Spouse or friend involvement
4. Take Off Pounds Sensibly (TOPS): [telephone number]
5. Weight Watchers: [telephone number]
6. Professional weight-control program: [telephone number]

intrusive interventions to most elaborate. In accord with the preceding information about effectiveness of various approaches to weight control, some people can lose weight effectively with relatively minimal guidance. For these individuals, the first two to three steps may provide all the encouragement they need. On the other hand, many other individuals may benefit from more structured interventions, including assistance from widely available self-help or commercial programs. The most intensive level of intervention (and the most effective), the sixth step, pertains to professional programs. These programs are generally directed by psychologists. They incorporate the 8–9 elements noted above for state-of-the-art/science treatments of obesity. In other words, the best of the professional programs (the sixth step) will meet the definition for long-term, intensive cognitive–behavioral treatment.

Psychologists who are consulting to physicians can give them a version of Exhibit 1 as a handout when accompanying an educational talk about the treatment of obesity (e.g., a workshop used to generate referrals). The psychologist can then review each of the hierarchical steps and provide suggestions for using each step. More specifically, physicians would be encouraged to talk with their patients about what they have tried in the past as the first step. Generally, people who have attempted to lose weight many times, and have used a variety of approaches without notable success, could proceed directly to Step 6. Patients who have not made many serious attempts to lose weight could be advised to attempt Steps 1, 2, or 3 and then return for a follow-up visit to the physician 2 or 3 months later. If they have not made progress on weight control (e.g., approximately 1/2 to 1 pound weight-loss per week for individuals starting at least 20% over ideal body weight), then Steps 4 through 6 would be recommended. It would be most helpful and appropriate for psychologists to identify the best professional programs in their area for physicians to use in their Step 6 referrals.

It seems worthwhile to know a few more details about the six steps in this plan before providing a lecture or workshop advocating its adoption:

1. Self-directed attempts? Physicians can ask their patients what approaches they have used to lose weight. They can discuss each major weight-loss effort and determine if the patient may be willing to try one of them again or if the patient is looking for something new. If the patient wishes additional direction, the physician can proceed to Step 2.

2. Increase exercise. It is sometimes useful for physicians to recommend dramatic increases in exercise. Many patients do not realize that a daily brisk 30-minute walk might do them a world of good. A knowledgeable physician can help them understand that such efforts might increase their metabolic rates (e.g., Donahoe, Lin, Kirschenbaum, & Keesey, 1984) and greatly facilitate weight-loss attempts (Hill, 1995; Wadden, 1995). This brief education could be followed by discussion about the feasibility and usefulness of joining health clubs or going for regular walks in the morning. For weight-loss purposes, it is helpful to recommend that patients attempt to exercise at least once per day, every day. This is in keeping with recent recommendations from the American College of Sports Medicine (1991), the *U.S. Department of Agriculture* (1995), and Kirschenbaum (1994). As the physician discusses this and other options with his or her patient, it is also useful to recommend some self-help reading about nutrition, exercise, and weight loss. Exhibit 1 includes some recommended books that are readily available.

3. Spouse or friend involvement. Physicians can make the point that weight controllers tend to maintain exercise better if they exercise with a friend or their spouse (e.g., Dishman, 1988).

4. and 5. Take Off Pounds Sensibly (TOPS) and Weight Watchers. Physicians can provide specific recommendations as to the type of nonprofessional programs that he or she believes will be the most effective and reasonable. The two programs that I recommend are the self-help program, Take Off Pounds Sensibly (TOPS), and Weight Watchers. Both of these programs are very well established (among the oldest self-help programs in the country), and both provide responsible information at reasonable costs. They're also widely available. On the other hand, patients should be warned that most people have great difficulty sustaining their involvement in nonprofessional programs. Most patients drop out of these programs within several weeks

or months (Volkmar et al., 1981). However, they can work for some people some of the time (Stuart & Guire, 1979).

6. Professional weight-control program. A professional approach to losing weight is offered in many major metropolitan areas, usually at hospitals or universities. As noted previously, the best examples of these programs are the ones that provide appropriate intensive cognitive–behavioral treatment and long-term care (Kirschenbaum & Fitzgibbon, 1995; Perri, Nezu, & Viegener, 1992; Wadden, 1995).

SUPPORTING WEIGHT LOSS EFFORTS

In addition to implementing a hierarchical weight-control plan, the second major issue about which some physicians could use some assistance pertains to acknowledging and supporting their patients' weight-loss efforts (cf. Hall et al., 1988; Shapiro et al., 1992). My colleagues and I believe that it is important to help physicians understand the distinction between double messages and encouragement. More specifically, double messages include comments such as, "You look much better!" Although this is intended to provide encouragement, it is concurrently critical. The critical aspect is the underlying message that the person looked much worse previously. An alternative method of encouragement would be to say something like, "Congratulations! What have you been doing?" This approach engages the patient in a dialogue about the effort, thereby suggesting its importance. It may also prove very helpful for physicians to make notes in their charts about the patient's specific efforts to lose weight. Periodic comments from authority figures like physicians can be very supportive if provided in a consistently positive fashion (Putnam et al., 1994; Sweet et al., 1991). This support, in turn, can increase the probability of meaningful behavior change (Hall et al., 1988).

THERAPEUTICALLY CONFRONTING DENIAL

A third issue, one with which many physicians seem to struggle, is denial. Many overweight people have become masters at denying the magnitude and importance of their weight status (Kirschenbaum et al., 1992). The natural tendency, and the one that seems to be followed by many physicians, is to criticize, rather directly, patients' ostensible lack of concern regarding their health. These parentally styled remarks tend to produce denigration and avoidance of the physician (cf. Hall et al., 1988; Shapiro et al., 1992). Negative feedback tends to be avoided rather than embraced (Stockton & Morran, 1981). Physicians, like most nonpsychologists, seem generally unaware of this perspective.

Instead of the parentally styled critical approach, a more informative approach often produces better outcomes (e.g., DiMatteo et al., 1993). For example, the physician could express concern about the patient's health status and the way it may affect her or him in the years to come. This concern, coupled with an appropriate referral, may lead to an increased readiness of the patient to change. In fact, the results of several studies suggest that when people devise specific plans to manage challenging behavioral regimens, they adhere more closely to those plans (e.g., Kirschenbaum & Flanery, 1984; Putnam et al., 1994).

CONCLUSIONS AND FUTURE DIRECTIONS

In summary, physicians often find it rather useful to have specific recommendations that they can provide to their patients about appropriate ways to lose weight. They also seem to benefit from education about how to acknowledge their patients' efforts at weight loss and how to confront, therapeutically, denial of obesity. The research evidence suggests that supportive, informative interactions, accompanied by specific plans for change, should enhance commitment and change.

It would, of course, be most helpful to have additional research investigating the actual usefulness of the strategy outlined in this chapter. For example, workshops could be conducted with groups of physicians. In the experimental workshops, these specific recommendations could be provided. In the comparison workshop, similar information could be provided without including the hierarchical plan and handout. It would be helpful to include some follow-up sessions to check on the implementation of these recommendations in the experimental condition.

Research could focus on the extent to which the patients to whom physicians made these specific recommendations actually changed behavior over time. This could include investigating changes in weight, percentage fat, and other health-risk factors over long periods of time (at least 1 year, ideally 3–5 years).

The evidence presented in this chapter would suggest that the experimental workshops would produce better outcomes for at least some of the patients to whom they were applied. Because this would be a relatively minimal type of intervention, however, these recommendations alone would not be expected to lead to dramatic weight losses for most of the people to whom they were offered (cf. Meyers et al., 1980). Additional research on weight-loss recommendations that could be used by primary care physicians would be quite useful (e.g., Williams & Duncan, 1976). Perhaps physicians could use some elements that are incorporated in state-of-the-art/science treatments offered in professional programs to the advantage of at least some of their patients.

RECOMMENDED READING

References marked with an asterisk indicate books that are technically oriented and recommended for health care professionals.

Bennion, L. H., Bierman, E. L., & Ferguson, J. M. (1991). *Straight talk about weight control.* Fairfield, OH: Consumer Report Books.

Brody, J. (1987). *Jane Brody's nutrition book.* New York: Bantam Books.

*Brownell, K. D., & Foreyt, J. P. (Eds.). (1986). *Handbook of eating disorders.* New York: Basic Books.

Fletcher, A. M. (1994). *Thin for life.* Shelburne, VT: Chapters.

Kirschenbaum, D. S. (1994). *Weight loss through persistence: Making science work for you.* Oakland, CA: New Harbinger Publications.

*Kirschenbaum, D. S., Johnson, W. G., & Stalonas, P. M. (1987). *Treating childhood and adolescent obesity.* New York: Wiley.

Perri, M. G., Nezu, A. M., & Viegener, B. J. (1992). *Improving the long-term management of obesity.* New York: Wiley.

Stunkard, A. J., & Wadden, T. A. (1993). *Obesity: Theory and therapy.* New York: Raven Press.

REFERENCES

American College of Sports Medicine. (1991). *Guidelines for exercise testing and prescription* (4th ed.). Philadelphia: Lea & Febiger.

Andres, R. (1989). Does the "best" body weight change with age? In A. J. Stunkard & A. Baum (Eds.), *Perspectives in behavioral medicine: Eating, sleeping, and sex* (pp. 100–108). Hillsdale, NJ: Erlbaum.

Baum, J. G., Clark, H. B., & Sandler, J. (1991). Preventing relapse in obesity through posttreatment maintenance systems: Comparing the relative efficacy of two levels of therapists support. *Journal of Behavioral Medicine, 14,* 287–302.

Beliard, B., Kirschenbaum, D. S., & Fitzgibbon, M. L. (1992). Evaluation of an intensive weight control program using *a priori* criteria to determine outcome. *International Journal of Obesity, 16,* 505–517.

Bennett, G. A. (1986). Behavior therapy for obesity: A quantitative review of the effects of selected treatment characteristics on outcome. *Behavior Therapy, 17,* 554–562.

Berg, F. (1993). *Health risks of obesity.* Hettinger, ND: Healthy Living Institute.

Blackburn, G. L., & Rosofsky, W. (1992). Making the connection between weight loss, dieting, and health: The 10% solution. *Weight Control Digest* [Professional ed.], *2,* 124–127.

Bray, G. A. (1985). Complications of obesity. *Annals of Internal Medicine, 103*, 1052–1062.

Bray, G. A. (1993). Use and abuse of appetite-suppressant drugs in the treatment of obesity. *Annals of Internal Medicine, 119*, 707–713.

Brownell, K. D. (1993). Whether obesity should be treated. *Health Psychology, 12*, 339–341.

Brownell, K. D., & Jeffery, R. W. (1987). Improving long-term weight loss: Pushing the limits of treatment. *Behavior Therapy, 18*, 353–374.

Conviser, J. H., Kirschenbaum, D. S., & Fitzgibbon, M. L. (1990, April). *Toward clinically effective weight control programs: Efficient long-term evaluation of an intensive program.* Paper presented at the meeting of the Society of Behavioral Medicine, Chicago.

DiMatteo, M. R., Sherbourne, C. D., Hays, R. D., Ordway, L., Kravitz, R. L., McGlynn, E. A., Kaplan, S., & Rogers, W. H. (1993). Physicians' characteristics influence patients' adherence to medical treatment: Results from the Medical Outcomes Study. *Health Psychology, 12*, 93–102.

Dishman, R. K. (Ed.), (1988). *Exercise adherence: Its impact on public health.* Champaign, IL: Human Kinetics Books.

Donahoe, C. P., Lin, D. H., Kirschenbaum, D. S., & Keesey, R. E. (1984). Metabolic consequences of dieting and exercising in the treatment of obesity. *Journal of Consulting and Clinical Psychology, 48*, 869–877.

Fatis, M., Weiner, A., Hawkins, J., & Van Dorsten, B. (1989). Following-up on a commercial weight loss program: Do the pounds stay off after your picture has been in the newspaper? *Journal of the American Dietetic Association, 89*, 547–548.

Hall, J. A., Roter, D. L., & Katz, N. R. (1988). Meta-analysis of correlates of provider behavior in medical encounters. *Medical Care, 26*, 1–19.

Hill, J. O. (1995). The role of exercise in weight maintenance. In D. B. Allison & F. X. Pi-Snunyer (Eds.), *Obesity treatment: Establishing goals, improving outcomes, and reviewing the research agenda* (pp. 127–132). New York: Plenum.

Jeffery, R. W., & Wing, R. R. (1983). Recidivism and self-cure of smoking and obesity: Data from population studies. *American Psychologist, 38*, 852.

Kirschenbaum, D. S. (1987). Self-regulatory failure: A review with clinical implications. *Clinical Psychology Review, 7*, 77–104.

Kirschenbaum, D. S. (1994). *Weight loss through persistence: Making science work for you.* Oakland, CA: New Harbinger Publications.

Kirschenbaum, D. S., & Fitzgibbon, M. L. (1995). Controversy about the treatment of obesity: Criticisms or challenges? *Behavior Therapy, 26*, 43–68.

Kirschenbaum, D. S., Fitzgibbon, M. L., Martino, S., Conviser, J. H., Rosendahl, E. H., & Laatsch, L. (1992). Stages of change in successful weight control: A clinically derived model. *Behavior Therapy, 23*, 623–635.

Kirschenbaum, D. S., & Flanery, R. C. (1984). Toward a psychology of behavioral contracting. *Clinical Psychology Review, 4*, 597–618.

Kirschenbaum, D. S., & Tomarken, A. J. (1982). On facing the generalization problem: The study of self-regulatory failure. In P. C. Kendall (Ed.), *Advances in cognitive behavioral research and therapy* (Vol. 1, pp. 121–200). San Diego, CA: Academic Press.

Korsch, B. M., & Francis-Negrete, V. (1972). Doctor–patient communication. *Scientific American, 227,* 66–74.

Meichenbaum, D., & Turk, D. C. (1987). *Facilitating treatment adherence: A practitioner's guidebook.* New York: Plenum.

Meyers, A. W., Cuvillier, C., Stalgaitis, S., & Cooke, C. J. (1980). An evaluation of self-help treatment programs for weight loss. *The Behavior Therapist, 3,* 25–26.

National Heart, Lung, and Blood Institute. (1992). Obesity education initiative takes a high risk in a population approach. *Infomemo, 1,* 16–17.

Orne, C. M., & Binik, Y. M. (1987). Recidivism and self-cure of obesity: A test of Schacter's hypothesis in diabetic patients. *Health Psychology, 6,* 467–475.

Perri, M. G., McAllister, D. A., Gange, J. J., Jordan, R. C., McAdoo, W. G., & Nezu, A. M. (1988). Effects of four maintenance programs on the long-term management of obesity. *Journal of Consulting and Clinical Psychology, 56,* 529–534.

Perri, M. G., Nezu, A. M., Patti, E. P., & McCann, K. L. (1989). Effect of length of treatment on weight loss. *Journal of Consulting and Clinical Psychology, 57,* 450–452.

Perri, M. G., Nezu, A. M., & Viegener, B. J. (1992). *Improving the long-term management of obesity: Theory, research, and clinical guidelines.* New York: Wiley.

Pi-Sunyer, F. X. (1993). Medical hazards of obesity. *Annals of Internal Medicine, 119,* 655–660.

Putnam, D. E., Finney, J. W., Barkley, P. L., & Bonner, M. J. (1994). Enhancing commitment improves adherence to a medical regimen. *Journal of Consulting and Clinical Psychology, 62,* 191–194.

Schachter, S. (1982). Recidivism and self-cure of smoking and obesity. *American Psychologist, 37,* 436–444.

Shapiro, D. E., Boggs, S. R., Melamed, B. G., & Graham-Pole, J. (1992). The effect of varied physician affect on recall, anxiety, and perceptions in women at risk for breast cancer: An analogue study. *Health Psychology, 11,* 61–66.

Silverstone, T. (1993). The place of appetite-suppressant drugs in the treatment of obesity. In A. J. Stunkard & T. A. Wadden (Eds.), *Obesity: Theory and therapy* (2nd ed., pp. 275–286). New York: Raven Press.

Stockton, R., & Morran, D. K. (1981). Feedback exchange, in personal growth groups: Received acceptance as a function of valence, session, and order of delivery. *Journal of Counseling Psychology, 28,* 490–497.

Stuart, R. B., & Guire, K. (1979). Some correlates of weight loss through behavior modification. *International Journal of Obesity, 3*, 87–96.

Sweet, J. J., Rozensky, R. H., & Tovian, S. M. (Eds.). (1991). *Handbook of clinical psychology in medical settings.* New York: Plenum.

U.S. Department of Agriculture. (1995). *Nutrition and your health: Dietary guidelines for Americans* (Publication No. 96-402-519). Washington, DC: U.S. Government Printing Office.

Volkmar, F. R., Stunkard, A. J., Woolston, J., & Bailey, B. A. (1981). High attrition rates in commercial weight reduction programs. *Archives of Internal Medicine, 141*, 426–428.

Wadden, T. A. (1995). What characterizes successful weight maintainers? In D. B. Allison & F. X. Pi-Snunyer (Eds.), *Obesity treatment: Establishing goals, improving outcomes, and reviewing the research agenda* (pp. 103–112). New York: Plenum.

Wadden, T. A., Foster, G. D., Letizia, K. A., & Stunkard, A. J. (1992). A multicenter evaluation of a proprietary weight reduction program for the treatment of marked obesity. *Archives of Internal Medicine, 152*, 961–966.

Williams, A. E., & Duncan, B. (1976). A commercial weight-reducing organization: A critical analysis. *Medical Journal of Australia, 1*, 781–785.

Williamson, D. F. (1995). Prevalence and demographics of obesity. In K. D. Brownell & C. G. Fairburn (Eds.), *Eating disorders and obesity: A comprehensive handbook* (pp. 391–395). New York: Guilford Press.

Wolf, A. M., & Colditz, G. A. (1994). The cost of obesity: The U.S. perspective.

13

SUBSTANCE USE PROBLEMS IN PRIMARY CARE MEDICAL SETTINGS: IS THERE A PSYCHOLOGIST IN THE HOUSE?

BRUCE S. LIESE, BELINDA A. VAIL, and KIMBERLY A. SEATON

The use of alcohol, tobacco, and illicit drugs is pervasive in the United States, and excessive use of these psychoactive substances contributes to the health problems of millions of men, women, and children. The physical sequelae of these health problems have traditionally been treated in primary care medical settings. However, most primary care physicians feel unprepared to deal with the psychological and behavioral manifestations of substance use.

In this chapter, it is argued that health psychologists should be actively involved in the treatment of substance use problems because these problems involve psychological (cognitive, behavioral, and affective) processes that directly influence health and physical well-being. It is further argued that primary care physicians will welcome health psychologists offering to help in the management of their patients with substance use problems.

PREVALENCE OF SUBSTANCE USE AND ASSOCIATED PROBLEMS

Millions of Americans use psychoactive substances every day. According to a recent National Household Survey on Drug Abuse conducted by the Substance Abuse and Mental Health Services Administration (1993), 68% of Americans over the age of 12 drank alcohol in the past year, 32.1% smoked cigarettes, 12.7% used illicit drugs, 4.7% used smokeless tobacco, and 4.5% used prescription drugs for nonmedical use. Furthermore, 84.6% of respondents said they had used alcohol *at some time in their lives*, 72.7% had smoked cigarettes, 37% had used illicit drugs, 14.1% had used smokeless tobacco, and 12.5% had used prescription drugs for nonmedical purposes. Although these data do not specifically reflect problematic use, they certainly reflect the pervasiveness of drug and alcohol use in the United States.

In another important study, Regier et al. (1993) examined the prevalence of psychopathology and substance use disorders. These investigators reported results of the National Institute of Mental Health's Epidemiologic Catchment Area study, a collaborative project involving five research groups and over 20,000 respondents. Regier et al. (1993) found that 28.1% of their sample had some alcohol, drug, or mental disorder within the preceding year. Approximately 10% reported substance use disorders; 7.4% specifically reported alcohol use disorders, and 3.1% reported drug use disorders.

Regier et al. (1993) also compared service utilization in the treatment of mental disorders with that of substance use disorders. They found that more than 50% of individuals with schizophrenia, bipolar disorder, somatization disorder, and panic disorder received formal treatment, whereas only 23% of individuals with substance use disorders received formal treatment for their disorders. Approximately 11% of individuals with substance use disorders received services from drug or alcohol treatment facilities, and 9.9% received treatment in general medical settings. This study established that most Americans with substance use disorders do not receive formal treatment.

HEALTH PROBLEMS ASSOCIATED WITH EXCESSIVE SUBSTANCE USE

Excessive psychoactive substance use may result in profound health problems. It is important for health psychologists to be knowledgeable about the health problems associated with excessive substance use.

Alcohol

Alcohol is a psychoactive drug that has a variety of effects, depending on the drinker's physiology, expectations, circumstances, and environment. Small amounts of alcohol can produce the desired effects of sedation, relaxation, and disinhibition. But substantially larger doses may produce cognitive impairment, poor judgment, labile mood, slurred speech, *ataxia* (difficulty walking), coma, respiratory failure, and death (Barker & Whitfield, 1991). Chronic or heavy use may impair peripheral nerve function and destroy brain cells, potentially resulting in memory loss and reduced learning capability (Schuckit, 1991).

Alcohol is a major contributor to heart disease, the leading cause of death in the United States (Friedman, 1990; Schuckit, 1991). Alcohol appears to be a direct cardiac toxin that contributes to fat deposition on the heart muscle and a subsequent decrease in the ability of the heart to beat effectively. Acutely, alcohol increases heart rate and the volume of blood pumped by the heart. It causes skin vessels to dilate, leading to loss of body heat (despite the warm sensation experienced by the drinker). Over time, alcohol may cause an increase in the drinker's blood pressure and cholesterol and hasten the development of cholesterol plaques in the coronary arteries. When a coronary artery is occluded by pieces of these plaques, a myocardial infarction may result.

Alcohol is a direct gastric irritant that induces a highly acidic state in the stomach. With chronic use, alcohol may lead to inflammation and ulcer formation in the esophagus and stomach. Even young drinkers may experience vague or chronic unexplained abdominal pain. Because teenagers are seen infrequently by physicians and rarely disclose their alcohol consumption, this abdominal pain is typically undiagnosed.

Acute inflammation of the liver (*hepatitis*) and fatty liver infiltrates are often seen in heavy drinkers. Contrary to popular belief, even social drinkers may develop these liver problems, which may lead to *cirrhosis* and liver cancer. Cirrhosis is the replacement of normal liver cells by fibrous tissue, with the eventual loss of liver function. Because a large percentage of blood passes through the liver before returning to the heart, cirrhosis causes an accumulation of fluid in the abdomen (*ascites*) and dilation of other large vessels that return blood to the heart. Some of the vessels may become enlarged, rupture, and produce massive hemorrhage into the throat and stomach. Alcohol is also one of the leading causes of *pancreatitis*, a dangerous inflammation of the pancreas that causes severe abdominal pain (Schuckit, 1991).

Other organ systems may also be adversely affected by heavy alcohol consumption (Schuckit, 1991). Production of red and white blood cells may be decreased. *Gout*, a condition characterized by painful inflammation of the joints, results from decreased uric acid secretion. Testosterone levels may also decrease, leading to sexual dysfunction in males. The acid–base balance of the body may be disrupted, leading to an array of vitamin and mineral deficiencies. Alcohol-dependent individuals have cancer rates 10 times greater than those of the general public, with an increased risk of mouth, throat, esophagus, stomach, liver, pancreas, and breast cancers.

Alcohol harms more than just those individuals who drink excessively. At least 50% of fatal automobile accidents are alcohol related, and a majority of victims are innocent passengers, pedestrians, and other drivers who have not been drinking. Women who drink during early pregnancy may place their babies at risk for *fetal alcohol syndrome*, characterized by mental retardation, cardiac anomalies, abnormal facial features, and genital malformation (McKenzie & Kipke, 1992).

Cigarettes

Nicotine, the addictive ingredient in cigarettes, is a powerful central nervous system stimulant and depressant. The acute physiological effects of nicotine include increased heart rate, blood pressure, and an increased demand for oxygen by the heart. Peripheral vessels vasoconstrict, and skeletal muscles relax. Some additional effects of nicotine are decreased appetite and the release of endogenous opiates (Holbrook, 1991).

The risks of smoking are well documented; the mortality rate for smokers is 70% higher than for nonsmokers. Adverse effects are primarily seen in the respiratory and cardiovascular systems, but other systems are affected as well. The most publicized adverse effect in smokers is the development of lung cancer. However, smoking is also implicated in cancers of the mouth, larynx, esophagus, stomach, pancreas, kidney, bladder, and cervix (Newcomb & Carbone, 1992).

Chronic obstructive pulmonary disease, chronic bronchitis, emphysema, and respiratory infections are closely associated with smoking (Sherman, 1992). Mild pulmonary function abnormalities may be seen even in teenagers who smoke (Holbrook, 1991). Cigarette smoke paralyzes the *cilia* (tiny hairlike structures) lining the respiratory tract while it simultaneously increases mucous production. Without the effective action of the cilia, clearance of the bronchial tracts is impaired. Cigarette smoke also interferes with the immune mechanism of the respiratory tract, potentially resulting in direct damage and an inability to protect against disease. Over time, the *alveoli* (tiny air sacs in the lungs) may rupture, leading to emphysema (McKenzie & Kipke, 1992).

The effects of cigarette smoke on the heart and blood vessels are equally dangerous (McBride, 1992). Smoking increases heart rate and blood pressure while constricting peripheral arteries. It also increases cholesterol circulating in the bloodstream, potentially leading to a rapid increase in arteriosclerosis. Tobacco and diabetes account for the majority of leg amputations from peripheral vascular disease. Tobacco and hypertension are the leading contributors to coronary artery disease and myocardial infarction (Holbrook, 1991; McBride, 1992). Tobacco smoke also decreases skin elasticity, which leads to premature wrinkling. In heavy smokers, the risk of developing impotence is heightened (McKenzie & Kipke, 1992).

As with alcohol, the dangers of smoking extend beyond the risks to the smoker. Substantial evidence has demonstrated that environmental smoke is dangerous to nonsmokers (Byrd, 1992). For example, children living with smokers are more likely than those living with nonsmokers to develop ear and nasal infections, pneumonia, and eczema. The heart rate of a pregnant woman's fetus increases when she smokes. Pregnant women smokers are more likely to miscarry and have underweight infants, and their babies are more likely to die from sudden infant death syndrome (Byrd, 1992).

Illicit Drugs

Marijuana. The acute (short-term) effects of marijuana primarily involve the central nervous system. Marijuana produces mild elation and relaxation, distortion of time, increased sensitivity to auditory and visual cues, and impairment of learning and cognitive functioning. A user's appetite often increases (McKenzie & Kipke, 1992), and mild increases in heart rate and blood pressure are likely, as well as marked redness of the eyes and increased body temperature (Mendelson, 1991). Chronic use may lead to decreased motivation levels (*amotivational syndrome*) and depression. Mood swings, anxiety, delusions, and paranoia may develop with extremely heavy use (D'Lugoff & Hawthorne, 1991).

Over time, the most severe effect of marijuana is probably damage to the lungs. The irritation from the smoke leads to cellular changes in the bronchial wall, bronchospasms, and bronchitis. Definite decreases in lung capacity and function occur with regular use (Mendelson, 1991). Other organ systems are less affected, but there is a decrease in fertility and sex drive with chronic use (D'Lugoff & Hawthorne, 1991).

Cocaine. Cocaine is a particularly dangerous and powerful central nervous system stimulant. Its effects include hyperalertness, anxiety, anorexia, labile affect, insomnia, paranoia, agitation, and heightened sensual awareness. Initially, cocaine causes an increase in blood pressure and heart rate that may advance to potentially fatal cardiac arrhythmias. Cocaine is a potent vasoconstrictor and may also lead to coronary artery spasm and sudden death by myocardial infarction. Users will occasionally develop seizures and stroke. When ingested nasally, cocaine causes membrane drying and atrophy that may lead to septal perforation. Cocaine also may cause reflex congestion and chronic sinusitis. Deeper in the respiratory tract, it produces more severe symptoms of fluid or blood accumulation in the lungs (Mendelson, 1991). Many of the side effects of cocaine are idiosyncratic and not dose related, making even occasional use dangerous. For some individuals, cocaine becomes highly addictive.

The recent development of crack cocaine has resulted in a dramatic increase in cocaine use in the United States (Schulz, 1993). Crack is a smokable cocaine derivative that is far less expensive than powder cocaine. The term *crack* comes from the crackling sound made by this drug when it is smoked (D'Lugoff & Hawthorne, 1991). In addition to the risks associated with powder cocaine use, crack seems to be more addictive and may lead to life-threatening lung symptoms with heavy use.

Opioids. Opioids such as heroin, codeine, and Demerol are used medically to manage pain and produce mild sedation. The physical effects of opioids include increased body temperature, heart rate, respiratory rate, and blood pressure. These drugs are abused primarily for their euphoric effects, but their use presents several risks: decreased digestive-tract motility, anorexia, constipation, and respiratory depression. Overdose can result in the fatal failure to initiate breathing. Withdrawal symptoms may be intense and influenza-like, including nausea, vomiting, cough, rhinorrhea, sweating, and twitching (Mendelson, 1991; Schuckit & Segal, 1991).

Phencyclidine. Phencyclidine (PCP) is a drug developed for veterinary medicine that produces variable responses. In low doses, it produces excitement, agitation, and analgesia. However, the toxic dose is very close to the dose producing desired effects, so overdose is common. Individuals who overdose may manifest psychological and physical effects. Psychological effects include disorganized thinking, body-image distortions, and feelings of estrangement. Physical side effects include vomiting, hypersalivation, muscle rigidity, convulsions, fever, coma, and death (Mendelson, 1991).

Hallucinogens. Hallucinogens, or psychedelics, like LSD and psilocybin are drugs that produce visual, auditory, tactile, and olfactory hallucinations (Schulz, 1993). Like PCP, hallucinogens may produce time distortions, confusion, and paranoia. When their judgment becomes impaired, users become endangered because they mistake illusions for reality. Thus, users may experience panic attacks and "bad trips" (McKenzie & Kipke, 1992; Mendelson, 1991).

Inhalants. Because they are inexpensive and easily acquired, inhalants, such as glue, paint, gasoline, lighter fluid, and paint thinner are most commonly used by young people. The acute symptoms of inhalant intoxication are similar to alcohol intoxication (D'Lugoff & Hawthorne, 1991). Impulsive behavior, confusion, and a general loss of inhibition are common. When the user is too confused to quit inhaling, oxygen depletion may occur, with resulting seizures or cardiorespiratory arrest (McKenzie & Kipke, 1992). Chronic use is believed to produce multiple organ damage.

PSYCHOLOGICAL PROBLEMS ASSOCIATED WITH SUBSTANCE USE DISORDERS

Recent evidence has demonstrated that individuals with substance use disorders are likely to have significant coexisting psychological problems. Regier et al. (1990) surveyed individuals with lifetime mental disorders and found that 28.9% had coexisting drug and alcohol disorders, 22.3% had coexisting alcohol disorders, and 14.7% had other drug disorders. These investigators found that individuals with alcohol use disorders had a 36.6% prevalence rate of other mental disorders. This figure was much higher (53.1%) in individuals with other drug use disorders.

Regier et al. (1990) found that the risk of substance use disorders varies with specific psychiatric diagnoses. Compared with the general public, the risk of a substance use disorder increases 4.6 times with schizophrenia, 29.6 times with antisocial personality disorder, 1.7 times with anxiety disorders, and 2.5 times with obsessive–compulsive disorder. In their study, Regier et al. (1990) also investigated the risk of psychiatric problems among particular drug users. They found that mental disorders increased by 2.3 times with alcohol use disorders, 3.8 times with marijuana, 11.3 times with cocaine, 6.7 times with opiates, 10.8 times with barbiturates, 6.2 times with amphetamines, and 8.0 times with hallucinogens. These data were consistent with other findings that cocaine addicts have a higher prevalence of depression, bipolar disorder, and attention deficit disorder than the general public (Group for the Advancement of Psychiatry, 1991). Rounsaville, Weissman, Kleber, and Wilber (1982) reported that opiate addicts have a heightened lifetime risk of psychiatric disorders (86.9%), with depression the most common disorder (53.9%). Ross, Glaser, and Germanson (1988) found high lifetime rates of antisocial personality disorder (46.9%), anxiety disorders (61.9%), affective disorders (33.7%), and psychosexual disorders (34.5%) among individuals with substance use problems. Given these data, indicating widespread psychological problems associated with substance use disorders, it becomes even more important that psychologists attend to substance use problems.

SUBSTANCE USE PROBLEMS IN PRIMARY CARE MEDICAL SETTINGS

It is well established that substance use disorders are common in primary care medical settings. For example, Bradley (1994) reported that between 11% and 20% of patients in general medical clinics have alcohol use disorders. In family practice clinics, these figures range from 8% to 16%, and in obstetrics and gynecology clinics, 12% to 16% of patients have alcohol use disorders (Bradley, 1994).

Unfortunately, it is also well established that physicians tend to focus on physical symptoms and problems rather than on underlying substance use problems (Chappel, 1992). In a study by Pursch (1978), 75% of physicians were unable to deal effectively with alcohol-troubled patients. Difficulties were attributed to inadequate training, unresolved personal or family substance use problems, negative experiences with addicted patients, rigid personality styles, lack of empathy, and fear of loss of collegial support.

Although brief interventions by primary care physicians have been found to be effective (Bien, Miller, & Tonigan, 1993; Schwartz, 1992), most physicians feel ill-prepared or uncomfortable treating substance use problems. Their training almost exclusively focuses on physical and life sciences (including biology, chemistry, physiology, pathology, pharmacology, and microbiology) and stresses the need to cure or control illness. Consequently, physicians generally prefer not to treat substance use problems that are not immediately curable. Goodwin (1981) characterized the situation poignantly:

> Like the employer, the alcoholic's doctor (if there is one) is in a good position to identify a drinking problem early. Doctors are notoriously slow to take advantage of this. Sometimes the patient has to show up drunk, jaundiced, with his liver down to his pelvis, before it occurs to the physician to ask whether he drinks. Why so unobserving? One reason is that doctors don't know much about alcoholism. The subject isn't brought up much in medical school. Doctors don't like to see alcoholics. They don't know what to do with them when they see them. . . . "Stay away from my door" is the message sent out by many doctors, and alcoholics get the message. (p. 121)

Editorials in the *Journal of the American Medical Association* (Bowen & Sammons, 1988; Delbanco, 1992) and elsewhere concur with Goodwin's claims. Bowen and Sammons (1988) referred to the alcohol-abusing patient as "a challenge to the profession" (p. 2267). Delbanco (1992) asked, "Where are their doctors?" (p. 702). Both editorials highlighted deficiencies in the substance abuse curricula of medical schools. Bowen and Sammons additionally pointed out that inadequate attention has been given to the educational needs of 500,000 physicians already in practice. In an article in *Science* entitled "The Neglected Disease in Medical Education," Holden (1985) described physicians as "notoriously deficient when it comes to early diagnosis and intervention with alcoholic patients. . . . And no wonder: they never learned much about the disease in medical school" (p. 742). And, in summarizing the empirical literature, Maly (1993) estimated that as many as 90% of addicted patients are undiagnosed by primary care physicians.

A physician's lack of training may be only one obstacle preventing him or her from addressing substance use problems. There is evidence suggesting that physicians' negative attitudes toward addicted patients also create substantial obstacles. It seems that physicians succumb to the same negative stereotypes of addicted patients as society at large (e.g., that such patients are "derelicts" or "skid row bums").

Denial and poor motivation are thought by some physicians to be chronic, inherent characteristics of patients with substance use disorders; however, this assumption is not empirically supported. Instead, these perceptions may be a function of poor doctor–patient relationships. Hanna (1991) found that patients who admitted to drinking problems were treated negatively by their doctors. In response, these patients were more likely to resist doctors' suggestions and report less satisfaction with treatment.

Even when their patients reveal overt signs and symptoms of alcohol problems, many physicians ignore the diagnosis, neglect to make appropriate referrals, or are pessimistic about potential behavioral change. Physicians may avoid addicted patients because of lack of training or role models, heavy time demands, the risk of making a socially stigmatized diagnosis, and the frustrations of managing a chronic illness (Delbanco, 1992). This avoidance is especially unfortunate, given that alcohol-dependent individuals who achieve long-term abstinence reduce their mortality rates to those of nondependent individuals (Bullock, Reed, & Grant, 1992). Similar reductions in morbidity and mortality rates have been found for people who abstain from smoking for extended periods of time (U.S. Department of Health and Human Services, 1990).

HEALTH PSYCHOLOGISTS AND THE TREATMENT OF SUBSTANCE USE PROBLEMS

Unfortunately psychologists, like physicians, generally have not become involved in the treatment of substance use problems. In fact, the American Psychological Association (APA) existed for more than 100 years before the creation of its Division on Addictions in 1994. Before the recent establishment of APA's College of Professional Psychology, there had been no mechanism for certifying psychologists to treat addictive behaviors. Furthermore, few doctoral training programs have provided even minimal training regarding substance use problems.

According to Matarazzo (1980), health psychology is primarily concerned with the "promotion and maintenance of health, the prevention and treatment of illness, and the identification of etiologic and diagnostic correlates" (p. 815). Given this definition, health psychologists should be ideally suited to provide services to individuals with substance use problems. Psychologists interested in addressing these problems will find abundant opportunities in primary care medical settings. Such opportunities may provide an important niche for health psychologists competing in an increasingly competitive market.

Liese and Chiauzzi (1995) listed six categories of activities for addressing substance use problems: (a) screening, (b) conceptualization, (c) assessing motivation to change, (d) intervention, (e) consultation and referral, and (f) follow-up and relapse prevention. It is strongly recommended that health psychologists get involved in the full range of substance use treatment activities.

Screening for Substance Use Problems

Substance use problems may be difficult to detect because of their insidious onset and associated social stigma. Screening is essential; substance use problems that are not detected are not likely to be treated. The best strategy for detecting substance use problems is to simply ask, "Have you ever had problems with drug or alcohol use?" followed by questions about recency, quantity, and frequency of substance use (Cyr & Wartman, 1988). Given the profound health consequences of substance use problems, it is imperative that *all* psychologists ask their patients about substance use.

Several standardized screening instruments also exist for the initial evaluation of persons with substance use disorders. The CAGE (Ewing, 1984) is among the most commonly cited screening instruments for alcohol problems. CAGE is an acronym for the following four questions:

1. Have you ever felt the need to Cut down on your drinking?
2. Have people ever Annoyed you by criticism of your drinking?
3. Have you ever felt Guilty about your drinking?
4. Have you ever taken a morning Eye-opener to steady your nerves or get rid of a hangover?

These four questions can be administered in less than a minute and consistently have established high sensitivity (80% range) and specificity

(85% range). Individuals who endorse two or more items are likely to have alcohol use problems.

The Michigan Alcoholism Screening Test (MAST; Selzer, 1971) is another important screening instrument. The MAST consists of 24 questions and has a demonstrated sensitivity of 90% and a specificity of 80% (Selzer, 1971). A shortened version of the MAST (SMAST; Selzer, Vinokur, & van Rooijen, 1975) consists of 13 items. The SMAST has a demonstrated sensitivity of 70% and a specificity of 80%. Regardless of the specific method used, psychologists are strongly encouraged to screen for substance use problems.

Conceptualizing Individuals With Substance Use Problems

The case conceptualization (Beck, Wright, Newman, & Liese, 1993) involves the process of gathering data to establish an accurate and comprehensive understanding of individuals with substance use problems. The case conceptualization should include background information, presenting problem and current functioning, psychiatric diagnoses, developmental profile (including family history of substance use problems), and cognitive–behavioral profile. The case conceptualization is essential for effective treatment planning (Liese, 1994; Liese & Beck, 1996; Liese & Franz, 1996).

The fourth edition of the *Diagnostic and Statistical Manual of Mental Disorders* (DSM–IV; American Psychiatric Association, 1994) provides well-validated diagnostic criteria for diagnosing and conceptualizing psychiatric and substance use problems. The DSM–IV distinguishes between substance abuse and dependence. *Abuse* is defined as a maladaptive pattern of use leading to significant impairment or distress (e.g., failure to fulfill responsibilities and legal, social, or interpersonal problems). *Dependence* is more severe than abuse, often involving tolerance, withdrawal, use of increasing amounts of a substance, and persistent desire for a substance despite significant substance-related problems. These two categories of the DSM–IV, however, may exclude certain individuals with mild or idiosyncratic substance use problems. In addition to these two categories, some authors (e.g., Bradley, 1994) have proposed that substance use problems be conceptualized on a continuum from *none* or *mild* to *severe*.

Numerous methods are available for assessing substance use problems. Most rely on self-report instruments or structured interviews; however, reports of significant others (i.e., *collaterals*) and biochemical tests may also be useful. Sobell, Toneatto, and Sobell (1994) provided an excellent review of the most practical, useful methods for assessing substance use disorders. They outlined six areas for assessment: (a) recent substance use, (b) antecedents and consequences of use, (c) substance use history, (d) psychiatric comorbidity or other life problems, (e) medical problems, and (f) barriers or potential barriers to change. Health psychologists are encouraged to become familiar with these assessment methods.

Assessing Motivation to Change

Despite well-known medical, legal, and psychological consequences, millions of people persist in their cigarette smoking, excessive alcohol consumption, and use of illicit drugs. Prochaska, DiClemente, and Norcross (1992) have made an enormous contribution to the field of addictions with their conceptual model for understanding the complex process of change (i.e., the stages-of-change model). In their model, Prochaska et al. distinguish among five levels of motivation: *precontemplation, contemplation, preparation, action*, and *maintenance*. Individuals who are least motivated to change are understood to be in the precontemplation stage. In the contemplation stage, individuals have begun to admit that they may have problems. Those in preparation have concluded that they have problems and plan to make changes to resolve these problems. In the action stage, individuals have recently begun to modify their undesired behaviors. And in the maintenance stage, individuals have successfully sustained changes for at least 6 months.

Individuals' motivation levels should largely influence the types of interventions selected for them. After determining motivation to change, the psychologist's challenge is to facilitate movement toward the next stage of change. For example, relatively unmotivated individuals (i.e., precontemplators) are likely to benefit most from nonjudgmental, empathic listening that focuses attention on problems associated with substance use. In contrast, individuals who have recently and willingly made changes might benefit from direct advice about how to maintain changes. The work of Miller and Rollnick (1991) has become extremely important as a model for applying the stages of change. Their text, *Motivational Interviewing*, serves as an excellent manual for psychologists assisting individuals at all stages of change.

Intervention

Treatment for substance use problems may be provided on an inpatient or outpatient basis, brief or long-term, individual or group, oriented toward insight or change, structured or unstructured, and focused on the individual or on the family. Theoretical approaches guiding treatment vary widely, and they include concepts and strategies from cognitive, behavioral, psychodynamic, medical, and spiritual models. Rotgers, Keller, and Morganstern (1996) recently edited a text that describes the theories and techniques of five intervention models: 12-step treatment (e.g., Alcoholics Anonymous), psychoanalytic therapy, family therapy, behavioral therapy, and motivational interviewing. Beck and his colleagues (Beck et al., 1993; Liese, 1994; Liese & Beck, 1996; Liese & Franz, 1996) have applied cognitive therapy to the treatment of addictive disorders.

Presently, there is not unequivocal evidence for the efficacy of any one substance use treatment approach over the others. Large-scale clinical trials, sponsored by the National Institute on Alcohol Abuse and Alcoholism and the National Institute on Drug Abuse, are under way to test the efficacy of the most promising approaches. Health psychologists are encouraged to critically evaluate the substance use treatment literature in order to become knowledgeable about the most effective strategies.

Consultation and Referral

Consultation and referral are extraordinarily important activities in managing individuals with substance use problems. Health psychologists addressing these problems may serve as consultants *to* other service providers, or they may request consultation *from* other service providers. For example, a health psychologist might conduct a psychological evaluation on a heavy drinker referred *by* a physician. That psychologist might also refer a patient with a substance use problem *to* the same physician for the medical management of depression.

In order for health psychologists to be effective in addressing substance use disorders, it is essential that they be familiar with treatment options available in the community. For example, the levels of care for substance use treatment can range from relatively brief outpatient treatment to extremely intensive inpatient treatment. The health psychologist wishing to refer a patient with a substance use problem needs to accurately understand these levels of care, as well as the types of clinicians that provide such care.

Support groups (e.g., Alcoholics Anonymous, Rational Recovery, Moderation Management, and S.M.A.R.T. Recovery) provide important services to individuals with substance use problems. These groups are readily available and free of charge. Some offer training in various interpersonal and introPersonal skills, whereas others provide primarily social support. Again, it is essential for health psychologists to be knowledgeable about these services and to encourage patients with substance use problems to use them.

Follow-Up and Relapse Prevention

Relapse is extremely common in persons recovering from substance use problems (Marlatt & Gordon, 1985). After treatment has been initiated and change has occurred, it is important for health psychologists to follow up and offer relapse-prevention services.

Marlatt and Gordon (1985), in their classic text, provide a comprehensive review of the relapse process. Relapse prevention efforts generally focus on eight major areas: (a) identification of high-risk situations, (b) understanding relapse as a process rather than as an event, (c) development of a supportive network, (d) coping with craving and pressures to use substances, (e) maintaining emotional balance, (f) clarifying maladaptive thinking that may trigger usage, (g) altering or eliminating environmental cues for substance use, and (h) coping with stressful life events.

SUMMARY AND RECOMMENDATIONS

Millions of Americans use psychoactive substances in ways that cause them substantial harm. Unfortunately, only a small proportion of these individuals receive formal help for their substance use problems. In this chapter, we have described the scope of substance use, and we have argued that health psychologists should be addressing substance use problems, because these problems have profound implications for health. The following are five specific recommendations for health psychologists:

1. Learn as much as possible about the medical and psychological aspects of substance use and keep current with the ever-evolving addiction literature.
2. Learn about the full spectrum of treatments for substance use problems. Become familiar with popular modalities (e.g., 12-step programs) as well as psychologically based treatments (e.g., cognitive–behavioral models).
3. Identify and address substance use problems in "traditional" psychotherapeutic settings (e.g., private practice). At the very least, reliably ask all new patients about their substance use attitudes and behaviors.
4. Market psychological services to primary care physicians who see a large volume of patients with substance use problems. Learn about their needs vis-à-vis the psychological care of their addicted patients. Collaborate with primary care physicians by providing consultation services to their patients. Use primary care physicians as consultants.

5. Participate in professional activities related to substance use problems. Join the APA's Division (50) on Addictions. Attend continuing education programs on substance use sponsored by the APA and other professional organizations. Consider proficiency certification in treating substance use disorders by the recently formed APA College of Professional Psychology.

In 1980, Matarazzo declared that "health psychology and behavioral health appear to be ideas whose time has come" (p. 816). Today it seems that the marriage between health psychology and substance use treatment is an idea whose time has come.

REFERENCES

American Psychiatric Association. (1994). *Diagnostic and statistical manual of mental disorders* (4th ed.). Washington, DC: Author.

Barker, L. R., & Whitfield, C. L. (1991). Alcoholism. In L. R. Barker, J. R. Burton, & P. D. Zieve (Eds.), *Principles of ambulatory medicine* (3rd ed., pp. 245–277). Baltimore: Williams & Wilkins.

Beck, A. T., Wright, F. D., Newman, C. F., & Liese, B. S. (1993). *Cognitive therapy of substance abuse*. New York: Guilford Press.

Bien, T. H., Miller, W. R., & Tonigan, J. S. (1993). Brief interventions for alcohol problems: A review. *Addiction, 88,* 315–336.

Bowen, O. R., & Sammons, J. H. (1988). The alcohol-abusing patient: A challenge to the profession. *Journal of the American Medical Association, 260,* 2267–2270.

Bradley, K. A. (1994). The primary care practitioner's role in the prevention and management of alcohol problems. *Alcohol Health and Research World, 18,* 97–104.

Bullock, K. D., Reed, R. J., & Grant, I. (1992). Reduced mortality risk in alcoholics who achieve long-term abstinence. *Journal of the American Medical Association, 267,* 668–672.

Byrd, J. C. (1992). Environmental tobacco smoke: Medical and legal issues. *Medical Clinics of North America, 76,* 377–378.

Chappel, J. N. (1992). Attitudes toward the treatment of substance abusers. In J. G. Lowinson, P. Ruiz, R. B. Millman, & J. G. Langrod (Eds.), *Substance abuse: A comprehensive textbook* (pp. 983–996). Baltimore: Williams & Wilkins.

Cyr, M. G., & Wartman, S. A. (1988). The effectiveness of routine screening questions in the detection of alcoholism. *Journal of the American Medical Association, 259,* 51–54.

Delbanco, T. L. (1992). Patients who drink too much: Where are their doctors? *Journal of the American Medical Association, 267,* 702–703.

D'Lugoff, B., & Hawthorne, J. (1991). Use and abuse of illicit drugs and substance abuse. In L. R. Barker, J. R. Burton, & P. D. Zieve (Eds.), *Principles of ambulatory medicine* (3rd ed., pp. 278–290). Baltimore: Williams & Wilkins.

Ewing, J. A. (1984). Detecting alcoholism: The CAGE questionnaire. *Journal of the American Medical Association, 252,* 1905–1907.

Friedman, H. S. (1990). Alcohol and hypertension. *Alcohol Health and Research World, 14,* 313–319.

Goodwin, D. W. (1981). *Alcoholism: The facts.* New York: Oxford University Press.

Group for the Advancement of Psychiatry. (1991). Substance abuse disorder: A psychiatric priority. *American Journal of Psychiatry, 148,* 1291–1300.

Hanna, E. Z. (1991). Attitudes toward problem drinkers, revisited: Patient–therapist factors contributing to the differential treatment of patients with alcohol problems. *Alcoholism: Clinical and Experimental Research, 15,* 927–931.

Holbrook, J. H. (1991). Tobacco. In J. D. Wilson, E. Baunwald, K. J. Isselbacher, R. A. Petersdorf, A. S. Fauci, & K. R. Root (Eds.), *Harrison's principles of internal medicine* (12th ed., pp. 2158–2161). New York: McGraw-Hill.

Holden, C. (1985). The neglected disease in medical education. *Science, 229,* 741–742.

Liese, B. S. (1994). Brief therapy, crisis intervention and the cognitive therapy of substance abuse. *Crisis Intervention, 1,* 11–29.

Liese, B. S., & Beck, A. T. (1996). Back to basics: Fundamental cognitive therapy skills for keeping drug-dependent individuals in treatment. In J. J. Boren, L. S. Onken, & J. D. Blaine (Eds.), *Beyond the therapeutic alliance: Keeping drug dependent individuals in treatment* (National Institute on Drug Abuse Research Monograph, pp. 210–235). Rockville, MD: National Institute on Drug Abuse.

Liese, B. S., & Chiauzzi, E. (1995). Alcohol and drug abuse. *Home study self-assessment program* (Monograph No. 189). Kansas City, MO: American Academy of Family Physicians.

Liese, B. S., & Franz, R. A. (1996). Treating substance use disorders with cognitive therapy: Lessons learned and implication for the future. In P. M. Salkovskis (Ed.), *Frontiers of cognitive therapy* (pp. 470–508). New York: Guilford Press.

Maly, R. C. (1993). Early recognition of chemical dependence. *Primary Care, 20,* 33–50.

Marlatt, G. A., & Gordon, J. R. (Eds.). (1985). *Relapse prevention: Maintenance strategies in the treatment of addictive behavior.* New York: Guilford Press.

Matarazzo, J. D. (1980). Behavioral health and behavioral medicine: Frontiers for a new health psychology. *American Psychologist, 35,* 807–817.

McBride, P. E. (1992). The health consequences of smoking: Cardiovascular diseases. *Medical Clinics of North America, 76,* 333–353.

McKenzie, R. G., & Kipke, M. D. (1992). Substance use and abuse. In S. B. Friedman, M. Fisher, & S. K. Schonberg (Eds.), *Comprehensive adolescent health care* (pp. 765–786). St. Louis, MO: Quality Medical Publications.

Mendelson, J. H. (1991). Commonly abused drugs. In J. D. Wilson, E. Baunwald, K. J. Isselbacher, R. A. Petersdorf, A. S. Fauci, & K. R. Root (Eds.), *Harrison's principles of internal medicine* (12th ed., pp. 2155–2158). New York: McGraw-Hill.

Miller, W. R., & Rollnick, S. (1991). *Motivational interviewing: Preparing people to change addictive behavior.* New York: Guilford Press.

Newcomb, P. A., & Carbone, P. P. (1992). The health consequences of smoking: Cancer. *Medical Clinics of North America, 76,* 305–331.

Prochaska, J. O., DiClemente, C. C., & Norcross, J. C. (1992). In search of how people change: Applications to addictive behaviors. *American Psychologist, 47,* 1102–1114.

Pursch, J. A. (1978). Physicians' attitudinal changes in alcoholism. *Alcoholism: Clinical and Experimental Research, 2,* 358–361.

Regier, D. A., Farmer, M. E., Rae, D. S., Locke, B. Z., Keith, S. J., Judd, L. L., & Goodwin, F. K. (1990). Comorbidity of mental disorders with alcohol and other drug abuse: Results of the Epidemiologic Catchment Area (ECA) study. *Journal of the American Medical Association, 264,* 2511–2518.

Regier, D. A., Narrow, W. E., Rae, D. S., Manderscheid, R. W., Locke, B. Z., & Goodwin, F. K. (1993). The de facto US mental and addictive disorders service system: Epidemiologic Catchment Area prospective 1-year prevalence rates of disorders and services. *Archives of General Psychiatry, 50,* 85–94.

Ross, H. E., Glaser, F. B., & Germanson, T. (1988). The prevalence of psychiatric disorders in patients with alcohol and other drug problems. *Archives of General Psychiatry, 45,* 1023–1031.

Rotgers, F., Keller, D. S., & Morganstern, J. (Eds.). (1996). *Treating substance abuse.* New York: Guilford Press.

Rounsaville, B. J., Weissman, M. M., Kleber, H., & Wilber, C. (1982). Heterogeneity of psychiatric diagnosis in treated opiate addicts. *Archives of General Psychiatry, 39,* 161–166.

Schuckit, M. A. (1991). Alcohol and alcoholism. In J. D. Wilson, E. Baunwald, K. J. Isselbacher, R. A. Petersdorf, A. S. Fauci, & K. R. Root (Eds.), *Harrison's principles of internal medicine* (12th ed., pp. 2146–2151). New York: McGraw-Hill.

Schulz, J. E. (1993). Illicit drugs of abuse. *Primary Care: Clinics in Office Practice, 20,* 221–230.

Schwartz, J. L. (1992). Methods of smoking cessation. *Medical Clinics of North America, 76,* 451–476.

Selzer, M. L. (1971). The Michigan Alcoholism Screening Test: The quest for a new diagnostic instrument. *American Journal of Psychiatry, 127,* 1653–1658.

Selzer, M. L., Vinokur, A., & van Rooijen, L. (1975). A self-administered Short Michigan Alcoholism Screening Test (SMAST). *Journal of Studies on Alcohol, 36,* 117–126.

Sherman, C. B. (1992). The health consequences of smoking: Pulmonary diseases. *Medical Clinics of North America, 76,* 355–375.

Sobell, L. C., Toneatto, T., & Sobell, M. B. (1994). Behavioral assessment and treatment planning for alcohol, tobacco, and other drug problems: Current status with an emphasis on clinical applications. *Behavior Therapy, 25,* 533–580.

Substance Abuse and Mental Health Services Administration. (1993). *National household survey on drug abuse: Main findings 1991* (DHHS Publication No. SMA 93-1980). Washington, DC: Government Printing Office.

U.S. Department of Health and Human Services. (1990). *The health benefits of smoking cessation* (DHHS Publication No. CDC 90-8416). Washington, DC: Government Printing Office.

14

ATTENTION DEFICIT HYPERACTIVITY DISORDER AND LEARNING DISABILITIES IN THE PEDIATRICIAN'S OFFICE

JAN L. CULBERTSON

Attention deficit hyperactivity disorder (ADHD) and learning disabilities are two of the most common neurodevelopmental disorders of childhood, and children with these disorders present frequently to the pediatrician for diagnosis and treatment. It is common for specialists in developmental and behavioral pediatrics or child neurology to indicate that referrals for ADHD now total 50% to 75% of their practices (B. A. Shaywitz & Shaywitz, 1991). Physician involvement in the management of more chronic handicapping conditions, such as learning disabilities, has also increased dramatically in conjunction with the decrease in acute, life-threatening illnesses among the pediatric population (S. E. Shaywitz, Shaywitz, Fletcher, & Escobar, 1990).

Not only the specialists, however, are involved in management of ADHD and learning disabilities. Both the growing movement toward managed care and the increased focus on primary care are leading primary care pediatricians to attempt to diagnose and treat ADHD and learning disabilities in their offices rather than refer to specialists. With capitation, there is often a financial disincentive to refer to specialists, such as psychologists, who can provide a more comprehensive and appropriate level of care for ADHD and learning disabilities. The disincentive for referral sets the stage for possible misdiagnosis, failure to diagnose, or inappropriate management, due to the pediatrician's often cursory training with regard to ADHD and learning disabilities. At this time in our history, more than ever before, there is a need to explore ways in which pediatricians and psychologists can work together to provide optimal care for children with these two common childhood disorders.

A pediatrician's office often is the point of entry to the health care system for parents who have questions about their children's behavioral and learning problems as well as their medical problems. There are many possible reasons why questions about ADHD and learning disabilities are so often presented to a medical doctor rather than a psychologist. For instance, the pediatrician is one of the first professionals with whom parents develop a relationship, and this relationship may extend over many years as the pediatrician follows a child's growth and development. The physician–parent relationship often results in a high level of trust that leads parents to bring even nonmedical concerns about their child to the office visit. Second, parents have greater access to pediatricians than to psychologists and, therefore, become accustomed to bringing their concerns to physicians before seeking out other professionals. Pediatricians often are seen as the professionals who coordinate referrals to other professionals when needed. Finally, there may be less stigma associated with having a medical problem than a mental or behavioral problem, leading parents to try to "medicalize" their child's behavioral and learning problems. The implication is that if the child's problem is medical, it may not reflect as negatively on the parents' genetic endowment or their parenting practices.

For these reasons, psychologists are, to a large degree, dependent on pediatricians to screen for ADHD and learning disabilities and to make referrals. This chapter explores the scope of the problem, as to prevalence of ADHD and learning disabilities, review of diagnostic and management approaches that represent the current state of our knowledge about best practice methods, and a discussion that contrasts and compares the roles of pediatricians and psychologists in the diagnosis and treatment of both disorders. Suggestions are made for collaboration between psychologists and pediatricians, with a focus on contributing their respective knowledge and skills to achieve optimal care for children with ADHD and or learning disabilities.

PREVALENCE OF ADHD AND LEARNING DISABILITIES

Both ADHD and learning disabilities are disorders that occur commonly in the general population. Prevalence estimates for ADHD among school-age children range from 3% to 5% (Barkley, 1990), and estimates for learning disabilities range from 4% to 6% (Chalfant, 1989; Hynd & Cohen, 1983). Both disorders are being diagnosed with increasing frequency as public awareness increases and as public agencies (such as schools) provide both recognition and appropriate educational services for these disorders. The number of students identified as having a learning disability tripled between 1976 and 1982 (Reynolds, 1990), and students with learning disabilities now constitute about 50% of the children who are served in special education programs in public schools (U.S. Department of Education, 1991). Attention deficit hyperactivity disorder also is being diagnosed more frequently than a decade ago (Safer & Krager, 1994; B. A. Shaywitz & Shaywitz, 1991), and the concomitant use of psychostimulant medication as the treatment of choice for this disorder is on the rise. A recent survey of Baltimore County, Maryland, schools revealed a dramatic increase in stimulant medication use among public school students, from 1.07% in 1971 to 3.58% in 1993 (Safer & Krager, 1994), with the greatest increase being at the secondary level.

Given the prevalence rates of ADHD and learning disabilities, these disorders quite likely make up a significant percentage of the referrals to pediatricians. This underscores the need to improve pediatricians' awareness of appropriate diagnostic and treatment approaches for these disorders and to highlight the role that psychologists can play in managing patients with ADHD or learning disabilities.

DIAGNOSIS AND MANAGEMENT OF ADHD

Recently published *Diagnostic and Statistical Manual of Mental Disorders* (DSM–IV; American Psychiatric Association, 1994) nosology for ADHD recognizes the empirical support for three primary subtypes: predominantly inattentive type, predominantly hyperactive–impulsive type, and combined type. The essential feature of ADHD is a "persistent pattern of inattention and/or hyperactivity–impulsivity that is more frequent and severe than is typically observed in individuals at a comparable level of development" (American Psychiatric Association, 1994, p. 78). Children with ADHD have been characterized as having deficient rule-governed behavior, behavioral disinhibition, and variability in task performance, in addition to the primary symptoms of inattention and excessive motor activity (Barkley, 1990).

The diagnosis of ADHD is made primarily by history and observation rather than by diagnostic tests. This has led many pediatricians to view ADHD as a diagnosis that can be made in a brief office visit merely by questioning the mother and observing the child. In fact, only the most severely hyperactive and impulsive children with ADHD are likely to squirm and fidget in the doctor's presence, perhaps due to illness or fear of a painful medical procedure if they "misbehave." Many children can suppress their overactive and impulsive behavior for a brief period of time or in settings where adults are closely watching their behavior. The constraints inherent in a physician's office visit raise the risk of the pediatrician misdiagnosing or failing to diagnose ADHD when it is present.

Diagnosis of ADHD is made even more complex and time-consuming by developmental influences that can affect the symptom picture and by the possible co-occurrence of other disorders that present in a fashion similar to ADHD. The professional must understand these developmental processes and must conduct an assessment that is detailed enough to rule in or rule out comorbid disorders, to develop an effective treatment plan. Failure to do so results in increased risk for misdiagnosis or underdiagnosis of ADHD. Several factors that complicate the diagnostic picture are discussed in the following sections.

Developmental Influences on Symptom Presentation

The presence of developmental factors can lead to misdiagnosis if care is not taken to obtain a detailed clinical history and chronology of symptom presentation. For instance, about 40% of children up to 4 years of age are considered to have significant symptoms of hyperactivity and inattention for brief periods (3 to 6 months), but few go on to have ADHD (Palfrey, Levine, Walker, & Sullivan, 1985). Young children whose symptoms persist for 12 months or longer are at greater risk to have ADHD than those whose symptoms are of briefer duration (Campbell, 1990; Campbell & Ewing, 1990). To distinguish normal developmental patterns from clinically significant symptoms of ADHD, professionals must consider both the duration and severity of symptoms to obtain an accurate diagnosis. Similar arguments can be made for developmental influences during adolescent years, when milder presentations of symptoms may still interfere significantly with functioning. Adolescents may no longer display the "motor-driven" quality that identifies their younger cohorts with ADHD, but a careful interview may reveal that adolescents continue to experience a subjective feeling of restlessness and significant problems with attentional focus (Brown & Borden, 1986). Both the age and developmental stage of the child must be considered, to make an accurate diagnosis.

Comorbid Disorders That Masquerade as ADHD or Complicate the Presenting Picture

ADHD has been subtyped not only according to the dimensions of inattention, hyperactivity, and impulsivity but also according to the presence or absence of learning and behavioral problems that are often comorbid with ADHD. For instance, the comorbidity between ADHD and learning disabilities has been estimated to range from 15% to 38%, depending on the stringency of diagnostic criteria used to define the learning disability (Semrud-Clikeman et al., 1992). Various researchers have reported that 50% to 65% of clinic-referred children with ADHD also meet diagnostic criteria for oppositional–defiant disorder (Barkley, DuPaul, & McMurray, 1990; Barkley, Fischer, Edelbrock, & Smallish, 1990; Loney & Milich, 1982). Herein lies one of the problems with diagnosis of ADHD in the pediatrician's office. A brief office visit and a screening approach to diagnosis are not conducive to making fine differential diagnoses among the various disorders that may be comorbid with ADHD.

Need for a Broad-Based Assessment

Accurate diagnosis is facilitated by use of multiple assessment methods, gathering information from multiple informants, and demonstrating that symptoms are present across multiple settings, as suggested by Shelton and Barkley (1993). The multimethod component refers to the range of assessment approaches needed to provide the best overview of the child's functioning:

1. Direct observation of the child (e.g., in the classroom, on the playground, on the bus, at home, and during structured and unstructured activities). Direct observations in the clinic setting can be done by using one of the observational paradigms devised for children suspected of having ADHD, such as the Restricted Academic Situation Observation (Barkley, 1990) or the Child Behavior Checklist—Direct Observation Form (Achenbach, 1986).
2. Use of age-normed behavioral checklists, completed by at least two or three informants, such as the parent, teacher, child self-report, or day care teacher. These checklists provide a yardstick for determining if the child's symptom severity is excessive for his or her age or developmental level. If the child's mental functioning is below an IQ of 85, mental age comparisons rather than chronological age comparisons should be used. Use of a clinical cutoff at the

97th percentile (2 standard deviations above the mean) on normed behavioral rating scales will identify children whose symptoms are more deviant from the norm, are likely to persist for several years, and will be more predictive of later adjustment (DuPaul, 1990).

3. Review of primary symptoms of ADHD to determine not only their presence but also their severity. Use of a structured-interview format based on *DSM–IV* diagnostic criteria will be useful.

4. Detailed clinical interview to obtain history and to screen for symptoms of comorbid disorders (e.g., learning disability, oppositional–defiant disorder, conduct disorder, internalizing disorders).

5. Laboratory measures of vigilance and impulsivity, to refine the observations of the primary symptoms of ADHD. Measures such as the continuous performance test paradigm from the Gordon Diagnostic System (Gordon & Mettelman, 1988) or the Conners' Continuous Performance Test computer program (Conners, 1994) might be used. The continuous performance test laboratory measures have been shown empirically to discriminate between children with and without ADHD (Barkley, DuPaul, & McMurray, 1990).

The assessment components just discussed would constitute a basic evaluation for ADHD. If comorbid disorders, such as learning disabilities, were suspected, a more detailed psychoeducational evaluation might be necessary, including intellectual, academic achievement, and perceptual processing measures. Likewise, if oppositional–defiant disorder is suspected, further assessment of the nature and severity of the behavioral disturbance must be done. A psychologist also might opt to provide a brief therapeutic intervention, such as parent–child interaction therapy (Eyberg & Boggs, 1989), to address relational and behavior management issues while observing changes in the ADHD symptoms as a function of treatment of the oppositional behavior problems. Symptoms of an oppositional disorder may include agitation and overactivity that are misconstrued as ADHD; if this is the case, these symptoms often diminish or disappear during and after a treatment program designed to address the behavior disorder, especially in preschool children.

Thus, the multimethod, multi-informant, multisetting assessment will provide the basis for a more accurate diagnosis than assessments based on more narrow parameters, as are often used by pediatricians. However, the pediatrician contributes important medical information as part of the diagnostic workup and management of children with suspected ADHD, as described in the next section.

Medical Consultation With ADHD

Pediatricians provide helpful medical information through reviewing a child's genetic background, pre- and perinatal events, and developmental and medical history, as well as the child's current health, nutritional status, and sensorimotor development (Barkley, 1990). The pediatric exam can rule out medical conditions that present with symptoms similar to ADHD, such as thyroid dysfunction (Weiss, Stein, Trommer, & Refetoff, 1993) and adrenal overactivity. Likewise, the medical examination will assess for associated soft neurological signs, motor incoordination (Barkley, DuPaul, & McMurray 1990; McMahon & Greenberg, 1977; S. E. Shaywitz & Shaywitz, 1988; Szatmari, Offord, & Boyle, 1989b), enuresis or encopresis (Stewart, Pitts, Craig, & Dieruf, 1966), sleep problems (Kaplan, McNichol, Conte, & Moghadam, 1987; Stewart et al., 1966; Trommer, Hoeppner, Rosenberg, Armstrong, & Rothstein, 1988), otitis media (Mitchell, Aman, Turbott, & Manku, 1987), and asthma and allergies (Hartsough & Lambert, 1985; Szatmari, Offord, & Boyle, 1989a), all of which have been reported to occur at a higher rate in children with ADHD. The physician also will obtain a thorough individual and family medical history, to determine the presence of tics or Tourette's syndrome, seizure disorder, and other medical problems that might contraindicate the use of psychostimulant medications. Finally, if a trial of stimulant medication is appropriate, the pediatrician plays an important role in monitoring the dosage level and effectiveness of the medication while remaining alert for side effects (such as appetite suppression, weight loss, or liver dysfunction) that might be harmful. Laboratory studies, such as blood work, urinalysis, chromosome studies, electroencephalograms, evoked potential studies, magnetic resonance imaging, or computerized axial tomograms, are not used routinely in the evaluation of children with ADHD but are used only if the physical exam or medical history suggest that these diagnostic studies are necessary to determine the presence of a treatable medical problem (Barkley, 1990).

DIAGNOSIS AND MANAGEMENT OF LEARNING DISABILITIES

In contrast to the diagnosis of ADHD, which depends largely on history and observations, the diagnosis of learning disability is established on the basis of performance on tests of ability and achievement. This diagnostic process requires specialized knowledge about cognitive, linguistic, and perceptual processing abilities. Learning disabilities have been conceptualized as an inability to learn in children who otherwise have normal or above normal intellectual ability (B. A. Shaywitz & Shaywitz, 1991). The definition of learning disabilities in the Education for All Handicapped Act of 1975 remains the most widely accepted. According to this law, diagnosis of learning disabilities is based on whether a child does not achieve commensurate with his or her own age and ability when provided with appropriate educational experiences and whether the child has a severe discrepancy between achievement and intellectual ability in one of seven areas, including listening, thinking, speaking, reading, writing, spelling, or doing mathematical calculations. Most state guidelines for implementing this law require that the professional demonstrate a child's failure to achieve; demonstrate the presence of psychological processing disorders that are presumed to underlie academic learning; rule out several exclusionary criteria (i.e., mental retardation; educational, economic, or cultural disadvantage; or emotional disturbance); and demonstrate a severe discrepancy between achievement and intellectual ability in one of the seven areas listed earlier (Chalfant, 1984). Although there is much controversy about the definition and diagnostic criteria for learning disabilities, it is basically a psychoeducational rather than a medical diagnosis.

Present-day conceptualization of learning disabilities suggests that it is a heterogeneous set of disorders with different subtypes, based on either the underlying processing deficits (e.g., linguistic, neurocognitive, or visuospatial reasoning deficits) or the clinical presentation of symptoms (e.g., reading, mathematics, written language, or social emotional deficits). To date, over 100 different subtyping classification models have been published based on achievement, neurocognitive, or neurolinguistic variables (Hooper & Willis, 1989). Assessment of children suspected of having a learning disability must include measures that carefully examine the pattern of strengths and deficits in information processing, to determine the subtype of that child's learning deficits. A clear delineation of the learning disability subtype provides a foundation for development of an appropriate educational plan and curriculum for each child.

From the foregoing discussion, it is clear that diagnosis of a learning disability requires detailed evaluation of a child's intellectual, academic, linguistic, perceptual processing, and perceptual–motor abilities to determine whether there is a learning disability, what processes underlie the learning disability, and how to intervene. It is not sufficient merely to establish an IQ–achievement discrepancy; rather, the psychologist must also examine a range of information-processing abilities to determine a profile of the child's strengths and weaknesses. Although pediatricians are an important member of the multidisciplinary team of professionals needed to assess for a learning disability, their assessment methods are not sufficient for making a diagnosis or providing the information necessary to develop an appropriate educational intervention plan.

Pediatricians play an important role in ruling out basic sensory acuity deficits before psychoeducational evaluation and assessing the integrity of the child's motor system. Pediatricians also provide important etiological information about children who have a learning disability, through review of pre- and perinatal risk factors and other medical factors that can have an impact on learning and development. The pediatrician who is aware of the definition and primary symptoms of learning disabilities can facilitate a referral for evaluation and can act as an advocate for the child and family with the school system. The pediatrician provides unique and important information to the diagnostic process, but the primary contributor to this process is the psychologist.

PSYCHOLOGISTS' ROLE IN COLLABORATING WITH PEDIATRICIANS ABOUT ADHD AND LEARNING DISABILITIES

Psychologists who develop a collaborative relationship with pediatricians may offer several types of training or provide information that can facilitate the management of children with ADHD or learning disabilities:

1. Provide a workshop or brief training sessions about normal child development and developmental influences on the symptom presentation of ADHD and learning disabilities.
2. Provide training about the primary symptoms of ADHD and learning disabilities, contrasted with common comorbid disorders. The primary symptoms may be condensed into a brief checklist or questionnaire that can be used readily in the office.
3. Offer training on use of appropriate screening measures for ADHD and learning disabilities and suggest decision rules about when it is appropriate to refer for further evaluation based on the screening results. For instance, screening measures such as the Conners parent and teacher questionnaires (Conners, 1989) are useful for ADHD, and an academic-screening test such as the Wide Range Achievement Test—3 (Wilkinson, 1993) is useful for screening academic progress in reading decoding, mathematics calculation, and spelling. Training may be provided to the pediatrician or to other professionals in the pediatric office (e.g., nurse practitioners) in the use of these measures or symptom checklists. Psychologists should include information about how to order appropriate screening tests for office practice.

4. Provide a roadmap for how to obtain essential information through the school system. For instance, inform the pediatrician about who should be contacted to determine if a child already has had psychometric assessment in the school system or if the child is currently receiving special education services. If the child is receiving special education, explain how the pediatrician can obtain a copy of the child's psychoeducational test results and the individualized educational plan records that detail the special education category and placement decisions regarding the child.

5. Provide suggestions for when it is appropriate to refer a child for further assessment and which professionals would be most helpful to answer specific referral questions (e.g., a speech/language pathologist may provide important information regarding the impact of language deficits on the child's learning disability).

6. Psychologists also can play an active role in forming alliances with pediatricians in the community for informal information sharing, cross-referral, and assistance in management (particularly with learning disabilities and ADHD). For instance, children with ADHD often respond better to a dual intervention that combines psychostimulant medication and behavioral treatment (e.g., parent-training programs or individual or group counseling for the child). The dual intervention approach is best carried out with collaboration between the pediatrician and psychologist.

7. Provide training about the rights and privileges afforded children and parents under the current special education and disability laws, such as the Individuals With Disabilities Education Act of 1990 or the Americans With Disabilities Act of 1990. Encourage the pediatrician to be an advocate for the child and family through providing information about rights to a free and appropriate education and the availability of potential diagnostic and treatment resources.

In addition to these factors, it is helpful for psychologists to remain aware of the contributions that pediatricians make in terms of their knowledge about medical aspects of learning disabilities and ADHD, their longitudinal knowledge about the child and family, and their probable rapport with the child and family. As mentioned earlier, parents often perceive less of a stigma in seeing a medical doctor compared with a psychologist. The pediatrician can be helpful in defusing that stigma associated with a possible mental or behavioral problem and facilitate the family in following through on the referral.

In conclusion, the trend toward greater involvement of primary care pediatricians in managing disorders such as learning disabilities and ADHD in the primary health care arena is of concern due to the increased risk for misdiagnosis or failure to diagnose these complex disorders. However, psychologists can and must make efforts to build the alliances that make such a trend workable and, most of all, provide the most optimal level of care for children and their families.

REFERENCES

Achenbach, T. M. (1986). *Manual for the Child Behavior Checklist—Direct Observation Form.* Burlington: University of Vermont, Department of Psychiatry.

American Psychiatric Association. (1994). *Diagnostic and statistical manual of mental disorders* (4th ed.). Washington, DC: Author.

Americans With Disabilities Act of 1990, 42 U.S.C.A. §12101 *et seq.* (West, 1993).

Barkley, R. A. (1990). *Attention deficit hyperactivity disorder.* New York: Guilford Press.

Barkley, R. A., DuPaul, G. J., & McMurray, M. B. (1990). Comprehensive evaluation of attention deficit disorder with or without hyperactivity as defined by research criteria. *Journal of Consulting and Clinical Psychology, 58,* 775–789.

Barkley, R. A., Fischer, M., Edelbrock, C. S., & Smallish, L. (1990). The adolescent outcome of hyperactive children diagnosed by research criteria: I. An 8 year follow-up study. *Journal of the American Academy of Child and Adolescent Psychiatry, 29,* 546–557.

Brown, R. T., & Borden, K. A. (1986). Hyperactivity at adolescence: Some misconceptions and new directions. *Journal of Clinical Child Psychology, 15,* 194–209.

Campbell, S. B. (1990). *Behavior problems in preschoolers: Clinical and developmental issues.* New York: Guilford Press.

Campbell, S. B., & Ewing, L. J. (1990). Follow-up of hard-to-manage preschoolers: Adjustment at age 9 years and predictors of continuing symptoms. *Journal of Child Psychology and Psychiatry and Allied Disciplines, 36,* 870–889.

Chalfant, J. C. (1984). *Identifying learning disabled students: Guidelines for decision-making.* Burlington, VT: Northeast Regional Resource Center.

Chalfant, J. C. (1989). Learning disabilities: Policy issues and promising approaches. *American Psychologist, 44,* 392–398.

Conners, C. K. (1989). *Manual for Conners' Rating Scales (Conners' Teacher Rating Scales, Conners' Parent Rating Scales).* North Tonawanda, NY: Multi-Health Systems.

Conners, C. K. (1994). *Conners' Continuous Performance Test computer program.* North Tonawanda, NY: Multi-Health Systems.

DuPaul, G. J. (1990). *The ADHD Rating Scale: Normative data, reliability, and validity*. Unpublished manuscript, University of Massachusetts Medical Center, Worcester.

Education for All Handicapped Children Act of 1975, Pub. L. No. 94-142. 89 Stat. 773. (1975).

Eyberg, S. M., & Boggs, S. R. (1989). Parent training for oppositional–defiant preschoolers. In C. E. Schaefer & J. M. Briesmeister (Eds.), *Handbook of parent training: Parents as cotherapists for children with behavior problems* (pp. 105–132). New York: Wiley.

Gordon, M., & Mettelman, B. B. (1988). The assessment of attention: I. Standardization and reliability of a behavior-based measure. *Journal of Clinical Psychology, 44,* 682–690.

Hartsough, C. S., & Lambert, N. M. (1985). Medical factors in hyperactive and normal children: Prenatal, developmental, and health history findings. *American Journal of Orthopsychiatry, 55,* 190–210.

Hooper, S. R., & Willis, W. G. (1989). *Learning disability subtyping: Neuropsychological foundations, conceptual models, and issues in clinical differentiation*. New York: Springer-Verlag.

Hynd, G. W., & Cohen, M. (1983). *Dyslexia: Neuropsychological theory, research, and clinical practice*. New York: Grune & Stratton.

Individuals With Disabilities Education Act of 1990, Pub. L. No. 101-476. 104 Stat. 1142. (1990).

Kaplan, B. J., McNichol, J., Conte, R. A., & Moghadam, H. K. (1987). Sleep disturbance in preschool age hyperactive and nonhyperactive children. *Pediatrics, 80,* 839–844.

Loney, J., & Milich, R. (1982). Hyperactivity, inattention, and aggression in clinical practice. In D. Routh & P. Wolraich (Eds.), *Advances in developmental and behavioral pediatrics* (Vol. 3, pp. 113–147). Greenwich, CT: JAI Press.

McMahon, S. A., & Greenberg, L. M. (1977). Serial neurologic examination of hyperactive children. *Pediatrics, 59,* 584–587.

Mitchell, E. A., Aman, M. G., Turbott, S. H., & Manku, M. (1987). Clinical characteristics and serum essential fatty acid levels in hyperactive children. *Clinical Pediatrics, 26,* 406–411.

Palfrey, J. S., Levine, M. D., Walker, D. K, & Sullivan, M. (1985). The emergence of attention deficits in early childhood: A prospective study. *Developmental and Behavioral Pediatrics, 6,* 339–348.

Reynolds, C. R. (1990). Conceptual and technical problems in learning disability diagnosis. In C. R. Reynolds & R. W. Kamphaus (Eds.), *Handbook of psychological and educational assessment of children* (pp. 571–592). New York: Guilford Press.

Safer, D. J., & Krager, J. M. (1994). The increased rate of stimulant treatment for hyperactive/inattentive students in secondary schools. *Pediatrics, 94,* 462–464.

Semrud-Clikeman, M., Biederman, J., Sprich-Buckminster, S., Lehman, B. K., Faraone, S. V., & Norman, D. (1992). Comorbidity between ADDH and learning disability: A review and report in a clinically referred sample. *Journal of the American Academy of Child and Adolescent Psychiatry, 31,* 439–448.

Shaywitz, B. A., & Shaywitz, S. E. (1991). Comorbidity: A critical issue in attention deficit disorder. *Journal of Child Neurology,* 6(Suppl. #1), S13–S22.

Shaywitz, S. E., & Shaywitz, B. A. (1988). Attention deficit disorder: Current perspectives. In J. F. Kavanaugh & T. J. Truss, Jr. (Eds.), *Learning disabilities: Proceedings of the national conference* (pp. 369–523). Parkton, MD: York Press.

Shaywitz, S. E., Shaywitz, B. A., Fletcher, J. M., & Escobar, M. D. (1990). *Journal of the American Medical Association, 264,* 998–1002.

Shelton, T. L., & Barkley, R. A. (1993). Assessment of attention deficit hyperactivity disorder in young children. In J. L. Culbertson & D. J. Willis (Eds.), *Testing young children: A reference guide for developmental, psychoeducational, and psychosocial assessments* (pp. 290–318). Austin, TX: PRO-ED.

Stewart, M. A., Pitts, F. N., Craig, A. G., & Dieruf, W. (1966). The hyperactive child syndrome. *American Journal of Orthopsychiatry, 36,* 861–867.

Szatmari, P., Offord, D. R., & Boyle, M. H. (1989a). Correlates, associated impairments, and patterns of service utilization of children with attention deficit disorders: Findings from the Ontario child health study. *Journal of Child Psychology and Psychiatry, 30,* 205–217.

Szatmari, P., Offord, D. R., & Boyle, M. H. (1989b). Ontario child health study: Prevalence of attention deficit disorder with hyperactivity. *Journal of Child Psychology and Psychiatry, 30,* 219–230.

Trommer, B. L., Hoeppner, J. B., Rosenberg, R. S., Armstrong, K. J., & Rothstein, J. A. (1988). Sleep disturbances in children with attention deficit disorder [Abstract]. *Annals of Neurology, 24,* 322.

U.S. Department of Education. (1991). *Thirteenth annual report to Congress on the implementation of the Individuals With Disabilities Education Act* (OCLC #25000254). Washington, DC: Author.

Weiss, R. E., Stein, M. A., Trommer, B., & Refetoff, S. (1993). Attention-deficit hyperactivity disorder and thyroid function. *Journal of Pediatrics, 123,* 539–545.

Wilkinson, G. S. (1993). *The Wide Range Achievement Test: 1993 edition administration manual.* Wilmington, DE: Wide Range.

III

PSYCHOLOGISTS IN TERTIARY CARE SETTINGS

INTRODUCTION

Often surprising to the public, to referring physicians, and even to psychologists, is the extent to which psychologists practice in tertiary care settings or are involved in trend-setting research into the understanding and treatment of acute or chronic life-threatening diseases. Although we chose to focus on only six clinical specialty areas in this text, psychologists can be found in most medical settings, on many treatment teams, caring for patients suffering from a myriad of illnesses.

In chapter 15, "Pediatric Oncology: Medical Crisis Intervention," Gerald P. Koocher focuses on the acute psychological and physiological distress symptoms experienced by otherwise psychologically well adjusted individuals coping with the diagnosis and treatment of childhood cancer. Reminding the psychologist not to interpret the patient or family responses to illness from the framework of psychopathology, Koocher furnishes guidelines for both providing crisis counseling and helping patient and families adapt to long-term survival.

Bruce G. Bender describes the clinical services of psychologists in chapter 16, "Establishing a Role for Psychology in Respiratory Medicine," and introduces the importance of psychological programming for those suffering from respiratory disorders, by highlighting the prevalence of these illnesses. He describes the treatment program at the National Jewish Center for Immunology and Respiratory Medicine and expands on psychologically based treatment protocols and their clinical efficacy.

Early detection of Alzheimer's disease is often hampered by common behavioral affects of aging and depression. In chapter 17, "The Role of

Clinical Neuropsychology in the Assessment and Care of Persons With Alzheimer's Disease," Alfred W. Kaszniak explores the critical role that psychologists can take in health care and geriatric settings to help with early detection. He outlines important criteria for accurate assessment, as well as interventions that will help patients and their families cope with Alzheimer's long-term affects.

In chapter 18, "Quality of Life and Adjustment in Renal Disease: A Health Psychology Perspective," Petra Symister and Ronald Friend provide a review of the quality-of-life issues for those who suffer from end-stage renal disease. Symister and Friend discuss both kidney transplant patients and those treated by hemodialysis and the process of psychological adjustment to the range of medical and surgical treatments. Research and clinical approaches to adherence to medical treatment regimes also are discussed.

In chapter 19, "Health Psychology and the Field of Urology," Steven M. Tovian covers a range of topics, from research ideas to practitioner interventions to collaborative suggestions for advocacy in a clinical area not often associated with psychologists, urology. Tovian defines types of adult urinary incontinence, the effects of incontinence on quality of life, and psychological treatments for the emotional sequelae of these disorders. Another disorder encountered in urological practice, erectile dysfunction, is also discussed from medical and psychological perspectives. Tovian offers suggestions for psychologists wishing to market their clinical services to urologists.

Tiffany M. Field, in chapter 20, "Touch Therapies for Pain Management and Stress Reduction," describes research studies and clinical interventions using touch therapy, massage, to reduce anxiety and stress in infants who are premature or who have been exposed to cocaine or HIV; children with a range of problems, such as diabetes, burns, or posttraumatic stress disorder; and adults who are HIV-positive. Clinical changes in anxiety were also found in those providing the massages, whether they were volunteer "grandparent therapists" or the parents of ill children. Field discusses proposed underlying biological mechanisms that explain the clinical utility of this approach to stress reduction.

Jacqueline Dunbar-Jacob and Elizabeth A. Schlenk, in chapter 21, "Treatment Adherence and Clinical Outcome: Can We Make a Difference?" describe the research outcomes of the level to which patients fail to comply with both their medication and behavioral treatment regimes and the health problems that ensue when patients do not follow treatment. Although most research has concentrated on the adverse outcomes of noncompliance with medication regimes, Dunbar-Jacob and Schlenk provide evidence that suggests that noncompliance with behavioral regimes (e.g., failure to follow diet plans) also adversely affects patients' health and adds to health care costs. Areas of research in this critical field of health care are suggested.

15

PEDIATRIC ONCOLOGY: MEDICAL CRISIS INTERVENTION

GERALD P. KOOCHER

The adventure begins in a relatively uneventful manner, as childhood medical problems go: a few bruises, a low-grade fever, a bruise or "athletic injury" that seems to worsen, a prolonged nosebleed, and curious minute red lines on the skin, which you will soon learn to identify as *petechiae*. The almost-casual visit to the pediatrician leads to a recommendation for "a few more tests." Then the diagnosis hits full-force: acute lymphoblastic leukemia, osteogenic sarcoma, Hodgkin's disease. The roller coaster ride begins bringing the threat of death, the hope of proven treatments, the necessity of an amputation or invasive surgical procedure, the promise of a "normal life down the road," the rocky course of high-dose chemotherapy. At times, the wait for information seems maddeningly slow. At other points, it seems that changes in medical status and the pace of interventions proceed at breakneck speed. All this in quest of a cure that is a real possibility for more than 70% of the children diagnosed with the most common forms of pediatric cancer.

What are psychologists doing in this setting? These events present especially intense coping challenges to both pediatric patients and their

213

families. The emotional toll taken by these stresses is often sufficient to trigger acute psychological and physiological distress symptoms in individuals who are otherwise well adjusted. Symptoms affecting physically healthy family members may include anxiety, depression, difficulty concentrating, insomnia, sibling school phobia, and the inability to attend to important work- or family-related needs. Behavioral problems also occur among the child and adolescent cancer patients, including anxiety, depression, conditioned reflex vomiting, school refusal, and resistance or nonadherence to recommended medical regimens. The existing health care system is generally oriented to respond reactively, rather than preventively, with respect to emotional distress and is not well equipped to assist patients and families psychologically during these crises. Too often, health and mental care providers tend to function in parallel, rather than synchronous, interaction.

That is to say, mental health care does not make an effort to communicate or coordinate services with the physicians treating the medical condition. Too often, mental health professionals approach such patients in much the same manner as they would a client with entrenched neurotic symptoms. In so doing, the practitioner might attempt to explore early trauma or peel back layers of unconscious material, all the while ignoring the surface issues and illness-related stresses the patient and family must face.

Physicians managing the medical aspects of such cases are dedicated specialists but seldom talk with community-based mental health care providers serving a patient's family, and the psychological clinicians based outside the medical setting frequently lack a meaningful understanding of the illness, course and side effects of treatment, and medical prognosis that constitute their patient's reality. As a result, integrated approaches addressing both health and mental health needs of people in the midst of medical crisis are all too rare. Neither mental health professionals nor their patients can accept a continuation of such patterns of service.

Many mental health clinicians have noted the need for psychologists to prepare to work in health care settings. Perhaps the best known is Cummings (1995), who noted, "The future professional psychologist will be primarily a health psychologist who will require retraining to acquire an enabling attitude for success and a knowledge of the growing body of efficient–effective therapies" (p. 14).

Leading pediatric oncology treatment centers are ahead of the curve on this issue. Perhaps it is the appealing nature of children or the wish to spare them discomfort that has propelled development of psychosocial services in pediatric oncology treatment centers. Whatever the reason, the advent of high-dose-chemotherapy protocols and the resulting increases in both medical side effects and survivorship, which began in the 1970s, have resulted in important roles for psychologists in such centers around the country, as both behavioral scientists and practicing clinicians.

Psychologists and other mental health practitioners have provided an array of important behavioral and psychosocial interventions for children with cancer across at lease five domains: crisis-oriented therapies, psychoeducational interventions, improved relief of symptoms, tolerance of stressful procedures, and programs to improve the adaptation of long-term survivors. Outcome research has consistently demonstrated the enhancements to quality of life provided by psychosocial intervention. So valuable are these contributions, they are now routinely incorporated as integral elements of the medical care system. They have become required services in nearly every comprehensive pediatric oncology treatment center. This chapter summarizes some of the more recent developments in such programs and illustrates in detail what psychologists are doing in such sites as both scientists and practitioners.

CRISIS-ORIENTED PSYCHOTHERAPIES

Although restoring patients to a prior level of functioning may be feasible in some clinical populations, such restoration is an inadequate, if not unrealistic, goal for most patients facing medical crises. The child with cancer will face painful and invasive testing, arduous chemotherapy, daunting medical side effects, and considerable uncertainty. The clinician who approaches these patients with the goal of restoring them to a prior level of functioning denies the very real life-changing nature of medical crises and risks alienating patients and families by minimizing these challenges, communicating unrealistic expectations, or interpreting their responses from the framework of psychopathology (Shapiro & Koocher, 1996).

The psychological landscape of most lives is permanently altered by a brush with cancer, even if in positive ways. However, returning to "the way things were" is simply not possible. This is not to say that restoring a sense of normalcy is impossible, but rather that patients and family members must come to a new personal homeostasis and understanding of what constitutes normality for them. The goal of the medical crisis intervention is to help the patient optimize functioning socially, occupationally, and in management of the medical aspects of the disease (Pollin, 1995).

Four a priori clinical assumptions are critical when working with patients who are struggling with medical crises. First, human responses to medical crises rarely represent psychopathology in the traditional sense. Rather, anyone facing the extreme stress of illness may react with a host of psychological distress symptoms, including those frequently associated with mental illness: dissociation, denial, and the so-called vegetative symptoms often indicative of anxiety disorders and major depression. Such people in medical crisis, however, do not warrant the same treatment approach as the patient experiencing the same symptoms independent of medical distress (Pollin, 1995). A pathologizing model and long-term treatment plan are seldom warranted. Rather, an approach that helps normalize the distress (under the circumstances), focuses on the illness, and emphasizes an intensive short-term or brief, intermittent intervention model is most likely to be helpful and well received.

Second, there is a continuum of social, occupational, and biomedical functioning that demands consideration. Imagine, for example, two adolescents with the same chronic, life-threatening illness. One may stay in touch with peers over the phone, even when bedridden, continue to invest energy in schoolwork, and talk openly about the illness. The other may find changes in her or his appearance (e.g., hair loss or amputation) devastating and retreat into social isolation, seeking home tutoring rather than a return to school and focusing energy on high-violence video games. Functional coping responses to the same illness and symptoms may be radically different, and although the observer might prefer one coping strategy over the other, neither can be described as pathological per se or useful for everyone (Shapiro & Koocher, 1996).

Third, a child's responses to serious medical illness cannot be understood in a vacuum. The patient's relationships at home, school, work, and in the neighborhood are often affected by illness. As in systems theory, we assume that changes in one part of the patient's personal ecology (e.g., the onset of illness) resonate throughout the entire system. Therefore, it is necessary to assess and work toward optimal functioning in every social system with which the patient interacts. The psychotherapist must be prepared to shift between individual and family meetings and must be able to consult with school personnel and members of the medical team as the child's medical treatment progresses. Intervention must be contextual to the site, the coping tasks required, and the developmental level of the child.

Finally, we assume that the duration of a given crisis will vary from disease to disease, symptom to symptom, and person to person. Cancer treatment can be a series of turbulent periods broken up by periods of relative calm. This unfolding natural history or course of the illness has implications for the frequency, duration, and intensity of psychological treatment. Psychotherapeutic intervention may prove to be a one-time course of sessions, or a series of clusters of interventions that are linked to treatment events (e.g., diagnosis, reintegration to school, relapse, survivorship issues, or terminal care).

PSYCHOEDUCATIONAL AND FAMILY INTERVENTIONS

Psychologists have been instrumental in developing psychoeducational programs to enhance the coping of children with cancer. Research focused on understanding developmental stressors and coping processes has led to interventions that facilitate coping by both child patients and their families. These strategies and techniques are often rather simple to implement, although not a part of routine training for most physicians. Hence, they would not be readily available without psychologists working in these settings.

School Reintegration

Maintaining as normal a life as possible is important for medically ill children, just as the ability to continue or resume work is a concern for chronically ill adults. Several investigations by psychologists have shed light on strategies for school reintegration. One example is a 1992 study by Katz, Varni, Rubinstein, and Blew in Southern California, which evaluated the effectiveness of a comprehensive school reintegration intervention. A total of 49 children (age 5–17 years), newly diagnosed with cancer, received a comprehensive school reintegration consisting of supportive counseling, educational presentations, systematic liaison between the hospital and the school, and periodic follow-ups. Children, their parents, and teachers rated their perceptions of the utility and value of the intervention approach. Evaluations were uniformly very positive, providing support for the social validity of the school reintegration approach for children with newly diagnosed cancer.

Social Support

For a child or adolescent who has undergone prolonged hospitalization, has become weakened and lost hair as a result of chemotherapy, or suddenly feels very different from peers, self-esteem loss and a sense of social isolation or stigma can be overwhelming. Varni and his colleagues (Varni, Katz, Colegrove, & Dolgin, 1993, 1994) have focused attention on issues of social support as a key issue in fostering coping of children with cancer. In 1993, they conducted a prospective investigation to determine whether explicit social skills training could enhance the psychological and social adjustment of children with newly diagnosed cancer. A total of 64 children (age 5–13 years) with newly diagnosed cancer were randomized to either a social skills training experimental treatment group or a school reintegration standard treatment group. Children who received explicit training in social skills reported higher perceived classmate and teacher social support at a 9-month follow-up, by comparison with pretreatment levels. At the same time, parents reported a decrease in internalizing and externalizing behavior problems and an increase in school competence among the children.

Another report on this same clinical population (Varni et al., 1994) described 30 children (age 8–13 years) who were evaluated for depressive symptoms, state anxiety, trait anxiety, social anxiety, general self-esteem, and perceived social support from classmates, parents, teachers, and friends. Perceived classmate, parent, and teacher social support correlated with the psychologic adjustment parameters in the direction of greater support predicting lower psychologic distress and higher self-esteem. Perceived classmate social support was the most consistent predictor of the ill child's adaptation.

Children's Understanding of Cancer

How children understand their illness and necessary treatments can be an important factor in their ability to cope. Bearison, Sadow, Granowetter, and Winkel (1993) reported on the kinds of causal attributions that pediatric cancer patients and their parents make about cancer. Their beliefs were systematically examined to determine whether different types of attributions were associated with different coping strategies. A total of 20 pediatric oncology patients (age 4 to 19 years) were interviewed to determine the kinds of attributions they made (if any) about their cancer. The parents also were interviewed, concerning their causal attributions of their child's cancer. The parents then completed the Strategies for Coping With Illness—Parents' Scale to determine their coping strategies. Pediatric oncology nurses rated the children's coping strategies. Findings indicate that both patients and parents who made external types of attributions coped significantly better than did those who made internal types of attributions or simply accepted the physicians' advice that the cause of pediatric cancers was unknown (i.e., who made no attributions).

Springer (1994) evaluated whether preschoolers with cancer are more or less likely than their healthy counterparts to consider illness a form of punishment for misdeeds (i.e., *imminent justice*). Seventeen 4–5-year-olds with cancer rejected imminent justice as a general cause of illness, both in themselves and in others, just as frequently as 17 age-matched healthy controls did. Both groups also rejected imminent justice in cases where misbehavior was prolonged. Children with cancer demonstrated a view of illness causality based on greater differentiation between themselves and other people, in that they were more likely than healthy controls to accept imminent justice as a cause of illness in themselves but not others and vice versa. Nearly all of the children with cancer who accepted imminent justice as a general cause of illness in themselves also attributed their cancer specifically to imminent justice.

These findings are among the latest in a long series of studies that inform both physicians and psychosocial support staff about how to explain these illnesses and their treatments to children of all ages (for detailed discussion in historical perspective, see Koocher, 1986b; Koocher & MacDonald, 1992; Slavin, O'Malley, Koocher, & Foster, 1981).

Family Coping in General

Mental health professionals have been highly successful in getting pediatric oncologists to recognize that when a child has cancer, the family must be considered the psychological unit of treatment. In an excellent article, Kazak and Nachman (1991) discussed select research studies on adjustment to childhood cancer and organized them within a social ecological framework, including consideration of social systems larger than the family. They used childhood cancers as an example and presented family research agendas relevant to cancer and other childhood chronic diseases. Research questions pertained to the ill child, siblings, parents, families, social support networks, education and health care systems, and policy and societal attitudes. Recommendations for research were suggested, and the importance of considering normalcy, family development, and methodology in research on ill children and their families is also discussed.

Horwitz and Kazak (1990) assessed 25 preschool (3–5-year-old) siblings and families of children with cancer and 25 preschool siblings and families of healthy children, by means of standardized measures of child adjustment and family adaptability and cohesion (including the Child Behavior Checklist and the Family Adaptability and Cohesion Evaluation Scale—II). Siblings' behavior, social competence, and self-perceptions in the oncology family group were in keeping with published norms and did not differ significantly from the comparison group. The oncology family group had more extreme levels of adaptability, and mothers were more likely to describe sibling pairs as alike. There was a negative correlation between behavior problems and adaptability and cohesion in the oncology group.

Unfortunately, there are times when surviving family members, including children, must cope with the loss of a loved one from cancer. Coping with a cancer death can be an agonizing experience, but once again this is an area of science and practice where there are many positive contributions by behavioral scientists (Koocher, 1986a).

Coping With the Death of a Child

Many books and papers have been published also on coping with the death of a child. Some recent work, however, has focused on a preventive approach. Koocher (1994) described a preventive-intervention program for families that suffered the loss of a child from cancer and other causes. Using a manualized intervention designed to mobilize mutual support among those who had shared the loss and guide the mourning process, interveners were able to provide significant benefit to families over the course of three sessions lasting 2–2 1/2 hours each. Once again, the model involved a normalizing focus on the loss event from the intervener's perspective.

SYMPTOMATIC RELIEF

Psychologists have been actively involved in the development of biobehavioral models (Andersen, Kiecolt-Glaser, & Glaser, 1994) and intervention protocols designed to assist patients in coping with the rigors of cancer therapies, ranging from control of nausea and vomiting symptoms to improved pain control (Koocher, 1985; Schulz & Masek, 1996). Some of these interventions are described in the next section of this chapter, but many involve simple adaptations of well-known behavioral techniques such as systematic desensitization procedures, applied in a context specific to pediatric oncology.

IMPROVED TOLERANCE OF STRESSFUL PROCEDURES

Before one can successfully intervene to reduce stress during medical procedures, it is important to understand the child's perspective. Bearison and Pacifici (1989) described the schematic organization of children's knowledge of the routine procedures they experience when being treated for cancer (leukemia). A total of 27 leukemia patients (age 4–17 years) participated in the study. The effects of several independent variables, including age, duration of treatment, prognostic condition, and gender, were tested on the participants' cognitive organization and recall of their experiences in oncology clinics relative to their experiences of other common recurrent events in their lives. Interview data showed that the participants demonstrated well-organized knowledge about the events they experienced in oncology clinics, particularly the administration of chemotherapy.

Venipuncture and bone marrow aspirations are two of the most frequent and distressing procedures to which children with cancer are subjected. Dahlquist, Power, Cox, and Fernbach (1994) examined the relationship between children's distress during invasive cancer procedures and parent anxiety, parent disciplinary attitudes, and parent behavior during the medical procedure. Sixty-six 2- to 17-year-olds with cancer and their parents were evaluated during a routine (but nonetheless painful) bone marrow aspiration. Significantly higher levels of distress existed for children under 8 years. Patterns of relationships with parent variables also varied by age. Young children's distress was positively associated with parental reassurance, ignoring, and agitation before the procedure and with information giving during the procedure. Older children's distress was negatively associated with parental distraction during the procedure. The substantial age differences in the correlations between child distress and parenting practices demonstrate the young child's greater dependence on caregivers for emotional regulation and control.

Manne et al. (1995) examined the impact of three coping behaviors (non-procedure-related statements and behaviors, information seeking, and requests for modifications in the procedure) exhibited during stressful medical procedures performed on 45 children (age 3–10 years) undergoing cancer treatment. By means of videotaped recordings of venipuncture, the relationship among the three coping behaviors and between coping and distress were investigated. Because age was associated with both distress and coping, age was partialed out when computing correlations. Coping behaviors were independent (i.e., not correlated). A pattern of consistent, weak-to-moderate associations was noted between non-procedure-related behaviors and reductions in both concurrent and subsequent distress. These results illustrate that studies of children's coping should be sensitive to developmental issues and show the special value of a psychological approach to the problem.

In an 1990 study, Manne, Redd, Jacobsen, and Gorfinkle, at Memorial Sloan Kettering Cancer Institute, reported on a behavioral intervention incorporating parent coaching, attentional distraction, and positive reinforcement to control child distress during invasive cancer treatment. Children who had previously required physical restraint to complete venipuncture were alternately assigned to either a behavioral intervention or an attention-control condition. Child distress behaviors were recorded, and self-reports of parent, child, and nurse distress were obtained. Parents and nurses also rated child distress. Results of planned comparisons indicate that observed child distress, parent-rated child distress, and parent ratings of his or her own distress were significantly reduced by behavioral intervention and were maintained across the course of three intervention trials. The use of physical restraint to manage child behavior was also significantly reduced. Child self-reported pain and nurse ratings of child distress were not significantly affected.

These are but a few illustrations of the contributions that psychologists have made in helping children with cancer to cope with difficult treatments. In so doing, they are also helping to calm anxious parents and relieve the pressures on physicians and nurses as well.

IMPROVED COPING FOR LONG-TERM SURVIVORS

Because the early reports on long-term survivors of childhood cancer focused on the uncertainty of outcome as a stressor (Koocher & O'Malley, 1981), psychological research has had a profound impact on the actual course of medical treatment for children with cancer. For example, psychologists were leaders in emphasizing the importance of honest and direct communication regarding the cancer diagnosis, to promote coping (Koocher & O'Malley, 1981; Spinetta, Rigler, & Karon, 1974). In addition, pediatric neuropsychology has led to important changes in the course of treatment for acute lymphoblastic leukemia (ALL), the most common form of childhood cancer.

Leukemia cells too often find sanctuary from curative chemotherapy in the fluids of the central nervous system, where the blood–brain barrier blocks passage of medications. The result may be a central nervous system relapse of ALL among children who were otherwise effectively treated. Irradiating the brain is one way of killing cancer cells that may escape the chemotherapy, but such treatments can also cause neurological damage. Pediatric psychologists were the first to document such sequelae in detail.

For example, Waber and her colleagues (Waber, Bernstein, Kammerer, & Tarbell, 1992; Waber, Gioia, Paccia, & Sherman, 1990) are among a group of pediatric neuropsychologists who have documented the devastating consequences that cranial irradiation can have on the developing brain. In controlled studies comparing children with ALL and other cancers that did not require brain irradiation, they described severe neuropsychological diagnoses and established dose and age relationships. Their research showed that high does of radiation to the brain were especially damaging in children under 36 months of age. They also documented female sex as a risk factor for cognitive delay in the aftermath of cranial irradiation for ALL. Because of such research, treatment protocols have been modified to minimize the amount of radiation used in treating newly diagnosed children with ALL. Baseline neuropsychological assessment and follow-up for long-term educational and learning problems are now routine components of treatment protocols for pediatric ALL.

Following early reports on the importance of open communication in families confronting childhood cancer (Koocher & O'Malley, 1981; Spinetta et al., 1974), Claflin and Barbarin (1991) examined the effects of parents telling young children less about the diagnosis, treatment, and prognosis of cancer than older children and adolescents. A total of 43 children diagnosed with cancer reported on information disclosed to them at diagnosis, their causal attributions, illness-related stress, and coping strategies. In keeping with parental reports, 18 children age under 9 years were told less than 15 children age 9–13 years and 10 adolescents age 14–18 years. Young children's reports of illness impact differed from those of older children and adolescents only with respect to school and social domains. Younger children reported fewer cognitive strategies than older children and adolescents. Even though young children were told much less than older children, they reported similar levels of distress. Claflin and Barbarin concluded that nondisclosure failed to mask the salient and distressing aspects of the illness.

CONCLUSION

The message to be gleaned from this overview is that psychologists are doing quite a bit in pediatric oncology settings. As both behavioral scientists and practitioners, psychologists are making significant contributions to health status and quality of life. These contributions involve both traditional and crisis-oriented interventions, as well as cognitive, behavioral, and neuropsychological approaches, to resolve the difficulties patients commonly encounter in the course of cancer treatment. The full magnitude of the impact psychology has had in these settings is evident in the fact that psychological components are routine parts of all major pediatric oncology treatment settings and research programs. The National Cancer Institute's research grant reviewers routinely expect that psychological and quality-of-life factors will be addressed in applications for funding. The American Cancer Society added a doctoral level psychologist as a vice president for behavioral science research in 1994, and its board of directors voted in 1995 to increase set-aside funds for psychosocial and behavioral research. The influence of psychology and psychologists in pediatric oncology settings over the past 25 years has been highly significant. So, what are we doing here? Plenty!

REFERENCES

Andersen, B. L., Kiecolt-Glaser, J. K., & Glaser, R. (1994). A biobehavioral model of cancer, stress, and disease course. *American Psychologist, 49,* 389–404.

Armstrong, F. D. (1995). Commentary: Childhood cancer. *Journal of Pediatric Psychology, 20,* 417–421.

Bearison, D. J., & Pacifici, C. (1989). Children's event knowledge of cancer treatment. *Journal of Applied Developmental Psychology, 10,* 469–486.

Bearison, D. J., Sadow, A. J., Granowetter, L., & Winkel, G. (1993). Patients' and parents' causal attributions for childhood cancer. *Journal of Psychosocial Oncology, 11,* 47–61.

Claflin, C. J., & Barbarin, O. A. (1991). Does "telling" less protect more? Relationships among age, information disclosure, and what children with cancer see and feel. *Journal of Pediatric Psychology, 16,* 169–191.

Cummings, N. A. (1995). Impact of managed care on employment and training: A primer for survival. *Professional Psychology: Research and Practice, 26,* 10–15.

Dahlquist, L. M., Power, T. G., Cox, C. N., & Fernbach, D. J. (1994). Parenting and child distress during cancer procedures: A multidimensional assessment. *Children's Health Care, 23,* 149–166.

Horwitz, W. A., & Kazak, A. E. (1990). Family adaptation to childhood cancer: Sibling and family systems variables. *Journal of Clinical Child Psychology, 19,* 221–228.

Katz, E. R., Varni, J. W., Rubenstein, C. L., & Blew, A. (1992). Teacher, parent, and child evaluative ratings of a school reintegration intervention for children with newly diagnosed cancer. *Children's Health Care, 21,* 69–75.

Kazak, A. E., & Nachman, G. S. (1991). Family research on childhood chronic illness: Pediatric oncology as an example. *Journal of Family Psychology, 4,* 462–483.

Koocher, G. P. (1985). Promoting coping with illness in childhood. In J. C. Rosen & L. J. Solomon (Eds.), *Prevention in health psychology* (pp. 217–223). Hanover, NH: University Press of New England.

Koocher, G. P. (1986a). Coping with a death from cancer. *Journal of Consulting and Clinical Psychology, 54,* 623–631.

Koocher, G. P. (1986b). Psychosocial care of the child during acute cancer treatment. *Cancer, 58,* 468–472.

Koocher, G. P. (1994). Preventive interventions following a child's death. *Psychotherapy: Theory, Research, and Practice, 31,* 377–382.

Koocher, G. P., & MacDonald, B. L. (1992). Preventive intervention and family coping with a child's life threatening or terminal illness. In T. J. Akamatsu, M. A. P. Stephens, S. E. Hobfoll, & J. H. Crowther (Eds.), *Family health psychology* (pp. 67–88). Washington, DC: Hemisphere.

Koocher, G. P., & O'Malley, J. E. (1981). *The Damocles syndrome: Psychosocial consequences of surviving childhood cancer.* New York: McGraw-Hill.

Manne, S. L., Bakeman, R., Jacobsen, P. B., & Redd, W. H. (1993). Children's coping during invasive medical procedures. *Behavior Therapy, 24,* 143–158.

Manne, S. L., Lesanics, D., Meyers, P., Wollner, N., Steinherz, P., & Redd, W. (1995). Predictors of depressive symptomatology among parents of newly diagnosed children with cancer. *Journal of Pediatric Psychology, 20,* 491–510.

Manne, S. L., Redd, W. H., Jacobsen, P. B., & Gorfinkle, K. (1990). Behavioral intervention to reduce child and parent distress during venipuncture. *Journal of Consulting and Clinical Psychology, 58*, 565–572.

Pollin, I. (1995). *Medical crisis counseling: Short-term therapy for long-term illness.* New York: Norton.

Schulz, M., & Masek, B. (1996). Medical crisis intervention with children and adolescents with chronic pain. *Professional Psychology: Research and Practice, 27*, 121–129.

Shapiro, D. E., & Koocher, G. P. (1996). Goals and time considerations in outpatient medical crises intervention. *Professional Psychology: Research and Practice, 27*, 109–120.

Slavin L., O'Malley J. E., Koocher, G. P., & Foster D. J. (1981). Communication of the cancer diagnosis to pediatric patients: Impact on long-term adjustment. *American Journal of Psychiatry, 139*, 179–183.

Spinetta, J. J. Rigler, D., & Karon, M. (1974). Personal space as a measure of a dying child's sense of isolation. *Journal of Consulting and Clinical Psychology, 42*, 751–756.

Springer, K. (1994). Beliefs about illness causality among preschoolers with cancer: Evidence against imminent justice. *Journal of Pediatric Psychology, 19*, 91–101.

Varni, J. W., Katz, E. R., Colegrove, R., & Dolgin, M. (1993). The impact of social skills training on the adjustment of children with newly diagnosed cancer. *Journal of Pediatric Psychology, 18*, 751–767.

Varni, J. W., Katz, E. R., Colgrove, R., & Dolgin, M. (1994). Perceived stress and adjustment of long-term survivors of childhood cancer. *Journal of Psychosocial Oncology, 12*, 1–16.

Waber, D. P., Bernstein, J. H., Kammerer, B. L., & Tarbell, N. J. (1992). Neuropsychological diagnostic profiles of children who received CNS treatment for acute lymphoblastic leukemia: The systematic approach to assessment. *Developmental Neurology, 8*, 1–28.

Waber, D. P., Gioia, G., Paccia, J., & Sherman, B. (1990). Sex differences in cognitive processing in children treated with CNS prophylaxis for acute lymphoblastic leukemia. *Journal of Pediatric Psychology, 15*, 105–122.

16

ESTABLISHING A ROLE FOR PSYCHOLOGY IN RESPIRATORY MEDICINE

BRUCE G. BENDER

Asthma is a chronic inflammation of the lung airways characterized by shortness of breath and wheezing. This disease affects about 12 million Americans, including 4 million children. Annually, asthma accounts for approximately 15 million physician visits, 479,000 hospitalizations, 1.2 million emergency room visits, and 10 million missed school days (S. T. Weiss et al., 1992). According to the Centers for Disease Control (1995), the morbidity and mortality associated with asthma have been on the rise in recent years. The number of asthma deaths has progressively increased since 1982 from 3,000 to 5,000 per year, with mortality significantly higher in African Americans.

The incidence of psychological difficulty is increased in asthmatic children. However, the rate of psychological disorder is not increased for all groups of asthmatic children (Kashani, Konig, Shepperd, Wilfley, & Morris, 1988; Klinnert, in press). Rather, there appears to be a generalized increase in problems of adaptation, self-esteem, and social confidence that may affect many asthmatic children, while actual psychological disorder is increased only among children with severe asthma (Bussing, Halfon, Benjamin, & Wells, 1995; Graham, Rutter, Yule, & Pless, 1967; Hamlett, Pelligrini, & Katz, 1992; Klinnert, in press). In one study of 81 asthmatic children, MacLean, Perrin, Gortmaker, and Pierre (1992) stratified the children into groups having mild, moderate, or severe asthma. Comparison of scores from the Child Behavior Checklist (Achenbach & Edelbrock, 1983) among these groups indicated that behavioral problems were increased and social competence decreased only in the group with severe asthma. Graham et al. (1967) similarly concluded almost 30 years ago that psychiatric disturbance is slightly increased among all asthmatic children, but particularly so in those with more severe asthma.

In this chapter, I review the psychologist's role in respiratory medicine. Particular emphasis is given to the currently changing place for psychological services as disease-management models redefine how tertiary care is delivered. I argue that the continued inclusion of psychological services in such settings will depend on several factors, including the ability of psychologists to demonstrate that untreated psychological disorders undermine successful medical treatment, that psychological intervention is cost-effective and improves treatment response, and that psychology's tradition of outcome research offers a means for continued reevaluation of multidisciplinary management of respiratory disease. I review evidence for each of these assertions.

WHY PSYCHOLOGICAL SERVICES ARE NECESSARY IN THE TERTIARY CARE MEDICAL SETTING

National Jewish Center for Immunology and Respiratory Medicine, a Denver-based tertiary care center, typically receives those patients with difficult-to-control asthma, often characterized by repeated emergency room visits and hospitalizations, chronic need for systemic steroids, and annual medical care costs in excess of $15,000. Because psychological disorders are increased in this high-risk asthma group (Todd, 1995) and often interfere with medical management (Bender & Klinnert, in press; Klinnert, in press), psychological assessment and intervention represent a primary service area at National Jewish Center.

The central role of psychosocial staff at National Jewish Center continues because of the high need for direct psychological intervention in this patient population. In response to the health care revolution taking place in the United States, significant changes are occurring in all health care centers. These dramatic changes require that psychology redefine its place in tertiary health care settings. The average length of hospitalization for a patient at National Jewish Center today is less than half of what it was 5 years ago, a change directly resulting from limitations imposed by the health insurance and managed care industries. Consequently, the delivery of health care to severe, chronically asthmatic patients at National Jewish Center is changing. Most immediately apparent is the change of primary treatment setting from inpatient hospitalization to day-treatment program. The highly structured day program provides education and training about chronic disease, medical evaluation and treatment, and psychosocial evaluation and treatment, in a manner that significantly reduces costs as compared with the inpatient program.

The relationship between psychological disorder and chronic disease is complex and interactive. At first glance, it appears fairly obvious that the imposition of chronic disease represents an enormous stressor, which can induce psychological difficulty, most frequently depression (Mrazek, 1985; Yellowless, Haynes, Potts, & Ruffin, 1988). However, the causal relationship is not uni directional. The preexistence of a psychological disorder also can contribute to poorly controlled, and, consequently, more severe disease. Nonadherence to essential medical care, in particular, can result from the patient's, or the patient's family's, psychological difficulties, exacerbating the illness and causing excessive, inappropriate, and expensive overuse of health care services.

Although the pharmacologic means for effective asthma management are readily available, treatment failure and excessive emergency room visits and hospitalizations occur largely because of patient nonadherence. In some cases, treatment nonadherence is directly related to psychological disorder. Studies using new microchip technologies, which allow investigators to document the exact date and time when patients use aerosolized medications, have revealed that much of the necessary anti-inflammatory medication prescribed to the patient is not taken as directed (Milgrom et al., 1995). As physicians increase the frequency of prescribed dosages, to gain better control of the disease, patients actually become less adherent (Coutts, Gibson, & Paton, 1992). Children from dysfunctional families are more nonadherent than other patients in their use of asthma medications (Bender et al., 1995). However, even seemingly stable and cooperative patients can be markedly nonadherent with medications essential to the control of their asthma (Milgrom, Bender, Sarlin, & Leung, 1994). The absence of necessary health care behavior, then, contributes to dangerously out-of-control asthma, a finding that is particularly prevalent among inner-city African Americans (Greineder, Loane, & Parks, 1995), which can result in asthma-related death (Strunk, Mrazek, Fuhrmann, & La Brecque, 1985).

Tertiary care psychological services then are a necessary component of disease management in the tertiary care medical setting. Mental health professionals with developed expertise can most effectively provide such services. Furthermore, when these services are provided within the tertiary care setting in collaboration with medical caregivers, they are more likely to result in an effective change in health care behavior and quality of life than those provided in settings with no connection to the patients' health care (Bender & Klinnert, in press). Such multidisciplinary approaches to asthma treatment at National Jewish Center are characterized by the following examples:

Working with conflicted families with a history of poor management of a child's asthma requires that the psychologist understand the behaviors necessary for optimal self-management and the best approaches for helping families to share responsibility for the various components of disease control.

When a depressed adolescent declines to adhere to a medication regimen as an act of angry rebellion, the psychologist must have an understanding of the function of various medications, assist in removing the sources of resistance, and help the adolescent to plan to take the medication at times and places that avoid embarrassment.

An adult patient with chronic obstructive pulmonary disease complains that a particular medication causes depression. The psychologist may assist in assessing whether the medication or other disease-related factors are contributing to the affective concerns and may discuss alternative medications with the prescribing physician.

When a 4-year-old child becomes highly anxious about a scheduled invasive procedure necessary for evaluation of lung damage, a psychologist knowledgeable about the procedure can help alleviate some of the concern by enabling the child to practice the procedure with a doll and by advising the parents about discussions they may have with their child in the days leading up to the procedure.

A patient appears to lose some memory and motor skills in the period immediately after a severe respiratory arrest. The psychologist may be asked to help evaluate the neurological and functional implications of this event and to help plan a program of remediation.

STUDIES EXAMINING THE INFLUENCE OF PSYCHOLOGICAL INTERVENTIONS ON DISEASE OUTCOME

Not all initiatives targeting health care behavior have been successful. Numerous asthma education programs have been studied to determine the effects of increased patient knowledge on disease morbidity. In many cases, providing patients with better knowledge about asthma has been found to be insufficient to change behavior without the inclusion of additional behavioral or psychological interventions. Although asthma-education programs increase knowledge about asthma and its appropriate care, evidence that education intervention alone significantly alters health care behavior is at best mixed. Some support can be found for the effect of asthma education on reducing health care use (Bolton, Tilley, Kuder, Reeves, & Schultz, 1991; Osman et al., 1994), but a meta-analysis analyzing results across 11 education-intervention studies concluded that such teaching programs do not reduce morbidity outcomes, including rate of school absenteeism and frequency of hospitalization and emergency room visits (Bernard-Bonnin, Stachenko, Bonin, Charette, & Rousseau, 1995). Other investigators have similarly concluded that asthma education alone is ineffective in changing health care behavior and morbidity (Rubin, Bauman, & Lauby, 1989; Tettersell, 1993).

Although asthma-education programs by themselves are generally insufficient to change health care behavior and outcome, they are a necessary component of a multidisciplinary effort to improve asthma self-management. When asthma education is combined with other psychologically based approaches to changing health care behavior, the intervention becomes more effective. Several psychoeducational interventions exemplify this approach, using asthma education within individually tailored and administered programs administered by a health care giver, usually a nurse. The introduction of a new caregiver who is sympathetic to the patient can have a powerful influence on health care behavior. In one study, 53 high-risk asthmatic children with histories of repeated emergency room visits and hospitalizations were enrolled in an intensive self-management program (Greineder et al., 1995). In addition to direct asthma education, these children and their families met individually with, and received regular telephone contact from, an outreach nurse. This intervention, distinct from other education programs in its inclusion of a relationship with a care giver unavailable to patients outside the program, resulted in a 79% reduction in emergency room visits, an 86% reduction in hospitalizations, and an average savings of over $1,600 for each patient. Because all patients received the same health maintenance organization medical care before, during, and after the program, these changes were attributed solely to the psychoeducational intervention. In another study, 47 adult asthmatics with multiple hospitalization histories were randomly assigned to a routine-care control group or an intervention group receiving intensive, individual counseling and education on self-management strategies (Mayo, Richman, & Harris, 1990). The intervention group alone demonstrated a dramatic reduction in hospitalizations. Although both of these programs were presented as primarily educational interventions, they included an educator/counselor who played a central role in advising, encouraging, instructing, and motivating patients. Given the convincing evidence that offering factual information to chronically ill patients does not by itself change behavior (Tettersell, 1993), the importance of this therapeutic figure should not be underestimated.

The psychological component of other psychoeducational intervention programs has been more clearly recognized and labeled. Creer and colleagues at the University of Ohio have used a social learning theory model to design intensive health care behavior interventions for asthmatic patients. These investigators have repeatedly demonstrated that a combination of education, specific instruction, and strategic-problem-solving training can result in decreased frequency and severity of asthma exacerbations, use of the medical care system, and treatment cost. Evaluating a behavioral and educational program for asthmatic adults, Kotses et al. (1995) randomly assigned 76 subjects to either a treatment group or a waiting-list control group. Patients in the treatment group participated in a 7-week program providing education and training that included an emphasis on self-management and problem solving. In a 6-month follow-up, patients were found to experience less frequent asthma attacks, reduced medication use, and improved overall self-management skills. In a second report, the investigators demonstrated a significant cost-benefit from this intervention program: The cost of administering the program to each patient was $208, with an average cost savings of $475.

A similar intervention was equally effective with asthmatic children. Twenty families with asthmatic children were randomly assigned to a control group or an intervention group, receiving 2 months of education and training in self-management and problem solving. A social learning theory model provided the framework within which the patient was helped to select appropriate behavioral options, depending on the nature of symptoms and environment in which they were experienced. An 18-month follow-up indicated both a significant improvement in asthma, relative to the baseline period, and reduced school absenteeism and health-care-related expenditures (Creer et al., 1988).

Other psychological interventions have also been used with chronically ill patients, successfully altering morbidity. Such services become more essential with increasing asthma severity. For high-risk asthmatic patients, the higher frequency of psychopathology and widespread failure to adhere to health-promoting self-management techniques underscore the essential inclusion of direct psychological services. However, psychological services must be tailored specifically to the disease population if they are to efficiently alter health care behavior. Improved asthma symptoms have been demonstrated in response to family therapy (Gustafsson, Kjellman, & Cederblad, 1986; Gustafsson, Kjellman, Ludvigsson, & Cederblad, 1987; Lask & Matthew, 1979); relaxation training (Leher, Isenberg, & Hochron, 1986); biofeedback (Kotses et al., 1991; Mussell & Harley, 1988); and hypnosis (Murphy et al., 1989); but the use of such techniques in isolation from a larger program of intervention is likely to be ineffective in the long run.

In the treatment of children with severe, poorly controlled asthma, psychological interventions must focus on the entire family system and on the full spectrum of behaviors required for effective asthma management (Bender & Klinnert, in press). Adherence in asthma involves not only taking medications with appropriate technique and at the correct times but also working in a partnership with a physician, pursuing environmental controls of asthma triggers, and recognizing and treating asthma symptoms when they occur. For many families of children with out-of-control asthma, overwhelming problems in living take precedence over attending to the specific needs of their asthmatic child. These can include markedly dysfunctional families with a variety of financial, social, and psychological needs. Intervention requires the involvement of mental health providers, who can help to address a range of problems that face these families. With such families, interventions must focus on specific, manageable problems and provide an arena within which to address the family's motivation to change. Discussion of family problems and interactions occur in the context of the behaviors required in the asthmatic child's care, the cost of medication, the shared responsibilities of various family members, and the actions required when an exacerbation of asthma symptoms occurs. When clearer lines of communication and clarification of responsibilities related to the asthmatic child are directly addressed, the intervention is likely to improve the effective and efficient management of the illness.

ENSURING THE FUTURE OF PSYCHOLOGY IN TERTIARY CARE SETTINGS

The future of psychology in tertiary health care centers will depend at least in part on its ability to change health care behavior. To do this, psychologists must (a) be highly knowledgeable about the disease they are helping to treat, (b) be present as a member of the treatment team in the health care setting, and (c) demonstrate that the services they offer are definable, effective, and result in cost savings.

The managed care preference to contract for psychological services with a mental health provider group separate from all medical services conflicts directly with the model of subspecialty psychological services integrated with the medical health care system. The provision of general practice psychological services is unlikely to result in significant changes in health care behavior or to alter the course of chronic illness.

Such an approach may be less costly in the short run but ineffective in the long run. A telephone conversation or two between psychologist and physician, perhaps followed by a letter summarizing the mental health consultation, cannot replace the ongoing collaboration between psychological and medical caregivers in the medical care setting. The mental health practitioner who is located in the treatment facility is much more effectively positioned to develop psychological interventions integrated with other health care. For example, in one hospital-based asthma program, the psychological intervention included identification of the patient's health beliefs, tailoring of prescribed treatment to specific patient characteristics, negotiating a behavioral contract between patient and physician, and, where indicated, problem-focused family therapy (Weinstein, 1995). Such innovative multidisciplinary programs can occur only when the psychological caregiver understands the disease and its treatment and has a direct voice in patient care and treatment planning.

Demonstrating the Cost-Effectiveness of Psychological Services

Cost-effective interventions are those that provide a reasonably effective outcome that is judged to be worth the cost involved, whereas a cost-saving intervention actually results in money saved (Doubilet, Weinstein, & McNeil, 1986). From the perspective of a disease-management planner, then, the judgment of cost-effectiveness may depend on debatable criteria. Nonetheless, the decision as to whether psychological interventions are worth the cost is likely to rest on whether (a) a demonstrable change occurs and (b) the change can be achieved within a reasonable period of time or number of sessions. Open-ended psychotherapy sessions lasting many months with nonspecific goals are less likely to be well received than interventions with specific objectives (e.g., to increase medication adherence, to improve judgment about avoiding environmental triggers of respiratory distress, or to reduce conflict among family members in order to achieve better coordination of an asthmatic child's care) and a session- or time-limited length. It is unreasonable to expect that all psychological interventions should necessarily be cost saving. However, in some instances, this will be so. The interventions described above, which yielded improved symptom control, also resulted in large cost savings. Changing behavior in low-to-moderate-risk asthmatics saved an average of $475 per patient (Kotses et al., 1995), whereas the intervention with high-risk, frequently hospitalized patients saved $1,642 per patient (Greineder et al., 1995). Although economic benefit cannot be allowed to become the sole criteria for behavioral medicine, those instances in which cost savings are achieved become powerful arguments in its favor (Friedman, Sobel, Myers, Caudill, & Benson, 1995).

The Importance of Continued Outcome Research

The inclusion of psychological services in tertiary care settings will depend on the demonstration of their direct impact on health care, including cost-effectiveness. With training and experience in outcome research, many psychologists are well equipped to conduct the research necessary to demonstrate the impact of psychological interventions. Such investigative efforts have several advantages: First, they require the investigator to clearly structure, define, and standardize the intervention, not only allowing for the measurement of the services' impact but also facilitating the "packaging" of interventions, making them more clearly understood, thus appealing to managed care contractors, and more easily duplicated in multiple health care settings. Second, such research establishes that psychological services can change health care behavior, improve the effectiveness of medical interventions, and save money. Finally, systematic investigation of the effect of psychological interventions on chronic illness can, in the best tradition of the science of psychology, result in an ongoing process of refinement and reevaluation of the intervention.

Comparison across studies of the effectiveness of various psychological and psychoeducational interventions is difficult because of large methodological variability. Individual studies have been weakened by failure to include an appropriate control group, to clearly define the patient sample or intervention, to use objective outcome measures, or to extend patient follow-up to a sufficient interval to adequately evaluate outcome (Bender & Klinnert, in press; Bernard-Bonnin et al., 1995). Creer, Wigal, Kotses, and Lewis (1990) argued that if studies of the impact of self-management interventions on treatment of asthma are to include the scientific merit necessary to stand up to peer review, and if the results of these investigations are to receive widespread acceptance, they must meet a number of criteria: (a) participants recruited in an unbiased fashion, with well-defined asthma and in numbers sufficient to allow appropriate statistical analysis; (b) random assignment to treatment and control groups; (c) use of clearly described and standardized treatments; (d) use of well-defined, valid, and reliable outcome measures; (e) collection of sufficient follow-up data; and (f) appropriate interpretation of data, including distinguishing between statistical and clinical significance.

CONCLUSION

Psychologists can continue to own an important role in the treatment of asthma and other chronic diseases, particularly in tertiary care settings, where severe, difficult-to-control illnesses are often accompanied by the presence of psychological problems. However, in today's climate of cost-effectiveness and efficiency, psychologists must demonstrate their ability to directly enhance medical treatment, increase efficiency, and reduce costs. In many regards, psychologists are poised to take a leading role as experts in health care behavior intervention, which can result in more effective and efficient medical treatment. The strong research background that defines much of psychology also equips psychologists with the ability to evaluate treatment outcomes and determine which combination of psychological and medical interventions result in most effective and cost-efficient disease control. To do this effectively in a tertiary care setting, such as National Jewish Center, psychologists must be knowledgeable about the disease and have full faculty membership. With specialized knowledge and skills, and integrated into the treatment setting, psychologists will be able to design, implement, and study innovative programs that can change health care behavior and improve treatment of chronic disease.

REFERENCES

Achenbach, T. M., Edelbrock, C. S. (1983). Manual for the Child Behavior Checklist and Revised Child Behavior Profile. Burlington: University of Vermont, Department of Psychiatry.

Bender, B., & Klinnert, M. (in press). Psychological correlates of asthma severity and treatment outcome. In H. Kotses & A. Harver (Eds.), *Behavioral contributions to the management of asthma*. New York: Dekker.

Bender, B., Milgrom, H., Bowry, P., Gabriels, R., Ackerson, L., & Rand, C. (1995). Asthmatic children's adherence with aerosolized medications. *American Journal of Respiratory and Critical Care Medicine, 151*, A352.

Bernard-Bonnin, A., Stachenko, S., Bonin, D., Charette, C., & Rousseau, E. (1995). Self-management teaching programs and morbidity of pediatric asthma: A meta-analysis. *Journal of Allergy and Clinical Immunology, 95*, 34–41.

Bussing, R., Halfon, N., Benjamin, B., & Wells, K. B. (1995). Prevalence of behavior problems in U.S. children with asthma. *Archives of Pediatric and Adolescent Medicine, 149*, 565–572.

Centers for Disease Control. (1995). Asthma—United States, 1982–1992. *Morbidity and Mortality Weekly Report, 43*, 952.

Coutts, J. A., Gibson, N. A., & Paton, J. Y. (1992). Measuring compliance with inhaled medication in asthma. *Archives of Disease in Childhood, 67*, 332–333.

Creer, T. L., Backial, M., Burns, K. L., Leung, P., Marion, R. J., Miklich, D. R., Morrill, C., Taplin, P. S., & Ullman, S. (1988). Living with asthma:

I. Genesis and development of a self-management program for childhood asthma. *Journal of Asthma, 25,* 335–362.

Creer, T. L., Wigal, J. K., Kotses, H., & Lewis, P. (1990). A critique of 19 self-management programs for childhood asthma: Part II. Comments regarding the scientific merit of the programs. *Pediatric Asthma, Allergy, and Immunology, 4,* 41–55.

Doubilet, P., Weinstein, M. C., & McNeil, B. J. (1986). Use and misuse of the term "cost effective" in medicine. *New England Journal of Medicine, 314,* 23–25.

Friedman, R., Sobel, D., Myers, P., Caudill, M., & Benson, H. (1995). Behavioral medicine, clinical health psychology, and cost offset. *Health Psychology, 14,* 509–518.

Graham, P. J., Rutter, M., Yule, W., & Pless, I. B. (1967). A psychosomatic disorder? *British Journal of Preventive and Social Medicine, 21,* 78–85.

Greineder, D. K., Loane, K. C., & Parks, P. (1995). Reduction in resource utilization by an asthma outreach program. *Archives of Pediatric and Adolescent Medicine, 149,* 415–420.

Gustafsson, P. A., Kjellman, N. M., & Cederblad, M. (1986). Family therapy in the treatment of severe childhood asthma. *Journal of Psychosomatic Research, 30,* 369–374.

Gustafsson, P. A., Kjellman, N. M., Ludvigsson, J., & Cederblad, M. (1987). Asthma and family interaction. *Archives of Disease in Childhood, 62,* 258–263.

Hamlett, K. W., Pelligrini, D. S., & Katz, K. S. (1992). Childhood chronic illness as a family stressor. *Journal of Pediatric Psychology, 17,* 33–47.

Kashani, J. H., Konig, P., Shepperd, J. A., Wilfley, D., & Morris, D. A. (1988). Psychopathology and self-concept in asthmatic children. *Journal of Pediatric Psychology, 13,* 509–520.

Klinnert, M. D. (in press). The psychology of asthma in the school-aged child. In J. Kember & J. Bemporand (Eds.), *Handbook of child and adolescent psychiatry: The grade school child.* New York: Wiley.

Kotses, H., Bernstein, I. L., Bernstein, D. I., Reynolds, R. V. C., Korbee, L., Wigal, J. K., Ganson, E., Stout, C., & Creer, T. L. (1995). A self-management program for adult asthma: Part I. Development and evaluation. *Journal of Allergy and Clinical Immunology, 95,* 529–540.

Kotses, H., Harver, A., Segreto, J., Glaus, K. D., Creer, T. L., & Young, G. A. (1991). Long-term effects of biofeedback-induced facial relaxation on measures of asthma severity in children. *Biofeedback and Self Regulation, 16,* 1–22.

Lask, B., & Matthew, D. (1979). Childhood asthma. A controlled trial of family psychotherapy. *Archives of Disease in Childhood, 54,* 116–119.

Lehrer, P. M., Isenberg, S., & Hochron, S. M. (1986). Asthma and emotion: A review. *Journal of Asthma, 30,* 5–21.

MacLean, W. E., Perrin, J. M., Gortmaker, S., Pierre, C. B. (1992). Psychological adjustment of children with asthma: Effects of illness severity and recent stressful life events. *Journal of Pediatric Psychology, 17*, 159–171.

Mayo, P. H., Richman, J., & Harris, H. W. (1990). Result of a program to reduce admissions for adult asthma. *Annals of Internal Medicine, 112*, 864–871.

Milgrom, H., Bender, B., Ackerson, L., Bowry, P., Smith, B., & Rand, C. (1995). Children's compliance with inhaled asthma medications. *Journal of Allergy and Clinical Immunology, 95*, 217.

Milgrom, H., Bender, B., Sarlin, N., & Leung, D. Y. M. (1994). Difficult to control asthma: The challenge posed by noncompliance. *American Journal of Asthma and Allergy for Pediatricians, 7*, 141–146.

Mrazek, D. A. (1985). Childhood asthma: The interplay of psychiatric and psychological factors. *Advances in Psychosomatic Medicine, 14*, 16–32.

Murphy, A. I., Karlin, R., Hochron, S., Lehrer, P. M., Swartzman, L., & McCann, B. (1989). Hypnotic susceptibility and its relationship to outcome in the behavioral treatment of asthma: Some preliminary data. *Psychological Reports, 65*, 691–698.

Mussell, M. J., & Harley, J. P. (1988). Trachea-noise biofeedback in asthma: A comparison of the effect of trachea-noise biofeedback, a bronchodilator, and no treatment on the rate of recovery from exercise- and eucapnic hyperventilation-induced asthma. *Biofeedback and Self Regulation, 13*, 219–234.

Osman, L. M., Abdalla, M. I., Beattie, J. A. G., Ross, S. J., Russell, I. T., Friend, J. A., Legge, J. S., & Douglas, J. G. (1994). Reducing hospital admission through computer supported education for asthma patients. *British Medical Journal, 308*, 568–571.

Strunk, R. C., Mrazek, D. A., Fuhrmann, G. S., & LaBrecque, J. F. (1985). Physiologic and psychological characteristics associated with deaths due to asthma in childhood: A case controlled study. *Journal of the American Medical Association, 254*, 1193–1198.

Tettersell, M. J. (1993). Asthma patients' knowledge in relation to compliance with drug therapy. *Journal of Advanced Nursing, 18*, 103–113.

Todd, W. E. (1995). New mindsets in asthma: Interventions and disease management. *Journal of Care Management, 1*, 2–8.

Weinstein, A. G. (1995). Clinical management strategies to maintain drug compliance in asthmatic children. *Annals of Allergy, Asthma, and Immunology, 74*, 304–310.

Weiss, S. T., Tosteson, T. D., Segal, M. R., Tager, I. B., Redline, S., & Speizer, F. E. (1992). Effects of asthma on pulmonary function in children: A longitudinal population-based study. *American Review of Respiratory Disease, 145*, 58–64.

Yellowless, P. M., Haynes, S., Potts, N., & Ruffin, R. E. (1988). Psychiatric morbidity in patients with life-threatening asthma: Initial report of a controlled study. *Medical Journal of Australia, 149*, 246–249.

17

THE ROLE OF CLINICAL NEUROPSYCHOLOGY IN THE ASSESSMENT AND CARE OF PERSONS WITH ALZHEIMER'S DISEASE

ALFRED W. KASZNIAK

Clinical neuropsychologists are being employed in increasing numbers within medical settings in which they provide clinical services to neurologic patients and consultation to neurologists. Among the most frequent requests for neuropsychological consultation within such settings are those concerning persons with known or suspected dementia, particularly Alzheimer's disease (AD). The term *dementia* refers to a syndrome, caused by brain dysfunction, of acquired intellectual impairment that is of sufficient severity to interfere with social or occupational functioning. According to most definitions (e.g., Bayles & Kaszniak, 1987; Cummings & Benson, 1992), the syndrome of dementia involves deterioration in two or more of the following domains of psychological functioning: memory, language, visuospatial skills, judgment or abstract thinking, and emotion or personality. In studies of dementia in various countries, prevalence rates have ranged from 2.5% to 24.6% for persons over the age of 65 (see Ineichen, 1987). Differences in dementia definitions, sampling techniques, and sensitivity of instruments used to identify cases may account for the variability in estimates of the prevalence of dementia. Cummings and Benson (1992), calculating the average of prevalence estimates across studies, suggest that approximately 6% of persons over the age of 65 have severe dementia, with an additional 10% to 15% having mild-to-moderate dementia. The prevalence of the syndrome of dementia is age related, doubling approximately every 5 years after age 65 (Jorm, Korten, & Henderson, 1987). Not surprisingly, the prevalence of dementia is higher among hospital and nursing home residents than among those living within the community (for reviews, see Kramer, 1986; Smyer, 1988).

The dementia syndrome can be associated with more than 50 different causes of brain dysfunction (Haase, 1977; Katzman, 1986). Alzheimer's disease accounts for the largest proportion of all causes, with published reports varying from a low of 22% to a high of 70% of all dementia patients receiving diagnoses of AD (for review, see Cummings & Benson, 1992). However, in some community surveys (particularly, although not exclusively, those in Japan and China), dementia associated with cerebrovascular disease is reportedly more common than AD (Folstein, Anthony, Parhad, Duffy, & Gruenberg, 1985; Li, Shen, Chen, Zhao, & Li, 1989; Rorsman, Hagnell, & Lanke, 1986; Shibayama, Kasahara, & Kobayashi, 1986). It is unclear whether differences in reported relative prevalence reflect methodological variation across studies or actual regional and international disparities. Despite differences in the relative prevalence estimates provided by epidemiological investigations, there is agreement that AD and vascular dementia are the most frequent causes of age-associated dementia (Roman, 1991). Alzheimer's disease and vascular dementia are also the most frequent diagnoses made of patients referred for comprehensive assessment because of memory complaints (Thal, Grundman, & Klauber, 1988).

Clinical neuropsychology is the applied science dealing with the cognitive and behavioral manifestations of human brain dysfunction. Its primary concern is with the assessment, diagnosis, management, and rehabilitation of patients with developmental and acquired brain dysfunction. As greater numbers of individuals are surviving into older age (Myers, 1990), the prevalence of dementing illness has increased (Manton, 1990). Accordingly, research and practice in the clinical neuropsychology of dementia has also increased dramatically, particularly over the past 2 decades (La Rue, 1992; Poon, Kaszniak, & Dudley, 1992). Neuropsychological consultation now plays a critical role in identifying the presence of the syndrome of dementia, contributes to differential neurologic diagnosis of the many possible causes of dementia, and aids in the treatment and clinical management of dementing illness. Clinical neuropsychologic consultation with the person having known or suspected dementia may be performed to address any or all of the following aims (see Albert & Moss, 1988; Bayles & Kaszniak, 1987; La Rue, 1992; Zec, 1993): (a) identification of the presence of cognitive impairment and patterns of impairment relevant to differential diagnosis; (b) provision of information to health care providers, patients, and family members, concerning specific strengths and deficits in cognitive functions and their practical implications; (c) assessment of treatment effects or disease progression; and (d) provision of, or recommendations for, treatment and management of cognitive and behavior problems.

IDENTIFICATION OF THE PRESENCE AND PATTERN OF COGNITIVE IMPAIRMENT

The clinical neuropsychologist has available a large number of standardized tests that have known reliability and sensitivity in the detection of cognitive deficits that result from either focal or diffuse brain damage (Kolb & Whishaw, 1995; Lezak, 1995; Spreen & Strauss, 1991). These tests have been designed to assess specific aspects of a wide range of cognitive functioning, including general intellectual ability, memory functions, orientation and attention, language functions, perceptual functions, visual–motor constructional ability, abstract and conceptual reasoning, and so-called executive functions (i.e., goal formulation, planning, and the execution of goal-directed plans). Because many such tests meet psychometric criteria of acceptable reliability and validity, they provide accurate procedures for describing the cognitive strengths and weaknesses of a person. Accurate description is important in detecting the presence of (particularly mild) dementia and in determining whether the pattern of deficits is consistent with that expected in some particular dementia etiology. According to the *Diagnostic and Statistical Manual of Mental Disorders* (American Psychiatric Association, 1994), the diagnosis of Dementia of the Alzheimer's Type requires that the following criteria be met: (a) presence of multiple cognitive deficits, including memory impairment and at least one other impairment (e.g., aphasia, apraxia, agnosia, or disturbed executive functioning); (b) a gradual onset and progressive course of deterioration; and (c) exclusion of all other possible causes of dementia (e.g., cerebrovascular disease, Huntington's disease, Parkinson's disease, or brain tumor) by history, physical examination, and laboratory tests. In addition, the impairment must significantly interfere with social or occupational functioning, must represent a significant decline from a previous level of functioning, and must not occur exclusively during the course of *delirium* (an acute confusional state, most often due to systemic physical illness). An increasingly large body of research (for review, see Zec, 1993) has demonstrated the reliability and validity of neuropsychological assessment procedures in detecting the multiple cognitive deficits of AD in its early stages and in documenting the course of deterioration. Research has also shown that particular patterns of relatively impaired and preserved areas of cognitive functioning are associated with different dementia etiologies, such as AD versus Huntington's disease (for review, see Butters, Salmon, & Butters, 1994).

In neurologic and psychiatric practice, clinical screening for cognitive deficit in older adults is typically done through brief mental status tests, such as the Mini-Mental State Examination (MMSE; Folstein, Folstein, & McHugh, 1975). However, brief mental status tests typically have substantial *false-negative* (identifying a cognitively impaired person as normal) rates in detecting cognitive impairment (Nelson, Fogel, & Faust, 1986), particularly for individuals who are more highly educated (O'Connor, Pollitt, Hyde, Miller & Fellowes, 1989). There is also evidence for low education increasing the probability of *false-positive* errors (misclassifying normal individuals as cognitively impaired), particularly when the individual in question has less than 9 years of education (Anthony, LaResche, Niaz, Voh Koroff, & Folstein, 1982; Murden, McRae, Kaner, & Bucknam, 1991).

Most psychometric tests used in neuropsychological assessment contain a range of item difficulty, so that test scores ideally approximate a normal distribution when administered to individuals in the general population. This can provide for greater sensitivity to mild or subtle cognitive deficits than what is provided by mental status screening tests on which most normal individuals achieve near-perfect scores (e.g., Crum, Anthony, Bassett, & Folstein, 1993). Appropriately selected neuropsychological tests can reveal subtle cognitive impairments in neurologic patients who show no evidence of deficit on mental status screening tests (e.g., Bondi, Kaszniak, Bayles, & Vance, 1993). The ability of neuropsychological test batteries to reliably assess the pattern of performance across different domains of cognitive functioning may be particularly important in evaluating persons with high premorbid intellectual functioning (Naugle, Cullum, & Bigler, 1990). In such persons, performance can be at or above general-population normative expectation on all tests, yet a comparison of performance across different tests may reveal a pattern consistent with deterioration characteristic of a particular dementing illness, such as AD.

GENERAL CONSIDERATIONS IN THE NEUROPSYCHOLOGICAL ASSESSMENT OF OLDER ADULTS

Given the age-associated prevalence of most dementing illnesses, the majority of persons referred for neuropsychological assessment because of suspected or known dementia will be older adults. Clinical and experimental psychologists have been responsible for generating a large body of research concerning the psychological changes of normal aging, which has important implications for the interpretation of neuropsychological assessment results. The competent neuropsychological evaluation of older persons requires particular knowledge of research concerning those aspects of aging that impact on the conduct and interpretation of psychological testing.

Sensory Changes With Aging

One significant aspect of aging, influencing both selection of test materials and their interpretation, concerns sensory changes characteristic of normal aging, as well as age-related sensory disorders. Changes in auditory functioning with age have been well documented (Corso, 1985; Fozard, 1990; Schieber, 1992). Decreased auditory acuity, particularly for high frequencies (termed *presbycusis*), occurs with increasing age and affects the perception of speech. Word comprehension thus becomes increasingly difficult with advancing age. Older individuals can become handicapped in speech comprehension and oral communication due to these deficits (Pickett, Bergman, & Levitt, 1979; Plomp & Mimpen, 1979). In some cases, older adults with hearing loss may be mistakenly presumed to be confused or demented (Becker, 1981).

The prevalence of hearing loss in those over 75 years of age has been estimated to be 50% (Plomp, 1978). Hearing loss occurring early in life can be associated with late-life paranoid psychosis (Cooper, 1976), and the association between hearing loss and emotional disturbance, particularly depression, in the elderly has been documented (e.g., O'Neil & Calhoun, 1975). Hearing loss in an older person can clearly affect the results of verbal tests of cognitive status, leading to inaccurate interpretations of test performance (e.g., Peters, Potter, & Scholer, 1988). Weinstein and Amsel (1986) administered a mental status questionnaire, with and without the tester's voice amplified to compensate for hearing loss, to a group of institutionalized older adults with hearing impairment. They found that 33% of the individuals were reclassified as being less severely demented when amplification was used. Roccaforte, Burke, Bayer, and Wenger (1992) similarly found diminished hearing to be associated with lower scores on a telephone-administered version of a commonly used mental status screening test. Auditory acuity screening is thus an important component of any neuropsychological evaluation of an older individual. Note that screening for auditory impairment can effectively be accomplished, even in institutionalized older adults with dementia (Ciurlia-Guy, Cashman, & Lewsen, 1993).

Older persons are also quite susceptible to auditory masking, making the perception of speech difficult when there is background noise (Storandt, 1994). Finally, the rate of auditory information processing slows with age (Lima, Hale, & Myerson, 1991) and is even further slowed in dementing illness, such as AD (Tomoeda, Bayles, Boone, Kaszniak, & Slauson, 1990). In conducting a neuropsychological examination of an older person, it is therefore important to take precautions to maximize auditory comprehension. These include making sure that the patient is wearing any prescribed hearing aids, securing a quiet examination room, speaking somewhat (although not dramatically) more slowly, maintaining eye contact (so that comprehension may be aided by watching the examiner's lips), and (for examiners with high-pitched voices) possibly using a lower-pitched voice than usual. Patients with dementing illness may experience additional impairment of higher level aspects of auditory perception. For example, persons with AD show impaired recognition of meaningful nonverbal sounds, even when high-frequency hearing is within normal limits for age and verbal comprehension (Rapcsak, Kentros, & Rubens, 1989).

Similarly, there is an age-related decline in visual acuity (Johnson & Choy, 1987; Kosnik, Winslow, Kline, Rasinski, & Sekuler, 1988) and a decline in the amount of light that is transmitted through the lens of the eye (due to cataracts or clouding of the lens; Lerman, 1983). As reviewed by Owsley and Sloane (1990) and Schieber (1992), visual capability begins to decline during the 4th decade of life, with, by 65 years of age, about half of all people showing a visual acuity of 20/70 or less. Blindness or other serious visual problems affect more than 7% of the population between 65 and 75 years of age and 16% of those over age 75. Age-associated visual impairment appears to be greater among aging women, as compared with men, and ability to read, watch television, and engage in other visual activities is reduced. Reduced visual capacity has been reported to contribute to apparent disorientation and behavioral deterioration in older adults (O'Neil & Calhoun, 1975). Given the age-related changes in visual functioning and the age-related prevalence of various visual disorders, it is important to consider the possible impact of visual impairment on any cognitive test that requires processing of visual information. Thus, older adults may require higher levels of illumination and larger printed verbal information than younger adults. Uncorrected visual impairment would appear to have the potential for contributing to errors on any cognitive task involving visual information processing, thus potentially increasing false-positive rates in the identification of cognitive impairment.

In some cases of AD and other dementias, the predominant or presenting symptoms may be visual. Research applying visual psychophysical testing, neuro-ophthalmologic examination, and electrophysiologic testing of the visual system (Rizzo et al., 1992) has suggested that these visual impairments result primarily from cortical disease rather than retinocalcarine dysfunction. The most common visual complaints in AD are problems relating to visuospatial functioning (e.g., not bumping into things when walking, finding door handles or other common objects, finding their way in surroundings, sewing, locating the next word or line of print; for review, see Mendez, Tomsak, & Remler, 1990). Until the later stages of dementia, AD patients and their caregivers less frequently complain of difficulties in visually identifying objects, faces, or scenes (Cogan, 1985).

Physical Disability in Older Age

Clearly, another factor to be considered is the possible contribution of any physical disability (e.g., neuromuscular disorder or severe arthritis) to below-expectation performance on any cognitive task. Mental status examination procedures, for example, have poorer ability to discriminate demented from nondemented subjects with some physical disability versus those without such disability (Jagger, Clarke, & Anderson, 1992). The contribution of physical disability is of particular concern when evaluating the oldest old, as it has been estimated that 29% of all persons over age 85 suffer from severe disability (Kunkel & Applebaum, 1992). In neuropsychologically evaluating the person who has a physical disability, the neuropsychologist must rely on those tests that are not likely to be influenced by the person's particular physical impairments.

Response Slowing and Aging

Both simple and choice reaction time show progressive slowing from early through late adulthood (Lima et al., 1991; Wilkinson & Allison, 1989). One obvious implication of this observation is that older adults will take longer to complete various neuropsychological testing procedures than younger adults (Storandt, 1994). This suggests that it may be necessary to take more frequent breaks during a neuropsychological examination session, when evaluating older, particularly ill or frail adults. Although healthy older people are unlikely to fatigue more rapidly than younger adults during average-length (e.g., 2 1/2 hr) testing sessions

(Cunningham, Sepkoski, & Opel, 1978), older persons in poor health are likely to fatigue quickly. The slowing of response speed with aging has other implications for neuropsychological assessment. For example, response slowing may result in slight underestimations of ability (Storandt, 1977) on tasks such as the Arithmetic and Block Design subtests of the Wechsler Adult Intelligence Scale–Revised (Wechsler, 1981) that assign bonus points for faster performance. Examiners therefore often "test the limits" by allowing an older person to continue working on the task after standard cutoff times have elapsed, to get a more complete picture of that person's cognitive strengths and deficits.

Need for Age-Appropriate Normative Data

Another important factor in the interpretation of neuropsychologic test performance is the fact that for both healthy people and people with cerebral disorders, performance on many tests is negatively correlated with adult age (Albert, 1988; Albert, Heller, & Milberg, 1988; Heaton, Grant, & Mathews, 1986; Kaszniak, 1990; Kaszniak, Garron, Fox, Bergen, & Huckman, 1979; La Rue, 1992; Mittenberg, Seidenberg, O'Leary, & DiGiulio, 1989; Moehle & Long, 1989; Petersen, Smith, Kokmen, Ivnik, & Tangalos, 1992; Reitan & Wolfsen, 1986; Vannieuwhirk & Galbraith, 1985). Age relationships with commonly used neuropsychological measures are particularly strong for tests of abstraction and complex problem-solving performance (Elias, Robbins, Walter, & Schultz, 1993). Such age relationships imply the necessity of using age-appropriate normative data when interpreting neuropsychological test performance. A particular problem has been the relative lack of adequate normative data on most neuropsychological tests for the oldest old (i.e., those over age 85; Albert, 1981; Erickson, Eimon, & Hebben, 1992; Kaszniak, 1987; Zec, 1990). Recently, however, relatively large scale normative studies have been published for some of the more commonly used neuropsychological tests, extending norms to over age 90 (Ivnik et al., 1992a; 1992b; 1992c; Malec, Ivnik, & Smith, 1993; VanGorp, Satz, Kiersch, & Henry, 1986). A comprehensive listing of neuropsychological and other cognitive test norms for older adults can be found in Erickson, Eimon, and Hebben (1994).

Need for Education-Appropriate Normative Data

Another factor to be considered is that performance on various neuropsychological tests is correlated with the person's educational background and other indicators of premorbid intellectual functioning (e.g., Barona, Reynolds, & Chastain, 1984; Heaton et al., 1986; Kaszniak et al., 1979). The availability of normative data for particular tests (Heaton, Grant, & Mathews, 1991; Malek et al., 1992), allowing a comparison of an individual to norms for the persons same age (by half-decade) and number of years of formal education, have helped to reduce the impact of this factor on interpretation of assessment results. However, such age- and education-specific normative data is not available for all neuropsychologic tests used in clinical practice, necessitating considerable caution when interpreting performance of any person who is either much more, or much less, educated than the average for the normative sample with which she or he is being compared.

The relationship between education and neuropsychological test performance is particularly problematic in the assessment of possible mild dementia in older adults. Research applying a neuropsychological paradigm-based criterion for identifying dementia (i.e., defective performance on memory testing and tests of at least two other areas of cognitive functioning) in community-resident older adults has classified as demented a significantly higher percentage of those participants with 8 or less years of education, compared with those with more than 8 years of education (Stern et al., 1992). Although this may indicate a greater false-positive rate for neuropsychological identification of dementia in less educated persons, it is also possible that rates of dementia are truly higher among those with little education (for discussion, see Berkman, 1986). Adding a measure of functioning in activities of daily living to the neuropsychological paradigm-based diagnosis may reduce the likelihood of false-positive identification of dementia in less educated people (Pittman et al., 1992).

EVIDENCE SUPPORTING THE VALIDITY OF NEUROPSYCHOLOGICAL DETECTION OF ALZHEIMER'S DISEASE

Much of the increasingly large body of research in the neuropsychology of dementia has focused on an understanding of the nature of cognitive dysfunction in Alzheimer's disease (for review, see Nebes, 1992). Other research has focused on the diagnostic utility of neuropsychological testing in differentiating dementia from normal aging and in distinguishing among the different causes of dementia (for review, see La Rue, 1992; La Rue, Yang, & Osato, 1992; Parks, Zec, & Wilson, 1993). The majority of diagnostic studies have examined the differentiation between normal aging and dementia. Most of these studies (e.g., Bayles, Boone, Tomoeda, Slauson, & Kaszniak, 1989; Eslinger, Damasio, Benton, & Van Allen, 1985; Huff et al., 1987; Kaszniak, Wilson, Fox, & Stebbins, 1986; Storandt, Botwinick, Danziger, Berg, & Hughes, 1984) have compared healthy older people with those having clinically diagnosed AD (of mild-to-moderate dementia severity) on a battery of neuropsychological tests. Results are consistent in showing AD patients to have deficits in two or more areas of cognitive functioning assessed by the tests, with the largest deficits seen on tests of ability to learn new information and retain this information over time.

Studies concerned with the differentiation of very mildly demented probable AD patients from healthy elderly people (Knopman & Ryberg, 1989; Morris et al., 1991; Welsh, Butters, Hughes, Mohs, & Heyman, 1991) have shown that measures of recent memory, particularly those involving delayed recall of newly learned material, are most discriminating. In one study (Morris et al., 1991), the neuropsychologic differentiation of normal older adults from those with very mild cognitive impairment was supported by subsequent postmortem histopathologic evidence of AD in all of those neuropsychologically classified as mildly impaired and in none of those classified as normal elderly. Also, Flicker, Ferris, and Reisberg (1991) reported that tests of recent memory have high sensitivity and specificity in discriminating mildly impaired individuals who cognitively decline at 2-year reexamination from those who do not. Despite this encouraging data for the application of neuropsychological testing, particularly of memory functioning, in the detection of very mild dementia, high sensitivity can be at the cost of lower specificity. Neuropsychological assessment batteries specifically designed or selected for the detection of mild dementia are correlated with participant educational level (Ganguli et al., 1991) and can clearly be affected by physical disability, visual or auditory impairment, psychiatric illness (including depression), and limited facility with the English language (O'Connor, Pollitt, Hyde, Miller, & Fellowes, 1991). Therefore, caution in the clinical interpretation of neuropsychological test results is necessary when any of these confounding conditions is present.

Overall, the available research indicates that neuropsychological assessment, particularly when measures of delayed recall are included, makes an important contribution to the identification of mild dementia, when interpreted within the context of other clinical data (e.g., informant-based history of cognitive decline, evidence of impairment in instrumental activities of daily living, educational background, assessment for depression, sensory impairment, or other factors than dementing illness to account for impaired performance). Due to the lower sensitivity of mental status screening tests, such as the MMSE, for detecting mild as compared to moderate-to-severe degrees of cognitive impairment (for review, see Tombaugh & McIntyre, 1992), neuropsychological testing may be particularly helpful when there is a history of apparent cognitive decline, but where a brief mental status test is performed within normal limits.

DIFFERENTIAL DIAGNOSIS OF DEMENTIA VERSUS DEPRESSION

A particularly difficult clinical problem involves the differential diagnosis of persons who present with signs of both cognitive impairment and depression. It must be determined whether the person is experiencing cognitive difficulty secondary to a depressive disorder or has developed a depressive syndrome secondary to a dementing illness, such as AD.

On the basis of available research, it has been estimated that between 1% and 31% of patients diagnosed as having a progressive dementing illness may actually be suffering from depression with associated cognitive deficits (Katzman, Lasker, & Bernstein, 1988). It has been estimated that 20% of older depressed patients may have cognitive deficits sufficiently severe as to merit the term *dementia syndrome of depression* (La Rue, D'Elia, Clark, Spar, & Jarvik, 1986). There are significant clinical risks associated with errors in differential diagnosis. Mistakenly diagnosing an irreversible dementing illness in a person actually suffering from depression deprives the person of appropriate treatment (psychologic and pharmacologic) and risks further deterioration of function. There are also risks associated with misdiagnosing a progressive dementing illness as depression. These include inappropriate treatment and the failure to provide prognostic information that would permit the patient and family members the opportunity to prepare for the consequences of progressive dementing illness.

Diagnosis is also complicated by the fact that dementing illnesses and depression often coexist. Teri and Wagner (1992) noted that published prevalence estimates of depressive syndromes in AD range from 0 to 86% with the majority of studies reporting rates in the 17%–29% range. Once a person has been diagnosed as having probable AD, symptoms of depression may go unrecognized. Because patients with coexisting depression and AD can expect to benefit from treatment of their depression (for review of the evidence for this conclusion, see Teri & Wagner, 1992), failure to diagnose and treat depression in an AD patient may result in unnecessary emotional, physical, and social discomfort. Patients with coexistent depression and AD have also been found more likely to exhibit delusions, various behavior problems such as restlessness and agitation, and greater impairment of instrumental activities of daily living than AD patients without depression (see Kaszniak & Christenson, 1994).

Neuropsychological assessment has an important role to play in the differential diagnosis of dementia and depression in older adults, as reviewed in detail by Kaszniak and Christenson (1994). Psychologists have contributed to the development and validation of various interview-based and self-report measures of depressive symptoms that are appropriate for use with older, cognitively impaired individuals (see Kaszniak &

Scogin, 1995). In addition, research has supported the validity of particular patterns of neuropsychological test performance, particularly involving different aspects of memory (e.g., rate of forgetting, free recall vs. recognition, or response to semantic organization of material to be remembered) as important contributors in the effort to differentiate the cognitive effects of dementia and depression. Despite such encouraging data, caution must be exercised in the interpretation of neuropsychological assessment results for persons with signs of both dementia and depression. The long-term prognosis of such patients is quite variable (i.e., some showing remission of both depression and cognitive impairment with effective depression treatment and some showing progressive dementia in long-term follow-up), and neuropsychological assessment may not be helpful in clarifying prognosis (Nussbaum, Kaszniak, Allender, & Rapcsak, 1995). Differential diagnosis in this area remains a necessarily interdisciplinary endeavor, with physicians and other health care providers also playing important roles. Complex interactions exist among biological aspects of illness, medications (both psychotropic and nonpsychotropic), age-related changes in pharmacokinetics and pharmacodynamics, and a variety of psychologic and social factors that influence the occurrence and nature of both cognitive and affective symptoms in older adults (see Cummings & Benson, 1992; Depression Guideline Panel, 1993).

PROVISION OF INFORMATION TO HEALTH CARE PROVIDERS, PATIENTS, AND FAMILY MEMBERS

Neuropsychological assessment can also be helpful to patients and their caregivers (whether personal or professional) in assisting them to understand the patient and in reducing anxiety and confusion (see Lezak, 1995). In my experience, this can be one of the most valuable aspects of neuropsychological consultation. Patients and their family members are often understandably distressed by the cognitive and behavioral changes that have provoked the request for consultation. Even when, as in AD, there is no available treatment to reverse or arrest the disorder, persons can be comforted by gaining an understanding of which specific functions are impaired and which remain fairly intact. It can be particularly important to identify and accurately describe patterns of cognitive strengths and deficits as early as possible in the course of a progressive dementing illness. Persons early in the course of AD may have relatively severe impairment of memory but considerably more intact functioning in language comprehension and expression, conceptual reasoning, and judgment. Therefore, the capacity of such persons to make decisions concerning necessary future plans (e.g., disposition of their estate or wishes concerning future medical and long-term care) may remain intact at this early stage. Providing the patient and family members with accurate assessment information can allow the person to make decisions and plans before the progression of illness renders him or her incompetent to do so.

There is also some evidence (e.g., LaBarge, Rosenman, Leavitt, & Cristiani, 1988) to suggest that mildly demented persons can improve their utilization of coping mechanisms and identify strategies to compensate for memory loss when they are given information concerning their specific cognitive strengths and deficits (derived from neuropsychological testing), within the context of brief supportive counseling. Again, it is important that such information be provided as early as possible to the person with a progressive dementing illness such as AD, because insight and the ability to maintain awareness of cognitive deficits may be lost with illness progression (Kaszniak & Christenson, 1996; McGlynn & Kaszniak, 1991a, 1991b).

ASSESSMENT OF DISEASE PROGRESSION AND TREATMENT EFFECTS

Dementing illnesses are typically progressive in their effects on cognitive functioning. Neuropsychological consultation can play an important role in assessing the severity of dementia and in tracking disease progression (for purposes of guiding caregivers and adjusting goals of clinical management). When mildly demented probable AD patients are compared with moderately demented individuals (Hill, Storandt, & LaBarge, 1992; Welsh, Butters, Hughes, Mohs, & Heyman, 1992), moderately demented patients show more severe memory impairment (often at the "basement" of the measurement range of the memory test) and an increased number and severity of deficits in other areas of cognitive functioning. The severity of recent memory deficits, particularly delayed recall, early in the course of AD, renders memory tests less useful (because of basement effects) for staging the severity of dementia across individuals (Welsh et al., 1992) or for tracking the progression of dementia over time (Kaszniak et al., 1986). Neuropsychological measures of other aspects of cognitive functioning (e.g., recognition memory, verbal fluency, confrontation naming, and praxis) appear better for staging dementia severity or tracking dementia progression (Kaszniak et al., 1986; Welsh et al., 1992).

Information concerning the differential sensitivity and specificity of neuropsychological tests for the initial detection versus the staging or tracking of dementia severity has important implications for the choice of outcome measures to evaluate intervention efficacy (see Berg et al., 1992). Neuropsychological tests, when carefully selected (e.g., according to criteria such as reliability, sensitivity to change, absence of marked basement effects, brevity, and high face validity), can play a very important role in the evaluation of medication or other intervention trials for patients with dementing illness (see Flicker, 1988). Clinical neuropsychologists have therefore been critical collaborators in the design and execution of such clinical trials.

As already noted, most dementing illness involves a progressive deterioration in cognitive functioning. Therefore, the documentation of deterioration is an important task in any clinical evaluation of an individual with possible AD or other dementia. The most direct approach to obtaining such evidence would be to compare performance on neuropsychological tests over time. In most instances, however, prior test scores are unavailable at the time when an initial assessment is made of an individual suspected of having a dementing illness. In such cases, the neuropsychologist has to rely on a history of progressive cognitive deterioration, obtained from a close relative or other informant. Relatives appear able to provide valid reports of progressive deterioration in dementia patients. McGlone et al. (1990) compared older adults with complaints of memory difficulty who later showed evidence of progressive dementia (as determined by 8- to 24-month neuropsychological reassessment) with those with memory complaints but without evidence of progressive dementia. The two groups of patients reported comparable numbers of memory complaints. However, when relatives rated memory change over time, the first group of patients, who did not show evidence of dementia, did not differ significantly from healthy elderly controls (without memory complaints), whereas the second group of patients, who did show evidence of progressive dementia, were rated by their relatives as having become significantly worse. Furthermore, the relatives' assessments of patients' memory were significantly intercorrelated with objective-memory-test scores, and not with patients' depression. This later observation is of importance because other research has shown self-reported memory complaints in healthy older adults to be more closely correlated with depressed mood than with objective-memory-test performance (e.g., Bolla, Lindgren, Bonaccorsy, & Bleecker, 1991). Research concerning the retrospective accounts of dementia symptoms, obtained from relatives of patients referred to a memory-disorders clinic, has also shown that relatives' reports are reasonably reliable over a 4- to 17-month test–retest interval (La Rue, Watson, & Plotkin, 1992). Bayles and Tomoeda (1991), in a study of 99 AD patients and their caregivers, also found that caregiver reports of memory and linguistic communication symptoms were significantly correlated with patients' performance on select corresponding items of a linguistic-communication test battery. Although such results encourage the use of caregiver interview data for assessing the presence of multiple cognitive deficits, it has also been found that relatives' reports are influenced by the nature of the relationship to the patient. For example, La Rue, Watson, and Plotkin (1992) found that spouses of memory-impaired patients reported lower levels of impairment than did younger relatives. Thus, neuropsychologists will often include more than one family informant or a family consensus approach, to increase the accuracy of conclusions about the presence and range of cognitive impairments in persons suspected of dementia. When no reliable informant is available, the clinician may have to rely on a qualitative evaluation of neuropsychological assessment results, to determine whether the pattern of cognitive deficits is more consistent with a dementing illness or with relatively focal or diffuse nonprogressive cerebral disease. Although patients with focal cerebral damage (e.g., left-hemisphere stroke) can show neuropsychological evidence of deficits in more than one area of cognitive functioning (e.g., language, memory, or executive functioning; Beeson, Bayles, Rubens, & Kaszniak, 1993), the pattern of deficits across tests differs from that of AD patients (Bayles et al., 1989).

TREATMENT AND MANAGEMENT OF COGNITIVE AND BEHAVIOR PROBLEMS

Neuropsychological consultation can also make important contributions to the clinical management of patients with AD or other dementing illness. Identification of relatively intact cognitive functioning can assist in developing plans for sharing daily responsibilities between the patient and others in their environment (see La Rue, Yang, & Osato, 1992). Conversely, neuropsychological documentation of particular deficits can direct caregivers to areas where the patient will require additional supervision or assistance. For example, Henderson, Mack, and Williams (1989), in a study of patients with probable AD, found that neuropsychologically documented visuoconstructive deficits (equating patients with vs. without visuospatial deficits for degree of memory impairment) significantly predicted real-world spatial disorientation (i.e., caregiver-reported episodes of getting lost, failing to recognize familiar environments, and wandering). Although research results to date have been mixed, neuropsychological evaluation may also be able to make contributions to decisions regarding whether the patient can safely continue in potentially risky activities such as driving (for review, see Kaszniak, Keyl, & Albert, 1991).

Finally, neuropsychologists and clinical geropsychologists have made important contributions to the design and delivery of interventions to reduce behavioral problems in AD and other dementing illnesses. Fisher and Carstensen (1990) reviewed available empirical studies of various behavior-management procedures that have been successfully applied in reducing behavior problems (e.g., aggressiveness or agitation) in dementia. Although continuing research needs to be directed toward answering questions concerning predictors of who will respond best to behavioral interventions and how treatment gains can be maintained in the face of progressive dementia, results to date have encouraged the application of behavioral interventions with persons having Alzheimer's and other dementing illnesses. Psychologists with training in behavioral treatment methods remain those best qualified to deliver such interventions. As recently reviewed by Teri and McCurry (1994), there exist a small number of studies that have reported effectiveness of cognitive–behavioral therapy in reducing coexistent depression in outpatients with progressive dementias, such as AD. Note that in the ongoing study by Teri and colleagues (described in Teri & McCurry, 1994), cognitive–behavior therapy for depression in AD patients also resulted in an improvement of caregiver's mood, even though treatment did not specifically focus on the caregiver. Teri and McCurry speculated that increased patient-management skill (caregivers were taught behavioral strategies for improving patient mood by increasing pleasant events, decreasing unpleasant events, and using behavioral problem-solving strategies to alter depression-related contingencies), the availability of regular support (eight 60-minute training sessions, once per week), and the reduced depression in their family member with dementia may explain the added caregiver benefits.

Within long-term-care settings, where large numbers of AD patients with more advanced dementia reside, psychologists have also been involved in providing behavioral interventions aimed at increasing sensory stimulation, maintaining social activity, and reducing particular problem behaviors (e.g., incontinence). The few available studies that have evaluated psychotherapeutic interventions with nursing home residents have suggested improvements in depression, social interaction, and patient self-concept (for review, see Terri & McCurry, 1994).

SUMMARY AND CONCLUSION

It is clear that psychologists have much to offer, both in assessment and intervention, to persons with AD or related dementias and their caregivers. Research evidence supports the reliability and validity of neuropsychological assessment in the early detection of dementia, in contributions to differential diagnosis, in the evaluation of disease progression and treatment trials, and in providing accurate descriptive information to patients and their caregivers. Furthermore, although the available body of research is still small, there is also growing research support for the role of psychological, particularly behavioral and cognitive–behavioral, interventions in the treatment and management of mood and behavioral problems of AD patients. The contributions of psychologists within neurological settings serving persons with AD, both in conducting necessary research and in the direct delivery of clinical service, have been substantial. The success of these efforts, to date, argues for an expanding role for psychology within this area of tertiary medical care.

REFERENCES

Albert, M. S. (1981). Geriatric neuropsychology. *Journal of Consulting and Clinical Psychology, 49,* 835–850.

Albert, M. S. (1988). Assessment of cognitive function. In M. S. Albert & M. B. Moss (Eds.), *Geriatric neuropsychology* (pp. 57–81). New York: Guilford Press.

Albert, M. S., Heller, H. S., & Milberg, W. (1988). Changes in naming ability with age. *Psychology and Aging, 3,* 173–178.

Albert, M. S., & Moss, M. B. (Eds.). (1988). *Geriatric neuropsychology.* New York: Guilford Press.

American Psychiatric Association. (1994). *Diagnostic and statistical manual of mental disorders* (4th ed.). Washington, DC: Author.

Anthony, J. C., LaResche, L., Niaz, U., Von Koroff, M. R., & Folstein, M. F. (1982). Limits of the 'Mini-Mental State' as a screening test for dementia and delerium among hospital patients. *Psychological Medicine, 12,* 397–408.

Barona, A., Reynolds, C., & Chastain, R. (1984). A demographically based index of premorbid intelligence for the WAIS–R. *Journal of Consulting and Clinical Psychology, 52,* 885–887.

Bayles, K. A., Boone, D. R., Tomoeda, C. K., Slauson, T. J., & Kaszniak, A. W. (1989). Differentiating Alzheimer's patients from the normal elderly and stroke patients with aphasia. *Journal of Speech and Hearing Disorders, 54,* 74–87.

Bayles, K. A., & Kaszniak, A. W. (1987). *Communication and cognition in normal aging and dementia.* Boston: College-Hill/Little, Brown.

Bayles, K. A., & Tomoeda, C. K. (1991). Caregiver report of prevalence and appearance order of linguistic symptoms in Alzheimer's patients. *The Gerontologist, 31,* 210–216.

Becker, G. (1981). *The disability experience: Educating health professionals about disabling conditions.* Berkeley: University of California Press.

Beeson, P. M., Bayles, K. B., Rubens, A. B., & Kaszniak, A. W. (1993). Memory impairment and executive control in individuals with stroke-induced aphasia. *Brain and Language, 45,* 253–275.

Berg, L., Miller, J. P., Bary, J., Rubin, E. H., Morris, J. C., & Figiel, G. (1992). Mild senile dementia of the Alzheimer type: 4. Evaluation of intervention. *Annals of Neurology, 31*, 242–249.

Berkman, L. F. (1986). The association between educational adjustment and mental status examinations: Of etiologic significance for senile dementia or not? *Journal of Chronic Disease, 39*, 171–174.

Bolla, K. I., Lindgren, K. N., Bonaccorsy, C., & Bleecker, M. L. (1991). Memory complaints in older adults: Fact or fiction? *Archives of Neurology, 48*, 61–64.

Bondi, M. W., Kaszniak, A. W., Bayles, K. A., & Vance, K. T. (1993). The contributions of frontal system dysfunction to memory and perceptual abilities in Parkinson's disease. *Neuropsychology, 7*, 89–102.

Butters, M. A., Salmon, D. P., & Butters, N. (1994). Neuropsychological assessment of dementia. In M. Storandt & G. R. VandenBos (Eds.), *Neuropsychological assessment of dementia and depression in older adults: A clinician's guide* (pp. 33–59). Washington, DC: American Psychological Association.

Ciurlia-Guy, E., Cashman, M., & Lewsen, B. (1993). Identifying hearing loss and hearing handicap among chronic care elderly people. *The Gerontologist, 33*, 644–649.

Cogan, D. G. (1985). Visual disturbances with focal progressive dementing disease. *American Journal of Ophthalmology, 100*, 68–72.

Cooper, A. F. (1976). Deafness and psychiatric illness. *British Journal of Psychiatry, 129*, 215–226.

Corso, J. F. (1985). Communication, presbycusis, and technological aids. In H. K. Ulatowska (Ed.), *The aging brain: Communication in the elderly* (pp. 33–51). San Diego, CA: College-Hill Press.

Crum, R. M., Anthony, J. C., Bassett, S. S., & Folstein, M. F. (1993). Population-based norms for the Mini-Mental State Examination by age and educational level. *Journal of the American Medical Association, 269*, 2386–3291.

Cummings, J. L., & Benson, D. F. (1992). *Dementia: A clinical approach* (2nd ed.). Stoneham, MA: Butterworth-Heinemann.

Cunningham, W. R., Sepkoski, C. M., & Opel, M. P. (1978). Fatigue effects on intelligence test performance in the elderly. *Journal of Gerontology, 33*, 541–545.

Depression Guideline Panel. (1993). *Depression in primary care: Volume 1. Detection and diagnosis: Clinical Practice Guideline, Number 5* (AHCPR Publication No. 93-0550). Rockville, MD: Public Health Service, Agency for Health Care Policy and Research.

Elias, M. F., Robbins, M. A., Walter, L. J., & Schultz, N. R. (1993). The influence of gender and age on Halstead–Reitan Neuropsychological Test performance. *Journal of Gerontology: Psychological Sciences, 48*, P278–P281.

Erickson, R. C., Eimon, P., & Hebben, N. (1992). A bibliography of normative articles on cognitive tests for older adults. *The Clinical Neuropsychologist, 6*, 98–102.

Erickson, R. C., Eimon, P., & Hebben, N. (1994). A listing of references to cognitive test norms for older adults. In M. Storandt & G. R. VandenBos (Eds.), *Neuropsychological assessment of dementia and depression in older adults: A clinician's guide* (pp. 183–197). Washington, DC: American Psychological Association.

Eslinger, P. J., Damasio, A. R., Benton, A. L., & Van Allen, M. (1985). Neuropsychologic detection of abnormal mental decline in older persons. *Journal of the American Medical Association, 253,* 670–674.

Fisher, J. E., & Carstensen, L. L. (1990). Behavior management of the dementias. *Clinical Psychology Review, 10,* 611–629.

Flicker, C. (1988). Neuropsychological evaluation of treatment effects in the elderly: A critique of tests in current use. *Psychopharmacology Bulletin, 4,* 535–556.

Flicker, C., Ferris, S. H., & Reisberg, B. (1991). Mild cognitive impairment in the elderly: Predictors of dementia. *Neurology, 41,* 1006–1009.

Folstein, M. F., Anthony, J. C., Parhad, I., Duffy, B., & Gruenberg, E. M. (1985). The meaning of cognitive impairment in the elderly. *Journal of the American Geriatrics Society, 33,* 228–235.

Folstein, M. F., Folstein, S., & McHugh, P. R. (1975). Mini-mental state: A practical method for grading the cognitive state of patients for the clinician. *Journal of Psychiatric Research, 12,* 189–198.

Fozard, J. L. (1990). Vision and hearing in aging. In J. E. Birren & K. W. Schaie (Eds.), *Handbook of the psychology of aging* (3rd ed., pp. 150–170). New York: Van Nostrand Reinhold.

Ganguli, M., Ratcliff, G., Huff, F. J., Belle, S., Kancel, M. J., Fisher, L., Seaberg, E. C., & Kuller, L. H. (1991). Effects of age, gender, and education on cognitive tests in a rural elderly community sample: Norms from the Monongahela Valley Independent Elders Survey. *Neuroepidemiology, 10,* 42–52.

Haase, G. R. (1977). Diseases presenting as dementia. In C. E. Wells (Ed.), *Dementia* (2nd ed., pp. 27–67). Philadelphia: Davis.

Heaton, R. K., Grant, I., & Mathews, C. G. (1986). Differences in neuropsychological test performance associated with age, education, and sex. In I. Grant & K. M. Adams (Eds.), *Neuropsychological assessment of neuropsychiatric disorders* (pp. 100–120). New York: Oxford University Press.

Heaton, R. K., Grant, I., & Mathews, C. G. (1991). *Comprehensive norms for an expanded Halstead–Reitan Battery: Demographic corrections, research findings, and clinical applications.* Odessa, FL: Psychological Assessment Resources.

Henderson, V. W., Mack, W., & Williams, B. W. (1989). Spatial disorientation in Alzheimer's disease. *Archives of Neurology, 46,* 391–394.

Hill, R. D., Storandt, M., & LaBarge, E. (1992). Psychometric discrimination of moderate senile dementia of the Alzheimer type. *Archives of Neurology, 49,* 377–380.

Huff, F. J., Becker, J. T., Belle, S. H., Nebes, R. D., Holland, A. L., & Boller, F. (1987). Cognitive deficits and clinical diagnosis of Alzheimer's disease. *Neurology, 37,* 1119–1124.

Ineichen, B. (1987). Measuring the rising tide. How many dementia cases will there be by 2001? *British Journal of Psychiatry, 150,* 193–200.

Ivnik, R. J., Malec, J. F., Smith, G. E., Tangalos, E. G., Petersen, R. C., Kokmen, E., & Kurland, L. T. (1992a). Mayo's Older Americans Normative Studies: Updated AVLT norms for ages 56 to 97. *The Clinical Neuropsychologist, 6* (Suppl.), 83–104.

Ivnik, R. J., Malec, J. F., Smith, G. E., Tangalos, E. G., Petersen, R. C., Kokmen, E., & Kurland, L. T. (1992b). Mayo's Older Americans Normative Studies: WAIS–R norms for ages 56 to 97. *The Clinical Neuropsychologist, 6* (Suppl.), 1–30.

Ivnik, R. J., Malec, J. F., Smith, G. E., Tangalos, E. G., Petersen, R. C., Kokmen, E., & Kurland, L. T. (1992c). Mayo's Older Americans Normative Studies: WMS–R norms for ages 56 to 94. *The Clinical Neuropsychologist, 6* (Suppl.), 49–82.

Jagger, C., Clarke, M., & Anderson, J. (1992). Screening for dementia: A comparison of two tests using receiver operating characteristics (ROC) analysis. *International Journal of Geriatric Psychiatry, 7,* 659–665.

Johnson, M. A., & Choy, D. (1987). On the definition of age-related norms for visual function testing. *Applied Optics, 26,* 1449–1454.

Jorm, A. F., Korten, A. E., & Henderson, A. S. (1987). The prevalence of dementia: A quantitative integration of the literature. *Acta Psychiatrica Scandinavica, 76,* 465–479.

Kaszniak, A. W. (1987). Neuropsychological consultation to geriatricians: Issues in the assessment of memory complaints. *The Clinical Neuropsychologist, 1,* 35–46.

Kaszniak, A. W. (1990). Psychological assessment of the aging individual. In J. E. Birren & K. W. Schaie (Eds.), *Handbook of the psychology of aging* (3rd. ed., pp. 427–445). San Diego, CA: Academic Press.

Kaszniak, A. W., & Christenson, G. D. (1994). Differential diagnosis of dementia and depression. In M. Storandt & G. R. VandenBos (Eds.), *Neuropsychological assessment of dementia and depression in older adults: A clinician's guide* (pp. 81–117). Washington, DC: American Psychological Association.

Kaszniak, A. W., & Christenson, G. D. (1996). Self-awareness of deficit in patients with Alzheimer's disease. In S. R. Hameroff, A. W. Kaszniak, & A. C. Scott (Eds.), *Toward a science of consciousness: The first Tucson discussions and debates* (pp. 227–242). Cambridge, MA: MIT Press.

Kaszniak, A. W., Garron, D. C., Fox, J. H., Bergen, D., & Huckman, M. (1979). Cerebral atrophy, EEG slowing, age, education, and cognitive functioning in suspected dementia. *Neurology, 29,* 1273–1279.

Kaszniak, A. W., Keyl, P., & Albert, M. (1991). Dementia and the older driver. *Human Factors, 33,* 527–537.

Kaszniak, A. W., & Scogin, F. R. (1995). Assessing for dementia and depression in older adults. *The Clinical Psychologist, 48*(2), 17–24.

Kaszniak, A. W., Wilson, R. S., Fox, J. H., & Stebbins, G. T. (1986). Cognitive assessment in Alzheimer's disease: Cross-sectional and longitudinal perspectives. *Canadian Journal of Neurological Sciences, 13*, 420–423.

Katzman, R. (1986). Alzheimer's disease. *New England Journal of Medicine, 314*, 964–973.

Katzman, R., Lasker, B., & Bernstein, N. (1988). Advances in the diagnosis of dementia: Accuracy of diagnosis and consequences of misdiagnosis of disorders causing dementia. In R. D. Terry (Ed.), *Aging and the brain* (pp. 17–62). New York: Raven Press.

Knopman, D. S., & Ryberg, S. (1989). A verbal memory test with high predictive accuracy for dementia of the Alzheimer type. *Archives of Neurology, 46*, 141–145.

Kolb, B., & Whishaw, I. Q. (1995). *Fundamentals of human neuropsychology (4th ed.)*. New York: Freeman.

Kosnik, W., Winslow, L., Kline, D., Rasinski, K., & Sekuler, R. (1988). Visual changes in daily life throughout adulthood. *Journal of Gerontology, 43*, P53–P70.

Kramer, M. (1986). Trends of institutionalization and prevalence of mental disorders in nursing homes. In M. S. Harper & B. D. Lebowitz (Eds.), *Mental illness in nursing homes: Agenda for research* (DHHS Publication No. ADM 86-1459, pp. 7–26). Rockville, MD: National Institute of Mental Health.

Kunkel, S. R., & Applebaum, R. A. (1992). Estimating the prevalence of long-term disability for an aging society. *Journal of Gerontology: Social Sciences, 47*, S253–S260.

LaBarge, E., Rosenman, L. S., Leavitt, K., & Cristiani, T. (1988). Counseling clients with mild senile dementia of the Alzheimer's type: A pilot study. *Journal of Neurological Rehabilitation, 2*, 167–173.

La Rue, A. (1992). *Aging and neuropsychological assessment*. New York: Plenum.

La Rue, A., D'Elia, L. F., Clark, E. O., Spar, J. E., & Jarvik, L. F. (1986). Clinical tests of memory in dementia, depression, and healthy aging. *Journal of Psychology and Aging, 1*, 69–77.

La Rue, A., Watson, J., & Plotkin, D. A. (1992). Retrospective accounts of dementia symptoms: Are they reliable? *The Gerontologist, 32*, 240–245.

La Rue, A., Yang, J., & Osato, S. (1992). Neuropsychological assessment. In J. E. Birren, R. B. Sloane, & G. D. Cohen (Eds.), *Handbook of mental health and aging* (2nd. ed., pp. 643–670). San Diego, CA: Academic Press.

Lerman, S. (1983). An experimental and clinical evaluation of lens transparency and aging. *Journal of Gerontology, 38*, 293–301.

Lezak, M. D. (1995). *Neuropsychological assessment* (3rd ed.). New York: Oxford University Press.

Li, G., Shen, Y. C., Chen, C. H., Zhao, Y. W., & Li, S. R. (1989). An epidemiological survey of age-related dementia in an urban area of Beijing. *Acta Psychiatrica Scandinavica, 79,* 557–563.

Lima, S. D., Hale, S., & Myerson, J. (1991). How general is general slowing? Evidence from the lexical domain. *Psychology and Aging, 6,* 416–425.

Malec, J. F., Ivnik, R. J., & Smith, G. E. (1993). Neuropsychology and normal aging: The clinician's perspective. In R. W. Parks, R. F. Zec, & R. S. Wilson (Eds.), *Neuropsychology of Alzheimer's disease and other dementias* (pp. 81–111). New York: Oxford University Press.

Malec, J. F., Ivnik, R. J., Smith, G. E., Tangalos, E. G., Petersen, R. C., Kokmen, E., & Kurland, L. T. (1992). Mayo's Older Americans Normative Studies: Utility of corrections for age and education for the WAIS–R. *The Clinical Neuropsychologist, 6* (Suppl.), 31–47.

Manton, K. G. (1990). Mortality and morbidity. In R. H. Binstock & L. K. George (Eds.), *Handbook of aging and the social sciences* (3rd ed., pp. 64–90). San Diego, CA: Academic Press.

McGlone, J., Gupta, S., Humphrey, D., Oppenheimer, S., Mirsen, T., & Evans, D. R. (1990). Screening for early dementia using memory complaints from patients and relatives. *Archives of Neurology, 47,* 1189–1193.

McGlynn, S. M., & Kaszniak, A. W. (1991a). Unawareness of deficits in dementia and schizophrenia. In G. P. Prigatano & D. Schacter (Eds.), *Awareness of deficit after brain injury: Clinical and theoretical issues* (pp. 84–110). New York: Oxford University Press.

McGlynn, S. M., & Kaszniak, A. W. (1991b). When metacognition fails: Impaired awareness of deficit in Alzheimer's disease. *Journal of Cognitive Neuroscience, 3,* 184–189.

Mendez, M. F., Tomsak, R. L., & Remler, B. (1990). Disorders of the visual system in Alzheimer's disease. *Journal of Clinical Neuro-ophthalmology, 10,* 62–69.

Mittenberg, W., Seidenberg, M., O'Leary, D. S., & DiGiulio, D. V. (1989). Changes in cerebral functioning associated with normal aging. *Journal of Clinical and Experimental Neuropsychology, 11,* 918–932.

Moehle, K. A., & Long, C. J. (1989). Models of aging and neuropsychological test performance decline with aging. *Journal of Gerontology: Psychological Sciences, 44,* P176–P177.

Morris, J. C., McKeel, D. W., Storandt, M., Rubin, E. H., Price, J. L., Grant, E. A., Ball, M. J., & Berg, L. (1991). Very mild Alzheimer's disease: Informant-based clinical, psychometric, and pathologic distinction from normal aging. *Neurology, 41,* 469–478.

Murden, R. A., McRae, T. D., Kaner, S., & Bucknam, N. E. (1991). Mini-Mental State Exam scores vary with education in Blacks and Whites. *Journal of the American Geriatric Society, 39,* 149–155.

Myers, G. C. (1990). Demography of aging. In R. H. Binstock & L. K. George (Eds.), *Handbook of aging and the social sciences* (3rd ed., pp. 19–44). San Diego, CA: Academic Press.

Naugle, R. I., Cullum, C. M., & Bigler, E. D. (1990). Evaluation of intellectual and memory function among dementia patients who were intellectually superior. *The Clinical Neuropsychologist, 4*, 355–374.

Nebes, R. D. (1992). Cognitive dysfunction in Alzheimer's disease. In F. I. M. Craik & T. A. Salthouse (Eds.), *The handbook of aging and cognition* (pp. 373–446). Hillsdale, NJ: Erlbaum.

Nelson, A., Fogel, B. S., & Faust, D. (1986). Bedside cognitive screening instruments: A critical assessment. *Journal of Nervous and Mental Disease, 174*, 73–83.

Nussbaum, P. D., Kaszniak, A. W., Allender, J., & Rapcsak, S. (1995). Depression and cognitive decline in the elderly: A follow-up study. *The Clinical Neuropsychologist, 9*, 101–111.

O'Connor, D. W., Pollitt, P. A., Hyde, J. B., Miller, N. D., & Fellowes, J. L. (1989). The reliability and validity of the Mini-Mental State in a British community survey. *Journal of Psychiatric Research, 23*, 87–96.

O'Connor, D. W., Pollitt, P. A., Hyde, J. B., Miller, N. D., & Fellowes, J. L. (1991). Clinical issues relating to the diagnosis of mild dementia in a British community survey. *Archives of Neurology, 48*, 530–534.

O'Neil, P. M., & Calhoun, K. S. (1975). Sensory deficits and behavioral deterioration in senescence. *Journal of Abnormal Psychology, 84*, 579–582.

Owsley, C., & Sloane, M. E. (1990). Vision and aging. In F. Boller & J. Grafman (Eds.), *Handbook of neuropsychology* (Vol. 4, pp. 229–249). Amsterdam: Elsevier.

Parks, R. W., Zec, R. F., & Wilson, R. S. (Eds.). (1993). *Neuropsychology of Alzheimer's disease and other dementias*. New York: Oxford University Press.

Peters, C. A., Potter, J. F., & Scholer, S. G. (1988). Hearing impairment as a predictor of cognitive decline in dementia. *Journal of the American Geriatric Society, 36*, 981–986.

Petersen, R. C., Smith, G., Kokmen, E., Ivnik, R. J., & Tangalos, E. G. (1992). Memory function in normal aging. *Neurology, 42*, 396–401.

Pickett, J. M., Bergman, M., & Levitt, M. (1979). Aging and speech understanding. In J. M. Ordy & K. Brizzee (Eds.), *Aging: Vol. 10. Speech systems and communication in the elderly* (pp. 167–186). New York: Raven Press.

Pittman, J., Andrews, H., Tatemichi, T., Link, B., Struening, E., Stern, Y., & Mayeux, R. (1992). Diagnosis of dementia in a heterogeneous population: A comparison of paradigm-based diagnosis and physician's diagnosis. *Archives of Neurology, 49*, 461–467.

Plomp, R. (1978). Auditory handicap of hearing impairment and the limited benefit of hearing aids. *Journal of the Acoustical Society of America, 63*, 533–549.

Plomp, R., & Mimpen, A. M. (1979). Speech reception threshold for sentences as a function of age and noise level. *Journal of the Acoustical Society of America, 66*, 1333–1342.

Poon, L. W., Kaszniak, A. W., & Dudley, W. N. (1992). Approaches in the experimental neuropsychology of dementia: A methodological and model review. In M. Bergner, K. Hasegawa, S. Finkel, & T. Nishimura (Eds.), *Aging and mental disorders: International perspectives* (pp. 150–173). New York: Springer.

Rapcsak, S. Z., Kentros, M., & Rubens, A. (1989). Impaired recognition of meaningful sounds in Alzheimer's disease. *Archives of Neurology, 46,* 1298–1300.

Reitan, R. M., & Wolfsen, D. (1986). The Halstead–Reitan Neuropsychological Test Battery and aging. *Clinical Gerontologist, 5,* 39–61.

Rizzo, J. F. III, Cronin-Golumb, A., Growdon, J. H., Sorkin, S., Rosen, T. J., Sandberg, M. A., Chiappa, K. H., & Lessell, S. (1992). Retinocalcarine function in Alzheimer's disease: A clinical and electrophysiological study. *Archives of Neurology, 49,* 93–101.

Roccaforte, W. H., Burke, W. J., Bayer, B. L., & Wenger, S. P. (1992). Validation of a telephone version of the Mini-Mental State Examination. *Journal of the American Geriatrics Society, 40,* 697–702.

Roman, G. C. (1991). The epidemiology of vascular dementia. In A Hartman, W. Kuschinsky, & S. Hoyer (Eds.), *Cerebral ischemia and dementia* (pp. 9–15). Berlin: Springer-Verlag.

Rorsman, B., Hagnell, O., & Lanke, J. (1986). Prevalence and incidence of senile and multi-infarct dementia in the Lundby study: A comparison between the time periods 1947–1957 and 1957–1972. *Neuropsychobiology, 15,* 122–129.

Schieber, F. (1992). Aging and the senses. In J. E. Birren, R. B. Sloane, & G. D. Cohen (Eds.), *Handbook of mental health and aging* (pp. 251–306). San Diego, CA: Academic Press.

Shibayama, H., Kasahara, Y., & Kobayashi, H. (1986). Prevalence of dementia in a Japanese elderly population. *Acta Psychiatrica Scandinavica, 74,* 144–151.

Smyer, M. A. (1988). The nursing home community. In M. A. Smyer, M. D. Cohn, & D. Brannon (Eds.), *Mental health consultation in nursing homes* (pp. 1–23). New York: New York University Press.

Spreen, O., & Strauss, E. (1991). *A compendium of neuropsychological tests: Administration, norms, and commentary.* New York: Oxford University Press.

Stern, Y., Andrews, H., Pittman, J., Sano, M., Tatemichi, T., Lantigua, R., & Mayeux, R. (1992). Diagnosis of dementia in a heterogeneous population: Development of a neuropsychological paradigm-based diagnosis of dementia and quantified correction for the effects of education. *Archives of Neurology, 49,* 453–460.

Storandt, M. (1977). Age, ability level, and method of administering and scoring the WAIS. *Journal of Gerontology, 32,* 175–178.

Storandt, M. (1994). General principles of assessment of older adults. In M. Storandt & G. R. VandenBos (Eds.), *Neuropsychological assessment of demen-*

tia and depression in older adults: A clinician's guide (pp. 7–32). Washington, DC: American Psychological Association.

Storandt, M., Botwinick, J., Danziger, W. L., Berg, L., & Hughes, C. P. (1984). Psychometric differentiation of mild senile dementia of the Alzheimer type. *Archives of Neurology, 41*, 497–499.

Strub, R. L., & Black, F. W. (1988). *Neurobehavioral disorders: A clinical approach*. Philadelphia: Davis.

Teri, L., & McCurry, S. M. (1994). Psychosocial therapies. In C. E. Coffey & J. L. Cummings (Eds.), *Textbook of geriatric neuropsychiatry* (pp. 661–682). Washington, DC: American Psychiatric Press.

Teri, L., & Wagner, A. (1992). Alzheimer's disease and depression. *Journal of Consulting and Clinical Psychology, 60*, 379–391.

Thal, L. J., Grundman, M., & Klauber, M. R. (1988). Dementia: Characteristics of a referral population and factors associated with progression. *Neurology, 38*, 1083–1090.

Tombaugh, T. N., & McIntyre, N. J. (1992). The Mini-Mental State Examination: A comprehensive review. *Journal of the American Geriatrics Society, 40*, 922–935.

Tomoeda, C. K., Bayles, K. A., Boone, D. R., Kaszniak, A. W., & Slauson, T. J. (1990). Speech rate and syntactic complexity effects on the auditory comprehension of Alzheimer patients. *Journal of Communication Disorders, 23*, 151–161.

VanGorp, W. G., Satz, P., Kiersch, M. E., & Henry, R. (1986). Normative data on the Boston Naming Test for a group of normal older adults. *Journal of Clinical and Experimental Neuropsychology, 8*, 702–705.

Vannieuwhirk, R. R., & Galbraith, G. G. (1985). The relationship of age to performance on the Luria–Nebraska Neuropsychological Battery. *Journal of Clinical Psychology, 41*, 527–532.

Wechsler, D. (1981). *Manual for the Wechsler Adult Intelligence Scale—Revised*. New York: Psychological Corporation.

Weinstein, B. E., & Amsel, L. (1986). Hearing loss and senile dementia in the institutionalized elderly. *Clinical Gerontologist, 4*, 3–15.

Welsh, K., Butters, N., Hughes, J., Mohs, R., & Heyman, A. (1991). Detection of abnormal memory decline in mild cases of Alzheimer's disease using CERAD neuropsychological measures. *Archives of Neurology, 48*, 278–281.

Welsh, K., Butters, N., Hughes, J., Mohs, R., & Heyman, A. (1992). Detection and staging of dementia in Alzheimer's disease: Use of the neuropsychological measures developed for the consortium to establish a registry for Alzheimer's disease. *Archives of Neurology, 49*, 448–452.

Wilkinson, R. T., & Allison, S. (1989). Age and simple reaction time: Decade differences for 5, 325 subjects. *Journal of Gerontology: Psychological Sciences, 44*, P29–P35.

Zec, R. F. (1990). Neuropsychology: Normal aging versus early AD. In R. E. Becker & E. Giacobini (Eds.), *Alzheimer disease: Current research in early diagnosis* (pp. 105–117). New York: Taylor & Francis.

Zec, R. F. (1993). Neuropsychological functioning in Alzheimer's disease. In R. W. Parks, R. F. Zec, & R. S. Wilson (Eds.), *Neuropsychology of Alzheimer's disease and other dementias* (pp. 3–80). New York: Oxford University Press.

18

QUALITY OF LIFE AND ADJUSTMENT IN RENAL DISEASE: A HEALTH PSYCHOLOGY PERSPECTIVE

PETRA SYMISTER and RONALD FRIEND

Although much research has focused on chronic illnesses such as cancer and cardiovascular disease, there are other chronic illnesses that have not received adequate attention or resources. One of these areas of research concerns end-stage renal disease (ESRD). In 1991, over 230,000 people were treated for this disease (National Institutes of Health [NIH], 1993), and unfortunately, the number of individuals beginning treatment continues to grow. Currently $8.59 billion, a vast sum, is expended on ESRD treatment. With an aging U.S. population, the projected number of patients by the year 2000 is expected to be 300,000 (NIH, 1993). Given the pervasiveness of ESRD treatment, health psychology and behavioral medicine can make an important contribution to the quality of life and rehabilitation of these patients. However, research and grant support in this area are sadly lacking, in relation to what is found for the more "popular" illnesses, such as cardiovascular disease and cancer. In this chapter, we review some current psychosocial research on ESRD patients, focusing on quality of life, adjustment processes, adherence, and survival. Because renal patients suffer a loss of autonomy and become more dependent on family and medical staff, we emphasize the influence of personal control and interpersonal relations in patients' adjustment to treatment and illness.

MISCONCEPTIONS OF THE QUALITY OF LIFE

Before reviewing the quality of life of end-stage renal disease patients and how it can be improved, it might be fruitful to discuss the way in which outside observers view the life of these patients. In a society that fosters individualism, the ideology of individual control and responsibility for one's life is a strong cultural and psychological force. However, the onset of chronic renal disease is characterized by individuals being forced to relinquish control to life-sustaining treatment. It is therefore not surprising that healthy individuals, who in their everyday lives attempt to maintain as much individual personal control as possible, view the prospect of dialysis treatment and resulting loss of control as one of the worse things that can happen to someone. This image of dialysis patients tied daily to their machines was portrayed in the *New York Times* headline, "A Bleak U.S. Report on Kidney-Failure Patients" (1993). The article presented a dismal outlook for these patients due to the fact that treatment effectiveness is not being maximized, because individuals are often already critically ill by the time they receive dialysis. Moreover, the article's image of patients' day-to-day living once dialysis has started was an equally somber depiction. The renal patient's life was described as one that is difficult, owing to the complex dietary regimen, abundant treatment side effects, and emotional stress that accompany renal replacement therapy ("Bleak U.S. report," 1993)

But is the woeful undertone of this article merely a representation of the projections of healthy people, projections of their own fears and uncertainties, or is it an expression of the actual realities and experiences of dialysis patients? How poor is the quality of life of ESRD patients? Is it really as bleak as the headlines of the *New York Times* portray? We have reason to believe that it is not, as we address in our next section.

A glance at the survival statistics may give some insight into the reasons for the bleak portrayal of the lives of these patients. When one looks at the number of years that patients survive after starting treatment, it becomes apparent that White patients survive longer than Black patients, for the 30-year-old and under patients. However, over-30-year-old Black patients survive longer than White patients of this age group. At any rate, for both groups, the expected survival is well below normal. A comparison of the expected survival of ESRD patients to that of the

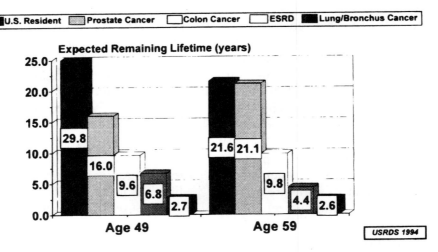

Figure 1. Expected remaining lifetime for selected U.S. populations. ESRD = end-stage renal disease. From "Annual Data Report," by United States Renal Data System, 1993, *American Journal of Kidney Diseases, 22*, p. 26. Copyright 1993 by W. B. Saunders Company. Reprinted with permission.

normal population is presented in Figure 1. Generally, a 59-year-old diagnosed with ESRD can only expect to survive an average of 4.4 more years, whereas healthy people will survive an average of 21.6 more years in this age category (United States Renal Data System [USRDS], 1994).

COMPARISONS WITH OTHER ILLNESSES

A comparison of the expected survival at age 59 of ESRD patients with the survival of patients of other chronic illnesses can be used to evaluate the length of time patients live with this disease (see Figure 1). Although ESRD patients survive nearly twice as long as lung cancer patients, the former only live half as long as individuals with colon cancer and one fifth as long as those diagnosed with prostate cancer (USRDS, 1993).

It is perhaps this knowledge of the dramatic cut in life expectancy that accompanies renal failure that accounts for the way these patients are pictured. These survival figures, however, are improving, and dialysis units are presently reporting patients who have survived as long as 25 years while on dialysis. Therefore, the quality of life of patients may not be so bleak as the *New York Times* reports and as the survival statistics suggest.

DEFINING QUALITY OF LIFE

It must be more than the duration of these patients' lives that causes people to see their existence as bleak. The perception of the quality of that existence is also responsible. What is meant by quality of life? The many ways in which quality of life is defined are represented in the literature. Measures of the quality of life of dialysis patients, in particular, usually include either one or more variables, which are sometimes combined to form an overall quality-of-life score (Bihl, Ferrans, & Powers, 1988; Churchill, Wallace, Ludwin, Beecroft, & Taylor, 1991; Simmons, Anderson, & Kamstra, 1984). Some of these variables are considered objective. Objective measures are usually physical measures and refer to areas of the patients' life that can be rated and generally agreed on by persons other than the patient. Measures of illness severity and employment status are examples of objective quality-of-life measures. On the other hand, subjective quality-of-life measures are usually psychological in nature and are often assessed by a questionnaire or interview given to the patient. Measures of depression and anxiety are examples of subjective quality-of-life measures.

QUALITY-OF-LIFE STUDIES OF END-STAGE RENAL DISEASE

The lives of ESRD patients are sustained by one or more treatment modalities. Patients, in fact, have a variety of modalities from which to choose, each with its own unique features. Therefore, patients can tailor their treatment to complement aspects of their life that they value. The modalities vary considerably in the amount of control they allow patients, the time flexibility they provide, and the level of interaction and dependence on medical staff, family, and other patients they require. The four major treatments are in-center hemodialysis, in which patients are dialyzed three times per week for several hours in a hospital setting; home hemodialysis, in which the same procedure is carried out in the patient's home or workplace; continuous ambulatory peritoneal dialysis (CAPD), in which patients are dialyzed daily using a solution inserted into their peritoneal cavity that extracts waste products through an osmotic process; and kidney transplantation. Transplantation is considered a treatment, because medications such as immunosuppressants must be taken after surgery to reduce the likelihood of graft rejection. In fact, the probability of graft failure even after 7 years is still as high as 50%, and it is not unusual for patients to have changed from one treatment modality to another, including those with failed transplants (McGee & Bradley, 1994). With this variety of modalities, an important issue becomes, How different is the quality of life across treatment options?

Although there are several studies that are concerned with the ways in which the quality of life differs as a function of modality, getting an idea of which treatment is best can be difficult because many of the findings are not in agreement. Most do agree, however, that transplant

EXHIBIT 1
Multiple Measures of Quality of Life

Objective	Subjective
Evans et al. (1985)	
Functional impairment	Well-being
Ability to work	Psychological affect
	Life satisfaction
Bremer, McCauley, Wrona, and Johnson (1989)	
Days in hospital	Positive affect
Hours spent seeking health care per week	Negative affect
Hours spent sleeping each night	Affect balance
No. of activities given up	General affect
Income	Well-being
Level of pain	Overall life
Days since intercourse	Hard/easy
Days since orgasm	Tied down/free
% more tired	Helpless/independent
% employed	Satisfactions (e.g., standard of living, friends, health, and religion)

patients have the highest quality of life (Levenson & Glocheski, 1991), but the collective body of research regarding the order in which the remaining treatments fall is equivocal. An inspection of these studies, however, uncovers methodological differences that may account for discrepant findings. So, we turn to the most methodologically sound studies for an accurate comparison of the different treatment groups with each other and with the normal population.

The two important studies addressing the quality-of-life issue are Evans et al. (1985) and Bremer, McCauley, Wrona, and Johnson (1989), and there are several reasons that these studies are important. First, both studies used adequate sample sizes. The Evans et al. study contains 859 patients, whereas the Bremer et al. study contained 489 patients. Second, the samples were diverse; a total of 12 centers in both urban and rural settings, both academic and nonacademic, were surveyed. Third, both studies were careful to control for case mix. This is the most important difference between these studies and others that looked at quality of life across modalities. *Case mix* refers to the varied composition of the treatment groups that is likely to confound comparisons. By taking variables on which treatment groups differ, such as age, race, and sex, into account, lack of homogeneity in composition between groups on these variables is controlled for. Finally, these studies used multiple measures of objective and subjective quality of life (see Table 1). Objective measures included functional ability and labor participation, whereas subjective

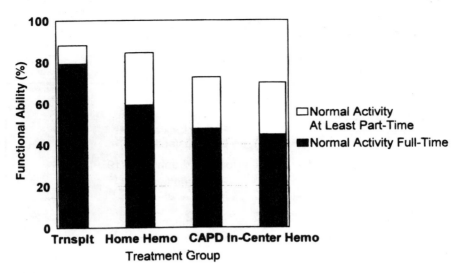

Figure 2. Functional status. Trnsplt = transplant, Home Hemo = home hemodialysis, CAPD = continuous ambulatory peritoneal dialysis, In-Center Hemo = in-center hemodialysis. Data are from Evans et al., (1985).

measures were represented by positive and negative affect and satisfaction with life. National norms were available for some of these scales, making comparisons with ESRD patients possible.

Comparisons With the Healthy Population

Renal patients showed a small-to-moderate reduction in objective quality of life when compared with the healthy population. With 100% on the Karnofsky Index (Mor, Laliberte, Morris, & Wiemann, 1984), designating the average functional status of a healthy sample, the majority of patients in the four modality groups either took part in normal physical activities "sometimes" or retained a level of physical activity that was nearly normal: transplanted, 88.1%; home hemodialysis, 84.4%, CAPD, 72.5%, and in-center hemodialysis 69.9% (see Figure 2). It is in regard to employment that ESRD patients differed. Patients showed a dramatic drop in labor participation, from 67.1% before illness onset (compared with 63.8% in the general population) to 33.5% after becoming ill. As can be seen, transplantation patients had a 53.5% labor participation rate (see Figure 3).

In summary, transplant patients were able to do more activities and were more likely to work, but all groups were able to maintain around 70% of their previous (healthy) activity levels (Bremer et al., 1989; Evans et al., 1985).

A surprising fact is that patients' subjective quality of life was similar to the national standards of healthy populations. On well-being,

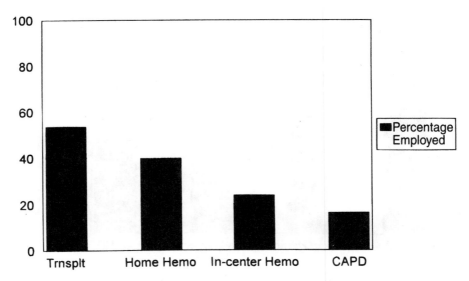

Figure 3. Employment status of renal patients. Trnsplt = transplant, Home-Hemo = home hemodialysis, In-Center Hemo = in-center hemodialysis, CAPD = continuous ambulatory peritoneal dialysis. Data are from Evans et al. (1985).

psychological affect, and life satisfaction, the healthy population averaged within 1 point of the ESRD group (healthy group $M = 11.77$, $SD = 2.21$ vs. ESRD group $M = 11.09$, $SD = 2.72$, on a 15-point scale measuring well-being; healthy group $M = 5.68$, $SD = 1.12$ vs. ESRD group $M = 5.33$, SD 1.25, on a 7-point scale measuring psychological affect; healthy group $M = 5.55$, $SD = 1.25$ vs. ESRD group 5.25, $SD = 1.62$, on a 7-point scale measuring life satisfaction). These differences were small, and individual differences within groups were much larger than were those between ESRD and normal samples.

Comparisons Within the Renal Patient Group

Just as there was very little difference between ESRD patients and the healthy population, there was also very little difference between patients in the various modalities, except on labor participation. With regard to objective quality of life, transplanted patients had the highest percentage of employed members, at 53.5%, followed by 39.6% of home hemodialysis, 23.7% of in-center hemodialysis, and 16.2% of CAPD patients (see Figure 3). When asked about their ability to work, as measured by the question, "Are you now able to work for pay full-time, part-time or not at all?" the groups responded in similar fashion, with transplants showing the greatest ability (62.30%), followed by home hemodialysis (54.80%), in-center hemodialysis (44.80%), and CAPD (27.80%). In general, the transplant group, whether it was a first, second,

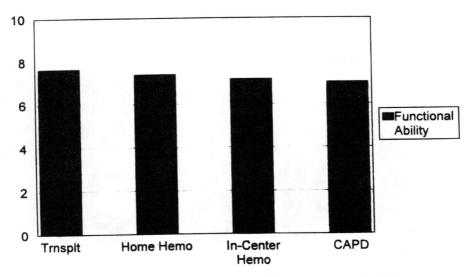

Figure 4. Functional ability of renal patients. Trnsplt = transplant, Home Hemo = home hemodialysis, CAPD = continuous ambulatory peritoneal dialysis, In-Center Hemo = in-center hemodialysis. Data are from Evans et al. (1985).

or later transplant, followed by the home hemodialysis group, showed the most meaningful difference in employment status from the in-center hemodialysis group and the CAPD group.

Regarding functional status, the transplanted group showed the least impairment on a scale of 1 to 10, with 10 representing normal functioning, followed by home hemodialysis, in-center hemodialysis, and CAPD (7.63, 7.37, 7.15, and 7.00, respectively). These were significant differences among groups, but inspection of the scores shows that the magnitude of these differences was small (see Figure 4).

For the remaining objective quality-of-life indicators, patients again displayed significant differences among groups. In the number of hours each night spent sleeping, the number of days since last having sexual intercourse, the number of days since last having an orgasm, fatigue level, time spent pursuing medical attention, amount of activities given up, and income level, there were significant differences among groups. The differences that existed among groups on the variables, hours of sleep per night and number of activities given up, were small. However, the differences among groups on the remaining variables were significantly large. It is easy to understand how the nature of the treatments could contribute to these differences. For example, it is not surprising that transplant patients and home hemodialysis patients would have higher incomes than patients in the other groups, because the former are not required to visit the hospital for treatment as often as patients in the other treatment groups and can therefore find or retain jobs more easily. There were no differences, however, between groups on the number of days hospitalized and the level of pain experienced (Bremer et al., 1989).

On subjective indicators, well-being (possible score range = 2.0–15.0, sample range = 10.4–12.18) and psychological affect (possible score range = 1.0–7.0, sample range = 5.09–5.72), transplant patients scored highest, followed by home hemodialysis, CAPD, and in-center hemodialysis patients, but the differences appear minute. For life satisfaction (possible score range = 1.0–7.0, sample range = 4.99–5.90), transplant patients still scored highest but were followed by CAPD, home hemodialysis, and then in-center hemodialysis groups. As indicated, the scores again were not vastly different. To clarify, the scores were statistically different from each other, but they were not very large.

On negative affect, the groups differed slightly from the U.S. norm but not from each other. Similarly for positive affect, treatment groups did not differ from one another, with the exception of the transplant group and the home hemodialysis group. Analyses showed that patients in all groups scored the same as healthy individuals, with home hemodialysis patients scoring slightly higher than the normal population. However, the most interesting finding concerning this scale was that transplant patients who experienced successful transplants either on the first attempt or a later attempt scored much higher on positive affect than the normal U.S. population.

For the final subjective quality-of-life indicators (see Table 1), all of which were based on 7-point scales, the treatment groups did not differ significantly from each other, except on the adjective pair, tied down/free, and on satisfaction with health (see Figure 5). High scores on the first scale indicated that the patient felt free, and high scores on the second scale indicated that the patient was highly satisfied with her or his health. Transplant patients and self-administered hemodialysis patients, whose treatments provide increased control for them, not surprisingly, experienced the greatest freedom, similar to that of the healthy population. However, the differences were not large among treatment groups, and all groups felt more free than tied down. All groups, with the exception of the transplant group, were significantly less satisfied with their health than were healthy individuals (see Figure 6).

COMPARING QUALITY OF LIFE ACROSS CHRONIC ILLNESSES

Are the responses of these ESRD patients unique, or do they characterize the experiences of all chronically ill patients? When we compare the measurements of psychological variables, such as mental health,

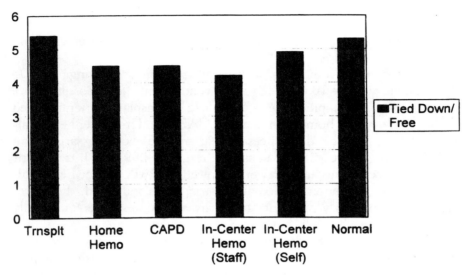

Figure 5. Scores on the tied down/free scale. Trnsplt = transplant, Home-Hemo = home hemodialysis, CAPD = continuous ambulatory peritoneal dialysis, In-Center Hemo (Staff) = staff-administered treatment; In-Center Hemo (Self) = patient-administered treatment; Normal = healthy population. Data are from Bremer, McCauley, Wrona, and Johnson (1989).

emotional ties, depression, loss of control, anxiety, and general positive affect, patients with ESRD are not very different from patients with skin disorders, diabetes, cancer, or arthritis, and like ESRD patients, patients in the other groups show no significant differences on these variables when compared with the healthy population (Cassileth et al., 1984).

In summary, research comparing the quality of life of various treatments shows some advantage of transplantation and home dialysis over in-center hemodialysis and CAPD, with the two former modalities reporting higher objective quality of life and somewhat higher subjective quality of life. Compared with the healthy population, renal patients show a drop in objective quality of life with a matching (lower) satisfaction with health. With regard to subjective quality-of-life measures, renal patients report minimally less quality of life than the healthy population, with little differences among modalities. However, individual variations within each treatment are substantial. This raises the question as to whether different treatments are important and have substantial benefits. Why does transplantation, which provides substantially more control and flexibility than other forms of treatment, not provide substantial improvement in subjective quality of life? One explanation from the nephrology community, which views subjective quality-of-life measures pejoratively, is that these measures lack validity (Nissenson, 1994). On the other hand, social psychologists report that measures of subjective well-being are indeed reliable and valid (Diener, 1995).

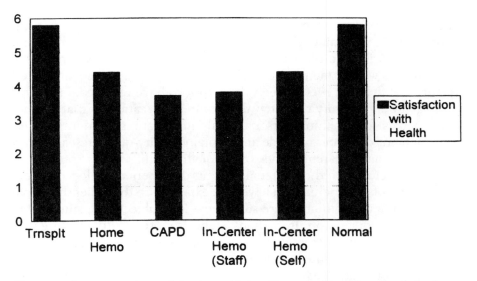

Figure 6. Scores on the satisfaction with health scale. Trnsplt = transplant; CAPD = continuous ambulatory peritoneal dialysis; In-Center Hemo (Staff) = staff-administered treatment. In-Center Hemo (Self) = patient-administered treatment; Normal = health population. Data are from Bremer, McCauley, Wrona, and Johnson (1989).

Perhaps a more fruitful answer to this paradoxical finding can be found by approaching these results from a theoretical perspective. A major problem in quality-of-life research is that it is descriptive and lacks theory to guide its findings and research. Recently, Diener (1995) developed a theory of subjective well-being that explains the low correlations observed between "resources," such as money and status, which may be considered objective measures, and subjective well-being. According to his theory, resources only predict subjective well-being if they help a person achieve their personal goals. To the extent that there is a congruence between a person's resources and the goals for which he or she strives, subjective well-being will be high. If there is a mismatch between resources and personal goals, then poor subjective well-being will occur. This social psychological theory, perhaps, can help explain this paradox. Modes of treatment can be conceived as resources to attain personal goals. Thus, for instance, if continuing to work is an important goal for a patient, then transplantation or home dialysis may be an important resource that contributes to subjective quality of life. If other goals predominate, such as countering isolation or having frequent available health care, then in-center hemodialysis may improve subjective quality of life, by providing patients with the resources of social interaction, social support, and health care, which the dialysis personnel can provide. Thus, two patients with different personal goals and with different treatment may report near equivalent subjective quality of life. Furthermore, a patient who, for medical reasons, needs to transfer to in-hospital treatment may relinquish previously important goals that were compatible with the old treatment and develop new goals compatible with the new treatment, thereby maintaining congruence and their quality-of-life level, even though their options have changed. From this vantage, it is necessary to match the features of treatments that can act as resources for reaching personal goals important to patients. Thus, development of theory to guide and explain quality-of-life research may help to explain apparent paradoxes in quality of life.

In conclusion, although renal patients do experience a loss of objective quality of life, including a lower life expectancy, the belief that renal patients undergoing dialysis are suffering a low subjective quality of life may be a misconception. It, perhaps, stems from the faulty labeling that healthy individuals project onto these patients. Forty years ago, a person who suffered renal failure had little chance of survival, and unfortunately, that image of renal disease has yet to fade. Despite advances in therapies and a decrease in mortality, patients are still perceived as being tied to a life of pain and suffering. This is not to belittle the fact that renal failure is a serious condition with many treatment side effects, but many patients whose lives are sustained by this treatment have learned to cope with the change in health status. Recall the *New York Times* article that portrayed patients as adjusting poorly. A letter from a dialysis patient was printed in response to that article and argued that patients are able to adjust to a life on dialysis. The response agreed that there was a change in lifestyle but maintained that renal patients adjust to what they are able to accomplish as chronically ill individuals. The letter was entitled "Life Can Continue After Kidney Failure," and the respondent stated the following:

> End-stage renal disease is indeed serious and disabling. . . . But a substantial part of the dialysis patient population leads reasonably productive, comfortable and long lives. For example, I am 65 years old and have been on dialysis for almost three years. I use a therapy known as peritoneal dialysis through a cycler machine in my home. . . . I go to work every day—albeit a five-hour workday—and lead a restrained but active social, community and family life. I am substantially free of discomfort and pain almost all the time, although my energy level and appetite are clearly down. (Marqusee, 1993, p. A26)

PROCESS OF PSYCHOLOGICAL ADJUSTMENT

The different modalities (transplantation, home hemodialysis, CAPD, and in-center hemodialysis) reflect a continuum of behavioral control over treatment, which provides a convenient method for observ-

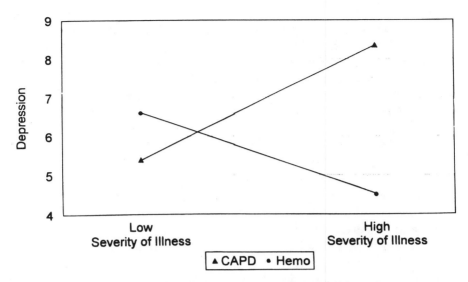

Figure 7. Burden of self-care in seriously ill patients. CAPD = continuous ambulatory peritoneal dialysis, Hemo = in-center hemodialysis. Data are from Eitel, Hatchett, Friend, Griffin, and Wadhwa (1995).

ing how different amounts of control can influence psychological adjustment (Eitel, Friend, Griffin, & Wadhwa, 1995). In one of the first thorough investigations, Devins and colleagues (Devins et al., 1982; Devins, Binik, Hollomby, Barre, & Guttman, 1981) found no relation between treatment control and depression. However, measures of psychological control (internal locus of control, health locus of control, and self-efficacy) strongly predicted depression and helplessness. Several other studies also found no effect of treatment control on psychological adjustment (Christensen, Smith, Holman, & Gregory, 1990; Sacks, Peterson, & Kimmel, 1990). These studies tend to parallel those comparing various treatment modalities and quality of life. Other studies found that control over nontreatment factors is strongly related to psychological adjustment (Devins et al., 1981; Sacks et al., 1990). One possible explanation is that situational or contextual variables interact with treatment control to influence psychological adjustment (Christensen et al., 1990).

Eitel, Hatchett, Friend, Griffin, and Wadhwa (1995) reasoned that as illness severity increases, the burden of controlling one's treatment, as in CAPD, would increase depression (see Figure 7). They predicted that depression would increase for CAPD patients with increasing disease severity, but not for in-center hemodialysis patients whose treatment was administered by hospital personnel.

Their results supported this hypothesis. As the severity of illness increased for CAPD patients, depression also increased. In keeping with Devin's previously reported work, mediational analyses indicated that seriously ill CAPD patients reported that the illness interfered in their social relations. They responded that others did not understand how seriously ill they were and that their illness disrupted their social relations. Interestingly, for in-center hemodialysis patients, depression decreased with increasing severity illness. Seriously ill in-center hemodialysis patients may have received more support and understanding from hospital staff, and fewer demands and expectations may have been placed on them by others because of the severity of their illness.

An additional study showed the relationship between illness severity and psychological well-being. Christensen, Turner, Slaughter, and Holman (1989) found patients with high-illness impairment to be less depressed and anxious when they had supportive families. For patients who had less illness impairment, the relationship between their well-being and perceived family support was not significant.

Most studies on adjustment in the renal area are cross-sectional. In one of the few prospective studies, Hatchett, Friend, Symister, and Wadhwa (1996), expanded on Eitel, Hatchett, Friend, Griffin, and Wadhwa's (1995) finding that patients reported that they were not well understood by others. Hatchett et al. assessed the patients' perceptions of family and medical staff demands and expectations placed on them regarding their responsibilities for everyday routine functions and medical care. Hatchett et al. hypothesized that the inability to meet these expectations regarding their ability to cope and fulfill routine functions would lead to poorer adjustment. Hatchett et al. assessed patients' expectations toward family and medical staff at two time points, separated by 2 months. Additionally, they assessed depression, hopelessness, satisfaction with quality of life, and illness intrusiveness at the same two time points. Results showed that discrepant expectations perceived by the patient predicted subsequent decreases in adjustment. Furthermore, an alternative hypothesis, that the more poorly adjusted patients would come to distort or misperceive the expectations of others, was not supported. Perceptions that family and friends did not understand the patient's illness, as measured by discrepant expectations, were much stronger predictors of adjustment than were social support measures. Many renal patients report a lack of energy. This may contribute to interpersonal conflict in the family regarding the fulfillment of routine functions. Hatchett et al. suggested that modifying interpersonal expectations between patient and families may improve adjustment.

ADHERENCE

Adherence to medical regimens is an area of great concern because of the difficulties that many renal patients experience in following dietary and fluid-intake restrictions. Earlier research focused on predictors; sociodemographic factors such as age, gender, and education; and personality factors such as internal locus of control and denial (Binik et al., 1982; Schneider, Friend, Whitaker, & Wadhwa, 1991). It is now understood that demographic and personality factors are inconsistently related to adherence (Binik et al., 1982; Schneider et al., 1991). More recent studies focus on the cognitive, emotional, and interpersonal processes that underlie compliance (Christensen et al., 1990; Schneider et al., 1991). Note that similar to other illnesses with complex regimens, there is little consistency in adherence from one area to the other; patients who adhere to their fluid regimen, for example, do not necessarily adhere to their dietary or medication regimen (Cummings, Becker, Kirscht, & Levin, 1981; Eitel, Friend, et al., 1995; Lamping & Campbell, 1989). There are generally few "good" or "poor" compliers.

Rosenbaum and Ben-Ari Smira (1986) proposed a self-regulating model in which resourcefulness (self-control skills) combined with various cognition (attributions of effort and success to one's past compliance) to predict future compliance. Resourcefulness assesses the ability to delay gratification and self-efficacy as personal skills. They found that patients with resourcefulness were more likely to label their past adherence as successful and due to their own effort. These attributions led to expectations of self-efficacy, which in turn predicted future fluid intake. Schneider et al. (1991) made the distinction between resourcefulness and locus of internal control. Whereas *resourcefulness* refers primarily to a repertoire of self-control skills, *locus of control* refers to a set of beliefs about whether behavior and consequences are internally or externally controlled. Schneider et al. replicated Rosenbaum and Ben-Ari Smira's model but assessed beliefs about control rather than self-control skills. They also hypothesized that negative emotions, such as anger, depression, and anxiety, would undermine cognitive control and therefore adherence to fluid intake. However, their results indicated that belief about control did not influence perceptions of success and effort. Furthermore, negative emotions did not undermine patients' ability to comply. However, the attribution and self-efficacy aspects of the model strongly supported Rosenbaum and Ben-Ari Smira's model. Attributions of effort and success to past compliant behavior appear to influence feelings of self-efficacy, which in turn are related to fluid control. These studies suggest that fluid intake is a cognitive-control problem and that interventions that encourage patients to make internal attributions to past adherence behavior will increase efficacy expectations. Thus, interventions to change compliance should encourage patients to attach these cognitive labels to their compliant behaviors.

A third study attempted to generalize Rosenbaum and Ben-Ari Smira's (1986) model to dietary and medication compliance. Eitel,

Friend, Griffin, and Wadhwa (1995) once again replicated the results with fluid compliance, but the model did not hold up for dietary and medication compliance. This suggested that different processes may underlie different adherence regimens. It is possible that unlike fluid intake, which is frequently and publicly monitored by the medical staff, dietary and medication compliance may not be well monitored. Also, the need for a nourishing protein diet to maintain body mass (Lindsay, Spanner, & Heidenheim, 1994) while maintaining potassium, sodium, and phosphorous control may be particularly difficult to achieve.

Christensen and his colleagues (1990) also approached adherence from a control perspective. Their person/environment model related preference for control or behavioral involvement with features of the treatment that are in keeping with such preferences. They found that self-care home patients who were high in preference for behavioral involvement in care showed greater dietary compliance, as measured by serum potassium levels, than those low in preference for behavioral compliance. The obverse was found was for patients whose hemodialysis was staff-administered. Among these patients, patients low in behavioral involvement complied better than those high in behavioral involvement. Similar results were obtained with fluid compliance, but they were not as strong.

An additional study by Christensen, Smith, Turner, and Cundick (1994) concerned coping and compliance. In this study, coping was defined by two behaviors, namely, information vigilance and active coping (behavioral involvement). Among in-center patients, higher information vigilance was associated with poorer dietary compliance, whereas self-care home patients showed an association between higher information vigilance and greater dietary compliance. The Information × Modality interaction was not significant for medical compliance.

In many of these studies, the proposed models or hypotheses hold up for some areas of compliance but not others, even for the same sample. Lamping, Campbell, and Churchill (1988); Eitel, Friend, Griffin, and Wadhwa (1995); and Cummings et al. (1981) noted the "crazy quilt" phenomena, in which one patient may comply on fluid levels but not on potassium, or vice versa. There appears to be no consistency in compliance, and very few patients are compliant on everything. The models described above, and their predictive capacities, often occur for some measures of compliance and not for others. For instance, Rosenbaum and Ben-Ari Smira's (1986) self-regulatory model was replicated by Schneider et al. (1991) and Eitel, Friend, Griffin, and Wadhwa (1995) for fluid compliance but not for dietary compliance. The Person × Environment interaction model appeared to be more predictive for potassium than it was for fluid intake. One possible explanation would be that compliance is very much determined by situational factors and that the obstacles to complying for fluid levels may be different than that for dietary compliance or medication. Cummings et al. (1981) reported that thirst was most important for fluid levels, whereas being reminded and obtaining prescription appeared to be important for medication. Very different sets of situational variables may be implicated. Concepts such as resourcefulness, which should have some generality, may not be predictive, unless the specific situations are identified as in the Lewinian model of behavior f(PE). Future research needs to conceive adherence in situational terms and identify characteristics of compliance situations.

THE NEED FOR PSYCHOLOGICAL INTERVENTIONS TO IMPROVE CARE

In one of the earliest studies, Foster, Cohn, and McKegney (1973) observed that poor social relations between the dialysis staff and patients influenced the survival of patients. Friend, Singletary, Mendell, and Nurse (1986), in a study of 126 patients at Harlem Hospital Center in New York City, compared those who participated in a patient-controlled support group with a control group of patients who did not. The two groups did not differ in etiology of renal disease or among demographic factors. Survival was substantially greater among patients participating in the support group than those who did not, even after controlling for 13 psychosocial and medical factors. Furthermore, when patients who expired during the first 6 months of dialysis were excluded from analysis— presumably the sickest patients—the results remained substantially significant. The results of this study are in keeping with experimental studies of cancer patients (Grossarth-Maticek, 1980; Spiegel, Bloom, Kraemer, & Gottheil, 1989) that compared social assistance and support groups with a usual-care control group. Cassileth et al. (1984), however, found no differences in survival rate between cancer patients who had high, medium, or low psychosocial assets, assessed by questionnaire, which included measures of both social ties and personality measures of depression, hopelessness, and life satisfaction. However, as social psychologists have forcefully demonstrated in their discipline, actual group and situational forces are considerably more powerful predictors of behavior than is assessment of individual differences.

Several studies that assessed individual differences in psychosocial assets produced conflicting results. Burton, Kline, Lindsay, and Heidenheim (1986) found that depression predicted survival. Devins et al. (1990), in contrast, found that it did not. Christensen, Wiebe, Smith, and Turner (1994), on the other hand, found that perceived family social support, not depression, predicted survival. Peterson et al. (1991) found that family support, however, did not predict survival but that depression (minus the somatic symptoms) distinguished between a group of survivors and nonsurvivors. However, Kimmel, Weihs, and Peterson (1993) reviewed the literature on depression and survival and concluded that measures of cognitive depression that exclude symptoms might predict depression. Friend et al. (1986) found that psychiatric illness diagnoses (which included depression) before dialysis or while on dialysis predicted poorer survival rates. In summary, strong supportive relations may influence survival rates in chronically ill patients. Peer support groups may influence patient survival by increasing compliance; facilitating coping skills, including optimism; reducing stress; and improving immune function (Boyer, Friend, Chlouverakis, & Kaloyanides, 1990; Kimmel et al., 1993; Plough & Salem, 1982). However, the relation between depression and survival is still equivocal.

CONCLUSION

Psychological and educational interventions to improve patient care and adjustment are few and far between in ESRD. With the exception of mostly case studies to change fluid compliance (Barnes, 1976; Cummings et al., 1981; Hegel, Ayllon, Thiel, & Oulton, 1992), there are few, if any, intervention studies designed to improve patient quality of life and adjustment (Devins et al., 1982). Given the number of ERSD patients and the enormous expenditure of funds, there is a clear need for such interventions. Presently, most research funding is for medical interventions. For example, the recent development and availability of recombinant erythropoietin (EPO) to correct anemia provide an important advance in the physical treatment of ESRD patients. Renal patients suffer substantially from loss of energy and fatigue, resulting from deficiency in endogenous erythropoietin, a hormone responsible for maintaining normal red blood cells. Although the advent of EPO signaled an important new phase in the treatment of anemia, some expectations regarding its influence have not been realized. It was expected that substantially more patients would become active, remain employed, or become reemployed. However, there are many additional reasons why patients continue to feel fatigued. Physical interventions do not always have a direct or desired impact.

The Canadian EPO study, a double-blind EPO trial, indicated that the recombinant drug resulted in improvement in exercise tolerance, increased strength, reduced fatigue, and fewer complaints of severe physical symptoms. There were also moderate improvements in depression and global psychosocial and physical well-being. Other studies showed that patients on EPO are not more likely to return to work, as was initially expected with the introduction of EPO therapy. This suggests that other factors are preventing this from occurring. Furthermore, correlations between changes in hemoglobin and the fatigue and physical functioning were low (.32 and .31, respectively), indicating that additional factors were contributing to fatigue and lack of energy. Although EPO is no doubt important for improving the physical condition of ESRD patients, there is not always a direct or strong relation between improvements in physical or objective conditions and subjective and psychological well-being. Recall also that the variance in well-being among maintenance therapies—transplantation, hemodialysis, and CAPD—is, in fact, far larger than the variance among treatment effects, indicating that many transplanted patients report worse quality of life than hemodialysis patients and that many hemodialysis patients report a better quality of life than do transplanted patients. In the case of EPO, why are the psychological or quality-of-life benefits not always commensurate with the dramatic changes that EPO provides in physically correcting for anemia? Some have suggested that the EPO dose needs to be increased but that physicians are reluctant to do so. Another approach, one that we prefer, argues the need for explicit and systematic psychological interventions to supplement the benefits accruing from medical interventions.

It is interesting to compare the effects of EPO treatment on work with a psychosocial intervention to maintain labor participation (Rasgon et al., 1993). The patients in this study were not receiving EPO. They were blue-collar workers who needed to expend considerable physical energy as a part of their work (see Figure 8). Rasgon et al. (1993) instituted an intensive predialysis program with medical staff that encouraged patients and family to remain working, by teaching them how to integrate their work and personal lives with ESRD treatment. Of the patients who received this psychosocial intervention, 47% continued working while on dialysis, in contrast to 24% of patients of a comparison group who were not provided with the intervention. This result draws attention to the important impact that psychosocial interventions alone can have. If such interventions were coupled with medical interventions, such as EPO treatment, they both could maximize the benefits that accrue from each. Given the multiple causes of fatigue and loss of energy, psychological and physical, patients need to be taught what to realistically expect and what to attribute or not attribute their energy level to as they receive medical treatment. Research reveals that interventions that fully explain the rationale for complex treatments improve patient adjustment (Taylor, 1995). Without parallel systematic psychological intervention, changes from physical intervention may be misperceived or misinterpreted, and benefits may not be maximized. How physical

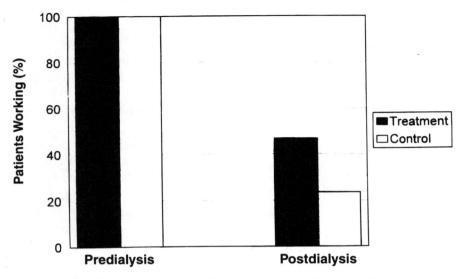

Figure 8. Blue-collar work status of end-stage renal disease patients. Data are from Rasgon et al. (1993).

changes and treatment modalities are subjectively experienced, how they translate psychologically, and what interpretations patients make may be crucially important to realizing the benefits of these changes and modalities. Given the large contribution of psychological factors to the subjective well-being and adjustment of ESRD patients, health psychology and behavioral medicine have an important role to play in the treatment of these patients.

REFERENCES

Barnes, M. R. (1976). Token economy control of fluid overload in a patient receiving hemodialysis. *Journal of Behavior Therapy and Experimental Psychiatry, 7,* 305–306.

Bihl, M. A., Ferrans, C. E., & Powers, M. (1988). Comparing stressors and quality of life of dialysis patients. *American Nephrology Nurses' Association Journal, 5,* 27–36.

Binik, Y. M., Baker, A. G., Kalogeropoulos, D., Devins, G. M., Guttman, R. D., Hollomby, D. J., Barre, P. E., Hutchison, T., Prud'homme, M., & McMullen, L. (1982). Pain, control over treatment, and compliance in dialysis and transplant patients. *Kidney International, 21,* 840–848.

A bleak U.S. report on kidney-failure patients. (1993, November 4). *The New York Times,* p. A17.

Boyer, C. B., Friend, R., Chlouverakis, G., & Kaloyanides, G. (1990). Social support and demographic factors influencing compliance of hemodialysis patients. *Journal of Applied Social Psychology, 20,* 1902–1918.

Bremer, B. A., McCauley, C. R., Wrona, R. M., & Johnson, J. P. (1989). Quality of life in end-stage renal disease: A reexamination. *American Journal of Kidney Diseases, 13*, 200–209.

Burton, H. J., Kline, S. A., Lindsay, R. M., & Heidenheim, A. P. (1986). The relationship of depression to survival in chronic renal failure. *Psychosomatic Medicine, 48*, 261–269.

Cassileth, B. R., Lusk, E. J., Strouse, T. B., Miller, D. S., Brown, L. L., Cross, P. A., & Tenaglia, A. N. (1984). Psychosocial status in chronic illness: A comparative analysis of six diagnostic groups. *The New England Journal of Medicine, 331*, 506–511.

Christensen, A. J., Smith, T. W., Holman, J. M., Gregory, M. C. (1990). Type of hemodialysis and preference for behavioral involvement: Interactive effects on adherence in end-stage renal disease. *Health Psychology, 9*, 225–236.

Christensen, A. J., Smith, T. W., Turner, C. W., & Cundick, K. E. (1994). Patient adherence and adjustment in renal dialysis: A Person × Treatment interactive approach. *Journal of Behavioral Medicine, 17*, 549–566.

Christensen, A. J., Turner, C. W., Slaughter, J. R., & Holman, J. M. (1989). Perceived family support as a moderator psychological well-being in end-stage renal disease. *Journal of Behavioral Medicine, 12*, 249–265.

Christensen, A. J., Wiebe, J. S., Smith, T. W., & Turner, C. W. (1994). Predictors of survival among hemodialysis patients: Effect of perceived support. *Health Psychology, 13*, 521–525.

Churchill, D. N., Wallace, J. E., Ludwin, D., Beecroft, M. L., & Taylor, D. W. (1991). A comparison of evaluative indices of quality of life and cognitive function in hemodialysis patients. *Controlled Clinical Trials, 12*, 159–167.

Cummings, K. M., Becker, M. H., Kirscht, J. P., & Levin, N. W. (1981). Intervention strategies to improve compliance with medical regimens by ambulatory hemodialysis patients. *Journal of Behavioral Medicine, 4*, 111–127.

Devins, G. M., Binik, Y. M., Gorman, P., Dattel, M., McClosky, B., Oscar, G., & Briggs, J. (1982). Perceived self-efficacy, outcome expectancies, and negative mood states in end-stage renal disease. *Journal of Abnormal Psychology, 91*, 241–244.

Devins, G. M., Binik, Y. M., Hollomby, D. J., Barre, P. E., & Guttman, R. D. (1981). Helplessness and depression in end-stage renal disease. *Journal of Abnormal Psychology, 90*, 531–545.

Devins, G. M., Mann, J., Mandin, H., Paul, L. C., Hons, R. B., Burgess, E. D., Taub, K., Schorr, S., Letourneau, P. K., & Buckle, S. (1990). Psychosocial predictors of survival in end-stage renal disease. *Journal of Nervous and Mental Disease, 178*, 127–133.

Diener, E. (1995). Resources, personal strivings, and subjective well-being: A nomothetic and idioic approach. *Journal of Personality and Social Psychology, 68*, 926–935.

Eitel, P., Friend, R., Griffin, K., & Wadhwa, N. K. (1995). *Cognitive control and consistency in compliance*. Manuscript submitted for publication.

Eitel, P., Hatchett, L., Friend, R., Griffin, K. W., & Wadhwa, N. K. (1995). Burden of self-care in seriously ill patients: Impact on adjustment. *Health Psychology, 14,* 457–463.

Evans, R. W., Manninen, D. L., Garrison, L. P., Hart, G., Blagg, C. R., Gutman, R. A., Hull, A. R., & Lowrie, E. G. (1985). The quality of life of patients with end-stage renal disease. *The New England Journal of Medicine, 312,* 553–559.

Foster, F., Cohn, G., & McKegney, F. (1973). Psychobiological factors and individual survival on chronic renal hemodialysis—A two-year follow-up: Part I. *Psychosomatic Medicine, 35,* 64–81.

Friend, R., Singletary, Y., Mendell, N. R., & Nurse, H. (1986). Group participation and survival among patients with end-stage renal disease. *American Journal of Public Health, 76,* 670–672.

Grossarth-Maticek, R. (1980). Social psychotherapy and course of the disease: First experiences with cancer patients. *Psychotherapy and Psychosomatics, 33,* 129–138.

Hatchett, L., Friend, R., Symister, P., & Wadhwa, N. (1996). *Interpersonal expectations and adjustment to chronic illness*. Manuscript submitted for publication.

Hegel, M. T., Ayllon, T., Thiel, G., & Oulton, B. (1992). Improving adherence to fluid restrictions in male hemodialysis patients: A comparison of cognitive and behavioral approaches. *Health Psychology, 11,* 324–330.

Kimmel, P. L., Weihs, K., & Peterson, R. A. (1993). Survival in hemodialysis patients: The role of depression. *Journal of the American Society of Nephrology, 4,* 12–27.

Lamping, D. L., & Campbell, K. A. (1989). A methodological study of hemodialysis compliance criteria. *Journal of Compliance in Health Care, 4,* 117–134.

Lamping, D., Campbell, K., & Churchill, D. (1988, November). *Consistency and stability of hemodialysis compliance criteria*. Paper presented at the meeting of the Association for the Advancement of Behavior Therapy, New York.

Levenson, J. L., & Glocheski, S. (1991). Psychological factors affecting end-stage renal disease: A review. *Psychosomatics, 32,* 382–389.

Lindsay, R. M., Spanner, E., & Heidenheim, P. A. (1994). Dietary requirements of renal patients and their impact on quality of life. In H. McGee & C. Bradley (Eds.), *Quality of life following renal failure: Psychosocial challenges accompanying high technology medicine* (pp. 265–273). Chur, Switzerland: Harwood Academic.

Marqusee, J. E. (1993, November). Life can continue after kidney failure [Letter to the editor]. *The New York Times,* p. A26.

McGee, H., & Bradley, C. (1994). Quality of life following renal failure: An introduction to the issues and challenges. In H. McGee & C. Bradley (Eds.),

Quality of life following renal failure: Psychosocial challenges accompanying high technology medicine (pp. 1–22). Chur, Switzerland: Harwood Academic.

Mor, V., Laliberte, L., Morris, J. N., & Wiemann, M. (1984). The Karnofsky performance status scale: An examination of its reliability and validity in a research setting. *Cancer, 53,* 2002–2007.

National Institutes of Health. (1993). Morbidity and mortality of dialysis. *National Institutes of Health Consensus Statement, 11,* 1–33.

Nissenson, A. R. (1994). Measuring, managing, and improving quality in the end-stage renal disease treatment setting: Peritoneal dialysis. *American Journal of Kidney Disease, 24,* 368–375.

Peterson, R. A., Kimmel, P. L., Sacks, C. R., Mesquita, M. L., Simmens, S. J., & Reiss, D. (1991). Depression, perception of illness and mortality in patients with end-stage renal disease. *International Journal of Psychiatry in Medicine, 21,* 343–354.

Plough, A. L., & Salem, S. (1982). Social and contextual factors in the analyses of mortality in end-stage renal disease: Implications for health policy. *American Journal of Public Health, 72,* 1293–1295.

Rasgon, S., Schwankovsky, L., James-Rogers, A., Widrow, L., Glick, J., & Butts, E. (1993). An intervention for employment maintenance among blue-collar workers with end-stage renal disease. *American Journal of Kidney Diseases, 22,* 403–412.

Rosenbaum, M., & Ben-Ari Smira, K. B. (1986). Cognitive and personality factors in the delay of gratification of hemodialysis patients. *Journal of Personality and Social Psychology, 51,* 357–364.

Sacks, C. R., Peterson, R. A., & Kimmel, P. L. (1990). Perception of illness and depression in chronic renal disease. *American Journal of Kidney Diseases, 15,* 31–39.

Schneider, M. S., Friend, R., Whitaker, P., & Wadhwa, N. K. (1991). Fluid noncompliance and symptomatology in end-stage renal disease: Cognitive and emotional variables. *Health Psychology, 10,* 209–215.

Simmons, R. G., Anderson, B. A., & Kamstra, B. A. (1984). Comparison of quality of life of patients on continuous ambulatory peritoneal dialysis, hemodialysis, and after transplantation. *American Journal of Kidney Diseases, 9,* 253–255.

Spiegel, D., Bloom, J. R., Kraemer, H. C., & Gottheil, E. (1989). Effect of psychosocial treatment on survival of patients with metastatic breast cancer. *The Lancet, 2,* 888–891.

Taylor, S. E. (1995). *Health psychology.* New York: McGraw-Hill.

United States Renal Data System. (1993). Annual data report. *American Journal of Kidney Diseases, 22* (Suppl. 2), S1–S118.

United States Renal Data System. (1994). Annual data report. *American Journal of Kidney Diseases, 24* (Suppl. 2), S1–S181.

19

HEALTH PSYCHOLOGY AND THE FIELD OF UROLOGY

STEVEN M. TOVIAN

The role of clinical psychologists in medical settings is expanding significantly to include a wide range of medical problems (Sweet, Rozensky, & Tovian, 1991). This chapter highlights two problem areas that offer research and practice opportunities for clinical health psychologists working in adult urological medicine. These areas in urology involve urinary incontinence (UI) and erectile dysfunction (ED).

URINARY INCONTINENCE

Urinary incontinence presents concerns for public health professionals, physicians, nurses, and psychologists because of its high incidence, its medical implications, and its psychological sequelae. It also imposes a large financial burden on the patient, his or her family, and society. The number of patients with urinary incontinence who are not successfully treated, either medically or psychologically, remains surprisingly high because of several factors, including the following:

underreporting by patients; underrecognition as a significant clinical problem by health providers; lack of education of health providers regarding new research findings; inadequate staffing in long-term-care settings; and persistent major gaps in understanding the natural history, pathophysiology, and most effective treatments of the common forms of UI. The amount of basic research, as well as research focusing on prevention, is meager (National Institutes of Health Consensus Conference, 1988).

Definition

Incontinence is a symptom, not a disease (Orzeck & Ouslander, 1987), and can result from pathologic, anatomic, or physiologic conditions within the urinary system or elsewhere in the body. Urinary incontinence is a condition in which involuntary loss of urine can be a social or hygienic problem and is objectively demonstrable (Ory, Wyman, & Yu, 1986). Many causes of UI can be reversed, such as infection, atrophic vaginitis, acute confusional states, restrictions in mobility, fecal impaction, and the side effects of drugs. Longer term or permanent causes of UI include diabetes, stroke, cerebral palsy, multiple sclerosis, prostate enlargement, cancer, spinal cord injuries, and birth defects such as spinal bifida (American Association of Retired Persons and Simon Foundation for Continence, 1993). Depending on the underlying cause, the bladder may malfunction in different ways, resulting in several types of UI.

Prevalence

It is estimated that over 10 million Americans suffer from UI (American Association of Retired Persons and Simon Foundation for Continence, 1993). Urinary incontinence may be underreported because of the stigma attached to the disorder and because of the inherent difficulty in measuring its occurrence. Among the population between 15 and 64 years of age, the prevalence of UI in men ranges from 1.5% to 5% and in women ranges from 10%–25% (Thomas, Plymat, Blannin, & Meade, 1980). In one series of randomly selected women (30–59 years old), 26% reported having experienced UI as a social or hygienic problem (Elving, Foldspang, Lain, & Mommens, 1989; Resnick, Welte, Scherr, Branch, & Taylor, 1986).

Among the more than 1.5 million U.S. nursing facility residents, the prevalence of UI is 50% or higher, with episodes generally occurring more than once per day (Urinary Incontinence Guideline Panel, 1992).

Costs

A reportedly conservative estimate (Hu, 1990) of the direct costs of caring for persons of all ages with incontinence is $7 billion annually in the community and $3.3 billion in nursing homes (based on 1987 dollars). If guidelines and protocols for improved treatment of UI were followed, Hu et al. (1992) estimated that there would be a savings of $105 per episode in the outpatient setting and $535 in the inpatient setting, for stress incontinence (to be discussed later) alone. From 1990 hospital discharge figures, Hu et al. (1991) noted that there were 53,000 patients discharged with a primary diagnosis of stress incontinence, of which 38,000 were less than 65 years of age. If existing guidelines and protocols for stress incontinence in individuals under age 65 were followed, the total estimated savings would be approximately $20.3 million per year. If guidelines and protocols for overflow UI among individuals under age 65 discharged from hospitals in 1990 were followed, the total estimated savings would be an additional $21.5 million per year (Hu et al., 1991).

Absorbent pads and undergarments, either disposable or reusable, are widely used by persons with UI, and their widespread use is reflected by growth of the market of disposable pads and adult undergarments from $99 million in 1972 to $496 million in 1987 (Urinary Incontinence Guideline Panel, 1992). These costs contribute to about half of the direct-care costs for incontinence among residents in nursing homes (Sowell, Schnelle, Hu, & Traughbers, 1987).

From a public health and financial viewpoint, when considering the costs of service use, medical supplies, and absorbent paper products, for example, UI clearly presents a far-reaching and costly health care problem.

Medical, Psychological, and Social Impact

Less than half of those individuals with UI living in the community consult health care providers about the problem (American Association of Retired Persons and Simon Foundation for Continence, 1993). Urinary incontinence is rarely detected and reported by hospital personnel, making its true extent and clinical impact difficult to assess. Instead, many people with UI turn prematurely to the use of absorbent materials and supportive aids, without having their condition properly diagnosed and treated. The long-term use of absorbent products should occur only after a basic evaluation of the person's incontinence by a physician. Dependence on caregivers increases as incontinence worsens, and the homebound frequently use indwelling catheters and other supportive devices, which increase the risk of urinary tract infections, morbidity, and mortality (Urinary Incontinence Guideline Panel, 1992).

The psychosocial impact of UI imposes a burden on individuals, their families, and health care providers. Individuals with UI are often depressed and embarrassed about their problem, appearance, and even odor. Consequently, excursions outside the home, social interactions with friends and family, and sexual activity may be restricted or avoided secondary to UI.

Types

Urge incontinence is the sudden and intense desire to urinate, with the inability to suppress the urge long enough to reach a toilet (Orzeck & Ouslander, 1987). Involuntary voiding is preceded by a warning of a few seconds to a few minutes. Leakage is periodic, but frequent, with a moderate-to-large volume (Resnick & Yalla, 1985). *Stress incontinence,* more common in women than in men (Mohr, Rogers, Brown, & Stark-weather, 1983; Resnick & Yalla, 1985), occurs when physical stress on the abdomen (e.g., coughing, sneezing, and laughing) causes excess pressure in the bladder, which overrides the bladder's normal restraint (Orzeck & Ouslander, 1987). The volume leaked is small to moderate (Resnick & Yalla, 1985). *Overflow incontinence* is the leakage of small amounts of urine without the urge to void (Orzeck & Ouslander, 1987). This occurs when the weight of the urine in the bladder overcomes the outlet resistance, and the excess amount runs off, but the bladder remains full (Resnick & Yalla, 1985). *Total (reflex) incontinence* is a complete absence of bladder control, with either continuous or periodic leakage. When leakage is periodic, it is frequent, with a moderate volume (Resnick & Yalla, 1985). *Functional incontinence* is the loss of urine resulting from an inability or unwillingness to use the toilet appropriately. Factors that contribute to functional incontinence may include deficits of mobility, mental status, motivation, or environmental barriers (Burgio & Engel, 1987). *Iatrogenic incontinence* occurs after surgery or due to the effects of medication combinations (Resnick & Yalla, 1985). *Complex (mixed) incontinence* occurs when a person experiences simultaneously more than one type of incontinence. An example is the development of urge incontinence in someone with a history of stress incontinence (Resnick & Yalla, 1985).

Causes

Urinary incontinence itself is a symptom, not a disorder (Orzeck & Ouslander, 1987). It has many predisposing factors and is associated with impaired physiological or psychological functioning (Resnick & Yalla, 1985; Trombini, Rossi, Umilta, & Baccarani, 1982; Yarnell et al., 1982).

Urinary incontinence affects individuals of all ages but is most prevalent among the elderly. As a result, UI is commonly and mistakenly attributed to the aging process. The elderly are more likely to have conditions that predispose them to incontinence or contribute to the causes of incontinence. For example, conditions such as decreased bladder capacity, decreased capacity of the urethral muscle to keep the bladder neck closed, increased frequency of bladder contractions, and increased postvoid residuals can contribute to UI and are seen in the elderly (American Association of Retired Persons and Simon Foundation for Continence, 1993; Burgio & Engel, 1987). However, many of these conditions can be controlled or avoided when properly identified. Other risk factors include childbearing, directly related to the delivery experience and number of children delivered vaginally, weakening the muscles of the pelvic floor; prostate surgery, with removal of all or part of the prostate gland secondary to prostate cancer or benign prostatic hyperplasia; and disease processes such as multiple sclerosis, stroke, Parkinson's disease, and cerebral palsy. Additionally, birth defects affecting the bladder or nervous system (i.e., spinal bifida) can be associated with UI (American Association of Retired Persons and Simon Foundation for Continence, 1993).

Urinary incontinence is not a normal aspect of aging, nor is it irreversible. Some transient or temporary causes of UI include delirium; urinary tract infection; vaginitis; use of pharmaceuticals (e.g., sedative hypnotics, diuretics, anticholinergics, alpha-adrenergics, and calcium channel blockers); severe depression; excessive urine production; restricted mobility; and stool impaction. Information about the causes of UI are available from Orzeck and Ouslander (1987) and from the *Clinical Practice Guidelines: Urinary Incontinence in Adults* from the Agency for Health Care Policy and Research (Urinary Incontinence Guideline Panel, 1992).

Assessment

Assessment in the treatment of UI includes characterization of the incontinence, identification of mechanisms of urine loss, and evaluating the emotional and behavioral responses to UI and its causes, as well as a possible psychological treatment regimen, if appropriate. The clinical health psychologist would do well to assess the adaptive tasks that must be accomplished by any medical patient (Moos, 1977). The psychologist should assess how the patient is coping with possible pain, incapacitation, and other symptoms. The patient's coping style in response to special assessment and treatment procedures unique to UI, as well as how the patient is developing and maintaining adequate relationships with the health care staff, is important. In the light of the nature of UI, whether the patient is maintaining a reasonable emotional balance, preserving a satisfactory self-image, and maintaining a sense of competence and mastery should be assessed. Also, whether the patient is preserving relationships with family and friends, and how the patient is preparing for an uncertain future, need to be determined.

Psychological and behavioral assessment for UI should follow a physician's thorough medical examination. An excellent review and summary of the medical assessment, including a discussion of the measurement of urodynamics (physiological measurements of bladder pressure and sphincter activity) are available in the *Clinical Practice Guidelines: Urinary Incontinence in Adults*, from the Agency for Health Care Policy and Research (Urinary Incontinence Guideline Panel, 1992). Again, this review should help the psychologist to be a well-informed member of the health care team.

Burgio and Engel (1987) provided a thorough review of behavioral assessment techniques that can be used by the psychologist when working in collaboration with physicians and nurses in the area of UI. Although the authors limit their discussion to geriatric populations, their methods can be generalized to other populations as well.

Burgio and Engel (1987) used techniques involving interview guidelines, mental status evaluations, bladder records or symptom diaries, and assessment of mobility and toileting skills. According to the Burgio and Engel (1987), interview guidelines need to take into account antecedents of incontinence, descriptions of incontinent episodes, and the consequences of UI. As mentioned previously, there are different types of UI, and each type may have its own unique antecedents and consequences for the patient. Interviews with significant others and other family members are also important.

Voiding habits and continence can be disrupted by depression or cognitive deficits, such as confusion, disorientation, and memory impairment. Burgio and Engel (1987) recommended use of the Mini-Mental State Examination (Folstein, Folstein, & McHugh, 1975) with acutely ill patients, as a brief measure of mental status. Depression may be evaluated by interview and other structured devices, such as the Beck Depression Inventory (Beck, 1972). Referral to a neuropsychologist for a more thorough cognitive evaluation may also be warranted.

Burgio and Engel (1987) also provided examples of bladder records or symptom diaries, which document patterns of UI on a day-to-day basis. Records provide a source of data to diagnose causes of UI and a means to assist in evaluating progress and treatment effectiveness. Finally, observations of mobility and assessment of toileting skills can be used to assess whether environmental barriers or physical handicapping conditions exacerbate or cause UI. As the expert in behavioral and psychological assessments, the psychologist can become a valuable member of the diagnostic team.

Psychological Aspects

Each person who suffers from incontinence feels differently about it and reacts with varying degrees of emotional distress. Tovian, Rozensky, Sloan, and Slotnik (1995) summarized numerous studies identifying the psychological aspects of incontinence.

Depression may be the most commonly reported reaction (Cuhna, 1986; Macaulay, Stern, Holmes, & Stanton, 1987; Ouslander, 1982; Stone & Judd, 1978; Sutherland, 1976; Tovian & Rozensky, 1985). Both agitated and retarded symptoms of depression are common (Yu, 1987), and Macaulay et al. (1987) reported that 25% of patients viewed life as not worth living because of their incontinence. Actual embarrassment and fear of possible public embarrassment from "accidents" or others noticing urine odor are also very pertinent psychological factors in the everyday management of incontinence (Dobson, 1973; Mitteness, 1987; Norton, 1982; Stone & Judd, 1978). Symptom complexes, including shame, humiliation, or damaged self-image are frequently experienced by the incontinent patient (Mitteness, 1987; Norton, 1982; Sadler, 1982; Stone & Judd, 1978). Anxiety, irritability, frustration, and anger have also been identified among incontinent patients (Tovian & Rozensky, 1985). Those patients with catheters, for example, tend to be constantly aware of its presence and are often fearful of others noticing the odor of urine (Roe & Brocklehurst, 1987).

Hafner, Stanton, and Guy (1977) asserted that roughly one third of all incontinence patients would benefit from psychological intervention. Given this estimate, as well as the figure of over 10 million known suffers of UI (Berkman, 1986), there would appear to be a large number of people in need of the health psychologist's clinical and research expertise.

Quality of Life

Work. In some cases, people with incontinence find it difficult to obtain a job and even more difficult to hold one (Dobson, 1973; Norton, 1982). Norton also reported that patients can lose their jobs or have to change employment because of the restriction of activities due to their incontinence. Fear and worry of leakage or odor can impair work concentration.

Social aspects. Many people rearrange their physical and social environments to accommodate their incontinence (Mitteness, 1987). The feelings of isolation often are reinforced due to a self-induced social withdrawal because of fears of being "found out" (Breakwell & Walker, 1988; Mitteness, 1987; Norton, 1982). Ouslander et al. (1987) found that people with incontinence in nursing homes felt that they had fewer close friends or talked with friends less often but that, in actuality, they engaged in activities as frequently as others.

Home life. One often unavoidable artifact of incontinence is dependency, especially for the elderly. This is reflected in their difficulties with activities of daily living, such as shopping, housekeeping, and hygiene (Noelker, 1987; Norton, 1982). More help is then needed from spouses and other family members (Ekelund & Rundgren, 1987). Many incontinent people fear entering a marriage, either because of fear of rejection by the spouse once they are told of the incontinence or because of possible awkwardness of the sexual aspect of the relationship (Dobson, 1973; Norton, 1982).

Reactions of Caregivers

Institutional caregivers. Mitteness (1987) believes that physicians often hold the attitude that UI is inevitable in old age and untreatable and, therefore, relegate the management of the incontinent patients to nurses. In a survey, Yu and Kaltreider (1987) found that the nursing personnel had both positive and negative feelings toward UI, feeling sympathy toward the patients as victims while experiencing stress due to the tedious maintenance of the incontinent patients.

Home caregivers. Living with a person who suffers from incontinence can have negative effects on family relations (Jakovac-Smith, 1988). The tasks involved in caring for the incontinent are tiring, difficult, and upsetting (Noelker, 1987), and there is a reluctance to talk openly about the subject (Dobson, 1973; Tovian & Rozensky, 1985). For this reason, caregivers are often unsure as to whether they are caring properly for their incontinent relative (Noelker, 1987). Because of the many tasks and time requirements, the caregivers' social activities may be restricted (Noelker, 1987). This nonmedical issue, the restriction of the caregiver's social activities, can often lead to a nursing home placement for the incontinent relative. Such a decision may be medically unnecessary for the patient (Jakovac-Smith, 1988). Although many relatives are willing to provide this home care, they may need regular relief and support (Dobson, 1973).

Treatment

The treatment of UI falls within four areas: behavioral, pharmacologic, surgical, and supportive devices (including catheters and absorbent pads and garments). A combination of interventions may be used, depending on the patient's needs and physician's diagnosis. For this chapter, discussion focuses on the behavioral interventions that fall into the scope of practice of clinical health psychologists. Thorough reviews of all treatment options for UI, including their risks, benefits, and outcome, are discussed in the *Clinical Practice Guidelines: Urinary Incontinence in Adults* (Urinary Incontinence Guideline Panel, 1992).

Behavioral Techniques

Behavioral techniques include bladder training, habit training (timed voiding), prompted voiding, pelvic muscle exercises, and biofeedback. Behavioral techniques show improvement ranging from complete dryness to reductions of wetness (Urinary Incontinence Guideline Panel, 1992). Improved bladder control can occur in cognitively impaired individuals (McCormick, Scheve, & Leahy, 1988; Schnelle, 1990). Behavioral techniques have no reported side effects, do not limit future treatment options, and can be used in combination with other therapies for UI.

Some limitations, however, are noteworthy in published results determining the effectiveness of behavioral interventions with UI. These include use of different outcome criteria, variability and frequency of treatment sessions, variability of comprehensiveness in training procedures, absence or variability in follow-up data, use of heterogeneous samples, and lack of standardized terminology for various behavioral techniques. These are important issues when considering future directions for clinical health psychologists in research with UI. Despite these limitations, behavioral interventions appear to be most effective for urge UI and stress UI. Behavioral interventions are not effective for patients with overflow UI (Urinary Incontinence Guideline Panel, 1992).

Bladder training. Bladder training (also termed *bladder retraining*) consists of three primary components: education, scheduled voiding, and positive reinforcement. The education program usually combines written, visual, and verbal instruction that addresses physiology and pathophysiology. The voiding schedule uses a progressively increased interval between mandatory voidings, with concomitant distraction or relaxation techniques. The person is taught to delay voiding consciously. If the patient is unable to delay voiding between schedules, one approach is to adjust this schedule and start the timing from the last void. Another option is to keep the prearranged schedule and disregard the unscheduled void between schedules. Finally, positive reinforcement is provided. More specific details regarding bladder-training programs, such as optional time involving voiding intervals, are available in the *Clinical Practice Guidelines: Urinary Incontinence in Adults* (Urinary Incontinence Guideline Panel, 1992). Fantl et al. (1991), in a randomized controlled study, reported that 12% of the women who underwent bladder training became continent, and 75% improved to at least a 50% reduction in the number of incontinent episodes. This form of training has been used to manage

UI due to bladder instability. However, studies indicate that this training may also control stress incontinence (Burgio, Whitehead, & Engel, 1985; Burton et al., 1988; Fantl et al., 1990; Rose, Baigis-Smith, Smith, & Newman, 1990).

Habit training. Habit training, or timed voiding, is scheduled toileting on a planned basis. The goal is to keep the person dry by telling them to void at regular intervals. Attempts are made to match the voiding intervals to the person's natural voiding schedule. Unlike bladder training, there is no systematic effort to motivate the patient to delay voiding and resist urge. Studies indicate improvement in patients (Colling, Ouslander, Hadley, Campbell, & Eisch, 1991; Engel et al., 1990; Schnelle, Newman, & Fogarty, 1990). In one controlled study on habit training, when 51 nursing home residents who were identified with an electronic monitoring device, Jarvis (1981) found that 86% of the participants improved their UI over baseline levels, when compared with control groups.

Prompted voiding. Prompted voiding is a supplement to habit training and attempts to teach the incontinent person to discriminate their incontinence status and to request toileting assistance from caregivers. There are three elements to prompted voiding: monitoring (the person is checked by caregivers on a regular basis and asked to report if wet or dry), prompting (the person is asked or prompted to try to use the toilet), and reinforcement (the person is praised for maintaining continence and for attempting to toilet). Prompted voiding has been shown to be effective in dependent or cognitively impaired nursing home incontinent patients (Colling et al., 1991; Engel et al., 1990; Hu et al., 1991; Schnelle, 1990).

Pelvic muscle exercises. Pelvic muscle exercises, also called *Kegel exercises*, improve urethral resistance through active exercise of the pubococcygeus muscle. The exercises strengthen the voluntary periurethral and pelvic muscles. The contraction inherent in the exercise exerts a closing force on the urethra and increases muscle support to the pelvic visceral structures (Urinary Incontinence Guideline Panel, 1992).

Pelvic muscle exercises have been shown to be effective with women with stress incontinence (Castleden, Duffin, Asher, & Yeomanson, 1985; Klarskov, Gerstenberg, & Hald, 1986); with men after prostate surgery (Burgio, Stutzman, & Engel, 1989); and after multiple surgical repairs in women (Baigis-Smith, Smith, Rose, & Newman, 1989; Burgio & Engel, 1990). This exercise is often coupled with pharmacologic therapy (Wells et al., 1991; Brody, 1985) and biofeedback (Burgio, Robinson, & Engel, 1986), to maximize results.

Biofeedback. Biofeedback uses electronic or mechanical instruments to relay information to patients about their physiologic activity.

It aims to alter bladder dysfunction by teaching people to change physiologic responses that mediate bladder control (Burgio & Engel, 1990). Display of this information, through auditory or visual displays, forms the core of the biofeedback procedure (Schwartz, 1987).

Biofeedback is often used with other behavioral and medical procedures; such studies report a range of 54%–95% improvement across different patient groups (Urinary Incontinence Guideline Panel, 1992). For women, a biofeedback device, called a *perineometer*, attaches by cable to a sensor that is inserted into the vagina. The sensor comes in contact with the pubococcygeus muscle and shows the strength of the muscle, the ability of the muscle to relax, and the level of control of that muscle (Burns, Marack, Duttmar, & Bullogh, 1985).

Burgio et al. (1986) found that 92% of the biofeedback patients significantly reduced incontinence, but only 55% of the patients without biofeedback achieved a reduction. Similarly, Shepherd, Montgomery, and Anderson (1983) found that 91% of the patients receiving biofeedback improved or were cured, whereas only 55% of those who did not use the perineometer improved.

Smith, Smith, Rose, and Kaschak (1987a) found that patients in an outpatient clinic improved by 75% when using a clinical perineometer for diagnosis and a personal perineometer for home use. Smith, Smith, Rose, and Kaschak (1987b) obtained similar results with homebound senior citizens, using a portable perineometer. Perry, Hullett, and Bollinger (1987) used computerized software (for diagnostic evaluations), home trainers, and patient telephone reports (to assure greater compliance). All 31 of their patients had marked improvement, with 100% symptom reduction and elimination of urinary incontinence. A replication with 56 new patients found 99.95% improved and 98% cured (Perry, Hullett, & Bollinger, 1988).

Biofeedback increases the effectiveness of Kegel exercises, because the patient can observe progress and learn from past attempts at controlling the muscle (Burgio et al., 1986). Henderson and Taylor (1987) found that as pubococcygeal strength increases, the amount and occurrence of urine loss, use of the devices to protect clothing, and patient concern about the problem decrease.

Behavioral techniques in outpatient adults. Combined analyses were conducted on 22 studies that dealt with all behavioral interventions on outpatient basis (Urinary Incontinence Guideline Panel, 1992). The studies were standardized along measures of efficacy, reflecting the percentage of wetness and dryness. Results indicated that the average percentage reduction in incontinence frequency at the end of behavioral treatments was 64.6%, with a 95% confidence interval range of from 58.8% to 70.4%. Additional randomized controlled trials (Burns, Pranikoff, Nochajski, Desotelle, & Harwood, 1990; Fantl et al., 1991) and a randomized but not controlled study (Wells et al., 1991), all with women in outpatient settings, suggested that behavioral techniques result in subjective cure/improvement rates of 70%–77%, with improvements maintained for at least 6 months.

Behavioral techniques in the nursing home. The severity of UI in nursing home residents is often aggravated by the effects of institutionalization, declining medical conditions, and inconsistent nursing care. Nevertheless, a similar combined analysis of 428 persons studied in nursing homes using habit training and prompted voiding (Urinary Incontinence Guideline Panel, 1992) suggested that patients were dry 70% of the time at baseline and rose 81% after behavioral treatments during daytime hours only. These techniques have the potential to reduce the costs and improve the quality of life for long-term-care patients, as well to as serve as an important place of intervention for clinical health psychologists.

Appliances and garments. When incontinence is severe or cannot be reversed, appliances and garments are comfortable ways of managing (Burton, Pearce, Burgio, & Engel, 1988). For those patients using these products for management only, it should be remembered that a concurrent medical problem exists (Ory et al., 1986). Therefore, the clinical health psychologist should insist on concurrent medical therapeutic procedures (Mohr et al., 1983). Alvero and Gartley (1985) provided a thorough list of the various devices that are available (pad and pant systems, absorbent pants, adult undergarments, bed protection pads, drip collectors, condom catheters, intermittent catheterization, and Foley catheters).

Additional Psychological Treatment Issues

Self-help and patient education. Given the proper selection of clients, appropriate goal setting, and patient compliance, self-help programs can be very effective in the treatment of chronic illnesses. Under the self-help paradigm, skills are taught to an active participant who assumes partial responsibility for designing and administering her or his own treatment. By these learning skills, some individuals can assume considerable responsibility necessary for the self-management of their chronic illness (Tobin, Reynolds, Holroyd, & Creer, 1986).

"I Will Manage" is a Simon Foundation program based on the principles of self-help. It is hosted by both lay and professional persons. The program is divided into four sessions: "Incontinence in America Today" (an introduction), "The Urologic System, Fixing It When It Fails," "Managing Incontinence With Products and Devices," and "Dealing Effectively With the Psychological Aspects of Incontinence." The program's format is designed to accomplish two goals: (a) to present practical multidisciplinary information on incontinence and (b) to encourage people to share their experiences and develop the confidence to make changes in their life ("I Will Manage" self-help groups, Simon Foundation for Continence, 1991). This patient-education approach assumes that much of the psychosocial distress accompanying incontinence is largely a result of a lack of knowledge concerning incontinence, its causes and treatment, and the health care system. Empirical evidence of the efficacy of this approach would be useful. Given the large psychosocial component of this self-help program, there is a defined role in which the psychologist may become involved.

Supportive group therapy. The second goal inherent in the self-help paradigm, that of encouraging people to share their experiences, is also important in another treatment modality, supportive group therapy. The effectiveness of supportive group therapy has been reviewed, in the context of such medical problems as cancer (Telsch & Telsch, 1985) and cardiac surgery (Bond et al., 1979). Researchers in group therapy (e.g., Yalom & Greaves, 1977) maintain that the support offered and the opportunity to express needs, concerns, and fears are the salient ingredients in the group therapy experience. Both support and catharsis are therapeutic tools used to diminish mood disturbance, improve relationship distress, and enhance adjustment. A common therapeutic strategy is to enlist patients in becoming active in the group process, where group members are encouraged to express problems, concerns, and feelings and to share personal methods of coping. In this way, it is expected that members will serve as peer models for one another. The therapeutic mechanism of community and mutuality in group therapy would seem especially relevant to the social problems of UI patients. This therapeutic approach may also be useful for the needs of the home caregiver. To date, however, there have been no published studies of the effectiveness of supportive group therapy with UI patients or their families.

Coping skills approach. The coping skills approach involves structured training in specific cognitive, behavioral, and affective competencies for managing the disruptive effects of UI. The coping skills approach assumes that the distress experienced in managing the effects of illness and disability is partially due to a limited or ineffective skills repertoire. Rozensky and Tovian (1985) suggested the use of self-instruction techniques, which help individuals with UI learn constructive self-talk and avoid negativistic thinking. Rozensky and Tovian also proposed assertiveness techniques and progressive relaxation approaches to be used by UI patients in distressing social situations. For example, the use of covert reinforcement and structured exposure to feared situations could be applied to the problems of social withdrawal and social phobia seen among UI patients. Learning both cognitive and behavioral coping strategies may enhance adjustment by expanding coping repertoires, thereby increasing one's perception of control; a problem that is very relevant to the UI patient. Among the coping skills area, Rozensky and Tovian also recommended stress inoculation training and problem-solving strategies. The coping skills techniques may be used in group- or individual-treatment formats. There exist no controlled studies examining the effectiveness of individual or combinations of cognitive–behavioral therapeutic interventions with UI patients.

ERECTILE DYSFUNCTION

Definition and Prevalence

Erectile dysfunction is defined as a persistent or recurrent, partial or complete, failure to attain or maintain sufficient penile erections for satisfactory sexual functioning to occur with subsequent marked distress and interpersonal difficulty (American Psychiatric Association, 1994). It is estimated that more than 10 million American men experience erectile dysfunction, with the prevalence of ED increasing with age as a result of physical and mental illnesses with concomitant prescription drug use that is common during the middle and later years of life. The incidence of ED is estimated to be found in at least 10% of the male population at age 50, 20% by age 60, 30% at age 70, and 40% at age 80 (Ackerman, 1992). Using a biopsychosocial model, ED is not seen as either organic or psychogenic but, rather, is perceived as an interacting set of variables, requiring assessment of cognitive, behavioral, and interpersonal factors as well as physical factors for effective treatment. The psychological consequences of ED include depression, performance anxiety, and relationship distress (Ackerman, 1995; Ackerman & Carey, 1995).

Causes

The clinical health psychologist needs to be aware of the many biological risk factors associated with ED. Diseases of the endocrine, vascular, and neurologic systems should be carefully screened before or after any referral to the psychologist (Ackerman & Carey, 1995). Some common medical conditions that are associated with ED are presented in the Appendix. Like UI, ED is not a result of natural aging.

Many medications prescribed for various physical and mental disorders can impair erectile dysfunctioning as well as sexual desire.

Medications such as antihypertensive agents, anticholinergics, and drugs used in the treatment of psychiatric disorders (i.e., phenothiazines, benzodiazepines, and antidepressants) can be associated with ED (Ackerman, 1995). Some medications associated with ED also are presented in the Appendix.

Assessment

Ackerman (1992; Ackerman & Carey, 1995) provided excellent reviews on the role of the psychologist in establishing a multidisciplinary research-based clinical program for the evaluation and treatment of ED. Ackerman noted that the primary role of the psychologist in the assessment of ED is to provide insights about patient behaviors, thoughts, affect, and the psychosocial data through interview and assessment protocols. Screening for psychological dysfunction, substance abuse, cognitive distortions, personality disorders, or life-stress events known to adversely affect erectile functioning can be accomplished through clinical interviews and self-report questionnaires such as the Minnesota Multiphasic Personality Inventory, Beck Depression Inventory, and the Short Marital Adjustment Test (Lock & Wallace 1959). According to Ackerman, men who are either married or report a significant other should be interviewed individually and conjointly to ascertain corroborative information regarding sexual performance and relationship factors.

The Miami Sexual Dysfunction Protocol (MSDP; Ackerman, Helder, & Antoni, 1989) is a broad, semistructured interview format designed for use in medical settings to help organize information taken from the sexual dysfunctional male and his partner. Another important skill that the psychologist brings to the evaluation of ED is the ability to elicit concise information regarding sexual functioning while creating a relaxed, trusting atmosphere (Ackerman & Carey, 1995). Having an organized protocol, such as the MSDP, helps to facilitate the collection of baseline data for clinical training and research purposes in a relaxed atmosphere.

Ackerman and Carey (1995) recommended a thorough evaluation of past and current erectile functioning (i.e., description of the presenting complaint and its duration, frequency, and nature of onset), once rapport has been established. Other relevant information includes masturbatory fantasies, sexual drive, sexual techniques, and sexual knowledge. Frequency and outcome attempts at intercourse should be reviewed, as well as coping effort for unsuccessful attempts. Questions pertaining to sexual orientation, sexual deviations, and past sexual abuse should be included. Occasionally, special treatment circumstances such as vasoactive injection therapy or penile implant surgery require the psychologist to assess misconceptions, attitude, or unrealistic expectations, to maximize treatment outcome.

Ackerman (1992) highlighted the importance of assessing the absence or presence of morning erections, quality of erections, and ejaculatory ability. Ackerman (1992) noted that the final step in the assessment process involves the patient returning to the urologist for 2 consecutive nights of in-hospital Rigiscan diagnostic monitoring. Rigiscan monitoring involves the assessment of erectile functioning, including rigidity and tumescence at the base and tip of the penis and duration of these events throughout the sleep cycle.

Treatment

Ackerman, Montague, and Morganstern (1994) outlined treatment options for ED. Treatment options will depend on the suspected cause of the ED. If the causes are psychological or behavioral in nature, sex therapy will be a crucial component or sole method of treatment. If relationship problems exist, conjoint therapy is recommended with or before sex therapy. Testosterone replacement therapy is used only when there is clear evidence of hormonal insufficiency. If the ED developed after medications were prescribed, cessation or substitution of those medications may be attempted. Ackerman et al. (1994) also reviewed possible medicinal approaches with Yohimbine HCl and Frental, and they concluded that these drugs provide nothing more than placebo effects at best.

In addition, Ackerman et al. (1994) thoroughly reviewed invasive therapeutic options such as injection methods with Pavaverine HCl, vascular surgery, and implant prosthesis. Although injection methods continue to be the first-line treatment option for ED, Ackerman et al. noted that patients undergoing any of these invasive procedures often will require adjunct psychological support and psychoeducational therapy, with a psychologist experienced with ED, to ensure the technical success of these procedures.

PROGRAM DEVELOPMENT

The general purpose of integrating clinical health psychology into urology programs is to enhance patient care. From the previous discussion, it is clear that the clinical health psychologist can offer a full spectrum of services to multidisciplinary programs treating urological disorders. In addition to direct interventions involving individual assessment and psychotherapy in response to patients' psychological reactions to urological disorders, the clinical health psychologist can provide specialized interventions involving biofeedback and behavioral treatments to individuals, families, and professional caregivers, in medical settings and nursing homes. In addition to individual-treatment modalities, the clinical health psychologist can provide and supervise supportive and self-help group interventions to both patients and their families. As a member of a multidisciplinary health care team or in a specific urology program, the clinical health psychologist can also provide consultation in regular staff meetings to medical staff, regarding particular problems involving adherence to medical treatment or patient reactions to stressful medical procedures, often experienced with urology problems, such as UI and ED.

Psychology and Surgery Interface

Clinical health psychologists working in medical settings will find themselves consulting with surgeons in this tertiary field of urology. In communicating with surgeons, written reports need to be prompt, concise, and free of psychological jargon (Ackerman, 1992; Adams, 1992). Reports should begin with a direct and concise answer to the restated referral question, followed by brief and equally concise data to support that answer. Recommendations for specific interventions need to be stated succinctly and early in the report. Contradictions for specific medical interventions should be clearly noted, with evidence for potential problems delineated (Ackerman, 1992). Lengthy reports discussing test results are too often obscure to the surgeon and answer questions that are not asked but fail to answer those that are obvious (Adams, 1992).

The clinical health psychologist working in urology needs to become familiar also with the surgical procedures used. A request to observe a surgical procedure, or "scrub" for a procedure, is an excellent way to demonstrate a willingness to learn firsthand about a given intervention, as well as to become a "member of the team." A clinical health psychologist working in a surgical specialty such as urology needs to relate to both the nature of a surgeon's work and the patient's surgical experience, expectancies, fears, and consequences (Adams, 1992).

Research Interface

Engaging in psychosocial research with urological problems can provide the clinical health psychologist scholarly recognition in the medical setting and a place on a multidisciplinary medical team. Working with a urologist or gynecologist as a co-investigator, for example, is also an effective means of establishing and maintaining referral sources, as well as a presence in urology programs.

Marketing Issues

In marketing services to relevant medical departments and professionals, the clinical health psychologist must be aware of his or her training and experience with urological problems, as well as those sociopolitical issues that exist in any medical setting (Sweet et al., 1991). Establishing professional relationships with nurse-clinicians and physicians in such tertiary areas as urology, gynecology, surgery, and oncology (especially those involving prostate cancer) may involve the psychologist's offering to present at medical grand rounds or notifying various medical staff about their interest and experience with urology patients. Major medical centers often have broad multidisciplinary programs that cross over various specialties, such as programs in geriatrics or women's health, for example, which can serve as a place for membership for a clinical health psychologist interested in UI, for example.

Finally, as a result of their training and expertise, clinical psychologists in medical settings can be instrumental in the necessary and increased efforts needed to inform and educate the public about urological problems. The public should be aware that a problem such as incontinence, for example, is not inevitable or shameful but is often treatable and always manageable. The psychology profession would appear to be a crucial link in any comprehensive, multidisciplinary attempts to design effective patient-education programs about the prevention, assessment, and treatment of urological problems such as UI and ED. Given the approximately 3,000 psychologists employed as faculty in medical schools (Clayson & Mensh, 1987), contributions from clinical health psychologists would also appear to be crucial in efforts to educate other medical professionals about the psychological evaluation and treatment of those who suffer from urological dysfunctions.

Appendix
Factors Associated With Erectile Dysfunction

Endocrine
Diabetes
Increased estrogen
Decreased testosterone

Neurologic
Epilepsy (including temporal lobe)
Multiple sclerosis
Peripheral neuropathy
Spinal cord injury
Stroke

Penile
Trauma
Peyronie's disease

Prostatic
Prostatitis
Prostate cancer treatment

Lifestyle
Alcohol use
Tobacco use
Recreational and illicit drug use

Psychologic
Anxiety
Depression
Stress
Marital discord

Vascular
Atherosclerosis

Pharmacological agents
Addictive substances
Antihypertensive agents
Endocrine agents
Psychotropic agents
Antihypertensive agents
Chemotherapy agents
Histamine-receptor antagonists

Adapted from Ackerman, Montague, & Morganstern (1994).

REFERENCES

Ackerman, M. D. (1992). Consultation with clinical urology: Expanded roles for health psychologists. *The Health Psychologist, 14*, 3–4.

Ackerman, M. D. (1995). Behavioral approaches to assessing erectile dysfunction. *The Behavior Therapist, 18*, 31–34.

Ackerman, M. D., & Carey, M. P. (1995). Psychology's role in the assessment of erectile dysfunction: Historical precedents, current knowledge, and methods. *Journal of Consulting and Clinical Psychology, 63*, 862–876.

Ackerman, M. D., Helder, L. H., & Antoni, M. H. (1989, March). *The Miami sexual dysfunction protocol.* Poster presented at the Tenth Annual Scientific Session of the Society of Behavioral Medicine, San Francisco.

Ackerman, M. D., Montague, D. K., & Morganstern, S. (1994, March). Impotence: Help for erectile dysfunction. *Patient Care*, pp. 22–56.

Adams, D. B. (1992). Medical and surgical interface: Problems with philosophy and nosology. *Psychotherapy Bulletin, 27(2)*, 23–25.

Alvero, J., & Gartley, W. A. (1985). Products and devices for managing incontinence. In C. B. Gartley (Ed.), *Managing incontinence* (pp. 81–92). Ottawa, IL: Jameson Books.

American Association of Retired Persons and Simon Foundation for Continence (1993). *Promoting continence: Educating older Americans about incontinence.* Washington, DC: American Association of Retired Persons.

American Psychiatric Association (1994). *Diagnostic and statistical manual of mental disorders* (4th ed.). Washington, DC: Author.

Baigis-Smith, J., Smith, D. A., Rose, M., & Newman, D. K. (1989). Managing urinary incontinence in community-residing elderly persons. *The Gerontologist, 29,* 229–233.

Beck, A. (1972). *Depression: Its causes and treatment.* Philadelphia: University of Pennsylvania Press.

Berkman, S. (1986, November). Those embarrassing ailments: Here's help! *Good Housekeeping,* pp. 318–319.

Bond, G. R., Borman, L. D., Bankoff, E. A., Daiter, S., Lieberman, M. A., & Videka, L. M. (1979). The self-help, mutual support group. In M. A. Lieberman & L. D. Borman (Eds.), *Self-help groups for coping with crisis* (pp. 489–526). San Francisco: Jossey-Bass.

Breakwell, S. L., & Walker, S. N. (1988). Differences in physical health, social interaction, and personal adjustment between continent and incontinent homebound aged women. *Journal of Community Health Nursing, 5*(1), 19–31.

Brody, J. E. (1985, June 5). Personal health. *The New York Times,* p. 47.

Burgio, K. L., & Engel, B. T. (1987). Urinary incontinence; Behavioral assessment and treatment. In L. L. Carstensen and B. A. Edelstein (Eds.), *Handbook of clinical gerontology.* New York: Pergamon Press.

Burgio, K. L., & Engel, B. T. (1990). Biofeedback-assisted behavioral training for elderly men and women. *Journal of the American Geriatrics Society, 38,* 338–340.

Burgio, K. L., Robinson, J. C., & Engel, B. T. (1986). The role of biofeedback in Kegel exercise training for stress urinary incontinence. *American Journal of Obstetrician Gynecology, 154,* 58–64.

Burgio, K. L., Stutzman, R. E., & Engel, B. T. (1989). Behavioral training for prostatectomy urinary incontinence. *Journal of Urology, 141,* 303–306.

Burgio, K. L., Whitehead, W. E., & Engel, B. T. (1985). Urinary incontinence in the elderly: Bladder–sphincter biofeedback and toilet skills training. *Annals of Internal Medicine, 103,* 507–515.

Burns, P. A., Mareck, M. A., Duttmar, S. S., & Bullogh, B. (1985). Kegel's exercises with biofeedback therapy for stress incontinence. *Nurse Practitioner, 4,* 28–33.

Burns, P. A., Pranikoff, K., Nochajski, T., Desotelle, P., & Harwood, M. K. (1990). Treatment of stress incontinence with pelvic floor exercises and biofeedback. *Journal of the American Geriatrics Society, 38,* 341–344.

Burton, J. R., Pearce, K. L., Burgio, K. L., Engel, B. T. (1988). Behavioral training for urinary incontinence in elderly ambulatory patients. *Journal of the American Geriatrics Society, 36,* 693–698.

Castleden, C. M., Duffin, H. M., Asher, M. J., & Yeomanson, C. W. (1985). Factors influencing outcome in elderly patients with urinary incontinence and detrusor instability. *Age and Aging, 14*, 303–307.

Clayson, D., & Mensh, I. (1987). Psychologists in medical schools: The trials of emerging political activism. *American Psychologist, 42*, 859–862.

Colling, J. C., Ouslander, J., Hadley, B. J., Campbell, E. B., & Eisch, J. (1991). *Patterned urge-response toileting for incontinence.* Portland: Oregon Health Sciences University.

Cuhna, U. V. (1986). Antidepressants: Their uses in nonpsychiatric disorders of aging. *Geriatrics, 41*(10), 63–71.

Dobson, P. (1973). Urinary incontinence: Social aspects. *Physiotherapy, 59*, 358–359.

Ekelund, P., & Rundgren, A. (1987). Urinary incontinence in the elderly with implications for hospital care consumption and social disability. *Archives of Gerontology and Geriatrics, 6*, 11–18.

Elving, L. B., Foldspang, A., Lain, G. W., & Mommens, S. (1989). Descriptive epidemiology of urinary incontinence in 3,100 women age 30–59. *Scandinavian Journal of Urology and Nephrology, 125*, 37–43.

Engel, B. T., Burgio, L. D., McCormick, K. A., Bergman, S., & Williams, J. P. (1990). Behavioral treatment of incontinence in the long-term care setting. *Journal of the American Geriatrics Society, 38*, 361–363.

Fantl, J. A., Wyman, J. F., Harkins, S. W., & Hadley, E. C. (1990). Bladder training in the management of lower tract urinary dysfunction in women: A review. *Journal of the American Geriatrics Society, 38*, 329–332.

Fantl, J. A., Wyman, J. F., McClish, D. K., Harkins, S. W., Elswick, K. K., Taylor, J. R., Hunt, W. G., Dunn, L. J., & Bump, R. C. (1991). Efficacy of bladder training in older women with urinary incontinence. *Journal of the American Medical Association, 265*, 609–613.

Folstein, M. F., Folstein, S. E., & McHugh, P. R. (1975). Mini-mental state exam: A practical method for grading the cognitive state of patients for clinicians. *Journal of Psychiatric Research, 12*, 189–198.

Hafner, R. J., Stanton, S. L., & Guy, J. (1977). A psychiatric study of women with urgency and urgency incontinence. *British Journal of Urology, 49*, 211–214.

Henderson, J. S., & Taylor, K. H. (1987). Age as a variable in an exercise program for the treatment of simple urinary stress incontinence. *British Journal of Obstetrics and Gynecology, 96*, 266–272.

Hu, T. W. (1990). Impact of urinary incontinence on health-care costs. *Journal of the American Geriatrics Society, 38*, 292–295.

Hu, T. W., Gabelko, K., Weis, K. A., Dionko, A. C., McCormick, K. A., & Fogarty, T. E. (1992). Urinary incontinence: Treatment patterns, costs, and clinical guidelines. *Journal of the American Medical Association, 10*, 184–186.

Hu, T. W., Igou, J. F., Kaltreider, D. L., Yu, L. C., Rohner, T. J., Dennis, P. J., Craighead, W. E., Hadley, E. C., & Ory, M. G. (1991). A clinical trial of behavior therapy to reduce urinary incontinence in nursing homes: Outcome and implications. *Journal of the American Medical Association, 261,* 2656–2662.

The Simon Foundation for Continence (1991). *"I Will Manage" self-help groups.* (Simon Foundation, P.O. Box 815, Wilmette, IL 60091)

Jakovac-Smith, D. A. (1988). Continence restoration in the homebound patient. *Nursing Clinics of North America, 23,* 207–218.

Jarvis, G. J. (1981). A controlled trial of bladder drill and drug therapy in the management of detrusor instability. *British Journal of Urology, 53,* 565–566.

Klarskov, P., Gerstenberg, T. C., & Hald, T. (1986). Bladder training in females with urge incontinence and stable detrusor function. *Scandinavian Journal of Urology and Nephrology, 20,* 41–46.

Locke, H., & Wallace, K. (1959). Short marital adjustment and prediction tests: Their reliability and validity. *Marriage and Family Living, 21,* 251–255.

Macaulay, A. J., Stern, R. S., Holmes, D. M., & Stanton, S. L. (1987). Micturition and the mind: Psychological factors in the aetiology and treatment of urinary symptoms in women. *British Medical Journal, 294,* 540–543.

McCormick, K. A., Scheve, A. S., & Leahy, E. (1988). Nursing management of urinary incontinence in geriatric inpatients. *Nursing Clinics of North America, 23,* 231–264.

Mitteness, L. S. (1987). The management of urinary incontinence by community-living elderly. *The Gerontological Society of America, 27*(2), 285–293.

Mohr, J. A., Rogers, J., Jr., Brown, T. N., & Starkweather, G. (1983). Stress urinary incontinence: A simple and practical approach to diagnosis and treatment. *Journal of the American Geriatrics Society, 31,* 476–478.

Moos, R. H. (1977). *Coping with physical illness.* New York: Plenum.

National Institutes of Health Consensus Development Conference Statement. (1988, October). *Urinary incontinence in adults, 7,* 1–11.

Noelker, L. S. (1987). Incontinence in elderly cared for by family. *The Gerontological Society of America, 27*(7), 194–200.

Norton, C. (1982). The effects of urinary incontinence in women. *International Rehabilitative Medicine, 4*(1), 9–14.

Ory, M. G., Wyman, J. F., & Yu, L. C. (1986). Psychosocial factors in urinary incontinence. *Clinics in Geriatric Medicine, 2,* 657–671.

Orzeck, S., & Ouslander, J. G. (1987). Urinary incontinence: An overview of causes and treatment. *Journal of Enterostomal Therapy, 14*(1), 20–27.

Ouslander, J. G. (1982). Physical illness and depression in the elderly. *Journal of the American Geriatrics Society, 30,* 593–599.

Ouslander, J. G., Morishita, L., Blaustein, J., Orzeck, S., Dunn, S., & Sayre, J. (1987). Clinical, functional, and psychosocial characteristics of an incontinent nursing home population. *Journal of Gerontology, 42,* 631–637.

Perry, J. D., Hullett, L. T., & Bollinger, J. R. (1987, November). Urinary incontinence treated by EMG biofeedback method. *Gerontological Society of America.*

Perry, J. D., Hullett, L. T., & Bollinger, J. R. (1988, March). EMG Biofeedback treatment of incontinence. *Biofeedback Society of America, 3,* 84–89.

Resnick, N. M., Welte, T. T., Scherr, P., Branch, L., & Taylor, J. (1986). Urinary incontinence in community dwelling elderly: Prevalence and correlates. *Proceedings of the International Continence Society, 1,* 76–78.

Resnick, N. M., & Yalla, S. V. (1985). Management of urinary incontinence in the elderly. *The New England Journal of Medicine, 313,* 800–805.

Roe, B. H., & Brocklehurst, J. C. (1987). Study of patients with indwelling catheters. *Journal of Advanced Nursing, 12,* 713–718.

Rose, M. A., Baigis-Smith, J., Smith, D., & Newman, D. (1990). Behavioral management of urinary incontinence in homebound older adults. *Home Healthcare Nurse, 8,* 10–15.

Rozensky, R. H., & Tovian, S. M. (1985). Strategies for a full life. In C. B. Gartley (Ed.), *Managing incontinence* (pp. 58–69). Ottowa, IL: Jameson Books.

Schnelle, J. F. (1990). Treatment of urinary incontinence in nursing home patients by prompted voiding. *Journal of the American Geriatrics Society, 38,* 356–360.

Schnelle, J. F., Newman, D. R., & Fogarty, T. (1990). Management of patient continence in long-term care nursing facilities. *The Gerontologist, 30,* 373–376.

Schwartz, M. S. (1987). *Biofeedback: A practitioner's guide.* New York: Guilford Press.

Shepherd, A. M., Montgomery, E., & Anderson, R. S. (1983). Treatment of genuine stress incontinence with a new perineometer. *Physiotherapy, 69,* 113.

Smith, D., Smith, J., Rose, M., & Kaschak, D. (1987a). Control of urinary incontinence in the acutely ill home patient. *Proceeds of the International Continence Society, 2,* 56–60.

Smith D., Smith J., Rose M., & Kaschak, D. (1987b). Kegel's exercise, biofeedback and relaxation training for the treatment of urinary incontinence in a community setting. *Proceedings of the International Continence Society, 2,* 61–65.

Sowell, V. A., Schnelle, J. F., Hu, T. W., & Traughbers, B. (1987). A cost comparison of five methods of managing urinary incontinence. *QRB. Quality Review Bulletin, 13,* 411–414.

Stone, C. B., & Judd, G. E. (1978). Psychogenic aspects of urinary incontinence in women. *Clinical Obstetrics and Gynecology, 21,* 807–815.

Sutherland, S. S. (1976). The psychology of incontinence. In F. L. Willington (Ed.), *Incontinence in the elderly* (pp. 13–27). London: Academic Press.

Sweet, J. J., Rozensky, R. H., & Tovian, S. M. (1991). *Handbook of clinical psychology in medical settings.* New York: Plenum.

Telsch, C. F., & Telsch, M. J. (1985). Psychological approaches for enhancing coping among cancer patients: A review. *Clinical Psychology Review, 5,* 325–345.

Thomas, T. M., Plymat, K. R., Blannin, J., & Meade, T. W. (1980). Prevalence of urinary incontinence. *British Medical Journal, 21,* 1243–1245.

Tobin, D. L., Reynolds, R. V. C., Holroyd, K. A., & Creer, T. L. (1986). Self-management and social learning theory. In K. A. Holroyd & T. L. Creer (Eds.), *Self-management of chronic disease: Handbook of clinical interventions and research* (pp. 29–58). Orlando, FL: Academic Press.

Tovian, S. M., & Rozensky, R. H. (1985). Building inner confidence. In C. B. Gartley (Ed.), *Managing incontinence* (pp. 48–57). Ottowa, IL: Jameson Books.

Tovian, S. M., Rozensky, R. H., Sloan, T. B., & Slotnik, G. M. (1995). Adult urinary incontinence: Assessment, intervention, and the role of clinical health psychology in program development. *Journal of Clinical Psychology in Medical Settings, 1,* 339–362.

Trombini, G., Rossi, N., Umilta, C., & Baccarani, C. P. (1982). Experimental stress and systomanometric recordings of patients with primary enuresis: A preliminary report. *Perceptual and Motor Skills, 54,* 771–777.

Urinary Incontinence Guideline Panel. (1992, March). *Urinary incontinence in adults: Clinical practice guidelines* (ACHPR Publication No. 92-0038). Rockville, MD: Public Health Service.

Wells, A. J., Rink, C. A., Dionko, A. C., Lawson, A. L., Neal, D. E., & Hoopes, J. M. (1991). Pelvic muscle exercises for stress urinary incontinence in elderly women. *Journal of the American Geriatrics Society, 38,* 296–299.

Yalom, I. D., & Greaves, C. (1977). Group therapy with the terminally ill. *American Journal of Psychiatry, 134,* 396–400.

Yarnell, J. W. G., Voyle, G. J., Sweetnam, P. M., Milbank, J., Richards, C. J., & Stephenson, T. P. (1982). Factors associated with urinary incontinence in women. *Journal of Epidemiology and Community Health, 36,* 58–63.

Yu, L. C. (1987). Incontinence stress index: Measuring psychological impact. *Journal of Gerontological Nursing, 13*(7), 18–24.

Yu, L. C., & Kaltreider, D. L. (1987). Stressed nurses dealing with incontinent patients. *Journal of Gerontological Nursing, 13*(1), 27–30.

20

TOUCH THERAPIES FOR PAIN MANAGEMENT AND STRESS REDUCTION

TIFFANY M. FIELD

Touch therapy is listed in the *Ayur-Veda*, the earliest known medical text from India (around 1800 B.C.), along with diet and exercise, as primary healing practices of that time. Exotic uses of massage in contemporary cultures have been described by Older (1982). He noted that in New Zealand, the pre-European Maori mothers massaged their children's noses to improve their shape, and they massaged their legs to lengthen and straighten them. In Cuba, garlic and oil massages are prepared and applied to the stomach after "a meal lodged in the stomach where it caused pain and fever" (Older, 1982, p. 86). In Samoa, massage is used for every disorder from diarrhea to migraine headache, using a mixture of coconut milk, flowers from trees, plants, and roots of grasses (Older, 1982). Touch therapies such as massage are used in many parts of the

This research was supported by National Institute of Mental Health (NIMH) Research Scientist Award MH00331 and NIMH Research Grant MH46586.

world for managing pain and reducing stress. The United States, though a latecomer to this field, is beginning to use touch therapies for wellness and chronic illness at all ages. This chapter is a review of recent data on the use of touch therapies.

Life's stressors begin as early as the prenatal period. In many countries, such as India, pregnant women are massaged several times daily for relaxation and to reduce their anxiety levels. This therapy is considered beneficial for both the pregnant woman and her fetus. We at the Touch Research Institute have been teaching the significant others of pregnant women to massage the women during pregnancy and labor. Ultrasound images taken after the massages reveal some very happy responses from the fetus. Most of them like the massage, as can be seen by their smiles on ultrasound. When we coded fetal movements, we found a normalization of activity level. This may relate to the reduced anxiety and depression in the mothers. In addition, during labor, the need for medication and for cesarean section by these mothers decreased, and the neonatal outcome was superior.

TOUCH THERAPIES FOR INFANTS

Premature infants. Some pregnancies, unfortunately, end in premature deliveries, and the babies are treated in the neonatal intensive care unit. We found many years ago that one could give babies in the neonatal intensive care unit a 15-minute massage three times a day for 10 days while they were still in the incubator (by putting one's hands through the incubator portholes and massaging them; Field et al., 1986; Scafidi et al., 1990). We were able to document a 47% weight gain for the treatment infants compared with the control infants, and they were hospitalized for 6 days less at a hospital cost savings of $10,000 per infant. If all 450,000 preterm infants born per year received this treatment, $4.5 billion in hospital costs would be saved per year. We also found an elevation in their norepinephrine and epinephrine levels (Kuhn et al., 1991), suggesting that we were able to facilitate the natural increase in these catecholamines at this stage in life.

Our assessments of these infants at 1 year suggested that they were still advantaged in terms of their weight, and they also showed greater gains on the Bayley Scales of Infant Development (Field, Scafidi, & Schanberg, 1987). On the Bayley Mental Scale, their scores averaged 12 points higher; on the Bayley Motor Scale, they averaged 13 points higher. Massaging these infants for 10 days in the first few days after birth seemed to lead to the infants being more responsive. The infants gained more weight as newborns, became more responsive, and apparently elicited more stimulation from their parents. That cycle then led to later growth and developmental gains.

Cocaine-exposed infants. Another infant that is seen very often in the neonatal intensive care unit is the cocaine-exposed baby. In a study on these infants, we were able to show similar weight gain in those who received massage therapy (Wheeden et al., 1993). These infants also showed superior motor behavior. In explaining the mechanism involved in weight gain, we assessed vagal tone. The vagus (1 of the 10 cranial nerves) slows heartbeat during tasks that require attention, and it enhances gastric motility and facilitates the release of food-absorption hormones such as insulin. When we measured vagal activity and insulin levels, we noted increases after the massage. The massaged infants did not eat more food, and they did not sleep more, so they were not conserving calories. Rather, the weight gain seems to have been mediated by an increase in vagal activity, which in turn increased metabolic activity by increasing the release of food-absorption hormones (at least insulin).

HIV-exposed infants. Another infant who is frequently treated on the neonatal intensive care unit is the HIV-exposed infant. In this study, we hypothesized that the mothers of HIV infants would be willing and reliable massage therapists, partly because the mothers might have some feeling of guilt for having transmitted HIV to their infants (Scafidi & Field, 1995).

We often teach parents to massage their infants for two reasons: (a) We find that parents' anxiety levels are highly related to their feeling helpless about their infant's or their child's condition. Helping with their infant's treatment will typically decrease the parents' anxiety levels and make them feel like they are contributing to the treatment. (b) The continuing daily massages are not practically or economically feasible without the parents' providing these.

One surprising result of this study was the 100% compliance from the mothers, most especially because our low-income, low-educated population in Miami is typically noncompliant. The mothers massaged their infants every day for the first 2 months of life. The massaged infants' weight gain was significantly greater than that of the control group, and the massaged group showed significantly fewer stress behaviors.

TOUCH THERAPY FOR HIV-POSITIVE ADULTS

In a related study that we did on HIV-positive adults, we found a significant increase in natural killer cells after 20 days of massage (Ironson et al., 1996). For 1 month, 29 gay men (20 of whom were HIV-positive) were massaged. A subset of 11 of the HIV-positive participants served as a within-participant control group (1 month with and 1 month without massages). Major immune findings for the effect of the month of massage included a significant increase in natural killer cell number, natural killer cell cytoxity, soluble CD_8, and the cytotoxic subset of CD_8 cells. There was no change in HIV disease progression markers (i.e., CD_4, CD_4/CD_8 ratio, beta-2 microglobulin, and neopterin). Major neuroendocrine findings, measured through urine specimens collected over a 24-hr period, included a significant decrease in cortisol and nonsignificant trends toward decrease of catecholamines. There were also significant decreases in anxiety and increases in relaxation, which were significantly correlated with increases in natural killer cell number. Thus, an increase in cytotoxic capacity apparently is associated with massage. Because natural killer cells are the front line of defense in the immune system, combating the growth and proliferation of viral and cancer cells, the HIV patients who received the massage might be expected to experience fewer opportunistic infections, such as pneumonia, which often are fatal for them.

"GRANDPARENT" VOLUNTEERS MASSAGING INFANTS

The question remained as to how to deliver this intervention cost-effectively, because not too many nursing or medical staff have time to massage infants. So we used volunteer grandparents. We were surprised to find that the grandparents were also benefiting. They reported a better sense of well-being, a significant decrease in depression after the 1-month period of massaging the infants, an increase in their self-esteem, and a decrease in their urinary cortisol levels. We then compared their giving massage with their receiving massage. They gave infant massages for a month and then received massages for a month, or vice versa. We found that the grandparent volunteers benefited more from giving the massage than from receiving the massage. Their affect and self-esteem improved, as did their lifestyle habits (e.g., they reported drinking fewer cups of coffee per day, they made more social phone calls, and they made fewer trips to the doctor's office).

TOUCH THERAPIES FOR CHILDREN

Asthmatic children. In studies where we used parents as therapists, such as with asthmatic children, the parents were asked to give the massages for 15 minutes before bedtime each night for a 1-month period (Field et al., 1996). Typically the parents' anxiety decreased, the child's anxiety decreased, and the child's affect improved. This may have contributed to the significant increase noted in peak air flow (the gold standard measure that physicians use for determining the clinical improvement of asthmatic children).

Diabetic children. In diabetic children, the gold standard is blood-glucose levels. Those levels decreased significantly from a high level of 159 to a level of 118, which is within the normal range for blood-glucose levels in children (Field, Delamater, Shaw, & LaGreca, 1995). The improvement in the diabetic children's clinical condition also may have related to the decrease in their anxiety levels and the associated decrease in cortisol levels.

Burn children. Burn patients are reporting lower anxiety levels at the end of their first and last treatments 5 days later, after a 30-minute treatment each day, and an associated decrease in cortisol levels (Field, Peck, Burman, & Krugman, 1995). Pain has also decreased by Day 5, as reported on a faces scale, showing painful expressions, and depression is decreased, probably because of the decrease in pain. Postburn patients, whose problem is not only pain but also itching, are reporting a decrease in their pain and itching on the McGill Pain Adapted Scale for Children (Melzack, 1987).

Autistic children. Another sample we have been working with are autistic children. They have been described as being extremely sensitive to touch and typically disliking being touched. However, we have noted surprisingly little resistance to their being massaged. Massage may not be aversive to them because it is predictable and does not involve social relations. In our study on autistic children, their off-task behavior in the classroom decreased after a 10-day period of massage, and their relating to their teachers increased (Field et al., 1996).

Children suffering from posttraumatic stress disorder. Many children showed symptoms of posttraumatic stress disorder (PTSD) after Hurricane Andrew. A number of these children had shown acting-out problems in the classroom, which were then exacerbated by Hurricane Andrew. We massaged a group of children two times per week for 5 weeks after the hurricane (Field, Seligman, Scafidi, & Schanberg, 1996). We compared them with a video control group of children, who watched a relaxing video. After the 5-week period, we observed a decrease in depression in the massage therapy group but not in the video control group. We also saw a decrease in their anxiety, and their drawing problems decreased. Drawings often tell the best story. For example, a girl (Ashley) drew a picture of a girl on the first day. The picture was very small, had dark colors, and had no facial features (see Figure 1). By the last day, she drew a birthday party, with bright colors, balloons, sunshine, birds, and all of her friends (see Figure 2). A very clear change in her affect was reflected in the change in her drawings.

Child and adolescent psychiatric patients. In Field et al. (1992) a 30-minute back massage was given daily for a 5-day period to 52 hospitalized depressed and adjustment-disordered children and adolescents. Compared with a control group, who viewed relaxing videotapes,

Ashley

Figure 1. A drawing by Ashley on the first day of massage therapy.

the massaged participants were less depressed and anxious and had lower saliva cortisol levels after the massage sessions. In addition, nurses rated the participants as being less anxious and more cooperative on the last day of the study, and nighttime sleep increased over this period. Finally, urinary cortisol and norepinephrine levels decreased, but only for the depressed participants.

TOUCH THERAPIES FOR ADULTS

Fibromyalgia syndrome. Thirty adults suffering from fibromyalgia syndrome were randomly assigned to a massage therapy group, a transcutaneous electrical stimulation group, or a transcutaneous electrical stimulation–no current group for 30-minute treatment sessions two times per week for 5 weeks (Sunshine et al., in press). The massage therapy participants reported lower anxiety and depression, and their cortisol levels were lower immediately after the therapy sessions on the first and last days of the study. The TENS group showed similar changes, but only after therapy on the last day of the study. The massage therapy group improved on the dolorimeter measure of pain. They also reported less pain last week, less stiffness and fatigue, and fewer nights of difficulty sleeping. Thus, massage therapy was the most effective therapy with these fibromyalgia patients.

Figure 2. A drawing by Ashley after 5 weeks of massage therapy.

Job stress. In the job-stress study, we massaged staff and faculty at the medical school for 15-minute lunch periods, in massage chairs in their offices (Field, Ironson, et al., 1995). These massage sessions involved deep pressure in the back, shoulders, neck, and head. We were somewhat concerned that people might be even more sleepy than usual at the time of day after massage. However, we found instead that they reported heightened alertness, much like a runner's high. This led us to recording electroencephalograms (EEG) before, during, and after the massage sessions. We found that alpha levels significantly decreased during massage, in contrast to what happens during relaxation and, of course, during sleep, when alpha levels significantly increase. This decrease combined with increased theta and decreased beta waves suggested a pattern of heightened alertness. We then assessed whether this EEG pattern of heightened alertness translated into performance, by adding a math computation task. The computation time was almost half, and the computation accuracy almost doubled, after the massages, suggesting that 15-minute massages during the lunch hour can enhance alertness and job performance.

UNDERLYING MECHANISMS

These, then, are the improvements that we have noted after massage therapy. Some of the changes were unique to the clinical condition being studied, such as increased peak air flow in arthritis or decreased glucose levels in diabetes. However, across all of these studies, we observed decreases in anxiety, depression, stress hormones (cortisol), and catecholamines. The underlying mechanism may relate to increased parasympathetic activity. The pressure stimulation associated with touch increases vagal activity, which in turn lowers psychological arousal and stress hormones. The pressure is critical, for if a person is lightly stroked, she or he usually finds it aversive, because it is too much like a tickle stimulus. The decreased stress hormones, in turn, have a positive impact on immune function. The parasympathetic state (enhanced vagal tone) also enhances alertness and performance on cognitive tasks and reduces stress. Given that most diseases are exacerbated by stress and that massage therapy alleviates stress, receiving massages should probably be high on the health priority list, along with diet and exercise, as it was around 1800 B.C. in India.

REFERENCES

Field, T. (in press). Infants of depressed mothers. *Infant Behavior and Development*.

Field, T., Delamater, A. M., Shaw, K. H., & LaGreca, A. (1995). *Massage therapy reduces glucose levels in children with insulin-dependent diabetes*. Manuscript in preparation.

Field, T., Henteleff, T., & Mavunda, K. (1994). [Asthmatic children have less anxiety and respiratory problems after touch therapy]. Unpublished raw data.

Field, T., Ironson, G., Pickens, J., Nawrocki, T., Fox, N., Scafidi, F., Burman, I., & Schanberg, S. (1995). *Massage effects on job stress, EEG, and math computations*. Manuscript submitted for publication.

Field, T., Morrow, C., Valdeon, C., Larson, S., Kuhn, C., & Schanberg, S. (1992). Massage reduces anxiety in child and adolescent psychiatric patients. *Journal of the American Academy of Child and Adolescent Psychiatry, 31*, 124–131.

Field, T., Peck, M., Burman, I., & Krugman, S. (1995). *Massage therapy reduces anxiety in children with burns*. Manuscript in preparation.

Field, T., Scafidi, F., & Schanberg, S. (1987). Massage of preterm newborns to improve growth and development. *Pediatric Nursing, 13*, 385–387.

Field, T., Schanberg, S. M., Scafidi, F., Bauer, C. R., Vega-Lahr, N., Garcia, R., Nystrom, J., & Kuhn, C. M. (1986). Tactile/kinesthetic stimulation effects on preterm neonates. *Pediatrics, 77*, 654–658.

Field, T., Seligman, S., Scafidi, F., & Schanberg, S. (in press). *Alleviating posttraumatic stress in children following Hurricane Andrew*.

Field, T., Taylor, S., Quintino, O., Kuhn, C., & Schanberg, S. (1995). *Massage reduces anxiety and pain in women during labor*. Manuscript in preparation.

Ironson, G., Field, T., Kumar, A., Price, A., Kumar, M., Hansen, K., & Burman I. (in press). Relaxation through massage is associated with decreased distress and increased serotonin levels. *International Journal of Neuroscience*.

Kuhn, C., Schanberg, S., Field, T., Symanski, R., Zimmerman, E., Scafidi, F., & Roberts, J. (1991). Tactile kinesthetic stimulation effects on sympathetic and adrenocortical function in preterm infants. *Journal of Pediatrics, 119,* 434–440.

Older, J. (1982). *Touching is healing.* New York: Stein & Day.

Scafidi, F., & Field, T. (1995). *Massage therapy improves behavior in neonates born to HIV-positive mothers.* Manuscript submitted for publication.

Scafidi, F., Field, T., Schanberg, S., Bauer, C., Tucci, K., Roberts, J., Morrow, C., & Kuhn, C. M. (1990). Massage stimulates growth in preterm infants: A replication. *Infant Behavior and Development, 13,* 167–188.

Sunshine, W., Field, T., Quintino, O., Fierro, K., Kuhn, C., Burman, I., & Schanberg, S. (in press). Fibromyalgia benefits from massage therapy and transcutaneous electrical stimulation. *Journal of Clinical Rheumatology.*

Wheeden, A., Scafidi, F. A., Field, T., Ironson, G., Bandstra, E., Schanberg S., & Valdeon, C. (1993). Massage effects on cocaine-exposed preterm neonates. *Journal of Developmental and Behavioral Pediatrics, 14,* 318–322.

21

TREATMENT ADHERENCE AND CLINICAL OUTCOME: CAN WE MAKE A DIFFERENCE?

JACQUELINE DUNBAR-JACOB and ELIZABETH A. SCHLENK

The costs of nonadherence to pharmacological therapies have been estimated to be as high as $100 billion annually (Grahl, 1994). A significant portion of those costs is attributed to the management of untoward clinical outcomes and to lost productivity. If, in addition to pharmacological treatment, one also considers nonpharmacological interventions, the costs of nonadherence is even higher, although it is unclear by how much. Nevertheless, evidence linking lifestyle behaviors to an excess prevalence of chronic disorders and to premature mortality (Belloc, 1973; Breslow & Enstrom, 1980; Matarazzo, 1984; U.S. Public Health Service, 1991) suggests the costs of nonadherence to behavioral therapies would also be high.

Although nonadherence has been identified as a problem at least since the time of Plato, attention to the role of adherence in moderating treatment effects has been much more recent. Indeed, it has just been over the past 2 decades that the Food and Drug Administration began to require the monitoring of adherence in drug-efficacy trials. Even today, no such standard is universally applied to nonpharmacological interventions.

Not surprisingly then, little is known about the degree of adherence necessary to effect a therapeutic outcome for known therapies. Only a limited number of studies have addressed a minimum adherence level necessary to effect a clinically meaningful outcome (e.g., De Geest, 1996; Haynes et al., 1976). The *Physicians' Desk Reference* (1996) notes the degree of clinical impact seen at varying levels of adherence to a standard prescription only for one drug, cholestyramine. The relationship between adherence to behavioral therapies and clinical outcomes is even less well known.

In the next sections, we review the limited existing knowledge about the relationship between adherence and clinical outcomes. Several therapies are reviewed: (a) prescribed medication, (b) therapeutic exercise, (c) therapeutic diets, (d) homework, (e) appointment keeping, and (f) multicomponent regimen. Six clinical outcomes across these therapeutic modalities were considered: (a) mortality; (b) hospitalization; (c) morbidity, including complications; (d) relapse; (e) symptom relief; and (f) health status. To identify studies for this review, a MEDLINE search was initiated for English-language, empirical studies, reporting an adherence–outcome relationship, published between 1977 and 1994. The search yielded 116 articles. We chose only those articles that examined differences in clinical outcomes between adhering and nonadhering groups. Interestingly, these articles rarely addressed overlapping therapies and outcomes. Thus, the majority of findings are based on single studies.

THE EFFECT OF ADHERENCE TO MEDICATION ON CLINICAL OUTCOMES

The treatment modality for which the effect of nonadherence on outcomes has been studied the most is drug treatment. Adherence in these studies generally was assessed by means of discontinuing medication, urine assays, serum drug levels, self-report, pill counts, physician or nurse ratings, or pharmacy refills. These methods each tend to overestimate adherence. Three studies used electronic monitors to assess adherence (Cheung et al., 1988; Cramer, Mattson, Prevey, Scheyer, & Ouellette, 1989; Granstrom, 1985). The electronic monitors record each medication-taking event onto a microprocessor chip, permitting an assessment of adherence over time as well as patterns of medication taking. Numerous studies did not identify the assessment method.

Prevention of Relapse

Good adherence to prescribed medication regimen was significantly associated with prevention of relapse in several chronic disorders. Most particularly, adherence prevented relapse in the treatment of tuberculosis (Dupon & Ragnaud, 1992); epilepsy (Cramer et al., 1989; Reynolds, 1987); childhood leukemia (Klopovich & Trueworthy, 1985); schizophrenia (Leff et al., 1989; Mantonakis, Jemos, Christodoulou, & Lykouras, 1982); and alcoholism (Fawcett et al., 1984, 1987; Pisani, Fawcett, Clark, & McQuire, 1993). Good adherence was also associated with prevention of symptomatic, but not asymptomatic, relapse in duodenal ulcer disease (Boyd, Wilson, & Wormsley, 1983). Adherence to antibiotics, as assessed by urine antibiotic assay, was not associated with a reduction in recurrence of otitis media in 295 patients treated for the infection (Reed, Lutz, Zazove, & Ratcliffe, 1984).

Symptom Relief

Symptom relief also was found to be significantly associated with adherence in a number of conditions. Adherence was associated with reductions in inflammation in peptic esophageal stenosis (Starlinger, Appel, Schemper, & Schiessel, 1985); symptoms of schizophrenia (Verghese et al., 1989); depressed mood among manic–depressed patients (Connelly, Davenport, & Nurnberger, 1982); and pain among chronic-pain patients (Berndt, Maier, & Schutz, 1993). Although hypertension is asymptomatic, good blood pressure control was associated with good adherence to medication regimen (e.g., Fletcher, Deliakis, Schoch, & Shapiro, 1979; Haynes, Gibson, Taylor, Bernholz, & Sackett, 1982; McKenney, Munroe, & Wright, 1992). This observation also was made for patients when hypertension is comorbid with diabetes (Kravitz et al., 1993).

Good adherence is not, however, always associated with improvement of symptoms. For example, although pulmonary symptoms were alleviated with adherence to medication for patients with chronic bronchitis, they were not alleviated for those with asthma (Dompeling et al., 1992). Surprisingly, progression of visual-field defect also was not affected by adherence among persons with open-angle glaucoma (Granstrom, 1985). In this latter study, adherence was examined by means of an electronic medication monitor and defined as the proportion of time that dose intervals exceeded 8 hours during two 3-week periods.

Health Status

Adherence with prescribed medications has also been examined for its effect on health status, but in few disorders. For patients with hypertension, clinical health status and perceived health status were both associated with adherence to medical regimen, although functional status was not (Given, Given, & Simoni, 1979). Additionally, in the area of rheumatoid arthritis, adherence with treatment, as measured by self-report, was not associated with health status or functional class (Taal, Rasker, Seydel, & Wiegman, 1993), although adherence was associated with pain relief in at least one study (Dunbar-Jacob, Kwoh, et al., 1996). However, self-report generally overestimates adherence. Thus, it is not clear whether a relationship was absent or whether the ability to detect a relationship was compromised by an inaccurate measure of adherence, self-report.

Morbidity

Morbidity was found to be associated with adherence to medication in a number of conditions. Cures for urinary-tract infections among the elderly were associated with adherence to antibiotics in a study in which electronic medication monitors were used to assess adherence (Cheung et al., 1988). Both number of dosing events and dosage intervals, targeting 12 hours between doses, were considered. In chronic conditions, morbidity has also been associated with adherence. For example, poorer adherence was associated with bronchial responsiveness and functional expiratory volume (FEV_1) among patients with chronic bronchitis (Dompeling et al., 1992).

Even with life-threatening conditions, nonadherence not only has been observed, but has been found to lead to poorer outcomes. For example, nonadherent transplant patients have a poorer clinical course. Greater proportions of persons with kidney transplants who adhere poorly return to dialysis (Kalil, Heim-Duthoy, & Kasiske, 1992); develop renal impairment in pregnancy (O'Donnell et al., 1985); and reject their transplanted organs (Rovelli et al., 1989; Schweizer et al., 1990). Just small deviations from prescribed immunosuppressive therapy were linked to late rejection and other untoward events (De Geest, 1996). Poorer outcomes related to poor adherence are also seen among psychiatric disorders. Depressed elderly (Cole, 1985) and manic–depressive patients (Connelly et al., 1982) who were nonadherent were shown to have a poorer course of illness than compliant patients.

Nonadherence to medications taken prophylactically or to manage risk factors has also been associated with increases in morbidity. Hypertensive patients who were nonadherent demonstrated a greater risk of incurring coronary heart disease events (Psaty, Koepsell, Wagner, LoGerfo, & Inui, 1990). Nonadherence to prophylactic medications for infectious disease has also resulted in greater disease occurrence. For example, significantly more cases of tuberculosis were seen among nonadherent persons on prophylactic medication regimen in a study of Southeast Asian refugees (Nolan, Aitken, Elarth, Anderson, & Miller, 1986). Similarly, a greater incidence of malaria was seen in poor adherers to prophylactic drugs among Dutch travelers to Africa (Wetsteyn & de Geus, 1993).

Thus, nonadherence to medication has been associated with significant and costly morbidity in the few studies where it has been examined. The excess morbidity crosses the range of acute, chronic, preventive, and life-threatening conditions.

Hospitalization

Excess hospitalization rates may be a consequence of poor adherence with a number of conditions. First are the major mental health disorders. These include manic–depressive disorder treated with lithium (Connelly et al., 1982) and schizophrenia (Gaebel & Pietzcker, 1985). Hospitalization rates have also been higher among poor adherers attending general medical clinics, including excess rates of drug-related hospitalizations, that is, when too much or too little medication is taken (Cowen, Jim, Boyd, & Gee, 1981). Not only were hospitalization rates higher in this population but the length of hospitalization also was greater, with an average of 7 days for poor adherers, compared with 4 days for adherent controls. Rehospitalization rates were higher for poor adherers with alcoholism (Fawcett et al., 1987) and with hypertension (Maronde et al., 1989).

Mortality

Death itself has been associated with poor adherence. Among 1,000 patients with epilepsy, 25% of cases of sudden death were associated with low adherence (Lip & Brodie, 1992). Mortality also was associated with poor adherence to asthma regimen (Robertson, Rubinfeld, & Bowes, 1992) and posttransplant medications (Lanza, Cooper, Boyd, & Barnard, 1984; Schweizer et al., 1990). Furthermore, among patients with hemotologic malignancies, adherence was associated with survival (Richardson, Shelton, Krailo, & Levine, 1990).

Thus, the weight of the evidence indicates that good adherence to medication therapies will prevent relapse, alleviate symptoms, reduce morbidity, reduce hospitalizations, and reduce mortality. Efforts to enhance adherence to medications among various populations is likely to have significant clinical as well as economic impact. However, the evidence for this effort remains to be gathered.

THE EFFECT OF ADHERENCE TO THERAPEUTIC DIETS ON CLINICAL OUTCOMES

Very few studies have examined the extent of adherence to therapeutic diets and its relationship to clinical outcomes. The studies that were identified in this review addressed patients with diabetes (Fishbein, 1985; Mulrow, Bailey, Sonksen, & Slavin, 1987; White, Kolman, Wexler, Polin, & Winter, 1984); multiple sclerosis (Swank & Dugan, 1990); phenylketonuria (Peat, 1993); and myocardial infarction (Singh, Niaz, Ghosh, Singh, & Rastogi, 1993). Dietary adherence was typically measured by self-report, although physician ratings (Fishbein, 1985) and serum phenylalanine levels (Peat, 1993) were also used in one study each.

Nonadherence to low-fat diets was associated with mortality for both patients with myocardial infarction (Singh et al., 1993) and multiple sclerosis (Swank & Dugan, 1990). It was further associated with other cardiac endpoints in the cardiac patients and with deterioration among the multiple sclerosis patients. Nonadherence to diabetic diets was associated with diabetic ketoacidosis (Mulrow et al., 1987; White et al., 1984) and an excess of hospital admissions (Fishbein, 1985; White et al., 1984) and emergency room visits (White et al., 1984), but adherence was not associated with glycosylated hemoglobin or weight loss in the lone study that examined these clinical parameters (Mulrow et al., 1987). Finally, among pregnant women with phenylketonuria, poor perinatal outcomes were associated with poor dietary adherence, including low birth weight and microencephalophy (Peat, 1993).

THE EFFECT OF ADHERENCE TO THERAPEUTIC EXERCISE ON CLINICAL OUTCOMES

Few studies exist also that examine the relationship of adherence to therapeutic exercise and clinical outcomes. Five studies were identified, addressing sway in elderly women (Lichtenstein, Shields, Shiavi, & Burger, 1989); incontinence (Bishop, Dougherty, Mooney, Gimotty, & Williams, 1992); and postoperative rehabilitation for orthopedic conditions (R. B. Hawkins, 1989; R. J. Hawkins & Switlyk, 1993; Rives, Gelberman, Smith, & Carney, 1992). Overall, poor adherence to therapeutic exercise regimen was associated with negative outcomes. Postsurgically, poorly adhering patients demonstrated poorer range of motion (R. J. Hawkins & Switlyk, 1993); less joint extension (Rives et al., 1992); poorer functional ability (R. J. Hawkins & Switlyk, 1993); and greater recurrence of the presurgical condition (R. B. Hawkins, 1989), when contrasted with adhering patients. Thus, these studies support the value of adherence to postsurgical exercise in the reduction of symptoms and the incidence of relapse. Adherence to group exercise improved change in sway among elderly women also (Lichtenstein et al., 1989). Interestingly, however, adherence to a pelvic muscle exercise program was not related to maximum intravaginal pressures in a sample of parous, continent women (Bishop et al., 1992). Thus, overall, the literature suggests that adherence to exercise is related to improved clinical outcomes when symptoms and relapse prevention are considered.

THE EFFECT OF ADHERENCE TO PRESCRIBED HOMEWORK ON CLINICAL OUTCOMES

Homework is typically prescribed in the behavioral therapies for medical conditions, as a means of promoting skill and generalization, as well as a means of directly managing selected conditions. Conditions in which homework is routinely prescribed, where studies on the impact of adherence were undertaken, include agoraphobia (Edelman & Chambless, 1993); anxiety disorder (Nelson & Borkovec, 1989); obsessive–compulsive disorder (O'Sullivan, Noshirvani, Marks, Monteiro, & Lelliott, 1991); marital therapy (Holtzworth-Munroe, Jacobson, DeKlyen, & Whisman, 1989); substance abuse (Ingram & Salzberg, 1990); incontinence associated with spina bifida (King, Currie, & Wright, 1994); chronic constipation and soiling (Loening-Baucke, 1989); encopresis (Rappaport, Landman, Fenton, & Levine, 1986); defecation disorders (Taitz, Wales, Urwin, & Molnar, 1986); urinary incontinence (Oldenburg & Millard, 1986); hand function in cerebral palsy (Law & King, 1993); and amblyopia (Lithander & Sjöstrand, 1991). As can be seen, the studies examining adherence to homework and clinical outcomes primarily lie in domains of the anxiety disorders and elimination disorders.

Although adherence to homework was associated with reduction in self-reported rituals among patients with obsessive–compulsive disorder (O'Sullivan et al., 1991) and with a reduction in fear among agoraphobic patients (Edelman & Chambless, 1993), adherence to homework was not associated with positive results in other studies. For example, avoidance was not reduced among persons with agoraphobia (Edelman & Chambless, 1993), and therapist- and self-reports did not reflect a reduction of anxiety among persons with generalized anxiety disorder (Nelson & Borkovec, 1989).

Still within the mental health realm are marital therapy and treatment of substance abuse. Adherence to homework was associated with posttherapy marital satisfaction (Holtzworth-Munroe et al., 1989). However, adherence was not associated with the development of assertive behavior among residents of a substance abuse treatment center (Ingram & Salzberg, 1990).

The impact of adherence to homework was more clear among patients with elimination disorders. Improvements in soiling were associated with adherence in all studies (King et al., 1994; Loening-Baucke, 1989; Rappaport et al., 1986; Taitz et al., 1986). However, children with chronic constipation and soiling, while reducing soiling frequency with adherence to the homework, did not show differences in bowel movements per week when compared with the nonadherers (Loening-Baucke, 1989). Success was also associated with adherence to homework among women with urge incontinence who were treated with bladder retraining with and without biofeedback (Oldenburg & Millard, 1986). Thus, adherence to homework associated with programs designed for elimination disorders apparently plays a significant role in the outcome of treatment, at least when symptoms are considered. Data are not available on other outcomes, such as relapse, morbidity, or hospitalization.

Adherence to homework, measured by parental report, was associated with cure rates in children with amblyopia (Lithander & Sjöstrand, 1991). The limited data available also suggest that adherence to a home program for children with cerebral palsy was associated with hand function when adherence was measured by parental ratings, but not by therapist ratings (Law & King, 1993). This may suggest that parent ratings of adherence are more accurate that clinician estimates, which the data on medication adherence would suggest (e.g. Caron & Roth 1968). Thus, measurement method may be an important factor in the ability to detect an effect of adherence on clinical outcome, when examining how extensively patients carry out homework assignments.

The weight of the evidence suggests that adherence to homework may be important in symptom reduction. However, the relationships are not consistent across disorders or measurement methods. Thus, more work is needed to evaluate the effect of adherence to homework in terms of clinical outcomes. It would be particularly important to determine the level of adherence necessary to obtain desired outcomes as well, to avoid burdening patients with unnecessary activity. There are no data at present on the level of adherence to homework assignments necessary to promote optimal outcomes.

THE EFFECT OF ADHERENCE TO APPOINTMENTS ON CLINICAL OUTCOMES

The relationship of appointment keeping to clinical outcomes has been examined in a number of studies. Unkept appointments were associated with mortality among transplant patients (Schweizer et al., 1990);

among patients receiving sclerotherapy for variceal bleeding (Nakamura et al., 1991); as well as patients with hematologic malignancies (Richardson et al., 1990). Nonadherence to appointments was also associated with organ rejection (Schweizer et al., 1990) and return to dialysis (Kalil et al., 1992), among transplant recipients, as well as relapse among patients with schizophrenia (Leff et al., 1989).

Appointment keeping has shown mixed results on symptom reduction in selected psychiatric disorders. Patients with anorexia who attended visits and completed treatment were more likely to have improved functioning (Steiner, Mazer, & Litt, 1990). Session attendance was associated with mood, social adjustment, and problem improvement among suicidal patients but was not associated with physician ratings of progress, suicidal ideation, or repeat overdose (Hawton et al., 1981). Indeed, in one study of psychiatric patients, adherence to appointment keeping was negatively associated with reductions in psychopathology (Bowden, Schoenfeld, & Adams, 1980). Clearly the relationship between therapy-session attendance and outcomes is uncertain at best and may be related to the type of patient or the specific outcome being evaluated.

Appointment keeping in behavioral treatment was related to cure among children with defecation disorders (Taitz et al., 1986) and to hand function among children with cerebral palsy (Law & King, 1993). On the other hand, adherence to appointments when the treatment is focused on medical therapies is less clearly important. Visit attendance was not related to weight loss or glycosylated hemoglobin among patients with non-insulin-dependent diabetes mellitus (Mulrow et al., 1987), nor was it related to the number of days until otitis media was cleared (Reed et al., 1984). Furthermore, appointment keeping was positively associated with FEV_1 among children with cystic fibrosis (Patterson, Budd, Goetz, & Warwick, 1993).

Of interest is the finding of negative associations between appointment keeping adherence and clinical outcomes in the Mulrow et al. (1987) and Reed et al. (1984) studies. One possible explanation could be that patients with fewer symptoms are less likely to feel the need for clinical contacts than patients who are feeling less well. Thus, it would be the more distressed patients who maintain their clinical visits. This finding needs further examination, particularly in the light of whether follow-up of missed visits is important to the patient's outcome.

THE EFFECT OF ADHERENCE TO MULTICOMPONENT REGIMEN ON CLINICAL OUTCOMES

Many patients within the health care system find themselves on multicomponent regimens. Persons with multiple disorders will be treated for each concurrently. Many of the chronic disorders have multiple components to their treatment regimen. Most commonly, these consist of medication, diet, exercise, and regular clinic visits. The question is whether adherence to the regimen as a whole is related to outcome.

Five studies examined adherence to the regimen among persons with diabetes. The findings were mixed. Adherence was related to glycosylated hemoglobin in studies with children (Auslander, Anderson, Bubb, Jung, & Santiago, 1990); adolescents (Hanson, Henggeler, & Burghen, 1987); and adults (Kravitz et al., 1993). On the other hand, two studies with children and adolescents found that adherence to the regimen was not related to glycosylated hemoglobin (Johnson, Freund, Silverstein, Hansen, & Malone, 1990; Johnson et al., 1992). Differing methods of assessing adherence were used between the studies; in some cases, the method was not specified. The exact nature of the regimen also was not specified. It is possible, then, that these differences in findings were due to different measurement methods for adherence or to differences in treatment efficacy.

Nonadherence to the diabetic regimen also was associated with diabetic ketoacidosis among pregnant diabetic women (Montoro et al., 1993). Nonadherence to more general prenatal recommendations was found to be related to perinatal mortality (Moawad, Lee, Fisher, Ferguson, & Phillippe, 1990). Indeed approximately one third of avoidable infant deaths were attributable to maternal nonadherence in this study.

Two studies examined adherence to multicomponent regimen for cystic fibrosis among children and disease-specific clinical outcomes (Patterson et al., 1993; Sanders, Gravestock, Wanstall, & Dunn 1991). No effect of adherence was found when physician rating of clinical status was examined. However, a positive association was found for appointment keeping and FEV_1. Once again, adherence appears to be related to differing parameters of a given disorder.

It is interesting that throughout these studies, little attention has been given to outcomes beyond those biological outcomes specific to the disease or to symptoms, with the exception of studies on medication adherence. Little attention has been given to such important and costly outcomes as relapse, preventable morbidity, hospitalization, or general health status. No data to date exist on the effect of improving adherence on clinical outcomes. Multiple studies examaining the adherence–outcome relationship for specific regimen within and between disorders are necessary. Clearly, much research is needed before one can determine the effect of adherence or of improving adherence to medical and behavioral regimen on disease outcomes or before acceptable levels of adherence can be set for specific regimen in specific disorders.

ADHERENCE AS AN INDEPENDENT FACTOR IN CLINICAL OUTCOMES

As interest has grown in the role of levels of adherence as a moderator of clinical outcomes, so too has interest been generated on the effect of adherence behaviors directly on outcomes. This interest was sparked by findings in the Coronary Drug Project (CDP)—a multicenter, randomized, double-blind clinical trial examining the efficacy of cholesterol lowering in post-myocardial infarction patients (Coronary Drug Project Research Group, 1980). The data suggested that cardiac mortality was associated with adherence regardless of whether the patient was on active drug or placebo. These findings sparked an examination of the direct effect of adherence, that is adherence independent of prescribed treatment, in a number of the multicenter studies thereafter. A review of those findings follows.

Before examining the studies directly, it is important to consider dimensions of the studies that could confound an interpretation of the adherence–outcome relationship. Of particular importance is the design of the study. First, a study of the direct effect of adherence on outcome calls for a placebo-controlled trial. A direct effect of adherence can be identified only if it is found when a nonactive or placebo treatment is examined. Second, the trial should be double-blind to reduce the likelihood of bias in the assessment or ascertainment of outcomes. A double-blind trial would reduce also the likelihood of placebo-treated participants obtaining additional intervention, which could act on the main outcome, outside the domain of the study. Such intervention could be participant initiated or could be primary care physician initiated. It would be most likely if the perception was that the participant was unlikely to receive benefit from the trial. And last, the assessment of adherence should be accurate and blinded from the investigator who was assessing clinical endpoints. This would also reduce bias in evaluating the relationship of the two variables.

In this discussion, then, only double-blind, placebo-controlled studies with blinded ascertainment of outcomes were reviewed. Five trials that evaluated the adherence–outcome relationship were identified. Three addressed cardiovascular disease or risk: the CDP (Coronary Drug Project Research Group, 1980); the Lipid Research Clinics Coronary Primary Prevention Trial, (LRC-CPPT, Lipid Research Clinics Program, 1984); and the Beta-Blocker Heart Attack Trial (BHAT; Gallagher, Viscoll, & Horwitz, 1993; Horwitz et al., 1990).

One addressed granulocytopenia (Pizzo et al., 1983), and one addressed alcoholism (Fuller, Roth, & Long, 1983). The outcome in each of the cardiovascular studies was mortality. For the granulocytopenia study, reduction in fever or infection was the outcome of interest, whereas abstinence was the outcome of interest for the alcoholism trial.

Clearly, the hardest endpoint would be mortality. For two of the three cardiovascular trials, an association was found between death and adherence, regardless of treatment assignment. That is, even in the placebo group, participants who adhered were more likely to survive than participants who did not adhere. The LRC-CPPT study found no effect on either morbidity or mortality (cardiovascular events) of adhering to placebo, although the active drug reduced events. Each of these studies used a pill count in some form. The LRC-CPPT and the BHAT both used blinded packet or pill counts. Still, reliance was on the participant to return unused packets or pills, to ascertain the number that had been consumed between appointment intervals. Pill counts have not been strongly related to event-monitored assessment of medication adherence and have been shown to overestimate adherence when compared with event monitoring (Hamilton, 1996). Thus, a question could be raised about the sensitivity with which adherence was assessed in both trials.

More problematic was the assessment of adherence in the CDP. The design paper of the trial indicates that adherence was assessed by clinician report (Coronary Drug Project Research Group, 1973). Using her or his own estimate, the clinician was advised to place the patient in one of three adherence categories: 80%–100%, 20%–80%, or less than 20%. If the clinician was unable to make an estimate, a pill count was performed. Adherence for the groups was then calculated, using the midpoint of the category. Thus, the estimate of adherence could very well be confounded by the clinician's estimate of the patient's clinical status, with patients who were doing well more likely to be seen as adhering.

Measurement method may also have been a factor in the assessment of an adherence–outcome relationship in the granulocytopenia study and the alcohol study. Pizzo et al. (1983) found a relationship between adherence to antibiotics and reduction in fever or infection. In this case, adherence was assessed by means of self-report. One might question whether patients who developed a fever, an infection, or a potentially salient symptom or who experienced a morbid event would have been more likely to acknowledge poor adherence, regardless of treatment assignment, than those who had no untoward events. As noted, self-reported adherence has been very poorly associated with the more sensitive event monitoring of adherence, with the bias in the direction of overestimation of adherence through self-report (Dunbar-Jacob, Berg, et al., 1996).

The alcoholism study used two measures of adherence: a riboflavin marker in anabuse and placebo and appointment-keeping rates. Appointment-keeping rates were associated with adherence, regardless of assignment to anabuse or placebo. But adherence assessed through the riboflavin marker was not associated with outcome. Again, one has to examine the sensitivity of the marker. Riboflavin has a very short half-life. Thus, adherence assessed through this method would only address the period immediately preceding the clinic visit, not the interval between visits (Rudd, Ahmed, Zachary, Barton, & Bonduelle, 1990). Research using event monitoring has suggested that patients are more likely to adhere just before and just after a clinic visit. Thus, the marker would bias the ascertainment of adherence toward an overestimate of actual behavior.

Thus, three studies reported a relationship between adherence and outcome, regardless of treatment assignment, suggesting a direct effect of adherence. Two studies had negative findings, suggesting that adherence does not have a direct effect on clinical outcome. Although each of the studies was double-blind and placebo controlled, adherence measurement varied between studies, with, however, each study using assessment techniques that themselves introduce bias. There are sufficient, yet conflicting, data to make this an important issue for further study. If such a direct effect is found, then efforts to promote adherence would assume central importance in the management of clinical disorders. If it is not found to exist, then it is more important to define levels of adherence necessary for desirable outcomes for specific regimens and disorders and to promote adherence to those levels. Further studies, however, require the use of sensitive and accurate assessment strategies.

DISCUSSION

It is interesting that so little work has been carried out on the relationship of adherence to clinical outcome. Numerous studies also have been devoted to identifying factors that contribute to adherence and, to a lesser extent, to identifying strategies that promote or remediate adherence. One assumes that improvements in adherence will lead to improvements in outcomes. Yet, there are little data available to indicate how clinically effective these efforts are. What data are available, however, support adherence–outcome relationships and suggest that efforts to enhance adherence should lead to improvements in clinical outcomes.

Clearly, more research needs to be conducted on the adherence–outcome relationship. The studies reported here suggest that low levels of adherence have a significant and costly impact on the patient's health, medical care utilization, and at times mortality. Yet there are limited data for any particular disease.

Studies on the direct effects of adherence, though interesting, are conflicting and few in number. The existing studies used assessment methods that confound the interpretation of their findings. The examination of a direct effect of adherence on outcome requires a study in the context of a double-blind, placebo-controlled trial. Design strategies need to minimize investigator and participant bias in the assessment of outcomes, as well as the assessment of adherence.

One of the difficulties in examining the role of adherence in clinical outcomes has been the assessment of adherence itself. Biological assays tend to address behavior over a limited period of time and are insensitive to individual variations in adherence patterns. Clinical estimates have been shown to be no better than chance (Caron & Roth, 1968; Mushlin & Appel, 1977; Roth, Caron, & Hsi, 1971). Patient self-reports overestimate compliance, often quite significantly (Dunbar-Jacob, Berg, et al., 1996). Daily diaries or records are dependent on the patients' willingness to report deviations from the prescription and willingness to complete the diary itself. Furthermore, diaries themselves have been shown to promote behavior change through their increased emphasis on self-monitoring. Newer methods of assessment include electronic pill monitors, activity monitors, diaries, and other devices that record on microchips the date and time of the event of interest. Though not error free, these devices represent a leap forward in the assessment of adherence to prescribed therapies. It is through these newer assessment techniques that a clearer picture of the relationship between both overall adherence, as well as patterns of adherence, and clinical outcomes will emerge.

Data on the effects of adherence to treatment regimen on clinical outcomes are promising, though not easily found. Few studies have been carried out with any particular disorder. New studies are needed that address the impact as well as the degree of adherence necessary to influence clinical outcome. Data supporting the direct effect of adherence on outcomes, although interesting, are inconsistent and have been limited to studies of mortality. Further research that takes into account the design flaws of earlier studies is needed to elucidate this potentially clinically important relationship.

REFERENCES

Auslander, W. F., Anderson, B. J., Bubb, J., Jung, K. C., & Santiago, J. V. (1990). Risk factors to health in diabetic children: A prospective study from diagnosis. *Health and Social Work, 15,* 133–142.

Belloc, N. B. (1973). Relationship of health practices and mortality. *Preventive Medicine, 2,* 67–81.

Berndt, S., Maier, C., & Schutz, H. W. (1993). Polymedication and medication compliance in patients with chronic non-malignant pain. *Pain, 52,* 331–339.

Bishop, K. R., Dougherty, M., Mooney, R., Gimotty, P., & Williams, B. (1992). Effects of age, parity, and adherence on pelvic muscle response to exercise. *Journal of Obstetric, Gynecologic, and Neonatal Nursing, 21,* 401–406.

Bowden, C. L., Schoenfeld, L. S., & Adams, R. L. (1980). A correlation between dropout status and improvement in a psychiatric clinic. *Hospital and Community Psychiatry, 31,* 192–195.

Boyd, E. J. S., Wilson, J. A., & Wormsley, K. G. (1983). Effects of treatment compliance and overnight gastric secretion on outcome of maintenance therapy of duodenal ulcer with ranitidine. *Scandinavian Journal of Gastroenterology, 18,* 193–200.

Breslow, L., & Enstrom, J. E. (1980). Persistence of health habits and their relationship to mortality. *Preventive Medicine, 9,* 469–483.

Caron, H. S., & Roth, H. P. (1968). Patients' cooperation with a medical regimen: Difficulties in identifying the noncooperator. *Journal of the American Medical Association, 203,* 922–926.

Cheung, R., Sullens, C. M., Seal, D., Dickins, J., Nicholson, P. W., Deshmukh, A. A., Denham, M. J., & Dobbs, S. M. (1988). The paradox of using a 7 day antibacterial course to treat urinary tract infections in the community. *British Journal of Clinical Pharmacology, 26,* 391–398.

Cole, M. G. (1985). The course of elderly depressed out-patients. *Canadian Journal of Psychiatry, 30,* 217–220.

Connelly, C. E., Davenport, Y. B., & Nurnberger, J. I., Jr. (1982). Adherence to treatment regimen in a lithium carbonate clinic. *Archives of General Psychiatry, 39,* 585–588.

Coronary Drug Project Research Group. (1973). The Coronary Drug Project: Design, methods, and baseline results. *Circulation, 47*(Suppl. 3), 1–50.

Coronary Drug Project Research Group. (1980). Influence of adherence to treatment and response of cholesterol on mortality in the Coronary Drug Project. *New England Journal of Medicine, 303,* 1038–1041.

Cowen, M. E., Jim, L. K., Boyd, E. L., & Gee, J. P. (1981). Some possible effects of patient noncompliance. *Journal of the American Medical Association, 245,* 1121.

Cramer, J. A., Mattson, R. H., Prevey, M. L., Scheyer, R. D., & Ouellette, V. L. (1989). How often is medication taken as prescribed? A novel assessment technique. *Journal of the American Medical Association, 261,* 3273–3277.

De Geest, S. (1996, March). Assessment of adherence in heart transplant recipients. In J. Dunbar-Jacob (chair), *Adherence in chronic disease.* Seminar conducted at the Fourth International Congress of Behavioral Medicine. Washington, DC.

Dompeling, E., Van Grunsven, P. M., Van Schayck, C. P., Folgering, H., Molema, J., & Van Weel, C. (1992). Treatment with inhaled steroids in asthma and chronic bronchitis: Long-term compliance and inhaler technique. *Family Practice, 9,* 161–166.

Dunbar-Jacob, J., Berg, J., Boehm, S., DeGeest, S., & Hamilton, G. (1996, March). In J. Dunbar-Jacob (chair), *Adherence in chronic disease.* Seminar presented at the Fourth International Congress of Behavioral Medicine, Washington, DC.

Dunbar-Jacob, J., Kwoh, C. K., Rohay, J., Burke, L., Sereika, S., & Starz, R. (1996, March). *Adherence and functional outcomes in rheumatoid arthritis.* Paper presented at the Fourth International Congress of Behavioral Medicine, Washington, DC.

Dupon, M., & Ragnaud, J. M. (1992). Tuberculosis in patients infected with Human Immunodeficiency Virus 1: A retrospective multicentre study of 123 cases in France. *Quarterly Journal of Medicine, 85,* 719–730.

Edelman, R. E., & Chambless, D. L. (1993). Compliance during sessions and homework in exposure-based treatment of agoraphobia. *Behaviour Research and Therapy, 31,* 767–773.

Fawcett, J., Clark, D. C., Aagesen, C. A., Pisani, V. D., Tilkin, J. M., Sellers, D., McQuire, M., & Gibbons, R. D. (1987). A double-blind, placebo-controlled trial of lithium carbonate therapy for alcoholism. *Archives of General Psychiatry, 44,* 248–256.

Fawcett, J., Clark, D. C., Gibbons, R. D., Aagesen, C. A., Pisani, V. D., Tilkin, J. M., Sellers, D., & Stutzman, D. (1984). Evaluation of lithium therapy for alcoholism. *Journal of Clinical Psychiatry, 45,* 494–499.

Fishbein, H. A. (1985). Precipitants of hospitalization in insulin-dependent diabetes mellitus (IDDM): A statewide perspective. *Diabetes Care, 8*(Suppl. 1), 61–64.

Fletcher, S. W., Deliakis, J., Schoch, W. A., & Shapiro, S. H. (1979). Predicting blood pressure control in hypertensive patients: An approach to quality-of-care assessment. *Medical Care, 17,* 285–292.

Fuller, R., Roth, H., & Long, S. (1983). Compliance with disulfiram treatment of alcoholism. *Journal of Chronic Diseases, 36,* 161–170.

Gaebel, W., & Pietzcker, A. (1985). One-year outcome of schizophrenic patients: The interaction of chronicity and neuroleptic treatment. *Pharmacopsychiatry, 18,* 235–239.

Gallagher, E. J., Viscoli, C. M., & Horwitz, R. I. (1993). The relationship of treatment adherence to the risk of death after myocardial infarction in women. *Journal of the American Medical Association, 270,* 742–744.

Given, B., Given, C. W., & Simoni, L. E. (1979). Relationships of processes of care to patient outcomes. *Nursing Research, 28,* 85–93.

Grahl, C. (1994). Improving compliance: Solving a $100 billion problem. *Managed Health Care,* S11–S13.

Granstrom, P. A. (1985). Progression of visual field defects in glaucoma: Relation to compliance with pilocarpine therapy. *Archives of Ophthalmology, 103,* 529–531.

Hamilton, G. (1996, March). Event monitoring of adherence in a hypertension trial. In J. Dunbar-Jacob (Chair), *Adherence in chronic disease*. Seminar conducted at the Fourth International Congress of Behavioral Medicine, Washington, DC.

Hanson, C. L., Henggeler, S. W., & Burghen, G. A. (1987). Model of associations between psychosocial variables and health-outcome measures of adolescents with IDDM. *Diabetes Care, 10*, 752–758.

Hawkins, R. B. (1989). Arthroscopic stapling repair for shoulder instability: A retrospective study of 50 cases. *Arthroscopy: The Journal of Arthroscopic and Related Surgery, 5*, 122–128.

Hawkins, R. J., & Switlyk, P. (1993). Acute prosthetic replacement for severe fractures of the proximal humerus. *Clinical Orthopaedics and Related Research, 289*, 156–160.

Hawton, K., Bancroft, J., Catalan, J., Kingston, B., Stedeford, A., & Welch, N. (1981). Domiciliary and out-patient treatment of self-poisoning patients by medical and non-medical staff. *Psychological Medicine, 11*, 169–177.

Haynes, R. B., Gibson, E. S., Taylor, D. W., Bernholz, C. D., & Sackett, D. L. (1982). Process versus outcome in hypertension: A positive result. *Circulation, 65*, 28–33.

Haynes, R. B., Sackett, D. L., Gibson, E. S., Taylor, D. W., Hackett, B. C., Roberts, R. S., & Johnson, A. L. (1976). Improvement of medication compliance in uncontrolled hypertension. *Lancet, 1*, 1265–1268.

Holtzworth-Munroe, A., Jacobson, N. S., DeKlyen, M., & Whisman, M. A. (1989). Relationship between behavioral marital therapy outcome and process variables. *Journal of Consulting and Clinical Psychology, 57*, 658–662.

Horwitz, R. I., Viscoli, C. M., Berkman, L., Donaldson, R. M., Horwitz, S. M., Murray, C. J., Ransohoff, D. F., & Sindelar, J. (1990). Treatment adherence and risk of death after a myocardial infarction. *Lancet, 336*, 542–545.

Ingram, J. A., & Salzberg, H. C. (1990). Effects of *in vivo* behavioral rehearsal on the learning of assertive behaviors with a substance abusing population. *Addictive Behaviors, 15*, 189–194.

Johnson, S. B., Freund, A., Silverstein, J., Hansen, C. A., & Malone, J. (1990). Adherence–health status relationships in childhood diabetes. *Health Psychology, 9*, 606–631.

Johnson, S. B., Kelly, M., Henretta, J. C., Cunningham, W. R., Tomer, A., & Silverstein, J. H. (1992). A longitudinal analysis of adherence and health status in childhood diabetes. *Journal of Pediatric Psychology, 17*, 537–553.

Kalil, R. S. N., Heim-Duthoy, K. L., & Kasiske, B. L. (1992). Patients with a low income have reduced renal allograft survival. *American Journal of Kidney Diseases, 20*, 63–69.

King, J. C., Currie, D. M., & Wright, E. (1994). Bowel training in spina bifida: Importance of education, patient compliance, age, and anal reflexes. *Archives of Physical Medicine and Rehabilitation, 75*, 243–247.

Klopovich, P. M., & Trueworthy, R. C. (1985). Adherence to chemotherapy regimens among children with cancer. *Topics in Clinical Nursing, 7*, 19–25.

Kravitz, R. L., Hays, R. D., Sherbourne, C. D., DiMatteo, M. R., Rogers, W. H., Ordway, L., & Greenfield, S. (1993). Recall of recommendations and adherence to advice among patients with chronic medical conditions. *Archives of Internal Medicine, 153*, 1869–1878.

Lanza, R. P., Cooper, D. K. C., Boyd, S. T., & Barnard, C. N. (1984). Comparison of patients with ischemic, myopathic, and rheumatic heart diseases as cardiac transplant recipients. *American Heart Journal, 107*, 8–12.

Law, M., & King, G. (1993). Parent compliance with therapeutic interventions for children with cerebral palsy. *Developmental Medicine and Child Neurology, 35*, 983–990.

Leff, J., Berkowitz, R., Shavit, N., Strachan, A., Glass, I., & Vaughn, C. (1989). A trial of family therapy v. a relatives group for schizophrenia. *British Journal of Psychiatry, 154*, 58–66.

Lichtenstein, M. J., Shields, S. L., Shiavi, R. G., & Burger C. (1989). Exercise and balance in aged women: A pilot controlled clinical trial. *Archives of Physical Medicine and Rehabilitation, 70*, 138–143.

Lip, G. Y. H., & Brodie, M. J. (1992). Sudden death in epilepsy: An avoidable outcome? *Journal of the Royal Society of Medicine, 85*, 609–611.

Lipid Research Clinics Program. (1984). The Lipid Research Clinics Coronary Primary Prevention Trial results: II. The relationship of reduction in incidence of coronary heart disease to cholesterol lowering. *Journal of the American Medical Association, 251*, 365–374.

Lithander, J., & Sjöstrand, J. (1991). Anisometropic and strabismic amblyopia in the age group 2 years and above: A prospective study of results of treatment. *British Journal of Ophthalmology, 75*, 111–116.

Loening-Baucke, V. (1989). Factors determining outcome in children with chronic constipation and faecal soiling. *Gut, 30*, 999–1006.

Mantonakis, J. E., Jemos, J. J., Christodoulou, G. N., & Lykouras, E. P. (1982). Short-term social prognosis of schizophrenia. *Acta Psychiatrica Scandinavica, 66*, 306–310.

Maronde, R. F., Chan, L. S., Larsen, F. J., Strandberg, L. R., Laventurier, M. F., & Sullivan S. R. (1989). Underutilization of antihypertensive drugs and associated hospitalization. *Medical Care, 27*, 1159–1166.

Matarazzo, J. D. (1984). Behavioral health: A 1990 challenge for the health sciences professions. In J. D. Matarazzo, S. M. Weiss, J. A. Herd, N. E. Miller, & S. M. Weiss (Eds.), *Behavioral health: A handbook of health enhancement and disease prevention* (pp. 3–40). New York: Wiley.

McKenney, J. M., Munroe, W. P., & Wright, J. T., Jr. (1992). Impact of an electronic medication compliance aid on long-term blood pressure control. *Journal of Clinical Pharmacology, 32*, 277–283.

Moawad, A. H., Lee, K. S., Fisher, D. E., Ferguson, R., & Phillippe, M. (1990). A model for the prospective analysis of perinatal deaths in a perinatal network. *American Journal of Obstetrics and Gynecology, 162,* 15–22.

Montoro, M. N., Myers, V. P., Mestman, J. H., Xu, Y., Anderson, B. G., & Golde, S. H. (1993). Outcome of pregnancy in diabetic ketoacidosis. *American Journal of Perinatology, 10,* 17–20.

Mulrow, C., Bailey, S., Sonksen, P. H., & Slavin, B. (1987). Evaluation of an Audiovisual Diabetes Education Program: Negative results of a randomized trial of patients with non-insulin-dependent diabetes mellitus. *Journal of General Internal Medicine, 2,* 215–219.

Murphy, G., Tzamaloukas, A. H., Quintana, B. J., Gibel, L. J., & Avasthi, P. S. (1989). Clinical significance of hemodialysis performed during the course of continuous ambulatory peritoneal dialysis. *International Journal of Artificial Organs, 12,* 303–306.

Mushlin, A. I., & Appel, F. A. (1977). Diagnosing potential noncompliance: Physicians' ability in a behavioral dimension of medical care. *Archives of Internal Medicine, 137,* 318–321.

Nakamura, R., Bucci, L. A., Sugawa, C., Lucas, C. E., Gutta, K., Sugimura, Y., & Sferra, C. (1991). Sclerotherapy of bleeding esophageal varices using a thrombogenic cocktail. *American Surgeon, 57,* 226–230.

Nelson, R. A., & Borkovec, T. D. (1989). Relationship of client participation to psychotherapy. *Journal of Behavior Therapy and Experimental Psychiatry, 20,* 155–162.

Nolan, C. M., Aitken, M. L., Elarth, A. M., Anderson, K. M., & Miller, W. T. (1986). Active tuberculosis after isoniazid chemoprophylaxis of Southeast Asian refugees. *American Review of Respiratory Disease, 133,* 431–436.

O'Donnell, D., Sevitz, H., Seggie, J. L., Meyers, A. M., Botha, J. R., & Myburgh, J. A. (1985). Pregnancy after renal transplantation. *Australian and New Zealand Journal of Medicine, 15,* 320–325.

Oldenburg, B., & Millard, R. J. (1986). Predictors of long term outcome following a bladder re-training programme. *Journal of Psychosomatic Research, 30,* 691–698.

O'Sullivan, G., Noshirvani, H., Marks, I., Monteiro, W., & Lelliott, P. (1991). Six-year follow-up after exposure and clomipramine therapy for obsessive compulsive disorder. *Journal of Clinical Psychiatry, 52,* 150–155.

Patterson, J. M., Budd, J., Goetz, D., & Warwick, W. J. (1993). Family correlates of a 10-year pulmonary health trend in cystic fibrosis. *Pediatrics, 91,* 383–389.

Peat, B. (1993). Pregnancy complicated by maternal phenylketonuria. *Australian and New Zealand Journal of Obstetrics and Gynaecology, 33,* 163–165.

Physicians' desk reference. (50th ed.). (1996). Oradell, NJ: Medical Economics.

Pisani, V. D., Fawcett, J., Clark, D. C., & McQuire, M. (1993). The relative contributions of medication adherence and AA meeting attendance to abstinent outcome for chronic alcoholics. *Journal of Studies on Alcohol, 54*, 115–119.

Pizzo, P. A., Robichaud, K. J., Edwards, B. K., Schumaker, C., Kramer, B. S., & Johnson, A. (1983). Oral antibiotic prophylaxis in patients with cancer: A double-blind randomized placebo-controlled trial. *Journal of Pediatrics, 102*, 125–133.

Psaty, B. M., Koepsell, T. D., Wagner, E. H., LoGerfo, J. P., & Inui, T. S. (1990). The relative risk of incident coronary heart disease associated with recently stopping the use of beta-blockers. *Journal of the American Medical Association, 263*, 1653–1657.

Rappaport, L., Landman, G., Fenton, T., & Levine, M. D. (1986). Locus of control as predictor of compliance and outcome in treatment of encopresis. *Journal of Pediatrics, 109*, 1061–1064.

Reed, B. D., Lutz, L. J., Zazove, P., & Ratcliffe, S. D. (1984). Compliance with acute otitis media treatment. *Journal of Family Practice, 19*, 627–632.

Reynolds, E. H. (1987). Early treatment and prognosis of epilepsy. *Epilepsia, 28*, 97–106.

Richardson, J. L., Shelton, D. R., Krailo, M., & Levine, A. M. (1990). The effect of compliance with treatment on survival among patients with hematologic malignancies. *Journal of Clinical Oncology, 8*, 356–364.

Rives, K., Gelberman, R., Smith, B., & Carney, K. (1992). Severe contractures of the proximal interphalangeal joint in Dupuytren's disease: Results of a prospective trial of operative correction and dynamic extension splinting. *Journal of Hand Surgery, 17*, 1153–1159.

Robertson, C. F., Rubinfeld, A. R., & Bowes, G. (1992). Pediatric asthma deaths in Victoria: The mild are at risk. *Pediatric Pulmonology, 13*, 95–100.

Roth, H. P., Caron, H. S., & Hsi, B. P. (1971). Estimating a patient's cooperation with his regimen. *American Journal of Medical Sciences, 262*, 269–273.

Rovelli, M., Palmeri, D., Vossler, E., Bartus, S., Hull, D., & Schweizer, R. (1989). Noncompliance in organ transplant recipients. *Transplantation Proceedings, 21*, 833–834.

Rudd, P., Ahmed, S., Zachary, V., Barton, C., & Bonduelle, D. (1990). Improved compliance measures: Applications in an ambulatory hypertensive drug trial. *Clinical Pharmacology and Therapeutics, 48*, 676–685.

Sanders, M. R., Gravestock, F. M., Wanstall, K., & Dunne, M. (1991). The relationship between children's treatment-related behaviour problems, age and clinical status in cystic fibrosis. *Journal of Paediatrics and Child Health, 27*, 290–294.

Schweizer, R. T., Rovelli, M., Palmeri, D., Vossler, E., Hull, D., & Bartus, S. (1990). Noncompliance in organ transplant recipients. *Transplantation, 49*, 374–377.

Singh, R. B., Niaz, M. A., Ghosh, S., Singh, R., & Rastogi, S. S. (1993). Effect on mortality and reinfarction of adding fruits and vegetables to a prudent diet in the Indian experiment of infarct survival (IEIS). *Journal of the American College of Nutrition, 12,* 255–261.

Starlinger, M., Appel, W. H., Schemper, M., & Schiessel, R. (1985). Long-term treatment of peptic esophageal stenosis with dilatation and cimetidine: Factors influencing clinical result. *European Surgical Research, 17,* 207–214.

Steiner, H., Mazer, C., & Litt, I. F. (1990). Compliance and outcome in anorexia nervosa. *Western Journal of Medicine, 153,* 133–139.

Swank, R. L., & Dugan, B. B. (1990). Effect of low saturated fat diet in early and late cases of multiple sclerosis. *Lancet, 336,* 37–39.

Taal, E., Rasker, J. J., Seydel, E. R., & Wiegman, O. (1993). Health status, adherence with health recommendations, self-efficacy and social support in patients with rheumatoid arthritis. *Patient Education and Counseling, 20*(2–3), 63–76.

Taitz, L. S., Wales, J. K. H., Urwin, O. M., & Molnar, D. (1986). Factors associated with outcome in management of defecation disorders. *Archives of Disease in Childhood, 61,* 472–477.

U.S. Public Health Service. (1991). *Healthy People 2000: National health promotion and disease prevention objectives* (Full report). Washington, DC: Author.

Verghese, A., John, J. K., Rajkumar, S., Richard, J., Sethi, B. B., & Trivedi, J. K. (1989). Factors associated with the course and outcome of schizophrenia in India: Results of a two-year multicentre follow-up study. *British Journal of Psychiatry, 154,* 499–503.

Wetsteyn, J. C. F. M., & de Geus, A. (1993). Comparison of three regimens for malaria prophylaxis in travellers to east, central, and southern Africa. *British Medical Journal, 307,* 1041–1043.

White, K., Kolman, M. L., Wexler, P., Polin, G., & Winter, R. J. (1984). Unstable diabetes and unstable families: A psychosocial evaluation of diabetic children with recurrent ketoacidosis. *Pediatrics, 73,* 749–755.

IV

PSYCHOLOGISTS IN DISEASE PREVENTION AND HEALTH PROMOTION

INTRODUCTION

The major cause of wellness is behavior that guarantees a healthy lifestyle. On the other hand, those choices or actions that put one in physical jeopardy or increase the chances of becoming ill, usually in the future, can be seen as contributors to some diseases or the major cause of others. The common factor, whether looking at health promotion or disease prevention, is behavior. Whether behavior is defined as doing something (e.g., lighting up a cigarette) or making a choice (e.g., to engage in unsafe sexual practices, even just once), no other profession is more qualified to speak to wellness than psychology; the profession that studies and treats behavior and thoughts. In this section, we look at four of the many topics areas in which psychologists help in the prevention of disease and the promotion of health.

In chapter 22, "African American Women, Their Families, and HIV/AIDS," Debra Greenwood and colleagues use a case-study approach to highlight the importance of a family-therapy-oriented approach to the emotional and social problems faced by women and their families. Greenwood et al. detail the staggering incidence statistics and emotional toll of HIV/AIDS on the African American family. The family's role in adaptation to environmental stress and in the development of effective coping strategies is presented, along with a structural-ecosystems-therapy approach that is designed to foster a sense of empowerment within the family.

In chapter 23, "Revolution in Health Promotion: Smoking Cessation as a Case Study," James O. Prochaska begins by documenting the costs of cigarette smoking—costs that include human suffering and the financial burden of illness and premature death. Prochaska describes a stage paradigm for change and then applies it to a smoking cessation program. The outcome of a large-scale, clinical trial comparing several treatment methods is presented, and the results for smoking cessation are offered as a model for health-promotion programs, to impact entire populations by preventing chronic diseases and premature death.

G. Alan Marlatt's chapter 24, "Reducing College Student Binge Drinking: A Harm-Reduction Approach," discusses a health problem that finds a significant percent of undergraduate students engaged in the episodic drinking of five or more drinks on a single occasion. Marlatt presents the research results of his alcohol-harm-reduction approach, designed to move those with harmful drinking problems along the behavioral continuum toward abstinence. This approach is based on the belief that any movement toward less harmful behavior is in the right direction, even if abstinence is not met. Other unrelated prevention programs are discussed under the umbrella of harm reduction.

The last chapter in the Disease Prevention and Health Promotion section, chapter 25, "Strategies to Reduce the Risk of HIV Infection, Sexually Transmitted Diseases, and Pregnancy Among African American Adolescents," by John B. and Loretta Sweet Jemmott, reviews a research program on various interventions for those high-health-risk behaviors. This chapter on community interventions exemplifies the kinds of innovative community programs that can be designed by combining research with practice. The authors review programs targeted at male African American adolescents to reduce sexually transmitted diseases and pregnancy among teenagers. They describe a series of innovative programs and outline research methodologies aimed at finding out which elements of these programs are particularly salient. In addition to outlining effective interventions for practitioners, this chapter shows how research can be used to help craft effective community programs.

22

AFRICAN AMERICAN WOMEN, THEIR FAMILIES, AND HIV/AIDS

DEBRA GREENWOOD, JOSÉ SZAPOCZNIK, SCOTT MCINTOSH,
MICHAEL ANTONI, GAIL IRONSON, MANUEL TEJEDA,
LAVONDA CLARINGTON, DEANNE SAMUELS, and
LINDA SORHAINDO

The rate of AIDS among African American women is 15 times that of White women (Centers for Disease Control and Prevention, 1995). In Dade County, Florida, alone, there are approximately 5,000 African American women and girls over the age of 12 with AIDS (Department of Health and Rehabilitative Services, 1995). These figures primarily represent inner-city women who have been devastated for decades by poverty, drug addiction, and the sequelae of crime and family disruption—historical problems in certain segments of the African American community.

Much like other catastrophic illnesses, HIV/AIDS does not only affect the infected woman. The impact of the infection reverberates to her social network, particularly her family.

This work was supported by National Institute of Mental Health Grant 1 R01 MH51402 to José Szapocznik and Debra Greenwood, coprincipal investigators.

The impact of HIV/AIDS on the family is of particular importance (Boyd-Franklin et al., 1995; Landau-Stanton, Clements, & Stanton, 1993; Shelton, Greenwood, & Szapocznik, in press; Walker, 1991). Indeed, family researchers and therapists identify the family as the unit of care, in that the family is the unit to receive and give care. In HIV, as in all other matters that affect an African American woman, to more fully understand the individual, one must understand her family, culture, and environmental context (cf. Szapocznik & Kurtines, 1993). For people affected by HIV/AIDS, the family plays a particularly crucial role (cf. Szapocznik, 1995). Given that in times of illness or distress, the family unit is typically called on to support its member in need, the added stress of HIV may tax the ability of African American families to effectively cope with these additional demands, particularly because many are already living under very stressful conditions.

Although it is well known that discrete, traumatic events (e.g., natural disasters) can negatively impact psychosocial adaptation, some researchers have argued that chronic stressful life conditions may more negatively impact psychosocial adaptation than discrete life events (Krause, 1986; McLanahan, 1983; Sherbourne, 1988). Several studies have identified being poor, African American, female, and a single parent as sources of chronic life stress (G. W. Brown, Craig, & Harris, 1985; Smith, 1985). Another source of stress for African American families is the marginalization that they experience because the preferences, needs, and special circumstances of African American families are peripheral to the concerns of most Americans (Smith, 1985). Pierce (1975) characterized the societal stress that African Americans face as living in an environment where racism and subtle oppression are ubiquitous rather than an occasional misfortune. Although racism is a constant, salient stressor in the lives of African Americans (Boyd-Franklin, 1989; Smith, 1985), other social problems, such as lack of education, low incomes, and unsafe neighborhoods co-occur. In this chapter, we review the environmental stresses on these women and how African American families tend to respond to these stresses. We also present a therapeutic model, adapted for the special characteristics of the African American family. Throughout, we provide a sense of the real-life challenges they face and how their families respond.

ENVIRONMENTAL CHALLENGES

In our work with low-income, African American, postpartum women, we have found that lack of financial resources is a problem that is frequently reported as troubling to their life. One of the manifestations of their poverty is the unsafe neighborhoods in which many of the women live. One of our HIV-seropositive women, Belinda, a recovering crack cocaine addict, told of how she felt victimized in her neighborhood. She told us that she had tried to reach out to her neighbors who had few, if any, food stamps by sharing her own food with them. She was disappointed and angered to learn that those to whom she had been kind were also stealing food from her kitchen: "It really hurt me that some of the very same people I helped when they didn't have nothin' [sic] are now stealing from me." This experience embittered her and fostered a sense of mistrust of her neighbors, heightening her sense of isolation.

Our women also frequently report that one of their greatest fears with regard to HIV is the unsanctioned disclosure of their HIV status within their neighborhoods. Our women have spoken to us about the negative, disparaging remarks their neighbors and family members have made about known seropositives in their community. Another of our women, Ruth, observed, "My sister is real nice to my cousin who is HIV-positive—to his face. But when he leaves, she throws the glass away that he drunk [sic] from. I don't want her treating me like that. That's why I don't tell her about me." And from Tasha, "You don't know what's it like to hear them talk about 'those people' who got that HIV thang [sic] like they's [sic] dogs. They ain't never gonna talk about me like that!" Clearly, for many of our women, the environment poses yet another set of stressors, in that in addition to the unsafe neighborhoods and poverty with which the women must contend, ignorance about HIV in their social context translates into fear of stigmatization and isolation, should their HIV status become known.

However, there are families that remain supportive of their HIV-affected member, despite difficult circumstances. Lynn Collins is a 23-year-old African American woman with three children. The older two children reside with her grandmother in Texas. Lynn and her youngest child live with Lynn's parents (mother and stepfather) and her younger siblings. Although Lynn and her mother have had disagreements about some of the choices Lynn has made in her life (e.g., three unplanned pregnancies), Lynn's mother, Donna, has been supportive of Lynn since becoming aware of Lynn's HIV diagnosis. Lynn works part-time, rears her child, and contributes financially to the household. The family lives in a modest home in the inner city.

THE FAMILY'S ROLE IN ADAPTATION TO ENVIRONMENTAL STRESS

What may be critical to families is their ability to respond and adapt to chronic and acute stress. For the family, this necessitates an appraisal of the stressful event(s), what Lazarus and Folkman (1984) called "primary appraisal" (pp. 31–32), their perception of other, competing stresses and strains and their perception of family resources. The perception of the family's capacity to manage the stress is a "secondary appraisal" (Lazarus, 1966, p. 23). Other elements that affect the family's capacity to manage stress include an assessment of resources, the duration of the stressor, and the disruptiveness of the stressor. In the Collins family, Donna's primary appraisal of Lynn's HIV status competed with the family's struggle to make ends meet and Donna's desire to launch Lynn's siblings into adolescence in such a way that they do not make the same kinds of mistakes Lynn did, that is, unmarried, teenage pregnancy. Donna and her husband monitor their younger children closely, even though they both work long hours to support the family. The ability of the Collins family to juggle competing stressors is illustrative of competence in coping with their reality.

African American families have demonstrated a unique ability to survive and overcome adverse societal conditions such as racism and discrimination (Billingsley, 1968; Hines & Boyd-Franklin, 1982). Much of this success can be attributed to the strength of African American families, that is, their flexibility and resilience and their cultural values (Hill, 1977; cf. Ogbu, 1981). The reliance on an extended network of family and friends allows for more effective sharing of scarce resources (Chatters, Taylor, & Jackson, 1985; R. J. Taylor, 1985). Caregiving burdens are frequently shared by several related or nonrelated "fictive," or "play," kin, thus relieving an individual from assuming an overwhelming responsibility. For example, in the Collins family, the Texas grandmother provides assistance to the family by caring for Lynn's two older children. By caring for the children, the grandmother makes a de facto financial contribution by relieving the family of some of its financial stress. Moreover, in this case, the grandmother's caring for the children is experienced by Donna and the family as compassionate emotional support. The reliance on extended family or nonrelated kin is an example of a family successfully making a secondary appraisal of its resources and galvanizing them to solve acute or chronic family-related problems.

A strong religious ethos is also cited as an important coping resource for African American families (Boyd-Franklin, 1989; D. R. Brown & Gary, 1987; Griffith, Young, & Smith, 1984). African American families often rely on prayer, their clergy, and their church congregation to provide not only a means of support from others but also a sense of meaningfulness and a refuge from the material world (R. J. Taylor & Chatters, 1986). Prayer is a very important part of life for the Collins family. Donna and her husband see to it that the family attends church regularly.

It is clear that the African American family has developed several effective mechanisms for coping with the stress faced in the extreme environmental conditions to which African Americans are often forced to adapt. As we have suggested above, one of these is the kinship network. In our work with African American families, to access the necessary family support on behalf of our clients, we carefully identify the complex web that can potentially provide social support or be a source of stress.

THE IMPORTANCE OF CORRECTLY IDENTIFYING THE AFRICAN AMERICAN FAMILY

Note that for African American families, the concept of family is often fluid, which suggests that our traditional definition of family needs to be expanded to reflect the reality of many African Americans, who do not limit their "family" to biological kin. For many African Americans, the family may include one's biological family (including extended family), significant others, and close friends. These close friends, or fictive kin, that is, people who are identified as relatives but who are not part of the biological family, are typically very important to one or more members of the family. Fictive kin relationships can be intergenerational. Thus, the daughter of one's play aunt may be referred to as one's *play cousin*.

To deliver care to the family or to appropriately identify family resources, it is important to accurately identify the family constellation. Without a clear, accurate picture of the members of the family, important, powerful, family figures may be overlooked, thus distorting the clinician's assessment of the family and its typical pattern of interactions.

In African American families, it is not unusual for many different types of family constellations to occur in the community. A friend or relative may temporarily live with a family for days, weeks, or even years, for a variety of reasons. The family may take in a boarder (who may or may not be a relative) to earn extra money. For example, in the case of Belinda, her ex-husband lived in the home with her, paid rent as if a boarder, yet functioned as an integral part of the family, in that he participated in child rearing and household decisions. Moreover, fictive kin may play an important role in a family, although they need not necessarily reside in the home. This cultural practice of broadening one's definition of family has important implications for researchers and clinicians who assess family composition or family functioning. Traditional methods of family identification, with their overemphasis on biological ties and neglect of function as an indication of family constellation, are often inappropriate for African American families.

Clinical Issues

Our clinical model is structural and strategic. It is concerned with identifying and changing maladaptive family interactions and promoting adaptive interactions within the family, as well as between the family and their social context. The model focuses on process rather than content. Whether the content is which football game to watch or who will take in Aunt Susie's youngest child, the model focuses on the nature of the interactions and not on their content.

If the family constellation is incomplete, the clinician may see incomplete or inaccurate interactions, especially in African American families, in which there is often a reluctance to involve family members with whom there are conflictive relationships. Therefore, it is important to ensure that all key people who contribute to the interactions are involved in both the assessment and intervention.

Research Issues

There is also a need for accurate assessment of the family for research purposes. Clinical and policy decisions are often based on research findings. Inaccurate assessment of the family constellation misrepresents the true nature of the family. There are also implications for generalizability. It is likely that certain interventions work better with certain kinds of family constellations than others. For that reason, it is important to accurately characterize the family constellation(s) within each study.

SOCIAL SUPPORT AND AFRICAN AMERICAN FAMILIES

As noted earlier, the African American family (such as the case of the Collins family) is often able to draw on the support of nuclear, extended, and nonbiological kin to assist in coping with stressful conditions. Several studies have documented the effectiveness of kin and nonkin support networks in African American families. For example, Lewis (1988) found that African American mothers of minor-aged children who frequently used extended kin networks or who had a supportive partner were less likely to report parental role strain than mothers without these supports.

D. R. Brown and Gary (1987) found that African American women with low perceived social support tended to have greater emotional distress irrespective of their stressful life events. In fact, the number of relatives who lived nearby was significantly related to a reduced level of emotional distress.

R. D. Taylor, Casten, and Flickinger (1993) found a positive association of kinship support with adolescent adjustment and more adequate parenting experiences in a sample of 125 African American adolescents from one- and two-parent homes. Single-parented adolescents reported that with more kinship support, their parents were more warm and accepting and more active in monitoring their behavior. These findings underscore the importance of social support in coping with a stressful life condition, the unique way women use support, and the importance of the family as a source of support.

FAMILY HASSLES AND FAMILY CONFLICT

Intense and intimate as are family relationships, they can be a source of support as well as a source of conflict. Among our HIV-seropositive mothers, we found that increased family hassles were related to an inappropriate family developmental level, in that families that were not adequately addressing the demands of their unique developmental stage also tended to report many family-related hassles.[1] Not surprisingly, families in which independent raters observed a high number of conflicts reported a high number of family hassles. Moreover, in families with poor conflict-resolution skills, seropositive mothers were less satisfied with their social support. This suggests that HIV-seropositive women may be cut off from an important source of support in their life, that is, their family, if the families are developmentally inadequate, have a high number of conflicts, report family-related hassles, or have difficulty resolving conflict in adaptive ways. In the Collins family, although Donna is supportive of Lynn, there have been reports of conflict over Donna's tendency to "overcontrol" Lynn's behavior at times. Lynn sometimes feels infantilized by Donna's overinvolvement in her life. Further research should explore if these variables—developmental level, number of conflicts, conflict-resolution skills, and reported hassles—covary in ways that suggest a syndrome of family problem behaviors in some families.

Clearly, African American women with HIV face many personal, family, and environmental challenges. Some of the problems they report, for example, lack of financial resources, family hassles, and a nonsupportive environment, may be amenable to treatment. Given the multidimensionality of their problems, however, an intervention that addresses the environmental, familial, and intrapersonal contexts of the women is indicated.

---

[1]By *development level* (see Szapocznik et al., 1991), we mean the appropriateness of the behaviors of each family member given their role and age (e.g., a parentified child who has too much responsibility, or a parent who fails to guide and assumes too little responsibility).

STRUCTURAL ECOSYSTEMS THERAPY

Structural ecosystems therapy (SET) is based on a systems approach pioneered by Szapocznik and colleagues in work with inner-city families (Kurtines & Szapocznik, 1996; Szapocznik, 1995; Szapocznik et al., in press). Structural-ecosystems-therapy targets interactions at the interface between the intrapersonal, familial, and environmental dimensions. It is designed to foster a sense of empowerment in the family as they learn to better negotiate their environment and to increase positive, supportive interactions among the woman and her family.

HIV-seropositive women and their families face numerous challenges: the HIV infection of the woman (about which the family may or may not be aware), environmental stresses and strains, family hassles, and problems in resolving family conflicts, among others. At the same time, many of these women and their families have important strengths: the flexible definition of family, which can serve to broaden the family's base of support, and a strong religious ethos. Based on our many years of experience with African American families at the Center for Family Studies, we believe that the necessary ingredients for an intervention to be successful with this population must address the challenges these women and their families face on many different levels.

The socioecological model on which SET is built is essentially an empowerment model. The therapist who works with the woman and her family seeks to teach them how to better negotiate their environment and how to better communicate and interact with each other. From our systems perspective, we believe that an ecological, structural model, which focuses on strengthening interactions, will result in improvements not only in family functioning but in intrapersonal functioning as well.

The goals of SET are as follows: (a) to identify patterns of interactions, (b) to strengthen supportive interactions, (c) to correct problematic interactions, and (d) to support the family in learning to better negotiate its environment. Just as we found problems in all three areas of context of the women—intrapersonal, (e.g., distress); familial (e.g., family conflicts and hassles); and environmental (e.g., financial need and poor neighborhoods)—SET addresses all three, in particular, the interface among them. The SET therapist identifies both supportive and problematic interactions in the family. Using a systems perspective, the therapist assesses how these interactions impact the family system in positive or negative ways. The therapist is very directive, yet diplomatic and strategic, in reinforcing supportive interactions and restructuring problematic interactions. For example, in the case of Donna's overinvolvement in Lynn's life, the SET therapist might reframe Donna's actions as expressions of her love and concern, thereby creating the opportunity for Donna to "express her love" in other ways. She might also recharacterize

Lynn's frustration as her desire to prove to her mother how well she has learned from her, thereby creating the opportunity for Lynn to explore, within a very positive frame, the possibility that Donna might step aside and allow Lynn to parent without interference.

In addition to identifying, supporting, and correcting family interactions, the SET therapist also identifies environmental stresses that negatively impact the family, as well as environmental supports that may serve to buffer some of the stress of the family. The therapist will help clarify the needs and aspirations of the family in improving their ability to cope with their environment. For example, Lynn has expressed a desire to enroll in school. The SET therapist might work alongside Lynn in identifying a potential area of study, identifying an appropriate school, and assisting in the enrollment process, as needed. The level of assistance will vary from individual to individual and family to family. Some people may require little more than information and supportive advice, whereas others may require assistance with filling out applications, making telephone calls, applying for financial aid, and so on. The SET therapist does whatever it takes to help the family to achieve its goals of improved family interaction and improved environmental negotiation.

CONCLUSION

The well-being of the woman with HIV or AIDS and her surviving children is often intimately tied to the well-being of her family. Families that are supportive and nurturing can provide both the woman and her children an atmosphere of acceptance that facilitates the personal growth and development of its members. We believe the SET approach to addressing the multifaceted context of African American, HIV-seropositive women and their families can offer viable alternatives to the environmental and familial stress that is far too common. It is our belief that interventions that are ecological and family based (e.g., SET) can help provide better family and environmental circumstances for HIV-affected women and children.

REFERENCES

Billingsley, A. (1968). *Black families in White America*. Englewood Cliffs, NJ: Prentice Hall.

Boyd-Franklin, N. (1989). *Black families in therapy: A multisystems approach*. New York: Guilford Press.

Boyd-Franklin, N., Aleman, J., Jean-Gilles, M., & Lewis, S. (1995). Cultural competency model: African American, Latino and Haitian families with pediatric HIV/AIDS. In N. Boyd-Franklin, G. Steiner, & M. Boland (Eds.), Children, families and AIDS/HIV: Psychosocial and psychotherapeutic issues (pp. 53–77). New York: Guilford Press.

Brown, D. R., & Gary, L. E. (1987, Winter). Stressful life events, social support networks, and the physical and mental health of urban Black adults. Journal of Human Stress, 165–174.

Brown, G. W., Craig, T. K., & Harris, T. O. (1985). Depression: Distress or disease? Some epidemiological considerations. British Journal of Psychiatry, 147, 612–622.

Centers for Disease Control and Prevention. (1995). HIV/AIDS Surveillance Report, 7(1), p. 18.

Chatters, L. M., Taylor, R. J., & Jackson, J. S. (1985). Size and composition of the informal helper networks of elderly Blacks. Journal of Gerontology, 40, 605–614.

Department of Health and Rehabilitative Services. (1995). HIV–AIDS reporting systems (HARS). State of Florida, Dade County Department of Public Health. HRS State Health Office, 1317 Winewood Blvd., Tallahassee, FL 32399-0700.

Griffith, E. E., Young, J. L., & Smith, D. L. (1984). An analysis of the therapeutic elements in a Black church service. Hospital and Community Psychiatry, 35, 464–469.

Hill, R. (1977). Informal adoption among Black families. Washington, DC: National Urban League Research Department.

Hines, P. M., & Boyd-Franklin, N. (1982). Black families. In M. McGoldrick, J. K. Pearce, & J. Giordano (Eds.), Ethnicity and family therapy (pp. 84–107). New York: Guilford Press.

Krause, N. (1986). Life stress as a correlate of depression among older adults. Psychiatry Research, 18, 227–237.

Kurtines, W. M., & Szapocznik, J. (1996). Structural family therapy in contexts of cultural diversity. In E. Hibbs & R. Jensen (Eds.), Psychosocial treatment research with children and adolescents. Washington, DC: American Psychological Association.

Landau-Stanton, J., Clements, C. D, & Stanton, M. D. (1993). Psychotherapeutic intervention: From individual through group to extended network. In J. Landau-Stanton & C. D. Clements (Eds.), AIDS, health, and mental health (pp. 214–266). New York: Brunner/Mazel.

Lazarus, R. S., & Folkman, S. (1984). Stress, appraisal, and coping. New York: Springer.

Lewis, E. (1988). Role strengths and gender role attitude among teenage mothers. Adolescence, 25, 709–716.

McLanahan, S. S. (1983). Family structure and stress: A longitudinal comparison of two-parent and female-headed families. Journal of Marriage and the Family, 45, 347–357.

Ogbu, J. U. (1981). Origins of human competence: A cultural–ecological perspective. *Child Development, 52,* 413–429.

Pierce, C. B. (1974). *All our kin: Strategies for Survival in a Black Community.* New York: Harper & Row.

Shelton, D., Greenwood, D., & Szapocznik, J. (in press). Family systems therapy with African American families coping with HIV/AIDS. In E. H. Johnson, H. Amaro, M. Antoni, J. Jemmott, & J. Szapocznik (Eds.), *AIDS in African Americans and Hispanics: The role of behavioral and psychosocial factors.* New York: Praeger.

Sherbourne, C. D. (1988). The role of social support and life stress events in the use of mental health services. *Social Science and Medicine, 27,* 1393–1400.

Smith, E. M. (1985). Ethnic minorities: Life stress, social support, and mental health issues. *Counseling Psychologist, 13,* 537–579.

Szapocznik, J. (1995). Research on disclosure of HIV status: Cultural evolution finds an ally in science. *Health Psychology, 14*(1), 4–5.

Szapocznik, J. (Ed.). (1996). *Structural ecosystems: Theory and practice.* Manuscript in preparation, University of Miami, Miami, FL.

Szapocznik, J., & Kurtines, W. M. (1993). Family psychology and cultural diversity: Opportunities for theory, research, and application. *American Psychologist, 48,* 400–407.

Szapocznik, J., Kurtines, W., Santisteban, D. A., Pantin, H., Scopetta, M., Mancilla, Y., Aisenberg, S., McIntosh, S., & Coatsworth, J. D. (in press). The evolution of a multisystemic structural approach for working with Hispanic families in culturally pluralistic contexts. In J. Garcia & M. C. Zea (Eds.), *Handbook of Latino psychology.* Needham Heights, MA: Allyn & Bacon.

Szapocznik, J., Rio, A. T., Hervis, O. E., Mitrani, V. B., Kurtines, W., & Faraci, A. M. (1991). Assessing change in family functioning as a result of treatment: The Structural Family Systems Rating Scale (SFSR). *Journal of Marital and Family Therapy, 17,* 295–310.

Taylor, R. D., Casten, R., & Flickinger, S. (1993). Influence of kinship social support on the parenting experiences and psychosocial adjustment of African-American adolescents. *Developmental Psychology, 29,* 382–388.

Taylor, R. J. (1985). The extended family as a source of support to elderly Blacks. *The Gerontologist, 25,* 488–495.

Taylor, R. J., & Chatters, L. M. (1986). Church-based informal support among elderly Blacks. *The Gerontologist, 26,* 637–642.

Walker, G. (1991). *In the midst of winter.* New York: Norton.

23

REVOLUTION IN HEALTH PROMOTION: SMOKING CESSATION AS A CASE STUDY

JAMES O. PROCHASKA

Health care costs in the United States total $1 trillion. Pharmaceuticals account for 7% of that total. Behavior accounts for 60%. With the way behavioral health is currently practiced, however, it impacts on only a small percentage of those costs. So there are huge unmet needs and great opportunities, but only if psychologists revolutionize the way they do science and the way they apply our science.

Smoking is an excellent case study, because it is so costly to individual smokers and to society. In the United States, approximately 47 million Americans continue to smoke. Over 400,000 preventable deaths per year are attributable to smoking (U.S. Department of Health and Human Services, 1990). Globally, the problem promises to be catastrophic. Of the people alive in the world today, 500 million are expected to die from

The research cited in this article was supported by National Cancer Institute Grants CA 27821, CA 50087, and CA 63745.

this single behavior, losing approximately 5 billion years of life to tobacco use (Peto & Lopez, 1990). If even modest gains could be made in behavioral science and the practice of smoking cessation, millions of premature deaths could be prevented, and billions of years of life could be preserved. Unfortunately, most smoking cessation programs have had little impact in reducing overall levels of smokers. This failure may be due to these programs' focus on achieving a specific outcome without reference to the larger process of how people come to stop a harmful, but engrained, behavior. This chapter describes a stage paradigm of smoking cessation and outlines how it can be integrated into sucessful interventions.

THE EFFICACY OF SMOKING CESSATION PROGRAMS

Currently, smoking cessation clinics have little impact. When offered for free by health maintenance organizations in the United States, such clinics recruit only about 1% of subscribers who smoke (Lichtenstein & Hollis, 1992). Such behavioral health services simply cannot make much difference if they treat such a small percentage of the problem.

Startled by such statistics, behavioral scientists took health-promotion programs into communities and work sites. The results are now being reported, and in the largest trials ever attempted, the outcomes are discouraging. In the Minnesota Heart Health project, for example, $40 million was spent with 5 years of intervention in four communities totaling 400,000 people. However, there were no significant differences between treatment and control communities on smoking, diet, cholesterol, weight, blood pressure, and overall risks for cardiovascular disease (Luepker et al., 1994).

What went wrong? The investigators speculate that they may have diluted their programs by targeting multiple behaviors. But the Community Intervention Trial for Smoking Cessation (COMMIT Research Group, 1995) had no effects with its primary target of heavy smokers and only a small effect with light smokers. Similarly, the largest work site cessation program produced no significant effects (Glasgow, Terborg, Hollis, Severson, & Boles, 1995).

A closer look at participation rates can probably account for the dismal results. In the Minnesota study, nearly 90% of smokers in both the treatment and control communities had processed media information about smoking in the past year (Lando et al., 1995). However, only about 10% had physicians intervene, and only about 3% participated in the most powerful behavioral programs, such as individualized and interactive clinics, classes, and contests. Behavioral scientists cannot have much impact on the health of our communities if they interact only with a small percentage of populations at high risk for disease and early death.

A NEW VISION FOR INTERVENTION STRATEGIES

There is an old interventionist rule that reads, if we don't like how our clients or our communities are acting, we need to change our behavior. Behavioral scientists cannot continue to offer only action-oriented cessation programs and expect the results to be better. A shift needs to be made, from an *action* paradigm to a *stage* paradigm, if psychologists are to interact with a much higher percentage of populations at risk. An action paradigm focuses on achieving a specific behavioral change, such as smoking cessation. The stage paradigm, however, construes behavior change as a process involving progress through six stages: precontemplation, contemplation, preparation, action, maintenance, and termination. Action is seen as one of the six stages, and it becomes integrated as part of the process of individual, community, or population change.

Precontemplation is the stage in which people are not intending to take action in the foreseeable future, usually measured as the next 6 months. People in this stage are often defensive and resistant, particularly against programs and persuasions designed to have them take action. They can also be demoralized by previous failures, and as a result, they tend to avoid reading, viewing, listening, or talking about their unhealthy habits. They certainly are not ready to enroll in action-oriented programs. Historically, psychologists labeled such individuals as *unmotivated, resistant,* or *not ready for therapy.* The reality is that psychologists were not ready for them, and were not motivated to match their needs. Without planned interventions, people in precontemplation can remain stuck in this stage for years.

In the contemplation stage, individuals are intending to take action in the next 6 months. They are more aware of the benefits of changing, but they are also acutely aware that change costs. The profound ambivalence they often experience can keep them contemplating for years. Chronic contemplators tend to substitute thinking for acting. In one sample, we found that less than 50% quit smoking for 24 hours over 12 months, even though all had initially intended to quit smoking for good in the next 6 months (Prochaska, DiClemente, Velicer & Rossi, 1993).

In the preparation stage, people are ready to participate in action-oriented interventions, because they are intending to take action in the next month and have taken some action in the past 12 months. They are more convinced that the pros outweigh the cons of quitting smoking, for example. These are the more motivated members of a population, though psychologists prefer the concept of preparation over motivation.

TABLE 1
Distribution of Smokers by Stage Across Four Different Samples

Sample	n	Stage		
		Precontemplation	Contemplation	Preparation
Random digit dial	4,144	42.1%	40.3%	17.6%
4 US work sites	4,785	41.1%	38.7%	20.1%
California	9,534	37.3%	46.7%	16.0%
RI high schools	208	43.8%	38.0%	18.3%

Note. RI = Rhode Island.

People often perceive motivation as something that happens to them, like hitting bottom, whereas preparation is perceived as more under personal control.

Action involves overt behavioral modification, such as stopping smoking, and is one of the reasons that change has been equated with action. Action is the stage in which people work the hardest, applying the most processes of change most frequently. In our research, we found that people have to work hard for about 6 months before they can ease up (Prochaska & DiClemente, 1983). One problem is that the public expects the worst to be over in a few weeks or a few months and ease their efforts too quickly. Such poor preparation is one of the reasons so many people relapse so quickly.

After about 6 months of concentrated action, people enter the maintenance stage. They continue to apply particular processes of change, but they do not have to work nearly as hard to prevent relapse. During maintenance, the most common risks for relapse are times of emotional distress, such as anger, anxiety, boredom, depression, and stress. People need to be adequately prepared to cope with such distress without resorting back to their unhealthy habits.

How long does the maintenance stage last? For some, it is a lifetime of maintenance. Others can totally terminate their unhealthy habits and experience zero temptations across all high-risk situations, with 100% confidence that they will never again resort back to their unhealthy habits.

INTEGRATING THE STAGE PARADIGM INTO PLANNED INTERVENTIONS

Let us examine how this stage paradigm can be applied to five of the most important phases of planned interventions.

Recruitment

Recall that action oriented cessation programs fail in this first phase of intervention. Table 1 reports results that can help explain such failures.

Across four different samples, it can be seen that 20% or less of smokers are in the preparation stage (Velicer et al., 1995). When action-oriented programs are advertised or announced, they explicitly or implicitly target less than 20% of a population. The other 80% plus are left on their own.

In one of the Minnesota Heart Health studies, smokers were randomly assigned to one of three recruitment methods for home-based cessation programs (Schmid, Jeffrey, & Hellerstedt, 1989). These announcements generated 1% to 5% participation rates, with a personalized letter doing the best.

In two home-based programs, with 5,000 smokers in each study, we reached out, either by telephone alone or by personal letters followed by telephone calls if needed, and recruited smokers to stage-matched interventions. Using these proactive recruitment methods and stage-matched interventions, we were able to generate participation rates of 82% to 85%, respectively (Prochaska, Velicer, Fava, & Laforge, 1995; Prochaska, Velicer, Fava, & Rossi, 1995). Such quantum increases in participation rates provide the potential to generate unprecedented impacts with entire populations of smokers.

Impact equals participation rate times efficacy or action. If a program produced 30% efficacy (such as long-term abstinence), historically it was judged to be better than a program that produced 25% abstinence. But a program that generates 30% efficacy but only 5% participation has an impact of only 1.5% (30% × 5%). A program that produces only 25% efficacy but 60% participation has an impact of 15%. With health-promotion programs, this would be a 1,000% greater impact on a high-risk population.

The stage paradigm would have us shift our outcomes from efficacy to impacts. To achieve such high impacts, psychologists need to shift from reactive recruitment, in which they advertise or announce their programs and react when people reach them, to proactive recruitments, in which they reach out to interact with all potential participants.

Proactive recruitment alone will not work. In the most intensive recruitment protocol to date, Lichtenstein and Hollis (1992) had physicians spend up to 5 minutes with each smoker, just to get them to sign up for an action-oriented cessation clinic. If that did not work, a nurse spent 10 minutes to persuade each smoker to sign up, followed by 12 minutes with a videotape and health educator and even a proactive counselor call, if necessary. The base rate was 1% participation. This proactive protocol resulted in 35% of smokers in precontemplation signing up. But only 3% showed up, and 2% finished up, and 0 ended up better off. With a combination of smokers in contemplation and preparation, 65% signed up, 15% showed up, 11% finished up, and some percentage ended up better off. To optimize impacts, behavioral scientists

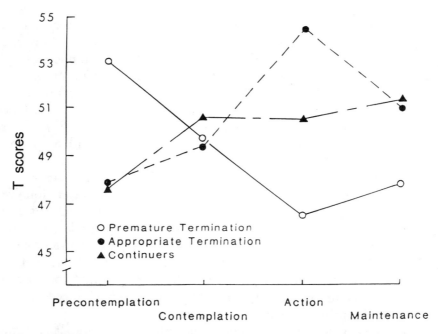

Figure 1. Pretherapy stage profiles for premature terminators, appropriate terminators, and continuers.

need to use proactive protocols to recruit participants to programs that match their stage.

RETENTION

One of the skeletons in the closet of psychotherapy and behavioral change interventions is their relatively poor retention rates. Across 125 studies, the average retention rate was only about 50% (Wierzbicki & Pekarik, 1993). Furthermore, this meta-analysis found few consistent predictors of which participants would drop out prematurely and which would continue in therapy. In studies on smoking, weight control, substance abuse, and a mixture of disorders (as listed in the *Diagnostic and Statistical Manual of Mental Disorders*; American Psychiatric Association, 1994) stage-of-change measures proved to be the best predictors of premature termination. Figure 1 contains the stage profile of three groups of psychotherapy participants: the pre-treatment-stage profile of the entire 40% who dropped out prematurely, as judged by their therapists, was that of patients in precontemplation. The 20% who terminated quickly but appropriately had a profile of patients in action. Using pre-treatment-stage-related measures, we were able to correctly classify 93% of the three groups (Medeiros & Prochaska, 1995).

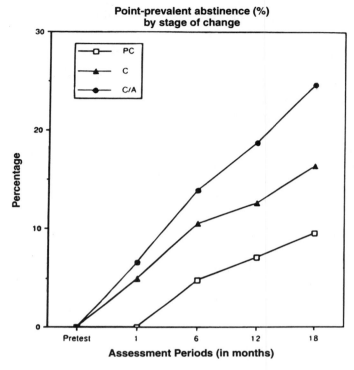

Figure 2. Percentage abstinent over 18 months for smokers in precontemplation (PC), contemplation (C), and preparation (C/A) stages before treatment (*N* = 570).

We simply cannot treat people with a precontemplation profile as if they were ready for action interventions and expect them to stay with us. Relapse-prevention strategies would be indicated with addicted clients who are taking action. But those in precontemplation are likely to need drop out-prevention strategies.

The best strategy we have found to promote retention is matching our interventions to stage of change. In four smoking cessation studies using such matching strategies, we found we were able to retain smokers in the precontemplation stage at the same high levels as those who started in precontemplation (Prochaska, 1994a).

Progress

The amount of progress participants make following health-promotion programs is directly related to the stage they were in at the start of the interventions. This *stage effect* is illustrated in Figure 2, where smokers initially in precontemplation show the smallest amount of abstinence over 18 months and those in preparation progress the most (Prochaska, DiClemente, & Norcross, 1992). Across 66 different predictions of progress, we found that smokers starting in contemplation were about two thirds more successful than those in precontemplation at 6-, 12-, and 18-month follow-ups. Similarly, those in preparation were about two thirds more successful then those in contemplation at the same follow-ups (Prochaska, Velicer, Fava, Rossi, & Laforge, 1995).

These results can be used clinically. A reasonable goal for each therapeutic intervention with smokers is to help them progress one stage. If over the course of brief therapy, they progress two stages, they will be about 2 2/3 times more successful at longer term follow-ups.

This strategy is being taught to nurses and physicians' assistants in Britain's National Health Care System. One of the first reports is a marked improvement in the morale of such health promoters intervening with all patients who smoke, abuse substances, and have unhealthy diets (Burton, L., personal communication, February 1996). These professionals now have strategies that match the needs of all of their patients, not just the minority prepared to take action. Furthermore, these professionals can see the majority progressing, where previously they saw most failing, when action was the only measure of movement.

Process

To help populations progress through the stages, we need to understand the processes and principles of change. One of the fundamental principles for progress is that different processes of change need to be applied at different stages of change. Classic conditioning processes, such as counterconditioning, stimulus control, and contingency control, can be highly successful for participants taking action but can produce resistance with individuals in precontemplation. With these individuals, more experiential processes, such as consciousness raising and dramatic relief, can move people cognitively and affectively and help them shift to contemplation (Prochaska, Norcross, & DiClemente, 1994).

We have reported in detail which processes are best matched to each stage (Prochaska, Norcross, & DiClemente, 1994). Space limitations will permit only a couple of examples of progress principles. Figure 3 contains the pros and cons of changing, across the stages of change, for 12 different behaviors from 10 different populations (Prochaska, Velicer, et al., 1994).

There are some remarkable consistencies across 12 diverse behaviors. With all 12, the cons of changing are evaluated as greater than the pros, by people in precontemplation. No wonder they are not intending to change. But this is not necessarily a rational or conscious process. With smokers in precontemplation, for example, their raw scores on the pros of quitting will usually be higher than their cons. It is only when we transform raw scores into standardized scores (as we do on the Minnesota

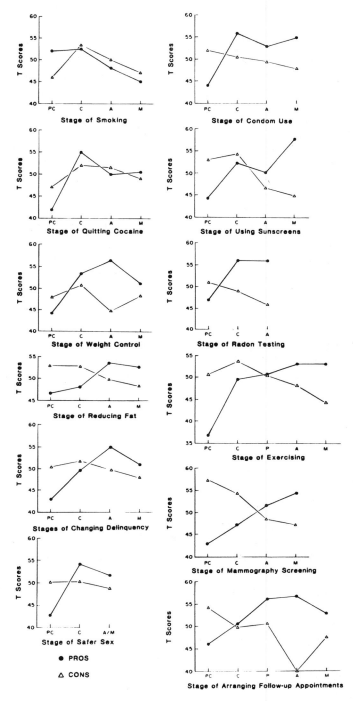

Figure 3. The pros and cons (in T scores) by stages of change for each of 12 problem behaviors. PC = precontemplation; C = contemplation; P = preparation; A = action; M = maintenance.

Multiphasic Personality Inventory or Wechsler Adult Intelligence Scale) that we see the clear pattern of cons greater than pros. Compared with smokers in other stages, those in precontemplation are underestimating the pros of quitting, overestimating the cons, and probably are not conscious of the process. No wonder we need to apply consciousness-raising techniques, such as feedback, to help them progress.

With all 12 problems, the pros are higher in contemplation than precontemplation, but there is no consistent pattern with the cons. With some behaviors, the cons of change increase as people begin to seriously think about taking action. So, one principle of progress is that the pros of changing must increase for people to move from precontemplation to contemplation.

With all 12 problems, the cons are lower in action than in contemplation. A second principle of progress, then, is that the cons of changing must decline as people move from contemplation to action.

We can be even more mathematical. Across all 12 behaviors, we discovered a strong principle of progress:

$$PC \rightarrow A \cong 1 \; SD \uparrow Pros.$$

To progress from precontemplation to action, the pros of changing increase approximately 1 standard deviation (Prochaska, 1994b).

We also discovered a weak principle:

$$PC \rightarrow A \cong 0.5 \; SD \downarrow Cons.$$

To progress from precontemplation to action, the cons of changing must decrease 0.5 standard deviation. One application of these principles would be to place twice as much emphasis on increasing the appreciation of the pros of changing than on decreasing the cons.

After 15 years of research, we have identified 14 variables that we intervene with, to accelerate progress across the first five stages of change (Prochaska, Norcross, & DiClemente, 1994). At any particular stage, we need to intervene with only a maximum of six variables. To help guide individuals at each stage of change, we have developed computer-based expert systems that can deliver individualized and interactive interventions to entire populations. These computer programs can be used alone or in conjunction with counselors.

Outcomes

In our first large-scale clinical trial, we compared four treatments: (a) one of the best home-based action-oriented cessation programs (standardized), (b) stage-matched manuals (individualized), (c) expert-system computer reports plus manuals (interactive), and (d) personalized counselors plus computers and manuals (personalized).

We randomly assigned by stage 756 smokers to one of the four treatments (Prochaska, DiClemente, Velicer, & Rossi, 1993). Note that we did not test our new treatments against placebo or no treatment controls. In our research, we test our hypotheses against the riskiest tests we can devise. That way, if our new treatments outperform one of the best tests available, then we can be more confident that we have something worth writing about, than if we outperform placebos or controls.

In the computer condition, participants completed, by mail or telephone, 40 questions, which were entered in our central computers and which generated feedback reports. These reports informed participants about their stage of change, their pros and cons of changing, and their use of change processes appropriate to their stages. At baseline, participants were given positive feedback on what they were doing correctly and guidance on which principles and processes they needed to apply more, to progress. In two progress reports, delivered over the next 6 months, participants also received positive feedback on any improvement they made on any of the variables relevant to progressing. Thus, demoralized and defensive smokers could begin progressing without having to quit and without having to work hard. Smokers in the contemplation stage could begin taking small steps, such as delaying their first cigarette in the morning for an extra 30 minutes. They could choose small steps that would increase their self-efficacy and help them become better prepared for quitting.

In the personalized condition, smokers received four proactive counselor calls over the 6-month intervention period. Three of the calls were based on the computer reports. Counselors reported much more difficulty in interacting with participants without any progress data. Without scientific assessments, it was much harder for both clients and counselors to tell whether any significant progress had occurred since their last interaction.

Figure 4 contains point-prevalence abstinence rates for each of the four treatment groups over 18 months, with treatment ending at 6 months (Prochaska et al., 1993). The two self-help-manual conditions paralleled each other for 12 months. At 18 months, the stage-matched-manual participants moved ahead. This is an example of a *delayed-action effect*, which we often observe with stage-matched programs. It takes time for participants in early stages to progress all the way to action. Therefore, some treatment effects, as measured by action, will be observed only after considerable delay. Nonetheless, it is encouraging to find treatments producing therapeutic effects even months and years after termination.

The computer-alone and personalized counselor conditions paralleled each other for 12 months. Then, the effects of the personalized

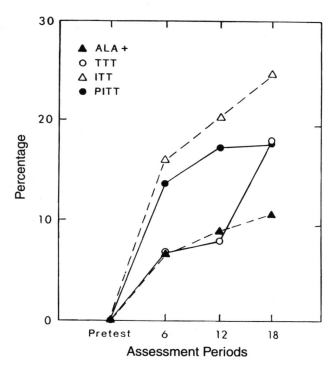

Figure 4. Point-prevalence abstinence (%) for four treatment groups at pretest and at 6, 12, and 18 months. ALA + = standardized manuals; TTT = individualized stage-matched manuals; ITT = interactive computer reports; PITT = personalized counselor calls.

counselor condition flattened out while the interactive computer condition effects continued to increase. We can only speculate as to the delayed differences between these two conditions. Participants in the personalized condition may have become somewhat dependent on the social support and social control of the counselor calling. The last call was after the 6-month assessment, and benefits would be observed at 12 months. Termination of the counselors could result in no further progress because of the loss of social support and control. The classic pattern in smoking cessation clinics is rapid relapse beginning as soon as the treatment is terminated. Some of this rapid relapse could well be due to the sudden loss of social support or social control provided by the counselors and other participants in the clinic.

In this clinical trial, smokers were recruited reactively. They called us in response to advertisements, announcements, and articles. How would their results compare with the smokers that we called to proactively recruit to our programs? Most people would predict that smokers who called us for help would succeed more than smokers who we called to help.

Figure 5 shows the remarkable results of comparing smokers in a study who called us (reactive; Prochaska et al., 1993) to those in a study

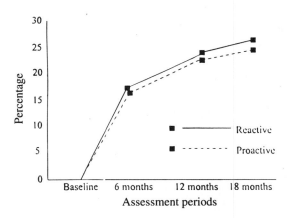

Figure 5. Point-prevalence abstinence rates for smokers recruitment by reactive versus proactive strategies and treated by stage-matched, home-based, expert-system computer reports.

that we called (proactive; Prochaska, Velicer, Fava, & Laforge, 1995). Both groups received the same home-based expert-system computer reports delivered over a 6-month period. Although the reactively recruited participants were slightly more successful at each follow-up, what is striking is how similar are the results.

CONCLUSION

If these results continue to be replicated, health-promotion programs will be able to produce unprecedented impacts on entire populations. We believe that such unprecedented impacts require scientific and professional shifts: (a) from an action paradigm to a stage paradigm, (b) from reactive to proactive recruitment, (c) from expecting participants to match the needs of our programs to having our programs match their needs, and (d) from clinic-based to community-based behavioral health programs that still apply the field's most powerful individualized and interactive intervention strategies.

With this type of revolution in health promotion, psychology and other health sciences and professions will be able to respond to the huge, unmet needs and the great opportunities related to the prevention of chronic diseases and premature death.

REFERENCES

American Psychiatric Association. (1994). *Diagnostic and statistical manual of mental disorders* (4th ed.). Washington, DC: Author.

COMMIT Research Group. (1995). Community Intervention Trial for Smoking Cessation (COMMIT): I. Cohort results from a four-year community intervention. *American Journal of Public Health, 85,* 183–192.

Glasgow, R. E., Terborg, J. R., Hollis, J. F., Severson, H. H., & Boles, S. M. (1995). Take heart: Results from the initial phase of a work-site wellness program. *American Journal of Public Health, 85,* 209–216.

Lando, H. A., Pechacek, T. F., Pirie, P. L., Murray, D. M., Mittelmark, M. B., Lichtenstein, E., Nothwehyr, F., & Gray, C. (1995). Changes in adult cigarette smoking in the Minnesota Heart Health Program. *American Journal of Public Health, 85,* 201–208.

Lichtenstein, E., & Hollis, J. (1992). Patient referral to smoking cessation programs: Who follows through? *The Journal of Family Practice, 34,* 739–744.

Luepker, R. V., Murray, D. M., Jacobs, D. R., Jr., Mittelmark, M. B., Bracht, N., Carlaw, R., Crow, R., Elmer, P., Finnegan, J., Folsom, A. R., Grimm, R., Hannan, P. J., Jeffrey, R., Lando, H., McGovern, P., Mullis, R., Perry, C. L., Pechacek, T., Pirie, P., Sprafka, J. M., Weisbrod, R., & Blackburn, H. (1994). Community education for cardiovascular disease prevention: Risk factor changes in the Minnesota Heart Health Program. *American Journal of Public Health, 84,* 1383–1393.

Medeiros, M. E., & Prochaska, J. O. (1995). *Predicting termination and continuation status in psychotherapy using the transtheoretical model.* Manuscript submitted for publication.

Peto, R., & Lopez, A. (1990). World-wide mortality from current smoking patterns. In B. Durstone & K. Jamrogik (Eds.), *The global war: Proceedings of the Seventh World Conference on Tobacco and Health* (pp. 62–68). East Perth, Western Australia: Organizing Committee of Seventh World Conference on Tobacco and Health.

Prochaska, J. O. (1994a, April). *Staging: A revolution.* Master science lecture presented at the annual meeting of the *Society for Behavioral Medicine,* Boston.

Prochaska, J. O. (1994b). Strong and weak principles for progressing from precontemplation to action based on twelve problem behaviors. *Health Psychology, 13,* 47–51.

Prochaska, J. O., & DiClemente, C. C. (1983). Stages and processes of self-change of smoking: Toward an integrative model of change. *Journal of Consulting and Clinical Psychology, 51,* 390–395.

Prochaska, J. O., DiClemente, C. C., & Norcross, J. C. (1992). In search of how people change: Applications to the addictive behaviors. *American Psychologist, 47,* 1102–1114.

Prochaska, J. O., DiClemente, C. C., Velicer, W. F., & Rossi, J. S. (1993). Standardized, individualized, interactive, and personalized self-help programs for smoking cessation. *Health Psychology, 12,* 399–405.

Prochaska, J. O., Norcross, J. C., & DiClemente, C. C. (1994). *Changing for good.* New York: Morrow.

Prochaska, J. O., Velicer, W. F., Fava, J., & Laforge, R. (1995). *Toward disease-state management for smoking: Stage-matched expert systems for a total managed care population of smokers.* Manuscript submitted for publication.

Prochaska, J. O., Velicer, W. F., Fava, J., & Rossi, J. (1995). *A stage-matched expert-system intervention with a total population of smokers.* Manuscript submitted for publication.

Prochaska, J. O., Velicer, W. F., Fava, J., Rossi, J., & Laforge, R. (1995). *Stage, interactive, dose-response, counseling, and stimulus-control computer effects in a total managed care population of smokers.* Manuscript submitted for publication.

Prochaska, J. O., Velicer, W. F., Rossi, J. S., Goldstein, M. G., Marcus, B. H., Rakowski, W., Fiore, C., Harlow, L., Redding, C. A., Rosenbloom, D., & Rossi, S. R. (1994). Stages of change and decisional balance for twelve problem behaviors. *Health Psychology, 13,* 39–46.

Schmid, T. L., Jeffrey, R. W., & Hellerstedt, W. L. (1989). Direct mail recruitment to house-based smoking and weight control programs: A comparison of strengths. *Preventive Medicine, 18,* 503–517.

U.S. Department of Health and Human Services. (1990). *The health benefits of smoking cessation: A report of the surgeon general* (DHHS Publication No. CDC 90–8416). Washington, DC: U.S. Government Printing Office.

Velicer, W. F., Fava, J. L., Prochaska, J. O., Abrams, D. B., Emmons, K. M., & Pierce, J. (1995). Distribution of smokers by stage in three representative samples. *Preventive Medicine, 24,* 401–411.

Wierzbicki, M., & Pekarik, G. (1993). A meta-analysis of psychotherapy dropout. *Professional Psychology: Research and Practice, 29,* 190–195.

24

REDUCING COLLEGE STUDENT BINGE DRINKING: A HARM-REDUCTION APPROACH

G. ALAN MARLATT

How many college students drink, and what are the problems they experience with alcohol? A recent random survey conducted with 1,595 students at the University of Washington (Lowell, 1993) provides illustrative data from a large public West Coast university with a total population of over 35,000 students. More than half the students were light drinkers or nondrinkers, but undergraduates tended to be more extreme in their drinking patterns than graduate students. Although there were more abstainers (28.6%) among undergraduates than graduate students (19.0%), among undergraduates there was a higher proportion (31%) of *binge drinkers* (defined as drinking five or more drinks on a single occasion) than among graduate students (17%). A significant minority of undergraduate students (11.4%) reported drinking more than eight drinks on a single occasion.

This research was supported in part by a Research Scientist Award AA00113 and MERIT Award AA05591.

Binge-drinking rates among undergraduate students may be even higher on other campuses. In one survey of drinking practices among freshman-class students at 14 colleges in Massachusetts, Wechsler and Issac (1992) found that over half the men (56%) and a third of women (35%) reported binge drinking. Over a third of the male and one quarter of the female binge drinkers reported engaging in unplanned sexual activity, compared with only 10% of non-binge drinkers. Binge drinkers were six times as likely to drive after consuming large quantities of alcohol and were twice as likely as non-binge drinkers to ride with an intoxicated driver (Wechsler & Issac, 1992).

National surveys reveal that American college students have a slightly higher annual prevalence of any alcohol use (88%) compared with their age peers who do not attend college (85%), 43% of college students report at least one episode of binge drinking in the past 2 weeks, compared with 34% of their age peers (Johnston, O'Malley, & Bachman, 1992). Other surveys indicate that heavy alcohol use is associated with a wide range of harmful consequences for college students, including school failure, relationship difficulties, vandalism, aggression, and date rape (Berkowitz & Perkins, 1986; Engs & Hanson, 1985). Alcohol-related accidents and injuries are the leading cause of death in this age group (National Institute on Alcohol Abuse and Alcoholism, 1984).

Adolescent drinking patterns change over time (Grant, Harford, & Grigson, 1988). Although drinking rates show a significant increase in the transition from high school to the college freshman year (Baer, Kivlahan, & Marlatt, 1994), heavy drinking declines as students get older and assume increased adult responsibilities (Fillmore, 1988; Jessor, Donovan, & Costa, 1991; Zucker, in press). Although the majority of young adults show this "maturing out" pattern over time, longitudinal studies have shown a continuity of drinking problems for a subset (approximately 30%) of heavy drinkers (Fillmore, 1988; Zucker, in press). Among identified risk factors for continued alcohol problems in this age population, environmental factors, such as residence (Larimer, 1992) and "party" settings (Geller & Kalsher, 1990; Geller, Russ, & Altomari, 1986), along with personal dispositional factors, such as family history of alcoholism (Sher, 1991) and history of conduct disorder (Jessor, 1984), have all been identified in the literature. Our prevention efforts, described below, are designed with these two goals in mind: (a) to reduce the harm of alcohol abuse in adolescents who show a pattern of binge drinking and (b) to prevent the development of alcohol dependence among high-risk drinkers.

BACKGROUND RESEARCH AND PRELIMINARY STUDIES

We developed our first alcohol-harm-reduction programs based on past research conducted in our laboratory on determinants of college student drinking (Marlatt, Baer, & Larimer, 1995). With our background and theoretical orientation in behavioral psychology and social cognitive theory, we were initially interested in psychosocial and environmental influences on drinking in this young population. Over the past 2 decades, our laboratory group conducted a series of studies in which college students consumed alcohol under controlled experimental conditions (Caudill & Marlatt, 1975; Collins & Marlatt, 1981; Collins, Parks, & Marlatt, 1985; Higgins & Marlatt, 1975; Marlatt, 1978; Marlatt, Kosturn, & Lang, 1975).

From these background research studies described above, we developed a cognitive–behavioral harm-reduction program for college student drinkers called the Alcohol Skills-Training Program (ASTP). We then conducted a controlled clinical trial to evaluate the impact of ASTP, presented in the form of an 8-week class (Kivlahan, Marlatt, Fromme, Coppel, & Williams, 1990). The design of this study called for random assignment of student drinkers ($N = 43$) to one of three conditions: the ASTP experimental group, a comparison group called the *Alcohol Information School*, or an assessment-only control group. Students were followed for a period of 1 year; a brief description of the study and the results follows.

Student volunteers were recruited to participate in the study by flyers, campus newspaper advertisements, and class announcements asking for participants who wanted to better understand or to change their drinking patterns. Participants who qualified were paid for their time and effort for participation. To qualify, participants needed to be heavy social drinkers, who reported at least one negative consequence of drinking and who indicated no more than mild physical dependence on the Alcohol Dependence Scale (Skinner & Horn, 1984). The sample of students who completed the study were 58% men and 42% women and averaged 23 years of age. On average, baseline drinking averaged 15 drinks per week, and participants reported, for the prior year, an average of 7.5 occasions of driving after consuming 4 or more drinks.

Students assigned to ASTP completed an 8-week course (each weekly class was 2 hours long). Groups of 8 students were led by male and female co-leaders. Each weekly session focused on a specific topic: (a) models of addiction and effects of drinking, (b) estimation of blood alcohol levels and setting drinking limits, (c) relaxation training and lifestyle balance, (d) nutritional information and aerobic exercise, (e) coping with high-risk drinking situations, (f) assertiveness training and drink-refusal skills, (g) an expectancy challenge, in which students consumed placebo beverages in Behavioral Alcohol Research Laboratory (BARLAB), and (h) relapse-prevention strategies for maintaining drinking-behavior changes. In each class, a cognitive–behavioral psychoeducational model was adopted, with didactic presentations and small-group discussions.

In the Alcohol Information School control condition, students received an 8-week course required by the State of Washington for those convicted of underage possession of alcohol or driving under the influence of alcohol. The program content was purely informational, and no new coping skills were taught. Lecture topics included physical and behavioral effects of alcohol, dispelling myths about alcohol, alcoholism problems, and legal aspects of alcoholism. In the assessment-only control group, students participated in all assessment and follow-up measures but received no prevention program until after the completion of the 1-year follow-up period. This control group provided data to assess the effects of completing the assessment forms and self-monitoring drinking.

The impact of the prevention programs was assessed by student evaluations, self-monitored drinking rates, and estimates of weekly drinking rates. Self-monitored drinking (daily drinking diaries) were scored by computer, to yield standard drinks per week and the peak (maximum) blood alcohol level reached each week. At baseline, before program entry, students reported an average of 15 drinks per week and a peak weekly blood alcohol level of 0.13% (0.10% or above defines legal intoxication in most states). At the 1-year follow-up, ASTP participants reported 6.6 drinks per week and a maximum blood alcohol level of 0.07%, compared with 12.7 drinks per week and a maximum blood alcohol level of 0.09%, for students in the Alcohol Information School and 16.8 drinks per week and 0.11% blood alcohol maximum for assessment-only controls. Measures of self-perceived drinking patterns (in which participants reported their drinking over a 90-day period) showed students in the ASTP to have reduced their drinking significantly more than the other two groups when assessed at the 1-year follow-up.

The results of this preliminary harm-reduction study were encouraging. Students involved in the research project reported that they significantly reduced their drinking, and participants in our ASTP condition showed the greatest changes at each follow-up period. Limitations included the small sample size, the use of only volunteer participants, and the lack of collateral reports to validate self-report measures of drinking (the issue of the validity of self-report and the use of collaterals is discussed further below). In addition, participant recruitment was difficult; as expected, students failed to respond to an invitation to participate in an "alcohol program." Once engaged, however, the evaluation feedback indicated that the ASTP was perceived as just as helpful as typical alcohol-education programs.

The second trial of our alcohol-harm-reduction approach was designed to evaluate the effectiveness of the ASTP program presented in different formats (Baer et al., 1992). Students ($N = 134$) were randomly assigned to one of three conditions: a classroom program (a replication of the ASTP program but reduced to six sessions from the original eight), a "correspondence course" (the ASTP program content presented in a written six-lesson format), and a single session of "professional advice," consisting of individual feedback and advice presented to the student. Although this third condition could be considered a minimal-contact control group, other studies indicated that even a single session of advice or motivational enhancement can have a significant impact on subsequent drinking behavior, even for those with serious alcohol problems (Edwards et al., 1977; Miller & Rollnick, 1991).

Student volunteers were again recruited from the campus population through flyers and newspaper ads, offering participation in a skills-training program to learn more about or change personal drinking patterns. As in the first study, participants were offered monetary compensation for the time and effort involved in participating in a research program with multiple assessment periods. To qualify, students needed to report at least one significant alcohol problem and at least 2 days of drinking on an average week with blood alcohol levels approaching 0.10% or above.

The sample of 134 students who enrolled in the program was slightly younger (average age = 21) than those in the first study. Over half of the sample consisted of women. Drinking patterns included an average of six drinking problems as assessed by the RAPI (Rutgers Alcohol Problem Inventory; White & La Bauvie, 1989); students reported drinking an average of 20 drinks per week spread over four drinking occasions (average drinks per occasion = 5, the lower cutoff for binge-level drinking). Estimated peak blood alcohol levels for weekly drinking averaged 0.14%. Students assigned to the correspondence-course format were least likely to complete the assignment; less than half completed all six assignments. Dropouts were less likely in the classroom-group condition, perhaps because of the peer support available in this format. The classroom condition was rated highest in the evaluation forms.

As in the first study, all students significantly reduced their alcohol consumption during the course of the intervention program. Average drinks per week declined overall from 12.5 to 8.5, and peak blood alcohol levels dropped from 0.14% to 0.10%. Reported reductions in drinking levels were maintained significantly over the 2-year follow-up period. At each assessment, participants in the classroom condition drank the least, although differences between the conditions only approached statistical significance. Note that the single session of professional advice showed results comparable to that of the more extensive prevention programs. On the basis of this finding, we decided to begin with a single session of advice as the first of a series of "stepped-care" options. Our major study investigating the effectiveness of a stepped-care prevention model is described next.

OVERVIEW OF THE LIFESTYLES '94 PROJECT

Rational for Stepped Care and Study Design

The Lifestyles '94 project was designed to replicate and extend our earlier studies of brief, harm-reduction programs with college student heavy drinkers. The Lifestyles '94 study differed in several ways from our earlier studies. First, we did not wish to bias the sample by advertising for volunteers for a research program but rather to apply this prevention to a cross-section of heavy drinkers in the college population. As a result, we screened all students in an entering college class and directly invited the heavier drinkers into a longitudinal study. Second, because we wished to test our interventions in a more preventive context, when students are younger and before problems develop, we focused on the 1st year in college (average age = 19) as the time for intervention (our previous samples were 3–4 years older, on average). Third, we wished to test if our brief, 1-hour feedback interview could be used as the first step in a graded program of interventions.

Our previous success with brief interventions suggested that motivational interventions such as feedback and advice may be sufficient to reduce harm associated with drinking among the college population. However, for those who did not respond, more intensive treatments were available. What is not clear is how to move students into more intensive and focused services. We felt that a brief, nonconfrontational feedback session might be the best first step in gaining rapport and access to students, hence facilitating the use of other, more intensive treatments as needed. Finally, the Lifestyles '94 study included specific research-design improvements (from our earlier studies), including a much larger sample size, longer term (4-year) follow-up, the use of collateral reporters to confirm self-reports of alcohol consumption, and the assessment and analysis of individual differences that might explain differential response to treatment. These individual-difference measures included gender, family history of alcoholism, history of conduct-disordered behavior, and type of student residence.

Procedure

Screening and Recruitment

In the spring of 1990, we mailed a questionnaire to all students who were accepted and had indicated an intention to enroll at the

University of Washington the next autumn term (by sending in $50 deposit), who were matriculating from high school, and who were not over 19 years of age. Each student was offered $5 and entrance into a drawing for prizes, for return of the questionnaires. Of 4,000 questionnaires sent, 2,179 completed forms were returned. Of these 2,179, 2,041 students provided usable questionnaires and indicated a willingness to be contacted for future research.

From the screening pool, a high-risk sample was selected. Students were considered high risk if they reported drinking at least monthly and consuming 5–6 drinks on one drinking occasion in the past month, or if they reported the experience of three alcohol-related problems on three to five occasions in the past 3 years, on the Rutgers Alcohol Problem Inventory (RAPI; White & Labouvie, 1989). These criteria identified approximately 25% of the screening sample ($n = 508$). An additional control sample was randomly selected from the pool of 2,041 responders, to provide a normative comparison group ($n = 151$). Because this sample was selected to represent normative practices, it was not restricted to those not previously screened as high risk. As a result, 33 individuals were selected both as high risk and as representing a normative comparison.

When they arrived on campus, students selected for the study were invited into a 4-year longitudinal study of alcohol use and other lifestyle issues, through a letter. Phone calls were used to ensure the receipt of the letter and to respond to questions. Students were asked to agree to be interviewed for approximately 45 minutes and to fill out questionnaires, for a $25 payment during the autumn academic term. Students in the high-risk group agreed also to be randomly assigned to receive or not receive individualized feedback the next academic quarter. All participants agreed to additional questionnaire assessments annually for payment. Of the 508 high-risk students invited, 366 were successfully recruited for the current study; 115 of 151 randomly selected participants were similarly recruited (26 students were in both groups). Comparisons on screening measures between those participants successfully recruited for the project and those not recruited revealed no significant differences in drinking rates (quantity and frequency), alcohol-related problems (RAPI scores), or gender.

Baseline and Follow-Up Assessments

The initial, or baseline, assessment was used to guide individual feedback sessions for those in the experimental group. The interview protocol was based on three standardized interviews: the Brief Drinker Profile (Miller & Marlatt, 1984); the Family Tree Questionnaire (Mann, Sobell, Sobell, & Pavan, 1985); and the Diagnostic Interview Schedule—

Child, or DIS–C (Helzer & Robins, 1988). From these protocols, we assessed typical drinking quantity and frequency, alcohol-related life problems, history of conduct disorder, *Diagnostic and Statistical Manual of Mental Disorders* (American Psychiatric Association, 1987) alcohol-dependency criteria, and family history of drinking problems and other psychopathology. Interviewers were trained members of our research staff. In addition, students completed questionnaires at baseline that included indexes of the type of living situation; alcohol expectancies; perceived risks; psychiatric symptomatology (assessed by the Brief Symptoms Inventory; Derogatis & Spencer, 1982); perceived norms for alcohol consumption; and sexual behavior.

Students completed follow-up assessments through mailed questionnaires in the spring of the 1st year in college and every autumn thereafter throughout college. At the time of this writing (March 1994), we have analyzed data from the junior-year assessment, 2 years after baseline assessment. Note that the 2-year assessment took place in the junior year for those students who pursued their college education continuously (all participants were followed regardless of enrollment or academic status). At each follow-up assessment, students reported their typical drinking patterns, drinking problems, and alcohol dependency, in addition to measures of alcohol expectancies, life events, and psychiatric symptomatology. Details of these assessments are described below.

Measures

Drinking rates. At all assessments, students used 6-point scales to report their typical drinking quantity, frequency, and the single greatest amount of alcohol consumption (peak consumption) over the past month. A second measure of drinking quantity and frequency was obtained at each follow-up assessment, by means of the Daily Drinking Questionnaire (Collins et al., 1985).

Alcohol-related problems and dependence. Alcohol-related problems were assessed with two different methodologies at each assessment. As a measure of harmful consequences, students completed the RAPI, rating the frequency of occurrence of 23 items reflecting alcohol's impact on social and health functioning over the past 6 months. Sample items include "Not able to do homework or study for a test," "Caused shame or embarrassment," and "Was told by friend or neighbor to stop or cut down drinking." The scale is reliable and accurately discriminates between clinical and normal samples (White & Labouvie, 1989). Students also completed the Alcohol Dependence Scale (ADS; Skinner & Horn, 1984), a widely used assessment of severity of dependence symptoms.

Other risk factors. Students were classified as family-history-positive if they reported either natural parent or a sibling as being an alcoholic or problem drinker and reported at least two identifiable problem-drinking symptoms for that individual. History of conduct problems was assessed from 14 items on the DIS–C that reflect common adolescent conduct problems, excluding alcohol or drug use (i.e., truancy, fighting, stealing, and school misconduct). These were coded as present or absent before age 18 and summed to form a scale. College residence was coded as living off campus, in the dormitory system, or in a fraternity or sorority (Greek) house.

Participants

The samples' drinking during high school and the transition into college have been described elsewhere (Baer et al., 1994). Of the 366 high-risk students recruited, 11 were removed from randomization because of extreme levels of drinking and drinking-related problems. These individuals were given our clinical intervention (described below) and referred for additional treatment. In addition, 7 participants returned questionnaires too late for the randomization. The final sample of 348 participants were randomly assigned to receive or not receive intervention. At baseline, before randomization, 63% of the sample of high-risk drinkers (188 women and 160 men) reported drinking at least "1–2 times a week"; 52.2% reported drinking as many as "three to four drinks" on a typical weekend evening of drinking; 61.4% reported binge drinking at least "five to six drinks" on a single drinking occasion during the previous month. On the RAPI, the sample reported an average of 7.5 ($SD = 5.86$) alcohol-related harmful consequences as having occurred at least once over the 6 months before the 1st-year autumn assessment; these students reported an average of 2.2 ($SD = 2.83$) problems occurring at least 3 to 5 times over this same period. Students reported an average of 2.5 ($SD = 1.94$) conduct incidents during childhood, although the distribution was predictably skewed. Most high-risk participants reported between 0 and 3 previous conduct incidents (72.1%). Fifty-three participants (12.9% of the sample) reported significant drinking problems in a first-degree relative (parent or sibling).

Motivational Interviewing

The motivational intervention provided in the winter of the 1st year of college was based on prior research with brief interventions among the college students described above (see also Baer et al., 1992) and motivational interviewing more generally (Miller & Rollnick, 1991).

Students assigned to receive an intervention were contacted first by phone and subsequently by mail to schedule a feedback interview (based on the data obtained the previous autumn term). Students were provided with alcohol-consumption-monitoring cards and asked to track their drinking for 2 weeks before their scheduled interview.

In the feedback interview, a professional staff member met individually with the student, reviewed their self-monitoring, and gave them concrete feedback about their drinking patterns, risks, and beliefs about alcohol effects. Drinking rates were compared with college averages, and risks for current and future problems (grades, blackouts, and accidents) were identified. Beliefs about real and imagined alcohol effects were addressed through discussions of placebo effects and the nonspecifics of the effects of alcohol on social behavior. Biphasic effects of alcohol were described, and the students were encouraged to question if "more alcohol is better." Suggestions for risk reduction were outlined.

The style of the interview was based on techniques of motivational interviewing. Confrontational communications, such as, "You have a problem, and you are in denial" are thought to create a defensive response in the client and were specifically avoided. Instead, we simply placed the available evidence to the client and sidestepped arguments. We sought to allow the student to evaluate their situation and begin to contemplate the possibility of change. "What do you make of this?" and "Are you surprised?" were common questions raised to students, to facilitate conversations about risk and the possibility of behavior change. The technique is quite flexible. Issues of setting (life in a fraternity), peer use, prior conduct difficulties, and family history were addressed only if applicable.

From a motivational interviewing perspective (Miller & Rollnick, 1991), students are assumed to be in a natural state of ambivalence and must come to their own conclusion regarding the need to change behavior and reduce risks. Thus, the goals of subsequent behavior changes were left to the student and not outlined or demanded by the interviewer. This style leaves responsibility with the client and, hence, treats all clients as thoughtful adults. Each student left the interview with a personalized feedback sheet, which compared their responses with college norms and listed reported problems, and a "tips" page, which described biphasic responses to alcohol and placebo effects and provided suggestions for reducing the risks of drinking. Each student was encouraged to contact the Lifestyles '94 project if they had any further questions or were interested in any additional services throughout college.

Results to Date

Early results of this brief intervention with college freshmen have been reported previously (Baer, 1993). In summary, those receiving the feedback interview reported less drinking than those in the control group at the 3-month follow-up. Longer term outcomes are described briefly here; a more thorough report of 2- and 3-year outcomes is currently being prepared. We have been generally successful in retaining the sample of students, with over 88% providing data at the 2-year follow-up assessment.

Multivariate analyses completed on 1- and 2-year postbaseline follow-up points revealed that although all students, on average, reported reduced drinking over time, significantly greater reductions were continually reported by those given the brief advice intervention. Furthermore, two different measures of alcohol-related problems (RAPI and ADS) revealed statistically significant differences between treatment and control groups, with results favoring the treatment group. Despite a general developmental trend of reporting fewer problems over time, examination of mean RAPI scores indicates that those given the brief intervention in the freshman year reported on average 3.3 harmful consequences from alcohol use by the junior year, compared with 4.7 for the high-risk control group. Our random group, which serves as a normative comparison for high-risk students, reported on average 2.4 problems at the junior-year assessment. Thus, these differences, if reliable, reflect meaningful harm reduction among those receiving the motivational intervention.

Analyses of individual differences that might relate to treatment response are complex: There are simply too many factors to analyze simultaneously and retain power to test all possible interactions. Therefore, a series of multivariate repeated-measures analyses of variance was completed, to evaluate each individual-difference factor (i.e., family history of alcoholism, conduct problem history, and type of university residence) as a main effect and in interaction with gender and treatment in the prediction of drinking trends. Both alcohol use rates and alcohol-related problems were evaluated as dependent measures. Analyses completed to date can be summarized by describing a few consistent trends in the data, pertaining to the report of alcohol-related problems. None of the individual-difference factors studied consistently interacted with treatment response: Our treatment seems effective for all students regardless of risk status. However, several trends in our data suggested that not all students are equally at risk, and therefore, treatment may be more important for certain individuals.

First, a family history of alcohol problems did not relate in any consistent fashion to changes to the self-report of drinking problems (no main effects or interactions). However, those with a history of conduct problems or delinquent behaviors reported more alcohol-related problems at all points in time (main effect). In addition, men living in fraternities reported more alcohol-related problems than women or those living elsewhere at all points in time (Sex × Residence interaction). Finally, compared with men, women reported greater decreases in problems over the 2-year follow-up time period (Sex × Time interaction).

The treatment effects described above and the individual differences in developmental trends sum or compile to create a risky picture for certain individuals, in particular, men with conduct histories living in the Greek system. For women, our prevention program appeared to enhance a downward developmental trend for drinking problems, regardless of residence. For men, a different and more troubling picture emerged. Men living in the Greek system reported more problems on average, and all men reported more consistent problems over time. Furthermore, all of these trends were exacerbated by a history of conduct difficulties, and roughly two thirds of those reporting conduct histories were men. As a result, individuals with multiple-risk profiles (men living in fraternities who also have a history of conduct problems) showed the most severe pattern of harmful drinking over time and the least decline. These individuals, therefore, may benefit the most from our preventive programming. For example, in this study, men in the Greek system who did not receive treatment represented our only subgroup in which alcohol-dependence scores actually increased during the first 2 years of college.

Our studies of college student drinking, described above, naturally are limited by the self-report nature of the data pertaining to alcohol use and estimates of blood alcohol levels. Although often criticized, self-reports of drinking behavior often show considerable reliability and validity under conditions of confidentiality and safety (Babor, Stephens, & Marlatt, 1987). We emphasize repeatedly to participants the confidential and nonevaluative nature of our data. Nevertheless, we cannot control completely for possible increases in the social desirability of reporting drinking reductions among those receiving treatment (and developing relationships with program staff), compared with those in the control condition. As a result of this concern, we have spent considerable effort in our latest study collecting confirmatory data from collateral reporters. Collateral data serves two general purposes. First, the procedure communicates to the participant an emphasis on accuracy and a check on self-report. A long history of research on "bogus pipeline" effects in social psychology suggests that this procedure should promote accurate reporting by subjects (Jones & Sigall, 1971). Second, collateral reports constitute a separate data source. With collateral reports, we can check if others perceive changes in our participants' drinking.

In our current longitudinal study, collateral data have provided support for our self-report data. We asked collaterals to rate fairly specific aspects of participants' drinking and the presence of low-level problems. Follow-up assessments resulted in reliable collateral assessments (both within collaterals and between participants and collaterals); reliability for some responses are above .70. Furthermore, these reports begin to confirm some behavioral differences based on self-report between treatment and control groups. In particular, collaterals perceive those in the treatment group as drinking less frequently and drinking to intoxication less often, compared with those in the control condition. These trends appear most evident when collaterals report on female participants, and less so with male participants. Treatment-group participants are also more likely to be seen as having decreased their drinking than are control participants. These data offer one important source of confirmatory evidence that our brief preventive intervention resulted in decreased drinking behavior.

HARM REDUCTION AND THE PREVENTION OF ALCOHOL ABUSE

Our work on the prevention of alcohol problems with college students is best conceptualized as a harm-reduction approach (Marlatt, Larimer, Baer, & Quigley, 1993). We believe that harm reduction provides a conceptual umbrella that covers a variety of previously unrelated programs and techniques in the addictive-behaviors field, including needle-exchange programs for injection-drug users, methadone maintenance for opiate users, nicotine replacement methods for smokers, weight management and eating-behavior-change programs for the obese, and safe-sex programs (e.g., condom distribution in high schools) to reduce the risk of HIV infection and AIDS (Marlatt & Tapert, 1993). Our work in the prevention of alcohol abuse in college students fits well within this domain.

Habits can be placed along a continuum of harmful consequences. The goal of harm reduction is to move the person with alcohol problems along this continuum: To begin to take "steps in the right direction" to reduce harmful consequences. It is important that the harm-reduction model accepts abstinence as the ideal or ultimate risk-reduction goal. But the harm-reduction model promotes any movement in the right direction along this continuum as progress, even if total abstinence is not attained.

Clearly, the excessive use of alcohol is associated with increasingly harmful consequences as consumption increases. Harm reduction is based on the assumption that by reducing the level of drinking, the risk of harm will drop in a corresponding manner. By this logic, total abstinence from alcohol would seem to be associated with the lowest level of harmful consequences. In some areas, however, the benefits of moderate drinking may outweigh the harm-reduction advantages offered by abstinence.

Moderate drinking can have both harmful and helpful consequences. Moderate-to-heavy drinking is reported to increase the risk associated with motor vehicle crashes, birth defects, and harmful interactions with certain medications; yet, it is also associated with reduced risk of cardiovascular disease (National Institute on Alcohol Abuse and Alcoholism, 1992). Given the mixed risks associated with moderate drinking, arguments have been presented on both sides concerning whether abstinence or moderation should be recommended to the public concerning the use of alcohol (Peele, 1993; Shaper, 1993).

Harm-reduction approaches are not limited to the type of individual clinical approaches or self-management training programs described in this chapter. Changes in the physical and social environment can also be implemented, along with public policy changes designed to minimize harm (e.g., legalization of needle-exchange programs). The best results occur when all three methods are combined. For example, to reduce the harm associated with automobile accidents, it is possible to develop better driver-training programs (individual self-management, or autoregulation); to construct safer automobiles and highways (changing the environment); and to introduce safety-enhancing public policies (e.g., reduced speed limit or enhanced enforcement programs). To reduce the harm of drunk driving, it is again possible to combine these three elements: programs mandated for the drunk driver (e.g., programs designed to modify drinking and avoid intoxicated driving); physical and social environmental changes (e.g., use of car ignition systems that are designed to foil the intoxicated driver and designated driver selection); and policy changes (e.g., reducing the blood alcohol minimum for legal intoxication while driving).

As documented in the present review, harm reduction can be applied to the secondary prevention of alcohol problems with moderation as the goal. In sharp contrast to the disease model and Twelve-Step programs that insist on abstinence as the First Step in dealing with any alcohol problem, harm reduction encourages a gradual "step-down" approach to reduce the harmful consequences of alcohol or other drug use. By stepping down the harm incrementally, drinkers can be encouraged to pursue proximal subgoals along the way to either moderation or abstinence.

REFERENCES

American Psychiatric Association. (1987). *Diagnostic and statistical manual of mental disorders* (3rd ed., rev). Washington, DC: Author.

Babor, T. F., Stephens, R. S., & Marlatt, G. A. (1987). Verbal report methods in clinical research on alcoholism: Response bias and its minimization. *Journal of Studies on Alcohol, 48,* 410–424.

Baer, J. S. (1993). Etiology and secondary prevention of alcohol problems with young adults. In J. S. Baer, G. A. Marlatt, & R. J. McMahon (Eds.), *Addictive behaviors across the lifespan* (pp. 111–137). Newbury Park, CA: Sage.

Baer, J. S., Kivlahan, D. R., & Marlatt, G. A. (1995). *High-risk drinking across the transition from high school to college. Alcoholism: Clinical and Experimental Research, 19*(1), 54–61.

Baer, J. S., Marlatt, G. A., Kivlahan, D., Fromme, K., Larimer, M., & Williams, E. (1992). An experimental test of three methods of alcohol risk reduction with young adults. *Journal of Consulting and Clinical Psychology, 60,* 974–979.

Berkowitz, A. D., & Perkins, H. W. (1986). Problem drinking among college students: A review of recent research. *Journal of American College Health, 35,* 1–28.

Caudill, B. D., & Marlatt, G. A. (1975). Modeling influences in social drinking: An experimental analogue. *Journal of Consulting and Clinical Psychology, 43,* 405–415.

Collins, R. L., & Marlatt, G. A. (1981). Social modeling as a determinant of drinking behavior: Implications for prevention and treatment. *Addictive Behaviors, 6,* 233–240.

Collins, R. L., Parks, G. A., & Marlatt, G. A. (1985). Social determinants of alcohol consumption: The effects of social interaction and model status on the self-administration of alcohol. *Journal of Consulting and Clinical Psychology, 53,* 189–200.

Derogatis, L. R., & Spencer, P. M. (1982). *The Brief Symptom Inventory (BSI): Administration, scoring, procedures manual—I.* Baltimore, MD: Johns Hopkins University of Medicine.

Edwards, G., Orford, J., Egert, S., Guthrie, S., Hawker, A., Hensman, C., Mitcheson, M., Oppenheimer, E., & Taylor, C. (1977). Alcoholism: A controlled trial of "treatment" and "advice." *Journal of Studies on Alcohol, 38,* 1004–1031.

Engs, R. C., & Hanson, D. J. (1985). The drinking-patterns and problems of college students: 1983. *Journal of Alcohol and Drug Education, 31,* 65–82.

Fillmore, K. M. (1988). *Alcohol use across the life course.* Toronto, Ontario, Canada: Alcoholism and Drug Addiction Research Foundation.

Geller, E. S., & Kalsher, M. J. (1990). Environmental determinants of party drinking: Bartenders vs. self-service. *Environment and Behavior, 22*(1), 74–90.

Geller, E. S., Russ, N. W., & Altomari, M. G. (1986). Naturalistic observations of beer drinking among college students. *Journal of Applied Behavior Analysis, 19,* 391–396.

Grant, B. F., Harford, T. C., & Grigson, M. B. (1988). Stability of alcohol consumption among youth: A national longitudinal study. *Journal of Studies on Alcohol, 49,* 253–260.

Helzer, J. E., & Robins, L. N. (1988). The Diagnostic Interview Schedule: Its development, evolution, and use. *Social Psychiatry and Psychiatric Epidemiology, 23*(6), 6–16.

Higgins, R. L., & Marlatt, G. A. (1975). Fear of interpersonal evaluation as a determinant of alcohol consumption in male social drinkers. *Journal of Abnormal Psychology, 84*, 644–651.

Jessor, R. (1984). Adolescent development and behavior health. In J. D. Matarazzo, S. M. Weiss, J. A. Herd, N. E. Miller, & S. M. Weiss (Eds.), *Behavior health: A handbook of health enhancement and disease prevention* (pp. 69–90). New York: Wiley.

Jessor, R., Donovan, J. E., & Costa, F. M. (1991). *Beyond adolescence: Problem behavior and young adult development.* New York: Cambridge University Press.

Johnston, L. D., O'Malley, P. M., & Bachman, J. G. (1992). *Smoking, drinking, and illicit drug use among American secondary school students, college students, and young adults, 1975–1991.* Washington, DC: National Institute on Drug Abuse.

Jones, E. E., & Sigall, H. (1971). The bogus pipeline: A new paradigm for measuring affect and attitude. *Psychological Bulletin, 76*, 349–364.

Kivlahan, D. R., Marlatt, G. A., Fromme, K., Coppel, D. B., & Williams, E. (1990). Secondary prevention with college drinkers: Evaluation of an alcohol skills training program. *Journal of Consulting and Clinical Psychology, 58*, 805–810.

Larimer, M. E. (1992). *Alcohol abuse and the Greek system: An exploration of fraternity and sorority drinking.* Unpublished doctoral dissertation, University of Washington, Seattle.

Lowell, N. (1993, December). *University life and substance abuse: 1993 survey* (Report No. 93-4) Seattle: University of Washington, Office of Educational Assessment.

Mann, R. E., Sobell, L. C., Sobell, M. B., & Pavan, D. (1985). Reliability of a family tree questionnaire for assessing family history of alcohol problems. *Drug and Alcohol Dependence, 15*, 61–67.

Marlatt, G. A. (1978). Behavioral assessment of social drinking and alcoholism. In G. A. Marlatt & P. E. Nathan (Eds.), *Behavioral approaches to alcoholism* (pp 35–37). New Brunswick, NJ: Rutgers Center of Alcohol Studies.

Marlatt, G. A., Baer, J. S., & Larimer, M. E. (1995). Preventing alcohol abuse in college students: A harm-reduction approach. In G. M. Boyd, J. Howard, & R. A. Zucker (Eds.), *Alcohol problems among adolescents: Current directions in prevention research* (pp. 147–172). Northvale, NJ: Erlbaum.

Marlatt, G. A., Kosturn, C. F., & Lang, A. R. (1975). Provocation to anger and opportunity for retaliation as determinants of alcohol consumption in social drinkers. *Journal of Abnormal Psychology, 84*, 652–659.

Marlatt, G. A., Larimer, M. E., Baer, J. S., & Quigley, L. A. (1993). Harm reduction for alcohol problems: Moving beyond the controlled drinking controversy. *Behavior Therapy, 24*, 461–504.

Marlatt, G. A., & Tapert, S. F. (1993). Harm reduction: Reducing the risks of addictive behaviors. In J. S. Baer, G. A. Marlatt, & R. J. McMahon (Eds.), *Addictive behaviors across the lifespan: Prevention, treatment, and policy issues* (pp. 243–273). Newbury Park, CA: Sage.

Miller, W. R., & Marlatt, G. A. (1984). *The Brief Drinker Profile*. Odessa, FL: Psychological Assessment Resources.

Miller, W. R., & Rollnick, S. (1991). *Motivational interviewing: Preparing people for change*. New York: Guilford Press.

National Institute on Alcohol Abuse and Alcoholism. (1984). *Report of the 1983 Prevention Planning Panel*. Rockville, MD: Author.

National Institute on Alcohol Abuse and Alcoholism. (1992). *Alcohol alert*. Rockville, MD: Author.

Peele, S. (1993). The conflict between public health goals and the temperance mentality. *American Journal of Public Health, 83*, 805–810.

Shaper, A. G. (1993). Editorial: Alcohol, the heart, and health. *American Journal of Public Health, 83*, 799–800.

Sher, K. J. (1991). *Children of alcoholics: A critical appraisal of theory and research*. Chicago: University of Chicago Press.

Skinner, H. A., & Horn, J. L. (1984). *Alcohol Dependence Scale* (ADS). Toronto, Ontario, Canada: Addiction Research Foundation.

Wechsler, H., & Issac, N. (1992). "Binge" drinkers at Massachusetts colleges. *Journal of the American Medical Association, 267*, 292–293.

White, H. R., & Labouvie, E. W. (1989). Towards the assessment of adolescent problem drinking. *Journal of Studies on Alcohol, 50*, 30–37.

Zucker, R. A. (in press). Alcohol involvement over the life span: A developmental perspective on theory and course. In L. S. Gaines & P. H. Brooks (Eds.), *Alcohol studies: A lifespan perspective*. New York: Springer.

25

STRATEGIES TO REDUCE THE RISK OF HIV INFECTION, SEXUALLY TRANSMITTED DISEASES, AND PREGNANCY AMONG AFRICAN AMERICAN ADOLESCENTS

JOHN B. JEMMOTT III and LORETTA SWEET JEMMOTT

Adolescence is a time of experimentation, as young people strive to develop their identity in preparation for adulthood. For many young people, it is a time of sexual experimentation. Unfortunately, the consequences of such experimentation far too often include increased risk of pregnancy and sexually transmitted disease (STD), including infection

Preparation of this manuscript was supported in part by National Institute of Mental Health Grants R01-MH45668 and R01-MH52035 and National Institute of Child Health and Human Development Grant U01-HD30145.

with human immunodeficiency virus (HIV), the virus that causes acquired immunodeficiency syndrome (AIDS). In this chapter, we discuss the incidence of pregnancy, STD, and HIV among adolescents and research on strategies to prevent these problems.

PREGNANCY, SEXUALLY TRANSMITTED DISEASE, AND HIV INFECTION AMONG ADOLESCENTS

Pregnancy

More than three fourths of American adolescents have had sexual intercourse by the time they are 19 years of age (Centers for Disease Control [CDC], 1991; Hatcher et al., 1994; Sonenstein, Pleck, & Leighton, 1989). Much of this sexual activity occurs without protection against pregnancy and STDs, and lack of protection is especially likely among adolescents who are sexually active during early adolescence (Pratt, Mosher, Backrach, & Horn, 1984; Taylor, Kagay, & Leichenko, 1986; Zelnik, Kantner, & Ford, 1981). One in eight women age 15 to 19 years in the United States becomes pregnant each year, a figure that has changed little since the late 1970s (Hatcher et al., 1994). In 1991, about 1.1 million pregnancies occurred among those age 15 to 19 years, and another 57,000 pregnancies occurred among women age 14 years or younger. Roughly 85% of teenage pregnancies are unintended (Jones et al., 1986; Pratt et al., 1984; Zelnik et al., 1981). Pregnancy is particularly likely during adolescents' initial sexual intercourse experiences, when contraceptive use is especially unlikely (Jones et al., 1986; Pratt et al., 1984; Taylor et al., 1986; Zelnik & Kantner, 1980). One half of all initial adolescent premarital pregnancies occur within the first 6 months after initiation of coitus; 20% occur in the 1st month alone (Zabin, Kantner, & Zelnik, 1979).

Sexually Transmitted Diseases

The problem of pregnancy among adolescents has much in common with the problem of STDs. Obviously, the two problems share a common pathway: They are both caused by sexual behavior. The structural variables that predict pregnancy also predict STDs. Just as there is concern about adolescent pregnancy, there is concern about STDs among adolescents. Although the use of latex condoms can reduce substantially the risk of STD (CDC, 1988; Stone, Grimes, & Magder, 1986), most sexually active adolescents do not use condoms consistently (Hingson, Strunin, Berlin, & Heeren, 1990; L.S. Jemmott & Jemmott, 1990; Keller et al., 1991; Sonenstein et al., 1989). Rates of syphilis, gonorrhea, and hospitalization for pelvic inflammatory disease have been highest among adolescents and decline exponentially with age (Bell & Holmes, 1984). About two thirds of all STDs occur among persons who are 24 years of age or younger (CDC, 1995b).

There are important consequences of STDs. The immediate consequences of STDs can be physical discomfort and embarrassment. However, STDs are often asymptomatic, particularly in women: The adolescent may not know she is infected. Sexually transmitted diseases are sexist. The consequences for women are more substantial than those for men. These more long-term consequences include pelvic inflammatory disease, infertility, cervical cancer, ectopic pregnancy, chronic pelvic pain, and infections passed on to newborns (CDC, 1995b).

Human Immunodeficiency Virus

The STD that is now of greatest concern is HIV, which causes AIDS. A diagnosis of AIDS is accompanied by a truly dismal prognosis. As of June 1995, over 295,000 deaths had been attributed to AIDS (CDC, 1995a). But this represents only part of the problem, for an estimated 1 million people in the United States have been infected by HIV (CDC, 1990), and these people will also develop AIDS. Human immunodeficiency virus infection is transmitted by exposure to infected blood, semen, and vaginal secretions, usually through sexual activities or the sharing of hypodermic needles and other drug paraphernalia by injection-drug users. Human immunodeficiency virus can also spread from infected mothers to their newborns in the womb or during birth, but for the most part, it is the behavior of individuals that creates their risk of HIV infection. To be sure, adolescents represent less than 1% of all reported AIDS cases in the United States (CDC, 1995a). But this statistic may underestimate the potential for HIV infection among adolescents. Young adults in their twenties constitute 18% of all AIDS cases, and because several years typically elapse between the time a person is infected with HIV and the appearance of clinical signs sufficient to warrant a diagnosis of AIDS, many of these young adults were infected during adolescence. The consequences of HIV and AIDS are disability and death.

Inner-City African American Adolescents

The risks associated with unprotected sexual activity are especially great among inner-city African American adolescents. Whether one considers self-reported sexual activities, unintended pregnancy rates, or

STD rates, the statistics on these youths are especially grim. Studies have indicated that African American adolescents, compared with White adolescents, are younger at first coitus (Taylor et al., 1986; Zelnik et al., 1981). Inasmuch as younger adolescents who are having sex for the first time are particularly unlikely to use any contraception (Zelnik et al., 1981), it is not surprising that African Americans are less likely than are Whites to use any contraception at first coitus.

The adolescent pregnancy rate is more than twice as high among African Americans as among Whites. For example, in 1988, 25% of African American female adolescents 15 to 19 years of age and 11% of their White counterparts became pregnant (Henshaw, 1992). In part, the higher rates among African Americans are explained by socioeconomic status (SES) differences. Low SES is associated with increased pregnancy rate, and African Americans are more likely to be of lower SES. Sexually transmitted diseases are substantially more common among African Americans than among Whites. For instance, in 1994, the gonorrhea rates among African American male and female adolescents 15 to 19 years of age were, on average, more than 28-fold higher than those in White adolescents 15 to 19 years old (CDC, 1995b). There are no known biologic reasons to explain why racial or ethnic factors alone would affect risk for STDs. Rather, race and ethnicity are risk makers that correlate with other more fundamental determinants of health status, including poverty, access to quality health care, health-care-seeking behavior, illicit drug use, and living in communities with high prevalence of STDs (Cates, 1987; CDC, 1995b; Hatcher et al., 1994).

The issue becomes even more pressing when it is considered that African American adolescents, particularly those who reside in inner-city areas, would also be at risk for infection with HIV. Although in the United States, the largest number of reported AIDS cases have involved White men who engaged in same-gender sexual activities, AIDS has levied a heavy toll on African Americans (CDC, 1995a). Seroprevalence surveys of civilian applicants for military service, women's health clinics, and Job Corps entrants (CDC, 1990) have indicated higher rates of HIV infection among African Americans as compared with Whites. African Americans are also overrepresented among reported AIDS cases. About 34% of AIDS cases in the United States have involved African Americans (CDC, 1995a), who constitute only 12% of the United States population (U.S. Bureau of Census, 1989). The disparity in reported AIDS cases is particularly great among women and children. As of June 1995, African American women accounted for 55% of adult female AIDS cases, whereas White women accounted for only 24%. More than one half of children under 13 years of age who have AIDS are African American. Compared with White pediatric AIDS cases, African American cases are more likely to have a mother who was exposed due to injection-drug use or heterosexual contact (CDC, 1995a). The prevalence of injection-drug use in the inner city also heightens the risk of HIV infection for African American adolescent residents. Although the adolescents themselves may not use injection drugs—indeed, some data (Turner, Miller, & Moses, 1989) indicate that injection drug use among adolescents is rare—they may have sexual relationships with injection-drug users or with individuals who have had sex with such potentially infected persons. The elevated adolescent pregnancy and STD rates, the potential for sexual involvement with injection drug users, and the potential for perinatally transmitted HIV infection all suggest the urgent risks among African American adolescents.

THEORETICAL FRAMEWORK

A common feature of pregnancy and STD, including HIV, is that they are tied to personal behavior, which suggests the possibility that through the use of behavioral interventions it may be possible to curb these risks. Our research has attempted to develop culture-sensitive, developmentally appropriate, theory-based interventions to curb these risks among inner-city adolescents. A solid theoretical framework is important to intervention research. Theory can be used in the development of intervention activities. Theory can be used to direct attention to the modifiable psychological determinants of risk behavior. By measuring the putative theory-based mediators of intervention-induced behavior change, a better conceptual understanding of risk behavior will emerge. While maintaining an emphasis on a theory-based approach to risk reduction, our research has also focused on practical questions regarding the most effective way to intervene to reduce risk of HIV infection.

As an organizing conceptual framework, our research has drawn on the *theory of planned behavior* (Ajzen, 1991; Madden, Ellen, & Ajzen, 1992), which is an extension of the more widely known *theory of reasoned action* (Ajzen & Fishbein, 1980; Fishbein & Ajzen, 1975; Fishbein, Middlestadt, & Hitchcock, 1994). The theory of reasoned action has been used successfully to predict and explain a broad range of health-related behaviors, including breast self-examination (Temko, 1987); smoking cessation (Fishbein, 1982); weight control (Schifter & Ajzen, 1985); infant feeding (Manstead, Profitt, & Smart, 1983); and contraceptive use (Davidson & Jaccard, 1979). According to the theory, behavior is the result of a specific intention to perform that behavior. A *behavioral intention* is seen as determined by attitude toward the specific behavior, the person's overall positive or negative feeling toward performing the behavior, and by subjective norm regarding the behavior, the person's perception of whether significant others would approve or disapprove of him or her performing the behavior. Thus, people intend to perform a behavior when they evaluate that behavior positively and when they believe significant others think they should perform it. A valuable feature of the theory is that it directs attention to why people hold certain attitudes and subjective norms. *Attitude* toward behavior is seen as reflecting behavioral beliefs, salient beliefs about the consequences of performing the act, and the person's negative or positive evaluation of those consequences. *Subjective norms* are seen as the product of salient beliefs about what specific reference persons or groups think should be done regarding the behavior and the person's motivation to comply with these referents.

According to the theory of reasoned action, attitudes and subjective norms are the sole direct determinants of intentions. Although other variables may affect intentions, these effects are indirect, mediated by the effects of the variables on the attitudinal component, the normative component, or both. However, Ajzen (1985, 1991; Ajzen & Madden, 1986; Madden et al., 1992; Schifter & Ajzen, 1985) recently argued for an exception to the general rule that all variables external to the theory of reasoned action have their effects on intentions and behavior by influencing the attitudinal and normative components. A fundamental assumption of the theory of reasoned action is that its predictive power is greatest for behaviors that are fully under the volitional control of individuals. Ajzen proposed the theory of planned behavior to account for behaviors that are subject to forces that are beyond individuals' control. For instance, performance of the behavior might depend on another person's actions, or the behavior might be performed in the context of strong emotions. Under such circumstances, Ajzen reasoned, prediction of intentions might be enhanced by considering not only attitudes and subjective norms, but *perceived behavioral control.* Defined as the perceived ease or difficulty of performing the behavior, perceived behavioral control reflects past experience as well as anticipated impediments, obstacles, resources, and opportunities.

Perceived behavioral control has affinity with the social–cognitive theory construct of *perceived self-efficacy,* or individuals' conviction that they can perform a specific behavior (Bandura, 1986, 1989, 1994; O'Leary, 1985). In fact, much of what is known about perceived behavioral control comes from research on perceived self-efficacy by Bandura and associates. What the theory of planned behavior does is to place the construct of perceived self-efficacy or perceived behavioral control within a more general framework of the relations among beliefs, attitudes, intentions, and behavior (Ajzen, 1991). Perceived behavioral control is determined by *control beliefs*—beliefs about factors that facilitate or inhibit perfor-

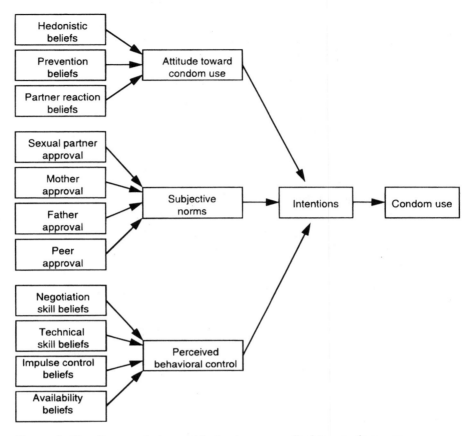

Figure 1. The theory of planned behavior as applied to condom use.

mance of the behavior. We hypothesized that the theory of planned behavior would be valuable to an understanding of sexual risk behavior. Sexual behaviors are performed in the context of strong emotions, and safer sex practices are not always under the individual's direct control because they may require a sexual partner's cooperation. In this view, in addition to inducing positive attitudes and supportive subjective norms, it might be useful to increase perceived behavioral control to implement safer sex practices.

As illustrated in Figure 1, we have applied the theory of planned behavior to HIV-risk-associated sexual behavior. As shown in the figure, the behavior, in this case, condom use, is a function of the intention to use condoms. Consistent with the theory of planned behavior, condom-use intention is determined by attitude toward condoms, subjective norms regarding condoms, and perceived behavioral control over condom use. This reflects our hypothesis that people intend to use condoms when they evaluate condom use positively, when they believe significant others think they should use condoms, and when they feel confident in their ability to implement condom use.

Attitudes and Behavioral Beliefs

Several behavioral beliefs may affect attitude toward condoms. Elicitation surveys conducted with inner-city African American adolescents suggest the importance of three behavioral beliefs in particular. The most obvious perhaps is *prevention beliefs*, or beliefs about whether the use of condoms will prevent pregnancy, STD, and HIV infection. *Hedonistic beliefs*, or beliefs about the effects of condoms on sexual enjoyment, are also likely to be important to condom-use attitude. Thus, to the extent that adolescents believe that using a condom ruins sexual enjoyment, their attitude toward using a condom should be negative. Several studies have tied such beliefs to condom use or intentions to use condoms (Catania et al., 1989; Hingson et al., 1990; L. S. Jemmott & Jemmott, 1992; Valdiserri, Arena, Proctor, & Bonati, 1989). The third type of behavioral belief is *partner-reaction beliefs*, or beliefs about how sexual partners will react to condom use.

Subjective Norms and Normative Beliefs

Subjective norms are determined by *normative beliefs*, which are beliefs about whether salient reference persons or groups would approve or disapprove of the person's engaging in the behavior. People may modulate their risk-associated behavior as a function of their beliefs about how significant others would view it (Fishbein & Middlestadt, 1989). Quite apart from the person's beliefs about other consequences of the behavior—as might be reflected in hedonistic beliefs, for example—if significant others disapprove of a risk behavior, the person may be less likely to engage in that behavior than if they approve of the behavior. The key referents that emerged in elicitation surveys include sexual partner, mother, father, other family members, and peers or friends. It is often argued that sexual partners are more important for women than for men and that they are singularly important in the case of ethnic minority women. Women's relative power in the relationship and their dependency on it (Guttentag & Secord, 1983; Milan & Kilmann, 1987) are likely to affect sexual risk behavior. Studying an African American female adolescent clinic sample, Ager, Shea, and Agronow (1982) found that partner opposition to, or reluctance to use, birth control was a factor in respondents' nonuse of contraception, a common finding in adolescent samples (Thompson & Spanier, 1978; Zabin & Clark, 1981). Studies have also indicated that friends or peers, parents, and other family members may affect adolescents' sexual risk behavior (Fox & Inazu, 1980; Furstenberg, 1971; Handelman, Cabral, & Weisfeld, 1987; Hofferth & Hayes, 1987; Milan & Kilmann, 1987; Morrison, 1985; Nathanson & Becker, 1986).

Perceived Behavioral Control, Self-Efficacy, and Control Beliefs

We have distinguished among four types of control beliefs, which are hypothesized to influence perceived behavioral control. *Negotiation-skill beliefs* concern adolescents' confidence that they can convince a sexual partner to use condoms. Thus, inducing more positive attitudes toward condoms among some African American adolescent women might not increase their intentions to use condoms because of their negotiation-skill beliefs—their perceptions that they may not be able to convince their sexual partner to use a condom. In this connection, it might be important to increase the adolescent's skill at convincing her partner to use a condom. This might result in greater perceived behavioral control or self-efficacy regarding condom use. In fact, there is evidence that behavioral programs that enhance adolescents' interpersonal skills (which should increase their self-efficacy) have produced significant changes in patterns of contraceptive use and unintended pregnancy (Schinke, Gilchrist, & Small, 1979). An intervention that increased assertiveness also increased use of condoms during anal intercourse among White gay men (Kelly et al., 1989). Another study found that a skill-building intervention increased condom use during insertive anal intercourse among White gay men (Valdiserri, Lyter, et al., 1989).

Availability beliefs concern whether adolescents feel confident that they can have condoms available for use when they need them. This would include their beliefs about the financial cost of condoms and beliefs about the appropriateness of carrying condoms. *Impulse-control, or self-control, beliefs* concern adolescents' confidence that they can control themselves in the midst of a sexual encounter to use condoms. *Technical-skill beliefs* concern adolescents' confidence that they can use condoms with facility, that is, without fumbling or ruining the mood. The focus here is on adolescents' confidence about their abilities, not on their actual abilities. Presumably, confidence and actual skill are correlated, but we are focusing on the belief. To the extent that people believe that they have the requisite skills and resources to use condoms, they should perceive greater control over performance of that behavior.

Variables External to the Theory

The theory of planned behavior does not include many variables that traditionally have been studied in attempts to understand preventive health behavior. Attitudes, subjective norms, and perceived behavioral control are viewed as the sole determinants of intentions and behaviors. The effects on intentions and behaviors of other variables are seen as mediated by their effects on the attitudinal component, the normative component, the perceived-control component, or all three. Thus, for instance, low socioeconomic background, low parental education, belonging to a nonintact or female-headed household, and residing in households with a larger number of children have been linked to heightened sexual activity, lower contraceptive use, and lack of condom use among adolescents (Brown, 1985; Fox & Inazu, 1980; Hofferth & Hayes, 1987; Hogan, Astone, Kitagawa, 1985; Hogan & Kitagawa, 1985; Zelnik et al., 1981). The theory of planned behavior holds that these variables that are external to the model would affect specific behavioral intentions and behaviors by influencing attitudes toward those behaviors, subjective norms regarding them, and perceptions of control over them. In this way, the theory can accommodate variables that are external to it (Ajzen, 1991; Fishbein & Middlestadt, 1989). Behavioral interventions, too, would constitute external variables. Hence, their effects on sexual risk behaviors and intentions would depend on their impact on the attitudinal component, the normative component, the perceived-control component, or all three. Accordingly, our interventions are designed to affect these components.

INTERVENING WITH INNER-CITY AFRICAN AMERICAN ADOLESCENTS

In this section, we discuss studies that are illustrative of our approach to sexual behavior intervention research. This research has emphasized risk of HIV infection, but it is also relevant to pregnancy prevention and STD prevention more broadly. The first study focused on inner-city African American male adolescents (J. B. Jemmott, Jemmott, & Fong, 1992). We were interested in this population for several reasons. First, inner-city African American male adolescents are considered difficult to reach and difficult to maintain in intervention trials. No HIV-risk-reduction intervention studies had been focused on them. In addition, as alluded to earlier, they are at high risk of contracting and spreading STDs, including HIV. For the most part, research on adolescents' sexual behavior has focused on female adolescents. Male adolescents, especially African American male adolescents, typically have been left out of the picture. This is especially troublesome because, aside from abstinence, the most advocated means of protecting against sexually transmitted HIV infection is the male's use of a condom.

The study was designed to test the effectiveness of an intervention on sexual risk behavior and theory-based putative mediators of such behavior among inner-city African American male adolescents. We were also interested in a practical question regarding how HIV-risk-reduction interventions should be implemented with African American male adolescents, namely, whether the gender of the educational facilitator or health educator would moderate effectiveness of the intervention. It is often reasoned that it is important to match the race and gender of participants and facilitators, to maximize the effectiveness of an intervention with ethnic minority individuals. The facilitator of a similar race and gender might have greater credibility, might be able to establish rapport more rapidly, and may have a deeper understanding of pertinent aspects of the participants' lives. According to this line of reasoning, African American male adolescents may be more receptive to behavior-change recommendations if they come from African American male facilitators, as compared with African American female facilitators. We tested that hypothesis.

The participants were 157 inner-city African American male adolescents from Philadelphia who were recruited from a local medical center, community-based organizations, and a local high school. They volunteered for a risk-reduction project, designed to understand African American male youths' behaviors that may create risks such as unemployment, truancy, teenage pregnancy, and STDs, especially AIDS, and to find ways to teach African American male youth how to reduce these risks. The overwhelming majority of the participants (97%) were currently enrolled in school, and their median grade in school was between 9th and 10th grade. Their chief risk was from heterosexual activities, particularly failure to use condoms. Although the mean age of the sample was only 14.6 years, about 83% of the participants reporting having had coitus at least once. About 21% of respondents who had coitus in the past 3 months reported that they never used condoms during those experiences, and only 30% reported always using condoms. Few (less than 5%) participants reported ever engaging in same-gender sexual behavior or injection drug use.

The adolescents were assigned randomly to an HIV-risk-reduction condition or a control condition on career opportunities and to a small group of about 6 boys led by a specially trained male or female African American facilitator. The adolescents in the HIV-risk-reduction condition received an intensive 5-hour intervention. The intervention included videotapes, games, and exercises designed to influence AIDS-related knowledge, behavioral beliefs, attitudes, and perceived behavioral control supportive of safer sex practices. The intervention materials and activities were selected not only to influence the putative theoretical mediators, but also to be interactive and enjoyable. For example, participants played AIDS Basketball, a game in which the adolescents were divided into two teams that earned points by correctly answering factual questions about AIDS. In this game, which adolescents find especially entertaining, there are two-point questions, three-point bonus questions, and one-point foul shot questions. One video, *The Subject Is AIDS*, presented factual information about AIDS. It was narrated by an African American woman and had a multiethnic cast. Another video, *Condom Sense*, addressed negative attitudes toward the use of condoms and hedonistic beliefs. It attacked the idea that sex is substantially less pleasurable when a condom is used. A major character is an African American man who tries to convince a basketball buddy that his girlfriend's request that they use condoms during sex is reasonable. The intervention also addressed perceived behavioral control. A condom exercise focused on familiarity with condoms and the steps involved in the correct use of them. Participants engaged in role-playing situations depicting potential problems in trying to implement safer sex practices, including abstinence.

To control for Hawthorne effects, to reduce the likelihood that effects of the HIV-risk-reduction intervention could be attributed to nonspecific features, including group interaction and special attention, adolescents randomly assigned to the control condition also received a 5-hour intervention. Structurally similar to the HIV-risk-reduction intervention, the control condition involved culturally and developmentally appropriate videotapes, exercises, and games regarding career opportunities. For example, the participants played Career Basketball, in which teams earned points for correctly answering questions about careers and job hunting. This control intervention was designed to be both enjoyable and valuable. Although career-opportunity participants did not learn about AIDS, given the high unemployment among inner-city African American male adolescents, the goal was to provide information that would be valuable to them as they plan their future.

Adolescents in both conditions completed questionnaires before, immediately after, and 3 months after the intervention. These questionnaires were administered not by the facilitators who implemented the interventions, but by project assistants. The project assistants, who were trained African American community residents, emphasized the importance of being honest. The participants signed an agreement, pledging to answer the questions as honestly as possible—a procedure that has been shown to yield more valid responses on sensitive issues. The project assistants told the participants that their responses would be used to create programs for other African American adolescents like themselves and that the programs would be effective only if they answered the questions honestly. In this way, we sought to pit the social responsibility motive against the social desirability motive. In addition, the Marlowe–Crowne Social Desirability Scale (Crowne & Marlowe, 1964) was used to measure the tendency of participants to describe themselves in favorable, socially desirable terms. Analyses of covariance (ANCOVAs), controlling for preintervention measures, revealed that adolescents who received the HIV-risk-reduction intervention subsequently had greater AIDS knowledge, less favorable attitudes toward HIV-risk-associated sexual behaviors, and reduced intentions for such behaviors, compared with adolescents in the control condition. In addition, they expressed more favorable hedonistic beliefs and stronger perceived behavioral control regarding condom use than did their counterparts in the control condition. In summary, these analyses on postintervention data made clear that we achieved changes on theoretically relevant variables thought to mediate behavior change immediately after the intervention. The next question was whether the intervention resulted in less sexual-risk behavior. A 3-month follow-up assessment was designed to address this question.

An important threat to the validity of studies like ours, involving several data-collection points, is the possibility of participant attrition, particularly differential attrition from conditions. Attrition reduces generalizability, and differential attrition from conditions clouds causal interpretation of treatment effects. We allocated participant reimbursement so as to increase the likelihood that participants would return for follow-up. The participants could have received a total of $40. They received $15 at the end of the intervention session, which involved an 8-hour time commitment, and they received $25 at the 3-month follow-up, which involved a 2-hour commitment. Questions are sometimes raised about paying participants in HIV-intervention studies. However, we believe that an important advantage of paying the participants is that it increases the diversity of the sample. If participants are not paid, then only those highly interested in risk reduction are likely to volunteer. By reimbursing participants, we recruit not only the highly interested, but also those who are volunteering just for the money; hence, a broader population.

Of the original participants, 150 completed follow-up questionnaires 3 months after the intervention, a return rate of 95.5%. ANCOVA, controlling for preintervention sexual behavior, indicated that adolescents in the HIV-risk-reduction condition reported less HIV-risk-associated sexual behavior in the 3 months postintervention than did those in the control condition. This analysis was done on a composite risky sexual behavior score, which combined responses to several sexual behav-

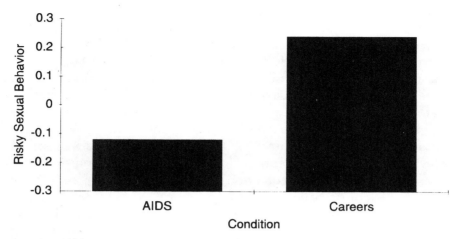

Figure 2. Mean adjusted 3-month follow-up risky sexual behavior among African American male adolescents by condition.

ior questions. Because the behaviors had different means and standard deviations, the responses were standardized to z scores. The composite score was the mean z score. The adjusted means are shown in Figure 2.

Additional ANCOVAs were performed on the specific behaviors that comprised the composite risky sexual behavior score. As shown in Table 1, the participants in the HIV-risk-reduction condition, compared with those in the control condition, reported having coitus less frequently and with fewer women, they reported using condoms more consistently during coitus, and fewer of them reported engaging in heterosexual anal intercourse. In addition, the HIV-risk-reduction-intervention partici-

TABLE 1
Adjusted Means for Specific Sexual Behaviors, by
Experimental Condition

| | Condition | |
| | HIV-risk-reduction | Career opportunities |
Sexual behavior		
Coitus	0.5	0.6
Days had coitus	2.2**	5.5
Coital partners	0.9***	1.8
Rated condom-use frequency	4.4*	3.5
Days did not use condom during coitus	0.6***	2.4
Heterosexual anal sex	0.1*	0.3

Note. For each variable, the preintervention measure was partialed out of the 3-month follow-up measure. Coitus and heterosexual anal sex were coded 0 = did not engage in the behavior in the past 3 months and 1 = did engage in the behavior in the past 3 months. The number of self-reported days on which the participants had coitus ranged from 0 to 50. The number of self-reported coital partners ranged from 0 to 9. Condom-use frequency was rated on 5-point scale from *never* (1) to *always* (5). The number of self-reported days on which the participants had coitus without using a condom ranged from 0 to 19.
*$p < .02$. **$p < .008$. ***$p < .003$.

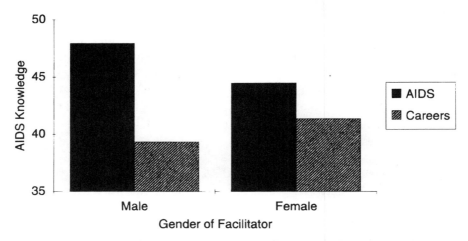

Figure 3. Mean adjusted postintervention AIDS knowledge among African American male adolescents by condition and facilitator gender.

pants still had greater AIDS knowledge and weaker intentions for sexual risk behavior in the next 3 months than did the other participants. Marlowe-Crowne Social Desirability Scale scores were unrelated to preintervention, 3-month follow-up, or amount of change in self-reports of risky sexual behavior. In addition, scores were unrelated to pre, post, or follow-up intentions and attitudes or to changes in these variables.

We had expected Condition × Gender of Facilitator interactions such that the effects of the HIV-risk-reduction intervention would be enhanced with African American male facilitators. Surprisingly, we did not find consistent support for this hypothesis. Consonant with the hypothesis, analyses on the postintervention questionnaire revealed a Condition × Gender of Facilitator interaction such that the HIV-risk-reduction intervention caused a greater increase in AIDS knowledge among participants who had a male facilitator than among those who had a female facilitator (see Figure 3). On the other hand, this interaction was not evident on postintervention measures of hedonistic beliefs, attitudes, perceived behavioral control, or intentions or on 3-month follow-up AIDS knowledge. In addition, the effects of the HIV-risk-reduction intervention on attitudes and sexual behavior measured at the 3-month follow-up were significantly *stronger* with female facilitators than with male facilitators, which was opposite to the predicted result (see Figure 4).

This study indicates that a relatively brief intervention can have impact on theory-based mediators of behavior change and self-reported sexual risk behavior among African American adolescents. Since this initial study, our research has proceeded in two directions. The study raised the question of whether particular conceptual variables are particularly important to achieving behavior change. Thus, one line of work seeks to identify the particular conceptual variables that are most important to achieving intervention-induced sexual risk behavior change. The lack of consistent effects of facilitator gender and the fact that the study included only male adolescents leave unanswered some practical questions about the best way to intervene with inner-city African American adolescents to reduce their sexual risk behavior. A second line of research seeks to elucidate whether the effectiveness of HIV-risk-reduction behavioral interventions is moderated by characteristics of facilitators, such as gender and race.

J. B. Jemmott, Jemmott, Spears, Hewitt, and Cruz-Collins (1992) conducted a study that focused more directly on the conceptual variables that mediate African American female adolescents' intentions to use condoms. J. B. Jemmott, Jemmott, Spears, et al. compared the effects on condom-use intentions of three interventions: (a) a social–cognitive intervention designed to increase hedonistic beliefs and perceived behavioral control regarding condoms, (b) an information-alone intervention designed to increase general AIDS knowledge and specific prevention beliefs, and (c) a general health-promotion intervention designed to provide information about health problems other than AIDS. The subjects were 19 sexually active African American adolescent women from an inner-city family planning clinic. As in the J. B. Jemmott, Jemmott, and Fong (1992) study, all interventions lasted the same amount of time and involved the use of videos and small-group exercises and games.

Analysis of covariance ANCOVA revealed that although participants in both the social–cognitive condition and the information-alone condition scored significantly higher in AIDS knowledge and prevention beliefs than did those in the health-promotion condition, participants in the social–cognitive condition registered significantly greater intentions to use condoms than did those in the other two conditions. In

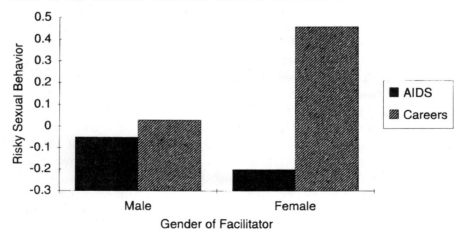

Figure 4. Mean adjusted 3-month follow-up risky sexual behavior among African American male adolescents by condition and facilitator gender.

addition, participants in the social–cognitive condition, as compared with the other conditions, reported significantly greater perceived self-efficacy and behavioral control and more favorable hedonistic beliefs—the two hypothesized mediators of the effects on condom-use intentions of the intervention. Thus, the study indicates that intervention-induced increases in AIDS knowledge and prevention beliefs do not portend changes in plans for sexual risk behavior. In addition, it highlights the importance of self-efficacy and hedonistic expectancies. The sample size was small, thus, it might be argued that the implications are limited. However, significance tests take sample size into account. In this sense, the fact that the intervention had significant effects on intentions and other theoretically relevant variables is impressive.

In another study bearing on conceptual variables, L. S. Jemmott and Jemmott (1992) evaluated an HIV-risk-reduction program for inner-city adolescent women, implemented by a community-based organization, the Urban League of Metropolitan Trenton. The three-session, 5-hour HIV-risk-reduction program drew on the studies by J. B. Jemmott, Jemmott, and Fong (1992) and J. B. Jemmott, Jemmott, Spears, et al. (1992) and used many of the same activities. The intervention, implemented by an African American female facilitator, addressed perceived behavioral control, hedonistic beliefs, and prevention beliefs. The 109 adolescent women who participated in the program scored higher in AIDS knowledge, registered more favorable prevention beliefs and hedonistic beliefs, expressed greater self-efficacy and perceived behavioral control, and scored higher in intentions to use condoms after the program, as compared with before it. Additional analyses indicated that increases in perceived self-efficacy, behavioral control, and hedonistic beliefs predicted increases in intentions to use condoms, whereas increases in general AIDS knowledge and specific prevention beliefs did not. One weakness of the study is that the changes in intentions might not reflect intervention effects, but history. L. S. Jemmott and Jemmott (1992) reasoned that history was an unlikely explanation, because the women participated in intervention groups that were run sequentially over a 6-month period. In this view, it is unlikely that events besides the intervention activities could have occurred between preintervention and postintervention and increased scores for these multiple-intervention groups. Although history cannot account for the differential predictive power of perceived self-efficacy and hedonistic beliefs, as compared with AIDS knowledge and prevention beliefs, the fact that the study did not include a control group that did not receive HIV-risk-reduction interventions limits the ability to draw causal inferences about intervention effects.

J. B. Jemmott, Jemmott, and Hacker (1992) tested the theory of planned behavior as a model of intentions to use condoms among 179

African American (72%) and Latino (19%) inner-city adolescents who attended a minority youth health conference organized by the Urban League of Metropolitan Trenton. Participants completed a confidential preconference questionnaire. Hierarchical multiple regression analysis was used to test the theory of planned behavior. In the first step, condom-use intentions were regressed on attitudes and subjective norms. The squared multiple correlation (.31) was statistically significant, as were the regression coefficients for attitudes and subjective norms. According to the theory of reasoned action, only attitude and subjective norm have direct effects on intentions. Thus, perceived behavioral control should not be significantly related to intentions if attitudes and subject norm are in the regression equation. However, in keeping consistent with the theory of planned behavior, in Step 2 of the hierarchical regression analysis, perceived behavioral control contributed a significant increment (.19) to the squared multiple correlation. Behavioral beliefs about the effects of condoms on sexual enjoyment, normative beliefs regarding sexual partners' and mothers' approval, and control beliefs regarding technical skill at using condoms were associated with condom-use intentions. These results suggest the utility of the theory of planned behavior for understanding condom-use decisions among inner-city African American adolescents.

Group Demographics

The second line of research focused on practical questions about the best way to intervene with inner-city African American adolescents. We were interested in pursuing further the issue of gender of facilitator. Gender of facilitator did not have consistent effects in the J. B. Jemmott, Jemmott, and Fong (1992) study, a result that may have occurred because the study included only male adolescents. Perhaps gender of facilitator is more important if the intervention participants are female adolescents. The literature on disclosure of personal information would suggest that men and women prefer to discuss personal or embarrassing information with a woman rather than a man and that this preference for female confidantes is particularly strong among women (Bennett & Dickinson, 1980; Noller & Callan, 1990). A second issue of interest was the race of the facilitator. We tested the hypothesis that an intervention with African American adolescents would be more effective if the facilitator were African American, as compared with White. Another issue the study addressed was the gender composition of the group. Interventions dealing with sexual behavior of adolescents may be more effective if implemented in single-sex groups. The advantage of single-sex groups may be particularly great for female adolescents. Thus, we tested whether the effectiveness of the intervention would vary depending on whether the group contained participants of only one gender or both male and female adolescents.

The participants were 506 seventh- and eighth-grade African American adolescents recruited from the public junior high schools and elementary schools of Trenton, New Jersey (J. B. Jemmott, Jemmott, & Fong, 1995). They volunteered for a health-promotion project, designed to reduce the chances that teenagers will develop devastating health problems, including cardiovascular diseases, cancers, and AIDS. Although the mean age of the participants was only 13.1 years, about 55% of respondents reported having experienced coitus at least once, and about 31% of all respondents reported having coitus in the past 3 months. About 25% of those reporting coitus in the past 3 months indicated that they never used condoms during those experiences, whereas 30% indicated that they always used condoms during those experiences.

The adolescents were assigned randomly to either an HIV-risk-reduction condition or the control condition and to a small group that was either homogeneous or heterogeneous in gender and that was led by a specially trained male or female facilitator who was African American or White. Adolescents in the HIV-risk-reduction condition received a 5-hour intervention designed to influence variables theoretically important to behavior change and to be meaningful and culturally and developmentally appropriate for young, inner-city African American adolescents. From a theoretical perspective, the intervention was designed (a) to increase perceived self-efficacy/behavioral control regarding the ability to implement condom use, including confidence that they could get their partner to use one; (b) to address hedonistic beliefs to allay participants' fears regarding adverse consequences of condoms on sexual enjoyment; and (c) to increase general knowledge of AIDS and STDs and specific beliefs regarding the use of condoms to prevent sexually transmitted HIV infection. As in our previous intervention studies, videotapes, games, and exercises were used to facilitate learning and active participation.

Participants in the control condition received an intervention targeting behaviors (e.g., dietary and exercise habits and cigarette smoking) that affect the risk of certain health problems other than AIDS. These health problems, including cardiovascular disease, hypertension, and certain cancers, are leading causes of morbidity and mortality among African Americans (Gillum, 1982; Ibrahim, Chobanian, Horan, & Roccella, 1985; Page & Asire, 1985). Structurally similar to the HIV-risk-reduction intervention, the general health-promotion intervention also lasted 5 hours and used culturally and developmentally appropriate videotapes, exercises, and games to reinforce learning and to encourage active participation.

Before, immediately after, 3 months after, and 6 months after the intervention the participants completed questionnaires of intentions, hedonistic beliefs, prevention beliefs, perceived self-efficacy to use condoms, and AIDS knowledge. The Marlowe–Crowne Social Desirability Scale, included in the preintervention questionnaire, was used to measure the tendency of participants to describe themselves in favorable, socially desirable terms. Adolescents in the HIV-risk-reduction condition subsequently expressed stronger intentions to use condoms; had more favorable beliefs about the effects of condoms on sexual enjoyment and about the ability of condoms to prevent pregnancy, STD, and AIDS; had greater perceived self-efficacy to use condoms; and had greater knowledge about AIDS than did those in the control condition, controlling for preintervention measures of the particular dependent measure. Of the original participants, 489 (97%) took part in the 3-month follow-up, and 469 (93%) took part in the 6-month follow-up. The effects of the HIV-risk-reduction intervention on the conceptual variables were sustained over the 6-month time interval. At both follow-ups, participants in the HIV-risk-reduction intervention scored higher on intentions to use condoms, AIDS knowledge, hedonistic beliefs, and perceived self-efficacy to use condoms than did the participants in the health-promotion condition. Although there were no significant effects of the HIV-risk-reduction intervention on self-reports of unprotected coitus at the 3-month follow-up, there was a significant effect at the 6-month follow-up: Adolescents who had received the HIV-risk-reduction intervention reported fewer days on which they had coitus without using a condom in the past 3 months than did those who had received the health-promotion intervention, controlling for preintervention self-reports.

Pearson product–moment correlations and multiple regression analyses revealed that scores on the Marlowe–Crowne Social Desirability Scale were unrelated to self-reports of condom use preintervention, at the 3-month follow-up, or at the 6-month follow-up or to changes in self-reports of condom use from preintervention to the 3-month or 6-month follow-up. Marlowe–Crowne Social Desirability scores were also unrelated to preintervention, postintervention, 3-month follow-up, or 6-month follow-up intentions to use condoms or to changes in intentions. Moreover, hierarchical multiple regression analyses revealed that the scores did not interact with experimental condition to affect self-reported condom use or intentions at postintervention, 3-month follow-up, or 6-month follow-up. The scores were also unrelated to self-reported condom use, intentions, or changes in these variables in the subsample of adolescents in the AIDS condition.

Analyses also examined whether effects of the intervention varied as a function of race of the facilitator, gender of the facilitator, gender of the participants, and gender composition of the intervention groups. We tested these interactions on four classes of variables: (a) the participants' perceptions of the intervention—how much they liked it, how much they talked, and how much they felt they learned; (b) the facilitators' perceptions of how much the participants liked it, talked, and learned from the intervention; (c) AIDS knowledge test, prevention beliefs, hedonistic beliefs, intentions, and perceived behavioral control; and (d) self-reported unprotected sexual intercourse. Results revealed that none of the interactions were statistically significant. Race of the facilitator, the gender of the facilitator, the gender of the participants, and the gender composition of the intervention group did not moderate facilitators' reports of how the participants reacted to the intervention or participants' own reports of their reactions to the interventions: How much they liked it, how much they talked, and how much they felt they had learned. In addition, these factors did not moderate effects of the intervention on AIDS knowledge, prevention beliefs, hedonistic beliefs, perceived self-efficacy, intentions, or self-reports of unprotected coitus. The effects of the HIV-risk-reduction intervention were about the same, irrespective of the race of the facilitator, the gender of the facilitator, the gender of the participants, and the gender composition of the intervention group.

CONCLUSION

First, these studies suggest that intensive 1-day interventions can influence theory-based motivational determinants of sexual risk behavior among inner-city African American adolescents, including African American male adolescents. Second, the studies suggest that it is possible to influence self-reports of unprotected coitus among inner-city African American adolescents, including African American male adolescents. Third, the present results suggest that the influence of the race and gender of facilitators or health educators may be more complex than previously assumed.

The lack of effects of race of facilitator is particularly surprising. In theory, African American facilitators should have a better grasp of the language, values, and experiences of African American adolescents, they should be better able to adapt prevention strategies to suit the adolescents, they should be less likely to offend the adolescents by using inaccurate and pernicious group stereotypes, and they should be able to establish rapport more readily and rapidly. This should presumably translate into better intervention outcomes. Yet, we found that race matching did not enhance intervention effects.

Although one possible explanation for this is that race matching is less important than previously assumed, a number of additional explanations should also be considered. First, perhaps the race matching did not matter because the intervention itself was culturally sensitive. All of the intervention materials had been selected to be culturally appropriate. Second, the activities were highly structured and engaging, which would have minimized the importance of individual facilitators. Third, all facilitators trained together, which may have served to calibrate their behavior. The training of the facilitators emphasized the importance of implementing the interventions according to the protocol, which might have further minimized any differences among facilitators with different characteristics. Thus, the culturally sensitive nature of the intervention and the strict nature of the facilitator-training protocol may have attenuated any effects of facilitator race. In the absence of such training, if culturally inappropriate materials had been used, and if the intervention had been less highly structured, differences in facilitator behavior by race might have emerged. Under such circumstances, results might have been different from those observed in the present study. This, of course, is an empirical question.

The significant effects of the interventions studies cannot be explained as a simple result of special attention received by the adolescents in the HIV-risk-reduction-intervention conditions. Participants in the control conditions (whether career opportunities or general health promotion) received the same amount of attention as those in the HIV-risk-reduction condition. Participants in the HIV-risk-reduction and control interventions went through similar activities that lasted the same amount of time.

By its very nature, sexual risk behavior is private behavior and, consequently, must be assessed with indirect measures. Thus, in our studies, *self-reports* of sexual risk behaviors, not sexual risk behaviors, were examined. Interpretations of findings should include consideration of the possibility that the participants' reports of their sexual practices might have been to some degree unintentionally or intentionally inaccurate. On several grounds, however, confidence about the accuracy of the responses in the present experiment is warranted. The fact that participants were asked to recall sexual risk behavior over a relatively brief period of time (i.e., 3 months) would facilitate their ability to recall their behavior. In addition, we used a number of techniques to make it less likely that participants in the present study would minimize or exaggerate reports of their sexual experiences, (a) code numbers rather than names were used on the questionnaires, (b) facilitators were not involved in any way in the administration of questionnaires, (c) the importance of responding honestly was emphasized, and (d) participants were assured that their responses would be kept confidential, and they signed an agreement to respond honestly. In addition, if concern about how they would be viewed by others influenced respondents' reports of their sexual behavior, the adolescents who were higher in the need for social approval might have differed from the other adolescents in self-reported sexual risk behavior or in the change in their reports after the HIV-risk-reduction intervention. However, analyses in the J. B. Jemmott, Jemmott, and Fong (1992) study and the J. B. Jemmott, Jemmott, and Fong (1995) study revealed that preintervention and follow-up self-reports of sexual risk behavior and the change in reported behavior were unrelated to social desirability response bias. Nevertheless, interpretations of our findings should include consideration of the possibility that the participants' self-reports might have been inaccurate.

In future research, it would be valuable to include other measures of sexual risk behavior. Another approach to assessing sexual risk behavior would be to measure physiological proxy variables that are indicative of unprotected sexual intercourse. For example, clinically documented STDs (e.g., chlamydia, gonorrhea, and syphilis) would provide valuable information. Still, note that even STD testing is not a perfect measure of unprotected sexual intercourse because it underestimates the actual frequency of unprotected sexual intercourse. Although a positive STD test establishes that unprotected sexual intercourse has occurred, a negative test result does not rule out the possibility that unprotected sexual intercourse has occurred. The test could be negative, not because of the practice of safer sex or abstinence, but because of unprotected sex with a partner who was not infected.

One common argument against HIV-risk-reduction education programs for adolescents and children has been that exposing them to information about sex will encourage them to engage in sexual activity. Our data, however, provide some evidence that the opposite may be true. Adolescents who received the HIV-risk-reduction intervention were less likely to engage in sexual activity, and those who did were more likely to engage in safe sexual activity. Thus, the fear that providing adolescents with information about AIDS will result in greater sexual activity is perhaps simply a fear.

Given the widely recognized potential risk of pregnancy and STD, including HIV, among inner-city African American adolescents, the results of these studies are encouraging. They suggest that relatively brief but intensive intervention can have significant impact on sexual risk behavior and theory-based mediators of such behavior among African American inner-city adolescents. We are optimistic that continued work along these lines will increase understanding of the social psychology of sexual risk behavior and will reduce the problems of pregnancy and STD, including HIV, among African American adolescents.

REFERENCES

Ager, J., Shea, F., & Agronow, S. (1982). Method discontinuance in teenage women. In I. Stuart & C. Wells (Eds.), *Pregnancy in adolescence* (pp. 236–263). New York: Van Nostrand Reinhold.

Ajzen, I. (1985). From intentions to actions: A theory of planned behavior. In J. Kuhl and J. Beckmann (Eds.), *Action-control: From cognition to behavior,* (pp. 11–39). Heidelberg: Springer.

Ajzen, I. (1991). The theory of planned behavior. *Organizational Behavior and Human Decision Processes, 50,* 179–211.

Ajzen, I., & Fishbein, M. (1980). *Understanding attitudes and predicting social behavior.* Englewood Cliffs, NJ: Prentice Hall.

Ajzen, I., & Madden, T. (1986). Prediction of goal-directed behavior: Attitudes, intentions, and perceived behavioral control. *Journal of Experimental Social Psychology, 22,* 453–474.

Bandura, A. (1986). *Social foundations of thought and action: A social cognitive theory.* Englewood Cliffs, NJ: Prentice Hall.

Bandura, A. (1989). Perceived self-efficacy. In V. M. Mays, G. W. Albee, & S. F. Schneider (Eds.), *Primary prevention of AIDS: Psychological approaches* (pp. 128–141). Newbury Park, CA: Sage.

Bandura, A. (1994). Social cognitive theory and exercise of control over HIV infection. In R. DiClemente & J. Peterson (Eds.), *Preventing AIDS: Theory and practice of behavioral interventions* (pp. 25–60). New York: Plenum.

Bell, T. A., & Holmes, K. K. (1984). Age-specific risks of syphilis, gonorrhea, and hospitalized pelvic inflammatory disease in sexually experienced U.S. women. *Sexually Transmitted Diseases, 7,* 291.

Bennett, S. M., & Dickinson, W. B. (1980). Student–parent rapport and parent involvement in sex, birth control, and venereal disease education. *Journal of Sex Research, 16,* 114–130.

Brown, S. V. (1985). Premarital sexual permissiveness among Black adolescent females. *Social Psychology Quarterly, 48,* 381–387.

Catania, J. A., Dolcini, M. M., Coates, T. J., Kegeles, S. M., Greenblatt, R. M., Puckett, S., Corman, M., & Miller, J. (1989). Predictors of condom use and multiple partnered sex among sexually-active adolescent women: Implications for AIDS-related health interventions. *Journal of Sex Research, 26,* 514–524.

Cates, W., Jr. (1987). Epidemiology and control of sexually transmitted diseases: Strategic evolution. *Infectious Disease Clinics of North America, 1,* 1–23.

Centers for Disease Control. (1988). Condoms for the prevention of sexually transmitted diseases. *Morbidity and Mortality Weekly Report, 37,* 133–137.

Centers for Disease Control. (1990). *National HIV seroprevalence surveys: Summary of results. Data from serosurveillance activities through 1989.* Atlanta, GA: Author.

Centers for Disease Control. (1991). Premarital sexual experience among adolescent women—United States, 1970–1988. *Morbidity and Mortality Weekly Report, 39,* 929–932.

Centers for Disease Control and Prevention (CDC). (1995a). *HIV/AIDS Surveillance Report, 7*(1), 1–34.

Centers for Disease Control and Prevention (CDC). (1995b). *Sexually transmitted disease surveillance, 1994,* Atlanta, GA: Author.

Chu, S., Buehler, J., & Berkelman, R. (1990). Impact of the human immunodeficiency virus epidemic on mortality in women of reproductive age. *Journal of the American Medical Association, 264,* 225–229.

Crowne, D., & Marlowe, D. (1964). *The approval motive.* New York: Wiley.

Davidson, A. R., & Jaccard, J. J. (1979). Variables that moderate the attitude-behavior relation: Results of a longitudinal survey. *Journal of Personality and Social Psychology, 37,* 1364–1376.

Fishbein, M. (1982). Social psychological analysis of smoking behavior. In J. R. Eiser (Ed.), *Social psychology and behavioral medicine* (pp. 179–197). New York: Wiley.

Fishbein, M., & Ajzen, I. (1975). *Belief, attitude, intention and behavior.* Boston: Addison-Wesley.

Fishbein, M., & Middlestadt, S. (1989). Using the theory of reasoned action as a framework for understanding and changing AIDS-related behaviors. In V. Mays, G. Albee, & S. Schneider (Eds.), *Primary prevention of AIDS: Psychological approaches* (pp. 93–110). Newbury Park, CA: Sage.

Fishbein, M., Middlestadt, S., & Hitchcock, P. J. (1994). Using information to change sexually transmitted disease-related behaviors: An analysis based on the theory of reasoned action. In R. DiClemente & J. Peterson (Eds.), *Preventing AIDS: Theory and practice of behavioral interventions* (pp. 61–78). New York: Plenum.

Fox, G. L., & Inazu, J. K. (1980). Patterns and outcomes of mother-daughter communication about sexuality. *Journal of Social Issues, 36,* 7–29.

Furstenberg, F. F. (1971). Birth control experience among pregnant adolescents: The process of unplanned parenthood. *Social Problems, 19,* 192–203.

Gillum, R. F. (1982). Coronary heart disease in Black populations: I. Mortality and morbidity. *American Heart Journal, 104,* 839–843.

Guttentag, M., & Secord, P. F. (1983). *Too many women?* Beverly Hills, CA: Sage.

Handelman, C. D., Cabral, R. J., & Weisfeld, G. E. (1987). Sources of information and adolescent sexual knowledge and behavior. *Journal of Adolescent Research, 2,* 455–463.

Hatcher, R. A., Trussell, J., Stewart, F., Stewart, G. K., Kowal, D., Guest, F., Cates, W., Jr., & Policar, M. S. (1994). *Contraceptive technology* (16th ed., rev.). New York: Irvington.

Henshaw, S. K. (1992). *U.S. teenage pregnancy statistics*. New York: Alan Guttmacher Institute.

Hingson, R. W., Strunin, L., Berlin, B., & Heeren, T. (1990). Beliefs about AIDS, use of alcohol and drugs, and unprotected sex among Massachusetts adolescents. *American Journal of Public Health, 80*, 295–299.

Hofferth, S., & Hayes, C. (1987). *Risking the future (Vol. 2)*. Washington, DC: National Academy Press.

Hogan, D. P., Astone, N. M., & Kitagawa, E. M. (1985). Social and environmental factors influencing contraceptive use among Black adolescents. *Family Planning Perspectives, 17*, 165–169.

Hogan, D. P., & Kitagawa, E. M. (1985). The impact of social status, family structure, and neighborhood on the fertility of Black adolescents. *American Journal of Sociology, 90*, 825–855.

Ibrahim, M., Chobanian, A. V., Horan, M., & Roccella, E. J. (1985). Hypertension prevalence and the status of awareness, treatment, and control in the United States: Final report of the Subcommittee on Definition and Prevalence of the 1984 Joint National Committee on Detection, Evaluation, and Treatment of High Blood Pressure. *Hypertension, 7*, 453–468.

Jemmott, J. B. III, Jemmott, L. S., & Fong, G. T. (1992). Reductions in HIV-risk-associated sexual behaviors among Black male adolescents: Effects of an AIDS prevention intervention. *American Journal of Public Health, 82*, 372–377.

Jemmott, J. B. III, Jemmott, L. S., & Fong, G. T. (1995). *Reducing the risk of AIDS in Black adolescents: Evidence for the generality of intervention effects*. Unpublished manuscript, Princeton University, Princeton, NJ.

Jemmott, J. B. III, Jemmott, L. S., & Hacker, C. I. (1992). Predicting intentions to use condoms among African American adolescents: The theory of planned behavior as a model of HIV risk associated behavior. *Journal of Ethnicity and Disease, 2*, 371–380.

Jemmott, J. B. III, Jemmott, L. S., Spears, H., Hewitt, N., & Cruz-Collins, M. (1992). Self-efficacy, hedonistic expectancies, and condom-use intentions among inner-city Black adolescent women: A social cognitive approach to AIDS risk behavior. *Journal of Adolescent Health, 13*, 512–519.

Jemmott, J. B. III, & Miller, S. M. (in press). Women's reproductive decisions in the context of HIV infection. In A. O'Leary & L. S. Jemmott (Eds.), *Women and AIDS: Issues in coping and caring*. New York: Plenum.

Jemmott, L. S., & Jemmott, J. B. III. (1990). Sexual knowledge, attitudes, and risky sexual behavior among inner-city Black male adolescents. *Journal of Adolescent Research, 5*, 346–369.

Jemmott, L. S., & Jemmott, J. B. III. (1992). Increasing condom-use intentions among sexually active inner-city Black adolescent women: Effects of an AIDS prevention program. *Nursing Research, 41*, 273–279.

Jones, E. F., Forrest, J. D., Goldman, N., Henshaw, S. Lincoln, R., Rosoff, J. I., Westoff, C. F., & Wulf, D. (1986). *Teenage pregnancy in industrialized countries*. New Haven, CT: Yale University Press.

Keller, S. E., Barlett, J. A., Schleifer, S. J., Johnson, R. L., Pinner, E., & Delaney, B. (1991). HIV-relevant sexual behavior among a healthy inner-city heterosexual adolescent population in an endemic area of HIV. *Journal of Adolescent Health, 12,* 44–48.

Kelly, J. A., Lawrence, J. S., Hood, H. V., & Brasfield, T. L. (1989). Behavioral intervention to reduce AIDS risk activities. *Journal of Consulting and Clinical Psychology, 57,* 60–67.

Madden, T. J., Ellen, P. S., & Ajzen, I. (1992). A comparison of the theory of planned behavior and the theory of reasoned action. *Personality and Social Psychology Bulletin, 18,* 3–9.

Manstead, A. S. R., Profitt, C., & Smart, J. L. (1983). Predicting and understanding mothers' infant-feeding intentions and behaviors. *Journal of Personality and Social Psychology, 44,* 657–671.

Milan, R. J., & Kilmann, P. R. (1987). Interpersonal factors in premarital contraception. *Journal of Sex Research, 23,* 289–321.

Morrison, D. (1985). Adolescent contraceptive behavior: A review. *Psychological Bulletin, 98,* 538–568.

Nathanson, C. A., & Becker, M. H. (1986). Family and peer influence on obtaining a method of contraception. *Journal of Marriage and the Family, 48,* 513–526.

Noller, P., & Callan, V. J. (1990). Adolescents' perceptions of the nature of their communication with parents. *Journal of Youth and Adolescence, 19,* 349–362.

O'Leary, A. (1985). Self-efficacy and health. *Behavioral Research and Therapy, 23,* 437–451.

Page, H. S., & Asire, A. J. (1985). *Cancer rates and risks* (NIH Publication No. 85-691, 3rd ed.). Bethesda, MD: National Institutes of Health.

Pratt, W., Mosher, W., Bachrach, C., & Horn, M. (1984). Understanding U. S. fertility: Findings from the National Survey of Family Growth, Cycle III. *Population Bulletin, 39,* 1–42.

Schifter, D. E., & Ajzen, I. (1985). Intention, perceived control, and weight loss: An application of the theory of planned behavior. *Journal of Personality and Social Psychology, 49,* 843–851.

Schinke, S. P., Gilchrist, L. D., & Small, R. W. (1979). Preventing unwanted adolescent pregnancy: A cognitive behavioral approach. *American Journal of Orthopsychiatry, 49,* 81–88.

Sonenstein, F. L., Pleck, J. H., & Leighton, C. K. (1989). Sexual activity, condom use and AIDS awareness among adolescent males. *Family Planning Perspectives, 21,* 152–158.

Stone, K. M., Grimes, D. A., & Magdeer, L. S. (1986). Personal protection against sexually transmitted diseases. *American Journal of Obstetrics and Gynecology, 155*, 180–188.

Taylor, H., Kagay, M., & Leichenko, S. (1986). *American teens speak: Sex myths, TV, and birth control.* New York: Planned Parenthood Federation of America.

Temko, C. (1987). Seeking medical care for a breast cancer symptom: Determinants of intentions to engage in prompt or delay behavior. *Health Psychology, 6*, 305–328.

Thompson, L., & Spanier, G. (1978). Influence of parents, peers and partners on the contraceptive use of college men and women. *Journal of Marriage and the Family, 40*, 481–492.

Turner, C., Miller, H., & Moses, L. (1989). *AIDS: Sexual behavior and intravenous drug use.* Washington, DC: National Academy Press.

U.S. Bureau of the Census. (1989). Projects of the population of the United States, by age, sex, and race: 1988–2080. *Current population reports* (Series P-25, No. 1018). Washington, DC: U.S. Government Printing Office.

Valdiserri, R. O., Arena, V. C., Proctor, D., & Bonati, F. A. (1989). The relationship between women's attitudes about condoms and their use: Implications for condom promotion programs. *American Journal of Public Health, 79*, 499–503.

Valdiserri, R. O., Lyter, D. W., Leviton, L. C., Callahan, C. M., Kingsley, L. A., & Rinaldo, C. R. (1989). AIDS prevention in homosexual and bisexual men: Results of a randomized trial evaluating two risk reduction interventions. *AIDS, 3*, 21–26.

Zabin, L., & Clark, S. D., Jr. (1981). Why they delay: A study of teenage family planning clinic patients. *Family Planning Perspectives, 13*, 205–217.

Zabin, L., Kantner, J., & Zelnik, M. (1979). The risk of adolescent pregnancy in the first months of intercourse. *Family Planning Perspectives, 11*, 215–226.

Zelnik, M., Kantner, J. F., & Ford, K. (1981). *Sex and pregnancy in adolescence.* Beverly Hills, CA: Sage.

V

PSYCHOLOGISTS AS
HEALTH CARE PROVIDERS

INTRODUCTION

The last chapter in the book, chapter 26, "Expanding Roles in the Twenty-First Century," is written by six psychologists whose experiences and expertise provide both an overview of issues confronting the science and practice of psychology and a vision of the profession's future. Patrick H. DeLeon et al. strongly suggest that the profession is in need of individuals who understand the "big picture" of health care from a public policy vantage point. By taking steps to place psychology in the public eye and assuring that we take into account the societal and political forces that shape health care, research, and educational funding, only then can our relatively young profession hope to prosper. The chapter presents the various perspectives from the various authors' uniques perspectives from which to view psychologists' role as health care providers.

From a scientific perspective, DeLeon et al. challenge the field to address and mend the schism between scientists and practitioners. Issues are discussed that if not attended to, will impede even the best trained scientific psychologist from finding meaningful employment or that will interfere with the important contributions the field can make to society at large.

From a practice perspective, the chapter looks at the effects of congressional action (or inaction) and the corporatization of health care through various managed care paradigms to encourage the field to continue its evolution. DeLeon et al. believe that sticking to the field's identity as only a mental health field would go against the current of today's health care changes.

A section next reviews the educational and training issues that will influence the very survival of the field. DeLeon et al. point to the uniqueness of the scientist/practitioner tradition in the education of clinical psychologists and how psychologists provide not only health care but also new knowledge to the understanding of illness. The chapter discusses advocacy to ensure continued funding for the training of psychologists and for public information about the role of psychology, to guarantee our inclusion in the twenty-first century's health care system.

Looking at psychology's goals in the public interest, the chapter next highlights several projects of the American Psychological Association. Conferences on psychosocial and behavioral factors in women's health, projects on violence—both youth violence and male violence against women—and the Public Interest Directorate's involvement in occupational safety and workplace stress are reviewed.

Next, the chapter discusses the importance of psychology's expanding its scope of practice to include the authority to prescribe medication. The reasons for this expanded role are outlined, and levels of training are suggested to prepare psychologists for this new role.

The chapter, and the book, ends with a timely reflection on the rapid maturation of the relatively young field of psychology. By proactively addressing society's needs, psychology can not only improve the human condition but also make for itself, and our colleagues in the field, unlimited opportunities.

26

EXPANDING ROLES IN THE TWENTY-FIRST CENTURY

PATRICK H. DELEON, WILLIAM C. HOWELL,
RUSS NEWMAN, ANITA B. BROWN,
GWENDOLYN PURYEAR KEITA, and JOHN L. SEXTON

I (Patrick DeLeon) have had the opportunity to serve on Capitol Hill for slightly more than 2 decades, and without question, it has been a very satisfying and stimulating experience. For those of us who work in a public sphere, we know, however, that at some point we will leave. The experience is a constant reminder of how personal and how "temporary" the political/public policy process is. In each case, it seems not long ago that some other very impressive individual served in an important capacity, whether this be for the Appropriations, Finance, or Labor and Human Resources Committee. Although I am a chief of staff, I am unaware of who served in that capacity for the previous chairpersons.

This represents a fundamentally different way of looking at the world, or at one's professional identity, than many of our colleagues

The views expressed do not necessarily reflect those of the U.S. Army, Navy, or Department of Defense.

typically do. Working within the political process, the philosophy of doing what can be done to improve society and, in all candor, not really worrying very much about that which can not be influenced was adopted. The public policy/political process is truly evolutionary in nature. Over the years, it has become evident that it cannot be controlled by any one individual or special interest group. Furthermore, when one leaves Capitol Hill, one has truly left!

BARRIERS

Over the past 2 decades, it has become very clear that although our colleagues in psychology—whether they be clinicians, researchers, or educators—are extraordinarily intelligent and professionally competent individuals, at the same time, they are surprisingly narrow in their perspective. If one seeks a researcher in a given area, it is true that a nationally renowned psychologist, with the appropriate expertise, who will truly do an outstanding job, can readily be found. But if one asks that individual about an important public policy issue in an area that is not directly relevant to his or her expertise, as a 12-year-old might say, "They do not have a clue."

Consider an image of a raft, with seven or eight distinguished psychologists on it, going down the Amazon River. Our colleagues know a considerable amount about their individual areas of expertise. And yet, none of them have ever been on a raft before, let alone on the Amazon River, where there are poisonous snakes, crocodiles, and many other creatures that, simply described, are not the type that one wants to put one's hands near. So this raft, with all of them on it—for none of them can get off—eventually will come to a waterfall. Some of our colleagues will vigorously expound as to why the raft should go right over the waterfall. They will argue, very forcefully, that they know, in their heart of hearts, from their personal experiences, that rafts go over waterfalls. That they should just proceed and see what happens. In this case, however, not only will the raft go over that waterfall, it will go down about 2,000 feet—straight down. Our colleagues are correct. The raft will go down. But none of the occupants will remain on the raft. They will become dinner for this crocodile or perhaps be hung up on a rock waiting for the birds to come. But because this has not been their personal experience, our traveling companions really do not believe the inevitable will happen. They really do not.

Psychology, as a profession, at this point in its evolution (for all of us are on that raft), is in need of individuals who possess the "bigger picture"—specifically, individuals with a public policy perspective. Perhaps they will not be quite as skilled as some of our colleagues about a particular research design, or as knowledgeable about how to conduct specific types of clinical therapies, but they will know something about rafts and waterfalls. We need to listen to individuals who appreciate the notion of "fording rivers," rather than blindly going over the waterfall and then wondering why eventually one hits bottom rather forcefully. Our collective lack of a public policy perspective is what may well be our profession's most significant weakness (DeLeon, 1988).

It is particularly unfortunate that many of us simply do not understand that we need this type of companion. We need colleagues who appreciate the specific place and societal context in which we find ourselves today. We do not need "friends" proclaiming, "Right, I have heard about 'fording.' We all 'hop off' right here and swim. Let the raft go first, and then we will just follow right behind." Or "Let us sit near those crocodiles, they are sound asleep. We'll just sit there for a while and rest." This is the image of our profession we should carry with us as we think about the evolving health care arena. Without question, we are maturing; however, this still is the image that comes to mind. We do not believe that most of our colleagues possess the big picture. Psychologists do not truly appreciate the societal or political context in which they live today.

Our profession is still very young. We are just beginning to mature. Our membership is maturing in both age and numbers. We are maturing in clinical techniques, research methodologies, and administrative responsibilities. Perhaps most significantly, we are finally beginning to mature in the public's eye (Resnick, DeLeon, & VandenBos, in press).

Approximately 2 decades ago, in 1977, the last state in the nation licensed psychologists as independent practitioners—in the terminology of today, as *health care providers*. That was not that long ago. As a youthful and evolving profession, we do not appreciate that it was not that long ago that most other professionals did not know that we existed. They could not, because until we became licensed, we did not exist as a "profession." The notion of having our own "scope of practice" and the concept of being one of the "educated professions"—these simply did not exist for us not that long ago.

Another fundamental concept, the significance of which many of us do not seem to understand, is that as individuals, we are extraordinarily fortunate. Our average income is $68,000; in contrast, our nation's median household income is less than $31,000. Realistically, this means that most of us live in families that possess at least two times the resources of the average American family. Educationally, we have no peer. As psychologists, we possess advanced degrees, with the doctorate taking, on average, more than 7 years to obtain. By comparison, nearly 80% of our nation's adult population possess less than a baccalaureate degree

(79.7%). Other studies suggest that nearly 20% of U.S. adults cannot read; they are functionally illiterate. Psychologists really represent society's elite. And yet, most of us do not realize how truly fortunate we are. Psychology has a major, not a tangential, responsibility to use its education in a manner that directly benefits society. We can no longer passively sit back and expect someone else to fulfill our responsibilities. As individuals, we often act as though we are paraprofessionals, not professionals. We act as though we have no control over our own destiny. Perhaps we view ourselves as an isolated professor in a small department, within a major university. The chair of a psychology department may complain that she or he does not possess the authority to make programmatic decisions. Yet, many psychology departments actually possess greater faculty resources than comparable law schools. Psychology chairs have greater resources than many deans. We often do not act as if we have the resources or the authority. We do not act as though we are an integral component of the university system or, more important, of society.

Even the American Psychological Association (APA) Board of Directors does not seem to appreciate the significance of having psychologists serve in high-level administrative positions, such as president of a university. In those positions, one establishes policy. The former APA treasurer, Judith Albino, was the president of the University of Colorado. At that policy level, she helped establish the priorities for the university and for each of its campuses. She would discuss with us the responsibility and challenges of providing high-quality education to citizens throughout the state, including rural Colorado. She conceptualized using the most up-to-date technology to deliver quality education and quality health care to those who traditionally would not have access. That is the type of dialogue that we should be having at the level of the APA board of directors and at APA's annual conventions. Unfortunately, however, this is quite rare. A defining element of a profession is an appreciation for how fast the world is evolving. By definition, professionals grasp the bigger picture and their societal responsibilities.

Within health care, skilled dermatologists, located at the Tripler Army Medical Center in Hawaii, can today perform quality consultations for patients on Guam. The visual resolution is that clear. The technology exists that allows health care providers and patients to effectively interact even though separated by thousands of miles. We suggest that this technology revolution, and that is what it is, demands a quantitatively different way of conceptualizing how to provide quality health care. It represents both a challenge and an exciting opportunity. Unfortunately, psychology does not appreciate the magnitude of required change, or more concretely, is not capitalizing on the advances in technology in a proactive fashion. There is no limit to how we can evolve as a profession.

However, we must seize the opportunity to develop our own substantive agenda (DeLeon, Sammons, & Sexton, 1995).

The most significant barrier facing psychology today is the profession's collective lack of vision. At times, psychologists can be so verbally assertive that they do not allow others to show us how little they (the psychologists) know. They do not appreciate that psychologists do not see the bigger picture. They simply do not listen to what society is saying. For example, teenage pregnancy has become a major problem in the United States. Of any industrialized nation in the world the United States has the highest incidence of teenage pregnancy. The American Medical Association understands this. The American Academy of Pediatrics understands this. The popular media vividly portrays a major role for the physician in addressing teenage pregnancy. However, teenage pregnancy is a behavioral phenomenon. It is the behavioral scientists who are, and who should be, on the cutting edge of developing prevention programs that work. Psychology should not continue to allow the medical profession to take credit for its accomplishments. The same situation is true for teenage violence and smoking cessation—both represent major public health hazards facing our nation today.

Another fundamental concept, which one serving on Capitol Hill quickly learns to appreciate, is the allocation of economic resources. Psychologist Debra Dunivin, a former APA congressional science fellow, investigated the amount of support provided by Medicare for training physicians. The reports varied considerably, ranging from $9 billion to $26 billion annually. By comparison, over each of the past several years, there has only been $2.5 million appropriated for mental health clinical training. Consider, $2.5 million to be shared by the five core mental health disciplines, contrasted with perhaps as much as $26 billion targeted for medical (and other health provider) training. Not surprisingly, psychology has historically not sought training support from Medicare. A Harvard medical school scholar and expert on stress physiology recently reported that 60% to 80% of visits to physicians involve stress-related problems that patients can help cure with self-care. Where is psychology in this emerging field of stress management? Surely, it has as much, or more to offer than medicine does (DeLeon, Frank, & Wedding, 1995).

The APA Practice and Education directorates are now beginning to address psychology's potential eligibility for Medicare's Graduate Medical Education initiative. However, at the same time, our professional training institutions remain blissfully unaware of what they are missing and what modifications they might ultimately have to make in their training programs to establish eligibility. Our educational institutions simply do not understand the bigger picture. They are not asking for their "fair share" of these substantial training resources. Health psychology, in particular, could be very responsive to Medicare's fundamental mission of providing high-quality health care to the elderly. Yet, as a profession, psychologists continue to be blissfully unaware of what potential training and service delivery resources they are missing.

The National Institutes of Health (NIH) develop an agenda from personal interaction between and among senior staff, and what emerges over the years is a picture of their personal pragmatic priorities. Personal involvement is the key. Our NIH colleague, Norman Anderson, is a perfect example. His behavioral science background will significantly influence how he ultimately recommends that funding be allocated. He may decide to focus on historically underserved populations, or he may not. However, until psychologists pay attention to what senior staff and institute directors believe should be the priorities of their individual institutes at the programmatic policy level, their profession (psychology) will never understand how the NIH is evolving. They will constantly react; they will not be proactive. They must become personally involved with policymakers. Unfortunately, they do not seem to conceptually understanding this.

To cite another concrete example, for the past decade, witnesses on behalf of the National Institute of Dental Research (NIDR) have consistently raised issues that many would consider to be within the domain of psychology. They discussed problems such as getting patients to see a dentist, problems with compliance, and emotional issues surrounding treating children. For NIDR, these are "dental issues"; for psychologists, they represent "behavioral health." Psychology has much to offer to the mission of NIDR. But psychologists must learn to listen to the institute's leadership rather than continuing to ignore this potential source of significant support. The same is also true for each of the other institutes, for example, the National Institute of Child Health and Human Development, the National Cancer Institute, and the National Institute of Nursing Research. The same underlying policy message exists.

Let us now focus on a related evolution occurring within health care: Psychology does not conceptually understand the significance of the fact that today 25% of doctoral level nursing faculty possess their degree in psychology. Over the next decade, there will be an increasing number of advanced-practice nurses, trained by these behavioral scientists, functioning throughout the health care arena in a wide variety of roles. Many aspects of advanced-practice nursing are, by definition, health psychology. But at the conceptual level, psychologists are not thinking about where the health care system is going. Psychologists do not understand that "they are we." We do not routinely have the type of interdisciplinary discussions that we should have. Once again, the only barrier preventing psychology from participating in these crucial interdisciplinary discussions is ourselves. We talk to ourselves excessively, but not about what is evolving in the real world. We do not systematically address society's needs, and we do not personally interact with those who set health care policy.

In many ways, psychologists seem to professionally agree that the American Medical Association should claim teenage pregnancy and teenage violence as their exclusive domain. They do not publicly proclaim the importance of the psychosocial aspects of working with families with diabetes. We psychologists do not insist that because more than half of the visits to primary health care providers are for psychosocial reasons, our practitioners should be actively involved. We do not argue in the public domain that a very high percentage of emergency room visits are primarily for psychological reasons or have psychological underpinnings. Perhaps we simply do not know how to assert our clinical value. We do not seem to even try. We often do not act like professionals, willing to accept clinical responsibilities. Yet we are starting to learn. Conceptually, we are beginning to think of ourselves as one of the health professions and as possessing a societal responsibility. This represents real progress. Over the years, psychologists have begun to understand that this nation's elected officials will be responsive to the needs of those who truly address society's problems—if and when they can see the contributions being made.

SOLUTIONS

Psychologists must become more personally involved in the public policy/political process. They must understand that their societal responsibilities include becoming intimately involved with those who establish public policy, including health care policy. From a policy perspective, mental health care is but a very small component of health care. Health care represents approximately one third of our nation's economy, and providers per se are only a subset of the total industry (Prospective Payment Assessment Commission, 1996; Samuelson, 1995).

We recently reviewed a report from the Library of Congress (1995) describing the composition of the 104th Congress (1995–1996). We were interested in learning how many members of Congress actually possessed a health care background. In the Senate, there is one physician and one social worker; 2% of the Senate have any firsthand experience as health care providers. In contrast, 54% of the Senate possess law degrees. If one has taught or taken a course in law school, it becomes readily evident that lawyers do not think the way psychologists think. The legislative process, in particular, expects the active participation of those with opposing views. It can be quite adversarial. Personal involvement is critical. In the Senate, those who establish health care policies definitely do not have any personal experience in providing mental health care. And unless they took a course in psychology at the undergraduate level or read about our research in the popular media, they may not be familiar with psychology.

In the House of Representatives, a very similar picture exists. The House has 4 physicians (1 of whom is a psychiatrist), 1 nurse, 2 dentists, 2 veterinarians, 1 pharmacist, and several social workers. During the last Congress, there was a psychologist, who hopefully will soon return. Of the 435 members in the House of Representatives, less than 15 have a health care background—approximately 3%. Simply stated, we should not expect our nation's elected officials to appreciate the nuances of providing mental health care or the potential broad clinical contribution of psychologists.

We think that one potential long-term solution is the APA Congressional Science Fellowship program. Over the past 2 decades, APA has been able to provide nearly 50 psychologists with the experience of working on Capitol Hill. This is a very positive approach. Not only have members of Congress and their staff been exposed to our colleagues' psychological expertise, a significant segment of the psychology profession has gained a firsthand glimpse of the political/public policy process. After their year of experience, the Fellows return to their universities and other employment settings, able to educate other psychologists about the all-important public policy process.

It has been our observation, however, that many of our colleagues often do not fully capitalize on the potential inherent in working on Capitol Hill. Over the years, there have been a number of psychologists working on Capitol Hill, on the personal staff, committee staff, and even as committee staff directors. Most of them refuse to identify themselves as psychologists and become quite defensive if the issue is raised.

We really do not understand this phenomena and sincerely hope that the APA Congressional Science Fellowship program will ultimately change this over time. Our training institutions must begin to systematically address the public policy process in a way that institutionally develops pride in public service. As psychologists, we should be proud of our profession and of what we can contribute to society. Unfortunately, too often we do not act proud. We do not regularly talk to elected officials or to policymakers in this program.

OPPORTUNITIES

Over the years, it has been extraordinarily difficult for psychology to convince the leadership of the NIH of the importance of the behavioral sciences to their fundamental mission. This is a very important objective, however, both for psychology and for our nation. Historically, almost all of the NIH directors have been physicians. Today there is a nurse, a dentist, and finally a psychologist. We must continue to collectively work to educate the NIH and those elected officials with oversight responsibilities regarding the importance of our behavioral science expertise. We can learn from professional nursing, now with its own National Institute of Nursing Research.

We must also learn to work collaboratively with those administrative psychologists who, for example, serve as directors of state mental health systems. Today a psychologist is the head of the state of California's mental health system. That governor understands the importance of psychology. Governors do not appoint individuals to their cabinet that they do not respect. Across the nation, there are a number of psychologists who serve in high-level administrative policy-setting positions. In all candor, however, we do not know very many of them. They frequently do not hold themselves out as psychologists, and equally important, we do not give them visibility within the profession.

By contrast, when a psychiatrist or other medical specialist is appointed to these important policy positions, they act as if they value their own profession. A physician was the director of the federal Office of Health Promotion and Disease Prevention. His strictly medical orientation was always evident. Behavioral health, however, was another matter. Psychologists must learn from the physicians. They must stop putting themselves down and, instead, learn to value their own expertise.

As an example, medicine can always find a position for their younger colleagues and actively mentors them for future leadership positions. Psychology does not do this. We do not find positions for new psychology graduates; we do not provide them with the experience of being deputy director of a community mental health center or health department.

We were very pleased, and in all candor quite surprised, that at the Opening Ceremony of the 1995 APA convention, a psychologist represented the mayor of New York. She had an impressive presence. What other psychologists are in potentially high visibility leadership positions? As a profession, psychologists must learn to value administrative expertise and to hold themselves out as possessing such. The clinical application of psychological knowledge is extraordinarily important. We must ensure that our nation's health care systems readily use our expertise.

Sometimes personal experiences speak volumes. Emergency rooms, to cite but one graphic example, are a place where the psychosocial aspects of health care are extraordinarily important. A decade ago, it became necessary for Patrick H. DeLeon's daughter to use an emergency room. At first, they said that she would be dead by morning, then that she would be brain-damaged for life. She is fine today, but the experience will never be forgotten. That is not the way anyone should be treated in an emergency room. Parents do not know how to deal with those blunt messages. No doubt there were well-intentioned professionals in that emergency room; however, they definitely did not know how to handle the psychosocial aspects of dealing with parents, especially those who had to explain to a sibling what might happen to his baby sister. Psychology has much to offer to families, and they must ensure that their expertise is utilized. There are many opportunities throughout the generic health care arena—far more than many of us appreciate.

One of the aspects of Robert J. Resnick's APA presidency that we have particularly come to admire has been his willingness to use the office on behalf of all of psychology. He has been willing to reach out and meet with people. From the very beginning, he has been particularly sensitive to the needs of our colleagues within the Department of Defense, perhaps because his son was on active duty. He has said to our military colleagues, "Tell me how you can use me!" That unusual message has been well received, and Dr. Resnick was recently awarded the U.S. Army's highest civilian recognition. Earlier APA presidents, such as Jack Wiggins, have also been willing to reach out and use the prestige of the office. President-Elect Dorothy Cantor will undoubtedly continue this tradition, particularly in addressing women's issues and inner-city needs. Although we do not really know how to most effectively use the office of our presidency, we are learning. Our association's leadership is actively attempting to have a real impact on society and on our nation's decision makers. We suggest that the availability of health care in our nation will continue to be a major agenda for the administration and for both nationally and locally elected officials in the years to come—an excellent forum for meaningful input.

The larger societal context is that in spite of managed care trends, our nation's health care costs continue to escalate faster than almost any other segment of the economy. The most recent figures suggest that in 1995, health spending exceeded $1 trillion for the first time in history (Prospective Payment Assessment Commission, 1996; Samuelson, 1995). Something has to be done. We are currently in the midst of major changes, and accordingly, we really cannot know with any sense of certainty how our health delivery system will ultimately evolve.

From the beginning of his administration, President Clinton made the enactment of comprehensive national health care reform legislation his highest priority. He has not yet succeeded, but in each of his State of the Union addresses, he continues to stress the importance of this issue. The Republican majority have made it clear that in time, they will have their own major health care legislation. Yet, it is too early to predict specifically how curtailing health care costs and increasing health care access will ultimately relate to reducing the national deficit. However, health care costs cannot continue to escalate. Radical changes are upon us.

Hopefully, we will soon see an era of systematically using objective data to make clinical decisions and to establish programmatic priorities. However, psychologists must not ignore our profession's history of aggressively fighting to retain the status quo. How dare someone try to tell our practitioners that what they have been doing for 40 years will not be reimbursed in the future? Listen to the intensity of our internal debates, particularly those surrounding managed care. Many of our practitioners simply refuse to understand that the world is moving forward. We refuse to understand the significance of clinical guidelines being required of the various medical specialties, including surgery. What has been happening throughout the generic health care arena is now just beginning to be experienced in mental health. Accountability is coming. Unfortunately, a sizable proportion of our practitioners simply refuse to believe the inevitable.

One of the important policy concepts that psychology is beginning to understand is that governmental entities will pay for services rendered by those health professionals whose training they have supported. The current buzzword is *primary health care provider*. Where are the training dollars for the next generation of primary health care providers? How will federal research activities relate to their practices? We are beginning to look at those federal statutes that address primary care to find out where, in fact, training resources exist. We are finally asking how we might obtain our fair share of these resources: Title VII of the health professions legislation and Medicare.

Over the years, we have been quite successful in having psychology statutorily recognized under an increasing number of health professions initiatives. This is very important. Few of us have ever read the federal health statutes or sought to obtain a comprehensive understanding of the Public Health Service Act. But as we have moved forward on new initiatives, two areas of caution have surfaced. First, we have not been careful in addressing how Congress actually defines our services. During the recent revisions of the health professions legislation, we were defined as being almost exclusively involved in mental health practice, expressly on par with social work and marriage and family therapists. In our judgment, this potentially very narrow definition is one that at the policy level, represents a distinct step backwards. A second concern is the apparent lack of interest in pursuing health professions initiatives that has been demonstrated by our professional training institutions.

To cite another graphic example, all of us are aware of the tremendous need for quality psychological care within our nation's nursing homes. Over the years, the administration, the Senate Special Committee on Aging, and the Institute of Medicine have released impressive reports noting the high incidence of residents with mental disorders; the importance of effectively addressing behavioral and environmental issues, including resident perception of social isolation; and, specifically, the relevance of biofeedback treatment for those being considered for admission. Similarly, numerous scientific studies have raised serious questions regarding the appropriateness of psychotropic medication usage (DeLeon & Wiggins, 1996).

Our nation's medical and nursing schools have come forth with proposals for "model teaching nursing homes," which would incorporate the most up-to-date clinical and research knowledge into patient care. At their suggestion, federal (and private foundation) funds have been made available to test out these models. But what psychology programs have been willing to get involved? Which of our schools have proposed a model *psychology-based* teaching nursing home? If our training institutions would get involved with this societal need, they would find the necessary resources, not only to provide the clinical care that is necessary but also to provide stipends for psychology interns and postdoctoral fellows (residents). When physical or dental care becomes necessary, one would expect the project managers to hire the necessary clinical expertise, not to provide it themselves. But historically, we have not thought this way.

By focusing on society's needs, we will learn that society will take care of us. In the health care arena, there is a tremendous range of possibilities, opportunities, and needs. Throughout the 1995 APA convention, speaker after speaker touched on some of the possibilities; it was fascinating. Our colleagues addressed the psychological needs of those with diabetes, those who require kidney dialysis, those who had premature births, and many other medical problems. However, there was a component missing: the involvement of our training programs. We did not hear our training institutions suggesting that with sufficient resources, they would provide the nation with the next generation of skilled clinicians who could competently care for our sons, daughters, or other loved ones.

Within the federal establishment, there is a programmatic entity entitled "centers of excellence." These represent a vehicle for ensuring a comprehensive, and often interdisciplinary, focus by training institutions on identified problems (or special populations). For example, there are centers of excellence focusing on the elderly, HIV patients, workplace violence, and teenage pregnancy. These represent a visual and tangible component of the federal government's programmatic planning and budgetary process. The Centers for Disease Control and Prevention (CDC) have been particularly adept in using this approach to explore their programmatic priorities. They allow the Department of Health and

Human Services to invest resources in targeted priorities and to promote interest among academic health centers and others in their priorities.

In Hawaii, we are currently interested in having a center of excellence designated to address public health issues surrounding volcanic emissions. Statistics suggest that on one of the Hawaiian islands, when the winds shift, there is a 15% increase in the use of emergency rooms, particularly by children—primarily for respiratory distress. Such a center would be an excellent example of the effectiveness of the public policy/political process in influencing NIH or CDC programmatic priorities. Psychology should similarly be actively involved in developing relevant public policy and public health priorities. Psychologists must learn to systematically focus on society's needs and use their unique expertise. They must learn to conceptualize in a manner that *visibly* allows others to appreciate their potential contributions. And most important, they must become involved in establishing their own agenda, highlighting what psychology has to contribute and sustaining that agenda at the local and national level for a prolonged period of time. By controlling the agenda, psychologists will ultimately serve themselves and society admirably.

For many psychologists, the prescription privilege agenda represents, above all else, a timely social policy agenda (DeLeon, Fox, & Graham, 1991). Psychologists are convinced that to significantly improve the quality of life for individuals either who require psychotropic medication or, perhaps more important, for whom psychotropic medication has been inappropriately prescribed, behavioral scientists must become intimately involved in this clinical decision-making process. The power to prescribe is equally the power not to prescribe or the power to ensure that medications are appropriately used. There is considerable data indicating that, for example, children, the elderly, women, people of color, and those residing in nursing homes, rural America, and inner-city ghettos are often inappropriately medicated.

Those of us supporting the prescription agenda are convinced that psychology's clinical and diagnostic skills can contribute significantly to ensuring that medications are appropriately used when necessary. Support within the profession for this policy agenda has been gradually building over the past decade, and at the 1995 APA Convention, our Council of Representatives, under Dr. Resnick's leadership, formally went on record overwhelmingly supporting prescription authority for appropriately trained psychologists. Five years earlier, at the 1990 Convention, the Council voted to establish an exploratory task force.

One must wonder, however, why so many of our colleagues felt that it was necessary, or appropriate, for the Council to even address this matter. As a profession, we have never adopted a formal Council policy expressing endorsement of biofeedback care, the use of projective techniques, or group therapy, for example. We have always taken the policy position that individual psychologists should not exceed their scope of competence and that our clinicians should be properly trained before engaging in specific clinical interventions. But for many, the pursuit of prescription privileges apparently represents a quantitative shift in psychology's fundamental self-image.

Rather then viewing the movement toward obtaining this particular clinical competence as opening up entirely new marketplaces or as allowing our clinicians to more comprehensively provide quality care, a number of our colleagues have expressed fears of medicalizing psychology and of deserting our fundamental behavioral science heritage. We suggest, in the alternative, that these colleagues have not been really thinking about what would be best for individual patients and, further, that they do not truly appreciate the extent to which our clinicians are currently very broadly involved in the generic health care arena. They really do not understand that as one of the health professions, psychology must be concerned with the patients' whole health picture.

As our practitioners obtain this new clinical responsibility, we will evolve into entirely new arenas, including providing care in nursing homes and ensuring that women have appropriate access to medications. We will undoubtedly develop new psychology specialties. No longer will we be able to ignore the clinical reality that less than 20% of psychotropic medications are provided by practitioners with substantial mental health training. We will instead possess the legal standing to address one of society's pressing needs. This is our responsibility, because we are among the leaders of society. This underlying concept is what we keep forgetting.

To those psychologists who seek to hold us back from obtaining prescription privileges and, thus, from expanding our clinical responsibilities, we would also point out that our profession must be very careful that mental health care per se is not deemed to be merely a very expensive specialty service that, in fact, can be competently provided by a wide range of professionals. Currently, we have considerable difficulty in convincing ourselves, not to mention policymakers, that there really is a qualitative difference between doctoral level providers and those with less training. In an era of constricting costs and finite budgets, why should those who "pay the bills" favor psychologists? More expensive care must be justified. We are facing very stiff competition from both extremes: from psychiatry, which considers us to be "public health hazards," and from lesser trained therapists, who stress how much more expensive we are.

Psychology must become more actively involved in policy-setting positions, thus determining how our expertise can most appropriately be used. Reimbursement-policy decisions will continue to be made, and we must strive to see psychologists actively involved in the decision-making process. Psychologists should seek to testify before the Senate Special Committee on Aging regarding the psychosocial expertise our profession could offer to the elderly. We should expect psychology-training programs to testify about their newest programs designed to improve the quality of life for the elderly. This is where psychology and APA must evolve, into the public policy arena. We must particularly get more active with the popular media, which has always had a major impact on our nation's expectations and priorities.

We have no doubt that our nation's health professions will rise to the occasion. Hopefully, psychology will be among them. Two decades ago, we started working closely with professional nursing. At that time, there were approximately 1,800 certified nurse midwives and several thousand nurse practitioners. Today, it is estimated that there are 50,000–75,000 advanced-practice nurses. Studies from the Office of Technology Assessment clearly indicate that the quality of care provided by advanced-practice nurses is excellent, comparable to that provided by physicians. We would challenge psychology to provide similar data. If psychology does not get actively involved in addressing society's health care needs, others will, and they will do very well. If we do not get involved, in all candor, we doubt that we will be missed. Our nation's health care system will continue to evolve, with or without us. The final choice is ultimately ours.

COMPLEMENTARY THOUGHTS

A Psychological Science Perspective

The questions of what is preventing psychology from being a more significant player in the nation's evolving health care system and what should be done about it have distinct parallels in the world of basic and applied science. Just as our health care providers bemoan the adverse impact of "outside forces" such as insurers, managed care companies, physicians, and politicians on their practice, researchers and academics wring their collective hands over the way psychological science is treated by the media, other disciplines, and the policymakers who control federal research dollars.

The failure of psychologists to grasp the big picture and to project ourselves into it; our lack of full appreciation for what we have to offer society; and our reluctance to get personally involved in the nasty business of advocating in the public arena—self-imposed barriers that limit psychology as *practice*—apply equally to psychological science.

To this list let us add just one more barrier: the culture gap that separates our scientists from our practitioners. Psychological practice should be informed on a continuing basis by psychological science, and vice versa, but we each seem to prefer sticking within our own communities and talking mostly to ourselves. Unless we can find better ways to share our respective knowledge and perspectives on human behavior, and to adopt a problem-solving rather than adversarial approach to controversial issues such as recovered/implanted memories and the criteria for treatment efficacy, we could wind up destroying the credibility of our discipline as both a practice and a science.

Returning to the original list, however, we would like to offer a few examples of barriers as they function outside the health care environment. Medical and nursing schools are not the only places where professional psychologists lose their identity (and we might well have included psychological researchers in epidemiology, neurology, and pediatrics departments among the medical illustrations). Engineering and computer science programs depend heavily on our cognitive and engineering psychologists for expertise in human factors; business schools use industrial/organizational, social, and quantitative psychologists to teach courses in management, organizational behavior, research design, and marketing; and psychologists are central to a host of hybrid programs such as neuroscience, cognitive science, educational technology, and occupational health. Clearly, therefore, other academic disciplines value what psychologists have to offer. One might expect this cross-fertilization to breed greater respect for the discipline than it does. The reason it does not is that our colleagues tend to adapt so completely to their environment that they no longer see themselves as psychologists.

Much the same thing happens in nonacademic settings where some of our scientists find work. They become principal engineers, human–computer interaction specialists, product development managers, or whatever the job title says, which is rarely *Psychologist*. Many even try to obscure the fact that they were trained in psychology, fearing stigmatization! So the opportunity to change psychology's image in the workplace and overcome the health care stereotype is lost because psychologists choose to become something else.

Of course, that same stereotype serves to keep many research psychologists out of these jobs in the first place. The high-tech industries, the communications and transportation fields, service industries, and the burgeoning world of technical training are but a few of the places where psychological expertise is sorely needed but largely unrecognized.

The stereotype barrier is just part of the problem. Another is our limited self-image. Why is not the field (most notably the graduate programs that train psychological scientists) doing more to prepare students for the kinds of applied opportunities that exist in the real world and will grow in the future rather than continuing to produce only traditional academicians for a shrinking market? Why are not faculties doing more to educate themselves and potential employers about these worlds of opportunity? Why are not our science professors building relationships with employing organizations, like the chemists, biologists, and physicists do? Why are we not training graduate students to appreciate the causal relationship between federal science policy and their future prospects as researchers or other career professionals?

The answer is a combination of resistance to change and a lack of vision. Like our health care provider counterparts, psychological scientists tend to adopt a myopic perspective on who they are, which prevents them from conceptualizing what they might be. In a world that is changing as rapidly as ours is, that could be fatal.

To this point, only barriers have been discussed, and no solutions offered. That is because the remedy becomes pretty obvious once one accepts the diagnosis. In a word, psychology needs to get out of some self-imposed ruts and broaden its horizons. As psychologists, we know this sort of change in mindset is a lot easier said than done. But it is high time we got started, and the place to begin is in our graduate schools. The APA Science Directorate has mounted one initiative toward this end, but it is far too early to tell what kind of reception it will receive there. Psychology's role in the twenty-first century, in science as in health care, can be pretty much whatever we choose to make it. If we ever wake up to that fact, our future can be bright indeed. If we do not, we have no one but ourselves to blame. And the clock is ticking.

A Practice Perspective

If we are on the metaphorical raft, the first thing we need to do is determine which way the current is moving. Although this may seem self-evident, we are aware of too many instances in which psychologists paddle upstream against the current. By contrast, if the profession is headed into new directions, we ought to know which way the current is flowing, to take best advantage of it. In other words, moving in the direction of the current and steering the raft to the profession's advantage seems entirely more reasonable than trying to paddle against the current.

In this context, we argue that sticking with a mental health focus for the profession would be akin to paddling against the current. This is not to say that psychology's past mental health focus has been an unimportant one. In fact, it has played a critical role in the profession's development. As a nascent profession, psychology's advocacy work to expand its activities in the mental health arena took advantage of a door that was already slightly open. It made perfect sense to move forward by pushing on that door rather than doors that were completely shut. And we have done quite well by becoming independent mental health providers in all the major publicly funded programs, such as Medicare, CHAMPUS, and Medicaid. The problem, however, is that we too often accept inclusion in the mental health world as our end goal rather than as an interim step on the way to an even more expansive future.

It is time to focus on that next step, a step that will be considerably aided if we are clear in which direction the water's current is flowing. To know that, we must first look at the big picture influencing health care. Despite the failure of Congress to enact a comprehensive health care reform plan, the very creation of the proposal begins to articulate the bigger picture. What is often overlooked is that legislation is only partly intended to stimulate change; it is in larger part intended to codify changes that have already taken place. The bigger picture, then, includes the fact that health care reform has been occurring for at least the past 15–20 years.

Among the significant changes that have been occurring in health care for some time now is the increasing integration and consolidation of the health care system. In other words, previously separate and fragmented pieces of the system are being joined together in the service of economic efficiency. This integration has been fueled over the years by a number of developments. First was the corporatization of health care. This was initially most evident in the for-profit hospital industry, which witnessed previously separate hospitals begin to chain together under one corporate umbrella.

Soon to follow was the rise of one particular form of health care corporate entity: the managed care company. One result of this development has been that previously separate and independent providers have been integrated together in panels or networks. Integration in health care was further facilitated by a period of mergers and acquisitions by health care corporate entities of all types. As one corporation joined with another and then another, greater consolidation in the industry resulted. Finally, we have witnessed legislative efforts at health care reform, which would have codified this integration but which also actually increased integration by virtue of the discussions and activities stimulated by the proposal themselves.

Two major trends of particular relevance to psychology have resulted from this integration. One is a transition from an emphasis on hospitals to a focus on health systems. These health systems, often comprising multiple hospitals as well as group practices, are equipped to provide the entire range of services: outpatient, partial hospitalization, residential treatment, inpatient treatment, after-care services, and even home health care. Because these systems and the services they provide are still usually "gated" by a medical staff organization and credentialing process, psychologists' membership on the medical staff and ability to be credentialed continue as important advocacy goals for the profession. In fact, this is even more important, because without medical staff membership and privileges in a health system format, psychologists stand to be excluded from the entire continuum of care rather than just prevented from providing inpatient treatment.

The other major trend that has resulted from increasing integration of the health care system, and the one that needs emphasizing, is the transition from an emphasis on specialty care to a focus on primary care. This is a particularly relevant direction of the current that psychology's raft must recognize to avoid paddling upstream. Because *primary care* has become somewhat of a buzzword, with multiple meanings, our own operational definition is provided here. For psychology's future directions, *primary care* is characterized broadly as prevention-oriented health care that integrates psychological and physical treatment. It is, without a doubt, much broader than mental health treatment, although it includes such treatment as a component part.

For psychology, we believe the emphasis on primary care is a significant and useful development. By virtue of our training and diverse capabilities, we are, or at least have the capacity to be, primary care providers. Yet those outside of our profession do not always see us as we see ourselves. The rude awakening we received on this point stems from efforts 2 years ago to have psychology included in a program sponsored by the U.S. Public Health Service called Putting Prevention Into Practice. It was a program intended to bring together prevention-oriented health professions in the context of a demonstration project. A letter was written to the PHS making psychology's best case for why we should be included in the program. Although the response to the letter recognized the valuable contribution of psychologists to health care, the PHS indicated that psychology did not meet the designated criteria for inclusion in the program. In particular, health professions who were to be included had to be able to provide immunization services and, according to the PHS, psychology did not. This conclusion seems especially ridiculous considering that 60% of visits to primary care physicians are actually for symptoms created by behavioral and psychological factors! Yet, in the context of the medical model in which health care remains entrenched, immunization equates with an inoculation. In reality, we have much work to do to change this unfortunate stereotype.

While we are affecting policy change, we must be emphasizing the actual primary care work psychologists do. We must continue to perform primary care activities. We must increase our work in primary care settings. And we must increase our collaboration with primary care providers. Only then will we begin to be seen by others as we see ourselves.

The last point we want to make has to do with one other obstacle to psychologists being recognized as true health care providers rather than as just mental health providers: The long-standing separation of physical health from behavioral and mental health, particularly for reimbursement purposes. Despite a generation of research that supports a decrease in health care costs as a result of psychological interventions, as long as behavioral and mental health care are carved-out of health care, the medical-cost offset can never be realized. Our ability to have an impact on health care in this way is also hampered by an insurance industry that views the financial bottom line on an annual or even quarterly basis. As a result, the industry sees little benefit to integrating psychological services with physical health services if the immediate costs go up and only create savings over time. Even Congress makes budget decisions from annual "scorable savings." In other words, unless savings are realized in the same budget as money is appropriated, cost savings cannot be accounted for.

Part of psychology's work, then, needs to target the decision makers, who must be persuaded of the overall and long-term benefit of including psychological services as a central part of health care services. The Practice Directorate of APA is presently initiating a demonstration project with Blue Cross and Blue Shield of Massachusetts to show the health and cost benefit of integrating psychological services within the traditional medical services for the treatment of breast cancer patients. Not only do we expect better overall health outcomes to result from the integration of services, but the actuarial model on which the project is based predicts a savings of $5 in health care costs for each $1 spent on psychological services. Armed with data such as we hope this project yields, we believe we can steer psychology's raft in a beneficial direction, aided, rather than impeded, by the current.

An Educational Perspective

From the barriers that can be identified as limiting the roles that psychologists should rightfully assume in the future of health care provision, three separate yet related problems immediately come to mind. First, there is poor recognition of the myriad of roles we currently fulfill and the amount of education and training that we represent. Whether we are delivering services, conducting research, teaching, consulting, or involved in administration, we bring to bear access to a whole body of psychological literature on human behavior and the knowledge that flows from that vast amount of information. Furthermore, training in clinical psychology is unique in its combination of practitioner as well as scientist skills, meaning that not only can we deliver services according to a variety of treatment models but also we are experienced in the theoretical development of these models, their empirical validation, and in training others to use them.

Psychology provides extensive training for many of the health care providers from other disciplines who are receiving funding for their training under legislation from which we are excluded. This illustrates the dangerous and defeating ways in which a lack of recognition of our skills and limited information about our position as the only doctoral trained mental health provider limit our roles. These factors contribute, in no small way, to significant decreases in the level of funding for psychology training, which is a second important barrier. Shutting down the pipeline of new psychologist providers and researchers further restricts the potential for continued contributions to health care that have historically been made by members of our field.

A third barrier is that of the conflicts between various players in the health care arena that divert energy and resources away from expanded and improved delivery of services. Interorganizational conflicts between national groups representing psychology often arise from historical events having little to do with common goals of enhancing the provision of psychological services, supporting the development and application of psychological science, and facilitating the production of well-trained psychologists. Intraorganizational struggles, among scientist, practitioner, and educator, to gain adequate resources for accomplishing our mission can result in a disconcerting lack of coordination of effort on issues of advocacy, public education, and membership participation. Finally, interdisciplinary conflicts between providers of health care, and especially between those disciplines traditionally involved in the delivery of mental health care, are rooted in historical differences in philosophy and training and in more recent financial restraints imposed on payment for services. These dividing issues cause us to fail to unite effectively in seeking a common goal, that is, increased access and funding for services and the removal of limitations to the delivery of care.

Solutions to these barriers include the provision of information to the public and to our nation's policymakers about psychology and its many contributions to health care. Advocacy aimed at increasing funding for training of psychologists and psychological research and seeking inclusion of psychologists as service providers is crucial. Links between organizations and individuals who share common ground in the provision of health care services, and common goals in the advancement of health care delivery to keep pace with the demands of the next century, must be developed and sustained. Continued leadership by our national governance in the development of a targeted and coordinated agenda is our most powerful weapon against further erosions in psychology's full participation in twenty-first century health care.

The issue of prescription privileges for psychologists is illustrative of how these barriers and solutions occur. As suggested earlier, arguments against prescription privileges are fueled by a lack of information about how psychotropic medications are currently being prescribed (i.e., mostly by general practice physicians with little mental health background or training); about the shortage of psychiatrically trained physicians, especially for underserved populations; and about the nature and extent of proposed training programs for psychologists. Furthermore, providing information to dispel some of the myths about prescription privileges leads to attitude change about the issue. Conflicts on all fronts have been probably the most consistent aspect of this endeavor. However, advocacy has successfully kept the issue alive and evolving and has given those of us involved with the experience a chance to demonstrate that the training of psychologists to prescribe is a feasible goal. Important links with those involved in a similar goal should be more fully explored. Clearly, this new role for psychologists offers an opportunity to expand the way in which health care is delivered.

A Public Interest Perspective

The American Psychological Association's Public Interest Directorate has been involved in several projects that attempt to show directly the importance of psychology in health. For example, at the request of the Committee on Women in Psychology, the Women's Programs Office convened a conference on Psychosocial and Behavioral Factors in Women's Health in May 1994. They are planning the second conference, a follow-up to the first, for September 1996. The September 1996 conference is titled "Psychosocial and Behavioral Factors in Women's Health: Research, Prevention, Treatment, and Service Delivery in Clinical and Community Settings." One of the major goals of these interdisciplinary conferences is to highlight the importance of psychosocial and behavioral factors in all aspects of women's health, including etiology, prevention, treatment, and rehabilitation. Although the specific focus is women's health, the points made are relevant to health in general.

In keeping with the conference goals, the Women's Programs Office is trying to broaden the definition of health to include psychosocial and behavioral factors. According to the U.S. Public Health Service, 7 of the 10 leading causes of death in the United States could be substantially reduced if people would change their behavior, namely adhere to medical regimens, eat proper diets, stop smoking, exercise, and stop abusing alcohol and other drugs. Psychology is the field that addresses behavior and behavior change and compliance with medical regimens. Moreover, research is beginning to show the importance of psychological well-being for recovery from major illnesses, including cardiovascular disease. Additionally, an accumulating body of research suggests that immune-related disease processes and immunological functioning are affected by psychological stress. Relatedly, psychological interventions have been shown to be effective in treating immune-related disease. These accumulating scientific data clearly indicate the importance of psychology in the treatment of, and recovery from, disease.

Another important area of women's health that is often overlooked is women's victimization in intimate relationships. A large number of women who report to emergency rooms are there because of intimate violence, yet health care providers continue to fail to ask about violence, even when there are clear indicators. Therefore, this issue is included in the women's health conference.

Violence in the United States, whether domestic violence, youth violence, or other types of violence, cannot be solved by legal and criminal interventions. The Public Interest Directorate has been involved in addressing broader issues of violence. Psychosocial factors and interventions are also critical and must be addressed. The Male Violence Against Women Task Force and the Youth Violence Commission were organized to address these issues. Reports that shed light on these issues are available from both groups.

The Public Interest Directorate also has been very involved in the issue of workplace, or occupational, stress. Over the past 6 or more years, they have been working with the National Institute of Occupational Safety and Health in a series of conferences on occupational stress, to increase the involvement of psychologists and to clearly show the importance of psychological stress in workplace issues. This focus has included highlighting the work, stress, and health connection. Again, the our goal is to showcase the importance of psychology to critical aspects of health and well-being. The message is not only for psychologists and other professionals, but for the media, government personnel, legislators, and the lay public.

A Prescribing Psychologist's Perspective

The authority to prescribe elevates a psychologist to the status of a full-service mental health provider capable not only of providing the traditional roles of psychological assessment and mental health counseling but also of providing the full spectrum of care for patients with mental disorders. This "one-stop mental health provider" not only makes good economic sense but also simplifies access problems and enhances the continuity of care for our patients. However, even given the obvious benefit to patients, the public sector, and the health care industry, significant barriers to prescriptive authority for psychologists remain.

One of the greatest potential benefits of psychologists prescribing is increased access for a number of underserved populations in the United States. In spite of the nearly $1 trillion spent on health care each year in this country, there continues to be large populations whose mental health needs are underserved. One of the largest of these populations is in rural America. In 90% of rural hospitals, where psychiatry is not present, who does the prescribing of psychotropics? Surveys (DeLeon, Sammons, & Sexton, 1995) show that it is probably someone who has not had sufficient training to accurately diagnose a mental disorder, and who knows relatively little about psychotropics for specific mental disorders. Even when the proper medication is prescribed, appropriate dosing is seldom attained. Additionally, 66% of the counties in the United States have no psychiatrists. In the state of Wyoming, one child psychiatrist might travel several hundred miles for consultations concerning pharmacologic intervention for children with mental disorders.

Another underserved group is the chronically mentally ill, a large contingent of our homeless population. In their 1990 report, the National Alliance of the Mentally Ill and the Public Citizen Health Research Group recommended that because psychiatrists have abandoned the public sector, psychologists, nurse practitioners, and physician assistants should be given special training and allowed to prescribe. The National Alliance of the Mentally Ill, with nationally recognized experts on the needs of the chronically mentally ill, continues to recommend that psychologists move aggressively to fill this significant health care void.

In contrast to our underserved populations, the United States also has overserved, or at least overmedicated, populations. For example, the use of Ritalin for "diagnosed" attention deficit disorder has reached an alarming rate, with as many as 15% (DeLeon, Sammons, & Sexton, 1995) of children in some elementary schools on this medication. This rate is in stark contrast to the 3% to 5% that the *Diagnostic and Statistical Manual of Mental Disorders* (American Psychiatric Association, 1994) suggests is the actual prevalence of ADD in our youth. Consider the value of prescribing psychologists who could accurately diagnose, use appropriate behavioral interventions, and also provide adjunctive pharmacologic therapy, including discontinuing drugs for incorrectly diagnosed children.

The elderly present a different type of challenge—sometimes underserved and sometimes overserved. Elderly individuals constitute 12% of our population but consume 40% of all psychotropics, primarily sedatives (DeLeon, Sammons, & Sexton, 1995). In our nursing homes, for example, a staggering 40% of the patients receive psychotropics

(DeLeon, Sammons, & Sexton, 1995). It is truly difficult to believe that the rate of mental illness among the elderly is that much greater than in the general population. In fact, the problem of overmedication for our elderly population has been addressed in the literature for years, with little apparent improvement. If one considers that by 2020, the number of licensed drivers over the age of 75 will double and that a significant percentage of these drivers are likely to be on some type of sedating medication, the roads will indeed be a hazardous place.

Solving the problem of unmet mental health care needs in our country will not be easy. Only one in three patients with a major depressive disorder seeks treatment. In the primary care setting, where these patients are most often seen, the diagnosis of depression is missed in about 55% of the cases (DeLeon, Sammons, & Sexton, 1995). These patients often present with chronic headaches, back pain, or gastrointestinal disturbances. And because their depression is often not diagnosed, it is often not treated. Thus, prescribing psychologists collaborating as mental health consultants would be an invaluable addition to the primary care team.

All indications are that these disparities in mental health care will only get worse if current trends continue. As the number of psychiatric patients increases, there are fewer psychiatrists to treat them. In the past 10 years, the medical profession has seen a significant decline, from 10% to 4%, in the number of medical school graduates that have chosen psychiatry as their specialty. With the "graying of America," the increased use of psychotropics, and the attrition of psychiatrists, the need for competent, comprehensive mental health care providers will only become greater.

What can psychologists do? The American Psychological Association's Ad Hoc Task Force on Psychopharmacology recommends that all psychologists receive one of three levels of training in psychopharmacology. The lowest level of training could best be completed in graduate school, with approximately 50 classroom hours.

The second level, possibly termed *collaborative practice*, would require more in-depth training and would prepare the psychologist to assist physicians, particularly primary care providers, in developing and monitoring medication-care plans for patients in need of psychotropic therapy. The third level would require considerably more classroom and practicum training and would prepare a psychologist for prescriptive privileges.

The opportunities are growing. Today, many physicians call on psychologists' knowledge to help them in selecting and managing the use of psychotropic agents. Managed health care will likely expand this already common practice. Because greater than 60% of all mental health patients are pharmacologically treated by nonpsychiatrists, the opportunity for collaborative-practice psychologists is great.

Across the country, psychologists are making progress in overcoming some of the barriers to obtaining prescriptive privileges. Programs to train psychologists to prescribe are already in the development process. Furthermore, a number of states have already completed or are working toward legislative action to license psychologists to prescribe. Those few psychologists who have earned prescriptive privileges know well the barriers but have successfully navigated around them. The needs are obvious and the opportunities abundant—it is now up to psychology to make them happen!

REFLECTIONS

Although a relatively young profession, psychology is rapidly maturing in numbers and breadth (i.e., scope) of practice. The next step is for the field to appreciate the importance of developing a broad vision, one that includes affirmatively addressing society's pressing needs. This is true for all aspects of psychology, including science, practice, education, and public interest. Our field possesses unlimited opportunities; the barriers are internal and self-imposed. Society is undergoing major and rapid changes; the challenge for psychology is to become a proactive participant in these developments. The future for psychology will be what we make it, no more and no less.

REFERENCES

American Psychiatric Association. (1994). *Diagnostic and statistical manual of mental disorders* (4th ed.). Washington, DC: Author.

DeLeon, P. H. (1988). Public policy and public service: Our professional duty. *American Psychologist, 43*, 309–315.

DeLeon, P. H., Fox, R. E., & Graham, S. R. (1991). Prescription privileges: Psychology's next frontier?

DeLeon, P. H., Frank, R. G., & Wedding, D. (1995). Health psychology and public policy: The political process. *Health Psychology, 14*, 493–499.

DeLeon, P. H., Sammons, M. T., & Sexton, J. L. (1995). Focusing on society's real needs: Responsibility and prescription privileges? *American Psychologist, 50*, 1022–1032.

DeLeon, P. H., & Wiggins, J. G. (1996). Prescription privileges for psychologists. *American Psychologist 51*(3), 225–229.

Library of Congress. (1995, May). CRS *report for Congress—Membership of the 104th Congress: A profile* (95-205 GOV). Washington, DC: Author.

Prospective Payment Assessment Commission. (1996, June). *Medicare and the American health care system.* (Report to Congress). Washington, DC: U.S. Government Printing Office.

Resnick, R. J., DeLeon, P. H., & VandenBos, G. R. (in press). Evolution of professional issues in psychology: Training standards, legislative recognition, and boundaries of practice. In J. R. Matthews & C. E. Walker (Eds.), *Beginning skills and professional issues in clinical psychology.* Needham Heights, MA: Allyn & Bacon.

Samuelson, R. J. (1995, October 25). Managed-care revolution. *The Washington Post,* p. A19.

INDEX

Ackerman, M. D., 303–304
Acquired immunodeficiency syndrome
    (AIDS), 315, 347–360,
    395–418
Acute lymphoblastic leukemia (ALL),
    222
AD. *See* Alzheimer's disease
Adaptation, 227
Addictive behaviors, 185, 389
ADHD. *See* Attention deficit
    hyperactivity disorder
Adherence, 278–281
    appointments and, 330–331
    clinical outcomes and, 324–338
    control and, 180
    diets and, 328
    exercise and, 328
    homework and, 329–330
    symptom relief and, 325
    treatment and, 323–338
Adolescents, 116, 317, 395–396. *See also*
    African Americans,
    adolescents
Advice, 382
Advocacy, 21, 121
African Americans, 43
    adolescents, 395–418
    families, 347
    health status of, 40
    women, 349–360, 395–404,
    410–411, 412
Aging, 44, 48. *See also specific problems,
    topics*
    AD and, 239–263
    age-related disorders, 243–244
    APA Task Force, 451
    behavioral science and, 52, 59, 61
    behavior and, 59
    cognition and, 48, 63–66
    control beliefs and, 49, 400
    demographics and, 10, 21, 59
    epidemiology and, 50
    health and, 59

    life-course models and, 39–52
    medication and, 62, 65
    memory function and, 63
    National Institute on Aging, 61
    normative data and, 61, 246–247
    psychotropics and, 450
    research objectives, 61, 62
    response slowing and, 245
    self-esteem and, 49
    Senate committee, 438, 441
    sensory changes with, 243–247
    stress and, 50
Agoraphobia, 142, 329
AIDS. *See* Acquired
    immunodeficiency syndrome
Alcohol, 334
    abuse problems, 177–194
    college students and, 377–392
    family history of, 387
    harm reduction and, 389–390
Alcoholics Anonymous, 189
Alcohol Skills Training Program
    (ASTP), 379
ALL. *See* Acute lymphoblastic leukemia
Alzheimer's disease (AD), 239–263
AMA. *See* American Medical
    Association
Ambulatory-care visits, 77
American Academy of Family
    Physicians, 90
American Biodyne, 28
American Medical Association
    (AMA), 433
American Psychological Association
    (APA), 2
    addiction division, 185
    Board of Directors, 430
    fellowship program, 434
    health pscychology and, 18
    Human Capital Initiative, 62
    planning and, 22
    presidency of, 436
    Presidential Miniconvention and, 3

American Psychological Association
(*continued*)
  primary care and, 91
  psychopharmacology and, 451
  public education and, 23, 434
  Public Interest Directorate, 448
Anderson, D. A., 16
Anemia, 283
Anxiety
  adherence and, 329
  appropriately treated, 139–141
  disorders, 133–148
  prevalence of, 92, 112
  primary care settings, 92, 135–137
  touch therapy and, 319
APA. *See* American Psychological
  Association
Appointments, adherence and, 330–331
Arthritis, 21, 138, 326
Asian Americans, 46
Assertiveness techniques, 301
Assessment methods, 119, 199
Asthma, 227, 233–234, 316
ASTP. *See* Alcohol Skills-Training
  Program
Attention deficit hyperactivity disorder
  (ADHD), 195–207, 450
  behavioral methods and, 221
  developmental influences on, 198
  diagnosis and management,
    197–201
  learning disabilities and, 197
  medication and, 120, 450
  pediatricians and, 195–207
  prevalence estimates for, 112, 197
  psychologist and, 203–205
  three primary subtypes, 197
Attitude, behavior and, 399
Autistic children, 317

Baby boomers, 59–60
Back pain, 33
Bar-coding system, 67
Barbarin, O. A., 221–222
Behavioral approach, 18
  aging and, 59–61
  biobehavioral models, 220
  checklist for, 199
  cognitive problems, 253–254
  control and, 400
  coping and, 221

costs and, 234
depression and, 155–157
disinhibition and, 197
health care and, 22, 133–148
improvement rates, 60–62, 299
intention and, 399
psychologist and, 91
risk factors, 79
Belar, C. D., 1
Binge drinking, 377–392
Biobehavioral models, 220
Biodyne, 28
Biofeedback, 233, 298–299, 305
Biopsychosocial model, 302
Birth cohorts, 41
Blacks. *See* African Americans
Books for Parents and Children, 116
Borderline personalities, 34
Bowen, O. R., 184
Brain dysfunction, 240
Breath, shortness of, 227
Bremer, B. A., 269
Brief counseling, 36, 103
Burn patients, 317
Burgio, K. L., 294

CAGE instrument, 186
Call-In Hour, 115–116, 124
Cameron, L., 69
Cancer, 19, 179
  chemotherapy, 217
  childhood, 222
  group therapy and, 301
  pediatric, 213–225
  prostate, 306
  self-esteem and, 217
Capitated systems, 16
Captivation, 196
Cardiac symptoms, 139
Cardiovascular disease, 333
Carpal tunnel syndrome, 33–34
Cartesian dualism, 29, 78
Carve-outs, 28–29
Case management, 36, 121
Catecholamines, 317
CDC. *See* Centers for Disease Control
Centers for Disease Control (CDC),
  227, 438
Center for Epidemiological Studies
  Depression Scale (CES-D),
  151

Center for Stress and Anxiety Disorder, 142

CES-D. *See* Center for Epidemiological Studies Depression Scale

Change, motivation for, 188

Charity care, 13

Chemotherapy, 217

Child Mental Health Evaluation Program, 121

Children. *See also specific topics*
    ADHD and, 120, 195–207, 450
    behavioral problems, 109–129
    developmental problems 114–117, 122
    diabetic, 317
    infants, 314–315
    sexual abuse and, 126
    socialization problems, 117
    touch therapies, 316–318

Chronic illness, 21, 273–275

Cicchetti, D. V., 153

Cigarettes, 180–181

Cirrhosis, 179

Claflin, D. J., 221–222

Clinical neuropsychology, 239–263

Clinical services, 10, 115–123

Clinton administration, 436

Cocaine, 181, 315

Cognitive approach
    aging and, 48, 63–66
    behavior problems and, 253–254
    cognitive deficits, 241–242
    control problems, 279
    depression and, 157–158
    development and, 48
    memory problems, 69
    potential in, 48

Cognitive–behavioral therapy, 167

Cohort theory, 44

Collaboration, 101–124. *See also specific topics*
    benefits of, 105–106
    health psychology and, 2–3
    integrated delivery systems and, 23
    model for, 92–96
    physicians and, 93
    power issues and, 105
    primary care and, 93

College students, 377–392

Committee on Women in Psychology, 448

Community consultation, 123–125

Community Mental Health Centers Act, 12

Compliance, coping and, 280

Comprehensive system, 119

Confusional states, 242

Congress, composition of, 433

Continued outcome research, 235

Control, adherence and, 180

Control beliefs, 49, 400

Coping
    compliance and, 280
    coping behaviors, 221
    depression and, 152
    long-term survivors, 222–223
    problems, 152
    skill approach, 301

Cornerly, P. B., 40

Coronary heart disease, 78, 138

Costs, of therapy
    cost-effectiveness, 22, 36, 234–235
    depression and, 92, 150
    fee-for-service, 13, 15, 23
    insurance industry, 13, 446
    managed care and, 32–33, 36
    offset phenomenon, 33, 446

Couples therapy, 122

Coyne, J. C., 151

Crazy-quilt phenomena, 280

Crisis-oriented therapy, 215–217

Cummings, K. M., 280

Delirium, 242

Dementia, 239–263

Denial, 171–172

Depression
    behavioral theory and, 155–157
    cognitive therapy and, 157–158
    coping and, 152
    costs associated with, 92, 150
    dementia and, 249–250
    disorders and, 134
    episodic, 134, 140
    Hamilton Scale, 140
    impairment and, 138
    incidence rates, 112
    primary care and, 149–162
    self-management model, 158
    sexuality and, 302
    stress and, 19
    substance use problems and, 183

Depression (*continued*)
    survival and, 281
    touch therapy and, 319
    tranquilizers and, 152
Developmental problems, 117, 122
Diabetes, 21, 138, 317
Diagnosis-related groups (DRGs), 28
*Diagnostic and Statistical Manual of Mental
        Disorders* (4th ed.; *DSM–IV*),
        120, 134, 152
Diet, 280, 313, 328, 368
Differentiation, integration and, 24
Direct observation, 199
Discrimination, 43, 352
Distress behaviors, 221
DRGs. *See* Diagnosis-related groups
Drotar, D., 109–119
Drugs. *See* Substance use
DSM-IV. *See* Diagnostic and Statistical
        Manual
Dysthymia, 134

Education for Handicapped Act, 202
Education methodologies, 18
Educator, function of, 18, 121
Eitel, P., 277–278, 280
Elderly. *See* Aging
End-stage renal disease (ESRD),
        265–287
Engel, B. T., 294
Environmental support, 351–352
Epidemiological research, 22, 49–50
EPO. *See* Erythropoietin
Erectile dysfunction, 302–304
Erythropoietin (EPO), 282
ESRD. *See* End-stage renal disease
Evans, R. W., 269
Executive functions, 241
Exercise, 170, 313

Family, 353–359
    conflict in, 355
    coping and, 219–220
    information to, 250–251
    intervention and, 217–220
    network and, 47
    role of, 43, 351–352
    stress and, 351–352
    therapy and, 122, 232

Family physician movement, 91
Fechner-Bates, S., 151–152
Feedback, 382
Fee-for-service models, 13, 15, 23
Financial factors. *See* Costs
Fong, G. T., 410–412, 416–417
Forrester, D., 31–32
Frank, R. G., 3
Friend, R., 277, 280

Gastrointestinal disorders, 138
Genetic factors, 21
Gillies, R. R., 16
Goodwin, D. W., 184
Gordon Diagnostic System, 200
Grandparent volunteers, 316
Griffin, K., 277, 280
Group therapy, 35, 301
Gynecology, 306

Habit training, 298
Hallucinogens, 182
Hamilton Scale for Depression, 140
Harm-reduction approach, 377–392
Hatchett, L., 277–278
Hawk, B. A., 111
Health care policy, 11, 141
Health insurance, 13, 446
Health maintenance organizations
        (HMOs), 12, 14, 16, 31
Heart disease, 21. *See also* Cardiovascular
        disease; Coronary heart disease
Hewitt, N., 410
HIV infection, 315, 347–360, 395–418
HMOs. *See* Health maintenance
        organizations
Holden, C., 185
Homework, adherence and, 329–330
Human Capital Initiative, 62
Human immunodeficiency virus (HIV),
        397. *See also* HIV infection
Huntington's disease, 241–242
Hypertension, 21, 236
Hypnosis, 233
Hypoglycemia, 33

Iatrogenics, 34
Imminent justice, 218

Impairment, 138
Incontinence, 289–301
Infants, 314–315
Inhalants, 182
Insurance industry, 13, 446
Integrated delivery systems, 15–18
Intellectual function, 48, 241
Interdisciplinary approach, 40, 438
Intergenerational models, 52
Internists, 101–108
Interpersonal therapy, 140, 157
Intervention. *See also specific disorders*
    protocols, 220
    race matching and, 415
    services and, 121
    strategies for, 363–364
    substance use and, 188–189
Interviewing, 382–387

Jemmott, J. B., 410–411, 416–417
Jemmott, L. S., 410–411, 416–417

Kasak, A. E., 219
Kaschak, D., 299
Katon, W., 139
Kielser, C. A., 14
Kinship network, 352

Learning disabilities, 195–205
Lewinian model, 281
Lewinsohn model, 156
Leventhal, H., 69
Lewinsohn, P. M., 155–156
Life-course models, 39–52
Life expectancy, 41
Lifestyle, 347
Linkages Project, 93
Long-term illness, 4, 18

Managed care organizations, 10, 28, 31
    business-driven, 30
    cost and, 28
    diagnosis-related groups, 28
    HMOs and, 16
    ownership of, 31
    preference for, 233
    trends in, 431
    usefulness of, 28, 32

Marital therapy, 122, 157, 329
Marlowe-Crowne Scale, 414
Massage, 313
Master's level therapists, 35
Matarazzo, J. D., 2, 186, 191
McCurry, S. M., 254
MedCo Behavioral Care Corporation, 28
Medical crises, 213–225
Medicare, 13, 41, 60, 431
Medication, 65–68, 79, 450
MedPartners, 32
Megaproviders, 10, 29–32
Melamed, B. G., 2
Memory, 230, 253. *See also* Dementia
Miami Sexual Dysfunction Protocol
    (MSDP), 303
Mind–body split, 2, 10, 22
Mini-Mental State Examination
    (MMSE), 242
Mixed anxiety–depressive disorder, 134
MMSE. *See* Mini-Mental State
    Examination
Moderation Management, 189
Motivational therapy, 95
Motor skills, 230
MSDP. *See* Miami Sexual Dysfunction
    Protocol
Mullikin Group, 31–32
Multicomponent regimen, 332
Multidisciplinary approach, 23, 202,
    234, 305
Multimethod component, 199
Multiple personality disorder, 34

National Cancer Institute, 432
National Institute of Child Health and
    Human Development, 432
National Institute of Nursing Research,
    432
National Institute on Aging, 61
National Institutes of Health (NIH),
    61, 432
National Institute of Mental Health
    (NIMH), 12
Native Americans, 46
Negative behavior, 125
Newman, R., 2
Nicotine, 180
NIH. *See* National Institutes of Health
NIMH. *See* National Institute of
    Mental Health

NOS. *See* Not otherwise specified
category
Not otherwise specified (NOS)
category, 134
Nursing home, 300
Nutrition, 166

OAA. *See* Older American Act
Obesity, 163–173
Obsessive–compulsive disorder, 134, 329
Occupational stress, 449
Older American Act (OAA), 41
Omnibus Budget Reconciliation Act, 12
Oncology, 306
Opioids, 182
Oppositional defiant disorder, 199

Pain management, 313
Panic disorder, 135, 142
Parenting, 115–118, 125, 221
Parkinson's disease, 241
Patient education, 250–251, 300
Pediatricians
ADHD and, 195–207
learning disabilities and, 195
oncologists and, 213–225
psychology and, 109–129, 203–205
training, 124
Phencyclidine, 182
Physical disability, 23, 138, 245
Physical equity model, 31
Physical exam, 118
Planned behavior, 399–401
PNI. *See* Psychoneuroimmunology
Posttraumatic stress disorder, 317
Power issues, collaboration and, 105
Precertification, 36
Pregnancy, 395–418, 431
Prevention beliefs, 401–402
Preventive services, 116
Primary care, 437. *See also specific disorder*
collaborative practice and, 93
definition of, 89, 90–91, 445
depression and, 149–162
mental health and, 77
psychological treatment, 141–145
psychologist and, 85–206
substance use and, 177–194
Problem solving, 301–302
Prochaska, J. O., 188
Prostate cancer, 305

Psychology. *See specific disorder, topic*
Psychoneuroimmunology, 19
Psychosexual disorders, 183
Psychosocial effects, 69
Psychotropics, 450
Public education, 23
Public Health Service Act, 437
Public Interest Directorate, 449
Punishment, 218

Quality of life, 265–287

Race, 41–46, 50. *See also specific group*
Race matching, 415
Rational Recovery, 189
Reasoned action, theory of, 399–400
Reducing stress, touch therapies and, 314
Referral process, 102–104
Regier, D. A., 178, 183
Regional Group Practices (RGPs), 30
Relapse prevention, 189
Relationship distress, 301, 302
Relaxation, 232, 301
Religion, 352
Renal disease, 265–287
Resnick, R. J., 436, 439
Resourcefulness, 279–281
Respiratory disorders, 227–238
Response rate, 245
RGPs. *See* Regional Group Practices
Riley, M. W., 44
Ritalin, 450
Ritual, 329
Rodham-Clinton proposal, 30
Rose, M., 299
Rosenbaum-Smira model, 279–280
Ross, M. J., 3
Rozensky, R. H., 2, 301

Sammons, J. H., 184
Schizophrenia, 183
School reintegration, 217
Screening instruments, 186
Self-care home patients, 279–280
Self-conception, 49
Self-efficacy, 400
Self-esteem, 49, 112, 217, 227, 316
Self-examination, 399
Self-help programs, 300–301
Self-management model, 158, 232–235

Senate Special Committee on Aging, 438, 441
SES. *See* Socioeconomic status
SET. *See* Structural ecosystems therapy
Sex education, 123
Sexual abuse, 121–126
Sexual disorders, 183
Sexually transmitted diseases (STDs), 395–418
Schneider, M. S., 279
Schwenk, T. L., 151
Shortell, S. M., 16–17
Siegel, L. J., 2
S.M.A.R.T. Recovery, 189
Smith, D., 299
Smith, J., 299
Smoking, 180, 361–375, 399
Sobell, L. C., 187–188
Social–cognitive theory, 400
Social confidence, 227
Social Desirability Scale, 414
Socialization problems, 117
Socially supportive processes, 47
Social phobia, 134
Social policy, 439
Social Security, 60
Social skills model, 156
Socioecological model, 356
Socioeconomic status (SES), 42–47, 73
Somatization, 33, 101
Spears, H., 410–411
Stage paradigm, 364–366
STD. *See* Sexually transmitted diseases
Stereotypes, 94
Sturm, R., 152–153
Stress
    age and, 50
    family and, 351–352
    hormones and, 317–318
    reduction, 313, 314
    tolerance of, 220
    training and, 302
Structural ecosystems therapy (SET), 355–357
Structural equation modeling, 70–71
Structural lags, 42
Subjective norms, 400–402
Substance use problems, 15, 329, 368
    addicted patients and, 185
    Americans and, 178
    intervention and, 188–189

personality disorder and, 183
primary care, 177–194
psychological problems and, 130
psychosexual disorders and, 183
schizophrenia and, 183
screening for, 186
Supply-side strategies, 15
Support groups, 79, 171, 301
Survival, 281–282
Symister, P., 278
Symptom Distress Checklist, 143

Tertiary care settings, 211–343. *See also specific therapies*
Thyroid dysfunction, 201
Tobacco, 177–194
Touch therapy, 313
    adults and, 318
    AIDS and, 315–316
    children and, 316–318
    infants and, 314–315
    managing pain and, 314
    massage and, 313
    stress and, 314
Tourette's syndrome, 201
Tranquilizers, 152
Traumatic injury, 79
Tricyclics, 157

Urology, 289–307
Utilization review, 36

Value, defined, 16
VandenBos, G. R., 13
Violence, 448
Visual–motor ability, 241
Vulnerability theory, 158

Wadhwa, N. K., 277–278, 280
Waiting list controls, 157
Wechsler Intelligence Scale, 246
Weight control, 163–173, 399
Wellness, lifestyle and, 347
Wells, K. B., 152–153
Wexler, B. E., 153
White, J., 143
Women in Psychology, 448

Yu, E. S. H., 46

ABOUT THE EDITORS

Robert J. Resnick, PhD, is Professor Emeritus of Psychiatry and Pediatrics and former Chair, Division of Clinical Psychology, Health Sciences Center, Virginia Commonwealth University. He is presently Professor of Psychology at Randolph-Macon College and maintains a pediatric health psychology practice. Dr. Resnick has been the recipient of the American Psychological Association's (APA) Division of Clinical Psychology Award for Distinguished Contributions to Clinical Psychology, the Society of Pediatric Psychology's Lee Salk Distinguished Service Award, the Department of the Army's Outstanding Civilian Service Medal, and the APA Award for Contributions to Applied Psychology as a Professional Practice. He is a Diplomate in Clinical Psychology and a Distinguished Practitioner in the National Academy of Practice. Dr. Resnick has held numerous elected offices in the APA, including the 1995–1996 presidency. He serves on the editorial boards of several journals and has published and presented widely in the areas of attention deficits and health policy.

Ronald H. Rozensky, PhD, is the Associate Chairperson of Psychiatry and Chief Psychologist at the Evanston Hospital. He is a Professor of Psychiatry and Behavioral Sciences and Adjunct Associate Professor of Psychology at Northwestern University and Medical School. Dr. Rozensky is a Diplomate in Clinical Psychology and a Distinguished Practitioner in the National Academy of Practice. He is founding editor of the *Journal of Clinical Psychology in Medical Settings* (Plenum) and coeditor of the *Handbook of Clinical Psychology in Medical Settings*. Dr. Rozensky is a past president of the Illinois Psychological Association and is a member of the APA's Council of Representatives. He received a 1995 APA Heiser Presidential Award in behalf of Professional Psychology. He serves as the APA's representative to the Joint Commission on Accreditation of Healthcare Organizations. Dr. Rozensky has published numerous chapters and articles on such topics as professional issues, credentialing, trauma, and health psychology.